Dr. iur. Bernhard Madörin
lic.oec. HSG Peter Bertschinger

**Rechnungslegung und Wirtschaftsprüfung /
Accounting and Auditing in Switzerland**

Band 4 A PRIMA VISTA

 Stämpfli Verlag AG Bern · 2009

Dr. iur. Bernhard Madörin
lic.oec. HSG Peter Bertschinger

Rechnungslegung und Wirtschaftsprüfung / Accounting and Auditing in Switzerland

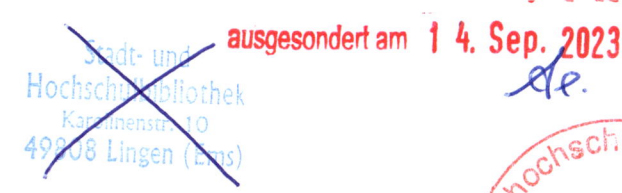

Stämpfli Verlag AG Bern · 2009

Zitiervorschlag:
Madörin/Bertschinger, Rechnungslegung und Wirtschaftsprüfung / Accounting and Auditing in Switzerland, A prima vista, 2009

Bibliografische Information der Deutschen Nationalbibliothek
Die Deutsche Nationalbibliothek verzeichnet diese Publikation in der Deutschen Nationalbibliografie; detaillierte bibliografische Daten sind im Internet über http://dnb.d-nb.de abrufbar.

Alle Rechte vorbehalten, insbesondere das Recht der Vervielfältigung, der Verbreitung und der Übersetzung. Das Werk oder Teile davon dürfen ausser in den gesetzlich vorgesehenen Fällen ohne schriftliche Genehmigung des Verlags weder in irgendeiner Form reproduziert (z. B. fotokopiert) noch elektronisch gespeichert, verarbeitet, vervielfältigt oder verbreitet werden.

© Stämpfli Verlag AG Bern · 2009

Gesamtherstellung:
Stämpfli Publikationen AG, Bern
Printed in Switzerland

ISBN 978-3-7272-9541-6

Für Pascale (B. Madörin)
Für Heidi (P. Bertschinger)

Vorwort

In letzter Zeit haben verschiedene negative wirtschaftliche Ereignisse in der Schweiz und im Ausland den Blick der Öffentlichkeit vermehrt auf die Arbeit der Revisionsstellen von Publikumsgesellschaften gelenkt; die Sensibilität gegenüber Rechnungslegung und Revision ist gestiegen. Dies kann als Chance für die Revisionsbranche betrachtet werden, welche früher in ihrer Bedeutung massiv unterschätzt wurde und daher fast in der Anonymität arbeitete. Heute jedoch wird deren Leistung ernst genommen. Auch eine präventive Wirkung ist durch diese erhöhte Aufmerksamkeit der Öffentlichkeit möglich und begrüssenswert. Diese «neue Position» dieses Gesellschaftsorgans macht es jedoch gleichzeitig unumgänglich, Neuerungen und damit natürlich auch Verbesserungen einzuführen, um das Vertrauen der Öffentlichkeit in die Revisionsstelle zu stärken und auch die Qualität der Revision selbst sowie die der Revisorinnen und Revisoren zu steigern. Dabei dürfen vor allem die Bedürfnisse der kleinen und mittleren Unternehmen (KMU) keinesfalls hintangestellt werden, da diese mit 99,7 % den Löwenanteil der schweizerischen Unternehmen stellen und für 66 % der Erwerbstätigen verantwortlich sind.[1]

Das neue Recht versucht, diesen Anforderungen gerecht zu werden: Für alle Gesellschaftsformen ist eine Revisionspflicht vorgesehen, die Aufgaben der Revisionsstelle wurden präzisiert und die fachlichen Anforderungen an die Revisorinnen und Revisoren sind neu definiert. Bezüglich der KMU ist zu beachten, dass ihnen eine Erleichterung bei der Revisionspflicht und dem Umfang der Revision zugebilligt wird, was neu mit dem Begriff eingeschränkte Prüfung bzw. Review ausgedrückt werden soll. Sodann darf unter bestimmten Bedingungen eine Prüfung auch unterbleiben. Ausserdem ist die Unabhängigkeit der Revisionsstelle eingehender geregelt und verschärft worden.

Mit der Neuregelung der Revision wurden vier Schutzziele gesetzlich verankert: Investorenschutz bei Publikumsgesellschaften, Schutz öffentlicher Interessen bei den wirtschaftlich bedeutsamen Unternehmen, Schutz der Personen mit Minderheitsbeteiligungen und Schutz der Gläubiger bei Privatgesellschaften.

---

1 BFS, Zahlen des Jahres 2001.

Das vorliegende Werk bietet eine umfassende Darstellung der neuen Bestimmungen und der ihnen zugrunde liegenden theoretischen und praktischen Hintergründe.

Zu besonderem Dank verpflichtet bin ich Frau Nadine Strub. Durch ihr Engagement und ihre kritische Auseinandersetzung mit der Materie hat sie wesentlich zum Gelingen dieses Buches beigetragen.

Dr. Bernhard Madörin

Preface

Swiss Auditing and Accounting is about to change significantly due to new legislation enacted at the end of 2005 by the Swiss parliament. They came into force on 1 January 2008. These are mainly:

1) Amendments to the Swiss Code of Obligations where auditors are concerned (Art. 727 to 731 CO). These articles now not only apply for Corporations (Ltd., AG, SA) but also to other types of legal organisations such as

    - Limited liability companies (LLC, GmbH, Sàrl)
    - Cooperatives
    - Associations
    - Foundations, etc.

2) New Swiss Auditor Oversight Act (AOA):
    - *Revisionsaufsichtsgesetz* (RAG)
    - Loi sur la surveillance de la révision (LSR)

3) Proposed new Accounting Law, CO 957 ff. (discussion in Swiss parliament)

We have decided to summarise the above mentioned auditing standards and other English material on business and statutory accounting in Switzerland in this book. Switzerland has a very internationally oriented economy. Swiss legislation is normally only available in German, French and Italian, three of the four Swiss official national languages. Only very few law texts are available in English (mostly unofficial translations by private organisations).

Therefore, there was need to translate important provisions of the Accounting and Auditing legislation in English. The texts presented in this book should give readers an insight in wording typically used in the business environment.

We are aware that most topics of this paper will develop dynamically and, therefore, the information is subject to change. Obviously, there are some strong links between statutory audits, the annual legal accounts and tax laws.

We appreciate any suggestions and recommendations for improving these English texts in possible future versions. As soon as more detailed guidelines are made available in the coming months and years by the Swiss government (in the form of laws, ordinances and court cases) or interpretations of the Swiss Institute of Certified Accountants (Treuhand-Kammer) and other professional bodies we will update this book accordingly.

Peter Bertschinger
lic.oec. HSG

Inhaltsübersicht

Vorwort	....	VII
Preface	....	VIII
Inhaltsübersicht	....	XI
Inhaltsverzeichnis	....	XIX
Abkürzungsverzeichnis	....	XLIX
Quellen	....	LVI

Teil A	Einführung / Introduction 1
Kapitel 1:	General business information on Switzerland 2
§ 1	Overview 2
§ 2	Political system 4
§ 3	Transportation and infrastructure 6
§ 4	Economic system 6
§ 5	Employment 7
§ 6	Financial services 9
§ 7	Forms of business organisation 10
Kapitel 2:	Einleitung 19
§ 1	Neues Recht 19
§ 2	Die Bedeutung einer sachgerechten Bilanz 20
§ 3	Die Revision 21

Teil B	Grundlagen des Rechnungswesens / Principles of accounting 23
Kapitel 1:	Buchführung 24
§ 1	Introduction and background 24
§ 2	Objectives, concepts and general principles of accounting 38
§ 3	Bookkeeping and preparation of financial statements 42
§ 4	Classification principles 46

XI

§ 5	Grundsätze der Ordnungsmässigkeit der Rechnungslegung	48
§ 6	Buchführung	51
§ 7	Grundsatz ordnungsmässiger Datenverarbeitung (GoD)	61
Kapitel 2:	Bilanz, Erfolgsrechnung und ergänzende Rechnungen	65
§ 1	Die Buchführungsvorschriften im Überblick	65
§ 2	Die Bilanz	68
§ 3	Die Erfolgsrechnung	108
§ 4	Der Anhang	118
§ 5	Kennzahlen	129
§ 6	Mittelflussrechnung	132
§ 7	Kostenrechnung	137
§ 8	Planungs- und Investitionsrechnung	139
Kapitel 3:	Individual company accounts in Switzerland	140
§ 1	Balance sheet	140
§ 2	Income statement	147
§ 3	Recognition criteria and valuation	154
§ 4	Special accounting areas	171
§ 5	Revaluation accounting	180
§ 6	Notes and additional statements	182
§ 7	Filing and publication of financial statements	197
§ 8	Sanctions	198
Teil C	**Revision / Auditing**	**201**
Kapitel 1:	Statutory auditing in Switzerland	202
§ 1	Audit requirements and appointment of auditors	202
§ 2	Qualifications of auditors	202
§ 3	Independence requirements including rotation	203
§ 4	Terms of mandate, resignation, etc. of auditors	213
§ 5	Duties of auditors	214

Inhaltsübersicht

§ 6	Standard form of audit report on the annual statutory accounts	215
§ 7	Audit report to the directors	219
§ 8	Education, certification and licensing	220
§ 9	Audits under the Swiss Merger Act (FusG)	221
§ 10	Over indebtedness and depositing the balance sheet	225
§ 11	Internal control and risk assessment	236
§ 12	Prohibition to reclaim contributions by shareholders (Art. 680 para. 2 CO)	241
§ 13	Swiss Audit Oversight Authority (RAG)	243
§ 14	Maintenance of audit secrecy	249
§ 15	Relief for small business (limited audit)	251
§ 16	Representation letters from Board and Management	255
Kapitel 2:	Grundlagen der Revision	257
§ 1	Gesetzliche Grundlagen	257
§ 2	Das neue Revisionsrecht im Überblick	257
§ 3	Aktienrechtliche Revision	265
§ 4	Gesellschaft mit beschränkter Haftung	266
§ 5	Genossenschaft	267
§ 6	Spezialerlasse	268
§ 7	Sonderprüfungen	268
§ 8	Prüfungsstandards PS (Soft law)	269
§ 9	Vereinsrechtliche Revision	269
§ 10	Stiftungsrechtliche Revision	273
§ 11	Vertragliche Revisionen	274
Kapitel 3:	Allgemeine Prüfungshandlungen	276
§ 1	Prüfungsverhalten	276
§ 2	Prüfungsmethoden	295
§ 3	Arbeitspapiere	299
§ 4	Gesetzliche Revision und interne Revision	299
§ 5	Ziele und Pflichten der Revisionsstelle	302

XIII

§ 6	Berichterstattung	305
§ 7	Standardbericht	324
§ 8	Abweichungen von der Standardberichterstattung	342
§ 9	Jahresbericht	354
§ 10	Umfassender Bericht (Erläuterungsbericht)	354
§ 11	Die Verantwortlichkeit der Revisionsstelle	356
Teil D	**Konsolidierung und Steuern / Consolidation and taxes**	**359**
Kapitel 1:	Consolidated financial statements in Switzerland	360
§ 1	Introduction and background	360
§ 2	Objectives, concepts and general principles	364
§ 3	Group concept and preparation of consolidated accounts	368
§ 4	Deferred taxation	372
Kapitel 2:	Von der Handelsbilanz zur Steuerbilanz	376
§ 1	Einleitung	376
§ 2	Formelle Vorschriften	376
§ 3	Materielle Vorschriften	377
Kapitel 3:	Tax summary about Switzerland	382
§ 1	Taxation of resident corporations	382
§ 2	Taxation of non-resident corporations	395
§ 3	Withholding tax	398
§ 4	Indirect taxes	401
Teil E	**Unternehmensform / Corporate form**	**405**
Kapitel 1:	Die Wahl der Gesellschaftsform für KMU unter besonderer Berücksichtigung der GmbH	406
§ 1	Einleitung	406
§ 2	Einzel- und Personengesellschaft und die GmbH	407
§ 3	Die jetzige Rechtswahl der GmbH	409
§ 4	Die Aktiengesellschaft und die GmbH	410
§ 5	Die GmbH im Konzern	412

	§ 6	Jährliche Arbeiten 412
Kapitel 2:		Die Unternehmensnachfolge (Exkurs) 415
	§ 1	Elemente der Unternehmensnachfolge 415
	§ 2	Familiäre Nachfolge 416
	§ 3	Ausserfamiliäre Nachfolge 420

Teil F   Rechtliche Aspekte / Legal aspects 425

Kapitel 1:		Neue Gesetzesbestimmungen und Erläuterungen 426
	§ 1	Das Recht der Aktiengesellschaft 426
	§ 2	Das Recht der Gesellschaft mit beschränkter Haftung 577
	§ 3	Das Recht der Genossenschaft 683
	§ 4	Änderung anderer Bestimmungen des Obligationenrechts 732
	§ 5	Das Recht des Vereins 752
	§ 6	Das Recht der Stiftung 766
	§ 7	Änderung bisherigen Rechts 779
	§ 8	Übergangsbestimmungen zum Gesetzesentwurf 01.082.... 798
	§ 9	Das Bundesgesetz über die Zulassung und Beaufsichtigung der Revisorinnen und Revisoren und damit einhergehende Änderungen bisherigen Rechts 811

Teil G   Anhänge und Unterlagen / Appendices and documents 885

Kapitel 1:		Bilanz, Erfolgsrechnung, Anhang, Vollständigkeitserklärung, Geschäftsbericht als Muster 886
	§ 1	Bilanz 886
	§ 2	Erfolgsrechnung 887
	§ 3	Anhang 888
	§ 4	Gewinnverwendungsvorschlag 890
	§ 5	Vollständigkeitserklärung 891
	§ 6	Rangrücktritt 892
	§ 7	Geschäftsbericht 895

§ 8	Die Generalversammlung	895
§ 9	Mittelflussrechnung	900
§ 10	Geschäfts- und Organisationsreglement	901
§ 11	Auftragsbestätigung	908
Kapitel 2:	Standardrevisionsunterlagen bei der AG für den Review	910
Kapitel 3:	Kurzfassung der Standardrevisionsunterlagen bei der AG für den Review	948
Kapitel 4:	Standardrevisionsunterlagen (Kurzfassung für Vereine etc.)	970
Kapitel 5:	Contents of Swiss Handbook on Auditing (HWP, MSA)	983
Kapitel 6:	Comparison of International Standards on Auditing (ISA) and Swiss Auditing Standards (SAS) / Schweizer Prüfungsstandards (PS) / Normes d'audit suisses (NAS)	988
Kapitel 7:	Financial reporting and audit oversight institutions in Switzerland	995
Kapitel 8:	Accounting glossary USA – UK – CH – D	997
Kapitel 9:	Accounting terms German - English	999
Kapitel 10:	Glossary to the Swiss Auditing Supervisory Act (RAG)	1010
Kapitel 11:	Syllabus of Swiss law test for foreign CPAs, CAs, WPs, RAs etc.	1013
§ 1	Proof of the required Knowledge of Swiss Law according to the Swiss Federal Auditor Oversight Act (AOA)	1013
§ 2	Oversight of Auditors - The legal position of the auditors in Switzerland	1013
§ 3	Business law, general part und special part (Contract law)	1014
§ 4	Company law	1014
§ 5	Social insurance law	1015
§ 6	VAT	1015
§ 7	Swiss and international corporate tax laws	1015
§ 8	What is special about Swiss audit reports	1015
§ 9	Special audits	1016

§ 10   Ordinary audit and limited statutory examination (ER)...1016
§ 11   Test..1016
Kapitel 12: Glossary Swiss Legal Terms (German-French-English)
– unofficial 1017
Sachregister 1078

Inhaltsverzeichnis

Vorwort VII
Preface VIII
Inhaltsübersicht XI
Inhaltsverzeichnis XIX
Abkürzungsverzeichnis XLIX
Quellen LVI

Teil A	**Einführung / Introduction** 1	
Kapitel 1:	General business information on Switzerland 2	
§ 1	Overview 2	
	I. Geography 2	
	II. Climate 2	
	III. History 2	
	IV. Languages 4	
	V. Population 4	
§ 2	Political system 4	
§ 3	Transportation and infrastructure 6	
§ 4	Economic system 6	
§ 5	Employment 7	
	I. Labour relations 7	
	II. Swiss Army 8	
	III. Salaries and benefits 8	
	IV. Foreign employees and expatriates 8	
§ 6	Financial services 9	
	I. General 9	
	II. Banks 9	
	III. Insurance companies 10	
§ 7	Forms of business organisation 10	

Inhaltsverzeichnis

		I.	Overview 10
		II.	Stock corporation (Ltd. / AG / SA) 12
		III.	Commercial register (HR) 14
		IV.	Other forms of business organisation 15
			1. Sole proprietorship 15
			2. General partnership (& Co.) 15
			3. Limited partnership (KG) 16
			4. Limited liability company (GmbH, Sàrl) 16
			5. Cooperative 16
			6. Ordinary partnership (Joint Venture) 17
			7. Foundation 17
			8. Branch 17
			9. Association 18
Kapitel 2:	Einleitung 19
§ 1	Neues Recht 19
§ 2	Die Bedeutung einer sachgerechten Bilanz 20
§ 3	Die Revision 21

Teil B   **Grundlagen des Rechnungswesens / Principles of accounting 23**

Kapitel 1:	Buchführung 24
§ 1	Introduction and background 24
	I.	Historical development of Swiss financial accounting 25
	II.	Accounting standards and standard setting 26
		1. The law relating to financial accounting (CO) 26
		2. Accounting and reporting recommendations (Swiss GAAP FER) 28
		3. Swiss Institute of Certified Accountants 31
		4. National securities exchange 33
	III.	Regulated industries 34

XX

		1.	Banking and insurance	34
		2.	Pension funds	36
		3.	Nationalised industries and governmental bodies	37
§ 2		Objectives, concepts and general principles of accounting		38
	I.	Principal users of accounts		38
	II.	Accounting concepts and standards		41
§ 3		Bookkeeping and preparation of financial statements		42
	I.	Bookkeeping		42
	II.	Uniform system of accounts		43
	III.	Duty to prepare an inventory		44
	IV.	Duty to prepare financial statements		44
§ 4		Classification principles		46
	I.	Completeness		46
	II.	Clarity and materiality of the financial statements		46
	III.	Consistency of presentation and valuation		46
	IV.	Prohibition of setting off assets and liabilities or expenses and income		47
§ 5		Grundsätze der Ordnungsmässigkeit der Rechnungslegung		48
	I.	Vollständigkeit		48
	II.	Klarheit		48
	III.	Vorsicht		49
		1.	Realisationsprinzip	49
		2.	Imparitätsprinzip	49
		3.	Niederstwertprinzip	50
	IV.	Fortführung (Going Concern)		50
	V.	Stetigkeit		50
	VI.	Bruttoprinzip (Verrechnungsverbot)		50
	VII.	Wesentlichkeit		51

§ 6	Buchführung	51
	I. Formelle Erfordernisse	51
	1. Hauptbuch	51
	2. Journal	51
	3. Eröffnungsbilanz	52
	4. Schlussbilanz	52
	a) Abschrift als unnötige Fehlerquelle	52
	b) Vorlage durch den Verwaltungsrat	52
	c) Einsicht in die Buchhaltung	53
	5. Erfolgsrechnung	53
	II. Belegablage	53
	1. Organisation der Belegablage	53
	2. Keine Buchung ohne Beleg	54
	III. Personelle Erfordernisse	55
	1. Bei der zu prüfenden Gesellschaft	55
	2. Bei der revidierenden Gesellschaft	56
	IV. Organisatorische Erfordernisse	57
	1. Das Organisationsreglement und das Geschäftsreglement	57
	a) Organisationsreglement	57
	b) Geschäftsreglement	58
	c) Formelle Voraussetzungen	58
	2. Keine statutarische Delegation	58
	3. Statutarische Delegation	60
	4. Schlussbemerkung	60
§ 7	Grundsatz ordnungsmässiger Datenverarbeitung (GOD)	61
	I. Einleitung	61
	II. Wichtige Aspekte	61
	III. Steuerliche Vorschriften	62
	IV. Schlussbemerkung	64

Kapitel 2:	Bilanz, Erfolgsrechnung und ergänzende Rechnungen		65
§ 1	Die Buchführungsvorschriften im Überblick		65
	I.	AG und GmbH	65
	II.	Die kaufmännische Buchführung	65
	III.	Die Bewertungsrichtlinien	66
		1. Grundlagen	66
		2. Die Bewertungsrichtlinien im Überblick	67
§ 2	Die Bilanz		68
	I.	Vorbemerkung	68
	II.	Der Kontenrahmen	70
	III.	Das Umlaufvermögen	71
		1. Flüssige Mittel und Wertschriften	71
		a) Kasse	71
		b) Postkonto	72
		c) Bankguthaben	72
		d) Übrige liquide Mittel	73
		e) Wertschriften kurzfristig realisierbar	73
		f) Verwaltung der liquiden Mittel	74
		2. Forderungen	76
		a) Debitoren (Forderungen aus Leistungen)	76
		b) Andere kurzfristige Forderungen	77
		aa) Gegenüber Dritten	77
		bb) Gegenüber Aktionären	77
		cc) Gegenüber staatlichen Stellen	78
		dd) Nicht einbezahltes Aktienkapital	78
		ee) Übrige Forderungen	79
		3. Vorräte und angefangene Arbeiten	80
		a) Warenlager	80
		b) Vorräte	81
		c) Angefangene Arbeiten	83

		4. Aktive Rechnungsabgrenzung 85

- IV. Das Anlagevermögen 86
    1. Abschreibungen 86
        a) Lineare Abschreibung 86
        b) Degressive Abschreibung 87
        c) Sofortabschreibungen 88
    2. Anlagespiegel 89
    3. Finanzanlagen 90
        a) Beteiligungspapiere 90
        b) Obligationen 90
        c) Langfristige Forderungen 91
    4. Mobile Sachanlagen 91
    5. Immobile Sachanlagen 92
        a) Immobilien 92
            aa) Sachenrecht 92
            bb) Obligationenrecht 92
            cc) Kaufvertrag 93
            dd) Kaufpreis 93
            ee) Marktsituation 94
            ff) Beschränkung des Grundstückerwerbs durch Ausländer 95
            gg) Prüfungshandlungen 95
        b) Einteilung der Immobilien 96
        c) Aufwertungen 96
    6. Immaterielle Sachanlagen 96
        a) Einleitung 96
        b) Voraussetzungen 97
    7. Aktivierter Aufwand und aktive Berichtigungsposten 98
- V. Das Fremdkapital 99
    1. Kurzfristiges Fremdkapital 99

a) Kreditoren (Verbindlichkeiten aus Lieferung und Leistung) 99
b) Anzahlungen von Kunden 99
c) Verbindlichkeiten gegenüber Aktionären 99
d) Bankverbindlichkeiten 100
e) Andere kurzfristige Verbindlichkeiten 101
f) Passive Rechnungsabgrenzung 101
g) Rückstellungen für absehbare Verpflichtungen 102
h) Rückstellungen für künftige Ersatzinvestitionen 102

2. Langfristiges Fremdkapital 103
   a) Langfristige Finanzverbindlichkeiten 103
   b) Andere langfristige Verbindlichkeiten 104
   c) Rückstellungen langfristig 104

VI. Das Eigenkapital 104
   1. Kapital 104
   2. Reserven 105
   3. Aufwertungsreserve 105
   4. Bilanzgewinn/Bilanzverlust (früher Gewinn- oder Verlustvortrag) 106
   5. Von der Steuerbilanz zur Handelsbilanz 107

§ 3 Die Erfolgsrechnung 108
   I. Vorbemerkung 108
   II. Der Aufwand 109
      1. Materialaufwand 109
      2. Handelswarenaufwand 109
      3. Aufwand für Dienstleistungen 109
      4. Personalaufwand 110
         a) Lohnaufwand 110
         b) Sozialversicherungsaufwand 110

				aa)	Lohnbuchhaltung	110
				bb)	Prüfungshandlung	111
				cc)	AHV/IV/EO/ALV	111
				dd)	UVG/BVG	112
		5.	Raumaufwand			112
		6.	Unterhalt und Reparaturen/Leasing			113
		7.	Fahrzeug- und Transportaufwand			113
		8.	Versicherungsaufwand			113
		9.	Energieaufwand			113
		10.	Verwaltungs- und Informatikaufwand			113
		11.	Werbeaufwand			114
		12.	Übriger Betriebsaufwand			114
		13.	Abschreibungen			114
		14.	Steuern			115
			a)	Ertragssteuer		115
			b)	Kapitalsteuer		115
			c)	Mehrwertsteuer		115
			d)	Eidgenössische Verrechnungssteuer		116
		15.	Ausserordentlicher und betriebsfremder Aufwand			117
	III.	Der Ertrag				117
		1.	Leistungsertrag			117
		2.	Bestandesänderungen (Vorräte)			118
		3.	Finanzerfolg			118
		4.	Liegenschaftsertrag			118
		5.	Ausserordentlicher und betriebsfremder Erfolg			118
§ 4	Der Anhang					118
	I.	Bürgschaften, Garantieverpflichtungen und Pfandbestellungen zugunsten Dritter (R)				119

	II.	Verpfändete oder abgetretene Aktiven sowie Aktiven unter Eigentumsvorbehalt zur Sicherstellung eigener Gesellschaftsverbindlichkeiten (R) 121
	III.	Nicht bilanzierte Leasingverbindlichkeiten (R) 122
	IV.	Brandversicherungswerte des Sachanlagevermögens (R) 123
	V.	Verbindlichkeiten gegenüber Vorsorgeeinrichtungen (R) 123
	VI.	Anleihensobligationen (NR) 124
	VII.	Wesentliche Beteiligungen (NR) 124
	VIII.	Auflösung stiller Reserven (R) 125
	IX.	Aufwertungen (R) 127
	X.	Eigene Aktien (NR) 127
	XI.	Kapitalerhöhungen (NR) 127
	XII.	Risikobeurteilung 128
	XIII.	Rücktritt der Revisionsstelle 128
	XIV.	Abweichungen von den Grundsätzen ordnungsgemässer Rechnungslegung (R) 128
§ 5		Kennzahlen 129
	I.	Eigenkapitalsquote 130
	II.	Anlageintensität 130
	III.	Goldene Bilanzregel 130
	IV.	Liquidität erster Stufe (Cash ratio/Zahlungsbereitschaft) 130
	V.	Liquidität zweiter Stufe (Quick ratio/Umsatzbedingte Liquidität) 131
	VI.	Liquidität dritter Stufe (Current ratio/Nettoumlaufvermögen (NUV) 131
	VII.	Bruttogewinn 131
	VIII.	Bruttogewinnmarge 131
	IX.	Umsatzrentabilität 132

Inhaltsverzeichnis

		X.	Kostenvergleich	132
§ 6	Mittelflussrechnung			132
§ 7	Kostenrechnung			137
	I.	Die Kostenartenrechnung		137
	II.	Kostenstellenrechnung		137
	III.	Kostenträgerrechnung		138
	IV.	Schlussbemerkung		138
§ 8	Planungs- und Investitionsrechnung			139
	I.	Kurzfristige Planungsrechnung		139
	II.	Langfristige Planung		139

Kapitel 3: Individual company accounts in Switzerland.................. 140

§ 1 Balance sheet... 140

    I. Minimum content.. 140

    II. Equity.. 142

        1. Share capital and participation capital............... 142

        2. Reserves.. 143

        3. Reserves for own shares 144

        4. Revaluation reserve 144

        5. Reserves provided for by the articles of incorporation... 145

        6. Reserves for employee welfare purposes........... 145

        7. Emergency reserves (Arbeitsbeschaffungsreserve) 145

        8. Relation between dividends and reserves 145

        9. Dividends, interest during construction (Bauzinsen)... 146

§ 2 Income statement 147

    I. Minimum content.. 147

    II. Net sales... 149

    III. Materials expenses.. 149

    IV. Personnel expenses 150

	V.	Depreciation	150
	VI.	Non-operating revenues and expenses	151
	VII.	Financial revenues and expenditure	151
	VIII.	Gains from the sale of fixed assets	152
	IX.	Extraordinary revenues and expenditure	152
	X.	Annual net income/loss	153
	XI.	Revenue items which need not be disclosed	153

§ 3 Recognition criteria and valuation 154
    I. Principles of the recognition of assets, liabilities and provisions 154
        1. Materiality 154
        2. Prudence (conservatism) and hidden reserves ... 154
        3. Continuance of the company's activities (going concern) 156
        4. Consistency of presentation and valuation 156
    II. Valuation principles 157
    III. Incorporation, capital increase and organisation costs 158
    IV. Fixed assets 158
        1. General principles 158
        2. Land 159
        3. Buildings 160
        4. Machinery, furniture and fixtures 160
        5. Intangible assets and merger goodwill 161
        6. Long-term loans 162
        7. Participations 162
    V. Current assets 163
        1. Inventories 163
        2. Long-term construction contracts 166
        3. Pre-paid expenses 167
        4. Cash 167

Inhaltsverzeichnis

		5.	Securities 168
		6.	Accounts receivable 169
		7.	Notes receivable 170
	VI.	Liabilities 170
	VII.	Provisions 171
§ 4	Special accounting areas 171
	I.	Lease accounting 171
	II.	Foreign currency translation 172
	III.	Research and development costs 174
	IV.	Government grants and subsidies 174
	V.	Financial instruments 175
	VI.	Deferred tax 175
	VII.	Factoring 176
	VIII.	Loans and receivables to shareholders and other related parties 176
	IX.	Trust agreements (fiduciary contracts) 176
	X.	Subsequent events 177
	XI	Pension accounting 178
	XII.	Prior period adjustments 180
§ 5	Revaluation accounting 180
	I.	Revaluation to avoid bankruptcy 180
	II.	Revaluation reserve 182
§ 6	Notes and additional statements 182
	I.	Notes on the accounts 182
		1.	Overview 182
		2.	Contingent liabilities 184
		3.	Pledged assets 185
		4.	Leasing obligations 186
		5.	Fire insurance value of fixed assets 186
		6.	Commitments to pension funds 186

		7.	Debentures 187
		8.	List of equity investments 187
		9.	Release of hidden reserves 188
		10.	Subject and amount of revaluations 190
		11.	Own shares 190
		12.	Authorised and contingent capital 192
		13.	Departures from certain generally accepted accounting principles 192
		14.	Disclosure of important shareholders 193
		15.	Consolidation and valuation principles in the consolidated accounts 193
		16.	Disclosure of management and board compensation in the notes 194
	II.	Asset movement schedule (*Anlagespiegel*) 196
	III.	Cash flow statement (*Geldflussrechnung*) 196
	IV.	Directors' report (*Geschäftsbericht*) 196
§ 7	Filing and publication of financial statements 197
§ 8	Sanctions 198

Teil C   Revision / Auditing 201

Kapitel 1: Statutory auditing in Switzerland 202

§ 1	Audit requirements and appointment of auditors 202
§ 2	Qualifications of auditors 202
§ 3	Independence requirements including rotation 203
	I.	New Company Law and Independence Rules effective 1 January 2008 205
	II.	Personal Independence 205
	III.	Employment Relationships 206
	IV.	Requirements for Auditors in-charge 206
	V.	Provision of Non-Audit Services 207
	VI.	Rotation requirements of the auditor in charge in an ordinary audit 208

XXXI

Inhaltsverzeichnis

VII.	When is this new legal requirement effective?	208
VIII.	Is this rotation also required for other forms of legal organisation in addition to corporations?	208
IX.	Are small corporations exempted from the rotation requirements?	208
X.	Are there special rules for quoted companies?	209
XI.	Will the Independence Rules of the Swiss Institute of 2001 be adapted?	209
XII.	Who is the „person that leads the audit"?	209
XIII.	How do we find out who the auditor in charge in the last years was?	210
XIV.	What are the rotation rules of the Swiss Stock Exchange (SIX)?	210
XV.	When can an auditor in charge which was rotated off resume the function again?	210
XVI.	Will the auditor in charge be registered in the Commercial Register?	210
XVII.	Will the ordinance of the Commercial Register be changed accordingly?	210
XVIII.	Are the rotation requirements also applicable for the auditor in charge who signs group audit opinions?	211
XIX.	What are the consequences of non-compliance?	211
XX.	What is the responsibility of the auditor in charge?	211
XXI.	Must the auditor in charge for the ordinary audit be qualified as admitted audit expert?	211
XXII.	Must the auditor in charge be an audit partner?	211
XXIII.	Must the title *dipl. Wirtschaftsprüfer* be mentioned under the name/signature and under the expression „Auditor in charge"?	212
XXIV.	Must the legal expression according to Art. 727b Sect. 2 CO „admitted audit expert" be	

			mentioned under the name of the auditor in charge in the audit report?...................................212
		XXV.	Are there similar or tougher rotation requirements abroad?..212
		XXVI.	What are the respective international IFAC rules?..212
		XXVII.	Who is responsible for the application of foreign rotation rules?...213
§ 4		Terms of mandate, resignation, etc. of auditors 213
§ 5		Duties of auditors 214
	I.	Individual company accounts..214
	II.	Consolidated financial statements...............................214
§ 6		Standard form of audit report on the annual statutory accounts..215
	I.	Individual company accounts..215
	II.	Consolidated financial statements...............................217
§ 7		Audit report to the directors 219
§ 8		Education, certification and licensing 220
§ 9		Audits under the Swiss Merger Act (FusG) 221
§ 10		Over indebtedness and depositing the balance sheet..........225
	I.	What does over indebtedness mean? 226
	II.	Why is over indebtedness a problem?.......................227
	III.	How does Swiss Company Law try to avoid over indebtedness? 227
		1.	Legal obligation to accounting in line with generally accepted accounting principles (Art. 662 to 679 CO) 228
		2.	Duty to prepare annual consolidated statements of account (Art. 663e CO) 229
		3.	Provisions for the board of directors in case of loss of capital (Art. 725 para. 1 CO):..................229
		4.	Provisions for the board of directors in case of over indebtedness (Art. 725 para. 2 CO): 229

		IV.	Are there two different kinds of over indebtedness?..230

- IV. Are there two different kinds of over indebtedness? 230
  1. Provisions for the auditors to convey a general assembly of the shareholders (Art. 729b para. 1 and Art. 699 para. 1 CO) or to notify the judge (Art. 729b para. 2 CO) 231
     - a) Calling a general meeting of shareholders by the auditors 231
     - b) Notification of the judge by the auditors 232
       - aa) Responsibility of the board of directors 233
       - bb) Responsibility of the auditors 233
- § 11 Internal control and risk assessment 236
  - I. Risk assessment 237
  - II. Existence of an internal control system (ICS) 238
- § 12 Prohibition to reclaim contributions by shareholders (Art. 680 para. 2 CO) 241
- § 13 Swiss Audit Oversight Authority (RAG) 243
- § 14 Maintenance of audit secrecy 249
- § 15 Relief for small business (limited audit) 251
- § 16 Representation letters from Board and Management 255

Kapitel 2: Grundlagen der Revision 257
- § 1 Gesetzliche Grundlagen 257
- § 2 Das neue Revisionsrecht im Überblick 257
  - I. Einleitung 257
  - II. Gründe zur Gesetzesrevision 258
  - III. Neue gesetzliche Regeln zur Revision 259
  - IV. Grundzüge der neuen gesetzlichen Regelungen 259
     - a) Opting-Out 260
     - b) Opting-Up/In 261
     - c) Opting-Down 261
  - V. Neue Aufgaben bei der ordentlichen Prüfung 261

		VI.	Unabhängigkeit	262
			a) Ordentliche Revision	262
			b) Eingeschränkte Revision	262
		VII.	Die Qualifikation des Revisors	262
		VIII.	Der Review (eingeschränkte Prüfung)	265
	§ 3	Aktienrechtliche Revision		265
	§ 4	Gesellschaft mit beschränkter Haftung		266
	§ 5	Genossenschaft		267
	§ 6	Spezialerlasse		268
	§ 7	Sonderprüfungen		268
	§ 8	Prüfungsstandards PS (Soft law)		269
	§ 9	Vereinsrechtliche Revision		269
		I.	Einleitung	269
		II.	Inhalt der Revision (ohne Erreichen der Grenzwerte)	270
		III.	Normalwortlaut des Vereinsrevisionsberichtes	271
			a) «An die Generalversammlung des Vereins . . .»	272
			b) «Als gesetzliche Revisionsstelle . . .»	272
			c) «. . . im Sinne der gesetzlichen Vorschriften»	272
		IV.	Ergänzungen	272
		V.	Zusammenfassung	273
	§ 10	Stiftungsrechtliche Revision		273
	§ 11	Vertragliche Revisionen		274
Kapitel 3:		Allgemeine Prüfungshandlungen		276
	§ 1	Prüfungsverhalten		276
		I.	Auftragsbestätigung	276
			1. Der gesetzliche Minimalauftrag	276
			2. Ergänzende Aufträge	279
		II.	Neumandate	279

	III.	Bestehende Mandate	281
	IV.	Verdeckte Gewinnausschüttung	282
		1. Begriff	282
		2. Verhalten	283
	V.	Beizug externer Berater	283
	VI.	Unabhängigkeit der Revisionsstelle	284
		1. Persönliche Unabhängigkeit	284
		2. Finanzielle Unabhängigkeit	285
		3. Strukturelle Unabhängigkeit	286
		4. Unabhängigkeit bei Revision und Buchführung	286
		5. Erwartungsunabhängige Haltung	287
	VII.	Rücktritt der Revisionsstelle	287
		1. Einfacher Rücktritt	287
		2. Problemhafter Rücktritt	288
	VIII.	Mögliche Überschuldung	288
		1. Die Feststellung	288
		2. Das Entstehen der Überschuldung (auch als Exkurs)	290
		3. Das Problem der faktisch «unbeschränkten Haftung» des Hauptaktionärs	293
		4. Der Rücktritt der Revisionsstelle	294
	IX.	Der «zugelassene Revisionsexperte»	295
§ 2	Prüfungsmethoden		295
	I.	Prüfungsweg	295
	II.	Prüfungsumfang	295
	III.	Direkte und indirekte Prüfung	296
	IV.	Prüfungstechniken	296
		1. Systematische Prüfungen	296
		2. Logische Prüfung	297
	V.	Überwachung des Mandates	298

§ 3	Arbeitspapiere		299
§ 4	Gesetzliche Revision und interne Revision		299
§ 5	Ziele und Pflichten der Revisionsstelle		302
	I. Ziele		302
	II. Pflichten		303
		1. Prüfungspflichten	303
		2. Meldepflichten	303
		3. Handlungspflichten	304
		4. Unterlassungspflichten	304
	III. Aktienbuch		304
§ 6	Berichterstattung		305
	I. Inhalt		305
		1. Standardbericht Treuhand-Kammer	306
		a) Bericht für die ordentliche Revision nach PS 700	306
		b) Bericht für die Review (prüferische Durchsicht) nach PS 910	307
		c) Uneingeschränkter Bericht über die prüferische Durchsicht nach ISA («International Standards on Auditing»)	308
		2. Standardbericht Treuhänderverband / B. Madörin	309
		3. Gesetzliche Berichterstattung der Revisionsstelle	309
	II. Der Revisionsbericht		311
		1. Ordentliche Revision	313
		2. Review	315
	III. «Grünes Licht»		317
	IV. «Oranges Licht»		318
	V. «Rotes Licht»		319
		1. Kapitalverlust	319
		2. Aufschub des Konkurses	321

	VI.	«Alarm» 321
§ 7		Standardbericht 324
	I.	Standardbericht für Review (Deutsch/Plural) 324
	II.	Standardbericht für Review (Deutsch/Singular) 325
	III.	Standardbericht für Review (Französisch/Plural) 326
	IV.	Standardbericht für Review (Französisch/Singular) 327
	V.	Standardbericht für Review (Italienisch/Plural) 328
	VI.	Standardbericht für Review (Italienisch/Singular) 329
	VII.	Standardbericht für Review für Stiftungen 329
	VIII.	Standardbericht für Vereine 331
		1. Kaufmännische Buchführung 331
		a) Ordentliche Revision 331
		b) Review 332
		2. Ohne Kaufmännische Buchführung 334
		a) Ordentliche Revision 334
		b) Review 335
	IX.	Standardbericht für Subventionierte (Kanton BS), Fassung 1998 336
	X.	Standardbericht für Genossenschaften 337
		1. Ordentliche Revision 338
		2. Review 338
	XI.	Standardbericht für GmbH 339
		1. Ordentliche Revision 339
		2. Review 340
	XII.	Standardbericht für Kollektivgesellschaften 340
		1. Ordentliche Revision 341
		2. Review 341
§ 8		Abweichungen von der Standardberichterstattung 342
	I.	Einführung 342

II.	Vorbehalte, Einschränkungen, Hinweise, Meldungen etc.		343
	1.	Vorbehalte	343
		a) Vorbehaltsfeindlicher Revisionsbericht	343
		b) Beispiel 1	343
		c) Beispiel 2	344
		d) Beispiel 3	345
		e) Der Anhang als Information	345
	2.	Einschränkungen	346
	3.	Hinweise	346
	4.	Meldung	347
	5.	Bemerkungen zur Geschäftslage	347
III.	Abweichungen (Einschränkungen)		348
	1.	Rechnungslegung	348
		a) Aussagekraft der Jahresrechnung	348
		b) Vollständigkeit	348
		c) Klarheit	348
		d) Bilanzvorsicht	349
		e) Fortführungswerte	349
		f) Verrechnungsverbot	349
		g) Stetigkeit	349
		h) Wesentlichkeit	349
	2.	Gesetzesverstösse	350
	3.	Mangelndes Handeln des Verwaltungsrates (Hinweis)	350
		a) Verlust von mehr als der Hälfte des Aktienkapitals und der Reserven	350
		b) Verlust des Eigenkapitals (Überschuldung)	350
	4.	Hinweise	350
		a) Formelle Überschuldung	350

			b) Dividende	351
			c) Rangrücktritt	351
		5.	Konklusion	351
		6.	Empfehlung der Revisionsstelle	352
		7.	Überschuldungsanzeige	352
	IV.	Problemhaftes Abweichen vom Standardbericht		352
§ 9	Jahresbericht			354
§ 10	Umfassender Bericht (Erläuterungsbericht)			354
	I.	Pflicht bei der ordentlichen Revision		354
	II.	Keine Erläuterungspflicht		355
§ 11	Die Verantwortlichkeit der Revisionsstelle			356

Teil D **Konsolidierung und Steuern / Consolidation and taxes** **359**

Kapitel 1: Consolidated financial statements in Switzerland 360

§ 1 Introduction and background 360

    I. Introduction 360

    II. Effects on companies 361

    III. Legislation and standards 361

        1. Duty to consolidate (Art. 663e para. 1 CO) 362

        2. Intermediate holding companies (Art. 663f para. 2 CO) 362

        3. Preparation of consolidated accounts (Art. 663g para. 3 CO) 363

        4. Publication of consolidated accounts (Art. 697h CO) 363

§ 2 Objectives, concepts and general principles 364

    I. Relevant objectives 364

    II. Underlying concepts and general principles 366

        1. General requirements 366

        2. Principles of consolidation 367

§ 3 Group concept and preparation of consolidated accounts .. 368

		I.	Consolidated accounts 368
		1. Duty to consolidate 368
		2. Preparation of consolidated accounts 370
		II.	Sub-consolidated accounts 371
	§ 4	Deferred taxation 372
		I.	Recommendation for deferred taxation 372
		II.	Temporary and permanent differences 373
		III.	Liability method 373
		IV.	Tax jurisdiction 374
		V.	Tax rate 375
Kapitel 2:	Von der Handelsbilanz zur Steuerbilanz 376
	§ 1	Einleitung 376
	§ 2	Formelle Vorschriften 376
	§ 3	Materielle Vorschriften 377
		I.	Die Abgrenzung zwischen Geschäfts- und Privatvermögen 377
		II.	Aktiven 378
		III.	Passiven 378
		IV.	Erfolgsrechnung 378
		V.	Konzernabschlüsse 379
		VI.	Vorschriften des Bundes 379
		1. Verdeckte Gewinnausschüttung 379
		2. Die Missbrauchsbestimmungen des Doppelbesteuerungsrechts 380
		3. Mantelhandel 380
Kapitel 3:	Tax summary about Switzerland 382
	§ 1	Taxation of resident corporations 382
		I.	Swiss tax liability 382
		II.	Determination of taxable income 382
		1. Financial statement income 382
		2. Gross income 383

XLI

			a)	Worldwide income 383
			b)	Capital gains 383
			c)	Exchange gains 383
			d)	Transactions with related parties 383
		3.	Deductions from gross income 384	
			a)	General business expense 384
			b)	Interest expense 384
			c)	Management and service fees paid to a foreign parent 385
			d)	Tax expense 385
			e)	Exchange losses 385
			f)	Depreciation 386
			g)	Inventory 386
			h)	Provision for bad and doubtful debts 386
			i)	Loss carry-forwards 387
			j)	Exclusions from taxable income 387
			k)	Holding company income 387
			l)	Foreign permanent establishments (foreign branches) and foreign real property profits 388
			m)	Contributions from shareholders 388
	III.	Tax-privileged corporations 388		
		1.	Holding companies 388	
		2.	Industrial or commercial holding companies 388	
		3.	Domiciliary companies 389	
		4.	Mixed companies (Swiss based) 389	
		5.	Service and international headquarters companies 389	
		6.	Tax rates applicable to tax privileged entities 390	
	IV.	Treaty benefits for Swiss resident corporations 390		
		1.	Eligibility 390	

		2.	Benefits	391
		3.	Anti-Abuse Provisions	391
	V.	Computation of corporate taxes		392
		1.	Income tax	392
		2.	Credits against income tax payable	392
	VI.	Assessment of corporate taxes		393
		1.	Federal tax	393
		2.	Cantonal taxes	393
	VII.	Withholding taxes on dividend distributions of Swiss corporations		393
	VIII.	Filing of tax returns, assessment of tax, tax litigation		394
		1.	Filing of tax returns	394
		2.	Assessment of tax	394
		3.	Payment of tax	394
		4.	Tax litigation	394
	IX.	Corporate reorganisations (mergers, acquisitions, spin-offs)		395
§ 2	Taxation of non-resident corporations			395
	I.	Liability to Swiss tax		395
		1.	Investment income from Swiss sources	396
		2.	Permanent establishment income	396
		3.	Swiss partnership income	396
		4.	Swiss real estate income	397
	II.	Determination of taxable income and capital of Swiss permanent establishments		397
	III.	Remittance of profits		397
§ 3	Withholding tax			398
	I.	Income subject to withholding tax		398
		1.	Interest	398
		2.	Profit Distributions	399

		II.	Exemptions from withholding tax 399
			1. Foreign source income 399
			2. Loan interest 399
			3. Interest on interbank loans between Swiss or foreign banks 399
			4. Interest on fiduciary deposits 400
			5. Branch profits 400
			6. Corporate restructuring 400
			7. Small amounts of income 400
			8. Interest on savings held by recognised pension funds 400
		III.	Withholding and reimbursement of tax 400
			1. Relief for Swiss resident taxpayers 401
			2. Relief for non-residents 401
	§ 4	Indirect taxes 401	
		I.	Value added tax (VAT) 401
		II.	Stamp duties 402
			1. Stamp duty on issues 402
			a) Issues or increases in capital stock 402
			b) Issues of bonds and money market paper 402
			2. Stamp duty on securities transactions 403
			a) Registered securities dealers 403
		III.	Real estate taxes 403

Teil E		**Unternehmensform / Corporate form** **405**
Kapitel 1:		Die Wahl der Gesellschaftsform für KMU unter besonderer Berücksichtigung der GmbH 406
	§ 1	Einleitung 406
	§ 2	Einzel- und Personengesellschaft und die GmbH 407
	§ 3	Die jetzige Rechtswahl der GmbH 409
	§ 4	Die Aktiengesellschaft und die GmbH 410

	I.	Gesetzliche Vinkulierung..410
	II.	Übrige Aspekte 411
§ 5	Die GmbH im Konzern 412
§ 6	Jährliche Arbeiten 412
	I.	Geschäftsabschluss 413
	II.	Steuererklärung 413
	III.	Gesellschafterversammlung 413
	IV.	Bankengerechtes Verhalten..414
Kapitel 2:	Die Unternehmensnachfolge (Exkurs)..............................415
§ 1	Elemente der Unternehmensnachfolge..............................415
	I.	Organisatorische Massnahmen 415
	II.	Steuerliche Konsequenzen 415
	III.	Rechtliche Aspekte 416
§ 2	Familiäre Nachfolge..416
	I.	Aktiengesellschaft..416
		1. Der Aktionärbindungsvertrag 416
		2. Der Ehe- und Erbvertrag..................................417
		3. Andere Verträge und Grundlagen....................417
	II.	Gesellschaft mit beschränkter Haftung 418
	III.	Einzelfirma..418
	IV.	Kollektiv- und Kommanditgesellschaft 419
	V.	Stiftung..419
§ 3	Ausserfamiliäre Nachfolge..420
	I.	Aktiengesellschaft..420
	II.	Gesellschaft mit beschränkter Haftung 421
	III.	Einzelfirma..422
	IV.	Kollektiv- und Kommanditgesellschaft 422
	V.	Stiftung..423

Teil F   **Rechtliche Aspekte / Legal aspects** **425**

Kapitel 1:   Neue Gesetzesbestimmungen und Erläuterungen 426

XLV

§ 1	Das Recht der Aktiengesellschaft	426
§ 2	Das Recht der Gesellschaft mit beschränkter Haftung	577
§ 3	Das Recht der Genossenschaft	683
§ 4	Änderung anderer Bestimmungen des Obligationenrechts	732
§ 5	Das Recht des Vereins	752
§ 6	Das Recht der Stiftung	766
§ 7	Änderung bisherigen Rechts	779
	I. Zivilgesetzbuch	779
	II. Schlusstitel: Anwendungs- und Einführungsbestimmungen	782
	III. Bundesgesetz über Schuldbetreibung und Konkurs	783
	IV. Bundesgesetz über Fusion, Spaltung, Umwandlung und Vermögensübertragung	784
	V. Bundesgesetz über das Internationale Privatrecht	790
	VI. Bundesgesetz über die Stempelabgaben	792
	VII. Bundesgesetz über die Verrechnungssteuer	795
	VIII. Bundesgesetz über die direkte Bundessteuer	796
	IX. Bundesgesetz über die Harmonisierung der direkten Steuern der Kantone und Gemeinden	797
§ 8	Übergangsbestimmungen zum Gesetzesentwurf 01.082	798
§ 9	Das Bundesgesetz über die Zulassung und Beaufsichtigung der Revisorinnen und Revisoren und damit einhergehende Änderungen bisherigen Rechts	811
	I. Das Bundesgesetz über die Zulassung und Beaufsichtigung der Revisorinnen und Revisoren	811
	II. Änderungen bisherigen Rechts	881
	1. Bundesgesetz über die Eidgenössische Finanzkontrolle	881
	2. Börsengesetz	882
Teil G	**Anhänge und Unterlagen / Appendices and documents**	**885**

Kapitel 1:	Bilanz, Erfolgsrechnung, Anhang, Vollständigkeitserklärung, Geschäftsbericht als Muster	886
§ 1	Bilanz	886
§ 2	Erfolgsrechnung	887
§ 3	Anhang	888
§ 4	Gewinnverwendungsvorschlag	890
§ 5	Vollständigkeitserklärung	891
§ 6	Rangrücktritt	892
§ 7	Geschäftsbericht	895
§ 8	Die Generalversammlung	895
§ 9	Mittelflussrechnung	900
§ 10	Geschäfts- und Organisationsreglement	901
§ 11	Auftragsbestätigung	908
Kapitel 2:	Standardrevisionsunterlagen bei der AG für den Review	910
Kapitel 3:	Kurzfassung der Standardrevisionsunterlagen bei der AG für den Review	948
Kapitel 4:	Standardrevisionsunterlagen (Kurzfassung für Vereine etc.)	970
Kapitel 5:	Contents of Swiss Handbook on Auditing (HWP, MSA)	983
Kapitel 6:	Comparison of International Standards on Auditing (ISA) and Swiss Auditing Standards (SAS) / Schweizer Prüfungsstandards (PS) / Normes d'audit suisses (NAS)	988
Kapitel 7:	Financial reporting and audit oversight institutions in Switzerland	995
Kapitel 8:	Accounting glossary USA – UK – CH – D	997
Kapitel 9:	Accounting terms German - English	999
Kapitel 10:	Glossary to the Swiss Auditing Supervisory Act (RAG)	1010
Kapitel 11:	Syllabus of Swiss law test for foreign CPAs, CAs, WPs, RAs etc.	1013
§ 1	Proof of the required Knowledge of Swiss Law according to the Swiss Federal Auditor Oversight Act (AOA)	1013

Inhaltsverzeichnis

§ 2	Oversight of Auditors - The legal position of the auditors in Switzerland	1013
§ 3	Business law, general part und special part (Contract law)	1014
§ 4	Company law	1014
§ 5	Social insurance law	1015
§ 6	VAT	1015
§ 7	Swiss and international corporate tax laws	1015
§ 8	What is special about Swiss audit reports	1015
§ 9	Special audits	1016
§ 10	Ordinary audit and limited statutory examination (ER)	1016
§ 11	Test	1016
Kapitel 12:	Glossary Swiss Legal Terms (German-French-English) – unofficial	1017
Sachregister		1078

Abkürzungsverzeichnis

a/o	ausserordentlich
Abs.	Absatz
AG	Aktiengesellschaft *Stock corporation*
AHV	Alters- und Hinterlassenenversicherung
ALV	Arbeitslosenversicherung
ARR	Accounting and Reporting Recommendations (FER, Switzerland)
AOA	Auditor Oversight Act *Revisionsaufsichtsgesetz*
aOR	Altes Obligationenrecht
Art.	Artikel
AV	Anlagevermögen
BAB	Betriebsabrechnungsbogen
BankG	Bundesgesetz vom 8. November 1934 über die Banken und Sparkassen (Bankengesetz, SR 952.0) *Federal Banking Act*
BankV	Verordnung zum Bankengesetz (Banking Ordinance)
BBl	Bundesblatt
BEHG	Bundesgesetz vom 24. März 1995 über die Börsen und den Effektenhandel (Börsengesetz, SR 954.1) *Swiss Stock Exchange Law (SESTA)*
BG	Bundesgesetz
BGE	Bundesgerichtsentscheid *Decisions of the Federal Supreme Court*
BiRiLiG	Bilanzrichtlinien-Gesetz *Accounting Directives Act in Germany*

Abkürzungsverzeichnis

BS	Kanton Basel-Stadt
BS	Balance Sheet *Bilanz*
BV	Bundesverfassung der Schweizerischen Eidgenossenschaft vom 18. April 1999 (SR 101)
BVG	Bundesgesetz vom 25. Juni 1982 über berufliche Alters-, Hinterlassenen- und Invalidenvorsorge (Berufsvorsorgegesetz, SR 831.40) *Pension Law in Switzerland*
CC	Swiss Civil Code *Zivilgesetzbuch*
CEO	Chief Executive Officer
CH	Confoederatio Helvetica
CHF	Schweizer Franken (Fr.) *Swiss Francs*
CO	Swiss Commerical Code, Code of Obligations *Obligationenrecht*
COGS	Cost of Goods Sold
Corp.	Corporation *Aktiengesellschaft*
CPA	Certified Public Accountant (USA)
E	Entwurf
EBIT	Earnings Before Interests and Taxes *Betriebsergebnis*
EBK	Eidgenössische Bankenkommission *Swiss Federal Banking Commission*
ED	Exposure Draft (FASB) *Entwurf zur Vernehmlassung*

L

Abkürzungsverzeichnis

EDV	Elektronische Datenverarbeitung
EFK	Eidgenössische Finanzkontrolle
EO	Erwerbsersatzordnung
etc.	et cetera
EU	Europäische Union *European Union*
EURL	Gesellschaftsrechtliche Richtlinien der EU *EU Directives*
EWR	Europäischer Wirtschaftsraum, *European Economic Area (EEA)*
f.	folgende (Seite)
ff.	fortfolgende (Seiten)
FAOA	Federal Audit Oversight Authority *Revisionsaufsichtsbehörde*
FASB	Financial Accounting Standards Board
FCF	Free Cash Flow
FCPA	Foreign Corrupt Practices Act (USA)
FDCB	Federal Act on Debt Collection and Bankruptcy *Schuldbetreibungs- und Konkursgesetz (SchKG)*
FER	Fachempfehlungen zur Rechnungslegung *Swiss Accounting Standards*
FIFO	First in first out
FINMA	Finanzmarktaufsichtsbehörde
FusG	Bundesgesetz vom 3. Oktober 2003 über Fusion, Spaltung, Umwandlung und Vermögensübertragung (Fusionsgesetz, SR 221.301)
GAAP	Generally Accepted Accounting Principles
GAAS	Generally Accepted Auditing Standards

LI

Abkürzungsverzeichnis

GmbH	Gesellschaft mit beschränkter Haftung *Limited liability company*
GoD	Grundsatz ordnungsmässiger Datenverarbeitung
GP	Going Public (Initial Public Offering) *Börseneinführung*
GV	Generalversammlung *General Meeting of Shareholders*
HB I	Handelsbilanz I, gesetzlicher Abschluss *statutory financial statements*
HB II	Handelsbilanz II für Konsolidierungszwecke *Balance Sheet for consolidation purposes (true and fair)*
HR	Handelsregister *Swiss Commercial Register*
HRB	Handbuch zur Revision und Buchhaltung
HRegV	Handelsregisterverordnung vom 7. Juni 1937 (SR 221.411)
HWP	Schweizer Handbuch der Wirtschaftsprüfung *Swiss Auditing Handbook*
IASB	International Accounting Standards Board
i.d.R.	in der Regel
IFRS	International Financial Reporting Standards
IKS	Internes Kontrollsystem
Inc.	Incorporated (USA) *Aktiengesellschaft*
IPO	Initial Public Offering *Börseneinführung*
IPRG	Bundesgesetz vom 18. Dezember 1987 über das internationale Privatrecht (SR 291)
IRSG	Bundesgesetz vom 20. März 1981 über internationale Rechtshilfe in Strafsachen (Rechtshilfegesetz, SR 351.1)

IS	Income Statement *Erfolgsrechnung*
ISA	International Standards on Auditing (Internationale Prüfungsstandards)
IV	Invalidenversicherung
KL	Konzernleitung *top management*
km	Kilometer
KMU	Kleine und mittlere Unternehmen
M&A	Mergers & Acquisitions
NR	Nationalrat
NSA	Swiss Auditing Standards *Normes d'audit suisses*
NYSE	New York Stock Exchange
OR	Bundesgesetz vom 30. März 1911 betreffend Ergänzung des Schweizerischen Zivilgesetzbuches (5. Teil: Obligationenrecht, SR 220)
p.a.	per annum (pro Jahr)
p.m.	per mense (pro Monat)
p.m.	pro memoria
POC	Percentage of Completion-Methode for long-term contracts *langfristige Fertigungsaufträge*
PP&E	Property, Plant and Equipment *Sachanlagen*
PS	Prüfungsstandard

Abkürzungsverzeichnis

PS	Partizipationsschein *Non voting participation certificate*
PVE	*Personalvorsorgeeinrichtung* Pension schemes
RAG	Bundesgesetz über die Zulassung und Beaufsichtigung der Revisorinnen und Revisoren (Revisionsaufsichtsgesetz, SR 221.302)
R&D	Research and Development *Forschungs- und Entwicklungskosten*
RHB	Revisionshandbuch (RHB 1992)
RLG	Rechnungslegungsgesetz
RVOG	Regierungs- und Verwaltungsorganisationsgesetz vom 21. März 1997 (SR 172.010)
SA	Société Anonyme *stock corporation, AG*
SARR	Swiss Accounting and Reporting Recommendations (FER)
SAS	Swiss Auditing Standards (PS)
SchKG	Schuldbetreibungs- und Konkursgesetz
SESTA	Federal Act on Stock Exchanges and Securities Trading (BEHG)
SFBC	Swiss Federal Banking Commission *Bankenkommission* (EBK)
SHAB	Schweizerisches Handelsamtsblatt *Swiss Trade Journal*
SPC	Swiss Penal Code *Schweizerisches Strafgesetzbuch (StGB)*
SR	Systematische Sammlung des Bundesrechts

StGB	Schweizerisches Strafgesetzbuch vom 21. Dezember 1937 (SR 311.0) *Swiss Penal Code*
SUVA	Schweizerische Unfallversicherungsanstalt
SIX	Swiss Stock Exchange
US GAAP	United States Generally Accepted Accounting Principles
UV	Umlaufvermögen
UVG	Bundesgesetz vom 20. März 1981 über die Unfallversicherung (Unfallversicherungsgesetz, SR 832.20)
VE	Vorentwurf
VR	Verwaltungsrat *Swiss Board of Directors*
VStrR	Bundesgesetz vom 22. März 1974 über das Verwaltungsstrafrecht (Verwaltungsstrafrechtsgesetz, SR 313.0)
WIR	Wirtschaftsring Genossenschaft
WP	Wirtschaftsprüfer *Certified Public Accountant in Germany*
dipl. WP	diplomierter Wirtschaftsprüfer *Swiss Federally Certified Accountant*
ZGB	Schweizerisches Zivilgesetzbuch vom 10. Dezember 1907 (SR 210)
Ziff.	Ziffer

LV

Quellen

Literatur

BERTSCHINGER PETER, Switzerland - Individual and Consolidated Accounts, in: TRANSACC - Transnational Accounting, Editors Prof. Dr. Dieter Ordelheide und KPMG Deutsche Treuhand-Gesellschaft, Düsseldorf, Palgrave, second edition 2001.

BERTSCHINGER PETER und ZENHÄUSERN MARKUS, Konzernabschlüsse verstehen - eine Darstellung für die Praxis, Verlag des Schweizerischen Kaufmännischen Verbandes, Teilauflage als Band 137 der Schriftenreihe der Treuhand-Kammer, Zurich 1996.

BÖCKLI PETER, Neuerungen im Verantwortlichkeitsrecht der Revisionsstelle, Zürich 1994.

BÖCKLI PETER, Revisionsstelle und Abschlussprüfung nach neuem Recht, Schriften zum Aktienrecht, Verlag Schulthess Juristische Medien AG, Zürich 2007.

BÖCKLI PETER, Schweizer Aktienrecht, Zürich, 3. Auflage, 2004.

BOEMLE MAX, Der Jahresabschluss, Zürich 1996.

BOEMLE MAX ET AL., Geld-, Bank- und Finanzmarkt-Lexikon der Schweiz, Zurich 2002.

BOEMLE MAX, Unternehmungsfinanzierung, 13 Auflage, Zürich 2002.

BRÜHLMANN A., Die Beutung der stillen Reserven nach dem revidierten Aktienrecht, Zürich 1996.

DESSEMONTET FRANÇOIS (Herausgeber), Introduction to Swiss Law, Kluwer / Schulthess, Zurich 2004.

FORSTMOSER PETER, Die Verantwortlichkeit des Revisors nach Aktienrecht, Zürich 1997.

HELBING CARL, Bilanz- und Erfolgsanalyse, Bern 1997.

HUTTER NORBERT, Ordner für kaufmännische Lehrlinge, herausgegeben vom Schweizerischen Treuhänderverband, Sektion Zürich (mit der freundlichen Genehmigung, einige Passagen wiederzugeben).

KÄLIN CHRISTIAN H., Switzerland Business & Investment Handbook, Orell Füssli Verlag, Zurich 2005.

LANGENSCHEIDT ALPMANN, Fachwörterbuch Kompakt Recht Englisch – Deutsch und Deutsch – Englisch, mit Einführung in das englische, amerikanische und deutsche Rechtssystem in beiden Sprachen, München 2006.

MADÖRIN BERNHARD, Buchprüfer werden staatlich geprüft, in: NZZ am Sonntag, Statements zum neuen Revisionsgesetz, 07. 12. 2003.

MADÖRIN BERNHARD, Das neue Revisionsrecht im Überblick, in: Jusletter vom 27. 06. 2005.

MADÖRIN BERNHARD, Der neue Revisionsbericht, in: NZZ Neue Zürcher Zeitung, Nr. 112 vom 17.05.1997.

MADÖRIN BERNHARD, Der Verein: Organisation und Recht, aktuelle Frage der Haftung, in: Der Treuhandexperte VI 2001, S. 392 ff., publiziert auf der Internetseite http://www.trex.ch.

MADÖRIN BERNHARD, Der Revisionsbericht der Revisionsstelle (Kommentar und Alternativen zur Revisionskammer), in: Der Treuhandexperte, Sondernummer 1996, S. 14 ff. und in I/1997, S. 12 ff.

MADÖRIN BERNHARD, Die direkten Steuern im gesamten System der Abgaben, in: Steuerbeilage Basler Zeitung 04. 03. 1994.

MADÖRIN BERNHARD, Die Kopiersteuer; Eine Erweiterung der Steuerlandschaft, in: Der Treuhandexperte II 1997, S. 90.

MADÖRIN BERNHARD, Die Revision eines Vereins, in: Der Treuhandexperte IV/1996, S. 154 ff..

MADÖRIN BERNHARD, Die steuerlich privilegierte Behandlung ausländisch beherrschter Gesellschaften in der Schweiz, in: IStR Internationales Steuerrecht Heft 14/1997, C.H. Beck Verlag, München und Frankfurt a. M. 1997.

MADÖRIN BERNHARD, Die steuerliche Behandlung grenzüberschreitender Gewinnausschüttungen unter besonderer Berücksichtigung des EG-Steuerrechts, Seminar des schweizerischen Treuhänderverbandes (Jahrestagung), Biel 29. 11. 1991, auszugsweise publiziert in: Der Treuhandexperte II/1992, S. 10 ff.

Quellen

MADÖRIN BERNHARD, Die steuerliche Behandlung grenzüberschreitender Gewinnausschüttungen, Internationales Treuhandseminar (Ordre des Experts comptable Steuerberaterkammer Südbaden, Schweiz. Treuhänderverband Nordwest-Schweiz), Strassburg 12.11.1991.

MADÖRIN BERNHARD, Die steuerliche privilegierte Behandlung ausländisch beherrschter Gesellschaften, Euromeeting, European Consultants Unit, Paris 30. 10. 1993.

MADÖRIN BERNHARD, Eine AG muss kein Vorteil sein, in: Steuerbeilage Basler Zeitung vom 26. 02. 1993.

MADÖRIN BERNHARD, Einen Verein gründen: Organisation und Rechte und Pflichten, in: Basler Zeitung, Ratstübli 16. 09. 1995, ausführlich publiziert in: Der Treuhandexperte II/1996, S. 54 ff..

MADÖRIN BERNHARD, Falsch bemessene Steuerfaktoren sind in Basel kaum erkennbar, in: Steuerbeilage Basler Zeitung vom 28. 02. 1992.

MADÖRIN BERNHARD, Freehold property in Switzerland, in: Business guide to Switzerland 18. 06. 1996.

MADÖRIN BERNHARD, Gesellschafts-, Steuer- und Sozialrecht, Internationales Treuhandseminar (Ordre des Experts comptable; Steuerberaterkammer Südbaden, Schweiz. Treuhänderverband Nordwest-Schweiz), Bad Krozingen 18. 05. 1995.

MADÖRIN BERNHARD Grenzüberschreitende Gewinnausschüttungen, in: Steuerbeilage Basler Zeitung vom 28. 02. 1992.

MADÖRIN BERNHARD, Handbuch zum Heimkontenrahmen BS, Herausgegeben vom Erziehungsdepartement BS, Ressort Dienste 1998.

MADÖRIN BERNHARD, Handbuch zur Revision und Buchhaltung (HRB), Helbing & Lichtenhahn Verlag, Basel 1998.

MADÖRIN BERNHARD, Ist eine Vorauszahlung sinnvoll?, in: Basler Zeitung, Ratstübli 21. 11. 1992, ausführlich publiziert in: Der Treuhandexperte, I/1993, S. 25 ff.

MADÖRIN BERNHARD, Kann man mit Schulden Steuern sparen?, in: Basler Zeitung, Ratstübli 12. 08. 1995.

MADÖRIN BERNHARD, Konkurse nehmen in der Schweiz zu, in: Basler Zeitung, Ratstübli 18. 11. 1995.

MADÖRIN BERNHARD, L'association: son organisation, les dispositions légales qui la concernent et la question de la responsabilité, plus actuelle que jamais, in: Der Treuhandexperte VI 2001, S. 396 ff.

MADÖRIN BERNHARD, L' Organe de révision, in: Der Treuhandexperte II 1997, S. 70.

MADÖRIN BERNHARD, Noch gibt es keine Panoramasteuer, in: Steuerbeilage Basler Zeitung, 28. 02. 1992.

MADÖRIN BERNHARD, Noch zahlreiche Nachteile gegenüber dem Ausland, in: Basler Zeitung, Stempelsteuer, 15. 09. 1992.

MADÖRIN BERNHARD, Standardrevisionsunterlagen, Helbing & Lichtenhahn Verlag, Basel 1998.

MADÖRIN BERNHARD, Steuerhinterziehung, in: Steuerbeilage Basler-Zeitung und andere Beiträge, 12. 02. 1991.

MADÖRIN BERNHARD, Stiftung mit wirtschaftlichem Zweck, in: Der Treuhandexperte IV/1995, S. 159 ff.

MADÖRIN BERNHARD, Stiftungen mit wirtschaftlichem Zweck verbieten?, in: Jusletter vom 14.12.2001.

MADÖRIN BERNHARD, Übersicht und Fallbeispiele zur Wirtschaftsprüfung, Helbing & Lichtenhahn Verlag, Basel 2003.

MADÖRIN BERNHARD, Umwandlung der Migros in eine Aktiengesellschaft, in: Basler Zeitung vom 21.08.1997, S. 1, 15 und 21.

MADÖRIN BERNHARD, Vielfältige Steuererklärungen – der Sonderfall Schweiz, in: Steuerbeilage Basler Zeitung vom 28. 02. 1992.

MADÖRIN BERNHARD, Von der Handelsbilanz zum steuerlichen Ergebnis in der Schweiz, Internationales Treuhandseminar (Ordre des Experts comptable Steuerberaterkammer Südbaden, Schweiz. Treuhänderverband Nordwest-Schweiz), Strassburg 12. 12. 1990.

MADÖRIN BERNHARD, Wie leicht Geld gespart werden kann, in: Steuerbeilage Basler Zeitung vom 26.02.1993.

MADÖRIN BERNHARD, Wohnsitz und Grundeigentum, Internationales Treuhandseminar (Ordre des Experts comptable; Steuerberaterkammer Südbaden, Schweiz. Treuhandverband Nordwest-Schweiz), Basel 03. 11. 1992.

NEUHAUS/ZUMOFFEN/FRUTTERO/VOYAME/RAEMY/JAVET/SCHERRER/-WATTER/MARTI,Verdeckte Gewinnausschüttungen, Schriftenreihe der Treuhand-Kammer, Band 150, Zürich 1997.

SCHWEIZERISCHE KAMMER DER WIRTSCHAFTSPRÜFER, STEUER- UND TREUHANDEXPERTEN (Hrsg.) Schweizer Handbuch der Wirtschaftsprüfung, 1998.

SCHWEIZERISCHE TREUHAND-KAMMER (Hrsg.), Revisionshandbuch der Schweiz, 1992.

STERCHI WALTER, Kontenrahmen KMU, Bern 1996.

TREUHAND-KAMMER, Schweizer Prüfungsstandards (PS), 2004.

Internet sources

- Swiss Stock Exchange (SIX), Zurich:

  www.six-group.ch

- Swiss Federal Banking Commission (SFBC), Berne/FINMA:

  www.ebk.admin.ch / www.finma.admin.ch

- Swiss Accounting Standards Setting Body, Swiss GAAP FER, Zurich:

  www.fer.ch

- Swiss Institute of CPAs and Tax Experts, Zurich:

  www.treuhand-kammer.ch

- Federation of Industrial and Service Groups in Switzerland (SwissHoldings), Berne, with IFRS Forum:

  www.industrie-holding.ch

Spezielle Materialien, Gesetze und Standards

Botschaft zur Revision des Obligationenrechts (GmbH-Recht sowie Anpassungen im Aktien-, Genossenschafts-, Handelsregister- und Firmenrecht), vom 19. Dezember 2001 (01.082)

Botschaft zur Änderung des Obligationenrechts (Revisionspflicht im Gesellschaftsrecht) sowie zum Bundesgesetz über die Zulassung und Beaufsichtigung der Revisorinnen und Revisoren, vom 23. Juni 2004 (zu 01.082)

Bundesgesetz über die Direkte Bundessteuer vom 14. Dezember 1990 (DBG, SR 642.11)

Bundesgesetz über die Harmonisierung der direkten Steuern der Kantone und Gemeinden vom 14. Dezember 1990 (StHG, SR 642.14)

Bundesgesetz über die Mehrwertsteuer vom 2. September 1999 (Mehrwertsteuergesetz, MWSTG, SR 641.20)

Bundesgesetz über die Stempelabgaben 27. Juni 1973 (StG, SR 641.10)

Bundesgesetz über die Verrechnungssteuer vom 13. Oktober 1965 (VStG, SR 642.21)

Bundesgesetz über die Zulassung und die Beaufsichtigung der Revisorinnen und Revisoren (Revisionsaufsichtsgesetz, RAG), Entwurf

Bundesratsbeschluss betreffend Massnahmen gegen die ungerechtfertigte Inanspruchnahme von Doppelbesteuerungsabkommen des Bundes vom 14. Dezember 1962 (SR 672.202)

Gesetz über die direkten Steuern des Kantons Basel-Stadt vom 22. Dezember 1949 (Steuergesetz, SG 640.100)

Obligationenrecht (GmbH-Recht sowie Anpassungen im Aktien-, Genossenschafts-, Handelsregister- und Firmenrecht) (OR), zwei Gesetzesentwürfe zu den jeweiligen Botschaften

Schweizer Prüfungsstandards (PS), Treuhand-Kammer, 2004

Swiss American Chamber of Commerce, Federal Act on the Licensing and Oversight of Auditors – Auditor Oversight Act (AOA) (English Translation of the Official Text), Zurich 2006.

Swiss American Chamber of Commerce, Swiss Code of Obligations Volume I, Swiss Contract Law, Articles 1 to 551 (English Translation of the Official Text), Zurich 2005.

Swiss American Chamber of Commerce, Swiss Code of Obligations, Volume II, Swiss Company Law, Articles 552 to 964 (English Translation of the Official Text), Zurich 2006.

Swiss American Chamber of Commerce, Swiss Code of Obligations, Volume III, Swiss Securities Law, Articles 965 to 1168 (English Translation of the Official Text), Zurich 2003.

Swiss American Chamber of Commerce, Swiss Civil Code, Volume I, Law of Persons and Family Law, Articles 1 to 456 (English Translation of the Official Text), Zurich 2008.

Swiss American Chamber of Commerce, Swiss Civil Code, Volume II, Inheritance Law and Property Law, Articles 457 to 977 (English Translation of the Official Text), Zurich 2008.

Swiss American Chamber of Commerce, Swiss Penal Code (English Translation of the Official Text), Zurich 2004.

Swiss American Chamber of Commerce, Swiss Merger Law (English Translation of the Official Text), Zurich 2003.

Swiss American Chamber of Commerce, Swiss Federal Act on Product Liability (English Translation of the Official Text), Zurich 1995.

Swiss American Chamber of Commerce, Swiss Cartel Law (English Translation of the Official Text), Zurich 2005.

Swiss American Chamber of Commerce, Swiss Federal Act on International Private Law (English Translation of the Official Text), Zurich 2004.

Swiss Banking – Compendium Edition 2006 – The Swiss Banking Sector, Swiss Bankers Association, Basel 2006.

Steuerrecht, Sammlung der Erlasse des Kantons Basel-Landschaft, herausgegeben von der Landeskanzlei 18.4.1995 (mit Änderungen)

Teil A

Einführung / Introduction

Kapitel 1:
General business information on Switzerland

§ 1   Overview

I.   Geography

Switzerland is a land locked country located in central Europe in the heart of the Alps. It is a small country, covering only about 41,300 square km. Switzerland is bordered on the north by France and Germany, on the east by Austria and Liechtenstein, on the south by Italy, and on the west by France.

One-quarter of Switzerland is covered by lakes, mountains or glaciers. There are many lakes in Switzerland; the largest are Lake Geneva (Genfersee, Lac Léman) and the Lake of Constance (Bodensee). The rivers Rhine and the Rhone both have their origin in Switzerland. It is also one of the most mountainous countries in Europe. Some of the peaks in the Swiss Alps reach up to 4,000 meters above sea level.

II.   Climate

The mountains and valleys cause many areas to have their own microclimates; therefore, Switzerland's climate varies by region. However, the climate is typically moderate with no excessive heat, cold, or humidity, with cooler temperatures at higher elevations. Daytime summer temperatures range from 18° to 30° C, and the winter daytime range is -1° to 4° C.

III.   History

Switzerland was originally inhabited by a Celtic tribe of Helvetians. In the 1st century BC, Julius Caesar conquered the Helvetians and named the region Helvetia. This land was later captured by the Burgundians and the Alamanni in the 4th century AD. Over the next several hundred years the land was again conquered by the Franks and eventually some of the land became part of the Holy Roman Empire of German Nation. The remaining portion of Switzerland became part of the Kingdom of Transjurane Burgundy.

The Holy Roman Emperor Rudolf I attempted to assert feudal rights in Switzerland. In order to defend themselves from these attacks, three cantons, *Uri, Schwyz* and *Unterwalden*, united to form a league of mutual defence on 1 August 1291 on the Rütli. They joined together to protect their independence. Other cities/cantons joined the league and it grew in power and strength. In September of 1499, the Treaty of Basel was signed. This treaty recognised the independence of Switzerland from the Roman Empire.

The Swiss mercenaries grew stronger and defeated Italian districts near the Ticino canton. However, they were defeated by the French in the early 16th century. This led to the introduction of Switzerland's neutrality policy. The Protestant Reformation greatly affected Switzerland. Many cities such as Zurich (reformer Zwingli), Berne, and Geneva (reformer Calvin) revolted against the Roman Catholic Church. The French Revolution spread into Switzerland in the 1790's. Within eight years the French occupied all of Switzerland. Napoleon unified the country and created the Helvetic Republic. He later allowed Switzerland to approve a new constitution, reinstating the cantons' self-governing policy.

The Congress of Vienna confirmed the perpetual neutrality of Switzerland and recognised 22 cantons in the Swiss territory. To this date the boundaries have barely changed.

The federal government gained additional power in 1847 when their troupes defeated the Sonderbund, a League of Catholic Cantons. In 1874 the constitution was ratified, which recognised Switzerland as a unified nation. Although it has been modified, this constitution is still in effect. Switzerland is currently comprised of 26 cantons. The official name of Switzerland is the "Swiss Confederation". The Latin name is Confoederatio Helvetica, abbreviated as CH (the international car identification of Switzerland). Therefore, the International Standard Organisation (ISO Code) for the Swiss national currency the Swiss franc is abbreviated CHF. Switzerland is not member of the Euro land, although the Euro currency (EUR) of the surrounding EU members is widely used in Switzerland, especially in border towns.

IV. Languages

There are four official languages in Switzerland: German, French, Italian and Romansh. 64% speak German, 19% speak French, 9% speak Italian, 1% speaks Romansh, and 7% speak other languages.

Swiss-German is spoken in a variety of dialects across Switzerland. This language is based on a version of Middle-High German. Swiss-German is rarely written; therefore, High German is the official written language. Most people speak at least one other language in addition to their native tongue. English is also very common in Switzerland, especially in the business community.

V. Population

The total population in Switzerland is slightly over 7 million. The largest cities include Zurich (population 350,000), Basel (population 190,000) and Geneva (population 180,000). Berne, the capital of Switzerland, is the fourth largest city, with a population of 130,000. The population is split equally between men with 49%, and women with 51%.

Switzerland is densely populated with 170 inhabitants per square km. Because much of Switzerland is uninhabitable (due to lakes and mountainous regions), the population density is actually 250 inhabitants per square km when disregarding the inhabitable regions.

Switzerland's population is composed of many different ethnic entities with 64% of German-Allemanic heritage, 19% French, 7% Italian, 1% Romansh and 9% Other. The religions are Roman Catholic 46%, Protestant 40%, Other 7%, None 7%.

§ 2 Political system

Each canton has its own constitution. However, they have only one parliamentary chamber and the number of representatives varies by canton. All issues that are not directly allocated to the Confederation are left up to the cantonal legislation. The Swiss are widely known for their democracy. Individuals may challenge a current law or present proposals for new laws. To make a change to the constitution, an obligatory referendum must be presented. The proposal must be accepted by an absolute majority of total votes cast and by a majority of cantons, for a referendum to pass. To oppose a newly passed law by parliament, an optional referendum can be presented. This requires the support of 50,000 voters or 8 cantons and must be filed within 3 months of the new law.

The Federal Parliament is responsible for the legislative duties of the federal government. It consists of two houses, the National Council (*Nationalrat*) and the Council of States/Cantons (*Ständerat*). Members of both houses are elected for four-year terms. The National Council consists of 200 members, which represent the people. The Council of States is composed of representatives from each canton. Both houses meet four times a year for three-week sessions in Berne.

To pass a law, a proposal is drafted by either house of parliament. If both houses approve the law it is sent to the Federal Council (*Bundesrat*) for implementation. As opposed to many other countries Switzerland does not have a presidential system. The Federal Council is formed by members of different parties, and therefore forms a coalition government.

The Federal Council is responsible for the executive duties of the federal government. The council consists of seven people who are elected by Parliament to four-year terms. Every year a new member of the council is elected to the position of chairman. A rotation for this position is customary.

There are several political parties in Switzerland. The four biggest ones are:

- The *Schweizerische Volkspartei* (SVP), a party formed by farmers, craftsmen and tradesmen; today predominantly supporting populist issues;
- The *Sozialdemokratische Partei der Schweiz* (SPS), a party originally formed by industrial workers and employees, supporting predominantly socialist issues;
- The *Freisinnige Partei der Schweiz* (FDP), a party originating form the liberal movement of the 19th and 20th centuries; supporting predominantly liberal economic issues;
- The *Christliche Volkspartei der Schweiz* (CVP), an originally Catholic conservative party; supporting predominantly family and society issues.

- The seven Federal Councillors are presently members of one of these four parties. Other parties of nation-wide recognition are:
- The *Grünen*, an ecological part;
- The *Evangelische Volkspartei* (EVP), the protestant counterpart to the CVP;
- The *Partei der Arbeit* (PdA), supporting communist issues.

§ 3   Transportation and infrastructure

Switzerland has a sophisticated transportation system. The country is easily accessible through multiple venues. Switzerland's rail and road systems are among the best in Europe. There are 69,000 km of main roads in Switzerland and 1,300 km of motorways. The train system is high speed and very reliable. There are multiple discount rail passes that are available, making travel much less expensive (*Halbtaxabo*).

Switzerland has three international airports located in Geneva-Cointrin, Zurich-Kloten and Basel-Mulhouse. The Geneva and Zurich airports have their own rail links to the city making access to airport more efficient.

The former Post and Telephone (PTT) ministry has now been split into The Post and SWISSCOM, a limited company that is listed on the Zurich Exchange.

§ 4   Economic system

Switzerland is a country of great economic and political stability. It is a highly industrialised country based upon a free enterprise economy in which government control is limited. State-owned industries are principally confined to some public utilities. With the exception of agriculture, government has rarely been willing to intervene in the functioning of the market economy.

Switzerland lacks significant natural resources with the exception of hydroelectric power. The most important industries are the production of machinery and precision instruments, metals, chemicals, pharmaceuticals, textiles, and consumer goods. Forty percent of the gross national product is accounted for by exports of goods and services. Because of its dependence on foreign trade, Switzerland has pursued a liberal trade policy with low tariffs and the avoidance of import restrictions. Swiss products in general are renowned for their high quality and precision.

Simultaneously with industrial growth, the service sector has become highly developed. Tourism, commerce, banking, and insurance have become significant elements in the Swiss economy and have a high degree of international interdependence. In particular, banking and insurance have grown thus strengthening the position of Zurich as a leading world financial centre.

As a country committed to open markets and freely convertible currencies, Switzerland has traditionally been the preferred location for the headquarters of many important international business organisations.

Switzerland was a founding member of the European Free Trade Association, (EFTA), which now includes only Switzerland, Iceland, and Norway. However, Switzerland and the other EFTA countries are associated with the European Union (EU) in many areas. There are no customs duties or other similar charges levied on cross-frontier transactions in industrial goods originating in EU or EFTA countries, but goods originating from countries other than the EU or EFTA are subject to customs duties if they are exported from Switzerland into EU countries, or vice versa. Goods may acquire Swiss origin if sufficient processing is carried out locally.

Switzerland is an active member of the World Trade Organisation (WTO) and has also concluded many bilateral trade agreements with third world countries. Switzerland does not belong to the European Monetary System. It is a member of the International Monetary Fund (IMF) and the United Nations (UN) since 2002.

§ 5 Employment

I. Labour relations

Switzerland has a well-trained and adaptable labour force, whose relations with management have been characterised by decades of labour peace. This has contributed to raising living standards to among the highest in the world. In 1937 a commitment was made to settle disputes dealing with labour negotiations by arbitration. This makes labour disputes quite uncommon and negotiations are very peaceful. All labour contracts must meet the legal minimum standards imposed by the law. Labour relations are based on the Federal Labour Law and Swiss Code of Obligations (CO, OR) as well as collective labour agreements (*Gesamtarbeitsverträge*), which require minimum vacation time and retirement ages. They are currently 65 for men and 63 for women.

In recent years, Switzerland has enjoyed a continually strong and vibrant labour market. The unemployment rate has been less than 4 percent and it is therefore significantly lower than in its neighbouring EU countries.

II. Swiss Army

Military service is required for all Swiss men between the ages of 20 and 50. All men must go through a 15-week recruitment training followed by 2 to 3 weeks of additional service every year. Compensation is received as usual from employers during military service. The Federal government makes a contribution to companies to help offset the cost (EO).

III. Salaries and benefits

The standard of living and salaries in Switzerland are very high. The cost of living is high but this is offset by higher salaries. However, there is no legal minimum wage in Switzerland. It is required by law that employees receive at least four weeks holidays. This is in addition to the 8 to 10 public holidays in Switzerland. It is normal for employers to offer benefit packages including retirement benefits.

IV. Foreign employees and expatriates

About 25 percent of the working population in Switzerland is foreign. Work permits are required for all foreign personnel.

Since the Bilateral Agreements between Switzerland and the European Union (EU) on 1 June 2004, Switzerland has had a dual recruitment system. Depending on the country of origin, i.e. whether the applicant is an EU/EFTA citizen or from other countries (the "third-country nationals"),

Kapitel 1: General business information on Switzerland

the requirements for obtaining a work permit and the necessary procedure, are different.

The Bilateral Agreements between Switzerland and the European Union included the Agreement on Free Movement of Persons (*Personenfreizügigkeitsabkommen*, Accord sur la libre circulation des personnes), which has it made much easier for EU/EFTA nationals to receive working permits.

§ 6   Financial services

I.   General

Switzerland offers many financial services. Switzerland's banks and insurance companies rank top in the world. The banking system in Switzerland is full service. Banks offer investment advice and act as portfolio managers over their clients' accounts. The breadth of the capital markets in Switzerland has been increasing over the last years. Switzerland also trades in specialised financial markets such as the precious metal market and the options and futures markets. Around 200,000 people are employed in the financial sector, more than half of them work for banks and almost half of the bank staff is employed with the big banks. Therefore, 200,000 financial sector employees represent only about 5% of the total Swiss workforce, however, they contribute about 14% of Swiss national product with the result that productivity per employee is about triple the national average.

II.   Banks

Swiss banks are widely known for their secrecy and security. Numbered accounts allow a customers identity to remain unknown expect for a few bank officers. However, secrecy is not in all cases guaranteed; it is disregarded in cases of criminal trials / offense and bankruptcy. There are two big universal banks in Switzerland which offer a wide variety of services, UBS and Credit Suisse. In addition to accepting deposits and financing loans, they offer private banking services (portfolio management, advisory, tax and services), asset management services (investment / mutual funds) and are active in investment banking business (trading of securities and foreign exchange, merger and acquisition, restructuring, etc.).

There are also about 25 cantonal banks, which offer more traditional services, such as saving accounts and mortgages. The biggest segment of Swiss banking is wealth and asset management. This activity forms part of the core business for 75% of all banks in Switzerland, the two big banks, some 90 private, regional, cantonal banks and 150 foreign banks. The volume of assets under management by Swiss banks amounted at the beginning of 2006 to over CHF 4,000 billion. Therefore, Switzerland is the world leader in wealth management, with a market share of one-third of international private client assets. The country's largest bank (UBS) is the world largest wealth manager with approximately USD 2,000 billion assets under management. Credit Suisse has more than USD 1,000 billion.

III. Insurance companies

Switzerland's insurance companies are some of the largest ones in the world (e.g. Zurich Financial Services, ZFS, and Winterthur, now part of the French AXA Group). They do much of their business outside of Switzerland; over half of their revenue comes from outside the country. A Federal license is required to conduct business in the insurance industry. Insurance companies invest most of their sizable portfolios into Swiss bonds and equities. This raises a substantial amount of money for Swiss capital markets.

§ 7 Forms of business organisation

I. Overview

There are two main types of companies in Switzerland, the stock corporation (*Aktiengesellschaft*, AG; société anonyme, SA) and the limited liability company (*Gesellschaft mit beschränkter Haftung*, GmbH, Société de responsabilité limitée, Sàrl). There are some 170,000 stock corporations. They constitute a substantial majority of Swiss companies, since that form of business organisation has a number of advantages over the limited liability company, but the rules and regulations governing them can be taken as applying equally to limited liability companies, unless specifically stated otherwise. According to estimates by the Federal Statistical Agency the number of corporations can be broken down approximately as follows:

- 12,000 holding companies.
- 10 corporations with more than 5,000 employees.
- 40 corporations with more than 2,000 employees.
- 300 corporations with more than 500 employees.
- 900 corporations with more than 200 employees.

Hence most of the registered corporations have only one employee or none at all. Only about 3,000 corporations have sales exceeding CHF 50 million; many of them are only trading, not manufacturing, concerns. In the French speaking region of Switzerland many corporations have been established for the sole purpose of holding a piece of real estate (*société immobilière*, SI).

The following types of business organisation are to be found in Switzerland:

- Stock corporations, limited companies (*Aktiengesellschaft*, AG).
- Corporations with unlimited partners (*Kommanditaktiengesellschaft*, KoAG).
- Sole proprietorships (*Einzelunternehmung*).
- General partnerships (*Kollektivgesellschaft* & Co.).
- Limited partnerships (*Kommanditgesellschaft*, KG).
- Limited liability companies (LLC) (*Gesellschaft mit beschränkter Haftung*, GmbH).
- Cooperatives (*Genossenschaft*).
- Ordinary partnerships, Joint ventures (*einfache Gesellschaft*).
- Foundations (*Stiftung*).
- Associations (*Verein*).
- Branches (*Zweigniederlassung, Sitz,* succursale, siège).

The legal form known as a trust in the Anglo-American world does not exist in Swiss law.

The number of entities registered in the Swiss Commercial Register as of 31 December 2006 was:

Simple partnerships (not registered)	unknown
Sole proprietorships/personal businesses	150,050
General partnerships	14,662
Limited partnerships	2,617
Stock corporations	175,459
Corporations with unlimited partners	12
Limited liability companies	92,448
Cooperatives	11,609
Associations	5,900
Foundations	18,641
Swiss Branches of Foreign Companies (estimated)	500
Total	471,898

II. Stock corporation (Ltd. / AG / SA)

As mentioned earlier, the stock corporation (AG) is by far the most important form of business organisation. It is also popular for small businesses and for a variety of business activities. A stock corporation has a fixed share capital and limited liability. The share capital has to be at least CHF 100,000; 20 percent or CHF 50,000 of which has to be paid up or contributed in kind. The voting shares have a nominal value of CHF 0.01 (1 Swiss centime, Rappen) or more. Both registered (Namenaktien) and bearer shares (Inhaberaktien) are common. Often the registered shares carry greater voting rights (for example, CHF 100 per share) than bearer shares (for example, CHF 1,000 per share). There are also non-voting shares called participation certificates (Partizipationsscheine, PS). They enjoy the same rights to dividend and liquidation payments but carry no voting rights. Often no share certificates are issued for private companies.

The main governing bodies of the stock corporation are as follows (German terminology in parenthesis):

- Shareholders' meeting (*Generalversammlung*, GV).
- Board of directors (*Verwaltungsrat*, VR).
- Officers:
  - Delegate of the board (*Delegierter des Verwaltungsrates*, Del.VR).
  - Management (*Geschäftsleitung*, GL).
  - Managers *(Direktoren)*.
  - Proxies with limited powers of signature (*Prokuristen*, p.p.a.).
- Auditors *(Revisionsstelle, Revisoren)*.

The delegate of the board is both a member of the board and head of the management team. He or she therefore has significant power in running the company. The role is similar to that of the chief executive officer (CEO) in the United States or the managing director in the United Kingdom. Switzerland does not have the German two-tier supervisory board system where the executive management team (*Vorstand*) is supervised by a board (the *Aufsichtsrat*) which includes outside directors and worker representatives (trade unions). However, more and more Swiss public companies are establishing an audit committee of outside board members.

The articles of incorporation have to include the firm's name (often in more than one language), the type of legal business organisation in abbreviated form (e.g. AG, SA, Ltd., Corp., GmbH, Sàrl), its legal domicile (residence), the objective of the company, and its capital stock (number of shares and nominal value per share category).

The annual general meeting of shareholders has to be held no later than six months after the balance sheet date as stated in the articles of incorporation. In 90 percent of all companies the balance sheet date will be the end of the calendar year, 31 December. The financial statements, including the auditors' report and the annual report of the directors, have to be sent to shareholders or made available at least 20 days (three weeks) before the general meeting. Therefore, the last day to issue audit reports is the 10 June.

Among other things the annual general meeting has the following obligations and rights:

- Approval of the financial statements.
- Approval of the company's annual report.
- Power of decision on the profit distribution (dividends) as proposed by the board of directors.
- Election of the board of directors and the auditors.
- Discharge of the board of directors.
- Changes in the articles of incorporation (statutes).
- Liquidation and winding up of the company.
- Mergers, demergers, capital increases, etc.

The board of directors has to consist of one or more individuals (no business organisations allowed as board members). The majority of the members have to be Swiss citizens and have to live in Switzerland.

The board of directors can entrust executive functions to one (or more) delegates of the board. Outside directors are common in public companies. Their duties and rights are usually set out in writing in a document known as the organisation rules (*Organisationsreglement*).

Corporations with unlimited partners (*Kommanditaktiengesellschaft*, KoAG) are very rare in practice. They are therefore not further discussed.

III. Commercial register (HR)

The commercial register (*Handelsregister*, HR) plays an important role in the commercial and business law. There are 26 cantonal commercial registers, which are co-ordinated by a federal agency to ensure uniformity. All changes in the data in the decentralised registers have to be published in the official Swiss Trade Journal (*Schweizerisches Handelsamtsblatt*, SHAB) which appears daily (also electronically e.g. by FACTIVA).

Excerpts are available on any company for a modest fee, to foreigners as well as Swiss nationals, also via private providers over the internet (e.g. TELEDATA). The information is restricted to the following, however, as financial statements and audit reports do not have to be filed:

- The company's name (*Firma*), domicile (*Domizil*) and legal business form.
- Its incorporation date and details of any changes in the information recorded in the register.
- The board members and other signatories, with their name and place of residence.
- The auditors (*Revisionsstelle*) (normally an audit firm) and their domicile.
- Total amount of capital; the number, nominal value and types of shares.
- Authorised or contingent share capital (in the case of corporations).

IV. Other forms of business organisation

1. Sole proprietorship

The business is carried out by one person alone, as in the case of a tradesman, farmer or a member of one of the liberal professions. If it reaches a certain size it has to be entered in the commercial register (more than CHF 100,000 in sales). The sole proprietorship's liability is unlimited. This type of establishment is normally used only for starting up of a business. These types of companies usually switch to stock corporation status later. After attaining entry in the commercial register, as a rule the sole proprietor will follow the same accounting rules as stock corporations. The financial accounts are mainly tax driven. About 150,000 sole proprietorships are listed in the commercial register.

2. General partnership (& Co.)

A general partnership is an association of two or more persons for a commercial purpose. The disadvantage is that the partners' liability is unlimited, i.e. all the partners are liable to the full extent of their personal fortune. All the partners have to be natural persons: Stock corporations may not become partners. The partnership has to be recorded in the commercial register. General partnerships normally use accounting rules similar to those of stock corporations. There are about 15,000 such partnerships in the commercial register.

3. *Limited partnership (KG)*

This is a similar form of business to the general partnership, except that the liability of one or more partners is limited to their equity share. This limit has to be stated in the commercial register. The general partners, whose liability is unlimited, must be private persons, whereas the limited partners may be either individuals or corporate investors. There are only about 3,000 limited partnerships in the commercial register. Limited partnerships normally follow much the same accounting rules as stock corporations.

4. *Limited liability company (GmbH, Sàrl)*

Most of the requirements of company law apply to limited liability companies. Previously the share capital could not exceed CHF 2 million. The names of the principal shareholders have to be stated in the commercial register. This form has therefore been less attractive in the past, as it was suitable only for a small company whose size would be signalled by the abbreviation GmbH after the name. The need to declare the main shareholders makes it doubly unattractive. Hence this form of business organisation was not extensively used. Even small businesses preferred the stock corporation alternative. Normally the same accounting and reporting rules apply as for stock corporations. The lack of enthusiasm for this corporate form is reflected in the fact that only about 3,000 were found in the commercial register about 15 years ago. Due to the changes and improvements of the law this number has dramatically increased to about 90,000 today.

5. *Cooperative*

There is no restriction on the number of members. The main object of a cooperative is to promote or secure its members' interests. This form of organisation is often used in agriculture, housing, insurance or the retail trade (e.g. the COOP retail chain). Unless the accounting rules for the relevant regulated industry apply, cooperatives follow the same accounting rules as stock corporations. There are about 12,000 cooperatives in the commercial register. They normally enjoy some forms of tax relief.

6. Ordinary partnership (Joint Venture)

This is an unstructured form of organisation or association between individuals and/or companies. It has no trading name and is established solely to carry out a specific project or joint venture (e.g. a construction contract). The accounting is normally done in the books of the joint venture partners. It cannot be entered in the commercial register.

7. Foundation

This is an amount of money or other assets (a fund) dedicated to a specific purpose. Normally the funds cannot be returned to the founder or sponsor. All foundations are supervised by cantonal or federal authorities so as to ensure that the assets and returns are properly used for the good of the beneficiaries. Virtually all pension funds in Switzerland are organised as foundations and are also subject to audit.

Special regulations govern the accounting, investment policies and financial reporting of pension funds (e.g. Swiss GAAP FER Accounting for pension funds). There are about 20,000 foundations on the commercial register; most of them pension funds, which are normally tax-exempt.

8. Branch

Those can be branches of foreign or domestic corporations, usually banks, insurance companies, airlines, etc. They are mostly taxed in the same way as stock corporations if they are owned by a corporation with a foreign head office. Often the accounting of the stock corporation as applied at the head office is adopted. There are no audit requirements for branches of foreign companies. The audit requirements apply only to the head office, which has to integrate the branch into its accounts. About 500 branches are listed in the commercial register.

9. *Association*

This is hardly used for business organisations but rather for sports clubs and not for profit organisations (NPOs). The biggest association is the World Football Association, Zurich (FIFA). Swiss GAAP FER 21 "Accounting for charitable, social non-profit organisations" was issued in 2003.

There are about 6,000 associations registered in the commercial register.

Kapitel 2:
Einleitung

§ 1   Neues Recht

Die Revision unterliegt einem starken Wandel. Gesetzgeberisch lag sie in einem jahrzehntelangen Winterschlaf, sie ist erst mit der Revision des Aktienrechts zu neuem Leben erwacht und hat mit dem neuen Revisionsrecht eine wahre Explosion erfahren. Die in der Lehre entwickelten Grundsätze wurden in das Gesetz aufgenommen. Nach dem gesetzgeberischen Innovationsschub folgten erste Entwicklungen in der Praxis, Lehre und Rechtsprechung. Das Handbuch zur Wirtschaftsprüfung erscheint in neuer Auflage mit quantitativen und qualitativen Erweiterungen, so wird namentlich ein neuer Normalwortlaut zum Revisionsbericht vorgeschlagen und eine Auftragsbestätigung der Revisionsstelle empfohlen. Die Bilanzskandale brachten offensichtliche Schwächen zu Tage, denen sich der schweizerische Gesetzgeber nicht entziehen konnte. So wurde das Revisionsrecht im Jahre 2005 neu definiert. Das neue Revisionsrecht gliedert sich in folgende drei Stufen.

1) Freiwillige KMU-Revision:

    Die freiwillige Revision ist vorgesehen für Kleingesellschaften mit bis zu neun Angestellten, sofern alle Kapitalinhaber damit einverstanden sind. Sie wird durchgeführt durch einen Revisor oder einen sog. «Zugelassenen Revisor».

2) Zwingende KMU-Revision:

    Die Revision als eingeschränkte Prüfung (Review) durch einen zugelassenen Revisor.

3) Ordentliche Revision:

    Die Revision als umfassende Prüfung durch einen «Zugelassenen Revisionsexperten» für wirtschaftlich bedeutende Unternehmen sowie für Gesellschaften mit kotierten Wertschriften für beaufsichtigte Revisionsexperten.

Das vorliegende Buch ist erklärend für Laienrevisoren und «zugelassene Revisoren», nicht aber für Revisionsexperten.

Neben der rechtlichen Seite der Revision erfordert die rasante wirtschaftliche Entwicklung ihren Tribut an den Revisor. Mit der Globalisierung der Wirtschaft, dem Internet und den wachsenden Möglichkeiten der EDV werden die Anforderungen an die Revision erhöht. Was früher einfach und logisch war, muss heute hinterfragt und neu beurteilt werden. Dazu gehört die wachsende Meinungsvielfalt. Gab es früher beispielsweise eine gefestigte Praxis zur Unternehmensbewertung, so sind heute viele Methoden bekannt und anerkannt, was letztlich dem Revisor keine Erleichterung verschafft. Im Gegenteil, bei verschiedenen Ergebnissen muss er sich an ein Resultat halten und dieses vertreten.

In diesem Umfeld kommt das vorliegende Buch auf die wesentlichen Grundsätze zurück und beschreibt die Revision aus einem einfacheren Ansatz: nicht als Fachwerk für eine Wissenschaft, sondern als Praktikerhandbuch für die Praxis. Das im Jahre 1995 erschienene «Handbuch zur Revision und Buchhaltung (HRB)» erscheint hier in überarbeiteter Form im Kontext des neuen Revisionsrechts.

§ 2 Die Bedeutung einer sachgerechten Bilanz

Der Geschäftsabschluss stellt hohe Anforderungen. Er dient nicht nur den Aktionären, sondern auch der Bemessung der öffentlichen Abgaben und Steuern. Die meisten Kleinunternehmen erstellen eine Bilanz und eine Erfolgsrechnung, welche sowohl den öffentlichen Abgaben als auch der wirtschaftlichen Betrachtungsweise dient (identische Steuer- und Handelsbilanz). Die Zahlen dieser Bilanz führen zu den Steuerfaktoren, werden aber auch zur Berechnung anderer Kosten herbeigezogen (Haftpflichtversicherungsprämien etc.).

Für die Erstellung eines Geschäftsabschlusses ist eine geordnete Buchhaltung unerlässlich. Diese muss vollständig, klar, wahr und insbesondere à jour sein. Nur so kommt man zum korrekten Ergebnis. Entspricht die Buchhaltung diesen Voraussetzungen, so bildet sie die Grundlage für betriebswirtschaftliche Entscheidungen des Unternehmens und dient der Gestaltung eines steueroptimalen Geschäftsabschlusses.

Kapitel 2: Einleitung

§ 3   Die Revision

Die Rechnungsprüfung (Revision) erstreckt sich auf folgende Feststellungen: Vorhandensein der Aktiven, Vollständigkeit der Passiven, angemessene Bewertung, Feststellung der Vollständigkeit der Einnahmen, Berechtigung der Ausgaben sowie Einhaltung der statutarischen und gesetzlichen Bestimmungen.

Die Prüfungsmethode (eine Verfahrensprüfung unter Berücksichtigung des internen Kontrollsystems oder eine Ergebnisprüfung) und das Prüfverfahren (Bestandesprüfung, Bewertungsprüfung, Verkehrsprüfung, Belegprüfung, rechnerische Prüfung, Abstimmprüfung, Übertragsprüfung, Totalprüfung, Zusammenhangsprüfung, Zahlenbeurteilung und Zahlenvergleich, kritische Durchsicht, Aktenstudium, Befragung und Besichtigung) sowie Prüfungsumfang und -auswahl (lückenlose oder stichprobenweise Prüfung, direkte oder indirekte Prüfung, progressive oder retrograde Prüfung) haben sich unter Berücksichtigung der Wesentlichkeit nach den vorliegenden Verhältnissen zu richten und sind von der Grösse der Institution abhängig.

Die «Interne Kontrolle», als zweiter Pfeiler der Revision, umfasst alle von der Geschäftsleitung (der eigentlichen Geschäftsführung) planmässig angeordneten Massnahmen, um einen ordnungsgemässen Ablauf des betrieblichen Geschehens zu sichern. Die Geschäftsleitung ist für die Anordnung und für die dauernde Wirksamkeit dieser Methoden und Massnahmen verantwortlich.

Das vorliegende Handbuch dient der Durchführung einer rechtskonformen Revision der Bilanz und Erfolgsrechnung sowie des Anhanges (im Sinne der eingeschränkten Revision.)

Teil B

Grundlagen des Rechnungswesens / Principles of accounting

Kapitel 1:
Buchführung

§ 1   Introduction and background

As in most of the continental European countries, Swiss accounting regulation derives from the Napoleonic Code. This system of law imposes on all companies certain requirements geared mainly to the protection of creditors. They include, but are not confined to, the following:

- Assets may normally be valued only at acquisition cost (the historical cost convention).

- Legal reserves have to be created before dividends can be paid, favouring internal financing through retained earnings.

The country's physical asset base suffered no destruction in the two World Wars. Additionally the currency, the Swiss franc (CHF), has remained quite stable for over 100 years. Switzerland has seen no hyperinflation, currency crises or currency reforms that have destroyed nominal values in other European countries. Many companies have been in existence for fifty years or more. The requirement of historical cost accounting has created significant hidden reserves for many companies.

The tax authorities use basically the same values as those stated in the statutory accounts as approved by the general meeting of the shareholders. Companies' management have therefore always sought to reduce net income, i.e. taxable profit, by understating assets in the individual company accounts and overstating liabilities. Minimal disclosure requirements have helped them conceal profits. In the past, the attitude of the fiscal authorities has always been very flexible regarding these practices, because indirect taxation (social, value-added tax (VAT), gas, withholding taxes, etc.) is a more important source of revenue than direct taxation (income taxes). Extensive income tax audits are rare.

Reliance on bank financing tends to reinforce such attitudes. Banks favour conservative accounting because it helps to reduce their risks. It also strengthens the power of management over minority shareholders and employees. Employees enjoy no right of representation in trade unions on the governing bodies of the organisations they work for.

Given these nowadays rather abnormal circumstances, the standards of accounting and financial reporting required in the individual company accounts are somewhat relaxed, notably in that the creation of hidden reserves is perfectly legal. Under the Corporations Act (CO) of 1992 their release has to be disclosed in the notes on the accounts. The Act also requires consolidated financial statements to be prepared, and audited.

In 1984 a Foundation for Accounting and Reporting Recommendations (*Stiftung für Fachempfehlungen zur Rechnungslegung,* Swiss GAAP FER) was set up to improve the standards of financial reporting, especially in consolidated accounts. The standards promulgated by the foundation follow internationally accepted accounting standards such as those of the IASB and the European Directives.

Multinational corporations provide substantially more than the statutory minimum accounting and reporting information. They normally issue consolidated financial statements fully audited by one of the Big Four international accounting firms. Most of such statements conform to the International Financial Reporting Standards (IFRS) of the International Accounting Standards Board (IASB). However, the individual company accounts of the parent company are drawn up under the terms of the Companies Act and do not normally comply with IFRS.

I. Historical development of Swiss financial accounting

Switzerland has a system of codified law typical of continental European countries. It has been influenced by the Napoleonic Code and by German law. Corporate Law is based upon the Code of Obligations (*Obligationenrecht*, CO).

The Code of Obligations (*Obligationenrecht*, CO) is set out in the fifth volume of the Swiss Civil Code. It governs all legal matters relating to commerce, finance and industry (business law), e.g. contracts, forms of business organisation, accounting and auditing, etc. It is the equivalent of company, business or commercial law as found in other countries.

The present version of the Code of Obligations was enacted in 1911, with minor revisions in 1936. It became obvious that the law had become out of date during the economic boom years after World War II, and major efforts had been under way for more than three decades to change the code. Not until the end of 1991 was there a majority in parliament willing to adopt the changes, which also affected accounting and auditing. After years of debate the revised law became effective as of 1992. Another proposal to bring the accounting law more in line with the true and fair concept was published at the end of 2005.

Banking confidentiality remains important in law. One reflection of this is the absence of any requirement upon privately owned companies to publish their financial statements.

The most extensive and authoritative history of Swiss accounting under the previous legislation is found in the Käfer commentary. In 1995 the Swiss government established a committee of experts in accounting and reporting (Groupe Mengiardi) to revise the Swiss Corporation and Company law and make it more compatible with European Directives. Their report was submitted in June 1998 and was published as a draft in October 1998. If adopted it would substantially expand the scope of accounting and reporting to all kinds of organisations and the related audit requirements. However, the draft law published at the end of 2005 for comment is subject to substantial change by parliamentary discussions. This most likely will take several years until the law will become fully effective.

II. Accounting standards and standard setting

1. *The law relating to financial accounting (CO)*

The legal requirements for accounting are very general in nature. All business organisations have to comply with the general rules embodied in Art. 957 to 964 of the Code of Obligations (CO). More stringent rules apply to corporations (Art. 662 to 677 CO). The relevant articles are listed in the table below. In general, however, the legal requirements are too broad to offer substantive guidance for effective corporate financial reporting.

The unusual feature of the existing statutory regime is the unrestricted freedom to use undisclosed (i.e. secret or hidden) reserves. Only when they are released does the existence of such reserves have to be disclosed.

Kapitel 1: Buchführung

Accounting requirements of the Swiss Code of Obligations (CO):

Art.	Requirement

General bookkeeping requirements affecting all companies
- 957 Bookkeeping requirements
- 958 Duty to prepare inventory, balance sheet and income statement
- 959 Generally accepted bookkeeping standards
- 960 Currency requirement (Swiss francs) and valuation
- 961 Duty to sign the accounts and inventory
- 962 Duty to retain records for ten years
- 963 Duty to publish accounts before court
- 964 Penalties for failure to comply with general bookkeeping requirements

Additional requirements on corporations
- 662 Duty to prepare directors' report and financial statements
- 662a Generally accepted accounting principles
- 663 Minimum format of the income statement
- 663a Minimum format of the balance sheet
- 663b Minimum format of the notes on the accounts
- 663b [bis] Compensation disclosures of public companies (new as of 1 January 2007)
- 663c Disclosure of shareholders of public companies (and conversion and option rights of each member of the board - new as of 1 January 2007)
- 663d Annual report
- 663e Duty to prepare consolidated financial statements
- 663f Exemption for sub-holding companies
- 663g Preparation of consolidated financial statements
- 663h Protection in cases of confidentiality
- 664 Incorporation costs
- 665 General valuation of fixed assets
- 665a Valuation of participations
- 666 Valuation of inventories
- 667 Valuation of securities
- 668 [Deleted]
- 669 Depreciation, value adjustments and provisions

670	Revaluation of participations and real estate
671	Allocation of reserves
671a	Reserve for own shares
671b	Revaluation reserve
672	Statutory reserve
673	Welfare reserve
674	Hidden reserves
675	Dividends
676	Construction dividends (*Bauzinsen*)
677	Payments to directors (*Tantièmes*)

To summarise, the major thrust of proposals for reform of company law (the Code of Obligations (CO)) are aimed at:

- Significantly greater disclosure requirements, e.g. in the notes.
- Cash flow statement.
- Revised accounting valuation rules, especially as regards the utilisation of hidden reserves.

Politically it proved impossible to introduce the concept of 'true and fair view'. Small businesses in particular feared that the abolition of hidden reserve accounting would mean increased demands on them from the tax authorities, employees and outside shareholders. Additionally it was felt that more sophisticated accounting systems were really needed. The compromise was that while hidden reserves could still be created and held secretly, only their release would need to be shown.

The leading commentaries on the corporation law are BÖCKLI and FORSTMOSER. The Swiss Institute of Certified Accountants (*Schweizerische Treuhand-Kammer*) has interpreted the legal requirements extensively in its Auditing Handbook (*Handbuch der Wirtschaftsprüfung*, Volume 2). New standards are published under www.treuhand-kammer.ch.

2. Accounting and reporting recommendations (Swiss GAAP FER)

As the reform of company law took so long, an initiative was launched by the Swiss Institute of Certified Accountants. Consequently the Swiss Foundation for Accounting and Reporting Recommendations (*Schweize-

rische Stiftung für Fachempfehlungen zur Rechnungslegung) was set up in 1984. The foundation is the legal body of the Technical Committee on Financial Accounting and Reporting Recommendations (*Fachkommission für Empfehlungen zur Rechnungslegung*) which, as an independent private institution, issues the Recommendations on Financial Accounting and Reporting (*Fachempfehlungen zur Rechnungslegung*, Swiss GAAP FER). Various economic interests are represented, such as employer/employee organisations, banks, insurance companies, industry, financial analysts, the media, academics, the tax authorities, accountants and auditors. The standard-setting body is organised as a foundation under federal supervision but funded by private parties with an interest in financial reporting. The funding is modest compared with that of Anglo-American standard-setting bodies. As the members receive no remuneration, the only expenses are those of printing, publishing, meetings, etc. About half the income derives from the sale of the standards. Big companies normally contribute a modest sum each year to ensure the foundation's independence.

Consolidated financial statements have been the foundation's first priority, because company law confines itself to the basic principles and lays down no detailed rules.

The table below lists the Swiss GAAP FER recommendations that have been issued so far after the restatement in 2006:

Swiss GAAP FER (valid as of 1 January 2007):

	Framework
1	Basics
2	Valuation
3	Presentation and format
4	Cash flow statement
5	[Deleted]
6	Notes
7	[Deleted]
8	[Deleted]
9	[Deleted]

Teil B: Grundlagen des Rechnungswesens / Principles of Accounting

10	Intangible assets
11	Taxes
12	Interim reporting
13	Leases
14	Consolidated financial statements of insurance companies
15	Related party transactions
16	Employee benefit obligations
17	Inventories
18	Tangible fixed assets
19	[Deleted]
20	Impairment
21	Accounting for charitable, social non-profit organisations
22	Long-term contracts
23	Provisions
24	Equity and transactions with shareholders
25	[Deleted]
26	Accounting for pension plans
27	Derivative financial instruments
28	[Deleted]
29	[Deleted]
30	Consolidated financial statements

The Recommendations on Financial Accounting and Reporting (ARR/ FER) are in two parts:

1) The recommendation itself (printed in bold type).

2) Explanations.

They are published in the three official languages of Switzerland (German, French and Italian) and also in English. Although the recommendations are not binding, they are the outcome of a broad consensus and widespread application is usual.

The first drafts are prepared by a project group of specialists in financial reporting. The results are refined by an executive committee and then discussed and approved by a commission of some thirty business people, as mentioned above. Once the proposals have been approved, an exposure draft is published and the views of interested parties are sought. After due consideration of the comments a final version is adopted and translations are prepared.

The recommendations take into consideration the guidelines of the European Directives and the International financial Reporting Standards (IFRS) of the IASB.

3. Swiss Institute of Certified Accountants

Formed in 1925, the Swiss Institute of Certified Public Accountants and Tax Experts (*Treuhand-Kammer*) deals on a private basis with accounting and auditing issues. The institute comprises not only public accountants (independent auditors, *dipl. Wirtschaftsprüfer*, WP, until called 1998 *dipl. Bücherexperte*) but also tax experts (*dipl. Steuerexperte*). It has both individual members and institutional members. There are some 4,000 individual members, about a quarter of them working as individual sole practitioners.

As mentioned above, tax consultants have also joined the institute. Similar training and certification programs are available to those seeking to attain the qualification of Certified Tax Expert (*dipl. Steuerexperte*).

The institute organises both basic education and continuing education programs for professionals, sets the professional examinations, issues auditing and accounting statements and promotes the interests of the profession as a whole.

The institute's publications program is quite extensive. The institute publishes the leading monthly professional journal *Der Schweizer Treuhänder*. It also issues a well-known series of professional and research monographs. Selected doctoral dissertations on accounting subjects from throughout Switzerland are included in this series. So far over 180 volumes have appeared.

An important product is the extensive four-volume Auditing Handbook (revised edition 1998), which contains accounting and auditing standards and interpretations. Although not legally binding, these find wide acceptance among accounting, legal and auditing professionals. Swiss accounting professionals are increasingly observing and implementing handbook recommendations, especially as regards the interpretation of the company law. Worries about exposure to professional liability claims have, however, acted as something of a brake on progress in this direction. In any case, it is imperative to ascertain the extent to which handbook recommendations have been followed in the work of preparation for the purposes of financial analysis, business negotiations or the evaluation of business opportunities. Due to the significant changes caused by the new audit legislation the Auditing Handbook will be revised in 2009.

Following the reform of company law in 1992 the Institute thoroughly revised the Auditing Handbook (*Schweizer Handbuch der Wirtschaftsprüfung*, abbreviated as HWP). Now with white covers, it runs to approximately 2,000 pages and is the leading reference source on accounting and auditing in Switzerland. In its entirety the handbook is available only in German and French (*Manuel Suisse d'Audit 1998, abbreviated* MSA, ed. Treuhand-Kammer, Zurich).

While the Auditing Handbook is concerned primarily with auditing procedures, its volume 1 covers generally accepted bookkeeping and accounting principles. As with other Swiss financial accounting practices, the recommendations in the handbook go well beyond the requirements of commercial law.

Since the handbook recommendations are close to internationally accepted accounting and financial reporting practice, there is broad agreement with its contents, in theory at least. At the same time, however, the handbook's recommendations are in no way binding for the management or the board of directors, and the accounting profession often has a difficult time persuading management to adopt them. Yet many accounting professionals feel that merely observing the requirements of company law could leave the auditor open to legal action for not meeting the handbook's more stringent standards. The fear of increased professional liability exposure has made the publication of the handbook somewhat controversial.

While the handbook annotates and explains all applicable provisions of the Code of Obligations (CO) in detail, it goes significantly beyond legal stipulations and sets forth underlying financial accounting conventions and professional accounting recommendations, so far as they exist.

4. *National securities exchange*

Before 1997 there has never been a federal law on dealing in securities. This has been the domain of the cantonal stock exchanges; the largest were Zurich, Basle and Geneva. There has been a consolidation into the fully automated Swiss Stock Exchange (SIX). SIX has decided that the IFRS should become the compulsory standard for all major publicly companies with listed shares.

As an important international financial centre Zurich has one of the more active securities exchanges on the European continent. In comparison with the volume of trading on the New York, Tokyo or London exchanges, Zurich's turnover is however quite modest. Continental European companies simply employ much less equity capital than their Anglo-American counterparts. Most of the funding of industry comes, as in Germany, from the major 'universal' (non-specialist) banks and not from equity issues. Consequently, continental European equity markets are considerably thinner than those in the United Kingdom and the United States. However, there has been an increasing trend for securitisation.

Most underwriting and secondary trading business in Zurich is conducted by the brokerage departments of the large commercial banks. This is taken into account when the Swiss Stock Exchange listing regulations are considered.

Despite the modest capacity for portfolio investments in corporate securities in the Zurich market, a number of large non-Swiss multinational corporations have arranged for their securities to be quoted on the Swiss Exchange for reasons of convenience. Also, many non-Swiss corporations and governmental organisations have issued bonds in Switzerland denominated in Swiss francs or Euros or US Dollars. Often these are arranged for institutional investors by way of private placements.

The regulations are fairly standard by continental European measures of comparison. The listing regulations in New York (NYSE and Nasdaq) are far more comprehensive and stringent with respect to accounting, auditing and financial reporting requirements.

Before 1997, the listing requirements used to be set by the Cantonal Exchanges. They have always been quite modest compared with the regulations of the Securities and Exchange Commission (SEC) in the United States. The same applies to the continuous reporting required of listed companies (see the Listing Rules of the Swiss Stock Exchange).

Only the shares of large multinational companies (such as Nestlé, Novartis, ABB, etc.) are listed on foreign stock exchanges (Frankfurt, London, etc.). Some of these companies also have quotations in the United States and are therefore required to meet the stringent filing and trading requirements of the Securities and Exchange Commission (SEC).

Due to the introduction of federal stock exchange regulations in 1997, the quality of accounting has significantly improved. The revised Companies Act also meant that consolidated accounts have to be prepared, and all companies whose shares are quoted, or which have debentures outstanding, have to publish consolidated financial statements, audited by suitably qualified auditors. Additionally, such companies have to publish full interim financial statements for the first half-year from 1998 on, thus significantly increasing and improving interim information.

III. Regulated industries

1. Banking and insurance

The banking industry is subject to quite extensive accounting, auditing and financial reporting regulation. The requirements of Swiss banking law are much more comprehensive and specific than those of the Code of Obligations (CO). One big difference from international accounting regulation is that banks and their auditors have to report to the Swiss Federal Banking Commission (*Eidgenössische Bankenkommission*, EBK, SFBC) in Berne, which is responsible for enforcing banking law. As of 1 January 2009 the banking and insurance regulators were merged into a new financial market oversight authority (FINMA). The reports are very comprehensive, confidential and are therefore not published. Mutual investment funds are regulated in much the same way as banks. The most important sources of law are:

- Federal Act on Banks and Savings Banks – BankL (*Bundesgesetz über die Banken und Sparkassen*, BankG).

- Ordinance regulating the Federal Law on Banks and Savings Banks – BankO (*Verordnung zum Bundesgesetz über die Banken und Sparkassen*, BankV).

- Federal Act on Stock Exchanges and Securities Trading (*Börsengesetz*, BEHG, SESTA)

As an independent federal administrative agency, the FINMA supervises banks and financial markets. This includes the supervision for:

- banks and brokers.
- licensed auditing companies that audit banks, securities traders or investment companies.
- investment funds (*Anlagefonds*).
- mortage bond business.
- stock exchanges (SIX and Berne Exchange, BEx).
- disclosures of share holdings in and public offers for listed companies.
- banks, brokers and fund managers with the aim of preventing and combating money laundering (*Geldwäschereigesetz*, GwG).
- insurance companies

The licensed Swiss auditing firms play a central role as instrument for insurance and banking supervision in Switzerland. This supervision system is essentially based on the split of responsibilities between the FINMA as the governmental supervisory agency and private auditing firms (basically the Big 4 +2) that are authorised by the FINMA to perform audits of banks and other financial institutions, the so called "dual (supervisory) system. Therefore, monitoring (both statutory and regulatory) is delegated to auditing firms, while general supervision and sanctioning are reserved exclusively to the FINMA. The banks audited bear the full cost of the audit.

The supervision exercised by auditing firms is the key means of bank client protection. Therefore, external bank auditors have to be adequately qualified and independent. The regulatory audit or Bank Law report (also called long-form audit report) has to be addressed to the board of directors of the bank. The audit firm has to the send report also to the FINMA. The

FINMA can also impose extraordinary audits of the bank by the banking auditors.

Although, banks have to comply with the accounting rules of the corporation law (Art. 662 to 670 CO), they are primarily governed by the provisons of Art. 6 of Bank-L (Swiss Banking Law, *Bankengesetz*, BaG) and the related Art. 23 to 28 of the implementing ordinance BankO (*Verordnung zum Bankengesetz*). More detailed information can be found in the FINMA Guidelines on Accounting Regulations.

Banks with global operations like UBS and Credit Suisse make use of international accounting standards (IFRS and US GAAP).

2. Pension funds

Employee pension funds have also been heavily regulated since 1986 under the Federal Pension Fund Act (BVG). The Act and detailed ordinances establishes a chart of accounts, valuation and investment policies, and requirements for audit by professional auditors and periodic review by professional actuaries. The requisite reporting to cantonal regulatory bodies and to beneficiaries is also quite stringent and formalised. The federal Acts and regulations are enforced by the Federal Social Insurance Agency (*Bundesamt für Sozialversicherung*, BSV).

The main laws are as follows:

- Federal Pension Fund Act (Bundesgesetz über die berufliche Alters-, Hinterlassenen- und Invalidtätsvorsorge, BVG).

- Ordinance governing the Regulation and Registration of Pension Funds (Verordnung über die Beaufsichtigung und die Registrierung der Vorsorgeeinrichtungen, BVV 1).

- Ordinance governing Pension Funds (Verordnung über die berufliche Alters-, Hinterlassenen- und Invaliditätsvorsorge, BVV 2).

The more important literature is: Carl Helbling, *Personalvorsorge und BVG, Zurich 2006*; Swiss Auditing Handbook, Volume 4, Zurich 1998 and FER 26 Accounting for pension schemes.

3. Nationalised industries and governmental bodies

Most countries in continental Europe, including Switzerland, have created State-owned enterprises to:

- Run public transport systems (e.g. railways, bus service, and ship transportation).
- Provide postal services.
- Supply domestic and industrial users with gas, water and electric power.

Governments often make substantial financial subsidies available (if and when necessary) to private enterprises whose survival is in the national interest or to companies that face unfair international competition. The *quid pro quo* usually entails a degree of government influence, if not control. Other regulated enterprises include nationalised industries (e.g. weapons) and governmental bodies.

These mostly nationalised industries have to follow accounting and reporting rules established by governmental agencies. These include, for example, the Swiss Federal Railways (*Schweizerische Bundesbahnen*, SBB), postal services (*Die Post*), pipelines, power stations and other utilities. The telephone services were privatised under the name of SWISSCOM in 1998 and listed on SIX Swiss Exchange. They use the International Accounting Standards (IFRS) in their consolidated financial statements.

The relevant legislation is the Railways Act (*Eisenbahngesetz*), the Shipping Act (*Schiffahrtsgesetz*), the Pipelines Act (*Rohrleitungsgesetz*) and the Emergency Public Services Act (*Landesversorgungsgesetz*).

Various regulations exist concerning governmental accounting for:

- The federal government and its agencies.
- The twenty-six cantonal governments, including their offshoots, for example cantonal banks.
- Municipalities / communes (approximately 2,760). Many cantons have a standard chart of accounts which is laid down in detailed accounting and reporting manuals.

§ 2 Objectives, concepts and general principles of accounting

I. Principal users of accounts

Most business activity in Switzerland is conducted by stock corporations. Some 170,000 figure on the commercial register. Only about 300 of them have their shares listed on a stock exchange. There are about another 300 with listed debenture bonds (*Obligationenanleihen*). Some stock corporations have both shares and bonds listed. It follows that over 99 percent of all corporations are privately owned, most of them by a single shareholder. They are therefore called one-man corporations (*Einmannaktiengesellschaften*) or wholly-owned subsidiaries of Swiss or foreign groups (*Tochtergesellschaften*). These companies are under no requirement to publish financial statements of any kind. The accounts are prepared mainly for the purpose of enabling the shareholder(s) to determine the dividend distribution. Profits are often retained. Shareholders in the company can often realise a tax-free capital gain upon the sale of their holding. When dividends are paid, both the company and the shareholder are liable for income tax (double taxation).

The statutory accounts are used only to assess income tax and determine the distribution of profit. For expenses to be tax-deductible they have to be included in the statutory accounts, i.e. recorded in the general ledger. As a result, the amounts on that tax return come directly from the statutory accounts. To small companies this is a significant administrative relief.

For outside shareholders with minority interest, the statutory accounts provide only minimal information about the stewardship of management. The limited disclosure and freedom to create hidden reserves has allowed management to cover up its misjudgements without difficulty. Dissident shareholders have the power to call for a special investigation (*Sonderprüfung*) if they suspect irregularities. Since the introduction of the 1 July 1992 corporation law, few investigations have been demanded. The courts have blocked many of those that have been initiated.

Statutory accounts, including a report by a recognised audit firm, are often prepared at the request of the banks, even though banks tend to ensure they get better information by monitoring the degree of risk their lending is exposed to (e.g. budgets, cash flow forecasts). All Swiss companies use these same statutory accounts for declaring their tax liability. The tax return will normally state the same net income and equity as the statutory accounts approved during the general meeting of shareholders in the company accounts.

Generally the financial statements of Swiss companies will include only a balance sheet, income statement and a brief section of notes with minimum disclosure. However, the trend is increasing among larger companies, especially those operating internationally, to present more comprehensive information.

The (voluntary) Swiss GAAP FER standards outline the components of individual and consolidated financial statements which should be included. Among the recommendations are the following:

1) The individual and consolidated financial statements should comprise a balance sheet, an income statement (profit and loss account) and cash flow and changes in equity statements as well as the notes (annex).

2) The cash flow statement should show the cash flow from operations in the consolidated financial statements, the cash flow from investing/divesting activities and the cash flow from financing activities.

3) The notes should disclose:
   a) The accounting policies applied in the accounts.
   b) Further details on other parts of the financial statements.
   c) Additional information not included elsewhere in the financial statements.

4) Alongside the amounts for the reporting year the financial statements must show the comparative figures for the previous year. If they are not comparable, an explanation is required.

In general, users have only a limited degree of access to the accounts of Swiss companies, since there is no requirement to publish accounts or file them in the commercial register. The only exceptions are quoted companies, banks, insurance companies and mutual investment funds. Financial institutions are also subject to strict supervision. They must file accounts with the relevant regulatory authorities (e.g. FINMA, the Swiss Stock Exchange (SIX). In addition, banks and insurance companies are required to publish their balance sheets in the Swiss Trade Journal (SHAB) and further newspapers, as specified in their articles of incorporation. These must be published annually, half-yearly or quarterly, depending on the size of the company.

All companies, even those not required to publish accounts, have to make the following documents available for inspection by shareholders:

1) Annual report of the directors.

2) Statutory audit report.

3) Balance sheet.

4) Income statement.

5) Notes on the accounts.

6) The board's proposal for profit appropriation.

They must be available at head offices and branches at least twenty days before the ordinary general meeting of shareholders, which must be held within six months after the balance sheet date.

Consequently, the primary users of published accounts are shareholders. As mentioned, most Swiss businesses are privately owned and therefore have few shareholders. Only about 300 companies, quoted on a Swiss stock exchange, have publicly traded shares. As in other continental European countries, only about 20 percent of the population hold quoted shares. The diversified holdings of institutional investors are more significant. Such investors, Swiss and foreign, include insurance companies, mutual funds, the pension funds of private and public employers. A significant role is played by foreign private investors whose portfolios are managed by Swiss banks.

Banks normally try to avoid investing a large amount in quoted industrial companies. When it does happen it is usually due to historical reasons or because the company had to be bailed out by the bank exchanging debt for equity. When the company is restored to financial health the bank will sell the shares as soon as possible.

Banks are the source of most external finance, in the form of short and long-term lending. Frequently they have access to detailed management accounts. Theoretically any creditor may apply directly to the company to see the balance sheet, the income statement, the notes and the auditors' report. However, the company may deny access by settling the debt. Other outsiders are not entitled to information concerning the performance and activities of the business.

The effect of the banks' position in the user profile is to incline accounting, access and disclosure towards their banks' interests, i.e. conservatism, the protection of the security of their investments and the servicing of debt. Big companies, responding to pressure from international capital markets, have been publishing more complete (consolidated) accounts. Hence the consolidated accounts are normally of much better quality than the individual company accounts with regard to disclosure. Most individual company accounts understate equity because they are tax-driven.

II. Accounting concepts and standards

Accounting and reporting standards are governed by the legal requirements of the company law which is part of the Code of Obligations (CO). The law was amended as of 1 July 1992 to bring it more into line with the European Directives. There is also a new project for revised Accounting legislation. The exposure draft was published for comment at the end of 2005.

Under the existing code, financial statements must be prepared in line with generally recognised commercial principles. According to Art. 662a CO the annual accounts in the individual financial statements should be prepared in accordance with recognised accounting principles in such a way as to offer the most reliable picture of the income and financial situation of the company (not a true and fair view). They should also include the previous year's figures. These recognised accounting principles, should follow the principles of:

- Completeness of the annual financial statements.
- Clarity and materiality of the financial statements.
- Prudence (conservatism).
- Going concern.
- Consistency in presentation and valuation.
- Prohibition of setting off assets and liabilities, as well as of setting off expenses and income (gross principle).

A regulation format is specified under the corporation law for minimum disclosure in the balance sheet and the income statement. The minimum level of disclosure required in the notes is also prescribed. This ensures a limited degree of standardisation.

In general, accounts must be prepared in accordance with 'recognised accounting principles', a term which is not defined in any detail. In practice, such principles are determined primarily by the accounting profession and laid down by the Swiss Institute of Certified Accountants, which publishes a comprehensive Auditing Handbook (HWP).

§ 3 Bookkeeping and preparation of financial statements

I. Bookkeeping

Under Art. 957 CO every firm entered in the cantonal commercial register is required to keep proper books of account. A stock corporation can be created only by entry into the register, and is automatically subject to the provisions of general accounting law as set out in Art. 957 to 964 CO. The most important rules, which are also applicable to stock corporations, are presented below. Every company is required to keep the necessary books of account, given the nature and extent of the business, to reflect its financial state properly and to determine liabilities and claims and the operating results of each year.

Some requirements are procedural only. For instance, Art. 957 CO requires every company to keep the necessary records and books of accounts, according to the nature of its business, and to prepare periodic (i.e. annual) balance sheets and income statements. Juridical interpretation of this article has expanded its applicability to include the maintenance of proper cost accounting systems when a manufacturing company is required to value work in progress and finished goods periodically. The accounting system therefore has elements of both financial accounting and cost accounting. Depending on the size and nature of the business, the accounting system may necessitate the following:

- Vouchers: original accounting documents.

- Inventory: list of assets (for example, stocks or fixed assets) at a period end, showing quantity on hand, description and value/cost.
- Journal: book with transactions entered in chronological order.
- General ledger: summary book of accounting.
- Subsidiary ledgers: ancillary books of accounting, for example payroll, debtors, etc.
- Balance sheet: assets and liabilities as at a period end and the resulting net assets (shareholders' equity).
- Income statement: income statement for a period, showing income and expenses by categories and the resulting profit/loss of the period.
- Cost accounting and calculation (to value work in progress and finished products and fixed assets manufactured internally).

II. Uniform system of accounts

As of 1 July 1992 a standard format was introduced for the accounts of stock corporations. The Code of Obligations (CO) requires additionally that accounts should be prepared in Swiss francs, that they should be complete and thorough and that they should give a clear picture of the trading position of the company, subject to the explicit acceptability of the creation and release of hidden reserves. However, under this current corporation law the net amount released has to be disclosed in the notes.

The accounts of companies are prepared on a basis consistent with that required by the fiscal authorities. If deductions are to be claimed they must be included in the accounts, which leads to a form of presentation which may not reflect the company's true commercial position.

Switzerland has no general chart of accounts such as those of other continental European countries (e.g. France). However, a recommended chart (*Kontenplan*) has been published on a voluntary basis (the former Käfer-Kontenplan has been revised in 1998). It is procedural only, as it is intended to provide bookkeepers with guidance on establishing a financial accounting system for a company. However, this chart of accounts was replaced by the new company law which took effect on 1 July 1993. A revised version of the Chart of Accounts was published in 1996 (*Kontenrahmen KMU*).

III. Duty to prepare an inventory

The inventory is the list of assets (not of inventories or stocks only) showing the items, their value and the totals (see also the special rules for corporations.) Other provisions of the Code of Obligations (CO) govern the running of internal control systems. For instance, Art. 958 CO requires companies to take annual inventories to ensure that the physical assets on the books are still in existence and that they are properly accounted for. For small companies inventories are determined on the basis of a stocktaking at year end. This exercise lists the identity of the articles, the quantity and the pricing, which are multiplied and added up to the total which is taken into the balance sheet. Under Swiss law the listing has to be signed. The stocktaking at year end can include counting, measuring, weighing, etc., the articles. If a (computerised) perpetual inventory accounting system is in use, each article should be counted at least once a year during the year. At the year end a listing is printed out.

All articles have to be inventoried at least once a year, normally at year end. The inventory sheets, including quantities and valuation per article, have to be signed by management. However, it is accepted practice to include items, or groups of items, at a pro memoria (*pro memoire*, p.m.) CHF 1.-. This is also permissible for tax purposes. It could lead to the accumulation of substantial hidden reserves in the individual company accounts.

IV. Duty to prepare financial statements

According to Art. 958 CO every company in the commercial register is required to prepare an inventory of assets and liabilities, a balance sheet as of the end of each financial year and an income statement for the year then ended. These records must be completed within a reasonable time, having due regard to the normal business practice of the enterprise. For stock corporations this means within less than five months after the balance sheet date.

Under Art. 662 CO the board of directors of a corporation has to prepare a business report for each year. This consists of the audited annual financial statements, the annual descriptive report and the consolidated financial statements where such statements are required by law. The annual financial statements consist of the income statement, the balance sheet and the notes.

Recorded transactions must be properly documented, and the documents underlying the preparation of financial statements must be preserved for at least ten years. Also, the internal accounting records of Swiss companies must be physically located in Switzerland and the financial statements must use (at least in their primary form) the national currency (Swiss francs). The records should be in one of the three main languages (German, French or Italian). English is widely used as well. In that case the tax authorities may ask the company to provide them with translation into a Swiss national language. Of course, supplementary or subsidiary records may be in other currencies. The tax authorities will only accept financial statements expressed in Swiss francs (except for foreign branches in Switzerland where a foreign currency is accepted).

Under Art. 960 CO the inventory sheets, the income statement and the balance sheet have to be prepared in the national currency, Swiss francs. This is also required by tax law. Rounding amounts to the nearest franc is possible. In consolidated accounts amounts are often rounded to the nearest thousand francs or to a million Swiss francs.

Under Art. 961 CO the inventory sheets, the income statement and the balance sheet must be signed by the persons responsible for the running of the company.

Under Art. 962 the books of account, the business correspondence and the accounting documents and vouchers have to be retained for a period of ten years. The balance sheet and the income statement must be preserved in their (signed) original form; other records may be preserved in some other form, provided they can be accessed at any time, i.e. for the ten-year retention period. Ancillary ledgers can therefore be maintained on microfilm or COM films (Computer Output on Microfilm) or burned into Compact Discs (CDs). Vouchers and accounting documents can even be maintained on magnetic information storage and retrieval systems (e.g. tape).

§ 4 Classification principles

I. Completeness

The financial statements should be complete and must not omit material information. All transactions should be fully entered in the bookkeeping system. Completeness includes the balances of the previous year being entered as the opening balances of the new financial year. The company is assumed to be a going concern. Either transactions are continuously booked from the beginning of the year to the end, or if this is not possible, e.g. with a permanent inventory system, a complete inventory taking has to be performed at year end to identify all existing assets and liabilities. Even if items are fully written off (e.g. for tax purposes) they should still be recorded at a *pro memoria* CHF 1.–.

II. Clarity and materiality of the financial statements

Clarity is a concept which also figures in the general accounting conventions mentioned in Art. 958 CO, which applies to all business organisations, including corporations. The items should be clearly and precisely stated. Also the additional information disclosed in the notes on the accounts should be self-explanatory and clear. Clarity is also achieved where a holding company prepares consolidated accounts and therefore provides an insight into the economic substance of the holding company and its subsidiaries (substance over form).

The materiality concept was introduced only with the revised company law of 1992. Previously there were no such guidelines. Lawyers argued before that only financial statements detailed right down to centimes could be accurate. Now there is no question about rounding the figures in financial statements to francs, ignoring centimes. In consolidated accounts it is in any case usual to round to the nearest thousand francs or, in the case of large groups, even to the nearest million.

III. Consistency of presentation and valuation

Consistency is important, so that prior year figures will be comparable. However, hidden reserve accounting makes the principle difficult to achieve. The presentation, the classification of headings, and the valuation and disclosure principles should be consistently applied. Any change should be explained and possibly quantified in the notes.

The annual financial statements are considered to have been prepared in accordance with the principle of consistency if in the current year the same accounting principles are applied as in the comparative period. Consistency relates to the presentation of the financial statements as a whole as well as to the content and the valuation of the individual account balances.

IV. Prohibition of setting off assets and liabilities or expenses and income

This gross principle is important for the sake of clarity in the financial statements. The structure of the balance sheet and income statement itself provides some guidance. The following have to be shown gross, for example:

- Accounts receivable and payable.
- Non-operating income and expense.
- Financial income and expenses.
- Extraordinary income and expenses.
- Gains on the sale of fixed assets (gross).
- Currency gains and losses.

However, it is accepted that the following may be shown in net form:

- Net sales (gross sales less sales deductions).
- Net fixed assets (cost less accumulated depreciation).
- Net receivables (gross receivables less allowance for doubtful accounts).
- Release of hidden reserves net (to be disclosed in the notes).

Any departure from consistency must be justified in the notes.

Teil B: Grundlagen des Rechnungswesens / Principles of Accounting

§ 5 Grundsätze der Ordnungsmässigkeit der Rechnungslegung

Die 7 Grundsätze der Ordnungsmässigkeit der Rechnungslegung sind:

1) Vollständigkeit
2) Klarheit
3) Vorsicht
4) Fortführung
5) Stetigkeit
6) Bruttoprinzip
7) Wesentlichkeit

I. Vollständigkeit

Dieser Grundsatz besagt, dass sämtliche Vermögensgegenstände, Schulden, Rechnungsabgrenzungsposten, Aufwendungen und Erträge im Jahresabschluss enthalten sein müssen.

Die Jahresrechnung muss somit vollständig sein. Das Weglassen bestimmter Verkaufserlöse zum Zwecke der Bildung stiller Reserven, die Aufstellung einer Erfolgsrechnung, die mit einem Bruttogewinn beginnt, oder das Weglassen wesentlicher Teile in der Bilanz sind unzulässig.

II. Klarheit

Der Grundsatz der Klarheit verlangt, dass zwei- oder mehrdeutige Begriffe in den verschiedenen Teilen der Bilanz vermieden werden müssen. Ebenfalls muss die Darstellung der Jahresrechnung übersichtlich und sachgerecht gruppiert sein und den Besonderheiten der Unternehmung Rechnung tragen.

Dieser Bilanzierungsgrundsatz hat vor allem formalen Charakter und betrifft auch die Gliederung der Bilanz und der Erfolgsrechnung. Eine Aktiengesellschaft muss die einmal gewählte Gliederung beibehalten, es sei denn, wirtschaftliche Gründe rechtfertigten ein Abweichen. Obwohl diese

Ausführungen hauptsächlich die geforderte Stetigkeit betreffen, sind sie auch im Rahmen der Klarheit anzubringen.

Dieser Bilanzierungsgrundsatz verlangt auch, dass die Saldi in der Eröffnungsbilanz des Geschäftsjahres mit den Schlusssaldi des Vorjahres übereinstimmen müssen. Die betragsmässige Identität der Saldi resultiert aus der doppelten Buchhaltung. Die Schlussbilanz eines Geschäftsjahres führt zur Eröffnungsbilanz des unmittelbar folgenden Geschäftsjahres.

III. Vorsicht

Der dritte Grundsatz, die Vorsicht, ist zugleich der wichtigste. Er bedeutet in erster Linie, dass Gewinne erst ausgewiesen werden dürfen, wenn sie sich realisieren (1), Aufwände dagegen schon dann, wenn sie sich für die Rechnungsperiode bloss aktualisieren (2). Aus dem Anschaffungswert-Prinzip (3) lässt sich herleiten, dass die Bewertung stets zu historischen Kosten (Kosten zum Zeitpunkt der Herstellung bzw. des Kaufes) geschehen muss.

Dieser Bilanzierungsgrundsatz verlangt, dass ein Unternehmen sich grundsätzlich nicht besser darstellen darf, als es tatsächlich dasteht. Das Vorsichtsprinzip umfasst das Realisationsprinzip, das Imparitätsprinzip und das Niederstwertprinzip.

1. Realisationsprinzip

Das Realisationsprinzip besagt, dass Gewinne nicht schon dann im Jahresabschluss erfasst werden dürfen, wenn sie nach Meinung des Unternehmens entstanden sind, sondern erst dann, wenn sie realisiert sind.

2. Imparitätsprinzip

Das Imparitätsprinzip besagt, dass noch nicht eingetretene Verluste bereits dann im Jahresabschluss ausgewiesen werden müssen, wenn sie vorhersehbar sind. Diese im Vergleich zum Realisationsprinzip ungleiche Behandlung (Imparität = Ungleichheit), wird als Imparitätsprinzip bezeichnet.

3. Niederstwertprinzip

Das Niederstwertprinzip gilt für die Vermögensbewertung und besagt, dass bei Vorliegen verschiedener möglicher Werte am Bilanzstichtag der niederste anzusetzen ist.

Im Niederstwertprinzip eingeschlossen ist das Anschaffungswert-Prinzip. Werte dürfen höchstens zu den Anschaffungs- oder wenn sie selbst hergestellt sind, zu den Herstellungskosten bilanziert werden. Dem Niederstwertprinzip (Kostenprinzip) muss auch dadurch Rechnung getragen werden, dass die Aktiven im Umlaufvermögen zum niedrigeren Marktwert zu bewerten sind, wenn der Kostenwert höher sein sollte.

IV. Fortführung (Going Concern)

Das neue Aktienrecht weist darauf hin, dass es in der Rechnungslegung normalerweise um Fortführungswerte geht. Erst wenn sich entweder ein Kapitalverlust oder eine Überschuldung abzeichnet oder der freiwillige Beschluss zur Auflösung des Unternehmens mit Liquidation gefasst wird, hat der Ausweis der Jahresrechnung zu Liquidationswerten zu erfolgen.

V. Stetigkeit

Der Grundsatz der Stetigkeit (Kontinuität) ist für die Sicherheit des Einblicks in die wirtschaftliche Lage des Unternehmens von erstrangiger Bedeutung. Dieser Grundsatz verlangt, dass die Zahlen von verschiedenen Perioden miteinander vergleichbar sein sollten. Andernfalls müssen die Darstellungsabweichungen im Anhang dargelegt und begründet werden.

VI. Bruttoprinzip (Verrechnungsverbot)

Nach dem Verrechnungsverbot dürfen Positionen der Aktivseite nicht mit Positionen der Passivseite der Bilanz und Aufwendungen nicht mit Erträgen in der Erfolgsrechnung verrechnet werden.

Das «Verrechnungs- und Saldierungsverbot» ist Bestandteil des Grundsatzes des Bruttoprinzipes. Es unterstreicht die Unzulässigkeit der Verrechnung.

Darin eingeschlossen ist auch die direkte Bebuchung der Eigenkapitalkonti. Diese können nur im Rahmen der Gewinnverbuchung und einer Kapitalerhöhung oder Kapitalherabsetzung verändert werden.

VII. Wesentlichkeit

Ein weiterer wichtiger Bilanzierungsgrundsatz, der neu in das Bilanzrecht aufgenommen wurde, ist der Grundsatz der Wesentlichkeit. Dieser Grundsatz besagt, dass dem Bilanzleser alle für die Beurteilung der Vermögens-, Finanz- und Ertragslage wesentlichen Informationen vermittelt werden müssen. Zugleich besagt der Grundsatz der Wesentlichkeit aber auch, dass alle unwesentlichen Informationen weggelassen werden dürfen bzw. vernachlässigt werden können.

Der Grundsatz der Wesentlichkeit («materiality») bedeutet somit auch, dass die Jahresrechnung den übrigen Grundsätzen insoweit widersprechen darf, als die dadurch bewirkte Unvollständigkeit oder Unklarheit für das Gesamtbild der Jahresrechnung nicht wesentlich ist.

§ 6 Buchführung

I. Formelle Erfordernisse

1. Hauptbuch

Eine ordnungsgemäss geführte Buchhaltung verlangt, dass ein Hauptbuch vorliegt. Das Hauptbuch ist i.d.R. ein Ausdruck aus einer mit EDV geführten Buchhaltung. Es empfiehlt sich, dass ein kompletter Satz fertig ausgedruckt vorliegt. Eine Abspeicherung auf EDV genügt im Prinzip auch. Oft ist es aber so, dass bei einem Generationenwechsel der EDV-Anlage die Kontenblätter nicht mehr ausgedruckt werden können. Mit Nachdruck sei deshalb empfohlen, als Revisor den ganzen Ausdruck aller Hauptbuchkonti zu verlangen.

2. Journal

Das Journal ist eine chronologische Liste aller Buchungen und schliesst am Schluss mit je einer Summe im Soll und im Haben ab. Beide Summen

Teil B: Grundlagen des Rechnungswesens / Principles of Accounting

müssen identisch sein. Auch hier sei an die Ausführungen des vorangegangenen Abschnitts erinnert; es empfiehlt sich, den kompletten Ausdruck zu verlangen.

3. *Eröffnungsbilanz*

Die Eröffnungsbilanz kann in der Regel mit einem einfachen Befehl eines EDV-Buchhaltungsprogrammes ausgedruckt werden. Ein Ausdruck muss vorliegen. Alle eröffneten Saldi müssen der Schlussbilanz des Vorjahres entsprechen und die Eröffnungsbilanz darf keinen Erfolg ausweisen.

Die Kontrolle dieser Bilanz gehört zu den Pflichtübungen der Revisionsstelle. Bei kleinen Unternehmen kommen leider immer noch fehlerhafte Programme und Bedienungsfehler vor.

4. *Schlussbilanz*

Sind alle Buchungen und die von der Revisionsstelle als wünschenswert erachteten Nachtragsbuchungen erfasst, erfolgt (nach dem Ausdruck des Hauptbuches, des Journals und der Eröffnungsbilanz) die Schlussbilanz.

Die Bilanz ist in Landeswährung zu erstellen und unter Angabe der Firmenbezeichnung zu unterzeichnen.

a) Abschrift als unnötige Fehlerquelle

Weit verbreitet ist die Abschrift von Schlussbilanzen durch die Revisionsstelle. Von solchen Arbeiten ist abzusehen.

Mit der Abschrift von Bilanz und Erfolgsrechnung entsteht eine unnötige Fehlerquelle, sowohl in mathematischer als auch in orthographischer Hinsicht.

b) Vorlage durch den Verwaltungsrat

Das Gesetz schreibt vor, dass der Verwaltungsrat Bilanz und Erfolgsrechnung vorlegt. Es ist geradezu widersprüchlich, wenn der Standardrevisionsbericht der Treuhandkammer diesen Passus expressis verbis in den Text aufnimmt und dann einem solchen Bericht Bilanz und Erfolgsrechnung mit identischem Schriftbild (d.h. erstellt durch die Revisionsstelle) folgen. Dies ist unverständlich und bereits formal wird diesem gesetzlichen Erfordernis nicht Rechnung getragen. EDV-Ausdrücke nutzen besser. Es gibt keine Additionsfehler und sie werden durch den Verwaltungsrat vorgelegt. Sie sind zudem kostengünstiger, da ein Arbeitsgang eingespart wird. Besonders problematisch wird es, wenn die Revisionsstelle in eigener Verantwortung mit der eigenen Darstellung der Bilanz und der Erfolgsrechnung zusätzlich Abschlussbuchungen vornimmt. Diese Buchungen sind dann nicht auf dem Hauptbuch und nicht im Journal erfasst. Werden sie nicht sofort nachgebucht, ergeben sich im Folgejahr unter Umständen Lücken oder die Eröffnungsbilanz ist ungenau.

c) Einsicht in die Buchhaltung

Letztlich gibt der Originalausdruck Einsicht in den Stand des Rechnungswesens. Auch mit einfachen Buchhaltungsprogrammen lassen sich klare Darstellungen erzielen und selbst bei einfachen Verhältnissen lässt sich eine einwandfrei gegliederte Bilanz zeigen. Man sollte sich nicht scheuen, die Ergebnisse der Buchhaltungsarbeit in Form eines EDV-Ausdruckes der Bilanz und Erfolgsrechnung zu zeigen.

5. Erfolgsrechnung

Mit dem Ausdruck der Bilanz erfolgt i.d.R. auch der Ausdruck der Erfolgsrechnung. Auch hier empfiehlt es sich, nichts abzuschreiben, sondern die Vorlage der EDV-Erfolgsrechnung zu gebrauchen.

Die Erfolgsrechnung ist in Landeswährung zu erstellen und unter Angabe der Firmenbezeichnung zu unterzeichnen.

II. Belegablage

1. Organisation der Belegablage

Die Belegablage ist eine der wesentlichen Voraussetzungen zur Revision. Ist sie geordnet, ist die Revision einfacher. Ist sie ungeordnet, nehmen die Schwierigkeiten zu und damit die Revidierbarkeit ab.

Oft anzutreffen sind umfangreiche Konstruktionen von Belegablagen und aufwendige Belegorganisationen. Für die Revision am vorteilhaftesten ist

Teil B: Grundlagen des Rechnungswesens / Principles of Accounting

eine einfache und nicht arbeitsintensive Variante: die chronologische Belegablage pro Bank-, Post- oder Kassenkonto. Hinter jedem Zahlungsausgang findet sich die Kreditorenrechnung, hinter jedem Zahlungseingang die Debitorenrechnung. Diese Belegablage kann ohne weiteres bewerkstelligt werden. Braucht der Betrieb eine alphabetische Ablage oder eine Ablage nach einer anderen Bezugsgrösse, so kann diese ohne weiteres mittels Kopien erreicht werden. Dieser Vorschlag ist nur eine allgemeine, vereinfachte Lösung und nicht individuell auf jeden Betrieb zugeschnitten. Für den Revisor bringt die vorgeschlagene Variante den Vorteil, dass er die Bank-, Post- oder Kassenordner durchblättern kann und sofort bei jeder Rechnung die geschäftsmässige Begründung erkennen kann. Für die Gesellschaft hat dies zur Folge, dass der Arbeitseinsatz für die Revision optimiert werden kann. Diese praktische Lösung ist vertretbar für Kleinunternehmen wie eingangs geschildert. Im Allgemeinen sind ca. 1–10 Bank- oder Postordner pro Jahr vorhanden. Damit ist eine Dimension beschrieben, welche auch den Prüfungsrahmen von 1–5 Revisionstagen umfasst und damit keine grosse Prüfungsorganisation erfordert.

2. Keine Buchung ohne Beleg

Es versteht sich von selbst, oder es sollte sich von selbst verstehen, dass jede Buchung durch einen Beleg dokumentiert sein sollte. Alle Buchungen der Geldkonti (Bank, Post, Kasse) müssen begründet sein, dies in der Regel durch Fakturen. Für einzelne Buchungen können diese nicht ausreichen; es müssen zusätzlich die entsprechenden Verträge eingesehen werden.

Es gibt wenige Buchungen ohne externen Beleg, so z.B. die Abschlussbuchungen. Diese werden am Ende des Buchungsjahres erstellt und gebucht. Diese Buchungen sind in der Regel nicht liquiditätswirksam. Abschlussbuchungen sind wie folgt näher zu umschreiben bzw. aufzuzählen:

- Abschreibungen,
- Bildung und Auflösung von Rückstellungen,
- Bildung und Auflösung der Warenlagerreserve,
- Erfassung der aktiven und passiven Rechnungsabgrenzungsposten,
- Anpassung von Wertberichtigungen,

Kapitel 1: Buchführung

- Anpassungen der Bewertungen (soweit sie nicht über die Wertberichtigung hinausgehen),
- Valutaausgleiche auf Fremdwährungskonti,
- Bildung von Debitoren und Kreditoren,
- Buchung von Zinsen,
- Verbuchung der steuerlich geforderten Privatanteile,
- Verbuchung der Mehrwertsteuer,
- Anpassung der Sozialabgaben,
- Anpassung des Prämienkontos der BVG,
- etc.

Bei diesen Buchungen ist es nicht so, dass kein Beleg vorliegt. In der Regel wird ein interner Beleg vorbereitet, der von der Buchhaltungsstelle erarbeitet wird. Dieser ist kein eigentlicher Beleg im ureigensten Sinne, der von einer ausserbetrieblichen Stelle kommt und die Buchung «belegt».

Wurde eine Buchung ohne Beleg oder nicht begründet vorgenommen, muss Aufklärung verlangt werden. Der Revisor darf dies nicht auf sich beruhen lassen. Er darf sich auch nicht mit der Überlegung begnügen, es sei genügend Eigenkapital da, um diesen Buchungsvorgang «abzudecken». Erfolgt keine Aufklärung, muss sich der Revisor gut überlegen, wie er sich verhalten soll. Handelt es sich um Bagatellbeträge, kann weiter revidiert werden, wobei erhöhte Aufmerksamkeit angebracht ist. Ist der Betrag wesentlich und erhält man keine befriedigende Antwort, empfiehlt sich eine Abklärung bei einem Fachmann.

Alle Belege und alle wesentlichen Grundlagen zur Jahresrechnung sowie die Jahresrechnung selbst sind während zehn Jahren aufzubewahren.

III. Personelle Erfordernisse

1. Bei der zu prüfenden Gesellschaft

Der Revisor hat zu analysieren, wer für die Buchhaltung zuständig ist, wer Buchungen vornimmt und wer für die Zahlungen verantwortlich ist.

Hat sich der Revisor davon überzeugt, dass die Buchhaltungsperson kompetent und erfahren ist, vereinfacht dies die Revision. Diese steht dann unter einem anderen Vorzeichen als wenn sich eine nicht sachverständige Person nebenberuflich darum gekümmert hat.

Wichtig ist auch, ob die Buchhaltungsperson sich auch um die Zahlungen kümmert. In Kleinunternehmen ist leider oft die Situation anzutreffen, dass sich ein und dieselbe Person um die Buchhaltung, die Zahlungen, die Debitoren, die Bank etc. kümmert. Der «Chef» achtet darauf, «dass der Karren läuft». An dieser Aufgabenteilung muss auch nicht gerüttelt werden. Zumindest jedoch sollte der Betriebsinhaber die Zahlungsaufträge unterschreiben und versenden. Er entbindet damit die Buchhaltungsperson von einer wesentlichen Aufgabe. Wenn Geld fehlt, fällt auf diesen dann kein Verdacht. In den meisten Fällen trifft ihn ohnehin keine Schuld. Die heutigen, vereinfachten Zahlungsaufträge erlauben es, Einzahlungsscheine auszutauschen, wodurch möglicherweise nicht berechtigte Personen Zahlungen erhalten. Es empfiehlt sich die direkte Übergabe bei der Poststelle, dies schützt die Postsendung vor Diebstahl.

2. Bei der revidierenden Gesellschaft

Der Revisor muss «Zugelassener Revisor» im Sinne des Gesetzes sein, womit die Laienrevision ausgeschlossen ist. Vorbei sind die Zeiten, in denen nach einer Addition der Bilanz das Prüfungsattest ausgestellt werden konnte. Vorbei ist auch die Zeit der anonymen Revisionsstellen. Die Revisionsstelle ist im Handelsregister publiziert. Die Verantwortlichkeit der Revisionsstelle hat damit an Bedeutung zugenommen. Wer sich nicht sicher fühlt, sollte sich von dieser Aufgabe lösen.

Die Befähigung wird neu gesetzlich konkretisiert (vgl. hinten V.). Erforderlich ist eine Berufsprüfung. Werden gewisse gesetzlich bestimmte Schwellenwerte überschritten, bedarf es eines «Zugelassenen Revisionsexperten».

Revisionen bei Kleinunternehmen werden oft durch Kleinrevisionsgesellschaften durchgeführt. Eine Person führt alle Revisionshandlungen durch und zeichnet für die Berichterstattung. Die angefügten Standardrevisionsblätter sollen dabei helfen, die wichtigsten Fragen aufzugreifen. Kann die grosse Mehrheit dieser Revisionsfragen mit «ja» beantwortet werden, kann i.d.R. eine problemlose Berichterstattung erfolgen, wobei diese Aussage zu 80 % zutreffen kann und nicht für alle individuellen

Fälle klar gegeben ist. Die Standardrevisionsblätter erlauben auch, die Revision zu einem wesentlichen Teil von einem Mitarbeiter durchführen zu lassen. Anhand der Revisionsnotizen kann der Vorgesetzte und damit der leitende Revisor die restliche Revisionsbeurteilung vornehmen und die Berichterstattung anweisen.

Bei Unsicherheiten sollte man sich nicht scheuen, einen Kollegen anzufragen. Oft ist eine kurze unverbindliche Stellungnahme nützlich und bewahrt vor einem folgenschweren Schritt. Unserer Meinung nach lassen sich durch einen solchen Dialog wesentliche Verantwortlichkeitsfragen vermeiden.

IV. Organisatorische Erfordernisse

Für die Buchführung ist der Verwaltungsrat zuständig. Zu seinen unentziehbaren Kompetenzen gehört u.a. die Ausgestaltung des Rechnungswesens. Die Revisionsstelle muss prüfen, ob ein Organisationsreglement vorliegt. Ein Reglement mit entsprechender statutarischer Delegation erlaubt eine bessere Übersicht und eine klarere Definition der Aufgaben. Andere Autoren sind besser berufen, hierüber zu berichten. Im Hinblick auf die landläufig fehlende statutarische Delegation und entsprechend fehlende Organisationsreglemente seien hier einige Ausführungen erlaubt.

Es ist anzumerken, dass neu bei der ordentlichen Revision (nicht jedoch beim Review) Verletzungen des Revisionsreglementes zu erwähnen sind (Art. 728c Abs. 1 OR).

1. Das Organisationsreglement und das Geschäftsreglement

a)   Organisationsreglement

Ein Organisationsreglement im Sinne des Obligationenrechts liegt vor, wenn die Geschäftsführung ganz oder zum Teil an eine untergeordnete Stelle übertragen wird, d.h., wenn Organfunktionen vom Verwaltungsrat an einzelne seiner Mitglieder und/oder Dritte delegiert werden. Eine Person übt dann eine Organfunktion aus, wenn sie in massgebender Weise an der Willensbildung der AG teilnimmt und korporative Aufgaben ausführt. Laut Art. 716b OR ordnet das Reglement die Geschäftsführung, bestimmt die hierfür erforderlichen Stellen, umschreibt deren Aufgaben und regelt insbesondere die Berichterstattung.

b) Geschäftsreglement

Ein Geschäftsreglement enthält keine Delegationsregelungen, sondern lediglich Anweisungen für die geschäftliche Tätigkeit und Vorschriften über die praktische Betriebsführung in technischer, kaufmännischer und rechtlicher Hinsicht.

c) Formelle Voraussetzungen

Während beim Erlass eines Geschäftsreglements keine besonderen Vorschriften zu beachten sind, müssen zur gültigen Kompetenzdelegation in einem Organisationsreglement die Voraussetzungen des Art. 716b OR beachtet werden:

1) das Organisationsreglement muss in der Form eines Verwaltungsratsbeschlusses ergehen (also schriftlich) und

2) die Statuten müssen den Verwaltungsrat ermächtigen, die Geschäftsführung nach Massgabe des Organisationsreglements ganz oder zum Teil an einzelne Mitglieder oder an Dritte zu übertragen.

2. Keine statutarische Delegation

Das in der Mustersammlung aufgeführte Geschäftsreglement eignet sich für kleine Unternehmen mit 1 bis 3 Verwaltungsräten (bei nur einem Verwaltungsrat erübrigen sich einige der Bestimmungen), wobei Verwaltungsrat und Geschäftsleitung identisch sind. Während es den Verwaltungsräten grosser Unternehmen nicht möglich ist, alle leitenden Funktionen selber wahrzunehmen, wird in einem kleinen Unternehmen eine Kompetenzdelegation nicht erforderlich sein. Insofern erübrigt sich auch ein Organisationsreglement. Hingegen erscheint es trotzdem sinnvoll, die wichtigsten Aufgaben und Kompetenzen dieser Verwaltungsrats- und Geschäftsführungseinheit in einem Geschäftsreglement aufzuzeichnen. Im Gegensatz zum Organisationsreglement, das die Delegation von Organkompetenzen an die Geschäftsführung bezweckt und daher zu seiner Gültigkeit einiger formeller Voraussetzungen bedarf, enthält das Geschäftsreglement lediglich Anweisungen für die geschäftliche Tätigkeit, insbesondere Vorschriften über die praktische Betriebsführung in technischer, kaufmännischer und rechtlicher Hinsicht, ohne Kompetenzen zu delegieren.

Auch wenn in mittleren und kleineren Unternehmen keine Kompetenzdelegation stattfindet (d.h. neben dem Verwaltungsrat keine Geschäftsstelle existiert), lohnt sich ein Blick ins Gesetz (insbesondere auf die Art. 716 ff. OR), dies vor allem im Hinblick auf die Haftung der Verwaltungsräte. Ist die Zahl der Verwaltungsräte klein, werden also beispielsweise vom Hauptaktionär, der selber Verwaltungsrat ist, nur noch zwei weitere Verwaltungsräte berufen, wird zwischen dem Hauptaktionärs-Verwaltungsrat und den von ihm berufenen Verwaltungsräten ein Machtgefälle bestehen. Da der Gesetzgeber befürchtete, ein übermächtiger Verwaltungsrat werde die AG lediglich als «verlängertes Ich» betrachten, die Bestimmung über die Firma möglichst in eigene Hände nehmen und die beiden berufenen Verwaltungsräte lediglich als stille Beisitzer behandeln wollen, was nicht immer den Gläubigerinteressen entsprechen wird, hielt er in Art. 716a OR diejenigen Aufgaben fest, die undelegierbar vom Verwaltungsrat zu erfüllen sind. Von Seiten kleiner Unternehmen wurde diese Regelung zum Teil heftig kritisiert. Man erachtete es als unpraktikabel, dass der Gesamtverwaltungsrat sich mit den genannten Kernkompetenzen zu befassen habe und dass eine Delegation an einen einzelnen Verwaltungsrat vom Gesetz nicht zugelassen werde. Von Seiten der Rechtslehre wird aber darauf hingewiesen, dass die Regelung des Art. 716a gerade für die Verwaltungsräte in kleineren und mittleren Unternehmen bestimmt ist. Die Aktionäre als Gesellschafter müssen mindestens einmal im Jahr zusammentreten. Weiter müssen sie dabei bestimmte Personen als Organ exklusiv mit der obersten Geschäftsführung beauftragen. Diese Personen wiederum müssen ihre exekutiven Hauptaufgaben unentziehbar und unübertragbar selbst wahrnehmen und für ihre Entscheidungen auch selbst geradestehen. Der Sinn der Regelung liegt nicht darin, dass der Verwaltungsrat möglichst viele Geschäfte gemeinsam erledige, sondern darin, dass alle Verwaltungsräte dafür haften. Im Hinblick auf die Haftung des Verwaltungsrates und der Haftung einer AG ganz allgemein empfiehlt sich eine klare Strukturierung und Zuweisung der einzelnen Kompetenzen. Will eine AG keine Geschäftsleitung einsetzen, werden also keine Organkompetenzen vom Verwaltungsrat delegiert, empfiehlt sich die Festlegung der einzelnen Aufgaben in einem Geschäftsreglement. Sobald Verwaltungsratskompetenzen delegiert werden, braucht die AG ein Organisationsreglement mit statutarischer Grundlage und Beispiel eines kombinierten Organisations- und Geschäftsreglements in der Mustersammlung.

3. Statutarische Delegation

Hat ein Unternehmen eine Grösse erreicht, die es dem Verwaltungsrat nicht mehr erlaubt, alle Organfunktionen selber wahrzunehmen, wird die Delegation von gewissen Aufgaben an eine Geschäftsleitungsstelle erforderlich. Diese Möglichkeit ist in Art. 716b OR explizit vorgesehen. Zu beachten ist bei der Erstellung eines Organisationsreglements zunächst die Einhaltung der Unübertragbarkeit der Kernkompetenzen gemäss Art. 716a OR. Ferner kann eine Delegation von Organfunktionen mit entlastender Wirkung nur an ein weiteres Organ, nicht aber auch an eine Hilfsperson erfolgen. Diese materielle Schranke hat vor allem haftungsrechtliche Konsequenzen. Liegt nämlich eine formell und materiell zulässige Kompetenzdelegation vor, so beschränkt sich die Haftung des Verwaltungsrats im Rahmen der delegierten Kompetenzen auf die gehörige Sorgfalt bei der Auswahl, der Beaufsichtigung und der Instruktion (sog. Drei-Curen-Haftung) derjenigen Personen, an die die Delegation erfolgte.

Insbesondere bei grösseren Unternehmen empfiehlt es sich, die Kompetenzdelegation und die Organisation in einem Organisations- und einem Geschäftsreglement (oder einem kombinierten Organisations- und Geschäftsreglement) zu regeln.

Auch ein Verwaltungsrat einer kleineren Aktiengesellschaft kann von der erleichterten Haftung profitieren, die er durch den Ausbau von Organisationsstrukturen mit statutarischer Delegation erreicht.

4. Schlussbemerkung

Ein Organisationsreglement mit statutarischer Delegation erlaubt eine klare Zuweisung der Kompetenzen und Aufgaben. Der erforderliche Aufwand sollte auch bei kleinen Aktiengesellschaften kein Hindernis sein. Hat man sich einmal grundsätzliche Überlegungen gemacht, dürften auch bessere Arbeitsabläufe in der Buchhaltung die Folge sein, was für die Revisionsstelle nur nützlich sein kann.

Ohne Regelung der Organisation und insbesondere ohne statutarische Kompetenzdelegation gibt es keine Haftungsreduktion für den Verwaltungsrat. Er ist für die Finanzbuchhaltung, die Debitoren- und Kreditorenbuchhaltung, die Belegablage, die Aufbewahrung der Geschäftsbücher, die Bilanz, die Erfolgsrechnung und den Anhang verantwortlich. Daran sei hier klar erinnert.

Kapitel 1: Buchführung

§ 7 Grundsatz ordnungsmässiger Datenverarbeitung (GoD)

I. Einleitung

Die meisten Gesellschaften setzen die EDV im Rechnungswesen ein, wobei Unterschiede zur manuellen Verarbeitung bestehen. Diese bewirken Veränderungen im Verhalten der buchführungspflichtigen Unternehmung und des Revisors.

Wie für die konventionell geführte Buchhaltung gelten auch für EDV-Buchhaltungen die obligationenrechtlichen Bestimmungen über die Ordnungsmässigkeit der Buchführung. Da die EDV-Buchhaltung anders abgewickelt wird als die konventionelle Buchhaltung, können sich andere Schwerpunkte bei der Sicherstellung der Ordnungsmässigkeit ergeben.

II. Wichtige Aspekte

Aspekte, die bei der Buchführung mit EDV zu berücksichtigen sind und aufgrund der speziellen Konzeption der EDV Beachtung erfordern, sind:

- Belegprinzip
- Journalisierung
- Kontenführung
- Aufbewahrung
- Prüfpfad

Belegprinzip: Die Dokumentation der Geschäftsvorfälle mittels Belegen ist Voraussetzung für eine korrekte Buchhaltung. Die Nachvollziehbarkeit der Buchungen muss gewährleistet sein.

Journalisierung: Die chronologische Aufzeichnung der Buchungen in einem Journal ist erforderlich. Es empfiehlt sich, Ende Jahr das Journal komplett auszudrucken.

Kontenführung: Die Transaktionen (Belegnummern und Kontierung) müssen identifizierbar sein. Ende Jahr empfiehlt sich der Ausdruck der Kontenblätter.

Aufbewahrung:	Die Aufbewahrung der Belege, der Programme und anderer Unterlagen muss von Gesetzes wegen erfolgen.
Prüfpfad:	Die Buchungen müssen vom Beleg zur Buchhaltung und von der Buchhaltung zum Beleg prüfbar sein.

Für Kleinunternehmen empfiehlt sich trotz nachhaltigem EDV-Boom eine traditionelle Aufbewahrung auf Papier. Die Aufbewahrungspflicht dauert zehn Jahre. Eine EDV-Generation dauert bloss drei bis sechs Jahre; für weiter zurückliegende Geschäftsfälle dürfte dann deshalb der Ausdruck auf Papier häufig Schwierigkeiten bereiten, z.B. weil Programme nicht mehr vorhanden sind oder das Betriebssystem gewechselt hat. Ein vorhandener Ausdruck beseitigt all diese Probleme.

III. Steuerliche Vorschriften

Die «Konferenz staatlicher Steuerbeamter» hat in Zusammenarbeit mit der Eidgenössischen Steuerverwaltung Richtlinien für die Ordnungsmässigkeit des Rechnungswesens unter steuerlichen Gesichtspunkten erlassen. Die Richtlinien sind auch massgebend für die Aufzeichnung von Geschäftsunterlagen auf Bild- oder Datenträgern und deren Aufbewahrung. Sie stammen aus dem Jahre 1979.

Gesetzlicher Ausgangspunkt sind die Vorschriften zur kaufmännischen Buchführung. Art. 962 OR äussert sich zur Pflicht über die Aufbewahrung der Geschäftsbücher und Art. 963 OR regelt die Editionspflicht. In Ergänzung zum Gesetz existiert eine Verordnung über die Aufzeichnung von aufzubewahrenden Unterlagen vom 2.6.1976.

Folgendes ist geregelt:

1) Betriebsrechnung und Bilanz sind im Original aufzubewahren
2) die übrigen Geschäftsbücher können auf Bildträgern aufgezeichnet werden
3) Geschäftskorrespondenz und Buchungsbelege können auf Bild- oder auf Datenträgern aufbewahrt werden.

Unter Bildträgern versteht man optische Aufzeichnungsmedien (z.B. Mikrofilm), Datenträger sind magnetische Datenträger (z.B. Bänder, Platten, Kassetten oder Disketten).

Die steuerlichen Richtlinien umfassen in formeller Sicht:

1) einen der Grösse und Eigenart des Unternehmens angepassten Aufbau des Rechnungswesens
2) die folgerichtige Behandlung aller buchungspflichtigen Geschäftsvorfälle
3) die Sicherung der Klarheit und Überprüfbarkeit des Rechnungswesens durch übersichtliche Aufzeichnungen
4) die lückenlose und geordnete Aufbewahrung
5) die Unterzeichnung von Inventar, Bilanz, Erfolgsrechnung und Anhang.

Die steuerlichen Richtlinien umfassen in materieller Sicht:

1) Buchungen nach tatsächlichen Verhältnissen,
2) rechnerische Richtigkeit,
3) Belegbarkeit der Buchungen und
4) einfache Ermittlung der Buchungen.

Die steuerlichen Richtlinien verlangen:

1) Aufzeichnungen über die EDV-Erfassung,
2) Ordnungsmässigkeit der Aufzeichnung,
3) Verfügbarkeit der Aufzeichnung,
4) Angaben über das Aufzeichnungsverfahren sowie
5) Wiedergabemöglichkeit der Aufzeichnung.

Die Richtlinien können bei der Eidgenössischen Steuerverwaltung, Hauptabteilung Mehrwertsteuer, bezogen werden (in D/F/I).

IV. Schlussbemerkung

Trotz wesentlicher Verbesserungen der Buchhaltungsprogramme in den letzten Jahren lassen einzelne Lösungen immer noch zu wünschen übrig. Die Einzelarbeitsplatzlösungen mit Kosten eines Monatssalärs eines Buchhalters für die Anschaffung eines Buchhaltungsprogrammes bereiten keine Probleme. Diese Programme sind ausgereift, leicht zu bedienen und funktionsfähig. Programme im Bereich bis CHF 1'000.– sind hingegen oft nicht ausgereift. Ihr Verbreitungsgrad ist nicht sehr weit und damit ist keine Kontrolle der Praxis vorhanden. Es sind oft auch Programme von Einzelpersonen ohne breite unternehmerische Abstützung. Diese Programme leiden oft an elementaren Fehlern:

- Additionsfehler
- fehlende Journalisierung
- keine klare Zuweisung von Buchung Soll und Haben
- mangelnde Nennung des Gegenkontos
- unterschiedliche Ergebnisse in der Bilanz und in der Erfolgsrechnung
- mangelnde Erfassung der Eröffnungsbilanz
- keine klare Zuweisung der Buchungsdaten (Buchungen des Folgejahres)
- kein formeller Abschluss der Buchhaltung (Schliessung der Bücher)
- etc.

Diese Aufzählung ist nicht abschliessend. Auf jeden Fall lohnt sich der Kauf eines guten Produktes. Meistens betragen die Lohnkosten des Buchhalters ein Vielfaches der Kosten eines guten Programms. In wenigen Monaten ist das bessere und teurere Programm durch die effizientere Arbeitsweise des Buchhalters amortisiert. Ein qualitativ taugliches EDV-Programm erlaubt auch dem Revisor eine Vereinfachung der Arbeiten.

Alle Belege und alle wesentlichen Grundlagen zur Jahresrechnung und die Jahresrechnung selbst sind während zehn Jahren aufzubewahren. Wie erwähnt, empfiehlt sich deshalb ein Papierausdruck, für den Fall, dass die Programme später nicht mehr kompatibel sind.

Kapitel 2:
Bilanz, Erfolgsrechnung und ergänzende Rechnungen

§ 1   Die Buchführungsvorschriften im Überblick

I.   AG und GmbH

Gleich zu Beginn sei hier erwähnt, dass AG und GmbH aufgrund des Verweises von Art. 801 OR für den Geschäftsbericht (Bilanz, Erfolgsrechnung, Anhang) identische Regelungen haben.

II.   Die kaufmännische Buchführung

Die handelsrechtlichen Normen sind Bundesrecht. Wer verpflichtet ist, seine Firma in das Handelsregister einzutragen, also dort wo Einzelfirmen, Personengesellschaften und Handelsgesellschaften erfasst werden, ist gehalten, eine Buchhaltung zu führen. Die hier interessierenden juristischen Personen umfassen insbesondere die Aktiengesellschaft (AG) und die Gesellschaft mit beschränkter Haftung (GmbH).

Zur kaufmännischen Buchführung gehören Inventar, Betriebsrechnung und Bilanz. Das Gesetz begnügt sich mit einer Regelung von weniger als 10 Artikeln und verweist neben der Wahrheit und Klarheit auf die allgemein anerkannten kaufmännischen Grundsätze.

Dazu gehören im Allgemeinen:
- eine systematisch und zeitgemäss organisierte Buchhaltung;
- die Nachprüfbarkeit;
- die Vollständigkeit;
- ein angemessener Ausbau des Rechnungswesens mit Journal, Hauptbuch und Hilfsbüchern;

und im Besonderen:
- das Kostenwertprinzip und die Bewertung zum Anschaffungspreis;

Teil B: Grundlagen des Rechnungswesens / Principles of Accounting

- das Realisationsprinzip;

- das Prinzip der Bilanzwahrheit, welche mit Ausnahme der stillen Reserven Geltung hat sowie

- das «Imparitätsprinzip», diesem Prinzip folgend, sind erkennbare Risiken in den Büchern zu berücksichtigen.

III. Die Bewertungsrichtlinien

1. Grundlagen

Das Handelsrecht ist durch Bewertungsobergrenzen geprägt, welche dem Vorsichtsprinzip Rechnung tragen. Das Vorsichtsprinzip kann deshalb zu stillen Reserven führen, welche das Gebot der Richtigkeit und Wahrheit beeinträchtigen.

Alle Werte sind zu Fortführungswerten zu bilanzieren («*Going Concern*»).

Die Bewertungsrichtlinien und die Buchführungsvorschriften des Aktienrechts gehen weiter. Das Umlaufvermögen ist zu Verkehrswerten und das Anlagevermögen zu Anschaffungs- oder Herstellungswerten (unter Berücksichtigung angemessener Abschreibungen) zu bilanzieren.

Das Warenlager, die Halb- und Fertigfabrikate und die angefangenen Arbeiten sind zu Gestehungskosten oder zum tieferen Marktwert zu bewerten. Für die Lagerbuchhaltung gibt es verschiedene Methoden zur Ermittlung der massgebenden Werte; «FiFo» (first in first out), «Lifo» (last in first out), «Hifo» (highest in first out) oder «tieferer Marktwert».

Die Wertpapiere sind zum Durchschnittskurs des Monats vor Bilanzstichtag zu bilanzieren. Die Eidgenössische Steuerverwaltung gibt jedes Jahr eine sog. eidgenössische Kursliste heraus, welche diesen Kurs jeweils per 31. Dezember ermittelt. Die Möglichkeit der Höherbewertung von Börsenpapieren führt zu einer Durchbrechung des Realisationsprinzips. Bei Wertpapieren ohne Kurswert ist höchstens der Einstandspreis als Bewertung zulässig.

Zu einem wichtigen Bewertungsprinzip gehört auch die «Gruppenbewertung». In einem Bilanzposten, der sich aus mehreren einzelnen Positionen zusammensetzt, erfolgt die Bewertung insgesamt, ohne jede Position für sich zu betrachten. So kann im Bilanzposten «Aktien», der sich aus verschiedenen Aktienpositionen zusammensetzt, eine Gesamtbewertung erfolgen. Ist somit der Vermögensnachweis der Bank im Total höher als die ausgewiesene Sammelposition, muss keine Bewertungskorrektur erfolgen. Eine Bewertung zu Einzelpositionen könnte zu einem anderen Ergebnis führen, da sie strenger ist.

Das Handelsrecht lässt der Buchführung einen weiten Spielraum. Besonders die Bildung von stillen Reserven führt dazu, dass faktisch dem Aktionär Rechte vorenthalten werden können. Andererseits ist die Auflösung von stillen Reserven bei Aktiengesellschaften im Anhang auszuführen. Gewinne können minimiert werden, was zur Folge hat, dass nur kleinere oder gar keine Gewinnausschüttungen erfolgen. Die schweizerische Rechtsprechung ist im Hinblick auf die Ausschüttung einer angemessenen Dividende äusserst zurückhaltend.

2. Die Bewertungsrichtlinien im Überblick

Bilanzpositionen	Bilanzierbarer Höchst- bzw. Mindestwert
Organisationskosten und Stempelsteuer (Art. 664 OR)	Kostenwert unter Abzug von linearen Abschreibungen von 20 % p.a.
Dauernd dem Betriebe dienende Anlagen, Anlagegüter und immaterielle Vermögenswerte (Art. 665 OR) (von Dritten gekauft oder selbst erzeugt)	Herstellungswert oder Anschaffungswert abzüglich der den Umständen entsprechenden angemessenen Abschreibungen
Rohmaterialien, Halb- und Fertigfabrikate und andere zur Veräusserung bestimmte Vermögensstücke (Art. 666 OR) (von Dritten gekauft oder selbst erzeugt)	Anschaffungswert oder Herstellungswert oder geltender Preis (Verkaufspreis) am Bilanzstichtag je nachdem, welcher tiefer ist (Niederstwertprinzip)
Wertpapiere mit Kurswert (Art. 667 Abs. 1 OR)	Durchschnittskurs des Monats vor dem Bilanzstichtag

Wertpapiere ohne Kurswert (Art. 667 Abs. 2 OR)	Anschaffungswert unter Berücksichtigung allfälliger Wertverminderungen
Ausgegebene Obligationen (Art. 669 OR) (hier pro memoria aufgeführt)	Passivierung zum vollen Rückzahlungsbetrag, Aktivierung des Disagios pro rata temporis
Rückstellungen (Art. 669 OR)	für erkennbare Risiken, auch für erst später zu erwartende Vermögenseinbussen

§ 2 Die Bilanz

I. Vorbemerkung

Für die Bilanz gilt stets die Gleichung: Aktiva = Passiva. Beide Seiten der Bilanz haben demnach stets die gleiche Summe aufzuweisen. Die doppelte Buchhaltung ist auf dieser Bilanzgleichung aufgebaut und spiegelt die folgende unterschiedliche Betrachtungsweise wider:

- Die Passivseite der Bilanz zeigt die Herkunft des im Unternehmen investierten Kapitals auf (Mittelherkunft).

- Die Aktivseite der Bilanz enthält das Vermögen, das heisst die Verwendung des Kapitals auf der Passivseite, und gibt damit ein Bild der Investierung (Mittelverwendung).

BILANZ

Aktiva: Mittelverwendung

- Anlagevermögen
- Umlaufvermögen

Passiva: Mittelherkunft

- Eigenkapital
- Fremdkapital

Die Bilanz ist aus revisionstechnischer Sicht das zentrale Instrument. Die Revision erfolgt einmal jährlich. Dabei werden ein Zeitpunkt (mittels der Bilanz) und ein Zeitraum (mittels der Erfolgsrechnung) geprüft. Die Bilanz kann auch als eine einfache Vermögenszusammenstellung per Stichtag verstanden werden, ohne direkten Bezug zur Erfolgsrechnung. Entsprechend einfach kann sie auch ermittelt werden. Die «Bilanz zu Liquidationswerten», welche bei besonderen Situationen zu erstellen ist, löst sich ebenfalls von der Buchhaltung und ist eine einfache Vermögenszusammenstellung. Da die Bilanz auch von Personen, welche nicht buchführungssachverständig sind, gelesen wird, muss sie umso mehr vom Revisor verstanden und analysiert werden. Bei richterlichen Beurteilungen wird die Bilanz besser verstanden als eine kompliziertere Erfolgsrechnung oder Mittelflussrechnung.

Im Normalfall geht die Bilanz (sowie die Erfolgsrechnung) als rechnerisches Ergebnis (Ergebnis 1) aus der Buchhaltung hervor. Sie ist ein mathematisches Ergebnis der Buchungen innerhalb der Bilanz und der Erfolgsrechnung. In diesem Fall ist sie als Endergebnis eingefügt in das rechnerische Umfeld der Buchhaltung. Für die Revision muss sie durch den Revisor in diesem Sinne als Ergebnis 1 nachvollzogen werden können. Als Ergebnis 2 muss sie als Vermögenszusammenstellung (wie ein Inventar) mit entsprechend notwendigem Ausweis und Bestand des Eigenkapitals analysiert werden.

Der international gebräuchliche Standardbericht der Treuhandkammer führt auf, dass die Prüfung nach Stichproben zu erfolgen hat. Im Bereich der Bilanz als Prüfung der einzelnen Bilanzpositionen ist meines Erachtens eine Stichprobenkontrolle ungenügend. Eine weitgehend vollständige Bestandeskontrolle aller Bilanzpositionen scheint – auch für den Review – unerlässlich. Alle ausgewiesenen Aktiven und Passiven sollten geprüft werden. Eine stichprobenweise Annäherung darf es nur in wenigen Positionen geben, welche die Zuverlässigkeit der Gesamtbeurteilung der Bilanz nicht beeinträchtigen dürfen. Man muss sich ganz klar vor Augen halten, dass im Falle von Haftungsfragen als erstes die Fragen auftauchen: «Haben Sie den Bestand dieser Position geprüft?» «War das Aktivum Ihrer Meinung nach vorhanden?» Mit Sicherheit wirft dann auch gerade diejenige Position Probleme auf, welche nur rudimentär geprüft worden ist oder die man das nächste Mal näher anschauen wollte. Wir führen deshalb hier unsere Empfehlung einer vollständigen Kontrolle an, welche bei Kleinunternehmen keine grosse Aufgabe bieten sollte und auch von der zu prüfenden Gesellschaft (durch Vorlage einer Dokumentation) im Wesentlichen vorbereitet werden kann.

II. Der Kontenrahmen

Jahrzehntelang hat der so genannte «Käfer-Kontenrahmen» (benannt nach Prof. Karl Käfer) das Bild aller Buchhaltungen geprägt. 1996 ist der neue «KMU-Kontenrahmen» publiziert worden. Dieser ist mittlerweile etabliert und Darstellungen nach dem alten Kontenplan sind nur noch selten anzutreffen.

Für die Rechnungslegung nach Aktienrecht spielt der Kontenrahmen keine Rolle. Wichtig ist nur, dass die Mindestgliederungsvorschriften eingehalten werden. Darauf wird später noch eingegangen.

Die Klassierung und Gruppierung ist i.d.R. in einer Dezimalklassifikation vorzunehmen und diese folgt dem Kontenrahmen. Zur Anwendung gibt es keine Vorschriften.

- Kontenklasse: 1
- Kontenhauptgruppe: 10
- Kontengruppe: 100
- Konto: 1000 (4–6 stellig)

Die Kontennummer sollte mindestens 4 Stellen, maximal aber 6 Stellen umfassen. Die ersten 4 Stellen der Kontennummer entsprechen der Zuordnung in die betreffenden Klassen, Kontenhauptgruppen und Kontengruppen. Sofern 4-stellige Konten für eine ausreichende Gliederung genügen, müssen keine Detailgruppen eröffnet werden. Die 5. und 6. Stelle der Kontennummer ist für eine weitere Feinunterteilung der Konten innerhalb der Kontengruppen bestimmt.

Als Minimalanforderung sollen die eröffneten Konti den entsprechenden Klassen und Gruppen zugeteilt werden können. Je nach Umfang der Buchhaltung, müssen die erforderlichen Kontengruppen geführt werden.

Die Erläuterung der einzelnen Bilanzposten und Erfolgsrechnungsposten folgt keinem Kontenrahmen explizit, sie richtet sich aber teilweise nach dem KMU-Kontenrahmen.

Das Aktienrecht sieht eine Minimalgliederung vor. Demnach könnte man sich mit wenigen Konti begnügen. Es spricht von selbst, dass diese Minimalgliederung als Kontenrahmen in vielen Fällen auch für Kleinunternehmen nicht genügt. Das Gebot, dass die Buchhaltung einen möglichst sicheren Einblick in die wirtschaftliche Lage des Unternehmens geben soll, fordert einen detaillierten Kontenplan, dies auch bei Kleingesellschaften. Der Kontenplan muss der Grösse des Unternehmens angepasst sein. Für die Bilanzierung können die Konti als Einzelkonti oder zusammengefasst ausgewiesen werden. Bei einer Zusammenfassung darf die gesetzlich geforderte Mindestgliederung gemäss Gesetz nicht unterschritten werden. Eine Bilanz und Erfolgsrechnung ist nach den Gliederungsvorschriften des Aktienrechts am Schluss anzuführen (Muster hinten im Anhang).

III. Das Umlaufvermögen

Bei der Beschreibung der wichtigsten Konti wird im nachfolgenden Aufbau dem KMU-Kontenrahmen gefolgt. Die Aufzählung erhebt keinen Anspruch auf Vollständigkeit. Es werden vielmehr nur die gebräuchlichsten Konti erläutert.

1. *Flüssige Mittel und Wertschriften*

a) Kasse

Jeder Betrieb führt eine Kasse zur Bezahlung der notwendigen Barausgaben. In der Regel bereitet die Führung des Kassabuches wenig Probleme. Die Buchungen im Hauptbuch müssen den Eintragungen des Kassabuches entsprechen.

Bei grösserem Kassaverkehr muss klar organisatorisch definiert sein, wer zur Kassa Zugang hat und wer für die Eintragungen im Kassabuch verantwortlich ist.

Grössere Kassavorgänge, welche erheblich über dem durchschnittlichen Kassabestand liegen, sollten geprüft werden. Besonderes Augenmerk gilt einem solchen Vorgang, wenn er kurz nach oder kurz vor dem Bilanzstichtag erfolgt.

Die Bestandeskontrolle per Bilanzstichtag der Kassa ist im Zeitpunkt der Revision meistens nicht möglich. Als Ersatzprüfung dient hier die Saldokontrolle am Prüfungstag. Ein eigentlicher Kassasturz dürfte nur in wenigen Fällen angebracht sein. Ist das Kassabuch à jour und klar geführt, dürfte der wesentliche Teil der Prüfung für diesen Posten durchgeführt sein. Erst wenn die Kasse ein wesentliches Bilanzaktivum ist (über 1 % relativ oder absolut mehr als CHF 10'000.– der Bilanzsumme), empfiehlt sich ein Blick in die Kasse oder den Tresor.

b)   Postkonto

Das Postkonto oder Postcheckkonto lässt sich bei der Bestandesprüfung einfach durch die Jahresendbescheinigung prüfen.

Es ist angebracht zu fragen, wer Unterschriftsberechtigung hat und in welchem Rahmen. Bei Kleinunternehmen ist oft eine Einzelunterschrift des Betriebsinhabers anzutreffen. Einzelunterschriften des Personals sind selten und sollten eher durch Kollektivunterschrift zu zweit ersetzt werden, wobei auch eine Koppelung von Personengruppen möglich ist.

c)   Bankguthaben

Die Bestandesprüfung der Bankaktiven bereitet in der Regel wenig Aufwand. Sämtliche Bankkonti sind im Bestand zu prüfen und müssen mit den Banksaldi des Hauptbuches übereinstimmen. Als Revisor kann man von der zu prüfenden Gesellschaft ein komplettes Set aller Banken verlangen. Oft eignen sich die von den Banken erstellten Verzeichnisse. Gebräuchlich sind auch (bei einem gewissen Umfang) spezielle Erklärungen der Banken über alle geführten Bankverbindungen.

Es kann vorkommen, dass der Banksaldo nicht identisch ist mit dem Buchsaldo. Meistens liegt die Differenz in einem Posten, welcher bereits in der Buchhaltung gebucht ist. Als Beispiel sei eine Bankcheckbelastung genannt: Buchung altes Jahr, bei der Bank belastet im Folgejahr mit Valuta Vorjahr. Hier empfiehlt sich eine Buchung über transitorische Aktiven oder Passiven. Es ist einfacher, wenn alle Banksaldi (gemäss Bankauszug) exakt mit der Buchhaltung übereinstimmen.

Für die Bankkonti muss kein eigentliches Bankbuch (analog eines Kassabuches) geführt werden. Es genügt eine vollständige und chronologische

Belegablage in der Folge des monatlichen (oder quartalsweisen) Kontoauszuges der Bank. Alle Bewegungen gemäss Bankkontoauszug müssen durch einen Beleg dokumentiert sein.

Viele verschiedene Bankkonti verursachen mehr Kosten und erschweren die Übersicht. Die anzutreffenden diversen Konti für jede Sache sind als «Kässeli-Denken» überholt (siehe folgend f). Es braucht nicht für jede Liegenschaft ein eigenes Konto; ein Konto genügt. Damit werden eine bessere Übersicht und eine einfachere sowie effizientere Revidierung erreicht. Schliesslich erlaubt dies auch eine bessere Liquiditätsplanung. Es ist nachteilig, ein Konto im Minus mit teuren Zinsen und ein anderes Konto im Plus mit wenig Zinsertrag zu haben.

Auch hier ist es angebracht zu fragen, wer eine Unterschriftsberechtigung hat und in welchem Rahmen. Bei Kleinunternehmen ist oft eine Einzelunterschriftsberechtigung des Betriebsinhabers anzutreffen. Einzelunterschriftsberechtigungen des Personals sind selten und sollten eher durch Kollektivunterschrift zu zweit ersetzt werden. Problematisch ist eine Berechtigung des Buchhalters. Eine Zeichnungsberechtigung des Buchhalters ist grundsätzlich nicht zu empfehlen. Bei ihm würden dann die Kompetenzen für die Zahlung und für die Verbuchung zusammenfallen, was ein erhöhtes Risiko darstellt.

d) Übrige liquide Mittel

Übrige kurzfristige Geldanlagen können ebenfalls durch einfache Bankunterlagen geprüft werden. In dieser Position sind i.d.R. Callgelder, Eurogeldanlagen, Festgelder etc. bilanziert.

e) Wertschriften kurzfristig realisierbar

Als Wertschriften bezeichnet man Aktien, Obligationen, Optionen oder andere Wertpapiere neuerer Finanzanlageinstrumente.

In diesem Konto werden nur kurzfristig realisierbare Positionen erfasst, diese müssen daher einen Börsenwert aufweisen.

In dieser Gruppe sind die Wertschriftenbestände aufzuführen. Kurzfristige Finanzanlagen (liquide Mittel) werden in der Gruppe Barmittel (4) eingegliedert.

Teil B: Grundlagen des Rechnungswesens / Principles of Accounting

f) Verwaltung der liquiden Mittel

Die Zusammenlegung der Mittel und diverser Bankkonti mit gemeinsamer Verwaltung können den Wertschriftenertrag erhöhen und die Liquidität verbessern. Oft wird für verschiedene Zwecke oder Objekte jeweils ein eigenes Bank- oder Postkonto geführt, z.B. pro Liegenschaft eines. Eine solche Aufsplitterung verteilt die Liquidität und es kann vorkommen, dass für ein Konto ein geringer Ertragszins resultiert und für das zweite Konto sogar ein teurer Kontokorrentzins bezahlt werden muss. Die Buchhaltung eignet sich, hier Ordnung zu schaffen. Verschiedene Bankkonti werden überflüssig, da an deren Stelle verschiedene Buchhaltungskonti geschaffen werden können. Es genügt, wenn die Aktiven (Sollkonto) gemeinsam bestehen, währenddem die Habenseite aufgeteilt ist.

Beispiel: «Kässeli-Denken» (vereinfacht dargestellt)

AKTIVEN		PASSIVEN	
Bank 1	100		
Bank 2	200		
Bank 3	300	Eigenkapital	600
AUFWAND		ERTRAG	
		Liegenschaftsertrag	600

Beispiel: Konzentrierte Liquidität:

AKTIVEN		PASSIVEN	
Bank	600	Eigenkapital	600
AUFWAND		ERTRAG	
		Liegenschaftsertrag 1	100
		Liegenschaftsertrag 2	200
		Liegenschaftsertrag 3	300

Mit der zweiten Variante ist klar ersichtlich, welche Liegenschaft wie viel Ertrag bringt. Die Konzentration der Mittel auf einem Konto erlaubt eine bessere Liquidität.

Wertpapiere sind in aller Regel bei einer Bank deponiert und die Bestandesprüfung erfolgt meistens über den Depotauszug der Bank, Abweichungen sind möglich. Höhere Buchwerte als Bankwerte sind nicht möglich und müssen korrigiert werden. Tiefere Buchwerte sind zulässig und ergeben sich, wenn der Einstandswert gegenüber der Bankbewertung zum Bilanzstichtag tiefer liegt. Eine Notwendigkeit zur Aufwertung besteht nicht und ist auch oft nicht gewollt. Der Ausweis von nicht realisierten Buchgewinnen – und damit eine oft nicht gewünschte steuerliche Belastung – wird vermieden. Umgekehrt können auch Aufwertungen gewünscht sein, um ausgewiesene Verluste zu kompensieren. Damit wird eine Steuerplanung verfolgt und z.B. der Verlust von verrechenbaren Geschäftsverlusten aus Vorjahren vermieden.

Die kaufmännische Buchführung erlaubt im Sinne des Prinzips der Vorsicht, dass solche nicht realisierten Buchgewinne nicht ausgewiesen werden müssen. Beim Aktienrecht ergibt sich dies aus der speziellen Bewertungsvorschrift von Art. 667 OR.

Die Eidgenössische Steuerverwaltung gibt jedes Jahr eine Kursliste heraus. Die dort publizierten Werte entsprechen dem durchschnittlichen Kurs des Monats Dezember. Für alle Aktiengesellschaften mit Bilanz per 31. Dezember sind dort somit die höchstzulässigen Bilanzwerte ersichtlich. Die Kursliste erscheint auch auf dem Internet.

Werden von Jahr zu Jahr die Wertschriften neu bewertet, müssen Richtlinien dokumentiert werden, welche eine klare Bewertungsregel zeigen. Das Gebot der Stetigkeit verlangt, dass Wertschriften jedes Jahr gleich oder nach gleichen Grundsätzen zu bewerten sind. Abweichungen sind im Anhang zu erwähnen (z.B.: Wertschriften zu 80 % der Börsenwerte, Vorjahr 90 %).

Die zulässige Bewertung zum Börsenwert ist eine Abweichung des Grundsatzes der Bewertung zu Anschaffungskosten. Damit wird das Kostenanschaffungsprinzip wie auch das Realisationsprinzip durchbrochen. Im Hinblick auf die rasche Realisierbarkeit von frei handelbaren Börsenpapieren bedeutet dies eine vertretbare Lösung.

Wertschriften, die als Sicherheiten dienen, müssen im Anhang aufgeführt werden. Es ist deshalb besonders auf den Depotauszug der Bank zu achten. Die Bezeichnung «Pfanddepot» für verpfändete Aktien ist üblich.

Eher selten werden bei Kleinunternehmungen Wertpapiere langfristig und strategisch gehalten, was nicht heissen soll, dass sie lange im Portefeuille der Gesellschaft sind. Dann sind sie im Anlagevermögen zu bilanzieren. In der Regel handelt es sich bei Aktien und Obligationen um eine Alternative zum Sparkonto. Damit gehören diese Posten zum Umlaufvermögen.

2. Forderungen

a) Debitoren (Forderungen aus Leistungen)

Debitoren sind bis zum Bilanzstichtag noch nicht bezahlte, jedoch bereits in Rechnung gestellte Fakturen an Kunden. Per Bilanzstichtag muss eine Debitorenliste vorliegen. Für alle einzelnen Posten muss eine gestellte Rechnung existieren. Als Prüfungshandlung empfiehlt sich hier eine Stichprobenkontrolle. Aus der Debitorenliste werden 2–5 % (oder die grössten Posten) der Debitoren ausgewählt. Zu diesen Posten sind die Fakturen und der Zahlungseingang nachzuweisen. Im Zeitpunkt der Revision dürften noch nicht alle bezahlt sein. Diese Kontrolle zeigt aber, wie viel Prozent der Debitoren bezahlt sind und wie hoch die Debitorenverluste sind. Daraus ergibt sich die Höhe des Delkrederes.

Die Debitoren sind einige der ganz wenigen Posten der Bilanz, welche sich nach dem Stichprobenprinzip prüfen lassen.

Bei den Debitoren ist von angefangenen Arbeiten oder Debitoren mit Fakturalauf kurz nach Bilanzstichtag klar abzugrenzen. Alle Debitoren müssen per Bilanzstichtag eine Faktura aufweisen und in Versand sein. Alles andere gehört nicht hierher, sondern allenfalls zu den angefangenen Arbeiten. Alle Versuche, das Bilanzbild durch Debitoren des folgenden Geschäftsjahres zu beschönigen, sind nicht zu tolerieren.

Einer Prüfung bedarf auch das Verfalldatum der Debitoren. Gibt es mehrere Debitoren, welche bezüglich des durchschnittlichen Zahlungsziels erheblich zurückliegen, so muss dies näher geprüft werden. Liegt die Summe dieser kritischen Debitoren mindestens 50 % innerhalb des Delkrederes (von 5–10 % des Debitorengesamtbestandes), so ist dies angemessen. Wird das ganze Delkredere konsumiert, muss näher analysiert werden. Bestehen Prozessrisiken, muss das Delkredere erhöht werden oder (und) es muss eine Rückstellung für die Prozesskosten gebildet werden.

In der Praxis der Steuerbehörden haben sich folgende Delkredereansätze entwickelt:

- 5 % Debitoren Schweiz
- 10 % Debitoren Ausland
- 15 % Debitoren Ausland in Fremdwährung

Darüber hinausgehende Wertberichtigungen müssen i.d.R. begründet werden.

b)   Andere kurzfristige Forderungen

Neben den klassischen Guthaben aus Umsatz kann es auch noch andere kurzfristige Forderungen geben.

aa)   Gegenüber Dritten

In diese Rubrik gehören kurzfristige Darlehen und dergleichen. Oft sind diese Forderungen im Zeitpunkt der Revision bereits bezahlt.

bb)   Gegenüber Aktionären

Das Gesetz verlangt ausdrücklich, dass Forderungen gegenüber Aktionären besonders bilanziert werden müssen. Gerade in Kleinaktiengesellschaften bestehen rege Kontokorrentbeziehungen zwischen Eigentümern und Aktiengesellschaft. Der Revisor muss deshalb das Aktienbuch konsultieren und sich Gewissheit darüber verschaffen, dass Forderungen und Guthaben an und von Aktionären separat bilanziert sind. Eine Unterschrift auf die Kopie des Kontoblattes (Kontokorrentbestätigung) ist empfehlenswert. Gerade wenn mehrere Aktionäre existieren, werden damit klare Verhältnisse geschaffen, welche nur nützlich sein können.

Sind die Forderungen gegenüber Aktionären langfristig, erfolgt die Bilanzierung im Anlagevermögen.

cc) Gegenüber staatlichen Stellen

Hier sind mehrere Positionen denkbar.

Die Mehrwertsteuer ist eine mögliche Aktivposition. Meist ist die Mehrwertsteuer eine Schuld aus dem Umsatz. Es kann aber auch sein, dass in Zeiten grösserer Investitionen ein Guthaben resultiert. Der Revisor sollte die Mehrwertsteuerabrechnung einsehen und die Zusammenstellung der Jahreskontrolle auf ihre Plausibilität hin prüfen. Das Mehrwertsteuergesetz verlangt, dass einmal pro Jahr der deklarierte Umsatz mit der Buchhaltung abgestimmt wird. Der Umsatz laut Mehrwertsteuerdeklaration ist identisch mit der Buchhaltung oder die Abweichung muss sich schlüssig erklären lassen. Aus diesen Dokumenten erfolgt der Bilanzierungsnachweis.

Hierher gehört auch die Forderung gegenüber der eidgenössischen Steuerverwaltung in der Form der eidgenössischen Verrechnungssteuer. Vom Bruttozinsertrag auf inländischen Schuldnern erfolgt eine Reduktion von 35 % als Quellensteuer, welche rückforderbar ist. Es empfiehlt sich, die Quellensteuer jährlich zurückzuverlangen, auch bei kleinen Beträgen. Man muss sich dann nie überlegen, ob der Antrag bereits gestellt wurde oder nicht. Als Bilanzierungsnachweis dient hier somit die Kopie des eingereichten Formulars 25 (früher R 25). Durch ein konsequentes Verlangen dieser Unterlagen wird auch vermieden, dass die Rückforderung verjährt, was nach nur drei Jahren der Fall ist. Oft finden sich in solchen aktivierten Guthaben bereits verjährte Quellensteuern aus Zinserträgen, welche ausgebucht werden müssen.

Die Abrechnung aller Sozialabgaben, AHV, IV, BVG (inkl. Pensionskasse), UVG etc. kann zu Guthaben führen.

dd) Nicht einbezahltes Aktienkapital

Diese Aktivforderung der Gesellschaft wird unter kurzfristigem Aspekt hier im Umlaufvermögen bilanziert und unter langfristigem Aspekt im Anlagevermögen.

Die Frage der Bonität dieser Forderung ist durch den Revisor zu prüfen. Oft besorgt der Revisor bei Kleingesellschaften die Steuerangelegenheiten für die Gesellschaft und den Alleinaktionär oder Hauptaktionär. Er kennt somit ganz genau die persönliche finanzielle Situation und kann die Bonität exakt beurteilen. Dieses Wissen ist gut, kann aber dem Revisor in Verantwortlichkeitsprozessen auch zum Problem werden.

ee) Übrige Forderungen

Bei Kleinunternehmen verbreitet sind WIR-Guthaben. Diese sollten betriebswirtschaftlich und bilanztechnisch nicht zu hoch sein. WIR-Guthaben sind sehr beschränkt liquid. Haben sie einen wesentlichen Anteil in der Bilanz, muss eine Bewertungskorrektur Platz haben. Der Bilanzierungsnachweis erfolgt über den WIR-Kontoauszug.

Kautionen für Fahrzeuge, Telecom, Leasing etc. können aktiviert werden. Es empfiehlt sich, Buch zu führen, da sich sonst nach ein paar Jahren niemand mehr zu erinnern vermag, wofür Kaution gestellt wurde. Die Kaution muss dann abgeschrieben werden und das Geld geht verloren. Der Bilanzierungsnachweis erfolgt i.d.R. über einen Vertrag oder Kaufbeleg.

Beispiel: Liste von Kautionen

- Telecom PTT, Telefonkaution, 13.6.96,   CHF 1'000.–
  Tel. Nr.: 866 12 17
  (rückzahlbar mit Löschung der Telefonnummer)

- Leasing Kaution, Fiat Panda, BS Nr. 318212   CHF 1'000.–
  (rückzahlbar 17.7.99 mit letzter Rate)

- Getränke Automaten AG, 14.4.95, Barkaution   CHF   500.–
  (rückzahlbar mit Entfernung des Getränkeautomaten)

                                                CHF 2'500.–

Prämienkontokorrent bei Versicherungsgesellschaften und dergleichen fallen in diese Aktivposition. Der Bilanznachweis erfolgt über Kontoauszüge. Das BVG-Prämienkonto muss vom Revisor eingesehen werden, da eine diesbezügliche Schuld im Anhang ausweispflichtig ist.

Teil B: Grundlagen des Rechnungswesens / Principles of Accounting

3. Vorräte und angefangene Arbeiten

a) Warenlager

Bei Kleinunternehmen ist i.d.R. eine Lagerbuchhaltung nicht vorhanden. Das Warenlager muss deshalb als Inventur einmal pro Jahr aufgenommen werden.

Das Problem besteht darin, dass der Revisor meistens am Inventurtag nicht anwesend ist. Das Inventar muss aber durch den Revisor geprüft werden. An einem Revisionstag sind deshalb einige Inventarposten im Stichprobenprinzip auf ihre Plausibilität nachzuprüfen. Geprüft werden kann, ob ein entsprechender Wareneinkauf besteht oder ob ein Warenverkauf erfolgt ist. Diese Prüfung ist nur bei identifizierbarer Ware (z.B. mit Seriennummer) möglich. Somit kann retrospektiv die Glaubhaftigkeit des Inventars annäherungsweise ermittelt werden, so z.B. durch die Berechnung der Bruttogewinnmarge.

Kann der Revisor am Inventurtag nicht anwesend sein, so ist bei vertretbarer Ware später nur noch eine Plausibilitätsprüfung möglich. So kann sich der Revisor an einem Bilanzstichtag über das aktuelle Inventar einen Überblick verschaffen und mit dem historischen Inventar am Bilanzstichtag vergleichen.

Das Warenlager muss bzgl. Branche und Umsatz eine Logik aufweisen. Verderbliche Ware kann z.B. nicht mit mehr als 5–10 % eines Jahreseinkaufs bilanziert sein. Inventarisierte Ware aus dem Vorjahr ist besonders zu analysieren.

Bei schwächerem Geschäftsgang wird oft versucht, den Ausweis von Verlusten durch Erhöhung des Warenlagers zu vermeiden. Hier ist deshalb besondere Vorsicht geboten.

Die pauschale Ermittlung des Warenlagers ist nicht zulässig. Sie ist nur dort möglich, wo das Warenlager eine untergeordnete Bedeutung hat, z.B. 1–5 % der Bilanzaktiven ausmacht. Sie kann auch möglich sein, wenn offensichtlich ist, dass das Warenlager effektiv wesentlich mehr wert ist, als bilanziert wurde. Beispiel: Der Juwelier bilanziert seit Jahren den Rohgoldvorrat mit CHF 30'000.– und ein Blick in den Tresor zeigt, dass mehrere Kilobarren vorhanden sind.

Wenn die pauschale Warenlagerermittlung zu keinem vertretbaren Resultat führt, müssen überprüfbare Warenlagerlisten vorhanden sein. Es empfiehlt sich, diese durch die verantwortliche Person oder durch den Verwaltungsrat unterzeichnen zu lassen.

Das Warenlager wird i.d.R. zu Einstandspreisen bewertet. Die einzelnen Warenlagerposten werden zum Einkaufspreis eingesetzt. Dies ist eine einfache und leicht nachvollziehbare Methode. Sie wird in der Regel genügen und ist die hauptsächlich angewandte Bewertungsmethode bei Kleinunternehmen. Neben dieser Methode gibt es noch andere Berechnungsschemata, wir verweisen auf das HWP.

Das Steuerrecht lässt eine Warenlagerreserve von 1/3 zu, das heisst, es kann pauschal ein Bewertungseinschlag erfolgen ohne Nachweis der Notwendigkeit. In Zeiten der Hochkonjunktur wurde von diesem Instrument Gebrauch gemacht. In den rezessiven Zeiten sind die Kleinunternehmen oft nicht mehr in der Lage, die volle Warenlagerreserve zu bilden. Die Warenlagerreserve kann auch zur Steuerplanung eingesetzt werden, indem die Bildung und Auflösung des Warenlagerreservedrittels dem ausgewiesenen Geschäftsausgang angepasst wird. Solche Veränderungen müssen i.d.R. in der Steuererklärung bei der Angabe zur Bewertung des Warenlagers deklariert werden. Sie sind aber auch im Anhang zur Bilanz anzugeben, da eine Änderung eine Abweichung von der Stetigkeit bedeutet, welche ausweispflichtig ist (z.B.: Warenlagerreserve 80 % zu Einstand, Vorjahr 66 %).

Für die buchhalterische Berücksichtigung empfiehlt sich im Hinblick auf die Stetigkeit eine relative Bezugsgrösse (1/3) und keine absolute (CHF 100,000.–). Die absolute Änderung der relativen Bezugsgrösse führt zu einem im Anhang ausweispflichtigen Tatbestand (Veränderungen der Reserven, sofern die Auflösung wesentlich ist).

b)   Vorräte

Bei Kleinunternehmen wird das Warenlager oft in wenigen Positionen aufgenommen. Solange das Lager übersichtlich ist, genügt dies. Ist es umfangreich, erfolgt die Gliederung wie folgt:
- Vorräte Handelswaren
- Vorräte Rohstoffe
- Vorräte Werkstoffe
- Vorräte Hilfs- und Verbrauchsmaterial

- Pflichtlager
- Waren in Konsignation
- Fertigfabrikate
- Halbfabrikate

Kapitel 2: Bilanz, Erfolgsrechnung und ergänzende Rechnungen

Beispiel Vorräte (Einteilung):

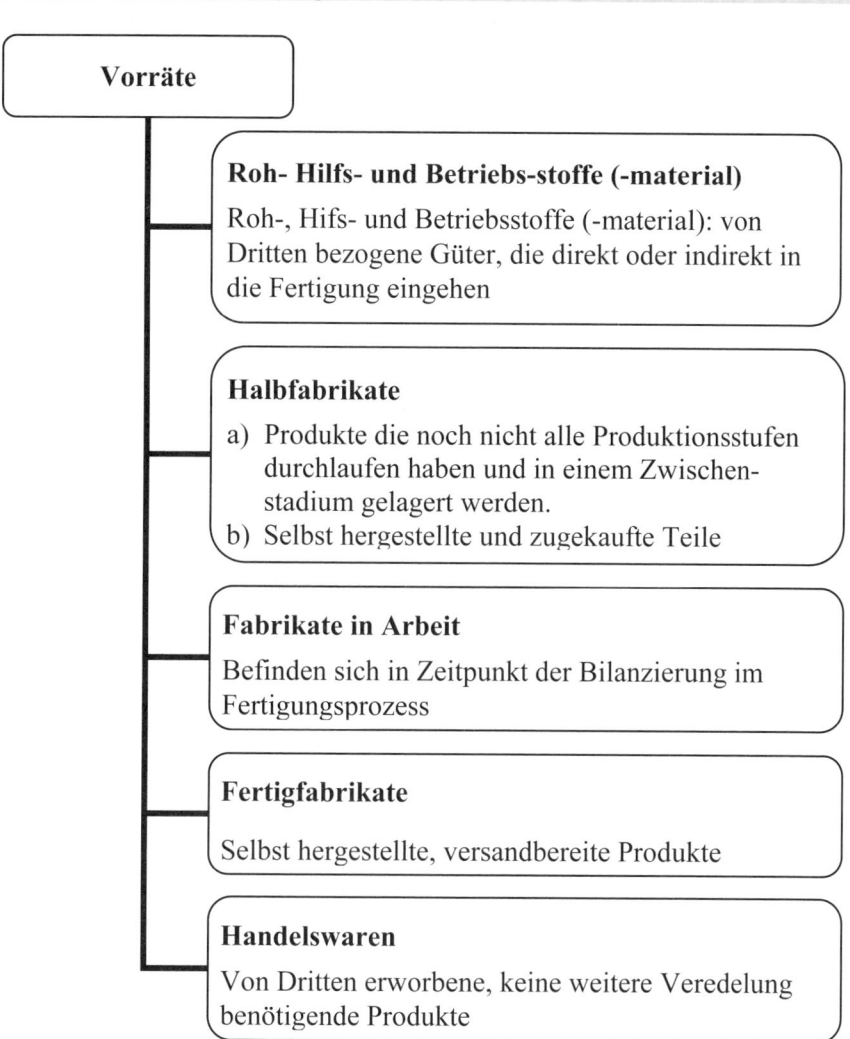

- **Vorräte**
  - **Roh- Hilfs- und Betriebs-stoffe (-material)**
    Roh-, Hifs- und Betriebsstoffe (-material): von Dritten bezogene Güter, die direkt oder indirekt in die Fertigung eingehen
  - **Halbfabrikate**
    a) Produkte die noch nicht alle Produktionsstufen durchlaufen haben und in einem Zwischenstadium gelagert werden.
    b) Selbst hergestellte und zugekaufte Teile
  - **Fabrikate in Arbeit**
    Befinden sich in Zeitpunkt der Bilanzierung im Fertigungsprozess
  - **Fertigfabrikate**
    Selbst hergestellte, versandbereite Produkte
  - **Handelswaren**
    Von Dritten erworbene, keine weitere Veredelung benötigende Produkte

c) Angefangene Arbeiten

Die Bewertung angefangener Arbeiten möchten wir an dieser Stelle noch etwas näher ausführen. Diese Position kann nicht als Spielball zur Bilanzkosmetik benutzt werden. Auch hier muss betont werden, dass pauschale Bewertungen unzulässig sind. Je kritischer eine Bilanz im Eigenkapitalausweis ist, desto eher ist der Verwaltungsrat geneigt, diese Position aufzuwerten. Für eine korrekte Bilanzierung ist eine genaue Erfassung unerlässlich. Damit ist eine Unterlage gefordert, welche folgende Angaben enthalten sollte:

1) die namentliche Nennung der mit den angefangenen Arbeiten betrauten Personen

2) die Stundenansätze zu Selbstkosten dieser Mitarbeiter

3) die geleisteten Stunden dieser Mitarbeiter für dieses Projekt

4) alle verarbeiteten Materialien.

Oft liegen bei Kleinunternehmen solche detaillierten Beschriebe nicht vor. Es können dann auch andere Aufzeichnungen geeignet sein, um den Bestand zu erfassen. Die Bestandesprüfung erfolgt anhand der Nachprüfung dieser Aufzeichnungen oder auch in der Einsicht von Fakturen des Folgejahres, welche am Bilanzstichtag vorhanden sind und bereits in Rechnung gestellt wurden. Dabei kann es natürlich nicht angehen, das Geschäftsjahr durch angefangene Arbeiten zu beschönigen, quasi den latenten Ertrag zu buchen, aber die latenten Aufwendungen nicht zu erfassen (z.B. bereits gelieferte Ware, die noch nicht in Rechnung gestellt ist).

Es ist auch zu berücksichtigen, dass bei einer Bilanzierung von angefangenen Arbeiten eine stetige Bewertung zu erfolgen hat. Abweichungen dieser Bewertung müssen im Anhang ausgewiesen werden. Für Kleinunternehmen empfiehlt es sich deshalb, hier besser nicht zu aktivieren.

Wichtig ist auch, dass genügend Liquidität vorhanden ist, um die angefangenen Arbeiten zu Ende zu führen. Dieser Punkt verdient umso mehr Beachtung, je langfristiger die angefangenen Arbeiten sind. Nur wenn die ganze Finanzierung möglich erscheint, kann aktiviert werden. Die Revisionsstelle ist keine Investitionsprüfungsstelle. Sie hat nicht zu beurteilen, ob die angefangenen Arbeiten zu einem erfolgsversprechenden Produkt führen werden. Dafür ist der Verwaltungsrat zuständig. Er kann aber eine Bilanzierung zu Erstellungskosten nur zulassen, wenn die Fertigstellung oder Fertigung absehbar ist, dies vor allem aus finanzieller Sicht.

Art. 666 Abs. 1 und 2 OR lautet:

«*^{1}Rohmaterialien, teilweise oder ganz fertig gestellte Erzeugnisse sowie Waren dürfen höchstens zu den Anschaffungs- oder den Herstellungskosten bewertet werden.*

^{2}Sind die Kosten höher als der am Bilanzstichtag allgemein geltende Marktpreis, so ist dieser massgebend.»

Damit soll auf die höchstzulässige Bewertung zum Marktwert hingewiesen werden. Dies bietet Probleme. Angefangene Arbeiten haben oft keinen Marktwert. Die Arbeiten können meistens nur von der Firma selbst fertig gestellt werden. Für einen Dritten sind sie nicht brauchbar. Angefangene Bauten, EDV-Programme, Waren, Einrichtungen, Möbel etc. sind für Dritte kaum verwertbar. Sofern es sich um regelmässige Leistungen handelt, dürfte die Aktivierung nicht problematisch sein. Aufgrund der Erfahrung finden diese Arbeiten Eingang in den Fertigungsprozess und gelangen auf den Markt. Im Zeitpunkt der Revision dürfte auch bereits schon ein Teil fertig gestellt und verkauft sein. Probleme bieten sich bei längerfristigen Projekten. Entsprechend steigen die Anforderungen an die Ermittlung der Werte der angefangenen Arbeiten. Unter Umständen empfiehlt sich ein Hinweis im Anhang.

Beispiel:

Hinweis: Angefangene Arbeiten sind zu Herstellungskosten bilanziert. Ein objektiver Marktwert konnte nicht ermittelt werden.

4. Aktive Rechnungsabgrenzung

Unter diese Position fallen buchhaltungsmässige Abgrenzungen, die fast ausschliesslich temporaler Natur sind, also eine zeitlich genaue Abgrenzung von einem zum anderen Geschäftsjahr zum Inhalt haben. Klassische Beispiele sind bereits bezahlte Versicherungsprämien und Mieten, welche jedoch erst das Folgejahr betreffen (bereits bezahlter Aufwand des folgenden Jahres).

Die transitorischen Aktiven sind kein Sammelsurium von diversen Aktiven und Guthaben, dafür müssen andere Konti verwendet werden.

Buchhaltungsmässig lösen sich die transitorischen Aktiven kurz nach Beginn des neuen Jahres auf, dann muss das Konto auf Null stehen.

Die Bestandeskontrolle erfolgt durch eine Stichprobenkontrolle. In der Regel empfiehlt es sich, die grösseren Posten zu analysieren.

IV. Das Anlagevermögen

1. Abschreibungen

Die im Umlaufvermögen bilanzierten Werte werden in der Regel mit integrierten Bewertungskorrekturen bilanziert, währenddem die im Anlagevermögen bilanzierten Werte zu Anschaffungskosten mit Abschreibungen und entsprechenden Wertberichtigungen bilanziert werden.

Umlaufvermögen ./. oder + Bewertungskorrektur = Bilanziertes UV

Anlagevermögen ./. Abschreibungen = Bilanziertes AV

oder: Anlagevermögen + Zugänge ./. Abgänge ./. Abschreibungen = Bilanziertes AV

Die einzelnen ausgewiesenen Konti des Anlagevermögens können netto nach Abschreibung ausgewiesen werden. Dies ist üblich. Zulässig ist auch die Führung eines separaten Wertberichtigungskontos, das dann auf der Bilanzaktivseite als Minusposten erscheint. Diese Bilanzierungsart empfiehlt sich vor allem bei Liegenschaften. Damit sind dann auf einen Blick Anschaffungswert und Wertberichtigung ersichtlich, was insbesondere bei geplanten Verkäufen für die Berechnung der Grundstückgewinnsteuer praktisch ist.

Die Abschreibungen müssen planmässig und stetig sein. In der Regel wird die steuerliche Abschreibungstabelle angewandt, und zwar der degressive Abschreibungssatz; dieser ist doppelt so hoch wie der lineare.

a) Lineare Abschreibung

10 % linear: 10 % Abschreibung pro Jahr auf dem Anschaffungswert, somit beträgt der Restwert nach 10 Jahren CHF 0.– (10 x 10 % = 100 %).

Die Abschreibung mit linearen Sätzen erfordert eine detaillierte Abschreibungsliste. Damit besteht Gewähr für eine Anlagekartei. Diese Abschreibungsmethode ist aufwendig und deshalb seltener anzutreffen.

b) Degressive Abschreibung

20 % degressiv: 20 % Abschreibung pro Jahr auf dem Restwert, somit beträgt der Restwert nach 1 Jahr 80 %, nach 2 Jahren 64 %, nach 3 Jahren 51,2 % etc. und somit nie 0.

Bei degressiver Abschreibung kann das Konto ohne Detail geführt werden. Die neuen Anschaffungen werden hinzugebucht und Ende Jahr wird vom ausgewiesenen Endwert abgeschrieben, meistens unter Beachtung der steuerlichen pro-rata-temporis-Abschreibungsvorschrift. Ein Kauf im Juni führt zur halben Abschreibung (6/12) im ersten Jahr, im zweiten wieder zur ganzen (12/12).

Mit Anwendung der degressiven Methode und der Beachtung der steuerlichen Abschreibungssätze ist die Abschreibung planmässig, stetig und meistens auch für die Bewertungskorrektur genügend.

Einige Steuergesetze sowie die Praxis erlauben, dass Abschreibungen nachgeholt werden können. Dies sieht konkret so aus, dass zur Vermeidung eines Verlustausweises die Abschreibungen nicht gebucht werden. Ist in einem späteren Jahr die Ertragsentwicklung so positiv, dass früher unterlassene Abschreibungen nachgeholt werden können, führt dies dann zu doppelten Abschreibungen (die laufenden und die nachgeholten). Was steuerlich in einigen Kantonen möglich ist, muss auf die handelsrechtliche Zulässigkeit überprüft werden. Als erstes bedingt die Nichtbuchung der Abschreibungen im Anhang bezüglich Stetigkeit einen Hinweis.

Beispiel:

Anhang: Die periodischen und planmässigen Abschreibungen auf Immobilien von CHF 10,000.– wurden nicht gebucht.

Als zweites muss das Anlagegut so weit abgeschrieben sein, dass der Buchwert unter dem Verkehrswert liegt. Ist dies nicht der Fall, muss abgeschrieben werden. Notwendige Abschreibungen müssen immer gebucht werden.

Als drittes müssen die später nachgeholten Abschreibungen wieder im Anhang bezüglich Abweichung zur Stetigkeit erwähnt werden.

Teil B: Grundlagen des Rechnungswesens / Principles of Accounting

Beispiel:

Anhang: Die Abschreibungen auf Immobilien beinhalten die periodischen und planmässigen Abschreibungen des laufenden Jahres, wie auch diejenigen des Vorjahres in Höhe von CHF 10,000.– (Nachholung).

c) Sofortabschreibungen

Einige Kantone erlauben steuerlich Sofortabschreibungen. Diese gestalten sich in der Regel wie folgt: 1. Jahr 80 %, 2. bis 4. Jahr keine, 5. Jahr 20 %. Damit trotz den (sich zeitlich durchmischenden) Abschreibungen von verschiedenen Werten (Gegenständen und Rechten) die Buchhaltung ohne das Führen einer separaten Anlagebuchhaltung transparent bleibt, empfiehlt sich, pro Jahr ein eigenes Konto zu führen, also z.B. Mobilien A (Kt. 1510.0 für im Jahre 2000 erworbene Gegenstände), Mobilien B (Kt. 1510.1 für im Jahre 2001 erworbene Gegenstände) etc. So ist sofort erkennbar, auf welchen Gegenständen gerade welche Abschreibungen erfolgen. Betrachten wir beispielsweise das Buchhaltungsjahr 2004. In diesem erfolgt auf den im Jahre 2000 gekauften Mobilien gerade die restliche Abschreibung von 20 % und auf den im Jahre 2004 erworbenen die erste Abschreibung von 80 %, die übrigen Mobilienkonti verändern sich in diesem Jahr nicht.

Kapitel 2: Bilanz, Erfolgsrechnung und ergänzende Rechnungen

Buchhaltungsjahre

	Jahr 2000	Jahr 2001	Jahr 2002	Jahr 2003	Jahr 2004	Jahr 2005
Mobilien A 1510.0 (seit 2000)	100 % −80 % = 20 %				20 % −20 % = 0 %	
Mobilien B 1510.1 (seit 2001)		100 % −80 % = 20 %				20 % −20 % = 0 %
Mobilien C 1510.2 (seit 2002)			100 % −80 % = 20 %			
Mobilien D 1510.3 (seit 2003)				100 % −80 % = 20 %		
Mobilien E 1510.4 (seit 2004)					100 % −80 % = 20 %	
Mobilien F 1510.5 (seit 2005)						100 % −80 % = 20 %

2. Anlagespiegel

Für eine einfache Darstellung der Anlagen empfiehlt sich ein Anlagespiegel. Diese Arbeit kann schnell und problemlos durchgeführt werden. Auf einen Blick lässt sich die Entwicklung der Anlagegüter darstellen.

Diese Darstellung wird ebenfalls in der Steuerdeklaration verlangt. Sie sieht vereinfacht wie folgt aus:

Teil B: Grundlagen des Rechnungswesens / Principles of Accounting

Stand 1.1.	Zugang	Stand vor Abschreibung	Abschreibung	Stand nach Abschreibung
Mobilien 100	0	100	40	60
Immobilien 100	0	100	7	93

3. Finanzanlagen

Bei Kleinunternehmen sind die Finanzanlagen meistens kurzfristiger Natur. Es handelt sich um vorhandene Liquidität, welche zur Erzielung eines Ertrages (Finanzertrages) in Obligationen und Aktien oder anderen Börsenpapieren angelegt wird. Selten sind deshalb Finanzanlagen im Anlagevermögen.

Zur Prüfung verweisen wir auf die Ausführungen zu den kurzfristigen Anlagen. Bei der Bewertung muss darauf hingewiesen werden, dass hier historische Anschaffungskosten unter Vornahme der notwendigen Abschreibungen massgebend sind.

a) Beteiligungspapiere

Zu den Beteiligungspapieren gehören Wertpapiere mit Vermögens- oder Mitwirkungsrechten, wie Aktien oder Partizipationsscheine. Damit von einer Beteiligung gesprochen werden kann, braucht es eine gewisse Quote (prozentualer Anteil an den gesamten Aktien der Gesellschaft). Kleinere Einheiten werden eher im Umlaufvermögen bilanziert.

Zur Prüfung verweisen wir auf die Ausführungen zu den kurzfristigen Anlagen. Bei der Bewertung muss darauf hingewiesen werden, dass hier historische Anschaffungskosten unter Vornahme der notwendigen Abschreibungen massgebend sind.

b) Obligationen

Obligationen sind Wertpapiere mit einem festen nominellen Kapital, welches i.d.R. verzinst wird.

Bei Kleinunternehmen sind die Obligationen trotz mehrjähriger Laufzeit meistens kurzfristiger Natur. Es handelt sich um vorhandene Liquidität, welche zur Erzielung eines Ertrages (Finanzertrages) in Obligationen und Aktien oder anderen Börsenpapieren angelegt wird. Selten sind deshalb Obligationen im Anlagevermögen anzutreffen.

Zur Prüfung verweisen wir auf die Ausführungen zu den kurzfristigen Anlagen. Bei der Bewertung muss darauf hingewiesen werden, dass hier historische Anschaffungskosten unter Vornahme der notwendigen Abschreibungen massgebend sind.

c) Langfristige Forderungen

Zu den langfristigen Forderungen gehören in der Regel Darlehen.

Zu den Bewertungen und zur Prüfung wird auf die Ausführungen zu den kurzfristigen Finanzanlagen verwiesen.

4. Mobile Sachanlagen

Als zweites wichtiges Anlagegut nach den Immobilien folgen die Mobilien. Kleinere Investitionen (geringer als CHF 1'000.–) werden meistens über den Aufwand ausgebucht und finden keinen Eingang in die Bilanz. Grössere Investitionen werden aktiviert, in die Bilanz aufgenommen und sukzessive abgeschrieben.

Die mobilen Sachanlagen werden gemäss KMU-Kontenrahmen wie folgt eingeteilt:

- Maschinen und Apparate Produktion (150.0)
- Mobiliar und Einrichtungen (151.0)
- Büromaschinen, EDV-Anlagen, Kommunikationssysteme (152.0)
- Fahrzeuge (153.0)
- Werkzeuge und Geräte (154.0)
- Lagereinrichtungen (155.0)

Hier soll keine Wiederholung der Ausführungen zum Kontenrahmen angebracht werden. In der Regel bereitet die Zuweisung der Begriffe keine besonderen Schwierigkeiten.

Mobilien werden meistens gekauft, für die Prüfung muss deshalb der Kaufvertrag eingesehen werden (mindestens sollte dies bei wesentlichen Neuerwerbungen erfolgen).

5. *Immobile Sachanlagen*

a) Immobilien

Für Kleinunternehmen bedeutet die Betriebsliegenschaft oft das wesentliche Aktivum des Betriebes, es ist das wirtschaftliche Dach. Die meisten Betriebsabläufe finden darin statt. Einerseits ist es Spargelegenheit; der erwirtschaftete Cashflow, das gesparte Geld, wird zur Amortisation der Hypotheken verwendet. Durch den Wegfall der Fremdfinanzierungskosten wird schnell eine Rendite von 4–5 % erwirtschaftet. Andererseits dient die Betriebsliegenschaft auch als Finanzierungsmittel. Die Hypotheken werden erhöht, damit betriebliche Investitionen finanziert werden können.

Aus der wesentlichen Bedeutung dieses Bilanzaktivums heraus erfolgt hier ein kleiner Exkurs zum Thema Immobilien und eine vertiefte Erläuterung.

aa) Sachenrecht

Ausgangspunkt für den Erwerb von Grundeigentum in der Schweiz ist der Eintrag eines Grundstückes im Grundbuch. Ist eine Liegenschaft eingetragen, darf auf das Bestehen des zivilrechtlichen Eigentums vertraut werden. Die Grundbuchämter sorgen für die aktuellen Eintragungen. Die teilweise im Ausland anzutreffende Unsicherheit mit entsprechenden Überraschungen ist nicht mit der hiesigen Situation vergleichbar. Im Grundbuch werden Liegenschaften (und seit 1963 auch Stockwerkeigentum) registriert.

bb) Obligationenrecht

Für den sachenrechtlichen Eintrag bedarf es einer Grundlage. Diese bildet in der Regel der Grundstückkauf. Der Grundstückkauf ist nur mit einem öffentlich beurkundeten Vertrag rechtsgültig. Der Vertrag wird vor einem Notar abgeschlossen, sei dies ein privat tätiger Notar oder ein Amtsnotar, was vom jeweiligen Kanton abhängt. Die Nichtbeachtung der Form hat die Nichtigkeit des Vertrages zur Folge. Auch das Vereinbaren von Vorverträgen, Reservationen etc. unterliegt dem Formzwang.

cc) Kaufvertrag

In den meisten Fällen erwirbt man in der Schweiz Grundeigentum durch Kauf. Als wesentlicher Inhalt sollte der Vertrag folgende Angaben enthalten:

- Käufer und Verkäufer
- Objekt (Nummer der Liegenschaftsparzelle) mit Beschrieb
- Kaufpreis

Damit sind die wesentlichen Elemente festgehalten. Meistens enthalten die Verträge noch Bestimmungen über die Fälligkeit des Kaufpreises, über das gesetzliche Pfandrecht des Staates, über den Übergangszeitpunkt (Antritt), über allfällige Mietverträge, über die Grundstückgewinnsteuer und über die Gewährleistung.

Vielfach erfolgt vor der Unterzeichnung der Verträge eine Anzahlung an den Verkäufer, verbunden mit einer Reservation oder einem einfachen schriftlichen Vertrag. Da diese Dokumente nicht über die erforderliche Form verfügen, haben sie keine direkt durchsetzbaren juristischen Auswirkungen.

Die Aktivierungsfähigkeit von Anzahlungen muss deshalb geprüft werden. Ist im Zeitpunkt der Revision der Kauf im Folgejahr schon vollzogen, kann im Rahmen der Kaufpreisabwicklung aktiviert werden. Ist dies noch nicht der Fall, ist eine nähere Untersuchung erforderlich.

dd) Kaufpreis

Die Immobilienpreise sind in der Schweiz gegenüber dem Ausland relativ hoch. Dies hat mehrere Gründe. Zum einen liegt es an der Währung. Der Schweizer Franken ist gegenüber dem Ausland überbewertet. Ein weiterer Grund liegt in den Bauvorschriften. Eine strenge Reglementierung sieht detaillierte Zonenvorschriften vor. Die in den 60er Jahren grosszügig dimensionierten Baulandzonen werden, im Hinblick auf die stark korrigierte Entwicklung der schweizerischen Bevölkerung, laufend zurückgezont. Weiter existieren Baunormen, die eine Leichtbauweise nicht zulassen. Billigbauten sind kaum anzutreffen. Die Bausubstanz wird im Hinblick auf ein Gebäudealter von bis zu hundert Jahren (bei Wohnhäusern) erstellt. Für industrielle Bauten liegen andere Werte vor. Vor allem aus diesen Gründen ist Grundeigentum in der Schweiz nicht günstig. Zum Kaufpreis kommen, je nach Kanton, Handänderungssteuern von 0,4–3 % sowie Notariatskosten von ca. 2,5 % hinzu.

ee) Marktsituation

Die Entwicklung der Grundstückpreise hat in der Vergangenheit eine kontinuierliche Zunahme der Preise gezeigt. In den 80er Jahren hatten Hochkonjunktur und Inflation zusätzlich die Liegenschaftspreise in die Höhe gedrückt. Mit gesetzgeberischen Massnahmen wurde im Jahre 1989 der Liegenschaftsmarkt gedämpft. Ein Veräusserungsverbot innerhalb von 5 Jahren seit Erwerb, sowie eine Pfandbelastungsgrenze von 80 % des Kaufpreises innerhalb von 3 Jahren seit Erwerb, haben den Liegenschaftsmarkt seinerzeit vehement gebremst. Die weitere Korrektur in Richtung Beruhigung und Dämpfung der Überhitzung kam dann später viel stärker ohne dirigistische staatliche Massnahmen. Die Rezession zu Beginn der 90er Jahre führte zu einem starken Einbruch der Immobilienpreise. Man darf davon ausgehen, dass sich die Preise um 20–30 % reduziert haben. Die Mutationen sind stark zurückgegangen. Die seinerzeitigen gesetzlichen Massnahmen wurden aufgehoben. Der Markt befindet sich jetzt in einer Stabilisierungsphase. Es ist damit zu rechnen, dass mit der zunehmenden Erholung der Wirtschaft die Preise anziehen werden.

Bei der Bewertung ist deshalb der aktuellen Marktsituation Rechnung zu tragen. Das Anlagevermögen wird zu Anschaffungswerten abzüglich Abschreibungen bilanziert. Gefordert ist auch die Bilanzierung zu Fortführungswerten («*going concern*»). Damit ist es möglich, dass der Bilanzwert über dem effektiven Wert liegt. Die aktuelle Marktsituation greift aber in die Gesamtsituation des Unternehmens ein, so auch bei der Hypothezierung. Die Bank wird bei der Berechnung der Belastungsgrenze nur mit Marktwerten operieren. Wird dadurch die Liquidität eingeschränkt, so ist dies zu berücksichtigen, und zwar auch durch die Revisionsstelle. Die mangelnde Liquidität kann dazu führen, dass gewisse Projekte nicht mehr zu Ende geführt werden können, dies kann sich dann in der Bewertung niederschlagen.

ff) Beschränkung des Grundstückerwerbs durch Ausländer

In diesem Zusammenhang ist auf das Bundesgesetz über den Erwerb von Grundstücken durch Personen im Ausland zu verweisen, welches den Erwerb stark einschränkt. Eine beschränkte Liberalisierung der Situation erfolgte aufgrund verschiedener bilateraler Abkommen mit der EU.

gg) Prüfungshandlungen

Bei neu bilanzierten Liegenschaften ist zu überprüfen, ob ein Kaufvertrag und ein Grundbuchauszug vorliegen.

Bei bereits bilanzierten Liegenschaften ist (je nach Situation) alle 2–4 Jahre ein Grundbuchauszug zu bestellen und zu prüfen. Zu prüfen ist insbesondere, ob die Liegenschaft immer noch im Eigentum der Gesellschaft steht. Weiter gibt der Grundbuchauszug Auskunft über die Grundpfandtitel. Die im Auszug erwähnten Schuldbriefe sollten in der Regel bei der kreditgebenden Bank deponiert sein, dies muss grundsätzlich so sein. Anderenfalls ist zu untersuchen, wo sich die Urkunde befindet. Ist sie im Safe der Gesellschaft, braucht es keine weiteren Handlungen. Damit liegt eine betriebseigene Liquiditätsreserve vor. Ist der Titel anderweitig deponiert, liegt in der Regel eine Sicherheit für eine Schuld vor. Ein entsprechender Hinweis «Abtretung von Bilanzaktiven zugunsten eigener oder fremder Schulden» muss im Anhang aufgeführt sein.

Bei bereits bilanzierten Liegenschaften ist der Wert zu prüfen. Wurde die Liegenschaft kontinuierlich abgeschrieben, dürften in der Regel stille Reserven bestehen (Verkehrswert höher als Bilanzwert). Erfolgten keine Abschreibungen mehr (z.B. um den Ausweis von Verlusten zu vermeiden), hat eine Verkehrswertprüfung zu erfolgen. Diese kann summarisch durch den Revisor erfolgen oder auch durch einen Architekten oder Immobiliensachverständigen durchgeführt werden. Dabei genügt für eine erste Beurteilung eine einfache kostengünstige Analyse. Zeigt diese einen Wert über dem Bilanzwert, so ist die Bewertung in Ordnung, liegt dieser Wert darunter, muss detailliert bewertet werden.

Liegenschaftskäufe während den Hochpreisjahren 1980–1990 müssen besonders kritisch beurteilt werden. Aufgrund der geschilderten Marktveränderungen können hier Bewertungskorrekturen bis zu 35 % notwendig sein.

b)   Einteilung der Immobilien

Die Immobilien werden i.d.R. wie folgt eingeteilt:

- Geschäftsliegenschaften
- Fabrikgebäude
- Werkstattgebäude
- Lagergebäude
- Ausstellungs- und Verkaufsgebäude
- Büro- und Verwaltungsgebäude
- Wohnhäuser
- unbebaute Grundstücke.

c)   Aufwertungen

Liegenschaften können bei entsprechender Werthaltigkeit bis zum Gestehungswert erfolgswirksam aufgewertet werden. Dies wird gemacht, um Verlustausweise zu verhindern oder steuerlich die Verrechenbarkeit von Vorjahresverlusten nicht zu verlieren. Darüber hinausgehende Aufwertungen sind nur beschränkt möglich (vgl. hinten Kapitel VI. 3). Voraussetzung für die Aufwertung ist, dass der Verkehrswert mindestens dem neuen Buchwert entspricht.

6.   *Immaterielle Sachanlagen*

a)   Einleitung

Immaterielle Anlagen haben eine zunehmende Bedeutung. Auch im privaten Konsum haben existentielle Güter eine abnehmende Bedeutung. Dienstleistungen und ideelle Werte machen einen zunehmenden Anteil aus. Gleich verhält es sich bei vielen Betrieben. Die Sachanlagenintensität ist abnehmend, währenddem der Aufwand für Know-how und betriebliches «Human capital» enorm steigt. Beispielsweise ist häufig nicht mehr der Maschinenpark von zentraler Bedeutung, sondern effiziente Betriebsabläufe. Die buchhaltungsmässige Notwendigkeit, solche immateriellen Investitionen zu aktivieren, kann zum Bedürfnis werden. Es ist jedoch klar zu betonen, dass dies nur sehr beschränkt möglich ist. Der zukünftige Nutzen der Immaterialgüter und Rechte muss vorhanden sein. Wenn in Kursen dem Personal erklärt wird, wie eine Steuererklärung auszufüllen ist, so ist dies nicht aktivierbar. Wenn jedoch Mitarbeiter ein EDV-Programm herstellen, das Steuererklärungen verarbeitet, so ist dies aktivierbar.

Die Aktivierung von selbst erarbeiteten immateriellen Gütern sollte sehr zurückhaltend eingesetzt werden. Anders ist es bei käuflich erworbenen immateriellen Gütern. Diese können unter Vornahme der notwendigen Abschreibungen zum Kaufpreis aktiviert werden.

Immaterielle Anlagegüter werden wie folgt eingeteilt:

- Patente und Rezepte,
- Marken, Muster und Modelle,
- Lizenzen, Konzessionen,
- Urheberrechte und
- Goodwill.

b) Voraussetzungen

Forschungs- und Entwicklungskosten können unter bestimmten Umständen aktiviert werden. Diese Aktivierung ist aber nur dann möglich, wenn sie einer bestimmten Struktur zugeordnet werden kann. Diese kurze Beschreibung setzt nach den allgemeinen Vorschriften der Buchführung eine Erfassung der geleisteten Arbeit voraus. Damit ist eine Urkunde gefordert, welche folgende Angaben enthalten sollte:

1) die Nennung mit Namen der mit dieser Entwicklung betrauten Personen
2) die Stundenansätze zu Selbstkosten dieser Mitarbeiter
3) die geleisteten Stunden dieser Mitarbeiter für dieses Projekt
4) einen Produktebeschrieb, der Auskunft über den derzeitigen Stand der Entwicklung gibt
5) die Marktchancen des Produktes
6) die aktuellen Verkaufszahlen.

Eine pauschale Aktivierung ist unzulässig. Die Überlegung «man hat schon sehr viel daran gearbeitet, dann wird es wohl sehr viel wert sein» darf nicht angestellt werden.

7. *Aktivierter Aufwand und aktive Berichtigungsposten*

Der KMU-Kontenrahmen empfiehlt für den aktivierten Aufwand eine separate Gruppe. Dies hat den Vorteil, dass der Bilanzleser sofort erkennt, welcher Aufwand aktiviert wurde. Damit ist klar ersichtlich, um wie viele Bilanzaktiven der Aufwand geschmälert wurde. Oft ist die Praxis anzutreffen, dass aktivierter Aufwand den Aufwandkonti belastet wird, also der Aufwand netto nach Korrektur erscheint.

Dies entspricht der klassischen Lehre, wonach eine Erhöhung des Warenlagers zu einer Verminderung des Warenaufwandes führt. Dies ist auch logisch: Wird nicht alle eingekaufte Ware verkauft, verbleibt der nicht verkaufte Teil als Warenlager. Damit werden nicht alle Wareneinkäufe zu Aufwand, sondern der nicht verkaufte Anteil wird zu Warenlager.

Oft ist ein separates Bestandesänderungskonto im Warenaufwand anzutreffen. Dies dient dem Bilanzleser (und Erfolgsrechnungsleser) als gute Information. Sofort ist ersichtlich, welche Bestandesänderung verbucht wurde. Diesem Prinzip folgend ist es auch sinnvoll, aktivierten Aufwand separat in der Erfolgsrechnung auszuweisen, dies anstelle einer versteckten Aufwandsminderung. Man muss sich sogar fragen, ob eine Praxis ohne separaten Ausweis nicht dem Verrechnungsverbot widerspricht. Eine Aktivierung von Aufwand über das Aufwandkonto führt immer zu einem Nettoausweis. Eine separate Buchung über ein eigenes Konto zeigt den Bruttoaufwand zu 100 % und den aktivierten Aufwand ganz separat.

In diesen Bereich fallen folgende Posten:

- Gründungs- und Organisationsaufwand
- Forschungs- und Entwicklungsaufwand
- übriger aktivierter Aufwand.

V. Das Fremdkapital

1. *Kurzfristiges Fremdkapital*

a)   Kreditoren (Verbindlichkeiten aus Lieferung und Leistung)

Die Kreditoren sind die bis zum Abschlussdatum gestellten Rechnungen von Lieferanten und anderen Personen. Die Kreditoren werden i.d.R. einzeln gebucht und im Passivkonto sowie in einem Aufwandkonto erfasst. Die Ende Jahr gebuchten Kreditoren lösen sich in den ersten 1–3 Monaten nach Bilanzabschluss wieder auf; dies wenn sie bezahlt worden sind. Das Kreditorenkonto hat deshalb einmal pro Jahr im Saldo CHF 0.–. Es kann sein, dass es sich nicht ganz auflöst und ein Saldo «mitgezogen» wird. Es empfiehlt sich hier abzuklären, worum es sich handelt. Der Klarheit willen sollte sich das Konto auflösen und dann nur die neuen Kreditoren per Ende Jahr enthalten. Für die Revision muss eine Kreditorenliste vorliegen. Diese sollte mit dem Konto übereinstimmen und die Zahlungen sollten im neuen Jahr ersichtlich sein. Im neuen laufenden Jahr muss geprüft werden, ob nicht Kreditoren bezahlt werden, welche per Abschlusstag des Vorjahres als Kreditoren hätten verbucht werden sollen. Dann ist zu analysieren, weshalb diese nicht auf der Kreditorenliste standen.

Zu den Kreditoren zählen nicht nur Forderungen von Lieferanten, sondern auch solche von Sozial- und anderen Versicherungsgesellschaften, von Finanzverwaltungen etc. Diese Schulden wurden unter «andere kurzfristige Verbindlichkeiten» erfasst (siehe e).

b)   Anzahlungen von Kunden

Sofern Vorauszahlungen von Kunden vorliegen, empfiehlt sich eine separate Bilanzierung.

c)   Verbindlichkeiten gegenüber Aktionären

Das Gesetz verlangt ausdrücklich, dass Forderungen von Aktionären gesondert bilanziert werden, dies sowohl auf der Aktiv- als auch auf der Passivseite. Das setzt voraus, dass der Revisor das Aktienbuch einsieht. Bei Kleinunternehmen sind meistens 100 % der Aktionäre bekannt, was die Situation vereinfacht, jedoch die Prüfungspflichten nicht einschränkt.

Bei kleinen Aktiengesellschaften ist der Aktionär eng mit seinem Betrieb verbunden (häufig ist er sogar Alleinaktionär), weshalb sich oft eine rege Kontokorrentbeziehung ergibt. Für den Revisor führt dies zur doppelten Schwierigkeit. Er muss einerseits die Aktiengesellschaft und andererseits noch zusätzlich die Situation des Aktionärs kritisch prüfen, dies wenn die Aktiengesellschaft diesem gegenüber eine Forderung hat. In Konsequenz führt dies zur doppelten Prüfung. Es genügt nicht, nur festzustellen, dass eine Forderung besteht, sondern es muss auch die Aktionärsforderung hinsichtlich Bewertung geprüft werden.

Die steuerlichen Vorschriften verlangen eine Verzinsung der Forderungen der AG.

d) Bankverbindlichkeiten

Was bei der Aktivseite gilt, ist auch für die Passivseite massgebend.

Die Bestandesprüfung der Bankpassiven bereitet in der Regel wenig Aufwand. Sämtliche Bankkonti sind im Bestand zu prüfen und müssen mit den Banksaldi des Hauptbuches übereinstimmen. Als Revisor kann man von der zu prüfenden Gesellschaft ein komplettes Set aller Banken verlangen. Oft eignen sich die von den Banken erstellten Verzeichnisse. Gebräuchlich sind auch bei einem gewissen Umfang spezielle Erklärungen der Banken über alle geführten Bankverbindungen.

Es kann vorkommen, dass der Banksaldo nicht identisch ist mit dem Buchsaldo. Meistens liegt die Differenz in einem Posten, welcher bereits in der Buchhaltung gebucht ist. Als Beispiel sei eine Bankcheckbelastung genannt: Buchung altes Jahr, bei der Bank belastet im Folgejahr, Valuta Vorjahr. Hier empfiehlt sich eine Buchung über transitorische Aktiven oder Passiven vorzunehmen. Es ist einfacher, wenn alle Banksaldi gemäss Bankauszug exakt mit der Buchhaltung übereinstimmen.

Für die Bankkonti muss kein eigentliches Bankbuch geführt werden. Es genügt eine vollständige und chronologische Belegablage. Alle Bewegungen gemäss den Bankkontoauszügen müssen durch einen Beleg dokumentiert sein.

Viele verschiedene Bankkonti verursachen mehr Kosten und erschweren die Übersicht.

Es ist auch hier angebracht zu fragen, wer Unterschriftsberechtigung hat und in welchem Rahmen. Bei Kleinunternehmen ist oft Einzelunterschrift des Betriebsinhabers anzutreffen. Einzelunterschriften des Personals sind selten und sollten eher durch Kollektivunterschrift zu zweit ersetzt werden.

e) Andere kurzfristige Verbindlichkeiten

In diesen Bilanzposten gehören alle kurzfristigen Verbindlichkeiten. Meistens liegen hier Verträge oder Saldobestätigungen vor. Der Bilanzposten muss sich klar aufschlüsseln. Enthält er mehrere Positionen, müssen diese ersichtlich sein. Positionen, die sich im Verlaufe von 1–2 Jahren nicht auflösen, sind näher zu prüfen.

Es kann empfehlenswert sein, eine Bestätigung zu verlangen. Dies muss im Dialog mit der Verwaltung geschehen. Es kann unangenehm für die Gesellschaft sein, einen Dritten daran zu erinnern, dass er noch ein Guthaben hat. Es kann aber auch gut für die Revisionsstelle sein, zu wissen, dass hier nicht noch mehr Forderungen figurieren.

f) Passive Rechnungsabgrenzung

Die passive Rechnungsabgrenzung (transitorische Passiven) darf nur klar definierte Buchungen enthalten wie:

- Zahlungseingänge im alten Jahr, welche im Folgejahr als Ertrag zu verbuchen sind (Beispiel: Zahlungseingang schon Ende Dezember 2004 für Miete Januar 2005);
- Sachaufwand im alten Jahr, welcher erst im Folgejahr zur Zahlung fällig wird (Beispiel: zeitlich abgegrenzter Zinsaufwand mit Fälligkeit nach Abschlussdatum).

Die Buchungen auf das Konto «Transitorische Passiven» sind klar von den Buchungen auf «Kreditoren» (fällige oder fakturierte Verpflichtungen) und «Rückstellungen» (absehbare Verpflichtungen, deren zeitlicher Anfall und betragliche Höhe jedoch nicht klar bestimmt werden kann) zu unterscheiden.

g) Rückstellungen für absehbare Verpflichtungen

Die betriebswirtschaftlich notwendigen Rückstellungen für «absehbare Verpflichtungen», deren zeitlicher Anfall und genaue Höhe ungewiss ist, sollen in dem Jahr, in welchem diese Verpflichtung entstanden oder erkannt worden ist, als Aufwand der Erfolgsrechnung belastet werden (klassischer Fall: hängiger Prozess mit ungewissem Ausgang). Sobald das Motiv, das zur Bildung der Rückstellung geführt hat, wegfällt, sollte die Rückstellung erfolgswirksam aufgelöst werden.

Das Obligationenrecht lässt auch noch Rückstellungen für bloss mögliche Risiken zu. Der Eintritt dieser Risiken und die Betragshöhe dieser Rückstellungen sind ungewiss, im Gegensatz zu absehbaren Ereignissen. Die Grenze solcher Rückstellungen findet sich für Kleinunternehmen schnell im Steuerrecht. Aufgrund der Identität von Steuer- und Handelsbilanz werden solche Rückstellungen oft vom Fiskus nicht anerkannt. Die Wahrscheinlichkeit des Ereignisses muss ein gewisses Gewicht haben, damit die steuerliche Akzeptanz vorhanden ist.

h) Rückstellungen für künftige Ersatzinvestitionen

Diese Verbuchung ist bei Kleinunternehmen sehr selten anzutreffen.

Der Sinn dieser Rückstellungen liegt darin, vorhersehbare Ersatzinvestitionen (Maschinenpark, Grossreparaturen, Revisionen, etc.), die zur Erstellung der Leistung notwendig sind und alle paar Jahre anfallen, periodengerecht (in Form vorweggenommener Abschreibungen) der Erfolgsrechnung zu belasten. Die Rückstellung kann in gewissem Sinne mit dem Wertberichtigungskonto zur Aktivseite verglichen werden, welches die kumulierten, periodisch verbuchten Abschreibungen beinhaltet.

Die Bildung und Auflösung dieser Rückstellungen muss betriebswirtschaftlich notwendig sein. Die Verwendung dieser Rückstellungen sollte mit der Investitionsrechnung im Einklang sein.

Beispiel:

Zu erwartende Ersatzinvestition: Spezialfahrzeug CHF 70'000.–

geschätzte Nutzungsdauer: 7 Jahre

vorzunehmende Rückstellung (anstelle der Abschreibungen):
CHF 10'000.– p.a.

Kumulierte Rückstellungen Anfang 7. Jahr: CHF 60'000.–

Offerte für Spezialfahrzeug, Kauf Ende 7. Jahr:	*CHF 77'000.–*
in Höhe der Rückstellungen einbehaltene Mittel	*./. CHF 60'000.–*
einbehaltener Zinsertrag auf diesen Mitteln, geschätzt	*./. CHF 5'000.–*
Ausgaben im 7. Jahr	*CHF 12'000.–*

Für die künftige Ersatzinvestition (Voranschlag z.B. CHF 84'000.–, geplante Nutzungsdauer 6 Jahre) ist ab dem 8. Jahr eine jährliche Rückstellung in der Höhe von CHF 14'000.– zu bilden.

Wie schon zu Beginn erwähnt, ist diese Verbuchung selten anzutreffen. Sie ist i.d.R. auch nicht steuerlich anerkannt. Da bei Kleinunternehmen Steuerbilanz und Handelsbilanz identisch sind, ist diese Verbuchung dort selten.

2. *Langfristiges Fremdkapital*

Langfristiges Fremdkapital sind i.d.R. Schulden, welche auf lange Sicht bestehen und meistens auch eine längere Fälligkeit haben. Schulden, die seit längerer Zeit bestehen, müssen nicht langfristig sein. Ein seit längerer Zeit bestehender Kontokorrentkredit ist meistens kurzfristig. Eine neu aufgenommene Hypothek ist langfristig.

a) Langfristige Finanzverbindlichkeiten

Langfristige Finanzverbindlichkeiten sind bei Kleinaktiengesellschaften meistens Hypotheken auf der Geschäftsliegenschaft. Zu denken ist aber auch an langfristige Bankdarlehen oder Darlehen Dritter.

Als Prüfungshandlung empfiehlt sich die Saldokontrolle; bei Bankschulden mit Zins- und Saldoausweis. Allenfalls ist eine Saldobestätigung des Gläubigers einzufordern.

Als weitere Prüfungshandlung empfiehlt sich der Beizug der Verträge. Langfristige Finanzverbindlichkeiten sind oft von quantitativer Bedeutung, weshalb meistens schriftliche Verträge vorliegen. Es ist gut zu wissen, ob in diesen Verträgen Vertragselemente enthalten sind, die für das Unternehmen wichtig sind. Schliesslich geben diese noch Auskunft, ob Sicherheiten bestehen. Allenfalls führt dies zu einem Hinweis im Anhang («Zur Sicherung eigener Verpflichtungen abgetretene Aktiven»).

b) Andere langfristige Verbindlichkeiten

Andere langfristige Finanzverbindlichkeiten sind hier aufzuführen, zu denken ist dabei z.B. an eine WIR-Hypothek.

Auch hier ist als Prüfungshandlung die Saldokontrolle mittels Zins- und Saldoausweis sowie das Studium der Vertragsunterlagen angebracht.

c) Rückstellungen langfristig

Die betriebswirtschaftlich notwendigen langfristigen Rückstellungen für absehbare Verpflichtungen, deren zeitlicher Anfall und genaue Höhe ungewiss ist, sollen in dem Jahr, in welchem diese Verpflichtung entstanden oder erkannt worden ist, als Aufwand der Erfolgsrechnung belastet werden. Sobald das Motiv, das zur Bildung der Rückstellung geführt hat, wegfällt, sollte die Rückstellung erfolgswirksam aufgelöst werden.

Steuerlich müssen solche Rückstellungen oft detailliert begründet werden.

VI. Das Eigenkapital

1. Kapital

Das Kapital weist i.d.R. keine Buchungen aus. Es bleibt konstant und kann sich nur durch einen Beschluss der Generalversammlung mit Kapitalerhöhung oder Kapitalherabsetzung verändern. Das buchhaltungsmässig ausgewiesene Kapital muss dem statutarischen Kapital entsprechen, was auch durch einen entsprechenden Handelsregisterauszug belegt wird.

Das Aktienkapital der AG beträgt mindestens CHF 100'000.–, bei Gesellschaften, die vor dem 1. Januar 1985 gegründet worden sind, CHF 50'000.–.

Das Stammkapital der GmbH beträgt mindestens CHF 20'000.–.

Kapitel 2: Bilanz, Erfolgsrechnung und ergänzende Rechnungen

2. Reserven

Die gesetzlichen Reserven werden durch die Einlagen aus Gewinnen geäufnet.

«*Fünf Prozent des Jahresgewinnes sind der allgemeinen gesetzlichen Reserve zuzuweisen, bis diese 20 Prozent des einbezahlten Aktienkapitals erreicht.*» (Art. 671 Abs. 1 OR)

Ebenso sind der allgemeinen Reserve «*10 Prozent der Beträge, die nach Bezahlung einer Dividende von 5 Prozent als Gewinnanteil ausgerichtet werden [zuzuweisen]*» (Art. 671 Abs. 2 Ziff. 3 OR).

«*Die allgemeine Reserve darf, soweit sie die Hälfte des Aktienkapitals nicht übersteigt, nur zur Deckung von Verlusten [. . .] verwendet werden [. . .].*» (Art. 671 Abs. 3 OR, auszugsweise)

Die gesetzliche Reserve wird sich deshalb nur im Rahmen der Gewinnverbuchung verändern. Wenn Verlustvorträge ausgewiesen sind, empfiehlt sich die Auflösung oder Teilauflösung der gesetzlichen Reserven. Das ausgewiesene Eigenkapital ist somit klar dargestellt.

3. Aufwertungsreserve

Auf die Aufwertungsreserve möchten wir hier nur kurz eingehen. Sie ist in Art. 671b OR geregelt und darf als gesetzgeberisches Missgeschick bezeichnet werden. Die Praxis hat dazu noch keine klare Lösung entwickelt. Durch die zulässige Aufwertung von Liegenschaften und Beteiligungen bis zum Marktwert sollte der Aktiengesellschaft ermöglicht werden, formell ausgewiesene Verschuldungen durch Aufwertung zu verhindern. Nach Aufwertung durch erfolgswirksame nicht-liquide Auflösung von stillen Reserven wäre damit die Verschuldung vermieden. Das Gesetz verlangt nun aber die Verbuchung einer Aufwertungsreserve auf der Passivseite, womit wieder ein buchmässiger Aufwand verbunden ist.

Die Buchungen sehen wie folgt aus:

1) Liegenschaft (Bilanz) *an* Aufwertung (Erfolgsrechnung)

2) Aufwertungsreservenbildung (Erfolgsrechnung) *an* Aufwertungsreserve (Bilanz)

   oder (und in der Regel):

3) Liegenschaft (Bilanz) an Aufwertungsreserve (Bilanz) (somit erfolgsneutral).

Im Ergebnis wird die ursprünglich beabsichtigte erfolgswirksame Aufwertung zur erfolgsunwirksamen Bilanzsummenerhöhung.

Das Prinzip der Bilanzierung der Vermögensgegenstände zu Anschaffungskosten gilt als obere Wertgrenze (Art. 665 OR) und wird durch die Aufwertungsmöglichkeit (Art. 670 OR) durchbrochen. Die Aufwertung ist zulässig, wenn die Hälfte des Aktienkapitals und der gesetzlichen Reserven nicht mehr gedeckt ist. Der Posten Aufwertungsreserve führt den Betrag der Aufwertung an. Die Aufwertung ist nur zulässig, wenn die Revisionsstelle zuhanden der Generalversammlung schriftlich bestätigt, dass die gesetzlichen Bestimmungen eingehalten sind.

4. Bilanzgewinn/Bilanzverlust (früher Gewinn- oder Verlustvortrag)

Jedes Jahr muss der Erfolg der Erfolgsrechnung und damit der Bilanz (hier: Bilanzgewinn) verbucht werden. Die Bilanz wird, per Ende des Geschäftsjahres, vor der Gewinnverbuchung dargestellt. Diese Gewinnverbuchung wird nach Ablauf des Geschäftsjahres durch den Vorschlag zur Gewinnverwendung durch den Verwaltungsrat eingeleitet und daraufhin durch die Generalversammlung beschlossen. Das Buchungsdatum ist der Tag der GV und bei beschlossener Dividende der Tag der Auszahlung (Fälligkeit) oder der Tag der Gutschrift auf dem Kontokorrent des Aktionärs (oder der Aktionäre).

Der Gewinnvortrag (ohne allfällige Tantième) stellt sich i.d.R. wie folgt dar:

Gewinnvortrag (nach letzter GV und Gewinnverbuchung)

+ laufender Gewinn

− Einlage in die gesetzlichen Reserven

− ausbezahlte Dividende

= **Gewinnvortrag neu**

Kapitel 2: Bilanz, Erfolgsrechnung und ergänzende Rechnungen

5. Von der Steuerbilanz zur Handelsbilanz

Es kommt immer wieder vor, dass die vorgelegte Bilanz bei der Steuerverwaltung zu Korrekturen führt und in der vorgelegten Form nicht akzeptiert wird. Da die Kleinunternehmen i.d.R. eine Jahresrechnung führen, also Identität der Handelsbilanz mit der Steuerbilanz besteht, müssen solche Änderungen unter Umständen korrigiert werden. Gewisse EDV-Programme erlauben eine Änderung im Vorjahr. In solchen Fällen bereitet die Korrektur keine Probleme, es wird die bereits erstellte Jahresrechnung korrigiert. Ein entsprechender Hinweis im Protokoll zur nächsten Generalversammlung ist empfehlenswert: «Aufgrund einer steuerlichen Korrektur wird die Jahresrechnung in der nun vorliegenden Form, mit korrigiertem Gewinnverwendungsvorschlag, von allen Aktionären genehmigt.» Sollte aufgrund abgeschlossener und journalisierter Jahresabläufe keine Korrektur mehr möglich sein, muss eine Korrektur im laufenden Jahr erfolgen. Erste Möglichkeit ist die Nachbuchung über ausserordentlichen Erfolg unter Korrektur in der Steuererklärung. Eine von der Steuerverwaltung nicht akzeptierte Rückstellung, welche aufgelöst werden muss, führt zu höherem Gewinn. Wird diese Auflösung im Folgejahr gebucht, muss dies in der Steuererklärung abgezogen werden, da sonst im Ertrag die im Vorjahr nicht tolerierte Rückstellung noch einmal besteuert würde. Eine solche Nachbuchung setzt einen entsprechenden Hinweis im Anhang voraus.

Abweichung ordnungsgemässer Rechnungslegung:

Die Rückstellung Forschungskosten CHF 20'000.–, welche im Vorjahr gebildet wurde, wurde von der Steuerverwaltung nicht akzeptiert. Sie wurde nun erfolgswirksam aufgelöst, um die Identität von Steuerbilanz und Handelsbilanz wiederherzustellen.

Eine zweite Möglichkeit besteht darin, direkt das Eigenkapital zu bebuchen, was mit Ausnahme statutarisch beschlossener Kapitalveränderungen unzulässig ist. Auch hier ist ein Hinweis im Anhang erforderlich.

Abweichung ordnungsgemässer Rechnungslegung:

Die Rückstellung Forschungskosten CHF 20'000.–, welche im Vorjahr gebildet wurde, wurde von der Steuerverwaltung nicht akzeptiert. Sie wurde nun direkt über das Eigenkapital aufgelöst, um die Identität von

Teil B: Grundlagen des Rechnungswesens / Principles of Accounting

Steuerbilanz und Handelsbilanz wiederherzustellen. Buchung: Rückstellung an Gewinnvortrag.

§ 3 Die Erfolgsrechnung

I. Vorbemerkung

In Verbindung mit der Bilanz ist am Ende des Geschäftsjahres die Erfolgsrechnung aufzustellen. Diese enthält die Gegenüberstellung der Aufwendungen und Erträge des Unternehmens. Übersteigen die Erträge die Aufwendungen, ergibt sich ein Gewinn. Sind umgekehrt die Aufwendungen höher als die Erträge, entsteht ein Verlust. Unabhängig davon, ob der Saldo zwischen Aufwendungen und Erträgen einen Gewinn oder einen Verlust darstellt, wird dadurch das Eigenkapital eines Unternehmens verändert: Ein Gewinn erhöht das Eigenkapital, währenddem ein Verlust das Eigenkapital vermindert. Der Saldo der Erfolgsrechnung widerspiegelt die Eigenkapitalveränderung in der Bilanz.

Bei der Bilanz empfiehlt sich eine lückenlose Prüfung aller Bilanzpositionen (Bewertung). Einzelne Bilanzpositionen werden durch Stichproben geprüft, z.B. Debitoren. Währenddem eine lückenlose Prüfung der Bilanzpositionen, bei Kleinunternehmen ca. 15–60 Konti, mit vertretbarem Zeitaufwand möglich ist, ist dies bei der Erfolgsrechnung nicht möglich und nicht angebracht. Es gibt auf dem Erfolgsrechnungskonto keinen bewertbaren Saldoendbestand. Der Saldo ist vielmehr eine Summe aller Einzelpositionen auf einem Konto. Die Erfolgsrechnung zeigt den Erfolg eines Zeitraumes (Geschäftsjahr), währenddem die Bilanz ein Ausweis eines Tages ist (Bilanzstichtag). Aus diesem Grund basiert die Revision der Erfolgsrechnung immer auf Stichproben.

Bei Kleinaktiengesellschaften mit der Zielvorgabe der Revision in 1–5 Personentagen, werden i.d.R. nicht mehr als 1–10 Ordner an Zahlungsverkehr vorliegen. Aus diesem Grund genügt oft eine kritische Durchsicht des Belegmaterials mit Stichproben; Beleg zu Buchung und Buchung zu Beleg.

Kapitel 2: Bilanz, Erfolgsrechnung und ergänzende Rechnungen

II. Der Aufwand

Die Ausführungen zum Aufwand sind kurz und beschränken sich auf das aus Revisionssicht Erwähnenswerte. Für weitere Angaben des Buchungsinhaltes konsultiere man ein Lehrbuch zur Einführung in die Buchhaltung, welches die verschiedenen Aufwandkonti beschreibt.

1. Materialaufwand

Im Materialaufwand sind alle Aufwendungen enthalten, die zur betrieblichen Herstellung benötigt werden. Er beinhaltet:

- Wareneinkauf
- Bestandesänderung

Die Bestandesänderung führt bei der Zunahme des Warenlagers zu einer Verminderung des Wareneinkaufs. Nicht der ganze Wareneinkauf hat sich so zu Aufwand gebildet, sondern ein Teil des Einkaufs besteht Ende Jahr als Warenlager, als Wert, und führt daher nicht zum Wertverzehr. Da alle Wareneinkaufsrechnungen laufend als Aufwand gebucht werden, führt die Bestandesänderung zu einer Aufwandminderung. Wir verweisen hier auf die Ausführungen zur Bilanz, Position Warenlager und auf den Anhang, Rubrik Stetigkeit.

Die Bestandesänderung kann im Konto Wareneinkauf gebucht werden. Besser und klarer ist der Ausweis über ein eigenes Konto.

2. Handelswarenaufwand

Werden die Waren nicht zur Herstellung von Gütern verwendet, sondern zum Wiederverkauf, so erscheinen sie als Handelswarenaufwand.

Bezüglich der Bestandesänderung Ende Jahr (Inventar) verweisen wir auf die vorangegangenen Ausführungen.

3. Aufwand für Dienstleistungen

Hier werden alle Aufwendungen für Dienstleistungen gebucht. Dafür können mehrere Konti benützt werden.

Teil B: Grundlagen des Rechnungswesens / Principles of Accounting

4. Personalaufwand

Der Personalaufwand gliedert sich wie folgt:

a) Lohnaufwand

Der eigentliche Lohnaufwand beinhaltet alle Salärzahlungen an das Personal. Wird keine Lohnbuchhaltung geführt, kann pro Mitarbeiter ein Lohnkonto geführt werden. Die Finanzbuchhaltung übernimmt dann die Funktion der Lohnbuchhaltung und genügt damit den gesetzlichen Erfordernissen der staatlichen Sozialabgaben. Pro Monat werden somit die Nettolohnzahlungen auf diesem Konto gebucht. Ende Jahr werden die Arbeitnehmerbeiträge dazugebucht. Als Ergebnis erscheint der Bruttolohn. Schliesslich empfiehlt es sich, den Bruttolohn in einem Betrag auf ein Lohnsammelkonto zu buchen. Das einzeln geführte Lohnkonto hat damit den Saldo 0.–, währenddem das Lohnsammelkonto mit 1–9 Buchungen, je nach Anzahl Arbeitnehmer (1–9), den ganzen Bruttolohnaufwand enthält. Diese Methode hat den Vorteil, dass im Ausweis der Erfolgsrechnung nicht erscheint, wer wie viel verdient. Das Konto des einzelnen Arbeitnehmers erscheint nicht oder mit Saldo 0.–, und die Lohnbuchhaltung ist korrekt geführt.

Prüfungshandlung: Prüfung der AHV-Jahreslohnbescheinigung in Übereinstimmung mit dem ausgewiesenen Jahreslohnaufwand.

b) Sozialversicherungsaufwand

Der Sozialversicherungsaufwand enthält die Arbeitgeberbeiträge für AHV, IV, EO, ALV, UVG und BVG. Sofern der Betrieb eine Krankentaggeldversicherung abgeschlossen hat, sind die entsprechenden Prämien auch hier erfasst.

aa) Lohnbuchhaltung

Bestehen neben der Buchhaltung klare Aufzeichnungen über die Salärzahlungen, z.B. in Form einer Lohnbuchhaltung oder von Lohnaufzeichnungen, kann auf eine Bruttoverbuchung der Löhne verzichtet werden. Ist man nicht sicher, ob die Aufzeichnungen für die Abrechnung der Sozialversicherungen genügen, erkundigt man sich am besten bei der zuständigen Ausgleichskasse.

Kapitel 2: Bilanz, Erfolgsrechnung und ergänzende Rechnungen

bb) Prüfungshandlung

Der Arbeitgeber muss dem Arbeitnehmer einen Lohnausweis aushändigen. Ein vollständig ausgefüllter Lohnausweis zeigt das Bruttoeinkommen, die Abzüge der AHV, IV, EO, ALV, UVG und BVG und das steuerbare Nettoeinkommen. Dieses Nettoeinkommen kann vom tatsächlich ausbezahlten Lohn abweichen. Es können noch weitere Abzüge des Arbeitgebers möglich sein für zusätzliche, nicht obligatorische Unfallversicherungen oder Kollektivkrankentaggeld-Versicherungen, welche steuerlich nicht absetzbar sind. Zu prüfen ist deshalb, ob die Sozialversicherungsabgaben korrekt aufgeführt wurden. In der Regel genügt ein Blick in die Lohnbuchhaltung und die Jahreslohnsummendeklaration an die AHV-Ausgleichskasse. Bei Zahlungsrückständen ist ein Kontoauszug der Ausgleichskasse zu bestellen und mit dem Posten Kreditor AHV zu überprüfen.

cc) AHV/IV/EO/ALV

Man unterscheidet:

- Alters- und Hinterbliebenenversicherung
- Invalidenversicherung
- Erwerbsersatzordnung
- Arbeitslosenversicherung.

Diese Abgaben sind eine Mischform von Versicherungen und Steuern. Währenddem bei den privaten Versicherungen ein Konnex von Risiko und Leistung in Form einer abgestuften Prämie besteht, ist dies bei der AHV und IV nur in beschränktem Masse der Fall. Ab einem Einkommen von CHF 77'400.– (2005) ist das rentenbildende Maximum erreicht. Die darüber liegenden Beiträge dienen nicht mehr dem Pflichtigen selber, sondern zur allgemeinen Finanzierung der Altersvorsorge und haben somit Steuercharakter. Weiter ist der erwerbstätige Rentner für sein CHF 16'800.– übersteigendes Einkommen ebenfalls AHV-beitragspflichtig (sog. Solidaritätsbeitrag), ohne dass sich seine AHV-Rente verbessert. Ähnlich liegt der Fall bei der Erwerbsersatzordnung und der Arbeitslosenversicherung, wobei der Selbständigerwerbende keine Beiträge an die Arbeitslosenversicherung entrichtet, aber konsequenterweise auch keine Leistungen beziehen kann.

Beim Lohnempfänger ist der Bruttolohn Basis für die richtige Bemessung der Sozialversicherungsabzüge, wobei beschränkte Spesenvergütungen möglich sind.

dd) UVG/BVG

- Unfallversicherungsgesetz
- Bundesgesetz über die berufliche Alters-, Hinterlassenen- und Invalidenvorsorge

Währenddem bei der AHV, IV, EO und ALV staatliche Organisationen mit der Anwendung dieser Gesetze betraut sind, erfolgt dies beim BVG und UVG über private Versicherer unter Aufsicht des Bundes. Risiko und Leistung stehen in einem Konnex in Form einer individuellen Prämie. Es gibt eine sehr grosse Vielfalt in der Ausgestaltung. Einige Pensionskassen verlangen von ihren Mitgliedern (sprich Lohnempfängern) fixe, andere wiederum leistungsbezogene Prämien (sog. Beitragsprimat im Gegensatz zum Leistungsprimat).

Es ist deshalb zu prüfen, ob ein Anschlussvertrag für das BVG vorliegt. Zwingend ist festzustellen, ob Prämienausstände bestehen. Ist dies der Fall, hat ein entsprechender Hinweis im Anhang zu erfolgen. Die Einsichtnahme in den Prämienkontoauszug der Vorsorgeeinrichtung ist unerlässlich.

Eine summarische Prüfung, ob die Sozialversicherungsbeiträge abgeführt werden, ist notwendig.

Im Zuge der Devaluation von Wertschriften ist zu prüfen, ob Nachschusspflichten gegenüber Pensionskassen infolge von Deckungslücken bestehen.

5. *Raumaufwand*

Hier sind alle Aufwendungen erfasst, die den Raumaufwand betreffen.

Prüfungshandlungen:

- Sind zwölf Monatsmieten erfasst?
- Ist die Heiz- und Nebenkostenabrechnung erfasst?

6. Unterhalt und Reparaturen/Leasing

Unterhalt und Reparaturen sind hier zu buchen.

Bestehen Leasingverträge, ist hier der Aufwand zu erfassen. In der Regel werden die laufenden Leasingraten als Aufwand erfasst. Die noch nicht bezahlten Leasingraten erscheinen im Anhang.

Weniger üblich ist die Erfassung der ganzen Leasingverbindlichkeit in den Passiven, die Aktivierung des Leasinggutes und die Behandlung der laufenden Zahlungen als Aufwand. Diese Methode ist bei Kleinunternehmen selten anzutreffen.

7. Fahrzeug- und Transportaufwand

Alle Fahrzeugaufwendungen sind hier zu buchen.

Probleme ergeben sich hier vor allen Dingen aus steuerlichen Abgrenzungen, namentlich aus der Zulässigkeit der Fahrzeugaufwendungen. Mancher Inhaber eines Kleinunternehmens hat sich steuerlich zum Ziel gesetzt, möglichst wenig zu verdienen, wobei dann für Repräsentationspflichten mindestens zwei Fahrzeuge der oberen Preisklasse notwendig sind. Ohne das Gebiet der Revision allzu sehr zu verlassen, soll hier erwähnt werden, dass solche Ausgangssituationen für einen konstruktiven Dialog mit der Steuerverwaltung ungünstig sind. Die Diskussion der Privatanteile an Fahrzeugspesen hat sich seit der neuen Regelung bei der Mehrwertsteuer entschärft. Nach Abzug der Privatanteile ist der Saldo als Fahrzeugaufwand ersichtlich.

8. Versicherungsaufwand

Hierunter fallen alle Versicherungsaufwendungen.

9. Energieaufwand

Hier werden alle Aufwendungen für Energie erfasst.

10. Verwaltungs- und Informatikaufwand

Hierunter fallen alle Verwaltungs- und Informatikaufwendungen.

Teil B: Grundlagen des Rechnungswesens / Principles of Accounting

11. Werbeaufwand

Hierunter fallen alle Werbeaufwendungen.

12. Übriger Betriebsaufwand

Hier ist der übrige Betriebsaufwand zu erfassen.

13. Abschreibungen

Abschreibungen müssen planmässig auf dem Anlagevermögen verbucht werden. Es handelt sich dabei um nichtliquiditätswirksame Buchungen. Abschreibungen werden i.d.R. am Schluss des Geschäftsjahres gebucht.

In der Steuerpraxis haben sich folgende Abschreibungssätze entwickelt (hier als Auswahl):

30 % Maschinen und Apparate

25 % Mobiliar und Einrichtungen

40 % Büromaschinen, EDV, Kommunikationsanlagen

40 % Fahrzeuge

45 % Werkzeuge und Geräte

25 % mobile Lagereinrichtungen

15 % Hochregallager

20 % feste Einrichtungen und Installationen

3 % Geschäftshäuser (Land und Gebäude)

4 % Gebäude des Gastgewerbes

7 % Fabrikgebäude (Land und Gebäude)

Diese Abschreibungssätze gelten für die degressive Abschreibung. Für die lineare Abschreibung sind die Sätze zu halbieren. Ein Merkblatt hierzu kann bei der kantonalen oder eidgenössischen Steuerverwaltung bezogen werden.

Kapitel 2: Bilanz, Erfolgsrechnung und ergänzende Rechnungen

14. Steuern

Hier werden die jährlich anfallenden Steuern auf Ertrag und Kapital gebucht. Bei Kleinunternehmen werden i.d.R. die Steueraufwendungen mit der Zahlung der Steuerforderungen als Aufwendungen gebucht. Diese einfache Methode ist bei Kleinunternehmen praktisch.

Es können auch die aus dem laufenden Geschäftsjahr anfallenden Steuern als Aufwand gebucht werden. Es handelt sich also um Steuerrechnungen, die je nach dem kantonalen Steuersystem erst im folgenden Jahr veranlagt und fällig werden. Damit werden die Steuerperioden gerecht abgegrenzt.

a) Ertragssteuer

Aufgrund der korrekt ausgefüllten Steuererklärung veranlagt die Steuerverwaltung die Ertragssteuer. Der Ertrag geht aus der Buchhaltung bzw. der Erfolgsrechnung hervor. Zu prüfen ist deshalb, ob eine Steuererklärung für den Kanton und für den Bund (Formular 103) abgegeben wurde. Bei den meisten Kantonen wird eine ertragsintensive Steuer auf dem ausgewiesenen Reingewinn erhoben. Die Bundessteuer ist linear (8,5 %).

b) Kapitalsteuer

Alle Jahre wird mit einem Vermögensstichtag (1. Januar) die Kapitalsteuer bemessen. Auch diese Steuer steht in direkter Beziehung zu anderen Abgaben. Die Kapitalhöhe ist massgebend für die Berechnung der Ertragsintensität (Ertrag dividiert durch Kapital). Je höher die Ertragsintensität, desto höher die progressive Ertragssteuer. Je höher das Kapital, desto tiefer die Ertragsintensität, desto tiefer die Ertragssteuer.

Mit der Unternehmenssteuerreform 1998 wurde beim Bund die bei den Kapitalgesellschaften und Genossenschaften erhobene Kapitalsteuer beseitigt, die Gewinnsteuer durch einen Proportionaltarif von 8,5 % bestimmt und die Emissionsabgabe (mit einer Freigrenze von CHF 250'000.–) auf 1 % gesenkt.

c) Mehrwertsteuer

Die Buchhaltung ist für die Bemessung der Mehrwertsteuer relevant. Massgebend sind die vier Quartalsdeklarationen oder die zwei Semesterdeklarationen. In der Kontrolle muss der Jahresumsatz des Geschäftsabschlusses mit dem abgerechneten Umsatz übereinstimmen. Wird die Mehrwertsteuer effektiv abgerechnet, ist sie erfolgsneutral. Wird sie pauschal abgerechnet, erscheint sie als Aufwand. Stellt der Steuerrevisor Abweichungen fest, meldet er dies der kantonalen Steuerverwaltung, was zu unliebsamen Nach- und Strafsteuern führen kann. Hat sich bis anhin die Kontrolle durch die Eidgenössische Steuerverwaltung auf den Umsatz (Warenumsatz) beschränkt, so werden die Beamten bei der Mehrwertsteuer infolge des Vorsteuerabzuges auch den gesamten Aufwand prüfen. Bei der Besteuerung zum Pauschalsteuersatz entfällt die Aufwandsprüfung. Der Geschäftsabschluss wird somit durch die kantonale Steuerverwaltung für die Einkommenssteuer geprüft, sodann folgt die Begutachtung für die direkte Einkommenssteuer des Bundes und zuallerletzt die kritische Prüfung durch die Eidgenössische Steuerverwaltung für die Mehrwertsteuer.

Für den Revisor bedeutet dies eine Prüfung der Mehrwertsteuerabrechnungen. In der Regel genügt die Vorlage der Quartals- oder Semesterabrechnungen mit der Jahreszusammenstellung, welche den Bezug zur Jahresbuchhaltung zeigt. Je nach Branche tut der Revisor aber gut daran, sich Besonderheiten bei speziellen Umsatz- oder Vorsteuerberechnungen näher anzusehen.

d) Eidgenössische Verrechnungssteuer

Mit der dreifachen Prüfung bzw. Prüfungsmöglichkeit ist der Reigen der Abgaben noch nicht abgeschlossen. Die Eidgenössische Steuerverwaltung, Hauptabteilung Verrechnungssteuer und Stempelabgaben, kann ebenfalls untersuchen, ob die Erlasse über die Verrechnungssteuer und Stempelabgaben eingehalten sind. Ein korrekt verbuchter Lohn mit Abführen der Sozialbeiträge kann unter dem Gesichtspunkt der Angemessenheit bei der Verrechnungssteuer zu Problemen führen. So werden überhöhte Saläre, welche eine verrechnungssteuerbelastete Dividendenausschüttung verhindern, nicht toleriert. Die Problemstellung besteht in der Regel für Aktiengesellschaften und Gesellschaften mit beschränkter Haftung und behandelt die Frage, ob die Aufwendungen auch tatsächlich geschäftlicher Natur und angemessen sind.

Als Beispiel sei hier angefügt, dass in einem Unternehmen der Betriebsinhaber regelmässig zu Lasten des Geschäftes ein Jahressalär von CHF 200'000.– verbuchen konnte. In einem ausserordentlich guten Geschäftsjahr entschliesst er sich, einen Bonus in Form einer ausserordentlichen Gratifikation auszuzahlen und das Salär auf CHF 300'000.– zu erhöhen. Eine solche Erhöhung kann unter diesen Umständen eventuell von der Steuerverwaltung nicht akzeptiert werden. Die Steuerverwaltung könnte von einem ordentlichen Salär von CHF 200'000.– ausgehen, zuzüglich zulässiger Gratifikation von CHF 40'000.–, womit ein Salär von CHF 240'000.– erreicht wird. Die darüber hinausgehenden CHF 60'000.– könnten als verdeckte Gewinnausschüttung qualifiziert werden. Dieses theoretische Beispiel soll zeigen, wie ein Salär unter dem Gesichtspunkt der eidgenössischen Verrechnungssteuer als «nicht geschäftsmässig begründet» betrachtet werden kann. Selbstverständlich ist dieses Beispiel nur theoretisch und kann nicht auf konkrete Tatsachen übertragen werden.

Der Revisor hat sich somit auch darüber Klarheit zu verschaffen, ob verrechnungssteuerpflichtige verdeckte Gewinnausschüttungen vorliegen. Ist dies der Fall, bedarf es einer Steuerrückstellung. Oft ist die verdeckte Gewinnausschüttung für den Revisor nicht ersichtlich. Ist sie aber nach den normalen Umständen erkennbar, muss er auf eine entsprechende Rückstellung hinweisen oder Gewissheit haben, dass genügend Eigenkapital und Liquidität vorhanden sind, um dieser Eventualverpflichtung nachzukommen.

15. Ausserordentlicher und betriebsfremder Aufwand

Ausserordentliche und betriebsfremde Aufwände müssen von Gesetzes wegen separat erfasst werden.

III. Der Ertrag

1. Leistungsertrag

Im Ertrag wird der ganze Umsatz erfasst. Je nach Art des Gewerbes erscheint dieser in Form von:

- Produktionsertrag
- Handelsertrag
- Dienstleistungsertrag

Vollständigkeitsprüfungen können selten durchgeführt werden. Bei gewissen Branchen sind Jahresumsatzboni üblich. Aufgrund solcher Vergütungen kann geprüft werden, ob der Umsatz oder Umsatzteile vollständig erfasst sind.

2. *Bestandesänderungen (Vorräte)*

Bestandesänderungen werden im Warenaufwand erfasst.

Der KMU-Kontenrahmen empfiehlt für Bestandesänderungen eine separate Gruppe. Dies ist deshalb von Vorteil, weil der Bilanzleser so sofort erkennt, welcher Aufwand aktiviert wurde (vgl. die Ausführungen zum Warenaufwand).

3. *Finanzerfolg*

Im Finanzerfolg sind die Zinserträge enthalten. Hier kann geprüft werden, ob die Rückerstattung der Verrechnungssteuer mittels Deklaration des ganzen Ertrages dem gebuchten Ertrag entspricht.

4. *Liegenschaftsertrag*

Die Liegenschaftsrechnung wird meistens separat geführt. Ausgewiesen wird der Liegenschaftserfolg.

5. *Ausserordentlicher und betriebsfremder Erfolg*

Ausserordentliche und betriebsfremde Erträge müssen von Gesetzes wegen separat erfasst werden.

§ 4 Der Anhang

Die dreiteilige Jahresrechnung – sie besteht stets aus Erfolgsrechnung, Bilanz und Anhang – soll eine möglichst zuverlässige Beurteilung der Vermögens- und Ertragslage gewähren. Ein wichtiges Element dazu ist der Anhang, welcher zahlreiche Informationen enthält, die aus der Jahresrechnung selbst nicht ersichtlich sind.

Der Anhang ist eine der wesentlichen Neuerungen zur Rechnungslegung bei der AG (seit dem neuen Aktienrecht) und der GmbH. Er ist dazu da, zusätzliche Informationen aufzunehmen, die für eine möglichst zuverlässige Beurteilung der Vermögens- und Ertragslage wichtig sind. Dazu gehören z.b. der Beschrieb über die Aktivierung von angefangenen Arbeiten und dergleichen. Durch solche Informationen kann der Leser ein verbessertes Bild erhalten. Diese Lösung, zusätzliche Informationen in einem Anhang anzufügen, ist zudem viel eleganter, als Einschränkungen im Bericht der Revisionsstelle vorzunehmen. Solche können durch einen Hinweis im Anhang überflüssig werden.

Um der Bedeutung innerhalb der Kleinaktiengesellschaft Rechnung zu tragen, werden die 14 Punkte im Anhang wie folgt eingeteilt:

- R = relevant für Kleinunternehmen
- NR = eher nicht relevant für Kleinunternehmen

I. Bürgschaften, Garantieverpflichtungen und Pfandbestellungen zugunsten Dritter (R)

Art. 663b Ziff. 1 OR lautet: [Der Anhang enthält:] *«den Gesamtbetrag der Bürgschaften, Garantieverpflichtungen und Pfandbestellungen zugunsten Dritter;»*

Die Gesellschaft muss hier die Bürgschaften deklarieren, die sie für Dritte eingegangen ist. Der Ausweis klassischer Bürgschaften sollte keine besonderen Fragen aufwerfen.

Weiter müssen die Garantieverpflichtungen angegeben werden. Dabei handelt es sich nicht um die üblichen Garantien aus Leistungen. Zu den nicht darstellungspflichtigen Garantien zählen zum Beispiel die 5-jährige Garantie für die Erstellung von Bauten (Art. 371 Abs. 2 OR) oder eine vertragliche Garantie von 2 Jahren auf gekaufte bewegliche Sachen. Ausweispflichtig sind vielmehr vertragliche Garantien in besonderen Garantieverträgen, wenn z.B. eine Firma im Rahmen einer gemeinsamen Leistung für die Leistungen des Partners einsteht. Solche Garantieverträge sind bei Kleinaktiengesellschaften eher selten anzutreffen.

Anzugeben ist auch eine Pfandbestellung zugunsten eines Dritten. Darunter fällt insbesondere das Zurverfügungstellen einer betrieblichen Liegenschaft als Sicherheit für einen Dritten. Oft handelt es sich um den Allein-

oder Hauptaktionär. Dieser erhält aufgrund einer Sicherheit der Aktiengesellschaft einen privaten Kredit. Solche Vorgänge sind im Anhang darzulegen.

Auszuweisen ist der Betrag der Verpfändung (oder Garantie), nicht aber der effektiv beanspruchte Teil. Es geht um den Nennwert der zur Verfügung gestellten Sicherheit (Verhältnis AG/Sicherungsnehmer), nicht um das Verhältnis Sicherungsnehmer/Sicherungsbeanspruchender. Freilich kann als zusätzliche Information dieser Betrag angegeben werden.

Beispiel:

Angabe: Grundpfandbrief CHF 100'000.– auf Liegenschaft Dornenweg 1 in Basel, im 4. Rang verpfändet (Pfandbeanspruchung zur Zeit CHF 50'000.–).

Oder Minimalangabe: CHF 100'000.–.

Prüfungshandlungen:

- Vollständigkeitserklärung
- Einsicht in den Grundbuchauszug (Eintrag von Grundpfandtiteln)
- Einsicht in den Vermögensnachweis der Bank (Bezeichnung als Pfanddepot oder dergleichen)
- Prüfung, ob im Aufwand eine Gebühr für Bankgarantien erscheint
- andere geeignete Prüfungen.

Nicht anzugeben sind Sicherheiten, welche die Gesellschaft von Dritten erhalten hat. Ein solcher Hinweis kann aber sehr nützlich oder sogar für die möglichst zuverlässige Beurteilung der Vermögens- und Ertragslage notwendig sein. Hier empfiehlt sich ein Hinweis am Ende des Anhanges.

II. Verpfändete oder abgetretene Aktiven sowie Aktiven unter Eigentumsvorbehalt zur Sicherstellung eigener Gesellschaftsverbindlichkeiten (R)

Art. 663b Ziff. 2 OR lautet: [Der Anhang enthält:] *«den Gesamtbetrag der zur Sicherung eigener Verpflichtungen verpfändeten oder abgetretenen Aktiven sowie der Aktiven unter Eigentumsvorbehalt;»*

Anzugeben sind alle abgetretenen Aktiven zugunsten der Sicherstellung eigener Passiven. Die beiden häufigsten Fälle sind die Hypotheken und der Kontokorrentkredit. Bei den Hypotheken werden regelmässig Grundpfandtitel auf der Liegenschaft errichtet und diese als Sicherheit der Bank verpfändet. Obwohl das Gesetz nur die Deklaration des Gesamtbetrages verlangt, dürfte dies für eine möglichst zuverlässige Beurteilung der Vermögens- und Ertragslage kaum dienen. Es empfiehlt sich vielmehr eine detailliertere Angabe.

Beispiel:

Angabe: Grundpfandbrief CHF 100'000.– auf Liegenschaft Dornenweg 1 in Basel, im 4. Rang verpfändet (Pfandbeanspruchung zurzeit CHF 50'000.–).

Oder Minimalangabe: CHF 100'000.–.

Oft wird auch ein Kredit bei einer Bank durch die Kleinaktiengesellschaft beansprucht. Sofern keine realen Sicherheiten (Grundpfand etc.) vorliegen, verbleibt dem Betrieb oft als einzige Möglichkeit, die Debitoren abzutreten (Debitorenzession).

Beispiel:

Angabe: Debitoren abgetreten zugunsten der Bank XY als Sicherheit für den Kontokorrentkredit (abgetretene Debitoren CHF 100'000.– = Bilanzausweis, beanspruchter Kredit = CHF 50'000.– = Bilanzausweis).

Oder Minimalangabe: CHF 100'000.–

Prüfungshandlungen:
- Vollständigkeitserklärung

- Einsicht in den Grundbuchauszug (Eintrag von Grundpfandtiteln)
- Einsicht in den Vermögensnachweis der Bank (Bezeichnung als Pfanddepot oder dergleichen)
- Prüfung, ob im Aufwand eine Gebühr für Bankgarantien erscheint
- andere geeignete Prüfungen.

Nicht anzugeben sind Pfandsicherheiten, die die Gesellschaft von Dritten erhalten hat. Ein solcher Hinweis kann aber sehr nützlich oder sogar für die möglichst zuverlässige Beurteilung der Vermögens- und Ertragslage notwendig sein. Hier empfiehlt sich ein Hinweis am Schluss des Anhanges.

III. Nicht bilanzierte Leasingverbindlichkeiten (R)

Art. 663b Ziff. 3 OR lautet: [Der Anhang enthält:] *«den Gesamtbetrag der nichtbilanzierten Leasingverbindlichkeiten;»*

Anzugeben ist die Restsumme der noch nicht bezahlten Leasingverbindlichkeiten. Bei Kleinunternehmen besteht die gängige Buchungspraxis darin, die laufenden Leasingzahlungen als Aufwand zu erfassen. Selten wird der volle Leasingbetrag in den Passiven ausgewiesen. Aus diesem Grund müssen die noch offenen Leasingraten im Anhang ausgewiesen werden. Angesichts der wirtschaftlichen Bedeutung des Leasings und der zukünftigen Verpflichtungen des Unternehmens aus Leasingverträgen ist dies eine sinnvolle Angabe.

Beispiel:

Angabe: CHF 14'400.– (144 Raten à 100.– p.m.)

oder Minimalangabe: CHF 14'400.–

Prüfungshandlung:

- Einsicht in die Leasingverträge

Nicht anzugeben sind die restlichen Raten aus anderen längerfristigen Verträgen wie Mietverträgen, Kaufabnahmeverpflichtungen (100 Stück pro Jahr zu CHF 100.– während 5 Jahren), Arbeitsverträgen (5-Jahres-Verträgen), Konventionalstrafen etc.

IV. Brandversicherungswerte des Sachanlagevermögens (R)

Art. 663b Ziff. 4 OR lautet: [Der Anhang enthält:] «*die Brandversicherungswerte der Sachanlagen;*»

Anzugeben sind die Brandversicherungswerte. Die Information dient dazu, einen vertieften Einblick in die Bilanz zu gewinnen. Meistens umfassen die Versicherungen den Neuwert. Damit sollte der Versicherungswert wesentlich höher sein als der bilanzierte Wert.

Ein Problem liegt oft darin, dass bei Kleinaktiengesellschaften kombinierte Versicherungen angeboten werden. Sie umfassen meistens eine Absicherung des Warenlagers, des Mobiliars, von zur Aufbewahrung übergebenen Gegenständen etc. bei Wasser- und Feuerschaden. Das versicherte Warenlager (Umlaufvermögen) gehört nicht zu den ausweispflichtigen Werten (Anlagevermögen). Anstelle langer Überlegungen zu Anteilen etc., empfiehlt sich ein pragmatischer Hinweis.

Beispiel:

Angabe: Versicherungswert für Mobiliar und Warenlager CHF 100'000.– (kombinierte Versicherung).

Oder Minimalangabe: CHF 75'300.– (bei genauer Ermittlung).

Prüfungshandlung:
- Einsicht in den Versicherungsordner

V. Verbindlichkeiten gegenüber Vorsorgeeinrichtungen (R)

Art. 663b Ziff. 5 OR lautet: [Der Anhang enthält] «*Verbindlichkeiten gegenüber Vorsorgeeinrichtungen;*»

Auszuweisen sind die gegenüber der Vorsorgeeinrichtung bestehenden Schulden. Bei Kleinunternehmen ist häufig ein Anschlussvertrag mit einer

Sammelstiftung vorhanden. Der Zahlungsverkehr erfolgt seitens der Versicherungsgesellschaft über ein Prämienkonto. Anzugeben sind die Verbindlichkeiten. Aus der Sicht der Stetigkeit empfiehlt sich z.B. auch die Angabe eines Guthabens, welches wegen eines Personaleintritts entstanden ist. Nicht dazu gehören die Konti Mutationsgewinne und Sondermassnahmen. Diese Beträge gehören nicht dem vorsorgepflichtigen Unternehmen. Oft sind die Verbindlichkeiten in den Kreditoren per Ende Jahr erfasst. Diese Information sollte im Anhang angeführt werden.

Beispiel:

Angabe: CHF 2'344.– (in Kreditoren erfasst)

oder

Angabe: CHF 2'234.– (Guthaben in TA)

oder Minimalangabe: CHF 2'344.–

VI. Anleihensobligationen (NR)

Art. 663b Abs. 1 Ziff. 6 OR lautet: [Der Anhang enthält:] *«die Beträge, Zinssätze und Fälligkeiten der von der Gesellschaft ausgegebenen Anleihensobligationen;»*

Kleinunternehmen führen diese Position nicht.

VII. Wesentliche Beteiligungen (NR)

Art. 663b Ziff. 7 OR lautet: [Der Anhang enthält:] *«jede Beteiligung, die für die Beurteilung der Vermögens- und Ertragslage der Gesellschaft wesentlich ist;»*

Kleinunternehmen führen diese Position selten. Anzugeben sind die wesentlichen Beteiligungen. Denkbar ist eine (meist 100 %-ige) Beteiligung an einer Tochtergesellschaft oder das Halten einer Minderheitenbeteiligung an einem befreundeten oder nahe stehenden Unternehmen. Beispiel: Ein Treuhandunternehmen hält eine 10 %-Beteiligung an einem Versicherungsberatungsbüro. Sofern der Ausweis für die Aktiengesellschaft nachteilig ist, kann er weggelassen werden.

Kapitel 2: Bilanz, Erfolgsrechnung und ergänzende Rechnungen

Beispiel:

Angabe: 100 % Tochter-AG, Basel

20 % Provisions-AG, Basel

Prüfungshandlungen:

- Nachfragen
- Vollständigkeitserklärung einfordern
- überprüfen, ob es Finanzerträge aus Tochtergesellschaften gibt
- abklären, wie viele Telefonnummern an der Firmenadresse existieren

VIII. Auflösung stiller Reserven (R)

Art. 663b Ziff. 8 OR lautet: [Der Anhang enthält:] «den Gesamtbetrag der aufgelösten Wiederbeschaffungsreserven und der darüber hinausgehenden stillen Reserven, soweit dieser den Gesamtbetrag der neugebildeten derartigen Reserven übersteigt, wenn dadurch das erwirtschaftete Ergebnis wesentlich günstiger dargestellt wird;»

Diese Angaben betreffen Kleinunternehmen eher selten. In der Regel werden die Umlaufvermögen aktuell bewertet und die Sachanlagen degressiv zum Einstandswert abgeschrieben. Eigentliche stille Reserven bilden sich damit bei den Liegenschaften und im Warenlager (wobei 1/3 steuerliche Reserve ist). Die absolute Veränderung des Warenlagers führt bei Beibehaltung der relativen Warenlagerreserve von einem Drittel zu einer Veränderung. Sofern dieser Betrag wesentlich ist, muss er angeführt werden. Wird ein fixer Betrag in der Warenlagerreserve beibehalten, ist die Darstellung nicht mehr stetig und bedarf einer Angabe im Anhang.

Warenlager 1996	600.–	Warenlager 1997	300.–	wesentliche Auflösung
Reserve 1996	200.–	Reserve 1997	100.–	100.–
				als Angabe
Buchwert	400.–	Buchwert	200.–	

Teil B: Grundlagen des Rechnungswesens / Principles of Accounting

Warenlager 1996	600.-	Warenlager 1997	300.-	Abweichung von der Stetigkeit
Reserve 1996	200.-	Reserve 1997	200.-	100.-
Buchwert	400.-	Buchwert	100.-	Fixe Warenlagerreserve

Die Darstellung des Warenlagers soll den Ausweisbedarf aufzeigen. Bei den Kleinunternehmen kann dies gegeben sein (sofern wesentlich und insgesamt Reserven aufgelöst wurden).

In unserem Beispiel (erster Teil) führt dieses zu folgendem Ausweis:
Angabe: CHF 100.-

Eine Aufstellung der stillen Reserven wird oft nicht geführt. Dies ist auch zulässig, solange keine Aufwertungen erfolgen. Erst bei Aufwertungen muss diese Arbeit gemacht werden, beziehungsweise für das Vorjahr noch nachgeholt werden.

Die Aufstellung könnte wie folgt aussehen:

Buchwert	Aktienrechtlicher Höchstwert	Stille Reserven	Stille Reserven Vorjahr	Veränderung
Wertschriften 100	150	50	10	+40
Vorräte 400	600	200	100	+100
Rückstellung 100	0	100	0	+100
Total		350	110	+240

In diesem Beispiel haben alle stillen Reserven zugenommen.

Prüfungshandlung:
- Aufstellung der stillen Reserven prüfen

IX. Aufwertungen (R)

Art. 663b Ziff. 9 OR lautet: [Der Anhang enthält:] «*Angaben über Gegenstand und Betrag von Aufwertungen;*»

In dieser Position müssen Aufwertungen von Liegenschaften und Beteiligungen deklariert werden. Es sind zugleich die beiden einzigen Ausnahmen, bei denen Anlagegüter aufgewertet werden dürfen. Sonst gelten Niederstwertprinzip und Anschaffungskostenprinzip, unter Beachtung planmässiger Abschreibungen. Aufwertungen sind nur zulässig, um eine Unterbilanz zu beseitigen.

Beispiel:

Angabe: Liegenschaft Dornenweg 1 um CHF 100.– aufgewertet.

Oder Minimalangabe: Immobilien CHF 100.–

Prüfungshandlung:
- Aufwertungen analysieren

X. Eigene Aktien (NR)

Art. 663b Ziff. 10 OR lautet: [Der Anhang enthält:] «*Angaben über Erwerb, Veräusserung und Anzahl der von der Gesellschaft gehaltenen eigenen Aktien, einschliesslich ihrer Aktien, die eine andere Gesellschaft hält, an der sie mehrheitlich beteiligt ist; anzugeben sind ebenfalls die Bedingungen, zu denen die Gesellschaft die eigenen Aktien erworben [...] hat*».

Kleinunternehmen führen diese Position in der Regel nicht.

XI. Kapitalerhöhungen (NR)

Art. 663b Ziff. 11 OR lautet: [Der Anhang enthält:] «*den Betrag der genehmigten und der bedingten Kapitalerhöhung*».

Kleinunternehmen führen diese Position in der Regel nicht.

XII. Risikobeurteilung

Neu hat der Verwaltungsrat eine Risikobeurteilung vorzunehmen. Über diese Durchführung ist im Anhang zu berichten (siehe hinten Art. 663b OR). Damit ist ein «Internes Kontrollsystem» (IKS) Bestandteil der Geschäftsführung.

XIII. Rücktritt der Revisionsstelle

Bei einem vorzeitigen Rücktritt der Revisionsstelle hat der Verwaltungsrat die Gründe offen zu legen, weshalb die Revisionsstelle ihr Mandat vorzeitig beendet hat (siehe hinten Art. 663b OR).

XIV. Abweichungen von den Grundsätzen ordnungsgemässer Rechnungslegung (R)

Art. 663b Ziff. 12 OR lautet: [Der Anhang enthält:] «*die anderen vom Gesetz vorgeschriebenen Angaben.*»

In dieser Vorschrift liegt die Crux. Man ist rasch geneigt, mit der Angabe der Punkte 1–13 den Anhang als komplett zu betrachten. Deklarationspflichtig sind jedoch auch die Abweichungen von der ordnungsgemässen Rechnungslegung.

Abweichungen von Grundsätzen ordnungsmässiger Rechnungslegung:
- Unternehmungsfortführung
- Stetigkeit der Darstellung
- Bewertungen
- Verrechnungsverbot

Dies führt dazu, dass folgende Vorgänge hier deklariert werden müssen, sofern sie wesentlich sind:
- Änderung der Abschreibungssätze
- Änderung der Warenlagerreserve (1/5 anstelle 1/3)
- Änderung des Kontenplanes

- Entscheid, neu angefangene Arbeiten zu aktivieren oder nicht mehr zu aktivieren
- Entscheid, eine Sofortabschreibung vorzunehmen
- Verbuchung von Provisionen im Warenertrag anstatt als gesonderte Ertragsminderung
- Entscheid, die Immobilien nicht abzuschreiben
- Änderung des Delkrederes (10 % anstelle 5 %)
- Änderung der Darstellung der Erfolgsrechnung (neu mehrstufig)
- etc.

Es sind primär die Änderungen der Stetigkeit, die hier zur Angabe führen.

Denkbar sind auch andere Angaben, die dem Bilanzleser dienen, wie z.B. Informationen über Steuern.

Beispiel:

Versteuerte stille Reserven 31.12.2002	CHF 676'000.–
Auflösung versteuerte stille Reserven 2003	CHF 226'000.–
Versteuerte stille Reserven 31.12.2003	CHF 450'000.–

steuerlicher Verlustvortrag gemäss Veranlagung 2003, somit per 31.12.2003 CHF 501'994.–

Obwohl wesentlich, erfolgen solche Angaben in der Praxis selten.

§ 5 Kennzahlen

Bilanzkennzahlen stellen Richtwerte dar. Diese Kennzahlen sollten permanent jedes Jahr ausgerechnet werden. Auf diese Weise erhält man einen vertieften Einblick in die wirtschaftliche Gesamtsituation eines Unternehmens. Selbstverständlich kann es notwendig sein, bei bestimmten wirtschaftlichen Gegebenheiten das Zahlenmaterial zu verdeutlichen und transparenter zu machen.

Nachdem Bilanz und Erfolgsrechnung erstellt sind, können diese durch Kennzahlen näher analysiert werden. Es ist eigentlich schade, dass die

Teil B: Grundlagen des Rechnungswesens / Principles of Accounting

ganze Arbeit der Buchhaltung mit der Bilanz und Erfolgsrechnung enden soll. Auf der einen Seite bieten Kennzahlen sinnvolle weitere Informationen, auf der anderen Seite können zu viele Kennzahlen die Übersicht erschweren. Aus diesem Grund sollte eine Konzentration auf 10 Kennzahlen erfolgen, die permanent mit jeder Jahresrechnung ausgerechnet werden sollten.

I. Eigenkapitalsquote

Eigenkapital dividiert durch Bilanzsumme.

Diese Verhältniszahl drückt aus, wie viel Eigenkapital ausgewiesen ist. Je höher die Zahl, desto gesünder ist die Eigenkapitalausstattung.

II. Anlageintensität

Anlagevermögen dividiert durch Bilanzsumme.

Diese Verhältniszahl drückt aus, wie viel Anlagevermögen ausgewiesen ist: Die Zahl besagt nichts darüber, ob ein Unternehmen gesund ist oder nicht. Je höher das Anlagevermögen ist, desto investitionsintensiver ist das Unternehmen. Eine Zunahme der Verhältniszahl von einem Jahr zum anderen bedeutet, dass die Investitionen zugenommen haben.

III. Goldene Bilanzregel

Die goldene Bilanzregel verlangt, dass langfristiges Anlagevermögen durch langfristiges Kapital gedeckt sein sollte und dass kurzfristiges Fremdkapital kurzfristigem Umlaufvermögen entspricht.

Kennzahlen dazu (Ziff. IV bis VI):

IV. Liquidität erster Stufe (Cash ratio/Zahlungsbereitschaft)

Sofort greifbare Mittel dividiert durch kurzfristige Verbindlichkeiten.

Diese Zahl drückt aus, wie die Verbindlichkeiten gedeckt sind. Je höher die Zahl, desto eher können die Verbindlichkeiten bezahlt werden.

Richtwert: 15–30 %

Kapitel 2: Bilanz, Erfolgsrechnung und ergänzende Rechnungen

V. Liquidität zweiter Stufe (Quick ratio/Umsatzbedingte Liquidität)

Zahlungsmittelbestand und Forderungen dividiert durch kurzfristige Verbindlichkeiten.

Diese Zahl drückt aus, wie die Verbindlichkeiten gedeckt sind. Je höher die Zahl, desto eher können die Verbindlichkeiten bezahlt werden. Hier werden nicht nur die kurzfristigen Verbindlichkeiten einbezogen, sondern alle liquiden Mittel und die Debitoren.

Richtwert: 100 %

VI. Liquidität dritter Stufe (Current ratio/Nettoumlaufvermögen (NUV)

Umlaufvermögen dividiert durch kurzfristige Verbindlichkeiten.

Diese Zahl drückt aus, wie die Verbindlichkeiten gedeckt sind. Je höher die Zahl, desto eher können die Verbindlichkeiten bezahlt werden. Hier werden nicht nur die kurzfristigen Verbindlichkeiten einbezogen, sondern das ganze Umlaufvermögen.

Richtwert: 150–200 %

VII. Bruttogewinn

Umsatz minus direkter Aufwand (bei Waren: Warenverkauf minus Wareneinkauf).

Die Zahl zeigt, welcher Betrag erwirtschaftet wurde, um die übrigen Aufwendungen zu decken.

VIII. Bruttogewinnmarge

Bruttogewinn dividiert durch Umsatz.

Die Zahl zeigt, welcher Betrag bei einem Umsatz prozentmässig übrig bleibt. Je höher die Quote ausfällt, desto besser.

Teil B: Grundlagen des Rechnungswesens / Principles of Accounting

IX. Umsatzrentabilität

Gewinn dividiert durch Umsatz.

Diese Zahl zeigt, wie viel Gewinn pro Franken Umsatz entsteht.

X. Kostenvergleich

Die wichtigsten Aufwendungen der Erfolgsrechnung sollten miteinander verglichen werden. Man reduziert die Erfolgsrechnung auf ca. 5–15 Posten, welche zusammen alle Aufwendungen erfassen, und vergleicht diese auf einer Tabelle über mehrere Jahre.

§ 6 Mittelflussrechnung

Das Gesetz verlangt, dass nach den Grundsätzen ordnungsgemässer Rechnungslegung eine möglichst zuverlässige Beurteilung der Vermögens- und Ertragslage erreicht werden soll.

Neben der ordnungsgemäss erstellten Bilanz und Erfolgsrechnung gehört zur notwendigen Beurteilung auch die Analyse der finanziellen Situation und der Liquidität des Unternehmens.

In Kleinunternehmen wird dies anhand der wichtigsten Kennzahlen zu Bilanz, Erfolgsrechnung und Liquidität beurteilt. Für grössere Unternehmen braucht es eine Mittelflussrechnung. Für Kleinunternehmen ist eine Mittelflussrechnung in aller Regel entbehrlich.

Die Bilanz kann teilweise Auskunft über den Mittelfluss geben.

Beispiel:

BILANZ 1

Aktiva: Mittelverwendung

- Umlaufvermögen
- Anlagevermögen

Kapitel 2: Bilanz, Erfolgsrechnung und ergänzende Rechnungen

Passiva: Mittelherkunft

- Eigenkapital
- Fremdkapital

Die Bilanz 1 zeigt das Grundprinzip.

BILANZ 2

Aktiva: Mittelverwendung

- Umlaufvermögen 200
- Anlagevermögen 0

Passiva: Mittelherkunft

- Eigenkapital 200
- Fremdkapital 0

So sieht die Startbilanz aus. 200 Kapital, 200 Bank. Mittelherkunft und Mittelverwendung sind klar ersichtlich.

BILANZ 3

Aktiva: Mittelverwendung

- Umlaufvermögen
- Anlagevermögen 200

Passiva: Mittelherkunft

- Eigenkapital 200
- Fremdkapital

Die Bilanz 3 zeigt eine Investition, die mit Eigenmitteln finanziert wird.

BILANZ 4

Aktiva: Mittelverwendung

- Umlaufvermögen

- Anlagevermögen 300

Passiva: Mittelherkunft

- Eigenkapital 200
- Fremdkapital 100

Die Bilanz 4 zeigt eine weitere Investition von 100, die mit Fremdkapital finanziert wird.

So einfach wie hier zeigen sich die Verhältnisse in der Praxis nicht. Eine Mittelflussrechnung kann notwendig werden. Die hier gezeigten Vorgänge betreffen nur Bilanzvorgänge. Für die Mittelflussrechnung sind aber die Vorgänge der Erfolgsrechnung miteinzubeziehen.

Zur Bestimmung, wie sich bestimmte Mittel bewegt haben, müssen bei der Mittelflussrechnung sog. «Fonds» gebildet werden. Ein solcher kann z.B. die «flüssigen Mittel» (das heisst Bargeld, Post-/Bankguthaben, jederzeit in Geld umwandelbare Wertschriften) oder «flüssige Mittel und Forderungen» umfassen.

In der Mittelflussrechnung wird jetzt dargestellt, wie sich diese Mittel bewegt haben.

Mittelzufluss:

- Finanzierung, d.h. Zufuhr von Mitteln (z.B. aus Kapitalerhöhungen, Zuschüssen der Eigentümer usw.)
- Desinvestition, d.h. Zufluss von Mitteln aus dem Verkauf von Anlagevermögen

Mittelabfluss:

- Definanzierung, d.h. Abfluss von Mitteln (z.B. durch Zahlung von Dividenden, Kapitalrückzahlungen etc.)
- Investition, d.h. Abfluss von Mitteln durch Kauf von Anlagevermögen (z.B. Fahrzeuge, Maschinen, Immobilien, Tochterfirmen usw.)

Je nach Fonds ist auch die Aufnahme von Darlehen ein Mittelzufluss, resp. die Rückzahlung eines solchen ein Mittelabfluss.

Die Bewegung des Fonds kann jetzt direkt (Zunahmen der Mittel minus Abnahmen derselben) oder aber indirekt (das heisst Reingewinn +/− der fonds-wirksamen Bewegungen) berechnet werden. In der Regel macht man beide Berechnungsarten, um so eine Kontrolle für die Richtigkeit zu erhalten.

Wichtigste Kennzahl innerhalb der Mittelflussrechnung ist der Cashflow. Der Cashflow ist der ausgewiesene Gewinn zuzüglich Abschreibungen. Die Zahl gibt somit Auskunft über die aus dem betrieblichen Erfolg erwirtschafteten Geldmittel. Die Abschreibungen sind nicht liquiditätswirksam, kosten in diesem Sinne kein Geld und werden deshalb zum Gewinn dazugezählt. Ist der Cashflow positiv, kann Geld (Cash) für neue Investitionen erwirtschaftet werden. Ist der Cashflow negativ (= Cash loss), können keine Investitionen aus dem laufenden Ertrag erwirtschaftet werden. Der Cashflow sollte nicht mehr als 1–2 Jahre lang negativ sein. In der Regel müssen danach Kapitalerhöhungen folgen oder die Geschäftsausrichtung muss neu definiert werden.

Direkte Berechnung des Cashflow:

liquiditätswirksamer Ertrag

./. liquiditätswirksamer Aufwand

= Cashflow (+) / Cash loss (–)

Indirekte Berechnung des Cashflow:

Erfolg

+ liquiditätsunwirksamer Aufwand (z.B. Abschreibungen)

./. liquiditätsunwirksamer Ertrag (z.B. Ertrag aus Eigenherstellung)

= Cashflow (+) / Cash loss (–)

Bei Kleinunternehmen ist die Erstellung einer Mittelflussrechnung i.d.R. nicht nötig. Sinnvoll kann aber die Darstellung des Cashflow sein. Die Mittelflussrechnung kann in einer weiteren Stufe die Bilanz miteinbeziehen und die Veränderung integrieren. So führt die Zunahme der Kreditoren zu einem Kapitalfluss.

Für eine vereinfachte erweiterte Berechnung ergibt sich folgendes Schema:

Erster Ausgangspunkt:

Erfolgsrechnung

Erfolg

+ Abschreibungen

= Mittelfluss aus betrieblicher Tätigkeit (= Cashflow NUV)

Zweiter Ausgangspunkt:

Bilanz

Cashflow NUV

+ Abnahme Umlaufvermögen oder ./. Zunahme Umlaufvermögen

+ Abnahme Anlagevermögen (Liquidierung, Desinvestition)

oder

./. Zunahme Anlagevermögen

+ Zunahme Fremdkapital oder ./. Abnahme Fremdkapital

= Mittelfluss (= Cashflow Geld)

Aus dieser einfachen Zusammenstellung lässt sich erkennen, was aus betrieblicher Tätigkeit an Mitteln erwirtschaftet wird, was an Mitteln aus der Reduktion von Aktiven absorbiert wurde und was an Mitteln durch Zunahme des Fremdkapitals beschafft werden konnte.

Wenn sich eine Zunahme der Fremdverschuldung zeigt, sollte eine Mittelflussrechnung erstellt werden und eine kritische Analyse der Bilanz und Erfolgsrechnung erfolgen. Die Kennzahlen sollten berechnet und am Schluss gewürdigt werden. Nach dieser klaren Situationsanalyse muss beurteilt werden, wie es weitergehen soll.

Kapitel 2: Bilanz, Erfolgsrechnung und ergänzende Rechnungen

§ 7 Kostenrechnung

Die Kostenrechnung ist eine bei Kleinunternehmen selten geführte Rechnung. Sie wird hier nur ansatzweise erläutert.

Wenn wir die Finanzbuchhaltung verlassen, kommen wir zum ersten Schritt der Betriebsbuchhaltung und Kostenrechnung.

Die Kostenrechnung wird dazu führen, dass die in der Buchhaltung entstandenen Aufwendungen erfasst, analysiert und ausgewertet werden. Nicht der Erfolg der Unternehmung als Ganzes steht im Vordergrund, sondern die Kosten und Erträge pro Leistungseinheit.

I. Die Kostenartenrechnung

Die Kostenartenrechnung gliedert die Kosten nach Arten. Sie beantwortet die Frage nach der Art der entstandenen Kosten. In der Regel führen die Zahlen der Finanzbuchhaltung als Aufwandarten zu den Kostenarten.

Gewisse Abgrenzungen können sich ergeben. Diese sind aber detailliert zu erklären. Solche Abgrenzungen führen dazu, dass nicht liquide und nicht erfolgswirksame Elemente zu Kosten werden.

Bei der betrieblichen Buchführung ist das am besten bekannte Beispiel der Eigenlohn des Unternehmers. Massgebende Abgrenzungen können sich bei Abschreibungen, Zinsen oder latenten Rückzahlungsverpflichtungen ergeben.

Das Erfassen der Kostenarten ist i.d.R. einfach.

II. Kostenstellenrechnung

Als zweiter Schritt in der Betriebsrechnung folgt die Kostenstellenrechnung. Diese gibt Antwort auf die Frage, wo die Kosten entstanden sind.

Dieser Bereich erfordert eine Zuordnung der entstandenen Kosten mit einem Betriebsabrechnungsbogen (BAB) auf die einzelnen Kostenstellen. Hauptproblem ist die Definition der Kostenstelle und der Vorkostenstelle.

Es empfiehlt sich, nicht zu viele Kostenstellen zu definieren, da sonst der Aufwand für die Erstellung zu gross ist. Am einfachsten orientiert man sich an den vorhandenen Sparten und Strukturen. In der Regel sind dies pro Betrieb 1–4 Kostenstellen.

Neben den Kostenstellen (Hauptkostenstellen) sind noch Vor- und Hilfskostenstellen zu definieren, auch hier empfiehlt sich Zurückhaltung.

Im Ergebnis wissen wir, wie viele Kosten pro Kostenstelle entstanden sind.

III. Kostenträgerrechnung

Die Kostenträgerrechnung schliesslich gibt Antwort auf die Frage, wofür die Kosten entstanden sind. Es handelt sich um die Kombination von Kosten und Ertrag.

Zuerst steht aber das Ermitteln der Kostenträger im Vordergrund. Es muss also dargelegt werden, wie viele Einheiten (Kostenträger) sich pro Kostenstelle ergeben.

Als Antwort erhalten wir somit, wie viele Kosten sich pro Einheit ergeben. Das Ergebnis der Kostenrechnung ist die Aufteilung aller entstandenen Kosten pro Kostenstelle und Kostenträger.

Hierfür müssen zuerst die Erträge aufgeteilt werden. Sie werden den einzelnen Kostenstellen zugeschrieben. Somit werden sich alle Erträge in der Summe auf die verschiedenen Kostenstellen verteilen. Am Schluss ergibt sich daraus das rechnerische Ergebnis von Kosten pro Kostenträger und Ertrag pro Kostenträger und damit Gewinn oder Verlust pro Kostenträger. Damit wird klar ersichtlich, wo die Stärken und Schwächen des Betriebs liegen.

IV. Schlussbemerkung

Ziele der Kosten- und Leistungsrechnung sind:

- Verbesserung der Kostentransparenz
- Ausweis der Leistungen
- Schaffung eines Führungsinstrumentes
- Ermittlung differenzierter Kennzahlen
- Beurteilung der Wirtschaftlichkeit

Kapitel 2: Bilanz, Erfolgsrechnung und ergänzende Rechnungen

Ein erstes Hauptziel für den Betrieb ist die Führung einer einheitlich geführten Finanzbuchhaltung. Ein weiteres Ziel kann in der Einführung einer Kostenrechnung liegen. Hier sind vor allen Dingen die grösseren Betriebe und Institutionen angesprochen.

§ 8 Planungs- und Investitionsrechnung

Die Planungs- und Investitionsrechnung ist eine bei Kleinunternehmen nur selten geführte Rechnung. Sie wird hier ansatzweise kurz erläutert.

Die Planungsrechnung und die Investitionsrechnung sind Entwicklungen für die Zukunft.

I. Kurzfristige Planungsrechnung

Wesentlichen Bestandteil der kurzfristigen Planung bildet das Jahresbudget, das in eine Planerfolgsrechnung und eine Planbilanz ausmündet. Daraus werden die kurzfristigen Finanzpläne für die monatlichen Einnahmen und Ausgaben abgeleitet. Finanzielle Engpässe sollen rechtzeitig erkannt werden und voraussehbare Mittelüberschüsse zinsgünstig angelegt werden können.

II. Langfristige Planung

Grundlage für die langfristige Planung ist die Unternehmensstrategie mit klar definierten Zielsetzungen. Damit die notwendigen Massnahmen ergriffen werden können, entstehen für den Betrieb die folgenden Aufgaben:

- Rechtzeitiges Erkennen von Ersatzinvestitionen
- Ausarbeitung von Vorschlägen für Rationalisierungs- und Erweiterungsinvestitionen
- Ausleuchten von Investitionsvorhaben in Bezug auf den betrieblichen Gesamtablauf
- Berechnung von Investitionsvorhaben
- Treffen von Investitionsentscheiden und umfassende Vorbereitung
- Kontrolle der ausgeführten Investitionen

Kapitel 3:
Individual company accounts in Switzerland

§ 1   Balance sheet

I.   Minimum content

The basic format of the balance sheet required under Art. 663a CO is shown in the following table:

Basic minimum format of the balance sheet
under Swiss law (Art. 663a CO)

ASSETS	AKTIVEN
Cash	Flüssige Mittel
Accounts receivable: trade[2]	Forderungen aus Lieferungen und Leistungen
Accounts receivable: other[2]	Andere Forderungen
Inventories	Vorräte
Pre-paid expenses	Rechnungsabgrenzungsposten
Total current assets	**Umlaufvermögen**
Financial assets[2]	Finanzanlagen
of which participations in other companies	*davon* Beteiligungen
Property, plant and equipment	Sachanlagen
Intangible assets	Immaterielle Anlagen
Incorporation, capital increase and organisation costs	Gründungs-, Kapitalerhöhungs- und Organisationskosten
Own shares	Eigene Aktien

[2] Of which due to and due from group companies and major shareholders.

Unpaid share capital	Nicht einbezahltes Aktienkapital
Total fixed assets	**Anlagevermögen**
LIABILITIES AND SHAREHOLDERS' EQUITY	**PASSIVEN**
Accounts payable - trade[3]	Schulden aus Lieferungen und Leistungen
Accounts payable - other[3]	Andere kurzfristige Verbindlichkeiten
Accrued liabilities	Rechnungsabgrenzungsposten
Long-term liabilities[3]	Langfristige Verbindlichkeiten
Provisions	Rückstellungen
Total liabilities	**Fremdkapital**
Share capital	Aktienkapital
Participation capital	Partizipationskapital
Legal reserves (general reserves)	Gesetzliche Reserven (allgemeine Reserven)
Statutory reserves	Statutarische Reserven
Other reserves (free reserves)	Übrige Reserven (freie Reserven)
Revaluation reserves	Aufwertungsreserven
Reserve for own shares	Reserve für eigene Aktien
Retained profits (accumulated losses)	Bilanzgewinn (Bilanzverlust)
Total shareholders' equity	**Eigenkapital**

The most important asset and liability headings are examined in detail below. The equity accounts are discussed below.

---

[3] Of which due to and due from group companies and major shareholders.

II. Equity

Shareholders' equity normally includes the following items:

1) Share capital: ordinary shares, registered or bearer.
2) Participation capital: participation certificates are non-voting shares.
3) General reserves: legal reserves from the assignment of profits, and share premiums or additional paid-in capital in excess of par.
4) Free or special reserves.
5) Undistributed earnings carried forward: retained earnings.
6) Net profit/loss for the year.

Preference shares are seldom encountered in Swiss corporations. Treasury stock (own shares) has to be capitalised and a corresponding reserve must be set up (see below).

1. *Share capital and participation capital*

Under Art. 621 CO the minimum share capital of a stock corporation is CHF 100,000. The shares may be bearer or registered. Both may be issued at the same time. They can be converted from one type into the other provided the articles of incorporation permit it. The minimum nominal value is set at CHF 0.01 (one centime, *Rappen*). Thus shares without par value may not be issued. On the incorporation of the company a minimum of 20 percent of the nominal value must be paid-in on registered shares. Bearer shares must be fully paid-in. In all cases the minimum paid-in capital must not be less than CHF 50,000. The unpaid amount has to be capitalised in the assets and termed unpaid share capital.

It is also possible to contribute assets (contribution in kind) instead of paying the share capital in cash so long as a special audit report on the valuation is prepared. Participation capital does not carry any voting rights; otherwise it is equivalent to normal shares. However, it may not exceed double the amount of the normal voting share capital.

2. Reserves

Legal reserves – general reserves

Art. 671 para. 1 CO requires certain allocations of profit to non-distributable reserves. These are normally called legal reserves or general reserves. The allocation must be as follows:

1) Five percent of the annual profit must be allocated to the general reserve until it reaches 20 percent of the paid-in share capital.

2) Also, once the 20 percent level has been reached, the following must be allocated to this reserve (in brackets: section):

   a) Any surplus over par value on the issue of new shares (additional paid-in capital in excess of par value, sometimes called a share premium), after deduction of the cost of the issue, to the extent that such surplus is not used for depreciation or welfare purposes.

   b) The excess of the amount which was paid-in on cancelled shares over any reduction in the issue price of replacement shares.

   c) Ten percent of the amounts which are distributed as a share of (annual) profits after payment of a dividend of 5 percent of the share capital.

3) To the extent that it does not exceed half the share capital, the general reserve should be used only to cover losses or for measures which are sure to assure the company's survival in times when business is poor; to counteract unemployment, or to soften its consequences (Art. 671 para. 3 CO).

4) The provisions of Art. 671 para. 2 sect. 3 CO, and para. 3 do not apply to companies whose principal object is to hold a participating interest in other companies (holding companies) (Art. 671 para. 4 CO).

According to Art. 671 para. 2 sect. 1 CO, value adjustments can be made directly to reserves. For example, overvalued participations are often directly value-adjusted by charging the amount to additional paid-in capital (share premium). The amount therefore does not affect the income statement as an (unusual) expense. In principle the annual general meeting of shareholders has to approve this treatment. Shareholders and the boards tend to favour it because no accumulated losses are created which would prevent the payment of dividends in future years. These direct charges to reserves (reserve accounting) should, however, be explained in the notes (reserve accounting).

Similarly all financing costs relating to a capital increase (e.g. emission stamp duty or bank commission) are normally also charged to the share premium, thus reducing the amount shown as additional paid-in capital.

Companies often stop making additional contributions to legal reserves out of profits when they reach 50 percent of share capital, because the general meeting of shareholders has the power to distribute such amounts as dividends.

Holding companies normally cease allocations at 20 percent. This rule has been introduced because it was argued that the subsidiaries already have to accrue legal reserves. On a consolidated basis the allocation would be doubled if the holding company allocated on the same basis as the operating company.

3. Reserves for own shares

Under the new company law, companies are allowed to acquire their own shares if freely disposable equity (i.e. reserves) to the amount necessary for the purpose is available and if the total par value of the shares does not exceed 10 percent of the capital (Art. 659 CO).

Under Art. 659a CO the company must create a separate reserve to an amount corresponding to the acquisition value of its own shares held. This should ensure that no dividends can be paid in the respective amounts. This also applies to the parent if a subsidiary acquires the shares of its parent. In the event of disposal or cancellation of own shares, the reserve for treasury stock may be dissolved to the full amount of their acquisition value (Art. 671a CO).

If own shares are not disposed of within one year of acquisition the federal tax authorities might consider the price paid in excess of par value as a hidden dividend distribution to shareholders, subject to the withholding tax of 35 percent. Hence any acquisition of own shares should be discussed beforehand with tax consultants.

4. Revaluation reserve

The revaluation reserve required by Art. 670 CO may be released only by conversion into share capital or by the depreciation or disposal of the revalued assets (Art. 671b CO).

5. Reserves provided for by the articles of incorporation

The articles of incorporation may provide that amounts higher than 5 percent of the annual profit shall be allocated to the reserve and that the reserve shall amount to more than 20 percent of the paid-in share capital required by law (Art. 672 para.1 CO).

They may provide for the creation of further reserves and determine their purpose and use (Art. 672 para. 2 CO).

6. Reserves for employee welfare purposes

The articles of incorporation may specify that reserves may be set aside for the founding and support of institutions intended to promote the welfare of employees of the company (Art. 673, 674 para. 3 CO). This is rare in practice because in Switzerland pension funds are separate from and independent of the employer and are fully funded. Contributions are therefore normally expensed and paid over to the pension fund (in cash). This is normally fully tax deductible.

7. Emergency reserves (Arbeitsbeschaffungsreserve)

These are tax-driven reserves that are created in good times. They can be drawn upon during an economic downturn. Normally a corresponding (restricted) cash deposit is capitalised, which can be used to prevent unemployment. The government will also reimburse the company for the income taxes it originally paid.

8. Relation between dividends and reserves

No dividend may be declared until the allocations to the legal reserve (Art. 671 to 671b CO) and to the reserves required by the company's articles of incorporation (Arts 672 para. 1 CO) have been made in accordance with the law and the articles of incorporation (Art. 674 para. 1 CO). The board of directors proposes to the general meeting of shareholders the amount it proposes to pay out in dividends and the allocations it intends to make to reserves. The auditors have to examine the proposals and state their opinion as to whether they are in line with the law and the company's articles of incorporation. This should also include an assessment of whether the company is able to finance the dividend, i.e. whether it has the necessary liquidity at its disposal.

Only when an affirmative audit report is available can the general meeting decide upon the distribution of profit. Thirty-five percent of the dividend (gross amount) has to be paid to the Department of Withholding Tax at the federal tax office in Berne within 30 days. Swiss shareholders can reclaim this tax in full if they declare the dividend income in their tax return. Foreign shareholders can claim most of the tax back under the terms of their country's double taxation treaty with Switzerland. If no treaty has been concluded or the dividend income has not been declared properly or not has been reclaimed within normally 3 years the tax is lost. Such unclaimed withholding tax generates considerable income for the Swiss government, indicating that it is not reclaimed.

The general meeting of shareholders may create other reserves which are required neither by law nor by the articles of incorporation or which go beyond their requirements to the extent that it is:

- Necessary for replacement purposes.
- Justified having regard to the continuing prosperity of the company or the distribution of a dividend as even-handedly as possible, taking into account the interests of all shareholders.

Even where there is no such provision in the articles of incorporation, the general meeting of shareholders may also create reserves from the balance sheet profit for the establishment and support of institutions intended to promote the welfare of employees of the company, or for other welfare purposes.

Minority shareholders are not very well protected, as it is difficult to prove that the reserves are not in the best interests of the company. The difficulty is increased by the limited nature of the disclosure in the individual company accounts. Dissident shareholders have the right to demand a special investigation (*Sonderprüfung*) under the new company law.

9. Dividends, interest during construction (Bauzinsen)

Under Art. 676 CO the shareholders may receive a fixed rate of interest debited to the fixed asset account during the period of time which is required for preparation and construction until the company attains full operating capacity. Within these limits, the articles of incorporation (Art. 627 sect. 3 CO) must stipulate a date for the termination of interest payments. This means that not only interest costs on debt, but also dividends to shareholders, can be capitalised as fixed assets. This is common procedure with power generating corporations. Construction may take several years. No income statement is prepared until electricity is being produced. All costs incurred are capitalised during the period of construction. Swiss law therefore also allows dividends to be paid during the period of construction as long as the articles permit it. The dividends are also capitalised and later depreciated over the useful life of the plant.

§ 2 Income statement

I. Minimum content

Either the account format or the reporting format may be used for the income statement.

The minimum content of the income statement under Art. 663 CO is set (in account format) in the following table. Under Art. 663 CO the minimum content of the income statement (in the reporting format) is as shown in the following table. Although not mentioned in the law, the Anglo-American type of income statement, i.e. the cost of sales method, can also be used in the format shown in the following table.

Minimum account format of the income statement (Art. 663 CO)

Expenses	Revenues
Materials use	Net sales
Depreciation	
Personnel expense	
Financial expenses	Financial income
Non-operating expenses	Non-operating income
	Gain from sale of fixed assets
Extraordinary expenses	Extraordinary income
Annual net profit	Annual net loss
Total expenses (and annual net profit)	**Total income (and annual net loss)**

Minimum reporting format of the income statement (Art. 663 CO)
with German original text

Net sales	Erlös aus Lieferungen und Leistungen
− Materials use	− Material- und Warenaufwand
− Personnel expenses	− Personalaufwand
− Depreciation	− Aufwand für Abschreibungen
+ Non-operating revenues	+ betriebsfremde Erträge
− Non-operating expenses	− betriebsfremde Aufwendungen
+ Financial revenues	+ Finanzertrag
− Financial expenses	− Finanzaufwand
+ Gain from the sale of fixed assets	+ Gewinne aus Veräusserungen von Anlagevermögen
+ Extraordinary income	+ ausserordentliche Erträge
− Extraordinary expenses	− ausserordentliche Aufwedungen
= **Annual net profit/loss**	= **Jahreswinn/Jahresverlust**

Format of the income statement according to cost of sales method (FER 3)

	Net sales	Nettoumsatz
less	Cost of goods sold	Kosten der verkauften Produkte
	Gross margin	**Bruttomarge**
less	Selling and marketing expenses	Verkaufskosten
	General administrative expenses	Verwaltungskosten
	Research and development expenses	Forschungs- und Entwicklungskosten
	Operating profit	**Betriebsgewinn**
less	Financial expenses net [1]	Finanzaufwand netto
less	Extraordinary expenses net [1]	Ausserordentlicher Aufwand netto
	Profit before tax	**Gewinn vor Steuern**
less	Income tax	Ertragsteuern
	Annual net income/loss	**Jahresgewinn/Jahresverlust**

1) Gross amounts shown in the notes

This cost of sales format of the income statement is also permissible under FER 3, Presentation and Format Swiss GAAP. However, the following types of cost required by Art. 663 CO have to be shown in the notes:

- Materials expenses.
- Personnel expenses.
- Depreciation expenses.

II.   Net sales

This item comprises:

- The gross sales from the sale of merchandise own products and services.
- Operating ancillary sales (e.g. sales of scrap metal, license income).
- Sales deductions (returns, discounts, sales discounts, losses incurred on doubtful accounts, etc.).
- Currency gains and losses closely connected with sales transactions.

It should not, however, include the increase/decrease in work in progress and finished goods inventories and capitalised fixed assets manufactured by the company. Although this item is not mentioned in the law it should be disclosed separately if it is material. These items are valued at manufacturing cost and not at sales price, i.e. they do not include a profit margin. If these items are not material they may be included under other operating income.

III.   Materials expenses

This item includes:
- Purchased merchandise, raw and auxiliary materials etc., and changes in the position as compared with the previous year (increases and decreases).
- Purchases of components.
- Differences in inventory of purchased materials.

- Inventory value adjustments because of obsolescence, losses, damage, price decline, etc.
- Direct freight costs, customs duties, etc.
- Purchase price deductions such as returns, discounts, sales discounts etc.
- Currency gains and losses closely connected with purchase transactions.
- General value adjustments for tax purposes (hidden reserves in stocks).

IV. Personnel expenses

This item comprises:
- Salaries and wages, provisions and other employee remuneration.
- Legal and voluntary social expenses, including old age insurance pension costs, etc.
- Cost of hiring temporary staff.
- Creation of accrued liabilities for unpaid salaries, bonuses, holiday entitlement, overtime, etc.

V. Depreciation

This item comprises:
- Systematic and unscheduled depreciation on tangible fixed assets such as buildings, equipment, machinery, etc.
- Amortisation and write-downs of intangible fixed assets such as patents, trade marks, copyrights, licenses, goodwill, etc.

Value adjustments of current assets should not be included here.

VI. Non-operating revenues and expenses

Differentiating between operating, non-operating and extraordinary revenues and expenses is not easy. Revenues and expenses must be shown gross. 'Non-operating' means that the expense is not related to the objectives (goal) of the company as stated in its articles of incorporation. Examples are:

- Rents from non-operating property holdings by a manufacturing company.
- Royalty income and expenses.

VII. Financial revenues and expenditure

Financial revenues comprise:

- Interest from bank accounts, notes receivable, loans receivable, etc.
- Interest and dividends on marketable securities.
- Gains from the sale of securities.
- Gains from reversal of downward value adjustments (write-downs) of financial assets.
- Realised and unrealised gains on financial assets in foreign currency.

Unrealised gains should be stated only if there is no doubt as to their realisability.

Financial expenses comprise:

- Interest paid/accrued on bank account overdrafts, notes payable, loans payable, etc.
- Interest on debenture loans.
- Losses on the sale of securities.
- Losses from value adjustments to financial assets.
- Realised and unrealised losses on financial assets in foreign currency.

Unrealised losses should be recognised as soon as the loss becomes evident, i.e. when it appears probable.

This item should not, however, include rent revenues / expenses or lease revenues / expenses, etc. These should be shown separately under separate headings if material or, if not, under other operating revenues / expenses or possibly under non-operating revenues / expenses.

VIII.   Gains from the sale of fixed assets

When fixed assets are sold, only gains have to be disclosed. It is understood that hidden reserves are often realised by selling property or other fixed assets (for example from the employer company to its pension funds). This would be disclosed separately under this heading. It should be borne in mind that significant tax effects may result. For example, many cantons levy special property turnover taxes (*Handänderungssteuern*) and capital gains taxes (*Grundstückgewinnsteuern*) on such transactions. These taxes should be included in tax expenses. They are shown in gross, not deducted directly from the gain (net of tax).

IX.   Extraordinary revenues and expenditure

Extraordinary revenues are defined as a gain from non-recurring transactions, which are not related to the normal course of business. Examples of extraordinary revenue might include:

- A large payment received following a patent infringement case.
- An extraordinary gain resulting from an insurance payout for the loss of a building which was not rebuilt. Sometimes this is deferred for tax purposes as a provision for replacement (*Ersatzbeschaffungsreserve*).

Extraordinary expenses are defined as losses on non-recurring transactions, which are not related to the normal course of business. Examples of extraordinary expenses might include:

- A fire that destroyed inventories which were not insured.
- A tax penalty or fine that was imposed on the company.
- A large product liability case that was lost.

It is very difficult to distinguish between non-operating and extraordinary items. The use of extraordinary expenses should therefore be confined to items, which are:

- Rare
- Non-recurring
- Material in amount
- Unusual for the company, given its size and business purpose

So that such items can be assessed it is recommended that their nature should be disclosed, especially in the notes.

X.   Annual net income/loss

This is the annual result of all operating revenues minus operating expenses, all non-operating revenues minus non-operating expenses, all financial revenues minus financial expenses, and all extraordinary revenues minus extraordinary expenses, minus tax.

XI.   Revenue items which need not be disclosed

International accounting standards require many more income statement items to be disclosed on the face of the income statement or in the notes. These include, for example:

- Net operating result.
- Net financial result.
- Changes in work in progress and finished goods.
- Capitalised fixed assets manufactured internally.
- Income before tax.
- Income tax.
- Details of personnel expenses.

Teil B: Grundlagen des Rechnungswesens / Principles of Accounting

§ 3 Recognition criteria and valuation

I. Principles of the recognition of assets, liabilities and provisions

1. *Materiality*

Materiality is a qualitative aspect influenced by subjective judgments. The question is what amount and/or omission will influence the decision to buy the investment, keep it or sell it. It may also involve the shareholders' approval of the financial statements or other decisions. Often the amounts concerned are taken into consideration alongside other balance sheet items or heads of the income statement, i.e.:

- Total assets.
- Shareholders' equity.
- Net sales.
- The net result.

It also depends whether net income is affected by the item or not (net of tax).

All items which influence the valuation and presentation of the annual financial statements or their individual items to such an extent that the decision of a user of the financial statements might be influenced are to be considered material. Where the said criteria are an inadequate basis on which to judge whether an item is material or not, it may be useful to form a conclusion as to materiality by viewing the item in question in relation to appropriate key figures. If the accumulation of immaterial items amounts to a significant influence on the reliability of the financial statements, this factor is to be taken into consideration.

2. *Prudence (conservatism) and hidden reserves*

Continental European countries, especially in Switzerland, have always stressed prudence as a key accounting concept. If quantitative decisions have to be taken the more conservative alternative is chosen. The key concept is that assets should not be overstated and liabilities should not be understated, so that equity is not overstated. This approach suits creditors such as the banks, since it reduces the risk their lending or investment is exposed to. It also minimises the tax bill, employee demands and the accountability of management and board. Bad decisions are not as visible as they might otherwise be; losses can silently be made good from hidden reserves. Even for the government there are perceptible advantages. The tax flow is more consistent. It is lower when the company is in a phase of expansion. Sooner or later, however, the accumulation of hidden reserves will lead to tax liabilities, if only in the end upon liquidation.

It is obvious that the measurement of assets and risks is very much a matter of judgment. Continental European managers and auditors tend to be more conservative in their outlook than their Anglo-American counterparts.

Swiss statute and tax law has always favoured the creation of hidden reserves in the individual financial statements. Only in consolidated accounts does the concept of a true and fair view enter into consideration.

It will not have escaped notice that the concept of conservatism is markedly at odds with the requirement of clarity. However, it is clearly the overriding principle.

The financial statements are prepared in accordance with the principle of prudence if:

1) Income is accounted for only when the goods have been delivered or, correspondingly, the service has been performed, and, when other types of income are recognised, only when payment has been received or an irrevocable claim exists, or, in general, where the circumstances support the recognition (the realisation principle).

2) Losses and risks, which are recognisable but not yet incurred are already provided for if the cause relates to the period under review or a prior period. This is so, even if they become known after the balance sheet date but before the financial statements have been issued (the principle of conservatism).

3) Independently of the valuation principles applied in the financial statements, the market value of inventories and work in process at the balance sheet date is taken into account if it is lower than the value determined according to the valuation rules (the lower of cost or market principle).

3. Continuance of the company's activities (going concern)

The going concern principle is also a very important concept. If the company is unable to continue (e.g. owing to bankruptcy), or is voluntarily discontinued (e.g. upon liquidation), then the valuation basis has to be changed. Strict application of the historical cost convention is necessary with a going concern, thereby giving rise to hidden reserves (owing to the effect of inflation). In a discontinuance of operations the assets are normally valued at fair market prices, less deferred tax, liquidation costs, etc.

The individual company accounts and the consolidated financial statements are based on the assumption that it is possible for the company to continue as a going concern for the foreseeable future (next twelve months). The continuation of the company as a going concern cannot be assumed if the dissolution of the company is anticipated or apparent, or if curtailments of a significant portion of the company's operations are planned or appear to be necessary.

Valuation problems in the event of liquidation or bankruptcy are treated in more detail below.

4. Consistency of presentation and valuation

Consistency is important if prior year figures are to be comparable. However, hidden reserve accounting makes the principle difficult to fully implement in Switzerland. The basis of presentation, classification of items, valuation and disclosure should be consistent. Any change should be explained and possibly quantified in the notes. However, the principle is overridden by the company's ability to create hidden reserves. Therefore, in the individual company accounts departures are highlighted only when hidden reserves are released. Examples would be:

- Netting income and expenditure.
- Failure to apply depreciation in a year of loss.
- A change in depreciation method.
- A change in the method of inventory valuation.

The annual financial statements are considered to have been prepared in accordance with the principle of consistency if in the current year the same accounting principles are applied as in the period under comparison. Consistency relates to the presentation of the financial statements as a whole and not just to the content and the valuation of the individual account balances.

II. Valuation principles

There are few of the restrictive valuation principles found in other countries. Depreciation must be applied, value adjustments made and provisions set aside to the extent required by recognised accounting principles in business (Art. 669 CO).

According to Art. 669 para. 1 CO 'Provisions are to be created particularly to cover uncertain contingent liabilities and potential losses from business transactions pending.' The code continues as follows:

For purposes of replacement, the board of directors may take additional depreciation, make value adjustments and provisions and refrain from dissolving provisions, which are no longer justified. Hidden reserves exceeding the above are permitted to the extent justified with regard to the continuing prosperity of the company or the distribution of a dividend as equal as possible, taking into account the interests of the shareholders (Art. 669 paras 2 and 3 CO).

This is the well known 'hidden reserve statute' (*stille Reserven*). Since the Code of Obligations stipulates only maximum accounting values (*Höchstwertprinzip*), undervaluation of assets and/or overstatement of liabilities can be implemented almost completely at management's discretion.

The auditors must be notified in detail of the creation and/or release of replacement reserves and any additionally created hidden reserves.

Such hidden reserves are sometimes also called latent or undisclosed reserves. To a large extent they are also accepted by the tax authorities. For example, one-third of inventories are deductible. In the canton of Zurich 80 percent depreciation of tangible fixed assets with a limited useful life is allowed in the year of acquisition, and the remaining 20 percent after five years. This single-stage depreciation is admissible in the tax accounts only if it is accounted for in the individual statutory accounts as well. The same canton permits an allowance for doubtful debt of 10 percent on domestic trade receivables and 20 percent on foreign receivables. Normally the tax return is identical to the statutory financial statements.

III. Incorporation, capital increase and organisation costs

Under Art. 664 CO the costs of incorporation, capital increase and organisation resulting from the establishment, expansion or reorganisation of the business may be included in the balance sheet as an asset. They have to be shown separately and amortized within five years at most. Such costs would include the stamp duty on the issued capital (1 percent at present).

IV. Fixed assets

1. General principles

Under Art. 663a CO the following items are included in fixed assets:
- Financial assets (including investments in other companies)
- Property
- Plant and equipment (tangible fixed assets)
- Intangible assets

Included in tangible fixed assets are normally:
- Land
- Buildings
- Machinery
- Equipment
- Vehicles
- Office furniture, computers
- Construction in progress

Under Art. 665 CO the maximum value of fixed assets is the acquisition or production cost less the required depreciation. This clearly reflects the historical cost convention. It means that an asset can be capitalised only at original cost. It also implies a very conservative approach, indicating that "depreciation, value adjustments and provisions" must be effected to the extent required by generally accepted accounting principles. Acquisition cost is determined on the basis of suppliers' invoices. Depreciation is determined by the method of depreciation and the estimated useful life of the assets. Tax considerations mean that often steep depreciation (from book values) is applied over a short period of time.

For certain categories of assets a portfolio approach to valuation is adopted which emphasises the reduced importance, by comparison with other European countries, of the principle of separate valuation in individual accounts.

2. Land

This category includes purchased land at acquisition cost on the basis of a contract which needs registration in the land register of the local authority in whose area the land is situated. In addition the following costs can also be capitalised:

- Estate agents' commission
- Conveyance fees
- Valuation costs
- Relevant property transfer taxes
- The cost of bringing the land to the condition required

At acquisition, land is stated on the balance sheet at purchase price. In later years it has to be valued at the lower of acquisition cost or net realisable value. In the past years downward value adjustments have not been required for land. Inflation has meant that property prices have been constantly increasing; therefore, depreciation is not normally applied to land.

Depressed property prices mean that devaluation may eventually become necessary if the property market continues to deteriorate (permanent impairment of value). A portfolio approach is often used in the individual company accounts, where losses on certain pieces of land are compensated by gains in other items.

The value of land does not need to be disclosed separately. It is invariably included with that of the related buildings, as separation is often impracticable.

3. Buildings

Buildings are normally shown at acquisition or production cost less depreciation. The following costs can be included in production cost:

- Expenses for architects and engineers
- Cost of excavation, etc.

Interest arising during the construction period can be capitalised.

Depreciation is determined mainly by tax law. The rate may vary from 2 percent to 4 percent of acquisition cost per year. It can be doubled if the depreciation is calculated from the book value. The canton of Zurich allows a particularly favourable depreciation rate (see above). To qualify as tax-deductible these amounts have to be booked through the statutory accounts.

A portfolio approach to valuation is often used in the individual company accounts, where losses on certain buildings are compensated by gains in other items.

The book value of the building does not need to be shown separately. Usually it is included under a heading 'Land and buildings' or 'Property' as no separation is feasible.

However, the fire insurance value has to be disclosed in the notes. The value is derived from the (often semi-governmental) insurance company's annual fire insurance premium invoice, based on an inflation index for rebuilding costs. It more or less reflects the current replacement cost of a new building that would have to be reimbursed in the event of destruction by fire. It therefore does not necessarily reflect the fair market value of the building (the depreciated value) because the insurance is geared to the new replacement building. Additionally, the land does not need to be insured.

Mortgaged property also has to be disclosed in the notes, but only at its book value. As property normally is mortgaged the book value is visible.

4. Machinery, furniture and fixtures

These are valued at acquisition cost according to the suppliers' invoices. The following can also be capitalised:

- Freight, custom duties, etc.
- Freight insurance
- The cost of installation

Interest during the construction period can be capitalised. However, the above costs are seldom capitalised (mainly for tax reasons). Sometimes a fixed percentage is added to the purchase price, e.g. 2 percent, based on experience. Discounts received are deducted from the purchase price.

Tools and other machines with a relatively low value are expensed directly, as they may have a short useful life. Normally only items higher than CHF 1,000 to CHF 10,000 are capitalised. Additionally, no tax requirements would limit direct write-offs.

Depreciation is often applied using the straight-line method based on acquisition cost. Normally the tax rates are used, which are rather generous. The tax depreciation rate can be doubled if the depreciation is calculated on the book value. For example, say the useful life is five years. Straight line depreciation of the acquisition cost would be 20 percent. The rate from the book value would be 40 percent. This second method does not require an indirect means of recording cumulative depreciation or a fixed assets register. More conservative depreciation methods are allowed in the canton of Zurich.

Additional depreciation is allowed for statutory accounting purposes. Some companies even value their fixed assets at a *pro memoria* CHF 1. However, the tax authorities may not allow the full depreciation amounts as tax-deductible.

The insurance value for all tangible fixed assets and the mortgaged amounts have to be disclosed in the notes.

5. *Intangible assets and merger goodwill*

Intangible assets have to be shown separately in the balance sheet. They could include purchased intangible assets such as:

- Concessions, cartel quotas (*Kontingente*) and similar rights
- Patents, recipes, copyrights
- Franchises, trade marks

- Goodwill (if the assets and liabilities of a partnership or of a sole proprietor are acquired at more than the fair market value of the assets and assumed liabilities and through a legal merger)
- Electronic data processing software (if not capitalised with the related hardware)

The differentiation from organisation cost according to Art. 664 CO is vague. Internally generated intangible values (e.g. development costs) can therefore also be capitalised. However, the costs claimed have to be substantiated (hours spent, expenses, etc.). The determination of acquisition cost is based on suppliers' invoices or contracts. Amortisation is determined by the method of depreciation and the estimated useful life of the assets. It is normally quite short (three to five years). Because of tax considerations intangibles are often directly expensed. Amortisation is normally taken on a linear basis over five years. If the value of the assets diminish (permanent impairment), a complete write-off is recorded.

Research and development costs are rarely capitalised in practice. Sometimes project-related development costs are. They may also be included in inventories, work in progress, fixed assets, organisation costs or deferred charges. However, their value should be monitored and, in the event of impairment, immediately written off. Because research and development costs are rarely capitalised, Swiss accounting literature barely addresses the subject.

6. *Long-term loans*

Long-term loans are stated at nominal value. If repayment is uncertain the nominal value is adjusted directly. Interest-free loans are normally discounted to their present value.

7. *Participations*

Participations are long-term equity stakes in other companies that give a certain degree of control. Voting rights of 20 percent or more will normally ensure such control (Art. 664a para. 3 CO). Any participation that is essential to an assessment of the company's financial situation and income should be shown in the notes according to Art. 663b no. 7 CO.

Participations are normally an investment in the capital of:
- Stock corporations (shares)
- Limited liability companies
- Cooperatives

Acquisition cost is normally derived from purchase agreements or bank statements. If the intrinsic (fair market) value is less than acquisition cost, value adjustments become compulsory to reflect the long-term value impairment. In the case of quoted companies the intrinsic value is calculated from stock exchange prices. the value of privately held companies is more difficult to determine. Value is derived from capitalised future net profits (price/earnings ratio) and the fair market value of the non-operating assets less deferred taxation. Estimated future distributable net profits are capitalised at an interest rate, which takes into consideration the risk-free interest rates of federal bonds and additionally the long-term risk of the investment (e.g. 8 to 12 percent).

A portfolio approach is often used in the valuation of the individual participations, where losses on certain items are compensated by gains in others.

The equity method may not be used in the individual company accounts if the value exceeds acquisition cost. The goodwill in a participation can be written off for tax purposes only when the participation is not financially sound (continuing losses, little or no equity left, etc.).

Long-term investments in the shares of companies constituting less than 20 percent of the capital and/or votes are stated at the lower of cost or intrinsic value.

V.   Current assets

1.   *Inventories*

Inventories include raw materials, work in progress and finished goods, as well as merchandise. Under Art. 666 CO they are all valued at no more than the acquisition cost or manufacturing cost. If the cost is higher than the market value at the date of the balance sheet, then market value would be used (lower of cost or market, or net realisable value).

Value adjustments for obsolete items should be based on a consistent formula. For tax purposes, the net value can additionally be reduced by one third. This has to be recorded in the statutory accounts in order to be tax-deductible. Inventories normally also include goods out on consignment or held by agents.

Instead of the specific identification method the following cost flow assumptions can be used:

- (Weighted) average cost
- First in – first out (FIFO)
- Last in – first out (LIFO)

The average cost method is the most commonly used in practice.

No definition of capitalisable acquisition or manufacturing cost is offered in the legislation. Many companies include only a few of the elements of cost, in order to reduce profits for tax purposes (e.g. only variable material cost). The Swiss Institute of Certified Accountants has defined the upper limit of cost which can be included in inventories (see Auditing Handbook, 1998, volume 1, page 147). It includes all acquisition costs that accrue until the inventories are in the company's warehouse (or have been brought to the intended location) such as:

- Invoice price of purchased merchandise, raw and ancillary materials, etc., and invoice price of components purchased.

Plus purchasing costs such as:

- Direct freight.
- Customs duties.
- Less purchase price deductions such as:
- Returns.
- Discounts.
- Sales discounts.
- Volume bonuses, etc.

Manufacturing costs of work in progress and finished goods include all production costs that accrue until the inventories are ready for sale (or brought to the intended condition), such as:

- Acquisition cost of raw, ancillary and packaging materials, supplies and purchased components, as mentioned above
- Materials overheads
- Direct labour costs
- Labour overheads
- Manufacturing overheads
- Product-related development, testing and construction costs
- Patent and manufacturing-related royalty costs

Manufacturing costs can include both variable and fixed costs, such as:
- Fuel and power
- Rents
- Insurance premiums
- Repairs
- Small tools
- Salaries of manufacturing management
- Planned (systematic) depreciation (but not extraordinary depreciation)
- Interest on debt (but not calculated interest on equity)
- Scrap

The above costs should be charged on the basis of normal production volume. Costs on idle capacity must not be included.

Not capitalisable are:
- General and administrative costs
- Selling costs
- The cost of sales warehouses or stores
- Sales provisions to agents
- Other acquisition costs

However, provisions and other acquisition costs may be capitalised as prepaid expenses (for example, in the case of large construction contracts).

Storage costs are not capitalisable unless the inventories have to mature in the course of time, as in the case of cheese, whisky, wine and timber. Similarly, property companies can capitalise interest on land under development and/or construction in progress.

As mentioned above, the tax authorities do not prescribe any particular method of valuation. They are often very flexible if only a few of the above components are capitalised. To qualify as tax-deductible the statutory accounts have to show the same valuations as the tax return. From the stated value (lower of cost or market) the tax authorities grant additional tax relief of one-third (*Warenreservendrittel*) on the inventory. Inventories are therefore normally understated by comparison with international standards. This means that there are often significant hidden reserves in the individual company accounts. In the consolidated accounts these allowances are normally reversed after calculating deferred tax on the item.

Valuation at selling price is only rarely used, e.g. for readily marketable goods, such as gold ingots. This selling price may be above the acquisition or production cost. When it is lower a value adjustment is necessary (lower of cost or market).

In certain industries other methods are used, e.g. retail companies are allowed to value inventories at the selling price less profit margin.

Only one amount of total inventories net of deductions has to be disclosed in the balance sheet. Pledged inventories have to be disclosed in the notes at their book value.

2. Long-term construction contracts

No specific accounting requirements prevail. Swiss GAAP FER 22 has more details on this topic. For tax purposes the completed contract method is normally applied. This method defers the realisation of the profit and revenues to the date when the project is completed. The same method is normally used for the statutory accounts as well.

The percentage of completion method (PoC) is admissible but rarely used. The following conditions have to be met:
- The contract must be clearly defined, the accounting system sophisticated and the profit secure. For a speculative contract the method is unacceptable.

- The company must be able to estimate the percentage of completion of the contract in a reliable manner.
- At the balance sheet date a claim for compensation must exist.
- Care should be taken with fixed price contracts or if cost-plus contracts have been agreed.

However, under the both the percentage of completion method and the completed contract method recognised losses have to be provided for immediately.

3. Pre-paid expenses

Pre-paid expenses are expenses paid normally in advance for a future period. At the balance sheet date the item has not been used or consumed (e.g. insurance or rent paid in advance). Pre-paid expenses have to be disclosed separately in the balance sheet.

Non-material items are commonly expensed but not capitalised. This is a way of understating assets (hidden reserves) which is often accepted for both statutory and tax accounting purposes.

4. Cash

According to Art. 663a CO liquid funds (cash) must be disclosed as a separate item under current assets. They comprise petty cash (coins, bank notes, foreign currencies), checks and money orders, postal and current bank accounts (checking or savings) in Swiss francs and foreign currency that are valued at year-end exchange rates. The valuation is usually at nominal values. Often cash also includes cash equivalents such as short-term deposits with banks (call money, twenty-four hour deposits, etc.). They can also be in the form of fiduciary deposits with banks.

Tied-up cash (e.g. blocked funds in a bank escrow account) should be disclosed. Under Art. 663b para. 2 CO ledged funds should also be disclosed in the notes. If a company has a loan from its bank, or an overdraft, all assets held at the bank are automatically pledged in favour of the bank under the terms of the general contractual arrangements with most banks.

Although most banks provide checking account facilities with current accounts, checks are seldom used in making payments. Even the banks themselves discourage it, since substantial fees are charged for cashing and depositing checks. Normally bank and postal transfers are made direct via the sophisticated giro clearing system. It can be done manually by sending the bank a payment order which indicates the payee and their bank or postal account number. Companies normally send a magnetic tape or diskette to the bank with electronically stored payee information on it. The quality of these automatic payment systems is very high. Electronic on-line banking is very important today.

5. *Securities*

Quoted securities which form current assets may be valued at cost or their average stock exchange price during the month preceding the date of the balance sheet. They may not be valued at more than the higher of these two values. The company can therefore choose whether to value the securities at market or at cost. The market valuation is often used where portfolios are managed by outside investment managers (banks) who after some time are no longer able to define cost because of the frequent portfolio changes. Income is then booked as the change in the market value compared with the previous year. A portfolio approach is often used in the individual company accounts, where losses on some items are compensated by gains on others.

Securities include quoted shares and bonds as well as precious metals, in the form of ingots or coin, with commodity prices (gold, platinum, silver). It is permissible to state marketable securities at values exceeding acquisition cost under Art. 667 para. 1 CO.

It is argued that these securities could easily be sold before the year end and then bought back in the new year to realise the same effect. Often the rates of the federal tax authorities are used. They are the average rates of the month of December, published in January the following year in a separate booklet. However, the tax authorities also recognise the valuation at acquisition costs of securities, which are lower than market value. Unrealised gains are therefore not liable to tax if they do not appear in the statutory accounts.

Unquoted securities are to be valued no higher than acquisition cost less the necessary value adjustments (Art. 667 para. 2 CO). If permanent value impairment becomes obvious, write-downs are necessary. Sometimes it is necessary to undertake a separate evaluation of the company that has issued the securities.

Unrealised losses are taken to the income statement immediately and are tax deductible. Subsequent recoveries can be recognised for both accounting and tax purposes.

No disclosure is required by law under the heading 'Securities', although it is normally shown separately in the balance sheet.

6. *Accounts receivable*

Trade accounts receivable have to be shown separately under current assets under the terms of Art. 663a CO. These are invoices unpaid at year end sent to customers in the ordinary course of business (customer receivables for the delivery of goods or services). They are reduced by debtors who are not collectible in a general allowance for doubtful debt (*Delkredere*). Tax law allows specific and general deductions for doubtful accounts. A full provision is accepted on specifically identified amounts where recovery is questionable or the amounts are long overdue. It is not necessary, however, for the debtor company to have entered into bankruptcy proceedings. After adjustments to specific items, an additional provision for bad debt, normally 5 percent of domestic debtors and 10 percent on foreign accounts, is acceptable. The canton of Zurich even allows double these percentages for tax purposes if the amounts are also deducted in the statutory accounts.

Disclosure of the amounts deducted by way of allowance for bad debts is not required. Some companies nevertheless disclose the amount on the face of the balance sheet as a deduction of receivables (allowance). Sometimes the allowance for doubtful debts is overstated (hidden reserves).

Inter-company receivables within the same group have to be disclosed separately in the balance sheet of the parent and subsidiary companies or in the notes. Also, amounts due from major shareholders should be shown, under Art. 663a para. 4 CO.

Other current receivables would normally include receivables from government authorities, especially concerning claims for domestic and foreign withholding tax refunds or VAT. They also have to be adjusted if the nominal value is no longer fully collectable.

7. *Notes receivable*

Promissory notes are rarely used for the delivery of goods and services. They may be used for foreign customers who are not credit worthy. Notes are normally discounted immediately and deposited with banks. The resulting contingent liability in the event of default is often disclosed in the notes.

If the notes are held until maturity they may be reclassified as long-term. Notes receivable from related parties have to be disclosed separately in the balance sheet or in the notes, under the terms of Art. 663a para. 4 CO.

VI. Liabilities

Current liabilities normally include:

- Trade accounts payable. This item would include unpaid invoices for purchased goods and services as well as purchases of fixed assets. Accounts payable to related parties have to be disclosed separately in the balance sheet or in the notes (Art. 663a para. 4 CO).
- Fiscal and social liabilities such as tax due, social security and old age insurance taxes due, pension contributions, salaries, etc.
- Accrued expenses.
- Deferred revenues.

Long-term liabilities normally include:

- Mortgages
- Debenture bonds, etc.

Liabilities are stated at the nominal value, which has to be repaid. Even if the market value is lower (e.g. the interest rate is well below the market rate) no adjustment is made. Liabilities to pension funds have to be disclosed in the notes.

VII. Provisions

The relevant legislation is Art. 669 para. 1 to 3 CO. Long-term general provisions are created for multiple reasons and are often tax-driven:

- Product warranty and liability (normally 2 percent of total sales can be accrued for tax purposes)
- Pending lawsuits, including tax contingencies
- Repairs
- Maintenance
- Advertising and marketing costs (e.g. planned campaigns, catalogues, etc.)

Normally no special provision is made for staff dismissals. Swiss law provides only for very short periods of notice:

- One month for employees with less than one year of service
- Two months for employees with two to nine years' service
- Three months for employees with over ten years' service

Normal employment contracts provide for three months for rank-and-file employees and six months for middle management. Top management contracts sometimes specify longer periods.

Severance costs are accrued only after a decision has been taken to lay employees off. However, mostly the costs of overtime and holiday entitlement not used up within the period are accrued. They would partly cover lay-off costs.

Provisions for taxes are normally included in accrued (short-term) liabilities. Sometimes, however, no distinction is drawn between short and long-term provisions.

§ 4 Special accounting areas

I. Lease accounting

Leasing is less widespread in Switzerland than in other countries. The reason may be that favourable depreciation rates on fixed assets are available for tax purposes. Most leasing contracts are operating leases. Here lease fees (rent) are expensed.

Only rarely are capital leases encountered. Sometimes they are capitalised as leased assets in the balance sheet of the lessee and depreciated over the lease period. At the same time a leasing obligation is set up under short and/or long-term liabilities. The monthly payment is regarded as partly interest expense and partly as a reduction in the liability. For the arrangement to qualify as a capital lease one of the following has to apply (Swiss GAAP FER 13):

- At the end of the period of the lease, ownership of the goods or property passes to the lessee.
- There is a purchase option under which the lessee can acquire the leased property for a nominal sum.
- The period of the lease is more than 75 percent of the useful life.
- The discounted lease payments are at least 90 percent of the fair market value.

These requirements are generally in line with international accounting standards.

Under Swiss law, leases that are not included in the balance sheet have to be shown in the notes (total of the unpaid leasing fees).

II. Foreign currency translation

There are no specific legal requirements regarding foreign currency translation. The federal tax authorities publish exchange rates that are to be used for tax purposes. These are the average of rates in the December before the balance sheet date. However, companies may use other rates (e.g. year-end rates as published by the major banks) if they wish.

With regard to the translation of foreign currencies into Swiss francs in the individual company accounts, Recommendation No. 2 (*Fachmitteilung* Nr. 2, *Fremdwährungen im Einzelabschluss*, ed. Treuhand-Kammer Zurich, Zurich 1990) of the Swiss Institute of Certified Accountants prefers all assets and liabilities stated in foreign currencies to be translated into Swiss francs at the current (i.e. balance sheet date) rate. The only exception is fixed assets and long-term liabilities, which are normally translated at the historical rate. As for the income statement treatment of the consequences of this method of translation, provisions are required with regard to any translation losses on long-term liabilities. Translation gains are often deferred until they are realised. This would apply, for example, to foreign branches with accounts in foreign currency. Such accounts must be translated into Swiss francs at the Swiss head office.

This recommendation also appears in the Auditing Handbook. It proposes four methods for the translation of foreign currency balances at year end:

- Current/non-current
- Monetary/non-monetary
- Modified monetary
- Current rate

In applying these methods it is necessary to ensure that, in general, the imparity principle is respected (i.e. the recognition of unrealised losses and deferral of unrealised gains) and that assets are stated at the lower of cost or market value. The following guidelines are recommended for individual balance sheet items:

1) Cash and sight deposits and overdrafts may be translated at the year-end rate, since the gains and losses can be considered realised.

2) Other short-term assets and liabilities, e.g. accounts receivable and payable: Unrealised gains and losses can be offset to arrive at a net position which, if a gain, should be deferred as a provision.

3) Inventories: Care should be taken to ensure that the translation method applied does not result in a higher amount than historical cost in Swiss francs. Normally the valuation is done at the time the foreign currency invoice is received and booked to creditors at the actual exchange rate, and not adjusted at year end.

4) Marketable securities: Since such securities can be adjusted to the year-end market price (under Art. 667 para. 1 CO), the related exchange rate gain or loss may be recorded as well, even if it is an unrealised gain.

5) Long-term loans receivable and payable. Unrealised gains and losses can be offset, provided they are in the same currency and of the same

maturity. A net gain would be deferred as a provision and a net loss recognised in accordance with the imparity principle.

6) Fixed assets that belong to foreign branches are translated into Swiss francs at historical rates. Translation at current rates would also be acceptable.

7) Long-term investments are normally translated at historical rates, even if the value of the foreign currency has deteriorated permanently. Such translation at current rates is normally more conservative. The investment is stated at the lower of cost or intrinsic value.

III. Research and development costs

Research and development costs normally include the following types of cost:

- Personnel expenses (payroll of the research and support staff)
- Materials expenses (materials used up for research purposes, e.g. drugs, chemicals, etc.)
- Depreciation expenses (depreciation of research computers, equipment and buildings)
- Overheads applicable to research and development departments

Such costs are normally expensed. They are not normally shown on the face of the income statement because the income statement has to show the types of cost (materials, personnel, etc.) required by company law.

IV. Government grants and subsidies

Government grants and subsidies are rare in Switzerland and normally take the form of favourable tax treatment. Some cantons grant other tax concessions or make land available at modest prices.

The construction of civil defence protection shelters used to be subsidised by central government. Such subvention is normally deducted from the related assets, thus reducing future depreciation charges. It is also possible to book a provision and release it over future periods.

Often no disclosure of government grants and subsidies is to be found in individual financial statements. Subsidies towards tangible fixed assets are usually booked directly to the respective assets, thereby reducing the asset book value and future depreciation. Sometimes the subsidies are shown as a provision and released to the income statement over the period required by the government contract. Amounts are seldom stated as extraordinary income.

V. Financial instruments

There is no specific guidance in the law or in the Auditing Handbook (HWP) on the treatment of financial instruments, except in the banking industry. Swiss GAAP FER 5 Off balance sheet items, mentions that disclosure in the notes is necessary of unusual business transactions pending and related risks. For example, purchase or sales commitments for goods or commodities, including futures, financial instruments such as currency or interest rate swaps, forward foreign exchange transactions etc. Recognizable losses from these transactions have to be accrued unless they represent hedging transactions.

It is not only banks and insurance companies that operate on the international financial markets. Large multinational companies have professional treasury departments, which habitually apply banking standards to their operations. They also follow international accounting standards (e.g. the IAS standards 32 and 39 on financial instruments). FER 5 deals with off-balance sheet instrument and is increasingly applied especially in group accounts. FER 27 on derivative financial instruments is applicable as of 1 January 2007.

VI. Deferred tax

Deferred tax is very seldom applied in the individual financial statements. These normally show the same amounts as the tax return. Deferred tax accounting is therefore normally applied only in the consolidated accounts, to achieve a true and fair view of the financial situation and results of operations. See FER 30 for deferred taxation in consolidated financial statements.

VII. Factoring

Factoring means the transfer of receivables to a financial institution (a bank or specialist factoring company). The factor manages the accounting of the receivables. This includes also sending out reminders to the debtors. The receivables are thus booked out of the company. Sometimes the risk of doubtful accounts (*Delkredere*) is also transferred. No disclosure is necessary, even if the factoring company has a right of recourse against the seller of the receivables.

VIII. Loans and receivables to shareholders and other related parties

Under the company law, loans and receivables to shareholders and related parties (individuals and companies) under common control have to be disclosed. This is important, as they could be granted without observing the arm's-length principle.

They might in fact constitute a repayment of share capital. This would be in contravention of Art. 680 para. 2 CO, which prohibits the shareholders' capital being returned. It might additionally be construed by the tax authorities as a concealed dividend, subject to 35 percent withholding tax (54% of the net amount "received"), especially if the shareholder is unwilling or unable to repay the loan from the company (construed dividend payment). This tax is due by the company which has to charge it to the recipient / shareholder. See also FER 15 Related party transactions.

IX. Trust agreements (fiduciary contracts)

A trust agreement is a fiduciary legal transaction by which a person gives assets (e.g. an investment, receivable, etc.) to a trustee. The risk remains with the trustor. The trustee, however, appears to third parties as the owner of the assets.

Interest and income from the assets are credited to the trustor. After the contract has expired the trustee returns the assets to the trustor.

These transactions are particularly frequent in private asset management. For a trust contract to be recognised by the tax authorities, it must be satisfy the following conditions:

1) There must be a written agreement between trustor and trustee dating from the commencement of the transaction.
2) All risks and costs have to be borne by the trustor.
3) In addition, the trustee receives a small commission, which should not be, less than two-thousandths of the fair market value of the asset.
4) The assets and liabilities, as well as the income they produce, must be clearly identified as trust assets in the books of the trustee, preferably on the face of the balance sheet, below the line or in the notes on the accounts.

It is recommended that the trust assets and liabilities should be shown in the notes.

X. Subsequent events

Events that take place after the balance sheet date but before the adoption of the balance sheet and/or the audit report have to be disclosed in the financial statements. They normally involve only losses incurred. If the reason for the loss relates to the past year, then a loss provision or value adjustment is necessary. Typical examples are:

- The bankruptcy of an account receivable, which was included in the year-end balance sheet.
- A dispute dating back to the previous year which is resolved by an adverse court decision in the new year.
- Raw materials ordered through a firm commitment to purchase but where there is a sharp fall in price the following year.

If an event bears no relation to the previous year it can be accounted for by disclosing it in the notes of the accounts. Examples might be:

- The uninsured portion of damage from a thunderstorm.
- A ship that sank this year.

- A sharp decline in a foreign currency to which the company is exposed.

However, prudent accounting would usually suggest setting up provisions as of the last balance sheet date.

XI   Pension accounting

Swiss companies are required by the Pension Fund Act (*Bundesgesetz für berufliche Vorsorge*, BVG) to establish independent legal entities in order to keep the assets held in favour of the beneficiaries separate from those of the employer. These entities normally take the form of foundations or, in rare cases, cooperatives. If no such legal vehicle is created – for instance, if the size of the company does not warrant it – the company can join a mutual pension scheme run by a life insurance company or a bank. Companies normally treat the actual amounts paid or due to the pension fund during the year as period expense. For tax purposes there is generally no limit upon the employer contribution. Therefore, if the company's profits are on the high side, extra payments are made to reduce it, and it is the reduced profit that appears in the statutory accounts.

If the pension fund is under-funded, i.e. if it shows a deficit of assets compared with the actuarial liabilities, the employer will make a provision because of a sense of moral obligation towards its former employees (constructive obligation).

The practice of allocating incurred costs to future periods is virtually unknown in Switzerland in the statutory accounts given the conservative approach to all accounting. As mentioned above, it is not uncommon for large single payments to be made into pension funds over and above current requirements, usually to take advantage of a tax deduction.

Hidden reserves in pension funds are often not regarded as deferred assets of the employer. Employers are not permitted to take them back into the balance sheet and income statement as foreign companies frequently do. Pension funds are strictly regulated under cantonal supervision. Moreover, the board of trustees of pension foundations will consist of both employer and employee representatives. The latter could block such transactions. Only in extreme circumstances could an employer mobilise these excess funds. Separate employer reserves (*Arbeitgeberbeitragsreserven*) have to be shown in the pension fund's balance sheet, which can be used to pay the employer's contribution until they are exhausted. The employer would not capitalise the respective deferred assets (less deferred taxes). However, in merger and acquisition situations such 'hidden reserves' are regarded as assets of the target company. The issue is controversial, because it can be argued that such funds belong to the employees of the company taken over. Specialist advice and the approval of the government regulatory bodies are necessary before changes can be introduced in pension funds.

As mentioned, surpluses cannot be repaid to the contributing company. Even the scope for investing such funds in the employer company is very limited. The following are possibilities:

- Current account payable of the employer
- Short-term loan to the employer
- Long-term loan to the employer
- Investments in bonds of the employer or its subsidiaries
- Investments in shares or non-voting shares of the employer or its subsidiaries

All nominal investments (loans and current accounts) have to carry interest at market rates. The investment limits are very restrictive. Loans should normally be secured by a mortgage or other means. Securities should preferably be marketable and should not exceed certain levels. If such investments exist, the auditors of the employer have to confirm with the cantonal authorities that the employer has recorded the same amount of debt and that the employer is a going concern (i.e. has more assets than liabilities).

Pension fund expenses do not have to be disclosed in the income statement of the employer. The employer's contributions are normally included in personnel expenses.

Under Art. 663b para. 5 CO the total liability to the pension fund has to be disclosed separately in the notes on the accounts, with comparative figures for the previous year (see 3.8).

Swiss GAAP FER 16 was reissued as of 1 January 2007 requires that deficit in pension funds be recorded as provisions in the employer balance sheet.

XII. Prior period adjustments

It is very rare for Swiss companies to adjust prior years' retained earnings in the individual financial statements in order to correct prior year errors, or to restate for the effect of an accounting change. All such items are adjusted through the income statement. In exceptional circumstances, if the tax authorities will not allow depreciation or other deductions, then a credit is booked directly to retained earnings. This would, however, be disclosed under changes in the equity.

§ 5 Revaluation accounting

I. Revaluation to avoid bankruptcy

There is no requirement to provide information on the effects of changes in the price level in individual financial statements. In the individual financial statements this information is virtually never disclosed. Only write-backs of past depreciation can be booked as income. If the revaluation exceeds historical cost a revaluation reserve has to be set up, as explained below.

Where, owing to losses shown in the balance sheet, half the capital and statutory reserves are no longer covered, property or shareholdings whose real (intrinsic) value has risen above acquisition or production cost may be revalued to no more than the balance sheet deficit for the purpose of eliminating such shortfall (Art. 670 CO).

Only property and equity investments in other companies (participations) may be revalued. Substantial hidden reserves may be created under these headings because they have to be valued at historical acquisition cost. Many companies have been holding property for fifty years or more, which has to be valued at the original purchase cost. Often it includes prime sites in the town centre, which are thus considerably understated in the balance sheet. Some major companies acquired holdings in cities over 100 years ago, for example, at CHF 0.50 a square meter. The value of such land has increased to over CHF 5,000 a square meter nowadays, mainly due to inflation. Under the historical cost convention companies may not adjust the now meaningless acquisition cost to current values in the individual financial statements.

Only where the business is in difficulty, i.e. over indebted in the terms of Art. 725 CO where liabilities exceed assets is an increase allowed. Of course, the company can always mobilise the hidden reserves by way of selling the assets.

In the event of revaluation the following must be disclosed in the notes:
1) The subject, e.g. the piece of property or participation concerned.
2) The amount of the revaluation (the extent of the increase).
3) The date of the revaluation (normally the balance sheet date).
4) Reference to the special audit report required, which must be the work of specialist auditors.
5) Reference to the valuation report, which must also be from experts.

In the case of property revaluation a professional estate agent will be engaged to value the land and buildings on the basis of capitalised earnings, the substance (replacement cost), comparable transactions near by, land prices, etc.

Similar valuations are undertaken for equity investments in subsidiaries and/or affiliated companies, on the basis of capitalised estimated earnings, equity at fair market values, share prices in the case of public companies, etc. Obviously these valuations will be arrived at conservatively and provision for deferred taxation will be deducted.

An example of revaluation of property and equity investment is shown in the following table. In the case of marketable equity investments revaluation to market value is permissible in accordance with Art. 667 CO. The profit can be stated as an unrealised gain in the income statement.

	Real estate	Investment
Acquisition cost	1,000	800
Book value	800	200
Current value	1,500	700
Possible revaluation with income effect	200	500
Possible revaluation without income effect under Art. 663b para. 9 CO	500	0

The revaluation of 500 has to be booked to a special equity account named 'Revaluation reserves'. It cannot be distributed until the revaluation is reversed or the assets are sold. Thus it is not possible to credit the amount to the income statement or to use it to reduce accumulated losses.

II. Revaluation reserve

The amount of the revaluation should be shown separately as a revaluation reserve. The revaluation reserve is permissible only if the auditors confirm in writing to the general meeting of shareholders that the legal requirements have been met in terms of Art. 670 CO. The revaluation reserve required by Art. 670 may be released only by conversion into capital, or by depreciation, or by the disposal of the revalued assets (Art. 671b CO).

§ 6 Notes and additional statements

I. Notes on the accounts

1. Overview

Under Art. 663b CO a certain minimum level of disclosure is required in the notes on the accounts. Under the old company law only two items of information had to be disclosed apart from the balance sheet and income statement: The insurance value of property and the total amount of contingent liabilities. These items were normally disclosed on the face of the balance sheet as footnotes below the balance sheet total. The fire insurance value reflected the replacement cost of buildings, as land itself needs no fire insurance. This amount was derived from the company's fire insurance policy. Virtually all buildings in Switzerland must have compulsory insurance as regulated by the government. The details are the responsibility of the cantons (political subdivisions). Many cantons have a government-owned insurance company. Given the limited information and often understated book values disclosed in Swiss financial statements, analysts sometimes used the insurance figures to estimate the hidden reserves in real estate.

For example, Company X disclosed in its parent company financial statements for a *pro memoria* book value for its property holdings of CHF 1. In a footnote to the balance sheet, however, it mentions that the fire insurance value of the property of the holding company (a headquarters building on Lake Zurich) is approximately CHF 93 million. This value would have been disclosed not to reveal the company's hidden reserves, but to demonstrate that the building was properly insured.

The footnotes in most Anglo-American countries grew to voluminous length, running to ten or twenty pages of the annual report. Eventually they could no longer be placed at the foot of the balance sheet and had to appear as an appendix, or annex, to the financial statements. They then became known as notes on the accounts.

The current company law (Art. 663b CO) requires 14 items of information to be disclosed in the notes. International accounting standards, including the Fourth and Seventh EU Directives and the International Financial Reporting Standards promulgated by the International Accounting Standards Board require much more disclosure than the Swiss requirements. Swiss GAAP FER 6 "Notes" is fairly comprehensive and recommends additional disclosure in accordance with international standards.

The disclosures in the notes must be audited by the company's auditors. Comparative figures are required (Art. 662a para. 1 CO).

The mandatory information to be disclosed in the notes under Art. 663b CO is listed in following table:

Minimum contents of notes (Art. 663 CO) in individual annual accounts

1. The total amount of guarantees, indemnity liabilities and pledges in favour of third parties.
2. The total amount of assets pledged or assigned for the securing of own liabilities, as well as of assets with retention of title. It is understood that only book values need be disclosed.
3. The total amount of liabilities from leasing not included in the balance sheet. According to the interpretation of the Swiss Institute in its Auditing Handbook (HWP) this is required only for financial leases.
4. The fire insurance value of fixed assets (in a single amount only).
5. Liabilities to pension funds of the employees of the company.

6   The amounts, interest rates and maturities of debentures (*Obligationenanleihen*) issued by the company.

7   Any participation which is essential to an accurate assessment of the company's financial situation and income. A participation is defined as an equity investment in another company commanding at least 20% of the voting rights, according to Art. 665a para. 3 CO.

8   The total amount of hidden reserves released (under Art. 669 para. 2 CO) and other hidden reserves (Art. 669 para. 3) to the extent that such total amount exceeds the total amount of the newly created reserves of that kind, if thereby the business result appears considerably more favourably.

9   Information on the subject and the amount of any revaluations (Art. 670 CO).

10 Information on the acquisition or disposal and on the number of own shares held by the company, including its shares held by another company in which it has a majority participation. Equally, the circumstances in which the company has acquired or disposed of its own shares should be disclosed (Art. 659 to 659b CO).

11 The amount of the authorised capital increase (Art. 651 to 651a CO) and of the capital increase subject to conditions (Art. 653 to 653i CO).

12 Information on the completion of a risk assessment (by the Board of Directors) – new as of 2008.

13 As applicable, the reasons that led to the premature resignation of the auditors – new as of 2008.

14 The other information required by law.

2.   Contingent liabilities

Under Art. 663b para. 1 CO the 'total amount of guarantees and securities in favour of third parties' has to be disclosed in the notes on the financial statements. Normally only a single amount is disclosed. The following items are included as contingent liabilities:

- Guarantees
- Securities given in favour of third parties.
- Dividend guarantees to minority shareholders of subsidiaries

- Obligations arising from the sale of receivables with recourse
- Obligations arising from joint ventures in the form of partnerships where the partners' liability is unlimited

The following need not normally be disclosed:

- Pending purchase or sales commitments
- Obligations arising from endorsed promissory notes
- Commitments arising from fixed assets on order
- The portion of subsidiaries' share capital not yet paid-in
- Subordinated loans receivable
- Comfort letters for the debt of subsidiaries (provided their substance is not a guarantee)
- Penalties in contracts
- Trust agreements

3. Pledged assets

Under Art. 663b para. 2 CO the 'total amount of assets pledged against own debts and those where ownership is restricted' has to be disclosed in the notes. The book value of such assets has to be disclosed, not the current value, which would be more relevant. A single amount for all assets which serves as security is sufficient. Examples are:

- Property that serves as security for a loan at book value
- Pledged inventories
- Securities, term deposits, current accounts, etc., that are deposited or held with a bank if the bank has granted a loan to the company, or an overdraft (according to the general agreement between banks and their customers all assets with the bank serve automatically as collateral)
- Receivables pledged to banks or financial institutions
- Fixed assets that have been acquired under a hire-purchase agreement, where the asset is entered in a government public register, until it has been paid for in full (in Switzerland there is an official register in

which the ownership of goods bought on hire-purchase can be recorded)
- Capitalised financial leases

4. Leasing obligations

Under Art. 663b para. 3 CO the 'total amount of the lease obligations that are not included in the balance sheet' (as liabilities) has to be disclosed in the notes. It is understood that only finance leases are involved. Operating leases do not need to be disclosed, as they are not recognised as liabilities in the balance sheet.

The sum of the outstanding future lease fee payments must be disclosed (the number of outstanding payments times the leasing fee).

5. Fire insurance value of fixed assets

Under the Art. 663b para. 4 CO the 'fire insurance value of fixed assets' must be disclosed in the notes. Sometimes two values are shown:
- Fire insurance value of buildings
- Fire insurance value of machinery, equipment, etc.

Disclosure is not required by international standards and this requirement is therefore unique to Switzerland.

6. Commitments to pension funds

Under Art. 663b para. 5 CO 'obligations towards pension funds' must be disclosed in the notes. Pension funds have to be established as separate legal units such as foundations or cooperatives to protect the beneficiaries. Such organisations are subject to considerable regulation and government scrutiny. The pension contributions of employees and employers (normally contributory, defined contribution plans) have to be funded, i.e. cash payments must be transferred to the pension fund. Strict investment policies apply. Share, bond and loan investments in the employer company are restricted or must be secured (normally against property).

Investments by the pension fund in the employer company are normally financial debts which have to earn interest.

The employer has to disclose the total debt to the fund. It may consist of:
- Current accounts
- Short-term loans
- Long-term loans (e.g. a loan secured by a mortgage)

7. *Debentures*

Under Art. 663b para. 6 CO the following information has to be disclosed in the notes: The 'amounts, interest rates and maturities of outstanding debenture bonds'. Debentures are defined as follows:

1) Public bonds issued in relatively small amounts, e.g. CHF 1,000 to CHF 5,000
2) Medium to long-term maturities
3) Total issue mostly in sizeable amounts of CHF 10 million or more
4) Publicly placed and traded on stock exchanges
5) Companies that have issued such bonds are subject to consolidation and publication requirements in the same way as those with quoted shares

Not considered as debentures are private placements with the following characteristics:

1) In high denominations, e.g. units of CHF 50,000 to CHF 100,000.
2) Normally first-class issuers.
3) Mostly sophisticated (institutional) investors.
4) No special prospectus requirements for creditors.
5) No public quotation or trading on a stock exchange.
6) Limited consolidation and disclosure requirement.

8. *List of equity investments*

Under Art. 663b para. 7 CO 'each equity investment that is material to an understanding of the financial position and results of the company' must be disclosed in the notes. Important investments are shares held in subsidiaries which are controlled and therefore consolidated or those with a significant influence where the company holds more than 20 percent of the voting rights of the investee. Investments carrying less than 20 percent of the voting rights should be included where the investment is material to the balance sheet of the investor. An investment is a long-term financial (fixed) asset which is not held on a merely temporary basis. In the consolidated accounts, obviously, only non-consolidated investments are capitalised in the balance sheet as fixed assets. The consolidated investments are eliminated in the consolidation. For each investment the following information needs to be disclosed:

1) Legal name (*Firma*) as stated in the articles and the commercial register.

2) Legal domicile where the company has its registered office.

3) Country of incorporation.

4) Percentage of capital held.

5) If other than the above, additionally the percentage of voting rights held.

9. *Release of hidden reserves*

Under Art. 663b para. 8 CO the 'total amount of hidden reserves released must be disclosed if the amount exceeds the newly created hidden reserves and if the amount is material to the results as shown in the income statement'. Hidden reserves in this legal sense are:

- The excess of acquisition cost over the book value. The acquisition cost, however, may not exceed the fair market value.

- Not, however, the difference between current value and acquisition cost.

Such hidden reserves can exist under almost any balance sheet heading except nominal share capital. They are created by understating assets (e.g. inventories, fixed assets, receivables) or overstating liabilities (provisions, accrued liabilities, etc.). It is difficult to calculate the extent to which hidden reserves have been released if no sophisticated accounting system is available. The release is calculated by deducting the higher hidden reserves at the beginning of the year from the balance of hidden reserves at the end of the year, making due allowance for deferred taxation. In principle companies have to prepare shadow financial statements to calculate the hidden reserves. Swiss subsidiaries of groups, foreign or domestic, normally use the accounts they have prepared for consolidation purposes to generate these figures. It is accepted that any accounting standards which require a true and fair view will rule out the creation of significant hidden reserves. Such standards would include:

- Swiss GAAP FER.

- Fourth and Seventh EU Directives translated into national law such as:

- German Accounting Directives Act (*Bilanzrichtlinien-Gesetz*, BiRiLiG).

- International Financial Reporting Standards (IFRS) of the IASB.

- United States Generally Accepted Accounting Principles (US GAAP).

The statutory (commercial and tax) accounts (referred to in Germany as *Handelsbilanz* I, HB I) are normally adjusted to group accounting policies on financial statements for consolidation purposes (*Handelsbilanz* II, HB II) after allowing for deferred taxation on the restated amounts. It is accepted practice to take the difference in the equity of HB I to HB II as hidden reserves net of tax. Invariably HB I is lower than HB II. If the opposite is the case, then HB I may be overstated and under Swiss law will be reduced to the HB II amount.

If the HB I profit is higher than the HB II profit in the income statement, the difference would be due to the release of hidden reserves, i.e. a reduction in hidden reserves compared with the previous year. If the amount materially influences the stated profit in the commercial accounts (HB I) the amount of released hidden reserves has to be disclosed in the notes on the commercial accounts. The gross amount of hidden reserves or the net amount (net of deferred tax) can be shown.

However, the creation of hidden reserves or their balance at year end need not be disclosed. This Swiss practice of disclosing the release of hidden reserves is unique. It stems from the fact that Switzerland has not had a currency reform for 100 years, has never allowed the revaluation of real estate above acquisition cost, except as mentioned below, and has enjoyed a liberal income tax regime and generous tax advantages.

10. Subject and amount of revaluations

Under Art. 663b para. 5 CO 'information about the subject and amount of revaluations' of certain fixed assets has to be presented in the notes. The information in the notes would normally include:

- The type of asset that has been revalued (property or investment in companies).
- The amount of the revaluation (the same as the amount of the revaluation reserve in the balance sheet).
- The date of the revaluation (normally the balance sheet date).
- The basis of the valuation (prudent current cost).
- A report by a suitably qualified specialist (e.g. an estate agent or a valuation report for companies).

This procedure is permissible only for property and equity investment in other companies.

11. Own shares

Art. 663b para. 10 CO requires disclosing in the notes:

"information on the acquisition or disposal and on number of own shares held by the company, including those held by a company in which it holds a majority of voting rights; additionally the circumstances must be disclosed in which the company has purchased or sold its own shares."

Hence the number and the amounts in Swiss francs of own shares on hand at year end, and movements in the figures during the year, must be disclosed in the notes. The summarised form of disclosure exemplified in the following table "Disclosure of own shares" could be used if the company buys and sells many own shares during the year (e.g. a public company with quoted shares).

Disclosure of own shares (Art. 663b para. 10 CO)

Own shares	Number	Amount (CHF)
Balance at 1 January 2006	1,000	500,000
Additions	50	30,500
Value adjustment		-120,000
Disposals	-60	-20,500
Balance at 31 December 2006	990	390,000

Under the old law companies were not allowed to hold their own shares. Inevitably all manner of arrangements were devised to circumvent the restriction. For instance the own shares might be held by a subsidiary company often domiciled in an offshore tax haven. Sometimes the company's bank would hold these own shares under a trust agreement at the nominal value.

This was necessary because public companies often issued convertible or option debentures and needed own shares in case the holders converted bonds or exercised options to acquire shares. It was not possible under the previous law, as it is now, to have authorised but unissued shares.

Own shares have to be capitalised as an asset in the balance sheet. The same procedure is adopted in the Fourth EU Directive. Under Anglo-American accounting principles own shares are deducted from shareholders' equity at cost. Under US GAAP and IFRS own shares are referred to as treasury stock. They are normally shares that have been bought back on the stock exchange. Such transactions reduce the cash position of the company and also the equity. Gains and losses on such transactions are directly debited or credited to additional paid-in capital (*Agio*) and therefore do not influence net income (in the United States this principle is summed up in the saying 'You can make money from dealing in own shares but not a profit').

The German or Continental view of treasury stock is that they are an asset. If their value is lower than cost a value adjustment is made through the income statement. If treasury stock is sold again the resultant gain is considered as income (also for tax purposes). Only if treasury stock is extinguished by way of a capital reduction is the resultant gain or loss considered an adjustment to additional paid-in share capital (*Agio*).

12. Authorised and contingent capital

Under Art. 663b para. 11 CO the 'amount of the authorised and contingent capital' must be disclosed in the notes. The concept of authorised and contingent capital was introduced into Swiss law only with the revised company law of 1992. The notes must state the proportion of the authorised and contingent capital as of the balance sheet date which has not been utilised (Art. 651 and 653 CO respectively). Such residual capital arises where the general meeting of shareholders has authorised the board of directors to increase the share capital (authorised capital) and/or where options and conversion rights relating to debentures have not been exercised by the balance sheet date.

This information is important in assessing the total amount of share capital and the shares outstanding and to assess the dilution of the shareholders' stake through such transactions. They must also be noted in the commercial register and in the company's articles.

13. Departures from certain generally accepted accounting principles

Under Art. 662a para. 3 CO 'departures from the principles of a going concern, of consistency in presentation and valuation and from the prohibition of netting amounts in the financial statements are permissible if they can be justified and must be disclosed in the notes on the accounts'. Examples would include:

- Netting financial expenditure and income.
- Failure to record depreciation one year.
- Owing to liquidity problems the going concern principle is in question.
- The method of valuing inventories has been changed.

However, the ability to create hidden reserves will always negate the above principles, including that of consistency. As long as hidden reserves can be created the company does not need to mention departures from consistency. Only when hidden reserves are released does the amount involved (income effect) have to be disclosed and departures from consistency mentioned in the notes as stated above.

14. *Disclosure of important shareholders*

Under Art. 663c para. 1 CO 'companies whose shares are listed on a stock exchange have to disclose the names of important shareholders and their stake (the percentage held) if their identity is known or should have been known'. Art. 663 para. 2 CO defines important shareholders as those shareholders or groups of shareholders legally connected through a shareholders' agreement that hold more than 5 percent of the votes of the company. If the articles of the company set a lower limit on the votes one shareholder may dispose of, then that percentage applies. For example, there are companies, which limit shareholdings to 2 percent per shareholder. In that case shareholders with 2 percent or more of the votes must be disclosed. Swiss public companies often have registered shares of low par value (e.g. CHF 100) which are controlled by the owning families. The investing public hold bearer shares of higher nominal value (e.g. CHF 500) or even non-voting participation certificates.

Such disclosure became mandatory as from 31 December 1993. Shareholders are not obliged to reveal major holdings to the company except as required by the Stock Exchange Regulations. Only the holders of registered shares will be known to the company through the share register. However, material holdings (representing more than 20 percent of the voting rights) must be disclosed by public companies in the list of investments which has to be included in the notes.

The disclosure of the stakes of corporate and private shareholders in the company was also a new requirement of the Stock Exchange Act (BEHG) which became effective in 1998.

15. *Consolidation and valuation principles in the consolidated accounts*

There has been criticism of the fact that the valuation principles need be disclosed only in the consolidated financial statements and not in the individual company accounts. It is difficult to assess the financial situation of a company and its results when the main accounting policies are not known.

16. Disclosure of management and board compensation in the notes

Under growing political pressure the Swiss parliament enacted the following amendment of the Swiss Corporation Law under the name of "Transparency amendment". This article which is only applicable for listed companies is applicable for financial years beginning on 1 January 2007 and reads as follows:

Art. 663b^{bis} CO requires "*Supplementary disclosures on compensations in the case of companies whose shares are listed on a stock exchange*" as follows:

"*^{1}Companies whose shares are listed on a stock exchange shall disclose in the notes to the balance sheet:*
1. *all compensations paid directly or indirectly to the members of the boards of directors;*
2. *all compensations paid directly or indirectly to persons whom the board of directors has fully or partially entrusted with the management (executive board);*
3. *all compensations paid directly or indirectly to the members of the advisory board;*
4. *compensations paid directly or indirectly to former members of the board of directors, the executive board, or the advisory board, if they are connected with their former activity in a body of the company or if they are not customary in the market;*
5. *compensations that are not customary in the market paid directly or indirectly to persons who are close to the persons mentioned in subparas 1 to 4.*

^{2}Compensations include, in particular:
1. *remunerations, wages, bonuses, and credit items;*
2. *profit sharings, turnover participations and other participations in the business result;*
3. *benefits in kind;*
4. *allocation of participations, conversion and option rights;*
5. *severance payments;*
6. *guarantees, indemnity obligations, pledges in favour of third parties and other securities;*
7. *waiver of claims;*

8. *payments establishing or increasing claims to benefits from pension plans;*
9. *any remuneration for additional work.*

³*Furthermore, the following shall be indicated in the notes to the balance sheet:*
1. *all outstanding loans and credits granted to the members of the board of directors, the executive board or the advisory board;*
2. *outstanding loans and credits granted, under conditions which are not customary in the market, to former members of the board of directors, the executive board and the advisory board;*
3. *outstanding loans and credits granted under conditions which are not customary in the market to persons who are close to the persons mentioned in subparts 1 and 2.*

⁴*The disclosures on compensations and credits must include:*
1. *the total amount for the board of directors and the amount attributed to each member indicating name and function;*
2. *the total amount for the executive board and the highest amount attributed to a member indicating his name and his function;*
3. *the total amount for the advisory board and the amount attributed to each member indicating name and function.*

⁵*Compensations and credits to close persons shall be disclosed separately. The names of the close persons need not be disclosed. Furthermore, the provisions on the disclosure of compensations and credits to members of the board of directors, the executive board and the advisory board shall apply by analogy."*

Additionally, Art. 663c CO was amended with a new disclosure requirement for board members and management of a public company:

"... participations in the company, as well as conversion and option rights of each member of the board of directors, of the management and the advisory board including participations of persons close to him or her, shall be disclosed (in the notes / annex of the parent company), including name and function of such member". This would include for example both the numbers of options and shares bought on the market (Stock exchange) as well as options and shares granted by the company under employment contracts.

II. Asset movement schedule (*Anlagespiegel*)

The Fourth EU Directive requires that changes in fixed assets are shown from the opening of the year to the closing balance in the individual company accounts. This applies to all fixed assets, including tangible, intangible and financial fixed assets. The amounts must be shown gross, i.e. acquisition cost, accumulated depreciation, etc. No such legal requirement exists in Switzerland. Swiss GAAP FER 18 requires such a listing of property, plant and equipment in the accounts.

III. Cash flow statement (*Geldflussrechnung*)

The Code of Obligations (CO) does not make cash flow or cash flow statements a requirement. This is in line with the Fourth and Seventh EU Directives, which impose no obligation to prepare and publish such information. Normally no such statement is prepared for the individual financial statements or parent company statement. However, in consolidated accounts almost all Swiss companies present consolidated cash flow statements.

Swiss GAAP FER 4 was issued in January 2007 and requires a cash flow statement also for the individual accounts.

IV. Directors' report (*Geschäftsbericht*)

Under Art. 662 CO the board of directors must prepare for each financial year a business report which consists of the audited annual financial statements, the annual report, and the consolidated financial statements if such statements are required by law. The annual financial statements consist of the income statement, the balance sheet and the notes on the accounts. All these have to be audited. However, in contrast to the requirements of the EU directives on the directors' report (*Lagebericht*), in Switzerland the directors' report does not need to be audited.

The contents of the directors' report to the shareholders are not defined. Often the reports are very short, merely repeating facts and figures, which can easily be derived from the financial statements.

§ 7 Filing and publication of financial statements

In general, users enjoy only limited access to the accounts of Swiss companies, since there is no requirement to publish or file them with the commercial registrar. The only exceptions are quoted companies, banks, insurance companies and mutual investment funds. The financial institutions are subject to strict supervision. They must file accounts with the regulatory authorities (FINMA, Swiss Stock Exchange, etc.). In addition, banks and insurance companies are required to publish their balance sheets in the Swiss Trade Journal (*Schweizerisches Handelsamtsblatt, SHAB*) and such other newspapers as their articles of association may require. These must appear annually, half-yearly or quarterly, depending on the size of the company.

Thus the publication of financial statements is very restricted. Under Art. 697h CO the annual financial statements and the consolidated financial statements, once approved by the general meeting of shareholders, must either be published in the official journal or a copy must be sent to any person requesting it, at his or her own expense, within one year of formal approval, if:

1) The company has bond issues outstanding.

2) Its shares are listed on a stock exchange.

For the above companies there is no size threshold. All public companies, and only public companies, have to publish their audited individual and (where applicable) consolidated accounts. The deadline is the end of June (six months after the balance sheet date – virtually all businesses take the calendar year as their financial year). Public companies normally provide a copy to anyone requesting it. Big companies normally make their full annual reports available in French and English as well as in German. The accounts are normally stored by database service companies on electronic media (Internet) and can be retrieved on screen (e.g. Teledata, Dun & Bradstreet) or are available in conventional printed form.

Other companies must make their annual financial statements, consolidated financial statements and auditors' reports available for inspection by creditors who can furnish evidence of an interest worthy of being protected. The courts decide in the event of dispute. Normally the company can avoid a creditor's inspection of the audited financial statements by paying the amount outstanding.

As only about 500 to 600 companies have bonds issued and/or quoted shares, extremely limited information is available on all other companies, including the 170,000 stock corporations whose accounts are not open to the public. This differs from the practice of most European countries, where all corporations must lodge their accounts in a commercial register to which everyone has access.

§ 8   Sanctions

Given that the duty to disclose their financial statements is limited to public companies, there are few sanctions upon a company that fails to prepare proper financial statements. The normal procedure is as follows where a company neglects to keep proper books of account or to produce financial statements.

Under Art. 699 CO the general meeting of shareholders must be convened by the board of directors. The ordinary meeting should take place annually within six months of the close of the financial year. Under Art. 700 para. 1 CO, the general meeting of shareholders must be summoned in the form provided for by the articles of incorporation at least twenty calendar days before the date of the meeting. For companies whose financial year is the same as the calendar year the latest day for the general meeting is therefore the 30 June following the calendar year end. The audit report and financial statements have to reach the shareholders before 10 June. The auditors thus need to be able to finish their work before 10 June if calendar year companies are to comply with the law.

If no financial statements are made available the auditors must remind the board, preferably in writing. When all measures have been exhausted, if the board has still not submitted the financial statements, the auditors will call a general meeting to inform the shareholders of the illegality. In one-person companies where there is only one shareholder and one board member at any one time, the shareholder may fail to attend the meeting. The auditors will ask a public notary to attend as well, to witness that no shareholder has shown up, and the auditors will resign at this meeting. At the same time they will communicate their resignation to the board, the commercial registrar and possibly the courts where there is a risk of bankruptcy. The court will then decide what to do next. The commercial registrar can close the company down with a court order and put it into liquidation and bankruptcy, the court appointing a receiver and an auditor.

Similarly, the tax authorities will remind the company to submit its tax return. However, the audit report does not need to be filed. If the return fails to materialise the company is assessed on an estimated basis. If the assessed tax is not paid the tax authorities can also have the company declared bankrupt and penalise the board members for failure to comply with the tax laws. Eventually the company will be struck from the commercial register: It will cease to exist and will be unable to transact any further business.

The main articles of the Swiss Penal Code (SPC, *Schweizerisches Strafgesetzgebuch*, StGB) relating to accounting and bookkeeping are as follows:

1) Art. 148 SPC Fraud.
2) Art. 152 SPC False information on businesses.
3) Art. 163 SPC Fraudulent bankruptcy.
4) Art. 166 SPC Negligent bookkeeping.

There have been only a few court judgments in these areas, most of them relating to bankruptcy cases and tax fraud.

Few companies have to publish their accounts (only banks, insurance companies and quoted companies). Where companies whose shares or debentures are listed fail to publish accounts the Swiss Stock Exchange (SIX) has the right to delist them and so debar errant companies from public trading. Similar measures would be taken by FINMA. Banks and insurance companies that neglect their duty to file audited accounts may find their license to operate being withdrawn by the regulatory agency.

Teil C

Revision / Auditing

Kapitel 1:
Statutory auditing in Switzerland

§ 1   Audit requirements and appointment of auditors

Auditing requirements are found mainly in Art. 727 to 731a of the Swiss Code of Obligations (CO), revised as of 1 January 2007. Some other legislation also refers to audit requirements (e.g. banking law). As stock corporations are by far the most important legal form of business the requirements for the auditing of stock corporations are treated here.

According to Art. 730 CO the general meeting of shareholders of every stock corporation (there are approximately 170,000) must appoint one or more auditors. At least one auditor must have his domicile, registered office or a registered branch office in Switzerland. Individual auditors or audit firms may be appointed. Public companies with quoted shares or debentures outstanding must have an audit firm under government oversight (Art. 7 RAG) usually one of the Big Four international accounting.

The auditors have to confirm their acceptance of the mandate in writing to the general meeting (assembly). The fact that they have done so has to be filed with the commercial registrar which makes this information public.

It is therefore possible to find out who the auditors of a stock corporation are; something, which would otherwise remain unknown because the accounts are not published. The Swiss domicile of auditors is important in order that correspondence may be addressed to an address in Switzerland.

§ 2   Qualifications of auditors

Under Art. 727a CO auditors must be qualified to fulfil their duty to the company to be audited. This means that they should have at least a basic knowledge of Swiss accounting, auditing, business law, taxation, etc. However, under Art. 727b CO public companies and those that are of a certain size have to appoint auditing experts as auditors (Art. 4 RAG) to perform an ordinary audit (full audit). These auditors must have special professional qualifications if at the company to be audited two of the following thresholds are exceeded in two consecutive years:

1) Balance sheet total of CHF 10 million.

2) Revenues of CHF 20 million.

3) Average annual number of employees 50.

or if

4) Consolidated financial statements have to be prepared.

5) Minority shareholders holding at least 10% of the shares require it.

The Law requires the following professional qualifications of auditing experts in the new Auditor Oversight Act (Art. 4 para. 2 RAG) as of 1 July 2007:

1) Swiss Certified Public Accountant (*dipl. Wirtschaftsprüfer*)

2) Swiss Certified Trust Expert (*dipl. Treuhandexperte*) or Swiss Certified Tax Expert (*dipl. Steuerexperte*) and Swiss Certified Expert in Accounting and Controlling (*dipl. Experte in Rechnungslegung und Controlling*) with five years' practical experience of auditing under the supervision of an audit expert.

3) Graduates of business/economics or law schools / universities (universities or *Fachhochschulen*) with twelve years' experience of auditing practice under the supervision of a Swiss Certified Public Accountant.

4) Persons who have acquired an equivalent foreign diploma as certified public accountant with the requisite experience and knowledge of Swiss law. Such qualifications would normally embrace Chartered Accountants (UK, Canada, Australia, etc.), Certified Public Accountants (United States), *Wirtschaftsprüfer* (Germany), *Experts Comptables Diplomés* (France), etc.

§ 3 Independence requirements including rotation

Under Art. 728 CO audit experts for ordinary audits must be independent of the board of directors and of any shareholder with a majority vote. In particular they must not be employees of the company to be audited, and they must not perform work for it that is incompatible with the auditing mandate. Swiss Certified Public Accountants have to observe the independence requirements of the Swiss Institute as published in the Auditing Handbook as well. Partners and staff of the Big Four audit firms also have to meet the independence requirements of the firm concerned, all of which substantially surpass the Swiss standards (because of SEC requirements).

Under Art. 2 lit. b RAG commercial companies etc. may also be appointed as auditors. They would have to ensure that the management and the personnel in charge of the assignment meet the qualification and independence requirements.

Art. 728 CO was revised in 2005. Therefore, the following new requirements apply most likely as of 1 July 2007. For the ordinary audits:

"[1] *The auditors must be independent and reach their audit opinion on an objective basis. Their independence may neither be impaired in actual fact nor based on appearances.*

[2] *In particular, independence shall not be reconcilable with:*
  1. *membership on the board of directors, another decision making function within the company, or an employment relationship with it;*
  2. *a direct participation of a considerable indirect participation in the share capital or a considerable claim or debt vis-à-vis the Company;*
  3. *a close relationship of the managing auditor with a member of the board of directors, or with the person in a decision making function, or with an important shareholder;*
  4. *participating in bookkeeping as well as the rendering of other services, giving rise to the risk of having to examine, as auditor, its own work;*
  5. *the acceptance of mandate that entails economic dependence;*
  6. *the conclusion of a contract with conditions that are not in line with the market, or of a contract by which the auditors acquire an interest in the audit result;*
  7. *the acceptance of valuable gift or special benefits.*

[3] *The provisions on independence shall apply to all persons involved in the audit. If the audit firm is a partnership or a legal entity, the provisions on independence shall also apply to the members of the supreme manag-*

ing or administrative body and to other persons in a decision making function of the audit firm.

⁴ Employees of the audit firm not involved in the audit may neither be a member of the board of directors nor have a decision making function in the Company to be audited.

⁵ The independence is also not guaranteed if persons not fulfilling the independence requirements are close to the audit firm, to persons involved in the audit, to members of the supreme managing or administrative body or other persons with a decision making function.

⁶ The provisions on independence shall also apply to companies that are under common management with the company to be audited of the audit firm."

I. New Company Law and Independence Rules effective 1 January 2008

On 1 January 2008, the new revised Code of Obligations (OR/CO) in Switzerland and the related new independence rules became effective. Audit professionals should be aware of the extended provisions of the revised rules and the revised Guidelines on Independence of the Swiss Institute such as:

II. Personal Independence

- Expansion of Covered Person concept: According to the Guidelines on Independence of the Swiss Institute all Partners in Switzerland (incl. Liechtenstein) are considered covered persons with regard to Swiss audit clients. Consequently, Swiss Partners are no longer allowed to hold mutual funds audited by the Swiss Firm. Such mutual funds should be disposed by 31 December 2007.

- Generally: Covered persons (all partners, all members of the audit team and all professionals (managers and partners) providing services to the audit client) and their immediate family members are prohibited from holding securities of that audit client. They are also not allowed

to have loans with that audit client (unless the audit client is a financial institution).
- All audit employees are prohibited from accepting an appointment as a member of the board of directors or position in a management function of any audit client.
- Close relationships: The auditor's independence can be compromised by a close relationship of any audit firm employee to a member of the Board of Directors, a person in a decision making function, or an important shareholder of an audit client. For members of the audit team and the chain of command such relationships are prohibited.
- Gifts and hospitality: Auditors should not accept valuable gifts or hospitality from our audit client, unless the value is insignificant (say below CHF 200). In any case we never accept cash.
- Rebates / discounts: Auditors should not accept discounts from an audit client that are under normal market conditions unless the value is insignificant (say below CHF 200).

Note: For SEC audit clients the rules are stricter. Generally, a covered person is prohibited from having financial relationships (including any kind of bank accounts!) with an SEC audit clients.

III. Employment Relationships

Cooling off periods for professionals that (a) work at an audit firm which join an audit client or (b) work at an audit client which join their audit firm are defined in the Article 11 of the Federal Act on the Licensing and Oversight of Auditors.

IV. Requirements for Auditors in-charge

- Licensing Requirements: The auditor in-charge (leitende/r Revisor/in, réviseur responsable) of audits of entities with financial years beginning on or after 1 January 2008 must have a provisional or definite license with the RAB. For audits that are performed at a specific point in time (e.g. audits of a capital increase or merger), the revised Code of Obligations (OR/CO) is in immediate effect and the auditor in-charge must have a provisional or definite license with the RAB as of the date of the audit.

- Rotation of auditor in-charge: The auditor in-charge of an ordinary audit must rotate after seven years and cannot resume this role until a further period of three years has elapsed.
- A public entity is not allowed to employ a person that was the auditor in-charge of that public entity during the past two years.

V. Provision of Non-Audit Services

Generally, the auditor is no longer allowed to perform bookkeeping, payroll services or other services where there is a risk that the auditor would audit their own work for audit clients that require an ordinary audit. Specifically auditors are prohibited to provide the following services:

- Bookkeeping / Payroll: Auditors are not allowed to perform bookkeeping, payroll or similar services.
- Valuations and fairness opinions are generally prohibited (valuations for tax purposes only are allowed).
- Representation of interests of a bank or similar institution that is an audit client with respect to the Oversight Authority (FINMA) is prohibited.
- Design and implementation of financial information technology systems that are used to generate information forming part of an audit client's financial statements is not allowed.
- Outsourcing of internal audit is not allowed. However, auditors may assist the audit client in certain areas.
- Tax services: Full outsourcing of tax and social security matters to employees of the audit firm are not allowed. Restrictions also apply to aggressive tax strategies which impact the financial statements unless such a strategy follows generally accepted tax practice or a ruling with tax autorities is obtained.

VI. Rotation requirements of the auditor in charge in an ordinary audit

Additionally, rotation rules were introduced in the new audit requirements as of 1 July 2007. The rotation of the auditor in charge is legally required under Art. 730a para. 2 CO as follows:

"In the ordinary audit the person which leads the audit can only perform this engagement for no more than seven years. This person can only resume the same engagement after a break period of three years."

As there are many questions surrounding the application of this new article the following are some tentative answers.

VII. When is this new legal requirement effective?

The Federal Council has determined the date when this new audit law will become effective (1 January 2008). According to Art. 7 of the transition provisions of the CO these regulations will be in force from the first business year that begins on or after the date when this law becomes effective (on 1 Januar 2015). The Federal Council will most likely issue a respective ordinance and determine as of when the rotation must apply (prospective).

VIII. Is this rotation also required for other forms of legal organisation in addition to corporations?

Yes, it also applies for limited liability companies (GmbH, Sàrl) according to Art. 818 sect. 1 CO), for cooperatives according to Art. 906 sect. 1 CO, for foundations according to Art. 83b Sect. 1 Swiss Civil Code (CC) (including ordinance of 24 August 2005), associations according to Art. 69b sect. 3 CC.

IX. Are small corporations exempted from the rotation requirements?

Yes, the rotation only applies for companies that require an ordinary audit. Companies with limited audits are not subject to these rotation requirements.

X. Are there special rules for quoted companies?

Yes, the Independence Rules of the Swiss Institute (2001 edition, new edition as of 1 January 2008) require the rotation in Rule 5 already since 2002 for listed companies and those financial institutes supervised by FINMA.

XI. Will the Independence Rules of the Swiss Institute of 2001 be adapted?

Yes, these were changed significantly and they were approved by the Swiss Institute's Board at the end of 2006. Additonally, it is possible that the Swiss Audit Oversight Authority (RAB) will issue an Ordinance on independence later.

XII. Who is the „person that leads the audit"?

Other similar expressions are:
- *verantwortlicher Prüfer*
- *(verantwortlicher) Mandatsleiter*
- *leitender Mitarbeiter*
- *leitender Revisor*
- *Prüfungsleiter*
- *Revisionsleiter*
- *leitender Bankrevisor (FINMA)*
- Engagement Partner
- Auditor in Charge

XIII. How do we find out who the auditor in charge in the last years was?

Only the check of the signed audit opinions can give a clear answer. These are available in the temporary files or in the archives of the audit firm. Possibly the client also has retained copies of the audit reports.

XIV. What are the rotation rules of the Swiss Stock Exchange (SIX)?

According to the SIX Rule for Corporate Governance (RCLG) Point 8.1 the duration of the audit engagement and the period of the auditor in charge have to be disclosed. This information has to be presented in the unaudited part of the annual report. With few exceptions the rotation rules of the Swiss Instituted have been followed (voluntarily).

XV. When can an auditor in charge which was rotated off resume the function again?

According to Art. 730a para. 2 second sentence CO an interruption period of three years is required (Cooling off period).

XVI. Will the auditor in charge be registered in the Commercial Register?

No, only the audit company (including branch office) will be recorded as statutory auditor for the corporations. So far this only applied for corporations. Now it also applies for foundations (which require an ordinary audit). This was also introduced for GmbHs, cooperatives, associations.

XVII. Will the ordinance of the Commercial Register be changed accordingly?

Yes, the statutory auditor will be recorded as in the past, with an additional remark such as:

- Statutory audit
- No audit requirement (opting out)

XVIII. Are the rotation requirements also applicable for the auditor in charge who signs group audit opinions?

Yes, according to Art. 731 CO this applies in the same way.

XIX. What are the consequences of non-compliance?

First of all, the Board of Directors of the company is responsible that the auditor in charge has not signed the audit opinion in this capacity for more than seven years. Whether the audited financial statements can be legally challenged in court because the auditor in charge was not rotated off correctly after seven years has still to be examined by lawyers and in the end by the judge.

XX. What is the responsibility of the auditor in charge?

The independence (in appearance) is not complied with if the rotation requirements are not observed. In principle, the audit report must be modified because of infraction of the legal independence rules.

XXI. Must the auditor in charge for the ordinary audit be qualified as admitted audit expert?

Yes, according to Art. 727b Sect. 2 CO and Art. 4 of the Swiss Auditor Oversight Act (RAG) (normally dipl. Wirtschaftsprüfer).

XXII. Must the auditor in charge be an audit partner?

No, the audit law does not know this term and function (this is the same for the leading bank auditor according to FINMA).

XXIII. Must the title *dipl. Wirtschaftsprüfer* be mentioned under the name/signature and under the expression „Auditor in charge"?

Yes, (if applicable) best practice of the big Swiss Audit Firms.

XXIV. Must the legal expression according to Art. 727b Sect. 2 CO „admitted audit expert" be mentioned under the name of the auditor in charge in the audit report?

This could become common practice. An alternative could be: „Auditor in charge and admitted audit expert".

XXV. Are there similar or tougher rotation requirements abroad?

Yes, most countries have introduced similar requirements. According to Sarbanes-Oxley Act 2002, Sec. 207 the period for foreign and US listed companies under SEC jurisdiction is five years.

XXVI. What are the respective international IFAC rules?

The IFAC rules require that the Lead audit engagement partner responsible for signing the report on the financial statements of the (listed) entity should be rotated after a pre-defined period, not to exceed seven years. The time out period should not be shorter than two years. Upon the initial application of these provisions, years of service prior to that date are counted in determining the number of years a partner has served an audit client. These provisions regarding rotation are to be implemented for financial years beginning on or after 1 January 2004. However, some degree of flexibility over timing of rotation may be necessary in certain circumstances, provided that safeguards measures are in place.

XXVII. Who is responsible for the application of foreign rotation rules?

In principle, the engagement partner (of the foreign country) is responsible. He or she must inform the local auditors on these foreign legal requirements.

§ 4   Terms of mandate, resignation, etc. of auditors

Under Art. 730a CO the maximum term of the mandate is three years. It ends at the general meeting of shareholders to which the last audit report is to be submitted. Re-election is possible. An auditor who resigns must explain the reason to the board directors, which must communicate it to the next general meeting of shareholders. The general meeting of shareholders may, at any time, remove an auditor. In addition, any shareholder or creditor may, by bringing a suit against the company, request the removal of an auditor unqualified for the position. The board of directors must notify the commercial registrar without delay of the termination of the mandate. If such notification is not lodged within thirty days the outgoing auditor may personally request the termination.

Under the new Art. 663b no. 13 CO the board of directors has to disclose in the notes to the annual accounts the reason why the auditors have resigned.

Under Art. 731b CO the commercial registrar, upon learning that a company has failed to appoint auditors, must set a time limit for the situation to be remedied. If the company fails to observe the deadline, a civil court judge must appoint the auditors for one business year on the request of the commercial registrar selecting the auditors at his or her discretion. Should these auditors resign, the commercial registrar will notify the judge accordingly. Provided the reasons are valid, the company may request the removal of the auditors appointed by the court.

§ 5 Duties of auditors

I. Individual company accounts

Under Art. 728 CO for an ordinary audit the auditors have to examine whether an internal control system (ICS) exists and the annual accounts as well as the proposed appropriation of retained earnings to satisfy themselves that they comply with the law and with the company's articles of incorporation. The board of directors should release to the auditors all requisite documents and provide them with all necessary information, in writing if so requested. This includes a 'representation letter' from the board attesting to the completeness of the liabilities shown, the truth of the valuations the existence of the assets and the correctness and completeness of the notes to the financial statements.

Under Art. 728b para. 2 CO the auditors must report the findings of their audit in writing to the general meeting of shareholders. They should recommend approval, with or without qualification, or rejection of the annual accounts. The report should name the persons in charge of the audit, and confirm that their qualifications and independence meet the requirements.

In the event of obvious over indebtedness, the auditors must notify the bankruptcy court should the board of directors fail to do so. Over indebtedness is defined by Art. 725 para. 2. CO as the total loss of the shareholders' equity where liabilities exceed assets.

II. Consolidated financial statements

Under Art. 728a CO the auditors are to examine the consolidated financial statements to ensure they comply with the law and principles of consolidation (*Regelwerk*) and that an internal control system (ICS) exists also in the group.

The board of directors has to deliver all required documents to the auditors and provide them with the necessary information on request, in writing. This includes a representation letter (Art. 730b para. 1 CO). According to Art. 728c para. 1 CO the auditors have to report non-compliance with the law or statutes in writing to the board of directors. In serious cases the auditors have to report this to the general meeting of shareholders.

According to Art. 731 para. 1 CO the general meeting of shareholders can only adopt the consolidated financial statements if the consolidated audit report has been submitted and the auditor is present. If no consolidated audit report is available the respective decisions of the general meeting of shareholders are not valid. Furthermore, the statutory audit report of the holding company must be qualified in respect of the missing consolidated financial statements.

If the auditor is absent the decisions can be challenged by a shareholder. However, the auditors can be absent, provided the shareholders make a unanimous decision accepting his absence. According to Art. 730b CO the auditors have to keep the group's secrets and are not allowed reporting confidential facts to individual shareholders or third parties.

According to Art. 728a CO the auditor's report the results of their audit in writing to the general meeting of shareholders. They recommend approval of the consolidated financial statements with or without qualifications, emphasis of matter etc., or adverse or disclaimer of opinion (rejection of the annual consolidated accounts to the directors, *Rückweisung an den Verwaltungsrat*). The consolidated audit report name of the person who managed the audit (auditor in charge, *leitender Revisor*), and confirms that the requirements concerning their qualifications and independence are fulfilled.

The Swiss Institute of Certified Public Accountants has published standard texts for unqualified consolidated audit opinion for corporations in the following languages: German, French, Italian and English (see Swiss Auditing Handbook, HWP, and Swiss Auditing Standards, PS).

§ 6 Standard form of audit report on the annual statutory accounts

I. Individual company accounts

The standard form of unqualified audit opinion (clean audit report) for use with corporations is as follows:

Standard audit report for *individual* annual statutory accounts:

Report of the Statutory Auditors to the General Meeting of ABC Ltd., Berne[4]

As statutory auditors, we have audited the accounting records and the financial statements (balance sheet, income statement and notes) of ABC Ltd. for the year ended 31 December 2006.

These financial statements are the responsibility of the board of directors. Our responsibility is to express an opinion on these financial statements based on our audit. We confirm that we meet the legal requirements concerning professional qualification and independence.

Our audit was conducted in conformity with Swiss Auditing Standards which require that an audit be planned and performed to obtain reasonable assurance about whether the financial statements are free from material misstatement. We have examined on a test basis evidence supporting the amounts and disclosures in the financial statement presentation. We have also assessed the accounting principles used, significant estimates made and the overall basis for our opinion. We believe that our audit provides a reasonable basis for our opinion.

In our opinion, the accounting records and the financial statements and the proposed appropriation of available earnings comply with Swiss law and with the company's articles of incorporation.

We recommend that the financial statements submitted to you be approved.

XYZ Audit Ltd.

A. Müller
Swiss Certified Accountant
Auditor in charge

B. Huber
Swiss Certified Accountant

Berne, 28 February 2007

---

[4] Source: Schweizer Handbuch der Wirtschaftsprüfung (HWP) and SAS / PS / NAS

> ***Enclosures:***
> *Financial statements consisting of:*
> • *Balance sheet*
> • *Income statement*
> • *Notes to the financial statements*
> • *Proposed appropriation of the available earnings*

II. Consolidated financial statements

The Swiss Institute has issued two versions of audit reports on consolidated financial statements.

In their audit opinion auditors normally refer to the set of standards applied (*Regelwerk*). One or more of the following true and fair standards are referred to in addition to compliance with the Swiss law (Swiss Code of Obligations):

1) Swiss GAAP FER

2) German Commercial Code (HGB, BiRiLiG)

3) International Financial Reporting Standards (IFRS) of the International Accounting Standards Board (IASB)

4) United States Generally Accepted Accounting Principles (US GAAP)

The second type of report, shown below, is required for public companies under the stock exchange requirements. Big groups already had anticipated this development and published true and fair view opinions generally in accordance with the IFRS standards.

Standard audit report for *consolidated* financial statements (true and fair view) in accordance with IFRS

Report of the Group Auditors to the General Meeting of ABC Ltd., Berne[5]

As group auditors, we have audited the consolidated financial statements of ABC Ltd. (balance sheet, income statement, cash flow statement, statement of changes in equity and notes) for the year ended 31 December 2006.

These consolidated financial statements are the responsibility of the board of directors. Our responsibility is to express an opinion on these consolidated financial statements based on our audit. We confirm that we meet the legal requirements concerning professional qualification and independence.

Our audit was conducted in conformity with Swiss Auditing Standards and International Standards on Auditing, which require that an audit be planned and performed to obtain reasonable assurance about whether the consolidated financial statements are free from material misstatement. We have examined on a test basis evidence supporting the amounts and disclosures in the consolidated financial statement presentation. We have also assessed the accounting principles used, significant estimates made and the overall basis for our opinion. We believe that our audit provides a reasonable basis for our opinion.

In our opinion, the consolidated financial statements give a true and fair view of the financial position, the results of operations and the cash flows in accordance with the International Financial Reporting Standards (IFRS) and comply with the law.

We recommend that the consolidated financial statements submitted to you be approved.

XYZ Audit Ltd.

---

[5] Source: Schweizer Handbuch der Wirtschaftsprüfung (HWP) and SAS / PS / NAS

A. Müller	B. Huber
Swiss Certified Accountant	*Swiss Certified Accountant*
Auditor in charge	

Zurich, 28 February 2007

Enclosures:

Consolidated financial statements consisting of:

• *Balance sheet*

• *Income statement*

• *Cash flow statement*

• *Statement of changes of equity*

• *Notes*

§ 7   Audit report to the directors

Art. 728b CO requires for ordinary audits that the audit experts must report not only to the shareholders (the short form auditors' report), but also to the board of directors. The report to the board should comment on the way they have carried out their task and the examination. Where companies had a sophisticated system of accounting records and internal controls the Swiss Institute of Certified Public Accountants proposed a standard short form of audit report. Under the new law a detailed report their will be required as of 2009. Art. 728b para. 1 CO requires:

"The auditors shall submit to the board of directors a comprehensive report with findings on the rendering of accounts, the internal control system as well as on the execution and result of the audit."

Management often requests the above-mentioned report in a management letter format in which important issues as identified by the auditors are highlighted and discussed. Comments of financial management are normally included. The board's audit committee discusses these management letters. Although Swiss companies are not required to have such committees there is a strong trend towards their establishment, following Anglo-American examples.

§ 8 Education, certification and licensing

Auditing has never been a major discipline at Swiss universities. In the past, practicing auditors were traditionally formed through a professional career path, starting as commercial apprentices and working their way up as bookkeeping clerks and accounting managers. Academic entrants into the profession were the exception. During the last decades, a shift took place. On one hand the influence of international comparisons suggested more and more the recruitment of academically trained persons. On the other hand professional junior colleges (e.g. *Fachhochschule*, FH, previously called *Höhere Wirtschaftsschule*, HWV) were established, and some universities intensified the studies in the fields of accounting and auditing.

Due to the lack of academic possibilities for education, in 1962 the Swiss Institute of Certified Accountants and Tax Experts (founded in 1925) introduced a series of courses that should prepare the aspirants for the professional exams as Certified Public Accountants (*dipl. Wirtschaftsprüfer*, formerly called *dipl. Bücherexperte*). These so-called *Kammerschule* courses were offered as evening and weekend lessons. In 1999 the Institute founded a business school (today called *Educaris*) that offers full day examination courses preparing for the exams as *dipl. Wirtschaftsprüfer* and *dipl. Steuerxperte* (Certified Tax Expert).

The exams for obtaining the diploma as *dipl. Wirtschaftsprüfer* stand under the supervision of the Federal Office of Professional Education and Technology (*Bundesamt für Berufsbildung und Technologie*, BBT). The procedure has been changed in recent years several times in order to facilitate the integration of academic aspirants whilst ascertaining the continuation traditional career paths at the same time.

Today, the exams are composed of two major steps. In a preparatory move, five written exams have to be taken in the subjects of Financial Accounting, Management Accounting and Controlling, Corporate Finance, Tax, and Auditing (*Modulprüfungen*).

After having passed all these more or less theoretical exams, the aspirant can apply for the diploma exam. In addition, at the time of registration for this exam the candidate must supply proof of a minimum of three years practical experience in the field of auditing after having obtained the prerequisites for entering the *Modulprüfungen* (academic degree, FH/HWV-Diplomas or equivalent).

This demanding final exam consists of a day-long written case study and oral exams in professional judgment as well as a short oral presentation of a current accounting topic. The goal of this final exam is to test the aptitude to apply the theoretical knowledge tested previously in the *Modulprüfungen* in practical cases. The success rate of this exam is about 70%, which indicates its severity. Due to the requirements of preparing education (academic of professional) and the requested practical experience in auditing the average age of a newly certified *Wirtschaftsprüfer* is about twenty-eight years.

The Swiss Institute requests its members to partake in auditing related events and courses as continuing professional education (CPE) after obtaining the diploma. This entails on average 60 "contact hours" annually in order to retain the qualification as dipl. Wirtschaftsprüfer. The Institute publishes a monthly journal *(Der Schweizer Treuhänder)* that contains a wide variety of articles regarding new developments in Accounting, Controlling, Tax, Business Law, Economics, and Auditing. All members of the Institute receive this publication, which also contains news about the Institute and the profession globally as part of their member fee. Furthermore, the Institute publishes a series of monographs and textbooks series that highlight topics related to Accounting and Auditing *(Schriftenreihe)*.

In principle, the professionals report their continued education in a self-assessment declaration, whereby the Institute has the right to review the correctness of such a declaration.

§ 9   Audits under the Swiss Merger Act (FusG)

The Federal Act on Merger, Demerger, Transformation and Transfer of Assets (Merger Act, MerA) was published only in the country's official languages German, French and Italian. The law was enacted on 3 October 2003 and became applicable as of 1 July 2005.

The Act governs the changes to legal structures of companies, general and limited partnerships, cooperative societies, associations, foundations and sole proprietorships through

- mergers (*Fusion*, fusion)
- demerger (*Spaltung*, scission)
- transformations (*Umwandlung*, transformation)
- transfers of Assets (*Vermögensübertragung*, transfert de patrimoine)

It ensures predictability and transparency and protects creditors and minority shareholders.

The merger of legal entities may occur by:

1) absorption of one legal entity by another (e.g. parent absorbs subsidiary company, vertical merger)
2) combination of legal entities to form a new legal entity (two sister companies combine, horizontal integration)

Art. 11 MerA on interim balance sheet requires:

"The legal entities involved shall draw up an interim balance sheet, if upon concluding the merger agreement, the date of the last balance sheet is more than six months older or if material changes in the financial position of the legal entities involved have occurred since the last balance sheet was made up."

As most Swiss legal entities have calendar year-ends, mergers must be consummated before 30 June in order to avoid required the establishment and auditing of an interim balance sheet as at 30 June of both entities to be merged.

Art. 15 MerA describes the legal audit requirements as follows:

"[1] If the acquiring legal entity is a capital company (e.g. AG, SA) or a cooperative society with shares, specially qualified auditors shall review the merger agreement, the merger report and the balance sheet underlying the merger of legal entities involved in the merger. The legal entities may appoint a joint auditor.

[2] Provided that all members consent, small and medium-sized enterprises may dispense with the requirement to appoint an auditor."

Kapitel 1: Statutory auditing in Switzerland

Art. 2 lit. e. MerA defines small and medium-sized enterprises as those:

"legal entities, which have not issued bonds, listed shares on the stock exchange, and furthermore, do not exceed two of the following thresholds during two consecutive financial years before adopting the resolution regarding the merger, demerger or transformation:
1. *total assets of CHF 20 million*
2. *revenue of CHF 40 million*
3. *an average of 200 full-time employees per annum."*

Art. 15 MerA further provides:

³ The legal entities involved shall provide the auditor with all relevant information and documents.

⁴ The auditor shall state in a written report:

a. whether the proposed capital increase of the acquiring legal entity is sufficient to protect the rights of the members of the transferring legal entity;

b. whether the share exchange ratio and the reasons why the method applied is adequate;

c. the method used to arrive at the exchange ratio and the reasons why the method applied is adequate;

d. if applicable, the relative importance attributed to each of the different methods applied to arrive at the exchange ratio;

e. any special circumstances that were to be considered in the valuation of the shares in arriving at the exchange ratio."

The merger audit report must be filed with the commercial register and therefore is public. The merger auditors need a special qualification as defined in Art. 727b para. 2 CO:

"The companies obligated to perform an ordinary audit shall appoint as auditor a licensed audit expert according to the provisions of the Law on Oversight of Auditors (RAG, LSR) dated 16 December 2005." Under this law a licensed audit expert is a licensed Swiss Accountant (*dipl. Wirtschaftsprüfer,* expert-comptable diplomé) or a foreign equivalent diploma with the necessary knowledge of Swiss law.

Art. 23 and 24 MerA simplifies the merger of capital companies (e.g. AGs, SAs) if the parent or the shareholder owns all voting shares of the affected company. In this case, no audit opinion has to be issued by a specially qualified auditor on the merger agreement and the merger balance sheet.

The audit requirements for demergers (Art. 40 MerA) are the same as for the merger (Art. 15 MerA).

Art. 62 MerA requires that a specially qualified auditor shall review the transformation plan, the transformation report (of the Directors) and balance sheet underlying the transformation. The auditor shall examine whether the requirements for the transformation have been met, and in particular, whether the legal status of the members will be preserved after the transformation.

A typical example of a transformation is the change of the legal form of a corporation (AG) to a limited liability company (GmbH) or vice versa.

A special case is the merger of entities which are in the situation of CO 725. Article 6 of MerA requires also an audit report in case of merger of legal entities with a capital loss or whose liabilities exceed its assets:

"[1] A legal entity which has lost half the sum of its nominal share of social capital and legal reserves or whose liabilities exceed its assets, may only merge with another legal entity, if the latter has freely utilizable equity in the amount of the shortfall, and where applicable, in the amount of the excess liabilities. This requirement does not apply insofar as the creditors of the legal entities involved in the merger agree to subordinate their claims to those of all other creditors.

[2] The supreme administrative or management body shall submit to the commercial register a confirmation from a specially qualified auditor, stating that the requirement pursuant to para. 1 has been complied with."

If no such "clean" audit report is delivered to the commercial register no registration will take place. If the merged companies go bankrupt later this will be especially scrutinised. Therefore, such audit reports are of rather high risk.

Similarly, audit opinions according to Art. 25 MerA should be avoided. Also here the protection of creditors and employees are prevalent:

"*¹ The acquiring legal entity shall secure claims of the creditors of the legal entities involved in the merger, if creditors so demand within three months after the merger becoming legally effective.*

The legal entities involved in the merger shall give notice to creditors of their rights three times in the Swiss Trade Journal (Gazette of Commerce, SHAB, FOSC). They are not required to publicise the merger in the Swiss Gazette of Commerce, if a specially qualified auditor confirms that there are no known or expected claims, which cannot be satisfied by the freely available assets or the legal entities involved."

Often, the claims of the Tax authorities, if any, are difficult to substantiate as they normally do not respond to the creditors calls. They may at any time require a tax audit.

Therefore, auditors should avoid the issue of such Art. 25 MerA audit reports.

Art. 108 MerA describes the (significant) responsibility and legal liability of merger auditors:

"Every person who is involved in the auditing of the merger, demerger, transformation or transfer of assets is liable to corporate persons, as well as to each individual member and creditor for any damage, which is caused wilfully or through negligence, while carrying out their duties." Reference is made to the provisions of Arts. 756, 759 and 760 CO which states:

"If several persons are liable for a damage, any one of them is liable jointly and severally with the others to the extent the damage is attributable to such person based on his own fault and the circumstances."

This obviously applies to the specially qualified auditor under the Merger Act.

§ 10   Over indebtedness and depositing the balance sheet

One of the most serious liability threats for Swiss statutory auditors are the worldwide unique obligations of auditors to declare an audit client bankrupt if he is over indebted. This is derived from the following provisions of the Swiss Code of Obligations (CO). If this duty is not observed properly the auditor himself is sued under Art. 755 CO (severally and unlimited liability).

Art. 725 CO is derived from the continental European (Napoleonic) laws covering the loss of capital and over indebtedness and the respective duty to notify the bankruptcy judge (court), the major concern of the law being the protection of the creditors:

"¹ If the last annual balance sheet shows that half of the share capital and the legal reserves are no longer covered, the board of directors shall without delay call a general meeting of shareholders and propose a financial reorganisation.

² In case of a substantiated concern of over indebtedness, an interim balance sheet must be prepared and submitted to a licensed (zugelassener) auditor for examination. If the interim balance sheet shows that the claims of the Company's creditors are neither covered if the assets are appraised at on-going business values nor at liquidation values, then the board of directors shall notify the judge unless creditors of the Company subordinate their claims to those of all other Company creditors to the extent of such insufficient coverage.

³ If the Company does not have any auditor, the licensed auditor shall be responsible for the notification obligations of the auditor charged with a limited audit."

Under Art 725a CO the bankruptcy judge upon being notified adjucates the bankruptcy or postpones it. He may appoint a curator. Art. 728c CO the statutory auditor has the following duty to notify:

"³ In the event of manifest over indebtedness (offensichtliche Überschuldung) of the Company, the auditors shall notify the judge if the board of directors fails to do so.

I. What does over indebtedness mean?

The assets do not cover the liabilities (anymore). There are three ways to create (or increase) over indebtedness:

1) Decrease the assets
2) Increase the liabilities

3) Indirectly by reducing the assets accordingly. E.g. a dividend payment out of free reserves or a decrease of share capital and repayment to the shareholders.

Therefore from a legal perspective there are theoretically three ways open in order to prevent companies from becoming over indebted:

1) Relating to the assets
Prudence, conservative valuation, which leads to upper valuation limits (e.g. Art. 665, 666, 667 CO)

2) Relating to the liabilities
Completeness, which leads to bottom valuation limits (Art. 669 CO)

3) Relating to equity
Very strict rules for the reduction of equity (Art. 732 to 735 CO)

II. Why is over indebtedness a problem?

Who should normally take the business risk? Who takes it if an over indebted company was allowed to carry on its business? What amount of losses do creditors suffer in Switzerland per year?

These figures do not include the losses of the creditors suffered because of suspension of bankruptcy proceedings due to lack of assets. And the losses of the creditors caused by non-opening the bankruptcy proceedings are not included either. The latter happens when the creditors know that there are no assets at all left in the company and that it is not even worthwhile to pay the advance payment for the opening of the bankruptcy proceedings.

The real losses can only be estimated. One third of all the opened bankruptcy proceedings in Switzerland are suspended due to lack of assets (*Konkurs mangels Aktiven eingestellt*). This concerns over three thousand bankruptcy proceedings a year. Bankruptcy specialists estimate the real losses of the creditors of the creditors to over CHF 10 billion per year.

III. How does Swiss Company Law try to avoid over indebtedness?

Swiss Company Law is taking several measures which are treated below:

1) Legal obligation to accounting in line with generally accepted accounting principles (Art. 662 to 679 CO)
2) Duty to prepare annual consolidated financial statements (Art. 663e CO)
3) Provisions for the board of directors in case of loss of capital (Art. 725 para. 1 CO)
4) Provisions for the board of directors in case of over indebtedness (Art. 725 para. 2 CO)
5) Provisions for the auditors to convey a general assembly of the shareholders (Art. 729b para. 1 and Art. 699 para. 1 CO) or to notify the bankruptcy judge (Art. 729b para. 2 CO)
6) Responsibility of the board of directors (Art. 754 CO)
7) Responsibility of the auditors (Art. 755 CO)

1. *Legal obligation to accounting in line with generally accepted accounting principles (Art. 662 to 679 CO)*

Financial statements must be prepared in line with generally accepted accounting principles. According to Art. 662a CO the annual accounts in the individual financial statements should be prepared in accordance with recognised accounting principles in such a way as to offer the most reliable picture of the income and financial situation of the company (not a true and fair view). These principles consist of:

- Completeness of the annual financial statements.
- Clarity and materiality of the financial statements.
- Prudence (conservatism).
- Going concern.
- Consistency in presentation and valuation.
- Prohibition of netting assets and liabilities, as well as of netting expenses and income (gross principle).

There is also a new project for revised Accounting legislation where the provisions regarding over indebtedness will be quite similar to the rules we have in the existing law.

2. *Duty to prepare annual consolidated statements of account (Art. 663e CO)*

Swiss company law has only required consolidated financial statements since 1994. There is a duty to consolidate with majority of votes (Art. 663e CO). Exceptions are made for intermediate holdings and small companies. This duty to prepare and audit consolidated accounts is another step of Swiss company law to recognise coming financial problems as early as possible.

3. *Provisions for the board of directors in case of loss of capital (Art. 725 para. 1 CO):*

What is a loss of capital? What are the duties of the board of directors?

They have to call a general meeting of shareholders without delay and to propose a financial reorganisation. This shows the prudence of Swiss company law, because the board of directors has to take these measures before the equity has been lost. This means that at this point in time, the liabilities are still fully covered.

Above the conservative accounting principles and then the duty to prepare annual consolidated statements were discussed. These provisions in case of capital loss represent therefore the third step of Swiss company law, which should protect the creditors from losses. The forth step for protection of the creditors is described below.

4. *Provisions for the board of directors in case of over indebtedness (Art. 725 para. 2 CO):*

What are the duties of the board of directors relating to this next step for protection of the creditors?

The elements are:

   1) a substantiated concern of over indebtedness.

2) prepare an interim balance sheet on on-going business values and at liquidation values.

3) submit this balance sheet to the auditors for examination.

IV. Are there two different kinds of over indebtedness?

Very often the liquidation value of assets is lower then the value of the assets on an on-going basis. The consequence of liquidation is therefore a sudden increase of over indebtedness. If the liabilities are neither covered at on-going values nor at liquidation values, then the board of directors shall notify the judge. This is called "depositing the balance sheet".

But there are still two last possibilities for the board of directors to get around the notification. One of them is mentioned in Art. 725 para. 2 CO. Notification of the judge is necessary unless creditors subordinate their claims to those of all other creditors to the extent of such insufficient coverage.

See a standard subordination contract below. The creditor signing this subordination contract is basically saying that he waives his rights of being paid as long as any other creditor can not be fully satisfied. This creates a new kind of liabilities which is close to equity. In case of liquidation, the assets of the company will first be distributed to the normal creditors. If they are paid in full and if the assets exceed these liabilities, the creditor that signed the subordination contract is satisfied next. If after his satisfaction there are still remaining assets, they will be used to pay the shareholders.

As mentioned there is another way out for the board of directors. Besides of the subordination contracts, the board of directors might achieve quick financial reorganisation by other means. This could be a waiver of a creditor or a capital increase with a surplus over par value etc.

The company is over indebted on a going concern basis and is even more over indebted on a liquidation basis. The board of directors does not have to notify the judge if creditors are subordinating their claims. What amount of liabilities has to be subordinated? Is it the smaller amount of over indebtedness on the basis of going concern? Or is it the bigger amount on the basis of the liquidation values?

Unfortunately the law is not answering the question in Art. 725 para. 2 CO. There is simply the wording "... to the extent of such insufficient coverage."

The question has not been decided yet. It could be argued, that the coverage of the smaller of the two amounts should do. The law itself asks for notification only if over indebtedness must be stated on both valuation criteria. If only one of the two valuation criteria shows an over indebtedness there does not have to be any notification. So why should it not be sufficient to subordinate liabilities in the amount to cover one of the two over indebtednesses?

There is by the way another - rather complicated - way out of the financial problems for the board of directors. Under Art. 725a CO the judge adjudicates the bankruptcy after being notified at the request of the board of directors or a creditor. There must be a prospect of a financial reorganisation. This means that if the board of directors has no quick solution to the financial problems and if he can not get subordinations of claims covering the over indebtedness but if he still has other real solutions in hand of which he thinks he could realise them within the short time limit of let's say three to six months, than he can ask the judge to postpone the bankruptcy.

Under Art. 725 para. 2 CO the bankruptcy judge may appoint a curator and either deprive the board of directors of its power to dispose, or make its decisions subject to the approval of the curator. The judge can even waive publication of the postponement if there is no danger for third parties.

In all other cases the bankruptcy proceedings will be opened and the company goes into liquidation.

1. *Provisions for the auditors to convey a general assembly of the shareholders (Art. 729b para. 1 and Art. 699 para. 1 CO) or to notify the judge (Art. 729b para. 2 CO)*

a) Calling a general meeting of shareholders by the auditors

If the board of directors fails to fulfil its duties of Art. 725 CO, the auditors shall report this to the general meeting of shareholders. This report has to be done in cases of violation of Art. 725 para. 1 and para. 2 CO.

In practice these general meetings of shareholders are rarely called by the auditors. Why? What can the auditors do at this meeting? They only can inform the shareholders that the board of directors should have called the general meeting because of a capital loss and should have proposed a financial reorganisation. And in case of substantiated concern of over indebtedness that the board of directors should have prepared an interim balance sheet and should have submitted it to the auditors and that he has not done that.

Never can the auditors make suggestions for or start the financial reorganisation by themselves. This is not their right and not their duty.

b)   Notification of the judge by the auditors

This is the most severe measure under the law. Under Art. 729b para. 2 CO the statutory auditors have the duty in the event of obvious over indebtedness and if the board of directors fails to notify the bankruptcy judge.

As mentioned, under Art. 725 para. 2 CO there are two kinds of over indebtednesses. The over indebtedness at the valuation on the on-going basis and the over indebtedness at the liquidation valuation. Art. 728c para. 3 CO seems to have a third category of over indebtedness, the so called obvious over indebtedness. It seems that the legislator made a difference between "normal" over indebtedness and "obvious" over indebtedness. Why this distinction?

The statutory auditors have to audit the accounts only once a year. This means that the auditors sometimes have no contact with their client for more than one year. But we have seen that in case of over indebtedness the reaction in order to prevent the company from becoming over indebted must be quick and must therefore be based on actual information which the auditors never have. Therefore, it is quite normal that the duty to notify the judge is mainly on the shoulders of the boards of directors. It is of course the board of directors that has actual information and control on the situation of the company.

Therefore, the legislator realised that this new duty for the auditors is strange. How can you ask a quick reaction of somebody who is never there? This is now the explication where the word "obvious" comes from. The legislator had to make a distinction between the duties of the board of directors and between the duties of the auditors. If we look at the discussions in parliament on this article, we can see that they said that "obvious" means that the auditors have to notify the judge "only when the over indebtedness is much clearer, much bigger, when it can not be denied anymore even if you look at the company in a optimistic way".

aa) Responsibility of the board of directors

The responsibility of the members of the board of directors should be a strong motivation for them to fulfil all their duties. But it is not certain whether this in practice really works. In fact, the members of the board rarely have to bear claims on responsibility against them. It is very natural that the claimant before starting litigation checks the wealth of the board members.

Anyway, Art. 754 para. 1 CO says that the members of the board of directors are liable for the damage caused by an intentional or negligent violation of their duties.

bb) Responsibility of the auditors

The same wording on the liability of the auditors is included in Art. 755 CO.

There is a big difference between the auditors and the board members. The auditors are very often companies or persons that have a liability insurance. Therefore they are "wealthy". So we have had an uneasy development for the auditors in Switzerland in the last years. There have been many actions against auditors. It is therefore very important to comply with these auditors' duties as carefully as possible.

Standard subordination contract:

Subordination Agreement

Made between ... (hereinafter referred to as "the corporate creditor")

and ... (hereinafter referred to as "the corporation")

<u>*Determinations*</u>

The balance sheet prepared as of ... and based upon valuations as a going concern give rise to reasonable grounds for assuming that corporate liabilities exceed assets.

or: *The balance sheet (or interim balance sheet) of the corporation prepared as of ....and based upon valuations as a going concern (possibly: and liquidation valuations) shows an over indebtedness in the amount of CHF ...*

or: *The losses reported in the balance sheet prepared as of ... and the poor performance of the business of the corporation give rise to the concern that the same may be over indebted.*

An interim balance sheet prepared according to valuations as a going concern and liquidation valuations would, in all probability, show such an over indebtedness that pursuant to Art. 725 para. 2 of the Swiss Code of Obligations (CO), the judge would have to be notified.

The Board of Directors expects that with the implementation of appropriate measures the over indebtedness can be overcome in the near future. In order that the Board of Directors must not notify the judge pursuant to Art. 725 para. 2 CO, the parties agree as follows:

1. *Claims of the corporate creditor in regards to the corporation, being in the amount of CHF ... as of (date) (possibly: including accrued and accruing interest) are subordinated in priority behind the claims of all existing and future company creditors.*

2. *The repayment of such debts as are the subject matter of the subordination is deferred for the duration of this agreement.*

The herein subordinated claims may neither be repaid in whole or in part, or by means of a set-off or novation, nor may the same be secured anew. A total or partial waiver of the said claims, or a total or partial transformation of the same into capital stock of the corporation remain excepted.

In the event of the bankruptcy of the corporate creditor, the corporation may set-off the herein subordinated claims against any claim which it has against the corporate creditor.

3. *This agreement is irrevocable and may not be terminated, save and except in the following circumstances:*

   a. *when according to the balance sheet (or interim balance sheet) which has been audited by the statutory auditors, the assets cover all of the corporate liabilities including the subordinated liabilities and the legal requirements concerning the submission of the auditor's report without reference to Art. 725 para. 2 CO are fulfilled;*

b. *in the event that the corporate creditor forever waives in writing the right to enforce the subordinated claim;*

c. *in the event that, by means of a set-off against the unpaid and payable capital contributions, the subordinated claims are transformed into capital stock;*

d. *in the event that another creditor of the corporation agrees, in the place of this subordination agreement, to a subordination, being for the same amount and equivalent to this subordination agreement.*

4. *This agreement has been approved by the Board of Directors of the corporation after having taken into consideration the credit-worthiness of the corporate creditor.*

5. *For the duration of this agreement the corporate creditor is not entitled to require that the Board of Directors refrain from notifying the judge concerning any over-indebtedness.*

6. *This agreement is subject to Swiss Law.*

7. *The registered headquarters of the corporation are to be considered as the place of jurisdiction.*

Place and Date: *The Parties:*

                      _____

                      The corporate creditor:

                      _____

                      The corporation:

                      _____

§ 11 Internal control and risk assessment

In Switzerland, the following important new laws and regulations resulted from the new Audit Oversight Act (RAG) and the changes in the Code of Obligation (CO):

1) Audit oversight board
2) Clear definition of independence of auditors (Art. 728 CO = ordinary audit and Art. 729 CO = limited audit/examination)
3) Audit objective Internal Control System (ICS)
4) Information on Risk Assessment in the notes to the financial statements

The original legal texts reads as follows:

Art. 663b no. 12 CO requires as of 2008 as additional disclosure in the financial statements:

"The notes shall include ...

12. information on the completion of a risk assessment;"

Art. 728a para. 1 no. 3 CO is an additional audit requirement:

"Duties of the auditors:

The auditors shall examine whether ...

3. an internal control system exists."

There were no changes within the duties of the Board of Directors and the Executive Board. However, the consideration here is to emphasise that the structuring of the accounting system and the financial controls, as well as the financial planning, are non-transferable duties of the Board of Directors (Art. 716a para. 1 no. 3 CO). The articles of incorporation may authorise the Board of Directors to fully or partially delegate the management to individual members or third parties in accordance with an organisation regulation (Art. 716b para. 1 CO). Thus, the Board of Directors can comprehensively or partially delegate the development and enhancement of Risk Assessment and ICS to the Executive Board.

I. Risk assessment

Risk Assessment (on which the necessary risk management measures will be decided) and Internal Controls are interrelated and integral components of Corporate Governance. Consequently, there are interdependencies between Risk Assessment and the Internal Control System. There are ambivalent statements which risks need to be addressed to meet the requirements of Art. 663b CO.

The Swiss Institute of Certified Accountant (*Treuhand-Kammer*) constituted a working group on the subject risk assessment, which has published an information paper by the end of 2007. This information paper provides the interpretation of this legal requirement by the Swiss Institute by giving further explanations on the content of the disclosures as well as the documentation to be prepared by the companies. It was the basis for audit guidance, in the form of an auditing standard and recommendations for auditors.

In principle, all Swiss companies are affected by the new corporation law and regulations. Exempt from these laws and regulations are sole proprietorships, simple partnerships, general partnerships and limited partnerships. There has been no final decision taken on whether foundations, which are subordinate to the BVG (i.e. pension funds), have to meet these requirements.

The following companies, which are subject to an ordinary or limited audit, are affected:

1) Corporations (Art. 728a CO)
2) Corporations with unlimited partners (Art. 764 CO)
3) Limited liability companies (Art. 818 CO)
4) Cooperatives (Art. 906 CO)
5) Associations (Art. 69b Swiss Civil Code (CC))
6) Foundations (Art. 83b CC)

What does "Information on the execution of a Risk Assessment" mean?
1) Disclosing the meeting date and including a statement that management held discussions in not expected to be enough.

2) Detailed discussion on the content of company risks and respective documentation and disclosure are expected.

Risk Assessment is the duty of the Board of Directors: a documented discussion on content of company risks must take place in a board meeting.

Auditors attest that there was a discussion on risks in the notes to the financial statements and that the Board of Directors has discussed and evaluated those risks (i.e. audit of formal aspects, not content).

1) The Board of Directors is informed about the significant risks of the enterprise.
2) The risk evaluation process is integrated into the strategy, budget and business processes.
3) The enterprise develops a culture, which identifies risks at an early stage and develops measures for risk management.

The Swiss Code of Best Practice recommends "an Internal Control System and a Risk Management aligned to the company's needs".

Risk can be defined as the threat that events or actions deter an enterprise to achieve its goals and/or successfully convert its strategies. The definition of risk refers to the enterprise risks, from which operational, financial reporting and compliance risks are derived.

The law requires that the enterprise has a governance mechanism and that risks are assessed, quantified and aggregated based on the company strategy. However, it is not required that risks are monitored and reported and that risk and control optimisations are implemented. Though, based on experiences of completed projects (particularly the monitoring and optimisation) are of significant value to the company.

Based on practical experience, it is critical that the projects are started as early because the projects usually are more time-consuming then expected, even when meeting the minimum requirements

II. Existence of an internal control system (ICS)

A position paper on Internal Controls of the Swiss Institute (*Treuhand-Kammer*) is available in German, French and English.

Art. 728a CO para. 1 no. 3 CO determines that the auditor examines whether an Internal Control System exists. Furthermore, Art. 728a para. 2 CO determines that the auditor considers the Internal Control System in planning and executing the audit. The consideration of internal controls in a financial statement audit has been in effect but has not been a regulatory law.

Based on the laws and regulations the following questions arise:

- What do "Internal Control System" and "exists" mean?
- In which way have auditors already considered internal controls in a financial statement audit and what does an examination of whether an ICS exists include?
- What are the roles and responsibilities?

The Federal Council clarified during the parliamentary debate on 1 December 2005 that

- the ICS only refers to internal controls over reliability of accounting and reporting, for example controls in the monthly / year-end closing or consolidation process. Controls in the area of compliance such as compliance with environmental laws and regulations and controls in the area of operation such as efficiency increase in production or service contribution are not addressed;
- the legislator does not provide any further guidance and provisions. The interpretation of the law and the design and implementation of the ICS is the responsibility of individual companies;
- the audit standards are to be defined by the audit profession. The Swiss Institute of Certified Accountants, therefore, first published a position paper to set the scope and constituted a task force "ICS", which was responsible for drafting a Swiss Auditing Standard "ICS".

What does "exist" mean? To answer this question it is important to consider the individual circumstances of the company when defining the scope and the design and implementation of the Internal Control System i.e. the size of the enterprise, the complexity of the business activities and the method of financing.

For the existence, it is important that:

- an ICS is established and auditable (i.e. documented)

- the ICS is aligned with business risks and activities
- the ICS is known by employees
- the ICS is implemented and operating as defined; it is therefore, for example, not sufficient that processes and controls are only documented, but not operating as defined, like in certain cases of ISO (International Standards Organisation guidelines)
- control awareness is high, control awareness generally increased during Internal Control projects due to the discussion on Internal Controls throughout the organisation, operationally active employees began to understand that their actions influence the financial reporting process.

It is not stipulated that a framework needs to be used. However, in practice the use of a framework is preferred such that there exists a systematic approach and a common language. This in particular is important for global companies. The COSO framework is the most widely used framework.

What does an examination include and what testing procedures are necessary in order to conclude whether an ICS exists?

- Analysis of the company / group (business model, markets, risks, etc.)
- Determining audit strategy and scope
- Analysis of the ICS in its entirety including documentation, i.e. controls over financial reporting on entity-level as well as on process-level is taken into consideration. Examples of entity-level controls are corporate policies and procedures, information and communication within the company and with third parties, or monitoring controls. Examples on process-level controls are segregation of duties, reconciliations or authorizations / approvals.
- To conclude on the design of the internal control system one generally first performs walk through tests. Then, further audit procedures such as spot-checks of single transactions or compliance with system specifications based on reconciliations, are performed to conclude that controls are implemented and operating as defined. However, there is no detailed operating effectiveness testing such as comprehensive or statistically relevant samples.
- Processes and controls that support the reliability of accounting and reporting have to be audited on a regular basis.

Audit reports are issued on Group level and for Swiss legal entities, which are subject to an ordinary audit, under the Code of Obligations. There is no auditor's report for foreign subsidiaries of a Swiss group. However, foreign subsidiaries can still be in scope although no auditor's report is issued. That is the case when those foreign subsidiaries are significant from a group perspective in order to conclude whether "an ICS exists" for the auditor's report on group level.

Each company in Switzerland has an ICS implemented. The question however is how developed, sustainable as well as documented is the ICS?

Many enterprises in Switzerland are between the development stages informal and formal, which outlines the lower range. Enterprises, which are subject to the US SOX 404 regulations, outline the upper range. The Swiss legal requirements are to be considered in-between – standardised.

We assume that small and medium-sized companies will aim for the legal minimum.

Larger companies may go further because

1) their most important competitors are subject to SOX 404

2) of their own will and interest

3) of pressures from creditors (banks), suppliers, clients and investors.

§ 12 Prohibition to reclaim contributions by shareholders (Art. 680 para. 2 CO)

Under Art. 680 para. 2 CO "The shareholder has no right to claim return of his contribution". Potential risks of violation of Art. 680 para. 2 CO are the following:

- Hidden profit distribution (with potential income tax consequences to the shareholders)

- Liquidity decrease: when withholding taxes / non refundable withholding taxes are requested by the Swiss Federal Tax Administration (EStV)

- Joint liability of the board of directors for unpaid withholding taxes

- Capital lost and/or over indebtedness, if the recoverability of the loan receivable / debtors (parent company / main shareholder or group companies) is insufficient and valuation allowances are required.

The following are indicators for violations of Art. 680 para. 2 CO:
1) The profits are retained (that is, no dividends are paid out, or from the tax standpoint, insufficient dividends are paid out).
2) The company retains the tax status of a management / domicile / holding company or does the company not provide any operative business transactions.
3) The company provides loans or other accounts receivable (e.g. current accounts, cash pool accounts) to the parent company/the main shareholder(s) or other group companies (SwissAir case).
4) The liquidity and recoverability of the parent company / the main shareholder(s) and/or the group are insufficient.
5) The parent company / major shareholder(s) / group companies neither have the intention nor the ability to pay back the loans / debts.
6) The company would ask for additional securities from third parties, if the company were to provide the same loan / current account to a third party (dealing at arm's length).
7) The loans / receivables from the parent company / major shareholder(s) or other group companies constitute the major part of all assets. (Additionally, please have a look at the concentration of risk: BGE 113 II 52ff. and securities taxes of the Swiss Federal Tax Administration (EStV).
8) The loan is provided without any written contract.
9) If a loan contract exists, there are no defined conditions with respect to the amortisation (pay back) or interest payments.
10) No interest will be paid on the loan or is the interests added to the receivables / loan (unpaid).
11) The interest rate is lower than the suggested minimum interest rate according to the leaflet of the Swiss Tax Authorities (EStV).

If one or more or even the majority of the indicators (answers to the above questions) results in a yes than the company most likely has violated Art. 680 para. 2 CO. The statutory audit report should contain an additional sentence with a matter of emphasis of these facts and circumstances. If the situation is serious, additional modifications might become necessary concerning violation of the law / emphasis of matters / qualifications / adverse or disclaimer of opinion that have to be considered:

- Art. 678 CO hidden dividend distribution
- Art. 660 and 717 CO equal treatment to shareholders
- Art. 732 capital decrease
- Art. 725 para. 2 CO liquidity / going concern / depositing the balance sheet
- bankruptcy

§ 13   Swiss Audit Oversight Authority (RAG)

The new Law on Auditor oversight (*Revisionsaufsichtsgesetz*, RAG) and the revision of the Code of Obligations (OR) in Switzerland were adopted by the Swiss parliament on 16 December 2005. By Federal Ordinance (*Verordnung*) of 18 October 2006 the Swiss Federal Council (*Bundesrat*, BR) appointed the five person board of directors of the Swiss Federal Auditor Oversight Authority (AOA) (*Schweizerische Revisionsaufsichtsbehörde,* RAB), Bern, for a four year period effective on 1 November 2006 as follows:

- As President of the Board of AOA: Hans Peter Walter (born 1944), Attorney, until 2004 Federal Judge, since then Professor for private and commercial law University of Berne.

- As Vice President of the Board of AOA: Thomas Rufer (born 1952), Swiss Federally Certified Accountant (*dipl. Wirtschaftsprüfer*), former Partner in charge of Arthur Andersen Switzerland, leading bank auditor.

- Eugen Haltiner (born 1948), Dr. oec., former President of the Federal Banking Commission (*Eidgenössische Bankenkommission*), Berne, former Member of the Executive Committee of UBS AG, Zurich/Basle.

- Alfred Stettler (born 1943), Prof. emer. in accounting, Dr. rer. pol., University (HEC) Lausanne.
- Peter R. Voser (born 1958), Chief Financial Officer (CFO) and Member of the Board of Directors of Royal Dutch Shell plc, England/Holland, former CFO of ABB Ltd., Zurich.

The executive Director of the Swiss Oversight Audit Authority is Frank Schneider, Swiss Federally Certified Accountant (*dipl. Wirtschaftsprüfer*), formerly with PricewaterhouseCoopers Zurich and New York and head of accounting and reporting enforcement at the Swiss Exchange (SIX). He has started his work on 1 January 2007.

The Chief Legal Counsel Reto Sanwald was appointed in February 2007. He was instrumental in drafting the new law.

The Swiss PCAOB is head quartered in Berne and employees some 20 staff.

The effective date was postponed to 1 January 2008. Although a provisional registration of individuals was started in summer 2007.

The implications of the new laws for audit firms and audited companies/organisations are extensive. They were expected to be implemented as of 2007 at the earliest. The new Law on audit supervision (RAG) should not only cover public limited companies (AG/SA) but also other legal structures, such as large limited liability companies (GmbH/Ltd.), cooperatives, foundations, associations, etc. About 300,000 legal entities will potentially be affected by the new Audit Supervision Law. Up until now, only about 170,000 corporations were subject to annual reporting and audit requirements. Thanks to numerous exceptions and facilitation provisions, smaller organisations (SME) will be largely exempt from the auditing requirement, so that their organisational freedom is not unduly restricted through additional legislation and guidelines.

In June 2004, the Federal Council introduced two new bills on annual audits in Switzerland for deliberation in parliament. One bill referred to the Federal Law on the Accreditation and Supervision of Auditors, called Law on Audit Supervision (RAG); the other one addressed the amendment of the Code of Obligations or Stock Corporation Law. Provisions for relief measures for Middle Market companies (SME) were foreseen: Limited audits or exemption under certain conditions.

These new laws reflect the direct impacts from national and international business failures and financial statement/reporting scandals, such as Enron and WorldCom in the USA, Flowtex (D), Ahold (NL), and Parmalat (I) in Europe, Erb Group, Suisse Romande Cantonal Banks and SAir Group in Switzerland.

In the USA, this led to the collapse of an internationally operating audit firm (Arthur Andersen). Shortly thereafter, the American Senate passed the Sarbanes-Oxley Act of 2002 (SOX). It mandates, inter alia, governmental supervision of the audit industry by establishing the Public Company Accounting Oversight Board (PCAOB), Washington, D.C., which has been active since the end of 2003.

This triggered extensive supervision and regulation of the big audit firms ('Big 4') in the USA and internationally. One focus are the rigorous independence rules and the supervision of auditors.

The Swiss PCAOB (federal supervision authority) is also designed to avoid or mitigate the extraterritorial application of the US or other PCAOBs. Without such a supervisory body, the Swiss auditors would have to disclose business secrets of their Swiss clients in the USA or abroad, which could qualify as a violation of the Swiss Penal Code (StGB). PCAOB registration of the US Big 4 was completed in the USA in October 2003. The international networks of the Big 4 were included simultaneously. The registration of the big Swiss audit firms with the US PCAOB took place in June 2004. Whether or not the US PCAOB will fully recognise the designated Swiss PCAOB remains to be seen. Such recognition depends on whether adequate qualitative and quantitative resources are available, and the board's willingness to impose and enforce sanctions for non-compliance.

Both bills were adopted almost unanimously by both chambers of parliament. The few remaining differences were settled at the end of 2005. This has cleared the way for an enactment in 2007. The audit section of the bill on Accounting and Audit (RRG) and certain directives of the Sarbanes-Oxley Act (concerning PCAOB) were largely integrated in the new laws. The supervision program to be carried out by a federal authority for auditors of companies or groups with listed shares or bonds or substantial role subsidiaries is of prime importance. The planned costs of the Swiss

PCAOB will be considerable. Internal compliance costs for the Swiss Big 4 will be high and increase audit costs by at least 20 percent. Personal liability and job-related consequences for senior auditors of SIX companies will also increase. This is comparable to similar Swiss Banking Commission (EBK / SFBC) requirements for leading bank auditors and the sanction system in the new Law on Financial Services Industry Regulation (FINMAG).

The hope for limited liability of auditors as a body (abolition of unlimited joint and several liability with the board of directors / management) has, regrettably, not yet materialised. This issue was addressed again in the proposed reform of the stock corporation law.

Analogous to the US PCAOB, the Swiss PCAOB will establish its own audit standards. As a self-regulatory measure, the Swiss Institute of Certified Accountants and Tax Consultants implemented the International Standards on Auditing (ISA) in the form of the Swiss Audit Standards (SAS, PS, NAS) as a self-regulatory measure, which became effective in 2005.

The EU Commission in Brussels introduced a tightened new 8th EU Directive on the supervision of auditors through European PCAOBs in March 2004.

As is generally known, the Swiss package of audit laws is only a first step. At the end of 2005, the accounting package was an update of the General Law on Accounting (Art. 957 to 964 CO), which is independent of a company's legal structure, followed. Hence, the preparatory work for the bill on Accounting and Audit (RRG) from 1998 was carried on and the Swiss GAAP FER will be adopted for about 500,000 Swiss organisations (AG, GmbH, foundations, associations etc.).

As of 2005, the consistently more stringent IFRS are mandatory for approximately 300 SIX companies. According to the RAG, these companies or groups must, in future, be audited by federally supervised audit firms with accredited audit experts.

The most important directives of these two Swiss bills on audit are summarised below. They were amply described in the statement of the Federal Council dated 23 June 2004. The parliamentary discussions only led to minor adjustments, thus yielding a largely consensual result.

The Federal Law on the Accreditation and Supervision of Auditors (Auditor Oversight Act, AOA; RAG) is administrative Federal legislation with the following provisions:

Content and purpose (Art. 1 RAG) are the rules of accreditation and supervision of individuals providing audit services and ensuring due compliance and quality of such services.

The new law defines audit services as audits and confirmations provided by accredited (licensed) audit experts (Art. 2 RAG) according to:

1) Swiss Civil Code, ZGB (new for associations, foundations)

2) Swiss Code of Obligations, OR (AG, new for GmbH, cooperatives, etc.)

3) new Merger Act, FusG (mergers and demergers / spin-offs) as of 1 July 2004

4) IPR (cross-border company relocations)

Public companies (Art. 2 lit. c RAG and Art. 727 para. 1 no. 1 CO) are entities

1) with listed participation documents (shares, participation certificates and profit participation shares)

2) with outstanding bonds

3) with at least 20% of the assets or sales in the consolidated accounts (important subsidiary or substantial role)

Such "public companies" are subject to extensive or full audits by federally supervised audit firms (complete audit, full audit, ordinary audit). Audit firms (Art. 2 lit. a and 6 RAG) must be registered in the Commercial Register. They are accredited for five years, provided the majority of the highest administrative body (VR) and the management (GL) of the audit firm are accredited as certified audit experts.

Audit experts (Art. 4 RAG) are accredited (licensed) as individuals, provided they have the required training and practical experience and a spotless record (*Leumund*). Swiss Certified Accountants (*dipl. Wirtschaftsprüfer*) are thus, in general, accredited. The accreditation is unlimited for individuals. Analogous to the Stock Corporation Law of 1991 (ordinance of the Federal Council dated 15 June 1992), other professions with corresponding practical experience can also apply for accreditation (Art. 4 RAG). Holders of foreign certificates must provide evidence of possessing the required knowledge of Swiss law (Commercial Law and Tax Law) und Art. 4 para. 2 lit. d RAG.

Filing for accreditation of federally supervised audit firms (Art. 10 RAG) follows a similar process as stipulated for the American supervisory authority (PCAOB), through registration of the audit companies including senior auditors of the approximately 300 to 500 SIX companies with listed shares and bonds (analogous to the FINMA for leading bank auditors) through the new Swiss Audit Supervision Authority in Berne (Swiss PCAOB).

The requirements for maintaining due registration or accreditation are:

1) Rotation of the leading auditors on the annual ordinary audit. According to the hitherto applicable independence guideline of the Swiss Institute of Certified Accountants and Tax Consultants, this period is currently limited to 7 years (SEC 5 years). This voluntary provision was adopted now in the Code of Obligations.

2) The fee income from any given client may only amount to max. 10 percent of the overall fee income of the audit firm (Art. 11 lit. a RAG).

3) Cooling-off of two years in the case of employment transfers of individuals with decision making power to and from audit clients (Art. 11 lit. b and c RAG).

For working papers the obligation to retain records is 10 years (SEC 7 years) in accordance with Art. 730c OR.

Routine reviews (of the quality control system of the audit firm and of the working papers of SWX audit engagements and major subsidiaries) through the Federal Supervisory Authority must be carried out at least every three years (Art. 17 RAG).

Federally supervised audit firms must grant access to their business locations to the supervisory authority at any time (unannounced inspections also outside of office hours according to Art. 14 para. 2 RAG).

The Federal Audit Supervision Authority (Swiss PCAOB) is a public institution with its head office in Berne (Art. 29 RAG). It is possible that it might ultimately report to a new authority (supervisory authority on banks, insurances, public companies, etc.) after the implementation of the integrated Law on Financial Services Industry Regulatory Agency (FINMAG). They include the former activities of the Swiss Federal Banking Commission (EBK / SFBC) and the Federal Office for Private Insurance (BPV).

The supervisory authority can impose monetary fines of up to CHF 100,000 for infractions (Art. 41 RAG), e.g. in the case of violation of independence rules. Tort fines may amount to as much as CHF 1 million, e.g. for violation of the documentation obligation or the obligation to retain records (Art. 42 para. 1 lit. c RAG) or in the case of refusal to provide information or access to the audit firm (Art. 42 para. 1 lit. b RAG).

Further sanctions provide for the revocation of the accreditation by means of a professional ban of the senior auditor or of the audit firm, in the case of a gross violation of the law or regulatory statutes (Art. 18 RAG).

In addition, administrative and legal assistance to national and international supervisory authorities (e.g. US PCAOB) according to Art. 27 RAG is planned.

For companies, the summary or limited audit is carried out according to Art. 727a CO. An exemption might be possible, if the headcount is less than 10 on an annual average, and if all shareholders agree (opting-out).

This involves additional new audit tasks for the external auditors. The details still need to be finalised.

§ 14 Maintenance of audit secrecy

Under Art. 730b para. 2 CO

"The auditors shall maintain secrecy on their findings as far as they are not obligated by law to disclose them. They shall preserve the business secrets of the Company when establishing their report and compulsory notifications and when providing information to the general meeting."

Therefore it contradicts Swiss law if an auditor of a Swiss company discloses information to foreign authorities, foreign auditors or foreign head offices/parent or other foreign parties. This could be in the form of producing documents such as emails, electronic files, fax, letter etc. or giving testimony by phone abroad.

The conflicting law provisions not only include the above mentioned article 730b CO under commercial laws but also a series of other Swiss laws including criminal laws such as:

1) Violation of data secrecy / privacy under Art. 12 and 35 DPL (Federal Law on Data Protection)

2) Violation of Swiss Employment Law protecting employee information under Art. 328b CO

3) Violation of the manufacturing and business secrecy under Art. 162 Swiss Penal Code (SPC)

4) Prohibition to perform illegal acts in favour of a foreign state which is protecting the sovereignty of Switzerland under Art. 271 para. 1 SPC. Pursuant to this article "whoever performs or furthers, without authorisation (by the competent Swiss authorities), on Swiss territory acts in favour of a foreign government or foreign party or foreign organisation) shall be imprisoned or in severe cases sentenced to penal servitude". Only the Swiss Department of Justice could grant waivers under Foreign legal assistance treaties, if any, with the respective country.

5) Prohibition of economic espionage under Art. 273 Swiss Penal Code (SPC) is also a provision to protect the sovereignty of the Swiss state on Swiss territory and the interests of the Swiss national economy.

6) Violation of professional secrets under Art. 321 Swiss Penal Code (SPC)

7) Violation of banking secrecy under Art. 47 Banking Act (BaG). This is probably the most severe. It applies to Swiss banks including board, management and employees, their auditors and certain other persons, to protect all information about the bank's clients, including their names and the mere fact that a certain person is a client of a bank or not. The violation of this banking secret is punishable by up to six month of imprisonment or fine. Similarly, Art. 43 SESTA (Stock Exchange and Securities Traders Act, BEHG) provides a widely analogous secrecy duty. Violations are punishable up to three years of prison or fine.

A consent or waiver by the audit client e.g. client's Board of Directors cannot cure some of these violations. Because also third party or even governmental interests are protected (e.g. bank client, debtors, creditors, business secrets etc.) a request of foreign authorities, parties and organisations must be treated under the provisions of Legal assistance treaties between the Swiss government (usually Justice department, FINMA) with the equivalent foreign governmental body. Consultation with specialised lawyers is normally required.

§ 15 Relief for small business (limited audit)

Under the amendment to the Code of Obligations decided on by the Swiss parliament on 16 December 2005 the concept of full (ordinary) and limited audit (examination) was introduced.

A full (ordinary) audit is required for public corporations (and limited liability companies, cooperatives) according to Art. 727 para. 1 and 2 CO for:

1) Public companies with:
   a) listed shareholding documents (shares, PS, GS)
   b) outstanding bonds
   c) at least 20 percent of the assets or sales of the consolidated accounts of a company according to a. or b. (important subsidiary of a listed group or substantial role).

2) Larger companies exceeding two of the following parameters for two consecutive years ("economically significant" companies, over 5,000 in Switzerland):
   a) total assets of CHF 10 million.
   b) sales revenues of CHF 20 million.
   c) employees of 50 on annual average.

3) Companies, which are required to submit consolidated accounts (Art. 663e CO).

4) If 10% of the shareholders (minorities) request this (opting-up).

5) If the articles of corporation provide for it.

6) If the general assembly has decided accordingly.

7) Possibly on account of market pressure, e.g. ordinary audit as required for banks as part of the credit agreement (opting-in).

This full or extensive ordinary audit, according to above-stated criteria 2 to 7, must at least be carried out by accredited audit experts.

This limited audit must at least be carried out by accredited (licensed auditors, (not necessarily, though, by accredited audit experts). Nevertheless, the rules concerning capital loss and over indebtedness (notification of bankruptcy) remain applicable in line with Art.725 CO. Furthermore, liability of auditors remains unlimited. In the case of a limited audit, the audit firm must also be independent (Art. 729 CO), but may, nevertheless, contribute book-keeping services and the preparation of accounts (which need to be disclosed in the audit report) as well as tax advisory services. Suitable organisational steps might need to be taken. Audit activities mostly consist of inquiries and analytical audit activities (Art. 729a CO). The audit report is therefore limited and only includes a negative assurance: "Based on our limited audit, nothing has come to our attention ...".

The differences between full (ordinary) and limited audit (examination) can be shown as follows:

Statutory Audit (Art. 727 CO)	Limited Audit (Art. 727a CO)
A) Similar expressions Full audit	A) Similar expressions Review, limited or summary audit (limited audit)
B) Application (most important criteria) 1) Publicly traded companies, characteristics: a. Ownership papers quoted on the stock exchange	B) Application Smaller companies / legal forms which do not fulfil the size criteria according to Art. 727 CO

b. Outstanding bonds	
c. Participation of at least 20 percent in the assets or the turnover of the group financial statements according to letter a or b	
2) Companies (including associations and foundations), which exceed two of the following sizes in two consecutive business years:	
a. Balance sheet sum of CHF 10 million.	
b. Annual turnover of CHF 20 million.	
c. Annual average of 50 full time positions	
3) Companies which must issue financial statements	
C) Professional requirements	**C) Professional requirements**
Strict requirements	Less stringent when applied to professional practice
Publicly traded companies: Government supervision,	Recognised (licensed) auditors (Art. 727c CO)
Recognised (licensed) audit experts (Art. 727b CO)	
D) Independence	**D) Independence**
High Standards (Art. 728 CO)	Reduced requirements (Art. 729 para. 2 CO):
Rotation of the lead auditor after seven years (Art. 730a CO)	Permissible to help in bookkeeping
	No requirement to rotate

E) Objective and scope of examination Largely comprehensive (Art. 728a CO)	**E) Objective and scope of examination** Brief, limited to specific audit procedures such as interviews, analytical audit procedures and related detailed tests (Art. 729a para. 2 CO)
F) Auditors' report Comprehensive audit report to the Board of Directors (detailed report) and short opinion to the general meeting (Art. 728b CO) Positively formulated confirmation in the audit opinion: «The financial statements are in accordance with the law and statutes…»	**F) Auditors' report** Short opinion to the general meeting (Art. 729b CO) Negatively formulated confirmation in the audit opinion: «… we have not come across any facts which would lead us to believe that the financial statements are not in accordance with law and statutes …»
G) Reporting obligation Notify the court if there is an obvious insolvency or the Board of Directors is incompetent (Art. 728c para. 3 CO)	**G) Reporting obligation** Same as statutory audit
H) Entry in the commercial register Name and domicile of the auditors	**H) Entry in the commercial register** Name and domicile of the auditors

§ 16 Representation letters from Board and Management

Representation letter

This representation letter is provided in connection with your audit of the financial statements (balance sheet, income statement and notes) of ABC Ltd. (the company) for the financial year ended 31 December 20 XX for the purpose of expressing an opinion as to whether the financial statements of ABC Ltd. as of 31 December 20XX and the result of its operations for the year ended comply with Swiss law and the company's articles of incorporation.

We acknowledge the responsibility of the Board of Directors for these financial statements which will be submitted to the General Meeting of the Shareholders for approval.

We confirm, to the best of our knowledge and belief, the following representations:

1. *The financial statements comply with the Swiss law and the company's articles of incorporation and are in this context free of material misstatements (including erroneous recording, valuation, presentation or disclosure and omissions).*

2. *We have made available to you all books of account, supporting documentation and business correspondence as well as all minutes of meetings of Shareholders, the Board of Directors and the committees of the Board of Directors. We have informed you of decisions that could have a significant effect on the financial statements but for which minutes are not yet available.*

3. *The company has complied with all aspects of contractual agreements that could have a material effect on the financial statements in the event of noncompliance. There has been no noncompliance with requirements of regulatory authorities (e.g. concerning direct taxes; value added taxes; social security; environmental protection) that could have a material effect on the financial statements in the event of noncompliance.*

4. *We are responsible for the set-up, implementation and maintenance of financial and internal control systems that are aimed at preventing and uncovering errors and fraudulent acts.*

We understand that the term "fraud" includes misstatements resulting from fraudulent financial reporting and misstatements resulting from misappropriation of assets. Misstatements resulting from fraudulent financial reporting involve intentional misstatements or omissions of amounts or disclosures in financial statements to deceive financial statement users. Misstatements resulting from misappropriation of assets involve the theft of company's assets, often accompanied by false or misleading records or documents in order to conceal the fact that the assets are missing.

4. *We have no knowledge of actual or suspected fraudulent acts that could have concerned our company.*

5. *We have disclosed to you the results of our assessment of the risks that the financial statements may be materially misstated as a result of fraud.*

6. *The Board of Directors and the management of the company are aware of the Swiss Corruption Penal Code (Schweizerischen Korruptionsstrafrecht/droit pénal suisse de la corruption, and especially among others, of Art. 100^{quater} and Art. 322ter etc. of the Swiss Penal Code (Schweizerischen Strafgesetzbuches (StGB)/Code pénal suisse (CP)) in connection with Art. 4a of the Federal Law Against Unfair Competition (Bundesgesetzes gegen den unlauteren Wettbewerb (UWG)/Loi fédérale contre la concurrence déloyale (LCD) and Art. 27 and 59 of the Swiss Federal Tax Law concerning the Direct Federal Income Taxes (Bundesgesetz über die direkte Bundessteuer (DBG)/Loi fédérale sur l'impôt fédéral direct (LIFD)). The legal and tax consequences of these laws are generally known in our company. Our board of directors and management has taken the necessary measures in time that our employees act in accordance with these legal requirements.*

Kapitel 2:
Grundlagen der Revision

§ 1   Gesetzliche Grundlagen

Übersicht Revision:

- Obligationsrecht
- Spezialerlasse
- Sonderprüfungen
- Nationale und internationale Prüfungsstandards

§ 2   Das neue Revisionsrecht im Überblick

I.   Einleitung

Die verschiedenen Börsenskandale haben die Vorschriften zur Revision verschärft, namentlich im angelsächsischen Recht. Diesem internationalen Trend hat sich die schweizerische Gesetzgebung angeschlossen. Im Herbst 2005 wurde das neue Recht von den Eidgenössischen Räten beschlossen. Dies führte zu einem tief greifenden Wandel in der Revisionsbranche, wobei sich zwei verschiedene Entwicklungen gegenüberstehen. Auf der einen Seite führt es im Bereich der qualifizierten Wirtschaftsprüfung zu einer Verstärkung der Aufgaben der Revisionsstelle, währenddem auf der anderen Seite für die KMUs eine Erleichterung gesucht wird; namentlich könnte ein Grossteil der Schweizer Firmen einige tausend Franken pro Jahr an Wirtschaftsprüfungshonoraren sparen, wenn ihre Rechnung nicht gemäss neuem Aktienrecht revidiert werden müsste, dies unter der Prämisse der Befreiung von Kleinstaktiengesellschaften.

Die nun vorliegende Gesetzesänderung basiert einerseits auf den Änderungen im Obligationenrecht im weiteren Sinne (Aktien-, GmbH-, Vereins- und Stiftungsrecht) und führt andererseits zu einem neuen Bundesgesetz über die Revisionsaufsicht (RAG). Letzteres betrifft diejenigen Gesellschaften, welche an der Börse kotiert sind oder an der Börse Anleihensobligationen ausstehend haben.

II. Gründe zur Gesetzesrevision

Die Gründe für die notwendigen Änderungen liegen in einer weltweiten Vertrauenskrise. Die Qualität der Rechnungslegungsnormen, vor allem der internationalen, haben gezeigt, dass diese mit gewissen Mängeln verbunden sind. Namentlich können hochwertige internationale Rechnungslegungsnormen nicht Konkurse internationaler Konzerne verhindern. Daran anzuschliessen ist, dass die Qualität der Prüfungsarbeiten in einer gewissen Kritik steht. Diese Kritik hat dazu geführt, dass zum Beispiel eine international anerkannte hochwertige Wirtschaftsprüfungsgesellschaft innert Monaten von der Bildfläche verschwunden ist. Solche mit Recht vorgetragenen Unzulänglichkeiten haben die Unabhängigkeit der Wirtschaftsprüfer in Frage gestellt. Dienen diese dem Unternehmer (von dem sie bezahlt werden) oder dem Umfeld?

Die Erwartungslücke (expectation gap) gegenüber der Wirtschaftsprüfung ist als allgemeiner Begriff bekannt. Sie drückt aus, dass in einer Revisionsgesellschaft ein sakrosanktes Urteil über die zu prüfende oder geprüfte Gesellschaft erwartet wird, währenddem der Revisionsstelle als so genanntes sekundäres Revisionsorgan nur eine bedingte Aufsicht zukommt. Zu diesem «expectation gap» ist nun der «accounting expectation gap» hinzugekommen. Dieser drückt aus, dass – wie oben ausgeführt – die internationalen Rechnungslegungsnormen grosse Spielräume haben, die eine Gesellschaft zu ihren Gunsten ausnützen kann. Die Öffentlichkeit als Bilanzleser ist nicht in der Lage, eine Bilanz im Rahmen dieser internationalen Rechnungslegungsnormen kritisch zu hinterfragen. Sie geht davon aus, dass diese Werte in den Jahresrechnungen richtig sind und im Zuge dieser Defizite wird die Selbstregulierung der Branche (der Wirtschaftsprüfer) von der Öffentlichkeit nicht mehr bedingungslos akzeptiert.

In anderen Ländern haben diese Veränderungen im Umfeld der Wirtschaftsprüfung bereits zu gesetzlichen Aktivitäten geführt, namentlich in den USA zum «Sarbanes-Oxley Act» im Jahre 2002. Daraus folgend ergaben sich im angelsächsischen Bereich grosse Änderungen und die internationalen Konzerne sind daran, diese Vorgaben in ihre Rechnungslegung umzusetzen, namentlich im Bereich der Risikoanalyse. Dieser Gesetzgebungsakt hat auch dazu geführt, dass die IOSCO-Arbeitsgruppe zur Übernahme der ISA-Richtlinien hinwirkt. Auch die 8. EU-Richtlinie wird ebenfalls überarbeitet. Bezüglich der Rechnungslegung wird in der EU und weiteren anderen Gremien eine Überarbeitung im Gesellschafts- und Wirtschaftsprüfungsrecht gefordert. Dieser Entwicklung können sich auch die in der Schweiz kotierten Gesellschaften nicht entziehen, soweit sie «nur» schweizerischem Recht unterliegen.

III. Neue gesetzliche Regeln zur Revision

Im Jahre 1991 ist das neue Aktienrecht in Kraft getreten. Nach einem jahrzehntelangen Stillstand der Rechtsentwicklung in der Rechnungslegung war die Gesetzesänderung dringend notwendig und hat in der Zwischenzeit guten Eingang gefunden. Die Adaption ist vollzogen. Bereits mit Abschluss der Revisionsarbeiten wurde offensichtlich, dass auch andere Institute des Gesellschaftsrechts einer Revision bedürfen. Im Jahre 1993 hat das Eidgenössische Justiz- und Polizeidepartement eine «Groupe de Réflexion» eingesetzt, welche den Handlungsbedarf auch bei anderen Gesellschaftsformen darlegte. Insbesondere wurde auch ein Gesetz zur Rechnungslegung vorgeschlagen und eine Systematisierung der Wirtschaftsprüfung.

Als weiterer bedeutender Meilenstein wurde ein Entwurf zu einem Rechnungslegungsgesetz (RRG) vorgelegt, der im Jahre 1998 zirkulierte. Der Entwurf wurde in einem breiten Vernehmlassungsverfahren nicht gut aufgenommen. Namentlich die geforderte absolute Identität von Steuerbilanz und Handelsbilanz wurde nicht goutiert. Das Gesetz wurde generell als KMU-untauglich qualifiziert.

Im Jahre 2001 ist neben den bereits erwähnten Finanzskandalen im Ausland auch unser grosser «Schweizer Fall» zutage getreten, der Zusammenbruch der «Swissair». Dies führte auch in der Politik zu Reaktionen.

Im Jahre 2003 beschloss das Eidgenössische Justiz- und Polizeidepartement den Revisionsteil vorweg neu zu revidieren und das Rechnungslegungsgesetz später in einer revidierten Fassung vorzulegen. Als Ergebnisse dieses Umfeldes zeigen sich die Entwürfe zu einem GmbH-Recht und zu einem neuen «Revisionsrecht».

IV. Grundzüge der neuen gesetzlichen Regelungen

Die Pflicht zur Revision wird rechtsform-unabhängig bezüglich der Kapitalgesellschaften. Die ursprünglich im RRG vorgesehene Regelung, dass alle Unternehmen unabhängig von ihrer Rechtsform revisionspflichtig sind, wurde fallen gelassen. Die Revisionspflicht bezieht sich auf alle Kapitalgesellschaften (AG, GmbH), wobei neu auch noch die Stiftung und der Verein hinzukommen.

Für «grössere» Gesellschaften und Unternehmungen gibt es erhöhte Anforderungen an die Abschlussprüfung. Darunter fallen Publikumsgesellschaften, welche in einem gesamtwirtschaftlichen Interesse liegen, sowie wirtschaftlich bedeutende Unternehmen. Weitere Ziele der Revision sind der Minderheiten- und der Gläubigerschutz.

Grundsätzlich gibt es zwei Arten der Prüfung: die ordentliche und die eingeschränkte Prüfung. Die ordentliche Prüfung ist bei den «grösseren» Unternehmungen Pflicht, sprich bei Gesellschaften, welche an der Börse kotiert sind. Weiter dazu gehören wirtschaftlich bedeutende Unternehmen. Hier müssen zwei von drei Kriterien während 2 Jahren erfüllt sein: ein Überschreiten der Bilanzsumme von 10 Mio. Franken, des Umsatzes von 12 Mio. Franken und mehr als 20 Vollzeitstellen. Der ordentlichen Prüfung unterliegen auch Gesellschaften, welche eine Konzernrechnung erstellen müssen.

Als neuer zweiter grosser Pfeiler im Revisionsrecht erscheint die eingeschränkte Prüfung. Diese kommt bei allen Gesellschaften zum Tragen, welche nicht die Kriterien für die ordentliche Prüfung erfüllen; jedoch nur bezüglich der Kapitalgesellschaften (AG, GmbH). Die eingeschränkte Prüfung ist bei den Vereinen und Stiftungen nicht möglich bzw. nicht vorgesehen.

Wahlmöglichkeit: Im Revisionsrecht existiert neu die Möglichkeit, dass Wahlrechte ausgeübt werden.

a) Opting-Out

Bei einer Kapitalgesellschaft (AG und GmbH), bei der nicht mehr als 10 Vollzeitstellen bestehen, können sämtliche Gesellschafter gemeinsam auf eine Revision verzichten, dies sofern es sich nicht um ein wirtschaftlich bedeutendes Unternehmen handelt. Faktisch dürfte das Opting-Out nicht zu oft praktiziert werden, da das Umfeld (wie z.B. Banken mit Kreditlimiten) oft eine Prüfung wünschen wird.

b)   Opting-Up/In

Im Rahmen des Minderheitenschutzes können Aktionäre, welche zusammen mindestens 10 % des Grundkapitals besitzen, eine ordentliche Prüfung verlangen. Auch können die Statuten eine solche generell vorschreiben.

Im Rahmen des Umfeldes, das höhere Prüfungen verlangt, kann auch anstelle einer eingeschränkten Revision eine ordentliche Revision vom Verwaltungsrat an die Revisionsstelle in Auftrag gegeben werden.

c)   Opting-Down

Sofern die Revision freiwillig ist, wie beim Opting-Out, können anstatt auf eine Prüfung völlig zu verzichten, auch Revisoren, die die fachlichen Anforderungen für die ordentliche Revision nicht erfüllen, Revisionen durchführen.

V.   Neue Aufgaben bei der ordentlichen Prüfung

Von Gesetzes wegen hat die Revisionsstelle eine neue Aufgabe zu übernehmen. Sie muss nämlich bestätigen, dass ein «Internes Kontrollsystem» (IKS) existiert. Diese fundamentale Änderung führt dazu, dass der Revisor neben der formellen und materiellen Prüfung der Bilanz und Erfolgsrechnung und damit des Rechnungswesens auch organisatorische Prinzipien eines Unternehmens analysieren muss. In dieser Tätigkeit eingeschlossen ist die Bestätigung mit dem Revisionsbericht, dass die Gesellschaft eine Risikobeurteilung vorgenommen hat, da diese im Anhang erläutert werden muss und der Anhang Bestandteil der Revision ist.

Als weitere zusätzliche Aufgabe muss die Revisionsstelle einen Bericht an den Verwaltungsrat vorlegen, der über den Inhalt der Revision Auskunft gibt. Dieses Instrument war früher der im Gesetz vorgesehene Erläuterungsbericht, welcher jedoch nur ab einer gewissen Gesellschaftsgrösse zwingend vorgeschrieben wurde. Der Bericht ist nunmehr bei allen ordentlichen Prüfungen Bestandteil der Berichterstattung der Revisionsstelle.

VI. Unabhängigkeit

Das alte Aktienrecht schrieb vor, dass die Revisionsstelle unabhängig sei, wobei sie die Definition der Revisionspraxis überliess. Dies hat dazu geführt, dass in den Berufsverbänden verschiedene Kataloge an Kriterien veröffentlicht wurden, welche jedoch insgesamt nicht befriedigten und teilweise der Besitzstandswahrung von Aufträgen dienten.

a) Ordentliche Revision

Bei der ordentlichen Revision führt das Gesetz auf, dass keine eigenen Arbeiten geprüft werden dürfen; dies als Generalklausel zu einem weiterfolgenden detaillierten Katalog. Damit verbunden ist, dass die Erstellung des Geschäftsabschlusses sowie die Buchführung oder die Mitwirkung bei der Buchführung ausgeschlossen sind. Weitere ausgeschlossene Dienstleistungen sind Arbeiten im Zusammenhang von Bewertungen, bei der Mitwirkung, bei der internen Revision und bei der Entwicklung von Finanzsystemen oder dergleichen. All diese letztgenannten Dienstleistungen sind unter die Generalklausel zu subsumieren.

b) Eingeschränkte Revision

Bei der eingeschränkten Revision gibt es keine formelle Generalklausel im Gesetz. Es wird aber speziell darauf hingewiesen, dass Mitwirkungen in der Rechnungslegung möglich sind, sofern eine personell und organisatorisch klar getrennte Arbeitsabwicklung besteht. Angaben im Revisionsbericht sind erforderlich, diese können auch im Anhang angeführt werden.

VII. Die Qualifikation des Revisors

Für börsenkotierte Gesellschaften wird eine staatlich beaufsichtigte Zulassungsstelle den Kriterienkatalog prüfen. Nur Unternehmen, welche eine solche Zulassungsverfügung erhalten haben, sind zur Revision dieser Gesellschaften befugt.

Der «zugelassene Revisionsexperte» darf die ordentliche und die eingeschränkte Revision vornehmen. Die berufliche Qualifikation geht in die gleiche Richtung wie beim heute bekannten «besonders befähigten Revisor».

Der «zugelassene Revisor» hat ähnliche berufliche Qualifikationen mitzubringen wie der Revisionsexperte, seine Praxisdauer ist jedoch nicht so umfassend.

Der Laienrevisor ist nur noch beim Verein möglich, und zwar nur, wenn es sich nicht um einen wirtschaftlich bedeutenden Verein handelt, sowie bei Gesellschaften, die sich zu einer freiwilligen eingeschränkten oder ordentlichen Revision entschlossen haben (Opting-Down).

Teil C: Revision / Auditing

Übersicht Prüfung	Revisor	Revision	AG	GmbH	Genossenschaft	Verein	Stiftung
Staatlich beaufsichtigtes Revisionsunternehmen	Qualifikation und Aufsicht	ordentliche	Kotierung/Anleihensobligationen	Kotierung/Anleihensobligationen	Kotierung/Anleihensobligationen	–	Kotierung/Anleihensobligationen (dispositiv)
Zugelassener Revisionsexperte	Qualifikation und Fachpraxis 5–12 Jahre	a) ordentliche Bilanz b) Zwischenbilanz bei Überschuldung	• Bilanzsumme CHF 10 Mio. • Umsatz CHF 20 Mio. Personal 50 10% der Aktionäre	• Bilanzsumme CHF 10 Mio. • Umsatz CHF 20 Mio. Personal 50 10% der Aktionäre	• Bilanzsumme CHF10 Mio. • Umsatz CHF 20 Mio. Personal 50 10% der Aktionäre	• Bilanzsumme CHF 10 Mio. • Umsatz CHF 20 Mio. Personal 50 10% der Aktionäre	• Bilanzsumme CHF 10 Mio. • Umsatz CHF 20 Mio. Personal 50 10% der Aktionäre
Zugelassener Revisor	Qualifikation und Fachpraxis 1 Jahr	a) Review b) freiwillige ordentl. Revision (opting up) c) Zwischenbilanz bei Überschuldung	alle übrigen	alle übrigen	alle übrigen	freiwillige Revision	alle übrigen
Revisor/ Laienrevisor	keine Regelung	a) Review b) freiwillige ordentl. Revision	Sofern auf Revision verzichtet werden kann: - Personal < 10 - 100% der Aktionäre (opting out)	Sofern auf Revision verzichtet werden kann: - Personal < 10 - 100% der Aktionäre (opting out)	Sofern auf Revision verzichtet werden kann: - Personal < 10 - 100% der Aktionäre (opting out)	freiwillige Revision	Sofern auf Revision verzichtet werden kann: - Personal < 10 - 100% der Aktionäre (opting out)
kein Revisor	–	–	- Personal < 10 - 100% der Aktionäre (opting out)	- Personal < 10 - 100% der Aktionäre (opting out)	- Personal < 10 - 100% der Aktionäre (opting out)	freiwillige Revision	- Personal < 10 - 100% der Aktionäre (opting out) (Pflicht)

VIII. Der Review (eingeschränkte Prüfung)

Neben der ordentlichen Revision, welche der bisherigen Revision materiell gleich kam, wurde neu – unter Berücksichtigung der Erweiterung der Prüfung des internen Kontrollsystems und des vorgesehenen Berichtes an den Verwaltungsrat – der Review eingeführt. Die eingeschränkte Prüfung kommt dem Review gleich, wie er z.B. im Prüfungsstandard 910 definiert worden ist.

Neben der generellen Vorgabe einer eingeschränkten Revision werden konkret folgende Handlungen nicht verlangt:

- Die Prüfung des internen Kontrollsystems,
- die Vorlage eines Berichtes an den Verwaltungsrat,
- die Meldung von Gesetzesverstössen.

Diese Erleichterungen führen dazu, dass auch der Bericht der Revisionsstelle klar auf den Charakter der eingeschränkten Revision hinweisen muss.

Die Anzeigepflicht bei Überschuldung bleibt, die Revisionsstelle behält ihre Organstellung. Die Zukunft wird zeigen, wie hier vorzugehen sein wird.

§ 3 Aktienrechtliche Revision

Zur aktienrechtlichen Revision sind hier die wichtigsten gesetzlichen Bestimmungen erwähnt (vgl. dazu die Prüfungsstandards 200):

Ordentliche Revision:

- OR 727   Ordentliche Revision
- OR 727a   Eingeschränkte Revision
- OR 727b   Anforderungen an die Revisionsstelle (bei ordentlicher Revision)
- OR 727c   Anforderungen an die Revisionsstelle (bei eingeschränkter Revision)
- OR 728   Unabhängigkeit der Revisionsstelle

Teil C: Revision / Auditing

- OR 728a   Gegenstand und Umfang der Prüfung
- OR 728b   Revisionsbericht
- OR 728c   Anzeigepflichten

Eingeschränkte Revision (Review):

- OR 729   Unabhängigkeit der Revisionsstelle
- OR 729a   Gegenstand und Umfang der Prüfung
- OR 729b   Revisionsbericht
- OR 729c   Anzeigepflicht

Allgemeines:

- OR 730   Wahl der Revisionsstelle
- OR 730a   Amtsdauer der Revisionsstelle
- OR 730b   Auskunft und Geheimhaltung
- OR 731   Abnahme und Rechnung und Gewinnverwendung
- OR 731a   Besondere Bestimmungen
- OR 731b   Mängel in der Organisation der Gesellschaft

Das Aktienrecht kennt die ausführlichsten Bestimmungen zur Revision. Hier wird von Anfang an von einer Dreiteilung in Kapitalgeber, Geschäftsführung (Verwaltung) und Revisionsstelle (Kontrolle) ausgegangen. Aufgrund dieser Aufteilung sind die Kontrollrechte der Revisionsstelle sehr weit gefasst.

§ 4   Gesellschaft mit beschränkter Haftung

Zu beachten sind wiederum die Prüfungsstandards 200. Hier die wichtigsten Bestimmungen des Obligationenrechts zur Revision der GmbH:

- OR 772   Begriff der GmbH
- OR 773   Stammkapital
- OR 782   Herabsetzung des Stammkapitals

- OR 798   Dividenden
- OR 801   Geschäftsbericht, Reserven und Offenlegung gemäss Aktienrecht (integraler Verweis)
- OR 804   Aufgabe der Gesellschafterversammlung (u.a. Genehmigung des Jahresberichts)
- OR 818   Revisionsstelle der GmbH gemäss Aktienrecht (integraler Verweis)

Aufgrund des integralen Verweises entspricht die Rechnungslegung und deren Prüfung derjenigen bei der Aktiengesellschaft.

Für die Berichterstattung kann der Standardbericht gemäss Aktienrecht verwendet werden.

§ 5   Genossenschaft

Die wichtigsten Bestimmungen zur Genossenschaft sind hier kurz aufgeführt (vgl. dazu die Prüfungsstandards 200):

- OR 856   Bekanntgabe der Bilanz
- OR 857   Auskunftsrecht
- OR 858   Erfolgsermittlung nach den Vorschriften über die kaufmännische Buchführung
- OR 859   Reingewinn = Genossenschaftsvermögen
- OR 860   Gesetzlicher Reservefonds
- OR 864   Anspruch bei Austritt
- OR 879   Befugnisse der Generalversammlung (u.a. Genehmigung der Jahresrechnung sowie Wahl der Revisionsstelle)
- OR 902   Erstellung der Jahresrechnung durch die Verwaltung
- OR 903   Anzeigepflicht bei Kapitalverlust, Erstellung einer Zwischenbilanz zu Liquidationswerten
- OR 906   Wahl der Revisionsstelle (integraler Verweis auf das Aktienrecht)

Teil C: Revision / Auditing

- OR 907   Prüfungspflicht
- OR 908   Mängel in der Organisation

Was bei der Aktiengesellschaft gilt, d.h. die Aufteilung von Kapitalgeber, Geschäftsführer und Kontrollstelle, gilt auch bei der Genossenschaft. Die Trennung von Kapital und Leitung bedingt auch hier die Notwendigkeit einer Revisionsstelle.

Für die Berichterstattung kann der Standardbericht gemäss Aktienrecht verwendet werden.

§ 6   Spezialerlasse

- Bundesgesetz über die Banken und Sparkassen (Bankengesetz, BankG, SR 952.0)
- Bundesgesetz über die Anlagefonds (Anlagefondsgesetz, AFG, SR 951.31)
- Bundesgesetz über die Alters- und Hinterlassenenversicherung (AHVG, SR 831.10)
- Bundesgesetz über die obligatorische Arbeitslosenversicherung und die Insolvenzentschädigung (AVIG, SR 837.0)
- Bundesgesetz über Krankenversicherung (KVG, SR 832.10)
- Bundesgesetz über die berufliche Alters-, Hinterlassenen- und Invalidenvorsorge (BVG, SR 831.40)

§ 7   Sonderprüfungen

- Bundesgesetz über die Seeschifffahrt unter Schweizer Flagge (Seeschifffahrtsgesetz, SR 747.30)
- Bundesgesetz Rohrleitungsanlagen zur Beförderung flüssiger oder gasförmiger Brenn- oder Treibstoffe (Rohrleitungsgesetz, RLG, SR 746.1)
- Bundesgesetz über die Vorbereitung der Krisenbekämpfung und Arbeitsbeschaffung (SR 823.31)

Kapitel 2: Grundlagen der Revision

- Bundesgesetz über die wirtschaftliche Landesversorgung (Landesversorgungsgesetz, LVG, SR 531)
- Bundesgesetz über die Unfallversicherung (UVG, SR 832.20)

§ 8 Prüfungsstandards PS (Soft law)

Die Prüfungsstandards sowie das Revisionshandbuch bzw. das «Schweizer Handbuch der Wirtschaftsprüfung (HWP)» sind sowohl Ausbildungs- und Lehrmittel sowie Nachschlagewerk und Entscheidungshilfen für alle revisionstechnischen Belange. Sie gelten als Qualitätsstandards der Revisionsbranche.

§ 9 Vereinsrechtliche Revision

I. Einleitung

Die gesetzliche Revision der Aktiengesellschaft ist mit dem neuen Aktienrecht auf eine klarere und bestimmtere gesetzliche Grundlage gestellt worden. Zu diesem Rechtsgebiet hat sich eine breite Wissenschaft, Literatur und Judikatur entwickelt. Die Revision des Vereins hingegen ist praktisch nicht dokumentiert, es existieren auch keine Prüfungsstandards dazu. Das liegt einerseits wohl daran, dass die Vereinsrevision keine gesetzliche, sondern eine rein statutarische ist. Es hängt alleine von den Vereinsmitgliedern ab, ob dieses Vereinsorgan bestehen soll oder nicht. In aller Regel wird der Entscheid darüber bei der Gründerversammlung gefällt. Ein zweiter Grund liegt in den geringen wirtschaftlichen Interessen. Die Vereinsrechnung ist in vielen Fällen eine bescheidene Einnahmen- und Ausgabenrechnung, welche oft durch ein Vereinsmitglied auf einfache Weise geprüft wird. Werden Mängel bei der Revision festgestellt, so lohnt es sich meist nicht, die Verantwortlichkeit der Revisionsstelle geltend zu machen. Die persönlichen Beziehungen im Vereinsleben tragen ebenfalls häufig dazu bei, dass die Haftungsansprüche letztlich nicht durchgesetzt werden.

Nach altem Recht war die Revision bloss eine statutarische, in der Folge richtete sich die Berichterstattung nur an die Mitglieder. Dritte hatten kaum Ansprüche gegenüber der Revisionsstelle. Mit der vorliegenden Revision wird nun die Prüfungspflicht der Vereine neu geregelt.

II. Inhalt der Revision (ohne Erreichen der Grenzwerte)

Das ZGB erwähnt in den neuen gesetzlichen Bestimmungen die aktienrechtlichen Normen. Sind die Grenzwerte nicht erreicht, gibt es keine subsidiäre Regelung, die die Revisionsstelle als Organ ansehen würde. Somit ist dann alleine auf die Statuten abzustellen. Fast alle Statuten begnügen sich damit, zu erwähnen, dass die jährliche Mitgliederversammlung den Revisor wählt, je nachdem wird noch erwähnt, dass er die Jahresrechnung prüft. Um den Inhalt der Revision zu ermitteln, sind die Statuten auszulegen. Was will mit der statutarisch vorgesehenen Revision erreicht werden? Ohne besondere protokollarische Vermerke dürfen wir davon ausgehen, dass mit der Revision eine Prüfung der Jahresrechnung und damit die Tätigkeit des Revisors nach anerkannter Lehre und Praxis gewünscht wird. Sind die relevanten Grenzwerte erreicht, ist die Revision nach Aktienrecht massgebend.

Die Prüfung orientiert sich nach den Grundsätzen der ordnungsmässigen Rechnungslegung. Diese Grundsätze richten sich aber nicht in erster Linie nach den Vorschriften des Aktienrechts, sondern nach den Bestimmungen über die kaufmännische Buchführung (Art. 957 ff. OR), dabei sind hier explizit aufgeführt:

1) die Notwendigkeit eines Inventars

2) das Erstellen einer Bilanz und einer Erfolgsrechnung

3) die Vollständigkeit

4) die Klarheit

5) die Übersichtlichkeit

6) den möglichst sicheren Einblick in die wirtschaftliche Lage des Geschäfts

7) das Erstellen der Bilanz in Landeswährung

8) die Bewertung höchstens zu dem Wert, der dem Aktivum für das Geschäft zukommt

All diese Grundsätze finden wir im Aktienrecht wieder, wobei dann die besonderen Rechnungslegungsvorschriften hinzukommen. Zum Vergleich seien hier die Vorschriften des Aktienrechts aufgeführt (Art. 622a OR):

1) die möglichst zuverlässige Beurteilung der Vermögens- und Ertragslage
2) die Vollständigkeit der Jahresrechnung
3) die Klarheit und Wesentlichkeit der Angaben
4) die Vorsicht
5) die Fortführung der Unternehmenstätigkeit
6) die Stetigkeit der Darstellung und Bewertung
7) die Unzulässigkeit der Verrechnung von Aktiven und Passiven sowie von Aufwand und Ertrag.

Die Ähnlichkeit der Grundsätze der Rechnungslegung nach Aktienrecht und nach den Vorschriften der kaufmännischen Buchführung lassen in der Folge zu, dass die nach Lehre und Praxis entwickelten Grundsätze der Aktienrevision für die Vereinsrevision übernommen werden dürfen. Nicht anwendbar sind die besonderen aktienrechtlichen Rechnungslegungsvorschriften, insbesondere die gesetzlichen Bewertungsvorschriften. Weiter ist ein Unterschied zu machen bei Vereinen, die zum Handelsregistereintrag verpflichtet sind (und damit den Vorschriften der kaufmännischen Buchführung unterliegen) und den Vereinen, die nicht dazu verpflichtet sind (und folglich keine gesetzlichen Bestimmungen zur Rechnungslegung kennen). Bei der ersten Gruppe ist der Inhalt der Revision nicht sehr weit von derjenigen der aktienrechtlichen Revision entfernt. Für die zweite Gruppe kann die Revision nach Aktienrecht nur ein leichter Wegweiser sein. Die Rechnungslegung orientiert sich anhand der Bedürfnisse und der Grösse des Vereins. Art. 957 OR dürfte hier insofern zur Hilfe stehen, als diejenigen Bücher ordnungsgemäss geführt werden müssen, die nach Art und Umfang nötig sind. Sei es eine einfache Ausgaben- und Einnahmenrechnung oder eine komplette doppelte Buchhaltung.

III. Normalwortlaut des Vereinsrevisionsberichtes

Wenn wir nun nach den Grundsätzen der aktienrechtlichen Revision prüfen, so kann auch die Berichterstattung jenen Grundsätzen folgen. Der

Normalwortlaut dient uns als Richtlinie; er hat jedoch den vereinsrechtlichen Modalitäten angepasst zu sein. Aus Bequemlichkeit wird oft der Text nach Aktienrecht verwendet, dabei dürften sich aber Ungereimtheiten ergeben.

a) «An die Generalversammlung des Vereins ...»

Der Verein kennt keine Generalversammlung, sondern eine Mitgliederversammlung. Es empfiehlt sich eine korrekte Wortwahl. Ein Ausnahmefall mag vielleicht dort vorliegen, wo in den Statuten die Mitgliederversammlung als Generalversammlung bezeichnet wird. Eine namhafte schweizerische Vereinigung macht von dieser Wortwahl Gebrauch. Eine Bezeichnung gemäss Vereinsrecht ist jedoch üblich und entsprechend im Bericht zu verwenden.

b) «Als gesetzliche Revisionsstelle ...»

Solange die Grenzwerte nicht erreicht sind, ist der Vereinsrevisor nicht gesetzliche Revisionsstelle, sondern statutarische. Der Text sollte dann auf diesen Umstand hinweisen.

c) «... im Sinne der gesetzlichen Vorschriften»

Bei Vereinen, die sich nicht in das Handelsregister eintragen müssen, seien sie de facto eingetragen oder nicht, gibt es keine gesetzlichen Vorschriften. Mit dem Vorhandensein der Eintragungspflicht gelten jedoch die Vorschriften der kaufmännischen Buchprüfung.

Im Kapitel «Berichterstattung» (Teil C, VIII, Seite 331 f.) wird ein Vorschlag für einen Standardbericht des Vereinsrevisors angeführt.

IV. Ergänzungen

Der Vorschlag bezieht sich nur auf den geläufigsten Normalwortlaut. Bei besonderen Situationen sind im Text entsprechende, sinngemässe Hinweise anzubringen. Überschuldung, wesentlicher Verstoss gegen die Grundsätze der kaufmännischen Buchführung und Verstösse gegen Gesetz und Statuten fordern entsprechende Berichterstattung.

Auch wenn das Vereinsrecht im Rahmen der freiwilligen Revision keine Vorschriften zur Zulassung und Unabhängigkeit kennt, scheint mir dies auch dort ein wesentlicher Pfeiler der Vereinsrevision zu sein. Die Anforderungen haben sich dabei nach den konkreten Umständen zu richten. Eine Laienrevision im Vereinswesen ist nach wie vor üblich und statthaft. Gewisse kaufmännische Grundkenntnisse sind jedoch erforderlich. Eine gewisse Unabhängigkeit ist notwendig. Je grösser der Verein, um so mehr sind erhöhte Anforderungen gefragt.

V. Zusammenfassung

Die Revision des Vereins ist ein nur wenig dokumentiertes Gebiet, dies obwohl die Schweiz ein ausgeprägtes Vereinsleben kennt. Dies liegt an der weit verbreiteten Laienrevision und an den oft bescheidenen wirtschaftlichen Interessen. Für wirtschaftlich bedeutende Vereine ist die Revision neu gesetzlich vorgeschrieben, im Übrigen bloss statutarisch bestimmt. Wie bisher bestehen Buchführungsvorschriften nur für Vereine mit Eintragungspflicht im Handelsregister. Dann sind die Bestimmungen über die kaufmännische Buchführung (Art. 957 ff. OR) massgebend. Als Richtlinie zur Revision im freiwilligen Bereich können Lehre und Praxis des Aktienrechts dienen, den besonderen vereinsrechtlichen Bestimmungen ist aber Rechnung zu tragen.

§ 10 Stiftungsrechtliche Revision

Bei der Revision von Stiftungen besteht eine neue Ausgangslage. Das ZGB erwähnt in den gesetzlichen Bestimmungen neu die Revision. Die Revisionsstelle ist neu Organ der Stiftung. Hier darf davon ausgegangen werden, dass nun mit der Revision eine Prüfung der Jahresrechnung und damit die Tätigkeit des Revisors nach anerkannter Lehre und Praxis gefordert wird, dies unabhängig von der Grösse der Stiftung.

Die Prüfung erfolgt somit nach den Grundsätzen der ordnungsmässigen Rechnungslegung. Diese Grundsätze richten sich aber nicht in erster Linie nach den Bestimmungen über die kaufmännische Buchführung (Art. 957 ff. OR / Art. 83a ZGB). Das Revisionsrecht der Stiftung richtet sich integral nach dem Aktienrecht (Art. 83b ZGB).

Wir gelangen somit zur ähnlichen Zielsetzung wie bei der Revision einer AG. Da die Stiftung im Handelsregister eingetragen werden muss, ist sie an die kaufmännischen Buchführungsvorschriften gebunden. Der Revisor bestätigt mit dem Vermerk «*Die Jahresrechnung entspricht dem Gesetz und der Stiftungsurkunde*», dass diese Vorschriften eingehalten sind (vgl. dazu Prüfungsstandard 200).

§ 11 Vertragliche Revisionen

Vertragliche Revisionen mit standardisierter Berichterstattung sind eher selten. Auf dem Gebiet der vertraglichen Revisionen sind vor allen Dingen Revisionen der Buchführung von Personengesellschaften angesprochen. Meistens sind hier die geschäftsführenden Personen mit den Inhabern identisch. Aus diesem Grund besteht ein permanenter Einblick in die Buchhaltung, weshalb das Bedürfnis einer externen Revisionsstelle nicht besteht. Sie ist vom Gesetz nicht vorgesehen. Wo Personen ohne Geschäftsführung beteiligt sind, ist oft im Gesellschaftsvertrag eine Revision vorgesehen. Eine entsprechende Formulierung im Vertrag ist empfehlenswert.

Bezüglich der Personengesellschaften sehen das Gesetz und die Praxis vor, dass sich die beteiligten Personen jederzeit über die Angelegenheiten der Gesellschaft orientieren können. Sie haben Einblick in die Geschäftsbücher und Akten der Gesellschaft. Diese Einsichtsrechte sind unentziehbar und können nicht beschränkt werden. Der Entwurf zum Rechnungslegungsgesetz (RRG) sah eine gesellschaftsunabhängige Prüfung vor, dies allgemein beim Erreichen von Grenzwerten. Dieser Entwurf wurde nicht umgesetzt.

Art. 541 Abs. 1 OR lautet: «*Der von der Geschäftsführung ausgeschlossene Gesellschafter hat das Recht, sich persönlich von dem Gange der Gesellschaftsangelegenheiten zu unterrichten, von den Geschäftsbüchern und Papieren der Gesellschaft Einsicht zu nehmen und für sich eine Übersicht über den Stand des gemeinschaftlichen Vermögens anzufertigen.*»

Inwieweit dieses Einsichtsrecht delegiert werden kann, ist nicht klar beantwortet. Begründete Ablehnungsgründe müssen gewährt sein. Eine pauschale Ablehnung sollte nicht rechtlich geschützt werden.

Vertragliche Revisionsstellen bei Personengesellschaften haben eine vorbeugende Wirkung. Sie dienen einer neutralen Revision sowie der Beratung und Unterstützung bei gesellschaftsrechtlichen Problemen.

Sporadisch eingesetzte Revisionsstellen haben in der Regel einen Sonderauftrag. Die Berichterstattung ist individuell.

Kapitel 3:
Allgemeine Prüfungshandlungen

§ 1 Prüfungsverhalten

I. Auftragsbestätigung

1. Der gesetzliche Minimalauftrag

Bei der Revisionstätigkeit werden zwei verschiedene Ausgestaltungsmöglichkeiten unterschieden: Zunächst gibt es die Revisionstätigkeit im Rahmen der gesetzlichen Vorschriften. Daneben besteht aber auch die Möglichkeit, der Revisionsstelle Aufgaben und Pflichten zu erteilen, die über das vom Gesetz Geforderte hinausgehen. Bei den Ausführungen zu diesem Titel wird nur von der ersten Variante ausgegangen. Die zweite Variante wird unter einem separaten Titel kurz behandelt.

Prüfungsgrundsätze (PS 210) sehen vor, dass eine Revisionsstelle eine Auftragsbestätigung ausstellen soll.

Die erwähnte Auftragsbestätigung soll enthalten:

1) Adressat
2) Bestätigung der Wahl als Abschlussprüfer
3) Zweck und Gegenstand der Prüfung
4) Zuständigkeit des Verwaltungsrates für die Buchführung
5) Prüfungsmethode (Stichprobe) und
6) Berichterstattung

Sie kann weitere Punkte enthalten:

7) Zusammenarbeit mit der internen Revision
8) Vollständigkeitserklärung
9) Planung der Prüfung
10) Vorbehalte zur definitiven Mandatsannahme

Damit sind die wesentlichen Punkte wiedergeben. Die Auftragsbestätigung ist sehr detailliert und ausführlich.

Als erstes stellt sich die Frage, ob die gesetzliche Revisionsstelle einer Aktiengesellschaft überhaupt eine Auftragsbestätigung ausstellen soll. Die Revisionsstelle ist neben der Generalversammlung und dem Verwaltungsrat drittes Organ der Aktiengesellschaft und somit steht fest, dass ihre Pflichten und ihre Haftung gesetzlich festgelegt sind und sich nicht durch ein abweichendes Bestätigungsschreiben verändern lassen. Die Revisionsstelle hat die Jahresrechnung zu prüfen und eine Empfehlung über Abnahme oder Rückweisung der Jahresrechnung abzugeben. Dass hier für die Revision teilweise Normen des Auftragsrechts (z.B. bezüglich der Honorarforderung) zur Anwendung gelangen, ändert an der Organfunktion und an den gesetzlich vorgeschriebenen Pflichten nichts. Sie hat die ihr gestellte Aufgabe auszuführen, wie es das Gesetz vorschreibt, ansonsten bleibt ihr nur der Rücktritt. Eine Alternative gibt es nicht. Die Wahl der Revisionsstelle erfolgt anlässlich der Generalversammlung, die der Willensbildung der Gesellschaft dient und für deren Durchführung der Verwaltungsrat zuständig ist. Dieser stellt fest, dass die Revisionsstelle gewählt worden ist. Die Willensbildung seitens der Revisionsstelle muss bereits vorher erfolgt sein. Eine Bestätigung nach der Wahl ist nicht mehr erforderlich. Bei gerichtlicher Anfechtung kann höchstens ein Richter darüber urteilen, ob die Wahl ordnungsgemäss erfolgt ist oder nicht. Somit stellt das hier diskutierte Dokument wohl keine Auftragsbestätigung dar, sondern höchstens eine Auftragsumschreibung einer gesetzlichen Pflicht (Hinweise zu den Aufgaben einer Revisionsstelle).

Sodann stellt sich die Frage, ob generell ein solches Schreiben an die zu prüfende Aktiengesellschaft gesandt werden soll. Es ginge dabei also um die Konkretisierung der Aufgaben als Revisionsstelle und damit um eine Individualisierung des Verhältnisses von Revisionsstelle und Aktiengesellschaft, wobei höchstens eine Ausdehnung der Pflichten und Haftung der Revisionsstelle erreicht werden kann, keinesfalls aber eine Einschränkung. Die Revisionsstelle gibt am Schluss ihrer Arbeiten den Revisionsbericht ab. Wie sie zu diesem Ergebnis kommt, ist einerseits durch das Gesetz, die Lehre und die Praxis vorgegeben. So geben anerkannte Richtlinien und Empfehlungen von Berufsverbänden Auskunft darüber, wie die Revision durchgeführt und was wie geprüft werden soll. Andererseits bestimmt die Gesellschaft und deren Vorgaben (Buchhaltung, Rechnungswesen, Geschäftstätigkeit etc.) die Vorgehensweise der Revisionsstelle. Die erste Vorgabe, der gesetzliche Auftrag, ist für alle Fälle gleich, jedoch ist die zweite Vorgabe, die konkreten Verhältnisse der Gesellschaft, in keinem Fall gleich. Durch das erwähnte Dokument sollen also eine generell abstrakte Aufgabe und eine individuell konkrete Ausgangslage in einer allgemeinen Muster-Umschreibung festgehalten werden. Dies ist eine ungünstige Konstellation. Es ist deshalb vorzuschlagen, auf ein Bestätigungsschreiben der oben erwähnten Art zu verzichten, zumindest soweit es die gesetzliche Erfüllung der Revisionstätigkeit betrifft.

Will man die Gesellschaft, und insbesondere den Verwaltungsrat, über die wesentlichen Grundsätze der Revision informieren, so empfiehlt es sich, eine kurze Broschüre über die Aktiengesellschaft mit dem Beschrieb der Aufgaben von Revisionsstelle und Verwaltungsrat abzugeben. Dort können diese Punkte aufgenommen werden und damit kann über die Tätigkeit der Revisionsstelle informiert werden. Damit wird aber nicht ein unnötiger Pflichtenkatalog geschaffen, sondern es bleibt bei einer allgemeinen Umschreibung ohne Konkretisierung. Davon unabhängig ist selbstverständlich die Korrespondenz zwischen Revisionsstelle und Verwaltungsrat, wie auch alle anderen Arten von Schriftstücken, Erklärungen und Dokumenten, die erarbeitet werden.

Schliesslich ist noch darauf hinzuweisen, dass mit einem solchen Dokument die Revisionsstelle zu Haftungsprozessen geradezu einlädt und für sich selbst eine denkbar schlechte Ausgangslage schafft. So soll das vorgeschlagene Dokument auf mögliche Problemfelder hinweisen, die von der Prüfung nicht abgedeckt werden. Wenn Problemfelder für die Revisionsfragen nicht relevant sind, hat die Revisionsstelle darüber nicht zu befinden. Sind sie relevant, müssen sie geprüft werden. Wie verhält es sich aber, wenn irrelevante Problemfelder später, in der ex-post-Betrachtung, revisionsrelevant erscheinen? Der Vorwurf an die Revisionsstelle ist dann nahe liegend. Je mehr die Revisionsstelle zu prüfen verspricht, desto grösser ist ihre Angriffsfläche bei Haftungsfragen. Die Gestaltung des individuellen Verhältnisses zwischen der Revisionsstelle und der Aktiengesellschaft sollte sich deshalb auf das Minimum, den Revisionsbericht, beschränken. Darüber hinausgehende Berichterstattungen (Erläuterungen, Erkenntnisse etc.) sollten aus dem konkreten Verhältnis hervorgehen.

Kapitel 3: Allgemeine Prüfungshandlungen

2. Ergänzende Aufträge

Wie eingangs erwähnt, besteht für eine Gesellschaft die Möglichkeit, einer Revisionsstelle Aufgaben und Pflichten aufzuerlegen, die über das gesetzliche Erfordernis hinausgehen. In solchen Fällen kann ein Bestätigungsschreiben, das den individuell ausgestalteten Aufgabenkatalog schriftlich festhält, sinnvoll sein. Die Revisionsstelle muss sich aber bei den festgehaltenen Aufgaben behaften lassen und kann sich später nicht mehr darauf berufen, dass das Gesetz weniger weit gehende Pflichten vorschreibe. Die Haftung der Revisionsstelle bezüglich solcher zusätzlicher Aufgaben beurteilt sich nach den Regeln über den Auftrag, wobei zu bemerken ist, dass diese vertragliche Haftung im Verhältnis Gesellschaft/Auftragnehmer vor allem bezüglich der Beweislast für die Revisionsstelle ungünstiger ist (beachte Exkulpationsbeweis) als die gesetzliche Revisionshaftung.

II. Neumandate

Die Voraussetzungen für die Annahme eines Mandates sind nachfolgend dargelegt.

Die Revisoren müssen im Sinne des Gesetzes befähigt sein, ihre Aufgabe bei der zu prüfenden Gesellschaft zu erfüllen, dies bedeutet, dass sie zugelassene Revisoren oder zugelassene Revisionsexperten sein müssen. Die Laienrevision ist nur gestattet, sofern die Gesellschaft durch Beschluss auf eine eingeschränkte Revision verzichten könnte Je grösser und komplexer die zu prüfende Gesellschaft ist, desto grösser sind auch die fachlichen Anforderungen, die an einen Revisor zu stellen sind. Mindestens sind jedoch auch in der Laienrevision Grundkenntnisse über Buchhaltung und Jahresabschluss, Vertrautheit mit wirtschaftlichen Zusammenhängen und den Grundsätzen ordnungsmässiger Rechnungslegung sowie gewisse Grundkenntnisse im Aktienrecht und Unternehmenssteuerrecht unerlässlich.

Bei der Gründung einer Aktiengesellschaft ist die Annahmeerklärung der Revisionsstelle in schriftlicher Form mit den Gründungsakten dem Handelsregister einzureichen. Bei einer bestehenden Gesellschaft erfolgt die Wahl, aber auch die Abberufung, anlässlich der Generalversammlung. Die Revisionsstelle kann für höchstens drei Jahre gewählt werden, wobei eine Wiederwahl zulässig ist.

Die Revisionsstelle steht in einem doppelten Verhältnis zur Gesellschaft. Auf der einen Seite ist der gesetzliche Prüfungsauftrag mit der angenehmen Seite einer Auftragserteilung (auftragsähnliches Verhältnis) und Honorarerwartung verbunden und auf der anderen Seite stehen klare Erwartungen des Umfeldes der Aktiengesellschaft, diese Jahresrechnung unabhängig und kritisch zu prüfen. Diesen Anforderungen gewachsen zu sein ist schwierig und mancher Revisor erfüllt diese Voraussetzungen nicht. Dabei liegen die Probleme oft weniger im fachlichen Bereich, als vielmehr in solchen der persönlichen Unabhängigkeit.

Unabhängig ist der Revisor dann, wenn er jederzeit ohne Reue vom Revisionsmandat zurücktreten kann, also darauf nicht angewiesen ist.

Bei Neumandaten kommt oft die Anfrage des Kostenrahmens als erste Hürde. Natürlich sucht man die Arbeit und das Mandat. Kostenprognosen sind zulässig und auch sinnvoll. Das Honorarbudget darf aber auf keinen Fall verbindlich und fix sein. Es darf eine unabhängige Prüfung nicht einschränken. Eine im Honorar beschränkte und somit billige Revision kann sehr teuer zu stehen kommen, wenn notwendige Kontrollen unterbleiben und sich anschliessend Haftungsfragen stellen. Anstehende Sanierungen können damit zu spät erkannt werden und zu kostspieligen Entwicklungen führen.

Als erster Schritt zur Abklärung der Verhältnisse gehört die Kommunikation mit dem Verwaltungsrat. Ohne die neuen Ansprechpartner zu brüskieren, gibt es einfache Kontrollmechanismen. Preiswert erhält die gesetzliche Revisionsstelle als erste nützliche Information ohne weiteres einen Betreibungsauszug. Zudem kann ein Handelsregisterauszug eingefordert werden. Hat die Revisionsstelle bereits mehrere Male gewechselt, muss dies hinterfragt werden.

Zu beachten ist, dass Revisionen in der Regel vor Ort stattfinden sollten. Dies erlaubt auch, einen Einblick in das Unternehmen zu gewinnen. Revisionen im Büro des Revisors mit Buchhaltung und Bankbelegen sind im ersten Jahr nicht angebracht.

Prüfungshandlung:
- Einsicht in das Protokoll zur Gründerversammlung (Wahl der Revisionsstelle)

An dieser Stelle sei auch erwähnt, dass der Verwaltungsrat eine gewisse Verantwortung für die Wahl der gesetzlichen Revisionsstelle hat. Bemerkt er Inkompetenz, muss er die Generalversammlung orientieren.

III. Bestehende Mandate

So wie Neumandate ihre Risiken haben, werfen auch bestehende Mandate ihre Probleme auf. Ansatzpunkt ist hier das gewachsene Vertrauen und die oft bestehende freundschaftliche Geschäftsbeziehung, welche kritische Ansätze untergehen lässt (es ist ja immer gut gegangen und die jetzige Krise wird auch gemeistert, wie schon oft). Ein Ende wird nicht gesetzt und kann mental oft nicht gesetzt werden. Derartige Krisensituationen gehören zu den komplexesten Situationen bei langjährigen Verhältnissen. Oft ist oder wird die Revisionsstelle zum Berater. Der Geschäftsabschluss wird von ihr so geformt, dass er «steht». Die Überschuldung (als Beispiel) wird durch Bilanzkosmetik vertuscht und dann mit gutem Gewissen mit Bericht der Revisionsstelle bestätigt. Oft werden noch Protokolle und Dokumente erstellt, die Glaubwürdigkeit und Überzeugung verschaffen sollen. Von derartigen Übungen ist ohne die Gewissheit und die absolute Überzeugung, Abstand zu nehmen. Es ist nicht die Aufgabe der Revisionsstelle, der Gesellschaft zu helfen, sondern sie zu prüfen. Dies muss sie sich immer vor Augen halten. Im Zweifel ist ein anderer Weg zu wählen.

Die jährliche Abschlussprüfung wird im Einvernehmen mit dem Mandanten zeitlich und sachlich vorbereitet. Die Vorbereitung beinhaltet im Wesentlichen eine sorgfältige Zeit- und Terminplanung sowie sachliche Vorbereitungsarbeiten sowohl seitens des Prüfers (Prüfungsplan, Durchsicht der Dauerakten und der Arbeitspapiere der letzten Revision, Vorbereitung der Arbeitspapiere), als auch seitens des Mandanten (Orientierung der Mitarbeiter, Bereitstellen der Jahresrechnung und aller prüfungspflichtiger Unterlagen).

Einzige Prüfungshandlung:
- Vorliegen eines Protokolls zur letzten Generalversammlung und Protokollierung der Wahl der Revisionsstelle.

IV. Verdeckte Gewinnausschüttung

1. Begriff

Verdeckte Gewinnausschüttungen sind nicht geschäftsmässig begründete Aufwendungen, oder anders gesagt, Aufwand zulasten der Erfolgrechnung ohne entsprechende geschäftsmässige Grundlage.

Der Begriff der verdeckten Gewinnausschüttung ist hauptsächlich im Steuerrecht dokumentiert. Die offene Gewinnausschüttung ist zulässig und üblich. Dabei handelt es sich i.d.R. um die Verbuchung und Auszahlung der ordentlichen Dividende: 65 % an den Aktionär und 35 % an die Eidgenössische Steuerverwaltung als Quellensteuer. Der Aktionär deklariert seine Dividende, versteuert diese und erhält die an den Bund gezahlte Verrechnungssteuer vom Kanton zurück. Um die Quellensteuer zu umgehen und die Versteuerung damit zu vermeiden, besteht immer der Anreiz, verdeckte Gewinnausschüttungen vorzunehmen. Der Phantasie solcher geldwerten Vorteile sind keine Grenzen gesetzt und die Steuerdoktrin hat dazu eine umfassende Literatur erarbeitet.

Verdeckte Gewinnausschüttungen als Beispiele:

- unentgeltlich erbrachte Warenlieferungen
- unentgeltlich erbrachte Dienstleistungen
- Leistungen aller Art zu untersetzten Preisen
- übersetzte Zinsgutschriften
- Gratis-Kredite
- etc.

Dabei sind solche verdeckte Leistungen steuerlich nur relevant, wenn sie an die Aktionäre oder nahe stehende Personen gehen. Gehen diese an unbeteiligte Dritte, so ist dies Sache der Gesellschaft. Meistens sind solche Geschäfte dann auch geschäftlich begründet (z.B. als Werbegeschenk, Spende oder Public Relation). Die aktienrechtliche Beurteilung folgt dem im Grundsatz.

Der Revisor, welcher solche verdeckten Gewinnausschüttungen sieht, muss analysieren, wie er sich verhalten soll. Als erstes muss er die möglichen Steuerfolgen eines solchen Vorganges berechnen und bei der Gesamtbeurteilung berücksichtigen. Verdeckte Gewinnausschüttungen reduzieren das Kapital. Ein zweites Problem kann auftauchen, wenn der Revisor zusätzlich zur Revision die Steuererklärung für die Gesellschaft erledigt. Es ist ohne weiteres möglich, dass damit die Frage der Gehilfenschaft zur Steuerhinterziehung aktuell wird – eine höchst schwierige Situation. Das dritte und grösste Problem wird auftreten, wenn die verdeckten Gewinnausschüttungen nicht gleichmässig an alle Aktionäre gehen. Spätestens hier werden die Probleme unüberbrückbar. Die Verantwortlichkeit des Revisors wird aktuell, wenn er nicht darüber berichtet. Sobald sich ein Aktionär hintergangen fühlt, folgen unweigerlich unangenehme Fragen an die Revisionsstelle.

2. *Verhalten*

Ein Revisor kann es sich nicht leisten, solchen Problemen aus dem Weg zu gehen. Er muss ganz klar zur Aufklärung des Sachverhaltes beitragen. Bagatellbeträge fordern erhöhte Aufmerksamkeit, wesentliche Beträge verlangen umfassende Aufklärung. Ist ihm der Sachverhalt klar, muss er überlegen, ob unter Berücksichtigung der Interessen aller Aktionäre und der Gläubiger der Gesellschaft eine ordentliche Berichterstattung erfolgen kann.

Die verdeckte Gewinnausschüttung verhindert einen ordnungsgemässen Gewinnverwendungsvorschlag (Gewinnausschüttung über Aufwand anstelle Gewinnvortrag) und führt zu einer inhaltlich unwahren Erfolgsrechnung (Gewinn als Aufwand). Ein Standardbericht in Kenntnis von verdeckten Gewinnausschüttungen ist inhaltlich nicht richtig (vgl. dazu Prüfungsstandard 240).

V. Beizug externer Berater

Der Beizug externer Berater ist ein Tabuthema. Jeder Revisor fühlt sich a priori sicher und scheut sich, externe Berater anzufragen. Es ist jedoch die Empfehlung abzugeben, in kritischen Situationen fremde Hilfe in Anspruch zu nehmen. Die Revisionsstelle ist an die gesetzliche Schweigepflicht gebunden, sie kann jedoch Fachleute, die ihrerseits an das Berufsgeheimnis gebunden sind, um Rat fragen.

Oft ist die Revisionsstelle nicht nur unabhängiges Kontrollorgan, sondern auch durch langjährige Aufgabenerfüllung geschätztes Beraterorgan. In solchen Beziehungsnetzen fehlt manchmal die notwendige Distanz. Bei problematischen Situationen sollte deshalb eine Fragestellung an einen unabhängigen Dritten nicht gescheut werden.

VI. Unabhängigkeit der Revisionsstelle

Nach neuem Recht ist die Frage der Unabhängigkeit ausführlicher behandelt worden und für die «Ordentliche Revision» und den «Review» unterschiedlich bestimmt.

Die Frage der Unabhängigkeit der Revisionsstelle ist ein Thema, welches die Treuhänder stark beschäftigt. Das Gesetz fordert unabhängige Revisoren. Treuhänder, welche diese Mandate ausüben, sind Generalisten für Kleinunternehmen und nicht nur auf dem Gebiete der Prüfungsrevision tätig; sie erledigen für die zu prüfende Aktiengesellschaft auch andere Mandate. Zwangsläufig haben Treuhänder ein wirtschaftliches Interesse daran, den Begriff der «Unabhängigkeit» nicht allzu strikte auszulegen.

Sicherlich kann der Gesetzgeber nicht verlangen, dass eine ganze Branche neu strukturiert wird. Es ist jedoch wünschenswert, wenn die Revisionsstellen künftig neutraler besetzt werden.

In einem nächsten Schritt soll der Begriff der Unabhängigkeit umschrieben werden, dies soweit sie für den Review gesetzlich umschrieben ist. Art. 728 OR umschreibt dies für die ordentliche Revision enger als Art. 729 OR für die eingeschränkte Revision, wobei die Zielsetzung für beide Revisionsrichtungen naturgemäss dieselbe sein muss.

1. Persönliche Unabhängigkeit

Unabhängig ist man als Revisor dann nicht, wenn enge persönliche oder verwandtschaftliche Beziehungen zwischen Revisor und Personen der Aktiengesellschaft (insbesondere dem Verwaltungsrat) bestehen. Damit besteht eine Parallelität zur ordentlichen Revision.

Die Personalunion von Verwaltungsrat und Revisionsstelle ist unmöglich. Darin eingeschlossen ist das Revisionsstellenmandat einer Prüfungs-AG, bei welcher der Verwaltungsrat der zu prüfenden AG angestellt ist. Darin eingeschlossen sind auch Doppelgesellschaften. Eine Beratungs-AG und eine Revisions-AG bieten keine Gewähr für eine unabhängige Revision bei engen Beziehungen zum Verwaltungsrat.

Das Problem der engen Beziehung ist bei Kleingesellschaften eine Crux. Gerade hier spielen persönliche Beziehungen eine bedeutende Rolle und ohne persönlichen Konnex schenkt der Verwaltungsrat als Alleinaktionär einem Unbekannten für die Revision nicht das nötige Vertrauen. Und wenn dann noch einem Verwandten oder Freund ein Auftrag in Form der Revision zugeschanzt werden kann, wird dies als Tugend angesehen. Hier muss ganz klar erkannt werden, dass das Aktienrecht keine Unterscheidung von grossen und kleinen Aktiengesellschaften macht. Gefordert ist allgemein eine unabhängige Revisionsstelle.

In die Rubrik der persönlich belasteten Revisionen gehören auch die sog. «Kreuzrevisionen» (diese sind bei Treuhandgesellschaften verbreitet): «Ich revidiere dich, du revidierst mich.» Solche Konstellationen genügen dem Erfordernis der Unabhängigkeit nicht. Solche Kreuzrevisionen sind auch in einer erweiterten Form (z.B. über die Verwaltung) unzulässig.

Die Unabhängigkeit erfordert, dass der Revisor jederzeit dem Verwaltungsrat uneingeschränkt seine Revisionsmeinung sagen kann, ohne auf Beziehungsnetze Rücksicht nehmen zu müssen. Ein Abbruch der geschäftlichen Beziehung muss jederzeit sofort möglich sein.

2. *Finanzielle Unabhängigkeit*

Als neutrale Revisionsstelle muss man jederzeit vollkommen finanziell unabhängig sein. Dies bedeutet, dass man zu keiner Zeit auf das Revisionshonorar angewiesen sein darf, sowohl vor der Prüfung als auch nach der Prüfung: Vor der Prüfung deshalb, um keiner Erwartungshaltung ausgesetzt zu sein. Der Revisor prüft, ohne durch das Revisionshonorar beeinflusst zu werden. Sowohl im zu hohen Revisionshonorar (als möglicher Ausgangspunkt für eine Gefälligkeitsprüfung), als auch im zu niedrigen Revisionshonorar (als faktische Einschränkung der Revision) liegt eine Gefahr. Aus diesem Grund dürfen Revisionshonorare in der Offerte nie verbindlich limitiert sein. Der gesetzliche Revisionsauftrag würde dadurch unzulässig eingeschränkt. Ein Revisionsmandat darf zu keiner wirtschaftlichen Abhängigkeit führen.

Zur finanziellen Unabhängigkeit gehören nicht nur das Honorar, sondern auch andere finanzielle Beziehungen. Darlehen von Personen der Revisionsgesellschaft an Personen der zu prüfenden Aktiengesellschaft und umgekehrt sind tabu.

Ausgeschlossen ist auch eine massgebliche Beteiligung des Revisors an der zu prüfenden Aktiengesellschaft. Eine Beteiligung von wenigen Prozenten dürfte jedoch in der Regel zulässig sein. Was darüber geht, beeinträchtigt die unabhängige Revision. Je höher die Beteiligung ist, desto grösser ist die Abhängigkeit des Revisors.

3. Strukturelle Unabhängigkeit

Die Revisionsstelle darf nicht strukturell mit der zu prüfenden Revisionsgesellschaft verbunden sein. Es kann sein, dass personelle, finanzielle oder andere Beziehungen bestehen, die einzeln betrachtet nicht die Unabhängigkeit gefährden, aber in der Summe dann zu einer Struktur führen, welche die Unabhängigkeit der Revisionsgesellschaft zu sehr einschränkt.

Beispiel: Revisor und Verwaltungsrat kennen sich seit dem Studium. Die Revision wird seit zwanzig Jahren vom gleichen Revisor durchgeführt. Der Revisor ist mit 10 % an der Aktiengesellschaft beteiligt. Der Schwiegervater des Revisors gewährte der Gesellschaft ein Darlehen (10 % der Passiven). Dieses Beziehungsgefüge muss nicht unbedingt die Unabhängigkeit beeinträchtigen, kann aber. Im Einzelfall ist dies zu analysieren.

4. Unabhängigkeit bei Revision und Buchführung

Werden Buchführung und Revision von in enger personeller Verbundenheit stehenden Personen ausgeführt, ist das Erfordernis der unabhängigen Revision nicht erfüllt. Es gibt Vorschläge, diese Kombination zuzulassen, sofern eine personelle Unabhängigkeit besteht. Unserer Meinung nach führen Buchführung und Revision in Personalunion oder über nahe stehende Gesellschaften primär zu einer nicht unabhängigen Revision. Dies muss nicht unbedingt zutreffen; der konkrete Einzelfall erfordert eine individuelle Betrachtung. Diese Ausgangslage führt aber zu einer Umkehrsituation. Die Revisionsstelle muss darlegen, dass sie trotz Buchführung unabhängig ist. Das neue Gesetz erlaubt für den Review das Mitwirken des Revisors bei der Buchführung, sofern das Risiko der Überprüfung eigener Arbeiten ausgeschlossen ist.

5. Erwartungsunabhängige Haltung

Die Unabhängigkeit ist dann nicht mehr gegeben, wenn gegenüber der Revisionsstelle eine Erwartungshaltung besteht, mit anderen Worten, wenn die Revisionsstelle den Eindruck hat, man erwarte von ihr mehr als nur die gesetzliche Revision, nämlich ein bestimmtes Ergebnis.

Der Revisor muss sich deshalb die Frage stellen, ob er auch das schlechtest mögliche Revisionsergebnis jederzeit der Verwaltung vortragen kann. Dass diese Mitteilung unangenehm ist, dürfte klar sein. In der Regel führt sie auch zur Beendigung des Mandates. Sie muss aber aus der Sicht des Revisors jederzeit verkraftbar erscheinen.

Die Frage der Unabhängigkeit ist abstrakt zwar klar formuliert, konkret kann dies jedoch meistens nur im Einzelfall beurteilt werden. Viele Umschreibungen dazu nützen nichts. Oft ist ein Element in der Beziehung Verwaltung/Revisor vorhanden, welches die Unabhängigkeit berührt. Dies schadet nicht und ist unvermeidlich. Am Schluss muss kritisch beurteilt werden. Letztlich geht es für die Revisionsstelle um eine Güterabwägung: Revision und Honorar oder keine Revision und kein Honorar. Im Hinblick auf die Verantwortung ist manchmal weniger mehr.

VII. Rücktritt der Revisionsstelle

Aus verschiedenen Gründen kann die Revisionsstelle geneigt sein, zurückzutreten. Der Schritt ist genau zu überlegen und kann mehr Probleme schaffen als lösen.

1. Einfacher Rücktritt

In der Regel können problemlose Rücktritte erfolgen, wenn das Revisionshonorar nicht bezahlt wird oder wurde. Die Revisionsstelle will nicht mehr handeln. Hat sich die Revisionsstelle nach Mahnungen etc. entschlossen, nicht mehr zu fungieren, empfiehlt sich eine rasche Beendigung mit Nachricht an die Gesellschaft und folgend an das Handelsregister.

Auch wenige Probleme bietet der Umstand, dass der Verwaltungsrat die erforderliche Jahresrechnung mit Buchhaltung und Geschäftsbericht nicht vorlegt. Die Revisionsstelle kann nicht mehr handeln.

Der Rücktritt ist schriftlich der Gesellschaft und dem Handelsregister anzuzeigen. In der Rücktrittserklärung muss eine Begründung aufgeführt sein. Neu ist bei vorzeitigem Rücktritt der Revisionsstelle der Grund im Anhang zu nennen.

2. *Problemhafter Rücktritt*

Der Rücktritt kann nicht dazu dienen, Problemen aus dem Weg zu gehen. Werden wesentliche Buchungsvorgänge nicht erläutert, bleibt nur die Anzeige der Revisionsstelle an die Generalversammlung. Dies wird von der Revisionsstelle erwartet und sie kann sich dem nicht durch Abgang entziehen. Aus der Sicht der Verantwortlichkeit der Revisionsstelle bringt eine Abwahl durch die Generalversammlung weitaus weniger Probleme als ein Rücktritt. Im ersten Fall kann die Revisionsstelle nicht mehr handeln, im zweiten Fall will sie nicht mehr handeln.

Problematisch sind deshalb Rücktritte in kritischen Situationen, so bei:

- Überschuldung
- verdeckter Gewinnausschüttung
- strafrechtlich relevantem Verhalten der Verwaltung
- Bestechungsversuchen der Verwaltung gegenüber der Revisionsstelle
- Rücktritt zur Unzeit
- etc.

Solche Situationen stellen hohe Ansprüche und die Revisionsstelle als Organ muss gemäss ihrem gesetzlichen Auftrag handeln. Dies kann dazu führen, dass Verwaltung und Revisionsstelle zu Gegenparteien werden.

VIII. Mögliche Überschuldung

1. *Die Feststellung*

In diesem Teil wird der Revisor auf die Problemstellung einer möglichen Überschuldung sensibilisiert (vgl. dazu Prüfungsstandards 290 und 570).

Stellt ein Revisor fest, dass eine mögliche Überschuldung vorliegt, so muss er handeln. Bei offensichtlicher Überschuldung ist der Richter zu benachrichtigen, und zwar unverzüglich nach Fristansetzung gegenüber der Verwaltung (dies sowohl bei der ordentlichen Prüfung als auch beim Review). Eine Überschuldung zeigt sich häufig noch nicht in einem Untergang der produktiven Bereiche. Oft funktionieren diese noch gut und gerade dies kann die Revisionsstelle dazu veranlassen, von den nötigen Vorkehren abzusehen. Solange Arbeit vorhanden ist und Aussicht auf Geschäfte und Umsatz besteht, wird Hoffnung auf Gesundung des Unternehmens gehegt werden. Zu berücksichtigen sind jedoch nicht nur die Arbeitsplätze des Betriebes, sondern auch die Interessen von Lieferanten und Kreditgebern, welche in der Zukunft noch mehr zu Schaden kommen werden und nur gestützt auf einen Prüfungsattest der Revisionsstelle weiter mitwirken.

In solchen Situationen gibt es nur zwei Varianten: sofort frisches Geld (Sacheinlagen genügen wegen mangelnder Liquidität häufig nicht) als Eigenkapital oder den Gang zum Richter mit Überschuldungsanzeige. Das frische Geld muss zu einer sofortigen Kapitalerhöhung mit Sanierung führen. Dies ist oft schwer möglich, da in serbelnden Kleinbetrieben der Betriebsinhaber seine ganzen Barreserven ins Geschäft investiert hat. Meistens naht deswegen doch das notwendige Ende. Der Gang zum Richter bedeutet jedoch nicht unbedingt die Liquidation. Der Richter kann auch bei einer Sanierung im Rahmen des Schuldbetreibungs- und Konkursverfahrens mitwirken. Scheuen Sie diesen Schritt nicht. Eine unabhängige richterliche Beurteilung über die Zukunftsfähigkeit des Unternehmens ist einer freundschaftlichen Beurteilung durch die vielleicht nicht mehr ganz unabhängige Revisionsstelle vorzuziehen. Die gerichtliche Sanierung bietet für die Revisionsstelle keine Haftungsfragen.

Sollte der Revisor bei einer notwendigen Überschuldungsanzeige unsicher sein oder hat er Zweifel und will nicht nur aufgrund von Zweifeln urteilen oder verurteilen, so sollte er dem Verwaltungsrat vorschlagen, eine kurze und summarische Beurteilung durch einen Dritten vornehmen zu lassen.

Beispiel Musterschreiben Revision an den Verwaltungsrat:

Sehr geehrte Herren

Die momentane Bilanz zeigt nicht gerade ein erfreuliches Ergebnis und es scheint ratsam für Ihre Gesellschaft, eine summarische Beurteilung der Finanzlage durch einen unabhängigen Experten vornehmen zu lassen. Die Einholung einer unabhängigen Beurteilung in einer kritisch erscheinen-

den Situation entspricht meiner Praxis und sie kann Ihnen und mir vielleicht neue Erkenntnisse bringen.

Beispiel Musterschreiben an einen unabhängigen Fachmann:

Sehr geehrter Herr Kollege

Ich bitte Sie freundlich um Prüfung der beigelegten Bilanz und Erfolgsrechnung. Wie beurteilen Sie die Situation? Ich bitte Sie, eine kurze Beurteilung zu verfassen, die Sie an Herrn Verwaltungsrat XX und in Kopie an mich richten wollen. Ihre Beurteilung soll summarisch sein und keine Revision beinhalten.

Die neutrale Beurteilung wird Bestätigung der Überschuldungsvermutung oder Entwarnung geben. Wir verweisen auf das Kapitel Berichterstattung.

2. Das Entstehen der Überschuldung (auch als Exkurs)

Eine Überschuldung liegt vor, wenn mehr Passiven als Aktiven bestehen. Das Kapitel der Überschuldung ist weit gefasst und insbesondere die Darstellung der Entstehung ist mit einem Beispiel ausführlich beschrieben. Dies aus zwei Gründen: Die Verantwortlichkeit der Revisionsstelle wird am häufigsten bei einer Insolvenz aktuell. Hier gilt also besonderes Augenmerk. Weiter ist die schleichende Verschuldung besonders schwierig zu erkennen. Ist bereits eine Überschuldung vorhanden oder ist es bloss eine vorübergehende schlechte aktuelle Geschäftslage?

In der Schweiz gibt es zurzeit viele Konkurse (mit hohen Verlustwerten). Oft sind es kleine Firmen, manchmal mittlere und grössere, die dann Eingang in die Berichterstattung der Medien finden. Die erhöhte Anzahl von zahlungsunfähigen Firmen ist eine aktuelle Zeiterscheinung und hängt mit der gegenwärtigen Konjunkturlage zusammen. Die Rezession der vergangenen Jahre ist noch nicht verdaut und die Anzeichen der wirtschaftlichen Erholung sind noch zu wenig deutlich, um die Krise zu meistern. Die leichte Verbesserung leidet am starken Schweizer Franken, der unsere stark exportorientierte Wirtschaft trifft. Die Folge dieser Situation ist eine Zunahme der Konkurse. Es bleibt zu hoffen, dass sich mit einem konjunkturell verbesserten Umfeld die Lage wieder zum Guten wendet. Bei der Variante des Konkurses ohne vorgängige Betreibung stellt der zahlungsunfähige Schuldner beim Gericht ein Konkursbegehren (sog. Insolvenzerklärung). Der Richter urteilt dann darüber, ob der Konkurs eröffnet wird. Zuerst muss die Überschuldung festgestellt werden. Wie stark diese ist, geht aus der Bilanz hervor. Eine geringe Überschuldung führt dazu, dass die Schuldner im Konkurs eine weitgehende Befriedigung erfahren dürfen. Leider ist dies in den seltensten Fällen so. Meist gehen viele Schuldner leer aus. Dies ist die Konsequenz mehrerer Umstände. Oft ist der Konkurs das Resultat eines jahrelangen Prozesses. Anstatt sich der kritischen Situation zu stellen, wird lamentiert und hinausgezögert, bis die Situation hoffnungslos ist und das Kartenhaus zusammenbricht. So gehen viele Gläubiger leer aus; eine frühzeitige Insolvenz hätte zu einer höheren Dividende geführt.

Beispiel:

Ein Unternehmen weist laufenden Umsatzrückgang mit gleich bleibenden Kosten aus. Um die laufenden Aufwendungen zu decken, werden der Betriebskredit der Bank wie auch die Hypothek auf der Betriebsliegenschaft ausgeschöpft. In der Bilanz wird auf der Liegenschaft nicht mehr abgeschrieben, um nicht zu viel Verlust auszuweisen. Ein neuer Manager wird eingesetzt, der ebenfalls Geld (mit einem Darlehen) einbringt. Um dann beispielsweise für einen Betriebsumbau weitere Finanzmittel zur Verfügung zu haben, wird bei der Bank ein Begehren um Hypothekarerhöhung gestellt. Diese verlangt eine Schätzung der Liegenschaft. Der Bericht des Schatzers zuhanden der Bank zeigt den jahrelangen Mangel im Unterhalt. Sanierungen sind notwendig, die Liegenschaft ist überbewertet. Die Bank verlangt weitere Eigenmittel des Unternehmers, die nicht vorhanden sind. Sie entschliesst sich, den Kredit und die Hypothek zu kündigen. Es kann kein weiterer Bankkredit organisiert werden, die Firma geht in Konkurs. Eine aktuelle Bilanz zeigt nun eine plötzliche Überschuldung. Die Liegenschaft ist zu einem wesentlich zu hohen Wert bilanziert, die Guthaben der Unternehmung sind gegenüber ihren Kunden etwas zu optimistisch gewesen und erfahren nun eine Korrektur.

Das kurze Beispiel soll zeigen, wie eine Intervention sich massiv auf die Guthaben der Gläubiger auswirken kann. Es soll nicht der Eindruck erweckt werden, dass der Entscheid über das Bestehen einer Unternehmung bei der Bank liegen würde. Die Finanzierung ist nur ein Teil. Diese bereitet keine Probleme, wenn der Betrieb gut geführt und das Rechnungswesen à jour ist. Es kann immer wieder vorkommen, dass ein Unternehmen in Konkurs gerät, sei es durch eine unvorhersehbare negative Entwicklung oder ausserordentliche Faktoren. Oft ist aber eine jahrelange Misswirtschaft diesem Ereignis vorausgegangen, weshalb den verantwortlichen Organen ein Vorwurf zu machen ist. Bis aber aus einem Vorwurf Verantwortung und aus Verantwortung klagbarer Schadenersatzanspruch entsteht, ist ein langer Weg. Und ob dann aus diesem Prozess bare Münze hervorgeht, steht auf einem ganz anderen Blatt. So muss für jeden Gläubiger gelten: «trau, schau wem».

Der Richter erhält vom zahlungsunfähigen Unternehmen oder von einem Gläubiger im Betreibungsverfahren den Antrag auf Konkurs. Sind alle Aktiven gänzlich verloren, so wird der Konkurs mangels Aktiven eingestellt. Sind noch Aktiven da, folgt das Konkursverfahren. Alle Aktiven und Passiven werden festgestellt. Daraus resultiert der Anteil, die Konkursdividende. Wegen der starken Belastung der Konkursämter kann dieses Verfahren längere Zeit dauern, je nach Umfang der Firma auch Jahre. Nach Bezahlung der Konkursdividende ist das Verfahren beendet und die Firma erloschen.

Nur die im Handelsregister eintragungspflichtigen Unternehmen unterliegen der Beitreibung auf Konkurs, so die Aktiengesellschaft, die Gesellschaft mit beschränkter Haftung, kaufmännische Kollektiv- und Kommanditgesellschaften sowie gewisse Einzelfirmen, um nur ein paar Beispiele zu nennen. Die anderen Personen, insbesondere natürliche Personen, unterliegen i.d.R. der Betreibung auf Pfändung. Hier werden nicht alle Aktiven und Passiven ermittelt, sondern es wird nur soviel gepfändet, als zur Tilgung der betriebenen Forderung(en) nötig ist.

Nicht immer braucht ein Konkurs ausgesprochen zu werden. Kann das Unternehmen glaubhaft machen, dass Aussicht auf einen Nachlassvertrag besteht, so gewährt der Richter diesem eine Nachlassstundung. Der Nachlassvertrag kommt zustande, wenn ihm eine (qualifizierte) Mehrheit der Gläubiger zustimmt und der Richter ihn bewilligt. Wird dem Nachlassgesuch entsprochen, erhalten die Gläubiger nur eine Dividende (z.B. 60 %) und das Unternehmen kann weiter bestehen. Dieser Weg ist aber regelmässig nur dann gangbar, wenn die Gläubiger bei einem Nachlass besserfahren als bei einem Konkurs, denn ansonsten würden die Gläubiger dem Nachlassvertrag sehr wahrscheinlich nicht zustimmen. Es ist also nicht gesagt, dass bei einer konkursiten Situation schon alles verloren ist. Oft wird aber nicht rechtzeitig gehandelt, was auf Kosten der Gläubiger geschieht. Langes Zuwarten führt dann nicht nur zum Verlust des Eigenkapitals, sondern auch des Fremdkapitals und damit letztendlich zum Verlust der meisten Forderungen.

Das Schuldbetreibungs- und Konkursgesetz wurde per 1.1.1997 revidiert. Das Grundprinzip wurde belassen. Die Revision hält am Bestehenden fest und führt einige neue Bausteine hinzu. Es bleibt zu hoffen, dass die wirtschaftliche Erholung anhält und damit die Zahl der Konkurse wieder abnimmt.

Mit dieser Darstellung soll gezeigt werden, dass bei einer Überschuldung meistens ein kontinuierlicher Vorgang vorliegt. Selten liegen plötzliche Insolvenzen vor. Gerade deshalb ist für den Revisor die Erkennung schwierig. «Es ist in der Vergangenheit immer gut gegangen, schwere Zeiten wurden überbrückt. Weshalb soll es jetzt nicht auch gut gehen?»

3. Das Problem der faktisch «unbeschränkten Haftung» des Hauptaktionärs

Bei Personengesellschaften werden immer wieder Fragen der Haftung gestellt. Tatsächlich ist es so, dass die Kollektivgesellschafter und Einzelfirmeninhaber unbeschränkt (und solidarisch) mit ihrem ganzen Vermögen für die Schulden der Gesellschaft haften.

Eine Insolvenz eines Partners führt dazu, dass sein Gesellschafteranteil in die Zwangsverwertung kommt. In aller Regel werden die verbleibenden Kollektivgesellschafter mit der Konkursverwaltung eine gütliche Einigung finden.

Somit beschränkt sich die Problematik auf die solidarische Haftung für Gesellschaftsschulden. Eine Überschuldung der Gesellschaft ist in der Regel auf einen kontinuierlichen Prozess zurückzuführen. Plötzliche Überschuldungen sind die Ausnahme (gehen z.B. aus versicherungsrechtlich nicht gedeckten Unfällen hervor). Damit beschränkt sich die Entstehung einer Überschuldung in aller Regel auf eine zeitlich längerfristige Entwicklung.

Wenn nunmehr versucht wird, die Überschuldung durch Umwandlung der Personengesellschaft in eine Aktiengesellschaft zu beschränken, so muss festgestellt werden, dass eine kontinuierliche Entwicklung einer Überschuldung auch mit einer Aktiengesellschaft in aller Regel nicht abgewendet werden kann. Meistens werden Bankkredite und andere Finanzierungen in Anspruch genommen. Solche frischen Gelder fliessen in aller

Regel nicht ohne eine Bürgschaft der Aktionäre in die Gesellschaft. In der Folge kann eine Überschuldung mit dem beschränkten Kapital der Gesellschaft nicht vermieden werden. Die Fälle sind selten, bei denen eine Aktiengesellschaft, welche sich in wenigen Händen befindet, in Konkurs gerät und die Aktionäre nicht auch in persönliche Haftung (z.B. aus Bürgschaft) genommen wurden. In den meisten Fällen führt dies zu Pfändungen oder zu einem Privatkonkurs. Wirft man einen Blick auf bestehende Kreditverträge, so muss man meistens feststellen, dass sich die Bank nicht mit dem Gesellschaftsvermögen als Sicherheit begnügt hat (beispielsweise fordert sie Grundpfandtitel der privaten Liegenschaft als Sicherheit).

Somit löst eine Aktiengesellschaft das Problem der Haftung oft nicht. Für ältere Verbindlichkeiten greift Art. 181 OR über die Geschäftsübernahme. Zwar besteht im Zeitpunkt der Gründung eine Beschränkung der Haftung für neue Gesellschaftsschulden, sobald sich aber Finanzierungsprobleme im Laufe der Entwicklung ergeben, besteht keine klare Haftungstrennung mehr. Damit lösen sich die Haftungsbeschränkungen auf.

Umso schwerer hat es der Revisor. Seine Beurteilung wirkt sich auch stark auf die privaten Verhältnisse des Aktionärs oder der Aktionäre aus. Mit einer Überschuldungsanzeige der AG ist oft auch der Privatkonkurs des Hauptaktionärs verbunden.

4. Der Rücktritt der Revisionsstelle

Die Niederlegung des Mandates durch die Revisionsstelle erfolgt in der Regel durch eingeschriebenen Brief an den Verwaltungspräsidenten zuhanden der Generalversammlung der Aktionäre. Dies muss insbesondere immer dann geschehen, wenn der Auftraggeber hinsichtlich Zeitdauer, Honorarkosten oder Prüfungsunterlagen Einschränkungen macht, die eine ausreichende Prüfung in Frage stellen.

Ist eine Revisionsstelle bereits im Handelsregister angemeldet, so muss sie ihren allfälligen Rücktritt dem Handelsregister auch melden. In der Regel verlangt das Register eine Begründung. Bei vorzeitigem Rücktritt bedarf es einer Offenlegung im Anhang.

Kapitel 3: Allgemeine Prüfungshandlungen

IX. Der «zugelassene Revisionsexperte»

Alle Gesellschaften, bei welchen zwei der nachstehenden Grössen in zwei aufeinander folgenden Geschäftsjahren überschritten werden, müssen sog. «zugelassene Revisionsexperten» wählen:

1) Bilanzsumme von CHF 10 Mio.
2) Umsatzerlös von CHF 20 Mio.
3) 50 Arbeitnehmer im Jahresdurchschnitt

§ 2 Prüfungsmethoden

Bei den Prüfungsmethoden sind die Prüfungsstandards 500 bis 593 zu berücksichtigen.

I. Prüfungsweg

Progressive Prüfung	Retrograde Prüfung
«vom Beleg in die Buchhaltung und bis zum Ergebnis in der Rechnungslegung	«vom Ergebnis in der Rechnungslegung in die Buchhaltung und zum Beleg»
(Beleg Buchhaltung→Rechnungslegung)	*(Rechnungslegung→Buchhaltung→Beleg)*
Prüfung der Vollständigkeit	Prüfung der Richtigkeit
Belegkontrolle	Ist die Buchung belegt?

II. Prüfungsumfang

Lückenlose Prüfung	Stichprobenweise Prüfung
Alle Geschäftsfälle werden vollumfänglich geprüft.	*Es wird nur eine Auswahl aller Geschäftsvorfälle geprüft.*

Anwendungen:	Anwendungen:
Lückenlose Prüfung erfolgt i.d.R. bei der Bilanz.	Bloss stichprobenweise Prüfung erfolgt i.d.R. bei der Erfolgsrechnung.
Lückenlose Prüfung erfolgt allgemein bei Unsicherheit.	

III. Direkte und indirekte Prüfung

Eine weitere Unterscheidung in der Art der Prüfung bildet die Gliederung in direkte und indirekte Prüfung:

Direkte Prüfung	Indirekte Prüfung
Die Buchungen werden unmittelbar mit dem entsprechenden Sachverhalt geprüft. Die Verbuchung wird ganz oder teilweise aufgrund der Buchungsbelege bis ins Einzelne nachgeprüft.	Der Prüfer beurteilt verschiedene Elemente des Jahresabschlusses aufgrund von Analysen und Überlegungen. Auch die Bildung von Kontrollsummen oder das Vergleichen und die Verwendung von Kennzahlen gehören zu den indirekten Prüfungshandlungen.
Das Prüfungsresultat kommt aufgrund von Nachprüfungen zustande.	Das Prüfungsresultat kommt aufgrund von Analysen zustande.

IV. Prüfungstechniken

1. Systematische Prüfungen

Prüfungstechnik	Beschreibung
Verkehrsprüfung	Prüfung der verbuchten Geschäftsvorfälle anhand der Belege. Prüfung der vollständigen Erfassung von Geschäftsfällen.
Totalprüfung/Detailprüfung	Feststellen der Richtigkeit einer Reihe gleichartiger Posten in einer Bilanzposition. Prüfung im Detail oder Total.

Kapitel 3: Allgemeine Prüfungshandlungen

Quellenprüfung	Lückenloses Verfolgen eines Geschäftsvorfalles vom Anfang bis zum Ende.
Kontierungsprüfung	Prüfung der Richtigkeit der aufgerufenen Konti bei der Belegverbuchung.
Übertragungsprüfung	Feststellung, ob die Zahlen korrekt auf die richtigen Konti übertragen wurden.
Bestandesprüfung	Reine Nachkontrolle. Feststellen des Vorhandenseins sowie des Eigentums (Aktiven) und der Vollständigkeit (Passiven).

2. Logische Prüfung

Prüfungstechnik	Beschreibung
Relationsprüfung	Prüfung basierend auf der zwingenden Abhängigkeit zwischen verschiedenen Positionen der Jahresrechnung. (Ein höherer Umsatz bedingt i.d.R. mehr Aufwand.)
Rechnerische Prüfung	Verifizieren durch Nachrechnen.
Bewertungsprüfung	Feststellen der vertretbaren Wertansätze für Aktiven und Passiven.
Verkehrsprüfung	Prüfung der Rechtmässigkeit und Erfassung von Geschäftsfällen innerhalb einer bestimmten Zeitperiode.
Kritische Durchsicht	Zum Festlegen der Stichprobe, zur Gewinnung des Überblicks, zur Abrundung eines Urteils.
Aktenstudium / Befragung	Prüfung buchmässig nicht erfasster Sachverhalte.

Nicht die Anwendung der einen oder der anderen Methode führt zum Ziel, sondern einzig die zweckmässige Kombination aller Prüfungsverfahren gewährleistet ein sicheres Prüfungsergebnis.

V. Überwachung des Mandates

Die Revisionsstelle hat, solange sie als solche amtet, das Mandat zu überwachen. Dafür ist eine zweckmässige Kontrollführung über die termingerechte Vorlage der Buchhaltung und des Jahresabschlusses für die Revision notwendig.

Es bedarf bei Revisionsgesellschaften einer Liste der zu revidierenden Gesellschaften. Sodann ist eine Fristenkontrolle zu führen, die orientiert, welche Gesellschaften ihre Jahresrechnung mit Buchhaltung und Geschäftsbericht vorgelegt haben und welche noch nicht. Das Gesetz verlangt eine Vorlage innerhalb von sechs Monaten nach Bilanzstichtag. Die Gesetzesvorschrift ist sanktionslos (lex imperfecta) und wird deshalb als blosse Ordnungsvorschrift aufgefasst. Für die Revisionsstelle bedeutet dies, dass erhöhte Aufmerksamkeit nach Ablauf der Frist gefordert ist. Laufende Ermahnungen müssen an den Verwaltungsrat folgen. Mindestens innerhalb eines Jahres nach Bilanzabschluss sollte die Revision durchgeführt sein. Von da an besteht die Vermutung, dass das Rechnungswesen nicht à jour und damit nicht aussagekräftig ist. Der Revisionsstelle steht selbstverständlich der Nachweis offen, dass dies nicht zutrifft. Damit soll nicht absolut gesagt sein, dass die Revisionsstelle von da an generell verantwortlich ist. Sie hat aber eine ungünstigere Ausgangslage und muss sich erklären.

Keine Revisionsgesellschaft kann es sich mehr leisten, Revisionsmandate nicht zu überwachen und «laufen zu lassen». Die notwendige Distanz wird nur durch einen Rücktritt erreicht. Die Revisionsstelle hat die Pflicht, offensichtlich überschuldete Gesellschaften beim Richter anzumelden, sofern der Verwaltungsrat nichts unternimmt. Dieser Pflicht kann sie nur durch eine einwandfrei geführte Fristenkontrolle nachkommen. Es gibt nichts Unangenehmeres, als von einem Gläubiger über den Konkurs einer Aktiengesellschaft orientiert zu werden, bei der man noch im Handelsregister als Revisionsstelle eingetragen ist und von der man seit längerer Zeit nichts mehr gehört hat. In diesem Zusammenhang ist auf die Prüfungsstandards 300 bis 399 über die Planung hinzuweisen.

Kapitel 3: Allgemeine Prüfungshandlungen

§ 3 Arbeitspapiere

Der Nachweis der Prüfungshandlungen wird durch die Arbeitspapiere und allenfalls durch den Erläuterungsbericht erbracht. Daneben gelten auch die Prüfungszeichen als Nachweis von Prüfungshandlungen. Arbeitspapiere und Prüfungsbericht ergänzen sich insofern, als der Revisor in der Lage sein muss, aus beiden zusammen das Prüfungsergebnis abzuleiten.

Gute Arbeitspapiere bedeuten ordentliche Arbeit und verlangen ein systematisches Vorgehen. Andererseits dürfen die Anforderungen an die Ausgestaltung der Arbeitspapiere nicht zu einem Formalismus führen, durch den die eigentliche Prüfung beeinträchtigt wird.

Die Arbeitspapiere sollten es einem fachkundigen Dritten ermöglichen, die Prüfung fortzuführen oder zu wiederholen bzw. aufgrund dieser Unterlagen einen Bericht abzugeben.

In der Praxis hat sich eine Zweiteilung in eigentliche Arbeitspapiere (jährliche Prüfungsnotizen) und Dauerakte ergeben.

Zu den Arbeitspapieren gehören:

1) Revisionsaufzeichnungen
2) übrige Schriftstücke

Zu den Dauerakten gehören:

1) allgemeine Schriftstücke wie Gesellschaftsstatuten, Verträge, Handelsregisterauszüge, Unterschriftsverzeichnis etc. sowie
2) Revisionsakten wie Prüfungsprogramm, Verzeichnis der Buchhaltungsakten, Kontenpläne, Grundbuch- und Registerauszüge etc.

Die im Anhang angeführten Standardrevisionsblätter sollen eine Richtlinie sein (vgl. dazu die Prüfungsstandards 230 über die Dokumentation).

§ 4 Gesetzliche Revision und interne Revision

Unter interner Kontrolle oder «Internem Kontrollsystem (IKS)» versteht man sämtliche betriebliche Massnahmen, die in einem Unternehmen angewendet werden, um das betriebliche Vermögen zu schützen, finanzielle

Fehlabwicklungen zu verhindern und damit die Genauigkeit und Zuverlässigkeit der Buchführung zu gewährleisten.

Die interne Kontrolle umfasst einerseits die automatische, selbsttätige Überwachung des betrieblichen Geschehens durch in die Arbeitsprozesse eingebaute Kontrollen sowie anderseits die Überwachungstätigkeit durch die Geschäftsleitung und das Kader oder durch die interne Revisionsstelle. Die Gesamtheit aller organisatorischen Regelungen, welche die interne Kontrolle gewährleisten sollen, nennt man internes Kontrollsystem (IKS).

Die interne Revision ist eine unabhängige Stelle (Abteilung) in der Unternehmung, welche meistens direkt dem Verwaltungsrat, zumindest aber der Geschäftsleitung, unterstellt sein soll. Sie nimmt nicht am Arbeitsprozess der Unternehmung teil und hat ihr gegenüber auch keine Weisungsbefugnis. Die einzige Aufgabe der internen Revision ist die Prüfungstätigkeit und die Berichterstattung an ihre vorgesetzte Stelle. Dabei kommen alle Prüfungsverfahren zum Tragen. Hauptsächlich aber setzt sich die interne Revision mit der Untersuchung von Arbeitsabläufen auseinander und beurteilt diese in Bezug auf die Verarbeitungssicherheit.

Kapitel 3: Allgemeine Prüfungshandlungen

```
                    ┌─────────────────────────┐
                    │       INTERNE           │
                    │      KONTROLLE          │
                    │                         │
                    │ (Gesamtheit der Siche-  │
                    │ rungsmittel in der Orga-│
                    │ nisation des Betriebes) │
                    └─────────────────────────┘
```

Selbsttätige Sicherung durch organisatorische Massnahmen	Überwachung durch Vorgesetzte und Beauftragte
durch die getroffene Organisation selbst: • Funktionentrennung • Regelung der Arbeitsabläufe • Systematisch eingebaute Kontrollen	durch Geschäftsleitung und Kader: Arbeitsvorgaben und -kontrollen im täglichen Arbeitsprozess
durch die Anwendung technischer Hilfsmittel: • Waagen, Formulare • Abschliessvorrichtungen • Rechen- und Datenverarbeitungsmaschinen	durch die interne Revision: in Grossbetrieben, in denen die Überwachung durch Geschäftsleitung und Kader nicht genügt

Anhand einer Risikobeurteilung ist zu definieren, welche konkreten Aufgaben im internen Kontrollsystem durchzuführen sind. Die Inhalte der Risikoprüfung sind im Anhang anzugeben (Art. 663b Ziff. 12 OR). Die Revisionsstelle hat bei der ordentlichen Prüfung zur Aufgabe, die Existenz eines internen Kontrollsystems zu hinterfragen (Art. 728a Ziff. 4 OR) sowie die Risikobeurteilung durchzuführen (Art. 728a Ziff. 5 OR). Beim Review gehört dies nicht zur Aufgabe der Revisionsstelle (Art. 729a OR). Es ist auf die Prüfungsstandards 400 bis 499 über die «Interne Kontrolle» hinzuweisen.

§ 5 Ziele und Pflichten der Revisionsstelle

I. Ziele

Hauptziel	
Erfüllung des gesetzlichen Auftrages.	Es dürfen keine Aufgaben der Verwaltung an die Revisionsstelle übertragen werden.
Weitergehende Bestimmungen können in den Statuten verankert werden (statutarische Revisionsbestimmungen).	Der gesetzliche Revisionsauftrag kann durch die Verwaltung nicht einschränkend bestimmt werden.

Nebenziel	
Vorbeugen von möglichen Fehlern und Mängeln in der Rechnungslegung (präventive Wirkung).	Ziel der Revisionsstelle ist nicht die Prüfung der Einhaltung von Vorschriften des Steuerrechts, Sozialversicherungsrechts etc., sondern nur derjenigen des OR.
Aufdecken von vorgekommenen Fehlern und Unregelmässigkeiten (detektive Wirkung).	

II. Pflichten

Die Revisionsstelle hat Prüfungspflichten, Meldepflichten, Handlungspflichten und eine Unterlassungspflicht:

1. Prüfungspflichten

1) Prüfung, ob Jahresrechnung und Buchhaltung übereinstimmen;
2) Prüfung, ob die Buchhaltung ordnungsgemäss geführt ist;
3) Prüfung, ob die Darstellung des Geschäftsergebnisses und der Vermögenslage den gesetzlichen und statutarischen Bewertungsgrundsätzen entspricht;
4) Prüfung, ob der Vorschlag der Verwaltung über die Gewinnverwendung Gesetz und Statuten entspricht.

Der Gedanke des Review kommt so zum Tragen, dass die Revisionsstelle prüft, ob Sachverhalte vorliegen, die ausschliessen, dass gesetzliche Vorschriften oder die Statuten nicht eingehalten sind. Die doppelte Verneinung führt zu einer viel weniger weit gehenden Prüfungspflicht als das alte Aktienrecht.

2. Meldepflichten

1) Bericht und Empfehlung an die Generalversammlung:
2) Die Revisionsstelle ist verpflichtet, über das Ergebnis ihrer Prüfungen zu berichten (Art. 729b OR).
3) Teilnahme und Auskunftserteilung an der Generalversammlung:
4) Die Revisionsstelle muss nicht an der Generalversammlung teilnehmen (Art. 731 OR), dies ist nur bei der ordentlichen Revision vorgesehen.
5) Mitteilung von Gesetzesverstössen und Statutenverletzungen: neu entfallen (bei Review)
6) Benachrichtigung des Konkursrichters bei offensichtlicher Überschuldung und Untätigkeit des Verwaltungsrates.

3. Handlungspflichten

1) Einberufung der Generalversammlung:
   neu entfallen (bei Review)

2) Teilnahme an der Generalversammlung:
   neu entfallen (bei Review)

3) Anzeigepflicht bei offensichtlicher Überschuldung:
   Die Revisionsstelle muss bei offensichtlicher Überschuldung den Richter benachrichtigen, sofern der Verwaltungsrat dies unterlässt.

4. Unterlassungspflichten

Schweigepflicht:

Die Revisoren unterliegen der gesetzlichen Schweigepflicht. Ohne Zustimmung der Gesellschaft dürfen sie keine Informationen weiterleiten. Das Mandat der gesetzlichen Revisionsstelle ist mit Eintrag im Handelsregister öffentlich, d.h. man weiss, wer revidiert, der Revisor darf jedoch nichts sagen.

III. Aktienbuch

Zu den Prüfungsaufgaben der Revisionsstelle gehört auch die Einsichtnahme in das Aktienbuch. Die Revisionsstelle muss prüfen, ob das Aktienbuch ordnungsgemäss geführt ist. Bei Kleinunternehmen dürfte dies nicht schwer fallen, zumal die wenigen Aktionäre oder der Alleinaktionär bekannt sind. Die Prüfung ist notwendig, um die Gewinnausschüttung zu kontrollieren. Sie darf als Dividende nur den Aktionären zukommen. Weiter muss die Revisionsstelle sich die Gewissheit verschaffen, dass aufgrund dieses Registers die Generalversammlung ordentlich einberufen werden kann.

§ 6 Berichterstattung

I. Inhalt

Infolge der Spaltung von ordentlicher Revision und dem Review ist eine Aufteilung in Revisionsbericht und Review die logische Folge. Hier wird auf die Berichterstattung zum Review eingegangen (vgl. dazu Prüfungsstandard 910).

Grundsatz im Review ist neu keine positive Beurteilung, sondern der Ausdruck eines Prüfungsurteils in Form einer doppelten Verneinung.

Der Revisionsbericht ist eine rein textliche Berichterstattung. Der Standardbericht äussert sich über das Rechnungswesen, nicht über das Unternehmen. Auch aus einem vorbehaltlosen Revisionsbericht lässt sich also nicht ablesen, ob das Unternehmen gesund ist. Der Bericht gibt auch keine Auskunft über die Zukunftsfähigkeit des Unternehmens. Er sagt auch nichts darüber, ob die Investitionen der Verwaltung sinnvoll sind. Seine Aussage beschränkt sich auf ein Attest über die Ordnungsmässigkeit der Buchhaltung und über das per Ende Geschäftsjahr ausgewiesene Eigenkapital. In diesem Sinne ist es auch möglich, einen Standardbericht ohne Einschränkung abzugeben, obwohl das Unternehmen auf einer verlustreichen Bahn fährt. Solange das Eigenkapital ausgewiesen ist und die Bewertung stimmt, hat die Revisionsstelle nichts anzufügen.

Die Revisionsstelle beurteilt nicht die Geschäftsführung, was neu ausdrücklich im Gesetz erwähnt ist (Art. 728a Abs. 2 OR). Die Revisionsstelle handelt nicht, solange die Gesellschaft nicht offensichtlich überschuldet ist, sie berichtet nur. Und solange die Buchhaltung einwandfrei geführt ist und die Bewertungsvorschriften eingehalten sind, hat sie nichts weiter zu sagen, sondern nur zu berichten (und zwar mit einem Standardbericht). Selbst wenn sie davon überzeugt ist, dass die Investitionen fehlschlagen werden, hat sie sich darüber auszuschweigen, solange die Bewertungen in Ordnung sind. Die Revisionsstelle prüft die Geschäftstätigkeit nicht.

Verstösse gegen Gesetz und Statuten meldet die Revisionsstelle dem Verwaltungsrat und erst in schweren Fällen der Generalversammlung, diesbezüglich besteht bei der ordentlichen Revision eine Pflicht (Art. 728c OR), beim Review nicht.

Man kann sich auch fragen, in welcher Form die Revisionsstelle berichten soll: in Form eines individuellen Briefes an die Generalversammlung oder in Form eines Standardberichtes? Seit längerer Zeit hat man sich für einen Standardbericht entschieden. Bei Verwendung des Standardberichtes gibt die Revisionsstelle zu erkennen, dass Buchhaltung und Jahresrechnung den gesetzlichen Vorschriften im Sinne eines Review entsprechen und dass das ausgewiesene Eigenkapital gemäss Rechnungslegung vorhanden ist – mehr nicht. Der Revisionsbericht ist, wie bereits ausgeführt wurde, kein Gütesiegel. Für Gütesiegel sind Rating-Agenturen zuständig, aber nicht die Revisionsstelle. Dies liegt auch daran, dass die Revisionsstelle einen zeitlich eng begrenzten Einsatz mit sehr geringen Steuerungsmöglichkeiten durchführt. Trotz der sehr strengen gesetzlichen Haftung ist diesem Umstand, den geringen Einwirkungsmöglichkeiten, Rechnung zu tragen.

Die zwei Standardberichte werden nachstehend beschrieben.

1.   Standardbericht Treuhand-Kammer

a)   Bericht für die ordentliche Revision nach PS 700

Der Standardbericht der Treuhand-Kammer wird nachstehend in der Fassung PS 700 des Jahres 2004 für die Jahresrechnung einer AG wiedergegeben.

Bericht der Revisionsstelle an die Generalversammlung der [Firmenbezeichnung] AG, [Domizil]

Als Revisionsstelle haben wir die Buchführung und die Jahresrechnung (Bilanz, Erfolgsrechnung und Anhang der [Firmenbezeichnung] AG für das am [Bilanzstichtag] abgeschlossene Geschäftsjahr geprüft.

Für die Jahresrechnung ist der Verwaltungsrat verantwortlich, während unsere Aufgabe darin besteht, diese zu prüfen und zu beurteilen. Wir bestätigen, dass wir die gesetzlichen Anforderungen hinsichtlich Zulassung und Unabhängigkeit erfüllen.

Unsere Prüfung erfolgte nach den Schweizer Prüfungsstandards, wonach eine Prüfung so zu planen und durchzuführen ist, dass wesentliche Fehlaussagen in der Jahresrechnung mit angemessener Sicherheit erkannt werden. Wir prüften die Posten und Angaben der Jahresrechnung mittels Analysen und Erhebungen auf der Basis von Stichproben. Ferner beurteilten wir die Anwendung der massgebenden Rechnungslegungsgrundsätze,

Kapitel 3: Allgemeine Prüfungshandlungen

> *die wesentlichen Bewertungsentscheide sowie die Darstellung der Jahresrechnung als Ganzes. Wir sind der Auffassung, dass unsere Prüfung eine ausreichende Grundlage für unser Urteil bildet.*
>
> *Gemäss unserer Beurteilung entsprechen die Buchführung und die Jahresrechnung sowie der Antrag über die Verwendung des Bilanzgewinnes dem schweizerischen Gesetz und den Statuten.*
>
> *Wir empfehlen, die vorliegende Jahresrechnung zu genehmigen.*
>
> *Datum / Revisionsstelle [Firmenbezeichnung] / [Domizil] / [Unterschriften]*
>
> *Beilage (insb. Jahresrechnung und Antrag über Verwendung des Bilanzgewinnes)*

Der dem neuen Revisionsrecht angepasste Bericht liegt noch nicht vor.

b)   Bericht für die Review (prüferische Durchsicht) nach PS 910

> **Bericht des Wirtschaftsprüfers an [Berichtsadressat] der [Firmenbezeichnung], [Domizil]**
>
> *Auftragsgemäss haben wir eine Review des Abschlusses [Abschlussart] der [Firmenbezeichnung] für das am [Bilanzstichtag] abgeschlossene Geschäftsjahr vorgenommen.*
>
> *Für den Abschluss [Abschlussart] ist [verantwortliches Organ] verantwortlich, während unsere Aufgabe darin besteht, aufgrund unserer Review einen Bericht über den Abschluss [Abschlussart] abzugeben.*
>
> *Unsere Review erfolgte nach dem Schweizer Prüfungsstandard 910 [und allfälligen internationalen Standards]. Danach ist eine Review so zu planen und durchzuführen, dass wesentliche Fehlaussagen im Abschluss [Abschlussart] erkannt werden, wenn auch nicht mit derselben Sicherheit wie bei einer Prüfung. Eine Review besteht hauptsächlich aus der Befragung von Mitarbeiterinnen und Mitarbeitern sowie analytischen Prü-*

Teil C: Revision / Auditing

> *fungshandlungen in Bezug auf die dem Abschluss [Abschlussart] zugrunde liegenden Daten. Wir haben eine Review, nicht aber eine Prüfung, durchgeführt und geben aus diesem Grund kein Prüfungsurteil ab.*
>
> *Bei unserer Review sind wir nicht auf Sachverhalte gestossen, aus denen wir schliessen müssten, dass der Abschluss [Abschlussart] kein den tatsächlichen Verhältnissen entsprechendes Bild der Vermögens-, Finanz- und Ertragslage der [Firmenbezeichnung] in Übereinstimmung mit [Angabe des Regelwerks, vgl. PS 120] vermittelt.*
>
> *Datum / Wirtschaftsprüfer [Firmenbezeichnung] / [Domizil] / [Unterschriften]*
>
> *Beilage*

Der dem neuen Revisionsrecht angepasste Bericht liegt noch nicht vor.

c)   Uneingeschränkter Bericht über die prüferische Durchsicht nach ISA («International Standards on Auditing»)

> **Bericht über die prüferische Durchsicht an ...**
>
> *Wir haben die beigefügte Bilanz der ABC Gesellschaft zum 31. Dezember 20XX sowie die Gewinn- und Verlustrechnung und die Kapitalflussrechnung für das an diesem Stichtag zu Ende gegangene Geschäftsjahr prüferisch durchgesehen. Für den Abschluss ist die Unternehmensleitung der Gesellschaft verantwortlich. Unsere Aufgabe ist es, auf der Grundlage unserer prüferischen Durchsicht einen Bericht über den Abschluss herauszugeben.*
>
> *Wir haben die prüferische Durchsicht in Übereinstimmung mit dem für Aufträge zur prüferischen Durchsicht geltenden ISA [bzw. Bezugnahme auf relevante nationale Prüfungsgrundsätze oder -gepflogenheiten] durchgeführt. Nach diesen Grundsätzen sind wir verpflichtet, die prüferische Durchsicht in einer Weise zu planen und durchzuführen, die mittelhohe Sicherheit darüber bietet, ob der Abschluss frei von wesentlich fal-*

Kapitel 3: Allgemeine Prüfungshandlungen

schen Aussagen ist. Eine prüferische Durchsicht beschränkt sich in erster Linie auf die Befragung von Mitarbeitern der Gesellschaft und analytische Prüfungshandlungen in Bezug auf finanzielle Daten und bietet deshalb weniger Sicherheit als eine Prüfung. Wir haben keine Prüfung durchgeführt und erteilen aus diesem Grund kein Prüfungsurteil.

Bei der Durchführung unserer prüferischen Durchsicht sind wir nicht auf Tatsachen gestossen, die uns zu der Annahme veranlassen, dass der beigefügte Abschluss kein den tatsächlichen Verhältnissen entsprechendes Bild [oder: nicht in allen wesentlichen Belangen angemessen dargestellt wird] in Übereinstimmung mit den IFRS vermittelt.

Datum   *PRÜFER*

Beilage

2.   *Standardbericht Treuhänderverband / B. Madörin*

Der Standardbericht des Treuhänderverbandes für die ordentliche Revision wurde in der aktuellen Fassung 1997 vorgeschlagen. Er beruht in weiten Teilen auf der Fassung, die vom Autor des vorliegenden Buches vorgeschlagen wurde (NZZ 1997, Der Treuhandexperte 1996; s. Quellen).

Der Bericht des Treuhänderverbandes ist kurz und bündig. Bei Kleinunternehmen ist der Standardbericht des Treuhänderverbandes geläufiger. Aufgrund der neuen gesetzlichen Ausgangslage wurde der Bericht im vorliegenden Buch überarbeitet.

3.   *Gesetzliche Berichterstattung der Revisionsstelle*

Die Berichterstattung für die Aktiengesellschaft umfasst nach Obligationenrecht:

    1) Prüfungsbestätigung des Gründungsprüfers (Art. 635a OR)

2) Bericht über die Prüfung des Zwischenabschlusses bei Erhöhung des Aktienkapitals aus Eigenkapital (Art. 652d Abs. 2 OR)

3) Prüfungsbestätigung der Revisionsstelle über die Prüfung des Kapitalerhöhungsberichtes (Art. 652f Abs. 1 OR)

4) Prüfungsbestätigung des Kapitalerhöhungsprüfers (Art. 653f OR, bei bedingter Kapitalerhöhung)

5) Prüfungsbestätigung des Kapitalerhöhungsprüfers (Art. 653i OR, Streichung der bedingten Kapitalerhöhung)

6) Bestätigung der Revisionsstelle bei Aufwertung von Grundstücken oder Beteiligungen (Art. 670 Abs. 2 OR)

7) Bericht des Sonderprüfers (Art. 697e OR)

8) Berichterstattung der Revisionsstelle zur Prüfung der Zwischenbilanz bei begründeter Besorgnis einer Überschuldung (Art. 725 Abs. 2 OR)

9) Bericht der Revisionsstelle (Art. 728b Abs. 2 und 729b OR)

10) Erläuterungsbericht zuhanden des Verwaltungsrates (Art. 728b Abs. 1 OR)

11) Meldung festgestellter Verstösse gegen das Gesetz, die Statuten oder Organisationsreglemente (Art. 728c OR)

12) Benachrichtigung des Richters bei offensichtlicher Überschuldung (Art. 729c OR)

13) Auskunftspflicht an der Generalversammlung (Art. 697 Abs. 1 OR)

14) Besonderer Revisionsbericht bei einer Kapitalherabsetzung (Art. 732 OR)

15) Bericht über die Prüfung von Liquidationsbilanzen (Art. 742 Abs. 1 OR, Art. 743 Abs. 5 OR)

16) Bestätigung im Zusammenhang mit der vorzeitigen Verteilung des Vermögens von Gesellschaften in Liquidation (Art. 745 Abs. 3 OR)

17) Bericht bei Sitzverlegung einer ausländischen Aktiengesellschaft in die Schweiz (Art. 163 Abs. 3 IPRG)

18) Berichterstattung des Konzernrechnungsprüfers (Art. 731a und 731a OR)

Kapitel 3: Allgemeine Prüfungshandlungen

Hier werden nur die geläufigsten Berichte erläutert. Für Spezialfälle verweisen wir auf die Prüfungsstandards (PS 700) der Treuhand-Kammer.

II.   Der Revisionsbericht

Das revidierte Aktienrecht ist am 1.7.1992 in Kraft getreten. Mit dieser Neuordnung wurde auch im Revisionshandbuch (RHB) ein neuer Text zur Berichterstattung der gesetzlichen Revisionsstelle an die Generalversammlung vorgeschlagen (RHB, S. 470 ff.). Der Standardbericht interessiert nur dort, wo die Revisionsstelle ohne besondere Vorkommnisse berichten kann. In den Prüfungsstandards (PS 700) werden diese Musterberichte aufgenommen.

Es stellt sich immer die Frage, was in einen Bericht integriert werden soll und was nicht. Soll er kurz und knapp sein oder weitere den Leser interessierende Elemente enthalten? Im Vorschlag RHB 1992 sowie im Prüfungsstandard 700 sind insbesondere folgende Punkte in den Bericht aufgenommen worden:

1) woraus sich die Jahresrechnung zusammensetzt,

2) wer für die Jahresrechnung verantwortlich ist,

3) welches die Aufgaben der Revisionsstelle sind,

4) die Unabhängigkeit der Revisionsstelle,

5) der Berufsstand,

6) der leitende Revisor sowie

7) die Prüfung nach den gesetzlichen Vorschriften.

Der erweiterte Text zur Berichterstattung (Der Schweizer Treuhänder, 4/1996, S. 15 ff.) wird im Wesentlichen wie folgt ergänzt:

8) die Verantwortlichkeit des Verwaltungsrates für die Jahresrechnung,

9) die Umschreibung der Aufgaben der Revisionsstelle,

10) die Umschreibung der Zuverlässigkeit der Berichterstattung,

11) die Methode der Prüfung (Stichproben),

12) die Anwendung der Rechnungslegungsgrundsätze und Bewertungsgrundsätze und

13) der Hinweis, dass die eigenen Prüfungen für die Bildung des Prüfungsurteils genügen.

Festzuhalten ist, dass eine Tendenz zur Erweiterung des Revisionstextes besteht. Die Motivation mag vielleicht einerseits darin liegen, den Revisor an seine wichtigsten Pflichten zu erinnern und andererseits den Leser des Revisionsberichtes darauf hinzuweisen, dass nie alle Faktoren der Revisionsstelle bekannt sind. Eine Unsicherheit bleibt. Damit wird im Bericht vorweg eine Haftungsbeschränkung gesucht. Weiter lehnt sich diese Berichterstattung auch an die internationalen Prüfungsstandards (ISA) an.

Gesetzliche Normen zur ordentlichen Revision:

Für den Review bestimmt sich die Prüfung nach Art. 729a OR:

1 Die Revisionsstelle prüft, ob Sachverhalte vorliegen, aus denen zu schliessen ist, dass:

  1. die Jahresrechnung nicht den gesetzlichen Vorschriften und den Statuten entspricht;

  2. der Antrag des Verwaltungsrats an die Generalversammlung über die Verwendung des Bilanzgewinnes nicht den gesetzlichen Vorschriften und den Statuten entspricht.

2 Die Prüfung beschränkt sich auf Befragungen und analytische Prüfungshandlungen.

3 Die Geschäftsführung des Verwaltungsrats ist nicht Gegenstand der Prüfung durch die Revisionsstelle.

Die Berichterstattung richtet sich nach Art. 729b OR:

1 Die Revisionsstelle erstattet der Generalversammlung schriftlich einen zusammenfassenden Bericht über das Ergebnis der Revision. Der Bericht enthält:

  1. einen Hinweis auf die eingeschränkte Natur der Revision;

  2. eine Stellungnahme zum Ergebnis der Prüfung;

  3. Angaben zur Unabhängigkeit und gegebenenfalls zum Mitwirken bei der Buchführung und zu anderen Dienstleistungen, die für die zu prüfende Gesellschaft erbracht wurden;

Kapitel 3: Allgemeine Prüfungshandlungen

4. Angaben zu den Personen, welche die Revision geleitet haben, und zu deren Zulassung.

2 Der Bericht muss von den Personen unterzeichnet werden, die die Revision geleitet haben.

Wir kommen damit zum Wortlaut des Berichts der Revisionsstelle:

1. Ordentliche Revision

Bericht der Revisionsstelle

An die Generalversammlung der AG

(Name und Adresse der Gesellschaft)

Wir haben die Jahresrechnung und Buchhaltung Ihrer Gesellschaft geprüft.

Die Jahresrechnung und die Gewinnverwendung entsprechen Gesetz und Statuten.

Wir bestätigen, dass wir die gesetzlichen Anforderungen an Zulassung und Unabhängigkeit erfüllen.

Wir empfehlen, die vorliegende Jahresrechnung zu genehmigen.

(Ort, Datum) (Rechtsgültige Firmierung mit Unterschrift der leitenden Revisoren)

Beilagen: Jahresrechnung und Antrag über die Gewinnverwendung

---

Dies genügt, um den gesetzlichen Anforderungen zu entsprechen. Alle übrigen Ergänzungen sowie die Aufgaben der Revisionsstelle sind aus dem Gesetz ersichtlich und eine weitere Erwähnung im Bericht ist nicht erforderlich. Wer für die Jahresrechnung verantwortlich ist, steht in

Art. 662 OR. Aus diesem Grund ist u.E. auch die Umschreibung der Art und Weise, wie die Prüfung zu erfolgen hat, eine unnötige Wiederholung des gesetzlichen Auftrages. Besonders kritisch zu hinterfragen ist der Hinweis auf die Methode der Prüfung (Stichproben). Wie uns das Revisionshandbuch lehrt, gibt es verschiedene Arten von Methoden, und die Erwähnung nur einer ist eine vom Gesetz nicht geforderte Einschränkung. Es kann sein, dass – je nach Gesellschaft – eine lückenlose Prüfung erforderlich ist. Eine Abweichung der Berichterstattung vom Normalwortlaut wäre die Folge und der Leser könnte dies bereits kritisch würdigen. Der Revisor sollte nicht durch den Wortlaut des Berichts beeinflusst werden. Er muss so prüfen, wie es die Vorschriften fordern. Die Prüfung nur aufgrund von Stichproben kann in bestimmten Fällen bereits zu Haftungsfragen führen.

Auch der Hinweis, dass die Prüfung genügend Grundlage für das Urteil bietet, ist eine rein textliche Erweiterung. Jedes Urteil bedarf einer Grundlage. Ist diese nicht vorhanden, kann nicht schlüssig abgeleitet werden. Ist sie vorhanden, kann entschieden werden. Dies sind Grundsätze methodischer Analytik, welche nicht in einen Revisionsbericht gehören.

Die Erweiterungen, wie sie sich zeigen, können in zwei Richtungen gehen; sie dienen dem Leser oder dem Verfasser. Wenn wir zuerst das Erste in die Beurteilung ziehen, so müssen wir uns fragen, ob der Leser durch die textlichen Erweiterungen mehr Nutzen zieht. Unserer Meinung nach ist dies nicht der Fall. Der Leser weiss beim Minimalwortlaut, dass geprüft wurde und welche Empfehlung abgegeben wurde. Dies genügt. Allein die Konklusion der Revisionsstelle interessiert. Der Rest steht im Gesetz und in den Akten der Revisionsstelle.

Ist die textliche Erweiterung reine Redundanz oder bringt sie der Revisionsstelle Haftungserleichterung? Es fragt sich somit, ob die Umschreibung als Einschränkung des gesetzlich Geforderten zu würdigen ist und damit eine Reduktion der Haftung zur Folge hat. Unseres Erachtens ist dies nicht der Fall. Der Text ist derart abstrakt gefasst, dass er nur allgemein gültigen Charakter hat und nicht zu entschuldbaren Haftungsmomenten führt. Ohnehin kommt der Revisionsbericht einer jährlichen Lebensbescheinigung für Aktiengesellschaften gleich. Einmal pro Jahr, in der Regel per Ende Jahr, wird erklärt, dass die Aktiengesellschaft existenzfähig ist. Alle Anmerkungen, Vormerkungen, Hinweise, Vorbehalte etc. sind nur beschränkt wirksam. Mit der Empfehlung, die Jahresrechnung zu genehmigen, wird der Bestand der Unternehmung aus der Sicht der Revisionsstelle manifestiert. So sind die textlichen Erweiterungen zu werten; sie ändern an der Haftung der Revisionsstelle nichts. Die Antwort auf die Frage nach dem Ausmass der Haftung kann nur das allgemeine Haftungsrecht liefern, das insbesondere die Frage stellt, ob ein Verschulden vorliegt. Ein solches kann durch allgemeine Umschreibungen nicht reduziert werden.

Die Entwicklungen im Haftungsrecht sind kritisch zu werten. Es besteht eine Tendenz zur Verschärfung. Das Missverhältnis von Honorar und Haftung akzentuiert sich. Es ist unbefriedigend, wenn beispielsweise das Tausendfache des Honorars als Schaden gefordert werden kann. Hier nützt nur eine künftige gesetzliche Beschränkung der Haftung der Revisionsstelle (z.B. auf 50 % der Bilanzsumme der revidierten Gesellschaft). Eine solche gesetzliche Beschränkung steht noch aus. Ein standardisierter, textlich erweiterter Revisionsbericht hingegen hat keinen Einfluss auf die Haftung.

Im Sinne der Klarheit und Prägnanz der Berichterstattung kann nur eine textliche Minimallösung für die Berichterstattung die beste Lösung sein.

Der Standardbericht des Schweizerischen Treuhänderverbandes folgt weitgehend diesen Überlegungen. Der Text ist im Kapitel Standardbericht wiedergegeben. Er beruht in weiten Teilen auf der von mir vorgeschlagenen Fassung (Der Treuhandexperte I 1997, S. 12 ff.). Konsequent werden nachfolgend Standardtexte für andere juristische Personen und Personengesellschaften vorgeschlagen, die dieser kurzen Fassung folgen.

2. Review

Vorstehend ist sowohl das Muster einer Review nach PS 910 wie das einer Prüfung nach den «International Standards on Auditing (ISA)» aufgeführt. Die Texte sind aufwändig. Ein schlanker Text könnte wie folgt lauten:

Teil C: Revision / Auditing

Beispiel:

> *Bericht der Revisionsstelle an die Generalversammlung der [Firmenbezeichnung]*
>
> *Wir haben die Jahresrechnung und die Buchhaltung Ihrer Gesellschaft als Review geprüft.*
>
> *Die Jahresrechnung und Gewinnverwendung entsprechen Gesetz und Statuten, soweit dies durch eine eingeschränkte Revision beurteilt werden kann.*
>
> *Wir bestätigen, dass wir die gesetzlichen Anforderungen an Zulassung und Unabhängigkeit erfüllen.*
>
> *[Ort und Datum] [Rechtsgültige Firmierung mit Unterschriften der Revisoren sowie Angabe der Zulassung]*
>
> *Beilage: Jahresrechnung und Antrag über die Gewinnverwendung*
>
> *Hinweis: Wir haben für die Gesellschaft folgende Dienstleistungen erbracht [Aufzählung]*

Ebenso konsequent hat die «Kommission für Wirtschaftsprüfung» für andere juristische Personen und zu Sonderberichterstattungen der AG weitere Standardtexte vorgeschlagen (Der Schweizer Treuhänder, Nr. 1–2/1998, S. 7 ff.). Es ist zuerst auf die früheren Ausführungen zu verweisen. Im Weiteren zeigen sich hier Ungenauigkeiten. Bei der GmbH wird angeführt: «*Als statutarische Kontrollstelle haben wir ...*» und bei der Stiftung sowie beim Verein: «*Als Revisionsstelle haben wir ...*». In allen drei Fällen handelt es sich um eine statutarische Revisions- oder Kontrollstelle. Eine konsequente Benützung des Wortes «statutarisch» wäre richtig gewesen. Weiter verwenden alle drei Standardtexte den Wortlaut: «*Wir bestätigen, dass wir die Anforderungen hinsichtlich Zulassung und Unabhängigkeit erfüllen.*» Um welche Anforderungen es sich handelt, wird nicht erwähnt. Diese Texte der Revisionsberichte wurden überarbeitet und nunmehr im Prüfungsstandard 700 präziser formuliert. Im Hinblick auf das neue Revisionsrecht werden neue Standardtexte folgen.

III. «Grünes Licht»

Die Berichterstattung erfolgt gemäss Art. 729b OR. Die Berichterstattung ist nach der Prüfung die wesentliche Aufgabe der Revisionsstelle. Damit gibt sie schriftlichen Bericht über das Ergebnis ihrer Prüfungen ab. Kernpunkt in der ordentlichen Revision ist die Empfehlung, die Jahresrechnung und Buchhaltung zu genehmigen. Dabei geht es nicht nur um eine Meinungsäusserung der Revisionsstelle dem Verwaltungsrat und den Aktionären gegenüber, sondern eine solche Erklärung ist auch für sehr viele Personen, die in einer Beziehung zur Aktiengesellschaft stehen, wichtig. Das Vertrauen gegenüber der Revisionsstelle ist Grundlage. Für den Review entfällt diese Beurteilung und sie obliegt allein den Aktionären.

Innerhalb von sechs Monaten seit Ende des Geschäftsjahres muss der Verwaltungsrat eine Bilanz vorlegen und diese muss auch geprüft sein. Diese Norm wird als Gebotsnorm angesehen. Es kann jedoch nicht darüber hinweggesehen werden, dass diese Frist eingehalten werden sollte und sicher nicht über das Geschäftsjahr hinaus toleriert werden kann. Die Revisionsstelle muss also dafür besorgt sein, dass sie bis sechs Monate nach Ende des Geschäftsjahres die Prüfung hat durchführen können, auf jeden Fall innerhalb von zwölf Monaten seit Geschäftsabschluss. Eine solche Erstreckung ist nur dann möglich, wenn die zu prüfende Gesellschaft nicht unter dem Manko an Aktualität leidet. Je grösser die Unternehmung, desto mehr muss die Buchhaltung à jour sein. Ein kleines Unternehmen mit wenigen Angestellten kann z.B. die Buchhaltung im zweiten Semester nach Geschäftsabschluss besorgen, wenn die Bank- und Kassabücher täglich geführt werden und der Verwaltungsrat den Überblick hat. Es kommt oft vor, dass Kleinbetriebe ihre Buchhaltung extern in Auftrag geben und die Buchführung dort nicht innerhalb von sechs Monaten erfolgt. Dies ist unter den genannten Umständen zulässig, auf jeden Fall müssen aber u.E. die Buchhaltung und der Revisionsbericht innerhalb von zwölf Monaten vorliegen. Weitergehende Verspätungen sind kaum zu akzeptieren und müssen bei der Revisionsstelle zum Handeln führen.

«Grünes Licht» und damit klares Signal besteht, wenn die Bilanz im Eigenkapital inklusive Reserven ohne Probleme besteht. Für eine kritische

Analyse geht man vom ausgewiesenen Eigenkapital aus und ergänzt dies um notwendige Korrekturen und kritische Positionen.

So reduziert man z.B. das ausgewiesene Eigenkapital um den Wert eines Aktivpostens, den man als kritisch betrachtet, beispielsweise ist die Forderung seit 3 Jahren unverändert bilanziert und damit scheint deren Einbringlichkeit fraglich. Eine weitere Korrektur in der Bewertung eines Anlagegutes ist notwendig, z.B. muss die Software abgeschrieben werden, da sie nur noch wenig tauglich ist. Nach den Korrekturen in den Aktiven müssen noch die Passiven ergänzt werden, so beispielsweise, wenn eine Bürgschaft voraussichtlich in Anspruch genommen wird. Dann wird die latente Schuld zur effektiven Schuld und muss dazu addiert werden. Ergeben sich nach dieser kritischen Beurteilung keine Probleme und ist das Eigenkapital noch ausgewiesen, kann eine Berichterstattung erfolgen.

IV.   «Oranges Licht»

Kapitalverlust: Art. 725 Abs. 1 OR lautet: *«Zeigt die letzte Jahresbilanz, dass die Hälfte des Aktienkapitals und der gesetzlichen Reserven nicht mehr gedeckt ist, so beruft der Verwaltungsrat unverzüglich eine Generalversammlung ein und beantragt ihr Sanierungsmassnahmen.»*

Eine erste Warnlampe leuchtet, wenn die Hälfte des Eigenkapitals (Aktienkapital und gesetzliche Reserven) durch Verluste verbraucht ist. Ist es formell durch eine ausgewiesene Bilanz dokumentiert, muss in der Berichterstattung auf dieses Ereignis hingewiesen werden. Der Verwaltungsrat muss Sanierungsmassnahmen in die Wege leiten oder geleitet haben.

Ganz klar muss gesagt werden, dass eine bloss kosmetische Veränderung in dieser Situation nicht genügt. Ein Hinweis, dass der Verwaltungsrat diese Situation erkannt hat und entsprechende Massnahmen eingeleitet hat, genügt nicht. Sehr oft ist die Revisionsstelle bei Kleinaktiengesellschaften geneigt, den Dingen freien Lauf zu lassen. Das geht nicht und im Zweifelsfalle muss der Revisor auf eine Kapitalerhöhung drängen. Die Revisionsstelle sollte auch an die eigenen Interessen denken. Wenn diese auf den hälftigen Kapitalverlust hingewiesen, aber nicht reagiert hat, ist sie Verantwortlichkeitsansprüchen, welche Gläubiger gegen sie geltend machen, schon ein gutes Stück ausgeliefert.

Bereits hier muss mit Nachdruck darauf hingewiesen werden, dass der Revisionsbericht kurz sein muss und sich auf das Wesentliche beschränken soll. Er kann nicht als Entschuldigungsschreiben dienen. Im Bericht wird beispielsweise erwähnt, dass die Revisionsstelle von gewissen notwendigen Massnahmen absieht, weil die Gegebenheiten doch nicht wirklich gravierend sind. Solche Angaben sind für die Revisionsstelle äusserst nachteilig: Überlebt die AG, interessiert der Hinweis niemanden, überlebt sie nicht, wird man den Revisor zur Verantwortung ziehen.

Das Signal «steht auch auf orange», wenn die Revisionsstelle die förmlich ausgewiesene Bilanz um kritische Bewertungen korrigiert und mehr als die Hälfte des Aktienkapitals verloren ist. Der Revisor hat daran zu denken, dass der Verwaltungsrat in kritischen Situationen geneigt ist, die Dinge zu optimistisch zu sehen. Gerade dann ist die Revisionsstelle besonders gefragt, ein unabhängiges Urteil abzugeben.

Es ist manchmal schwer, als Revisionsstelle zu handeln und Remedur zu ziehen. Doch sollte dies der Revisionsstelle leichter fallen als dem Verwaltungsrat. Ihr kritisches Urteil ist notwendig und gefragt. Schliesslich handelt sie nicht zum Schaden der Gesellschaft und der Aktionäre, geschweige denn zum Schaden der Gläubiger.

Sanierungsmassnahmen können folgendermassen aussehen:
- Verkauf verlustreicher Unternehmensteile
- Liquidation verlustreicher Betriebsteile
- Kostenreduktionen
- Umstrukturierungen
- Partnerschaften
- etc.

Anzumerken ist, dass auch unter dem Aspekt des neuen Revisionsrechts die Meldepflicht der Revisionsstelle weiter aktiv ist.

V. «Rotes Licht»

1. Kapitalverlust

Art. 725 Abs. 2 OR wurde neu formuliert und besagt zum Kapitalverlust Folgendes: *«Wenn begründete Besorgnis einer Überschuldung besteht, muss eine Zwischenbilanz erstellt werden und diese einem zugelassenen Revisor zur Prüfung vorgelegt werden. Ergibt sich aus der Zwischenbi-*

lanz, dass die Forderungen der Gesellschaftsgläubiger weder zu Fortführungs- noch zu Veräusserungswerten gedeckt sind, so hat der Verwaltungsrat den Richter zu benachrichtigen, sofern nicht Gesellschaftsgläubiger [...] zurücktreten.»

Ist das Eigenkapital nicht mehr vorhanden, kann die Jahresrechnung nicht mehr zur Abnahme empfohlen werden. Es bleibt nur noch die Rückweisung bzw. der Gang zum Konkursrichter. Gleiches gilt für den Review.

Sind noch stille Reserven vorhanden, müssen diese buchhaltungsmässig aufgelöst werden, um zu einem ausgeglichenen Ergebnis zu führen. Einen Text wie: *«die Bilanz ist zwar überschuldet aber in der Position Liegenschaften sind noch stille Reserven, weshalb auf die Benachrichtigung des Richters verzichtet werden kann»* erachten wir aus haftungsrechtlicher Sicht als ungünstig und zudem für den Bilanzleser als eine Zumutung. Wenn die Verluste so gross sind, dass das Eigenkapital nicht mehr gedeckt ist, muss aufgewertet werden, sofern dies möglich und zulässig ist. Dann muss eine kritische Beurteilung und im Anschluss daran eine klare Berichterstattung erfolgen. Wortspielereien im Revisionsbericht führen immer zu Problemen bei Haftungsfragen. Kein Richter wird verstehen, weshalb Sie trotz Überschuldung einen Revisionsbericht abgegeben haben. Suchen Sie die Lösung einer komplexen Situation nicht in der Formulierung des Revisionsberichts, sondern in der Buchhaltung.

Oft hat die Revisionsstelle das Gefühl, dem Verwaltungsrat und langjährigen Kunden «helfen» zu müssen. Man glaubt, mit einem zustimmenden Revisionsbericht eine kritische Zeit überbrücken zu können und dass nachher alles wieder besser geht. Die Revisionsstelle kann jedoch solche Probleme nicht lösen. Eine Remedur hilft mehr, als etwas anstehen zu lassen. Mit klaren Worten kann die Revisionsstelle eine Neuorientierung beim Verwaltungsrat bewirken, hierzu die folgenden Lösungsansätze:

- Kapitalerhöhung
- Rangrücktritterklärung
- Personalentscheide
- Partnerschaften
- Verkauf
- etc.

Solche Ansätze führen zur Überlebensfähigkeit des Unternehmens oder helfen, kritische Situationen im Moment zu überwinden.

2. Aufschub des Konkurses

Eröffnung oder Aufschub des Konkurses: Art. 725a OR lautet:

«^{1}*Der Richter eröffnet auf die Benachrichtigung hin den Konkurs. Er kann ihn auf Antrag des Verwaltungsrates oder eines Gläubigers aufschieben, falls Aussicht auf Sanierung besteht; in diesem Falle trifft er Massnahmen zur Erhaltung des Vermögens.*

^{2}*Der Richter kann einen Sachwalter bestellen und entweder dem Verwaltungsrat die Verfügungsbefugnis entziehen oder dessen Beschlüsse von der Zustimmung des Sachwalters abhängig machen. Er umschreibt die Aufgaben des Sachwalters.*

^{3}*Der Konkursaufschub muss nur veröffentlicht werden, wenn dies zum Schutze Dritter erforderlich ist.*»

Nicht jede Überschuldung führt zwangsläufig zum Ende und zum Konkurs. Der Richter kann bei Aussicht auf Sanierung einen Konkursaufschub gewähren. Damit ist auch klar gesagt, dass bei Überschuldung nicht die Revisionsstelle zu beurteilen hat, ob die Sanierung sinnvoll ist.

Ein Revisionstext «*Die Gesellschaft ist zwar überschuldet, doch zeigen die vom Verwaltungsrat durchgeführten Massnahmen Erfolg und es ist mit einer Gesundung des Unternehmens zu rechnen.*» geht trotz allem Optimismus am gesetzlichen Ziel vorbei. Der Richter ist dafür zuständig, und wenn man ihn mit Erfolgszahlen orientieren kann, wird er dem Konkursaufschub zustimmen.

Hier sei auch noch an die Möglichkeiten des SchKG erinnert, wie z.B. die Stundung oder der Nachlassvertrag (Prozentvergleich).

VI. «Alarm»

Die Anzeigepflichten bei der ordentlichen Revision bestimmen sich nach Art. 728c OR:

¹ Stellt die Revisionsstelle Verstösse gegen das Gesetz, die Statuten oder das Organisationsreglement fest, so meldet sie dies schriftlich dem Verwaltungsrat.

² Sie informiert zudem die Generalversammlung, wenn:

1. sie wesentliche Verstösse gegen das Gesetz oder die Statuten feststellt;

2. der Verwaltungsrat auf Grund der schriftlichen Meldung der Revisionsstelle keine angemessenen Massnahmen ergreift.

³ Ist die Gesellschaft offensichtlich überschuldet und unterlässt der Verwaltungsrat die Anzeige, so benachrichtigt die Revisionsstelle den Richter.

Für die Review ist Art. 729c OR massgeblich:

Ist die Gesellschaft offensichtlich überschuldet und unterlässt der Verwaltungsrat die Anzeige, so benachrichtigt die Revisionsstelle den Richter.

Ist das Unternehmen offensichtlich überschuldet, muss die Revisionsstelle handeln und den Richter benachrichtigen. Dann reissen alle Stricke. Die Revisionsstelle kann sich dieser Pflicht nicht entledigen. Sie muss handeln und wird verantwortlich, wenn sie es unterlässt.

Das Kriterium der offensichtlichen Überschuldung ist bisher nicht näher gesetzlich definiert worden (d.h. es gibt keine Legaldefinition). Ein Ansatz liegt darin, dass mindestens eine Überschuldung in der Höhe des Aktienkapitals vorliegen muss, wenn also ein Verlust des Aktienkapitals (inkl. gesetzliche Reserven) und eines weiteren zusätzlichen Verlustes in dieser gleichen Höhe vorliegt.

Beispiel:	
Aktienkapital	100'000.–
Reserven	50'000.–
	150'000.–
Verlust	200'000.–
Kapitalverlust	50'000.–

→ nicht offensichtlich

Kapitel 3: Allgemeine Prüfungshandlungen

Aktienkapital   100'000.–
Reserven   50'000.–
                   150'000.–

Verlust   251'000.–
Kapitalverlust   101'000.–

→offensichtlich

Dies ist als Vorschlag zu einer relativen Grösse zu verstehen. Ein absoluter Wert scheint uns als Massstab unangebracht. Sehr vieles hängt von der Unternehmensgrösse ab und ist damit relativ. Auch Bewertungsfragen sind immer in Relation zur Bilanz zu beurteilen. Das Kriterium der offensichtlichen Überschuldung im Massstab des Kapitals ist nur ein Hilfskriterium. Sie kann bei Kleinaktiengesellschaften mit mehreren Bilanzpositionen als mögliche Lösung angesehen werden. Existieren nur drei Bilanzposten (Verlust, Kreditoren, Aktienkapital), ist die Überschuldung sehr viel früher offensichtlich.

Die Revisionsstelle braucht bei diesem Schritt der Überschuldungsanzeige kein schlechtes Gewissen zu haben. Sie soll den Richter beurteilen lassen. Der Verwaltungsrat der Aktiengesellschaft kann darlegen, weshalb er der Meinung ist, dass keine Überschuldung vorliegt. Schlimmstenfalls geht der Revisionsstelle ein Mandat verloren; in ihrer Beurteilung muss sie sowieso unabhängig sein, d.h. auf dieses verzichten können.

Bis jetzt sind noch keine Fälle bekannt, bei denen die Revisionsstelle schadenersatzpflichtig wurde, weil sie bei offensichtlicher Überschuldung den Richter benachrichtigt hat. Weil sie in der zu revidierenden Gesellschaft auch den Kunden sieht, wird sie i.d.R. vor diesem Schritt zögern. Wenn dies bereits Thema ist, ist es meistens höchste Zeit. Wenn der Revisor nicht ganz sicher ist, sollte er ein bisschen Zeit und Geld investieren. Ein Treuhandkollege kann in kurzer Zeit eine neutrale Beurteilung abgeben. Dass die gesetzliche Revisionsstelle handeln muss, ist sie sich selbst, der Gesellschaft und deren Gläubigern schuldig.

Bei offensichtlicher Überschuldung muss die Revisionsstelle ihre Anzeigepflicht erfüllen. Vorgängig hat sie den Verwaltungsrat auf diese Handlungspflicht hinzuweisen. Unterlässt der Verwaltungsrat die Anzeige, obliegt sie der Revisionsstelle.

§ 7 Standardbericht

Die Revisionsstelle berichtet der Generalversammlung schriftlich über das Ergebnis ihrer Prüfung. Sie gibt an, ob die Buchführung und die Jahresrechnung sowie der Anhang dem Gesetz und den Statuten entsprechen, und wenn nicht, in welchen Punkten eine wesentliche Abweichung von den normativen Vorgaben festgestellt wurde. Sie äussert sich auch darüber, ob der Dividendenantrag (Antrag über die Verwendung des Bilanzgewinns) gesetzes- und statutenkonform ist.

Ein gesetzlich vorgesehener Revisionsbericht existiert nicht. Jede Revisionsstelle entscheidet frei, wie sie über die Ergebnisse ihrer Prüfung berichten will. In der Praxis hat sich ein Standardbericht entwickelt.

I. Standardbericht für Review (Deutsch/Plural)

Nachfolgend wird der Standardbericht des Schweizerischen Treuhänder-Verbandes (STV), vom Autor massgeblich geformt, in einer überarbeiteten Form für den Review wiedergegeben.

Bericht der Revisionsstelle an die Generalversammlung der [Name und Adresse der geprüften Gesellschaft]

Wir haben die Buchführung und die Jahresrechnung Ihrer Gesellschaft als Review geprüft. Die Bilanz per [Datum] weist eine Summe von CHF [Betrag] aus. Die Erfolgsrechnung [Jahr/Zeitraum] zeigt einen [Gewinn/Verlust] von CHF [Betrag].

Die Revision wurde von [Vorname, Name, Titel] geleitet. Wir bestätigen, dass wir die gesetzlichen Anforderungen hinsichtlich Zulassung und Unabhängigkeit erfüllen.

Die Buchführung und die Jahresrechnung [sowie der Antrag über die Verwendung des Bilanzgewinnes] entsprechen Gesetz und Statuten, soweit dies durch eine eingeschränkte Revision beurteilt werden kann.

[Ort, Datum]   *[Firma, Unterschrift und Name]*

Beilage(n):

– Jahresrechnung (Bilanz, Erfolgsrechnung, Anhang)

– [Antrag über die Verwendung des Bilanzgewinnes]

Hinweis: Wir haben für die Gesellschaft folgende Dienstleistungen erbracht [Aufzählung]

II. Standardbericht für Review (Deutsch/Singular)

Bericht des Revisors an die Generalversammlung der [Name und Adresse der geprüften Gesellschaft]

Ich habe die Buchführung und die Jahresrechnung Ihrer Gesellschaft als Review geprüft. Die Bilanz per [Datum] weist eine Summe von CHF [Betrag] aus. Die Erfolgsrechnung [Jahr/Zeitraum] zeigt einen [Gewinn/Verlust] von CHF [Betrag].

Ich bestätige, die gesetzlichen Anforderungen hinsichtlich Zulassung und Unabhängigkeit zu erfüllen.

Die Buchführung und die Jahresrechnung [sowie der Antrag über die Verwendung des Bilanzgewinnes] entsprechen Gesetz und Statuten, soweit dies durch eine eingeschränkte Revision beurteilt werden kann.

[Ort, Datum]   [Firma, Unterschrift und Name, Titel]

Beilage(n):

– Jahresrechnung (Bilanz, Erfolgsrechnung, Anhang)

– [Antrag über die Verwendung des Bilanzgewinnes]

Hinweis: Ich habe für die Gesellschaft folgende Dienstleistungen erbracht [Aufzählung]

Teil C: Revision / Auditing

III. Standardbericht für Review (Französisch/Plural)

Rapport de l'organe de révision à l'assemblée générale de [nom et adresse de la société contrôlée]

Nous avons vérifié en tant que review la comptabilité et les comptes annuels de votre société. Le total du bilan au [date] se monte à CHF [montant]. Le compte de profits et pertes [année/période] présente [un bénéfice/une perte] de CHF [montant].

Notre révision a été effectuée sous la direction de [nom, prénom, titre]. Nous attestons que nous remplissons les exigences légales concernant d'agrément et d'indépendance.

La tenue de la comptabilité et l'établissement des comptes annuels [ainsi que la proposition relative à l'emploi du bénéfice au bilan] sont conformes à la loi et aux statuts, dans la mesure où une révision au sommaire constitue une base suffisante pour former notre opinion.

[Lieu, date]   *[Raison sociale, signature et nom]*

Annexe(s):

– comptes annuels (bilan, compte de profits et pertes, annexe)
– [proposition relative à l'emploi du bénéfice au bilan]

Indications: Pour la société nous avons effectué les services suivants [liste]

Kapitel 3: Allgemeine Prüfungshandlungen

IV. Standardbericht für Review (Französisch/Singular)

Rapport de l'organe de révision à l'assemblée générale de [nom et adresse de la société contrôlée]

J'ai vérifié en tant que review la comptabilité et les comptes annuels de votre société. Le total du bilan au [date] se monte à CHF [montant]. Le compte de profits et pertes [année/période] présente [un bénéfice/une perte] de CHF [montant].

J'atteste que je remplis les exigences légales concernant d'agrément et d'indépendance.

La tenue de la comptabilité et l'établissement des comptes annuels [ainsi que la proposition relative à l'emploi du bénéfice au bilan] sont conformes à la loi et aux statuts, dans la mesure où une révision au sommaire constitue une base suffisante pour former une opinion.

[Lieu, date]   *[Raison sociale, signature et nom, titre]*

Annexe(s):

– comptes annuels (bilan, compte de profits et pertes, annexe)

– [proposition relative à l'emploi du bénéfice au bilan]

Indications: Pour la société j'ai effectué les services suivants [liste]

V. Standardbericht für Review (Italienisch/Plural)

Rapporto di revisione all'assemblea generale degli azionisti della [nome e indirizzo della società verificata]

Abbiamo verificato come rivista la contabilità e il conto annuale della vostra società.

Il bilancio del [data] presenta una somma di fr. [importo]. Il conto perdite e profitti del [anno/periodo] mostra un [utile/perdita] di fr. [importo].

La revisione è stata seguita dal signor [nome, cognome, titolo]. Confermiamo che adempiamo i requisiti richiesti dalle disposizioni legali concernenti indipendenza e abiliazione.

La tenuta della contabilità e i conti di chiusura [così come la proposta di distribuzione degli utili] rispettano le disposizioni legali e statutarie, in misura su rivista sommaria a base riconoscimento sufficiente per formare la nostra opinione.

[luogo e data]   [ditta, firma e nome]

Allegati:

– conti di chiusura (bilancio, conto perdite e profitti, allegato)

– [proposta di distribuzione degli utili]

Indicazione: Per la vostra impresa sono state effetuate seguenti servizi [conguaglio].

Kapitel 3: Allgemeine Prüfungshandlungen

VI. Standardbericht für Review (Italienisch/Singular)

Rapporto di revisione all'assemblea generale degli azionisti della [nome e indirizzo della società verificata]

Ho verificato come rivista la contabilità e il conto annuale della vostra società.

Il bilancio del [data] presenta una somma di fr. [importo]. Il conto perdite e profitti del [anno/periodo] mostra un [utile/perdita] di fr. [importo].

In qualità di revisore, confermo che adempio i requisiti richiesti dalle disposizioni legali concernenti indipendenza e abiliazione.

La tenuta della contabilità e i conti di chiusura [così come la proposta di distribuzione degli utili] rispettano le disposizioni legali e statutarie, in misura su rivista sommaria a base riconoscimento sufficiente per formare la mia opinione.

[luogo e data]   *[ditta, firma e nome, titolo]*

Allegati:

– *conti di chiusura (bilancio, conto perdite e profitti, allegato)*

– *[proposta di distribuzione degli utili]*

Indicazione: Per la vostra impresa sono state effetuate seguenti servizi [conguaglio].

VII. Standardbericht für Review für Stiftungen

(Zwingender Revisionsbericht für Stiftungen ohne Vorsorgezweck/kein Opting out)

Teil C: Revision / Auditing

Bericht der Revisionsstelle an den Stiftungsrat der [Name und Adresse der geprüften Stiftung]

Wir haben die Buchführung und die Jahresrechnung Ihrer Stiftung als Review geprüft. Die Bilanz per [Datum] weist eine Summe von CHF [Betrag] aus. Die Erfolgsrechnung [Jahr/Zeitraum] zeigt einen [Gewinn/ Verlust] von CHF [Betrag].

Die Revision wurde von [Vorname, Name, Titel] geleitet. Wir bestätigen, dass wir zugelassen und unabhängig sind.

Die Buchführung und die Jahresrechnung entsprechen dem Gesetz und der Stiftungsurkunde, soweit dies durch eine eingeschränkte Revision beurteilt werden kann.

[Ort, Datum]   *[Firma, Unterschrift und Name]*

Beilage: Jahresrechnung (Bilanz, Erfolgsrechnung)

Hinweis: Wir haben für die Gesellschaft folgende Dienstleistungen erbracht [Aufzählung].

oder

Bericht des Revisors an den Stiftungsrat der [Name und Adresse der geprüften Stiftung]

Ich habe die Buchführung und die Jahresrechnung Ihrer Stiftung als Review geprüft. Die Bilanz per [Datum] weist eine Summe von CHF [Betrag] aus. Die Erfolgsrechnung [Jahr/Zeitraum] zeigt einen [Gewinn/Verlust] von CHF [Betrag].

Ich bestätige, dass ich zugelassen und unabhängig bin.

Kapitel 3: Allgemeine Prüfungshandlungen

Die Buchführung und die Jahresrechnung entsprechen dem Gesetz und der Stiftungsurkunde, soweit dies durch eine eingeschränkte Revision beurteilt werden kann.

[Ort, Datum]   *[Firma, Unterschrift und Name, Titel]*

Beilage: Jahresrechnung (Bilanz, Erfolgsrechnung)

Hinweis: Wir haben für die Gesellschaft folgende Dienstleistungen erbracht [Aufzählung]

VIII. Standardbericht für Vereine

1. Kaufmännische Buchführung

(Freiwilliger oder statutarischer Revisionsbericht mit Eintragungspflicht im Handelsregister.)

a)   Ordentliche Revision

Bericht der Revisionsstelle an die Mitgliederversammlung des [Name und Adresse des geprüften Vereins]

Wir haben die Buchführung und die Jahresrechnung Ihres Vereins geprüft. Die Bilanz per [Datum] weist eine Summe von CHF [Betrag] aus. Die Erfolgsrechnung [Jahr/Zeitraum] zeigt einen [Gewinn/Verlust] von CHF [Betrag].

Die Revision wurde von [Vorname, Name, Titel] geleitet. Wir bestätigen, dass wir zugelassen und unabhängig sind.

Die Buchführung und die Jahresrechnung entsprechen Gesetz und Statuten.

Wir empfehlen Ihnen, die vorliegende Jahresrechnung zu genehmigen.

Teil C: Revision / Auditing

[Ort, Datum]   *[Firma, Unterschrift und Name]*

Beilage: Jahresrechnung (Bilanz, Erfolgsrechnung)

oder

Bericht des Revisors an die Mitgliederversammlung des [Name und Adresse des geprüften Vereins]

Ich habe die Buchführung und die Jahresrechnung Ihres Vereins geprüft. Die Bilanz per [Datum] weist eine Summe von CHF [Betrag] aus. Die Erfolgsrechnung [Jahr/Zeitraum] zeigt einen [Gewinn/Verlust] von CHF [Betrag].

Ich bestätige, dass ich zugelassen und unabhängig bin.

Die Buchführung und die Jahresrechnung entsprechen dem Gesetz und Statuten.

Ich empfehle Ihnen, die vorliegende Jahresrechnung zu genehmigen.

[Ort, Datum]   *[Firma, Unterschrift und Name, Titel]*

Beilage: Jahresrechnung (Bilanz, Erfolgsrechnung)

b)   Review

Bericht der Revisionsstelle an die Mitgliederversammlung des [Name und Adresse des geprüften Vereins]

Wir haben die Buchführung und die Jahresrechnung Ihres Vereins als Review geprüft. Die Bilanz per [Datum] weist eine Summe von CHF [Be-

trag] aus. Die Erfolgsrechnung [Jahr/Zeitraum] zeigt einen [Gewinn/ Verlust] von CHF [Betrag].

Die Revision wurde von [Vorname, Name, Titel] geleitet. Wir bestätigen, dass wir zugelassen und unabhängig sind.

Die Buchführung und die Jahresrechnung entsprechen Gesetz und Statuten, soweit dies durch eine eingeschränkte Revision beurteilt werden kann.

[Ort, Datum]   *[Firma, Unterschrift und Name]*

Beilage: Jahresrechnung (Bilanz, Erfolgsrechnung)

Hinweis: Wir haben für die Gesellschaft folgende Dienstleistungen erbracht [Aufzählung]

oder

Bericht des Revisors an die Mitgliederversammlung des [Name und Adresse des geprüften Vereins]

Ich habe die Buchführung und die Jahresrechnung Ihres Vereins als Review geprüft. Die Bilanz per [Datum] weist eine Summe von CHF [Betrag] aus. Die Erfolgsrechnung [Jahr/Zeitraum] zeigt einen [Gewinn/Verlust] von CHF [Betrag].

Ich bestätige, dass ich zugelassen und unabhängig bin.

Die Buchführung und die Jahresrechnung entsprechen dem Gesetz und Statuten, soweit dies durch eine eingeschränkte Revision beurteilt werden kann.

[Ort, Datum]   *[Firma, Unterschrift und Name, Titel]*

Teil C: Revision / Auditing

> Beilage: Jahresrechnung (Bilanz, Erfolgsrechnung)
>
> Hinweis: Ich habe für die Gesellschaft folgende Dienstleistungen erbracht [Aufzählung]

2.   Ohne Kaufmännische Buchführung

(Ohne Eintragungspflicht im Handelsregister)

a)   Ordentliche Revision

> **Bericht der Revisionsstelle an die Mitgliederversammlung des [Name und Adresse des geprüften Vereins]**
>
> *Wir haben die Buchführung und die Jahresrechnung Ihres Vereins geprüft. Die Bilanz per [Datum] weist eine Summe von CHF [Betrag] aus. Die Erfolgsrechnung [Jahr/Zeitraum] zeigt einen [Gewinn/Verlust] von CHF [Betrag].*
>
> *Die Revision wurde von [Vorname, Name, Titel] geleitet. Wir bestätigen, dass wir zugelassen und unabhängig sind.*
>
> *Die Buchführung und die Jahresrechnung entsprechen den Statuten.*
>
> *Wir empfehlen Ihnen, die vorliegende Jahresrechnung zu genehmigen.*
>
> [Ort, Datum]   [Firma, Unterschrift und Name]
>
> Beilage: Jahresrechnung (Bilanz, Erfolgsrechnung)

oder

> **Bericht des Revisors an die Mitgliederversammlung des [Name und Adresse des geprüften Vereins]**
>
> *Ich habe die Buchführung und die Jahresrechnung Ihres Vereins geprüft. Die Bilanz per [Datum] weist eine Summe von CHF [Betrag] aus. Die*

Kapitel 3: Allgemeine Prüfungshandlungen

> *Erfolgsrechnung [Jahr/Zeitraum] zeigt einen [Gewinn/Verlust] von CHF [Betrag].*
>
> *Ich bestätige, dass ich zugelassen und unabhängig bin.*
>
> *Die Buchführung und die Jahresrechnung entsprechen den Statuten.*
>
> *Ich empfehle Ihnen, die vorliegende Jahresrechnung zu genehmigen.*
>
> *[Ort, Datum]   [Firma, Unterschrift und Name, Titel]*
>
> *Beilage: Jahresrechnung (Bilanz, Erfolgsrechnung)*

b) Review

> **Bericht der Revisionsstelle an die Mitgliederversammlung des [Name und Adresse des geprüften Vereins]**
>
> *Wir haben die Buchführung und die Jahresrechnung Ihres Vereins als Review geprüft. Die Bilanz per [Datum] weist eine Summe von CHF [Betrag] aus. Die Erfolgsrechnung [Jahr/Zeitraum] zeigt einen [Gewinn/Verlust] von CHF [Betrag].*
>
> *Die Revision wurde von [Vorname, Name, Titel] geleitet. Wir bestätigen, dass wir zugelassen und unabhängig sind.*
>
> *Die Buchführung und die Jahresrechnung entsprechen den Statuten, soweit dies durch eine eingeschränkte Revision beurteilt werden kann.*
>
> *[Ort, Datum]   [Firma, Unterschrift und Name]*
>
> *Beilage: Jahresrechnung (Bilanz, Erfolgsrechnung)*
>
> *Hinweis: Wir haben für die Gesellschaft folgende Dienstleistungen erbracht [Aufzählung]*

oder

> **Bericht des Revisors an die Mitgliederversammlung des [Name und Adresse des geprüften Vereins]**
>
> *Ich habe die Buchführung und die Jahresrechnung Ihres Vereins als Review geprüft. Die Bilanz per [Datum] weist eine Summe von CHF [Betrag] aus. Die Erfolgsrechnung [Jahr/Zeitraum] zeigt einen [Gewinn/Verlust] von CHF [Betrag].*
>
> *Ich bestätige, dass ich zugelassen und unabhängig bin.*
>
> *Die Buchführung und die Jahresrechnung entsprechen den Statuten, soweit dies durch eine eingeschränkte Revision beurteilt werden kann.*
>
> *[Ort, Datum]   [Firma, Unterschrift und Name, Titel]*
>
> *Beilage: Jahresrechnung (Bilanz, Erfolgsrechnung)*
>
> *Hinweis: Ich habe für die Gesellschaft folgende Dienstleistungen erbracht [Aufzählung]*

IX. Standardbericht für Subventionierte (Kanton BS), Fassung 1998

Die Finanzkontrolle des Kantons Basel-Stadt hat Richtlinien für die Revision von subventionierten Institutionen erlassen. Diese beruhen im Wesentlichen auf meinen Vorschlägen zur Revision von Vereinen. Der Standardtext entspricht auch weitestgehend meiner Kurzformulierung. Obwohl dieser Standardtext nur für den Kanton Basel-Stadt Anwendung findet, ist er hier wiedergegeben:

Kapitel 3: Allgemeine Prüfungshandlungen

> **Bericht der Revisionsstelle an die Mitgliederversammlung der [Name und Adresse der geprüften Institution]**
>
> *Wir haben die Buchführung und die Jahresrechnung Ihrer Institution geprüft. Die Bilanz per [Datum] weist eine Summe von CHF [Betrag] aus. Die Erfolgsrechnung [Jahr/Zeitraum] zeigt einen [Gewinn/Verlust] von CHF [Betrag].*
>
> *Die Buchführung und die Jahresrechnung (sowie der Antrag über die Verwendung des Ergebnisses) entsprechen den allgemeinen kaufmännischen Buchführungsvorschriften sowie den Statuten.*
>
> *Nebst der ordentlichen Rechnungsprüfung wurde auch die Einhaltung des Subventionsvertrages geprüft. Der Leistungsauftrag wurde aufgrund der vertraglichen Abmachungen erfüllt. Die im Rahmen des Subventionsvertrages zugestandenen Rücklagen sind ebenso wie die Einlagen resp. die Entnahmen offen ausgewiesen.*
>
> *Wir empfehlen Ihnen, die vorliegende Jahresrechnung zu genehmigen.*
>
> *[Ort, Datum]*   *[Unterschrift und Name]*
>
> *Beilage: Jahresrechnung (Bilanz, Erfolgsrechnung und Anhang)*

X. Standardbericht für Genossenschaften

Nach neuem Recht ist dies wie bei der Aktiengesellschaft zu beurteilen.

(Gesetzlicher Revisionsbericht)

Teil C: Revision / Auditing

1. Ordentliche Revision

Bericht der Revisionsstelle an die Generalversammlung der [Name und Adresse der geprüften Genossenschaft]

Wir haben die Buchführung und die Jahresrechnung Ihrer Genossenschaft geprüft. Die Bilanz per [Datum] weist eine Summe von CHF [Betrag] aus. Die Erfolgsrechnung [Jahr/Zeitraum] zeigt einen [Gewinn/Verlust] von CHF [Betrag].

Die Revision wurde von [Vorname, Name, Titel] geleitet. Wir bestätigen, dass wir zugelassen und unabhängig sind.

Die Buchführung und die Jahresrechnung entsprechen Gesetz und Statuten.

Wir empfehlen Ihnen, die vorliegende Jahresrechnung zu genehmigen.

[Ort, Datum]   *[Firma, Unterschrift und Name]*

Beilage: Jahresrechnung (Bilanz, Erfolgsrechnung)

2. Review

Bericht der Revisionsstelle an die Generalversammlung der [Name und Adresse der geprüften Genossenschaft]

Wir haben die Buchführung und die Jahresrechnung Ihrer Genossenschaft als Review geprüft. Die Bilanz per [Datum] weist eine Summe von CHF [Betrag] aus. Die Erfolgsrechnung [Jahr/Zeitraum] zeigt einen [Gewinn/Verlust] von CHF [Betrag].

Die Revision wurde von [Vorname, Name, Titel] geleitet. Wir bestätigen, dass wir zugelassen und unabhängig sind.

Die Buchführung und die Jahresrechnung entsprechen Gesetz und Statuten, soweit dies durch eine eingeschränkte Revision beurteilt werden kann.

Kapitel 3: Allgemeine Prüfungshandlungen

> *[Ort, Datum]*   *[Firma, Unterschrift und Name]*
>
> Beilage: *Jahresrechnung (Bilanz, Erfolgsrechnung)*
>
> Hinweis: *Wir haben für die Gesellschaft folgende Dienstleistungen erbracht [Aufzählung]*

XI. Standardbericht für GmbH

Nach neuem Recht ist dies wie bei der Aktiengesellschaft zu beurteilen.

1. Ordentliche Revision

> **Bericht der Revisionsstelle an die Gesellschafterversammlung der [Name und Adresse der geprüften Gesellschaft mit beschränkter Haftung]**
>
> *Wir haben die Buchführung und die Jahresrechnung Ihrer Gesellschaft geprüft. Die Bilanz per [Datum] weist eine Summe von CHF [Betrag] aus. Die Erfolgsrechnung [Jahr/Zeitraum] zeigt einen [Gewinn/Verlust] von CHF [Betrag].*
>
> *Die Revision wurde von [Vorname, Name, Titel] geleitet. Wir bestätigen, dass wir zugelassen und unabhängig sind.*
>
> *Die Buchführung und die Jahresrechnung entsprechen Gesetz und Statuten.*
>
> *Wir empfehlen Ihnen, die vorliegende Jahresrechnung zu genehmigen.*
>
> *[Ort, Datum]*   *[Firma, Unterschrift und Name]*
>
> Beilage: *Jahresrechnung (Bilanz, Erfolgsrechnung, Anhang)*

2. Review

> **Bericht der Revisionsstelle an die Gesellschafterversammlung der [Name und Adresse der geprüften Gesellschaft mit beschränkter Haftung]**
>
> *Wir haben die Buchführung und die Jahresrechnung Ihrer Gesellschaft als Review geprüft. Die Bilanz per [Datum] weist eine Summe von CHF [Betrag] aus. Die Erfolgsrechnung [Jahr/Zeitraum] zeigt einen [Gewinn/Verlust] von CHF [Betrag].*
>
> *Die Revision wurde von [Vorname, Name, Titel] geleitet. Wir bestätigen, dass wir zugelassen und unabhängig sind.*
>
> *Die Buchführung und die Jahresrechnung entsprechen Gesetz und Statuten, soweit dies durch eine eingeschränkte Revision beurteilt werden kann.*
>
> *[Ort, Datum]   [Firma, Unterschrift und Name]*
>
> *Beilage: Jahresrechnung (Bilanz, Erfolgsrechnung, Anhang)*
>
> *Hinweis: Wir haben für die Gesellschaft folgende Dienstleistungen erbracht [Aufzählung]*

XII. Standardbericht für Kollektivgesellschaften

(Freiwilliger oder vertraglicher Revisionsbericht mit Eintragungspflicht der Gesellschaft im Handelsregister)

Kapitel 3: Allgemeine Prüfungshandlungen

1. Ordentliche Revision

Bericht der vertraglichen Revisionsstelle an die Gesellschafterversammlung des [Name und Adresse der geprüften Kollektivgesellschaft]

Wir haben die Buchführung und die Jahresrechnung Ihrer Gesellschaft geprüft. Die Bilanz per [Datum] weist eine Summe von CHF [Betrag] aus. Die Erfolgsrechnung [Jahr/Zeitraum] zeigt einen [Gewinn/Verlust] von CHF [Betrag].

Die Revision wurde von [Vorname, Name, Titel] geleitet. Wir bestätigen, dass wir zugelassen und unabhängig sind.

Die Buchführung und die Jahresrechnung entsprechen Gesetz und Statuten.

Wir empfehlen Ihnen, die vorliegende Jahresrechnung zu genehmigen.

[Ort, Datum] *[Firma, Unterschrift und Name]*

Beilage: Jahresrechnung (Bilanz, Erfolgsrechnung)

2. Review

Bericht der vertraglichen Revisionsstelle an die Gesellschafterversammlung des [Name und Adresse der geprüften Kollektivgesellschaft]

Wir haben die Buchführung und die Jahresrechnung Ihrer Gesellschaft als Review geprüft. Die Bilanz per [Datum] weist eine Summe von CHF [Betrag] aus. Die Erfolgsrechnung [Jahr/Zeitraum] zeigt einen [Gewinn/Verlust] von CHF [Betrag].

Die Revision wurde von [Vorname, Name, Titel] geleitet. Wir bestätigen, dass wir zugelassen und unabhängig sind.

> *Die Buchführung und die Jahresrechnung entsprechen Gesetz und Statuten, soweit dies durch eine eingeschränkte Revision beurteilt werden kann.*
>
> *[Ort, Datum]*   *[Firma, Unterschrift und Name]*
>
> *Beilage: Jahresrechnung (Bilanz, Erfolgsrechnung)*
>
> *Hinweis: Wir haben für die Gesellschaft folgende Dienstleistungen erbracht [Aufzählung]*

§ 8 Abweichungen von der Standardberichterstattung

I. Einführung

Die Revisionsstelle ist bei der ordentlichen Revision dazu angehalten, gleichzeitig eine Empfehlung auszusprechen, über die die Aktionäre sich theoretisch hinwegsetzen können, nämlich:

1) auf Genehmigung der Jahresrechnung ohne Einschränkung,

2) auf Genehmigung der Jahresrechnung mit Einschränkung oder

3) auf Rückweisung der Jahresrechnung an den Verwaltungsrat.

Hat die Prüfung ergeben, dass ein Rechnungsabschluss nur mit Einschränkungen zur Annahme empfohlen werden kann oder zur Abänderung an die Verwaltung zurückgewiesen werden muss, so ist der Wortlaut des Bestätigungsberichtes entsprechend anzupassen. Eine Weglassung der zu bestätigenden Punkte genügt nicht, sondern die festgestellten Mängel sind konkret als Einschränkung oder als Hinweis im Bericht aufzuführen.

Eine wichtige Einschränkung liegt z.B. vor, wenn die aktienrechtlichen Bewertungsvorschriften nicht oder nur teilweise eingehalten wurden und deshalb in der Bilanz wesentliche Positionen falsch dargestellt sind.

Ein wichtiger Hinweis ist derjenige auf Art. 725 OR, wenn es der Verwaltungsrat unterlassen hat, bei einer ausgewiesenen Überschuldung der Gesellschaft eine Zwischenbilanz zu Veräusserungswerten zu erstellen.

Kapitel 3: Allgemeine Prüfungshandlungen

Bei der eingeschränkten Revision ist die Revisionsstelle nicht mehr verpflichtet, die Empfehlung über Annahme oder Nicht-Annahme bzw. Rückweisung abzugeben. Falls sie jedoch im Rahmen ihrer Revision auf wesentliche Fehler stösst, ist sie gleichwohl gehalten, darüber zu berichten.

II. Vorbehalte, Einschränkungen, Hinweise, Meldungen etc.

Es ist an dieser Stelle noch einmal mit Nachdruck darauf hinzuweisen, dass der Revisionsbericht nicht dazu da ist, Revisions- und Buchhaltungsprobleme zu lösen. Der Bericht soll nicht, mit textlichen Erweiterungen, dazu dienen, eine mögliche Überschuldung zu übertünchen oder als Entschuldigungsschreiben die Revisionsstelle von ihrer Handlungspflicht (Anzeige der Überschuldung etc.) zu entbinden. Zu viel Text im Bericht zeigt eine problembeladene Revision. Viele Einschränkungen, Hinweise und Vorbehalte sind dann eher durch einen Bericht zu ersetzen, bei dem die Buchhaltung und Jahresrechnung nicht zur Genehmigung empfohlen wird. Eine solche Empfehlung ist auch im Rahmen des Review möglich.

1. Vorbehalte

a)   Vorbehaltsfeindlicher Revisionsbericht

Der Revisionsbericht ist vorbehaltsfeindlich. Er ist nicht dazu bestimmt, unter Vorbehalt erstattet zu werden. Die Revisionsstelle hat Prüfungs- und Berichterstattungspflicht. Dem kann sie sich nicht entziehen. Mit ihrem Urteil prüft sie die Jahresrechnung, welche sie zur Genehmigung empfiehlt, wobei die Möglichkeit zu einem Hinweis auf Mängel besteht. Sie muss im Rahmen ihrer Berichterstattung zu einem Urteil darüber kommen, ob eine Empfehlung zur Genehmigung an die Generalversammlung auszusprechen ist oder nicht.

b)   Beispiel 1

Eine Berichterstattung mit folgendem Text ginge an der gesetzlichen Prüfungs- und Berichterstattungspflicht vorbei:

«Die Jahresrechnung entspricht unter dem Vorbehalt einer Sanierung Gesetz und Statuten.»

Die Aktionäre, der Verwaltungsrat und die Gläubiger der Gesellschaft erwarten eine klare Beurteilung. Bei Unklarheiten muss die Revisionsstelle einen Bewertungseinschlag berechnen und daraus beurteilen, ob das ausgewiesene Kapital vorhanden ist oder ob gar eine offensichtliche Überschuldung vorliegt. Um diese Beurteilung kommt sie nicht umhin, auch nicht mit Vorbehalten.

c) Beispiel 2

Auch ein Vorbehalt über die Investition und deren Bewertung ist fraglich.

«Der Revisionsbericht steht unter dem Vorbehalt der Bewertung des Investitionsprojektes '<Ferienwohnungen in Spanien'>. Die Gesellschaft hat dort beträchtliche Investitionen geleistet und die Anlage steht in der zweiten von insgesamt vier Bauphasen. Eine abschliessende Beurteilung ist nicht möglich, da deren Bewertung von der zukünftigen Bewirtschaftung abhängt. Sollten sich die Planzahlen nicht realisieren, könnte die Vermutung bestehen, dass mehr als die Hälfte des Kapitals und der Reserven verloren ist. Wir weisen darauf hin, dass der Verwaltungsrat diesfalls entgegen den Bestimmungen von Art. 725 Abs. 1 OR es bisher unterlassen hat, die Generalversammlung über den Verlust von mehr als der Hälfte des Aktienkapitals und der gesetzlichen Reserven zu orientieren und Sanierungsmassnahmen zu beantragen.»

Solche langen Texte sind schwer leserlich und nicht praktikabel. Sie werfen ein ungutes Licht auf die Revisionsstelle. Es empfiehlt sich bloss eine klare Analyse. Ist genügend Kapital (Eigen- und Fremdkapital) vorhanden, um das Projekt zu Ende zu bauen? Wird eine Bilanzierung zu Gestehungskosten zulässig sein? Die Revisionsstelle darf davon ausgehen, dass die Verwaltung sinnvolle Investitionen vornimmt. Die Revisionsstelle ist nicht Investitionsprüfungsstelle. Nur bei offensichtlicher Fehlinvestition muss sie darüber berichten.

Mit einem Vorbehalt, und sei er auch noch so deutlich, kommt die Revisionsstelle nicht um ihre Verantwortung. Entscheidend ist vielmehr, ob die Jahresrechnung Gesetz und Statuten entspricht.

Kapitel 3: Allgemeine Prüfungshandlungen

d)   Beispiel 3

Auch ein Passus wie der folgende ist nicht behilflich:

«Die Aktivierung der Entwicklung von EDV-Programmen kann nicht vollständig beurteilt werden, da deren zukünftige Marktchancen offen sind. Falls die von der Verwaltung prognostizierten Umsatzzahlen nicht realisiert werden können, besteht Anlass zur Vermutung, dass die Bewertung zu hoch ist. Mit der Bewertungskorrektur kann mehr als die Hälfte des Aktienkapitals und der Reserven verloren sein. Wir machen in diesem Fall den Verwaltungsrat darauf aufmerksam, dass eine ausserordentliche Generalversammlung einberufen werden muss und dass Sanierungsmassnahmen beantragt werden müssen.»

Solche Formulierungen lösen das Problem nicht. Auch kann sich die Revisionsstelle nicht ihrer Verantwortung mit dem Hinweis entziehen, sie habe auf diesen kritischen Punkt in ihrem Bericht hingewiesen. Ist die Bewertung im Sinne der Rechnungslegung vertretbar, ist nichts dazu zu bemerken; ist die Bewertung nicht vertretbar oder nicht zulässig, hat sie darüber zu berichten. Ein Dilemma bleibt. Muss sie berichten und sagt sie nichts, verletzt sie ihre Pflicht. Berichtet sie, muss sie dies in aller Konsequenz des Gesetzes tun. Ein Text wie der vorherige liegt in der gefährlichen Mitte. Er zeigt dem Leser, dass Unsicherheiten bestanden hatten, und lädt bei einem allfälligen Konkurs gerade dazu ein, die Verantwortlichkeit der Revisionsstelle anzurufen. Gefordert ist also ein «vorbehaltloser» Bericht oder ein konsequenter Hinweis bzw. eine konsequente Einschränkung.

e)   Der Anhang als Information

Wie gesagt, ist der Revisionsbericht nicht dazu da, die Probleme einer kritischen Jahresrechnung zu lösen. Ein Ansatz, ein solches Problem wie oben dargestellt zu lösen, kann darin liegen, im Anhang diesen Bilanzposten näher zu umschreiben. Der Anhang ist dazu da, «andere wesentliche Angaben» anzuführen. Dazu kann der Beschrieb der Aktivierung eines wesentlichen Bilanzpostens zählen.

Gelangt die Revisionsstelle zum Schluss, dass die Bewertung zu optimistisch ist, muss sie eine Bewertungskorrektur machen. Führt diese Korrektur zu einer offensichtlichen Überschuldung, muss sie den Richter benachrichtigen.

2. Einschränkungen

Wenn die Revisionsstelle aufgrund ihrer Prüfungen zum Ergebnis kommt, dass alles ordnungsgemäss ist, kann sie einen vorbehaltlosen Bericht oder besser, einen Bericht ohne Einschränkung erstellen. Kommt sie nicht zu diesem Schluss, muss sie darüber Bericht erstatten. Die vom Standardbericht abweichende Berichterstattung ist nur notwendig, wenn die Ordnungswidrigkeit wesentlich ist.

Die geläufigsten Abweichungen sind als Textbeispiele nachfolgend aufgeführt. Die Aufzählung erhebt keinen Anspruch auf Vollständigkeit. Nicht jeder Textbaustein kann tel quel aufgenommen werden. So ist z.B. die Einschränkung auf die mangelnde Führung einer Mittelflussrechnung nur angebracht, wenn die Führung im Sinne des Gesetzes notwendig ist.

Weiter können auch Einschränkungen nicht nötig sein, wenn der Anhang bereits darüber Auskunft gibt. Wenn in der Position «Abweichungen zur ordnungsgemässen Rechnungslegung» ausgeführt wird, dass die Immobilien im Berichtsjahr nicht abgeschrieben wurden, so jedoch im Vorjahr, und damit eine Abweichung vom Erfordernis der Stetigkeit vorliegt, muss dieser Punkt im Revisionsbericht nicht mehr erwähnt werden. Wenn durch diese Nichtabschreibung andere wesentliche Merkmale, z.B. Verlust von mehr als der Hälfte des Aktienkapitals und der Reserven, berührt sind, muss der Revisionsbericht dies erwähnen.

3. Hinweise

Der Bericht der Revisionsstelle erfolgt mit oder ohne Einschränkungen. Einschränkungen sind bei Feststellung von wesentlichen Abweichungen von der ordnungsgemässen Rechnungslegung notwendig. Die Berichterstattung hat hier materiellen Inhalt. Demgegenüber stehen Hinweise, die blossen Informationscharakter haben.

- Einschränkungen: Gefahrensignal
- Hinweis: Information

Dies gilt sowohl für den Revisor als auch für den Leser des Revisionsberichtes.

Kapitel 3: Allgemeine Prüfungshandlungen

4. Meldung

Neben der Einschränkung und dem Hinweis gibt es als gesetzlich vorgesehene Variante noch die Meldung gemäss Art. 728c OR. Sie erfolgt seitens der Revisionsstelle bei Verstössen gegen Gesetz, Statuten oder Organisationsreglement. Beim Review entfällt dies; allenfalls liegt eine freiwillige Berichterstattung der Revisionsstelle vor.

5. Bemerkungen zur Geschäftslage

Nicht Aufgabe der Revisionsstelle ist es, sich über die Geschäftslage zu äussern. Für die Geschäftspolitik, die Strategie und das Leitbild des Unternehmens ist alleine der Verwaltungsrat zuständig. Auch hat sich die Revisionsstelle nicht über den wirtschaftlichen Sinn oder Unsinn von Investitionen zu äussern.

In einen Grenzbereich zu dieser Problematik gelangt man bei Fällen, wo sich die Revisionsstelle zur Liquidität äussert.

> **Beispiel:**
>
> *Wir weisen darauf hin, dass die vom Verwaltungsrat vorgeschlagene Dividende sich negativ auf die weitere Entwicklung der Gesellschaft auswirken könnte. Die Liquidität wird durch die Dividendenauszahlung wesentlich eingeschränkt* (sinngemäss aus RHB 1992).

Meiner Meinung nach ist eine solche Berichterstattung möglich, gehört aber nicht in den Aufgabenbereich der Revisionsstelle. Sie hat nicht zu beurteilen, ob genügend Liquidität vorhanden ist. Die Liquidität spielt nur dann eine Rolle, wenn sie für die Bewertung massgebend ist. So können angefangene Arbeiten nur dann zu Einstandspreisen bewertet werden, wenn genügend Liquidität vorhanden ist, damit diese Arbeiten auch zu Ende geführt werden können. Das Gleiche gilt z.B. für technische Entwicklungen. Die Revisionsstelle hat sich deshalb nicht zur Liquidität zu äussern, sondern zur Bewertung, sofern diese durch mangelnde Liquidität beeinflusst wird. Die Frage der Liquiditätsbeurteilung ist auch deshalb schwer durch die Revisionsstelle zu beurteilen, weil diese Liquidität massgeblich von Investitionen oder Desinvestitionen beeinflusst ist. Für Investitionen ist ausschliesslich die Verwaltung zuständig. Eine Beurteilung durch die Revisionsstelle führt zu einer Vermischung der Aufgaben.

III. Abweichungen (Einschränkungen)

1. Rechnungslegung

a) Aussagekraft der Jahresrechnung

Einschränkung: *Die Jahresrechnung gibt keinen genügenden Einblick für eine zuverlässige Beurteilung der Vermögens- und Ertragslage, da keine Mittelflussrechnung geführt wird.*

Einschränkung: *Die Jahresrechnung gibt keinen genügenden Einblick für eine zuverlässige Beurteilung der Vermögens- und Ertragslage, da die Bilanz und Erfolgsrechnung zu komprimiert ist und nicht alle Kontengruppen im Detail ausgewiesen sind.*

Einschränkung: *Die Jahresrechnung gibt keinen genügenden Einblick für eine zuverlässige Beurteilung der Vermögens- und Ertragslage, da keine Vorjahreszahlen aufgeführt sind.*

b) Vollständigkeit

Einschränkung: *Die Jahresrechnung ist nicht vollständig, da kein Anhang aufgeführt ist.*

Einschränkung: *Die Jahresrechnung ist nicht vollständig, da keine Kreditoren mit Stichtag des Geschäftsabschlusses gebucht sind.*

Einschränkung: *Die Jahresrechnung ist nicht vollständig, da der Geschäftsertrag nicht vollständig erfasst ist.*

c) Klarheit

Einschränkung: *Die Jahresrechnung ist nicht klar, da die buchmässige Anpassung des Warenlagers in der Erfolgsrechnung in den Abschreibungen anstatt im Warenaufwand erfasst ist.*

Einschränkung: *Die Jahresrechnung ist nicht klar, da angefangene Arbeiten erfasst sind, währenddem die latenten Aufwendungen (gelieferte und verarbeitete Leistungen, die aber noch nicht fakturiert sind) nicht entsprechend passiviert und erfasst sind.*

Kapitel 3: Allgemeine Prüfungshandlungen

d) Bilanzvorsicht

Einschränkung: *Die Jahresrechnung widerspricht dem Gebot der Vorsicht, da die Warenlagerbestände zum Marktwert und nicht zum tieferen Einstandswert bewertet sind.*

e) Fortführungswerte

Dazu kommen Hinweise oder Einschränkungen nur sehr selten vor. Anstelle der Fortführungswerte sind nur Liquidationswerte denkbar. Sind diese höher und entsprechend bilanziert, liegt ein Verstoss gegen das Niederstwertprinzip (vgl. lit. d Bilanzvorsicht) vor. Sind diese Liquidationswerte tiefer, können sie im Rahmen der Bilanzvorsicht ohne Verstoss gegen das «Prinzip der Bilanzierung zu Fortführungswerten» entsprechend Eingang in die Bilanz finden.

f) Verrechnungsverbot

Einschränkung: *Die Jahresrechnung widerspricht dem Verrechnungsverbot, da der Umsatz nicht brutto ausgewiesen, sondern bereits um Warenaufwendungen gekürzt ist.*

g) Stetigkeit

Einschränkung: *Die Jahresrechnung widerspricht dem Prinzip der Stetigkeit, da die Warenlagerbestände im Berichtsjahr zu 2/3 des Einstandswertes bewertet sind, währenddem im Vorjahr eine Bewertung zu 4/5 erfolgte.*

Einschränkung: *Die Jahresrechnung widerspricht dem Prinzip der Stetigkeit, da die Immobilien im Berichtsjahr nicht abgeschrieben wurden, im Vorjahr hingegen mit 7 % degressiv.*

h) Wesentlichkeit

Einschränkung: *Die Jahresrechnung widerspricht dem Prinzip der Wesentlichkeit, da im Anhang nur Beteiligungen mit einer Quote von 51 % aufgeführt sind, währenddem noch andere Beteiligungen mit weniger hohen Quoten im Bestand sind, die für das Unternehmen von strategischer Bedeutung und damit wesentlich sind.*

Einschränkung: *Die angefangenen Arbeiten sind zu Herstellungskosten bewertet. Ein Marktwert ist objektiv nicht ermittelbar.*

2. Gesetzesverstösse

Meldung: *Die Gesellschaft hat erhebliche Darlehen aus Medellin (Venezuela) erhalten, die sich geschäftsmässig nicht klar begründen lassen und auf strafrechtlich relevante Handlungen zurückzuführen sein könnten.*

3. Mangelndes Handeln des Verwaltungsrates (Hinweis)

a) Verlust von mehr als der Hälfte des Aktienkapitals und der Reserven

Hinweis: *Wir weisen darauf hin, dass es der Verwaltungsrat entgegen den Bestimmungen von Art. 725 Abs. 1 OR bisher unterlassen hat, die Generalversammlung über den Verlust von mehr als der Hälfte des Aktienkapitals und der gesetzlichen Reserven zu orientieren und ihr Sanierungsmassnahmen zu beantragen.*

(aus RHB 1992)

b) Verlust des Eigenkapitals (Überschuldung)

Hinweis: *Wir weisen darauf hin, dass es der Verwaltungsrat unterlassen hat, angesichts der ausgewiesenen Überschuldung eine Zwischenbilanz zu erstellen. Sollte die Zwischenbilanz zeigen, dass auch zu Veräusserungswerten eine Überschuldung besteht, müsste gemäss Art. 725 Abs. 2 OR der Richter benachrichtigt werden.*

(aus RHB 1992)

4. Hinweise

a) Formelle Überschuldung

Hinweis: *Wir halten fest, dass die Gesellschaft buchmässig überschuldet ist. In der gemäss Art. 725 Abs. 2 OR erstellten Zwischenbilanz zu Ver-*

Kapitel 3: Allgemeine Prüfungshandlungen

äusserungswerten sind indessen die Forderungen der Gläubiger durch die Aktiven gedeckt.

(aus RHB 1992)

b) Dividende

Hinweis: *Wir weisen darauf hin, dass die vom Verwaltungsrat vorgeschlagene Dividende sich negativ auf die weitere Entwicklung der Gesellschaft auswirken könnte. Die Liquidität wird durch die Dividendenauszahlung wesentlich eingeschränkt.*

(sinngemäss aus RHB 1992)

Hinweis: *Wir weisen darauf hin, dass die vom Verwaltungsrat vorgeschlagene Dividende sich negativ auf die weitere Entwicklung der Gesellschaft auswirken könnte. Die Gesellschaft verfügt nicht mehr über das betriebsnotwendige Eigenkapital.*

c) Rangrücktritt

Hinweis: *Wir halten ferner fest, dass auch die zu Veräusserungswerten erstellte Zwischenbilanz eine Überschuldung ausweist. Da für Guthaben in der Höhe von CHF [Betrag] Rangrücktritt erklärt wurde, hat der Verwaltungsrat gemäss den Bestimmungen von Art. 725 Abs. 2 auf die Benachrichtigung des Richters verzichtet.*

(aus RHB 1992)

5. *Konklusion*

Die Buchführung und die Jahresrechnung [sowie der Antrag über die Verwendung des Bilanzgewinnes] entsprechen mit Ausnahme der zuvor erwähnten Hinweise Gesetz und Statuten.

Oder absolut:

Die Buchführung und die Jahresrechnung (sowie der Antrag über die Verwendung des Bilanzgewinnes) entsprechen nicht Gesetz und Statuten.

6. Empfehlung der Revisionsstelle

Diese Empfehlung ist im Review nicht mehr vorgesehen. Werden in der Revision erhebliche Mängel festgestellt, ist meines Erachtens die Revisionsstelle gehalten, dennoch die Nichtgenehmigung zu empfehlen.

Wir empfehlen Ihnen, die vorliegende Jahresrechnung zu genehmigen.

Oder:

Wir empfehlen Ihnen, die vorliegende Jahresrechnung trotz der zuvor erwähnten Einschränkungen zu genehmigen.

Oder absolut:

Wir empfehlen Ihnen, die vorliegende Jahresrechnung aufgrund der zuvor erwähnten Hinweise nicht zu genehmigen.

7. Überschuldungsanzeige

Es ist auf oben Erwähntes (Ziff. 6) zu verweisen.

Wir empfehlen Ihnen, die vorliegende Jahresrechnung aufgrund der zuvor erwähnten Einschränkungen nicht zu genehmigen.

Wir sind weiter der Meinung, dass eine offensichtliche Überschuldung vorliegt, und haben deshalb den Richter benachrichtigt, da es die Verwaltung unterlassen hat, diesen Schritt einzuleiten.

IV. Problemhaftes Abweichen vom Standardbericht

Solange der Revisor den Standardbericht verwenden kann, ergeben sich keine Probleme. Die Probleme entstehen erst, wenn er davon abweicht und Einschränkungen darin enthalten sind. Das Problem liegt darin, dass die Revisionsstelle den Leser mit dem Anbringen von Einschränkungen darauf aufmerksam macht, wo Probleme sind. Führen diese Probleme später zu Folgen, kann man der Revisionsstelle eine Unterlassung vorwerfen.

Kapitel 3: Allgemeine Prüfungshandlungen

Beispiel:

Einschränkung: *Die angefangenen Arbeiten sind zu Gestehungskosten bewertet. Sie umfassen die Entwicklung eines EDV-Programmes im Bereiche der Telekommunikation. Dieser Bilanzposten kann in der Bewertung nicht abschliessend beurteilt werden, da die Marktchancen dieses Produktes noch nicht bestimmbar sind. Sollte das Produkt keine Marktfähigkeit haben, so muss die Entwicklung als Nonvaleur angesehen werden. In diesem Fall machen wir den Verwaltungsrat auf Art. 725 OR aufmerksam.*

Es stellt sich die Frage, welchem Zweck ein Hinweis dient. Die Revisionsstelle kann nie wissen, wie sich die Investitionen für das Unternehmen in der Zukunft zeigen. Die Revisionsstelle ist kein Investitionsprüfungsorgan. Diese Aufgabe kommt ihr nicht zu. Nur dort, wo die Investition offensichtlich nutzlos ist, kann sie einen Hinweis anfügen. Solche Fälle dürften die seltene Ausnahme sein und in der Regel hat die Revisionsstelle die Investitionen nur auf die Zulässigkeit ihrer Aktivierung zu überprüfen. In unserem Beispiel muss sie prüfen, ob es langfristig oder kurzfristig angefangene Arbeiten sind, ob die Gestehungskosten genau ermittelt sind und ob genügend Mittel da sind, um die Arbeiten zu Ende zu führen. Je grösser die Bilanzposition, desto höher sind die Anforderungen an die Ermittlung.

Wenn wir nun zur Formulierung des Hinweises zurückkehren, so müssen wir uns fragen, ob ein solcher notwendig ist. Ich verneine dies. Sind die Buchführungsvorschriften eingehalten, ist die Aktivierung in Ordnung, sind sie nicht eingehalten, muss eine Einschränkung erfolgen. Die Einhaltung der Buchführungsvorschriften kann nicht davon abhängig gemacht werden, ob in der Zukunft etwas gut geht oder nicht. Die Buchführungsvorschriften richten sich nach der Gegenwart und diese muss die Revisionsstelle beurteilen. In concreto ist ein Hinweis nicht gefordert, er würde die Revisionsstelle nur belasten. Wenn diese Investition in angefangene Arbeiten keinen Erfolg hat und deswegen die Gesellschaft in Konkurs gerät, ist offensichtlich, dass die Revisionsstelle diese fragwürdige Bilanzierung erkannt hat. Dass sie darüber berichtet hat, entschuldigt sie eben nicht in ihrem Urteil über die zulässige Aktivierung. Sagt sie nichts, kann ihr der Vorwurf gemacht werden, dass sie sich über diese kritische Bilanzierung nicht geäussert hat.

Welchen Weg soll nun die Revisionsstelle gehen? Ich neige dazu, nur über das absolut Notwendige zu berichten. Und wenn in einem Punkt die

Berichterstattung absolut notwendig ist, so soll sie klar und deutlich erfolgen. Wenn möglich, sollte der Verwaltungsrat angehalten werden, wichtige Punkte im Anhang zu erläutern. Bei jedem Hinweis der Revisionsstelle muss sich diese im Klaren sein, dass er ihr entgegengehalten werden kann.

§ 9 Jahresbericht

Der Jahresbericht ist der in Textform gefasste, ergänzende Bestandteil zur Jahresrechnung. Der Jahresabschluss ist nur dann komplett, wenn auch der Jahresbericht vorliegt. Im alten Aktienrecht war der Geschäftsbericht (jetzt Jahresbericht) nicht zwingend vorgeschrieben und man begnügte sich damit, im Protokoll zur Generalversammlung festzuhalten, dass dieser mündlich vorgetragen worden sei. Ist der textliche Jahresbericht zur möglichst zuverlässigen Beurteilung der Vermögens- und Ertragslage unerlässlich, kann der Revisor demnach seinen Bericht nicht ohne einen entsprechenden Hinweis abgeben.

Der Bericht lässt sich nicht aus der Buchhaltung ableiten. Aufgabe des Berichtes ist es, zusätzliche Informationen in allgemeiner Form zu vermitteln, die einen zusammenfassenden Überblick über die Gesamtlage der Aktiengesellschaft geben und ergänzende Aufschlüsse darüber liefern, ob sich das Unternehmen auf dem Markt behaupten und seinen Verpflichtungen nachkommen kann:

1) Bericht über den Geschäftsverlauf der Gesellschaft (wirtschaftliche Lage)
2) Bericht über die finanzielle Lage der Gesellschaft

Der Bericht sollte etwa ein bis zwei Seiten umfassen, kann aber auch ausführlicher sein.

§ 10 Umfassender Bericht (Erläuterungsbericht)

I. Pflicht bei der ordentlichen Revision

Der Erläuterungsbericht ist nur bei jenen Gesellschaften zu erstatten, die die Prüfung ihres Abschlusses «zugelassenen Revisionsexperten» anvertraut haben (Art. 728b Abs. 1 OR). In diesem Fall erstellt die Revisionsstelle dem Verwaltungsrat einen Bericht, in dem sie sowohl die Durchführung als auch das Ergebnis ihrer Prüfung näher erläutert. Man muss hinzufügen, dass sie dabei jene Einzelheiten ihrer Arbeit und ihrer Feststellungen in systematischer Weise darstellt, die in ihrem Bericht an die Generalversammlung – der ja bloss Schlussergebnisse und Empfehlungen enthält – nicht zum Ausdruck kommen können.

Der Erläuterungsbericht ist für den einzelnen Verwaltungsrat eine wesentliche Informationsquelle, auch deshalb, weil viele finanzielle Ereignisse und Zusammenhänge gerade einem in Rechnungslegung und Finanzsachen nicht besonders ausgebildeten Mitglied des Verwaltungsrates erst in der Gesamtdarstellung verständlich werden. Er muss insbesondere auch jenes Thema abdecken, das nach Aktienrecht neu ist, nämlich die Analyse über das «Interne Kontrollsystem».

Bei der konzernrechnungspflichtigen Obergesellschaft ist ein Konzernerläuterungsbericht zu erstatten; der Konzernprüfer kann ihn mit jenem der Obergesellschaft als Einzelgesellschaft zusammenfassen.

II. Keine Erläuterungspflicht

Eine Erläuterungspflicht für Aktiengesellschaften mit Review erachte ich als unnötige Aufgabe. Sinnvoll sind solche Angaben nur, sofern sie sich in repräsentativer Form über das Ergebnis der Prüfung äussern. Mehr sollte nicht enthalten sein und trifft dies doch zu, wird bereits ein Ansatz zum Angriff auf die Verantwortlichkeit eröffnet. Je mehr unerforderliche Angaben die Revisionsstelle macht, desto eher wird sie zur Rechenschaft gezogen. Je mehr sie sich auf die absolut notwendige Berichterstattung mit Prüfung konzentriert, desto mehr übersteht sie Probleme im Zusammenhang mit der Verantwortlichkeit.

Üblich sind auch sog. «Management-Letters». Sie kommen einem Erläuterungsbericht nahe und dienen dazu, festgestellte Ungereimtheiten darzulegen und Ziele der Verbesserung für das nächste Jahr festzulegen. In diesem Sinn sind solche Berichte sehr sinnvoll.

§ 11 Die Verantwortlichkeit der Revisionsstelle

Noch mehr als andere Fachpersonen ist der Revisor für seine Arbeit verantwortlich. Er muss seine Arbeit sorgfältig ausführen; er ist für den Schaden verantwortlich, den er durch sein Verschulden anderen zufügt.

Die Revisionsstelle hat zwei Verantwortlichkeiten:
1) die aktienrechtliche Verantwortlichkeit
2) die Verantwortlichkeit nach Auftragsrecht

Handelt die Revisionsstelle als Organ einer AG, ist die Haftungsgrundlage Art. 755 OR. Danach sind alle mit der Prüfung der Jahres- und Konzernrechnung, der Gründung, der Kapitalerhöhung oder Kapitalherabsetzung befassten Personen sowohl der Gesellschaft als auch den einzelnen Aktionären und Gesellschaftsgläubigern für den Schaden verantwortlich, den sie durch absichtliche oder fahrlässige Verletzung ihrer Pflichten verursachen. Diese Haftungsnorm gilt für die ordentliche wie für die eingeschränkte Revision, wobei die Voraussetzungen verschieden sind. Wird z.B. eine freiwillige ordentliche Revision durchgeführt (siehe Art. 727 Abs. 3 OR), so liegt Auftragsrecht vor und damit eine Vertragshaftung (welche i.d.R. strenger als die Organhaftung ist).

Übernimmt die Revisionsstelle Aufgaben ausserhalb der Organpflicht (z.B. Abschlussberatung, betriebswirtschaftliche Untersuchungen, Sonderrevisionen etc.), so sind Pflichtverletzungen nach Auftragsrecht (Art. 394 ff. OR) zu beurteilen.

Gerade diese Polarität von gesetzlicher Revisionsstelle und Auftragnehmer ist ein zweischneidiges Schwert. Auf der einen Seite ist der Revisor gesetzliche Revisionsstelle und prüft nach eigenem Ermessen. Andererseits ist die zu prüfende Gesellschaft auch sein Kunde. Sie bezahlt das Prüfungshonorar und vergibt oft noch weitere Aufträge wie Steuerberatung, Rechtsberatung etc. an die Revisionsstelle. Denn oft wird von der Verwaltung das vertiefte Wissen der Revisionsstelle geschätzt. Solche Aufträge können von der Revisionsstelle angenommen werden, sofern sie mit dem Prüfungsauftrag vereinbar sind. Das Problem liegt darin, dass die Revisionsstellen oftmals zu schnell den Eindruck haben, dass die Aufträge problemlos durchgeführt werden können. Je mehr Aufträge die Revisionsstelle für die zu prüfende Gesellschaft übernimmt, desto mehr Verantwortung übernimmt sie und desto mehr nimmt auch ihre Abhängigkeit zu.

Für die Revisionsstelle ist es am besten, wenn sie ihre übrigen Aufgaben vom Revisionsmandat losgelöst wahrnehmen kann. Tut sie es nicht, handelt sie auf eigene Gefahr und muss im Schadenfall nachweisen, dass sie nicht für den entstandenen Schaden verantwortlich ist (ihr obliegt der sog. Exkulpationsbeweis).

Teil D

Konsolidierung und Steuern / Consolidation and taxes

Kapitel 1:
Consolidated financial statements in Switzerland

§ 1   Introduction and background

I.   Introduction

In Switzerland, consolidated accounts play a much more important role for public companies than individual company accounts do. Although some 170,000 Swiss stock corporations are required to prepare individual company accounts and follow company law provisions, these individual company accounts are mostly tax driven. They disclose little and tend to follow conservative accounting policies aimed at avoiding or reducing income tax.

The history of consolidated accounts began with big multinational companies, which needed to finance themselves on domestic and international stock exchanges. One of these was Alusuisse, a big aluminum and chemical company. Alusuisse sought funds on the London financial markets in the nineteen-seventies, in order to finance a large expansion project in Australia. The London bankers requested audited consolidated financial statements for the whole group.

Alusuisse, therefore, has a long history of consolidated statements, which have undergone continual improvements since their introduction. The adoption of the Fourth and Seventh EC Directives in 1986 was followed by a switch towards the International Accounting Standards (IAS) of the International Accounting Standards Committee (IASC). Many other big Swiss companies followed this trend.

When Switzerland voted against joining the European Economic Area (EEA) in 1992 many public companies started to move their standards away from the EU Directives and towards the Anglo-American accounting standards. Almost all the big Swiss-based industrial multinationals have now adopted the International Financial Reporting Standards (IFRS) of the IASB in London. Some of the largest companies are also preparing to change to United States Generally Accepted Accounting Principles (US GAAP) as they have placed shares on US Stock Exchanges (e.g. NYSE).

An increasing number of Swiss groups have established holding companies in the last decades. The purpose of the holding company is to separate the operating activities in newly established subsidiary companies. As the Swiss operations have sometimes been limited compared to foreign operations the main emphasis of a holding company has been to:

- Provide worldwide headquarters with top management and staff.
- Promote investor relations.
- Manage investments in subsidiaries.
- Finance subsidiaries with debenture bonds.

II. Effects on companies

There are between 400 and 600 companies whose shares or debenture bonds are quoted on Swiss Stock Exchange (SIX). They represent less than 1 percent of all Swiss corporations and the majority are holding or parent companies which are required to prepare and publish consolidated financial statements. Publication can involve distributing printed annual reports to existing or potential shareholders or printing the consolidated accounts in the Swiss Federal Commercial Gazette. The latter method is, however, rarely used.

It is also estimated that there are about 12,000 privately held holding companies in Switzerland, all of which are too small to be required to prepare or publish consolidated accounts. Approximately 1,500 only are subject to consolidation requirements due to their size. However, only public companies need to publish consolidated accounts.

The requirements for consolidated accounts have some features in common with the Seventh Directive. The law prescribes when a consolidation has to take place but does not strictly regulate the methods of consolidation and valuation principles to be used. These must be disclosed in the annex to the accounts.

III. Legislation and standards

Under the provisions of the old Code of Obligations, effective until 30 June 1992, there were no requirements for consolidation. Certain rules were established after lengthy discussions in parliament; however, there are very few articles of the Swiss Code of Obligations (*Schweizerisches Obligationenrecht*, CO) which relate to consolidated accounts.

1. Duty to consolidate (Art. 663e para. 1 CO)

1) If the company has, by way of a majority of votes or other means, one or more companies under common control (a group) it must prepare consolidated accounts (consolidated accounts).

2) The company is excluded from the duty to consolidate if it, together with its subsidiaries, does not exceed two of the following criteria in two subsequent years:
   a) Balance sheet total of CHF 10 million.
   b) Net sales of CHF 20 million.
   c) 200 employees per annual average.

3) Consolidated accounts still have to be prepared, if:
   a) The company has debenture bonds outstanding.
   b) The company's shares are quoted on a stock exchange.
   c) Shareholders holding at least 10 percent of the share capital request them.
   d) It is necessary to receive a picture which is as reliable as possible of the financial position and the results of operations of the company.

2. Intermediate holding companies (Art. 663f para. 2 CO)

1) Any company included in the consolidated accounts of a parent company, which is established and audited according to Swiss law or equivalent foreign standards, is not required to prepare separate consolidated accounts if it makes the consolidated accounts of its parent known to its shareholders and creditors in the same way as its own individual company accounts.

2) Such a company is, however, required to establish separate consolidated accounts if it has to publish its individual company accounts (because of debenture bonds outstanding and shares quoted on stock exchanges) or if consolidated accounts are requested by shareholders who hold at least 10 percent of the share capital.

3. *Preparation of consolidated accounts (Art. 663g par. 3 CO)*

1) The consolidated accounts have to follow accepted (Swiss) accounting principles.

2) The company describes the applied consolidation and valuation principles in the annex to the consolidated accounts. If it deviates from these, it has to disclose this and give additional information necessary for a clear presentation of the financial position and results of operations of the group.

4. *Publication of consolidated accounts (Art. 697h CO)*

1) After consolidated accounts have been adopted by the general meeting of shareholders they, together with the group audit report, have to be published. Publication can either be in the Commercial Gazette or, if the following conditions apply, by giving a copy (free of charge) to anybody requesting it within a year after adoption if:

   a) The company has debenture bonds outstanding.

   b) The company's shares are quoted on a stock exchange.

2) The other companies have to show consolidated accounts and the audit report to creditors who have a genuine interest in them (where there is a dispute a judge decides).

As the legal coverage of this complex topic is limited to the basic requirements, the accounting profession's published interpretations were needed to clarify the position. Such interpretations are included in the Swiss Accounting and Reporting Recommendations (Swiss GAAP FER) and the Auditing Handbook (HWP).

§ 2 Objectives, concepts and general principles

I. Relevant objectives

Consolidated accounts have long been prepared on a more or less voluntary basis; Swiss company law has only required consolidated accounts since 1 July 1994. Because there was no federal stock exchange law the cantonal stock exchanges in Zurich, Basle and Geneva did not require consolidated financial information. Since 1996 such information, and the adherence to the FER recommendations, has become compulsory under the regulation of SIX.

Although not required by company law or stock exchange regulations such information was demanded by market forces. Bankers, accounting professionals, auditors, accountants, financial analysts, business journalists and others have pressured public companies to publish more meaningful information. Once such information was available demand grew for these reports to be audited by internationally experienced auditing firms.

Consolidated accounts are not used for profit distribution: Dividends can only be paid out of the current profits and available reserves shown in the holding company's individual company accounts. Swiss annual reports always have to disclose the holding company's statutory accounts, as shareholders base their decision on the proposed dividends on these individual company accounts.

Financial analysts often calculate the dividends paid out by the parent compared to the consolidated net profit (pay-out ratio). Compared to Anglo-American groups these ratios tend to be low (e.g. 20 to 30 percent) although they are increasing. Swiss companies only pay out the dividends once per year, normally one day after the general meeting of shareholders, and they are generally paid in cash (stock dividends are rare). The shareholders receive only 65 percent of the dividend in cash or as a capital reduction. The 35 percent withholding tax has to be deducted by the company and paid to the federal tax authorities. The shareholders can claim this tax back if they declare the dividend as income based on their tax return.

The consolidated accounts are not relevant for tax purposes. Switzerland is one of the few industrialised countries where it is not possible to offset the profits of one subsidiary against the losses of another in the same country through a consolidated tax return. The only way to achieve these tax benefits is by merging two Swiss group companies with each other (combination) or with the parent (absorption) in a legal merger (fusion) and therefore establishing head office and branch offices/operations.

After consolidation became compulsory under Swiss law in 1994, the tax authorities could access the consolidated accounts of a parent company. Additional information, which would make it more difficult for the parent or the Swiss subsidiaries to hide profits from the tax authorities, could become available. However, the tax authorities have hardly used this information up to now.

The duty to prepare, audit and publish consolidated accounts under the new company law can be summarized as follows.

There is a duty to consolidate with majority of votes (Art. 663e CO). Exceptions are made for intermediate holdings and small companies. Therefore there are fewer than approximately 1,500 companies which must consolidate and have their consolidated accounts audited by specially qualified auditors.

The rules concerning the preparation of consolidated accounts (Art. 663g CO) are very limited. They have to be drawn up according to commercially accepted accounting principles in Switzerland (*Grundsätze ordnungsmässiger Rechnungslegung*, GoR). However, those are not specified in detail. Swiss GAAP FER provides a possible set of acceptable standards. The annex to the consolidated accounts has to specify the consolidation and valuation principles used.

The disclosure requirements for audited consolidated accounts (Art. 697h CO) are also very limited. The consolidated accounts have to be published only if the company has shares or debenture bonds quoted. Less than 600 companies are involved.

Auditing of consolidated accounts (Art. 731 CO) is reserved for qualified auditors (normally Swiss Certified Accountants or those with an equivalent foreign degree or diploma). The auditors have to confirm that the consolidated accounts are in agreement with the law and that the consolidation and valuation principles, as disclosed in the annex, are actually applied. The abbreviated report is directed to the general meeting of shareholders which has to adopt the consolidated accounts in question.

Specific consolidation principles and methods are not mentioned in the law. However, Swiss GAAP FER provides minimal requirements.

FER was created in 1984 as a foundation under federal supervision. It consists of representatives from industry, banks, universities, politics etc. It has issued the recommendations shown in the following table in the three Swiss languages – German, French and Italian – and additionally English, after a due consideration process. All these standards apply to group as well as individual company accounts.

The Basic FER Statement was originally issued in December 1985 and restated as of March 1993 and January 2007. The recommendations are as follows:

- All companies which adopt the FER (English name: Accounting and Reporting Recommendations in Switzerland (ARR)) in their financial reporting are invited to state this in their financial statements. If this is the case, then the company should have their independent auditors examine and report the degree of compliance.

- All accounting and reporting recommendations should be applied to the individual and consolidated financial statements except where their use is expressly restricted by other Swiss GAAP FER.

- The recommendations do not deal with publication of individual or consolidated financial statements. This is dealt with by company law.

II. Underlying concepts and general principles

1. General requirements

Given that the Swiss Code of Obligations is very basic in respect of consolidated accounts, such consolidated accounts, according to the legal minimum, can omit a lot of the information normally required under international principles. However, the group accounts published in Swiss annual reports tend to follow the international true and fair view principle The management accounts, which top management uses to control the group internally, are often published.

Company law has no specific requirements as to consolidation methods. However, the private sector standard-setting body, Swiss GAAP FER, has issued standards on how consolidated statements should be prepared. FER 30 'Consolidated financial statements' (*Konzernrechnung*) was originally issued in September 1986 and restated as of March 1993 and 1 January 2007. The general recommendations are that the consolidated financial statements have to present a true and fair view of the group's financial position, its results and its cash flows. The original German wording as used in the Seventh Directive is: *'ein den tatsächlichen Verhältnissen entsprechendes Bild der Vermögens-, Finanz- und Ertragslage'*. Consolidated financial statements are the financial statements of a group of companies as defined by the scope of consolidation (*Konsolidierungskreis*).

2. *Principles of consolidation*

Although the parent and subsidiaries are separate legal entities and Switzerland, unlike Germany, does not have a group company law (*Konzernrecht*), the group is considered a fictitious legal entity. Each consolidated company is initially responsible for its own accounting and finance. However, the group management and board also have a duty to control the subsidiaries. In fact, the parent has to ensure that the subsidiaries have sufficient financing available and that they meet their obligations in Switzerland and abroad. It is extremely rare for Swiss parent companies not to bail out their subsidiaries when they are in financial difficulties. It is also quite unusual for public companies not to be supported by the big Swiss banks and/or industrial groups when they are in financial difficulties.

Other important concepts prevalent in Swiss consolidated accounts are going concern, substance over form, materiality, consistency, completeness, etc. These principles are particularly relevant to consolidated accounts and are therefore expanded here.

Materiality is a very important principle in consolidated accounts. Most Swiss multinational companies round their group account figures to the nearest CHF million. It is considered irrelevant to show thousand or even francs and centimes (*Rappen*) if a group shows a net turnover of CHF five to ten thousand million (five to ten billion). In addition, Swiss accounting firms use their materiality concepts to decide whether or not cumulative errors should be corrected or might result in qualifications to the consolidated accounts.

The going concern principle is of special importance for a group. If a going concern is no longer maintainable then a consolidation is no longer justified. A holding company where the continuation is no longer assured should immediately cease to prepare consolidated accounts as this would give a misleading impression.

§ 3 Group concept and preparation of consolidated accounts

I. Consolidated accounts

1. Duty to consolidate

The duty to consolidate is stated in Art. 663e para. 1 CO as follows: 'If the company, by majority vote or by another method, joins one or more companies under a common control (group of companies), it has to prepare annual consolidated accounts (consolidated financial statements).' This means in principle that only corporations (*Aktiengesellschaft*) have to consolidate as the article applies only to corporations. Also affected are corporations with one or more unlimited partners as shareholders (*Kommanditaktiengesellschaften*). However, these are very rare in Switzerland. Cooperatives (*Genossenschaft*) and small limited companies (*Genossenschaft mit beschränkter Haftung*) do not need to consolidate if they hold subsidiary companies. The latter are rare. However, there are some large retail organisations (e.g. Migros and COOP) which are cooperatives. They, however, consolidate on a voluntary basis.

An exception to the duty to consolidate, for small groups, is stated in Art. 663e para. 2 CO:

"The company is exempted from the duty to prepare consolidated financial statements if it, during two consecutive business years, together with its subsidiaries, does not exceed two of the following:

1) A balance sheet total of CHF 10 million.

2) Revenue of CHF 20 million.

3) An average annual number of employees of 200."

The above rule is reasonable to protect employees of big companies, although the employees might have difficulty in obtaining consolidated accounts from their employers. Even in big private and public groups employees are not represented on the boards of their employers. The figures for the balance sheet total and revenue under Art. 663e para. 2 CO are calculated on an unconsolidated level (gross method).

The consolidated financial statements include the parent company, the fully consolidated subsidiary companies, joint ventures (which are included according to the proportionate consolidation) and investments in associate companies (which are often included under the equity method). The parent's individual company accounts have to be established and audited even if there are consolidated accounts.

Small groups have to prepare consolidated accounts if the following exception (of the exception according to Art. 663e para. 3 CO) applies:

1) The company has outstanding bond issues.

2) The company's shares are listed on a stock exchange.

3) Shareholders representing at least 10 percent of the share capital request consolidated accounts.

4) It is necessary for assessing as reliably as possible the company's financial and income situation.

Public companies' duty to consolidate seems feasible as there are many shareholders or creditors who need special protection. It is estimated that there are less than 1,000 companies which are quoted with their shares or bonds. Although this is a small percentage of Swiss corporations as a whole (some 170,000) these companies are economically important and they are big employers.

The Swiss Stock Exchange has so far requested consolidated accounts since 1995. Under the new company law consolidated accounts have to be established, but only according to the minimal legal requirements. Consolidated accounts which show a true and fair view are only be required under the new quotation rules of the Swiss Stock Exchange (SIX) and the new stock exchange law (BEHG). Although minority rights are not very well covered in Swiss law, big minorities can now request consolidated financial statements (Art. 663e para. 3 no. 3 CO).

Point 4 of Art. 663e para. 3 CO is very vague. Company auditors could probably, in critical cases, request their clients to prepare consolidated accounts. If not, they might not be able to form an opinion on the valuation of the investments and loans to subsidiaries in the parent's balance sheet.

Under Swiss law (Art. 662 CO) the components of consolidated accounts are as follows:

1) Consolidated balance sheet.

2) Consolidated income statement.

3) Annex to the consolidated financial statements.

2. *Preparation of consolidated accounts*

Current company law provides little guidance as to how the consolidation should be carried out and presented in the annual report. The only rules available are the general rules given in the commercially accepted accounting principles (GoR). According to Art. 662a para. 1 CO these require that:

The financial statements (and the consolidated financial statements) have to follow the commercially accepted accounting principles in order to provide as reliable a picture as possible of the financial situation and results of the company. They also contain the previous year's figures.

The 'as reliable a picture as possible' required by para. 1 still allows reserves to remain hidden. This contradicts international accounting standards that require a true and fair view. Consolidated accounts that only are in conformity with Swiss law might therefore not present the financial situation and the results fairly. Thus they might not be equivalent to foreign requirements.

The requested comparative figures are internationally recognised. The regulations are in line with legal principles but are too vague for accounting practice. The materiality principle is mentioned in law for the first time: large groups with large figures in their financial statements can now round their figures to the nearest CHF 100,000 or CHF million, if applicable. Unnecessary detail is therefore eliminated and the statements are easier to read.

According to Art. 663h CO the consolidated accounts may omit data which could damage the interests of Switzerland and/or the company/ group. The auditors have to be informed of the reasons. There is insufficient evidence available to interpret the specific meaning of this general article. It could, for example, relate to disclosure of names of subsidiaries and/or non-consolidated participations although these companies would be included in the consolidated accounts.

The law does not distinguish whether the minimal structure of the financial statements and the valuation principles also apply for the consolidated accounts. This was confirmed by practical interpretation.

II. Sub-consolidated accounts

In principle every holding company (ultimate and intermediate parent) which is domiciled in Switzerland as a corporation has to prepare consolidated accounts according to Art. 663e para. 1 CO, unless it is exempted from consolidation.

Exception from the duty to consolidate is stated in Art. 663f CO for sub-holding (or intermediate) companies:

"A company included in the consolidated statements of a parent company that are prepared and audited according to the provisions of Swiss or equivalent foreign law need not prepare separate consolidated statements if it communicates the parent's consolidated statements in the same way as its own annual statement to its shareholders and creditors. It is, however, obliged to prepare separate consolidated statements if it is required to publish its annual report or if consolidated accounts are requested by shareholders representing at least 10 percent of the share capital."

The intermediate holding company's sub-consolidated consolidated accounts have to be included in its parent's consolidation as well as its individual company accounts. If the intermediate holding company has minority shares or bonds outstanding on a Swiss stock exchange it has to publish (sub-)consolidated financial statements.

The first question to ask is which foreign standards are equivalent. Possibilities include legal rules of a foreign country or professional standards issued by accountants' organisations. These could include American Generally Accepted Accounting Principles (US GAAP), International Financial Reporting Standards (IFRS), German Commercial Code (HGB) and EU Directives. However, some additional disclosures required under Swiss law are also necessary (e.g. fire insurance value of property, plant and equipment).

The intermediate holding company auditor will have to examine the foreign consolidated statements. According to Art. 663f CO, if no consolidation is prepared a comment should be made in the annex to the financial statements of the intermediate holding company referring to these foreign statements and where they are available. The intermediate holding company auditor has not only to judge whether the upper or ultimate consolidation is equivalent to Swiss standards, but also whether the group auditors of such consolidated accounts have an equivalent qualification to the specially qualified Swiss auditors (Art. 727b and 731a CO). These are normally Swiss Certified Auditors (*dipl. Wirtschaftsprüfer (WP)*). Obviously all qualified auditors in Europe and in Anglo-American countries would be equivalent (e.g. German *Wirtschaftsprüfer*, British Chartered Accountants (CAs), and United States Certified Public Accountants (US CPAs). The majority of these certified auditors are employed by big international accounting firms.

§ 4   Deferred taxation

I.   Recommendation for deferred taxation

Deferred taxation is not normally used in the individual company accounts which are usually the same as the tax return. Therefore, there are no temporary differences which would require deferred tax accounting.

Thus, deferred taxation normally relates only to consolidated accounts. FER 2 "Valuation" referred to the tax effect of accounting, although it was very vague in para. 9 where it says: 'Tax implications from revaluations should be taken into consideration.' Due to the lack of guidance Swiss companies followed IFRS and US GAAP standards in this respect.

FER 11 on income taxes in the consolidated accounts became effective in 1997. It describes the accrual of current and deferred income taxes. The accrual of current income taxes is derived from the requirements of calculating taxable net income. This includes the liability from assessed and non-assessed taxes, possible tax penalties and possible tax prepayments and tax credits.

Capital taxes (based on equity) and other fees have to be separated from income taxes. They are not related to the pre-tax profit, i.e. because they are not income taxes they are normally included in other operating expenses. The above-mentioned tax accruals are mostly carried out in the individual company accounts. Sometimes, however, they have to be adjusted for the balance sheet for consolidation purposes (HB II).

II. Temporary and permanent differences

If the tax basis is different from the financial accounting valuation method deferred taxes are accrued. The consolidated financial statements should give a true and fair view of the economic situation of the group but do not reflect the tax situation. This can lead to differences between the tax values and values used in the consolidated accounts.

Permanent differences can occur if certain transactions are included only in either the tax return or the consolidated accounts. Therefore, permanent differences do not reverse over the course of time. Typical examples are items that are not allowed for the tax return but included in the consolidated accounts. In Switzerland these are very rare. Temporary differences are those that are included at the same amount in the tax return and consolidated accounts but not in the same time period. Typical examples are differences arising from the application of different depreciation methods and useful lives. By accounting for deferred tax effects on temporary differences a relationship between profit before income taxes and the related tax expense is established.

III. Liability method

The annual accrual of deferred taxes provides for a comprehensive allocation of all income taxes from a balance sheet point of view. This liability approach refers to the individual balance sheet positions. These have the character of future tax-deductible assets (debit temporary differences) or future taxable liabilities (credit temporary differences). Accordingly they are classified as assets or liabilities.

Deferred taxes are accounted for by using the full tax rate (future tax rate if known or else the actual rate). This is normally around 20 to 30 percent in Switzerland. Changes in the tax rate or system are to be accounted for as deferred tax expenses or income of the year when they become known. All future income tax effects are included in the annual calculation of deferred taxes (comprehensive allocation method) independent from the time of reversal.

Accounting for deferred taxes should be governed by the principles of consistency and materiality. This means particularly that the method of calculation and presentation should be applied consistently. It should be explained in the annex to the consolidated financial statements.

IV. Tax jurisdiction

Income taxes should be accounted for separately in each accounting period for each tax jurisdiction. Debit and credit deferred tax items can only be netted in the same tax jurisdiction. Various levels can be distinguished when deferred taxes are calculated:

- Temporary differences in the individual financial statements for consolidation purposes arise because of differences between tax and group valuation. If a sub consolidation is prepared and a consolidated tax return prepared and filed, temporary differences are calculated at this sub consolidation level.
- Temporary differences arise from profit and loss consolidation entries (e.g. elimination of inter company profits in inventories or matching of inter company accounts receivable and payable).
- If profits are retained in the consolidated subsidiary companies or associated companies are accounted for under the equity method unless the retained earnings are not to be paid out in the foreseeable future.

If the temporary differences are calculated on an individual company or sub consolidation level existing accumulated tax losses and deferred tax assets can be applied to deferred tax liabilities. Deferred tax assets are only capitalisable if sufficient future profits can be generated. Therefore care should be taken when such assets are set up. Deferred tax assets from the elimination of inter company profits on intra group inventory transfers are always realised when these profits are realised. Swiss groups normally do not extensively capitalise deferred tax assets.

Under the comprehensive allocation method all temporary differences must be included in the calculation of deferred taxes independent of the time of reversal. Exceptions are temporary differences arising from goodwill and as un remitted retained earnings which are not paid out.

V. Tax rate

The annual calculation of deferred taxes is based on actual tax rates. For the individual company or sub consolidated group the actual tax rate of the relevant tax jurisdiction applies. For the calculation of deferred tax on consolidation entries affecting profit and loss the respective average tax rate of the group applies. It is also possible to apply a group average tax rate which has to be disclosed in the annex. For un remitted retained earnings of consolidated subsidiaries and associated companies under the equity method the non-recoverable part of the withholding tax (so-called *Sockelsteuern*) has to be accounted for. Discounting deferred income taxes is not allowed.

If income tax rates have changed compared to the prior year the tax assets and liabilities have to be adjusted accordingly.

Kapitel 2:
Von der Handelsbilanz zur Steuerbilanz

§ 1   Einleitung

Die Handelsbilanz bildet die Grundlage für die Steuerbilanz. Sie ist der Ausgangspunkt und führt unter Beachtung der steuerlichen Normen zur Steuerbilanz. In der Literatur wird davon gesprochen, dass die Steuerbilanz den «wirklichen Gewinn» zeigen soll (WALTER STUDER, Bilanzsteuerrecht, Basel 1968, 7). Letztlich lässt jede Bilanz nur eine beschränkte Beurteilung zu. Die eine ist beeinflusst durch das Vorsichtsprinzip, die andere ermittelt nur den steuerbaren Gewinn, welcher seinerseits durch eine Vielzahl von Normen eher abstrakten Charakter hat. Nur eine Gesamtbetrachtung unter Berücksichtigung der Zukunftsaussichten, der Arbeitsplätze, des Arbeitsklimas, der Soziologie des Unternehmens, der Wertschöpfung und der Umweltfaktoren ergibt letztlich eine schlüssige Beurteilung eines Unternehmens. Dabei kann der Gewinn eine bloss untergeordnete Bedeutung haben.

§ 2   Formelle Vorschriften

Neben den materiellen Vorschriften (auf die noch zurückgekommen wird) existieren formelle Vorschriften, welche zu beachten sind. Hier zu erwähnen sind:

1) *«Richtlinien für die Ordnungsmässigkeit des Rechnungswesens unter steuerlichen Gesichtspunkten sowie über die Aufzeichnung von Geschäftsunterlagen auf Bild- oder Datenträgern und deren Aufbewahrung»* (1979).

Es handelt sich um formelle Mindestanforderungen im EDV-Bereich. Die Vorschriften wurden von der sog. «Konferenz staatlicher Steuerbeamter» (dies sind die kantonalen Steuerbehörden) in Zusammenarbeit mit der Eidgenössischen Steuerverwaltung und dem Bundesamt für Justiz herausgegeben.

2) Daneben existieren die *«Richtlinien für die Ordnungsmässigkeit des Rechnungswesens»*, herausgegeben von der Konferenz staatlicher Steuerbeamter in Zusammenarbeit mit der Eidgenössischen Steuerverwaltung (ohne Mitwirkung des Bundesamtes für Justiz). Sie behandeln Grundlagen der Buchführung.

3) Letztlich seien noch die *«EDV-Richtlinien für Lohnaufzeichnungen»* der Schweizerischen Unfallversicherungsanstalt (SUVA) erwähnt. Es handelt sich dabei um Vorschriften für Lohnprogramme, welche auf Anfrage hin von der Schweizerischen Unfallversicherungsanstalt geprüft werden.

4) Weiter möchten wir hier noch auf das *«Merkblatt vom Januar 1980 betreffend Aufbewahrungs- und Aufzeichnungspflicht»*, welcher Steuerpflichtige mit selbständiger Erwerbstätigkeit unterstehen, hinweisen. Dieses Merkblatt beschreibt die Anforderungen an die Aufzeichnungen von Einnahmen und Ausgaben, wenn keine Buchführungspflicht besteht. Es wurde von der Eidgenössischen Steuerverwaltung (der damaligen Hauptabteilung Wehrsteuer) herausgegeben und hat immer noch Gültigkeit.

Häufig ist es unpraktisch, wenn verschiedene Behörden parallel Normen gestalten, welche das gleiche Gebiet betreffen.

§ 3 Materielle Vorschriften

I. Die Abgrenzung zwischen Geschäfts- und Privatvermögen

Das Geschäftsvermögen ist vom Privatvermögen zu unterscheiden. Die Abgrenzung ergibt sich aber nicht alleine aus Buchführung und Bilanz. Das schweizerische Steuerrecht geht von der wirtschaftlichen Betrachtungsweise aus. So kann Vermögen, welches im Zusammenhang mit der Geschäftstätigkeit eines Betriebes steht, steuerlich zu Geschäftsvermögen werden, obwohl dies nicht bilanziert ist und im Privatvermögen gehalten wird. Bei Kapitalgesellschaften gibt es hier im Allgemeinen keinen Konflikt. Ganz anders verhält es sich jedoch bei Personengesellschaften und Einzelfirmen.

II. Aktiven

Für das Umlaufvermögen ergeben sich meistens keine Probleme.

Für sämtliche Anlagegüter existieren verbindliche maximale Abschreibungssätze (linear oder progressiv).

Abschreibungen, welche infolge schlechten Geschäftsganges nicht verbucht werden konnten, können nachgeholt werden. Das Steuerrecht erlaubt hier eine Durchbrechung des Periodizitätsprinzipes. Ein entsprechender Vorbehalt in der Steuererklärung empfiehlt sich. Mit Umsetzung des StHG wird von dieser Möglichkeit mehr und mehr abgesehen.

Auf dem Warenlager kann generell eine steuerliche Reserve von 1/3 gebildet werden.

III. Passiven

Sie weisen das Fremd- und Eigenkapital aus. Rückstellungen sind nur sehr beschränkt möglich. Erfolgswirksame Reservenbildung ist nur in eng umschriebenen gesetzlichen Sonderpositionen möglich.

IV. Erfolgsrechnung

Auch im Steuerrecht ist die Erfolgsrechnung durch das Realisierungsprinzip und die Periodizität gekennzeichnet. Beide werden durch die Verlustrechnungen aus Vorjahren und der Möglichkeit, Abschreibungen (soweit als möglich) nachzuholen, durchbrochen.

Das Steuerrecht lässt nur unter einem sehr strengen Blickwinkel geschäftsmässig begründete Aufwendungen zu. Hier findet eine Kontrolle statt. Nicht begründete Aufwendungen, welche steuerlich zu einer unzulässigen Entreicherung der Gesellschaft führen, werden sanktioniert. Betroffen ist das Problem der verdeckten Gewinnausschüttungen, wovon später die Rede sein wird.

V. Konzernabschlüsse

Dem schweizerischen Steuerrecht sind Konzernabschlüsse, bis auf die Mehrwertsteuer (Gruppenbesteuerung), fremd. Eine steuerliche Konsolidierung findet nicht statt. Jedes Unternehmen ist für sich allein zu betrachten. Leistungen unter Konzerngesellschaften werden überprüft. Werden diese nicht zu marktkonformen Preisen abgerechnet (sog. Transferpreise), gelangen wir wieder in den Problemkreis der verdeckten Gewinnausschüttung.

Das Zivilrecht hingegen kennt eine Konzernrechnungspflicht. Die Konzernrechnung betrifft jedoch den Kreis des «zugelassenen Revisionsexperten», welcher hier explizit ausgeklammert wurde.

VI. Vorschriften des Bundes

1. Verdeckte Gewinnausschüttung

Die Problematik der verdeckten Gewinnausschüttung ist in allen Kantonen und auch beim Bund anzutreffen. Massstäbe zur steuerlichen Erfassung von verdeckten Gewinnausschüttungen wurden vor allen Dingen im Zusammenhang mit dem Bundesgesetz über die Verrechnungssteuer herausgebildet. Dort hat sich eine eigene Wissenschaft entwickelt.

Im Rahmen von verdeckten Gewinnausschüttungen werden sämtliche Rechtsgeschäfte zwischen wirtschaftlich verbundenen Unternehmen überprüft. Aus der endlosen Palette von Tatbeständen seien hier erwähnt:

- übersetzte Saläre
- übersetzte Akquisitionsprämien
- unzulässige Kommissionen und Provisionen
- übersetzte Rentenansprüche des Alleinaktionärs
- nicht-marktkonforme Mietzinse und Mietpreise
- Kaufgeschäfte ohne wirtschaftliche Grundlage
- überhöhte oder untersetzte Verzinsung von Aktiven und Passiven (steuerliche Zinssätze)
- unzulässige Lizenzvergütungen

- nicht verbuchte Erträge
- nicht dokumentierte Schmiergelder
- etc.

Gewinnausschüttungen von schweizerischen Aktiengesellschaften unterliegen einer 35% igen Quellensteuer. Werden solche verdeckten Gewinnausschüttungen von der Steuerverwaltung bemerkt, erfolgt eine Steuerbelastung, evtl. mit Nach- und Strafsteuern.

2. Die Missbrauchsbestimmungen des Doppelbesteuerungsrechts

Im Zuge internationaler Kritik bezüglich der Gewährung von kantonalen Steuerprivilegien hat sich die schweizerische Eidgenossenschaft bemüht, durch griffige Vorschriften hier entgegenzuwirken. Sobald Vorteile von Doppelbesteuerungsabkommen in Anspruch genommen werden, sind folgende Bedingungen zu erfüllen:

1) Zur Erfüllung vertraglicher Ansprüche im Ausland dürfen maximal 50 % der Bruttoerträge verwendet werden. Die verbleibenden 50 % dürfen nur noch durch geringe Verwaltungskosten reduziert werden.

2) Die Gesellschaften sind mit einem Mindest-Eigenkapital zu versehen und für Aktiven und Passiven gibt es Maximalzinsvorschriften. Diese stimmen im Wesentlichen mit den Vorschriften der verdeckten Gewinnausschüttung überein.

3) Es ist jährlich eine Pflichtausschüttung von 25 % der abkommensbegünstigten Erträge vorzunehmen. Die Gewinn-Thesaurierung ist unzulässig. Die Ausschüttung führt dazu, dass die schweizerische Quellensteuer abgeführt wird.

Kleinunternehmen sind selten mit diesem Problemkreis konfrontiert.

3. Mantelhandel

Der Verkauf einer Aktiengesellschaft in liquider Form führt dazu, dass 35 % vom Kaufpreis abzüglich Grundkapital steuerlich abgeschöpft werden.

Da die Emmissionsabgabe bis CHF 250'000.– Gründungskapital seit 1995 0 % beträgt, sind solche Käufe sehr selten geworden.

Es empfiehlt sich, eine Firmenneugründung der Übernahme einer bestehenden Gesellschaft vorzuziehen. Bei übernommenen Aktiengesellschaften ist nie genau bekannt, welche Forderungen noch offen sind. Dazu können auch massive latente Steuerforderungen gehören.

Kapitel 3:
Tax summary about Switzerland

§ 1 Taxation of resident corporations

In Switzerland, corporations are taxed on both their income and their capital (only cantonal). The Confederation, each canton and community (municipality) and, sometimes, churches have taxing jurisdiction. Certain types of corporations, including holding, domiciliary, and service companies, receive special tax treatment, as explained below. Usually, foreign controlled corporations operating in Switzerland are taxed in the same way as Swiss domestic corporations. Non-resident corporations with a branch in Switzerland are subject to tax on branch income and branch capital similar as resident corporations.

I. Swiss tax liability

Except for certain exempt organisations, all resident corporations, public or private, come within the scope of the corporate tax system. A corporation is considered resident if its place of incorporation or its business activities is in Switzerland. The place of incorporation is the place where the corporation is domiciled as shown in the articles. The place of business is the place from where its business activities are directed.

Corporations with branches in several cantons must apportion their total taxable Swiss income among the cantons concerned. The apportionment rules depend on the corporation's activity; for example, banks apply apportionment rules that are quite different from those applicable to public utilities or retail stores.

II. Determination of taxable income

1. Financial statement income

Swiss business enterprises are assessed on their net profit and net equity as shown by the statutory financial statements prepared in accordance with Swiss generally accepted accounting principles. Swiss business enterprises are not required to prepare special tax accounts, nor are they allowed to submit any financial statements other than those prepared by management and approved by the general meeting of the shareholders. Thus, the importance of the statutory financial statements may not be underestimated: they constitute basic taxpayer evidence and form the starting point for the determination of taxable income. The various adjustments made to statutory income to arrive at taxable income are discussed below.

2. *Gross income*

a) Worldwide income

A resident corporation is subject to income tax on its worldwide income from all sources, except as explained below.

b) Capital gains

Capital gains are included in the ordinary income of a corporation and are fully taxable except for real estate gains which are taxed separately in certain cantons (e.g. Zurich). There are no separate rates applicable to capital gains.

c) Exchange gains

Realised exchange gains are included in ordinary income; unrealised gains, however, are deferred as provisions until realised in accordance with current Swiss accounting practice.

d) Transactions with related parties

Related party transactions must be recorded at arm's-length prices. Any deficiency of income or excess of expense incurred vis-à-vis related parties represents a hidden profit distribution and will be included in taxable income. Examples of such hidden profit distributions are excessive compensation paid to a director-shareholder, interest-free or cheap loans made to shareholders, lease agreements with shareholders under terms regarded as unreasonable, loans from shareholders at unreasonably high rates of interest, and purchases or sales of merchandise involving unusual pricing arrangements.

In addition to being disallowed for income tax purposes, hidden profit distributions are subject to withholding taxes (see below.) Withholding taxes are paid by the corporation but ultimately borne by the recipient of the income. When the withholding tax charge is not transferred to the recipient, the benefit received must be grossed up for the purposes of calculating the add-back to taxable income of the deemed distribution. With withholding tax at 35%, the gross up is 153.85%, 35% of 153.85% being 53.85%.

3. Deductions from gross income

a) General business expense

Business expenses must be wholly and exclusively incurred for the purpose of the business in order to qualify as a deduction from taxable income. Commission payments, finders' fees, and the like are deductible to the extent that the name and address of the recipient is disclosed and the character of these payments as necessary expenses is properly documented.

b) Interest expense

Interest is a deductible business expense. However, interest expense incurred with affiliates will be scrutinised as to its deductible character and may be subject to limitations. The rate of interest used should reflect fair market terms and conditions. The Swiss tax authorities regularly publish guidelines as to the interest rates considered appropriate on Swiss franc loans and borrowings. Interest payments at rates exceeding fair market rates or recommended official rates are disallowed for income tax purposes and are also treated as distributions for withholding tax purposes.

The deduction of interest expense is further limited if the Swiss corporation is exclusively or substantially financed by loans from affiliates. Interest expense is deductible usually as a rule of thumb only to the extent that total indebtedness does not exceed six times equity. Any interest paid on indebtedness exceeding this amount is treated as a distribution.

c) Management and service fees paid to a foreign parent

The tests for deductibility of management and service fees are as follows (see OECD guidelines):

1) The payer must establish that (management) functions are assumed by the foreign parent company or head-office for the benefit of the Swiss operation.

2) The expenses must be necessary, reasonable, and at arm's-length prices.

3) The basis for allocation should be consistent and fair and should reflect sound business practice. Also, the expenses must be properly substantiated.

d) Tax expense

For Swiss income tax purposes, any tax expense incurred by a corporation is a tax-deductible expense, as follows:

Pre-tax income	1,000
Corporate income tax (federal, cantonal, communal) at statutory rate of 40% on 714	- 286
Net after-tax income, being the taxable income	714

Because of the deductibility of the tax expense, the effective tax rate (expressed as a percentage of pre-tax income) is consistently lower than the statutory rate. In the example shown, the statutory rate is 40% and the effective rate is 28.6% (corporate income tax divided through pre-tax income).

e) Exchange losses

Both realised and unrealised exchange losses are tax-deductible. In cross-currency transactions (for example, where the proceeds of borrowings in one foreign currency are used directly to extend loans in another) only the net unrealised exchange loss is deductible.

f) Depreciation

Depreciation is deductible if it is calculated using allowable rates. The methods of depreciation currently used are the straight-line and the declining-balance methods. Maximum allowable depreciation rates are given in tax authority circulars, although some cantons may allow accelerated depreciation (i.e. on-off depreciation to 20% of the original value).

The following are examples of the rates currently allowed when using the declining-balance method:

	of book value
Office buildings (excluding land)	4%
Office furniture and equipment	25%
Intangible assets	40%
Automobiles	40%
Computer hardware and software	40%

If the straight-line depreciation method (on acquisition cost) is used, the above rates are reduced by half. Assets having only a short life and those of small unit value are charged to income as operating expenses.

g) Inventory

Inventories must be carried at the lower of cost or market value. Cost may be determined using the FIFO, LIFO or average method. Furthermore, market value is calculated after taking into account adjustments for special risks, such as obsolescence, slow moving stocks, etc.

From this resultant value, an additional provision of one third may be taken. Obviously, this additional provision presents all the characteristics of a hidden reserve.

h) Provision for bad and doubtful debts

An allowance for bad and doubtful debts is allowed for all accounts receivable which are likely not to be recovered. The debtor's declaration of bankruptcy is not required. Generally, Swiss tax laws allow general provisions of up to 5% against domestic debtors and up to 10% against foreign debtors (in domestic currency). Provisions in excess of these percentages require substantiation.

i)   Loss carry-forwards

Swiss federal income tax laws allow losses to be carried forward for up to a maximum of seven years. The cantons generally allow the same deduction of prior year losses.

j)   Exclusions from taxable income

A reduction of, or exemption from, income tax is generally available for the following:

- Holding company income derived from major investments in other Swiss or foreign corporations.
- Foreign permanent establishment income and foreign branch profits.
- Profits distributed by a foreign partnership, provided that the business of the partnership is carried out abroad.
- Income and gains from foreign real property.
- Contributions by shareholders to equity and share premium accounts.

k)   Holding company income

Income derived from Swiss domestic or foreign subsidiaries is subject to Swiss taxes if received by the Swiss parent in form of dividend or liquidation proceeds. However, such income qualifies for relief, which is usually given in any of the following forms:

- A 95% exclusion from the tax base.
- Taxation at a reduced tax rate (7.8%; no cantonal taxes).
- A proportionate reduction of tax due.

Capital gains realised on the disposition of a qualifying interest in a domestic or foreign subsidiary or affiliate acquired after 1 January 1997 are also excluded from taxable income. The disposal before the year 2007 of such participations acquired previously were taxable.

l) Foreign permanent establishments (foreign branches) and foreign real property profits

Income attributable to foreign permanent establishments, foreign branches, and foreign real property is generally exempt from Swiss corporate income tax. A determining issue is the appropriateness of the method used to allocate net income between the Swiss head-office and the foreign branches. Losses incurred by such establishments or branches may be allowed as deductions against Swiss income, but a claw-back may apply if these losses are earned out within 7 years.

m) Contributions from shareholders

Contributions from shareholders in the form of singular payments or waivers are usually exempt from income tax in the hands of the recipient; frequently, however, they are characterised as capital contributions and, as a result, subject to stamp duty.

III. Tax-privileged corporations

Special rules, involving either exemption from or significant reduction of cantonal and/or federal taxes, apply to certain types of corporation, as follows.

1. *Holding companies*

These are entities which hold substantial investments in the capital of other corporations and their income comprises essentially dividend income. Provided that income other than dividend income (such as trading, interest and commission income) does not exceed a certain percentage of total income, the corporation will retain its status as a holding company and therefore be exempt from tax on income. The only exception hereof is income on real estate.

2. *Industrial or commercial holding companies*

These are normal commercial and industrial corporations which also hold equity investments in other corporations and which may qualify for relief from income taxes on their investment income. To qualify for such relief, the investment must represent at least 20% of the investee's share capital or have a carrying value of not less than CHF 2,000,000.

3. Domiciliary companies

These are entities engaged in any type of trading or financing operation abroad and the registered office in Switzerland is only carrying out limited administrative and no commercial activities. The transactions of the corporation must originate in or be supervised from places other than the registered office, and by some party or person other than the Swiss board, any individual Swiss director or any other Swiss party connected with the corporation's shareholder(s). Domiciliary companies may not have local staff and, normally, have transactions only with parties outside Switzerland. Total tax burden on its foreign sourced income: 9%-11%

4. Mixed companies (Swiss based)

Some cantons give favourable treatment to entities whose activities extend beyond the limitations of the domiciliary companies described above. In contrast to the domiciliary company, it can carry out not only administrative but also commercial activities in Switzerland, which are tolerated to the extent that they do not exceed 20% of the company's income and expense. The tax privileges generally take the form of exempting profits from trading outside Switzerland or taxing these profits at substantially reduced rates. The request for the determination of the tax status is usually made to the cantonal tax administration prior to formation of the corporation, each case being dealt with on its merits. The agreement thus reached is valid for as long as there is no change in the operational structures or circumstances on which the determination is based. Total tax burden on its foreign sourced income: 10%-12%.

5. Service and international headquarters companies

In the case of Swiss resident corporations providing group coordination or management services, including research and promotional activities, Swiss tax laws require that a share of profit accruing to the group be assessed at the level of the Swiss corporation. Because it is impracticable in many cases to determine the extent of the contribution of the Swiss resident corporation to the total profits of the group, the profit assessable in Switzerland is generally deemed to be equal, at a minimum, to 5% to 10% of total expenses (including the tax expense) incurred in the provision of the services. One sixth of the total local payroll cost is an alternative calculation method sometimes used.

For withholding tax purposes, a service company is required to recover all expenses incurred in connection with services performed for the group and to generate a net, distributable profit equal to 5% to 10% of all expenses, as follows:

Total recoveries from group companies, with a mark-up of 14.6%	1,146
Expenses incurred in the provision of services to group companies	- 1,000
Pre-tax income	146
Corporate income taxes, at, for example, 40% of 104	- 42
Net profit available for distribution (the taxable profit)	104

The net profit of 104 meets the minimum profit requirement in that it represents 10% of total expenses including tax expense (1,000 + 42 = 1,042).

6. *Tax rates applicable to tax privileged entities*

The charge to cantonal taxes varies from canton to canton and thus it is not possible to provide a complete overview. In general, income of holding and domiciliary companies is exempt from cantonal taxes. Federal income taxes are only reduced in the case of holding company income. Cantonal capital taxes in general are levied at lower rates in the case of holding and domiciliary companies.

IV. Treaty benefits for Swiss resident corporations

1. *Eligibility*

Switzerland has concluded over 70 tax treaties with foreign countries, and Swiss corporations are usually eligible for treaty benefits if:

1) They have their corporate residence in Switzerland or
2) They are the ultimate beneficial owners of the property producing the income in the foreign country.

2. *Benefits*

Benefits available under the various treaties include:

- For certain items of income, exemption from Swiss tax, with taxation in the country of source.
- The reduction or elimination of foreign withholding tax.
- The ability of Swiss corporations to claim a credit for foreign withholding taxes against Swiss income taxes payable (foreign tax credit).
- The protection against most forms of double taxation.

3. *Anti-Abuse Provisions*

Limitation of benefits:

The Misuse Decree of 1962 was introduced to prevent non-qualifying persons (corporate or private) from deriving the benefits of Swiss tax treaties by using Swiss resident corporations either as a conduit or as a means of unreasonably accumulating treaty-benefited income.

These anti-abuse provisions may be summarized as follows:

- Capital structure - The Swiss corporation must have a reasonable capital structure, with the ratio of interest-bearing debt to equity not exceeding 6 to 1 (often more stringent requirements must be met).
- Interest rate limitation - The rate of interest paid on borrowings from affiliates must not exceed the fair market rate. If there is no market, the safe haven rates published by the Federal Tax Authorities apply.
- Expense limitation - Tax-deductible expenses, such as interest, royalties and management fees paid to non-residents of Switzerland may not exceed 50% of the gross income benefiting from treaties. This limitation applies also to depreciation taken on tangible and intangible property acquired from non-residents.

- Distribution requirement - The Swiss Corporation is required to redistribute, in the form of a dividend, at least 25% of gross income benefiting from treaties.

Non-compliance with the above provisions prevents the Swiss corporation from claiming treaty benefit. Undue benefits obtained must be returned to the foreign tax authority via the Swiss authority in charge of supervising the correct implementation of Swiss income tax treaties.

V. Computation of corporate taxes

1. Income tax

Swiss federal income tax rates are flat at 8.5% statutory rate (7.8% effective rate).

Cantonal tax rates are either proportional or the progression is a function of yield (ROE), with fixed minimum and maximum rates. Because income taxes are tax-deductible, the effective tax rate, expressed as a percentage of pre-tax income, is considerably lower than the statutory rate. This is also valuable for the federal income tax.

2. Credits against income tax payable

A credit against income tax is generally granted for the following taxes paid:
- Swiss withholding tax - Where a Swiss taxpayer receives Swiss source investment income on which the payer deducted Swiss withholding tax, such withholding tax is either creditable against tax (both federal and cantonal) or refundable.
- Foreign withholding tax - For Swiss resident corporations, foreign withholding taxes generally represent a final charge in the foreign country unless tax treaty relief is available. For the non-recoverable amount of foreign withholding tax, most treaties provide for a credit against Swiss income tax, subject to certain limitations (*pauschale Steueranrechnung*, imputation forfaitaire.) There is no credit available for the underlying corporate income tax paid by the distributing entity. Swiss branches of foreign entities do not qualify for treaty relief as described above, even though they are treated in the same way as resi-

dent taxpayers in respect of taxes on income and capital attributable to their Swiss operations.

- Capital taxes - Capital taxes are levied by the cantons on total equity (capital and reserves), usually as of the end of the tax year. The aggregate flat tax rate is normally under 0.5%. The tax also applies to the contributed capital (dotation) of branches. In situations where branches do not have a formal contributed capital, the assessment basis for capital taxes is represented by a fixed percentage of the balance sheet totals.

VI. Assessment of corporate taxes

1. Federal tax

Significant changes to the way in which federal income tax is assessed became effective on 1 January 1995. For corporations, assessment by reference to prior periods of two years was abolished. Tax is now calculated on the basis of income earned during the business year and is assessed in the following business year.

2. Cantonal taxes

Each of the cantons has its own tax legislation and it is not possible to give details of each. However, most are similar to the federal system. A general alignment of the cantonal tax systems on the new federal system was accomplished on 1 January 2001.

VII. Withholding taxes on dividend distributions of Swiss corporations

Distributions of Swiss resident corporations are subject to withholding tax at the rate of 35%, the gross up rate is 54%. Swiss recipients may recover such withholding taxes in full. Recipients who reside abroad may obtain reimbursement under any relevant tax treaty.

VIII. Filing of tax returns, assessment of tax, tax litigation

1. Filing of tax returns

Tax return forms, which are sent out to all registered corporations at the beginning of each assessment period, are to be filed within the prescribed period (generally between March and June.) Extensions may normally be obtained without difficulty upon written request. Penalties for late filing take the form of automatic assessments, which may be appealed, only in certain limited situations.

2. Assessment of tax

The assessing agent reviews the tax return for reasonableness upon receipt. It is decided at that time whether further inquiry is required. When the tax return has been investigated to the satisfaction of the agent, a final assessment is issued, or a tax audit is initiated.

3. Payment of tax

Generally, taxes are payable on the basis of a provisional or final assessment, although payments on account may be required by cantonal regulations.

4. Tax litigation

In situations where a taxpayer believes that the assessment received is not made in accordance with applicable laws, an appeal may be filed. The time limit for appeal is usually thirty days. The filing of a written notice of appeal is a prerequisite for an appeal to be heard. The assessing authorities must reconsider all taxable elements, which may also result in other items being reconsidered which may be advantageous or disadvantageous to the taxpayer.

A further right of appeal exists to a cantonal administrative court, or, in certain cases, to the Swiss Federal Court, whose decision is final. In certain cantons the decision of the first appeal regarding cantonal taxes may be challenged.

IX. Corporate reorganisations (mergers, acquisitions, spin-offs)

Swiss income tax laws contained only a few fragmentary and poorly co-ordinated provisions governing corporate reorganisations. This was improved in connection with the Federal Merger Act (*Fusionsgesetz*, FusG).

The administrative practice followed by the various tax authorities is therefore of critical importance. Reorganisation treatment involving deferral of gain on transfers of assets, exemption from withholding tax, and reduction or exemption from stamp duty (see below), is generally available if the following requirements are met:

1) Non-recognition of the gain; i.e., transfer of assets and liabilities on the basis of existing book values.
2) Continuity of business operations and tax residency.
3) Continuity of ownership / interest at risk.

Obviously, there are many pitfalls in the area of corporate reorganisations. In recent times, acquisition techniques and financing methods used in corporate reorganisations have attained a high degree of sophistication. The tax problems associated with complex mergers and acquisitions are therefore extremely complicated. The presence of both Swiss domestic and foreign parties frequently introduces a further factor of complexity. In significant transactions, careful tax planners would typically seek and obtain an advance ruling from the competent tax authorities.

§ 2 Taxation of non-resident corporations

I. Liability to Swiss tax

Liability to Swiss tax arises when a non-resident entity:

- Receives investment income from Swiss sources.
- Maintains a permanent establishment in Switzerland.
- Is a partner in a Swiss partnership.
- Owns real estate in Switzerland.

- Receives interest secured by Swiss real estate.
- Receives commissions for its activities as intermediary for dealing in Swiss real estate.

1. Investment income from Swiss sources

See below.

2. Permanent establishment income

The following are considered permanent establishments:
- Branch, office or factory.
- Long-term building, construction, or installation project (more than 12 months).

A permanent establishment may also be created if a person in Switzerland habitually exercises authority to contract in the name of and on behalf of a foreign principal.

A foreign entity is not deemed to maintain a permanent establishment in Switzerland and is therefore not liable to Swiss taxes if it operates:
- A mere representative office.
- A warehouse where goods are stored for convenience of delivery.

Also, foreign corporations may retain the independent services of Swiss banks, lawyers, notaries, fiduciaries, accountants, and bookkeepers without attracting a liability to Swiss taxes on income, capital and profit distributions. Even a very broad range of contractual relationships of a non-resident corporation with Swiss based service providers is not sufficient to constitute a taxable presence in Switzerland. However, these services must be limited in scope, in particular if the activities are regulated.

3. Swiss partnership income

Swiss partnerships are fiscally transparent. The foreign partners are liable to Swiss income tax on their share of partnership profits and on their equity invested in the partnership. If the foreign partner is an individual, he or she will be liable to individual income tax and social security contributions; a foreign corporation will be liable to corporate income tax.

4. *Swiss real estate income*

A foreign corporation owning Swiss real estate is liable to Swiss taxes as follows:

- Real property transfer tax on the acquisition and disposition of Swiss real estate (only applied by a decreasing number of cantons).
- Income tax on net income derived from, and capital gains realised on the disposition of, Swiss real estate; a proportion of interest expense is tax deductible.
- Capital tax on the net asset value of the Swiss real estate.
- Where applicable, special property taxes imposed by the canton or community (municapility) in which the real estate is located.

II. Determination of taxable income and capital of Swiss permanent establishments

The foreign entity is liable to Swiss corporate income tax on income and capital attributable to the permanent establishment. In general, taxable income of a permanent establishment is determined on the basis of its separate financial statements as if it were a corporate entity separate from its head office.

III. Remittance of profits

Swiss-based permanent establishments may remit their net after-tax profits abroad free of Swiss withholding tax.

§ 3 Withholding tax

I. Income subject to withholding tax

Federal withholding tax is levied at source on income from movable capital, lottery gains and insurance benefits. Movable capital includes the following:

- Deposits with Swiss banks.
- Bonds and other similar negotiable debt instruments issued by a Swiss resident borrower.
- Shares and profit participation certificates issued by Swiss resident corporations.
- Units issued by Swiss resident investment funds.

1. Interest

Interest withholding tax is imposed on certain specific interest categories only, the most important being interest on deposits with Swiss banks. For withholding tax purposes, the term "Swiss bank" is broader than the regulatory definition, and may include resident finance corporations and any other corporate or individual person accepting customer deposits on a regular basis and paying interest in the same way as a professional deposit taker. Generally speaking, deposit takers are considered as banks for withholding tax purposes if they attract more than 12 interest-bearing customer deposits and expect to attain the number of 20 deposits within a period of three years.

Interest withholding tax is also imposed on interest derived from bonds and similar negotiable debt instruments issued by Swiss resident borrowers. A Swiss person is deemed to "issue bonds" if it pays interest to 10 persons or more on identical terms.

Withholding tax on interest secured on Swiss real estate paid by persons in or outside Switzerland is levied independently of normal withholding tax and, in certain instances, both withholding taxes could be levied cumulatively.

2. Profit Distributions

Profit distributions involve any benefit of a financial nature received by a shareholder or a person deemed to be an "associate" (other than the repayment of capital) and include:

- Ordinary dividends.
- Liquidation proceeds.
- Stock dividends.
- Constructive dividends.

Royalties, management fees, service fees, and technical assistance fees are not subject to Swiss withholding tax. However, if the payments are to an affiliate (whether or not a shareholder) and are deemed excessive, they are treated as a hidden distribution of profits subject to withholding tax.

II. Exemptions from withholding tax

The following income is exempt from withholding tax:

1. Foreign source income

Withholding tax is levied exclusively on Swiss source income. The residence of the situation of real estate securing the debt determines the source.

2. Loan interest

This includes a whole range of business and non-business loan transactions where the borrower is not a "bank" or the issuer of a debt security.

3. Interest on interbank loans between Swiss or foreign banks

This category includes a whole range of interbank transactions; a circular issued by the tax authorities provides a list of exempt transactions.

4. Interest on fiduciary deposits

If a bank acts as fiduciary agent (trustee) and deposits the funds with a foreign bank or invests them in Eurobonds for the exclusive risk and benefit of the investor, the interest derived there from and transferred to the customer is exempt.

5. Branch profits

Remittances of profits by a Swiss branch to its foreign head-office.

6. Corporate restructuring

Retained earnings of a corporation, which are transferred to the reserves of another entity of the same kind upon merger, transformation, or reorganisation.

7. Small amounts of income

Interest on savings accounts and deposits, if the interest is less than CHF 50 per annum.

8. Interest on savings held by recognised pension funds

Interest on deposits in insurance funds, welfare funds and similar institutions, which provide for old age, survivor and disability benefits.

III. Withholding and reimbursement of tax

The payer of the income is required to withhold 35% irrespective of whether the recipient is entitled to a full or partial refund. Payment of tax must be made on or before 30 days after maturity of the interest or dividend coupon. Relief may be obtained, depending on the residency of the taxpayer and the provisions of any relevant treaty, as follows:

1. Relief for Swiss resident taxpayers

For recipients who are Swiss residents, the withholding tax is a means to enforce compliance with Swiss tax reporting requirements.

Withholding tax is reimbursed by way of cash refunds to corporate taxpayers or credit against income tax payable by individual taxpayers, subject to the following conditions:

- The beneficiary must be a Swiss resident taxpayer.
- The beneficiary must report the asset and the income derived there from.

2. Relief for non-residents

For most non-resident recipients, Swiss withholding tax represents a final tax on investment income from Swiss sources. A tax treaty may, however, reduce the rate of tax or exempt the non-resident entirely.

Relief is available upon application for a refund to be filed by the recipient with its local tax authority. Formerly, the only exceptions for treaty reduction or exemption of the withholding tax at source were applicable to U.S. and Germany. The new measure – effective per 1 January 2005 – does equal the treatment of dividend payments within Switzerland as well as of cross-border dividend payments.

§ 4 Indirect taxes

I. Value added tax (VAT)

Value added tax (VAT) was introduced on 1 January 1995 and increased as of 1 January 1999 and 1 January 2001, replacing the existing sales tax. VAT is imposed on deliveries of goods and services, and the assessment system is broadly similar to those in force in the European Union.

The rates applied are as follows:

- Standard rate 7.6%.
- Reduced rate (food, medicine, water, etc.) 2.4%.
- Special rate (for hotel accommodation, introduced in October 1996) 3.6%.

II. Stamp duties

After the part revision of the law on stamp duties from 1 April 1993, they have been levied on the following transactions:

- Issues or increases of the capital stock of legal entities, bonus certificates, bond issues, and money market paper. Capital transfers to a branch are exempt.
- Transactions in Swiss and foreign securities effected by Swiss-based brokers or other registered securities dealers, including banks.

1. Stamp duty on issues

a) Issues or increases in capital stock

Duty is assessed at an ordinary rate of 1% on the fair market value of the capital contribution made, with the following exemptions:

- Shares issued in connection with mergers and other business combinations.
- The parts issued by investment trusts.
- Shares issued on the transfer of domicile of a foreign corporation to Switzerland.
- Capital contributions on incorporation of new companies of less than CHF 1,000,000, although there are some exceptions to this exemption.

b) Issues of bonds and money market paper

- Stamp duty is assessed on the issue price of debt securities at the rates indicated.
- On domestic bonds, notes, and mortgage bonds at 0.12% per annum.
- On domestic bank paper, medium-term notes, and certificates of deposit at 0.06% per annum.
- On domestic money market paper at 0.06% per day/360 days.

2. Stamp duty on securities transactions

a) Registered securities dealers

For the purpose of assessing stamp duty on securities transactions, the following are treated as registered securities dealers:

- Banks and bank-like entities.

- Individuals, corporations, or partnerships that buy and sell securities for customers or who act as intermediaries in the purchase and sale of dutiable securities.

- Investment fund managers.

- Other entities that report taxable securities with a value of more than CHF 10,000,000 in their balance sheet.

Securities on the transfer of which duty is assessed include:

- Securities such as bonds, shares, commercial paper and investment fund units of foreign issuers.
- Similar securities issued in Switzerland by non-residents.

Securities of Swiss residents are assessed at 0.015% of the transaction price and non-residents at 0.03%. However, the law contains numerous exceptions, such as in respect of transactions in money market paper, transactions between two foreign trading partners, and purchases by banks for their own purposes.

III. Real estate taxes

Certain cantons and communities levy an annual real estate tax based on the gross value of real estate, without deduction of mortgage or other debts that may be attached. The taxable value is normally lower than current market value and rates of tax range from 0.05% to 0.40%.

Teil E

Unternehmensform / Corporate form

Kapitel 1:
Die Wahl der Gesellschaftsform für KMU unter besonderer Berücksichtigung der GmbH

§ 1   Einleitung

Nachstehend soll vor allem die GmbH als mögliche Rechtsform für ein KMU dargestellt und in Vergleich zu anderen Gesellschaftsformen gesetzt werden. Als praktizierender Treuhänder möchte ich hier zentral «die GmbH als Kundin beim Treuhänder» behandeln. Dabei werden folgende Fragen näher behandelt:

1) Wie sich der Kunde zur GmbH-Gründung entscheidet

2) Partnerschaften in der GmbH

3) Die GmbH im Konzern

4) Jährliche Arbeiten des Treuhänders für den GmbH-Kunden

5) Steuern der GmbH

6) Abgabenrechtliche Probleme

Zu Beginn ein praktisches Beispiel: Zwei Personen erscheinen in einem Treuhandbüro (oder z.B. in einem Anwalts- bzw. Notariatsbüro). Sie stellen sich als Architekten vor, beide aktiv tätig in einer Personengesellschaft. Sie haben den Wunsch, eine AG zu gründen, um die Haftung zu beschränken. Zudem wollen sie einen Aktionärbindungsvertrag schliessen und die Aktien vinkulieren, damit diese nur erschwert übertragbar sind und das Unternehmen beim Austritt eines Partners zukunftsfähig bleibt.

Ein alltäglicher Fall, der eigentlich am kostengünstigsten über eine GmbH gelöst werden kann: Beschränkung der Haftung mit gesetzlich strenger Vinkulierung. Gleichwohl wird die AG das Rennen machen, und die Grundsätze einer vertieften juristischen Prüfung der Vor- und Nachteile von AG und GmbH verlieren sich im pragmatischen Lösungsansatz des Kunden. Nichtsdestotrotz soll die Rechtswahl mit einem kurzen Vergleich zu anderen Gesellschaftsformen unternehmerischer Tätigkeit analysiert werden.

§ 2 Einzel- und Personengesellschaft und die GmbH

Die GmbH war gesetzgeberisch als die AG des kleinen Mannes konzipiert. Diese Gesetzgebung ist deshalb auch auf Kleinunternehmen zugeschnitten. Die Kommanditgesellschaft oder Kollektivgesellschaft sowie auch die Einzelfirma bilden oft Ausgangspunkt für die Rechtswahl der GmbH. Währenddem der Vergleich AG und GmbH auf der Hand liegt, soll an dieser Stelle auch ein Vergleich Personengesellschaft und GmbH erfolgen, weil KMUs sich sehr stark in diesen Strukturen bewegen. Der Vergleich sei zudem erlaubt, weil damit stark abgabenrechtliche Probleme angeschnitten werden:

- Die unbeschränkte Haftung der *Kommanditgesellschaft oder Kollektivgesellschaft (sowie der Einzelfirma)* bildet oft Anlass für die Rechtswahl der GmbH. Dabei hat der Kunde den Konkurs vor Augen, der die Firma untergehen lässt, währenddem das Privatvermögen des Eigentümers der GmbH den Gläubigern entzogen ist und somit gerettet werden kann. Dieses Idealbild ist realitätsfremd. In den meisten mir bekannten Fällen ist der Unternehmer zu allem bereit, um sein Unternehmen zu stützen oder allenfalls zu retten. Als praktische Massnahmen dienen etwa Privateinlagen oder die Hinterlegung von Grundpfandtiteln, lastend auf der privaten Liegenschaft zur Absicherung von Bankkrediten der Gesellschaft. Die mangelnde Liquidität ist oft ein erstes und wichtiges Symptom eines kranken Unternehmens. Um diese zu verbessern, wird eine private Bürgschaft gegenüber der kreditierenden Bank eingegangen. Damit haben wir den gleichen Mechanismus der Vermischung der unterschiedlichen Vermögensmassen. Es versteht sich von selbst, dass mit solchen Tatsachen der Konkurs der GmbH auf das Privatvermögen einen erheblichen Einfluss hat, und die GmbH wird damit zur GmH, der Gesellschaft mit Haftung.

- Die *gesetzliche Haftung* bei den Sozialversicherungsbeiträgen und den Quellensteuern auf Salären bringt es mit sich, dass trotz Konkurses Forderungen nicht untergehen und gegenüber den geschäftsführenden Organen geltend gemacht werden können. Nach dem Konkurs herrscht während einiger Zeit trügerische Ruhe, bis sich die Ausgleichskassen melden. Allenfalls kommen Strafanzeigen nach den Sonderstraftatbeständen der AHV- und BVG-Gesetzgebung hinzu. Auch hier kann der Konkurs einen erheblichen Einfluss auf das Privatvermögen der Gesellschafter haben, zumal Sozialabzüge auf Salären substanziell und wesentlich sind. Es bedarf einiger Anstrengungen, dass ein KMU-Konkurs die GmbH isoliert betrifft.

- Die *wirtschaftliche Doppelbesteuerung* wird oft vernachlässigt, obwohl unter der Prämisse einer steueroptimalen Gestaltung des Geschäftsabschlusses faktisch die Besteuerung der GmbH und der Privatperson für das gleiche Substrat Erfolg und Vermögen reduziert werden kann. Es verbleibt jedoch eine Vermögens- und Einkommenssteuer sowie eine Kapital- und Gewinnsteuer, welche sich in einem Teilbereich addieren.

- Die *Bemessung der AHV* hat zur Folge, dass bei der juristischen Person (GmbH) der Unternehmerlohn mit 10,1 % belastet wird. Der Teil des Verdienstes, der das rentenbildende Maximum von derzeit CHF 74'160.– übersteigt, ist mangels Vorteilsbildung faktisch eine reine Steuer. Demgegenüber steht der Beitragssatz für Selbstständigerwerbende von 9,5 %. Was auf den ersten Blick als Vorteil für den Selbstständigerwerbenden aussieht, muss näher betrachtet werden. Die AHV-Gesetzgebung sieht vor, dass die an die AHV geleisteten Beiträge nicht als für die Bemessung der Beiträge absetzbare Unkosten gelten. Ein Einkommen von CHF 100'000.– mit einem bereits steuerlich abgezogenen AHV-Beitrag von CHF 9'500.– (hier 9,5 % von CHF 100'000.–) führt deshalb zu einer AHV-Bemessung von 9,5 % von CHF 109'500.–, was somit im Ergebnis wieder zum AHV-Satz für Unselbstständige von 10,1 % (auf CHF 100'000.–) führt. Die genaue Rechnung führt zu gleichwertigen Sätzen. Die 11. AHV-Revision sieht einen gleichen Satz für Selbstständige und Unselbstständigerwerbende vor, was tatsächlich zu einer Verschlechterung der Selbstständigen führt, da die notwendige systemkonforme Egalisierung der Bemessungsgrundlage unterbleibt.

- Die *Bemessung der ALV* hat zur Folge, dass der Unternehmerlohn zusätzlich gegen Arbeitslosigkeit versichert ist. Aber auch hier gibt es ein versicherbares Maximum von 106'800.–, währenddem die 1 %-Abgabe von CHF 106'800.– bis CHF 267'000.– eine reine Steuer ist. Diese Regelung wurde zwar mittlerweile aufgehoben, angesichts der Defizite der ALV könnte es jedoch zu einer Wiedereinführung kommen.

- Die *Bemessung der AHV* erlaubt ferner nicht, dass vorgeschobene GmbHs oder AGs eine Fakturierung als Selbstständigerwerbender an die eigene GmbH oder AG zulassen. Sie werden von den Ausgleichskassen nicht zugelassen und führen zu einer Nichtanerkennung der Selbständigkeit.

- Die *Mehrwertsteuer* möchte ich als eigentliche Crux im abgabenrechtlichen Bereich bezeichnen. Bei der GmbH ist die Behandlung kein Problem. Die GmbH bildet das Subjekt der Mehrwertsteuer und ist ein in sich geschlossener Kreis. Bei den Selbstständigerwerbenden (als Einzelunternehmer) ist nicht die Einzelfirma Subjekt, sondern die natürliche Person. Dies hat zur Folge, dass private Geschäfte, wie zum Beispiel das Vermieten der eigenen Ferienwohnung, zu mehrwertsteuerpflichtigen Erträgen führen. Ich möchte hier das Thema nicht weiter ausführen, jedoch zusammenfassend feststellen, dass betreffend Mehrwertsteuer eine eigene juristische Person Sinn macht.

- Die *gesetzliche Situation* ist ambivalent. Pro und Contra juristische Person versus natürliche Person stehen sich gegenüber. Zusammenfassend lässt sich feststellen, dass in einfacheren Verhältnissen die Personengesellschaft sehr tauglich ist, jedoch bei einer Expansion sehr bald aufgegeben werden muss.

Für die so genannten «freien Berufe» (wie Ärzte) sind GmbH oder AG als Erscheinungsbild fremd, aber häufig möglich. Rechtsanwälte können nicht innerhalb einer juristischen Person als solche praktizieren.

§ 3   Die jetzige Rechtswahl der GmbH

Die erwähnten Gründe führen dazu, dass der Unternehmer sich zur Rechtswahl einer juristischen Person entscheidet. Ich habe dabei in meiner 20-jährigen Praxis noch nie erlebt, dass der Kunde eine sorgfältige Analyse für und wider AG oder GmbH sucht. In den meisten Fällen bestehen klare Vorstellungen.

Diejenigen Personen, welche sich für die GmbH entscheiden, haben wenig Kapital und wollen mit CHF 20'000.– eine Gesellschaft gründen. Diese Unternehmen sind in der Regel noch nicht ertragsstark, weshalb eine kostengünstige Lösung gesucht werden soll, es besteht somit auch kein Bedarf an einer Revisionsstelle. Mit diesen Tatsachen erübrigen sich alle weiteren Überlegungen zu einer fundiert abgeklärten Wahl der Gesellschaftsform.

Diejenigen Unternehmer hingegen, welche sich für eine AG entscheiden, sind kapitalkräftiger und suchen die Lösung in einer anonymen Kapitalgesellschaft. In der Regel wollen sie mit dieser Rechtswahl auch dem Nimbus der billigen GmbH entgehen. Eine Beurteilung, welche weit verbreitet ist und auch eine gewisse Richtigkeit hat.

§ 4   Die Aktiengesellschaft und die GmbH

Die zahlenmässig stark gestiegenen GmbH-Gründungen lassen eine Steigerung der Attraktivität der GmbH vermuten. Tatsache ist jedoch, dass die GmbH unverändert dasteht, währenddem die AG durch die Revision erheblich unattraktiver geworden ist. Dazu gehören:

- Die Erhöhung des Mindestaktienkapitals,
- die gesteigerten Anforderungen an das Rechnungswesen und die Revision,
- die erhöhte Verantwortung des Verwaltungsrates.

Zu beachten ist, dass die Revision des GmbH-Rechts gerade mit der Einführung der im Revisionsentwurf zwingend vorgeschriebenen Revisionsstelle einen bedeutenden Kostenvorteil zugunsten der GmbH vernichtet. Es gibt selbstverständlich zahlreiche gute Gründe für diese Änderung.

I.   Gesetzliche Vinkulierung

- Die Übertragbarkeit der GmbH-Anteile nur mittels notarieller Urkunde wird oft als Nachteil erwähnt. Ich erachte dies jedoch überwiegend als Vorteil. So sind beispielsweise die Gesellschafterverhältnisse immer klar und unmissverständlich. Jeder Berater, der schon einmal eine Aktiengesellschaft verkauft hat, weiss zu berichten, wie die nachträgliche Erstellung eines Aktienbuches oft mühsam ist. Es fehlt die Geschichte der Gesellschafterverhältnisse, nicht alle notwendigen Indossamente lassen sich innerhalb der gebotenen Zeit einholen oder beispielsweise sind Zertifikate nicht auffindbar. Das Gesetz zwingt zur Klarheit. Die neu vorgesehene Schriftlichkeit führt zu einer Vereinfachung der Übertragbarkeit. Andererseits dürfte darunter auch das Erfordernis klar geführter Anteilsbücher leiden. In die gleiche Richtung

geht die jährliche Meldung der Stammkapitalhalter an das Handelsregisteramt, welche nun wegfällt.
- Die Vinkulierung von Aktien ist ein spezielles Fachgebiet. Bei der GmbH ist, als wohl einer der wichtigsten Vorteile, schon von Gesetzes wegen eine recht starke, ausbaubare Übertragungsbeschränkung vorhanden. Hier haben wir sicher einen der wichtigsten Vorteile für die KMU bei personenabhängigen Unternehmungen. Die GmbH taugt deshalb besonders gut bei langfristigen Partnerschaften. Weiter ist sie als Organisation gedacht, bei der die Gesellschafter zugleich im Geschäft aktiv tätig sind. In der Praxis kommt der GmbH nicht die Bedeutung zu, die ihr eigentlich zugedacht war.

II. Übrige Aspekte

Die **GmbH** wird auch unter dem neuen Recht noch einige wesentliche Abweichungen gegenüber der AG aufweisen.

- Die *Publizität* führt dazu, dass die Gesellschaftseigentümer bekannt sind.
- Das *liberierte Mindestkapital* beträgt bei der AG CHF 50'000.– und bei der GmbH CHF 20'000.– (neu ist nach dem jetzigen Vorentwurf das Erfordernis der vollen Liberierung).
- Die neuen Normen über die *Rechnungslegung* bei der GmbH führen dazu, dass diese bei AG und GmbH identisch sind. Zusammen mit der zwingenden Revisionsstelle bestehen im Rechnungswesen und in der Prüfung keine Unterschiede mehr.

Die Neuerungen werden also meiner Meinung nach die GmbH nicht attraktiver machen, so insbesondere nicht die neu notwendige Revisionsstelle, die erweiterte Rechnungslegung und das erhöhte liberierte Mindestkapital.

Viele ausländische Rechte kennen keine generelle Revision für kleine Gesellschaften (8. EU-RL: 5 Mio. Euro Umsatz, 50 Mitarbeiter). Insofern dürfte eine Pflicht der Revisionsstelle weitergehen als das EU-Recht.

§ 5   Die GmbH im Konzern

An dieser Stelle möchte ich kurz die **GmbH** im Konzern näher ausführen. Im Konzern, in der Regel ist die AG dort vorherrschend, hat jede Tochteraktiengesellschaft ihr juristisches Eigenleben:

- Der *Verwaltungsrat* dieser Tochtergesellschaften ist von Gesetzes wegen gefordert, die ihm unentziehbaren Aufgaben wahrzunehmen. Tatsache ist jedoch, dass die Oberleitung der Gesellschaft, um nur ein Beispiel zu nennen, oft gerade nicht dort wahrgenommen wird, sondern über die Konzernleitung, sei nun diese personell als Verwaltungsrat oder als Direktorium definiert. Damit stehen sich das juristische Gebot und die faktische Gegebenheit gegenüber. Eine Tochter-GmbH befreit aus diesem juristischen Dilemma. Es sei wohl angefügt, dass dazu wenig Problematik publik wird. Die Tochter-GmbH bietet jedoch eine klare, konsequente Lösung.

- Die *Tochter-GmbH* bietet im Moment auch den Vorteil, dass diese keiner Revisionsstelle bedarf. Die Mutter-AG aber unterliegt der Revisionspflicht, womit indirekt eine Prüfung erfolgt. Der Umfang der Prüfung dürfte sich aber in der Regel reduzieren, wobei sich dies von einem theoretischen Aspekt betrachtet, nicht absolut beurteilen lässt. Massgebend ist die Tatsache, wie weit die Bilanz und Erfolgsrechnung mit der Mutter-AG verflochten ist. Die Rechnungslegung erfolgt neu analog der AG und damit besteht die Pflicht zur Konsolidierung ab einem Umsatz von CHF 20 Mio. und einer Bilanzsumme von CHF 10 Mio. Aus diesem Grund spielt es keine Rolle, welche Rechtsform im Konzern sich findet, alleine entscheidend ist die Überschreitung der quantitativen Kriterien.

§ 6   Jährliche Arbeiten

Mit dem Thema der jährlichen Arbeiten des Treuhänders für die AG möchte ich die GmbH in weiteren Aspekten beleuchten.

I. Geschäftsabschluss

Die Anfertigung des *Geschäftsabschlusses*, also des buchhalterischen Abschlusses, ist eine der wesentlichen Tätigkeiten des Treuhänders für den GmbH-Kunden. Er beinhaltet die Verifizierung der betriebsintern geführten Buchhaltung oder die Führung der Buchhaltung selbst. Hinzu kommt eine steuerliche Optimierung der Bilanz und Erfolgsrechnung, wobei zu 99 % eine Identität von Steuer- und Handelsbilanz besteht. Die Arbeiten kommen einem Review gleich, weshalb neben der Revisionsstelle die Einführung eines Review, wie in anderen Rechtsgebieten üblich, ein praktischer Lösungsansatz wäre und das Dilemma der heute fehlenden Revisionsstellenpflicht Europa-tauglich lösen würde. Die nun neu eingeführte eingeschränkte Revision geht in diese Richtung.

II. Steuererklärung

Die *Steuererklärung* ist der dem Geschäftsabschluss folgende zweite Teil und die logische Konsequenz des steueroptimalen Geschäftsabschlusses.

Zur Frage der *Besteuerung* der GmbH sei darauf verwiesen, dass GmbH und AG identisch besteuert werden. Die Grundsätze des Unternehmenssteuerrechts finden ohne Unterscheidung Anwendung.

Die Besteuerung der GmbH-Anteile im *Vermögen* der Eigentümer richtet sich bei natürlichen Personen nach dem Vermögenssteuerwert. Diese Bewertung orientiert sich an einer Wegleitung des Bundes, welche unter Berücksichtigung von Buchwert, Verkehrswert und Ertragswert den Steuerwert festlegt.

III. Gesellschafterversammlung

Pro memoria sei hier auf die jährliche *Gesellschafterversammlung* hingewiesen, welche mit dem neuen Recht auf dem Zirkularweg zulässig werden sollte.

IV. Bankengerechtes Verhalten

Zu den regelmässigen Arbeiten gehören auch das Gespräch mit den Banken und die Sensibilisierung zu bankengerechtem Verhalten. Angesichts der negativen Erfahrungen der Kreditinstitute in der Vergangenheit mit ihren Kunden ist die zurückhaltende Gewährung von Limiten verständlich. Leider beobachte ich in letzter Zeit einen Würgegriff der Banken bei den KMUs. Ein Unterschied zwischen AG und GmbH für das Rating bei den Banken ist mir nicht bekannt. Die Ratingdokumente einiger Banken kenne ich, sie sehen nichts dergleichen vor. Die Kreditwürdigkeit richtet sich somit alleine nach wirtschaftlichen Kriterien. Die meisten Banken dürften einen Revisionsbericht verlangen. Ein allfälliges Opting-Out würde dem entgegenstehen.

Kapitel 2:
Die Unternehmensnachfolge (Exkurs)

Im Sinne eines Exkurses sind nachfolgend die Grundsätze der Unternehmensnachfolge umschrieben.

§ 1 Elemente der Unternehmensnachfolge

Die Überführung eines Unternehmens umfasst drei wesentliche Komponenten:

I. Organisatorische Massnahmen

Die notwendigen Führungs- und Entscheidungsstrukturen müssen geschaffen werden, damit das Unternehmen nahtlos überführt werden kann.

II. Steuerliche Konsequenzen

Wenn Unternehmen ihren Besitzer wechseln, fallen in der Regel Steuern an. Da die Steuerbelastung sehr gross sein kann, müssen sie beurteilt werden. Unter Umständen empfehlen sich daraus rechtliche Konstruktionen, welche die Steuerbelastung reduzieren können. Es ist aber zu beachten, dass komplizierte rechtliche Verhältnisse schwerfällig sein können, wenn sie nur das Ziel verfolgen, die Steuerbelastung zu minimieren. Je nachdem kann dann das höhere Ziel der Unternehmensnachfolge darunter leiden.

Je grösser das Unternehmen, desto wichtiger die betrieblichen Aspekte. Steuerliche Beurteilungen sind ein kleineres Element vom Ganzen. Je kleiner das Unternehmen, desto grösser sind die Möglichkeiten, auf steuerliche und rechtliche Fragen gestalterisch einzugehen. Die Flexibilität der Klein- und Mittelunternehmen spielt eine grosse Rolle. Wenn ein grosses, börsennotiertes Unternehmen ein anderes Unternehmen übernehmen will, treten zuerst die betriebswirtschaftlichen Überlegungen in den Vordergrund. Wie hoch ist der Preis, wie können wir die Mehrheit erlangen und wie gelangen wir in den Verwaltungsrat? Steuerliche Fragen treten in den Hintergrund. Was zählt, ist Einfluss und wirtschaftliche Potenz. Bei den kleineren Unternehmen ist die Bereitschaft grösser, sich mit den Fragen Recht und Steuern als sich gegenseitig gestaltende Komponenten auseinander zu setzen. Dies ist auch möglich, weil die wirtschaftliche Macht konzentriert ist und damit überhaupt erst die Möglichkeit von Varianten eröffnet wird.

III. Rechtliche Aspekte

Ein Unternehmen ist Bestandteil des Vermögens von Personen. Damit dieses übertragen werden kann, bedarf es rechtlicher Grundlagen.

§ 2 Familiäre Nachfolge

Zuerst wollen wir uns mit der Nachfolge innerhalb der Familie befassen. Für die Klein- und Mittelbetriebe ist dies eine verbreitete Variante. Es ist jedoch zu beachten, dass nur grob geschätzt 2/3 der Firmen den Übergang in die zweite Generation finden. Der Sprung in die Dritte Generation dürfte bei ca. 1/5 liegen. Viele werden verkauft, liquidiert oder scheitern in der betrieblichen Führung.

I. Aktiengesellschaft

Ist das Unternehmen in einer Aktiengesellschaft integriert, so kann das Unternehmen relativ einfach durch Übergabe der Aktien auf die Nachfolgegeneration übertragen werden.

Probleme bietet oft die Übergangsphase. Der Senior hat noch die Zügel in der Hand und der Junior hat noch nicht die wirtschaftliche Kompetenz an Sachwissen und Persönlichkeit erlangt. Hier sind bereits Verträge notwendig, die den Übergang vorbereiten.

1. Der Aktionärbindungsvertrag

Der Vertrag bindet die Aktionäre untereinander. Durch Kaufrechte, Vorkaufsrechte, Hinterlegung der Aktien etc. wird sichergestellt, dass die Aktien in einer Familienhand bleiben. Die Aktionäre bilden eine einfache Gesellschaft untereinander. Die Kaufrechte sind oft mit Bewertungsregeln verbunden. Ist die Übertragung von Aktien durch einen Nachlass bedingt, liegen erbvertragliche Elemente vor. In der Regel sind solche Verträge schriftlich abgefasst. Für die erbvertraglichen Teile sind öffentliche Urkunden notwendig, ansonsten sind diese ungültig.

2. Der Ehe- und Erbvertrag

Ist vorgesehen, das Unternehmen auf die zweite Generation zu übertragen, müssen ehegüterrechtliche und erbrechtliche Analysen vorgenommen werden. In einem Nachlass ist der überlebende Ehegatte, aufgrund der allgemeinen Lebenserwartung ist dies oft die Ehefrau, zusammen mit den Kindern erbberechtigt. Alle Aktien stehen zuerst im gemeinsamen Eigentum aller. Erst durch die Erbteilung werden die Quoten gebildet. Durch einen Ehevertrag, verbunden mit erbvertraglichen Bestimmungen, lässt sich die Unternehmensnachfolge gezielt planen. Beim Tod des Seniors wird durch klare Bestimmungen die kritische Zeit des Übergangs geleitet. Für diese Verträge braucht es öffentliche Beurkundung. In der Regel sind die beiden Ehepartner Vertragsparteien; wenn dann auch die Nachkommen miteinbezogen werden, sind auch diese Mitunterzeichner. Dies ist besonders dann erforderlich, wenn bei der Nachfolge ein Nachkomme eine aktivere Rolle spielt als der andere oder die anderen. Je nach Struktur des Unternehmens und nach den persönlichen Bedürfnissen der Familie werden die Aktien nur an den in der Geschäftsführung aktiven Nachkommen übertragen oder aber auch an alle mit einer Mehrheitsbeteiligung. Damit solche familiären Unternehmensnachfolgen bestehen, dürfen sie nicht den erbrechtlichen Pflichtteil der anderen Erben verletzen oder alle erklären sich durch einen Vertrag mit diesem Vorgehen einverstanden. Je breiter eine Nachfolge abgestützt ist, desto besser sind alle Beteiligten darauf vorbereitet und desto problemloser erfolgt der Übergang.

3. Andere Verträge und Grundlagen

Neben diesen beiden wichtigsten Grundlagen gibt es noch zahlreiche andere Dokumente, die nützlich sind. Ein Firmenleitbild legt die Ausrichtung des Unternehmens für die Zukunft fest. Die Strategie wird definiert. Es muss so ausformuliert sein, dass es sich der zukünftigen Entwicklung anpassen kann und auch abänderlich ist. Ein Organisationsreglement ist bereits durch das neue Aktienrecht vorgeschrieben. Es hilft, die Struktur festzulegen und die Arbeitsabläufe zu beschreiben. Auch hier muss der

Zukunft Rechnung getragen werden. Arbeitsverträge der aktiven Familienaktionäre legen das individuelle Arbeitsgebiet fest und zeigen damit auch, für welche Personen keine Tätigkeit vorgesehen ist.

II. Gesellschaft mit beschränkter Haftung

Es braucht nicht immer eine AG zu sein. Eine GmbH kann auch für diese Zwecke dienen. Mit der Revision des Aktienrechts gewinnt diese Rechtsform zunehmend an Bedeutung. Die GmbH ist ein bisschen schwerfälliger als die Aktiengesellschaft. Aber gerade dies braucht kein Nachteil zu sein. In der Familienaktiengesellschaft wird oft eine Schwerfälligkeit gesucht. Die Aktien sollen nicht frei handelbar sein, die aktive Mitarbeit von Aktionären wird in Verträgen definiert und erbrechtliche Beschränkungen sind stipuliert. All dies bietet die GmbH bereits von sich aus. Anstelle komplizierter Verträge für die Aktionäre genügen einfache Statuten der GmbH. Für die individuelle Unternehmensnachfolge ist dies mit einzubeziehen.

Auch hier sollten schlussendlich gleiche rechtliche Strukturen geschaffen werden, wie in der Aktiengesellschaft. Übertragung der Firmenanteile innerhalb der Familie, Erbverträge, Arbeitsverträge, Firmenleitbild, Organisationsreglement, etc.

III. Einzelfirma

Die Einzelfirma ist die am wenigsten rechtlich strukturierte Unternehmenseinheit. Ein einfacher Eintrag im Handelsregister lässt diese Unternehmensform bilden. Die Einzelfirma selbst kann nicht übertragen werden, sie ist an die Person des Unternehmers gebunden. In der Nachfolge werden Aktiven und Passiven, partiell oder integral, auf den neuen Eigentümer der Firma übertragen. Die alte Einzelfirma erlischt und eine neue entsteht. Diese Form ist oft in Kleinunternehmen anzutreffen. Für einfache Strukturen genügen einfache Lösungen. Die Übertragung erfolgt zu Lebzeiten als Verkauf oder Schenkung; innerhalb des Nachlasses als Erbteilung.

Auch hier empfiehlt es sich, die gleichen Rahmenbedingungen festzulegen, wie bereits schon erwähnt.

IV. Kollektiv- und Kommanditgesellschaft

Es kommt eher selten vor, dass eine Einzelfirma übertragen wird. Eher zeichnet sich bereits schon zu Lebzeiten eine Partnerschaft zwischen Senior und Junior, oder Junioren, ab. Zu Beginn steht ein gewöhnliches Arbeitsverhältnis, welches sich im Laufe der Zeit aufgrund des gewachsenen Vertrauensverhältnisses zu einer Partnerschaft entwickelt. Als Folge wird eine Kollektivgesellschaft gegründet: Meier & Sohn. Als rechtliche Grundlage genügt der gemeinsame Eintrag im Handelsregister. Gleichwohl empfiehlt sich bald einmal ein ausformulierter Kollektivgesellschaftsvertrag. Diese Form der Personengesellschaft ist sehr flexibel. Speziell in Bewertungsfragen und Gewinnverteilungen gibt es grosse Gestaltungsfreiräume. Dies gilt sinngemäss für die fast gleich geregelte Kommanditgesellschaft.

Besonderes Augenmerk ist darauf zu richten, dass Kollektivgesellschafter solidarisch und persönlich für die Schulden der Personengesellschaft haften. Es empfiehlt sich hier eine Kollektivunterschrift der Gesellschafter oder eine strenge und permanente Kontrolle. Insbesondere bei Todesfall eines Gesellschafters müssen die Erben rasch prüfen, ob sie die Gesellschaft weiterführen wollen. Vorhandenes Vermögen ist rasch verzehrt und anstelle dessen treten Schulden, die bei den Erben eingefordert werden.

Auch hier sind neben der rechtlichen Struktur des Unternehmens parallel dazu die ergänzenden Verträge auszuformulieren und zu vereinbaren, um die Unternehmensnachfolge in der Familie auf eine klare und sichere Grundlage zu binden.

V. Stiftung

Für die Unternehmensnachfolge braucht es immer einen rechtlichen Träger. Neben den Kapitalgesellschaften und den Personengesellschaften ist es auch möglich, das Unternehmen in eine Stiftung zu integrieren. Im Bereiche der öffentlichen Aufgaben kommt dies sehr oft vor: Spitäler, Museen, Kulturelle Institutionen, etc. sind in Stiftungen integriert. Dort bereitet dies keine Probleme. Es sind Aufgaben mit öffentlichem Interesse, welche über eine Stiftung wahrgenommen werden und damit der Kontrolle des Staates unterstehen. Teilweise wird dieses rechtliche Institut auch für die Unternehmensnachfolge verwendet. Ein Beispiel für viele: IKEA. Als Motivation zu dieser Lösung ist die ungelöste Familiennachfolge. Es findet sich keine herausragende Persönlichkeit, welche das unternehmerische Leitbild des Gründers weiter verwirklichen kann, oder ein Machtkampf in der Familie ist absehbar. Mit dem Parkieren des Unternehmens in der Stiftung und der damit verbundenen Übertragung auf eine neutrale Person glaubt man eine Lösung gefunden zu haben. Das Unternehmen ist unantastbar und geht infolge dessen seinen Weg. Es ist jedoch unverkennbar, dass damit auch eine Sackgasse vorprogrammiert ist. Das Unternehmen ist unausweichlich für ewig in der Stiftung. Es unterliegt der staatlichen Kontrolle durch die jährliche Prüfung. Anstelle von freiem Unternehmertum folgt halbstaatliches Wirtschaften. Bereits zeigen sich hier Konsequenzen. Die Stiftungen werden vermehrt besteuert. Anstelle einer steuerbefreiten Holdinggesellschaft tritt eine besteuerte Stiftung.

§ 3 Ausserfamiliäre Nachfolge

Ob ein Unternehmen innerhalb der Familie oder ausserhalb der Familie übertragen wird, führt im Ergebnis zum gleichen Ziel, nur der Weg ist anders. Der erste Weg ist in der Regel eine Übertragung durch Schenkung oder Erbschaft, womit erbrechtliche Fragen zu beurteilen sind. Der zweite Weg ist in der Regel entgeltlich, wobei gesellschaftsrechtliche und kaufrechtliche Fragen zu prüfen sind.

I. Aktiengesellschaft

Wird eine Aktiengesellschaft verkauft, so wechseln die Aktien den Besitzer. Der Kaufvertrag sollte die wichtigsten Punkte festhalten:

1) die Vertragsparteien (Käufer und Verkäufer, nicht die AG)
2) den Kaufsgegenstand (Anzahl Aktien)
3) die Zustimmung des Verwaltungsrates zum Eintrag in das Aktienbuch bei Namensaktien
4) den Kaufpreis, eventuell definiert durch Bewertungsschema
5) Sicherheiten bei Ratenkauf
6) Hinterlegung der Aktien bei sukzessiver Überführung
7) Gerichtsstandklausel, Schiedsgericht
8) Vinkulierung (Übertragungsbeschränkung)

Mit der Übertragung der Aktiengesellschaft können auch noch andere Problemkreise verbunden sein:

9) Unsicherheiten über Steuerfolgen, latente Steuern
10) Rentenverpflichtung der AG zugunsten des Verkäufers
11) Unsicherheiten für einzelne Aktiven oder Passiven in der Bewertung
12) Arbeitsverträge oder Beratungsverträge mit dem Verkäufer
13) Versicherungsverträge als Sicherheiten
14) Bankgarantien
15) Garantien für zukünftige Umsätze
16) Konkurrenzverbot
17) Firma als rechtlich geschützter Name
18) Marke als rechtlich geschütztes geistiges Eigentum

Die Aufzählung ist unvollständig und soll zeigen, wo allenfalls Probleme liegen können. Oft besteht ein gewisser zeitlicher Druck und nicht alle Dokumente können rechtzeitig vorbereitet werden. Rahmenverträge bieten hier provisorische Lösungen. Sie werden auch teilweise als Vorverträge bezeichnet. Zu beachten ist hier, dass diese voll wirksam sind. Entsteht Streit, ist der Vertrag dennoch wirksam. Meist handelt es sich nicht um einen wesentlichen Hauptpunkt, sondern um einen Nebenpunkt. Allenfalls muss der Richter darüber befinden.

II. Gesellschaft mit beschränkter Haftung

Die Überführung einer GmbH unterscheidet sich gegenüber der AG in einem wesentlichen Punkt: Sie bedarf der öffentlichen Urkunde. Man kann somit sagen, dass der Besitztitel einer GmbH stark vinkuliert ist, und zwar in einer Form, die in dieser Strenge bei der AG nie erreicht werden kann.

Ein weiteres Merkmal der GmbH ist das Recht zur Geschäftsführung des Gesellschafters. Einen Arbeitsvertrag braucht es also nicht, ist aber dennoch empfehlenswert, da das Gesetz nur minimale Vorschriften enthält.

Alle übrigen Punkte, wie sie für die AG aufgeführt sind, finden sinngemäss Anwendung.

III. Einzelfirma

Die Einzelfirma als Träger des Unternehmens kann nicht verkauft werden. Es ist aber möglich, alle Aktiven und Passiven einer Einzelfirma zu verkaufen, wobei Käufer eine neue Einzelfirma ist. Ein Kaufvertrag wird hier in aller Regel nicht die ganze Bilanz umfassen. Einzelne Aktiven werden vertraglich definiert: Goodwill, Warenlager, Mobiliar, etc. Damit handelt es sich um einen Kaufvertrag. Nach Übertragung des Unternehmens wird die verbleibende Einzelfirma gelöscht. Auch hier können umfassende Vertragskonzeptionen nötig sein.

IV. Kollektiv- und Kommanditgesellschaft

Der Weg zur Übertragung eines Unternehmens muss nicht immer eine Zäsur sein. Anstelle einer abrupten Übergabe kann eine sukzessive erfolgen. Für kleinere Unternehmen bietet hier die Kollektivgesellschaft eine gute Grundlage.

Der Kollektivgesellschaftsvertrag beinhaltet:

1) Die Parteien (Gesellschafter)

2) Den Zweck und den Namen der Gesellschaft

3) Die Kapitaleinlagen

4) Die Geschäftsführung

5) arbeitsvertragliche Elemente für die Gesellschafter

6) Monatsbezüge

7) Erfolgsbeteiligung

8) Dauer der Gesellschaft bzw. Kündigungsfristen

9) Gerichtsstand, Schiedsgericht

Anstelle einer Einkaufssumme des neuen Gesellschafters für seinen Eintritt kann auch für eine gewisse Zeit eine unterschiedliche Gewinnbeteiligung vorgesehen werden. Dies hat den Vorteil, dass der immaterielle Goodwill nicht mit einem Stichtag zur Besteuerung gelangt. Voraussetzung ist aber, dass er nicht quantifiziert ist.

Auch hier können weitere Verträge nötig sein.

V. Stiftung

Die Stiftung dient einem besonderen Zweck. In der Regel werden kulturelle oder gemeinnützige Aufgaben verfolgt. Die Stiftungen unterstehen dabei der staatlichen Aufsicht. Damit die Stiftung ihren Zweck verfolgen kann, benötigt sie Mittel. Sie erhält Vermögenswerte. Wenn also eine Stiftung zum Zweck hat, Not leidende Menschen zu unterstützen, und dafür eine entsprechende Geldsumme erhält, so ist dies unproblematisch. Wenn sie aber mit gleichem Zweck anstelle von Geld ein Unternehmen erhält, tauchen Probleme auf. Der erwirtschaftete Gewinn dient zur Verfolgung des Stiftungszweckes. Das Unternehmen selbst aber wird nicht mehr vom Unternehmer beherrscht. An dessen Stelle treten Stiftungsräte und Beamte als staatliche Kontrollorgane. Das unternehmerische Denken geht verloren und eine Quasi-Verstaatlichung ist die Folge. Unlösbar ist das Problem, wenn die Stiftung die Erhaltung des Unternehmens zum Zweck hat. Das Mittel, das Unternehmen, dient dem Zweck, das Unternehmen zu erhalten. Ein juristisches Perpetuum mobile. Das Unternehmen für die Ewigkeit für sich selbst in einer Stiftung. Dies ist keine brauchbare Lösung.

Teil F

Rechtliche Aspekte / Legal aspects

Kapitel 1:
Neue Gesetzesbestimmungen und Erläuterungen[6]

§ 1   Das Recht der Aktiengesellschaft

Erster Abschnitt: Allgemeine Bestimmungen

A. Begriff

Art. 620

1 Die Aktiengesellschaft ist eine Gesellschaft mit eigener Firma, deren zum voraus bestimmtes Kapital (Aktienkapital[7]) in Teilsummen (Aktien) zerlegt ist und für deren Verbindlichkeiten nur das Gesellschaftsvermögen haftet.

2 Die Aktionäre sind nur zu den statutarischen Leistungen verpflichtet und haften für die Verbindlichkeiten der Gesellschaft nicht persönlich.

3 Die Aktiengesellschaft kann auch für andere als wirtschaftliche Zwecke gegründet werden.

B. Mindestkapital

Art. 621

Das Aktienkapital muss mindestens 100 000 Franken betragen.

---

6   Basierend auf dem Entwurf des Bundesrates. Änderungen des National- und Ständerates sind nicht berücksichtigt, wohl aber im Gesetzestext.
7   Ausdruck gemäss Ziff. II 1 des BG vom 4. Okt. 1991, in Kraft seit 1. Juli 1992 (AS 1992 733 786; BBl 1983 II 745). Diese Änderung ist im ganzen Erlass berücksichtigt.

Kapitel 1: Neue Gesetzesbestimmungen und Erläuterungen

C. Aktien

I. Arten

Art. 622

1 Die Aktien lauten auf den Namen oder auf den Inhaber.

2 Beide Arten von Aktien können in einem durch die Statuten bestimmten Verhältnis nebeneinander bestehen.

3 Die Statuten können bestimmen, dass Namenaktien später in Inhaberaktien oder Inhaberaktien in Namenaktien umgewandelt werden sollen oder dürfen.

4 Der Nennwert der Aktie muss mindestens 1 Rappen betragen.[8]

5 Die Aktientitel müssen durch mindestens ein Mitglied des Verwaltungsrates[9] unterschrieben sein. Die Gesellschaft kann bestimmen, dass auch auf Aktien, die in grosser Zahl ausgegeben werden, mindestens eine Unterschrift eigenhändig beigesetzt werden muss.

II. Zerlegung und Zusammenlegung

Art. 623

1 Die Generalversammlung ist befugt, durch Statutenänderung bei unverändert bleibendem Aktienkapital die Aktien in solche von kleinerem Nennwert zu zerlegen oder zu solchen von grösserem Nennwert zusammenzulegen.

2 Die Zusammenlegung von Aktien bedarf der Zustimmung des Aktionärs.

---

8 Fassung gemäss Ziff. I des BG vom 15. Dez. 2000, in Kraft seit 1. Mai 2001 (AS 2001 1047; BBl 2000 4337 Ziff. 2.2.1 5501).

9 Ausdruck gemäss Ziff. II 3 des BG vom 4. Okt. 1991, in Kraft seit 1. Juli 1992 (AS 1992 733 786; BBl 1983 II 745). Diese Änderung ist im ganzen Erlass berücksichtigt.

III. Ausgabebetrag

Art. 624

1 Die Aktien dürfen nur zum Nennwert oder zu einem diesen übersteigenden Betrage ausgegeben werden. Vorbehalten bleibt die Ausgabe neuer Aktien, die an Stelle ausgefallener Aktien treten.
2–3 ...[10]

D. Aktionäre

Art. 625

Eine Aktiengesellschaft kann durch eine oder mehrere natürliche oder juristische Personen oder andere Handelsgesellschaften gegründet werden.

Nach geltendem Recht muss die Aktiengesellschaft bei der Gründung mindestens drei Aktionärinnen oder Aktionäre zählen. Wie in der GmbH will der Entwurf neu die Gründung von Einpersonenaktiengesellschaften ermöglichen (s. dazu die Ausführungen zu Art. 775 E OR). Mit der Neuformulierung wird überdies klargestellt, wer Aktionärin oder Aktionär sein kann (s. dazu die Ausführungen zu Art. 775 E OR). Die bisher in *Abs. 2* vorgesehene Sanktion kann entfallen; das Vorgehen beim Fehlen der vorgeschriebenen Organe wird künftig in Art. 731*b* E OR geregelt.

Die Zulassung von Einpersonengesellschaften in Art. 625 E OR findet ungeachtet der allgemeinen Verweisungsnorm in Art. 764 Abs. 2 OR keine Anwendung für *Kommanditaktiengesellschaften*, da für diese Rechtsform begriffsnotwendigerweise zwei Arten von Aktionären (gewöhnliche und unbeschränkt haftende Aktionäre) gegeben sein müssen[11]. Für die Gründung und den Bestand einer Kommanditaktiengesellschaft sind daher aus sachlichen Gründen stets zumindest zwei Aktionäre erforderlich.

---

10 Aufgehoben durch Ziff. I des BG vom 4. Okt. 1991 (AS 1992 733; BBl 1983 II 745).
11 ARTHUR MEIER-HAYOZ/PETER FORSTMOSER, Schweizerisches Gesellschaftsrecht, 8. Aufl., Bern 1998, § 17 N 2 und 22 ff.

Kapitel 1: Neue Gesetzesbestimmungen und Erläuterungen

E. Statuten

I. Gesetzlich vorgeschriebener Inhalt

Art. 626

Die Statuten müssen Bestimmungen enthalten über:

1. **die Firma und den Sitz der Gesellschaft;**
2. **den Zweck der Gesellschaft;**
3. **die Höhe des Aktienkapitals und den Betrag der darauf geleisteten Einlagen;**
4. **Anzahl, Nennwert und Art der Aktien;**
5. **die Einberufung der Generalversammlung und das Stimmrecht der Aktionäre;**
6. **die Organe für die Verwaltung und für die Revision;**
7. **die Form der von der Gesellschaft ausgehenden Bekanntmachungen.**

II. Weitere Bestimmungen

1. Im Allgemeinen

Art. 627

Zu ihrer Verbindlichkeit bedürfen der Aufnahme in die Statuten Bestimmungen über:

1. **Die Änderung der Statuten, soweit sie von den gesetzlichen Bestimmungen abweichen;**
2. **die Ausrichtung von Tantiemen;**
3. **die Zusicherung von Bauzinsen;**
4. **die Begrenzung der Dauer der Gesellschaft;**
5. **Konventionalstrafen bei nicht rechtzeitiger Leistung der Einlage;**
6. **die genehmigte und die bedingte Kapitalerhöhung;**

7. die Zulassung der Umwandlung von Namenaktien in Inhaberaktien und umgekehrt;
8. die Beschränkung der Übertragbarkeit von Namenaktien;
9. die Vorrechte einzelner Kategorien von Aktien, über Partizipationsscheine, Genussscheine und über die Gewährung besonderer Vorteile;
10. die Beschränkung des Stimmrechts und des Rechts der Aktionäre, sich vertreten zu lassen;
11. die im Gesetz nicht vorgesehenen Fälle, in denen die Generalversammlung nur mit qualifizierter Mehrheit Beschluss fassen kann;
12. die Ermächtigung zur Übertragung der Geschäftsführung auf einzelne Mitglieder des Verwaltungsrates oder Dritte;
13. die Organisation und die Aufgaben der Revisionsstelle, sofern dabei über die gesetzlichen Vorschriften hinausgegangen wird.

2. Im besonderen Sacheinlagen, Sachübernahmen, besondere Vorteile

Art. 628 (ursprünglicher Botschaftsentwurf)

1 Leistet ein Aktionär eine Sacheinlage, so müssen die Statuten den Gegenstand und dessen Bewertung sowie den Namen des Einlegers und die ihm zukommenden Aktien angeben.[12]

2 Übernimmt die Gesellschaft von Aktionären oder Dritten Vermögenswerte oder beabsichtigt sie solche Sachübernahmen, so müssen die Statuten den Gegenstand, den Namen des Veräusserers und die Gegenleistung der Gesellschaft angeben.[13]

3 Werden bei der Gründung zugunsten der Gründer oder anderer Personen besondere Vorteile ausbedungen, so sind die begünstigten Personen in den Statuten mit Namen aufzuführen, und es ist der gewährte Vorteil nach Inhalt und Wert genau zu bezeichnen.

---

12 Fassung gemäss Ziff. I des BG vom 4. Okt. 1991, in Kraft seit 1. Juli 1992 (AS 1992 733 786; BBl 1983 II 745).
13 Fassung gemäss Ziff. I des BG vom 4. Okt. 1991, in Kraft seit 1. Juli 1992 (AS 1992 733 786; BBl 1983 II 745).

Kapitel 1: Neue Gesetzesbestimmungen und Erläuterungen

4 Bestimmungen über Sachübernahmen können auch aufgehoben werden, wenn die Gesellschaft endgültig auf die Sachübernahme verzichtet.

Art. 628 (durch den Nationalrat bereinigte Version)

2 Übernimmt die Gesellschaft von Aktionären oder einer diesen nahestehenden Person Vermögenswerte oder beabsichtigt sie solche Sachübernahmen, so müssen die Statuten den Gegenstand, den Namen des Veräusserers und die Gegenleistung der Gesellschaft angeben.

Mit einer Ergänzung von Abs. 4 wird klargestellt, dass statutarische Bestimmungen über Sachübernahmen auch vor Ablauf der allgemeinen Frist von 10 Jahren gestrichen werden dürfen, wenn die Gesellschaft endgültig auf entsprechende Sachübernahme verzichtet.[14]

F. Gründung

I. Errichtungsakt

1. Inhalt

Art. 629

1 Die Gesellschaft wird errichtet, indem die Gründer in öffentlicher Urkunde erklären, eine Aktiengesellschaft zu gründen, darin die Statuten festlegen und die Organe bestellen.

2 In diesem Errichtungsakt zeichnen die Gründer die Aktien und stellen fest:

1. dass sämtliche Aktien gültig gezeichnet sind;

---

14 Die vorliegenden Erläuterungen beziehen sich ausschliesslich auf die ursprüngliche bundesrätliche Gesetzesversion und nicht auf die bereinigte Fassung durch den Nationalrat.

2. dass die versprochenen Einlagen dem gesamten Ausgabebetrag entsprechen;

3. dass die gesetzlichen und statutarischen Anforderungen an die Leistung der Einlagen erfüllt sind.

2. Aktienzeichnung

Art. 630

Die Zeichnung bedarf zu ihrer Gültigkeit:

1. der Angabe von Anzahl, Nennwert, Art, Kategorie und Ausgabebetrag der Aktien;

2. einer bedingungslosen Verpflichtung, eine dem Ausgabebetrag entsprechende Einlage zu leisten.

II. Belege

Art. 631

¹ Im Errichtungsakt muss die Urkundsperson die Belege über die Gründung einzeln nennen und bestätigen, dass sie ihr und den Gründern vorgelegen haben.

² Dem Errichtungsakt sind folgende Unterlagen beizulegen:

1. die Statuten;

2. der Gründungsbericht;

3. die Prüfungsbestätigung;

4. die Bestätigung über die Hinterlegung von Einlagen in Geld;

5. die Sacheinlageverträge;

6. bereits vorliegende Sachübernahmeverträge.

Die Regelung der Belege zum Errichtungsakt wird mit derjenigen des GmbH-Rechts in Übereinstimmung gebracht (s. dazu die Ausführungen zu Art. 777*b* E OR).

III. Einlagen

1. Mindesteinlage

Art. 632

1 Bei der Errichtung der Gesellschaft muss die Einlage für mindestens 20 Prozent des Nennwertes jeder Aktie geleistet sein.

2 In allen Fällen müssen die geleisteten Einlagen mindestens 50 000 Franken betragen.

2. Leistung der Einlagen

a. Einzahlungen

Art. 633

1 Einlagen in Geld müssen bei einem dem Bankengesetz[15] unterstellten Institut zur ausschliesslichen Verfügung der Gesellschaft hinterlegt werden.

2 Das Institut gibt den Betrag erst frei, wenn die Gesellschaft in das Handelsregister eingetragen ist.

b. Sacheinlagen

Art. 634

Sacheinlagen gelten nur dann als Deckung, wenn:

1. sie gestützt auf einen schriftlichen oder öffentlich beurkundeten Sacheinlagevertrag geleistet werden;

---

15 SR **952.0**

2. die Gesellschaft nach ihrer Eintragung in das Handelsregister sofort als Eigentümerin darüber verfügen kann oder einen bedingungslosen Anspruch auf Eintragung in das Grundbuch erhält;
3. ein Gründungsbericht mit Prüfungsbestätigung vorliegt.

c. Nachträgliche Leistung

Art. 634a

1 Der Verwaltungsrat beschliesst die nachträgliche Leistung von Einlagen auf nicht voll liberierte Aktien.

2 Die nachträgliche Leistung kann in Geld, durch Sacheinlage oder durch Verrechnung erfolgen.

3. Prüfung der Einlagen
a. Gründungsbericht

Art. 635

Die Gründer geben in einem schriftlichen Bericht Rechenschaft über:

1. die Art und den Zustand von Sacheinlagen oder Sachübernahmen und die Angemessenheit der Bewertung;
2. den Bestand und die Verrechenbarkeit der Schuld;
3. die Begründung und die Angemessenheit besonderer Vorteile zugunsten von Gründern oder anderen Personen.

b. Prüfungsbestätigung

Art. 635a

Ein zugelassener Revisor prüft den Gründungsbericht und bestätigt schriftlich, dass dieser vollständig und richtig ist.

Bei der Gründung einer Aktiengesellschaft ist der Gründungsbericht (vgl. Art. 635 OR) in jedem Fall – also auch dann, wenn die Gesellschaft über keine Revisionsstelle verfügt – durch eine unabhängige Fachperson zu überprüfen. Damit soll das Risiko betrügerischer Handlungen bei Sacheinlagen, Sachübernahmen, der Einräumung besonderer Vorteile (vgl. Art. 628 OR) und der Liberierung durch Verrechnung reduziert werden.

Art. 635a OR muss der Neukonzeption der Revision angepasst werden: Der heute vom Gesetz verwendete Begriff des «Revisors» würde nach der Neuregelung eine Person ohne besondere Fachausbildung bezeichnen. Unter Berücksichtigung der erheblichen Bedeutung der Gründungsprüfung ist jedoch eine fachliche Ausbildung vorauszusetzen, wie dies – wenn auch nicht hinreichend klar – bereits im geltenden Recht der Fall war (zu den Anforderungen an die Revisorinnen und Revisoren im geltenden Recht s. Art. 727a OR). Der Entwurf bleibt so nahe wie möglich beim bisherigen Recht und verlangt die Prüfung durch eine zugelassene Revisorin oder einen zugelassenen Revisor. Dadurch werden die fachlichen Anforderungen gegenüber der heutigen Rechtslage präzisiert: Es werden zwingend ein erfolgreicher Ausbildungsabschluss sowie eine einjährige Fachpraxis vorausgesetzt (s. Art. 5 E RAG). Im Interesse der Beschränkung der Gründungskosten verzichtet der Entwurf dagegen auf den zwingenden Beizug einer zugelassenen Revisionsexpertin oder eines zugelassenen Revisionsexperten (entsprechend einer besonders befähigten Revisorin oder eines besonders befähigten Revisors im geltenden Recht; s. Art. 4 E RAG sowie die Ausführungen dazu), obschon dies zur Verhinderung von Gründungsschwindeln an sich wünschbar wäre.

G. Eintragung in das Handelsregister
I. Gesellschaft

Art. 640

Die Gesellschaft ist ins Handelsregister des Ortes einzutragen, an dem sie ihren Sitz hat.

Neben dem Grundsatz der Eintragung der Gesellschaft ins Handelsregister am Ort ihres Sitzes (Abs. 1) regelt das geltende Recht in dieser Bestimmung auch die Anmeldung beim Handelsregister, deren Unterzeichnung sowie die Anmeldung der Personen, welche die Gesellschaft vertreten (Abs. 2 bis 4). Der Entwurf sieht dazu im Handelsregisterrecht eine einheitliche Regelung für alle Rechtsformen vor, wobei teilweise eine Ordnung auf Verordnungsstufe ermöglicht wird (s. Art. 929 Abs. 1 und 931*a* E OR sowie die Ausführungen zu diesen Bestimmungen). Die bisherigen *Abs. 2 bis 4* können daher gestrichen werden.

II. Zweigniederlassungen

Art. 641

Zweigniederlassungen sind unter Bezugnahme auf die Eintragung der Hauptniederlassung ins Handelsregister des Ortes einzutragen, an dem sie sich befinden.

Diese Bestimmung umschreibt im geltenden Recht den Inhalt der Eintragungen von Aktiengesellschaften im Handelsregister. Weil es sich dabei um Einzelheiten eher technischer Natur handelt, sieht der Entwurf eine Delegation zur Regelung in der Handelsregisterverordnung vor (s. dazu Art. 929 Abs. 1 E OR sowie die Ausführungen zu dieser Bestimmung).

Im neuen Artikel wird die Eintragung von Zweigniederlassungen ins Handelsregister geregelt (bisher Art. 642 OR). Zu Gunsten einer einheitlichen Ordnung im Handelsregisterrecht kann dabei auf eine Vorschrift zur Anmeldung (bisher Art. 642 Abs. 2 OR) verzichtet werden. (s. Art. 929

Abs. 1 und 931*a* E OR sowie die Ausführungen zu diesen Bestimmungen; ebenso Art. 778*a* E OR).

III. Sacheinlagen, Sachübernahmen, besondere Vorteile

Art. 642

Der Gegenstand von Sacheinlagen und die dafür ausgegebenen Aktien, der Gegenstand von Sachübernahmen und die Gegenleistung der Gesellschaft sowie Inhalt und Wert besonderer Vorteile müssen ins Handelsregister eingetragen werden.

Der Inhalt der Eintragung im Handelsregister soll neu grundsätzlich in der Handelsregisterverordnung festgehalten werden (s. Art. 929 Abs. 1 E OR). Das Erfordernis der Eintragung von Sacheinlagen, Sachübernahmen und besonderen Vorteilen ist jedoch materiellrechtlicher Natur. Die entsprechende Eintragungspflicht muss daher weiterhin auf Gesetzesstufe vorgesehen bleiben. Für die Rechtsfolgen der Verletzung der Eintragungspflicht sind die Umstände zu berücksichtigen, wie dies in der Literatur betreffend das Erfordernis der Angabe von Sacheinlagen, Sachübernahmen und besonderen Vorteilen in den Statuten aufgezeigt wurde[16] (die Eintragung im Handelsregister unterbleibt meist dann, wenn auch in den Statuten eine entsprechende Angabe fehlt, da die Statuten als Beleg für die Eintragung dienen).

H. Erwerb der Persönlichkeit

I. Zeitpunkt; mangelnde Voraussetzungen

Art. 643

1 Die Gesellschaft erlangt das Recht der Persönlichkeit erst durch die Eintragung in das Handelsregister.

2 Das Recht der Persönlichkeit wird durch die Eintragung auch dann erworben, wenn die Voraussetzungen der Eintragung tatsächlich nicht vorhanden waren.

---

16 s. PETER BÖCKLI, Schweizer Aktienrecht, 2. Aufl., Zürich 1996, N 103 ff.

3 Sind jedoch bei der Gründung gesetzliche oder statutarische Vorschriften missachtet und dadurch die Interessen von Gläubigern oder Aktionären in erheblichem Masse gefährdet oder verletzt worden, so kann der Richter auf Begehren solcher Gläubiger oder Aktionäre die Auflösung der Gesellschaft verfügen.

4 Das Klagerecht erlischt, wenn die Klage nicht spätestens drei Monate nach der Veröffentlichung im Schweizerischen Handelsamtsblatt angehoben wird.

Abs. 3 regelt die Auflösung der Gesellschaft durch den Richter bei Gründungsmängeln. Der letzte Satz sieht die Anordnung vorsorglicher Massnahmen vor und macht diese davon abhängig, ob bereits eine Klage in der Hauptsache rechtshängig ist. Da je nach den Regelungen des kantonalen Zivilprozessrechts vorsorgliche Massnahmen bereits vor diesem Zeitpunkt beantragt werden können, führt dies zu einer ungewollten Einschränkung. Der entsprechende Satz ist daher zu streichen.

II. Vor der Eintragung ausgegebene Aktien

Art. 644

1 Die vor der Eintragung der Gesellschaft ausgegebenen Aktien sind nichtig; dagegen werden die aus der Aktienzeichnung hervorgehenden Verpflichtungen dadurch nicht berührt.

2 Wer vor der Eintragung Aktien ausgibt, wird für allen dadurch verursachten Schaden haftbar.

III. Vor der Eintragung eingegangene Verpflichtungen

Art. 645

1 Ist vor der Eintragung in das Handelsregister im Namen der Gesellschaft gehandelt worden, so haften die Handelnden persönlich und solidarisch.

2 Wurden solche Verpflichtungen ausdrücklich im Namen der zu bildenden Gesellschaft eingegangen und innerhalb einer Frist von drei Monaten nach der Eintragung in das Handelsregister von der

Gesellschaft übernommen, so werden die Handelnden befreit, und es haftet nur die Gesellschaft.

J. Statutenänderung

Art. 647

Jeder Beschluss der Generalversammlung oder des Verwaltungsrates über eine Änderung der Statuten muss öffentlich beurkundet und ins Handelsregister eingetragen werden.

Auf Grund der einheitlichen Neuregelung der Eintragung ins Handelsregister im Handelsregisterrecht ist die vorliegende Bestimmung derjenigen im GmbH-Recht anzugleichen (es wird auf die Ausführungen zu Art. 780 E OR verwiesen; s. auch Art. 929 Abs. 1 und 931a E OR sowie Art. 932 OR).

K. Erhöhung des Aktienkapitals
I. Ordentliche und genehmigte Kapitalerhöhung
1. Ordentliche Kapitalerhöhung

Art. 650

¹ Die Erhöhung des Aktienkapitals wird von der Generalversammlung beschlossen; sie ist vom Verwaltungsrat innerhalb von drei Monaten durchzuführen.

² Der Beschluss der Generalversammlung muss öffentlich beurkundet werden und angeben:

1. den gesamten Nennbetrag, um den das Aktienkapital erhöht werden soll, und den Betrag der darauf zu leistenden Einlagen;
2. Anzahl, Nennwert und Art der Aktien sowie Vorrechte einzelner Kategorien;

3. den Ausgabebetrag oder die Ermächtigung an den Verwaltungsrat, diesen festzusetzen, sowie den Beginn der Dividendenberechtigung;
4. die Art der Einlagen, bei Sacheinlagen deren Gegenstand und Bewertung sowie den Namen des Sacheinlegers und die ihm zukommenden Aktien;
5. bei Sachübernahmen den Gegenstand, den Namen des Veräusserers und die Gegenleistung der Gesellschaft;
6. Inhalt und Wert von besonderen Vorteilen sowie die Namen der begünstigten Personen;
7. eine Beschränkung der Übertragbarkeit neuer Namenaktien;
8. eine Einschränkung oder Aufhebung des Bezugsrechtes und die Zuweisung nicht ausgeübter oder entzogener Bezugsrechte;
9. die Voraussetzungen für die Ausübung vertraglich erworbener Bezugsrechte.

3 Wird die Kapitalerhöhung nicht innerhalb von drei Monaten ins Handelsregister eingetragen, so fällt der Beschluss der Generalversammlung dahin.

2. Genehmigte Kapitalerhöhung

a. Statutarische Grundlage

Art. 651

1 Die Generalversammlung kann durch Statutenänderung den Verwaltungsrat ermächtigen, das Aktienkapital innert einer Frist von längstens zwei Jahren zu erhöhen.

2 Die Statuten geben den Nennbetrag an, um den der Verwaltungsrat das Aktienkapital erhöhen kann. Das genehmigte Kapital darf die Hälfte des bisherigen Aktienkapitals nicht übersteigen.

3 Die Statuten enthalten überdies die Angaben, welche für die ordentliche Kapitalerhöhung verlangt werden, mit Ausnahme der Angaben über den Ausgabebetrag, die Art der Einlagen, die Sachübernahmen und den Beginn der Dividendenberechtigung.

4 Im Rahmen der Ermächtigung kann der Verwaltungsrat Erhöhungen des Aktienkapitals durchführen. Dabei erlässt er die notwendigen Bestimmungen, soweit sie nicht schon im Beschluss der Generalversammlung enthalten sind.

b. Anpassung der Statuten

Art. 651a

1 Nach jeder Kapitalerhöhung setzt der Verwaltungsrat den Nennbetrag des genehmigten Kapitals in den Statuten entsprechend herab.

2 Nach Ablauf der für die Durchführung der Kapitalerhöhung festgelegten Frist wird die Bestimmung über die genehmigte Kapitalerhöhung auf Beschluss des Verwaltungsrates aus den Statuten gestrichen.

3. Gemeinsame Vorschriften

a. Aktienzeichnung

Art. 652

1 Die Aktien werden in einer besonderen Urkunde (Zeichnungsschein) nach den für die Gründung geltenden Regeln gezeichnet.

2 Der Zeichnungsschein muss auf den Beschluss der Generalversammlung über die Erhöhung oder die Ermächtigung zur Erhöhung des Aktienkapitals und auf den Beschluss des Verwaltungsrates über die Erhöhung Bezug nehmen. Verlangt das Gesetz einen Emissionsprospekt, so nimmt der Zeichnungsschein auch auf diesen Bezug.

3 Enthält der Zeichnungsschein keine Befristung, so endet seine Verbindlichkeit drei Monate nach der Unterzeichnung.

b. Emissionsprospekt

Art. 652a

1 Werden neue Aktien öffentlich zur Zeichnung angeboten, so gibt die Gesellschaft in einem Emissionsprospekt Aufschluss über:

1. den Inhalt der bestehenden Eintragung im Handelsregister, mit Ausnahme der Angaben über die zur Vertretung befugten Personen;
2. die bisherige Höhe und Zusammensetzung des Aktienkapitals unter Angabe von Anzahl, Nennwert und Art der Aktien sowie der Vorrechte einzelner Kategorien von Aktien;
3. Bestimmungen der Statuten über eine genehmigte oder eine bedingte Kapitalerhöhung;
4. die Anzahl der Genussscheine und den Inhalt der damit verbundenen Rechte;
5. die letzte Jahresrechnung und Konzernrechnung mit dem Revisionsbericht und, wenn der Bilanzstichtag mehr als sechs Monate zurückliegt, über die Zwischenabschlüsse;
6. die in den letzten fünf Jahren oder seit der Gründung ausgerichteten Dividenden;
7. den Beschluss über die Ausgabe neuer Aktien.

2 Öffentlich ist jede Einladung zur Zeichnung, die sich nicht an einen begrenzten Kreis von Personen richtet.

3 Bei Gesellschaften, die über keine Revisionsstelle verfügen, muss der Verwaltungsrat durch einen zugelassenen Revisor einen Revisionsbericht erstellen lassen und über das Ergebnis der Revision im Emissionsprospekt Aufschluss geben.

Bietet eine Gesellschaft neue Aktien öffentlich zur Zeichnung an, so hat sie einen Emissionsprospekt zu erstellen, der die wesentlichen Angaben zur Vermögens-, Finanz- und Ertragslage der Gesellschaft enthält.

Nach dem Entwurf ist es möglich, dass die emittierende Gesellschaft auf Grund eines Opting-out gemäss Art. 727a Abs. 2 E OR über keine Revisionsstelle verfügt. Wird jedoch eine öffentliche Emission durchgeführt, so ist es aus Gründen des Investorenschutzes unentbehrlich, dass eine geprüfte Jahresrechnung oder ein geprüfter Zwischenabschluss vorliegt. Bei Gesellschaften, die über keine Revisionsstelle verfügen, muss daher der Verwaltungsrat die Jahresrechnung oder den Zwischenabschluss nach *Abs. 3* durch eine zugelassene Revisorin oder einen zugelassenen Revisor prüfen lassen. Über das Ergebnis der Revision ist im Emissionsprospekt Aufschluss zu geben.

c. Bezugsrecht

Art. 652b

1 Jeder Aktionär hat Anspruch auf den Teil der neu ausgegebenen Aktien, der seiner bisherigen Beteiligung entspricht.

2 Der Beschluss der Generalversammlung über die Erhöhung des Aktienkapitals darf das Bezugsrecht nur aus wichtigen Gründen aufheben. Als wichtige Gründe gelten insbesondere die Übernahme von Unternehmen, Unternehmensteilen oder Beteiligungen sowie die Beteiligung der Arbeitnehmer. Durch die Aufhebung des Bezugsrechts darf niemand in unsachlicher Weise begünstigt oder benachteiligt werden.

3 Die Gesellschaft kann dem Aktionär, welchem sie ein Recht zum Bezug von Aktien eingeräumt hat, die Ausübung dieses Rechtes nicht wegen einer statutarischen Beschränkung der Übertragbarkeit von Namenaktien verwehren.

d. Leistung der Einlagen

Art. 652c

Soweit das Gesetz nichts anderes vorschreibt, sind die Einlagen nach den Bestimmungen über die Gründung zu leisten.

e. Erhöhung aus Eigenkapital

Art. 652d

1 Das Aktienkapital kann auch durch Umwandlung von frei verwendbarem Eigenkapital erhöht werden.

2 Die Deckung des Erhöhungsbetrags ist mit der Jahresrechnung in der von den Aktionären genehmigten Fassung und dem Revisionsbericht eines zugelassenen Revisors nachzuweisen. Liegt der Bilanzstichtag mehr als sechs Monate zurück, so ist ein geprüfter Zwischenabschluss erforderlich.

Auch diese Bestimmung muss der Tatsache angepasst werden, dass eine Aktiengesellschaft nach dem Entwurf nicht in jedem Fall über eine Revisionsstelle verfügt (s. Art. 727*a* Abs. 2 E OR).

Beabsichtigt die Gesellschaft im Rahmen einer ordentlichen oder genehmigten Kapitalerhöhung, das neue Aktienkapital durch Umwandlung von frei verwendbarem Eigenkapital zu liberieren, so hat sie die Deckung des Erhöhungsbetrages durch die genehmigte Jahresrechnung und den Revisionsbericht eines zugelassenen Revisors nachzuweisen. Gesellschaften mit einer Revisionsstelle, die den gesetzlichen Anforderungen genügt, verfügen ohne weiteres über den erforderlichen Revisionsbericht. Mit der Modifikation der vorliegenden Bestimmung wird für die Liberierung durch Eigenmittel ein Revisionsbericht auch von Gesellschaften verlangt, die über keine Revisionsstelle verfügen. Damit wird verhindert, dass es zu Scheinliberierungen mittels fiktiver Reserven kommt.

Liegt der Bilanzstichtag mehr als sechs Monate zurück, so ist ein von einer zugelassenen Revisorin oder einem zugelassenen Revisor geprüfter Zwischenabschluss erforderlich.

f. Kapitalerhöhungsbericht

Art. 652e

Der Verwaltungsrat gibt in einem schriftlichen Bericht Rechenschaft über:

1. die Art und den Zustand von Sacheinlagen oder Sachübernahmen und die Angemessenheit der Bewertung;
2. den Bestand und die Verrechenbarkeit der Schuld;
3. die freie Verwendbarkeit von umgewandeltem Eigenkapital;
4. die Einhaltung des Generalversammlungsbeschlusses, insbesondere über die Einschränkung oder die Aufhebung des Bezugsrechtes und die Zuweisung nicht ausgeübter oder entzogener Bezugsrechte;
5. die Begründung und die Angemessenheit besonderer Vorteile zugunsten einzelner Aktionäre oder anderer Personen.

g. Prüfungsbestätigung

Art. 652f

1 Ein zugelassener Revisor prüft den Kapitalerhöhungsbericht und bestätigt schriftlich, dass dieser vollständig und richtig ist.

2 Keine Prüfungsbestätigung ist erforderlich, wenn die Einlage auf das neue Aktienkapital in Geld erfolgt, das Aktienkapital nicht zur Vornahme einer Sachübernahme erhöht wird und die Bezugsrechte nicht eingeschränkt oder aufgehoben werden.

Erhöht eine Gesellschaft ihr Kapital auf dem Weg der ordentlichen oder genehmigten Kapitalerhöhung, so hat der Verwaltungsrat den Kapitalerhöhungsbericht (s. Art. 652e OR) im Allgemeinen durch die Revisionsstelle prüfen zu lassen (Ausnahmen s. Abs. 2).

Auch diese Bestimmung muss der Tatsache angepasst werden, dass eine Aktiengesellschaft nach dem Entwurf nicht in jedem Fall über eine Revisionsstelle verfügt (s. Art. 727a Abs. 2 E OR). Im Wortlaut des Gesetzes wird daher der Begriff der Revisionsstelle durch jenen der zugelassenen Revisorin bzw. des zugelassenen Revisors ersetzt. Dies schliesst nicht aus, dass gegebenenfalls die Revisionsstelle die Prüfung vornimmt.

h. Statutenänderung und Feststellungen

Art. 652g

1 Liegen der Kapitalerhöhungsbericht und, sofern erforderlich, die Prüfungsbestätigung vor, so ändert der Verwaltungsrat die Statuten und stellt dabei fest:

1. dass sämtliche Aktien gültig gezeichnet sind;
2. dass die versprochenen Einlagen dem gesamten Ausgabebetrag entsprechen;
3. dass die Einlagen entsprechend den Anforderungen des Gesetzes, der Statuten oder des Generalversammlungsbeschlusses geleistet wurden.

2 Beschluss und Feststellungen sind öffentlich zu beurkunden. Die Urkundsperson hat die Belege, die der Kapitalerhöhung zugrunde liegen, einzeln zu nennen und zu bestätigen, dass sie dem Verwaltungsrat vorgelegen haben.

3 Der öffentlichen Urkunde sind die geänderten Statuten, der Kapitalerhöhungsbericht, die Prüfungsbestätigung sowie die Sacheinlageverträge und die bereits vorliegenden Sachübernahmeverträge beizulegen.

i. Eintragung in das Handelsregister; Nichtigkeit vorher ausgegebener Aktien

Art. 652h

1 Der Verwaltungsrat meldet die Statutenänderung und seine Feststellungen beim Handelsregister zur Eintragung an.

2 Einzureichen sind:

1. die öffentlichen Urkunden über die Beschlüsse der Generalversammlung und des Verwaltungsrates mit den Beilagen;
2. eine beglaubigte Ausfertigung der geänderten Statuten.

³ Aktien, die vor der Eintragung der Kapitalerhöhung ausgegeben werden, sind nichtig; die aus der Aktienzeichnung hervorgehenden Verpflichtungen werden dadurch nicht berührt.

II. Bedingte Kapitalerhöhung
1. Grundsatz

Art. 653

¹ Die Generalversammlung kann eine bedingte Kapitalerhöhung beschliessen, indem sie in den Statuten den Gläubigern von neuen Anleihens- oder ähnlichen Obligationen gegenüber der Gesellschaft oder ihren Konzerngesellschaften sowie den Arbeitnehmern Rechte auf den Bezug neuer Aktien (Wandel- oder Optionsrechte) einräumt.

² Das Aktienkapital erhöht sich ohne weiteres in dem Zeitpunkt und in dem Umfang, als diese Wandel- oder Optionsrechte ausgeübt und die Einlagepflichten durch Verrechnung oder Einzahlung erfüllt werden.

2. Schranken

Art. 653a

¹ Der Nennbetrag, um den das Aktienkapital bedingt erhöht werden kann, darf die Hälfte des bisherigen Aktienkapitals nicht übersteigen.

² Die geleistete Einlage muss mindestens dem Nennwert entsprechen.

3. Statutarische Grundlage

Art. 653b

¹ Die Statuten müssen angeben:

1. den Nennbetrag der bedingten Kapitalerhöhung;

2. Anzahl, Nennwert und Art der Aktien;
3. den Kreis der Wandel- oder der Optionsberechtigten;
4. die Aufhebung der Bezugsrechte der bisherigen Aktionäre;
5. Vorrechte einzelner Kategorien von Aktien;
6. die Beschränkung der Übertragbarkeit neuer Namenaktien.

2 Werden die Anleihens- oder ähnlichen Obligationen, mit denen Wandel- oder Optionsrechte verbunden sind, nicht den Aktionären vorweg zur Zeichnung angeboten, so müssen die Statuten überdies angeben:

1. die Voraussetzungen für die Ausübung der Wandel- oder der Optionsrechte;
2. die Grundlagen, nach denen der Ausgabebetrag zu berechnen ist.

3 Wandel- oder Optionsrechte, die vor der Eintragung der Statutenbestimmung über die bedingte Kapitalerhöhung im Handelsregister eingeräumt werden, sind nichtig.

4. Schutz der Aktionäre

Art. 653c

1 Sollen bei einer bedingten Kapitalerhöhung Anleihens- oder ähnliche Obligationen, mit denen Wandel- oder Optionsrechte verbunden sind, ausgegeben werden, so sind diese Obligationen vorweg den Aktionären entsprechend ihrer bisherigen Beteiligung zur Zeichnung anzubieten.

2 Dieses Vorwegzeichnungsrecht kann beschränkt oder aufgehoben werden, wenn ein wichtiger Grund vorliegt.

3 Durch die für eine bedingte Kapitalerhöhung notwendige Aufhebung des Bezugsrechtes sowie durch eine Beschränkung oder Aufhebung des Vorwegzeichnungsrechtes darf niemand in unsachlicher Weise begünstigt oder benachteiligt werden.

5. Schutz der Wandel- oder Optionsberechtigten

Art. 653d

1 Dem Gläubiger oder dem Arbeitnehmer, dem ein Wandel- oder ein Optionsrecht zum Erwerb von Namenaktien zusteht, kann die Ausübung dieses Rechtes nicht wegen einer Beschränkung der Übertragbarkeit von Namenaktien verwehrt werden, es sei denn, dass dies in den Statuten und im Emissionsprospekt vorbehalten wird.

2 Wandel- oder Optionsrechte dürfen durch die Erhöhung des Aktienkapitals, durch die Ausgabe neuer Wandel- oder Optionsrechte oder auf andere Weise nur beeinträchtigt werden, wenn der Konversionspreis gesenkt oder den Berechtigten auf andere Weise ein angemessener Ausgleich gewährt wird, oder wenn die gleiche Beeinträchtigung auch die Aktionäre trifft.

6. Durchführung der Kapitalerhöhung
a. Ausübung der Rechte; Einlage

Art. 653e

1 Wandel- oder Optionsrechte werden durch eine schriftliche Erklärung ausgeübt, die auf die Statutenbestimmung über die bedingte Kapitalerhöhung hinweist; verlangt das Gesetz einen Emissionsprospekt, so nimmt die Erklärung auch auf diesen Bezug.
2 Die Leistung der Einlage durch Geld oder Verrechnung muss bei einem Bankinstitut erfolgen, das dem Bankengesetz [17] unterstellt ist.
3 Die Aktionärsrechte entstehen mit der Erfüllung der Einlagepflicht.

---

17 SR **952.0**

b. Prüfungsbestätigung

Art. 653f

1 Ein zugelassener Revisionsexperte prüft nach Abschluss jedes Geschäftsjahres, auf Verlangen des Verwaltungsrats schon vorher, ob die Ausgabe der neuen Aktien dem Gesetz, den Statuten und, wenn ein solcher erforderlich ist, dem Emissionsprospekt entsprochen hat.

2 Er bestätigt dies schriftlich.

Der Entwurf ersetzt den Begriff der besonders befähigten Revisorin bzw. des besonders befähigten Revisors durch jenen der zugelassenen Revisionsexpertin bzw. des zugelassenen Revisionsexperten (vgl. dazu die Erläuterungen zu Art. 4 E RAG). Die vorliegende Bestimmung muss daher entsprechend angepasst werden.

c. Anpassung der Statuten

Art. 653g

1 Nach Eingang der Prüfungsbestätigung stellt der Verwaltungsrat in öffentlicher Urkunde Anzahl, Nennwert und Art der neu ausgegebenen Aktien sowie die Vorrechte einzelner Kategorien und den Stand des Aktienkapitals am Schluss des Geschäftsjahres oder im Zeitpunkt der Prüfung fest. Er nimmt die nötigen Statutenanpassungen vor.

2 In der öffentlichen Urkunde stellt die Urkundsperson fest, dass die Prüfungsbestätigung die verlangten Angaben enthält.

d. Eintragung in das Handelsregister

Art. 653h

Der Verwaltungsrat meldet dem Handelsregister spätestens drei Monate nach Abschluss des Geschäftsjahres die Statutenänderung an und reicht die öffentliche Urkunde und die Prüfungsbestätigung ein.

Kapitel 1: Neue Gesetzesbestimmungen und Erläuterungen

7. Streichung

Art. 653i

1 Sind die Wandel- oder die Optionsrechte erloschen und wird dies von einem zugelassenen Revisionsexperten in einem schriftlichen Prüfungsbericht bestätigt, so hebt der Verwaltungsrat die Statutenbestimmungen über die bedingte Kapitalerhöhung auf.

2 In der öffentlichen Urkunde stellt die Urkundsperson fest, dass der Prüfungsbericht die verlangten Angaben enthält.

In *Abs. 1* ersetzt der Entwurf den Begriff der besonders befähigten Revisorin bzw. des besonders befähigten Revisors durch jenen der zugelassenen Revisionsexpertin bzw. des zugelassenen Revisionsexperten (vgl. dazu die Erläuterungen zu Art. 4 E RAG).

Abs. 2 wurde ebenfalls redaktionell angepasst.

III. Vorzugsaktien

1. Voraussetzungen

Art. 654

1 Die Generalversammlung kann nach Massgabe der Statuten oder auf dem Wege der Statutenänderung die Ausgabe von Vorzugsaktien beschliessen oder bisherige Aktien in Vorzugsaktien umwandeln.

2 Hat eine Gesellschaft Vorzugsaktien ausgegeben, so können weitere Vorzugsaktien, denen Vorrechte gegenüber den bereits bestehenden Vorzugsaktien eingeräumt werden sollen, nur mit Zustimmung sowohl einer besonderen Versammlung der beeinträchtigten Vorzugsaktionäre als auch einer Generalversammlung sämtlicher Aktionäre ausgegeben werden. Eine abweichende Ordnung durch die Statuten bleibt vorbehalten.

3 Dasselbe gilt, wenn statutarische Vorrechte, die mit Vorzugsaktien verbunden sind, abgeändert oder aufgehoben werden sollen.

2. Stellung der Vorzugsaktien

Art. 656

1 Die Vorzugsaktien geniessen gegenüber den Stammaktien die Vorrechte, die ihnen in den ursprünglichen Statuten oder durch Statutenänderung ausdrücklich eingeräumt sind. Sie stehen im Übrigen den Stammaktien gleich.

2 Die Vorrechte können sich namentlich auf die Dividende mit oder ohne Nachbezugsrecht, auf den Liquidationsanteil und auf die Bezugsrechte für den Fall der Ausgabe neuer Aktien erstrecken.

L. Partizipationsscheine

I. Begriff; Anwendbare Vorschriften

Art. 656a

1 Die Statuten können ein Partizipationskapital vorsehen, das in Teilsummen (Partizipationsscheine) zerlegt ist. Diese Partizipationsscheine werden gegen Einlage ausgegeben, haben einen Nennwert und gewähren kein Stimmrecht.

2 Die Bestimmungen über das Aktienkapital, die Aktie und den Aktionär gelten, soweit das Gesetz nichts anderes vorsieht, auch für das Partizipationskapital, den Partizipationsschein und den Partizipanten.

3 Die Partizipationsscheine sind als solche zu bezeichnen.

II. Partizipations- und Aktienkapital

Art. 656b

1 Das Partizipationskapital darf das Doppelte des Aktienkapitals nicht übersteigen.

² Die Bestimmungen über das Mindestkapital und über die Mindestgesamteinlage finden keine Anwendung.

³ In den Bestimmungen über die Einschränkungen des Erwerbs eigener Aktien, die allgemeine Reserve, die Einleitung einer Sonderprüfung gegen den Willen der Generalversammlung und über die Meldepflicht bei Kapitalverlust ist das Partizipationskapital dem Aktienkapital zuzuzählen.

⁴ Eine genehmigte oder eine bedingte Erhöhung des Aktien- und des Partizipationskapitals darf insgesamt die Hälfte der Summe die bisherigen Aktien- und Partizipationskapitals nicht übersteigen.

⁵ Partizipationskapital kann im Verfahren der genehmigten oder bedingten Kapitalerhöhung geschaffen werden.

III. Rechtsstellung des Partizipanten

1. Im Allgemeinen

Art. 656c

¹ Der Partizipant hat kein Stimmrecht und, sofern die Statuten nichts anderes bestimmen, keines der damit zusammenhängenden Rechte.

² Als mit dem Stimmrecht zusammenhängende Rechte gelten das Recht auf Einberufung einer Generalversammlung, das Teilnahmerecht, das Recht auf Auskunft, das Recht auf Einsicht und das Antragsrecht.

³ Gewähren ihm die Statuten kein Recht auf Auskunft oder Einsicht oder kein Antragsrecht auf Einleitung einer Sonderprüfung (Art. 697a ff.), so kann der Partizipant Begehren um Auskunft oder Einsicht oder um Einleitung einer Sonderprüfung schriftlich zuhanden der Generalversammlung stellen.

2. Bekanntgabe von Einberufung und Beschlüssen der Generalversammlung

Art. 656d

1 Den Partizipanten muss die Einberufung der Generalversammlung zusammen mit den Verhandlungsgegenständen und den Anträgen bekanntgegeben werden.

2 Jeder Beschluss der Generalversammlung ist unverzüglich am Gesellschaftssitz und bei den eingetragenen Zweigniederlassungen zur Einsicht der Partizipanten aufzulegen. Die Partizipanten sind in der Bekanntgabe darauf hinzuweisen.

3. Vertretung im Verwaltungsrat

Art. 656e

Die Statuten können den Partizipanten einen Anspruch auf einen Vertreter im Verwaltungsrat einräumen.

4. Vermögensrechte

a. Im Allgemeinen

Art. 656f

1 Die Statuten dürfen die Partizipanten bei der Verteilung des Bilanzgewinnes und des Liquidationsergebnisses sowie beim Bezug neuer Aktien nicht schlechter stellen als die Aktionäre.

2 Bestehen mehrere Kategorien von Aktien, so müssen die Partizipationsscheine zumindest der Kategorie gleichgestellt sein, die am wenigsten bevorzugt ist.

3 Statutenänderungen und andere Generalversammlungsbeschlüsse, welche die Stellung der Partizipanten verschlechtern, sind nur zu-

Kapitel 1: Neue Gesetzesbestimmungen und Erläuterungen

lässig, wenn sie auch die Stellung der Aktionäre, denen die Partizipanten gleichstehen, entsprechend beeinträchtigen.

4 Sofern die Statuten nichts anderes bestimmen, dürfen die Vorrechte und die statutarischen Mitwirkungsrechte von Partizipanten nur mit Zustimmung einer besonderen Versammlung der betroffenen Partizipanten und der Generalversammlung der Aktionäre beschränkt oder aufgehoben werden.

b. Bezugsrechte

Art. 656g

1 Wird ein Partizipationskapital geschaffen, so haben die Aktionäre ein Bezugsrecht wie bei der Ausgabe neuer Aktien.

2 Die Statuten können vorsehen, dass Aktionäre nur Aktien und Partizipanten nur Partizipationsscheine beziehen können, wenn das Aktien- und das Partizipationskapital gleichzeitig und im gleichen Verhältnis erhöht werden.

3 Wird das Partizipationskapital oder das Aktienkapital allein oder verhältnismässig stärker als das andere erhöht, so sind die Bezugsrechte so zuzuteilen, dass Aktionäre und Partizipanten am gesamten Kapital gleich wie bis anhin beteiligt bleiben können.

M. Genussscheine

Art. 657

1 Die Statuten können die Schaffung von Genussscheinen zugunsten von Personen vorsehen, die mit der Gesellschaft durch frühere Kapitalbeteiligung oder als Aktionär, Gläubiger, Arbeitnehmer oder in ähnlicher Weise verbunden sind. Sie haben die Zahl der ausgegebenen Genussscheine und den Inhalt der damit verbundenen Rechte anzugeben.

2 Durch die Genussscheine können den Berechtigten nur Ansprüche auf einen Anteil am Bilanzgewinn oder am Liquidationsergebnis oder auf den Bezug neuer Aktien verliehen werden.

3 Der Genussschein darf keinen Nennwert haben; er darf weder Partizipationsschein genannt noch gegen eine Einlage ausgegeben werden, die unter den Aktiven der Bilanz ausgewiesen wird.

4 Die Berechtigten bilden von Gesetzes wegen eine Gemeinschaft, für welche die Bestimmungen über die Gläubigergemeinschaft bei Anleihensobligationen sinngemäss gelten. Den Verzicht auf einzelne oder alle Rechte aus den Genussscheinen können jedoch nur die Inhaber der Mehrheit aller im Umlauf befindlichen Genussscheintitel verbindlich beschliessen.

5 Zugunsten der Gründer der Gesellschaft dürfen Genussscheine nur aufgrund der ursprünglichen Statuten geschaffen werden.

N. Eigene Aktien

I. Einschränkung des Erwerbs

Art. 659

1 Die Gesellschaft darf eigene Aktien nur dann erwerben, wenn frei verwendbares Eigenkapital in der Höhe der dafür nötigen Mittel vorhanden ist und der gesamte Nennwert dieser Aktien 10 Prozent des Aktienkapitals nicht übersteigt.

2 Werden im Zusammenhang mit einer Übertragbarkeitsbeschränkung Namenaktien erworben, so beträgt die Höchstgrenze 20 Prozent. Die über 10 Prozent des Aktienkapitals hinaus erworbenen eigenen Aktien sind innert zweier Jahre zu veräussern oder durch Kapitalherabsetzung zu vernichten.

Kapitel 1: Neue Gesetzesbestimmungen und Erläuterungen

II. Folgen des Erwerbs

Art. 659a

1 Das Stimmrecht und die damit verbundenen Rechte eigener Aktien ruhen.

2 Die Gesellschaft hat für die eigenen Aktien einen dem Anschaffungswert entsprechenden Betrag gesondert als Reserve auszuweisen.

III. Erwerb durch Tochtergesellschaften

Art. 659b

1 Ist eine Gesellschaft an Tochtergesellschaften mehrheitlich beteiligt, so gelten für den Erwerb ihrer Aktien durch diese Tochtergesellschaften die gleichen Einschränkungen und Folgen wie für den Erwerb eigener Aktien.

2 Erwirbt eine Gesellschaft die Mehrheitsbeteiligung an einer anderen Gesellschaft, die ihrerseits Aktien der Erwerberin hält, so gelten diese Aktien als eigene Aktien der Erwerberin.

3 Die Reservebildung obliegt der Gesellschaft, welche die Mehrheitsbeteiligung hält.

Zweiter Abschnitt: Rechte und Pflichten der Aktionäre

A. Recht auf Gewinn- und Liquidationsanteil

I. Im Allgemeinen

Art. 660

1 Jeder Aktionär hat Anspruch auf einen verhältnismässigen Anteil am Bilanzgewinn, soweit dieser nach dem Gesetz oder den Statuten zur Verteilung unter die Aktionäre bestimmt ist.

Teil F: Rechtliche Aspekte / Legal aspects

2 Bei Auflösung der Gesellschaft hat der Aktionär, soweit die Statuten über die Verwendung des Vermögens der aufgelösten Gesellschaft nichts anderes bestimmen, das Recht auf einen verhältnismässigen Anteil am Ergebnis der Liquidation.

3 Vorbehalten bleiben die in den Statuten für einzelne Kategorien von Aktien festgesetzten Vorrechte.

II. Berechnungsart

Art. 661

Die Anteile am Gewinn und am Liquidationsergebnis sind, sofern die Statuten nicht etwas anderes vorsehen, im Verhältnis der auf das Aktienkapital einbezahlten Beträge zu berechnen.

B. Geschäftsbericht

I. Im Allgemeinen

1. Inhalt

Art. 662

1 Der Verwaltungsrat erstellt für jedes Geschäftsjahr einen Geschäftsbericht, der sich aus der Jahresrechnung, dem Jahresbericht und einer Konzernrechnung zusammensetzt, soweit das Gesetz eine solche verlangt.

2 Die Jahresrechnung besteht aus der Erfolgsrechnung, der Bilanz und dem Anhang.

2. Ordnungsmässige Rechnungslegung

Art. 662a

1 Die Jahresrechnung wird nach den Grundsätzen der ordnungsmässigen Rechnungslegung so aufgestellt, dass die Vermögens- und Ertragslage der Gesellschaft möglichst zuverlässig beurteilt werden kann. Sie enthält auch die Vorjahreszahlen.

2 Die ordnungsmässige Rechnungslegung erfolgt insbesondere nach den Grundsätzen der:

1. Vollständigkeit der Jahresrechnung;
2. Klarheit und Wesentlichkeit der Angaben;
3. Vorsicht;
4. Fortführung der Unternehmenstätigkeit;
5. Stetigkeit in Darstellung und Bewertung;
6. Unzulässigkeit der Verrechnung von Aktiven und Passiven sowie von Aufwand und Ertrag.

3 Abweichungen vom Grundsatz der Unternehmensfortführung, von der Stetigkeit der Darstellung und Bewertung und vom Verrechnungsverbot sind in begründeten Fällen zulässig. Sie sind im Anhang darzulegen.

4 Im Übrigen gelten die Bestimmungen über die kaufmännische Buchführung.

II. Erfolgsrechnung; Mindestgliederung

Art. 663

1 Die Erfolgsrechnung weist betriebliche und betriebsfremde sowie ausserordentliche Erträge und Aufwendungen aus.

2 Unter Ertrag werden der Erlös aus Lieferungen und Leistungen, der Finanzertrag sowie die Gewinne aus Veräusserungen von Anlagevermögen gesondert ausgewiesen.

3 Unter Aufwand werden Material- und Warenaufwand, Personalaufwand, Finanzaufwand sowie Aufwand für Abschreibungen gesondert ausgewiesen.

4 Die Erfolgsrechnung zeigt den Jahresgewinn oder den Jahresverlust.

III. Bilanz; Mindestgliederung

Art. 663a

1 Die Bilanz weist das Umlaufvermögen und das Anlagevermögen, das Fremdkapital und das Eigenkapital aus.

2 Das Umlaufvermögen wird in flüssige Mittel, Forderungen aus Lieferungen und Leistungen, andere Forderungen sowie Vorräte unterteilt, das Anlagevermögen in Finanzanlagen, Sachanlagen und immaterielle Anlagen.

3 Das Fremdkapital wird in Schulden aus Lieferungen und Leistungen, andere kurzfristige Verbindlichkeiten, langfristige Verbindlichkeiten und Rückstellungen unterteilt, das Eigenkapital in Aktienkapital, gesetzliche und andere Reserven sowie in einen Bilanzgewinn.

4 Gesondert angegeben werden auch das nicht einbezahlte Aktienkapital, die Gesamtbeträge der Beteiligungen, der Forderungen und der Verbindlichkeiten gegenüber anderen Gesellschaften des Konzerns oder Aktionären, die eine Beteiligung an der Gesellschaft halten, die Rechnungsabgrenzungsposten sowie ein Bilanzverlust.

IV. Anhang

1. Im Allgemeinen

Art. 663b

Der Anhang enthält:

1. den Gesamtbetrag der Bürgschaften, Garantieverpflichtungen und Pfandbestellungen zugunsten Dritter;

2. den Gesamtbetrag der zur Sicherung eigener Verpflichtungen verpfändeten oder abgetretenen Aktiven sowie der Aktiven unter Eigentumsvorbehalt;

3. den Gesamtbetrag der nichtbilanzierten Leasingverbindlichkeiten;

4. die Brandversicherungswerte der Sachanlagen;

5. Verbindlichkeiten gegenüber Vorsorgeeinrichtungen;

6. die Beträge, Zinssätze und Fälligkeiten der von der Gesellschaft ausgegebenen Anleihensobligationen;

7. jede Beteiligung, die für die Beurteilung der Vermögens- und Ertragslage der Gesellschaft wesentlich ist;

8. den Gesamtbetrag der aufgelösten Wiederbeschaffungsreserven und der darüber hinausgehenden stillen Reserven, soweit dieser den Gesamtbetrag der neugebildeten derartigen Reserven übersteigt, wenn dadurch das erwirtschaftete Ergebnis wesentlich günstiger dargestellt wird;

9. Angaben über Gegenstand und Betrag von Aufwertungen;

10. Angaben über Erwerb, Veräusserung und Anzahl der von der Gesellschaft gehaltenen eigenen Aktien, einschliesslich ihrer Aktien, die eine andere Gesellschaft hält, an der sie mehrheitlich beteiligt ist; anzugeben sind ebenfalls die Bedingungen, zu denen die Gesellschaft die eigenen Aktien erworben oder veräussert hat;

11. den Betrag der genehmigten und der bedingten Kapitalerhöhung;

12. Angaben über die Durchführung einer Risikobeurteilung;

13. allenfalls die Gründe, die zum vorzeitigen Rücktritt der Revisionsstelle geführt haben;

14. die anderen vom Gesetz vorgeschriebenen Angaben.

Neu ist der Verwaltungsrat gemäss *Ziff. 12* gehalten, im Anhang Angaben über die Durchführung einer Risikobeurteilung zu machen.

Die sich ständig ändernden Bedingungen im technischen, wirtschaftlichen, sozialen und politischen Umfeld beeinflussen die Risiken der zu prüfenden Gesellschaft. Diese Risiken sind vom Verwaltungsrat im Hinblick auf die Beurteilung der Jahresrechnung darzulegen.

Massnahmen, die im Hinblick auf diese Risiken getroffen werden, werden nach geltendem Recht in der Regel im Jahresbericht erläutert. Der Jahresbericht wird aber von der Revisionsstelle nicht geprüft; aus diesem Grund werden die entsprechenden Aussagen des Verwaltungsrates vom Entwurf in den Anhang verschoben und somit in die Prüfung durch die Revisionsstelle eingeschlossen (s. Art. 728a Abs. 1 Ziff. 5 E OR).

Es ist klarzustellen, dass die Risikobeurteilung nicht sämtliche Geschäftsrisiken erfasst, sondern nur die Erläuterung derjenigen Risiken, die einen wesentlichen Einfluss auf die Beurteilung der Jahresrechnung haben könnten. Solche Risiken können beispielsweise in den Bereichen der Branchenzugehörigkeit, der Grösse des Unternehmens, der technologischen Entwicklungen, der Arbeitsmarktverhältnisse, der Formen der Finanzierung und der Liquiditätslage, der Konkurrenzsituation, des Produktemixes, der internen Organisation, der Eigentümerstruktur, der externen Einflüsse von interessieren Dritten (Stakeholder) oder der Umwelt bestehen. Beispielsweise können Mängel eines Produkts zu einem Bewertungsrisiko bei den Produktevorräten und zu Erlösminderungen führen[18].

Gemäss *Ziff. 13* legt der Verwaltungsrat im Anhang die Gründe offen, die zum vorzeitigen Rücktritt der Revisionsstelle geführt haben. Damit wird im Rahmen der heutigen Vorschriften zur Offenlegung der Jahresrechnung (s. Art. 697*h* OR) über die Gründe informiert, warum die Revisionsstelle ihr Mandat vorzeitig beendet hat. Der Verwaltungsrat muss zudem die Generalversammlung vor der Neuwahl der Revisionsstelle über die Gründe der Rücktritts informieren (s. Art. 730*a* Abs. 3 E OR sowie die Ausführungen zu dieser Bestimmung).

Die bisherige Ziff. 12 wird durch den Einschub der beiden erläuterten Bestimmungen zur neuen *Ziff. 14*. Inhaltlich ändert sich die Vorschrift nicht.

---

18 Schweizer Handbuch der Wirtschaftsprüfung, Zürich 1998, Band 2, N 3.2412; Grundsätze der Abschlussprüfung (GzA), Zürich 2001, GzA 11, N 4.11, 4.23.

Kapitel 1: Neue Gesetzesbestimmungen und Erläuterungen

2. Zusätzliche Angaben bei Gesellschaften mit kotierten Aktien

a. Vergütungen

Art. 663b^{bis}[19]

1 Gesellschaften, deren Aktien an einer Börse kotiert sind, haben im Anhang zur Bilanz anzugeben:

1. alle Vergütungen, die sie direkt oder indirekt an gegenwärtige Mitglieder des Verwaltungsrates ausgerichtet haben;
2. alle Vergütungen, die sie direkt oder indirekt an Personen ausgerichtet haben, die vom Verwaltungsrat ganz oder zum Teil mit der Geschäftsführung betraut sind (Geschäftsleitung);
3. alle Vergütungen, die sie direkt oder indirekt an gegenwärtige Mitglieder des Beirates ausgerichtet haben;
4. Vergütungen, die sie direkt oder indirekt an frühere Mitglieder des Verwaltungsrates, der Geschäftsleitung und des Beirates ausgerichtet haben, sofern sie in einem Zusammenhang mit der früheren Tätigkeit als Organ der Gesellschaft stehen oder nicht marktüblich sind;
5. nicht marktübliche Vergütungen, die sie direkt oder indirekt an Personen ausgerichtet haben, die den in den Ziffern 1–4 genannten Personen nahe stehen.

2 Als Vergütungen gelten insbesondere:

1. Honorare, Löhne, Bonifikationen und Gutschriften;
2. Tantiemen, Beteiligungen am Umsatz und andere Beteiligungen am Geschäftsergebnis;
3. Sachleistungen;
4. die Zuteilung von Beteiligungen, Wandel- und Optionsrechten;
5. Abgangsentschädigungen;

---

[19] Eingefügt durch Ziff. I des BG vom 7. Okt. 2005 (Transparenz betreffend Vergütungen an Mitglieder des Verwaltungsrates und der Geschäftsleitung), in Kraft seit 1. Jan. 2007 (AS **2006** 2629 2632; BBl **2004** 4471).

6. Bürgschaften, Garantieverpflichtungen, Pfandbestellungen zugunsten Dritter und andere Sicherheiten;

7. der Verzicht auf Forderungen;

8. Aufwendungen, die Ansprüche auf Vorsorgeleistungen begründen oder erhöhen;

9. sämtliche Leistungen für zusätzliche Arbeiten.

3 Im Anhang zur Bilanz sind zudem anzugeben:

1. alle Darlehen und Kredite, die den gegenwärtigen Mitgliedern des Verwaltungsrates, der Geschäftsleitung und des Beirates gewährt wurden und noch ausstehen;

2. Darlehen und Kredite, die zu nicht marktüblichen Bedingungen an frühere Mitglieder des Verwaltungsrates, der Geschäftsleitung und des Beirates gewährt wurden und noch ausstehen;

3. Darlehen und Kredite, die zu nicht marktüblichen Bedingungen an Personen, die den in den Ziffern 1 und 2 genannten Personen nahe stehen, gewährt wurden und noch ausstehen.

4 Die Angaben zu Vergütungen und Krediten müssen umfassen:

1. den Gesamtbetrag für den Verwaltungsrat und den auf jedes Mitglied entfallenden Betrag unter Nennung des Namens und der Funktion des betreffenden Mitglieds;

2. den Gesamtbetrag für die Geschäftsleitung und den höchsten auf ein Mitglied entfallenden Betrag unter Nennung des Namens und der Funktion des betreffenden Mitglieds;

3. den Gesamtbetrag für den Beirat und den auf jedes Mitglied entfallenden Betrag unter Nennung des Namens und der Funktion des betreffenden Mitglieds.

5 Vergütungen und Kredite an nahe stehende Personen sind gesondert auszuweisen. Die Namen der nahe stehenden Personen müssen nicht angegeben werden. Im Übrigen finden die Vorschriften über die Angaben zu Vergütungen und Krediten an Mitglieder des Verwaltungsrates, der Geschäftsleitung und des Beirates entsprechende Anwendung.

Absatz 1 enthält eine Generalklausel, die sämtliche Vergütungen an Mitglieder des Verwaltungsrates und der Geschäftsleitung der Offenlegungspflicht unterstellt (siehe Ziff. 1.3.3). Mit der Wendung «direkt oder indirekt ausgerichtet» wird klargestellt, dass auch eine Vergütung anzugeben ist, die nicht durch die Gesellschaft selbst, sondern durch eine Konzerngesellschaft (Art. 663e Abs. 1 OR) oder über eine Drittperson ausgerichtet worden ist (zur Problematik der Umgehung durch die Zuwendung an nahe stehende Personen siehe hinten). Ausserdem wird damit verdeutlicht, dass das Transparenzgebot nach seinem Ziel und Zweck umfassend zu verstehen ist und nicht durch die Wahl einer besonderen Form oder Modalität der Ausrichtung der Vergütung umgangen werden kann (zur Problematik der Umgehung durch die Vereinbarung einer Vergütung für zusätzliche Arbeiten vgl. die Regelung in Art. 663bbis Abs. 2 Ziff. 9 E OR).

Wie in der Vernehmlassung vorgeschlagen (siehe Ziff. 1.2.2), wird im Entwurf ausdrücklich festgehalten, dass nicht nur die gegenwärtigen, sondern auch die früheren Mitglieder des Verwaltungsrates und der Geschäftsleitung von der Offenlegungspflicht erfasst sind. Offen zu legen sind ebenfalls sämtliche Vergütungen und Kredite an Personen, die im Laufe des Geschäftsjahres oder zu einem früheren Zeitpunkt aus dem Verwaltungsrat oder der Geschäftsleitung ausgeschieden sind. Damit wird verhindert, dass die Pflicht zur Offenlegung von Bezügen durch die Vereinbarung von langfristig geschuldeten Vergütungen umgangen werden kann.

Schliesslich beschränkt der Entwurf – wie ebenfalls in der Vernehmlassung angeregt (siehe Ziff. 1.2.2) – die Offenlegungspflicht nicht auf Vergütungen an die Mitglieder des Verwaltungsrates und der Geschäftsleitung selbst. Erfasst werden (in Übereinstimmung mit der Regelung gemäss RLCG) auch Zuwendungen, die an ihnen nahe stehende Personen ausgerichtet werden.

Der Begriff der nahe stehenden Personen wird auch in Artikel 678 OR über die Rückerstattungspflicht verwendet. Bei dieser Bestimmung geht es nach der Lehre ebenfalls darum, Umgehungsmöglichkeiten zu verhindern, indem auch Leistungen an Drittpersonen miterfasst werden, die in enger Beziehung zu den nach Artikel 678 Absatz 1 OR rückerstattungspflichtigen Aktionären oder Verwaltungsratsmitgliedern stehen. Unerheblich ist dabei, ob diese besondere Beziehung persönlicher, wirtschaftlicher, rechtlicher oder tatsächlicher Natur ist.

Absatz 2 führt in Ergänzung zur Generalklausel in Absatz 1 einzelne Beispiele offenlegungspflichtiger Vergütungen auf. Diese Aufzählung ist nicht abschliessend.

Anzugeben sind nach Absatz 2 insbesondere:

- *Honorare, Löhne, Bonifikationen und Gutschriften (Ziff. 1):* Mit Honoraren und Löhnen sind die typischen Fälle fester Entschädigungen an die Mitglieder des Verwaltungsrates und der Geschäftsleitung gemeint. Bonifikationen und Gutschriften stellen dagegen variable Vergütungen dar.

- *Tantiemen, Beteiligungen am Umsatz und andere Beteiligungen amGeschäftsergebnis (Ziff. 2).*

- *Sachleistungen (Ziff. 3):* Dabei handelt es sich um die in der Praxis oft ausgerichteten Zusatzleistungen, die nicht in der Ausrichtung oder Gutschrift von Bargeld bestehen (fringe benefits).

- *Die Zuteilung von Beteiligungen, Wandel- und Optionsrechten (Ziff. 4):*Anzugeben sind die im Geschäftsjahr zugeteilten Rechte, nicht aber derengesamter Bestand (anders hinten bei Art. 663c Abs. 3 E OR).

- *Abgangsentschädigungen (Ziff. 5):* Die Notwendigkeit der speziellen Angabe von Abgangsentschädigungen resultiert ebenfalls aus dem Anliegen,Interessenkonflikte zu vermeiden.

- *Bürgschaften, Garantieverpflichtungen, Pfandbestellungen zugunsten Dritter und andere Sicherheiten (Ziff. 6):* Der Grund für die Offenlegung dieser Geschäfte liegt in der mit ihnen verbundenen Übertragung des wirtschaftlichen Risikos auf die Gesellschaft. Der Wortlaut der Bestimmung ist weiter gefasst als derjenige von Artikel 663b Ziffer 1 OR, da der Pflicht zur Offenlegung nicht nur die zur Sicherung einer Forderung eingegangenen Eventualverbindlichkeiten, sondern sämtliche Verpflichtungen, welche die Funktion einer Sicherheit erfüllen (wie insbesondere auch ein Schuldbeitritt), zu unterstellen sind.

- *Der Verzicht auf Forderungen (Ziff. 7):* Da der Verzicht auf eine Forderung eine Vermögensverschiebung zu Lasten der Gesellschaft bewirkt, ist er ebenfalls offen zu legen.

- *Aufwendungen, die Ansprüche auf Vorsorgeleistungen begründen oder erhöhen (Ziff. 8):* In der Praxis durchaus üblich sind Aufstockungen der Personalvorsorgeleistungen, die von der Gesellschaft

Kapitel 1: Neue Gesetzesbestimmungen und Erläuterungen

zu Gunsten ihrer Verwaltungsrats- oder Geschäftsleitungsmitglieder getätigt werden. Da diese die Vermögenssituation der begünstigten Personen verbessern, sind sie ebenfalls anzugeben.

- *Sämtliche Leistungen für zusätzliche Arbeiten (Ziff. 9)*: Wie in der Vernehmlassung angeregt (siehe Ziff. 1.2.2), werden die Leistungen für zusätzliche Arbeiten besonders erwähnt. Damit kann die Pflicht zur Offenlegung von Vergütungen nicht dadurch umgangen werden, dass diese nicht als Entschädigung für die Mitwirkung im Verwaltungsrat oder in der Geschäftsleitung, sondern als Gegenleistung für andere Dienste vereinbart werden.

Absatz 3 verlangt die Offenlegung von Darlehen und weiteren Krediten, die eine besondere Form von Vergütungen darstellen können. Organkredite werden unter dem Gesichtspunkt von Corporate Governance allgemein als problematisch betrachtet.

Für die Modalitäten der Offenlegung von Vergütungen gelten folgende Grundsätze:

- *Vergütungen an Mitglieder des Verwaltungsrates und der Geschäftsleitung (Abs. 4)*: Anzugeben sind der Gesamtbetrag der Vergütungen für Verwaltungsrat und Geschäftsleitung, die individuellen Bezüge der einzelnen Verwaltungsratsmitglieder und der höchste auf ein Mitglied der Geschäftsleitung entfallende Betrag (siehe auch Ziff. 1.3.4). Soweit die Vergütungen individuell offen zu legen sind, müssen Name und Funktion der betreffendenPerson angegeben werden. Bei der Ermittlung der höchsten an ein Mitgliedder Geschäftsleitung ausgerichteten Entschädigung sind Vergütungen undKredite an nahe stehende Personen mitzuberücksichtigen, soweit diese funktional zumindest im weiteren Sinne eine Entschädigung für die Tätigkeit in der Geschäftsleitung darstellen.

- *Vergütungen an nahe stehende Personen (Abs. 5)*: Vergütungen und Kredite, die an Personen gewährt werden, die einem Mitglied des Verwaltungsrates oder der Geschäftsleitung nahe stehen, sind gesondert auszuweisen. Dabei müssen die Namen der nahe stehenden Personen nicht angegeben werden. Was die Angaben zu Vergütungen und Krediten betrifft, sind im Übrigen die Vorschriften für die Mitglieder des Verwaltungsrates und der Geschäftsleitung entsprechend anwendbar. Dies gilt für die Offenlegung von Gesamtbeträgen wie auch der individuellen Vergütungen: Angegeben werden müssen die Gesamtbeträge der Vergütungen für die den Mitgliedern des

Verwaltungsrates und Geschäftsleitung nahe stehenden Personen. Weiter müssen die Bezüge der Personen offen gelegt werden, die den Verwaltungsratsmitgliedern nahe stehen, gegliedert nach den einzelnen Mitgliedern und unter Nennung von deren Namen. Schliesslich sind die Entschädigungen an die Personen anzugeben, die dem Mitglied der Geschäftsleitung mit der höchsten Vergütung nahe stehen.

– *Massgeblicher Zeitpunkt*: Massgeblich für die Pflicht zur Offenlegung der Vergütungen ist der Zeitpunkt, in dem diese in der Rechnungslegung erfasst werden. Die entsprechenden Angaben erfolgen somit in demjenigen Geschäftsjahr, in dem die Vergütungen geschuldet sind.

Bei Krediten ist nicht der im Geschäftsjahr ausgerichtete Betrag massgeblich. Anzugeben sind vielmehr sämtliche noch ausstehenden Darlehen und Kredite, da den betreffenden Personen die Vorteile aus den gesamten Konditionen zugute kommen (Abs. 3).

Die Angaben zu Vergütungen und Krediten sind nach deren einzelnen Bestandteilen zu gliedern. Damit soll sichergestellt werden, dass die Aktionärinnen und Aktionäre die wesentlichen Informationen erhalten und ihre Kontrollrechte besser ausüben können.

V. Beteiligungsverhältnisse bei Gesellschaften mit kotierten Aktien

Art. 663c
1 Gesellschaften, deren Aktien[20] an einer Börse kotiert sind, haben im Anhang zur Bilanz bedeutende Aktionäre und deren Beteiligungen anzugeben, sofern diese ihnen bekannt sind oder bekannt sein müssten.

2 Als bedeutende Aktionäre gelten Aktionäre und stimmrechtsverbundene Aktionärsgruppen, deren Beteiligung 5 Prozent aller Stimmrechte übersteigt. Enthalten die Statuten eine tiefere prozentmässige Begrenzung der Namenaktien (Art. 685d Abs. 1), so gilt für die Bekanntgabepflicht diese Grenze.

3 Anzugeben sind weiter die Beteiligungen an der Gesellschaft sowie die Wandel- und Optionsrechte jedes gegenwärtigen Mitglieds des

---

20 Berichtigt von der Redaktionskommission der BVers [Art. 33 GVG – AS 1974 1051].

Kapitel 1: Neue Gesetzesbestimmungen und Erläuterungen

Verwaltungsrates, der Geschäftsleitung und des Beirates mit Einschluss der Beteiligungen der ihm nahe stehenden Personen unter Nennung des Namens und der Funktion des betreffenden Mitglieds.

Der Randtitel «Beteiligungsverhältnisse bei Publikumsgesellschaften» wird durch «Beteiligungsverhältnisse bei Gesellschaften mit kotierten Aktien» ersetzt. Diese Änderung wird notwendig, weil in Art. 727 Abs. 1 Ziff. 1 E OR der Begriff der Publikumsgesellschaft mit einem leicht abweichenden Begriffsinhalt verwendet wird.

Der heutige Artikel 663c OR regelt die Offenlegung von Beteiligungsverhältnissen bei Publikumsgesellschaften. Im Anhang zur Bilanz sind die bedeutenden Aktionärinnen und Aktionäre anzugeben. Der neue Absatz 3 verlangt, dass neben der Beteiligung bedeutender Aktionärinnen und Aktionäre inskünftig auch die Beteiligungen der gegenwärtigen und früheren Mitglieder des Verwaltungsrates und der Geschäftsleitung sowie der ihnen nahe stehenden Personen offen zu legen sind. In das Transparenzgebot eingeschlossen sind Wandel- und Optionsrechte, da diese u.U. gleichermassen die Geschäftsführung einzelner Personen beeinflussen können (siehe Ziff. 1.3.3).

Die Offenlegungspflicht darf sich nicht nur auf die jeweils im Geschäftsjahr erworbenen Rechte beschränken, sondern muss sämtliche bestehenden Beteiligungen umfassen. Um eine Beurteilung der Geschäftstätigkeit zu ermöglichen, hat die Offenlegung für sämtliche Mitglieder des Verwaltungsrates und der Geschäftsleitung individuell zu erfolgen.

Beteiligungen von Personen, die einem Mitglied des Verwaltungsrates oder der Geschäftsleitung nahe stehen, sind beim betreffenden Organmitglied anzugeben.

VI. Jahresbericht

Art. 663d

1 Der Jahresbericht stellt den Geschäftsverlauf sowie die wirtschaftliche und finanzielle Lage der Gesellschaft dar.

2 Er nennt die im Geschäftsjahr eingetretenen Kapitalerhöhungen und gibt die Prüfungsbestätigung wieder.

VII. Konzernrechnung

1. Pflicht zur Erstellung

Art. 663e

1 Fasst die Gesellschaft durch Stimmenmehrheit oder auf andere Weise eine oder mehrere Gesellschaften unter einheitlicher Leitung zusammen (Konzern), so erstellt sie eine konsolidierte Jahresrechnung (Konzernrechnung).

2 Die Gesellschaft ist von der Pflicht zur Erstellung einer Konzernrechnung befreit, wenn sie zusammen mit ihren Untergesellschaften zwei der nachstehenden Grössen in zwei aufeinander folgenden Geschäftsjahren nicht überschreitet:

1. Bilanzsumme von 10 Millionen Franken;
2. Umsatzerlös von 20 Millionen Franken;
3. 200 Vollzeitstellen im Jahresdurchschnitt;

3 Eine Konzernrechnung ist dennoch zu erstellen, wenn:

1. die Gesellschaft Beteiligungspapiere an einer Börse kotiert hat;
2. die Gesellschaft Anleihensobligationen ausstehend hat;
3. Aktionäre, die zusammen mindestens 10 Prozent des Aktienkapitals vertreten, es verlangen;
4. dies für eine möglichst zuverlässige Beurteilung der Vermögens- und Ertragslage der Gesellschaft notwendig ist.

Die vorliegende Bestimmung regelt die Pflicht zur Erstellung einer Konzernrechnung. In *Abs. 2 Ziff. 3* E OR erfolgt lediglich eine redaktionelle Anpassung an Art. 727 Abs. 1 Ziff. 2 lit. c E OR («Vollzeitstellen im Jahresdurchschnitt» statt «Arbeitnehmer»).

In *Abs. 3* werden die *Ziff. 1 und 2* an Art. 727 Abs. 1 Ziff. 1 lit. a und b E OR angepasst: Zum einen wird die Reihenfolge vertauscht (die Ziff. 2 des geltenden Rechts wird zur Ziff. 1), zum anderen wird der Begriff «Aktien» durch den umfassenderen Ausdruck der «Beteiligungspapiere» ersetzt (vgl. dazu die Ausführungen zu Art. 727 Abs. 1 Ziff. 1 lit. a E OR). Ziff. 3 bleibt unverändert.

Kapitel 1: Neue Gesetzesbestimmungen und Erläuterungen

2. Zwischengesellschaften

Art. 663f

¹ Ist eine Gesellschaft in die Konzernrechnung einer Obergesellschaft einbezogen, die nach schweizerischen oder gleichwertigen ausländischen Vorschriften erstellt und geprüft worden ist, so muss sie keine besondere Konzernrechnung erstellen, wenn sie die Konzernrechnung der Obergesellschaft ihren Aktionären und Gläubigern wie die eigene Jahresrechnung bekanntmacht.

² Sie ist jedoch verpflichtet, eine besondere Konzernrechnung zu erstellen, wenn sie ihre Jahresrechnung veröffentlichen muss oder wenn Aktionäre, die zusammen mindestens 10 Prozent des Aktienkapitals vertreten, es verlangen.

3. Erstellung

Art. 663g

¹ Die Konzernrechnung untersteht den Grundsätzen ordnungsmässiger Rechnungslegung.

² Im Anhang zur Konzernrechnung nennt die Gesellschaft die Konsolidierungs- und Bewertungsregeln. Weicht sie davon ab, so weist sie im Anhang darauf hin und vermittelt in anderer Weise die für den Einblick in die Vermögens- und Ertragslage des Konzerns nötigen Angaben.

VIII. Schutz und Anpassung

Art. 663h

¹ In der Jahresrechnung, im Jahresbericht und in der Konzernrechnung kann auf Angaben verzichtet werden, welche der Gesell-

schaft oder dem Konzern erhebliche Nachteile bringen können. Die Revisionsstelle ist über die Gründe zu unterrichten.

2 Die Jahresrechnung kann im Rahmen der Grundsätze der ordnungsmässigen Rechnungslegung den Besonderheiten des Unternehmens angepasst werden. Sie hat jedoch den gesetzlich vorgeschriebenen Mindestinhalt aufzuweisen.

IX. Bewertung

1. Gründungs-, Kapitalerhöhungs- und Organisationskosten

Art. 664

Gründungs-, Kapitalerhöhungs- und Organisationskosten, die aus der Errichtung, der Erweiterung oder der Umstellung des Geschäfts entstehen, dürfen bilanziert werden. Sie werden gesondert ausgewiesen und innerhalb von fünf Jahren abgeschrieben.

2. Anlagevermögen

a. Im Allgemeinen

Art. 665

Das Anlagevermögen darf höchstens zu den Anschaffungs- oder den Herstellungskosten bewertet werden, unter Abzug der notwendigen Abschreibungen.

b. Beteiligungen

Art. 665a

1 Zum Anlagevermögen gehören auch Beteiligungen und andere Finanzanlagen.

2 Beteiligungen sind Anteile am Kapital anderer Unternehmen, die mit der Absicht dauernder Anlage gehalten werden und einen massgeblichen Einfluss vermitteln.

3 Stimmberechtigte Anteile von mindestens 20 Prozent gelten als Beteiligung.

3. Vorräte

Art. 666

1 Rohmaterialien, teilweise oder ganz fertig gestellte Erzeugnisse sowie Waren dürfen höchstens zu den Anschaffungs- oder den Herstellungskosten bewertet werden.

2 Sind die Kosten höher als der am Bilanzstichtag allgemein geltende Marktpreis, so ist dieser massgebend.

4. Wertschriften

Art. 667

1 Wertschriften mit Kurswert dürfen höchstens zum Durchschnittskurs des letzten Monats vor dem Bilanzstichtag bewertet werden.

2 Wertschriften ohne Kurswert dürfen höchstens zu den Anschaffungskosten bewertet werden, unter Abzug der notwendigen Wertberichtigungen.

5. Abschreibungen, Wertberichtigungen und Rückstellungen

Art. 669

1 Abschreibungen, Wertberichtigungen und Rückstellungen müssen vorgenommen werden, soweit sie nach allgemein anerkannten kaufmännischen Grundsätzen notwendig sind. Rückstellungen sind insbesondere zu bilden, um ungewisse Verpflichtungen und drohende Verluste aus schwebenden Geschäften zu decken.

2 Der Verwaltungsrat darf zu Wiederbeschaffungszwecken zusätzliche Abschreibungen, Wertberichtigungen und Rückstellungen vornehmen und davon absehen, überflüssig gewordene Rückstellungen aufzulösen.

3 Stille Reserven, die darüber hinausgehen, sind zulässig, soweit die Rücksicht auf das dauernde Gedeihen des Unternehmens oder auf die Ausrichtung einer möglichst gleichmässigen Dividende es unter Berücksichtigung der Interessen der Aktionäre rechtfertigt.

4 Bildung und Auflösung von Wiederbeschaffungsreserven und darüber hinausgehenden stillen Reserven sind der Revisionsstelle im einzelnen mitzuteilen.

6. Aufwertung

Art. 670

1 Ist die Hälfte des Aktienkapitals und der gesetzlichen Reserven infolge eines Bilanzverlustes nicht mehr gedeckt, so dürfen zur Beseitigung der Unterbilanz Grundstücke oder Beteiligungen, deren wirklicher Wert über die Anschaffungs- oder Herstellungskosten gestiegen ist, bis höchstens zu diesem Wert aufgewertet werden. Der Aufwendungsbetrag ist gesondert als Aufwertungsreserve auszuweisen.

2 Die Aufwertung ist nur zulässig, wenn ein zugelassener Revisor zuhanden der Generalversammlung schriftlich bestätigt, dass die gesetzlichen Bestimmungen eingehalten sind.

Ist die Hälfte des Aktienkapitals und der gesetzlichen Reserven infolge eines Bilanzverlustes nicht mehr gedeckt, so dürfen zur Beseitigung der Unterbilanz bestimmte Aufwertungen vorgenommen werden (Art. 670 Abs. 1 OR).

Nach dem geltenden Art. 670 Abs. 2 OR muss die Revisionsstelle schriftlich zuhanden der Generalversammlung bestätigen, dass die gesetzlichen Bestimmungen hierzu eingehalten sind.

Auch diese Bestimmung muss der Tatsache angepasst werden, dass eine Aktiengesellschaft nach dem Entwurf nicht in jedem Fall über eine Revisionsstelle verfügt. (s. Art. 727a Abs. 2 E OR). Es wird daher eine Bestätigung durch eine zugelassene Revisorin oder einen zugelassenen Revisor verlangt. Dies schliesst nicht aus, dass gegebenenfalls die Revisionsstelle die erforderliche Bestätigung abgibt.

C. Reserven

I. Gesetzliche Reserven

1. Allgemeine Reserve

Art. 671

1 5 Prozent des Jahresgewinnes sind der allgemeinen Reserve zuzuweisen, bis diese 20 Prozent des einbezahlten Aktienkapitals erreicht.

2 Dieser Reserve sind, auch nachdem sie die gesetzliche Höhe erreicht hat, zuzuweisen:

1. ein bei der Ausgabe von Aktien nach Deckung der Ausgabekosten über den Nennwert hinaus erzielter Mehrerlös, soweit er nicht zu Abschreibungen oder zu Wohlfahrtszwecken verwendet wird;

2. was von den geleisteten Einzahlungen auf ausgefallene Aktien übrig bleibt, nachdem ein allfälliger Mindererlös aus den dafür ausgegebenen Aktien gedeckt worden ist;

3. 10 Prozent der Beträge, die nach Bezahlung einer Dividende von 5 Prozent als Gewinnanteil ausgerichtet werden.

3 Die allgemeine Reserve darf, soweit sie die Hälfte des Aktienkapitals nicht übersteigt, nur zur Deckung von Verlusten oder für Massnahmen verwendet werden, die geeignet sind, in Zeiten schlechten Geschäftsganges das Unternehmen durchzuhalten, der Arbeitslosigkeit entgegenzuwirken oder ihre Folgen zu mildern.

4 Die Bestimmungen in Abs. 2 Ziff. 3 und Abs. 3 gelten nicht für Gesellschaften, deren Zweck hauptsächlich in der Beteiligung an anderen Unternehmen besteht (Holdinggesellschaften).

5 Konzessionierte Transportanstalten sind, unter Vorbehalt abweichender Bestimmungen des öffentlichen Rechts, von der Pflicht zur Bildung der Reserve befreit.

2. Reserve für eigene Aktien

Art. 671a

Die Reserve für eigene Aktien kann bei Veräusserung oder Vernichtung von Aktien im Umfang der Anschaffungswerte aufgehoben werden.

3. Aufwertungsreserve

Art. 671b

Die Aufwertungsreserve kann nur durch Umwandlung in Aktienkapital sowie durch Wiederabschreibung oder Veräusserung der aufgewerteten Aktiven aufgelöst werden.

II. Statutarische Reserven

1. Im Allgemeinen

Art. 672

1 Die Statuten können bestimmen, dass der Reserve höhere Beträge als 5 Prozent des Jahresgewinnes zuzuweisen sind und dass die Reserve mehr als die vom Gesetz vorgeschriebenen 20 Prozent des einbezahlten Aktienkapitals betragen muss.

2 Sie können die Anlage weiterer Reserven vorsehen und deren Zweckbestimmung und Verwendung festsetzen.

Kapitel 1: Neue Gesetzesbestimmungen und Erläuterungen

2. Zu Wohlfahrtszwecken für Arbeitnehmer

Art. 673

Die Statuten können insbesondere auch Reserven zur Gründung und Unterstützung von Wohlfahrtseinrichtungen für Arbeitnehmer des Unternehmens vorsehen.

III. Verhältnis des Gewinnanteils zu den Reserven

Art. 674

1 Die Dividende darf erst festgesetzt werden, nachdem die dem Gesetz und den Statuten entsprechenden Zuweisungen an die gesetzlichen und statutarischen Reserven abgezogen worden sind.

2 Die Generalversammlung kann die Bildung von Reserven beschliessen, die im Gesetz und in den Statuten nicht vorgesehen sind oder über deren Anforderungen hinausgehen, soweit

1. dies zu Wiederbeschaffungszwecken notwendig ist;

2. die Rücksicht auf das dauernde Gedeihen des Unternehmens oder auf die Ausrichtung einer möglichst gleichmässigen Dividende es unter Berücksichtigung der Interessen aller Aktionäre rechtfertigt.

3 Ebenso kann die Generalversammlung zur Gründung und Unterstützung von Wohlfahrtseinrichtungen für Arbeitnehmer des Unternehmens und zu anderen Wohlfahrtszwecken aus dem Bilanzgewinn auch dann Reserven bilden, wenn sie in den Statuten nicht vorgesehen sind.

D. Dividenden, Bauzinse und Tantiemen
I. Dividenden

Art. 675

1 Zinse dürfen für das Aktienkapital nicht bezahlt werden.
2 Dividenden dürfen nur aus dem Bilanzgewinn und aus hierfür gebildeten Reserven ausgerichtet werden.[21]

II. Bauzinse

Art. 676

1 Für die Zeit, die Vorbereitung und Bau bis zum Anfang des vollen Betriebes des Unternehmens erfordern, kann den Aktionären ein Zins von bestimmter Höhe zu Lasten des Anlagekontos zugesichert werden. Die Statuten müssen in diesem Rahmen den Zeitpunkt bezeichnen, in dem die Entrichtung von Zinsen spätestens aufhört.

2 Wird das Unternehmen durch die Ausgabe neuer Aktien erweitert, so kann im Beschlusse über die Kapitalerhöhung den neuen Aktien eine bestimmte Verzinsung zu Lasten des Anlagekontos bis zu einem genau anzugebenden Zeitpunkt, höchstens jedoch bis zur Aufnahme des Betriebes der neuen Anlage zugestanden werden.

III. Tantiemen

Art. 677

Gewinnanteile an Mitglieder des Verwaltungsrates dürfen nur dem Bilanzgewinn entnommen werden und sind nur zulässig, nachdem die Zuweisung an die gesetzliche Reserve gemacht und eine Dividende

---

21 Fassung gemäss Ziff. I des BG vom 4. Okt. 1991, in Kraft seit 1. Juli 1992 (AS 1992 733 786; BBl 1983 II 745).

von 5 Prozent oder von einem durch die Statuten festgesetzten höheren Ansatz an die Aktionäre ausgerichtet worden ist.

E. Rückerstattung von Leistungen
I. Im Allgemeinen

Art. 678

1 Aktionäre und Mitglieder des Verwaltungsrates sowie diesen nahe stehende Personen, die ungerechtfertigt und in bösem Glauben Dividenden, Tantiemen, andere Gewinnanteile oder Bauzinse bezogen haben, sind zur Rückerstattung verpflichtet.

2 Sie sind auch zur Rückerstattung anderer Leistungen der Gesellschaft verpflichtet, soweit diese in einem offensichtlichen Missverhältnis zur Gegenleistung und zur wirtschaftlichen Lage der Gesellschaft stehen.

3 Der Anspruch auf Rückerstattung steht der Gesellschaft und dem Aktionär zu; dieser klagt auf Leistung an die Gesellschaft.

4 Die Pflicht zur Rückerstattung verjährt fünf Jahre nach Empfang der Leistung.

II. Tantiemen im Konkurs

Art. 679

1 Im Konkurs der Gesellschaft müssen die Mitglieder des Verwaltungsrates alle Tantiemen, die sie in den letzten drei Jahren vor Konkurseröffnung erhalten haben, zurückerstatten, es sei denn, sie weisen nach, dass die Voraussetzungen zur Ausrichtung der Tantiemen nach Gesetz und Statuten erfüllt waren; dabei ist insbesondere nachzuweisen, dass die Ausrichtung aufgrund vorsichtiger Bilanzierung erfolgte.

2 Die Zeit zwischen Konkursaufschub und Konkurseröffnung zählt bei der Berechnung der Frist nicht mit.

F. Leistungspflicht des Aktionärs
I. Gegenstand

Art. 680

1 Der Aktionär kann auch durch die Statuten nicht verpflichtet werden, mehr zu leisten als den für den Bezug einer Aktie bei ihrer Ausgabe festgesetzten Betrag.

2 Ein Recht, den eingezahlten Betrag zurückzufordern, steht dem Aktionär nicht zu.

II. Verzugsfolgen
1. Nach Gesetz und Statuten

Art. 681

1 Ein Aktionär, der den Ausgabebetrag seiner Aktie nicht zur rechten Zeit einbezahlt, ist zur Zahlung von Verzugszinsen verpflichtet.

2 Der Verwaltungsrat ist überdies befugt, den säumigen Aktionär seiner Rechte aus der Zeichnung der Aktien und seiner geleisteten Teilzahlungen verlustig zu erklären und an Stelle der ausgefallenen neue Aktien auszugeben. Wenn die ausgefallenen Titel bereits ausgegeben sind und nicht beigebracht werden können, so ist die Verlustigerklärung im Schweizerischen Handelsamtsblatt sowie in der von den Statuten vorgesehenen Form zu veröffentlichen.

3 Die Statuten können einen Aktionär für den Fall der Säumnis auch zur Entrichtung einer Konventionalstrafe verpflichten.

Art. 682

1 Beabsichtigt der Verwaltungsrat, den säumigen Aktionär seiner Rechte aus der Zeichnung verlustig zu erklären oder von ihm die in den Statuten vorgesehene Konventionalstrafe zu fordern, so hat er im Schweizerischen Handelsamtsblatt sowie in der von den Statuten vorgesehenen Form mindestens dreimal eine Aufforderung zur Einzahlung zu erlassen, unter Ansetzung einer Nachfrist von mindestens einem Monat, von der letzten Veröffentlichung an gerechnet. Der Aktionär darf seiner Rechte aus der Zeichnung erst verlustig erklärt oder für die Konventionalstrafe belangt werden, wenn er auch innerhalb der Nachfrist die Einzahlung nicht leistet.

2 Bei Namenaktien tritt an die Stelle der Veröffentlichungen eine Zahlungsaufforderung und Ansetzung der Nachfrist an die im Aktienbuch eingetragenen Aktionäre durch eingeschriebenen Brief. In diesem Falle läuft die Nachfrist vom Empfang der Zahlungsaufforderung an.

3 Der säumige Aktionär haftet der Gesellschaft für den Betrag, der durch die Leistungen des neuen Aktionärs nicht gedeckt ist.

G. Ausgabe und Übertragung der Aktien

I. Inhaberaktien

Art. 683

1 Auf den Inhaber lautende Aktien dürfen erst nach der Einzahlung des vollen Nennwertes ausgegeben werden.

2 Vor der Volleinzahlung ausgegebene Aktien sind nichtig. Schadenersatzansprüche bleiben vorbehalten.

II. Namenaktien

Art. 684

1 Die Namenaktien sind, wenn nicht Gesetz oder Statuten es anders bestimmen, ohne Beschränkung übertragbar.

2 Die Übertragung durch Rechtsgeschäft kann durch Übergabe des indossierten Aktientitels an den Erwerber erfolgen.

H. Beschränkung der Übertragbarkeit
I. Gesetzliche Beschränkung

Art. 685

1 Nicht voll liberierte Namenaktien dürfen nur mit Zustimmung der Gesellschaft übertragen werden, es sei denn, sie werden durch Erbgang, Erbteilung, eheliches Güterrecht oder Zwangsvollstreckung erworben.

2 Die Gesellschaft kann die Zustimmung nur verweigern, wenn die Zahlungsfähigkeit des Erwerbers zweifelhaft ist und die von der Gesellschaft geforderte Sicherheit nicht geleistet wird.

II. Statutarische Beschränkung
1. Grundsätze

Art. 685a

1 Die Statuten können bestimmen, dass Namenaktien nur mit Zustimmung der Gesellschaft übertragen werden dürfen.

2 Diese Beschränkung gilt auch für die Begründung einer Nutzniessung.

3 Tritt die Gesellschaft in Liquidation, so fällt die Beschränkung der Übertragbarkeit dahin.

Kapitel 1: Neue Gesetzesbestimmungen und Erläuterungen

2. Nicht börsenkotierte Namenaktien

a. Voraussetzungen der Ablehnung

Art. 685b

1 Die Gesellschaft kann das Gesuch um Zustimmung ablehnen, wenn sie hierfür einen wichtigen, in den Statuten genannten Grund bekanntgibt oder wenn sie dem Veräusserer der Aktien anbietet, die Aktien für eigene Rechnung, für Rechnung anderer Aktionäre oder für Rechnung Dritter zum wirklichen Wert im Zeitpunkt des Gesuches zu übernehmen.

2 Als wichtige Gründe gelten Bestimmungen über die Zusammensetzung des Aktionärskreises, die im Hinblick auf den Gesellschaftszweck oder die wirtschaftliche Selbständigkeit des Unternehmens die Verweigerung rechtfertigen.

3 Die Gesellschaft kann überdies die Eintragung in das Aktienbuch verweigern, wenn der Erwerber nicht ausdrücklich erklärt, dass er die Aktien im eigenen Namen und auf eigene Rechnung erworben hat.

4 Sind die Aktien durch Erbgang, Erbteilung, eheliches Güterrecht oder Zwangsvollstreckung erworben worden, so kann die Gesellschaft das Gesuch um Zustimmung nur ablehnen, wenn sie dem Erwerber die Übernahme der Aktien zum wirklichen Wert anbietet.

5 Der Erwerber kann verlangen, dass der Richter am Sitz der Gesellschaft den wirklichen Wert bestimmt. Die Kosten der Bewertung trägt die Gesellschaft.

6 Lehnt der Erwerber das Übernahmeangebot nicht innert eines Monates nach Kenntnis des wirklichen Wertes ab, so gilt es als angenommen.

7 Die Statuten dürfen die Voraussetzungen der Übertragbarkeit nicht erschweren.

b. Wirkung

Art. 685c

1 Solange eine erforderliche Zustimmung zur Übertragung von Aktien nicht erteilt wird, verbleiben das Eigentum an den Aktien und alle damit verknüpften Rechte beim Veräusserer.

2 Beim Erwerb von Aktien durch Erbgang, Erbteilung, eheliches Güterrecht oder Zwangsvollstreckung gehen das Eigentum und die Vermögensrechte sogleich, die Mitwirkungsrechte erst mit der Zustimmung der Gesellschaft auf den Erwerber über.

3 Lehnt die Gesellschaft das Gesuch um Zustimmung innert drei Monate nach Erhalt nicht oder zu Unrecht ab, so gilt die Zustimmung als erteilt.

3. Börsenkotierte Namenaktien

a. Voraussetzungen der Ablehnung

Art. 685d

1 Bei börsenkotierten Namenaktien kann die Gesellschaft einen Erwerber als Aktionär nur ablehnen, wenn die Statuten eine prozentmässige Begrenzung der Namenaktien vorsehen, für die ein Erwerber als Aktionär anerkannt werden muss, und diese Begrenzung überschritten wird.

2 Die Gesellschaft kann überdies die Eintragung in das Aktienbuch verweigern, wenn der Erwerber auf ihr Verlangen nicht ausdrücklich erklärt, dass er die Aktien im eigenen Namen und auf eigene Rechnung erworben hat.

3 Sind börsenkotierte[22] Namenaktien durch Erbgang, Erbteilung oder eheliches Güterrecht erworben worden, kann der Erwerber nicht abgelehnt werden.

---

22 Berichtigt von der Redaktionskommission der BVers [Art. 33 GVG – AS 1974 1051].

Kapitel 1: Neue Gesetzesbestimmungen und Erläuterungen

b. Meldepflicht

Art. 685e

Werden börsenkotierte Namenaktien börsenmässig verkauft, so meldet die Veräussererbank den Namen des Veräusserers und die Anzahl der verkauften Aktien unverzüglich der Gesellschaft.

c. Rechtsübergang

Art. 685f

1 Werden börsenkotierte Namenaktien börsenmässig erworben, so gehen die Rechte mit der Übertragung auf den Erwerber über. Werden börsenkotierte Namenaktien ausserbörslich erworben, so gehen die Rechte auf den Erwerber über, sobald dieser bei der Gesellschaft ein Gesuch um Anerkennung als Aktionär eingereicht hat.

2 Bis zur Anerkennung des Erwerbers durch die Gesellschaft kann dieser weder das mit den Aktien verknüpfte Stimmrecht noch andere mit dem Stimmrecht zusammenhängende Rechte ausüben. In der Ausübung aller übrigen Aktionärsrechte, insbesondere auch des Bezugsrechts, ist der Erwerber nicht eingeschränkt.

3 Noch nicht von der Gesellschaft anerkannte Erwerber sind nach dem Rechtsübergang als Aktionär ohne Stimmrecht ins Aktienbuch einzutragen. Die entsprechenden Aktien gelten in der Generalversammlung als nicht vertreten.

4 Ist die Ablehnung widerrechtlich, so hat die Gesellschaft das Stimmrecht und die damit zusammenhängenden Rechte vom Zeitpunkt des richterlichen Urteils an anzuerkennen und dem Erwerber Schadenersatz zu leisten, sofern sie nicht beweist, dass ihr kein Verschulden zur Last fällt.

d. Ablehungsfrist

Art. 685g

Lehnt die Gesellschaft das Gesuch des Erwerbers um Anerkennung innert 20 Tagen nicht ab, so ist dieser als Aktionär anerkannt.

4. Aktienbuch

a. Eintragung

Art. 686

1 Die Gesellschaft führt über die Namenaktien ein Aktienbuch, in welches die Eigentümer und Nutzniesser mit Namen und Adresse eingetragen werden.

2 Die Eintragung in das Aktienbuch setzt einen Ausweis über den Erwerb der Aktie zu Eigentum oder die Begründung einer Nutzniessung voraus.

3 Die Gesellschaft muss die Eintragung auf dem Aktientitel bescheinigen.

4 Im Verhältnis zur Gesellschaft gilt als Aktionär oder als Nutzniesser, wer im Aktienbuch eingetragen ist.

b. Streichung

Art. 686a

Die Gesellschaft kann nach Anhörung des Betroffenen Eintragungen im Aktienbuch streichen, wenn diese durch falsche Angaben des Erwerbers zustande gekommen sind. Dieser muss über die Streichung sofort informiert werden.

5. Nicht voll einbezahlte Namenaktien

Art. 687

1 Der Erwerber einer nicht voll einbezahlten Namenaktie ist der Gesellschaft gegenüber zur Einzahlung verpflichtet, sobald er im Aktienbuch eingetragen ist.

2 Veräussert der Zeichner die Aktie, so kann er für den nicht einbezahlten Betrag belangt werden, wenn die Gesellschaft binnen zwei Jahren seit ihrer Eintragung in das Handelsregister in Konkurs gerät und sein Rechtsnachfolger seines Rechtes aus der Aktie verlustig erklärt worden ist.

3 Der Veräusserer, der nicht Zeichner ist, wird durch die Eintragung des Erwerbers der Aktie im Aktienbuch von der Einzahlungspflicht befreit.

4 Solange Namenaktien nicht voll einbezahlt sind, ist auf jedem Titel der auf den Nennwert einbezahlte Betrag anzugeben.

III. Interimsscheine

Art. 688

1 Auf den Inhaber lautende Interimsscheine dürfen nur für Inhaberaktien ausgegeben werden, deren Nennwert voll einbezahlt ist. Vor der Volleinzahlung ausgegebene, auf den Inhaber lautende Interimsscheine sind nichtig. Schadenersatzansprüche bleiben vorbehalten.

2 Werden für Inhaberaktien auf den Namen lautende Interimsscheine ausgestellt, so können sie nur nach den für die Abtretung von Forderungen geltenden Bestimmungen übertragen werden, jedoch ist die Übertragung der Gesellschaft gegenüber erst wirksam, wenn sie ihr angezeigt wird.

3 Interimsscheine für Namenaktien müssen auf den Namen lauten. Die Übertragung solcher Interimsscheine richtet sich nach den für die Übertragung von Namenaktien geltenden Vorschriften.

J. Persönliche Mitgliedschaftsrechte

I. Teilnahme an der Generalversammlung

1. Grundsatz

Art. 689

1 Der Aktionär übt seine Rechte in den Angelegenheiten der Gesellschaft, wie Bestellung der Organe, Abnahme des Geschäftsberichtes und Beschlussfassung über die Gewinnverwendung, in der Generalversammlung aus.

2 Er kann seine Aktien in der Generalversammlung selbst vertreten oder durch einen Dritten vertreten lassen, der unter Vorbehalt abweichender statutarischer Bestimmungen nicht Aktionär zu sein braucht.

2. Berechtigung gegenüber der Gesellschaft

Art. 689a

1 Die Mitgliedschaftsrechte aus Namenaktien kann ausüben, wer durch den Eintrag im Aktienbuch ausgewiesen oder vom Aktionär dazu schriftlich bevollmächtigt ist.

2 Die Mitgliedschaftsrechte aus Inhaberaktien kann ausüben, wer sich als Besitzer ausweist, indem er die Aktien vorlegt. Der Verwaltungsrat kann eine andere Art des Besitzesausweises anordnen.

3. Vertreter des Aktionärs

a. Im Allgemeinen

Art. 689b

1 Wer Mitwirkungsrechte als Vertreter ausübt, muss die Weisungen des Vertretenen befolgen.

2 Wer eine Inhaberaktie aufgrund einer Verpfändung, Hinterlegung oder leihweisen Überlassung besitzt, darf die Mitgliedschaftsrechte nur ausüben, wenn er vom Aktionär hierzu in einem besonderen Schriftstück bevollmächtigt wurde.

b. Organvertreter

Art. 689c

Schlägt die Gesellschaft den Aktionären ein Mitglied ihrer Organe oder eine andere abhängige Person für die Stimmrechtsvertretung an einer Generalversammlung vor, so muss sie zugleich eine unabhängige Person bezeichnen, die von den Aktionären mit der Vertretung beauftragt werden kann.

c. Depotvertreter

Art. 689d

1 Wer als Depotvertreter Mitwirkungsrechte aus Aktien, die bei ihm hinterlegt sind, ausüben will, ersucht den Hinterleger vor jeder Generalversammlung um Weisungen für die Stimmabgabe.

2 Sind Weisungen des Hinterlegers nicht rechtzeitig erhältlich, so übt der Depotvertreter das Stimmrecht nach einer allgemeinen Weisung des Hinterlegers aus; fehlt eine solche, so folgt er den Anträgen des Verwaltungsrates.

3 Als Depotvertreter gelten die dem Bankengesetz[23] unterstellten Institute sowie gewerbsmässige Vermögensverwalter.

---

23 SR **952.0**

Teil F: Rechtliche Aspekte / Legal aspects

d. Bekanntgabe

Art. 689e

1 Organe, unabhängige Stimmrechtsvertreter und Depotvertreter geben der Gesellschaft Anzahl, Art, Nennwert und Kategorie der von ihnen vertretenen Aktien bekannt. Unterbleiben diese Angaben, so sind die Beschlüsse der Generalversammlung unter den gleichen Voraussetzungen anfechtbar wie bei unbefugter Teilnahme an der Generalversammlung.

2 Der Vorsitzende teilt die Angaben gesamthaft für jede Vertretungsart der Generalversammlung mit. Unterlässt er dies, obschon ein Aktionär es verlangt hat, so kann jeder Aktionär die Beschlüsse der Generalversammlung mit Klage gegen die Gesellschaft anfechten.

4. Mehrere Berechtigte

Art. 690

1 Steht eine Aktie in gemeinschaftlichem Eigentum, so können die Berechtigten die Rechte aus der Aktie nur durch einen gemeinsamen Vertreter ausüben.

2 Im Falle der Nutzniessung an einer Aktie wird diese durch den Nutzniesser vertreten; er wird dem Eigentümer ersatzpflichtig, wenn er dabei dessen Interessen nicht in billiger Weise Rücksicht trägt.

II. Unbefugte Teilnahme

Art. 691

1 Die Überlassung von Aktien zum Zwecke der Ausübung des Stimmrechts in der Generalversammlung ist unstatthaft, wenn damit die Umgehung einer Stimmrechtsbeschränkung beabsichtigt ist.

2 Jeder Aktionär ist befugt, gegen die Teilnahme unberechtigter Personen beim Verwaltungsrat oder zu Protokoll der Generalversammlung Einspruch zu erheben.

3 Wirken Personen, die zur Teilnahme an der Generalversammlung nicht befugt sind, bei einem Beschlusse mit, so kann jeder Aktionär, auch wenn er nicht Einspruch erhoben hat, diesen Beschluss anfechten, sofern die beklagte Gesellschaft nicht nachweist, dass diese Mitwirkung keinen Einfluss auf die Beschlussfassung ausgeübt hatte.

III. Stimmrecht in der Generalversammlung

1. Grundsatz

Art. 692

1 Die Aktionäre üben ihr Stimmrecht in der Generalversammlung nach Verhältnis des gesamten Nennwerts der ihnen gehörenden Aktien aus.

2 Jeder Aktionär hat, auch wenn er nur eine Aktie besitzt, zum mindesten eine Stimme. Doch können die Statuten die Stimmenzahl der Besitzer mehrerer Aktien beschränken.

3 Bei der Herabsetzung des Nennwerts der Aktien im Fall einer Sanierung der Gesellschaft kann das Stimmrecht dem ursprünglichen Nennwert entsprechend beibehalten werden.

2. Stimmrechtsaktien

Art. 693

1 Die Statuten können das Stimmrecht unabhängig vom Nennwert nach der Zahl der jedem Aktionär gehörenden Aktien festsetzen, so dass auf jede Aktie eine Stimme entfällt.

2 In diesem Falle können Aktien, die einen kleineren Nennwert als andere Aktien der Gesellschaft haben, nur als Namenaktien ausgegeben werden und müssen voll liberiert sein. Der Nennwert der übrigen

Aktien darf das Zehnfache des Nennwertes der Stimmrechtsaktien nicht übersteigen.[24]

3 Die Bemessung des Stimmrechts nach der Zahl der Aktien ist nicht anwendbar für:

1. die Wahl der Revisionsstelle;
2. die Ernennung von Sachverständigen zur Prüfung der Geschäftsführung oder einzelner Teile;
3. die Beschlussfassung über die Einleitung einer Sonderprüfung;
4. die Beschlussfassung über die Anhebung einer Verantwortlichkeitsklage.[25]

3. Entstehung des Stimmrechts

Art. 694

Das Stimmrecht entsteht, sobald auf die Aktie der gesetzlich oder statutarisch festgesetzte Betrag einbezahlt ist.

4. Ausschliessung vom Stimmrecht

Art. 695

Bei Beschlüssen über die Entlastung des Verwaltungsrates haben Personen, die in irgendeiner Weise an der Geschäftsführung teilgenommen haben, kein Stimmrecht.

Bei der Beschlussfassung über die Entlastung des Verwaltungsrats haben Personen, die in irgendeiner Weise an der Geschäftsführung teilgenom-

---

24 Fassung gemäss Ziff. I des BG vom 4. Okt. 1991, in Kraft seit 1. Juli 1992 (AS 1992 733 786; BBl 1983 II 745).
25 Fassung gemäss Ziff. I des BG vom 4. Okt. 1991, in Kraft seit 1. Juli 1992 (AS 1992 733 786; BBl 1983 II 745).

men haben, kein Stimmrecht; sie haben von Gesetzes wegen in den Ausstand zu treten (Art. 695 Abs. 1 OR).

Der Revisionsstelle ist es auf Grund der verschärften Vorschriften zur Unabhängigkeit generell untersagt, an der Geschäftsführung der von ihr geprüften Gesellschaft mitzuwirken (Art. 728 Abs. 2 Ziff. 1 und Art. 729 Abs. 1 E OR). *Abs. 2* wird daher überflüssig. Zur Vermeidung unzutreffender Interpretationen sollte die Bestimmung gestrichen werden (vgl. auch Art. 887 Abs. 2 E OR zum Genossenschaftsrecht).

IV. Kontrollrechte der Aktionäre

1. Bekanngabe des Geschäftsberichtes

Art. 696

1 Spätestens 20 Tage vor der ordentlichen Generalversammlung sind der Geschäftsbericht und der Revisionsbericht den Aktionären am Gesellschaftssitz zur Einsicht aufzulegen. Jeder Aktionär kann verlangen, dass ihm unverzüglich eine Ausfertigung dieser Unterlagen zugestellt wird.

2 Namenaktionäre sind hierüber durch schriftliche Mitteilung zu unterrichten, Inhaberaktionäre durch Bekanntgabe im Schweizerischen Handelsamtsblatt sowie in der von den Statuten vorgeschriebenen Form.

3 Jeder Aktionär kann noch während eines Jahres nach der Generalversammlung von der Gesellschaft den Geschäftsbericht in der von der Generalversammlung genehmigten Form sowie den Revisionsbericht verlangen.

2. Auskunft und Einsicht

Art. 697

1 Jeder Aktionär ist berechtigt, an der Generalversammlung vom Verwaltungsrat Auskunft über die Angelegenheiten der Gesellschaft

und von der Revisionsstelle über Durchführung und Ergebnis ihrer Prüfung zu verlangen.

2 Die Auskunft ist insoweit zu erteilen, als sie für die Ausübung der Aktionärsrechte erforderlich ist. Sie kann verweigert werden, wenn durch sie Geschäftsgeheimnisse oder andere schutzwürdige Interessen der Gesellschaft gefährdet werden.

3 Die Geschäftsbücher und Korrespondenzen können nur mit ausdrücklicher Ermächtigung der Generalversammlung oder durch Beschluss des Verwaltungsrates und unter Wahrung der Geschäftsgeheimnisse eingesehen werden.

4 Wird die Auskunft oder die Einsicht ungerechtfertigterweise verweigert, so ordnet sie der Richter am Sitz der Gesellschaft auf Antrag an.

V. Recht auf Einleitung einer Sonderprüfung

1. Mit Genehmigung der Generalversammlung

Art. 697a

1 Jeder Aktionär kann der Generalversammlung beantragen, bestimmte Sachverhalte durch eine Sonderprüfung abklären zu lassen, sofern dies zur Ausübung der Aktionärsrechte erforderlich ist und er das Recht auf Auskunft oder das Recht auf Einsicht bereits ausgeübt hat.

2 Entspricht die Generalversammlung dem Antrag, so kann die Gesellschaft oder jeder Aktionär innert 30 Tagen den Richter um Einsetzung eines Sonderprüfers ersuchen.

2. Bei Ablehnung durch die Generalversammlung

Art. 697b

1 Entspricht die Generalversammlung dem Antrag nicht, so können Aktionäre, die zusammen mindestens 10 Prozent des Aktienkapitals

oder Aktien im Nennwert von 2 Millionen Franken vertreten, innert dreier Monate den Richter ersuchen, einen Sonderprüfer einzusetzen.

2 Die Gesuchsteller haben Anspruch auf Einsetzung eines Sonderprüfers, wenn sie glaubhaft machen, dass Gründer oder Organe Gesetz oder Statuten verletzt und damit die Gesellschaft oder die Aktionäre geschädigt haben.

3. Einsetzung

Art. 697c

1 Der Richter entscheidet nach Anhörung der Gesellschaft und des seinerzeitigen Antragstellers.

2 Entspricht der Richter dem Gesuch, so beauftragt er einen unabhängigen Sachverständigen mit der Durchführung der Prüfung. Er umschreibt im Rahmen des Gesuches den Prüfungsgegenstand.

3 Der Richter kann die Sonderprüfung auch mehreren Sachverständigen gemeinsam übertragen.

4. Tätigkeit

Art. 697d

1 Die Sonderprüfung ist innert nützlicher Frist und ohne unnötige Störung des Geschäftsganges durchzuführen.

2 Gründer, Organe, Beauftragte, Arbeitnehmer, Sachwalter und Liquidatoren müssen dem Sonderprüfer Auskunft über erhebliche Tatsachen erteilen. Im Streitfall entscheidet der Richter.

3 Der Sonderprüfer hört die Gesellschaft zu den Ergebnissen der Sonderprüfung an.

4 Er ist zur Verschwiegenheit verpflichtet.

Teil F: Rechtliche Aspekte / Legal aspects

5. Bericht

Art. 697e

1 Der Sonderprüfer berichtet einlässlich über das Ergebnis seiner Prüfung, wahrt aber das Geschäftsgeheimnis. Er legt seinen Bericht dem Richter vor.

2 Der Richter stellt den Bericht der Gesellschaft zu und entscheidet auf ihr Begehren, ob Stellen des Berichtes das Geschäftsgeheimnis oder andere schutzwürdige Interessen der Gesellschaft verletzen und deshalb den Gesuchstellern nicht vorgelegt werden sollen.

3 Er gibt der Gesellschaft und den Gesuchstellern Gelegenheit, zum bereinigten Bericht Stellung zu nehmen und Ergänzungsfragen zu stellen.

6. Behandlung und Bekanntgabe

Art. 697f

1 Der Verwaltungsrat unterbreitet der nächsten Generalversammlung den Bericht und die Stellungnahmen dazu.

2 Jeder Aktionär kann während eines Jahres nach der Generalversammlung von der Gesellschaft eine Ausfertigung des Berichtes und der Stellungnahmen verlangen.

7. Kostentragung

Art. 697g

1 Entspricht der Richter dem Gesuch um Einsetzung eines Sonderprüfers, so überbindet er den Vorschuss und die Kosten der Gesellschaft. Wenn besondere Umstände es rechtfertigen, kann er die Kosten ganz oder teilweise den Gesuchstellern auferlegen.

Kapitel 1: Neue Gesetzesbestimmungen und Erläuterungen

2 Hat die Generalversammlung der Sonderprüfung zugestimmt, so trägt die Gesellschaft die Kosten.

K. Offenlegung von Jahresrechnung und Konzernrechnung

Art. 697h

1 Jahresrechnung und Konzernrechnung sind nach der Abnahme durch die Generalversammlung mit den Revisionsberichten entweder im Schweizerischen Handelsamtsblatt zu veröffentlichen oder jeder Person, die es innerhalb eines Jahres seit Abnahme verlangt, auf deren Kosten in einer Ausfertigung zuzustellen, wenn

1. die Gesellschaft Anleihensobligationen ausstehend hat;
2. die Aktien der Gesellschaft an einer Börse kotiert sind.

2 Die übrigen Aktiengesellschaften müssen den Gläubigern, die ein schutzwürdiges Interesse nachweisen, Einsicht in die Jahresrechnung, die Konzernrechnung und die Revisionsberichte gewähren. Im Streitfall entscheidet der Richter.

Dritter Abschnitt: Organisation der Aktiengesellschaft

A. Die Generalversammlung

I. Befugnisse

Art. 698

1 Oberstes Organ der Aktiengesellschaft ist die Generalversammlung der Aktionäre.

2 Ihr stehen folgende unübertragbare Befugnisse zu:

1. die Festsetzung und Änderung der Statuten;

2. die Wahl der Mitglieder des Verwaltungsrates und der Revisionsstelle;

3. die Genehmigung des Jahresberichtes und der Konzernrechnung;

4. die Genehmigung der Jahresrechnung sowie die Beschlussfassung über die Verwendung des Bilanzgewinnes, insbesondere die Festsetzung der Dividende und der Tantieme;

5. die Entlastung der Mitglieder des Verwaltungsrates;

6. die Beschlussfassung über die Gegenstände, die der Generalversammlung durch das Gesetz oder die Statuten vorbehalten sind. [26]

II. Einberufung und Traktandierung

1. Recht und Pflicht

Art. 699

1 Die Generalversammlung wird durch den Verwaltungsrat, nötigenfalls durch die Revisionsstelle einberufen. Das Einberufungsrecht steht auch den Liquidatoren und den Vertretern der Anleihensgläubiger zu.

2 Die ordentliche Versammlung findet alljährlich innerhalb sechs Monaten nach Schluss des Geschäftsjahres statt, ausserordentliche Versammlungen werden je nach Bedürfnis einberufen.

3 Die Einberufung einer Generalversammlung kann auch von einem oder mehreren Aktionären, die zusammen mindestens 10 Prozent des Aktienkapitals vertreten, verlangt werden. Aktionäre, die Aktien im Nennwerte von 1 Million Franken vertreten, können die Traktandierung eines Verhandlungsgegenstandes verlangen. Einberufung und Traktandierung werden schriftlich unter Angabe des Verhandlungsgegenstandes und der Anträge anbegehrt. [27]

---

26 Fassung gemäss Ziff. I des BG vom 4. Okt. 1991, in Kraft seit 1. Juli 1992 (AS 1992 733 786; BBl 1983 II 745).
27 Fassung gemäss Ziff. I des BG vom 4. Okt. 1991, in Kraft seit 1. Juli 1992 (AS 1992 733 786; BBl 1983 II 745).

4 Entspricht der Verwaltungsrat diesem Begehren nicht binnen angemessener Frist, so hat der Richter auf Antrag der Gesuchsteller die Einberufung anzuordnen.

2. Form

Art. 700

1 Die Generalversammlung ist spätestens 20 Tage vor dem Versammlungstag in der durch die Statuten vorgeschriebenen Form einzuberufen.

2 In der Einberufung sind die Verhandlungsgegenstände sowie die Anträge des Verwaltungsrates und der Aktionäre bekanntzugeben, welche die Durchführung einer Generalversammlung oder die Traktandierung eines Verhandlungsgegenstandes verlangt haben.

3 Über Anträge zu nicht gehörig angekündigten Verhandlungsgegenständen können keine Beschlüsse gefasst werden; ausgenommen sind Anträge auf Einberufung einer ausserordentlichen Generalversammlung oder auf Durchführung einer Sonderprüfung.

4 Zur Stellung von Anträgen im Rahmen der Verhandlungsgegenstände und zu Verhandlungen ohne Beschlussfassung bedarf es keiner vorgängigen Ankündigung.

3. Universalversammlung

Art. 701

1 Die Eigentümer oder Vertreter sämtlicher Aktien können, falls kein Widerspruch erhoben wird, eine Generalversammlung ohne Einhaltung der für die Einberufung vorgeschriebenen Formvorschriften abhalten.

2 In dieser Versammlung kann über alle in den Geschäftskreis der Generalversammlung fallenden Gegenstände gültig verhandelt und

Beschluss gefasst werden, solange die Eigentümer oder Vertreter sämtlicher Aktien anwesend sind.

III. Vorbereitende Massnahmen; Protokoll

Art. 702

1 Der Verwaltungsrat trifft die für die Feststellung der Stimmrechte erforderlichen Anordnungen.

2 Er sorgt für die Führung des Protokolls. Dieses hält fest:

1. Anzahl, Art, Nennwert und Kategorie der Aktien, die von den Aktionären, von den Organen, von unabhängigen Stimmrechtsvertretern und von Depotvertretern vertreten werden;
2. die Beschlüsse und die Wahlergebnisse;
3. die Begehren um Auskunft und die darauf erteilten Antworten;
4. die von den Aktionären zu Protokoll gegebenen Erklärungen.

3 Die Aktionäre sind berechtigt, das Protokoll einzusehen.

IV. Teilnahme der Mitglieder des Verwaltungsrates an des Verwaltungsrates

Art. 702a

Die Mitglieder des Verwaltungsrates sind berechtigt, an der Generalversammlung teilzunehmen. Sie können Anträge stellen.

Der Entwurf sieht vom Erfordernis ab, dass die Mitglieder des Verwaltungsrates mindestens eine Aktie halten müssen («Pflichtaktie»; s. Art. 707 Abs. 1 E OR). Auch wenn sie nicht Aktionärinnen oder Aktionäre sind, müssen sie dennoch an der Generalversammlung teilnehmen und Anträge stellen können.

V. Beschlussfassung und Wahlen

1. Im Allgemeinen

Art. 703

Die Generalversammlung fasst ihre Beschlüsse und vollzieht ihre Wahlen, soweit das Gesetz oder die Statuten es nicht anders bestimmen, mit der absoluten Mehrheit der vertretenen Aktienstimmen.

Art. 703 Randtitel

Geändert wird nur die Nummerierung des Randtitels.

2. Wichtige Beschlüsse

Art. 704

1 Ein Beschluss der Generalversammlung, der mindestens zwei Drittel der vertretenen Stimmen und die absolute Mehrheit der vertretenen Aktiennennwerte auf sich vereinigt, ist erforderlich für:

1. die Änderung des Gesellschaftszweckes;
2. die Einführung von Stimmrechtsaktien;
3. die Beschränkung der Übertragbarkeit von Namenaktien;
4. eine genehmigte oder eine bedingte Kapitalerhöhung;
5. die Kapitalerhöhung aus Eigenkapital, gegen Sacheinlage oder zwecks Sachübernahme und die Gewährung von besonderen Vorteilen;
6. die Einschränkung oder Aufhebung des Bezugsrechtes;
7. die Verlegung des Sitzes der Gesellschaft;
8. die Auflösung der Gesellschaft.

2 Statutenbestimmungen, die für die Fassung bestimmter Beschlüsse grössere Mehrheiten als die vom Gesetz vorgeschriebenen festlegen, können nur mit dem vorgesehenen Mehr eingeführt werden.

3 Namenaktionäre, die einem Beschluss über die Zweckänderung oder die Einführung von Stimmrechtsaktien nicht zugestimmt haben, sind während sechs Monaten nach dessen Veröffentlichung im Schweizerischen Handelsamtsblatt an statutarische Beschränkungen der Übertragbarkeit der Aktien nicht gebunden.

Nach dem bisherigen Recht gilt nur die Auflösung einer Aktiengesellschaft ohne Liquidation als wichtiger Beschluss, nicht aber die Auflösung mit Liquidation. Da die Auflösung jedoch in jedem Fall für alle an einer Gesellschaft beteiligten Personen von grösster Bedeutung sein kann, sollen für den Auflösungsbeschluss in Übereinstimmung mit dem GmbH-Recht stets die Anforderungen an wichtige Beschlüsse beachtet werden (vgl. Art. 808*b* Abs. 1 Ziff. 10 E OR). Die so genannte Auflösung ohne Liquidation (so insbesondere durch Fusion) wird zukünftig im Fusionsgesetz geregelt[28].

VI. Abberufung des Verwaltungsrates und der Revisionsstelle

Art. 705

1 Die Generalversammlung ist berechtigt, die Mitglieder des Verwaltungsrates und der Revisionsstelle sowie allfällige von ihr gewählte Bevollmächtigte und Beauftragte abzuberufen.

2 Entschädigungsansprüche der Abberufenen bleiben vorbehalten.

VII. Anfechtung von Generalversammlungsbeschlüssen

1. Legitimation und Gründe

Art. 706

1 Der Verwaltungsrat und jeder Aktionär können Beschlüsse der Generalversammlung, die gegen das Gesetz oder die Statuten verstossen, beim Richter mit Klage gegen die Gesellschaft anfechten.

---

28 s. Art. 18 und Art. 43 Abs. 2 E FusG; BBl 2000 4539 und 4548.

2 Anfechtbar sind insbesondere Beschlüsse, die

1. unter Verletzung von Gesetz oder Statuten Rechte von Aktionären entziehen oder beschränken;
2. in unsachlicher Weise Rechte von Aktionären entziehen oder beschränken;
3. eine durch den Gesellschaftszweck nicht gerechtfertigte Ungleichbehandlung oder Benachteiligung der Aktionäre bewirken;
4. die Gewinnstrebigkeit der Gesellschaft ohne Zustimmung sämtlicher Aktionäre aufheben.[29]

3–4 ...[30]

5 Das Urteil, das einen Beschluss der Generalversammlung aufhebt, wirkt für und gegen alle Aktionäre.

2. Verfahren

Art. 706a

1 Das Anfechtungsrecht erlischt, wenn die Klage nicht spätestens zwei Monate nach der Generalversammlung angehoben wird.

2 Ist der Verwaltungsrat Kläger, so bestellt der Richter einen Vertreter für die Gesellschaft.

3 Der Richter verteilt die Kosten bei Abweisung der Klage nach seinem Ermessen auf die Gesellschaft und den Kläger.

---

29 Fassung gemäss Ziff. I des BG vom 4. Okt. 1991, in Kraft seit 1. Juli 1992 (AS 1992 733 786; BBl 1983 II 745).
30 Aufgehoben durch Ziff. I des BG vom 4. Okt. 1991 (AS 1992 733; BBl 1983 II 745).

VIII. Nichtigkeit

Art. 706b

Nichtig sind insbesondere Beschlüsse der Generalversammlung, die:

1. **das Recht auf Teilnahme an der Generalversammlung, das Mindeststimmrecht, die Klagerechte oder andere vom Gesetz zwingend gewährte Rechte des Aktionärs entziehen oder beschränken;**
2. **Kontrollrechte von Aktionären über das gesetzlich zulässige Mass hinaus beschränken oder**
3. **die Grundstrukturen der Aktiengesellschaft missachten oder die Bestimmungen zum Kapitalschutz verletzen.**

Geändert wird nur die Nummerierung der Randtitel.

B. Der Verwaltungsrat

I. Im Allgemeinen

1. Wählbarkeit

Art. 707

1 Der Verwaltungsrat der Gesellschaft besteht aus einem oder mehreren Mitgliedern.

2 Ist an der Gesellschaft eine juristische Person oder eine Handelsgesellschaft beteiligt, so ist sie als solche nicht als Mitglied des Verwaltungsrates wählbar; dagegen können an ihrer Stelle ihre Vertreter gewählt werden.

Nach dem geltenden Recht müssen die Mitglieder des Verwaltungsrates Aktionärinnen oder Aktionäre sein (*Abs. 1*). Werden andere Personen in den Verwaltungsrat gewählt, so dürfen sie ihr Amt erst antreten, nachdem sie Aktionärinnen beziehungsweise Aktionäre geworden sind (*Abs. 2*). Zwar erscheint der Gedanke, dass die Mitglieder des Verwaltungsrates an der Gesellschaft beteiligt sein sollten, um das wirtschaftliche Risiko mitzutragen, grundsätzlich nach wie vor zutreffend. Für die Erfüllung der gesetzlichen Voraussetzung der Aktionärseigenschaft genügt allerdings das Eigentum an einer einzigen Aktie, die zudem treuhänderisch gehalten werden darf. Das Erfordernis einer «Pflichtaktie» kommt demzufolge einer blossen Formalie gleich und wurde daher in der Literatur zu Recht hinterfragt[31]. Anders als im Aktienrecht kann die Geschäftsführung in der GmbH sowohl nach dem geltenden Recht als auch nach dem Entwurf an Personen übertragen werden, die nicht Gesellschafterinnen oder Gesellschafter zu sein brauchen (s. Art. 812 OR; Art. 809 Abs. 1 E OR). Es wird vorgeschlagen, die Wahlvoraussetzungen für Mitglieder des Verwaltungsrates mit dem GmbH-Recht zu harmonisieren und auf das Erfordernis einer «Pflichtaktie» zu verzichten. In der Folge muss die Teilnahme der Mitglieder des Verwaltungsrats an der Generalversammlung klargestellt werden (s. Art. 702a E OR).

Art. 708

Aufgehoben

Nach Art. 708 OR müssen die Mitglieder des Verwaltungsrats mehrheitlich Personen sein, die in der Schweiz wohnhaft sind und das Schweizer Bürgerrecht besitzen. Für Holdinggesellschaften mit Beteiligungen im Ausland können Ausnahmen von dieser Regel bewilligt werden, wobei stets ein zur Vertretung der Gesellschaft befugtes Mitglied des Verwaltungsrates in der Schweiz wohnhaft sein muss. Diese Regelung erscheint in einer zunehmend internationalen Wirtschaft nicht mehr sachgerecht: Sie schafft einen Standortnachteil und kann Diskriminierungen von in der Schweiz lebenden Personen mit ausländischem Bürgerrecht bewirken. Der Entwurf schlägt daher vor, für die GmbH und die Aktiengesellschaft eine einheitliche Neuregelung zu schaffen (vgl. Art. 814 E OR). Es soll nur noch verlangt werden, dass eine der Personen, welche die Gesellschaft vertreten können, in der Schweiz Wohnsitz hat. Dabei kann es sich um ein Mitglied des Verwaltungsrates, aber auch um eine Direktorin oder einen

---

31 s. insbes. PETER BÖCKLI, Schweizer Aktienrecht, 2. Aufl., Zürich 1996, N 1467 ff.; PETER FORSTMOSER/ARTHUR MEIER-HAYOZ/PETER NOBEL, Schweizerisches Aktienrecht, Bern 1996, § 27 N 2 ff.; MARTIN WEHRLI, in: Kommentar zum schweizerischen Privatrecht, Obligationenrecht II, Basel und Frankfurt a.M. 1994, Art. 707 N 6 ff.

Direktor handeln (Art. 718 Abs. 3 E OR; es wird auf die Ausführungen zu Art. 814 E OR verwiesen).

2. Vertretung von Aktionärskategorien und -gruppen

Art. 709

1 Bestehen in Bezug auf das Stimmrecht oder die vermögensrechtlichen Ansprüche mehrere Kategorien von Aktien, so ist durch die Statuten den Aktionären jeder Kategorie die Wahl wenigstens eines Vertreters im Verwaltungsrat zu sichern.

2 Die Statuten können besondere Bestimmungen zum Schutz von Minderheiten oder einzelnen Gruppen von Aktionären vorsehen.

3. Amtsdauer

Art. 710

1 Die Mitglieder des Verwaltungsrates werden auf drei Jahre gewählt, sofern die Statuten nichts anderes bestimmen. Die Amtsdauer darf jedoch sechs Jahre nicht übersteigen.

2 Wiederwahl ist möglich.

Geändert wird nur die Nummerierung der Randtitel.

Art. 711

Aufgehoben

Das geltende Recht regelt in diesem Artikel die Anmeldung des Ausscheidens von Mitgliedern des Verwaltungsrates beim Handelsregister. Der Entwurf sieht in Bezug auf die Löschung von Personen, die als Mitglied eines Organs im Handelsregister eingetragen sind, eine einheitliche

Ordnung für alle juristischen Personen vor (s. Art. 938*b* E OR). Die vorliegende Bestimmung kann daher aufgehoben werden.

II. Organisation

1. Präsident und Sekretär

Art. 712

1 Der Verwaltungsrat bezeichnet seinen Präsidenten und den Sekretär. Dieser muss dem Verwaltungsrat nicht angehören.

2 Die Statuten können bestimmen, dass der Präsident durch die Generalversammlung gewählt wird.

2. Beschlüsse

Art. 713

1 Die Beschlüsse des Verwaltungsrates werden mit der Mehrheit der abgegebenen Stimmen gefasst. Der Vorsitzende hat den Stichentscheid, sofern die Statuten nichts anderes vorsehen.

2 Beschlüsse können auch auf dem Wege der schriftlichen Zustimmung zu einem gestellten Antrag gefasst werden, sofern nicht ein Mitglied die mündliche Beratung verlangt.

3 Über die Verhandlungen und Beschlüsse ist ein Protokoll zu führen, das vom Vorsitzenden und vom Sekretär unterzeichnet wird.

3. Nichtige Beschlüsse

Art. 714

Für die Beschlüsse des Verwaltungsrates gelten sinngemäss die gleichen Nichtigkeitsgründe wie für die Beschlüsse der Generalversammlung.

4. Recht auf Einberufung

Art. 715

Jedes Mitglied des Verwaltungsrates kann unter Angabe der Gründe vom Präsidenten die unverzügliche Einberufung einer Sitzung verlangen.

5. Recht auf Auskunft und Einsicht

Art. 715a

1 Jedes Mitglied des Verwaltungsrates kann Auskunft über alle Angelegenheiten der Gesellschaft verlangen.

2 In den Sitzungen sind alle Mitglieder des Verwaltungsrates sowie die mit der Geschäftsführung betrauten Personen zur Auskunft verpflichtet.

3 Ausserhalb der Sitzungen kann jedes Mitglied von den mit der Geschäftsführung betrauten Personen Auskunft über den Geschäftsgang und, mit Ermächtigung des Präsidenten, auch über einzelne Geschäfte verlangen.

4 Soweit es für die Erfüllung einer Aufgabe erforderlich ist, kann jedes Mitglied dem Präsidenten beantragen, dass ihm Bücher und Akten vorgelegt werden.

5 Weist der Präsident ein Gesuch auf Auskunft, Anhörung oder Einsicht ab, so entscheidet der Verwaltungsrat.

6 Regelungen oder Beschlüsse des Verwaltungsrates, die das Recht auf Auskunft und Einsichtnahme der Verwaltungsräte erweitern, bleiben vorbehalten.

Kapitel 1: Neue Gesetzesbestimmungen und Erläuterungen

III. Aufgaben

1. Im Allgemeinen

Art. 716

1 Der Verwaltungsrat kann in allen Angelegenheiten Beschluss fassen, die nicht nach Gesetz oder Statuten der Generalversammlung zugeteilt sind.

2 Der Verwaltungsrat führt die Geschäfte der Gesellschaft, soweit er die Geschäftsführung nicht übertragen hat.

2. Unübertragbare Aufgaben

Art. 716a

1 Der Verwaltungsrat hat folgende unübertragbare und unentziehbare Aufgaben:

1. die Oberleitung der Gesellschaft und die Erteilung der nötigen Weisungen;
2. die Festlegung der Organisation;
3. die Ausgestaltung des Rechnungswesens, der Finanzkontrolle sowie der Finanzplanung, sofern diese für die Führung der Gesellschaft notwendig ist;
4. die Ernennung und Abberufung der mit der Geschäftsführung und der Vertretung betrauten Personen;
5. die Oberaufsicht über die mit der Geschäftsführung betrauten Personen, namentlich im Hinblick auf die Befolgung der Gesetze, Statuten, Reglemente und Weisungen;
6. die Erstellung des Geschäftsberichtes[32] sowie die Vorbereitung der Generalversammlung und die Ausführung ihrer Beschlüsse;
7. die Benachrichtigung des Richters im Falle der Überschuldung.

---

32 Berichtigt von der Redaktionskommission der BVers [Art. 33 GVG – AS 1974 1051].

2 Der Verwaltungsrat kann die Vorbereitung und die Ausführung seiner Beschlüsse oder die Überwachung von Geschäften Ausschüssen oder einzelnen Mitgliedern zuweisen. Er hat für eine angemessene Berichterstattung an seine Mitglieder zu sorgen.

3. Übertragung der Geschäftsführung

Art. 716b

1 Die Statuten können den Verwaltungsrat ermächtigen, die Geschäftsführung nach Massgabe eines Organisationsreglementes ganz oder zum Teil an einzelne Mitglieder oder an Dritte zu übertragen.

2 Dieses Reglement ordnet die Geschäftsführung, bestimmt die hierfür erforderlichen Stellen, umschreibt deren Aufgaben und regelt insbesondere die Berichterstattung. Der Verwaltungsrat orientiert Aktionäre und Gesellschaftsgläubiger, die ein schutzwürdiges Interesse glaubhaft machen, auf Anfrage hin schriftlich über die Organisation der Geschäftsführung.

3 Soweit die Geschäftsführung nicht übertragen worden ist, steht sie allen Mitgliedern des Verwaltungsrates gesamthaft zu.

IV. Sorgfalts- und Treuepflicht

Art. 717

1 Die Mitglieder des Verwaltungsrates sowie Dritte, die mit der Geschäftsführung befasst sind, müssen ihre Aufgaben mit aller Sorgfalt erfüllen und die Interessen der Gesellschaft in guten Treuen wahren.

2 Sie haben die Aktionäre unter gleichen Voraussetzungen gleich zu behandeln.

Kapitel 1: Neue Gesetzesbestimmungen und Erläuterungen

V. Vertretung

1. Im Allgemeinen

Art. 718 (ursprünglicher Botschaftsentwurf)

1 Der Verwaltungsrat vertritt die Gesellschaft nach aussen. Bestimmen die Statuten oder das Organisationsreglement nichts anderes, so steht die Vertretungsbefugnis jedem Mitglied einzeln zu.

2 Der Verwaltungsrat kann die Vertretung einem oder mehreren Mitgliedern (Delegierte) oder Dritten (Direktoren) übertragen.

3 Eine der Personen, die die Gesellschaft vertreten können, muss Wohnsitz in der Schweiz haben. Hat kein zur Vertretung befugtes Mitglied des Verwaltungsrats Wohnsitz in der Schweiz, so muss ein Direktor mit Wohnsitz in der Schweiz mit der Vertretung der Gesellschaft betraut werden.

Art. 718 (durch den Nationalrat bereinigte Version)

3 Die Gesellschaft muss durch eine Person vertreten werden können, die Wohnsitz in der Schweiz hat. Dieses Erfordernis kann durch ein Mitglied des Verwaltungsrates oder einen Direktor erfüllt werden.

Der neue *Abs. 3* tritt an die Stelle von Art. 708 OR und stimmt mit Art. 814 E OR im GmbH-Recht überein. Es kann auf die Ausführungen zu diesen beiden Bestimmungen verwiesen werden.[33]

---

33 Die vorliegenden Erläuterungen beziehen sich ausschliesslich auf die ursprüngliche bundesrätliche Gesetzesversion und nicht auf die bereinigte Fassung durch den Nationalrat.

511

2. Umfang und Beschränkung

Art. 718a

1 Die zur Vertretung befugten Personen können im Namen der Gesellschaft alle Rechtshandlungen vornehmen, die der Zweck der Gesellschaft mit sich bringen kann.

2 Eine Beschränkung dieser Vertretungsbefugnis hat gegenüber gutgläubigen Dritten keine Wirkung; ausgenommen sind die im Handelsregister eingetragenen Bestimmungen über die ausschliessliche Vertretung der Hauptniederlassung oder einer Zweigniederlassung oder über die gemeinsame Vertretung der Gesellschaft.

3. Verträge zwischen der Gesellschaft und ihrer Vertreterin oder ihrem Vertreter

Art. 718b

Wird die Gesellschaft beim Abschluss eines Vertrages durch diejenige Person vertreten, mit der sie den Vertrag abschliesst, so muss der Vertrag schriftlich abgefasst werden. Dieses Erfordernis gilt nicht für Verträge des laufenden Geschäfts, bei denen die Leistung der Gesellschaft den Wert von 1000 Franken nicht übersteigt.

Der Vorentwurf sah in Anlehnung an das Recht der Europäischen Gemeinschaft[34] vor, dass Verträge zwischen einer Alleinaktionärin oder einem Alleinaktionär und der von dieser Person vertretenen Gesellschaft schriftlich abzuschliessen sind. Ausgenommen blieben Verträge des laufenden Geschäfts zu Marktbedingungen (Art. 717 Abs. 3 VE OR). Diese Regelung wurde in der Vernehmlassung überwiegend begrüsst, da sie der Rechtsklarheit und damit den Interessen aller Betroffenen diene. Es wurde jedoch eingewendet, es sei nicht einzusehen, wieso diese Bestimmung nur für Einpersonengesellschaften gelten solle. Auch sei die Einschränkung auf Verträge, die nicht zu Marktbedingungen abgeschlossen werden, zu wenig klar.

---

34 s. Art. 5 der 12. Richtlinie; 89/667/EWG; ABl Nr. L 395 vom 30.12.1989, S. 40 ff.

Der Entwurf nimmt diese Kritik auf und verlangt für Verträge zwischen der Gesellschaft und derjenigen Person, durch welche die Gesellschaft beim Vertragsschluss vertreten wird, allgemein die Schriftform[35]. Dabei muss ohne Belang bleiben, ob es sich um eine Einpersonengesellschaft handelt. Um den Anforderungen der Praxis gerecht zu werden, soll im Rahmen des laufenden Geschäfts bis zum Betrag von 1000 Franken auf die Schriftlichkeit verzichtet werden dürfen. Ohne besondere Form gültig sind demnach Kleinverträge im Bereich des üblichen Geschäfts der Gesellschaft. Die Freigrenze bezieht sich auf Preise, wie sie Dritten verrechnet werden. Der Wert der Leistung innerlich zusammenhängender Verträge ist zusammenzurechnen. Verträge, die Leistungen beinhalten, die sich nicht in Geld beziffern lassen, sind stets schriftlich abzufassen. Die vorgesehene Formvorschrift findet auch für die GmbH und die Genossenschaft Anwendung (Art. 814 Abs. 4 und 899*a* E OR).

4. Zeichnung

Art. 719

Die zur Vertretung der Gesellschaft befugten Personen haben in der Weise zu zeichnen, dass sie der Firma der Gesellschaft ihre Unterschrift beifügen.

5. Eintragung

Art. 720

Die zur Vertretung der Gesellschaft befugten Personen sind vom Verwaltungsrat zur Eintragung in das Handelsregister anzumelden, unter Vorlegung einer beglaubigten Abschrift des Beschlusses. Sie haben ihre Unterschrift beim Handelsregisteramt zu zeichnen oder die Zeichnung in beglaubigter Form einzureichen.

---

35 vgl. Art. 11 ff. OR. Vorbehalten bleiben weitergehende andere gesetzliche Formvorschriften.

6. Prokuristen und Bevollmächtigte

Art. 721

Der Verwaltungsrat kann Prokuristen und andere Bevollmächtigte ernennen.

Art. 719, 720 und 721 Randtitel

Geändert wird nur die Nummerierung der Randtitel.

VI. Haftung der Organe

Art. 722

Die Gesellschaft haftet für den Schaden aus unerlaubten Handlungen, die eine zur Geschäftsführung oder zur Vertretung befugte Person in Ausübung ihrer geschäftlichen Verrichtungen begeht.

Art. 722 Randtitel

Der Randtitel wird rein redaktionell modifiziert.

VII. Kapitalverlust und Überschuldung

1. Anzeigepflichten

Art. 725

1 Zeigt die letzte Jahresbilanz, dass die Hälfte des Aktienkapitals und der gesetzlichen Reserven nicht mehr gedeckt ist, so beruft der Verwaltungsrat unverzüglich eine Generalversammlung ein und beantragt ihr Sanierungsmassnahmen.

2 Wenn begründete Besorgnis einer Überschuldung besteht, muss eine Zwischenbilanz erstellt und diese einem zugelassenen Revisor zur Prüfung vorgelegt werden. Ergibt sich aus der Zwischenbilanz, dass die Forderungen der Gesellschaftsgläubiger weder zu Fortführungs- noch zu Veräusserungswerten gedeckt sind, so hat der Verwaltungsrat den Richter zu benachrichtigen, sofern nicht Gesellschaftsgläubiger im Ausmass dieser Unterdeckung im Rang hinter alle anderen Gesellschaftsgläubiger zurücktreten.

3 Verfügt die Gesellschaft über keine Revisionsstelle, so obliegen dem zugelassenen Revisor die Anzeigepflichten der eingeschränkt prüfenden Revisionsstelle.

Art. 725 Abs. 2 OR sieht vor, dass bei begründeter Besorgnis einer Überschuldung eine Zwischenbilanz erstellt und diese der Revisionsstelle zur Prüfung vorgelegt werden muss. Gegebenenfalls muss der Verwaltungsrat oder die Revisionsstelle (Art. 728*c* Abs. 3 und Art. 729*c* E OR) das zuständige Gericht über die Überschuldung informieren. Die Prüfung durch die Revisionsstelle bezweckt einerseits, die Beschönigung der finanziellen Situation zu verhindern, und andererseits, den gerichtlichen Entscheid über das weitere Vorgehen auf gesicherte Zahlen abzustützen.

Auch *Abs. 2* muss der Tatsache angepasst werden, dass eine Aktiengesellschaft nach dem Entwurf nicht in jedem Fall über eine Revisionsstelle verfügt (s. Art. 727*a* Abs. 2 E OR). Es wird daher vorgesehen, dass die Gesellschaft die Zwischenbilanz in jedem Fall durch eine zugelassene Revisorin oder einen zugelassenen Revisor prüfen lassen muss. Verfügt die Gesellschaft über eine entsprechend ausgestaltete Revisionsstelle, kann – wie bisher – diese die Revision vornehmen.

Verfügt die Gesellschaft über keine Revisionsstelle, so obliegen der zugelassenen Revisorin oder dem zugelassenen Revisor, die oder der mit der Prüfung der Zwischenbilanz betraut ist, nach *Abs. 3* dieselben Anzeigepflichten wie einer eingeschränkt prüfenden Revisionsstelle. Wer den Zwischenabschluss prüft, hat daher gemäss Art. 729*c* E OR das Gericht zu benachrichtigen, wenn die Gesellschaft offensichtlich überschuldet ist und der Verwaltungsrat die Überschuldungsanzeige unterlässt.

2. Eröffnung oder Aufschub des Konkurses

Art. 725a

1 Der Richter eröffnet auf die Benachrichtigung hin den Konkurs. Er kann ihn auf Antrag des Verwaltungsrates oder eines Gläubigers aufschieben, falls Aussicht auf Sanierung besteht; in diesem Falle trifft er Massnahmen zur Erhaltung des Vermögens.

2 Der Richter kann einen Sachwalter bestellen und entweder dem Verwaltungsrat die Verfügungsbefugnis entziehen oder dessen Beschlüsse von der Zustimmung des Sachwalters abhängig machen. Er umschreibt die Aufgaben des Sachwalters.

3 Der Konkursaufschub muss nur veröffentlicht werden, wenn dies zum Schutze Dritter erforderlich ist.

VIII. Abberufung und Einstellung

Art. 726

1 Der Verwaltungsrat kann die von ihm bestellten Ausschüsse, Delegierten, Direktoren und andern Bevollmächtigten und Beauftragten jederzeit abberufen.

2 Die von der Generalversammlung bestellten Bevollmächtigten und Beauftragten können vom Verwaltungsrat jederzeit in ihren Funktionen eingestellt werden, unter sofortiger Einberufung einer Generalversammlung.

3 Entschädigungsansprüche der Abberufenen oder in ihren Funktionen Eingestellten bleiben vorbehalten.

C. Die Revisionsstelle

I. Revisionspflicht

Die Vorschriften in Art. 727 und 727a E OR regeln die Verpflichtung zur Revision und Art der Revision (ordentliche Revision, s. Art. 728 ff. E OR, oder eingeschränkte Revision, s. Art. 729 ff. E OR).

1. Ordentliche Revision

Art. 727 (ursprünglicher Botschaftsentwurf)

1 Folgende Gesellschaften müssen ihre Jahresrechnung und gegebenenfalls ihre Konzernrechnung durch eine Revisionsstelle ordentlich prüfen lassen:

1. Publikumsgesellschaften; als solche gelten Gesellschaften, die:
   a. Beteiligungspapiere an einer Börse kotiert haben,
   b. Anleihensobligationen ausstehend haben,
   c. mindestens 20 Prozent der Aktiven oder des Umsatzes zur Konzernrechnung einer Gesellschaft nach lit. a oder b beitragen;
2. Gesellschaften, die zwei der nachstehenden Grössen in zwei aufeinander folgenden Geschäftsjahren überschreiten:
   a. Bilanzsumme von 6 Millionen Franken,
   b. Umsatzerlös von 12 Millionen Franken,
   c. 50 Vollzeitstellen im Jahresdurchschnitt;
3. Gesellschaften, die zur Erstellung einer Konzernrechnung verpflichtet sind.

2 Eine ordentliche Revision muss auch dann vorgenommen werden, wenn Aktionäre, die zusammen mindestens 10 Prozent des Aktienkapitals vertreten, dies verlangen.

3 Verlangt das Gesetz keine ordentliche Revision der Jahresrechnung, so können die Statuten vorsehen oder kann die Generalversammlung beschliessen, dass die Jahresrechnung ordentlich geprüft wird.

Art. 727 (durch den Nationalrat bereinigte Version)
2. Gesellschaften, die zwei der nachstehenden Grössen in zwei aufeinander folgenden Geschäftsjahren überschreiten:

   a. **Bilanzsumme von 10 Millionen Franken,**

   b. **Umsatzerlös von 20 Millionen Franken,**

Abs. 1 bestimmt, welche Gesellschaften ihre Jahresrechnung (s. dazu Art. 662 ff. OR) und gegebenenfalls (d.h. soweit die Pflicht zur Erstellung einer Konzernrechnung besteht, s. dazu Art. 663e ff. OR) ihre Konzernrechnung durch eine Revisionsstelle ordentlich prüfen lassen müssen. Die ordentliche Revision wird inhaltlich durch die Art. 728 ff. umschrieben.

Gemäss *Ziff. 1* müssen Publikumsgesellschaften ihre Jahresabschlüsse ordentlich revidieren lassen. Durch diese Bestimmung sollen alle Gesellschaften erfasst werden, die direkt oder indirekt durch eine Obergesellschaft den Kapitalmarkt beanspruchen. Das Gesetz definiert, welche Unternehmen als Publikumsgesellschaften im Sinne dieser Bestimmung gelten:

— Unter *lit. a* werden alle Gesellschaften erfasst, die Beteiligungspapiere an einer schweizerischen oder ausländischen Börse kotiert haben.

Der Begriff des Beteiligungspapiers wird aus der Börsengesetzgebung[36] übernommen. Unter Beteiligungspapieren werden demnach Aktien, Partizipationsscheine, Genussscheine und «andere Beteiligungspapiere» verstanden, welche die Berechtigten erfolgsabhängig am Ertrag der Gesellschaft partizipieren lassen. Unter «andere Beteiligungspapiere» fallen vor allem Wandelrechte und Erwerbsrechte auf Beteiligungspapiere (Optionen). Erfasst werden nicht nur Wertpapiere, sondern auch nicht verurkundete Rechte mit gleicher Funktion (sog. Wertrechte). Der Begriff der Beteiligungspapiere ist weit auszulegen, so dass auch künftige Entwicklungen im Börsenbereich miterfasst werden.

---

36 Art. 2 lit. a und e des Bundesgesetzes vom 24. März 1995 über die Börsen und den Effektenhandel (SR **954.1**) und Art. 2 der Verordnung der Übernahmekommission vom 21. Juli 1997 über öffentliche Kaufangebote (SR **954.195.1**).

Die in der Börsengesetzgebung ebenfalls erfassten Derivate werden meist durch Effektenhändler und nicht durch die Unternehmen selbst emittiert. Erstere unterstehen jedoch auf Grund von Art. 17 des Börsengesetzes einer besonderen Revision durch eine von der Eidg. Bankenkommission (EBK) anerkannte Revisionsstelle.

- Nach *lit. b* müssen Gesellschaften ihre Jahresrechnung ordentlich revidieren lassen, wenn sie Anleihensobligationen (vgl. dazu Art. 1156 ff. OR) ausstehend haben. Anleihensobligationen sind keine Beteiligungspapiere i.S.v. lit. a, weil die Obligationärinnen und Obligationäre unabhängig vom Erfolg der Gesellschaft eine fixe Verzinsung erhalten. Von lit. b werden sowohl börsenkotierte als auch nicht börsenkotierte Anleihensobligationen erfasst. Die Revisionspflicht für Gesellschaften, die nicht börsenkotierte Anleihen ausstehend haben, ist insofern gerechtfertigt, als diese Unternehmen trotz fehlender Börsenkotierung dennoch am (nicht institutionalisierten) Kapitalmarkt teilnehmen.

- Gemäss *lit. c* gelten Gesellschaften, die mindestens 20% der (konsolidierten) Aktiven oder des (konsolidierten) Umsatzes zur Konzernrechnung einer Gesellschaft nach lit. a oder b beitragen, ebenfalls als Publikumsgesellschaften. Damit müssen sich nicht nur die direkt am Kapitalmarkt engagierten Gesellschaften ordentlich revidieren lassen, sondern auch deren wesentliche Tochtergesellschaften.

Diese Bestimmung entspricht sinngemäss dem US-amerikanischen Sarbanes-Oxley Act und stellt einen kompatiblen Geltungsbereich der beiden Revisionsaufsichtssysteme sicher. Die Regelung ist aber auch in der Sache erforderlich: Die Revisionsaufsicht würde zu kurz greifen, wenn nur Revisionsunternehmen erfasst würden, welche die Konzernobergesellschaften prüfen, während Versäumnisse bei der Revision von Konzernuntergesellschaften, die wesentlich zum Gesamtergebnis beitragen, ohne Sanktion blieben. Für die Definition wesentlicher Beteiligungen hat sich die Schwelle von 20% sowohl im Schweizer Aktien- und Steuerrecht (vgl. Art. 665*a* OR und z.B. Art. 8 Abs. 2 DBG[37]) als auch international (so in den USA) etabliert.

Nach *Ziff. 2* müssen weiter diejenigen Gesellschaften ihre Jahresabschlüsse ordentlich prüfen lassen, die zwei der drei nachstehenden Grössen in zwei aufeinander folgenden Geschäftsjahren überschreiten:

- eine Bilanzsumme von 6 Millionen Franken;

---

[37] Bundesgesetz über die direkte Bundessteuer (DBG; SR **642.11**).

- einen Umsatzerlös von 12 Millionen Franken;
- 50 Vollzeitstellen im Jahresdurchschnitt.

Ziff. 2 erfasst mit den bewährten[38] Kriterien der Bilanzsumme, der Umsatzerlöse und der Vollzeitstellen im Jahresdurchschnitt die «wirtschaftlich bedeutenden Gesellschaften». Der Entwurf stellt auf die Kennziffern in zwei aufeinanderfolgenden Geschäftsjahren ab, um zu vermeiden, dass Gesellschaften, welche die Schwellenwerte auf Grund ausserordentlicher Geschäftsfälle einmalig überschreiten, nicht dazu gezwungen werden, ihre Jahresrechnung ordentlich revidieren zu lassen.

Ziff. 3 sieht vor, dass Gesellschaften, die zur Erstellung einer Konzernrechnung verpflichtet sind, ihre Jahres- *und* ihre Konzernrechnung ordentlich prüfen lassen müssen.

Die Pflicht zur *Erstellung einer Konzernrechnung* richtet sich nach Art. 663*e* Abs. 2 und 3 OR. Art. 727 E OR regelt lediglich die Frage der *Revision* der Jahres- und der Konzernrechnung. Gesellschaften, die von Gesetzes wegen eine Konzernrechnung zu erstellen haben, müssen diese ordentlich revidieren lassen. Der Entwurf geht in diesem Punkt nicht weiter als das geltende Recht (Art. 731*a* OR). Neu ist, dass Gesellschaften, die eine Konzernrechnung zu erstellen haben, auch ihre Jahresrechnung ordentlich prüfen lassen müssen. Dies gilt jedoch nur für die Konzernobergesellschaft, welche die Konzernrechnung zu erstellen hat; die in der Konzernrechnung erfassten Konzernuntergesellschaften werden von dieser Pflicht nicht erfasst.

Freiwillig erstellte Konzernrechnungen müssen nicht ordentlich revidiert werden; die Statuten können dies jedoch vorschreiben, oder die Generalversammlung kann dies beschliessen. Es steht den Gesellschaften zudem frei, Viertel- oder Halbjahresabschlüsse von Konzernrechnungen ordentlich oder eingeschränkt revidieren zu lassen (vgl. dazu Art. 65 des Kotierungsreglements der Schweizer Börse SWX, welche für Zwischenabschlüsse keine Revisionspflicht vorsieht).

Nach *Abs.* 2 können Aktionäre, die zusammen mindestens 10% des Aktienkapitals vertreten, verlangen, dass die Jahres- und gegebenenfalls die Konzernrechnung einer ordentlichen Revision unterzogen werden (Opting-up als Minderheitenrecht). Mit der Schranke einer Mindestbeteiligung von 10% sieht der Entwurf die für den Minderheitenschutz im Akti-

---

38 vgl. dazu Art. 663*e* Abs. 3 und Art. 727*b* Abs. 1 OR sowie Art. 2 lit. e FusG (SR **221.301**; BBl 2003 6691).

enrecht übliche Hürde vor (s. Art. 663e Abs. 3 Ziff. 3, 663f Abs. 2, 697b Abs. 1, 699 Abs. 3 und Art. 736 Ziff. 4 OR).

Nach *Abs. 3* können Gesellschaften, für die das Gesetz keine ordentliche Revision der Jahresrechnung verlangt, in den Statuten dennoch eine solche vorsehen (statutarisches Opting-up). Es ist aber auch möglich, dass die Generalversammlung auf Grund bestimmter Vorfälle in einem Geschäftsjahr eine ordentliche Prüfung in Einzelfall beschliesst (Opting-up durch Generalversammlungsbeschluss). Die Beschlussfassung durch die Generalversammlung unterliegt (ohne gegenteilige statutarische Bestimmung) in beiden Fällen dem gesetzlichen Beschlussquorum nach Art. 703 OR.

Zu den fachlichen Anforderungen der Revisionsstelle macht Abs. 3 keine Vorgaben (vgl. aber die Anforderungen gemäss Art. 727b und Art. 727c E OR). Die freiwillige ordentliche Prüfung der Jahresrechnung kann daher sowohl durch eine zugelassene Revisionsexpertin bzw. einen Revisionsexperten als auch durch eine zugelassene Revisorin bzw. einen Revisor erfolgen. In den Statuten oder im Beschluss der Generalversammlung kann diese Frage ausdrücklich geregelt werden. Sehen die Statuten nichts anderes vor, so gilt subsidiär die gesetzliche Regelung: Den Kapitalerhöhungsbericht beispielsweise muss in diesem Fall durch eine zugelassene Revisorin oder einen zugelassenen Revisor geprüft werden (s. Art. 652f Abs. 1 E OR).

Neben der freiwilligen ordentlichen Revision nach Abs. 3 steht es auch dem Verwaltungsrat offen, eine ordentliche Prüfung der Jahresrechnung oder eines Zwischenabschlusses durch eine Fachperson oder eine Person ohne Fachausbildung in Auftrag zu geben. Die beauftragten Revisorinnen und Revisoren stellen in diesem Fall kein Gesellschaftsorgan dar.

Für die Kommanditaktiengesellschaft enthält Art. 764 Abs. 2 OR eine weitgehende Verweisung auf das Aktienrecht. Da es sich dabei um einen sogenannt dynamischen Verweis handelt[39], gilt die neue Regelung der Revision und der Revisionsstelle der Aktiengesellschaft auch für die Kommanditaktiengesellschaft, soweit sich aus der gesetzlichen Regelung dieser Rechtsform nichts Besonderes ergibt. Der so genannten Aufsichtsstelle in der Kommanditaktiengesellschaft kommen jedoch weit umfas-

---

39 s. dazu HEINRICH KOLLER/HANSPETER KLÄY, Das Mittel der gesetzlichen Verweisung im Gesellschaftsrecht, in: Aktienrecht 1992–1997, Versuch einer Bilanz, Festschrift Rolf Bär, Bern 1998, S. 193 ff.

sendere Kompetenzen zu als der Revisionsstelle in der Aktiengesellschaft (s. Art. 768 f. OR)[40].

2. Eingeschränkte Revision

Art. 727a (ursprünglicher Botschaftsentwurf)

1 Sind die Voraussetzungen für eine ordentliche Revision nicht gegeben, so muss die Gesellschaft ihre Jahresrechnung durch eine Revisionsstelle eingeschränkt prüfen lassen.

2 Mit der Zustimmung sämtlicher Aktionäre kann auf die eingeschränkte Revision verzichtet werden, wenn die Gesellschaft nicht mehr als zehn Vollzeitstellen im Jahresdurchschnitt hat.

Art. 727a (durch den Ständerat bereinigte Version, neuer Abs. 3 und 4)

1 Sind die Voraussetzungen für eine ordentliche Revision nicht gegeben, so muss die Gesellschaft ihre Jahresrechnung durch eine Revisionsstelle eingeschränkt prüfen lassen.

2 Mit der Zustimmung sämtlicher Aktionäre kann auf die eingeschränkte Revision verzichtet werden, wenn die Gesellschaft nicht mehr als zehn Vollzeitstellen im Jahresdurchschnitt hat.

3 Der Verwaltungsrat kann die Aktionäre schriftlich um Zustimmung ersuchen. Er kann für die Beantwortung eine Frist von mindestens 20 Tagen ansetzen und darauf hinweisen, dass das Ausbleiben einer Antwort als Zustimmung gilt.

4 Haben die Aktionäre auf eine eingeschränkte Revision verzichtet, so gilt dieser Verzicht auch für die nachfolgenden Jahre. Jeder Aktionär hat jedoch das Recht, spätestens zehn Tage vor der Generalversammlung eine eingeschränkte Revision zu verlangen. Die Generalversammlung muss diesfalls die Revisionsstelle wählen.

---

40 s. dazu ARTHUR MEIER-HAYOZ/PETER FORSTMOSER, Schweizerisches Gesellschaftsrecht, 9. Aufl., Bern 2004, § 17 N 34 ff.

5 Soweit erforderlich passt der Verwaltungsrat die Statuten an und meldet dem Handelsregister die Löschung der Revisionsstelle an.

Sind die Voraussetzungen für eine ordentliche Revision gemäss Art. 727 E OR nicht gegeben, so muss die Gesellschaft ihre Jahresrechnung nach *Abs. 1* von einer Revisionsstelle eingeschränkt prüfen lassen.

Abs. 2 sieht im Interesse von KMU die Möglichkeit vor, auf eine Revision gänzlich zu verzichten (sog. Opting-out), wobei jedoch weiterhin eine rechtmässige Buchhaltung zu führen und ein Jahresabschluss zu erstellen sind. Folgende zwei Bedingungen müssen für den Verzicht auf eine Revision erfüllt werden:

– Das Unternehmen darf nicht mehr als zehn Vollzeitstellen im Jahresdurchschnitt haben, und

– sämtliche Aktionärinnen und Aktionäre müssen dem Verzicht zustimmen.

Diese Regelung beruht auf einer Abwägung aller betroffenen Interessen. Unter Berücksichtigung der Schutzziele der Revision muss das Opting-out auf kleine Unternehmen beschränkt bleiben. In Unternehmen mit mehr als zehn Vollzeitstellen ist zumindest eine eingeschränkte Revision durchzuführen. Deren Kosten fallen in dieser Unternehmensgrösse im Vergleich mit der gesamten Lohnsumme weniger ins Gewicht als in kleineren Betrieben.

Zumindest eine eingeschränkte Revision muss auch dann durchgeführt werden, wenn nicht alle finanziell am Eigenkapital beteiligten Personen einem Verzicht zustimmen. Dieses Zustimmungserfordernis ist unter Berücksichtigung der Beteiligung am Risikokapital zum Schutz der Eigentumsrechte unabdingbar. Qualifizierten Minderheiten muss zudem das Recht auf eine ordentliche Revision eingeräumt werden (s. Art. 727 Abs. 2 E OR).

Das Erfordernis der Zustimmung nach Abs. 2 bezieht sich auch auf allfällige Partizipantinnen und Partizipanten, die allerdings in Kleinunternehmen selten sind (s. Art. 656*a* Abs. 2 OR). Auch wenn die Partizipantinnen und Partizipanten an der Beschlussfassung der Generalversammlung über die Genehmigung der Jahresrechnung nicht mitwirken, dient eine Revision dennoch dem Schutz ihrer finanziellen Beteiligung.

Die Voraussetzungen des Verzichts auf eine Revision mögen auf den ersten Blick einschränkend erscheinen. Da Kleinunternehmen jedoch meist Einpersonengesellschaften oder Gesellschaften mit nur wenigen Beteiligten sind, stellt einvernehmliches Handeln die Regel dar. Die Voraussetzungen eines Opting-out dürften sich daher in kleineren Unternehmen im Allgemeinen gut erreichen lassen.

Die Zustimmung zum Verzicht auf eine Revision kann in Form eines Generalversammlungsbeschlusses erfolgen, sofern sämtliche Aktionärinnen und Aktionäre an der Versammlung teilnehmen und dem betreffenden Beschluss zustimmen. Ein Verzicht kann aber auch auf anderem Wege unter allen Beteiligten vereinbart werden.

Die eingeschränkt prüfende Revisionsstelle ist, wie die ordentlich prüfende Revisionsstelle, ein Gesellschaftsorgan. Auch sie hat das Recht bzw. die Pflicht:

- gegebenenfalls die Generalversammlung einzuberufen (Art. 699 Abs. 1 OR);
- das Gericht gegebenenfalls über die Überschuldung der Gesellschaft zu informieren (Art. 729*c* E OR);
- für Schaden einzustehen, der durch absichtliche oder fahrlässige Verletzung ihrer Pflichten entstanden ist (Art. 755 OR).

Was die Verantwortlichkeit betrifft, so ergeben sich aus dem Umstand, dass die Revisionsstelle nur eingeschränkt prüft, lediglich beschränkte Folgerungen: Die Revisionsstelle haftet auch bei der eingeschränkten Revision grundsätzlich unverändert gemäss Art. 755 ff. OR. Der einzige Unterschied zur Haftung bei der ordentlichen Revision besteht darin, dass die Aufgaben, für deren sorgfältige Erfüllung die Revisionsstelle haftet, bei der eingeschränkten Revision enger umschrieben werden.

Der Übergang von einer eingeschränkten zu einer ordentlichen Revision hat keine technischen Probleme zur Folge. Allerdings kann es vorkommen, dass gewisse Rechnungsposten auf Grund einer ordentlichen Revision neu eingeschätzt und berichtigt werden müssen.

Die Vorschriften zur eingeschränkten Revision beziehen sich ausschliesslich auf die Revision der Jahresrechnung (s. Wortlaut von Art. 727*a* Abs. 1 E OR). Wo das Gesetz eine andere Prüfung oder eine andere Bestätigung einer zugelassenen Revisorin oder eines zugelassenen Revisors verlangt (s. bspw. Art. 635*a* und 732 Abs. 2 E OR, Art. 15 Abs. 1 FusG), ist weder eine bloss eingeschränkte Prüfung noch ein Opting-out zulässig.

Auch die Möglichkeit einer nur eingeschränkten Revision der Konzernrechnung wird vom Entwurf nicht vorgesehen, da dies unter Berücksichtigung der meist recht komplexen Verhältnisse selbst in kleineren Konzernen sachlich nicht sinnvoll erscheint (vgl. dazu Art. 727 Abs. 1 Ziff. 3 E OR).

II. Anforderungen an die Revisionsstelle

Die Art. 727*b* und 727*c* E OR regeln die erforderliche Qualifikation für die Revisorin bzw. den Revisor (staatlich beaufsichtigtes Revisionsunternehmen, zugelassene Revisionsexpertin bzw. Revisionsexperte oder zugelassene Revisorin bzw. Revisor).

1. Bei ordentlicher Revision

Art. 727b

1 Publikumsgesellschaften müssen als Revisionsstelle ein staatlich beaufsichtigtes Revisionsunternehmen nach den Vorschriften des Revisionsaufsichtsgesetzes vom 16. Dezember 2005[41] **bezeichnen. Sie müssen Prüfungen, die nach den gesetzlichen Vorschriften durch einen zugelassenen Revisor oder einen zugelassenen Revisionsexperten vorzunehmen sind, ebenfalls von einem staatlich beaufsichtigten Revisionsunternehmen durchführen lassen.**

2 Die übrigen Gesellschaften, die zur ordentlichen Revision verpflichtet sind, müssen als Revisionsstelle einen zugelassenen Revisionsexperten nach den Vorschriften des Revisionsaufsichtsgesetzes vom 16. Dezember 2005 über die Zulassung und Beaufsichtigung der Revisorinnen und Revisoren bezeichnen. Sie müssen Prüfungen, die nach den gesetzlichen Vorschriften durch einen zugelassenen Revisor vorzunehmen sind, ebenfalls von einem zugelassenen Revisionsexperten durchführen lassen.

Publikumsgesellschaften müssen nach *Abs. 1 Satz 1* als Revisionsstelle ein staatlich beaufsichtigtes Revisionsunternehmen gemäss den Vorschriften des Revisionsaufsichtsgesetzes (s. Art. 4, Art. 6 und Art. 7 E RAG) bezeichnen.

---

41 SR **221.302** (BBl 2004 4139)

Abs. 1 Satz 2 schreibt vor, dass Publikumsgesellschaften neben der Prüfung der Jahresrechnung auch andere Prüfungen und Bestätigungen, die nach den gesetzlichen Vorschriften durch eine zugelassene Revisorin, einen zugelassenen Revisor, eine zugelassene Revisionsexpertin oder einen zugelassenen Revisionsexperten vorzunehmen sind (s. z.B. Art. 635*a* und 732 Abs. 2 E OR, Art. 15 Abs. 1 FusG), durch ein staatlich beaufsichtigtes Revisionsunternehmen durchführen lassen müssen.

Der Entwurf sieht beispielsweise vor, dass der Kapitalerhöhungsbericht durch eine zugelassene Revisorin oder einen zugelassenen Revisor geprüft werden muss (s. Art. 652*f* Abs. 1 E OR). Auf Grund von Abs. 1 Satz 2 müssen Publikumsgesellschaften diese Prüfung durch ein staatlich beaufsichtigtes Revisionsunternehmen vornehmen lassen, welches die fachlichen Anforderungen an eine zugelassene Revisionsexpertin oder einen zugelassenen Revisionsexperten erfüllt. Durch diese Regelung wird sichergestellt, dass in Publikumsgesellschaften neben der Revision der Jahresrechnung auch andere, teilweise sogar besonders sensible Revisionsdienstleistungen (so z.B. die genannte Kapitalerhöhungsprüfung) ebenfalls durch besonders qualifizierte und beaufsichtigte Personen vorgenommen werden.

Alle Gesellschaften, die nicht als Publikumsgesellschaften gelten, aber dennoch zu einer ordentlichen Revision verpflichtet sind (s. Art. 727 Abs. 1 Ziff. 2 und 3, Abs. 2 und Abs. 3 E OR), müssen nach *Abs. 2 Satz 1* als Revisionsstelle eine zugelassene Revisionsexpertin oder einen zugelassenen Revisionsexperten nach den Vorschriften des Revisionsaufsichtsgesetzes (s. Art. 4 und 6 E RAG) bezeichnen.

Sie müssen gemäss *Abs. 2 Satz 2* Prüfungen, die nach den gesetzlichen Vorschriften durch eine zugelassene Revisorin oder einen zugelassenen Revisor vorzunehmen sind (s. bspw. Art. 635*a* E OR), ebenfalls von einer zugelassenen Revisionsexpertin bzw. einem zugelassenen Revisionsexperten durchführen lassen. Auch hier werden die fachlichen Anforderungen für die besonderen Prüfungen dem Qualifikationsniveau der Revisionsstelle angepasst (vgl. dazu die Ausführungen zu Abs. 1 Satz 2). Beispielsweise muss die Prüfung des Kapitalerhöhungsberichts (s. Art. 652*f* Abs. 1 E OR) daher durch eine zugelassene Revisionsexpertin oder einen zugelassenen Revisionsexperten durchgeführt werden.

2. Bei eingeschränkter Revision

Art. 727c
Die Gesellschaften, die zur eingeschränkten Revision verpflichtet sind, müssen als Revisionsstelle einen zugelassenen Revisor nach den Vorschriften des Revisionsaufsichtsgesetzes vom 16. Dezember 2005[42] über die Zulassung und Beaufsichtigung der Revisorinnen und Revisoren bezeichnen.

Diejenigen Gesellschaften, die zur eingeschränkten Revision verpflichtet sind, müssen als Revisionsstelle eine zugelassene Revisorin oder einen zugelassenen Revisor nach den Vorschriften des Revisionsaufsichtsgesetzes (s. Art. 5 f. E RAG) bezeichnen. Für die besonderen Prüfungen gelten die in den jeweiligen gesetzlichen Vorschriften vorgegebenen fachlichen Qualifikationen (s. z.B. Art. 635*a* und 732 Abs. 2 E OR, Art. 15 Abs. 1 FusG).

Art. 727d

Aufgehoben

Der geltende Art. 727*d* OR enthält verschiedene Vorschriften, die dann zur Anwendung kommen, wenn eine Handelsgesellschaft oder eine Genossenschaft als Revisionsstelle gewählt wird. Die drei Absätze dieses Artikels werden voneinander getrennt und aus gesetzessystematischen Gründen neu gruppiert.

– Die Abs. 1 und 3 wurden in die Art. 728 und 729 E OR verschoben (vgl. die Ausführungen zu den genannten Vorschriften sowie Art. 2 lit. b E RAG). Der Entwurf schränkt die Revisionsstelle in ihrer Rechtsform nicht ein, sondern lässt ausdrücklich auch Revisionsstellen im Rechtskleid des Vereins und der Stiftung zu.

– Abs. 2 wurde in Art. 6 lit. c E RAG verschoben.

Der Artikel wird daher aufgehoben.

---

42 SR **221.302** (BBl 2004 4139)

Art. 727e

Aufgehoben

Art. 727e OR schreibt die Amtsdauer der Revisionsstelle sowie das Vorgehen bei Rücktritt, Abberufung und Löschung der Revisionsstelle aus dem Handelsregister vor. Die vier Absätze dieses Artikels werden ebenfalls aus gesetzessystematischen Gründen an anderer Stelle eingefügt.

- Abs. 1 wurde in den Art. 730a Abs. 1 E OR verschoben.
- Abs. 2 wurde in den Art. 730a Abs. 3 E OR verschoben (vgl. zudem Art. 663b Ziff. 13 E OR).
- Abs. 3 wurde in den Art. 730a Abs. 4 E OR verschoben. Die Abberufungsklage wird neu in Art. 731b E OR im Entwurf zur Revision des Rechts der GmbH für alle Gesellschaften einheitlich geregelt.
- Die Löschung der Revisionsstelle im Handelsregister wird neu in Art. 938b des Entwurfs zur Revision des Rechts der GmbH für alle Gesellschaften einheitlich geregelt.

Der Artikel wird daher aufgehoben.

III. Ordentliche Revision

1. Unabhängigkeit der Revisionsstelle

Art. 728 (ursprünglicher Botschaftsentwurf)

1 Die Revisionsstelle muss unabhängig sein und sich ihr Prüfungsurteil objektiv bilden. Die Unabhängigkeit darf weder tatsächlich noch dem Anschein nach beeinträchtigt sein.

2 Mit der Unabhängigkeit nicht vereinbar ist insbesondere:

1. **die Mitgliedschaft des Verwaltungsrats, eine andere Entscheidfunktion in der Gesellschaft oder ein arbeitsrechtliches Verhältnis zu ihr;**

2. eine direkte oder bedeutende indirekte Beteiligung am Aktienkapital oder eine wesentliche Forderung oder Schuld gegenüber der Gesellschaft;
3. eine enge Beziehung des leitenden Prüfers zu einem Mitglied des Verwaltungsrats, zu einer anderen Person mit Entscheidfunktion oder zu einem bedeutenden Aktionär;
4. das Mitwirken bei der Buchführung sowie das Erbringen anderer Dienstleistungen, durch die das Risiko entsteht, als Revisionsstelle eigene Arbeiten überprüfen zu müssen;
5. die Übernahme eines Auftrags, der zur wirtschaftlichen Abhängigkeit führt;
6. der Abschluss eines Vertrags zu nicht marktkonformen Bedingungen oder eines Vertrags, der ein Interesse der Revisionsstelle am Prüfergebnis begründet;
7. die Annahme von wertvollen Geschenken oder von besonderen Vorteilen.

3 Die Bestimmungen über die Unabhängigkeit gelten für alle an der Revision beteiligten Personen. Ist die Revisionsstelle eine Personengesellschaft oder eine juristische Person, so gelten die Bestimmungen über die Unabhängigkeit auch für die Mitglieder des obersten Leitungs- oder Verwaltungsorgans und andere Personen mit Entscheidfunktion.

4 Arbeitnehmer der Revisionsstelle, die nicht an der Revision beteiligt sind, dürfen in der zu prüfenden Gesellschaft weder Mitglied des Verwaltungsrates sein noch eine andere Entscheidfunktion ausüben.

5 Die Unabhängigkeit ist auch dann nicht gegeben, wenn Personen, die der Revisionsstelle, deren Arbeitnehmern oder dem Verwaltungsrat nahe stehen, die Unabhängigkeitsvoraussetzungen nicht erfüllen.

6 Die Bestimmungen über die Unabhängigkeit erfassen auch Gesellschaften, die mit der zu prüfenden Gesellschaft oder der Revisionsstelle unter einheitlicher Leitung stehen.

Art. 728 (durch den Nationalrat bereinigte Version)

5 Die Unabhängigkeit ist auch dann nicht gegeben, wenn Personen, die der Revisionsstelle, den an der Revision beteiligten Personen, den Mitgliedern des obersten Leistungs- oder Verwaltungsorgans oder anderen Personen mit Entscheidfunktion nahe stehen, die Unabhängigkeitsvoraussetzungen nicht erfüllen.

Abs. 1 enthält den Grundsatz, wonach die Revisionsstelle unabhängig sein und sich ihr Prüfungsurteil objektiv bilden muss. Die Unabhängigkeit darf weder tatsächlich (sog. «Independence in Fact») noch dem Anschein nach (sog. «Independence in Appearance») beeinträchtigt sein. Die Unabhängigkeit nach dem äusseren Erscheinen ist mit Blick auf das Ziel der Verlässlichkeit der Rechnungslegung und der Revision für Dritte von zentraler Bedeutung. Die Revision eines einwandfreien Abschlusses durch eine subjektiv unvoreingenommene Revisionsstelle ist für Dritte wertlos, wenn nach aussen hin die Glaubwürdigkeit der Revision durch Umstände beeinträchtigt wird, die den Anschein einer mangelnden Unabhängigkeit der Revisionsstelle begründen. Wie bereits die entsprechende Bestimmung im Aktienrecht von 1991 (vgl. Art. 727c OR[43]) zielen die Vorschriften des Entwurfs daher nicht nur darauf hin, die subjektive, innere Unabhängigkeit der Revisorinnen und Revisoren zu fordern; vielmehr gilt es auch, auf der objektiven, äusseren Ebene jeden Anschein der Abhängigkeit zu vermeiden. Nur so können Dritte in die Verlässlichkeit der Revision und der Jahresrechnung vertrauen. Die Bejahung des Anscheins einer ungenügenden Unabhängigkeit darf demzufolge nicht als ethischer Vorwurf einer effektiven inneren Befangenheit verstanden werden; dennoch hat ein entsprechender Anschein den Ausschluss der betroffenen Person von der Revision zur Folge.

Für die Beurteilung des äusseren Anscheins der fehlenden Unabhängigkeit ist auf die Würdigung der Umstände durch eine durchschnittliche Betrachterin oder einen durchschnittlichen Betrachter auf Grund der allgemeinen Lebenserfahrung abzustellen. Ein Anschein der fehlenden Unabhängigkeit kann sich insbesondere aus persönlichen Umständen ergeben.

---

[43] Botschaft über die Revision des Aktienrechts vom 23. Februar 1983, BBl 1983 845; BGE 123 III 31 ff., 32 f.; BGE 123 V 161 ff., 164 ff.

Abs. 2 enthält eine konkretisierende, nicht abschliessende Aufzählung von Tatbeständen, die mit der Tätigkeit als Revisionsstelle unvereinbar sind:

- Nach *Ziff. 1* darf die Revisionsstelle nicht Mitglied des Verwaltungsrates der zu prüfenden Gesellschaft sein, in dieser keine andere Entscheidfunktion wahrnehmen und in keinem arbeitsrechtlichen Verhältnis zu ihr stehen. Die beiden ersten Punkte stellen über die Unabhängigkeit hinaus sicher, dass die Aufgabenkreise der verschiedenen Gesellschaftsorgane sauber getrennt werden.

- *Ziff. 2* untersagt direkte oder bedeutende indirekte Beteiligungen am Aktienkapital oder wesentliche Forderungen oder Schulden gegenüber der zu prüfenden Gesellschaft. Bei den indirekten Beteiligungen ist an bedeutende Beteiligungen über Zwischengesellschaften u. dgl. zu denken. Indirekte Beteiligungen über Anlagefonds oder vergleichbare Vorsorgeeinrichtungen gelten nicht als unzulässige Beteiligung, wenn auf die Anlagepolitik keinerlei Einfluss genommen werden kann und der Anlagefonds bzw. die Vorsorgeeinrichtung nicht Revisionskunde der Revisionsstelle ist.

- Enge Beziehungen der leitenden Prüferin oder des leitenden Prüfers zu einem Mitglied des Verwaltungsrates, zu einer anderen Person mit Entscheidfunktion oder zu einem wesentlichen Aktionär der zu prüfenden Gesellschaft sind mit der Tätigkeit als Revisionsstelle nicht vereinbar und daher gemäss *Ziff. 3* unzulässig. Enge Beziehungen können sich dabei auf geschäftlicher oder persönlicher Grundlage ergeben.

- Eine Unvereinbarkeit kann sich insbesondere auch ergeben, wenn die Revisionsstelle neben der Revision noch andere Mandate der zu prüfenden Gesellschaft übernimmt. *Ziff. 4* untersagt daher die Erbringung von anderen Dienstleistungen an die zu prüfende Gesellschaft, wenn dadurch das Risiko der Überprüfung eigener Arbeiten entstehen würde, wie dies insbesondere bei der Mitwirkung in der Buchführung der Fall wäre (sog. Selbstprüfungsverbot). Weitere Anwendungsfälle dieser Bestimmung betreffen namentlich die Erstellung von Jahresabschlüssen, das Erbringen von Bewertungsdienstleistungen, die Entwicklung und Einführung von Finanzinformationssystemen und die Durchführung einer internen Revision. Steuerberatende Dienstleistungen sind insoweit zulässig, als es nicht zu einer Selbstüberprüfung kommt. Unvereinbar ist insbesondere die Beratung und Mitwirkung bei der Erstellung von komplexen internationalen Strukturen zu Zwecken der Steueroptimierung, die durch die Revisionsstelle zu beurteilen sind.

- Die Übernahme eines Auftrages, der zur wirtschaftlichen Abhängigkeit der Revisionsstelle von der zu prüfenden Gesellschaft führt, ist nach *Ziff.* 5 unzulässig. Darunter fallen sowohl Revisionsmandate als auch andere gemäss Ziff. 4 an sich erlaubte Aufträge. Ist die Revisionsstelle wirtschaftlich von der zu prüfenden Gesellschaft (oder von Gesellschaften und Personen, die mit dieser verbunden sind) abhängig, so wird sie dadurch in der Freiheit ihres Prüfungsurteils erheblich beeinträchtigt, da sie bei negativen Wertungen mit einem Entzug ihres Mandats rechnen muss. Vgl. dazu die ergänzende Sondervorschrift für Publikumsgesellschaften in Art. 11 lit. a E RAG.

- Mit dem Revisionsmandat unvereinbar ist nach *Ziff.* 6 der Abschluss eines Vertrags, der nicht marktkonforme Konditionen vorsieht oder der ein Interesse der Revisionsstelle am Prüfergebnis begründet. Zu denken ist insbesondere an erfolgsabhängige Honorarabsprachen, an die Gewährung ungewöhnlicher Rabatte, an zinsgünstige Darlehen oder an die Zusicherung einer Funktion in der zu prüfenden Gesellschaft (vgl. dazu die ergänzenden Sondervorschriften für Publikumsgesellschaften in Art. 11 lit. b, c und d E RAG). Verträge im Rahmen des Geschäftsbereichs der zu prüfenden Gesellschaft sind jedoch zulässig, sofern marktübliche Bedingungen bestehen.

- Nach *Ziff.* 7 ist die Annahme von wertvollen Geschenken oder von besonderen Vorteilen mit dem Revisionsmandat selbstverständlich nicht vereinbar. Nicht erfasst werden sollen Höflichkeitsgeschenke ohne grösseren Wert. Die Unvereinbarkeit der Einräumung besonderer Vorteile wurde vom Gesetzgeber im Rahmen der Beratungen des Fusionsgesetzes zur Klarstellung in Art. 727*c* Abs. 1 OR eingefügt und wird vom Entwurf übernommen.

Für die Revisionsstellen von Publikumsgesellschaften sieht der Entwurf zu einem Revisionsaufsichtsgesetz ergänzende, über die vorliegenden allgemeinen Vorschriften hinausgehende Normen zur Unabhängigkeit vor (s. Art. 11 E RAG).

Die Abs. 3 bis 6 regeln den Geltungsbereich der Bestimmungen über die Unabhängigkeit. Diese gelten gemäss *Abs. 3 Satz 1* für alle an der Prüfung beteiligten Personen. An der Revision beteiligt sind die leitende Prüferin oder der leitende Prüfer, die Mitglieder des Prüfungsteams sowie alle übrigen Personen, die Prüfungshandlungen vornehmen oder zu solchen beitragen. Ein solcher Beitrag liegt auch dann vor, wenn eine Person auf Grund einer ihr zustehenden Weisungsbefugnis in die Prüfung eingreift (z.B. ein Mitglied der Geschäftsleitung; vgl. dazu auch Abs. 5). Grundsätzlich ist nicht erheblich, ob die zur Prüfung beitragende Person durch einen Arbeitsvertrag oder durch ein Auftragsverhältnis mit der Revisionsstelle verbunden ist. Alleiniges Kriterium bildet der Beitrag zur Revision. Erfasst werden damit ebenfalls die Immobilienschätzerin, die in einem Auftragsverhältnis zur Revisionsstelle steht, oder der frühere Mitarbeiter, der sich selbständig gemacht hat und auf Auftragsbasis für gewisse Fachfragen beigezogen wird.

Ist die Revisionsstelle eine Personengesellschaft oder eine juristische Person, so bestimmt *Abs. 3 Satz 2*, dass die Vorschriften über die Unabhängigkeit auch für die Mitglieder des obersten Leitungs- oder Verwaltungsorgans und für andere Personen mit Entscheidfunktion gelten. Von dieser Bestimmung erfasst werden insbesondere auch die Mitglieder der Geschäftsleitung. Die Vorschrift ist auch für Revisionsstellen im Rechtskleid des Vereins oder der Stiftung anwendbar, soweit die Revisionstätigkeit im Rahmen der gesetzlich zulässigen Zwecke dieser Rechtsformen überhaupt statthaft ist.

Arbeitnehmerinnen und Arbeitnehmer der Revisionsstelle, die in keiner Weise an der Revision beteiligt sind, dürfen nach *Abs. 4* in der zu prüfenden Gesellschaft weder Mitglied des Verwaltungsrates sein noch eine andere Entscheidfunktion ausüben. Es würde aber zu weit führen, ihnen auch andere auftrags- oder arbeitsrechtliche Verhältnisse zu untersagen.

Gemäss *Abs. 5* ist die Unabhängigkeit auch dann nicht gegeben, wenn Personen, die der Revisionsstelle, deren Arbeitnehmerinnen und Arbeitnehmern oder dem Verwaltungsrat nahe stehen, die Unabhängigkeitsvoraussetzungen nicht erfüllen. Dies bedeutet Folgendes: Zwar kann und will das Gesetz Personen, die der Revisionsstelle nahe stehen, keine Auflagen für ihre Tätigkeiten oder ihre persönlichen Umstände machen. Falls aber eine Person, die der Revisorin oder dem Revisor nahe steht, einen Tatbestand verwirklicht, der mit der Revision einer bestimmten Gesellschaft unvereinbar wäre, entfällt auch die erforderliche Unabhängigkeit der Revisorin oder des Revisors. Mit der Unabhängigkeit der Revisionsstelle ist beispielsweise nicht vereinbar, dass:

— die Ehefrau des Revisors Mitglied des Verwaltungsrates der zu prüfenden Gesellschaft ist (Abs. 2 Ziff. 1 i.V.m. Abs. 5);
— der Bruder der Revisorin bei der Buchführung der zu prüfenden Gesellschaft mitwirkt (Abs. 2 Ziff. 4 i.V.m. Abs. 5);

– der Grossvater des Revisors Mehrheitsaktionär der zu prüfenden Gesellschaft ist (Abs. 2 Ziff. 2 i.V.m. Abs. 5).

Der Begriff der nahe stehenden Person stimmt inhaltlich mit demjenigen der «engen Beziehung» in Abs. 2 Ziff. 3 überein. Erfasst werden Partnerschaften sowie nahe verwandtschaftliche oder enge freundschaftliche Beziehungen. Massgebend für die Beurteilung einer Beziehung ist die Einschätzung der Umstände durch einen Dritten auf Grund der allgemeinen Lebenserfahrung; eine subjektiv empfundene Unabhängigkeit bleibt dabei ohne Belang.

Schliesslich bestimmt *Abs. 6*, dass die Bestimmungen über die Unabhängigkeit auch Gesellschaften erfassen, die mit der zu prüfenden Gesellschaft oder der Revisionsstelle unter einheitlicher Leitung stehen (Konzern). Die Bestimmungen über die Unabhängigkeit müssen demnach auch in den folgenden Verhältnissen beachtet werden:

– zwischen der Revisionsstelle und Gesellschaften, die mit der zu prüfenden Gesellschaft unter einheitlicher Leitung stehen;
– zwischen der zu prüfenden Gesellschaft und Gesellschaften, die mit der Revisionsstelle unter einheitliche Leitung stehen.

Beispielsweise darf die Revisionsstelle nicht über eine Tochtergesellschaft an der zu prüfenden Gesellschaft beteiligt sein. Auch darf ein Mitglied des Verwaltungsrats einer Tochtergesellschaft der Revisionsgesellschaft nicht gleichzeitig im Verwaltungsrat der zu prüfenden Gesellschaft Einsitz nehmen.

Die Vorschriften zur Unabhängigkeit werden durch folgende Mechanismen durchgesetzt:

– Die Generalversammlung der zu prüfenden Gesellschaft hat das Recht, die Revisionsstelle jederzeit abzuberufen (s. Art. 730*a* Abs. 4 E OR).

– Die Handelsregisterbehörden weisen die Eintragung der Revisionsstelle ab, wenn der Anschein der Abhängigkeit besteht.

Da für die Beurteilung des Anscheins der Abhängigkeit auf eine rein äussere, objektivierte Betrachtung abgestellt wird, gehört eine summarische Prüfung der erforderlichen Unabhängigkeit der Revisionsstelle zu den Aufgaben der Handelsregisterbehörden (s. im geltenden Recht

Art. 86*a* Abs. 1 HRegV)⁴⁴. Soweit für einen durchschnittlichen Betrachter der Anschein einer ungenügenden Unabhängigkeit besteht, ist die Eintragung der Revisionsstelle ins Handelsregister abzulehnen. Zu berücksichtigen sind dabei sowohl Umstände, die sich aus der eingereichten Anmeldung oder den Belegen ergeben, als auch solche, die den Registerbehörden auf andere Weise bekannt sind (z.B. enge verwandtschaftliche Beziehungen). Die Registerbehörden haben jedoch keine Nachforschungen anzustellen.

– Die Aktionärinnen und Aktionäre, Gläubigerinnen und Gläubiger sowie die Handelsregisterführerin und der Handelsregisterführer haben die Befugnis, dem Gericht die erforderlichen Massnahmen zu beantragen, wenn eine bereits im Handelsregister eingetragene Revisionsstelle sich als nicht unabhängig erweist (s. Art. 731*b* E OR Revision GmbH).

– Dem Verwaltungsrat obliegt die Pflicht, der Generalversammlung eine Revisionsstelle zur Wahl vorzuschlagen, welche die gesetzlichen Anforderungen an die Unabhängigkeit erfüllt. Zudem hat er einzugreifen, wenn er feststellt, dass diese Vorschriften nachträglich während der Mandatsdauer der Revisionsstelle nicht mehr eingehalten werden.

– Entsteht durch die nicht unabhängig durchgeführte Revision ein Schaden, so steht der Gesellschaft, den Aktionärinnen und Aktionären sowie Gläubigerinnen und Gläubigern die Einreichung einer Verantwortlichkeitsklage gegen die mit der Revision befassten Personen offen (Art. 755 OR).

2. Aufgaben der Revisionsstelle

a. Gegenstand und Umfang der Prüfung

Art. 728a (ursprünglicher Botschaftsentwurf)

1 Die Revisionsstelle prüft, ob:

---

44 SR **221.411**; s. auch BGE 123 III 31 ff., 33, 123 V 161 ff., 166, und die Weisung des Eidg. Amts für das Handelsregister vom 17.8.1994 über die Eintragungen von Revisoren ins Handelsregister und über die Unterlagen betreffend deren fachliche Befähigung, Ziff. III.2.

1. die Jahresrechnung und gegebenenfalls die Konzernrechnung den gesetzlichen Vorschriften, den Statuten und dem gewählten Regelwerk entsprechen;
2. der Antrag des Verwaltungsrats an die Generalversammlung über die Verwendung des Bilanzgewinnes den gesetzlichen Vorschriften und den Statuten entspricht;
3. die vom Gesetz verlangten Angaben gemacht werden;
4. ein funktionierendes internes Kontrollsystem existiert;
5. eine Risikobeurteilung vorgenommen wurde.

2 Die Geschäftsführung des Verwaltungsrats ist nicht Gegenstand der Prüfung durch die Revisionsstelle.

Art. 728a (durch den Nationalrat bereinigte Version, neuer Abs. 1bis)

1 Die Revisionsstelle prüft, ob:

1. die Jahresrechnung und gegebenenfalls die Konzernrechnung den gesetzlichen Vorschriften, den Statuten und dem gewählten Regelwerk entsprechen;
2. der Antrag des Verwaltungsrats an die Generalversammlung über die Verwendung des Bilanzgewinnes den gesetzlichen Vorschriften und den Statuten entspricht;
3. *...gestrichen*
4. ein internes Kontrollsystem existiert;
5. *...gestrichen*

2 Die Revisionsstelle berücksichtigt bei der Durchführung und bei der Festlegung des Umfanges der Prüfung das interne Kontrollsystem.

3 Die Geschäftsführung des Verwaltungsrats ist nicht Gegenstand der Prüfung durch die Revisionsstelle.

Abs. 1 umschreibt die Prüfungsaufgaben der Revisionsstelle:

– Sie hat gemäss *Ziff. 1* zu prüfen, ob die Jahresrechnung und gegebenenfalls die Konzernrechnung den gesetzlichen Vorschriften, den Statuten und dem gewählten Regelwerk entsprechen. Prüfungspflichtig sind die Erfolgsrechnung, die Bilanz und der Anhang (s. Art. 662 Abs. 2 OR). Als massgebliche gesetzliche Vorschriften gelten die für die Aktiengesellschaft anwendbaren Bestimmungen zur Buchführung und Rechnungslegung[45].

Hat die Gesellschaft ein bestimmtes Regelwerk wie etwa die Swiss GAAP FER oder die IAS/IFRS gewählt, so hat die Revisionsstelle ebenfalls zu prüfen, ob dieses vollumfänglich eingehalten wurde. Damit wird verhindert, dass sich eine Gesellschaft der Anwendung eines Rechnungslegungsstandards rühmt, obwohl die entsprechenden Normen nur selektiv befolgt wurden.

– Nach *Ziff. 2* ist weiter zu prüfen, ob der Antrag des Verwaltungsrats an die Generalversammlung über die Verwendung des Bilanzgewinnes den gesetzlichen Vorschriften und den Statuten entspricht.

– Gemäss *Ziff. 3* hat die Revisionsstelle weiter zu prüfen, ob die vom Gesetz verlangten Angaben gemacht werden (s. dazu Art. 663*b* Ziff. 14 E OR). Als Beispiele für solche Angaben seien die Hinweise zu Abweichungen von den Grundsätzen ordnungsmässiger Rechnungslegung (Art. 662*a* Abs. 3 OR) und die Offenlegung der Beteiligungsverhältnisse bei Gesellschaften mit kotierten Aktien erwähnt (Art. 663*c* OR). Mit dem offenen Wortlaut von Ziff. 3 wird sichergestellt, dass auch künftig vom Gesetz verlangte Angaben erfasst werden, so etwa die Offenlegung der Entschädigung der Mitglieder des Verwaltungsrates und der Geschäftsleitung sowie andere Angaben zur Corporate Governance.

– Die Revisionsstelle prüft gemäss *Ziff. 4*, ob ein funktionierendes internes Kontrollsystem (sog. IKS) existiert. Die Pflicht des Verwaltungsrats zur Schaffung interner Kontrollmechanismen ergibt sich aus seiner Verpflichtung, das Rechnungswesen der Gesellschaft so auszugestalten, dass die Grundsätze der ordnungsgemässen Buchführung und Rechnungslegung eingehalten werden (Art. 716*a* Abs. 1 Ziff. 3 i.V.m. Art. 662*a* sowie Art. 957 ff. OR).

---

[45] vgl. PETER BÖCKLI, Schweizer Aktienrecht, 2. Aufl., Zürich 1996, N 1809; PETER FORSTMOSER/ARTHUR MEIER-HAYOZ/PETER NOBEL, Schweizerisches Aktienrecht, Bern 1996, § 33 N 10; ROLF WATTER, in: Honsell/Vogt/Watter (Hrsg.), Basler Kommentar zum Schweizerischen Privatrecht, Obligationenrecht II, Art. 530–1186 OR, 2. Aufl., Basel 2002, Art. 728 N 1.

Die Revisionsstelle prüft, ob der Verwaltungsrat Massnahmen zur Sicherstellung einer ordnungsgemässen Buchführung und Rechnungslegung getroffen hat und ob diese Massnahmen eingehalten werden. Stellt sie fest, dass das IKS Mängel aufweist, so kompensiert sie diese durch eigene Prüfungshandlungen.

Die Prüfung des internen Kontrollsystems stellt an sich keine neue Prüfaufgabe der Revisionsstelle dar; der Entwurf erwähnt diesen Prüfaspekt allerdings im Gegensatz zum geltenden Recht ausdrücklich.

– Nach *Ziff. 5* prüft die Revisionsstelle, ob vom Verwaltungsrat eine Risikobeurteilung vorgenommen wurde.

Die Revisionsstelle stützt sich dabei auf die entsprechenden Aussagen des Verwaltungsrates im Anhang (s. dazu die Ausführungen zu Art. 663*b* Ziff. 12 E OR). Die verlangte Beurteilung durch die Revisionsstelle darf nicht als eine inhaltliche Prüfung verstanden werden; bestätigt wird lediglich, *dass* eine Risikobeurteilung vorgenommen wurde. Die Verantwortlichkeit für den Inhalt und die Art der Risikobeurteilung liegt beim Verwaltungsrat.

Die Prüfung der Geschäftsrisiken stellt keine neue Prüfaufgabe der Revisionsstelle dar; der Entwurf erwähnt diesen Prüfaspekt allerdings im Gegensatz zum geltenden Recht ausdrücklich.

Die Geschäftsführung des Verwaltungsrats bildet nach *Abs. 2* nicht Gegenstand der Revisionsaufgabe. Diese Bestimmung dient einer klaren Abgrenzung der Verantwortlichkeiten zwischen dem Verwaltungsrat und der Revisionsstelle. Der Revisionsstelle fehlen im Allgemeinen die Voraussetzungen, um die Angemessenheit und Zweckmässigkeit sowie die Ziele der Geschäftsführung beurteilen zu können. Vorbehalten bleiben jedoch die Anzeigepflichten nach Art. 728*c* E OR.

Die Verantwortung des Verwaltungsrats für die Erstellung eines Geschäftsberichts (s. Art. 716*a* Abs. 1 Ziff. 6 OR) wird durch die Revision der Jahres- und der Konzernrechnung ebenfalls nicht berührt. Es ist m.a.W. nicht die Aufgabe der Revisionsstelle, sondern des Verwaltungsrates, dafür besorgt zu sein, dass der Geschäftsbericht im Einklang mit den gesetzlichen und statutarischen Bestimmungen erstellt wird. Die Revisionsstelle hat den Verwaltungsrat lediglich darauf hinzuweisen, wenn sie diesbezügliche Mängel feststellt.

Kapitel 1: Neue Gesetzesbestimmungen und Erläuterungen

b. Revisionsbericht

Art. 728b (ursprünglicher Botschaftsentwurf)

1 Die Revisionsstelle erstattet dem Verwaltungsrat einen umfassenden Bericht mit Feststellungen über die Rechnungslegung, das interne Kontrollsystem sowie die Durchführung und das Ergebnis der Revision.

2 Die Revisionsstelle erstattet der Generalversammlung schriftlich einen zusammenfassenden Bericht über das Ergebnis der Revision. Der Bericht enthält:

1. eine Stellungnahme zum Ergebnis der Prüfung;
2. Angaben zur Unabhängigkeit;
3. Angaben zu den Personen, welche die Revision geleitet haben, und zu deren fachlichen Befähigung;
4. eine Empfehlung, ob die Jahresrechnung und die Konzernrechnung mit oder ohne Einschränkung zu genehmigen oder zurückzuweisen ist.

3 Beide Berichte müssen von den Personen unterzeichnet werden, die die Revision geleitet haben.

Art. 728b (durch den Nationalrat bereinigte Version)

2 Die Revisionsstelle erstattet der Generalversammlung schriftlich einen zusammenfassenden Bericht über das Ergebnis der Revision. Der Bericht enthält:

3. Angaben zur Person, welche die Revision geleitet hat, und zu deren fachlichen Befähigung;

3 Beide Berichte müssen von der Person unterzeichnet werden, die die Revision geleitet hat.

Die Revisionsstelle erstattet dem Verwaltungsrat gemäss *Abs. 1* einen umfassenden Bericht mit Feststellungen über die Rechnungslegung, das interne Kontrollsystem sowie die Durchführung und das Ergebnis der Revision. Die Stellung des Ergänzungsberichts nach geltendem Recht (s. Art. 729a OR) wird damit gestärkt.

Der Generalversammlung erstattet die Revisionsstelle auf Grund von *Abs. 2* schriftlich einen zusammenfassenden Bericht über das Ergebnis der Revision. Die nachfolgenden Ziffern umschreiben den Mindestinhalt dieses zusammenfassenden Revisionsberichts:

- Der Bericht enthält nach *Ziff. 1* eine Stellungnahme der Revisionsstelle zum Ergebnis der Prüfung gemäss der Umschreibung des Prüfungsgegenstands in Art. 728a E OR. Eine gegebenenfalls blosse negative Stellungnahme genügt nicht; festgestellte Mängel müssen aufgelistet werden.

- Die Revisionsstelle muss nach *Ziff. 2* Ausführungen zu ihrer Unabhängigkeit machen (s. Art. 728 E OR). Offen zu legen sind sämtliche Sachverhalte, die Grund zur Annahme geben könnten, die Unabhängigkeit sei beeinträchtigt. Aufzuzeigen sind in diesem Fall auch die ergriffenen Schutzmassnahmen. Der Wortlaut des Entwurfs bringt zum Ausdruck, dass die Revisionsstelle sich nicht mit einer floskelhaften Bestätigung der eigenen Unabhängigkeit begnügen darf, sondern sich nach den konkret vorliegenden Umständen mit allen Punkten auseinander setzen muss, die für Dritte den Anschein einer fehlenden Unabhängigkeit begründen könnten. Liegen keine solchen Sachverhalte vor, ist dies im Revisionsbericht zu bestätigen.

- Die Revisionsstelle nennt auf Grund von *Ziff. 3* diejenigen Personen, welche die Prüfung geleitet haben (so bereits im geltenden Recht; s. Art. 729 Abs. 2 OR), und macht Angaben zu deren fachlicher Befähigung (s. dazu Art. 4 und Art. 6 E RAG).

- Schliesslich enthält der Revisionsbericht gemäss *Ziff. 4* eine Empfehlung, ob die Jahresrechnung und gegebenenfalls die Konzernrechnung mit oder ohne Einschränkung zu genehmigen oder zurückzuweisen sind.

Abs. 3 schreibt vor, dass die Berichte nach den Abs. 1 und 2 von denjenigen Personen unterzeichnet werden müssen, welche die Revision geleitet haben. Als solche gelten die als Revisionsstelle gewählten oder innerhalb eines Revisionsunternehmens (vgl. dazu die Ausführungen zu Art. 2 lit. b E RAG) für das Revisionsmandat zuständigen natürlichen Personen.

Kapitel 1: Neue Gesetzesbestimmungen und Erläuterungen

c. Anzeigepflichten

Art. 728c (ursprünglicher Botschaftsentwurf)

1 Stellt die Revisionsstelle Verstösse gegen das Gesetz, die Statuten oder das Organisationsreglement fest, so meldet sie dies schriftlich dem Verwaltungsrat.

2 Sie informiert zudem die Generalversammlung, wenn:

1. sie wesentliche Verstösse gegen das Gesetz oder die Statuten feststellt;
2. der Verwaltungsrat auf Grund der schriftlichen Meldung der Revisionsstelle keine angemessenen Massnahmen ergreift.

3 Ist die Gesellschaft offensichtlich überschuldet und unterlässt der Verwaltungsrat die Anzeige, so benachrichtigt die Revisionsstelle das Gericht.

Art. 728c (durch den Nationalrat bereinigte Version)

2 Sie informiert zudem die Generalversammlung über Vorstösse gegen das Gesetz oder die Statuten, wenn:

1. diese wesentlich sind; oder

Stellt die Revisionsstelle im Rahmen ihrer Revisionstätigkeit Verstösse gegen das Gesetz, die Statuten oder das Organisationsreglement fest, so meldet sie dies gemäss *Abs. 1* schriftlich dem Verwaltungsrat.

Während nach Art. 728a Abs. 1 Ziff. 1 E OR nur zu prüfen ist, ob die Jahres- und die Konzernrechnung den für die Buchführung und Rechnungslegung massgeblichen Normen (Gesetz, Statuten, Regelwerk) entsprechen, ist die vorliegende Meldepflicht umfassenderer Natur. Die Revisionsstelle ist verpflichtet, sämtliche Verstösse gegen das Gesetz, die Statuten oder das Organisationsreglement dem Verwaltungsrat zu melden, wenn sie solche Verstösse feststellt. Welcher Art die verletzte Norm ist, bleibt dabei ohne Relevanz; so sind insbesondere sämtliche festgestellten Delikte gegen das Strafrecht zu melden. Die Revisionsstelle trifft jedoch ausserhalb des Rahmens ihrer Prüfungsaufgaben (Art. 728a E OR) keine

Nachforschungspflicht. Als einem Organ der Gesellschaft kommt ihr aber eine gewisse Treuepflicht zu, und sie hat daher auch zufällig aufgedeckte Rechtswidrigkeiten anzuzeigen.

Anders als im geltenden Recht (vgl. Art. 729*b* Abs. 1 OR) müssen neu auch Verstösse gegen das Organisationsreglement gemeldet werden. Namentlich Vorschriften zur Corporate Governance werden oftmals im Organisationsreglement des Verwaltungsrats niedergelegt. Stellt die Revisionsstelle bei der Durchführung ihrer Prüfung fest, dass die reglementarischen Vorgaben zur Organisation verletzt wurden, so hat sie dies zu melden.

Die Revisionsstelle informiert überdies nach *Abs. 2* in zwei Fällen die Generalversammlung. Zum einen ist sie gemäss *Ziff. 1* hierzu verpflichtet, wenn sie wesentliche Verstösse gegen das Gesetz oder die Statuten festgestellt hat, zum anderen muss sie gemäss *Ziff. 2* orientieren, wenn der Verwaltungsrat im Nachgang zu einer Meldung durch die Revisionsstelle (s. dazu Abs. 1) keine angemessenen Massnahmen ergreift. Die Vorschriften der Ziff. 1 und 2 stehen also in einem alternativen und nicht in einem kumulativen Verhältnis zueinander. Verstösse gegen das Organisationsreglement sind der Generalversammlung nicht zu melden, da Ersteres durch den Verwaltungsrat erlassen wurde.

Verunmöglicht der Verwaltungsrat der Revisionsstelle, sich an die Generalversammlung zu wenden, so hat die Revisionsstelle das Recht, eine solche unter Umgehung des Verwaltungsrates einzuberufen (Art. 699 Abs. 1 OR)[46].

Abs. 3 übernimmt den geltenden Art. 729*b* Abs. 2 OR, wonach die Revisionsstelle das Gericht zu benachrichtigen hat, wenn die Gesellschaft offensichtlich überschuldet ist und der Verwaltungsrat diese Anzeige unterlässt.

---

46 PETER FORSTMOSER/ARTHUR MEIER-HAYOZ/PETER NOBEL, Schweizerisches Aktienrecht, Bern 1996, § 33 N 66; ROLF WATTER, in: Honsell/Vogt/Watter (Hrsg.), Basler Kommentar zum Schweizerischen Privatrecht, Obligationenrecht II, Art. 530–1186 OR, 2. Aufl., Basel 2002, Art. 729*b* N 4.

IV. Eingeschränkte Revision (Review)

1. Unabhängigkeit der Revisionsstelle

Art. 729

1 Die Revisionsstelle muss unabhängig sein und sich ihr Prüfungsurteil objektiv bilden. Die Unabhängigkeit darf weder tatsächlich noch dem Anschein nach beeinträchtigt sein.

2 Das Mitwirken bei der Buchführung und das Erbringen anderer Dienstleistungen für die zu prüfende Gesellschaft sind zulässig. Sofern das Risiko der Überprüfung eigener Arbeiten entsteht, muss durch geeignete organisatorische und personelle Massnahmen eine verlässliche Prüfung sichergestellt werden.

Gemäss *Abs. 1* muss die Revisionsstelle unabhängig sein und sich ihr Prüfungsurteil objektiv bilden. Die Unabhängigkeit darf weder tatsächlich noch dem Anschein nach beeinträchtigt sein.

Die Zielsetzung der Unabhängigkeitsvorschriften ist bei der ordentlichen und bei der eingeschränkten Revision naturgemäss dieselbe. Das in Abs. 1 festgehaltene Prinzip der Unabhängigkeit muss daher aus sachlichen Gründen demjenigen für die ordentliche Revision entsprechen (vgl. Art. 728 Abs. 1 E OR). Im Unterschied zur ordentlichen Revision wird aber auf gesetzliche Konkretisierungen dieses Grundsatzes verzichtet. Die entsprechenden Vorgaben in Art. 728 Abs. 2 E OR können aber auch für die eingeschränkt prüfende Revisionsstelle eine Leitlinie darstellen: Eine Durchsicht dieser Vorschriften zeigt, dass die aufgeführten Unvereinbarkeitsgründe auch für eingeschränkt prüfende Revisionsstellen von Bedeutung sind, wenn nicht der Anschein einer offensichtlichen Befangenheit entstehen soll. Beispielsweise dürfen Revisorinnen und Revisoren weder im Verwaltungsrat der zu prüfenden Gesellschaft Einsitz nehmen (s. Art. 728 Abs. 2 Ziff. 1 E OR) noch mit der Mehrheitsaktionärin oder dem Mehrheitsaktionär verwandt sein (Ziff. 3) noch bedeutende Geschenke annehmen (Ziff. 7).

In einem wesentlichen Punkt werden bei der eingeschränkten Revision aber weniger strenge Anforderungen an die Unabhängigkeit gestellt: Mit Blick auf die Bedürfnisse der KMU nach Dienstleistungen «aus einer Hand» lässt *Abs. 2* ausdrücklich zu, dass die Revisionsstelle bei der Buchführung mitwirkt oder andere Dienstleistungen für die zu prüfende Gesellschaft erbringt. Sofern dadurch das Risiko der Überprüfung eigener Arbeiten entsteht, muss mittels geeigneter organisatorischer und personeller Massnahmen eine verlässliche Prüfung sichergestellt werden.

Die vorliegende Bestimmung ermöglicht es beispielsweise, dass dasselbe Revisionsunternehmen oder zwei Gesellschaften derselben Unternehmensgruppe sowohl an der Buchführung mitwirken als auch eine eingeschränkte Revision durchführen, wenn eine verlässliche Prüfung in organisatorischer und personeller Hinsicht dennoch sichergestellt ist. Die Arbeiten in der Buchführung und die eingeschränkte Revision dürfen aber nicht durch dieselbe Person oder dieselbe Personengruppe durchgeführt werden. Es steht in der Verantwortung der Revisionsstelle, unternehmensintern die geeigneten Massnahmen zu treffen.

Wirkt die Revisionsstelle bei der Buchführung mit oder erbringt sie andere Dienstleistungen, die zu einer Überprüfung eigener Arbeiten führen können, so soll diesbezüglich Transparenz bestehen: Die Revisionsstelle muss daher im Revisionsbericht entsprechende Ausführungen machen (s. dazu Art. 729*b* Abs. 1 Ziff. 3 E OR).

2. Aufgaben der Revisionsstelle

a. Gegenstand und Umfang der Prüfung

Art. 729a (ursprünglicher Botschaftsentwurf)

1 Die Revisionsstelle prüft, ob Sachverhalte vorliegen, aus denen zu schliessen ist, dass:

1. **die Jahresrechnung nicht den gesetzlichen Vorschriften und den Statuten entspricht;**

2. **der Antrag des Verwaltungsrats an die Generalversammlung über die Verwendung des Bilanzgewinnes nicht den gesetzlichen Vorschriften und den Statuten entspricht.**

2 Die Prüfung beschränkt sich auf Befragungen und analytische Prüfungshandlungen.

3 Die Geschäftsführung des Verwaltungsrats ist nicht Gegenstand der Prüfung durch die Revisionsstelle.

Kapitel 1: Neue Gesetzesbestimmungen und Erläuterungen

Art. 729a (durch den Nationalrat bereinigte Version)
2 Die Prüfung beschränkt sich auf Befragungen, analytische Prüfungshandlungen und angemessene Detailprüfungen.

Die Revisionsstelle prüft gemäss *Abs. 1*, ob Sachverhalte vorliegen, aus denen zu schliessen ist, dass:

- gemäss *Ziff. 1* die Jahresrechnung nicht den gesetzlichen Vorschriften und den Statuten entspricht (vgl. dazu bei der ordentlichen Revision Art. 728*a* Abs. 1 Ziff. 1 E OR);

- nach *Ziff. 2* der Antrag des Verwaltungsrats an die Generalversammlung über die Verwendung des Bilanzgewinns nicht den gesetzlichen Vorschriften und den Statuten entspricht (vgl. dazu bei der ordentlichen Revision Art. 728*a* Abs. 1 Ziff. 2 E OR).

Gemäss *Abs. 2* beschränkt sich die eingeschränkte Prüfung auf Befragungen und analytische Prüfungshandlungen. Für die nach Abs. 1 geforderten Feststellungen ist eine weniger eingehende Prüfung erforderlich als bei der ordentlichen Revision. Insbesondere finden keine eingehende Prüfung sämtlicher Einzelpositionen, keine Prüfung der Bewertungen und keine physische Bestandesaufnahme statt. Die eingeschränkte Revision ergibt im Vergleich mit der ordentlichen Revision eine weniger hohe Sicherheit in der Beurteilung der Frage, ob die durchgesehenen Unterlagen keine wesentlichen Fehlaussagen enthalten. Die von der Revisionsstelle abzugebende Zusicherung kann daher keine positive Bestätigung der Rechtskonformität der Jahresrechnung beinhalten, sondern beschränkt sich auf eine negative Feststellung des Fehlens von Sachverhalten, die auf eine mangelnde Rechtskonformität schliessen lassen.

Das Risiko, dass Verstösse gegen die gesetzlichen Vorschriften und die Statuten sowie wesentliche Fehlaussagen nicht aufgedeckt werden, ist bei der eingeschränkten Revision naturgemäss grösser als bei der ordentlichen Revision. Allerdings sind die Prüfungshandlungen so auszugestalten, dass das Risiko von Fehlaussagen gering ist.

Die ordentliche und die eingeschränkte Revision unterscheiden sich demnach zum einen in der Prüfungsintensität, zum andern werden bei der eingeschränkten Revision verschiedene Punkte nicht geprüft. Nicht untersucht wird, ob:

- die Jahresrechnung nach einem besonderen Regelwerk (Swiss GAAP FER, IAS/IFRS, etc.) erstellt wurde und ob dieses vollständig eingehalten wurde (vgl. Art. 728a Abs. 1 Ziff. 1 E OR bei der ordentlichen Revision);
- die vom Gesetz verlangten Angaben offen gelegt werden (vgl. Art. 728a Abs. 1 Ziff. 3 E OR);
- ein funktionierendes internes Kontrollsystem existiert (vgl. Art. 728a Abs. 1 Ziff. 4 E OR);
- eine Risikobeurteilung vorgenommen wurde (vgl. Art. 728a Abs. 1 Ziff. 5 E OR).

Abs. 3 entspricht Art. 728a Abs. 2 E OR (s. die Ausführungen dazu).

b. Revisionsbericht

Art. 729b (ursprünglicher Botschaftsentwurf)

1 Die Revisionsstelle erstattet der Generalversammlung schriftlich einen zusammenfassenden Bericht über das Ergebnis der Revision. Der Bericht enthält:

1. einen Hinweis auf die eingeschränkte Natur der Revision;

2. eine Stellungnahme zum Ergebnis der Prüfung;

3. Angaben zur Unabhängigkeit und gegebenenfalls zum Mitwirken bei der Buchführung und zu anderen Dienstleistungen, die für die zu prüfende Gesellschaft erbracht wurden;

4. Angaben zu den Personen, welche die Revision geleitet haben, und zu deren fachlicher Befähigung.

2 Der Bericht muss von den Personen unterzeichnet werden, die die Revision geleitet haben.

Art. 729b (durch den Nationalrat bereinigte Version)

1 Die Revisionsstelle erstattet der Generalversammlung schriftlich einen zusammenfassenden Bericht über das Ergebnis der Revision. Der Bericht enthält:

4. Angaben zur Person, welche die Revision geleitet hat, und zu deren fachlicher Befähigung.

2 Der Bericht muss von der Person unterzeichnet werden, die die Revision geleitet hat.

Die Revisionsstelle erstattet der Generalversammlung gemäss *Abs. 1* schriftlich einen zusammenfassenden Bericht über das Ergebnis der Revision. Die nachfolgenden Ziffern umschreiben den Mindestinhalt dieses zusammenfassenden Revisionsberichts:

- Zum Schutz der Aktionärinnen und Aktionäre sowie Dritter muss im Bericht gemäss *Ziff. 1* ein ausdrücklicher Hinweis auf die eingeschränkte Natur der Revision enthalten sein.

- Der Bericht enthält nach *Ziff. 2* eine Stellungnahme zum Ergebnis der Prüfung (s. dazu Art. 729a Abs. 1 E OR). Festgestellte Mängel müssen detailliert angegeben werden.

- Die Revisionsstelle muss gemäss *Ziff. 3* Ausführungen zu ihrer Unabhängigkeit machen. Besonders darzulegen sind sämtliche Sachverhalte, die Grund zur Annahme geben könnten, die Unabhängigkeit sei beeinträchtigt. So müssen alle Dienstleistungen der Revisionsstelle an die geprüfte Gesellschaft offen gelegt werden und insbesondere diejenigen, die zu einer Überprüfung eigener Arbeiten führen können (s. Art. 729 Abs. 2 E OR).

Im Rahmen der Ausführungen zur Unabhängigkeit sind gegebenenfalls auch die ergriffenen Schutzmassnahmen anzugeben, so insbesondere im Falle des Mitwirkens bei der Buchführung und beim Erbringen anderer Dienstleistungen.

- Die Revisionsstelle hat nach *Ziff. 4* die Personen zu nennen, welche die Prüfung geleitet haben. Sie macht dabei die erforderlichen Angaben zur fachlichen Befähigung (s. dazu Art. 5 und Art. 6 E RAG).

Die eingeschränkt prüfende Revisionsstelle erstellt keinen umfassenden Revisionsbericht zuhanden des Verwaltungsrats (vgl. Art. 728*b* Abs. 1 E OR). Im Gegensatz zum zusammenfassenden Revisionsbericht der ordentlich prüfenden Revisionsstelle enthält der Bericht der eingeschränkt prüfenden Revisionsstelle keine Empfehlung, ob die Jahresrechnung mit oder ohne Einschränkung zu genehmigen oder zurückzuweisen sei. Auf Grund des eingeschränkten Charakters der Revision muss dieser Schluss den Aktionärinnen und Aktionären überlassen bleiben.

Abs. 2 schreibt vor, dass der Revisionsbericht von denjenigen Personen unterzeichnet werden muss, welche die Revision geleitet haben (vgl. dazu die Ausführungen zu Art. 728*b* Abs. 3 E RAG).

c. Anzeigepflicht

Art. 729c

Ist die Gesellschaft offensichtlich überschuldet und unterlässt der Verwaltungsrat die Anzeige, so benachrichtigt die Revisionsstelle das Gericht.

Die Anzeigepflicht der eingeschränkt prüfenden Revisionsstelle beschränkt sich auf die Benachrichtigung des Gerichts, wenn die Gesellschaft offensichtlich überschuldet ist und der Verwaltungsrat diese Anzeige unterlässt (vgl. dazu die weitergehenden Anzeigepflichten der ordentlich prüfenden Revisionsstelle, Art. 728*c* E OR).

V. Gemeinsame Bestimmungen

Die Art. 730–731*a* E OR gelten sowohl für die ordentlich als auch für die eingeschränkt prüfende Revisionsstelle.

1. Wahl der Revisionsstelle

Art. 730 (ursprünglicher Botschaftsentwurf)
1 Die Generalversammlung wählt die Revisionsstelle.

Kapitel 1: Neue Gesetzesbestimmungen und Erläuterungen

> 2 Als Revisionsstelle können eine oder mehrere natürliche oder juristische Personen oder Personengesellschaften gewählt werden.
>
> 4 Wenigstens ein Mitglied der Revisionsstelle muss seinen Wohnsitz, seinen Sitz oder eine eingetragene Zweigniederlassung in der Schweiz haben.

> *Art. 730 (durch den Nationalrat bereinigte Version, neuer Abs. 2bis)*
>
> 3 Finanzkontrollen der öffentlichen Hand oder deren Mitarbeiter können als Revisionsstelle gewählt werden, wenn sie die Anforderungen dieses Gesetzes erfüllen. Die Vorschriften über die Unabhängigkeit gelten sinngemäss.

Abs. 1 sieht vor, dass die Revisionsstelle, wie im geltenden Recht, von der Generalversammlung gewählt wird. Dies entspricht der Umschreibung der zwingend der Generalversammlung zugewiesenen Befugnisse in Art. 698 Abs. 2 Ziff. 2 OR.

Als Revisionsstelle können nach *Abs. 2* eine oder mehrere natürliche oder juristische Personen oder Personengesellschaften gewählt werden. In der Praxis kommt die Wahl einer mehrgliedrigen Revisionsstelle eher selten vor; sie kann jedoch in gewissen Konstellationen sinnvoll sein. So kann es etwa vorkommen, dass verschiedene an einem Unternehmen beteiligte Personengruppen je eine Revisorin oder einen Revisor ihres Vertrauens beiziehen wollen. Es ist auch zulässig, dass eine Gesellschaft mehrere Revisionsstellen bezeichnet. So kann insbesondere einer zweiten Revisionsstelle ein beschränktes Mandat im Hinblick auf Erfordernisse des ausländischen Rechts erteilt werden. Die Beschränkung des Revisionsmandats ist aus Transparenzgründen und im Hinblick auf die Relevanz für die Verantwortlichkeit im Handelsregister offen zu legen.

Im Vergleich zum geltenden Recht verzichtet der Entwurf auf die Vorschrift, wonach Ersatzleute gewählt werden können (Art. 727 Abs. 1 Satz 2 OR). Die praktische Relevanz dieser Bestimmung hat sich als gering erwiesen. Im Rahmen der Privatautonomie soll es der Generalversammlung aber weiterhin offen stehen, Ersatzpersonen zu wählen. Eine gesetzliche Regelung erscheint jedoch auf Grund der bescheidenen Bedeutung nicht notwendig. Es sei hier aber festgehalten, dass das Erforder-

549

nis einer formellen Wahl durch die Generalversammlung auch für Ersatzmitglieder gilt.

Mehrgliedrige Revisionsstellen stehen in einem gewissen Spannungsverhältnis zum Prinzip der Einheit der Revisionsstelle als Organ[47]. Wird eine mehrgliedrige Revisionsstelle gewählt, so müssen sich die Mitglieder intern so organisieren und aufeinander abstimmen, dass die Einheit als Organ gewährleistet ist. Zweckmässig sind in diesem Fall besondere Bestimmungen in den Statuten nach Art. 731a E OR.

Hat die Gesellschaft mehrere Personen in die Revisionsstelle gewählt, so bilden diese das Organ in ihrer Gesamtheit und übernehmen dementsprechend alle dieselben gesetzlichen Pflichten.

Nach *Abs.* 3 muss wenigstens ein Mitglied der Revisionsstelle seinen Wohnsitz, seinen Sitz oder eine eingetragene Zweigniederlassung in der Schweiz haben.

Damit wird das geltende Recht übernommen (s. Art. 727 Abs. 2 OR). Die Auswirkungen des Personenfreizügigkeitsabkommens mit der Europäischen Union auf die Wohnsitzerfordernisse im Gesellschaftsrecht stehen derzeit noch nicht endgültig fest. Im Rahmen der parlamentarischen Beratung wird in dieser Frage der weiteren Entwicklung und den in Auftrag gegebenen Gutachten Rechnung zu tragen sein.

2. Amtsdauer der Revisionsstelle

Art. 730a (ursprünglicher Botschaftsentwurf)

1 Die Revisionsstelle wird für ein bis drei Geschäftsjahre gewählt. Ihr Amt endet mit der Abnahme der letzten Jahresrechnung. Eine Wiederwahl ist möglich.

2 Bei der ordentlichen Revision dürfen die Personen, die die Revision leiten, das Mandat längstens während fünf Jahren ausführen. Sie dürfen das gleiche Mandat erst nach einem Unterbruch von drei Jahren wieder aufnehmen.

3 Tritt eine Revisionsstelle zurück, so hat sie den Verwaltungsrat über die Gründe zu informieren; dieser teilt sie der nächsten Generalversammlung mit.

---

47 s. PETER BÖCKLI, Schweizer Aktienrecht, 2. Aufl., Zürich 1996, N 1792b.

Kapitel 1: Neue Gesetzesbestimmungen und Erläuterungen

4 Die Generalversammlung kann die Revisionsstelle jederzeit mit sofortiger Wirkung abberufen.

Art. 730a (durch den Nationalrat bereinigte Version)

2 Bei der ordentlichen Revision darf die Person, die die Revision leitet, das Mandat längstens während fünf Jahren ausführen. Sie darf das gleiche Mandat erst nach einem Unterbruch von drei Jahren wieder aufnehmen.

Art. 730a (durch den Ständerat bereinigte Version)

2 Bei der ordentlichen Revision einer Publikumsgesellschaft darf die Person, die die Revision leitet, das Mandat längstens während sieben Jahren ausführen. Sie darf das gleiche Mandat erst nach einem Unterbruch von drei Jahren wieder aufnehmen.

Abs. 1 Satz 1 sieht vor, dass die Revisionsstelle für die Revision von einem bis drei Geschäftsjahren gewählt wird. Ihr Amt endet gemäss *Satz 2* mit der Abnahme der letzten Jahresrechnung der jeweiligen Amtsperiode durch die Generalversammlung. Eine Wiederwahl ist nach *Satz 3* möglich.

Der Entwurf übernimmt das geltende Recht und verzichtet auf die zwingende Rotation der Revisionsstelle. Um Risiken vorzubeugen, die auf Grund einer zu grossen persönlichen Vertrautheit oder eines übermässigen Vertrauens entstehen können, sieht jedoch *Abs. 2* für die ordentliche Revision vor, dass diejenigen Personen, welche die Revision leiten, nach fünf Geschäftsjahren ausgewechselt werden müssen. Die ausgewechselten Personen dürfen das gleiche Mandat erst nach drei Jahren Wartezeit wieder aufnehmen (sog. Cooling-off Period). Für die eingeschränkte Revision gilt diese Vorschrift nicht.

Die Richtlinie der Treuhand-Kammer zur Unabhängigkeit schreibt eine Rotationspflicht der leitenden Prüferin bzw. des leitenden Prüfers nach 7

Jahren vor[48]. In den USA wird für börsenkotierte Gesellschaften eine Rotationspflicht nach 5 Jahren vorgesehen[49]. Die EU empfiehlt bisher eine Rotation nach spätestens 7 Jahren mit einer Karenzfrist von 2 Jahren[50], schlägt aber im Vorschlag zur neuen Prüferrichtlinie ebenfalls eine Rotation nach 5 Jahren vor[51]. Der Entwurf folgt damit der allgemeinen internationalen Entwicklung. Eine Recherche im Rahmen einer Studie der Zürcher Kantonalbank zur Corporate Governance in den Unternehmen des Swiss Market Index (SMI) hat 2003 erbracht, dass die aktuellen leitenden Prüferinnen und Prüfer ihre Funktion im Durchschnitt seit rund 4,7 Jahren ausüben[52]. Vereinzelt wurde allerdings eine Amtsdauer von bis zu 9 Jahren festgestellt. Die Vorschrift zur Rotation bezieht sich nicht auf die Revisionsstelle, sondern auf die Person, welche die Revision leitet. Abs. 2 ist daher auch dann zu beachten, wenn die leitende Prüferin oder der leitende Prüfer eine Anstellung bei einem andern Revisionsunternehmen annimmt. Tritt eine Revisionsstelle zurück, so teilt sie dem Verwaltungsrat gemäss *Abs. 3* die Gründe mit. Der Verwaltungsrat informiert sodann die nächste Generalversammlung. Tritt eine Revisionsstelle vorzeitig zurück, so legt der Verwaltungsrat die Gründe zudem im Anhang zur Jahresrechnung offen (Art. 663*b* Ziff. 13 E OR). Diese doppelte Information ist erforderlich, weil einerseits die nächste Generalversammlung nicht in jedem Fall erst nach Erstattung der Jahresrechnung stattfindet und andererseits der Adressatenkreis der Jahresrechnung (und damit des Anhangs) über die Generalversammlung hinausreicht (s. Art. 697*h* OR). Für die Generalversammlung ist es wesentlich, spätestens anlässlich der Neuwahl der Revisionsstelle zu erfahren, welches die Ursache der Demission war. Die zwingende Offenlegung der Gründe ist zudem von präventiver Wirkung und dient der indirekten Sicherung der Unabhängigkeit der Revisionsstelle von den Organen der zu prüfenden Gesellschaft.

---

48 Treuhand-Kammer, Richtlinien zur Unabhängigkeit, Zürich 2001, Ziff. 5.
49 Sec. 203 Sarbanes-Oxley Act. Sec. 207 Sarbanes-Oxley Act sieht allerdings vor, dass eine Studie über die Vor- und Nachteile der Rotation der Revisionsstelle erstellt werden soll. Diese Frage ist somit noch nicht definitiv beantwortet.
50 Empfehlung der Kommission vom 16. Mai 2002, Unabhängigkeit des Abschlussprüfers in der EU, Grundprinzipien, ABl. Nr. L 191 vom 19. Juli 2002, S. 22 ff., Ziff. 10.2.a.
51 Art. 40 lit. c des Vorschlags der EU-Kommission vom 16. März 2004 für eine neue Prüferrichtlinie (s. dazu hinten unter Ziff. 5).
52 Zürcher Kantonalbank, Corporate Governance in der Schweiz, Die SMI-Unternehmen in Vergleich, Zürich 2003.

Die Revisionsstelle ist frei, ihr Amt jederzeit durch Rücktritt zu beenden. Eine Demission zur Unzeit kann allerdings die Pflicht zur Ersetzung des daraus entstandenen Schadens begründen.

Abs. 4 erlaubt der Generalversammlung, die Revisionsstelle jederzeit mit sofortiger Wirkung abzuberufen.

3. Auskunft und Geheimhaltung

Art. 730b

1 Der Verwaltungsrat übergibt der Revisionsstelle alle Unterlagen und erteilt ihr die Auskünfte, die sie für die Erfüllung ihrer Aufgaben benötigt, auf Verlangen auch schriftlich.

2 Die Revisionsstelle wahrt das Geheimnis über ihre Feststellungen, soweit sie nicht von Gesetzes wegen zur Bekanntgabe verpflichtet ist. Sie wahrt bei der Berichterstattung, bei der Erstattung von Anzeigen und bei der Auskunftserteilung an die Generalversammlung die Geschäftsgeheimnisse der Gesellschaft.

Der Verwaltungsrat muss der Revisionsstelle gemäss *Abs. 1* alle Unterlagen übergeben und Auskünfte erteilen, die diese für die Erfüllung ihrer Aufgaben benötigt. Auf Verlangen sind die Auskünfte schriftlich zu erteilen. In der Praxis ist eine sog. Vollständigkeitserklärung des Verwaltungsrats zuhanden der Revisionsstelle üblich[53].

Auf Grund von *Abs. 2 Satz 1* ist die Revisionsstelle verpflichtet, das Geheimnis über ihre Feststellungen zu wahren, soweit sie nicht von Gesetzes wegen zur Bekanntgabe verpflichtet ist. Eine solche Verpflichtung besteht insbesondere betreffend:

- den Inhalt des Revisionsberichts und die Auskünfte gegenüber der Generalversammlung (Art. 728*b*, Art. 729*b* E OR sowie Art. 697 Abs. 1 und 2 OR);
- die gesetzlichen Anzeigepflichten (s. Art. 728*c* und Art. 729*c* E OR);

---

53 s. PETER BÖCKLI, Schweizer Aktienrecht, 2. Aufl., Zürich 1996, N 1811, m.w.N.; vgl. auch das Schweizer Handbuch der Wirtschaftsprüfung, Zürich 1998, Band 2, S. 157 ff.

- die Auskunft gegenüber der Sonderprüferin oder dem Sonderprüfer (s. Art. 697*d* Abs. 2 OR);
- die Einreichung der Unterlagen zur Zulassung als staatlich beaufsichtigtes Revisionsunternehmen (Art. 10 E RAG);
- die Auskunftspflichten und die Zutrittsgewähr gegenüber der Aufsichtsbehörde (s. Art. 14 E RAG);
- die Meldepflichten gegenüber der Aufsichtsbehörde (s. Art. 15 E RAG).

Satz 2 stellt klar, dass die Revisionsstelle im Rahmen der Berichterstattung, der Erstattung von Anzeigen und der Auskunftserteilung an die Generalversammlung die Geschäftsgeheimnisse der Gesellschaft zu wahren hat. Für die Auskunftspflicht der Revisionsstelle gegenüber der Aufsichtsbehörde (s. Art. 14 E RAG) gilt diese Einschränkung nicht, da die Aufsichtsbehörde zur Erfüllung ihrer Aufgaben auf eine umfassende Information angewiesen sein kann, dafür aber ihrerseits unter einer Geheimhaltungspflicht steht.

4. Dokumentation und Aufbewahrung

Art. 730c (vom Nationalrat neu geschaffener Artikel)

1 Die Revisionsstelle muss sämtliche Revisionsdienstleistungen dokumentieren und Revisionsberichte sowie alle wesentlichen Unterlagen mindestens während zehn Jahren aufbewahren. Elektronische Daten müssen während der gleichen Zeitperiode wieder lesbar gemacht werden können.

2 Die Unterlagen müssen es ermöglichen, die Einhaltung der gesetzlichen Vorschriften in effizienter Weise zu prüfen.

5. Abnahme der Rechnung und Gewinnverwendung

Art. 731

1 Bei Gesellschaften, die verpflichtet sind, ihre Jahresrechnung und gegebenenfalls ihre Konzernrechnung durch eine Revisionsstelle prü-

fen zu lassen, muss der Revisionsbericht vorliegen, bevor die Generalversammlung die Jahresrechnung und die Konzernrechnung genehmigt und über die Verwendung des Bilanzgewinns beschliesst.

2 Wird eine ordentliche Revision durchgeführt, so muss die Revisionsstelle an der Generalversammlung anwesend sein. Die Generalversammlung kann durch einstimmigen Beschluss auf die Anwesenheit der Revisionsstelle verzichten.

3 Liegt der erforderliche Revisionsbericht nicht vor, so sind die Beschlüsse zur Genehmigung der Jahresrechnung und der Konzernrechnung sowie zur Verwendung des Bilanzgewinnes nichtig. Werden die Bestimmungen über die Anwesenheit der Revisionsstelle missachtet, so sind diese Beschlüsse anfechtbar.

Bei Gesellschaften, die verpflichtet sind, ihre Jahresrechnung und gegebenenfalls ihre Konzernrechnung durch eine Revisionsstelle prüfen zu lassen, muss der Revisionsbericht gemäss *Abs. 1* vorliegen, bevor die Generalversammlung die Rechnung(en) genehmigen und über die Verwendung des Bilanzgewinnes beschliessen darf. Damit wird sichergestellt, dass die Aktionärinnen und Aktionäre diese Entscheide nur in Kenntnis der damit verbundenen finanziellen Konsequenzen fällen. Die Bestimmung gilt nicht für Gesellschaften, die an sich zur eingeschränkten Revision ihrer Jahresrechnung verpflichtet wären, die aber ein Opting-out vorgenommen haben (Art. 727*a* Abs. 2 E OR).

Wird eine ordentliche Revision durchgeführt, so muss die Revisionsstelle gemäss *Abs. 2 Satz 1* an der Generalversammlung anwesend sein. Den Aktionärinnen und Aktionären wird dadurch ermöglicht, Fragen an die Revisionsstelle zu richten (s. Art. 697 Abs. 1 OR). *Satz 2* sieht vor, dass die Generalversammlung durch einstimmigen Beschluss auf die Anwesenheit der Revisionsstelle verzichten kann. Fällt die Generalversammlung einstimmig einen entsprechenden Entscheid, so entfällt die Anfechtbarkeit nach Abs. 3 (s. dazu nachstehend).

In der Praxis wird insbesondere bei Kleingesellschaften bereits vor der Generalversammlung zwischen den Aktionärinnen und Aktionären abgesprochen, ob es der Anwesenheit der Revisionsstelle bedarf oder nicht.

Im Falle einer eingeschränkten Revision ist die Anwesenheit der Revisionsstelle an der Generalversammlung nicht notwendig.

Abs. 3 sanktioniert Verstösse gegen die Vorschriften in den Abs. 1 und 2: Liegt der Revisionsbericht nicht vor, so sind die Beschlüsse zur Genehmigung der Jahresrechnung und der Konzernrechnung sowie zur Verwendung des Bilanzgewinns nichtig. Werden die Bestimmungen über die Anwesenheit der ordentlich prüfenden Revisionsstelle missachtet, so sind die Beschlüsse anfechtbar.

6. Besondere Bestimmungen

Art. 731a

1 Die Statuten und die Generalversammlung können die Organisation der Revisionsstelle eingehender regeln und deren Aufgaben erweitern.

2 Der Revisionsstelle dürfen weder Aufgaben des Verwaltungsrates, noch Aufgaben, die ihre Unabhängigkeit beeinträchtigen, zugeteilt werden.

3 Die Generalversammlung kann zur Prüfung der Geschäftsführung oder einzelner Teile Sachverständige ernennen.

Abs. 1 hält das Recht der Gesellschaft fest, in den Statuten und durch Beschluss der Generalversammlung die Organisation der Revisionsstelle eingehender zu regeln und deren Aufgaben (in einem beschränkten Umfang) zu erweitern. Ergänzende Bestimmungen können bei mehrgliedrigen Revisionsstellen (s. die Ausführungen zu Art. 730 Abs. 2 E OR) sinnvoll sein, doch sind entsprechende Regelungen in der Praxis selten[54]. Ein Beispiel für die Erweiterung der Aufgaben der Revisionsstelle ist die Verpflichtung der Revisionsstelle, Zwischenrevisionen zu machen[55].

Eine Einschränkung der gesetzlichen Aufgaben der Revisionsstelle durch die Statuten ist grundsätzlich nicht zulässig. Unter der Bedingung, dass die Voraussetzungen eines Opting-out (Art. 727a Abs. 2 E OR) erfüllt werden, sind jedoch Einschränkungen möglich ([...]).

---

54 ROSMARIE ABOLFATHIAN-HAMMER, Das Verhältnis von Revisionsstelle und Revisor zur Aktiengesellschaft, Diss. Bern 1992, 31, m.w.N.; PETER BÖCKLI, Schweizer Aktienrecht, 2. Aufl., Zürich 1996, N 1837.
55 ROLF WATTER, in: Honsell/Vogt/Watter (Hrsg.), Basler Kommentar zum Schweizerischen Privatrecht, Obligationenrecht II, Art. 530–1186 OR, 2. Aufl., Basel 2002, Art. 731a N 3.

Art. 731a Abs. 1 E OR ist auch im Zusammenhang mit Art. 627 Ziff. 13 OR zu lesen. Entgegen Stellungnahmen in der Lehre[56] besteht zwischen diesen beiden Bestimmungen keine Diskrepanz: Generelle und über ein Geschäftsjahr hinaus geltende Bestimmungen sind gemäss Art. 627 Ziff. 13 OR in den Statuten niederzulegen. Für einmalige Anordnungen – etwa auf Grund besonderer Umstände oder Geschäftsvorfälle – genügt jedoch ein Beschluss der Generalversammlung; eine Änderung der Statuten bliebe hier ohne Sinn.

Abs. 2 schränkt die Erweiterung der Prüfaufgaben der Revisionsstelle insofern ein, als dieser weder Aufgaben des Verwaltungsrates (vgl. dazu Art. 716a Abs. 1 Ziff. 4 und 5 OR) noch solche zugeteilt werden dürfen, welche die Unabhängigkeit der Revisionsstelle beeinträchtigen können (vgl. dazu Art. 728 und Art. 729 E OR). Die Vermischung der Aufgaben und Verantwortlichkeiten dieser beiden Organe soll vermieden werden. Es handelt sich dabei um eine Vorschrift zur Corporate Governance.

Der Generalversammlung steht es gemäss *Abs. 3* offen, zur Prüfung der Geschäftsführung oder einzelner Teile davon Sachverständige zu ernennen. Auch diese Möglichkeit wird selten genutzt, kann sich aber unter Umständen als nützlich erweisen[57].

D. Mängel in der Organisation der Gesellschaft

Art. 731b

1 Fehlt der Gesellschaft eines der vorgeschriebenen Organe oder ist eines dieser Organe nicht rechtmässig zusammengesetzt, so kann ein Aktionär, ein Gläubiger oder der Handelsregisterführer dem Richter beantragen, die erforderlichen Massnahmen zu ergreifen. Der Richter kann insbesondere:

1. **der Gesellschaft unter Androhung ihrer Auflösung eine Frist ansetzen, binnen derer der rechtmässige Zustand wieder herzustellen ist;**
2. **das fehlende Organ oder einen Sachwalter ernennen;**

---

56 Statt vieler PETER FORSTMOSER/ARTHUR MEIER-HAYOZ / PETER NOBEL, Schweizerisches Aktienrecht, Bern 1996, § 8 N 82 f.
57 PETER BÖCKLI, Schweizer Aktienrecht, 2. Auflage, Zürich 1996, N 1839; PETER FORSTMOSER/ARTHUR MEIER-HAYOZ/PETER NOBEL, Schweizerisches Aktienrecht, Bern 1996, § 33 N 107.

3. die Gesellschaft auflösen und ihre Liquidation nach den Vorschriften über den Konkurs anordnen.

² Ernennt der Richter das fehlende Organ oder einen Sachwalter, so bestimmt er die Dauer, für die die Ernennung gültig ist. Er verpflichtet die Gesellschaft, die Kosten zu tragen und den ernannten Personen einen Vorschuss zu leisten.

³ Liegt ein wichtiger Grund vor, so kann die Gesellschaft vom Richter die Abberufung von Personen verlangen, die dieser eingesetzt hat.

Der Entwurf sieht eine vollständige Neuordnung des Vorgehens bei Mängeln in der Organisation der Gesellschaft vor. Eine Neuregelung erscheint aus den folgenden Gründen erforderlich:

– Bezeichnet eine Aktiengesellschaft selbst keine Revisionsstelle, so bestimmt der Richter nach Art. 727*f* OR eine Revisorin oder einen Revisor. Diese Vorschrift erwies sich jedoch in der Praxis als unzulänglich, da Revisorinnen und Revisoren ein Mandat meist nur gegen einen Kostenvorschuss annehmen und sich zudem die Möglichkeiten richterlicher Zwangsmassnahmen als unklar und ungenügend herausstellten.

– Im Rahmen der Revision des Vormundschaftsrechts sollen vormundschaftliche Massnahmen auf natürliche Personen beschränkt werden. Die Möglichkeit der Ernennung eines Beistandes für juristische Personen nach Art. 393 Ziff. 4 ZGB ist daher zu ersetzen.

– Die bisherigen rechtlichen Grundlagen für das Vorgehen bei Mängeln in der Organisation von Gesellschaften sind zahlreich und unübersichtlich und zudem ungenügend aufeinander abgestimmt[58].

Die vorliegende Bestimmung will eine einheitliche Ordnung für die Behebung und Sanktionierung sämtlicher Mängel in der gesetzlich vorgeschriebenen Organisation der Gesellschaft schaffen. Erfasst werden sowohl das Fehlen als auch die nicht rechtsgenügende Zusammensetzung obligatorischer Organe. Die Fälle der Durchsetzung zwingender Vorgaben werden gegenüber dem geltenden Recht nicht erweitert, sondern nur einheitlich geregelt. Unter diese Vorschrift fallen insbesondere die folgenden Tatbestände: Die Handlungsunfähigkeit eines Gesellschaftsorgans, das

---

58 s. Art. 625 Abs. 2, Art. 708 Abs. 4, Art. 727*e* Abs. 3, Art. 727*f* und Art. 740 Abs. 3 OR; Art. 393 Ziff. 4 ZGB; Art. 86 Abs. 1bis bis 3 HRegV.

Fehlen eines Verwaltungsrates (Art. 707 OR), das Fehlen eines Präsidenten des Verwaltungsrates (Art. 711 OR), das Fehlen einer Revisionsstelle (Art. 727 OR), das Verletzen der Anforderungen an die Befähigung und Unabhängigkeit der Revisionsstelle (Art. 727a ff. OR) sowie die Verletzung von Wohnsitzerfordernissen (Art. 718 Abs. 3 E OR und Art. 727 Abs. 2 OR).

Ähnlich wie bei der Auflösung der Gesellschaft aus wichtigem Grund (s. Art. 736 Ziff. 4 OR) muss dem Gericht ein hinreichender Handlungsspielraum gewährt werden, weil es die konkreten Umstände zu berücksichtigen gilt und weil sowohl vom Fehlen eines Organs als auch von Zwangsmassnahmen nicht nur die Gesellschaft und deren Aktionärinnen und Aktionäre, sondern auch Dritte berührt werden können (insbes. Gläubigerinnen und Gläubiger, Arbeitnehmerinnen und Arbeitnehmer).

Fehlt einer Gesellschaft eines der vorgeschriebenen Organe oder ist eines dieser Organe nicht rechtsgenügend zusammengesetzt, so soll eine Aktionärin oder ein Aktionär, eine Gläubigerin oder ein Gläubiger sowie die Handelsregisterführerin oder der Handelsregisterführer (vgl. Art. 941a E OR) dem Gericht beantragen können, die erforderlichen Massnahmen zu ergreifen (*Abs. 1*). Es liegt daraufhin beim Gericht, die Anordnungen zu treffen, die nach den Umständen zur Durchsetzung der zwingenden gesetzlichen Vorgaben geeignet erscheinen. Auf Grund der Interessen Dritter sowie der Öffentlichkeit besteht keine Bindung an allfällige spezifizierte Anträge der Parteien. Die Richterin oder der Richter kann insbesondere:

– der Gesellschaft unter Androhung ihrer Auflösung eine *Frist zur Wiederherstellung des rechtmässigen Zustandes* ansetzen (*Ziff. 1*);
– *das fehlende Organ ernennen* (*Ziff. 2*), so beispielsweise in andauernden Pattsituationen oder bei Handlungsunfähigkeit der einzigen Aktionärin oder des einzigen Aktionärs;
– als befristete Massnahme *eine Sachwalterin oder einen Sachwalter ernennen* (*Ziff. 2*)[59], wobei die Kompetenzen im Urteil zu bestimmen sind (bspw. die Führung der Geschäfte oder die Behebung eines Mangels);
– die *Gesellschaft auflösen* und ihre *Liquidation* nach den Vorschriften über den Konkurs anordnen (*Ziff. 3*).

Wird eine zwangsweise Liquidation angeordnet, so gelangen die Vorschriften über den Konkurs auch dann sinngemäss zur Anwendung, wenn

---

59 Die Ernennung eines Sachwalters wird bereits in Art. 725a OR vorgesehen.

die Gesellschaft nicht überschuldet ist. Eine entsprechende Zwangsmassnahme ist erforderlich, da sich in der Praxis gezeigt hat, dass Gesellschaften, die nach Art. 625 Abs. 2 OR durch das Gericht aufgelöst wurden, ihre Geschäftstätigkeit ungehindert fortsetzten.

Soweit dies sachlich notwendig ist, hat das Gericht die Dauer der getroffenen Massnahme festzusetzen (so insbesondere bei der Bestellung eines Organs und der Ernennung eines Sachwalters; *Abs. 2*). Es versteht sich von selbst, dass richterliche Anordnungen von der Generalversammlung weder widerrufen noch durch andere Beschlüsse derogiert werden dürfen[60].

Die Kosten sämtlicher Massnahmen sind durch die Gesellschaft zu tragen. Das Gericht kann diese auch verpflichten, den ernannten Personen (so der Revisionsstelle oder dem Sachwalter) einen Vorschuss zu leisten (*Abs. 2*).

Abs. 3 sieht zum Schutz der Gesellschaft vor, dass diese vom Gericht die Abberufung gerichtlich eingesetzter Personen verlangen kann, sofern dafür ein wichtiger Grund vorliegt.

Durch gesetzliche Verweisungen gelangt Art. 731*b* E OR auch für die GmbH und die Genossenschaft zur Anwendung (s. Art. 819 und 910*a* E OR). Für den Verein und die Stiftung sind auf Grund der Besonderheiten dieser Rechtsformen differenzierte Vorschriften zu schaffen (s. Art. 69*a* bzw. 83 E ZGB).

Vierter Abschnitt: Herabsetzung des Aktienkapitals

A. Herabsetzungsbeschluss

Art. 732

1 Beabsichtigt eine Aktiengesellschaft, ihr Aktienkapital herabzusetzen, ohne es gleichzeitig bis zur bisherigen Höhe durch neues, voll einzubezahlendes Kapital zu ersetzen, so hat die Generalversammlung eine entsprechende Änderung der Statuten zu beschliessen.

2 Sie darf einen solchen Beschluss nur fassen, wenn ein zugelassener Revisionsexperte in einem Prüfungsbericht bestätigt, dass die Forderungen der Gläubiger trotz der Herabsetzung des Aktien-

---

60 vgl. BGE 126 III 283 ff.

Kapitel 1: Neue Gesetzesbestimmungen und Erläuterungen

kapitals voll gedeckt sind. Der Revisionsexperte muss an der Generalversammlung anwesend sein.

3 Im Beschluss ist das Ergebnis des Prüfungsberichts festzustellen und anzugeben, in welcher Art und Weise die Kapitalherabsetzung durchgeführt werden soll.

4 Ein aus der Kapitalherabsetzung allfällig sich ergebender Buchgewinn ist ausschliesslich zu Abschreibungen zu verwenden.

5 Das Aktienkapital darf nur unter 100 000 Franken herabgesetzt werden, sofern es gleichzeitig durch neues, voll einzubezahlendes Kapital in der Höhe von mindestens 100 000 Franken ersetzt wird.

Der Entwurf formuliert *Abs. 2* redaktionell neu und ersetzt den Begriff der besonders befähigten Revisorin bzw. des besonders befähigten Revisors durch jenen der zugelassenen Revisionsexpertin bzw. des zugelassenen Revisionsexperten (vgl. dazu die [...] Erläuterungen zu Art. 4 E RAG). Materielle Änderungen ergeben sich daraus keine.

Abs. 3 wird ebenfalls redaktionell angepasst.

Abs. 5: Nach dem geltenden Recht darf das Aktienkapital in keinem Fall unter 100 000 Franken herabgesetzt werden. Dieser Wortlaut steht im Widerspruch zur Zulässigkeit der Herabsetzung auf null im Rahmen einer Sanierung, sofern das Kapital verbunden mit der Herabsetzung wieder erhöht wird. Die Wiedererhöhung muss jedoch gemeinsam mit der Herabsetzung erfolgen und die Schranke von 100 000 Franken beachten. Um einen grammatikalischen Widerspruch zur neuen Bestimmung über die Vernichtung von Aktien anlässlich einer Sanierung (Art. 732*a* E OR) zu vermeiden, wird Art. 732 Abs. 5 OR neu redigiert und damit die einzige Ausnahme von der Vorschrift zum Mindestkapital (Art. 621 OR) klar umschrieben.

B. Vernichtung von Aktien im Fall einer Sanierung

Art. 732a

1 Wird das Aktienkapital zum Zwecke der Sanierung auf null herabgesetzt und anschliessend wieder erhöht, so gehen die bisherigen Mitgliedschaftsrechte der Aktionäre mit der Herabsetzung unter. Ausgegebene Aktien müssen vernichtet werden.

561

2 Bei der Wiedererhöhung des Aktienkapitals steht den bisherigen Aktionären ein Bezugsrecht zu, das ihnen nicht entzogen werden kann.

Hat eine Gesellschaft einen Kapitalverlust i.S.v. Art. 725 Abs. 1 OR erlitten, so kann die Generalversammlung als Sanierungsmassnahme unter anderem einen so genannten «Kapitalschnitt» beschliessen. Ist nach einer objektiven Beurteilung das Aktienkapital vollständig verloren, so ist es möglich, dieses auf null herabzusetzen und zugleich wieder zu erhöhen, wobei die bisherigen Aktien vernichtet werden. In einem neueren Urteil hat das Bundesgericht entschieden, dass die bisherigen Aktionärinnen und Aktionäre ihre Gesellschafterstellung ungeachtet der Vernichtung ihrer Aktien beibehalten und selbst dann, wenn sie sich nicht an der Wiedererhöhung des Kapitals beteiligen, ein minimales Stimmrecht (d.h. zumindest eine Stimme) bewahren[61].

Auf Grund dieser Rechtsprechung entstehen Aktionärinnen und Aktionäre, die entgegen der Grundstruktur der Aktiengesellschaft nicht mehr am Aktienkapital beteiligt sind. Der Entscheid des Bundesgerichts wurde daher in der Literatur zu Recht kritisiert[62]. Die Gesellschafterstellung ist in der Kapitalgesellschaft zwingend mit einer Beteiligung am Risikokapital verbunden. Geht dieses Risikokapital verloren, muss dementsprechend auch die damit verbundene Beteiligung ein Ende finden. Personen, die weder am Aktienkapital noch am wirtschaftlichen Erfolg der Gesellschaft teilhaben, weisen kein sachlich begründetes Interesse an der Ausübung des Stimmrechts auf; eine frühere Beteiligung kann dazu nicht ausreichen. Die Einräumung des Stimmrechts an Personen, die über keine Aktien mehr verfügen, lässt eine Art «Phantom-Aktionärinnen» und «Phantom-Aktionäre» entstehen, denen eine gesetzlich nicht vorgesehene Rechtsstellung zukommt. Dies kann nicht nur eine Erschwerung der Sanierung zur Folge haben, sondern führt zu zahlreichen Rechtsfragen und praktischen Schwierigkeiten während der gesamten weiteren Dauer der Gesellschaft (bspw. bei einer Fusion).

Um diesen Problemen zu begegnen, sieht der Entwurf eine gesetzliche Ordnung der Vernichtung von Aktien im Rahmen einer Sanierung vor.

---

61 gl. BGE 121 III 420 ff., insbes. S. 429 ff., Erwägung 4c.
62 s. BERNHARD BODMER, Urteil der 1. Zivilabteilung des Bundesgerichtes vom 7. Juli 1995 in Sachen T. AG gegen E. AG und M. AG, in: SZW 68 (1996) 285 ff.; PETER BÖCKLI, Kapitalschnitt zwecks Sanierung: Untergang der alten Mitgliedschaftsrechte zufolge Kapitalherabsetzung, in: REPRAX 1/02 S. 1 ff.

Sämtliche Rechte, die aus der Beteiligung am Aktienkapital fliessen, sollen gemäss dessen Charakter als Risikokapital untergehen, wenn das Aktienkapital zufolge eines Kapitalverlustes als vollständig verloren betrachtet werden muss. *Abs. 1* hält demnach fest, dass die bisherigen Mitgliedschaftsrechte der Aktionärinnen und Aktionäre entfallen, wenn das Aktienkapital zum Zwecke der Sanierung auf null herabgesetzt und sogleich wieder erhöht wird (zum Übergangsrecht s. Art. 10 UeB.). Ausgegebene Aktien sind dabei zu vernichten. Diese Regelung bleibt auf Fälle beschränkt, in denen die Kombination einer Kapitalherabsetzung mit einer Kapitalerhöhung dem Zweck der Sanierung dient.

Der grundsätzlich nicht entziehbaren Rechtsstellung der Aktionärinnen und Aktionäre muss im Falle eines gänzlichen Kapitalverlustes dadurch Rechnung getragen werden, dass ihnen ein unbedingtes und unentziehbares Recht zugestanden wird, sich im Ausmass ihres bisherigen Aktienbesitzes an der Wiedererhöhung des Aktienkapitals zu beteiligen. *Abs. 2* räumt den bisherigen Aktionärinnen und Aktionären demgemäss bei der Wiedererhöhung des Aktienkapitals ein zwingendes und unentziehbares Bezugsrecht ein.

Eine Kapitalherabsetzung zu Sanierungszwecken kann nicht nur durch eine Vernichtung von Aktien, sondern auch durch eine Herabsetzung des Nennwerts der Aktien erfolgen. Dabei muss allerdings der Mindestnennwert von einem Rappen beachtet werden (Art. 622 Abs. 4 OR). Die Möglichkeit, den Nennwert im Fall einer Sanierung unter den gesetzlichen Mindestwert herabzusetzen, wurde im Zusammenhang mit der Reduktion des Mindestnennwerts von 10 Franken auf nur einen Rappen richtigerweise aufgegeben[63]. Ist selbst dieser Mindestnennwert nicht mehr durch Aktiven gedeckt, so erweist sich eine Vernichtung der bisherigen Aktien als zwingend. In Ergänzung zur Revision von Art. 622 OR schafft die vorliegende Bestimmung die nötige Rechtssicherheit für die Vernichtung bisheriger Aktien.

---

63 Zur Revision von Art. 622 Abs. 4 OR, s. BBl 2000 4493, 4568, 5501 ff., 6113; AB 2000 S S. 585 und 944, N S. 1317 und 1616; AS 2001 1047.

Teil F: Rechtliche Aspekte / Legal aspects

C. Aufforderung an die Gläubiger

Art. 733

Hat die Generalversammlung die Herabsetzung des Aktienkapitals beschlossen, so veröffentlicht der Verwaltungsrat den Beschluss dreimal im Schweizerischen Handelsamtsblatt und überdies in der in den Statuten vorgesehenen Form und gibt den Gläubigern bekannt, dass sie binnen zwei Monaten, von der dritten Bekanntmachung im Schweizerischen Handelsamtsblatt an gerechnet, unter Anmeldung ihrer Forderungen Befriedigung oder Sicherstellung verlangen können.

Art. 733 Randtitel

Geändert wird nur die Nummerierung des Randtitels.

D. Durchführung der Herabsetzung

Art. 734

Die Herabsetzung des Aktienkapitals darf erst nach Ablauf der den Gläubigern gesetzten Frist und nach Befriedigung oder Sicherstellung der angemeldeten Gläubiger durchgeführt und erst in das Handelsregister eingetragen werden, wenn durch öffentliche Urkunde festgestellt ist, dass die Vorschriften dieses Abschnittes erfüllt sind. Der Urkunde ist der Prüfungsbericht beizulegen.

Die Bestimmung wurde an die Terminologie von Art. 732 Abs. 2 und 3 E OR angepasst. Weiter wird die Nummerierung des Randtitels geändert.

Kapitel 1: Neue Gesetzesbestimmungen und Erläuterungen

E. Herabsetzung im Fall einer Unterbilanz

Art. 735

Die Aufforderung an die Gläubiger und ihre Befriedigung oder Sicherstellung können unterbleiben, wenn das Aktienkapital zum Zwecke der Beseitigung einer durch Verluste entstandenen Unterbilanz in einem diese letztere nicht übersteigenden Betrage herabgesetzt wird.

Geändert wird nur die Nummerierung des Randtitels.

Fünfter Abschnitt: Auflösung der Aktiengesellschaft

A. Auflösung im Allgemeinen

I. Gründe

Art. 736

Die Gesellschaft wird aufgelöst:

1. **nach Massgabe der Statuten;**
2. **durch einen Beschluss der Generalversammlung, über den eine öffentliche Urkunde zu errichten ist;**
3. **durch die Eröffnung des Konkurses;**
4. [64]**durch Urteil des Richters, wenn Aktionäre, die zusammen mindestens zehn Prozent des Aktienkapitals vertreten, aus wichtigen Gründen die Auflösung verlangen. Statt derselben kann der Richter auf eine andere sachgemässe und den Beteiligten zumutbare Lösung erkennen;**
5. **in den übrigen vom Gesetze vorgesehenen Fällen.**

---

64 Fassung gemäss Ziff. I des BG vom 4. Okt. 1991, in Kraft seit 1. Juli 1992 (AS 1992 733 786; BBl 1983 II 745).

565

Teil F: Rechtliche Aspekte / Legal aspects

II. Anmeldung beim Handelsregister

Art. 737

Erfolgt die Auflösung der Gesellschaft nicht durch Konkurs oder richterliches Urteil, so ist sie vom Verwaltungsrat zur Eintragung in das Handelsregister anzumelden.

III. Folgen

Art. 738

Die aufgelöste Gesellschaft tritt in Liquidation, unter Vorbehalt der Fälle der Fusion, der Aufspaltung und der Übertragung ihres Vermögens auf eine Körperschaft des öffentlichen Rechts.

B. Auflösung mit Liquidation

I. Zustand der Liquidation. Befugnisse

Art. 739

1 Tritt die Gesellschaft in Liquidation, so behält sie die juristische Persönlichkeit und führt ihre bisherige Firma, jedoch mit dem Zusatz «in Liquidation», bis die Auseinandersetzung auch mit den Aktionären durchgeführt ist.

2 Die Befugnisse der Organe der Gesellschaft werden mit dem Eintritt der Liquidation auf die Handlungen beschränkt, die für die Durchführung der Liquidation erforderlich sind, ihrer Natur nach jedoch nicht von den Liquidatoren vorgenommen werden können.

II. Bestellung und Abberufung der Liquidatoren

1. Bestellung

Art. 740

1 Die Liquidation wird durch den Verwaltungsrat besorgt, sofern sie nicht in den Statuten oder durch einen Beschluss der Generalversammlung anderen Personen übertragen wird.

2 Die Liquidatoren sind vom Verwaltungsrat zur Eintragung in das Handelsregister anzumelden, auch wenn die Liquidation vom Verwaltungsrat besorgt wird.

3 Wenigstens einer der Liquidatoren muss in der Schweiz wohnhaft und zur Vertretung berechtigt sein.

4 Wird die Gesellschaft durch richterliches Urteil aufgelöst, so bestimmt der Richter die Liquidatoren.[65]

5 Im Falle des Konkurses besorgt die Konkursverwaltung die Liquidation nach den Vorschriften des Konkursrechtes. Die Organe der Gesellschaft behalten die Vertretungsbefugnis nur, soweit eine Vertretung durch sie noch notwendig ist.

Das Verfahren zur gerichtlichen Ernennung einer Liquidatorin oder eines Liquidators mit Wohnsitz in der Schweiz wird durch die Regelung von Art. 731*b* E OR ersetzt. Der zweite Satz von Art. 740 Abs. 3 E OR ist daher zu streichen.

2. Abberufung

Art. 741

1 Die Generalversammlung kann die von ihr ernannten Liquidatoren jederzeit abberufen.

---

[65] Fassung gemäss Ziff. I des BG vom 4. Okt. 1991, in Kraft seit 1. Juli 1992 (AS 1992 733 786; BBl 1983 II 745).

567

² Auf Antrag eines Aktionärs kann der Richter, sofern wichtige Gründe vorliegen, Liquidatoren abberufen und nötigenfalls andere ernennen.

III. Liquidationstätigkeit

1. Bilanz. Schuldenruf

Art. 742

¹ Die Liquidatoren haben bei der Übernahme ihres Amtes eine Bilanz aufzustellen.

² Die aus den Geschäftsbüchern ersichtlichen oder in anderer Weise bekannten Gläubiger sind durch besondere Mitteilung, unbekannte Gläubiger und solche mit unbekanntem Wohnort durch öffentliche Bekanntmachung im Schweizerischen Handelsamtsblatt und überdies in der von den Statuten vorgesehenen Form von der Auflösung der Gesellschaft in Kenntnis zu setzen und zur Anmeldung ihrer Ansprüche aufzufordern.

2. Übrige Aufgaben

Art. 743

¹ Die Liquidatoren haben die laufenden Geschäfte zu beendigen, noch ausstehende Aktienbeträge nötigenfalls einzuziehen, die Aktiven zu verwerten und die Verpflichtungen der Gesellschaft, sofern die Bilanz und der Schuldenruf keine Überschuldung ergeben, zu erfüllen.

² Sie haben, sobald sie eine Überschuldung feststellen, den Richter zu benachrichtigen; dieser hat die Eröffnung des Konkurses auszusprechen.

³ Sie haben die Gesellschaft in den zur Liquidation gehörenden Rechtsgeschäften zu vertreten, können für sie Prozesse führen, Vergleiche und Schiedsverträge abschliessen und, soweit erforderlich, auch neue Geschäfte eingehen.

4 Sie dürfen Aktiven auch freihändig verkaufen, wenn die Generalversammlung nichts anderes angeordnet hat.

5 Sie haben bei länger andauernder Liquidation jährliche Zwischenbilanzen aufzustellen.

6 Die Gesellschaft haftet für den Schaden aus unerlaubten Handlungen, die ein Liquidator in Ausübung seiner geschäftlichen Verrichtungen begeht.

3. Gläubigerschutz

Art. 744

1 Haben bekannte Gläubiger die Anmeldung unterlassen, so ist der Betrag ihrer Forderungen gerichtlich zu hinterlegen.

2 Ebenso ist für die nicht fälligen und die streitigen Verbindlichkeiten der Gesellschaft ein entsprechender Betrag zu hinterlegen, sofern nicht den Gläubigern eine gleichwertige Sicherheit bestellt oder die Verteilung des Gesellschaftsvermögens bis zur Erfüllung dieser Verbindlichkeiten ausgesetzt wird.

4. Verteilung des Vermögens

Art. 745

1 Das Vermögen der aufgelösten Gesellschaft wird nach Tilgung ihrer Schulden, soweit die Statuten nichts anderes bestimmen, unter die Aktionäre nach Massgabe der einbezahlten Beträge und unter Berücksichtigung der Vorrechte einzelner Aktienkategorien verteilt.[66]

2 Die Verteilung darf frühestens nach Ablauf eines Jahres vollzogen werden, von dem Tage an gerechnet, an dem der Schuldenruf zum dritten Mal ergangen ist.

---

66 Fassung gemäss Ziff. I des BG vom 4. Okt. 1991, in Kraft seit 1. Juli 1992 (AS 1992 733 786; BBl 1983 II 745).

3 Eine Verteilung darf bereits nach Ablauf von drei Monaten erfolgen, wenn ein zugelassener Revisionsexperte bestätigt, dass die Schulden getilgt sind und nach den Umständen angenommen werden kann, dass keine Interessen Dritter gefährdet werden.

Der Entwurf ersetzt den Begriff der besonders befähigten Revisorin bzw. des besonders befähigten Revisors durch jenen der zugelassenen Revisionsexpertin bzw. des zugelassenen Revisionsexperten (vgl. dazu die Erläuterungen zu Art. 4 E RAG).

IV. Löschung im Handelsregister

Art. 746

Nach Beendigung der Liquidation ist das Erlöschen der Firma von den Liquidatoren beim Handelsregisteramt anzumelden.

V. Aufbewahrung der Geschäftsbücher

Art. 747

Die Geschäftsbücher der aufgelösten Gesellschaft sind während zehn Jahren an einem sicheren Ort aufzubewahren, der von den Liquidatoren, und wenn sie sich nicht einigen, vom Handelsregisteramt zu bezeichnen ist.

C. Auflösung ohne Liquidation
II. Übernahme durch eine Körperschaft des öffentlichen Rechts

Art. 751

1 Wird das Vermögen einer Aktiengesellschaft vom Bunde, von einem Kanton oder unter Garantie des Kantons von einem Bezirk oder von einer Gemeinde übernommen, so kann mit Zustimmung der General-

versammlung vereinbart werden, dass die Liquidation unterbleiben soll.

2 Der Beschluss der Generalversammlung ist nach den Vorschriften über die Auflösung zu fassen und beim Handelsregisteramt anzumelden.

3 Mit der Eintragung dieses Beschlusses ist der Übergang des Vermögens der Gesellschaft mit Einschluss der Schulden vollzogen, und es ist die Firma der Gesellschaft zu löschen.

Sechster Abschnitt: Verantwortlichkeit

A. Haftung

I. Für den Emissionsprospekt

Art. 752

Sind bei der Gründung einer Gesellschaft oder bei der Ausgabe von Aktien, Obligationen oder anderen Titeln in Emissionsprospekten oder ähnlichen Mitteilungen unrichtige, irreführende oder den gesetzlichen Anforderungen nicht entsprechende Angaben gemacht oder verbreitet worden, so haftet jeder, der absichtlich oder fahrlässig dabei mitgewirkt hat, den Erwerbern der Titel für den dadurch verursachten Schaden.

II. Gründungshaftung

Art. 753

Gründer, Mitglieder des Verwaltungsrates und alle Personen, die bei der Gründung mitwirken, werden sowohl der Gesellschaft als den einzelnen Aktionären und Gesellschaftsgläubigern für den Schaden verantwortlich, wenn sie

1. absichtlich oder fahrlässig Sacheinlagen, Sachübernahmen oder die Gewährung besonderer Vorteile zugunsten von Aktionären

oder anderen Personen in den Statuten, einem Gründungsbericht oder einem Kapitalerhöhungsbericht unrichtig oder irreführend angeben, verschweigen oder verschleiern, oder bei der Genehmigung einer solchen Massnahme in anderer Weise dem Gesetz zuwiderhandeln;

2. absichtlich oder fahrlässig die Eintragung der Gesellschaft in das Handelsregister aufgrund einer Bescheinigung oder Urkunde veranlassen, die unrichtige Angaben enthält;

3. wissentlich dazu beitragen, dass Zeichnungen zahlungsunfähiger Personen angenommen werden.

III. Haftung für Verwaltung, Geschäftsführung und Liquidation

Art. 754

1 Die Mitglieder des Verwaltungsrates und alle mit der Geschäftsführung oder mit der Liquidation befassten Personen sind sowohl der Gesellschaft als den einzelnen Aktionären und Gesellschaftsgläubigern für den Schaden verantwortlich, den sie durch absichtliche oder fahrlässige Verletzung ihrer Pflichten verursachen.

2 Wer die Erfüllung einer Aufgabe befugterweise einem anderen Organ überträgt, haftet für den von diesem verursachten Schaden, sofern er nicht nachweist, dass er bei der Auswahl, Unterrichtung und Überwachung die nach den Umständen gebotene Sorgfalt angewendet hat.

IV. Revisionshaftung

Art. 755 (ursprünglicher Botschaftsentwurf)

Alle mit der Prüfung der Jahres- und Konzernrechnung, der Gründung, der Kapitalerhöhung oder Kapitalherabsetzung befassten Personen sind sowohl der Gesellschaft als auch den einzelnen Aktionären und Gesellschaftsgläubigern für den Schaden verantwortlich, den sie durch absichtliche oder fahrlässige Verletzung ihrer Pflichten verursachen.

Art. 755 (durch den Nationalrat bereinigte Version, neuer Abs. 2)

1 Alle mit der Prüfung der Jahres- und Konzernrechnung, der Gründung, der Kapitalerhöhung oder Kapitalherabsetzung befassten Personen sind sowohl der Gesellschaft als auch den einzelnen Aktionären und Gesellschaftsgläubigern für den Schaden verantwortlich, den sie durch absichtliche oder fahrlässige Verletzung ihrer Pflichten verursachen.

2 Wurde die Prüfung von einer Finanzkontrolle der öffentlichen Hand oder von einem ihrer Mitarbeiter durchgeführt, so haftet das betreffende Gemeinwesen. Der Rückgriff auf die an der Prüfung beteiligten Personen richtet sich nach dem öffentlichen Recht.

B. Schaden der Gesellschaft

I. Ansprüche ausser Konkurs

Art. 756

1 Neben der Gesellschaft sind auch die einzelnen Aktionäre berechtigt, den der Gesellschaft verursachten Schaden einzuklagen. Der Anspruch des Aktionärs geht auf Leistung an die Gesellschaft.

2 Hatte der Aktionär aufgrund der Sach- und Rechtslage begründeten Anlass zur Klage, so verteilt der Richter die Kosten, soweit sie nicht vom Beklagten zu tragen sind, nach seinem Ermessen auf den Kläger und die Gesellschaft.

II. Ansprüche im Konkurs

Art. 757

1 Im Konkurs der geschädigten Gesellschaft sind auch die Gesellschaftsgläubiger berechtigt, Ersatz des Schadens an die Gesellschaft zu verlangen. Zunächst steht es jedoch der Konkursverwaltung zu, die Ansprüche von Aktionären und Gesellschaftsgläubigern geltend zu machen.

2 Verzichtet die Konkursverwaltung auf die Geltendmachung dieser Ansprüche, so ist hierzu jeder Aktionär oder Gläubiger berechtigt. Das Ergebnis wird vorab zur Deckung der Forderungen der klagenden Gläubiger gemäss den Bestimmungen des Schuldbetreibungs- und Konkursgesetzes [67] verwendet. Am Überschuss nehmen die klagenden Aktionäre im Ausmass ihrer Beteiligung an der Gesellschaft teil; der Rest fällt in die Konkursmasse.

3 Vorbehalten bleibt die Abtretung von Ansprüchen der Gesellschaft gemäss Art. 260 des Schuldbetreibungs- und Konkursgesetzes.

III. Wirkung des Entlastungsbeschlusses

Art. 758

1 Der Entlastungsbeschluss der Generalversammlung wirkt nur für bekanntgegebene Tatsachen und nur gegenüber der Gesellschaft sowie gegenüber den Aktionären, die dem Beschluss zugestimmt oder die Aktien seither in Kenntnis des Beschlusses erworben haben.

2 Das Klagerecht der übrigen Aktionäre erlischt sechs Monate nach dem Entlastungsbeschluss.

---

[67] SR **281.1**

Kapitel 1: Neue Gesetzesbestimmungen und Erläuterungen

C. Solidarität und Rückgriff

Art. 759

1 Sind für einen Schaden mehrere Personen ersatzpflichtig, so ist jede von ihnen insoweit mit den anderen solidarisch haftbar, als ihr der Schaden aufgrund ihres eigenen Verschuldens und der Umstände persönlich zurechenbar ist.

2 Der Kläger kann mehrere Beteiligte gemeinsam für den Gesamtschaden einklagen und verlangen, dass der Richter im gleichen Verfahren die Ersatzpflicht jedes einzelnen Beklagten festsetzt.

3 Der Rückgriff unter mehreren Beteiligten wird vom Richter in Würdigung aller Umstände bestimmt.

D. Verjährung

Art. 760

1 Der Anspruch auf Schadenersatz gegen die nach den vorstehenden Bestimmungen verantwortlichen Personen verjährt in fünf Jahren von dem Tage an, an dem der Geschädigte Kenntnis vom Schaden und von der Person des Ersatzpflichtigen erlangt hat, jedenfalls aber mit dem Ablaufe von zehn Jahren, vom Tage der schädigenden Handlung an gerechnet.

2 Wird die Klage aus einer strafbaren Handlung hergeleitet, für die das Strafrecht eine längere Verjährung vorschreibt, so gilt diese auch für den Zivilanspruch.

Siebenter Abschnitt: Beteiligung von Körperschaften des öffentlichen Rechts

Art. 762

1 Haben Körperschaften des öffentlichen Rechts wie Bund, Kanton, Bezirk oder Gemeinde ein öffentliches Interesse an einer Aktiengesellschaft, so kann der Körperschaft in den Statuten der Gesellschaft das Recht eingeräumt werden, Vertreter in den Verwaltungsrat oder in die Revisionsstelle abzuordnen, auch wenn sie nicht Aktionärin ist.

2 Bei solchen Gesellschaften sowie bei gemischtwirtschaftlichen Unternehmungen, an denen eine Körperschaft des öffentlichen Rechts als Aktionär beteiligt ist, steht das Recht zur Abberufung der von ihr abgeordneten Mitglieder des Verwaltungsrates und der Revisionsstelle nur ihr selbst zu.

3 Die von einer Körperschaft des öffentlichen Rechts abgeordneten Mitglieder des Verwaltungsrates und der Revisionsstelle haben die gleichen Rechte und Pflichten wie die von der Generalversammlung gewählten.[68]

4 Für die von einer Körperschaft des öffentlichen Rechts abgeordneten Mitglieder haftet die Körperschaft der Gesellschaft, den Aktionären und den Gläubigern gegenüber, unter Vorbehalt des Rückgriffs nach dem Recht des Bundes und der Kantone.

Achter Abschnitt: Ausschluss der Anwendung des Gesetzes auf öffentlich-rechtliche Anstalten

Art. 763

1 Auf Gesellschaften und Anstalten, wie Banken, Versicherungs- oder Elektrizitätsunternehmen, die durch besondere kantonale Gesetze gegründet worden sind und unter Mitwirkung öffentlicher Behörden verwaltet werden, kommen, sofern der Kanton die subsidiäre Haftung für deren Verbindlichkeiten übernimmt, die Bestimmungen

---

[68] Fassung gemäss Ziff. I des BG vom 4. Okt. 1991, in Kraft seit 1. Juli 1992 (AS 1992 733 786; BBl 1983 II 745).

über die Aktiengesellschaft auch dann nicht zur Anwendung, wenn das Kapital ganz oder teilweise in Aktien zerlegt ist und unter Beteiligung von Privatpersonen aufgebracht wird.

2 Auf Gesellschaften und Anstalten, die vor dem 1. Januar 1883 durch besondere kantonale Gesetze gegründet worden sind und unter Mitwirkung öffentlicher Behörden verwaltet werden, finden die Bestimmungen über die Aktiengesellschaft auch dann keine Anwendung, wenn der Kanton die subsidiäre Haftung für die Verbindlichkeiten nicht übernimmt.

§ 2 Das Recht der Gesellschaft mit beschränkter Haftung

Erster Abschnitt: Allgemeine Bestimmungen

A. Begriff

Art. 772

1 Die Gesellschaft mit beschränkter Haftung ist eine personenbezogene Kapitalgesellschaft, an der eine oder mehrere Personen oder Handelsgesellschaften beteiligt sind. Ihr Stammkapital ist in den Statuten festgelegt. Für ihre Verbindlichkeiten haftet nur das Gesellschaftsvermögen.

2 Die Gesellschafter sind mindestens mit je einem Stammanteil am Stammkapital beteiligt. Die Statuten können für sie Nachschuss- und Nebenleistungspflichten vorsehen.

Die Legaldefinitionen der Gesellschaftsformen im Obligationenrecht wurden verschiedentlich kritisiert[69]. Sie enthalten teilweise Unwesentliches,

---

69 s. insbes. PETER BÖCKLI, Schweizer Aktienrecht, 2. Aufl. Zürich 1996, N 38*b*; PETER FORSTMOSER/ARTHUR MEIER-HAYOZ/PETER NOBEL, Schweizerisches Aktienrecht, Bern 1996, § 1 N 4; zur GmbH vgl. WERNER VON STEIGER, in: Zürcher

erwähnen aber umgekehrt wichtige Strukturelemente nicht. Der Entwurf umschreibt den Begriff der GmbH neu und trägt dabei auch der neuen Konzeption dieser Rechtsform Rechnung. *Abs. 1* charakterisiert die Gesellschaft als solche, während *Abs. 2* der Mitgliedschaft der Gesellschafterinnen und der Gesellschafter gewidmet ist. Die gesetzliche Begriffsbestimmung kann ihrer Natur gemäss nur wenige kennzeichnende Züge der GmbH hervorheben und beansprucht daher keine Vollständigkeit. Ihre Rechtsrelevanz liegt vorab darin, im Hinblick auf die Interpretation des Gesetzes die Paradigmen zu verdeutlichen, die der (Neu-)Regelung der GmbH zu Grunde gelegt wurden.

Abs. 1 umschreibt die GmbH als eine personenbezogene Kapitalgesellschaft, an der eine oder mehrere Personen oder Handelsgesellschaften beteiligt sind. Wie dies allen Kapitalgesellschaften[70] eigen ist, ist die GmbH eine Körperschaft, d.h. eine Gesellschaft mit juristischer Persönlichkeit. Der GmbH kommt demnach eine eigene, von ihren Gesellschafterinnen und Gesellschaftern losgelöste rechtliche Existenz zu. Bereits die Legaldefinition zeigt auf, dass eine GmbH zukünftig auch als blosse Einpersonengesellschaft gegründet werden kann (dazu hinten die Ausführungen zu Art. 775 E OR). Als Kapitalgesellschaft verfügt die GmbH über ein in den Statuten bestimmtes Grundkapital. Die Mitgliedschaft der Gesellschafterinnen und Gesellschafter beruht auf einer Beteiligung an diesem so genannten Stammkapital. Der Umfang ihrer finanziellen Beteiligung bestimmt – zumindest im Grundsatz – auch die ihnen zukommenden Rechte. Die GmbH wird aber vom Entwurf klar als personenbezogene[71] Kapitalgesellschaft ausgestaltet. Dies bedeutet, dass die rechtliche Organisation der Gesellschaft zwar einerseits auf dem Bestehen eines in den Statuten festgelegten Grundkapitals (d.h. des Stammkapitals) aufgebaut ist, dass aber andererseits die Strukturen der Rechtsform erlauben, neben der finanziellen Beteiligung weitgehend auch die Persönlichkeit der Gesellschafterinnen und Gesellschafter sowie weitere konkrete Umstände zu berücksichtigen. Als personenbezogene Elemente des GmbH-Rechts seien hier – als Beispiele – die Möglichkeit statutarischer Nachschuss- und Nebenleis-tungspflichten, die strenge Beschränkung der Abtretbarkeit der

---

Kommentar V/5c, Zürich 1965, Einleitung, N 40 ff.; HERBERT WOHLMANN, GmbH-Recht, Basel und Frankfurt a.M. 1997, S. 9 ff.

70 Als Kapitalgesellschaften gelten die Aktiengesellschaft (AG), die Kommanditaktiengesellschaft und die GmbH.
71 Zu den Unterschieden zwischen personenbezogenen und kapitalbezogenen Gesellschaftsformen s. insbes. ARTHUR MEIER-HAYOZ/PETER FORSTMOSER, Schweizerisches Gesellschaftsrecht, 8. Aufl., Bern 1998, § 3 N 13.

Anteile (Vinkulierung) sowie die Austritts- und Ausschlussmöglichkeiten erwähnt.

Der Entwurf unterstreicht die personenbezogenen Elemente der GmbH und zielt auf eine klare Ausrichtung dieser Rechtsform auf die Bedürfnisse von Unternehmen mit einem eher kleinen Kreis von Gesellschafterinnen und Gesellschaftern. Er stellt die GmbH der stärker kapitalbezogenen[72] Aktiengesellschaft als Alternative für Gesellschaften mit einem engen Personenbezug zur Seite (dies können durchaus auch grössere Gesellschaften sein). Im Ergebnis erscheinen die beiden Rechtsformen deutlicher auf bestimmte Bedürfnisse ausgerichtet als unter dem Recht von 1936, und sie ergänzen einander gegenseitig. Das Bundesgesetz über die Fusion, Spaltung, Umwandlung und Vermögensübertragung (Fusionsgesetz)[73] wird zudem zukünftig einen Wechsel von einer Rechtsform in die andere erleichtern, wenn ein solcher auf Grund veränderter Bedürfnisse wünschenswert erscheint (so bspw. wegen des Wachstums eines Unternehmens).

Der Entwurf hebt in der Definition der GmbH weiter hervor, dass die Haftung für Verbindlichkeiten der Gesellschaft auf deren Vermögen beschränkt bleibt. Diese konsequente Haftungsbeschränkung stellt insofern eine wichtige Neuerung dar, als der Entwurf auf die bisherige subsidiäre Solidarhaftung aller Gesellschafterinnen und Gesellschafter in der Höhe des nicht (oder nicht mehr) liberierten Stammkapitals verzichtet (vgl. Art. 802 OR; s. dazu hinten den Kommentar zu Art. 794 E OR).

Abs. 2 hält fest, dass die Gesellschafterinnen und Gesellschafter mit mindestens je einem Stammanteil am Stammkapital beteiligt sind. Der Ausgestaltung der GmbH als Kapitalgesellschaft entsprechend, beruht die Mitgliedschaft also zwingend auf einer Beteiligung am Stammkapital. Während aber im geltenden Recht die gesamte Beteiligung einer Gesellschafterin oder eines Gesellschafters in nur einem Stammanteil zusammengefasst werden musste (s. Art. 774 Abs. 2 OR), soll jede Gesellschafterin und jeder Gesellschafter nach dem Entwurf neu über mehrere Anteile verfügen können ([...]).

---

72 Zur Aktiengesellschaft als grundsätzlich «kapitalbezogene Kapitalgesellschaft» s. etwa PETER FORSTMOSER/ARTHUR MEIER-HAYOZ/PETER NOBEL, Schweizerisches Aktienrecht, Bern 1996, § 2 N 22 f.; CHRISTOPH VON GREYERZ, Die Aktiengesellschaft, in: Schweizerisches Privatrecht, Bd. VIII/2, Basel und Frankfurt a.M. 1982, S. 14; KARL WIELAND, Handelsrecht, II. Band, München und Leipzg 1931, S. 2.

73 Botschaft des Bundesrates zum Fusionsgesetz: BBl 2000 4337 ff.

Abs. 2 weist weiter darauf hin, dass die Statuten für die Gesellschafterinnen und Gesellschafter Nachschuss- und Nebenleistungspflichten vorsehen können (s. Art. 795 ff. E OR). Erwähnt werden damit nur zwei bedeutende Pflichten. Die Gesellschafterinnen und Gesellschafter unterstehen darüber hinaus einer (dispositiven) gesetzlichen Treuepflicht, und können mit einem Konkurrenzverbot belastet werden (s. Art. 803 E OR). Die Möglichkeit, den Gesellschafterinnen und Gesellschaftern je nach den konkreten Bedürfnissen bestimmte Pflichten aufzuerlegen, entspricht der personenbezogenen Struktur der GmbH; demgegenüber dürfen den Aktionärinnen und Aktionären in der AG keine Pflichten auferlegt werden, die über die Liberierung ihrer Aktien hinausgehen (s. Art. 680 Abs. 1 OR)

Nach dem geltenden Recht steht die GmbH ausschliesslich für wirtschaftliche Zwecke offen (Art. 772 Abs. 3 OR), während die Aktiengesellschaft auch für ideelle Zielsetzungen verwendet werden kann (s. Art. 620 Abs. 3 OR). Die Einschränkung der GmbH auf wirtschaftliche Vorhaben lässt sich jedoch sachlich nicht begründen. Der Entwurf stellt die GmbH als Rechtsform auch für ideelle und gemeinnützige Zwecke zur Verfügung; der bisherige *Abs. 3* wird gestrichen. Auf eine Bestimmung zu den Verwendungszwecken der GmbH (in Anlehnung an Art. 620 Abs. 3 OR) wird verzichtet, weil einer solchen Vorschrift kein normativer Gehalt zukäme.

B. Stammkapital

Art. 773

Das Stammkapital muss mindestens 20 000 Franken betragen.

Das Stammkapital darf nach dem geltenden Recht nicht weniger als 20 000 und nicht mehr als zwei Millionen Franken betragen (Art. 773 OR). Gemäss dem Entwurf soll die obere Begrenzung auf zwei Millionen Franken entfallen, da sie das Wachstum einer GmbH beeinträchtigen kann. Im Interesse von Kleinunternehmen wird auf eine Erhöhung des gesetzlich verlangten Mindestkapitals verzichtet, doch soll das Stammkapital zukünftig in jedem Fall voll liberiert werden. [...].

Kapitel 1: Neue Gesetzesbestimmungen und Erläuterungen

C. Stammanteile

Art. 774

1 Der Nennwert der Stammanteile muss mindestens 100 Franken betragen. Im Falle einer Sanierung kann er bis auf einen Franken herabgesetzt werden.

2 Die Stammanteile müssen mindestens zum Nennwert ausgegeben werden.

Nach geltendem Recht beträgt der Mindestnennwert der Stammanteile 1 000 Franken. In *Abs. 1* wird dieser Betrag auf 100 Franken gesenkt. Eine weitergehende Senkung erscheint im Hinblick auf den personenbezogenen Charakter, die Ausgestaltung als Rechtsform für einen beschränkten Kreis von Beteiligten und die fehlende Kapitalmarktfähigkeit der GmbH nicht sachgerecht.

Im Fall einer Sanierung soll der Nennwert jedoch unter den allgemeinen Mindestwert bis auf einen Franken herabgesetzt werden können; es entstehen dadurch Sanierungs-Stammanteile. (s. dazu Art. 732*a* i.V.m. Art. 782 Abs. 4 E OR sowie die Ausführungen zu Art. 732*a* E OR).

Nach geltendem Recht kann jede Gesellschafterin und jeder Gesellschafter nur einen einzigen Stammanteil besitzen (Art. 774 Abs. 2 OR). Bei der Veränderung der Beteiligung einer Gesellschafterin oder eines Gesellschafters (d.h. bei der Veräusserung eines Teils der bisherigen Beteiligung oder bei einem Zuerwerb) muss demzufolge die Grösse der Stammanteile angepasst werden. Dies bedingt jedoch einen öffentlich zu beurkundenden Gesellschafterbeschluss über die Änderung der Statuten. Um Veränderungen der Beteiligungsverhältnisse zu erleichtern, kann nach dem Entwurf jede Gesellschafterin und jeder Gesellschafter mehrere Stammanteile besitzen.

Abs. 2 hält fest, dass die Stammanteile mindestens zum Nennwert ausgegeben werden müssen; eine so genannte Unterpari-Emission ist demnach wie bei den andern Kapitalgesellschaften unzulässig. Die vorliegende Bestimmung betrifft nur die Festsetzung des Ausgabebetrags; die Leistung der Einlagen (Liberierung) ist in Art. 777*c* E OR geregelt.

D. Genussscheine

Art. 774a

Die Statuten können die Schaffung von Genussscheinen vorsehen; die Vorschriften des Aktienrechts sind entsprechend anwendbar.

Der Entwurf sieht die Möglichkeit der Ausgabe von Genussscheinen vor. Er schliesst damit eine Lücke des geltenden Rechts. Für die Regelung kann auf die aktienrechtlichen Vorschriften verwiesen werden (Art. 657 OR).

E. Gesellschafter

Art. 775

Eine Gesellschaft mit beschränkter Haftung kann durch eine oder mehrere natürliche oder juristische Personen oder andere Handelsgesellschaften gegründet werden.

Einpersonengesellschaften sind bereits heute weit verbreitet. Zur Gründung einer GmbH sind allerdings immer noch mindestens zwei Personen erforderlich (Art. 775 Abs. 1 OR); die Praxis behilft sich dabei häufig mit dem Beizug von «Strohleuten».

Werden sämtliche Stammanteile nach der Gründung in der Hand einer einzigen Person vereinigt, kann der Richter nach Art. 775 Abs. 2 OR auf Antrag einer Gläubigerin oder eines Gläubigers die Gesellschaft auflösen, wenn der gesetzmässige Zustand nicht innerhalb einer angemessenen Frist wieder hergestellt wird.

Der Entwurf sieht vor, diese Klagemöglichkeit zu streichen und die Gründung einer GmbH durch eine einzige Person zuzulassen. Diese Neuerung bringt für die Praxis eine massgebliche Vereinfachung und entspricht überdies der 12. EG-Richtlinie auf dem Gebiet des Gesellschaftsrechts[74].

---

74 Richtlinie 89/667/EWG; ABl N°L 395 vom 30.12.1989, S. 40 ff.

Die Gründung von Einpersonengesellschaften soll zugleich auch für die Rechtsform der Aktiengesellschaft ermöglicht werden (s. Art. 625 E OR; zur Genossenschaft s. die Ausführungen zu Art. 831 E OR).

Neben der Zulassung der Gründung von Einpersonengesellschaften in der Rechtsform der GmbH stellt *Art. 775* des Entwurfs auch klar, wer Gesellschafterin bzw. Gesellschafter sein kann: Die Mitgliedschaft steht natürlichen und juristischen Personen sowie anderen Handelsgesellschaften (d.h. Kollektiv- und Kommanditgesellschaften) offen. Dies entspricht sowohl der Lehre als auch der bereits 1934 im Parlament vertretenen Auffassung[75].

F. Statuten

I. Gesetzlich vorgeschriebener Inhalt

Art. 776

Die Statuten müssen Bestimmungen enthalten über:

1. **die Firma und den Sitz der Gesellschaft;**
2. **den Zweck der Gesellschaft;**
3. **die Höhe des Stammkapitals sowie die Anzahl und den Nennwert der Stammanteile;**
4. **die Form der von der Gesellschaft ausgehenden Bekanntmachungen.**

Diese Bestimmung legt den so genannt «absolut notwendigen Inhalt» der Statuten fest. *Ziff. 1* und *4* werden unverändert aus dem geltenden Recht übernommen, während *Ziff. 2* redaktionell modifiziert wird (der «Gegenstand des Unternehmens» wird durch den «Zweck der Gesellschaft» ersetzt). In *Ziff. 3* nimmt der Entwurf ebenfalls eine terminologische Anpassung vor («Nennwert» statt «Betrag der Stammeinlage»). Da jede Gesell-

---

[75] AB 1934 N, S. 733 ff., insbes. S. 740 ff.; statt vieler CARL BAUDENBACHER, in: Kommentar zum Schweizerischen Privatrecht, Obligationenrecht II, Basel und Frankfurt a.M. 1994, Art. 772 N 13; LUKAS HANDSCHIN, Die GmbH, Ein Grundriss, Zürich 1996, § 4 N 2; ROLAND RUEDIN, Droit des sociétés, Bern 1999, N 428; HERBERT WOHLMANN, GmbH-Recht, Basel und Frankfurt a.M. 1997, S. 38.

schafterin und jeder Gesellschafter neu mehrere Stammanteile besitzen darf (vgl. die Ausführungen zu Art. 774 E OR), wird zusätzlich die Angabe der Anzahl der Stammanteile verlangt.

II. Bedingt notwendiger Inhalt

Art. 776a

1 Zu ihrer Verbindlichkeit bedürfen der Aufnahme in die Statuten Bestimmungen über:

1. **die Begründung und die Ausgestaltung von Nachschuss- und Nebenleistungspflichten;**
2. **die Begründung und die Ausgestaltung von Vorhand-, Vorkaufs- oder Kaufsrechten der Gesellschafter oder der Gesellschaft an den Stammanteilen;**
3. **Konkurrenzverbote der Gesellschafter;**
4. **Konventionalstrafen zur Sicherung der Erfüllung gesetzlicher oder statutarischer Pflichten;**
5. **Vorrechte, die mit einzelnen Kategorien von Stammanteilen verbunden sind (Vorzugsstammanteile);**
6. **Vetorechte von Gesellschaftern betreffend Beschlüsse der Gesellschafterversammlung;**
7. **die Beschränkung des Stimmrechts und des Rechts der Gesellschafter, sich vertreten zu lassen;**
8. **Genussscheine;**
9. **statutarische Reserven;**
10. **Befugnisse der Gesellschafterversammlung, die dieser über die gesetzlichen Zuständigkeiten hinaus zugewiesen werden;**
11. **die Genehmigung bestimmter Entscheide der Geschäftsführer durch die Gesellschafterversammlung;**
12. **das Erfordernis der Zustimmung der Gesellschafterversammlung zur Bezeichnung von natürlichen Personen, die für Gesellschafter, die juristische Personen oder Handelsgesellschaften sind, das Recht zur Geschäftsführung ausüben;**

Kapitel 1: Neue Gesetzesbestimmungen und Erläuterungen

13. die Befugnis der Geschäftsführer, Direktoren, Prokuristen sowie Handlungsbevollmächtigte zu ernennen;
14. die Ausrichtung von Tantiemen an die Geschäftsführer;
15. die Zusicherung von Bauzinsen;
16. die Organisation und die Aufgaben der Revisionsstelle, sofern dabei über die gesetzlichen Vorschriften hinausgegangen wird;
17. die Gewährung eines statutarischen Austrittsrechts, die Bedingungen für dessen Ausübung und die auszurichtende Abfindung;
18. besondere Gründe für den Ausschluss von Gesellschaftern aus der Gesellschaft;
19. andere als die gesetzlichen Auflösungsgründe.

2 Zu ihrer Verbindlichkeit bedürfen ebenfalls der Aufnahme in die Statuten von den gesetzlichen Vorschriften abweichende Regelungen:

1. der Beschlussfassung über die nachträgliche Schaffung von neuen Vorzugsstammanteilen;
2. der Übertragung von Stammanteilen;
3. der Einberufung der Gesellschafterversammlung;
4. der Bemessung des Stimmrechts der Gesellschafter;
5. der Beschlussfassung in der Gesellschafterversammlung;
6. der Beschlussfassung der Geschäftsführer;
7. der Geschäftsführung und der Vertretung;
8. zu den Konkurrenzverboten der Geschäftsführer.

Die gesetzliche Ordnung des GmbH-Rechts ist in wichtigen Fragen dispositiver Natur. Dies ermöglicht, eine auf die konkreten Umstände und die persönlichen Verhältnisse bezogene Ausgestaltung der Gesellschaft zu schaffen. Die in Art. 776*a* E OR aufgezählten wesentlichen Gestaltungselemente müssen gegebenenfalls zwingend in den Statuten vorgesehen werden. Die Bestimmung zeigt auf, in welchen Punkten von der gesetzlichen Ordnung der GmbH abgewichen werden kann. Der Normgehalt bleibt jedoch auf die Aufzählung des bedingt notwendigen Inhalts der

Statuten beschränkt; die materielle Regelung der einzelnen Optionen erfolgt stets in andern Bestimmungen.

Die Aufzählung von *Abs. 1* entspricht teilweise dem geltenden Recht (vgl. Art. 777 OR); sie wurde aber vervollständigt und den Neuerungen des Entwurfs angepasst. Sie umfasst die folgenden Punkte:

- *Ziff. 1:* Bestimmungen betreffend die Begründung und die Ausgestaltung von *Nachschuss- und Nebenleistungspflichten* (s. dazu Art. 795 ff. E OR). Für Einzelheiten zu Nebenleistungspflichten kann in den Statuten auf ein Reglement verwiesen werden (s. Art. 796 Abs. 3 E OR).

- *Ziff. 2:* Bestimmungen betreffend (statutarische) *Vorhand-, Vorkaufs- oder Kaufsrechte* der Gesellschafterinnen und der Gesellschafter sowie der Gesellschaft an Stammanteilen. Es handelt sich dabei um eine besondere Art von Nebenleistungspflichten (s. dazu Art. 796 f. E OR). Unbenommen bleibt die Vereinbarung vertraglicher Erwerbsvorrechte ausserhalb der Statuten.

- *Ziff. 3:* Bestimmungen betreffend ein *Konkurrenzverbot* für Gesellschafterinnen und Gesellschafter. Nehmen diese an der Geschäftsführung teil, so unterstehen sie dem Konkurrenzverbot für Geschäftsführerinnen und Geschäftsführer (vgl. dazu Abs. 2 Ziff. 8 sowie Art. 803 Abs. 2 und Art. 812 Abs. 3 E OR). Unbenommen bleibt die Vereinbarung vertraglicher Konkurrenzverbote ausserhalb der Statuten.

- *Ziff. 4:* Bestimmungen betreffend *Konventionalstrafen* für den Fall der Nichterfüllung oder der nicht rechtzeitigen Erfüllung statutarischer oder gesetzlicher Pflichten (s. dazu Art. 796 E OR betr. Nebenleistungspflichten). Unbenommen bleibt die Vereinbarung vertraglicher Konventionalstrafen ausserhalb der Statuten.

- *Ziff. 5:* Bestimmungen betreffend Vorrechte, die mit einzelnen Kategorien von Stammanteilen verbunden werden (*Vorzugsstammanteile*; s. dazu Art. 654 Abs. 1 und 656 OR i.V.m. Art. 799 E OR).

- *Ziff. 6:* Bestimmungen betreffend *Vetorechte*, die bestimmten Gesellschafterinnen oder Gesellschaftern gegen Beschlüsse der Gesellschafterversammlung eingeräumt werden (s. dazu Art. 807 E OR).

- *Ziff. 7:* Bestimmungen betreffend eine *Beschränkung des Stimmrechts* der Gesellschafterinnen und Gesellschafter (s. dazu Art. 806 Abs. 1 E OR) sowie Bestimmungen betreffend eine *Beschränkung des Rechts,* sich in der Gesellschafterversammlung vertreten zu lassen (s. dazu Art. 689 Abs. 2 OR i.V.m. Art. 805 Abs. 5 Ziff. 8 E OR).

- *Ziff. 8:* Bestimmungen betreffend *Genussscheine* (s. dazu Art. 657 OR i.V.m. Art. 774a E OR).

- *Ziff. 9:* Bestimmungen betreffend *statutarische Reserven* (s. Art. 672 f. OR i.V.m. Art. 801 E OR).

- *Ziff. 10:* Bestimmungen betreffend *Befugnisse der Gesellschafterversammlung*, welche dieser über die gesetzlichen Zuständigkeiten hinaus zugewiesen werden (s. Art. 810 Abs. 1 E OR). Ausgeschlossen ist die Übertragung von Aufgaben, die vom Gesetz zwingend einem andern Organ vorbehalten sind (s. insbes. Art. 810 Abs. 2 E OR und Art. 728 ff. OR i.V.m. 818 Abs. 2 E OR)

- *Ziff. 11:* Bestimmungen, die gewisse Entscheide der Geschäftsführerinnen und Geschäftsführer dem Erfordernis der *Genehmigung durch die Gesellschafterversammlung* unterstellen, sowie Bestimmungen, die den Geschäftsführerinnen und Geschäftsführern die Möglichkeit einräumen, einzelne Fragen der Gesellschafterversammlung zur Genehmigung vorzulegen (s. dazu Art. 811 E OR).

- *Ziff. 12* bedarf einer näheren Erläuterung: Wenn die Statuten nichts anderes vorsehen, sind alle Gesellschafterinnen und Gesellschafter zur *Geschäftsführung* befugt (Art. 809 Abs. 1 E OR). Geschäftsführerinnen und Geschäftsführer können jedoch nur natürliche Personen sein (Art. 809 Abs. 2 E OR). Für Gesellschafterinnen, die an sich zur Geschäftsführung befugt wären, die aber juristische Personen oder Handelsgesellschaften sind, muss daher eine Sonderregelung getroffen werden: Sie dürfen eine natürliche Person bezeichnen, die an ihrer Stelle das Recht zur Geschäftsführung ausübt. Damit das Interesse der übrigen Beteiligten an einer einvernehmlichen Geschäftsführung gewahrt bleibt, sollen die Statuten nach dem Entwurf vorsehen können, dass die Bezeichnung von Personen, die für juristische Personen oder Handelsgesellschaften das Recht zur Geschäftsführung ausüben, der Zustimmung der Gesellschafterversammlung bedarf (s. Art. 809 Abs. 2 E OR).

- *Ziff. 13:* Bestimmungen betreffend die Befugnis der Geschäftsführerinnen und Geschäftsführer, *Direktorinnen und Direktoren, Prokuristinnen und Prokuristen sowie Handlungsbevollmächtigte zu ernennen* (s. dazu Art. 804 Abs. 3 E OR).

- *Ziff. 14:* Bestimmungen betreffend die Ausrichtung von *Tantiemen* an die Geschäftsführerinnen und Geschäftsführer (s. dazu Art. 677 OR i.V.m. Art. 798*b* E OR).
- *Ziff. 15:* Bestimmungen betreffend die Zusicherung von *Bauzinsen* (s. dazu Art. 676 OR i.V.m. Art. 798*a* Abs. 2 E OR)
- *Ziff. 16:* Bestimmungen betreffend die Organisation und die Aufgaben der *Revisionsstelle*, sofern die Gesellschaft eine solche hat und sofern über die gesetzlichen Vorschriften hinausgegangen wird (s. dazu Art. 818 E OR i.V.m. Art. 731 Abs. 1 OR).
- *Ziff. 17:* Bestimmungen betreffend die Gewährung eines *statutarischen Austrittsrechts* sowie betreffend die Bedingungen für die Ausübung dieses Rechts und die auszurichtende Abfindung (s. dazu Art. 822 Abs. 2 und Art. 825 E OR)
- *Ziff. 18:* Bestimmungen betreffend besondere *Gründe*, die einen *Ausschluss* von Gesellschafterinnen und Gesellschaftern ermöglichen (s. dazu Art. 823 Abs. 2 E OR). Der Ausschluss aus wichtigen Gründen (Art. 823 Abs. 1 E OR) braucht in den Statuten nicht vorgesehen zu werden; es ist aber auch nicht zulässig, die entsprechende gesetzliche Regelung in den Statuten abzuändern.
- *Ziff. 19:* Bestimmungen betreffend *Auflösungsgründe*, die über die gesetzlich geregelten Fälle der Auflösung hinausgehen (s. dazu Art. 821 Abs. 1 Ziff. 1 E OR).

Abs. 2 enthält eine Liste der Punkte, in denen die Statuten (und nur die Statuten) eine von den gesetzlichen Vorschriften abweichende Regelung treffen können:

- *Ziff. 1:* Regelungen zur Beschlussfassung über die *nachträgliche Schaffung von neuen Vorzugsstammanteilen* (s. dazu Art. 654 Abs. 2 OR i. V. m. Art. 799 E OR).
- *Ziff. 2:* Regelungen zur *Übertragung der Stammanteile*. Dabei handelt es sich um Vinkulierungsvorschriften, die von der dispositiven, gesetzlich vorgegebenen Vinkulierungsordnung abweichen (s. dazu Art. 786 Abs. 2 und Art. 788 Abs. 5 E OR). Die Statuten können hingegen weder auf die Formvorschriften für die Abtretung (s. Art. 785) noch auf Eintragung der Gesellschafterinnen und Gesellschafter im Handelsregister (s. dazu Art. 791 E OR) verzichten; es ist indessen zulässig, die Abtretung der Form der öffentlichen Beurkundung zu unterstellen.

- *Ziff. 3:* Regelungen zur *Einberufung der Gesellschafterversammlung* (s. dazu Art. 805 Abs. 2 und 3 E OR).
- *Ziff. 4:* Regelungen zur *Bemessung des Stimmrechts* (Ausgabe im Stimmrecht privilegierter Stammanteile; s. Art. 806 2 E OR)
- *Ziff. 5:* Regelungen zur *Beschlussfassung* in der Gesellschafterversammlung (erforderliche Mehrheit, einschliesslich Anwesenheitserfordernisse; Stichentscheid; s. dazu Art. 808, 808*a* und 808*b* Abs. 2 E OR).
- *Ziff. 6:* Regelungen zur *Beschlussfassung der Geschäftsführerinnen und Geschäftsführer* (zur Beschlussfassung erforderliche Mehrheit, einschliesslich Anwesenheitserfordernisse; Stichentscheid; s. dazu Art. 809 Abs. 4 E OR).
- *Ziff. 7:* Regelungen zur *Geschäftsführung* (s. dazu Art. 809 Abs. 1 E OR) und zur *Vertretung* (s. dazu Art. 814 Abs. 2 E OR). Für Einzelheiten zur Vertretung kann auf ein Reglement der Geschäftsführerinnen und Geschäftsführer verwiesen werden.
- *Ziff. 8:* Regelungen betreffend das *Konkurrenzverbot* für Personen, die mit der Geschäftsführung befasst sind (s. dazu Art. 812 Abs. 3 E OR).

G. Gründung

I. Errichtungsakt

Art. 777

1 Die Gesellschaft wird errichtet, indem die Gründer in öffentlicher Urkunde erklären, eine Gesellschaft mit beschränkter Haftung zu gründen, darin die Statuten festlegen und die Organe bestellen.

2 In diesem Errichtungsakt zeichnen die Gründer die Stammanteile und stellen fest, dass:

1. sämtliche Stammanteile gültig gezeichnet sind;

2. die Einlagen dem gesamten Ausgabebetrag entsprechen;

3. die gesetzlichen und statutarischen Anforderungen an die Leistung der Einlagen erfüllt sind;

4. sie die statutarischen Nachschuss- oder Nebenleistungspflichten übernehmen.

Die vorliegende Bestimmung entspricht inhaltlich Art. 779 Abs. 1 und 2 OR, übernimmt jedoch den 1991 überarbeiteten und verbesserten Wortlaut sowie die Struktur der entsprechenden Regelung des Aktienrechts (Art. 629 OR).

Abs. 1 regelt die Errichtung der Gesellschaft durch die Gründerinnen und Gründer. Die Vorschrift entspricht inhaltlich dem geltenden Recht.

Abs. 2 führt den Inhalt des öffentlich zu beurkundenden Errichtungsaktes auf. Es handelt sich dabei um die gleichen Punkte wie bei der Gründung einer Aktiengesellschaft. Zusätzlich haben die Gründerinnen und Gründer in der GmbH gegebenenfalls festzuhalten, dass sie die vorgesehenen statutarischen Nachschuss- oder Nebenleistungspflichten übernehmen (Ziff. 4).

II. Zeichnung der Stammanteile

Art. 777a

1 Die Zeichnung der Stammanteile bedarf zu ihrer Gültigkeit der Angabe von Anzahl, Nennwert und Ausgabebetrag sowie gegebenenfalls der Kategorie der Stammanteile.

2 In der Urkunde über die Zeichnung muss hingewiesen werden auf statutarische Bestimmungen über:

1. **Nachschusspflichten;**

2. **Nebenleistungspflichten;**

3. **Konkurrenzverbote für die Gesellschafter;**

4. **Vorhand-, Vorkaufs- und Kaufsrechte der Gesellschafter oder der Gesellschaft;**

5. **Konventionalstrafen.**

Nach *Abs. 1* bedarf die Zeichnung der Stammanteile zu ihrer Gültigkeit der Angabe von Anzahl, Nennwert und Ausgabebetrag der Stammanteile; bestehen mehrere Kategorien von Stammanteilen, so ist auch die Kategorie anzugeben. Anders als bei der Zeichnung von Aktien (s. Art. 630 Ziff. 1 OR) ist die Angabe der Art der Anteile nicht erforderlich, da Stammanteile nur als Beweisurkunden oder Namenpapiere ausgestaltet werden können (s. Art. 784 Abs. 1 E OR).

Abs. 2 sieht vor, dass in der Urkunde über die Zeichnung zum Schutz der Gründerinnen und Gründer ausdrücklich darauf hingewiesen werden muss, wenn die Statuten Nachschuss- oder Nebenleistungspflichten, Konkurrenzverbote für Gesellschafterinnen und Gesellschafter (keiner Erwähnung bedarf das gesetzlich vorgesehene Konkurrenzverbot für Geschäftsführerinnen und Geschäftsführer), Vorhand-, Vorkaufs-, und Kaufsrechte an Stammanteilen sowie Konventionalstrafen zur Sicherung der Erfüllung gesetzlicher oder statutarischer Pflichten enthalten.

III. Belege

Art. 777b

1 Im Errichtungsakt muss die Urkundsperson die Belege über die Gründung einzeln nennen und bestätigen, dass sie ihr und den Gründern vorgelegen haben.

2 Dem Errichtungsakt sind folgende Unterlagen beizulegen:

1. die Statuten;

2. der Gründungsbericht;

3. die Prüfungsbestätigung;

4. die Bestätigung über die Hinterlegung von Einlagen in Geld;

5. die Sacheinlageverträge;

6. bereits vorliegende Sachübernahmeverträge.

Wie der geltende Art. 779 Abs. 3 OR verlangt *Abs. 1*, dass die Urkundsperson die Belege über die Gründung im Errichtungsakt einzeln nennen muss. Sie hat weiter zu bestätigen, dass diese Belege den Gründerinnen und Gründern sowie der Urkundsperson vorgelegen haben.

Abs. 2 führt die dem Errichtungsakt beizulegenden Belege auf. Es sind dies die Statuten, der Gründungsbericht, die Prüfungsbestätigung, die

Bestätigung über die Hinterlegung von Einlagen in Geld, allfällige Verträge betreffend Sacheinlagen sowie bereits vorliegende Verträge betreffend Sachübernahmen.

IV. Einlagen

Art. 777c

1 Bei der Gründung muss für jeden Stammanteil eine dem Ausgabebetrag entsprechende Einlage vollständig geleistet werden.

2 Im Übrigen sind die Vorschriften des Aktienrechts entsprechend anwendbar für:

1. **die Angabe der Sacheinlagen, der Sachübernahmen und der besonderen Vorteile in den Statuten;**
2. **die Eintragung von Sacheinlagen, Sachübernahmen und besonderer Vorteile ins Handelsregister;**
3. **die Leistung und die Prüfung der Einlagen.**

Diese Bestimmung enthält sämtliche Vorschriften betreffend die Einlagen für Stammanteile. Sie findet sowohl bei der Gründung als auch (durch Verweisung) bei Kapitalerhöhungen Anwendung (s. Art. 781 Abs. 3 E OR).

Nach *Abs. 1* ist für jeden Stammanteil bei der Gründung eine dem Ausgabebetrag (dazu vgl. Art. 774 Abs. 2 E OR) entsprechende Einlage vollständig zu leisten (Liberierung der Stammanteile). Nach geltendem Recht brauchen im Zeitpunkt der Gründung demgegenüber lediglich 50% der Einlagen geleistet zu werden (Art. 774 Abs. 2 OR); es besteht jedoch eine subsidiäre Solidarhaftung jeder Gesellschafterin und jedes Gesellschafters für den nicht liberierten Teil des gesamten Stammkapitals (Art. 802 OR). Der Entwurf schlägt einerseits vor, das bisherige Mindestkapital ungeachtet der seit 1936 eingetretenen Inflation auf bloss 20 000 Franken zu belassen, dies im Interesse kleinerer Unternehmen mit geringem Kapitalbedarf. Anderseits erscheint auch ein Verzicht auf die nicht ungefährliche subsidiäre Solidarhaftung der Gesellschafterinnen und Gesellschafter dringend. Beides ist allerdings im Hinblick auf den Schutz Dritter sachlich nur vertretbar, wenn dennoch stets gewährleistet bleibt, dass zumindest ein minimales Haftungssubstrat vorliegt. Der Entwurf verlangt daher eine vollständige Einbezahlung des Ausgabebetrags für die Stammanteile bei der Gründung beziehungsweise anlässlich einer Kapitalerhöhung. Angesichts des geringen Mindestkapitals ergeben sich daraus selbst für kleine Unternehmen im Allgemeinen keine wirklich wesentlichen Erschwernisse. Das Erfordernis einer stets vollständigen Liberierung der Stammanteile ermöglicht ferner verschiedene Vereinfachungen der Regelung der GmbH im Interesse der Praxis. Die Funktion der bisherigen Teilliberierung kann durch statutarische Nachschusspflichten (Art. 795 ff. E OR) erfüllt werden; dadurch lassen sich Doppelspurigkeiten im Gesetz vermeiden.

Abs. 2 verweist in drei Punkten auf das Aktienrecht, die für alle Formen von Kapitalgesellschaften übereinstimmend geregelt werden sollen, da sachliche Gründe für eine Differenzierung fehlen:

– *Ziff. 1:* Für die *Angabe von Sacheinlagen, Sachübernahmen und besonderen Vorteilen in den Statuten* verweist der Entwurf auf Art. 628 OR. Die weniger präzise und unvollständige Regelung für die GmbH (Art. 778 OR) kann demzufolge entfallen.

– *Ziff. 2:* Für die *Eintragung von Sacheinlagen, Sachübernahmen und besonderen Vorteilen in das Handelsregister* soll ebenfalls das Gleiche gelten wie in der Aktiengesellschaft (Art. 642 E OR; dazu hinten). Im Vergleich zum geltenden GmbH-Recht (Art. 781 Ziff. 6 OR) wird zusätzlich die Einräumung besonderer Vorteile erfasst.

– *Ziff. 3:* Das Konzept des geltenden GmbH-Rechts zur Sicherung der Aufbringung des Stammkapitals beruht vorab auf der subsidiären Solidarhaftung aller Gesellschafterinnen und Gesellschafter in der Höhe des gesamten Stammkapitals, soweit dieses nicht oder nicht gehörig liberiert wurde oder aus der Liberierung Rückleistungen und Bezüge erfolgten (s. Art. 802 OR). Die aus dem Aktienrecht bekannten Massnahmen zur Gewährleistung einer effektiven Liberierung des Grundkapitals fehlen jedoch (Hinterlegung von Bareinlagen; Gründungsbericht und Prüfungsbestätigung; Art. 633, 635 und 635*a* OR). Die Aufbringung des Kapitals ist nicht deshalb sichergestellt. Zudem ist die Regelung für die Gesellschafterinnen und Gesellschafter mit kaum zumutbaren Haftungsrisiken verbunden. Wie bereits erläutert, verzichtet der Entwurf auf die subsidiäre Haftung der Gesellschafterinnen und Gesellschafter für die Liberierung des Stammkapitals. Die Aufbringung des Stammkapitals muss daher durch dieselben Vorkehren gewährleistet werden wie in der Aktiengesellschaft. Die Durchsetzung einer einigermassen verlässlichen Liberierung erscheint zudem auch im Hinblick auf die geringen Anforderungen an das Mindestkapital (20 000 Franken) unerlässlich. Für die Leistung der Einlagen verweist der Entwurf daher auf die Art. 633 und 634 OR (nicht anwendbar ist Art. 634a OR; die Liberierung durch Verrechnung ist jedoch zulässig): Bareinlagen sind bei einer Depositenstelle zu hinterlegen, und für Sacheinlagen sind ebenfalls die Voraussetzungen des Aktienrechts zu beachten (unter Einschluss der durch die Literatur und Praxis entwickelten Kriterien zur Zulässigkeit von Sacheinlagen[76]). Entsprechend Art. 635 OR haben die Gründerinnen und Gründer in einem Bericht Rechenschaft zu geben über Sacheinlagen, Sachübernahmen, Liberierungen durch Verrechnung und die Einräumung besonderer Vorteile. Dieser Gründungsbericht ist durch einen Revisor zu prüfen (Art. 635a OR), und zwar auch in Gesellschaften, die über keine Revisionsstelle verfügen (vgl. Art. 818 E OR). In der Literatur wird darauf hingewiesen, dass kaum ein anderes Institut des Gesellschaftsrechts für Missbräuche derart anfällig ist, wie die so genannt qualifizierte Gründung[77] (d.h. die Gründung unter Sacheinlage, Sachübernahme, Verrechnung oder Einräumung besonderer Vorteile); die Erfahrungen der Handelsregisterbehörden bestätigen dies. Die vorgesehenen Massnahmen zum Schutz Dritter erscheinen daher unabdingbar (dies auch für Kleingesellschaften). Für die Unternehmen ergeben sich daraus genau besehen nur geringe Belastungen, da es sich um einmalige Aufwendungen handelt und weil sich die entsprechenden Kosten dadurch vermeiden lassen, dass auf Sacheinlagen und Sachübernahmen verzichtet wird.

H. Eintragung ins Handelsregister

I. Gesellschaft

Art. 778

Die Gesellschaft ist ins Handelsregister des Ortes einzutragen, an dem sie ihren Sitz hat.

Nach dieser Bestimmung ist eine GmbH in das Handelsregister des Ortes einzutragen, an dem sie ihren statutarischen Sitz hat (im geltenden Recht Abs. 1 von Art. 780 OR). Die Unterzeichnung der Anmeldung zur Eintragung wird vom Entwurf für alle juristischen Personen gemeinsam gere-

---

76 s. dazu die Mitteilung des Eidg. Amts für das Handelsregister vom 15. August 2001, REPRAX 2/01, S. 59 ff. (mit Hinweisen auf die Literatur).
77 HERBERT WOHLMANN, GmbH-Recht, Basel und Frankfurt a.M. 1997, S. 26.

gelt, ebenso das Verfahren zur Eintragung und die einzureichenden Belege (s. Art. 929 und 931*a* E OR); die entsprechenden Bestimmungen des GmbH-Rechts können daher gestrichen werden (Art. 780 Abs. 2 bis 4 OR).

II. Zweigniederlassungen

Art. 778a

Zweigniederlassungen sind unter Bezugnahme auf die Eintragung der Hauptniederlassung ins Handelsregister des Ortes einzutragen, an dem sie sich befinden.

Diese Bestimmung übernimmt den bisherigen Art. 782 Abs. 1 OR, wonach Zweigniederlassungen unter Bezugnahme auf die Eintragung der Hauptniederlassung in das Handelsregister des Ortes einzutragen sind, an dem sie sich befinden (der vorliegende Art. betrifft nur die Eintragungspflicht; zum Inhalt der Eintragung s. die Delegationsnorm in Art. 929 E OR; zur Art der Eintragung s. Art. 935 OR).

J. Erwerb der Persönlichkeit

I. Zeitpunkt; mangelnde Voraussetzungen

Art. 779

1 Die Gesellschaft erlangt das Recht der Persönlichkeit durch die Eintragung ins Handelsregister.

2 Sie erlangt das Recht der Persönlichkeit auch dann, wenn die Voraussetzungen für die Eintragung tatsächlich nicht erfüllt sind.

3 Waren bei der Gründung gesetzliche oder statutarische Voraussetzungen nicht erfüllt und sind dadurch die Interessen von Gläubigern oder Gesellschaftern in erheblichem Masse gefährdet oder verletzt worden, so kann das Gericht auf Begehren einer dieser Personen die Auflösung der Gesellschaft verfügen.

4 Das Klagerecht erlischt drei Monate nach der Veröffentlichung der Gründung im Schweizerischen Handelsamtsblatt.

Die Regelung des Erwerbs der Persönlichkeit durch die Gesellschaft entspricht im Grundsatz dem geltenden Recht (Art. 783 Abs. 1 OR); sie wird jedoch in Anlehnung an das Aktienrecht präzisiert und vervollständigt (vgl. Art. 643 OR). Nach *Abs. 1* erlangt die Gesellschaft das Recht der Persönlichkeit durch die Eintragung ins Handelsregister (wie bisher, s. Art. 783 Abs. 1 OR; zum genauen Zeitpunkt s. Art. 932 OR). Auf Grund der so genannt heilenden Wirkung der Eintragung wird die Gesellschaft nach *Abs. 2* auch dann rechtsfähig, wenn die Voraussetzungen für die Eintragung tatsächlich nicht erfüllt sind. *Abs. 3* räumt in diesem Fall jedoch den Gesellschafterinnen und Gesellschaftern sowie den Gläubigerinnen und Gläubigern das Recht ein, auf Auflösung der Gesellschaft zu klagen. Dieses Recht erlischt gemäss *Abs. 4* nach 3 Monaten.

II. Vor der Eintragung eingegangene Verpflichtungen

Art. 779a

1 Personen, die vor der Eintragung ins Handelsregister im Namen der Gesellschaft handeln, haften dafür persönlich und solidarisch.

2 Übernimmt die Gesellschaft innerhalb von drei Monaten nach ihrer Eintragung Verpflichtungen, die ausdrücklich in ihrem Namen eingegangen werden, so werden die Handelnden befreit, und es haftet nur die Gesellschaft.

Diese Bestimmung entspricht inhaltlich den heutigen Art. 783 Abs. 2 und 3 OR. Nach *Abs. 1* haften Personen persönlich und solidarisch, wenn sie vor der Eintragung der Gesellschaft ins Handelsregister in deren Namen handeln. Sie werden jedoch nach *Abs. 2* befreit, sofern die Gesellschaft die in ihrem Namen eingegangenen Verpflichtungen innerhalb von 3 Monaten nach der Eintragung übernimmt.

Kapitel 1: Neue Gesetzesbestimmungen und Erläuterungen

K. Statutenänderung

Art. 780

Jeder Beschluss der Gesellschafterversammlung über eine Änderung der Statuten muss öffentlich beurkundet und ins Handelsregister eingetragen werden.

Wie im geltenden Recht ist jeder Beschluss der Gesellschafterversammlung über eine Änderung der Statuten öffentlich zu beurkunden und im Handelsregister einzutragen (vgl. Art. 784 Abs. 1 und 785 Abs. 1 OR). Diese Regelung entspricht derjenigen für die Festsetzung der ursprünglichen Statuten bei der Gründung (vgl. Art. 777 Abs. 1 und 778 E OR).

Das geltende Recht sah in Art. 785 Abs. 2 OR vor, dass der Beschluss über eine Änderung der Statuten auch Dritten gegenüber (d.h. nicht nur gesellschaftsintern) unmittelbar mit der Eintragung in das Handelsregister rechtswirksam wird (der französische Gesetzestext lautet allerdings anders). Diese Vorschrift weicht von der allgemeinen Ordnung des Beginns der Wirksamkeit von Eintragungen im Handelsregister ab (s. Art. 932 OR). Sachlich überzeugende Gründe für eine Sonderregelung liegen jedoch nicht vor[78]; vielmehr sollen auch Statutenänderungen Dritten erst entgegengehalten werden können, sobald sie auf Grund der Eintragung im Handelsregister und der Publikation im Schweizerischen Handelsamtsblatt überhaupt davon Kenntnis erhalten. Art. 785 Abs. 2 OR ist daher zu streichen. Das Gleiche gilt für die Parallelnorm im Aktienrecht (Art. 647 Abs. 3 OR).

L. Erhöhung des Stammkapitals

Art. 781

1 Die Gesellschafterversammlung kann die Erhöhung des Stammkapitals beschliessen.

2 Die Ausführung des Beschlusses obliegt den Geschäftsführern.

---

78 s. auch die Kritik bei GUILLAUME VIANIN, L'inscription au registre du commerce, Diss. Freiburg 2000, S. 212 f. mit Verweisen.

3 Die Zeichnung und die Einlagen richten sich nach den Vorschriften über die Gründung. Für den Zeichnungsschein sind zudem die Vorschriften über die Erhöhung des Aktienkapitals entsprechend anwendbar. Ein öffentliches Angebot zur Zeichnung der Stammanteile ist ausgeschlossen.

4 Die Erhöhung des Stammkapitals muss innerhalb von drei Monaten nach dem Beschluss der Gesellschafterversammlung beim Handelsregister zur Eintragung angemeldet werden; sonst fällt der Beschluss dahin.

5 Im Übrigen sind die Vorschriften des Aktienrechts über die ordentliche Kapitalerhöhung entsprechend anwendbar für:

1. die Form und den Inhalt des Beschlusses der Gesellschafterversammlung;

2. das Bezugsrecht der Gesellschafter;

3. die Erhöhung des Stammkapitals aus Eigenkapital;

4. den Kapitalerhöhungsbericht und die Prüfungsbestätigung;

5. die Statutenänderung und die Feststellungen der Geschäftsführer;

6. die Eintragung der Erhöhung des Stammkapitals ins Handelsregister und die Nichtigkeit vorher ausgegebener Urkunden.

Die geltende Regelung der Erhöhung des Stammkapitals ist unpräzis (Art. 786 OR). Die Verweisung auf die für die Gründung geltenden Vorschriften bewirkt zudem, dass eine Kapitalerhöhung der Zustimmung sämtlicher Gesellschafterinnen und Gesellschafter bedarf[79]. Dieses Zustimmungserfordernis trägt der heutigen subsidiären Solidarhaftung für die Liberierung des gesamten Stammkapitals Rechnung, erschwert aber die Kapitalerhöhung stark. Da der Entwurf auf die bisherige subsidiäre Solidarhaftung der Gesellschafterinnen und Gesellschafter verzichtet, kann die Kapitalerhöhung erleichtert werden. Zugleich ist die gesetzliche Regelung praxisgerecht zu vervollständigen.

---

79 Statt vieler: WERNER VON STEIGER, in: Zürcher Kommentar V/5c, Zürich 1965, Art. 786 N 8; a.M. GAUDENZ G. ZINDEL/PETER R. ISLER, in: Kommentar zum schweizerischen Privatrecht, Obligationenrecht II, Basel und Frankfurt a.M. 1994, Art. 786 N 2.

Abs. 1 räumt der Gesellschafterversammlung die Möglichkeit ein, eine Erhöhung des Stammkapitals zu beschliessen. Die erforderliche Mehrheit beträgt mindestens zwei Drittel der vertretenen Stimmen und die absolute Mehrheit des gesamten stimmberechtigten Stammkapitals (s. Art. 808*b* Abs. 1 Ziff. 5 E OR). Die Kapitalerhöhung erfolgt in einem zweistufigen Verfahren: Während die Gesellschafterversammlung über den Grundsatz der Erhöhung, den Erhöhungsbetrag und allfällige Besonderheiten (Art. 650 Abs. 2 Ziff. 1–9 OR) entscheidet, obliegt die Durchführung des weiteren Verfahrens nach *Abs. 2* den Geschäftsführerinnen und Geschäftsführern. Sie haben die notwendigen Schritte zur Aufbringung des Kapitals zu unternehmen und die gesetzlich verlangten Feststellungen zu machen. Kommt die Erhöhung zu Stande, liegt es bei ihnen, die Statuten anzupassen und die Kapitalerhöhung beim Handelsregister zur Eintragung anzumelden.

Gemäss *Abs. 3* richten sich die Zeichnung und die Leistung der Einlagen nach den Vorschriften über die Gründung (d.h. nach Art. 777*a* und 777*c* E OR). Weiter sind die aktienrechtlichen Bestimmungen betreffend den Zeichnungsschein (Art. 652 OR) entsprechend anwendbar.

Abs. 3 schliesst ferner ein öffentliches Angebot zur Zeichnung der Stammanteile aus. Dies entspricht dem personenbezogenen und eher geschlossenen Charakter der GmbH sowie der Tatsache, dass die Stammanteile nie kapitalmarktfähig sind. Die Suche nach einzelnen zusätzlichen Gesellschafterinnen und Gesellschaftern in Fachblättern und Zeitungen gilt nicht als unzulässiges öffentliches Zeichnungsangebot im Sinne dieser Bestimmung. Auf Grund der fehlenden Kapitalmarktfähigkeit werden weiter auch die Möglichkeiten der genehmigten und der bedingten Kapitalerhöhung nicht in das GmbH-Recht übernommen.

Abs. 4 sieht für die Durchführung der Kapitalerhöhung eine Frist von 3 Monaten vor (ebenso das Aktienrecht, s. Art. 650 Abs. 3 OR). Diese Befristung will – so weit wie möglich – vermeiden, dass sich die Bedingungen und Umstände, die für den Entscheid der Gesellschafterversammlung von Bedeutung waren, bis zur effektiven Durchführung der Kapitalerhöhung wesentlich verändern. Massgebend für die Wahrung der Frist ist der Eingang der Anmeldung beim Handelsregister.

Abs. 5 bringt im Weiteren die Bestimmungen des Aktienrechts zur ordentlichen Kapitalerhöhung entsprechend zur Anwendung. Diese Verweisung ermöglicht es, auf eine Wiederholung der Regelung der Einzelheiten des Kapitalerhöhungsverfahrens zu verzichten. Sie umfasst die folgenden Punkte:

- *Ziff. 1* verweist für die *Form und den Inhalt* des Beschlusses der Gesellschafterversammlung auf Art. 650 Abs. 2 OR. Der Beschluss ist demnach aus Gründen der Rechtssicherheit öffentlich zu beurkunden.

- *Ziff. 2* verweist für das *Bezugsrecht* der Gesellschafterinnen und Gesellschafter auf Art. 652*b* OR. Weil die Kapitalerhöhung im Interesse der Praktikabilität zukünftig nicht mehr der Zustimmung sämtlicher Gesellschafterinnen und Gesellschafter bedarf, sind für den Schutz von Personen mit Minderheitsbeteiligungen die aktienrechtlichen Bestimmungen zum Bezugsrecht zur Anwendung zu bringen. Dadurch werden zudem die Lücken der geltenden Regelung (Art. 787 OR) geschlossen.

- *Ziff. 3* verweist für die Erhöhung des Stammkapitals aus *Eigenkapital* auf Art. 652*d* OR.

- Ziff. 4 verweist für den Kapitalerhöhungsbericht und die Prüfungsbestätigung auf Art. 652e und 652f OR.

Die Prüfungsbestätigung einer Revisorin oder eines Revisors ist nicht erforderlich, wenn in bar liberiert wird und weder Sachübernahmen vorgesehen sind noch das Bezugsrecht eingeschränkt oder aufgehoben wird (s. Art. 652*f* Abs. 2 OR). Auf eine Prüfungsbestätigung wird daher insbesondere in kleinen Unternehmen meist verzichtet werden können. Ist jedoch eine Prüfungsbestätigung erforderlich, so muss zum Schutz aller Beteiligten und Betroffenen auch dann eine solche eingeholt werden, wenn die Gesellschaft über keine Revisionsstelle verfügt (es braucht jedoch keine eigentliche Revisionsstelle geschaffen zu werden).

- *Ziff. 5* verweist für die *Statutenänderung* und die erforderlichen *Feststellungen* auf Art. 652g OR. Die im Aktienrecht dem Verwaltungsrat zugewiesenen Aufgaben obliegen in der GmbH den Geschäftsführerinnen und Geschäftsführern.

- *Ziff. 6* verweist für die *Eintragung im Handelsregister* und die *Nichtigkeit von Urkunden*, die *vor der Eintragung ausgegeben* werden, auf Art. 652*h* OR (zur Anmeldung beim Handelsregister, s. Art. 931*a* E OR).

M. Herabsetzung des Stammkapitals

Art. 782

1 Die Gesellschafterversammlung kann die Herabsetzung des Stammkapitals beschliessen.

2 Das Stammkapital darf in keinem Fall unter 20 000 Franken herabgesetzt werden.

3 Zur Beseitigung einer durch Verluste entstandenen Unterbilanz darf das Stammkapital nur herabgesetzt werden, wenn die Gesellschafter die in den Statuten vorgesehenen Nachschüsse voll geleistet haben.

4 Im Übrigen sind die Vorschriften über die Herabsetzung des Aktienkapitals entsprechend anwendbar.

Wie bereits die geltende Regelung (Art. 788 OR) verweist der Entwurf zur Herabsetzung des Stammkapitals weitgehend auf das Aktienrecht. Neu wird auch für die GmbH eine erleichterte Kapitalherabsetzung zu Sanierungszwecken ermöglicht (Art. 735 OR i.V.m. Art. 782 Abs. 4 E OR).

Abs. 1 hält den Grundsatz fest, wonach die Gesellschafterversammlung die Herabsetzung des Stammkapitals beschliessen kann. Dabei ist stets das gesetzliche Mindestkapital zu beachten (Art. 773 E OR): Das Stammkapital darf nach *Abs. 2* in keinem Fall unter 20 000 Franken herabgesetzt werden.

Für die erleichterte Kapitalherabsetzung zu Sanierungszwecken (s. Art. 735 OR i.V.m. Art. 782 Abs. 4 E OR) gilt nach *Abs. 3* eine Besonderheit: Liegt eine durch Verluste entstandene Unterbilanz[80] vor, so darf das Stammkapital zu deren Beseitigung nur herabgesetzt werden, wenn alle in den Statuten vorgesehenen Nachschüsse bereits voll geleistet wurden. Abgesehen von dieser Besonderheit geht die erleichterte Herabsetzung des Stammkapitals gleich von statten wie bei der Aktiengesellschaft. Für alles Weitere verweist *Abs. 4* auf die Art. 732 ff. OR. Das Erfordernis, wonach eine Kapitalherabsetzung nur beschlossen werden darf, wenn ein

---

[80] Zum Begriff der Unterbilanz s. PETER BÖCKLI, Schweizer Aktienrecht, 2. Aufl., Zürich 1996, N 1684g.

Revisionsbericht die Deckung der Forderungen bestätigt, muss auch von Gesellschaften beachtet werden, die keine Revisionsstelle haben.

Im geltenden Recht regelt Art. 782 OR der Eintragung von Zweigniederlassungen ins Handelsregister. Diese Bestimmung wird aufgehoben, wobei Abs. 1 teilweise in Art. 778*a* E OR integriert wird. Die Anmeldung zur Eintragung (Art. 782 Abs. 2 OR) soll neu für alle Rechtsformen einheitlich in Art. 931*a* E OR geordnet werden.

N. Erwerb eigener Stammanteile

Art. 783

1 Die Gesellschaft darf eigene Stammanteile nur dann erwerben, wenn frei verwendbares Eigenkapital in der Höhe der dafür nötigen Mittel vorhanden ist und der gesamte Nennwert dieser Stammanteile zehn Prozent des Stammkapitals nicht übersteigt.

2 Werden im Zusammenhang mit einer Übertragbarkeitsbeschränkung, einem Austritt oder einem Ausschluss Stammanteile erworben, so beträgt die Höchstgrenze 35 Prozent. Die über zehn Prozent des Stammkapitals hinaus erworbenen eigenen Stammanteile sind innerhalb von zwei Jahren zu veräussern oder durch Kapitalherabsetzung zu vernichten.

3 Ist mit den Stammanteilen, die erworben werden sollen, eine Nachschusspflicht oder eine Nebenleistungspflicht verbunden, so muss diese vor deren Erwerb aufgehoben werden.

4 Im Übrigen sind für den Erwerb eigener Stammanteile durch die Gesellschaft die Vorschriften über eigene Aktien entsprechend anwendbar.

Der Erwerb eigener Stammanteile durch die Gesellschaft vermindert deren Haftungssubstrat und kann den Schutz der Gläubigerinnen und Gläubiger erheblich beeinträchtigen. Die geltende Regelung des Erwerbs und der Pfandnahme eigener Anteile (Art. 807 OR) ist ungenügend; insbesondere fehlt eine klare Begrenzung. Der Entwurf lehnt sich an die Ordnung des Aktienrechts an (Art. 659 OR), wobei es aber die Eigenheiten der GmbH zu berücksichtigen gilt.

Nach *Abs. 1* darf die Gesellschaft eigene Stammanteile nur erwerben, wenn sie über das dafür erforderliche frei verwendbare Eigenkapital verfügt. Der Erwerb wird zudem auf 10% des Stammkapitals begrenzt (in Übereinstimmung mit dem Aktienrecht; s. Art. 659 Abs. 1 OR). In bestimmten Fällen kann sich diese Schranke jedoch als zu restriktiv erweisen. *Abs. 2* sieht daher eine Höchstgrenze von 35% vor, sofern die Stammanteile im Zusammenhang mit einem Austritt, einem Ausschluss oder einer Übertragbarkeitsbeschränkung (Vinkulierung) erworben werden. Diese Sondertatbestände sind abschliessend. Der Vorentwurf legte – wie im Aktienrecht (vgl. Art. 659 Abs. 2 OR) – die Höchstgrenze noch bei 20%fest. Der Entwurf trägt der in der Vernehmlassung geäusserten Kritik Rechnung und hebt die Schranke auf 35% an, um den Bedürfnissen von Unternehmen mit nur wenigen Gesellschafterinnen und Gesellschaftern Rechnung zu tragen. So soll namentlich auch der Austritt einer Person erleichtert werden, die über einen Drittel des Stammkapitals verfügt. Unter dem Gesichtspunkt des Kapitalschutzes erscheint die vorgesehene Grenze allerdings als hoch angesetzt. Damit eine Gefährdung der Gläubigerinnen und Gläubiger soweit wie möglich vermieden werden kann, müssen die über 10% des Stammkapitals hinaus erworbenen eigenen Stammanteile innerhalb von 2 Jahren wieder veräussert oder durch eine Kapitalherabsetzung (Art. 782 E OR) vernichtet werden.

Würde eine Gesellschaft Stammanteile erwerben, mit denen eine Nachschusspflicht verbunden ist, so würde sie selber zur Schuldnerin dieser Nachschusspflicht. Die Nachschüsse wären demzufolge uneinbringlich. Ähnliches gilt für Nebenleistungspflichten. *Abs. 3* setzt daher für den Erwerb eigener Stammanteile voraus, dass allfällige Nachschuss- oder Nebenleistungspflichten vor dem Erwerb aufgehoben werden.

Für alles Weitere verweist *Abs. 4* auf die Regelung des Erwerbs eigener Aktien (Art. 659*a* und 659*b* OR). Die Pfandnahme an eigenen Stammanteilen gilt, wie dort, nicht als Erwerb eigener Stammanteile.

Die Zuständigkeit zum Entscheid über den Erwerb eigener Stammanteile liegt grundsätzlich bei der Gesellschafterversammlung, doch kann diese die Geschäftsführerinnen und Geschäftsführer damit betrauen (s. Art. 804 Abs. 2 Ziff. 11 E OR).

Zweiter Abschnitt: Rechte und Pflichten der Gesellschafterinnen und Gesellschafter

A. Stammanteile

I. Urkunde

Art. 784

1 Wird über Stammanteile eine Urkunde ausgestellt, so kann diese nur als Beweisurkunde oder Namenpapier errichtet werden.

2 In die Urkunde müssen dieselben Hinweise auf statutarische Rechte und Pflichten aufgenommen werden wie in die Urkunde über die Zeichnung der Stammanteile.

Nach *Abs. 1* darf die Ausstellung einer Urkunde über Stammanteile nur in Form einer Beweisurkunde oder eines Namenpapiers im Sinne von Art. 974 ff. OR erfolgen. Auf Grund der Personenbezogenheit der Rechtsform der GmbH sind deren Anteile nicht kapitalmarktfähig: Die Stammanteile sind in der Regel nicht ohne die Zustimmung der Gesellschafterversammlung übertragbar (s. Art. 786 E OR). Die Gesellschafterinnen und Gesellschafter können einerseits mit Treuepflichten, Konkurrenzverboten sowie mit Nachschuss- und Nebenleistungspflichten belastet sein; andererseits sind sie zur Geschäftsführung zuständig, sofern die Statuten nichts anderes vorsehen (s. Art. 809 E OR). Eine derart ausgestaltete Mitgliedschaft eignet sich grundsätzlich nicht für eine Verbriefung in Wertpapieren. Der herrschenden Lehrmeinung zum geltenden Recht[81] folgend, soll jedoch die Ausgabe von Namenpapieren ermöglicht werden (demgegenüber untersagt das französische Recht die Ausgabe von Wertpapieren gänzlich[82]).

Abs. 2 verlangt, dass dieselben Hinweise auf statutarische Rechte und Pflichten in die Urkunde aufgenommen werden wie in die Urkunde über die Zeichnung der Stammanteile (s. Art. 777*a* Abs. 2 E OR).

---

81 s. insbes. PETER JÄGGI, in: Zürcher Kommentar V/7a, Zürich 1959, Art. 965 N 283; WERNER VON STEIGER, in: Zürcher Kommentar V/5c, Zürich 1965, Art. 789 N 16; nuanciert: A. JANGGEN/H. BECKER, in: Berner Kommentar VII/3, Bern 1939, Art. 789 N 7.

82 s. Art. L 223-11 und L 223-12 Code de Commerce.

Kapitel 1: Neue Gesetzesbestimmungen und Erläuterungen

II. Übertragung

1. Abtretung

a. Form

Art. 785

1 Die Abtretung von Stammanteilen sowie die Verpflichtung zur Abtretung bedürfen der schriftlichen Form.

2 In den Abtretungsvertrag müssen dieselben Hinweise auf statutarische Rechte und Pflichten aufgenommen werden wie in die Urkunde über die Zeichnung der Stammanteile.

Unter dem geltenden Recht bedarf die Abtretung von Stammanteilen der öffentlichen Beurkundung (Art. 791 Abs. 4 OR). Diese Formvorschrift soll die Rechtssicherheit bei der Abtretung von Stammanteilen gewährleisten, dies insbesondere im Hinblick auf allfällige Pflichten der Gesellschafterinnen und Gesellschafter. Es soll aber auch sichergestellt werden, dass die Erwerberinnen und Erwerber von Stammanteilen über ihre subsidiäre Solidarhaftung in der GmbH (s. Art. 802 OR) informiert werden.

Während der erste Expertenentwurf von 1996 auf eine öffentliche Beurkundung der Abtretung von Stammanteilen verzichtete[83], sah der Vorentwurf von 1999 dieses Erfordernis wiederum vor (Art. 791 Abs. 1 VE)[84]. Im Vernehmlassungsverfahren wurde die Notwendigkeit der öffentlichen Beurkundung allerdings bestritten; es wurde eingewendet, dass den damit verbundenen Kosten kein relevanter Vorteil gegenüber stehe.

Der Entwurf verzichtet auf das Erfordernis der öffentlichen Beurkundung: Nach *Abs. 1* bedürfen die Abtretung von Stammanteilen sowie die Verpflichtung zur Abtretung lediglich der schriftlichen Form (vgl. Art. 165 OR). Der Verzicht auf die öffentliche Beurkundung erscheint namentlich deshalb vertretbar, weil die bisherige subsidiäre Solidarhaftung der Gesellschafterinnen und Gesellschafter entfällt und sich demzufolge eine entsprechende Rechtsbelehrung beim Erwerb von Stammanteilen erübrigt. Im Hinblick auf die Rechte und Pflichten der Gesellschafterinnen und Gesellschafter muss bei der Abtretung von Stammanteilen jedoch die

---

[83] PETER BÖCKLI/PETER FORSTMOSER/JEAN-MARC RAPP, Reform des GmbH-Rechts, Zürich 1997, S. 26 und 84 ff.
[84] s. dazu Expertenbericht zum Vorentwurf, S. 52 ff.

Sicherheit und Transparenz der Rechtsnachfolge gewährleistet werden. In Anlehnung an den ersten Expertenentwurf kann die erforderliche Rechts- und Verkehrssicherheit durch die Eintragung der Gesellschafterinnen und Gesellschafter ins Handelsregister (Art. 791 E OR) geschaffen werden. Eine entsprechende Eintragung wird zwar schon im geltenden Recht verlangt (Art. 781 Ziff. 4 und 5 OR); sie ersetzt aber neu auch die Formvorschrift der öffentlichen Beurkundung der Abtretung von Stammanteilen. Bei der Eintragung von Erwerberinnen oder Erwerbern von Stammanteilen prüft das Handelsregisteramt die Abtretung allerdings nur in formellrechtlicher Hinsicht.

Nach *Abs. 2* müssen dieselben Hinweise auf statutarische Rechte und Pflichten in den Abtretungsvertrag aufgenommen werden wie in die Urkunde über die Zeichnung der Stammanteile (Art. 777*a* Abs. 2 E OR). Es mag als Doppelspurigkeit erscheinen, wenn der Entwurf die Angabe eines Hinweises auf statutarische Rechte und Pflichten sowohl in der Urkunde über die Stammanteile (Art. 784 Abs. 2 E OR) als auch im Abtretungsvertrag verlangt. Eine entsprechende Regelung erscheint indessen sinnvoll, weil einerseits in der Praxis häufig keine Urkunden für Stammanteile ausgestellt werden und andererseits ausgestellte Urkunden bei besonderen Erwerbsarten auch ohne Abtretungsvertrag übertragen werden (so beim Erbgang oder bei einer Fusion). In beiden Fällen sollen die Erwerberinnen und Erwerber in zweckmässiger Weise auf statutarische Rechte und Pflichten hingewiesen werden.

b. Zustimmungserfordernisse

Art. 786

1 Die Abtretung von Stammanteilen bedarf der Zustimmung der Gesellschafterversammlung. Die Gesellschafterversammlung kann die Zustimmung ohne Angabe von Gründen verweigern.

2 Von dieser Regelung können die Statuten abweichen, indem sie:

1. auf das Erfordernis der Zustimmung zur Abtretung verzichten;

2. die Gründe festlegen, die die Verweigerung der Zustimmung zur Abtretung rechtfertigen;

3. vorsehen, dass die Zustimmung zur Abtretung verweigert werden kann, wenn die Gesellschaft dem Veräusserer die Übernahme der Stammanteile zum wirklichen Wert anbietet;
4. die Abtretung ausschliessen;
5. vorsehen, dass die Zustimmung zur Abtretung verweigert werden kann, wenn die Erfüllung statutarischer Nachschuss- oder Nebenleistungspflichten zweifelhaft ist und eine von der Gesellschaft geforderte Sicherheit nicht geleistet wird.

³ Schliessen die Statuten die Abtretung aus oder verweigert die Gesellschafterversammlung die Zustimmung zur Abtretung, so bleibt das Recht auf Austritt aus wichtigem Grund vorbehalten.

Weitgehende Möglichkeiten, die Abtretung von Stammanteilen zu beschränken, sind für die GmbH charakteristisch; sie entsprechen deren Personenbezogenheit sowie der grossen Bedeutung der Zusammensetzung des Gesellschafterkreises in kleineren Gesellschaften. Da ein Ausscheiden – anders als in der Aktiengesellschaft – nicht nur durch die Veräusserung der Anteile, sondern auch durch Austritt aus wichtigen oder aus in den Statuten vorgesehenen Gründen (Art. 822 E OR) möglich ist, kann die Zulässigkeit der Beschränkung der Abtretbarkeit erheblich weiter gefasst werden als im Aktienrecht[85]. Der Entwurf bringt eine auf Praktikabilität und Klarheit bedachte Neuregelung, die den Gesellschaften einen breiten Gestaltungsfreiraum belässt, es aber erlaubt, auf eine eingehende Ordnung der Vinkulierung in den Statuten zu verzichten.

Nach *Abs. 1* bedarf die Abtretung von Stammanteilen der Zustimmung der Gesellschafterversammlung. Dieses Zustimmungserfordernis wird als Vinkulierung bezeichnet. Im Gegensatz zum Aktienrecht (Art. 684 Abs. 1 OR) sieht der Entwurf von Gesetzes wegen eine dispositive Vinkulierung vor, die keiner Konkretisierung in den Statuten bedarf. Wird nichts anderes vorgesehen, kann die Gesellschafterversammlung die Zustimmung zur Abtretung von Stammanteilen verweigern, ohne dafür Gründe angeben zu müssen.

Die Zuständigkeit zum Entscheid über die Zustimmung wird zwingend der Gesellschafterversammlung zugewiesen (Art. 804 Abs. 2 Ziff. 8 E OR). Dies entspricht der Personenbezogenheit der GmbH: Die Gesell-

---

85 Umfassend zur Vinkulierung im Aktienrecht s. HANSPETER KLÄY, Die Vinkulierung, Diss. Basel, Basel und Frankfurt a.M. 1997.

schafterinnen und Gesellschafter sollen selber entscheiden, wer in ihren Kreis aufgenommen wird. Der Entscheid stellt einen wichtigen Beschluss dar, der mit mindestens zwei Dritteln der vertretenen Stimmen und der absoluten Mehrheit des gesamten stimmberechtigten Stammkapitals gefasst werden muss (Art. 808*b* Abs. 1 Ziff. 4 E OR; das erforderliche Quorum wird gegenüber dem geltenden Recht leicht gesenkt; vgl. Art. 791 Abs. 2 OR). Dabei ist zu beachten, dass sich der Beschluss der Gesellschafterversammlung auf die Zustimmung zur Abtretung bezieht – nicht etwa auf deren Verweigerung (s. die Formulierung von Art. 808*b* Abs. 1 Ziff. 4 E OR). Erreicht der Beschluss nicht die erforderliche Mehrheit, gilt die Zustimmung als verweigert (vgl. aber Art. 787 Abs. 2 E OR).

In den Statuten kann eine abweichende Ordnung der Vinkulierung getroffen werden. Die Möglichkeiten, die dafür zur Verfügung stehen, werden in *Abs. 2* abschliessend aufgeführt. Der Entwurf gewährleistet damit die erforderliche Rechtssicherheit bei der Abtretung der Stammanteile und erleichtert die konkrete Ausgestaltung der Statuten. Als Alternative zur gesetzlich vorgegebenen Vinkulierung (Möglichkeit der Verweigerung der Zustimmung zur Abtretung ohne Angabe von Gründen) stehen die folgenden Varianten zur Verfügung, die zudem teilweise miteinander kombiniert werden können:

– Nach *Ziff. 1* kann auf das Erfordernis der *Zustimmung* zur Abtretung von Stammanteilen *verzichtet* werden. Dies erlaubt, Wechsel im Kreis der Gesellschafterinnen und Gesellschafter zu erleichtern, wenn dies auf Grund eines geringen Personenbezugs der Gesellschaft erwünscht ist.

– Nach *Ziff. 2* können die Statuten *Gründe* definieren, welche die Verweigerung der Zustimmung zur Abtretung rechtfertigen. Im Rahmen dieser Umschreibung bestehen zahlreiche verschiedene Gestaltungsmöglichkeiten: Die Statuten können bestimmte Gründe mehr oder weniger konkret umschreiben, so beispielsweise Konkurrenten- und Familienklauseln. Sie dürfen auch festlegen, dass keine Gesellschafterin und kein Gesellschafter eine Beteiligung von mehr als 20% am gesamten Stammkapital erwerben kann (Prozentklausel). Es ist ausserdem möglich vorzusehen, dass die Verweigerung der Zustimmung zur Abtretung nur aus wichtigen Gründen verweigert werden kann. Während in der Aktiengesellschaft die Statuten die Vinkulierungsgründe klar und bestimmt umschreiben müssen[86], sind in der GmbH auch in-

---

86 s. AB NR 1990, S. 1365 f.

haltlich offenere Formulierungen zulässig, da bei einer Verweigerung der Zustimmung zur Abtretung nicht zwingend ein Grund anzugeben ist (vgl. Abs. 1).
- Nach *Ziff. 3* können die Statuten vorsehen, dass die Zustimmung zur Abtretung verweigert werden darf, wenn die Gesellschaft der Veräusserin oder dem Veräusserer die *Übernahme* der Stammanteile zum wirklichen Wert anbietet. Eine entsprechende Regelung wird als Escape-clause bezeichnet. Sie bietet den Gesellschafterinnen und Gesellschaftern Gewähr dafür, dass sie aus der Gesellschaft ausscheiden können, wenn sie eine Erwerberin oder einen Erwerber für ihre Stammanteile finden.
- Nach *Ziff. 4* ist es zulässig, die Abtretung von Stammanteilen gänzlich *auszuschliessen*. Diese Möglichkeit besteht bereits nach geltendem Recht (Art. 791 Abs. 3 OR). Ein Ausschluss der Abtretung der Stammanteile ist im Hinblick auf den Rechtsschutz der Gesellschafterinnen und Gesellschafter allerdings nur darum vertretbar, weil in der GmbH ein Recht zum Austritt aus wichtigen Gründen gegeben ist (Art. 822 E OR). Die Zulässigkeit einer strikten Bindung der Gesellschafterinnen und Gesellschafter an die Gesellschaft kann jedoch in bestimmten, besonderen Fällen einem Bedürfnis entsprechen und interessante Gestaltungsmöglichkeiten eröffnen, so insbesondere für Konsortien und Joint Ventures.
- Nach *Ziff. 5* können die Statuten vorsehen, dass die Gesellschafterversammlung die Zustimmung zur Abtretung von Stammanteilen verweigern kann, wenn die Erfüllung statutarischer *Nachschuss- oder Nebenleistungspflichten* zweifelhaft ist und eine von der Gesellschaft geforderte Sicherheit nicht geleistet wird. Dieser Vinkulierungsgrund entspricht funktional der gesetzlichen Vinkulierung nicht voll liberierter Aktien (Art. 685 Abs. 1 OR). In der GmbH muss eine solche Regelung nur dann in den Statuen aufgenommen werden, wenn Nachschuss- oder Nebenleistungspflichten bestehen und die Gesellschaft die dispositive gesetzliche Vinkulierung (Verweigerung der Zustimmung zur Abtretung ohne Angabe von Gründen; Abs. 1) ausgeschlossen hat.

Die strenge Vinkulierung der Stammanteile in der GmbH ist für den Rechtsschutz der Gesellschafterinnen und Gesellschafter nicht unproblematisch, weil sie ein Ausscheiden aus der Gesellschaft auf dem Weg der Abtretung der Anteile unter Umständen unterbindet. Die Verweigerung der Zustimmung zur Abtretung ohne Angabe von Gründen zeichnet sich zwar durch den Vorteil einer einfachen Anwendung in der Praxis aus, doch lässt sich eine rechtsmissbräuchliche Verwendung nicht verhindern und zudem meist nicht nachweisen. Ein Ausschluss der Abtretbarkeit dürfte namentlich für Gesellschafterinnen und Gesellschafter, die natürliche Personen sind, oft mit einschneidenden Folgen verbunden sein. Wie bereits angesprochen wurde, können in der GmbH (im Unterschied zur Aktiengesellschaft) nur darum derart weitgehende Vinkulierungsmöglichkeiten eingeräumt werden, weil den Gesellschafterinnen und Gesellschaftern erforderlichenfalls ein Recht zum Austritt aus wichtigen Gründen zusteht (Art. 822 E OR). *Abs. 3* stellt klar, dass bei der Verweigerung der Zustimmung zur Abtretung von Stammanteilen stets ein Austritt aus wichtigen Gründen vorbehalten bleibt. Die vorliegende Bestimmung ist namentlich auch für die Interpretation von Art. 822 E OR von Bedeutung. Ist die Abtretung von Anteilen in einer Gesellschaft übermässig erschwert, so kann dies – je nach den persönlichen und sachlichen Gegebenheiten – einen wichtigen Grund für einen Austritt darstellen.

c. Rechtsübergang

Art. 787

1 Ist für die Abtretung von Stammanteilen die Zustimmung der Gesellschafterversammlung erforderlich, so wird die Abtretung erst mit dieser Zustimmung rechtswirksam.

2 Lehnt die Gesellschafterversammlung das Gesuch um Zustimmung zur Abtretung nicht innerhalb von sechs Monaten nach Eingang ab, so gilt die Zustimmung als erteilt.

Bedarf die Abtretung von Stammanteilen der Zustimmung der Gesellschafterversammlung, so wird die Abtretung nach *Abs. 1* erst mit dieser Zustimmung rechtswirksam. Die Vinkulierung der Stammanteile der GmbH ist demnach als eigentliche Übertragbarkeitsbeschränkung konzipiert, wie dies auch für nicht börsenkotierte Aktien der Fall ist (vgl. Art. 685*c* Abs. 1 OR): Ohne die erforderliche Zustimmung bleibt die Abtretung unwirksam (dies im Unterschied zur früheren «Spaltungstheorie» zur Übertragung von Aktien; vgl. insbes. BGE 90 II 235 ff.).

Im Interesse der betroffenen Gesellschafterinnen und Gesellschafter legt *Abs. 2* einen zeitlichen Rahmen fest, innerhalb dessen die Gesellschafterversammlung über ein Gesuch um Zustimmung zur Abtretung von Stammanteilen entscheiden muss. Lehnt die Gesellschafterversammlung ein Gesuch nicht binnen 6 Monaten nach dessen Eingang ab, so gilt die Zustimmung als erteilt. Für die Wahrung der Frist ist der Zugang des Entscheids an die Gesuchstellerin oder den Gesuchsteller massgebend. Mit 6 Monaten ist die Frist recht grosszügig bemessen, um der Gesellschaft für allenfalls erforderliche Abklärungen (bspw. zur Ausübung statutarischer Erwerbsvorrechte) genügend Zeit einzuräumen (das Aktienrecht sieht für nicht börsenkotierte Aktien eine Frist von 3 Monaten vor; Art. 685c Abs. 3 OR).

2. Besondere Erwerbsarten

Art. 788

1 Werden Stammanteile durch Erbgang, Erbteilung, eheliches Güterrecht oder Zwangsvollstreckung erworben, so gehen alle Rechte und Pflichten, die damit verbunden sind, ohne Zustimmung der Gesellschafterversammlung auf die erwerbende Person über.

2 Für die Ausübung des Stimmrechts und der damit zusammenhängenden Rechte bedarf die erwerbende Person jedoch der Anerkennung der Gesellschafterversammlung als stimmberechtigter Gesellschafter.

3 Die Gesellschafterversammlung kann ihr die Anerkennung nur verweigern, wenn ihr die Gesellschaft die Übernahme der Stammanteile zum wirklichen Wert im Zeitpunkt des Gesuches anbietet. Das Angebot kann auf eigene Rechnung oder auf Rechnung anderer Gesellschafter oder Dritter erfolgen. Lehnt die erwerbende Person das Angebot nicht innerhalb eines Monates nach Kenntnis des wirklichen Wertes ab, so gilt es als angenommen.

4 Lehnt die Gesellschafterversammlung das Gesuch um Anerkennung nicht innerhalb von sechs Monaten ab, so gilt die Anerkennung als erteilt.

5 Die Statuten können auf das Erfordernis der Anerkennung verzichten.

Für bestimmte Erwerbsarten ist die allgemeine Ordnung sowohl der Zustimmungserfordernisse (Art. 786 E OR) als auch des Rechtsübergangs (Art. 787 E OR) nicht geeignet. Art. 788 E OR sieht daher eine Sonderregelung für besondere Erwerbsarten[87] vor.

Werden Stammanteile durch Erbgang, Erbteilung, eheliches Güterrecht oder Zwangsvollstreckung erworben, so gehen nach *Abs. 1* sämtliche Rechte und Pflichten, die damit verbunden sind, ohne Zustimmung der Gesellschafterversammlung von Gesetzes wegen auf die Erwerberin oder den Erwerber über. Diese Regelung ist erforderlich, da bei den erwähnten Erwerbsarten die mit den Stammanteilen verbundenen Rechte aus sachlichen Gründen nicht mehr dem bisherigen Eigentümer oder der bisherigen Eigentümerin zugeschrieben werden können oder sollen. Es wird dadurch verhindert, dass die Rechte und Pflichten «herrenlos» werden.

Die Aufzählung der besonderen Erwerbsarten in *Abs. 1* ist nicht abschliessend zu verstehen. Vielmehr sind die in diesem Artikel vorgesehenen Sonderregelungen auch auf ähnliche Sachverhalte anzuwenden, sofern die Umstände und die Interessenlage einem der im Gesetz aufgezählten Fälle entsprechen[88].

Abs. 2 umschreibt die Rechtswirkungen der Vinkulierung für besondere Erwerbsarten. Da hier der Rechtsübergang als solcher nie der Zustimmung durch die Gesellschafterversammlung bedarf, beschränkt sich die Vinkulierung darauf, dass für die Ausübung des Stimmrechts und der damit zusammenhängenden Rechte die Anerkennung der erwerbenden Person als stimmberechtigte Gesellschafterin oder als stimmberechtigter Gesellschafter vorausgesetzt wird.

Nach *Abs. 3* darf die Gesellschafterversammlung ein Anerkennungsgesuch bei den erwähnten besonderen Erwerbsarten nur dann ablehnen, wenn die Gesellschaft der Gesuchstellerin oder dem Gesuchsteller die Übernahme der Stammanteile zum wirklichen Wert anbietet. Diese Regelung ist erforderlich, weil die Gesuchstellerin oder der Gesuchsteller die Stammanteile bereits erworben hat. Wird der neuen Eigentümerin oder dem neuen Eigentümer die Ausübung der Stimmrechte verweigert, so muss der betroffenen Person die Möglichkeit geboten werden, die erworbenen Stammanteile zum wirklichen Wert wieder zu veräussern.

---

87 Der Begriff der «besonderen Erwerbsarten» ist übernommen aus: HANSPETER KLÄY, Die Vinkulierung, Diss. Basel, Basel und Frankfurt a.M. 1997, S. 205 (zum Aktienrecht).
88 s. HANSPETER KLÄY, a.a.O., S. 205 ff., insbes. 207; PETER LUTZ, Vinkulierte Namenaktien, Diss. Zürich 1988, S. 171 f. (beide zum Aktienrecht).

Das Angebot der Gesellschaft zur Übernahme der Stammanteile zum wirklichen Wert kann auf eigene Rechnung, auf Rechnung anderer Gesellschafterinnen und Gesellschafter oder auf Rechnung Dritter erfolgen. Ein Angebot zur Übernahme durch die Gesellschaft setzt allerdings voraus, dass die Vorschriften über den Erwerb eigener Stammanteile erfüllt sind (Art. 783 E OR).

Macht die Gesellschaft ein Angebot zur Übernahme der Stammanteile zum wirklichen Wert, wird dessen Annahme vermutet, wenn das Angebot nicht innerhalb eines Monates nach Kenntnis vom wirklichen Wert abgelehnt wird (ebenso Art. 685*b* Abs. 6 OR). Der Gesuchstellerin oder dem Gesuchsteller steht es jedoch frei, die Übernahme abzulehnen und die Stammanteile zu behalten. Die berechtigte Person darf diesfalls nur diejenigen Rechte ausüben, die nicht mit dem Stimmrecht zusammenhängen (zur Eintragung im Aktienbuch s. Art. 790 Abs. 3 E OR). Allfällige Pflichten der Gesellschafterinnen und Gesellschafter müssen erfüllt werden.

Abs. 4 räumt der Gesellschaft für den Entscheid über ein Gesuch um Anerkennung eine Frist von 6 Monaten ein. Diese Frist entspricht derjenigen von Art. 787 Abs. 2 E OR. Geht der Gesuchstellerin oder dem Gesuchsteller innerhalb von sechs Monaten kein Entscheid zu, so gilt die Anerkennung als erteilt.

Nach *Abs. 5* kann in den Statuten für besondere Erwerbsarten auf das Erfordernis der Anerkennung der erwerbenden Person als stimmberechtigt verzichtet werden. Es ist auch möglich, nur einzelne besondere Erwerbsarten von diesem Erfordernis auszunehmen, so beispielsweise den erbrechtlichen Erwerb. Schliessen die Statuten die dispositive gesetzliche Vinkulierung aus (d.h. die Möglichkeit der Verweigerung der Zustimmung zur Abtretung ohne Angabe von Gründen; s. Art. 786 Abs. 1 und Abs. 2 Ziff. 1 E OR), so gilt ohne weiteres auch die Vinkulierung für besondere Erwerbsarten als aufgehoben.

3. Bestimmung des wirklichen Werts

Art. 789

1 Stellen das Gesetz oder die Statuten auf den wirklichen Wert der Stammanteile ab, so können die Parteien verlangen, dass dieser vom Gericht bestimmt wird.

2 Das Gericht verteilt die Kosten des Verfahrens und der Bewertung nach seinem Ermessen.

Beim Erwerb von Stammanteilen durch besondere Erwerbsarten setzt die Verweigerung der Anerkennung der Erwerberin oder des Erwerbers voraus, dass die Gesellschaft anbietet, die Stammanteile zum wirklichen Wert zu übernehmen (Art. 788 Abs. 3 E OR). Eine gleiche Regelung kann in den Statuten auch generell für die Abtretung von Stammanteilen vorgesehen werden (Art. 786 Abs. 2 Ziff. 3 E OR). Scheitert die Verständigung unter den beteiligten Parteien, so steht es ihnen nach *Abs. 1* stets offen, die Festsetzung des wirklichen Werts[89] durch das Gericht zu verlangen (vgl. Art. 685*b* Abs. 5 OR im Aktienrecht).

Abs. 2 räumt dem Gericht für die Verteilung der Kosten des Verfahrens und der Bewertung einen gewissen Freiraum ein, damit allen relevanten Umständen Rechnung getragen werden kann. Es ist dabei zu berücksichtigen, dass das Interesse für das Fernhalten unerwünschter Erwerberinnen und Erwerber bei der Gesellschaft liegt. Sie hat es auch zu vertreten, wenn sich die Bewertung ihrer Anteile als schwierig erweist. Sofern keine Gründe eine andere Zuteilung der Kosten rechtfertigen, sind diese daher grundsätzlich der Gesellschaft aufzuerlegen, wie dies im Aktienrecht der Fall ist (s. Art. 685*b* Abs. 5 Satz 2 OR). Eine andere Zuweisung kann namentlich dann angezeigt sein, wenn das Gericht angerufen wird, obschon die Gesellschaft eine seriöse und zutreffende Ermittlung des wirklichen Wertes durch neutrale Experten hat vornehmen lassen.

4. Nutzniessung

Art. 789a

1 Für die Bestellung einer Nutzniessung an einem Stammanteil sind die Vorschriften über die Übertragung der Stammanteile entsprechend anwendbar.

---

[89] Zur Bestimmung des wirklichen Wertes s. insbes. PETER BÖCKLI, Schweizer Aktienrecht, 2. Aufl., Zürich 1996, N 699 ff.; DERS., Neun Regeln der «Best Practice» für den Rückkauf nicht kotierter eigener Aktien, in: Der Schweizer Treuhänder 2001, S. 575 ff., insbes. 579 ff.; PETER LUTZ, Vinkulierte Namenaktien, Diss. Zürich 1988, S. 271 ff. (alle zum Aktienrecht).

2 Schliessen die Statuten die Abtretung aus, so ist auch die Bestellung einer Nutzniessung an den Stammanteilen ausgeschlossen.

Nach *Abs. 1* finden für die Bestellung einer Nutzniessung an einem Stammanteil die Vorschriften zur Übertragung der Stammanteile entsprechende Anwendung. Diese Verweisung betrifft die Form, die Zustimmungserfordernisse, den Rechtsübergang, die Regelung für besondere Erwerbsarten sowie gegebenenfalls die Bestimmung des wirklichen Werts (Art. 785–789 E OR; zur Ausübung des Stimmrechts durch den Nutzniesser s. Art. 806*b*).

Schliessen die Statuten die Abtretung von Stammanteilen aus (Art. 786 Abs. 2 Ziff. 4 E OR), so ist nach *Abs. 2* ebenfalls die Bestellung einer Nutzniessung daran ausgeschlossen. Dies ergibt sich aus dem Recht der Nutzniessung (s. Art. 745 ff. ZGB) und verhindert auch, dass der Ausschluss der Abtretbarkeit durch die Bestellung einer Nutzniessung umgangen wird. Es ist aber auch möglich, die Abtretung der Stammanteile zwar zuzulassen, die Einräumung einer Nutzniessung daran aber statutarisch auszuschliessen (Art. 786 Abs. 2 Ziff. 4 i.V.m. Art. 789*a* Abs. 1 E OR). Dies dürfte namentlich dann einem Bedürfnis entsprechen, wenn die Statuten Nachschuss- oder Nebenleistungspflichten vorsehen: Sind mit Stammanteilen statutarische Pflichten verbunden, kann dies im Falle der Begründung einer Nutzniessung schwerwiegende Probleme zur Folge haben, die mit der Zuordnung der Rechte und Pflichten an die Nutzniesserin oder den Nutzniesser beziehungsweise die Eigentümerin oder den Eigentümer zusammenhängen.

5. Pfandrecht

Art. 789b

1 Die Statuten können vorsehen, dass die Bestellung eines Pfandrechts an Stammanteilen der Zustimmung der Gesellschafterversammlung bedarf. Diese darf die Zustimmung nur verweigern, wenn ein wichtiger Grund vorliegt.

2 Schliessen die Statuten die Abtretung aus, so ist auch die Bestellung eines Pfandrechts an den Stammanteilen ausgeschlossen.

Die Bestellung eines Pfandrechts an einem Stammanteil ist nicht mit der Abtretung des Eigentums an den Pfandgläubiger gleichzusetzen. Dieser kann lediglich die Verwertung des Stammanteiles verlangen, falls der Pfandschuldner seinen Verpflichtungen nicht nachkommen sollte. Der Pfandgläubiger kann keine mit dem Stammanteil verbundenen Rechte ausüben. Das Stimmrecht und die damit zusammenhängenden Rechte verbleiben somit beim Pfandschuldner (Art. 905 Abs. 2 E ZGB).

Abs. 1 sieht daher vor, dass die Bestellung eines Pfandrechts an Stammanteilen nur dann der Zustimmung durch die Gesellschafterversammlung bedarf, wenn die Statuten dies ausdrücklich verlangen. Wird die Zustimmung vorbehalten, darf die Gesellschafterversammlung diese nur aus wichtigen Gründen verweigern. Der Entwurf will mit dieser Regelung ein Minimum an wirtschaftlicher Verfügbarkeit von Gesellschaftsanteilen gewährleisten. So soll es beispielsweise möglich sein, dass eine Gesellschafterin ihren Stammanteil für den Erwerb einer Eigentumswohnung verpfänden kann.

Abs. 2 entspricht Art. 899 Abs. 1 ZGB, wonach ein Recht nur dann verpfändet werden kann, wenn es übertragbar ist. Sofern die Statuten die Abtretung von Stammanteilen untersagen, fehlt es an dieser Voraussetzung. Die Bestellung eines Pfandrechtes an einem unübertragbaren Stammanteil ist daher ausgeschlossen.

III. Anteilbuch

Art. 790

1 Die Gesellschaft führt über die Stammanteile ein Anteilbuch.

2 In das Anteilbuch sind einzutragen:

1. die Gesellschafter mit Namen und Adresse;
2. die Anzahl, der Nennwert sowie allenfalls die Kategorien der Stammanteile jedes Gesellschafters;
3. die Nutzniesser mit Namen und Adresse;
4. die Pfandgläubiger mit Namen und Adresse.

3 Gesellschafter, die nicht zur Ausübung des Stimmrechts und der damit zusammenhängenden Rechte befugt sind, müssen als Gesellschafter ohne Stimmrecht bezeichnet werden.

4 Den Gesellschaftern steht das Recht zu, in das Anteilbuch Einsicht zu nehmen.

Abs. 1 auferlegt der Gesellschaft die Pflicht, ein Anteilbuch zu führen. Die Verantwortung für die korrekte Führung des Anteilbuches liegt (sofern die Statuten nichts anderes vorsehen) bei den Geschäftsführerinnen und Geschäftsführern (s. Art. 810 Abs. 1 E OR).

Abs. 2 legt den Inhalt des Anteilbuches fest. Einzutragen sind die Namen und die Adressen sämtlicher Gesellschafterinnen und Gesellschafter (*Ziff. 1*). Steht ein Stammanteil in gemeinschaftlichem Eigentum, so ist jede der daran berechtigten Personen als Gesellschafterin respektive als Gesellschafter einzutragen; weiter ist ein gemeinsamer Vertreter anzugeben (vgl. Art. 792 E OR). Im Anteilbuch zu verzeichnen sind ebenfalls die Anzahl und der Nennwert sowie allenfalls die Kategorien der Stammanteile jeder Gesellschafterin und jedes Gesellschafters (*Ziff. 2*). Demgegenüber ist die Auflistung der Beträge der von den einzelnen Gesellschafterinnen und Gesellschaftern auf ihre Stammanteile eingebrachten Leistungen im Allgemeinen nicht mehr erforderlich, da der Entwurf von einer vollen Liberierung der Stammanteile ausgeht (Art. 777*c* Abs. 1 E OR). Falls Stammanteile gestützt auf die Regelung des Übergangsrechts (noch) nicht voll liberiert wurden (vgl. Art. 3 UeB), müssen im Aktienbuch aber auch die erfolgten Einlagen angegeben werden (entsprechend dem bisherigen Recht; Art. 790 Abs. 1 OR). Ins Anteilbuch aufzunehmen sind ferner ebenfalls die Nutzniesserinnen und Nutzniesser sowie die Pfandgläubigerinnen und Pfandgläubiger (*Ziff. 3 und 4*).

Die Aufzählung der einzutragenden Tatbestände in Abs. 2 ist nicht abschliessender Natur. Es steht der Gesellschaft offen, weitere relevante Umstände einzutragen, so insbesondere bestehende Nachschuss- und Nebenleistungspflichten.

Abs. 3 stellt die Art der Eintragung von Personen klar, die ihre Stammanteile auf Grund besonderer Erwerbsarten nach Art. 788 E OR erworben haben und von der Gesellschaft nicht als stimmberechtigte Gesellschafterinnen oder Gesellschafter anerkannt wurden: Behalten sie ihre Stammanteile, so sind sie als Gesellschafterinnen ohne Stimmrecht beziehungsweise als Gesellschafter ohne Stimmrecht im Anteilbuch einzutragen.

Nach *Abs. 4* sind die Gesellschafterinnen und Gesellschafter berechtigt, Einblick in das Anteilbuch zu nehmen. Sie haben einen Anspruch darauf, in Erfahrung bringen zu können, mit wem zusammen sie eine Gesellschaft bilden.

Das Aktienrecht sieht vor, dass Eintragungen «im Aktienbuch gestrichen[90]» werden können, wenn sie durch falsche Angaben zu Stande gekommen sind (Art. 686a OR). Diese Regelung findet nach dem Entwurf für die GmbH keine Anwendung, weil hier die Möglichkeit offen steht, Gesellschafterinnen und Gesellschaftern aus wichtigen Gründen auszuschliessen (Art. 823 Abs. 1 E OR). Die Angabe falscher Informationen anlässlich eines Gesuches um Zustimmung zur Abtretung kann durchaus einen Grund darstellen, der einen Ausschluss zu rechtfertigen vermag. Eine Sonderregelung für eine Streichung aus dem Anteilbuch erscheint daher nicht sinnvoll.

IV. Eintragung ins Handelsregister

Art. 791

1 Die Gesellschafter sind mit Name, Wohnsitz und Heimatort sowie mit der Anzahl und dem Nennwert ihrer Stammanteile ins Handelsregister einzutragen.

2 Die Gesellschaft muss die Eintragung anmelden.

Die Gesellschafterinnen und Gesellschafter sind bereits nach dem geltenden Recht ins Handelsregister einzutragen (Art. 781 Ziff. 4 OR). Die Geschäftsführerinnen und Geschäftsführer müssen zudem dem Handelsregisteramt jedes Jahr eine Liste der Gesellschafterinnen und Gesellschafter einreichen und insbesondere die auf die Stammanteile erfolgten Leistungen angeben (Art. 790 Abs. 2 OR).

Der Entwurf verzichtet auf die Pflicht zur Einreichung einer Gesellschafterliste. An der Eintragung der Gesellschafterinnen und Gesellschafter ins Handelsregister ist dagegen aus folgenden Gründen festzuhalten: In Abkehr vom geltenden Recht (Art. 791 Abs. 4 OR) sieht der Entwurf für die Abtretung von Gesellschaftsanteilen vom Erfordernis der öffentlichen Beurkundung ab (Art. 785 Abs. 1 E OR; vgl. Kommentar zu dieser Bestimmung). Damit dennoch eine genügende Rechtssicherheit gewährleis-

---

90 Mit dem ungenauen Begriff der «Streichung im Aktienbuch» ist gemeint, dass die Anerkennung als Aktionärin oder als Aktionär nachträglich wieder aufgehoben werden kann.

tet werden kann, muss vorausgesetzt werden, dass die Abtretung von Stammanteilen durch die Eintragung der Gesellschafterinnen und Gesellschafter ins Handelsregister erfasst und zumindest formal geprüft wird (vgl. Art. 940 Abs. 1 OR). Die Eintragung der Gesellschafterinnen und Gesellschafter ins Handelsregister ist aber insbesondere auch darum erforderlich, weil mit der Gesellschafterstellung in der GmbH verschiedene Pflichten verbunden sein können, die auch für Dritte teilweise von Bedeutung sind; zu denken ist an die Treuepflicht, ein Konkurrenzverbot sowie an Nachschuss- und Nebenleistungspflichten. Einerseits liegt es im Interesse der Gesellschaft selbst, dass die verpflichteten Personen klar im Handelsregister festgehalten werden; andererseits sollen beispielsweise Gläubigerinnen und Gläubiger oder potenzielle Vertragspartnerinnen und Vertragspartner durch eine Einsichtnahme ins Handelsregister die für sie relevanten Informationen in Erfahrung bringen können. Es ist zu beachten, dass in der GmbH Wechsel im Kreis der Gesellschafterinnen und Gesellschafter eher selten sind; der Aufwand, der mit der Eintragung ins Handelsregister verbunden ist, dürfte daher gering sein und etwa demjenigen bei der Eintragung von Prokuristinnen und Prokuristen entsprechen.

Abs. 1 sieht die Eintragung der Gesellschafterinnen und Gesellschafter ins Handelsregister vor und präzisiert die einzutragenden Angaben (Name, Wohnsitz, Heimatort, Anzahl und Nennwert der Stammanteile).

Nach *Abs. 2* ist es Aufgabe der Gesellschaft, die erforderlichen Eintragungen beim Handelsregisteramt anzumelden. Es obliegt der Person, die den Vorsitz über die Geschäftsführung innehat, die Anmeldung sicherzustellen (s. Art. 810 Abs. 3 Ziff. 3 und 931*a* E OR).

V. Gemeinschaftliches Eigentum

Art. 792

Steht ein Stammanteil mehreren Berechtigten ungeteilt zu, so:

1 haben diese gemeinsam eine Person zu bezeichnen, die sie vertritt. Sie können die Rechte aus dem Stammanteil nur durch diese Person ausüben;

2 haften diese für Nachschusspflichten und Nebenleistungspflichten solidarisch.

Die Regelung betreffend gemeinschaftliches Eigentum an Stammanteilen gilt sowohl für Miteigentum als auch für Gesamteigentum. Ein gemeinschaftliches Eigentum kann sich insbesondere ergeben, wenn Stammanteile durch eine einfache Gesellschaft, eine Kollektiv- oder eine Kommanditgesellschaft gehalten werden; erwähnt sei auch der Erwerb eines Stammanteils durch eine Erbengemeinschaft.

Wenn ein Stammanteil im gemeinschaftlichen Eigentum mehrerer Personen steht, haben diese nach *Abs. 1* eine gemeinsame Vertreterin oder einen gemeinsamen Vertreter zu bezeichnen. Die Rechte aus dem Stammanteil können nur durch diese Person ausgeübt werden (so auch im geltenden Recht; s. Art. 797 OR).

Abs. 2 sieht vor, dass mehrere an einem Stammanteil berechtigte Personen solidarisch für statutarische Nachschuss- und Nebenleistungspflichten haften, die mit dem Stammanteil verbunden sind.

B. Leistung der Einlagen

Art. 793

1 Die Gesellschafter sind zur Leistung einer dem Ausgabebetrag ihrer Stammanteile entsprechenden Einlage verpflichtet.

2 Die Einlagen dürfen nicht zurückerstattet werden.

Abs. 1 auferlegt den Gesellschafterinnen und Gesellschaftern die Pflicht, eine dem Ausgabebetrag ihrer Stammanteile entsprechende Einlage zu leisten (Liberierungspflicht). Nach Art. 777c Abs. 1 E OR muss diese Einlage bei der Gründung vollständig geleistet werden (s. dazu die Ausführungen zu Art. 777c Abs. 1 E OR; zur Art der Liberierung s. die Erläuterungen zu Art. 777c Abs. 2 Ziff. 3 E OR).

Abs. 2 untersagt jede Rückerstattung von Einlagen (ebenso, wenn auch unklar formuliert, Art. 680 Abs. 2 OR im Aktienrecht). Zum Schutz der Gläubigerinnen und Gläubiger ist eine Rückleistung nur auf dem Weg einer Kapitalherabsetzung (Art. 782 E OR) zulässig.

C. Haftung der Gesellschafter

Art. 794

Für die Verbindlichkeiten der Gesellschaft haftet nur das Gesellschaftsvermögen.

Nach dem geltenden Recht unterliegen die Gesellschafterinnen und Gesellschafter einer subsidiären Solidarhaftung im Umfang des gesamten Stammkapitals, sofern dieses nicht voll einbezahlt oder durch Rückleistungen oder ungerechtfertigte Bezüge vermindert wurde (s. Art. 802 OR).

Dieses Haftungsmodell vermag sachlich nicht zu befriedigen: Die subsidiäre solidarische Haftung der Gesellschafterinnen und Gesellschafter soll die effektive Liberierung der Stammanteile sowie die Kapitalerhaltung gewährleisten. Eine Haftung für fremde Liberierungsschulden oder ungerechtfertigte Kapitalentnahmen durch andere Personen kann sich aber als stossend erweisen, so zum Beispiel, wenn eine Gesellschafterin, die ihren Stammanteil in bar liberiert hat, zur Verantwortung gezogen wird für eine nicht werthaltige Sacheinlage eines andern Gesellschafters. Auf Grund der subsidiären Solidarhaftung kann eine Gesellschafterin oder ein Gesellschafter zudem für das gesamte Stammkapital von beispielsweise 200 000 Franken haften müssen, obschon sie oder er einen Stammanteil von bloss 1000 Franken gezeichnet hat. Die subsidiäre Solidarhaftung ist für die Gesellschafterinnen und Gesellschafter mit Gefahren verbunden, die in der Praxis häufig verkannt werden, da oft zu Unrecht davon ausgegangen wird, dass in der GmbH dieselbe Haftungsbeschränkung besteht wie in der Aktiengesellschaft. Eine Neuregelung der Haftung der Gesellschafterinnen und Gesellschafter erscheint daher dringend.

Der Entwurf verzichtet auf die subsidiäre Solidarhaftung. Nach Art. 794 E OR soll für Verbindlichkeiten der Gesellschaft nur noch das Gesellschaftsvermögen haften. Die effektive Liberierung des Stammkapitals sowie die Kapitalerhaltung kann durch die Anwendung der entsprechenden Vorschriften des Aktienrechts dennoch gewährleistet werden. Von Bedeutung ist dabei namentlich die Prüfung von Sacheinlagen und Sachübernahmen sowie von Verrechnungstatbeständen (s. Art. 635 und 635a OR i.V.m. Art. 777c Abs. 2 Ziff. 3 E OR). Im Hinblick auf das geringe Mindestkapital (20 000 Franken; Art. 773 E OR) ist weiter eine vollständige Liberierung vorauszusetzen (Art. 777c Abs. 1 E OR). Die Anwendung der aktienrechtlichen Bestimmungen für Sacheinlagen, Sachübernahmen und die Liberierung durch Verrechnung mag zwar auf den ersten Blick als Belastung erscheinen, ist aber aus sachlichen Gründen notwendig und ermöglicht, auf die problematische subsidiäre Solidarhaftung des bisherigen Rechts zu verzichten.

Der Entwurf sieht vor, dass die Stammanteile stets vollständig zu liberieren sind (Art. 777c Abs. 1 E OR). Die bisherigen *Art. 799–801 OR* können gestrichen werden, da sie sich auf nur teilweise einbezahlte Stammanteile beziehen (Entrichtung von Verzugszinsen; Ausschluss säumiger Gesellschafterinnen und Gesellschafter; Verwertung von Anteilen; Haftung für den Ausfall).

D. Nachschüsse und Nebenleistungen

I. Nachschüsse

1. Grundsatz und Betrag

Art. 795

1 Die Statuten können die Gesellschafter zur Leistung von Nachschüssen verpflichten.

2 Sehen die Statuten eine Nachschusspflicht vor, so müssen sie den Betrag der mit einem Stammanteil verbundenen Nachschusspflicht festlegen. Dieser darf das Doppelte des Nennwertes des Stammanteils nicht übersteigen.

3 Die Gesellschafter haften nur für die mit den eigenen Stammanteilen verbundenen Nachschüsse.

Abs. 1 hält als Grundsatz fest, dass die Statuten die Gesellschafterinnen und Gesellschafter zur Leistung von Nachschüssen verpflichten können. Nachschusspflichtig sind die jeweiligen Gesellschafterinnen und Gesellschafter als solche. Die Nachschusspflicht ist demnach nicht mit bestimmten Personen verbunden, sondern mit den Stammanteilen (vorbehalten bleibt jedoch die Fortdauer der Nachschusspflicht beim Ausscheiden aus der Gesellschaft; s. Art. 795*d* E OR). Die verpflichteten Personen werden nicht etwa namentlich in den Statuten genannt, sondern bestimmen sich durch das Eigentum an den Stammanteilen, die mit einer Nachschusspflicht belastet sind.

Neben den herkömmlichen Verwendungszwecken der Nachschusspflicht übernimmt diese nach dem Entwurf auch die Funktion der bisherigen Teilliberierung des Stammkapitals. Dadurch lassen sich Doppelspurigkeiten im Gesetz vermeiden.

Nach *Abs. 2* müssen die Statuten den Betrag der mit einem Stammanteil verbundenen Nachschusspflicht festlegen. Sie können eine Nachschusspflicht sowohl für sämtliche als auch nur für einzelne Stammanteile vorsehen oder auf bestimmte Kategorien beschränken. Stets muss aber aus den Statuten klar hervorgehen, welche Stammanteile in welchem Umfang mit einer Nachschusspflicht belastet sind.

Während das geltende Recht Nachschusspflichten in beliebiger Höhe zuliess (Art. 803 Abs. 2 OR), beschränkt der Entwurf Nachschusspflichten auf das Doppelte des Nennwertes der Stammanteile, mit denen sie verbunden sind. Die gesetzliche Begrenzung will die Gesellschafterinnen und Gesellschafter im Hinblick auf sich ändernde Umstände vor einer übermässigen Bindung schützen. Dies erscheint notwendig, weil die Folgen einer Nachschusspflicht für die belasteten Personen denjenigen einer Bürgschaft nahe kommen können, ohne dass aber die Kautelen des Bürgschaftsrechts beachtet werden müssen[91]. Eine Limitierung ist namentlich auch im Interesse von Erwerberinnen und Erwerbern von Stammanteilen auf Grund des Erbrechtes erforderlich.

Die bisherige subsidiäre Solidarhaftung der Gesellschafterinnen und Gesellschafter für den nicht liberierten Teil des Stammkapitals (Art. 802 OR) soll mit der Revision aufgehoben werden. In Entsprechung dazu sieht *Abs. 3* vor, dass die Gesellschafterinnen und Gesellschafter nur für diejenigen Nachschüsse haften, die mit den eigenen Stammanteilen der verpflichteten Person verbunden sind.

In steuerrechtlicher Hinsicht ist bedeutsam, dass die GmbH für Zuwendungen ihrer Gesellschafter die Emissionsabgabe zu entrichten hat, ausser in jenen Sanierungsfällen, in denen die Emissionsabgabe erlassen werden kann. Werden solche Zuwendungen später zurückgegeben, unterliegen sie der Verrechnungssteuer und gegebenenfalls der Einkommenssteuer. Die steuerliche Situation ist somit dieselbe wie bei der Leistung und der Rückzahlung von Zuschüssen an Aktiengesellschaften.

---

[91] s. PETER BÖCKLI/PETER FORSTMOSER/JEAN-MARC RAPP, Reform des GmbH-Rechts, Zürich 1997, S. 100.

2. Einforderung

Art. 795a

1 Die Nachschüsse werden durch die Geschäftsführer eingefordert.

2 Sie dürfen nur eingefordert werden, wenn:
1. **die Summe von Stammkapital und gesetzlichen Reserven nicht mehr gedeckt ist;**
2. **die Gesellschaft ihre Geschäfte ohne diese zusätzlichen Mittel nicht ordnungsgemäss weiterführen kann;**
3. **die Gesellschaft aus in den Statuten umschriebenen Gründen Eigenkapital benötigt.**

3 Mit Eintritt des Konkurses werden ausstehende Nachschüsse fällig.

Nach geltendem Recht werden Nachschüsse durch die Gesellschafterversammlung eingefordert (Art. 810 Abs. 1 Ziff. 7 OR). Der Entwurf überträgt die Befugnis zur Einforderung in *Abs. 1* den Geschäftsführerinnen und Geschäftsführern, da es sich um eine Massnahme zur Abwendung eines Kapitalverlustes oder des Konkurses handelt, die im Rahmen der Geschäftsführung zu ergreifen ist.

Abs. 2 legt die Voraussetzungen fest, unter denen Nachschüsse eingefordert werden dürfen. Da die statutarische Nachschusspflicht neben den angestammten Funktionen auch jene der bisherigen Teilliberierung erfüllen kann, werden die Gründe, die eine Einforderung ermöglichen, gegenüber dem geltenden Recht erweitert.

– Nach *Ziff. 1* können Nachschüsse eingefordert werden, wenn die Summe von Stammkapital und gesetzlichen Reserven nicht mehr gedeckt ist. Die Einforderung von Nachschüssen ermöglicht es, beim Eintreten eines Kapitalverlustes die Eigenkapitalbasis der Gesellschaft zu verbessern (vgl. Art. 725 Abs. 1 OR i.V.m. Art. 820 Abs. 1 E OR).

– Nach *Ziff. 2* sollen Nachschüsse neu ebenfalls dann eingefordert werden können, wenn die Gesellschaft ihre Geschäfte ohne diese zusätzlichen Mittel nicht ordnungsgemäss weiterführen kann. Als Beurteilungsmassstab wird derjenige einer sorgfältigen Geschäftsführerin oder eines sorgfältigen Geschäftsführers vorausgesetzt. Die Nachschüsse dienen hier der Überwindung von Liquiditätsengpässen, doch darf mit Blick auf den Schutz der Gesellschafterinnen und Gesellschafter nicht jeder beliebige Bedarf an finanziellen Mitteln die Einforderung rechtfertigen. Für die Beurteilung der Zulässigkeit, Nachschüsse einzufordern, können etwa die folgenden Kriterien dienen:

– Die liquiden Mittel gehen so rasch verloren, dass kurzfristig die Zahlungsunfähigkeit bevorsteht.

– Die Gesellschaft bedarf liquider Mittel, hat aber grosse Schwierigkeiten, diese im erforderlichen Masse zu beschaffen. Sie hat ihre Kreditlimiten ausgeschöpft, und es sind keine neuen Kredite zu üblichen Bedingungen erhältlich. Die Verbindlichkeiten werden so spät wie möglich beglichen, und die Gläubigerinnen und Gläubiger sind nicht bereit, die Zahlungsfristen zu erstrecken. Sachwerte, die für die Geschäftstätigkeit der Gesellschaft nicht erforderlich sind, wurden schon veräussert oder sind nicht innert nützlicher Frist veräusserlich.

– *Ziff. 3* räumt die Möglichkeit ein, in den Statuten weitere Fälle zu umschreiben, in denen die Geschäftsführerinnen und Geschäftsführer ausstehende Nachschüsse einfordern können. Die Voraussetzungen sind dabei in den Statuten klar zu umschreiben. Es kann beispielsweise vorgesehen werden, dass Nachschüsse einverlangt werden dürfen, wenn dies zum Erwerb einer zusätzlichen Geschäftsliegenschaft erforderlich ist (dabei wäre klarzustellen, wie weit eine Finanzierung durch Fremdkapital erfolgen soll). Es ist auch zulässig, die Anforderungen für das Einverlangen von Nachschüssen zur Überbrückung von Liquiditätsengpässen weniger streng zu fassen, als dies aus *Ziff. 2* hervorgeht. *Ziff. 1* und *Ziff. 2* sind jedoch in dem Sinne als einseitig zwingend zu verstehen, als die Statuten die Anforderungen für das Einverlangen von Nachschüssen nicht erhöhen dürfen, da dadurch sowohl der Zweck von Nachschüssen als auch Interessen Dritter beeinträchtigt werden könnten.

Nach *Abs. 3* werden noch ausstehende Nachschüsse mit Eintritt des Konkurses fällig. Von diesem Zeitpunkt an sind nicht mehr die Geschäftsführerinnen und Geschäftsführer zur Einforderung zuständig, sondern die Konkursverwaltung.

Teil F: Rechtliche Aspekte / Legal aspects

3. Rückzahlung

Art. 795b

Geleistete Nachschüsse dürfen nur dann ganz oder teilweise zurückbezahlt werden, wenn der Betrag durch frei verwendbares Eigenkapital gedeckt ist und ein zugelassener Revisionsexperte dies schriftlich bestätigt.

Der Entwurf ersetzt den Begriff der besonders befähigten Revisorin bzw. des besonders befähigten Revisors durch jenen der zugelassenen Revisionsexpertin bzw. des zugelassenen Revisionsexperten (vgl. dazu die Erläuterungen zu Art. 4 E RAG).

4. Herabsetzung

Art. 795c

¹ Eine statutarische Nachschusspflicht darf nur dann herabgesetzt oder aufgehoben werden, wenn das Stammkapital und die gesetzlichen Reserven voll gedeckt sind.

² Die Vorschriften über die Herabsetzung des Stammkapitals sind entsprechend anwendbar.

Nach *Abs. 1* darf eine statutarische Nachschusspflicht nur dann herabgesetzt oder aufgehoben werden, wenn das Stammkapital und die gesetzlichen Reserven voll gedeckt sind. Diese Bestimmung will zum Schutz der Gläubigerinnen und Gläubiger verhindern, dass eine Nachschusspflicht in einem Zeitpunkt aufgehoben wird, in dem auf Grund eines Kapitalverlustes die Voraussetzungen der Einforderung der Nachschüsse nach Art. 795*a* Abs. 2 Ziff. 1 E OR erfüllt sind.

Für die Herabsetzung oder Aufhebung statutarischer Nachschusspflichten kommen nach *Abs. 2* die Vorschriften über die Herabsetzung des Stammkapitals entsprechend zur Anwendung (s. Art. 782 E OR sowie Art. 732 ff. OR).

5. Fortdauer

Art. 795d

1 Für Gesellschafter, die aus der Gesellschaft ausscheiden, besteht die Nachschusspflicht unter Vorbehalt der nachfolgenden Einschränkungen während dreier Jahre weiter. Der Zeitpunkt des Ausscheidens bestimmt sich nach der Eintragung ins Handelsregister.

2 Ausgeschiedene Gesellschafter müssen Nachschüsse nur leisten, wenn die Gesellschaft in Konkurs fällt.

3 Ihre Nachschusspflicht entfällt, soweit sie von einem Rechtsnachfolger erfüllt wurde.

4 Die Nachschusspflicht ausgeschiedener Gesellschafter darf nicht mehr erhöht werden.

Bestehen statutarische Nachschusspflichten, so kann die Erfüllung von Forderungen dadurch gefährdet werden, dass Gesellschafterinnen und Gesellschafter, auf deren Solvenz sich die Gläubigerinnen und Gläubiger verlassen haben, aus der Gesellschaft ausscheiden. *Abs. 1* sieht daher eine zeitlich beschränkte Fortdauer der Nachschusspflicht ausscheidender Personen vor. Die *Abs. 2–4* dienen demgegenüber dem Schutz der Verpflichteten, da diese nach ihrem Ausscheiden aus der Gesellschaft ohne Einfluss auf deren Geschäftsführung bleiben. Die Nachschusspflicht wird so weit eingegrenzt, wie dies mit dem Schutz der Gläubigerinnen und Gläubiger vereinbar ist. Im Hinblick auf diese beidseitigen Schutzziele der gesetzlichen Ordnung müssen abweichende statutarische Regelungen als ausgeschlossen gelten.

Nach *Abs. 1* besteht die Nachschusspflicht ausscheidender Gesellschafterinnen und Gesellschafter unter Vorbehalt der nachfolgend vorgesehenen Einschränkungen während dreier Jahre fort. Im Hinblick auf den Schutz der Gläubigerinnen und Gläubiger muss der Grund des Ausscheidens dabei ohne Bedeutung bleiben; d.h., die Fortdauer der Nachschusspflicht greift sowohl bei der Abtretung eines Stammanteils als auch bei einem Austritt oder einem Ausschluss Platz.

Die Frist von 3 Jahren wird gleich angesetzt wie die Frist, die der Entwurf des Bundesrates zum Fusionsgesetz in Art. 181 Abs. 2 E OR (betreffend die Übernahme eines Vermögens oder eines Geschäftes)[92] vorsieht. Sie beginnt mit der Eintragung des Ausscheidens einer Gesellschafterin oder eines Gesellschafters ins Handelsregister zu laufen (massgebend ist der Zeitpunkt der Veröffentlichung der Eintragung im Schweizerischen Handelsamtsblatt; (s. Art. 932 Abs. 2 OR).

Nach *Abs. 2* müssen ausgeschiedene Gesellschafterinnen und Gesellschafter Nachschüsse nur dann leisten, wenn die Gesellschaft in Konkurs fällt. Die Nachschusspflicht kann also nicht mehr zur Sanierung der Gesellschaft geltend gemacht werden (vgl. Art. 795*a* E OR), sondern nur noch zur Befriedigung der Gläubigerinnen und Gläubiger.

Die Nachschusspflicht ist an die Stammanteile gebunden und geht bei deren Veräusserung auf die Erwerberinnen oder Erwerber über (vgl. die Ausführungen zu Art. 795 E OR). Sie ist grundsätzlich durch die jeweiligen Gesellschafterinnen und Gesellschafter zu erfüllen. Nur falls eine Gesellschafterin oder ein Gesellschafter die Nachschüsse nicht zu leisten vermag, sollen ihre beziehungsweise seine Rechtsvorgängerinnen oder Rechtsvorgänger herangezogen werden können. *Abs. 3* sieht daher vor, dass die Nachschusspflicht entfällt, soweit sie von einer Rechtsnachfolgerin oder einem Rechtsnachfolger erfüllt wurde. Falls Stammanteile während der Frist von drei Jahren (Abs. 1) mehrmals veräussert wurden, sind gemäss dem Wortlaut der vorliegenden Bestimmung spätere Gesellschafterinnen und Gesellschafter vor früher ausgeschiedenen Personen zu erfassen. Die Nachschüsse, die gestützt auf Art. 795*d* E OR geleistet wurden, sind steuerlich gleich zu behandeln wie diejenigen nach Art. 795*a* E OR.

Abs. 4 stellt klar, dass die Nachschusspflicht ausgeschiedener Gesellschafterinnen und Gesellschafter nicht mehr erhöht werden darf. Erhöht die Gesellschafterversammlung die Nachschusspflicht, so wird der Umfang der Verpflichtung ausgeschiedener Gesellschafterinnen und Gesellschafter dadurch nicht berührt. Umgekehrt muss eine Herabsetzung oder Aufhebung der Nachschusspflicht auch ausgeschiedenen Gesellschafterinnen und Gesellschaftern zugute kommen.

---

92 s. BBl 2000 4493 und 4568.

II. Nebenleistungen

Art. 796

1 Die Statuten können die Gesellschafter zu Nebenleistungen verpflichten.

2 Sie können nur Nebenleistungspflichten vorsehen, die dem Zweck der Gesellschaft, der Erhaltung ihrer Selbstständigkeit oder der Wahrung der Zusammensetzung des Kreises der Gesellschafter dienen.

3 Gegenstand und Umfang wie auch andere nach den Umständen wesentliche Punkte einer mit einem Stammanteil verbundenen Nebenleistungspflicht müssen in den Statuten bestimmt werden. Für die nähere Umschreibung kann auf ein Reglement der Gesellschafterversammlung verwiesen werden.

4 Statutarische Verpflichtungen zur Zahlung von Geld oder zur Leistung anderer Vermögenswerte unterstehen den Bestimmungen über Nachschüsse, wenn keine angemessene Gegenleistung vorgesehen wird und die Einforderung der Deckung des Eigenkapitalbedarfs der Gesellschaft dient.

Die Möglichkeit statutarischer Nebenleistungspflichten gilt zwar als eines der Kennzeichen der GmbH (vgl. Art. 772 Abs. 2 E OR), wird jedoch im geltenden Recht nur fragmentarisch erfasst (vgl. Art. 777 Ziff. 2 OR). Der Entwurf füllt bestehende Regelungslücken und will einen hinreichenden Schutz der Gesellschafterinnen und Gesellschafter sicherstellen.

Abs. 1 hält den Grundsatz fest, wonach die Statuten die Gesellschafterinnen und Gesellschafter zu Nebenleistungen verpflichten können. Als Pflichtinhalt ist sowohl ein Tun als auch ein Unterlassen oder ein Dulden zulässig. Wie die Pflicht zu Nachschüssen können Nebenleistungspflichten mit sämtlichen oder nur mit bestimmten Stammanteilen verbunden werden.

Zum Schutz der betroffenen Personen ist die gesetzliche Regelung statutarischer Nebenleistungspflichten als zwingend zu verstehen. Dies steht jedoch der Vereinbarung rein vertraglicher Leistungspflichten nicht entgegen. Anders als bei vertraglichen Abmachungen zwischen den Gesellschafterinnen und Gesellschaftern ist bei statutarischen Nebenleistungspflichten die Gesellschaft selbst zur Durchsetzung befugt.

Nach *Abs.* 2 dürfen in den Statuten nur Nebenleistungspflichten vorgesehen werden, die dem Zweck der Gesellschaft, der Erhaltung ihrer Selbstständigkeit oder der Wahrung der Zusammensetzung des Kreises der Gesellschafterinnen und der Gesellschafter dienen. Die vorliegende Bestimmung will sachfremde Verpflichtungen ausschliessen, so etwa Pflichten, die gar nicht der Gesellschaft selbst, sondern den Partikularinteressen einzelner Personen dienen. Zulässig sind beispielsweise Belieferungs- oder Abnahmepflichten, das Recht zur Benutzung von Parkplätzen sowie Vorhand-, Vorkaufs- und Kaufsrechte an Stammanteilen. Während die Berechtigung aus Nebenleistungspflichten im Allgemeinen der Gesellschaft zusteht, können statutarische Erwerbsvorrechte an Stammanteilen zu Gunsten der Gesellschaft (s. aber Art. 783 E OR), der Gesellschafterinnen und Gesellschafter oder gewisser Dritter begründet werden, solange sie dem Zweck der Wahrung einer bestimmten Zusammensetzung des Kreises der an einem Unternehmen beteiligten Personen dienen.

Nebenleistungspflichten müssen in den Statuten klar und eindeutig umschrieben werden; zu bestimmen sind nach *Abs.* 3 der Gegenstand und der Umfang der vorgesehenen Pflichten. In die Statuten aufzunehmen sind aber auch weitere Punkte, die nach den konkreten Umständen von wesentlicher Bedeutung sind (so bspw. Befristungen und Bedingungen). Soweit jedoch eine detaillierte Regelung erforderlich ist, soll für die nähere Umschreibung auf ein Reglement der Gesellschafterversammlung verwiesen werden können.

Sämtliche statutarischen Bestimmungen, die funktional einer Nachschusspflicht gleichkommen, unterstehen nach *Abs.* 4 von Gesetzes wegen den Art. 795–795*d* E OR. Diese Regelung will eine Umgehung der Vorschriften für Nachschusspflichten verhindern.

III. Nachträgliche Einführung

Art. 797

Die nachträgliche Einführung oder Erweiterung statutarischer Nachschuss- oder Nebenleistungspflichten bedarf der Zustimmung aller davon betroffenen Gesellschafter.

| Kapitel 1: | Neue Gesetzesbestimmungen und Erläuterungen |

Werden nach erfolgter Gründung Nachschuss- oder Nebenleistungspflichten neu in die Statuten aufgenommen oder erweitert, so ist dafür die Zustimmung aller betroffenen Gesellschafterinnen und Gesellschafter notwendig. Personen, die der entsprechenden Änderung der Statuten nicht zustimmen, können keine zusätzlichen oder erweiterten Pflichten auferlegt werden.

E. Dividenden, Zinse, Tantiemen

I. Dividenden

Art. 798

1 **Dividenden dürfen nur aus dem Bilanzgewinn und aus hierfür gebildeten Reserven ausgerichtet werden.**

2 **Die Dividende darf erst festgesetzt werden, nachdem die dem Gesetz und den Statuten entsprechenden Zuweisungen an die gesetzlichen und statutarischen Reserven abgezogen worden sind.**

3 **Die Dividenden sind im Verhältnis des Nennwerts der Stammanteile festzusetzen; wurden Nachschüsse geleistet, so ist deren Betrag für die Bemessung der Dividenden dem Nennwert zuzurechnen; die Statuten können eine abweichende Regelung vorsehen.**

Nach *Abs. 1* dürfen Dividenden nur aus dem Bilanzgewinn und aus hierfür gebildeten Reserven ausgerichtet werden. Vor der Festsetzung der Dividenden müssen dem Bilanzgewinn nach *Abs. 2* die erforderlichen Zuweisungen an die gesetzlichen und statutarischen Reserven entnommen werden. Diese Regelung entspricht Art. 675 Abs. 2 und Art. 674 Abs. 1 OR.

Anders als im Vorentwurf wird in *Abs. 3* eine Regelung zur Verteilung der Dividenden vorgegeben. Der Entwurf will damit vermeiden, dass die Gesellschaften in den Statuten zwingend eigene Lösungen schaffen müssen. Im Unterschied zu den beiden vorangehenden Absätzen ist die Ordnung der Zuweisung der Dividenden aber dispositiver Natur: Sehen die Statuten nichts anderes vor (vgl. Art. 654 und 656 OR i.V.m. Art. 799 E OR), so sind die Dividenden im Verhältnis des Nennwerts der Stammanteile festzusetzen. Falls bereits Nachschüsse an die Gesellschaft geleistet wurden, so muss deren Betrag für die Berechnung der Dividenden dem Nennwert hinzugerechnet werden. Nicht zu berücksichtigen sind demgegenüber nicht eingeforderte, ausstehende oder zurückbezahlte Nachschüsse.

II. Zinse

Art. 798a

1 Für das Stammkapital und geleistete Nachschüsse dürfen keine Zinse bezahlt werden.

2 Die Ausrichtung von Bauzinsen ist zulässig. Die Vorschrift des Aktienrechts über Bauzinse ist entsprechend anwendbar.

Abs. 1 untersagt die Zahlung von Zinsen für das Stammkapital und geleistete Nachschüsse. Die Verzinsung von Eigenkapital stellt einen Verstoss gegen die Grundstruktur jeder Kapitalgesellschaft dar. Eine Ausrichtung von Zinsen ohne Rücksicht auf den Erfolg des Unternehmens könnte zu einer verpönten Rückerstattung der Einlagen führen (s. Art. 793 Abs. 2 E OR). Sie stünde auch im Widerspruch mit der Regelung der Rückzahlung geleisteter Nachschüsse (Art. 795*b* E OR).

Eine Ausnahme vom Verzinsungsverbot gilt nach *Abs. 2* einzig für so genannte Bauzinsen, die während des Aufbaus des Unternehmens bis zur Aufnahme des vollen Betriebes ausgerichtet werden. Wie nach geltendem Recht (Art. 804 Abs. 2 OR) sollen dazu die Vorschriften des Aktienrechts Anwendung finden (s. Art. 676 OR). Bauzinsen kommen allerdings in der Praxis ausserordentlich selten vor.

III. Tantiemen

Art. 798b

Die Statuten können die Ausrichtung von Tantiemen an Geschäftsführer vorsehen. Die Vorschriften des Aktienrechts über Tantiemen sind entsprechend anwendbar.

Das geltende Recht regelt die Ausrichtung von Gewinnanteilen an die Geschäftsführerinnen und Geschäftsführer nicht. Der Entwurf erlaubt die

Ausrichtung von Tantiemen ausdrücklich und verweist dazu auf die entsprechende Vorschrift des Aktienrechts (s. Art. 677 OR).

F. Vorzugsstammanteile

Art. 799

Für Vorzugsstammanteile sind die Vorschriften des Aktienrechts über Vorzugsaktien entsprechend anwendbar.

Das geltende Recht enthält keine Regelung von Vorzugsstammanteilen. Der Entwurf schliesst diese Lücke durch eine Verweisung auf das Aktienrecht (s. Art. 654 und 656 OR).

G. Rückerstattung von Leistungen

Art. 800

Für die Rückerstattung von Leistungen der Gesellschaft an Gesellschafter, Geschäftsführer sowie diesen nahe stehende Personen sind die Vorschriften des Aktienrechts entsprechend anwendbar.

Die Rückerstattung von Gewinnanteilen, die Gesellschafterinnen, Gesellschafter, Geschäftsführerinnen und Geschäftsführer ungerechtfertigterweise bezogen haben, ist im geltenden Recht unvollständig und teilweise abweichend vom Aktienrecht geregelt. Da Gründe für eine unterschiedliche Ordnung fehlen, verweist der Entwurf auf die aktienrechtlichen Bestimmungen (s. Art. 678 f. OR).

H. Geschäftsbericht, Reserven und Offenlegung

Art. 801

Für den Geschäftsbericht, für die Reserven sowie für die Offenlegung der Jahresrechnung und der Konzernrechnung sind die Vorschriften des Aktienrechts entsprechend anwendbar.

Die Anforderungen an die Rechnungslegung sind auf der Grundlage der wirtschaftlichen Gegebenheiten eines Unternehmens zu bestimmen; sie sind namentlich vom Umfang der Geschäftstätigkeit der Gesellschaft abhängig. Die Rechtsform bleibt demgegenüber weitgehend ohne Relevanz, was mit der Aufhebung der oberen Begrenzung des Stammkapitals noch verdeutlicht wird. Die Rechnungslegung muss demnach aus sachlichen Gründen für wirtschaftlich tätige Körperschaften unabhängig von ihrer Rechtsform möglichst einheitlich geregelt werden[93].

Entsprechend dem materiellen Erfordernis einer übereinstimmenden Ordnung verweist das geltende GmbH-Recht (Art. 805 OR) für die Bilanz und die Reservefonds auf die Bestimmungen des Aktienrechts. Wie der Bundesrat bereits anlässlich der Beantwortung einer parlamentarischen Anfrage dargelegt hat[94], beziehen sich diese Verweisungen seit der Revision des Aktienrechts auf die Vorschriften von 1991.

Der Entwurf formuliert die Verweisungsnorm neu. Für den Geschäftsbericht und die Reserven sind die Vorschriften des (geltenden) Aktienrechts entsprechend anwendbar (s. Art. 662 bis 670 OR bzw. Art. 671 bis 674 OR). Die aktienrechtlichen Bestimmungen sollen zudem auch für die Offenlegung herangezogen werden (s. Art. 697*h* OR). Diese zusätzliche Verweisung ist allerdings nur von beschränkter Tragweite, da die spezifischen Offenlegungsvorschriften für Publikumsgesellschaften infolge der mangelnden Kapitalmarktfähigkeit der GmbH belanglos bleiben. Auf Grund der Beschränkung der Haftung auf das Gesellschaftsvermögen sollen GmbH aber Gläubigerinnen und Gläubigern, die ein schützwürdiges Interesse nachweisen, dasselbe Einsichtsrecht gewähren wie Aktiengesellschaften (vgl. Art. 697*h* Abs. 2 OR).

---

93 s. Groupe de réflexion «Gesellschaftsrecht», Schlussbericht vom 24.9.1993, S. 12 und 81 (Bezugsquelle: Bundesamt für Bauten und Logistik, Vertrieb Publikationen, 3003 Bern; Art.-Nr. 407.020.d); Begleitbericht zum Vorentwurf eines Bundesgesetzes über die Rechnungslegung und die Revision [VE RRG], S. 69 und 98; PETER BÖCKLI/PETER FORSTMOSER/JEAN-MARC RAPP, Reform des GmbH-Rechts, Zürich 1997, S. 92 f.

94 AB 1995 N, S. 2269 f.

Kapitel 1: Neue Gesetzesbestimmungen und Erläuterungen

J. Zustellung des Geschäftsberichts

Art. 801a

1 Der Geschäftsbericht und der Revisionsbericht sind den Gesellschaftern spätestens zusammen mit der Einladung zur ordentlichen Gesellschafterversammlung zuzustellen.

2 Die Gesellschafter können verlangen, dass ihnen nach der Gesellschafterversammlung die von ihr genehmigte Fassung des Geschäftsberichts zugestellt wird.

Nach *Abs. 1* hat die Gesellschaft ihren Gesellschafterinnen und Gesellschaftern den Geschäfts- und den Revisionsbericht spätestens zusammen mit der Einladung zur ordentlichen Gesellschafterversammlung zuzustellen, um allen Beteiligten eine sachgerechte Vorbereitung zu ermöglichen (zur Frist für die Einberufung der Gesellschafterversammlung s. Art. 805 Abs. 3 E OR).

Nach *Abs. 2* ist den Gesellschafterinnen und Gesellschaftern auf Wunsch die von der Gesellschafterversammlung genehmigte Fassung des Geschäftsberichts zuzustellen.

K. Auskunfts- und Einsichtsrecht

Art. 802

1 Jeder Gesellschafter kann von den Geschäftsführern Auskunft über alle Angelegenheiten der Gesellschaft verlangen.

2 Hat die Gesellschaft keine Revisionsstelle, so kann jeder Gesellschafter in die Bücher und Akten uneingeschränkt Einsicht nehmen. Hat sie eine Revisionsstelle, so besteht ein Recht zur Einsichtnahme nur, soweit ein berechtigtes Interesse glaubhaft gemacht wird.

3 Besteht Gefahr, dass der Gesellschafter die erlangten Kenntnisse zum Schaden der Gesellschaft für gesellschaftsfremde Zwecke verwendet, so können die Geschäftsführer die Auskunft und die Einsichtnahme im erforderlichen Umfang verweigern; auf Antrag des Gesellschafters entscheidet die Gesellschafterversammlung.

4 Verweigert die Gesellschafterversammlung die Auskunft oder die Einsicht ungerechtfertigterweise, so ordnet sie das Gericht auf Antrag des Gesellschafters an.

Der Umfang des Auskunfts- und Einsichtsrechts ist im geltenden Recht von der Einsetzung einer «Kontrollstelle» (d.h. einer Revisionsstelle) abhängig und wird durch Verweisungen auf das Recht der einfachen Gesellschaft sowie der Aktiengesellschaft bestimmt (s. Art. 819 OR). Die Informationsrechte der Gesellschafterinnen und Gesellschafter und die Aufgaben der Revisionsstelle sind jedoch grundsätzlich unterschiedlich ausgerichtet und können einander nicht ersetzen. Die vorgesehenen Verweisungen sind zudem auch materiell unzulänglich[95].
Der Entwurf schlägt eine Neukonzeption vor, die den engen persönlichen Beziehungen in der GmbH Rechnung trägt und sich an den Vorschriften für die Mitglieder des Verwaltungsrates in der Aktiengesellschaft orientiert (vgl. Art. 715*a* OR); eine ähnliche Ordnung kennt auch das deutsche Recht (vgl. § 51*a* GmbHG). Die Auskunfts- und Einsichtsrechte der Gesellschafterinnen und Gesellschafter werden verbessert. Entsprechend der in der GmbH meist starken persönlichen Bindung der Beteiligten an das Unternehmen sollen die Informationsrechte weiter gehen als diejenigen der Aktionärinnen und Aktionäre. Dies steht in Übereinstimmung damit, dass die Gesellschafterinnen und Gesellschafter in der GmbH im Unterschied zu den Aktionärinnen und Aktionären einer Treuepflicht unterstehen (s. Art. 803 E OR).

Nach *Abs. 1* kann jede Gesellschafterin und jeder Gesellschafter von den Geschäftsführerinnen und Geschäftsführern Auskunft über sämtliche Angelegenheiten der Gesellschaft verlangen. Ob die Gesellschaft über eine Revisionsstelle verfügt oder nicht, bleibt dabei ohne Belang. Das Auskunftsrecht kann jederzeit ausgeübt werden. Es liegt bei den Geschäftsführerinnen und Geschäftsführern, eine sachgerechte Art der Auskunftserteilung zu wählen: Je nach den Umständen können sie eine Gesellschafterversammlung einberufen oder die gewünschten Auskünfte schriftlich erteilen. Bei mündlichen Anfragen ist auch eine mündliche Beantwortung möglich. Stets ist aber das Gebot der Gleichbehandlung zu beachten (s. Art. 813 E OR). Informationen, die für alle relevant sind, müssen daher im Allgemeinen sämtlichen Gesellschafterinnen und Gesellschaftern zugänglich gemacht werden (vorbehalten bleibt aber *Abs. 3*).

---

95 Zu allem eingehend: Expertenbericht zum Vorentwurf vom April 1999, S. 32.

Abs. 2 regelt das Recht der Gesellschafterinnen und Gesellschafter, in die Bücher und Akten der Gesellschaft Einsicht zu nehmen. Fehlt eine Revisionsstelle, so wird die Einsichtnahme zum Schutz der Beteiligten erleichtert: Während ein Recht zur Einsichtnahme grundsätzlich nur unter der Voraussetzung gegeben ist, dass ein berechtigtes Interesse glaubhaft gemacht wird, entfällt dieses Erfordernis, wenn die Gesellschaft über keine Revisionsstelle verfügt.

Abs. 3 sieht im Interesse der Gesellschaft eine Schranke vor, die sowohl für das Auskunftsrecht als auch für das Einsichtsrecht massgebend ist: Besteht die Gefahr, dass eine Gesellschafterin oder ein Gesellschafter die erlangten Kenntnisse zum Schaden der Gesellschaft für gesellschaftsfremde Zwecke verwendet, so darf die Auskunft beziehungsweise die Einsichtnahme soweit verweigert werden, als dies erforderlich ist. Verweigern die Geschäftsführerinnen und Geschäftsführer die Auskunft oder Einsichtnahme, steht es der betroffenen Gesellschafterin oder dem betroffenen Gesellschafter offen, das Begehren der Gesellschafterversammlung zum Entscheid zu unterbreiten. Verweigert die Gesellschafterversammlung die Auskunft oder Einsichtnahme ebenfalls, so kann sie nach *Abs. 4* auf Klage hin durch das Gericht angeordnet werden, falls die Verweigerung nicht gerechtfertigt erscheint.

L. Treuepflicht und Konkurrenzverbot

Art. 803

¹ Die Gesellschafter sind zur Wahrung des Geschäftsgeheimnisses verpflichtet.

² Sie müssen alles unterlassen, was die Interessen der Gesellschaft beeinträchtigt. Insbesondere dürfen sie nicht Geschäfte betreiben, die ihnen zum besonderen Vorteil gereichen und durch die der Zweck der Gesellschaft beeinträchtigt würde. Die Statuten können vorsehen, dass die Gesellschafter konkurrenzierende Tätigkeiten unterlassen müssen.

³ Die Gesellschafter dürfen Tätigkeiten, die gegen die Treuepflicht oder ein allfälliges Konkurrenzverbot verstossen, ausüben, sofern alle übrigen Gesellschafter schriftlich zustimmen. Die Statuten können vorsehen, dass stattdessen die Zustimmung der Gesellschafterversammlung erforderlich ist.

4 Die besonderen Vorschriften über das Konkurrenzverbot von Geschäftsführern bleiben vorbehalten.

Die personenbezogene Konzeption der GmbH erfordert gemäss den Bedürfnissen von Unternehmen mit einem kleineren Kreis von Beteiligten zumindest für den Regelfall eine Treuepflicht der Gesellschafterinnen und Gesellschafter. Das geltende Recht erwähnt die Treuepflicht als solche nicht, ordnet jedoch das Konkurrenzverbot als wohl wichtigste Konkretisierung der Treuepflicht (s. Art. 818 OR). Der Entwurf sieht eine flexible Regelung der Treuepflicht vor. Diese trägt den meist engen persönlichen Bindungen aller Beteiligten an das Unternehmen Rechnung und ist auch ein notwendiges Gegenstück zum Auskunfts- und Einsichtsrecht der Gesellschafterinnen und Gesellschafter (vgl. Art. 802 E OR sowie vorne die Ausführungen zu dieser Bestimmung).

Nach *Abs. 1* sind alle Gesellschafterinnen und Gesellschafter zur Wahrung des Geschäftsgeheimnisses verpflichtet. Sie müssen zudem nach *Abs. 2* alles unterlassen, was die Interessen der Gesellschaft beeinträchtigt, und dürfen insbesondere keine Geschäfte betreiben, die dem Zweck der Gesellschaft abträglich sind. Der Treuepflicht unterstehen auch nicht zur Geschäftsführung befugte Gesellschafterinnen und Gesellschafter. Der Entwurf ermöglicht jedoch, im Einzelfall eine andere Lösung zu treffen (s. dazu *Abs. 3*). Während einerseits der Kreis der treuepflichtigen Personen weit gefasst ist, wird andererseits die Tragweite der Treuepflicht im Interesse der Betroffenen dadurch beschränkt, dass für das Konkurrenzverbot eine Sonderregelung vorgesehen wird.

Im Gegensatz zur allgemeinen Treuepflicht besteht für Gesellschafterinnen und Gesellschafter, die nicht an der Geschäftsführung teilhaben, nach *Abs. 2* nur dann ein Konkurrenzverbot, wenn dies die Statuten ausdrücklich vorsehen (vgl. aber Art. 812 Abs. 3 E OR). Es ist unter anderem möglich, in den Statuten bloss einzelnen Gesellschafterinnen und Gesellschaftern ein Konkurrenzverbot aufzuerlegen.

Zur Vermeidung von Unsicherheiten sollte der sachliche und räumliche Geltungsbereich des Konkurrenzverbots in den Statuten klar bestimmt werden. Wird nichts Genaueres vorgesehen, bleibt das Konkurrenzverbot auf Tätigkeiten beschränkt, die zweifelsfrei im Bereich des statutarischen Gesellschaftszwecks liegen und die sich örtlich mit den bisherigen Aktivitäten der Gesellschaft überschneiden. Da es sich um ein Konkurrenzverbot gesellschaftsrechtlicher Natur handelt, kann das Verbot nur die jeweiligen

Gesellschafterinnen und Gesellschafter erfassen. Es ist daher unzulässig, das Konkurrenzverbot in den Statuten über das Ausscheiden aus der Gesellschaft hinaus zu erstrecken. Diese Begrenzung statutarischer Konkurrenzverbote schützt das wirtschaftliche Fortkommen der Gesellschafterinnen und Gesellschafter nach ihrem Ausscheiden. Sind weiter gehende Konkurrenzverbote erwünscht, so können diese nur auf vertraglicher Grundlage im Rahmen der bestehenden rechtlichen Schranken vereinbart werden (s. insbes. Art. 340 ff. OR).

Im Interesse einer möglichst grossen Flexibilität der Treuepflicht und des Konkurrenzverbots sieht *Abs. 3* vor, dass Tätigkeiten, die gegen die Treuepflicht oder ein allfälliges Konkurrenzverbot verstossen, dennoch ausgeübt werden dürfen, sofern die übrigen Gesellschafterinnen und Gesellschafter damit einverstanden sind. Um Streitigkeiten und Unsicherheiten vorzubeugen, wird die Zustimmung in Schriftform verlangt. Es soll aber auch offen stehen, statt der Zustimmung sämtlicher Gesellschafterinnen und Gesellschafter einen Mehrheitsentscheid genügen zu lassen. Die Statuten sollen daher festlegen können, dass die Gesellschafterversammlung über die Erteilung der Zustimmung entscheidet (dabei ist eine qualifizierte Mehrheit erforderlich; s. Art. 808*b* Abs. 1 Ziff. 7 E OR).

Die vorliegende Bestimmung regelt die Treuepflicht und das Konkurrenzverbot für Gesellschafterinnen und Gesellschafter. *Abs. 4* behält *Art. 812* E OR vor, der eine Sonderregelung für alle Personen vorsieht, die mit der Geschäftsführung befasst sind.

Dritter Abschnitt: Organisation der Gesellschaft

A.   Gesellschafterversammlung

I.   Aufgaben

Art. 804

1 Oberstes Organ der Gesellschaft ist die Gesellschafterversammlung.

2 Der Gesellschafterversammlung stehen folgende unübertragbare Befugnisse zu:

1. **die Änderung der Statuten;**
2. **die Bestellung und die Abberufung von Geschäftsführern;**

3. die Bestellung und die Abberufung der Mitglieder der Revisionsstelle und des Konzernrechnungsprüfers;

4. die Genehmigung des Jahresberichtes und der Konzernrechnung;

5. die Genehmigung der Jahresrechnung sowie die Beschlussfassung über die Verwendung des Bilanzgewinnes, insbesondere die Festsetzung der Dividende und der Tantieme;

6. die Festsetzung der Entschädigung der Geschäftsführer;

7. die Entlastung der Geschäftsführer;

8. die Zustimmung zur Abtretung von Stammanteilen beziehungsweise die Anerkennung als stimmberechtigter Gesellschafter;

9. die Zustimmung zur Bestellung eines Pfandrechts an Stammanteilen, falls die Statuten dies vorsehen;

10. die Beschlussfassung über die Ausübung statutarischer Vorhand-, Vorkaufs- oder Kaufsrechte;

11. die Ermächtigung der Geschäftsführer zum Erwerb eigener Stammanteile durch die Gesellschaft oder die Genehmigung eines solchen Erwerbs;

12. die nähere Regelung von Nebenleistungspflichten in einem Reglement, falls die Statuten auf ein Reglement verweisen;

13. die Zustimmung zu Tätigkeiten der Geschäftsführer und der Gesellschafter, die gegen die Treuepflicht oder das Konkurrenzverbot verstossen, sofern die Statuten auf das Erfordernis der Zustimmung aller Gesellschafter verzichten;

14. die Beschlussfassung darüber, ob dem Gericht beantragt werden soll, ein Gesellschafter aus wichtigem Grund auszuschliessen;

15. der Ausschluss eines Gesellschafters aus in den Statuten vorgesehenen Gründen;

16. die Auflösung der Gesellschaft;

17. die Genehmigung von Geschäften der Geschäftsführer, für die die Statuten die Zustimmung der Gesellschafterversammlung fordern;

18. die Beschlussfassung über die Gegenstände, die das Gesetz oder die Statuten der Gesellschafterversammlung vorbehalten oder die ihr die Geschäftsführer vorlegen.

3 Die Gesellschafterversammlung ernennt die Direktoren, die Prokuristen sowie die Handlungsbevollmächtigten. Die Statuten können diese Befugnis auch den Geschäftsführern einräumen.

Abs. 1 bezeichnet die Gesellschafterversammlung als oberstes Organ der Gesellschaft (im geltenden Recht Art. 808 Abs. 1 OR; vgl. Art. 698 Abs. 1 OR für die Aktiengesellschaft). Dies ist jedoch nicht im Sinne einer hierarchischen Überordnung über die andern Organe zu verstehen; vielmehr werden damit die der Gesellschafterversammlung zugewiesenen Aufgaben angesprochen: Als Versammlung der Anteilseigner und damit der Träger des wirtschaftlichen Risikos bleibt es ihr vorbehalten, die wichtigsten Grundsatzentscheide selbst zu treffen (s. die Auflistung in Abs. 2). Sie ist es auch, die die andern Organe der Gesellschaft bestellt und abberufen kann. Im Übrigen bestimmt sich das Verhältnis der Gesellschaftsorgane nach der so genannten Paritätstheorie[96,97], d.h. jedem Organ sind gemäss seiner Funktion spezifische Aufgaben zugewiesen, die ihm durch die andern Organe nicht entzogen werden können; die Organe sind einander insofern gleichgeordnet. Der Entwurf sieht – im Unterschied zum Aktienrecht – die Möglichkeit vor, durch Statutenbestimmungen einzelne wichtige Entscheide der Geschäftsführerinnen und Geschäftsführer dem Erfordernis der Genehmigung durch die Gesellschafterversammlung zu unterstellen (s. Art. 811 E OR). Es versteht sich von selbst, dass die Paritätstheorie von begrenzter Bedeutung bleibt, wenn zwischen der Gesellschafterversammlung und der Geschäftsführung personelle Identität besteht. Ist dies (namentlich in grösseren Gesellschaften) nicht der Fall, so erhält eine klare gesetzliche Zuteilung der Aufgaben und Verantwortlichkeiten auch in der GmbH grosse Bedeutung.

---

[96] s. dazu insbes. Werner von Steiger, in: Zürcher Kommentar V/5c, Zürich 1965, Vorbemerkungen zu Art. 808–819 N 5; ARTHUR MEIER-HAYOZ/PETER FORSTMOSER, Schweizerisches Gesellschaftsrecht, 8. Aufl., Bern 1998, § 18 N 69; eher im Sinne einer eingeschränkten Omnipotenztheorie HERBERT WOHLMANN, GmbH-Recht, Basel und Frankfurt a.M. 1997, S. 95 f.

[97] Der Gesetzgeber hat sich bereits bei der Aktienrechtsrevision von 1991 ausdrücklich für das Paritätsprinzip ausgesprochen: s. BBl 1983 II 841 f.; Protokoll der Kommission des Ständerates, Beratungen 1985–1988, S. 320 f.; Protokoll der Kommission des Nationalrates, Beratungen 1989–1990, S. 193 ff.

Abs. 2 enthält eine Liste der unübertragbaren Befugnisse der Gesellschafterversammlung:

- Nach *Ziff. 1* liegt die Zuständigkeit zur Änderung der Statuten bei der Gesellschafterversammlung (vorbehalten bleibt die Anpassung der Statuten anlässlich einer Kapitalerhöhung durch die Geschäftsführerinnen und Geschäftsführer (s. Art. 652g OR i.V.m. Art. 781 Abs. 5 Ziff. 5 E OR).

- Nach *Ziff. 2* ist die Gesellschafterversammlung zur Bestellung und Abberufung der Geschäftsführerinnen und Geschäftsführer zuständig. Dies gilt jedoch nur dann, wenn die Gesellschafterinnen und Gesellschafter nicht als solche ohne weiteres zur Geschäftsführung befugt sind (vgl. Art. 809 Abs. 1 E OR).

- Nach *Ziff. 3* ist die Gesellschafterversammlung zur Bestellung und Abberufung der Mitglieder der Revisionsstelle zuständig. Dies gilt auch dann, wenn freiwillig eine Revisionsstelle bezeichnet wird (vgl. Art. 818 E OR). Die Bestellung und Abberufung der Konzernrechnungsprüferinnen und Konzernrechnungsprüfer liegt bei der Gesellschafterversammlung der Muttergesellschaft.

- Nach *Ziff. 4* genehmigt die Gesellschafterversammlung den Jahresbericht und gegebenenfalls die Konzernrechnung.

- Nach *Ziff. 5* genehmigt die Gesellschafterversammlung die Jahresrechnung und befindet über die Verwendung des Bilanzgewinnes; sie setzt insbesondere die Dividenden und gegebenenfalls die Tantiemen fest.

- Nach *Ziff. 6* liegt es bei der Gesellschafterversammlung, die Entschädigung der Geschäftsführerinnen und Geschäftsführer zu bestimmen.

- Nach *Ziff. 7* liegt es in der Kompetenz der Gesellschafterversammlung, die Geschäftsführerinnen und Geschäftsführer zu entlasten.

- Nach *Ziff. 8* ist die Gesellschafterversammlung zuständig für den Entscheid über die Zustimmung zur Abtretung von Stammanteilen sowie – bei besonderen Erwerbsarten (s. Art. 788 E OR) – für die Anerkennung der Erwerberinnen und Erwerber als stimmberechtigte Gesellschafterinnen beziehungsweise stimmberechtigte Gesellschafter.

- Sehen die Statuten vor, dass die Bestellung eines Pfandrechts an Stammanteilen der Zustimmung der Gesellschaft bedarf, so ist nach *Ziff. 9* die Gesellschafterversammlung zum Entscheid zuständig.

- Nach *Ziff. 10* entscheidet die Gesellschafterversammlung über die Ausübung statutarischer Vorhand-, Vorkaufs- oder Kaufsrechte durch die Gesellschaft.

- Nach *Ziff. 11* bedürfen die Geschäftsführerinnen und Geschäftsführer für den Erwerb eigener Stammanteile einer Ermächtigung durch die Gesellschafterversammlung. Wurden eigene Stammanteile ohne entsprechende Ermächtigung erworben, kann die Gesellschafterversammlung nachträglich ihre Genehmigung erteilen. Die Befugnisse von Ziff. 10 und Ziff. 11 bleiben namentlich deswegen der Gesellschafterversammlung vorbehalten, weil sich aus einem Erwerb eigener Stammanteile unter Umständen eine wesentliche Verschiebung der Beherrschungsverhältnisse ergibt (nach Art. 783 Abs. 2 E OR können bis zu 35% des Stammkapitals erworben werden). Erteilt die Gesellschafterversammlung eine Ermächtigung oder Genehmigung für den Erwerb eigener Stammanteile, so ist darin sachnotwendigerweise auch die Zustimmung zur Abtretung der Stammanteile an die Gesellschaft eingeschlossen (dies, wenn die Statuten nichts anderes vorsehen, auch ohne dass Art. 808b Abs. 1 Ziff. 4 E OR beachtet werden muss[98]).

- Verweisen die Statuten für die nähere Regelung der Nebenleistungspflichten auf ein Reglement (s. Art. 796 Abs. 3 E OR), so bedarf dieses nach *Ziff. 12* der Genehmigung der Gesellschafterversammlung.

- Gesellschafterinnen und Gesellschafter sowie Geschäftsführerinnen und Geschäftsführer bedürfen für Tätigkeiten, die gegen die Treuepflicht oder ein allfälliges Konkurrenzverbot verstossen, grundsätzlich der Zustimmung aller übrigen Gesellschafterinnen und Gesellschafter (Art. 803 Abs. 3 und 812 Abs. 2 und 3 E OR). Falls die Statuten dies vorsehen, ist nach *Ziff. 13* stattdessen die Gesellschafterversammlung zur Erteilung der Zustimmung zuständig.

- Nach *Ziff. 14* hat allein die Gesellschafterversammlung darüber zu befinden, ob gegen eine Gesellschafterin oder einen Gesellschafters eine Klage auf Ausschluss aus wichtigem Grund eingereicht werden soll (vgl. Art. 823 Abs. 1 E OR).

- Sehen die Statuten vor, dass Gesellschafterinnen und Gesellschafter aus bestimmten Gründen aus der Gesellschaft ausgeschlossen werden können (Art. 823 Abs. 2 E OR), so entscheidet nach *Ziff. 15* die Gesellschafterversammlung über den Ausschluss.

---

98 s. dazu Anmerkung 58.

- Nach *Ziff. 16* liegt der Entscheid über die Auflösung der Gesellschaft bei der Gesellschafterversammlung (vorbehalten bleibt die Auflösung durch den Entscheid einer Behörde; vgl. Art. 731b i.V.m. Art. 819 sowie 821 E OR).

- Nach *Ziff. 17* ist die Gesellschafterversammlung zuständig zur Genehmigung von Geschäften der Geschäftsführerinnen und Geschäftsführer, soweit die Statuten ein entsprechendes Genehmigungserfordernis vorsehen.

- *Ziff. 18* sieht eine residuale Zuständigkeit der Gesellschafterversammlung für alle weiteren Fragen vor, die ihr vom Gesetz oder von den Statuen vorbehalten werden. Die Aufzählung der Kompetenzen in Art. 804 E OR ist also nicht abschliessender Natur. Der Entwurf erlaubt zudem, den Geschäftsführerinnen und Geschäftsführern in den Statuten die Möglichkeit einzuräumen, einzelne Fragen der Gesellschafterversammlung zur Genehmigung vorzulegen (Art. 811 Abs. 1 E OR).

Nach *Abs. 3* ernennt die Gesellschafterversammlung die Direktorinnen und Direktoren, die Prokuristinnen und Prokuristen sowie die Handlungsbevollmächtigten. Die Statuten können diese Befugnis auch den Geschäftsführerinnen und Geschäftsführern einräumen.

II. Einberufung und Durchführung

Art. 805

1 Die Gesellschafterversammlung wird von den Geschäftsführern, nötigenfalls durch die Revisionsstelle, einberufen. Das Einberufungsrecht steht auch den Liquidatoren zu.

2 Die ordentliche Versammlung findet alljährlich innerhalb von sechs Monaten nach Schluss des Geschäftsjahres statt. Ausserordentliche Versammlungen werden nach Massgabe der Statuten und bei Bedarf einberufen.

3 Die Gesellschafterversammlung ist spätestens 20 Tage vor dem Versammlungstag einzuberufen. Die Statuten können diese Frist verlängern oder bis auf zehn Tage verkürzen. Die Möglichkeit einer Universalversammlung bleibt vorbehalten.

4 Beschlüsse können auch schriftlich gefasst werden, sofern nicht ein Gesellschafter die mündliche Beratung verlangt.

5 Im Übrigen sind die Vorschriften des Aktienrechts entsprechend anwendbar für:

1. die Einberufung;
2. das Einberufungs- und Antragsrecht der Gesellschafter;
3. die Verhandlungsgegenstände;
4. die Anträge;
5. die Universalversammlung;
6. die vorbereitenden Massnahmen;
7. das Protokoll;
8. die Vertretung der Gesellschafter;
9. die unbefugte Teilnahme.

Der Entwurf folgt inhaltlich weitgehend der geltenden Regelung (Art. 809 OR). Nach *Abs. 1* ist die Gesellschafterversammlung grundsätzlich durch die Geschäftsführerinnen und Geschäftsführer einzuberufen. Wird die Geschäftsführung durch mehrere Personen ausgeübt, so obliegt die Einberufung der Person, die den Vorsitz der Geschäftsführung innehat (Art. 810 Abs. 3 Ziff. 1 E OR). Bleiben die Geschäftsführerinnen und Geschäftsführer untätig, so ist die Gesellschafterversammlung, nötigenfalls durch die Revisionsstelle, einzuberufen, falls die Gesellschaft über eine solche verfügt. Weiter sind auch Gesellschafterinnen und Gesellschafter, die zusammen mindestens 10% des Stammkapitals vertreten, berechtigt, die Einberufung einer Gesellschafterversammlung zu verlangen (Art. 699 Abs. 3 OR i.V.m. Art. 805 Abs. 5 Ziff. 2 E OR). Wird ihrem Begehren nicht innerhalb einer angemessenen Frist entsprochen, so können sie die Einberufung durch das Gericht verlangen. Nach der Auflösung der Gesellschaft steht das Einberufungsrecht den Liquidatorinnen und Liquidatoren zu.

Nach *Abs. 2* ist die ordentliche Gesellschafterversammlung wie bisher zwingend innerhalb von 6 Monaten nach Schluss des Geschäftsjahres durchzuführen. Ausserordentliche Versammlungen werden nach Massgabe der Statuten und bei Bedarf einberufen.

Für die Einberufung der Gesellschafterversammlung ist nach dem geltenden Recht (Art. 809 Abs. 4 OR) eine Frist von nur 5 Tagen zu beachten.

Gestützt auf die Vernehmlassungsergebnisse sieht der Entwurf in *Abs. 3* in Übereinstimmung mit dem Aktienrecht (Art. 700 Abs. 1 OR) eine Einberufungsfrist von 20 Tagen vor. Die bisherige Frist ist für eine seriöse Vorbereitung der Gesellschafterinnen und Gesellschafter oft zu kurz. Damit den konkreten Bedürfnissen aber Rechnung getragen werden kann, ist es möglich, die Einberufungsfrist in den Statuten zu verlängern oder bis auf 10 Tage zu verkürzen. Aus den gesetzlich vorgegebenen Einberufungsfristen ergeben sich auch für Unternehmen mit nur wenigen Gesellschafterinnen und Gesellschaftern keinerlei Nachteile, weil im Allgemeinen die Möglichkeit einer Universalversammlung gegeben ist. Eine Gesellschafterversammlung kann ohne Beachtung der Einberufungsfrist durchgeführt werden, wenn alle Gesellschafterinnen und Gesellschafter teilnehmen und damit einverstanden sind (s. Art. 701 OR i.V.m. Art. 805 Abs. 5 Ziff. 5 E OR). Dies wird bei kleineren Unternehmen regelmässig der Fall sein.

In Anlehnung an die aktienrechtliche Regelung der Beschlussfassung im Verwaltungsrat (Art. 713 Abs. 2 OR) ermöglicht *Abs. 4,* dass Beschlüsse der Gesellschafterversammlung auch schriftlich gefasst werden können (allenfalls ist ein Verzicht auf die Anwesenheit eines Revisors erforderlich, vgl. Art. 729c OR i.V.m. 818 Abs. 2 E OR). Da auf dem Zirkularweg keine Diskussion der Traktanden möglich ist, muss jeder Gesellschafterin und jedem Gesellschafter das Recht zustehen, eine mündliche Beratung zu verlangen.

Abs. 5 verweist für verschiedene Einzelheiten der Einberufung und Durchführung der Gesellschafterversammlung auf die Bestimmungen des Aktienrechts.

III. Stimmrecht

1. Bemessung

Art. 806

1 Das Stimmrecht der Gesellschafter bemisst sich nach dem Nennwert ihrer Stammanteile. Die Gesellschafter haben je mindestens eine Stimme. Die Statuten können die Stimmenzahl der Besitzer mehrerer Stammanteile beschränken.

2 Die Statuten können das Stimmrecht unabhängig vom Nennwert so festsetzen, dass auf jeden Stammanteil eine Stimme entfällt. In diesem

Fall müssen die Stammanteile mit dem tiefsten Nennwert mindestens einen Zehntel des Nennwerts der übrigen Stammanteile aufweisen.

3 Die Bemessung des Stimmrechts nach der Zahl der Stammanteile ist nicht anwendbar für:

1. die Wahl der Mitglieder der Revisionsstelle;
2. die Ernennung von Sachverständigen zur Prüfung der Geschäftsführung oder einzelner Teile davon;
3. die Beschlussfassung über die Anhebung einer Verantwortlichkeitsklage.

Entsprechend dem Modell der Kapitalgesellschaft verhält sich das Stimmrecht der Gesellschafterinnen und Gesellschafter grundsätzlich proportional zu ihrer Beteiligung am Grundkapital. Nach *Abs. 1* ist das Stimmrecht nach dem Nennwert der Stammanteile der Gesellschafterinnen und Gesellschafter zu bemessen, wobei jeder beteiligten Person zumindest eine Stimme zukommt. Die Statuten können jedoch die Stimmenzahl der Besitzerinnen und Besitzer mehrerer Stammanteile beschränken (statutarische Stimmrechtsbeschränkung).

Von der Proportionalität des Stimmrechts zum Umfang der Beteiligung am Stammkapital kann nach *Abs. 2* weiter dadurch abgewichen werden, dass Stammanteile mit unterschiedlichen Nennwerten ausgegeben werden, wobei die Statuten das Stimmrecht unabhängig vom Nennwert so festsetzen dürfen, dass auf jeden Stammanteil eine Stimme entfällt. Die Stammanteile mit einem tieferen Nennwert werden dadurch in ihrer Stimmkraft privilegiert. Um eine gänzliche Loslösung der Mitwirkungsrechte von der Beteiligung am Risikokapital auszuschliessen, sieht der Entwurf vor, dass unterschiedliche Nennwerte das Verhältnis 1 zu 10 nicht überschreiten dürfen (so auch Art. 693 Abs. 2 OR für die Aktiengesellschaft). Dieses Verhältnis muss jedoch nur dann beachtet werden, wenn die Statuten von der Bemessung des Stimmrechts nach dem Nennwert der Stammanteile abweichen.

Zur Sicherung der gesellschaftsinternen Kontrolle nimmt *Abs. 3* einzelne Beschlüsse der Gesellschafterversammlung von der Bemessung des Stimmrechts nach der Zahl der Stammanteile aus, so insbesondere die Wahl der Revisionsstelle.

2. Ausschliessung vom Stimmrecht

Art. 806a

1 Bei Beschlüssen über die Entlastung der Geschäftsführer haben Personen, die in irgendeiner Weise an der Geschäftsführung teilgenommen haben, kein Stimmrecht.

2 Bei Beschlüssen über den Erwerb eigener Stammanteile durch die Gesellschaft hat der Gesellschafter, der die Stammanteile abtritt, kein Stimmrecht.

3 Bei Beschlüssen über die Zustimmung zu Tätigkeiten der Gesellschafter, die gegen die Treuepflicht oder das Konkurrenzverbot verstossen, hat die betroffene Person kein Stimmrecht.

Die vorliegende Bestimmung regelt den Ausstand von Gesellschafterinnen und Gesellschaftern für bestimmte Beschlüsse, bei denen sich typischerweise Interessengegensätze zwischen der Gesellschaft und den Betroffenen ergeben können. So bleiben Personen, die an der Geschäftsführung teilgenommen haben, bei der Entlastung der Geschäftsführerinnen und Geschäftsführer vom Stimmrecht ausgeschlossen (*Abs. 1*). Bei Beschlüssen über den Erwerb eigener Stammanteile durch die Gesellschaft kommt den Veräussererinnen und Veräusserern kein Stimmrecht zu (*Abs. 2*). Weiter sind die betroffenen Personen bei Beschlüssen über die Zustimmung zu Tätigkeiten, die gegen die Treuepflicht oder ein Konkurrenzverbot verstossen (s. Art. 803 Abs. 3 und 812 Abs. 3 E OR), ebenfalls vom Stimmrecht ausgeschlossen (*Abs. 3*).

3. Nutzniessung

Art. 806b

Im Falle der Nutzniessung an einem Stammanteil stehen das Stimmrecht und die damit zusammenhängenden Rechte dem Nutzniesser zu. Dieser wird dem Eigentümer ersatzpflichtig, wenn er bei der Ausübung seiner Rechte nicht in billiger Weise auf dessen Interessen Rücksicht nimmt.

Kapitel 1: Neue Gesetzesbestimmungen und Erläuterungen

In Übereinstimmung mit der Ordnung des Zivilgesetzbuches (s. Art. 755 Abs. 2 ZGB) weist der Entwurf im Falle der Nutzniessung an Stammanteilen das Stimmrecht und die damit verbundenen Rechte den Nutzniesserinnen und Nutzniessern zu (ebenso Art. 690 Abs. 2 OR im Aktienrecht). Diese werden den Eigentümerinnen und Eigentümern aber ersatzpflichtig, wenn sie bei der Ausübung ihrer Rechte nicht in billiger Weise auf deren Interessen Rücksicht nehmen (zur Nutzniessung an Stammanteilen vgl. auch die Ausführungen zu Art. 789*a* E OR).

IV. Vetorecht

Art. 807 (ursprünglicher Botschaftsentwurf)

1 Die Statuten können Gesellschaftern ein Vetorecht gegen Beschlüsse der Gesellschafterversammlung einräumen. Sie müssen die Beschlüsse umschreiben, für die das Vetorecht gilt.

2 Die nachträgliche Einführung eines Vetorechts bedarf der Zustimmung aller Gesellschafter.

3 Das Vetorecht kann nicht übertragen werden.

Art. 807 (durch den Nationalrat bereinigte Version)

1 Die Statuten können Gesellschaftern ein Vetorecht gegen bestimmte Beschlüsse der Gesellschafterversammlung einräumen. Sie müssen die Beschlüsse umschreiben, für die das Vetorecht gilt.

Im Unterschied zum geltenden Recht enthält der Entwurf eine Bestimmung zum Vetorecht, da diesem sowohl in kleineren Unternehmen als beispielsweise auch in Konsortien eine erhebliche Bedeutung für eine bedürfnisbezogene Ausgestaltung der Entscheidungsprozesse zukommen dürfte. Nach *Abs. 1* können die Statuten allen oder einzelnen Gesellschafterinnen und Gesellschaftern ein Vetorecht gegen sämtliche oder bestimmte Beschlüsse der Gesellschafterversammlung einräumen. Die erfassten Beschlüsse sind in den Statuten klar zu umschreiben. Aus Praktikabilitätsgründen ausgeschlossen ist ein direktes Vetorecht gegenüber den

Entscheiden der Geschäftsführerinnen und Geschäftsführer. Weil die Statuten aber bestimmte Entscheide der Geschäftsführerinnen und Geschäftsführer der Genehmigung der Gesellschafterversammlung unterstellen können (s. Art. 811 Abs. 1 Ziff. 1 E OR), lässt sich indirekt dennoch ein Vetorecht realisieren, das bestimmte Entscheide im Rahmen der Geschäftsführung erfasst.

Nationalrat: Die bereinigte Fassung des Art. 807 Abs. 1 OR stellt klar, dass kein generelles Vetorecht gegen Beschlüsse der Gesellschafterversammlung gegeben ist, vgl. auch Amtl. Bull. vom 02.03.2005, 15.00 h.

Die Zulässigkeit eines Vetorechts mag den Bedürfnissen der Praxis in vielen Fällen entsprechen; dennoch darf nicht übersehen werden, dass die Gesellschaft durch Vetorechte unter Umständen blockiert wird. Sollen statutarische Vetorechte nicht gerade in denjenigen Fällen derogiert werden, für die sie vorgesehen sind, müssen gesellschaftsrechtliche Interventionsmöglichkeiten auf Situationen beschränkt bleiben, in denen die vorgeschriebenen Organe nicht mehr rechtskonform bestellt werden können (dazu Art. 731*b* i.V.m. Art. 819 E OR).

Nach *Abs.* 2 bedarf die nachträgliche Einführung eines Vetorechts der Zustimmung aller Gesellschafterinnen und Gesellschafter (falls ein Vetorecht bereits bei der Gründung vorgesehen wird, ist ohnehin ein Konsens erforderlich; s. Art. 777 Abs. 1 E OR). Diese Voraussetzung erscheint unabdingbar, weil durch Vetorechte die Willensbildung der Gesellschaft in einschneidender Weise verändert wird.

Auf Grund der Tragweite eines Vetorechts für alle Gesellschafterinnen und Gesellschafter und weil die Einräumung entsprechender Rechte regelmässig auf den persönlichen Verhältnissen beruht, sieht *Abs.* 3 vor, dass statutarische Vetorechte nicht übertragen werden können. Es handelt sich demnach um persönliche Rechte, die nicht mit dem Stammanteil verbunden sind und die mit dem Ausscheiden oder dem Tod der berechtigten Personen erlöschen. Soll der Rechtsnachfolgerin oder dem Rechtsnachfolger ebenfalls ein Vetorecht eingeräumt werden, so kann ein solches durch einvernehmliches Handeln (gemäss *Abs.* 2) erneut in die Statuten aufgenommen werden. Zudem besteht die Möglichkeit, ein Vetorecht zeitlich unbegrenzt einer juristischen Person zuzuteilen. Im Hinblick auf die Gefahren, die mit der personell wechselnden Berechtigung zur Ausübung eines Vetorechtes verbunden sind, dürfte das Bedürfnis nach entsprechenden Lösungen aber gering sein.[99]

V. Beschlussfassung

1. Im Allgemeinen

Art. 808

Die Gesellschafterversammlung fasst ihre Beschlüsse und vollzieht ihre Wahlen mit der absoluten Mehrheit der vertretenen Stimmen, soweit das Gesetz oder die Statuten es nicht anders bestimmen.

Während das geltende Recht für die Beschlussfassung in der Gesellschafterversammlung im Allgemeinen die absolute Mehrheit der abgegebenen Stimmen verlangt (Art. 808 Abs. 3 OR), stellt der Entwurf für die Ermittlung der Mehrheit auf die an der Gesellschafterversammlung vertretenen Stimmen ab. Der Unterschied wirkt sich dahingehend aus, dass Enthaltungen und ungültige Stimmzettel für die Berechnung der erforderlichen Mehrheit neu einzubeziehen sind. Mit dieser Änderung wird die Regelung mit jener des Aktienrechts in Übereinstimmung gebracht (vgl. Art. 703 OR), da keine Gründe für eine unterschiedliche Ordnung vorliegen.

2. Stichentscheid

Art. 808a

Der Vorsitzende der Gesellschafterversammlung hat den Stichentscheid. Die Statuten können eine andere Regelung vorsehen.

Diese Bestimmung sieht vor, dass der Vorsitzenden oder dem Vorsitzenden der Gesellschafterversammlung bei Stimmengleichheit der Stichentscheid zusteht. Es ist jedoch möglich, in den Statuten eine andere Regelung zu treffen und namentlich den Stichentscheid auszuschliessen.

---

99 Die vorliegenden Erläuterungen beziehen sich ausschliesslich auf die ursprüngliche bundesrätliche Gesetzesversion und nicht auf die bereinigte Fassung durch den Nationalrat.

3. Wichtige Beschlüsse

Art. 808b

1 Ein Beschluss der Gesellschafterversammlung, der mindestens zwei Drittel der vertretenen Stimmen und die absolute Mehrheit des gesamten stimmberechtigten Stammkapitals auf sich vereinigt, ist erforderlich für:

1. die Änderung des Gesellschaftszweckes;
2. die Einführung von stimmrechtsprivilegierten Stammanteilen;
3. die Erschwerung, den Ausschluss oder die Erleichterung der Übertragbarkeit der Stammanteile;
4. die Zustimmung zur Abtretung von Stammanteilen beziehungsweise die Anerkennung als stimmberechtigter Gesellschafter.
5. die Erhöhung des Stammkapitals;
6. die Einschränkung oder Aufhebung des Bezugsrechtes;
7. die Zustimmung zu Tätigkeiten der Geschäftsführer sowie der Gesellschafter, die gegen die Treuepflicht oder das Konkurrenzverbot verstossen;
8. den Antrag an das Gericht, einen Gesellschafter aus wichtigem Grund auszuschliessen;
9. den Ausschluss eines Gesellschafters aus in den Statuten vorgesehenen Gründen;
10. die Verlegung des Sitzes der Gesellschaft;
11. die Auflösung der Gesellschaft.

2 Statutenbestimmungen, die für die Fassung bestimmter Beschlüsse grössere Mehrheiten als die vom Gesetz vorgeschriebenen festlegen, können nur mit dem vorgesehenen Mehr eingeführt werden.

Die im geltenden Recht an verschiedenen Stellen vorgesehenen Vorschriften über besondere Mehrheiten für wichtige Beschlüsse (Art. 784 Abs. 2, Art. 791 Abs. 2, Art. 795, Art. 822 Abs. 3 OR) sollen in einer einzigen Bestimmung zusammengeführt werden. Nach *Abs. 1* ist für die aufgeführten wichtigen Beschlüsse die Zustimmung von mindestens zwei Drittel der an der Gesellschafterversammlung vertretenen Stimmen sowie die absolute Mehrheit des gesamten stimmberechtigten Stammkapitals erforderlich. Diese Regelung ist in dem Sinne einseitig zwingend, als die Statuten die Anforderungen an die Beschlussfassung wohl erhöhen (dazu *Abs. 2*), nicht aber herabsetzen dürfen. Anders als im Aktienrecht (vgl. Art. 704 Abs. 1 OR) wird die erforderliche Kapitalmehrheit nicht auf die an der Gesellschafterversammlung vertretenen Nennwerte bezogen, sondern auf das gesamte stimmberechtigte Stammkapital. Im Hinblick auf die Bedürfnisse von Unternehmen mit nur wenigen Beteiligten wird dadurch die Beschlussfassung in Abwesenheit einzelner Gesellschafterinnen oder Gesellschafter erschwert, um Missbräuche zu verhindern.

Als wichtige Beschlüsse, die nur mit der vorgesehenen qualifizierten Mehrheit gefasst werden können, gelten nach dem Entwurf die folgenden:

− die Änderung des Gesellschaftszwecks (*Ziff. 1*);

− die Einführung im Stimmrecht privilegierter Stammanteile (*Ziff. 2*);

− sämtliche Abweichungen von der dispositiven gesetzlichen Beschränkung der Abtretung von Stammanteilen (*Ziff. 3*);

− die Zustimmung zur Abtretung von Stammanteilen beziehungsweise (bei besonderen Erwerbsarten) die Anerkennung des Erwerbers als stimmberechtigte Gesellschafterin oder stimmberechtigter Gesellschafter (*Ziff. 4*) [100];

− die Erhöhung des Stammkapitals (*Ziff. 5*; das bisherige Erfordernis der Zustimmung aller Gesellschafterinnen und Gesellschafter kann aufgegeben werden, da die subsidiäre Solidarhaftung bis zur Höhe des gesamten Stammkapitals entfällt);

− die Einschränkung oder Aufhebung des Bezugsrechts (*Ziff. 6*);

---

100 Der Beschluss der Gesellschafterversammlung über eine Ermächtigung der Geschäftsführerinnen und Geschäftsführer zum Erwerb eigener Stammanteile (Art. 804 Abs. 2 Ziff. 11 E OR) schliesst sachnotwendigerweise die Zustimmung zur Übertragung der erworbenen Stammanteile an die Gesellschaft in sich. Da der Entwurf für diese Ermächtigung keine qualifizierte Mehrheit verlangt, ergibt sich eine Ausnahme von Art. 808*b* Abs. 1 Ziff. 4 E OR. Es ist aber möglich, in den Statuten die Ermächtigung zum Erwerb eigener Stammanteile ebenfalls dem Erfordernis einer qualifizierten Mehrheit zu unterstellen.

- die Zustimmung zu Tätigkeiten, die gegen die Treuepflicht oder ein Konkurrenzverbot verstossen (*Ziff. 7*; s. dazu Art. 803 Abs. 3, 812 Abs. 2 und 3 E OR sowie 804 Abs. 2 Ziff. 13 E OR);
- der Ausschluss einer Gesellschafterin oder eines Gesellschafters aus in den Statuten vorgesehenen Gründen sowie der Entscheid über die Einreichung eine Klage auf Ausschluss aus wichtigem Grund (*Ziff. 8*);
- die Verlegung des Sitzes der Gesellschaft (*Ziff. 9*);
- die Auflösung der Gesellschaft (*Ziff. 10*); soweit ein Widerruf des Auflösungsbeschlusses zulässig ist[101], müssen dafür dieselben Mehrheitserfordernisse erfüllt werden wie für den Auflösungsbeschluss[102].

Nach *Abs.* 2 können die Statuten für die Fassung bestimmter Beschlüsse grössere Mehrheiten festlegen als von Gesetzes wegen vorgeschrieben. Um zu verhindern, dass statutarisch Mehrheiten festgeschrieben werden, die sich später gar nicht erreichen lassen, wird für die Fassung entsprechender Beschlüsse diejenige Mehrheit verlangt, die eingeführt werden soll (ebenso Art. 704 Abs. 2 OR).

VI. Anfechtung von Beschlüssen der Gesellschafterversammlung

Art. 808c

Für die Anfechtung der Beschlüsse der Gesellschafterversammlung sind die Vorschriften des Aktienrechts entsprechend anwendbar.

Für die Anfechtung von Beschlüssen der Gesellschafterversammlung wird wie bisher (Art. 808 Abs. 6 OR) auf das Aktienrecht verweisen (s. Art. 706 bis 706*b* OR).

---

[101] s. BGE 123 III 473 ff., 126 III 283 ff. (beide Entscheide zum Aktienrecht, aber auch für die GmbH zutreffend).

[102] vgl. dazu die unterschiedlichen Erwägungen bei: PETER BÖCKLI, Schweizer Aktienrecht, 2. Aufl., Zürich 1996, N 1955*d*; PETER FORSTMOSER, Widerrufbarkeit des Auflösungsbeschlusses einer Aktiengesellschaft, in: SZW 70 (1998) S. 155.

Kapitel 1: Neue Gesetzesbestimmungen und Erläuterungen

B. Geschäftsführung und Vertretung

I. Bezeichnung der Geschäftsführer und Organisation

Art. 809 (ursprünglicher Botschaftsentwurf)

1 Alle Gesellschafter üben die Geschäftsführung gemeinsam aus. Die Statuten können die Geschäftsführung abweichend regeln.

2 Als Geschäftsführer können nur natürliche Personen eingesetzt werden. Ist an der Gesellschaft eine juristische Person oder eine Handelsgesellschaft beteiligt, so bezeichnet sie gegebenenfalls eine natürliche Person, die diese Funktion an ihrer Stelle ausübt. Die Statuten können dafür die Zustimmung der Gesellschafterversammlung verlangen.

3 Hat die Gesellschaft mehrere Geschäftsführer, so muss die Gesellschafterversammlung einen von ihnen mit dem Vorsitz betrauen.

4 Hat die Gesellschaft mehrere Geschäftsführer, so entscheiden diese mit der Mehrheit der abgegebenen Stimmen. Der Vorsitzende hat den Stichentscheid. Die Statuten können eine andere Regelung der Beschlussfassung durch die Geschäftsführer vorsehen.

Art. 809 (durch den Nationalrat bereinigte Version)

3 Hat die Gesellschaft mehrere Geschäftsführer, so muss die Gesellschafterversammlung den Vorsitz regeln.

Nach dem Vorentwurf musste die Geschäftsführung und die Vertretung in den Statuten geordnet werden (Art. 811 VE OR). Der Entwurf will die Möglichkeiten einer bedürfnisbezogenen Gestaltung nicht einschränken, sieht aber im Unterschied zum Vorentwurf dispositive gesetzliche Normen für die Geschäftsführung und Vertretung vor, um den Aufwand für die Rechtsberatung bei der Gründung von Kleinunternehmen möglichst gering zu halten. Diese gesetzliche Regelung orientiert sich dementsprechend an den typischen Umständen und Bedürfnissen in kleineren Unternehmen mit nur wenigen beteiligten Personen. Das Gesetz lässt jedoch

655

einen weiten Raum für eine geeignete Organisation in den Statuten, so namentlich für Gesellschaften mit einer grösseren Anzahl von Beteiligten.

Nach *Abs. 1* üben alle Gesellschafterinnen und Gesellschafter die Geschäftsführung gemeinsam aus. Sie treffen die hierfür notwendigen Entscheide im Rahmen ihrer Zusammenarbeit (vgl. *Abs. 4*), wie dies in Kleinunternehmen in der Praxis üblich ist. Soweit diese Regelung den konkreten Bedürfnissen nicht entspricht, können die Statuten die Geschäftsführung abweichend ordnen. Es ist namentlich möglich, die Geschäftsführung auf einzelne Gesellschafterinnen oder Gesellschafter zu beschränken oder an Dritte zu übertragen (im geltenden Recht s. Art. 811 Abs. 2 und Art. 812 Abs. 1 OR).

Eine persönlich zu verantwortende Mitwirkung bei der Willensbildung der Gesellschaft ist nur durch natürliche Personen möglich. *Abs. 2* hält daher fest, dass nur natürliche Personen als Geschäftsführerinnen und Geschäftsführer eingesetzt werden können, wie dies sinngemäss auch in allen andern Rechtsformen der Fall ist (vgl. insbes. Art. 707 Abs. 3 und 894 Abs. 2 OR)[103]. Für Gesellschafterinnen, die als solche nach *Abs. 1* oder nach der Ordnung der Statuten an sich zur Geschäftsführung berechtigt sind, die aber juristische Personen oder Handelsgesellschaften sind, muss eine Sonderregelung getroffen werden: Sie können eine natürliche Person bezeichnen, welche die Funktion einer Geschäftsführerin oder eines Geschäftsführers an ihrer Stelle ausübt. Damit sich die andern Gesellschafterinnen und Gesellschafter nicht mit Personen konfrontiert sehen, die für eine einvernehmliche Geschäftsführung aus irgendwelchen Gründen nicht geeignet erscheinen, können die Statuten vorsehen, dass für die Bezeichnung von Geschäftsführerinnen und Geschäftsführern durch juristische Personen oder Handelsgesellschaften die Zustimmung der Gesellschafterversammlung erforderlich ist (s. auch Art. 776*a* Abs. 1 Ziff. 12 E OR).

Obliegt die Geschäftsführung mehreren Personen, so muss die Gesellschafterversammlung nach *Abs. 3* eine von ihnen mit dem Vorsitz betrauen. Im Hinblick auf die Gewährleistung der Funktionstüchtigkeit der Organisation der Gesellschaft ist diese Vorgabe zwingender Natur. Der Vorsitz kann sowohl einer Gesellschafterin oder einem Gesellschafter als auch einer anderen Geschäftsführerin oder einem andern Geschäftsführer zugewiesen werden. Da die Bezeichnung der Person, welcher der Vorsitz

---

103 a.M. HANS MICHAEL RIEMER, Die Vereine, Berner Kommentar I/3/2, Bern 1990, Art. 69 N 14 f.; DERS., Die Stiftungen, Berner Kommentar I/3/3, Bern 1975, Art. 83 N 6. Diese Ansicht entspricht jedoch nicht der Praxis der Handelsregisterbehörden.

zukommt, nicht zu den unübertragbaren Aufgaben der Gesellschafterversammlung gehört (vgl. Art. 804 Abs. 2 E OR), können die Statuten die Wahl den Geschäftsführerinnen und Geschäftsführern überlassen.

Nationalrat: Nach der bereinigten Gesetzesversion kann auch ein Co-Präsidium vorgesehen werden, vgl. Amtl. Bull. vom 02.03.05 15.00 h.

Abs. 4 regelt die Beschlussfassung durch eine Mehrzahl von Geschäftsführerinnen und Geschäftsführern. Sehen die Statuten nichts anderes vor, entscheiden die an der Geschäftsführung beteiligten Personen mit der Mehrheit der abgegebenen Stimmen, wobei der Vorsitzenden oder dem Vorsitzenden der Stichentscheid zukommt. Die Statuten können beispielsweise Anwesenheitsquoren für bestimmte Beschlüsse festlegen oder auf den Stichentscheid verzichten.[104]

II. Aufgaben der Geschäftsführer

Art. 810

1 Die Geschäftsführer sind zuständig in allen Angelegenheiten, die nicht nach Gesetz oder Statuten der Gesellschafterversammlung zugewiesen sind.

2 Unter Vorbehalt der nachfolgenden Bestimmungen haben die Geschäftsführer folgende unübertragbare und unentziehbare Aufgaben:

1. die Oberleitung der Gesellschaft und die Erteilung der nötigen Weisungen;

2. die Festlegung der Organisation im Rahmen von Gesetz und Statuten;

3. die Ausgestaltung des Rechnungswesens und der Finanzkontrolle sowie der Finanzplanung, sofern diese für die Führung der Gesellschaft notwendig ist;

4. die Aufsicht über die Personen, denen Teile der Geschäftsführung übertragen sind, namentlich im Hinblick auf die Befolgung der Gesetze, Statuten, Reglemente und Weisungen;

---

104 Die vorliegenden Erläuterungen beziehen sich ausschliesslich auf die ursprüngliche bundesrätliche Gesetzesversion und nicht auf die bereinigte Fassung durch den Nationalrat.

5. die Erstellung des Geschäftsberichtes (Jahresrechnung, Jahresbericht und gegebenenfalls Konzernrechnung);

6. die Vorbereitung der Gesellschafterversammlung sowie die Ausführung ihrer Beschlüsse;

7. die Benachrichtigung des Gerichts im Falle der Überschuldung.

³ Wer den Vorsitz der Geschäftsführung innehat, beziehungsweise der einzige Geschäftsführer hat folgende Aufgaben:

1. die Einberufung und Leitung der Gesellschafterversammlung;

2. Bekanntmachungen gegenüber den Gesellschaftern;

3. die Sicherstellung der erforderlichen Anmeldungen beim Handelsregister.

Nach *Abs. 1* sind die Geschäftsführerinnen und Geschäftsführer in allen Angelegenheiten zuständig, die nicht nach Gesetz oder Statuten der Gesellschafterversammlung (oder gegebenenfalls der Revisionsstelle) zugewiesen sind (subsidiäre Generalkompetenz; sinngemäss ebenso Art. 716 Abs. 1 OR für die Aktiengesellschaft). Durch diese Regelung werden negative Kompetenzkonflikte verhindert.

Abs. 2 listet die Aufgaben der Geschäftsführerinnen und Geschäftsführer auf, die unter Vorbehalt von *Art. 811* E OR als unübertragbar und unentziehbar gelten (vgl. Art. 716a Abs. 1 OR für die Aktiengesellschaft). Die Geschäftsführer tragen namentlich die Verantwortung für die Oberleitung der Gesellschaft (*Ziff. 1 und 4*), die Festlegung der Organisation (*Ziff. 2*), die Ausgestaltung des Rechnungs- und Finanzwesens und die Erstellung des Geschäftsberichts (*Ziff. 3 und 5*), die Vorbereitung der Gesellschafterversammlung (*Ziff. 6*) sowie die Benachrichtigung des Gerichts im Falle der Überschuldung (*Ziff. 7*).

Abs. 3 nennt die besonderen Aufgaben der Person, die mit dem Vorsitz über die Geschäftsführung betraut ist. Hat die Gesellschaft nur eine einzige Geschäftsführerin oder einen einzigen Geschäftsführer, so obliegen die entsprechenden Pflichten dieser Person. Es handelt sich dabei um die Einberufung und Leitung der Gesellschafterversammlung, die Anordnung der erforderlichen Bekanntmachungen gegenüber den Gesellschafterinnen und Gesellschaftern sowie die Sicherstellung der Anmeldungen beim Handelsregister.

Kapitel 1: Neue Gesetzesbestimmungen und Erläuterungen

III. Genehmigung durch die Gesellschafterversammlung

Art. 811

1 Die Statuten können vorsehen, dass die Geschäftsführer der Gesellschafterversammlung:

1. bestimmte Entscheide zur Genehmigung vorlegen müssen;

2. einzelne Fragen zur Genehmigung vorlegen können.

2 Die Genehmigung der Gesellschafterversammlung schränkt die Haftung der Geschäftsführer nicht ein.

In der Aktiengesellschaft sind die Befugnisse der Generalversammlung und des Verwaltungsrates konsequent aufgeteilt, und die Generalversammlung vermag im Bereich der Geschäftsführung (aus Gründen der Verantwortlichkeit) keinerlei Aufgaben an sich zu ziehen (vgl. Art. 716*a* OR). Demgegenüber sieht der Entwurf für die GmbH zwei verschiedene Arten einer Genehmigungskompetenz der Gesellschafterversammlung vor: Die Statuten sollen bestimmen können, dass die Geschäftsführerinnen und Geschäftsführer der Gesellschafterversammlung bestimmte Entscheide zur Genehmigung vorlegen müssen (obligatorischer Genehmigungsvorbehalt; *Abs. 1 Ziff. 1*). Es soll aber auch offen stehen, in den Statuten anzuordnen, dass die Geschäftsführerinnen und Geschäftsführer der Gesellschafterversammlung einzelne Fragen freiwillig zur Genehmigung vorlegen dürfen (fakultativer Genehmigungsvorbehalt; *Abs. 1 Ziff. 2*). Diese Gestaltungsmöglichkeiten sind Ausdruck der flexiblen, personenbezogenen Organisationsstruktur der GmbH und entsprechen namentlich den Bedürfnissen kleiner und mittlerer Unternehmen.

So sehr ein Genehmigungsvorbehalt zu Gunsten der Gesellschafterversammlung den Bedürfnissen der Praxis entgegenkommen mag, so heikel kann er sich rechtlich betrachtet erweisen: Während die Geschäftsführerinnen und Geschäftsführer einer gesellschaftsrechtlichen Verantwortlichkeit unterliegen (s. Art. 754 OR i.V.m. Art. 827 E OR), fehlt für Entscheide der Gesellschafterversammlung jede entsprechende Haftung. Es gilt daher zu vermeiden, dass potenziell haftungsrelevante Entscheide zum Schaden Dritter an die Gesellschafterversammlung überstellt werden. Der Entwurf sieht keine eigentliche Verschiebung der Zuständigkeiten vor, sondern die Möglichkeit fakultativer oder obligatorischer Genehmigungskompetenzen. Die Geschäftsführerinnen und Geschäftsführer haben demnach stets selbst einen Entscheid zu treffen, den sie der Gesellschafterversammlung zur Genehmigung unterbreiten müssen beziehungsweise können. *Abs. 2* stellt klar, dass die Genehmigung der Gesellschafterversammlung die Haftung der Geschäftsführerinnen und Geschäftsführer grundsätzlich nicht berühren darf. Gesellschaftsintern kann die Genehmigung je nach den Umständen aber dennoch einer Entlastung gleichkommen (vgl. Art. 758 OR i.V.m. Art. 827 E OR).

Das statutarische Erfordernis der Genehmigung eines bestimmten Entscheids der Geschäftsführerinnen und Geschäftsführer durch die Gesellschafterversammlung bleibt ohne Einfluss auf die Vertretungsmacht der zeichnungsberechtigten Personen. Verträge, die ohne Genehmigung abgeschlossen werden, sind rechtsbeständig, solange die andere Vertragspartei nicht um das Fehlen einer erforderlichen Genehmigung wusste oder hätte wissen sollen.

IV. Sorgfalts- und Treuepflicht; Konkurrenzverbot

Art. 812

1 Die Geschäftsführer sowie Dritte, die mit der Geschäftsführung befasst sind, müssen ihre Aufgabe mit aller Sorgfalt erfüllen und die Interessen der Gesellschaft in guten Treuen wahren.

2 Sie unterstehen der gleichen Treuepflicht wie die Gesellschafter.

3 Sie dürfen keine konkurrenzierenden Tätigkeiten ausüben, es sei denn, die Statuten sehen etwas anderes vor oder alle übrigen Gesellschafter stimmen der Tätigkeit schriftlich zu. Die Statuten können vorsehen, dass stattdessen die Zustimmung durch die Gesellschafterversammlung erforderlich ist.

Nach *Abs. 1* müssen die Geschäftsführerinnen und Geschäftsführer ihre Aufgaben mit aller Sorgfalt erfüllen und die Interessen der Gesellschaft in guten Treuen wahren. Dies gilt auch für andere Personen, die mit der Geschäftsführung befasst sind (ebenso Art. 717 Abs. 1 OR für die Aktiengesellschaft).

Abs. 2 dehnt die Treuepflicht der Gesellschafterinnen und Gesellschafter (s. Art. 803 E OR) auf Geschäftsführerinnen und Geschäftsführer aus, die selbst nicht an der Gesellschaft beteiligt sind.

Während für Gesellschafterinnen und Gesellschafter nur dann ein Konkurrenzverbot besteht, wenn die Statuten dies vorsehen (s. Art. 803 Abs. 2 E OR), gilt für Geschäftsführerinnen und Geschäftsführer sowie für Dritte, die mit der Geschäftsführung befasst sind, gerade die umgekehrte Regelung: Sie unterstehen nach *Abs. 3* grundsätzlich einem Konkurrenzverbot, doch ist es möglich, dieses in den Statuten auszuschliessen. Es steht zudem offen, im Einzelfall eine Dispensation durch die schriftliche Zustimmung sämtlicher Gesellschafterinnen und Gesellschafter zu erwirken. Die Statuten können bestimmen, dass die Zustimmung zu konkurrenzierenden Tätigkeiten stattdessen durch die Gesellschafterversammlung erteilt wird (vgl. Art. 808*b* Abs. 1 Ziff. 7 E OR). Im Weiteren wird auf die Ausführungen zu Art. 803 Abs. 2 und 3 E OR hingewiesen.

Konkurrenzierende Tätigkeiten von Geschäftsführern und Gesellschaftern können zu steuerlichen Folgen bei der Gesellschaft und den Betroffenen führen. Das Bundesgericht hat entschieden, dass eine Aktiengesellschaft natürlichen Personen eine geldwerte Leistung erbringt, soweit diese für sie tätig sind und gleichzeitig einzelne in den Geschäftsbereich der Gesellschaft fallende Geschäfte auf eigene Rechnung abschliessen. Dies ist der Fall, wenn die Gesellschaft – namentlich einem geschäftsführenden Allein- oder Hauptaktionär[105] – eine konkurrenzierende Tätigkeit erlaubt und darauf verzichtet, die Gewinne aus Geschäften herauszuverlangen, die ihrer Natur nach der Gesellschaft zukommen. Solche Überlegungen müssen auch bei konkurrenzierenden Tätigkeiten von Geschäftsführern und Gesellschaftern von Gesellschaften mit beschränkter Haftung gelten.

V. Gleichbehandlung

Art. 813

Die Geschäftsführer sowie Dritte, die mit der Geschäftsführung befasst sind, haben die Gesellschafter unter gleichen Voraussetzungen gleich zu behandeln.

---

105 vgl. BGE vom 27.10.1997 in: Archiv für Schweizerisches Abgaberecht Bd. 67, S. 216 ff.

Der Grundsatz der Gleichbehandlung ist allgemein als wegleitendes Prinzip des Gesellschaftsrechts anerkannt[106]. Er ist auf zwei verschiedenen Ebenen von unterschiedlicher Tragweite:
– *Im Verhältnis zwischen den Gesellschafterinnen und Gesellschaftern:*

Bei der Normsetzung in den ursprünglichen Statuten sind Ungleichbehandlungen grundsätzlich zulässig, soweit sie mit den zwingenden gesetzlichen Vorschriften und den Strukturen der Rechtsform vereinbar sind. In diesem Rahmen erscheinen asymmetrische Ausgestaltungen im Allgemeinen als unproblematisch, da sämtliche Gründerinnen und Gründer den Statuten zustimmen müssen (vgl. Art. 777 Abs. 1 E OR). Die Möglichkeit einer Differenzierung der mit den einzelnen Stammanteilen verbundenen Rechte und Pflichten entspricht der personenbezogenen Struktur der GmbH (bspw. kann eine Nachschusspflicht mit einem Vetorecht kombiniert werden).

Als heikler erweist sich die nachträgliche Ungleichbehandlung durch eine Statutenänderung und durch andere Beschlüsse der Gesellschafterversammlung. Die Gesellschafterinnen und Gesellschafter werden diesbezüglich durch besondere Zustimmungserfordernisse für bestimmte Beschlüsse geschützt (vgl. Art. 797 E OR betr. die nachträgliche Einführung statutarischer Nachschuss- und Nebenleistungspflichten; Art. 807 Abs. 2 E OR für die nachträgliche Einführung eines Vetorechts). Darüber hinaus müssen Beschlüsse als anfechtbar gelten, wenn sie eine durch den Gesellschaftszweck nicht gerechtfertigte Benachteiligung einer Gesellschafterin oder eines Gesellschafters bewirken, ohne dass die Zustimmung der betroffenen Person vorliegt (s. Art. 706 Abs. 2 Ziff. 3 OR i.V.m. Art. 808c E OR).

– *Im Rahmen der Geschäftsführung:*

Art. 813 sieht zwingend vor, dass die Geschäftsführerinnen und Geschäftsführer sowie alle andern Personen, die mit der Geschäftsführung befasst sind, die Gesellschafterinnen und Gesellschafter unter gleichen Voraussetzungen gleich behandeln müssen (s. auch Art. 717 Abs. 2 und 854 OR). Dieses Gebot einer relativen Gleichbehandlung kann sowohl im Innenverhältnis der Gesellschaft als auch da, wo Gesellschafterinnen oder Gesellschafter der Gesellschaft als Dritte (bspw. als Käufer) gegenübertre-

---

106 s. bspw. CLAIRE HUGUENIN JACOBS, Das Gleichbehandlungsprinzip im Aktienrecht, Zürich 1994, S. 5; WERNER VON STEIGER, in: Schweizerisches Privatrecht VIII/1, Basel und Stuttgart 1976, S. 298 ff.; HERBERT WOHLMANN, GmbH-Recht, Basel und Frankfurt a.M. 1997, S. 40.

ten, von Bedeutung sein[107]. Es handelt sich dabei um eine zentrale Schutzbestimmung für Personen mit Minderheitsbeteiligungen.
Die Relativierung des Gleichbehandlungsgebots durch den Vorbehalt gleicher Voraussetzungen gewährt den erforderlichen Handlungsspielraum, um den konkreten personenbezogenen Beteiligungsverhältnissen Rechnung zu tragen. Entsprechend dem Konzept der Kapitalgesellschaft richtet sich die Gleichbehandlung zudem weitgehend nach dem Umfang der Beteiligung am Stammkapital.

VI. Vertretung

Art. 814 (ursprünglicher Botschaftsentwurf)

1 Jeder Geschäftsführer ist zur Vertretung der Gesellschaft berechtigt.

2 Die Statuten können die Vertretung abweichend regeln; für Einzelheiten kann auf ein Reglement verwiesen werden. Mindestens ein Geschäftsführer muss zur Vertretung befugt sein.

3 Eine der Personen, die die Gesellschaft vertreten können, muss Wohnsitz in der Schweiz haben. Hat kein zur Vertretung befugter Geschäftsführer Wohnsitz in der Schweiz, so muss ein Direktor mit Wohnsitz in der Schweiz mit der Vertretung der Gesellschaft betraut werden.

4 Für den Umfang und die Beschränkung der Vertretungsbefugnis sowie für Verträge zwischen der Gesellschaft und der Person, die sie vertritt, sind die Vorschriften des Aktienrechts entsprechend anwendbar.

5 Die zur Vertretung der Gesellschaft befugten Personen haben in der Weise zu zeichnen, dass sie der Firma der Gesellschaft ihre Unterschrift beifügen.

6 Sie müssen ins Handelsregister eingetragen werden. Sie haben ihre Unterschrift beim Handelsregisteramt zu zeichnen oder die Zeichnung in beglaubigter Form einzureichen.

---

107 s. dazu PETER FORSTMOSER/ARTHUR MEIER-HAYOZ/PETER NOBEL, Schweizerisches Aktienrecht, Bern 1996, § 39 N 42 ff.; Rolf Watter, in: Kommentar zum Schweizerischen Privatrecht, Obligationenrecht II, Basel und Frankfurt a.M. 1994, Art. 717 N 27 (beide zum Aktienrecht).

Art. 814 (durch den Nationalrat bereinigte Version)

3 Die Gesellschaft muss durch eine Person vertreten werden können, die Wohnsitz in der Schweiz hat. Dieses Erfordernis kann durch einen Geschäftsführer oder einen Direktor erfüllt werden.

Das geltende Recht geht von der gemeinsamen Vertretung der Gesellschaft durch alle Gründungsgesellschafterinnen und Gründungsgesellschafter aus (Art. 811 Abs. 1 und 3 OR); diese Regelung erwies sich jedoch als schwerfällig und nicht praxisgerecht. Nach dem Vorentwurf sollte die Vertretung zwingend in den Statuten bestimmt werden müssen (Art. 811 Abs. 1 VE OR). Um den Aufwand für die Rechtsberatung bei der Gründung gering zu halten, sieht der Entwurf demgegenüber eine dispositive Anordnung vor, die sich an den Bedürfnissen kleinerer Unternehmen orientiert (s. dazu auch die Ausführungen zu Art. 809 E OR): Nach *Abs. 1* ist jede Geschäftsführerin und jeder Geschäftsführer zur Vertretung der Gesellschaft berechtigt. Entsprechend den Bedürfnissen der Praxis werden für die Geschäftsführung und die Vertretung somit abweichende Regelungen getroffen (vgl. Art. 809 Abs. 1 E OR).

Nach *Abs. 2* steht es offen, die Vertretung in den Statuten abweichend zu regeln. Indessen muss mindestens eine Geschäftsführerin oder ein Geschäftsführer zur Vertretung befugt sein, damit gewährleistet bleibt, dass die Gesellschaft auf der Ebene der Geschäftsführung vertreten werden kann. Dieses Erfordernis gilt auch dann als erfüllt, wenn zwei Geschäftsführerinnen oder Geschäftsführer gemeinsam die Gesellschaft vertreten (mit Kollektivunterschrift zu zweien). Wird die Vertretung in den Statuten abweichend von den dispositiven gesetzlichen Vorschriften geregelt, so kann für die Einzelheiten auf ein Reglement der Gesellschafterversammlung oder der Geschäftsführerinnen und Geschäftsführer verwiesen werden.

Abs. 3 verlangt, dass die Gesellschaft durch eine der Personen vertreten werden kann, die Wohnsitz in der Schweiz hat. Anders als nach geltendem Recht (s. Art. 813 Abs. 1 OR) muss es sich dabei nicht zwingend um eine Geschäftsführerin oder einen Geschäftsführer handeln; es genügt auch eine Direktorin oder ein Direktor. Verfügt keine in der Schweiz wohnhafte Person über eine Einzelzeichnungsberechtigung, so kann das Wohnsitzerfordernis auch durch das Zusammenwirken mehrerer Personen erfüllt werden. Durch diese Regelung soll im Interesse der Transparenz der Unternehmensverhältnisse und zur Sicherung einer rechtsverbindlichen Kommunikation mit der Gesellschaft ein personeller Anknüpfungspunkt in der Schweiz gewährleistet werden, ohne dass sich daraus für die Praxis signifikante Einschränkungen ergeben.

Für den Umfang und die Beschränkung der Vertretungsbefugnis verweist *Abs. 4* (wie bereits Art. 814 Abs. 1 OR) auf das Aktienrecht (s. Art. 718*a* OR). Die Verweisung erfasst zudem auch die neue Regelung betreffend Verträge zwischen der Gesellschaft und der Person, durch die sie vertreten wird (s. Art. 718*b* E OR).

Nach *Abs. 5* haben die zur Vertretung der Gesellschaft befugten Personen (wie bisher) in der Weise zu zeichnen, dass sie der Firma der Gesellschaft ihre Unterschrift beifügen (vgl. Art. 815 Abs. 1 OR).

Die zur Vertretung befugten Personen müssen nach *Abs. 6* in das Handelsregister eingetragen werden (ebenso Art. 720 OR). Die Unterschrift ist beim Handelsregisteramt zu zeichnen oder die Zeichnung in beglaubigter Form einzureichen.[108]

VII. Abberufung von Geschäftsführern; Entziehung der Vertretungsbefugnis

Art. 815

1 Die Gesellschafterversammlung kann von ihr gewählte Geschäftsführer jederzeit abrufen.

2 Jeder Gesellschafter kann dem Gericht beantragen, einem Geschäftsführer die Geschäftsführungs- und Vertretungsbefugnis zu entziehen oder zu beschränken, wenn ein wichtiger Grund vorliegt, namentlich wenn die betreffende Person ihre Pflichten grob verletzt oder die Fähigkeit zu einer guten Geschäftsführung verloren hat.

3 Die Geschäftsführer können Direktoren, Prokuristen oder Handlungsbevollmächtigte jederzeit in ihrer Funktion einstellen.

---

108 Die vorliegenden Erläuterungen beziehen sich ausschliesslich auf die ursprüngliche bundesrätliche Gesetzesversion und nicht auf die bereinigte Fassung durch den Nationalrat.

4 Sind diese Personen durch die Gesellschafterversammlung eingesetzt worden, so ist unverzüglich eine Gesellschafterversammlung einzuberufen.

5 Entschädigungsansprüche der abberufenen oder in ihren Funktionen eingestellten Personen bleiben vorbehalten.

Nach *Abs. 1* kann die Gesellschafterversammlung von ihr gewählte Geschäftsführerinnen und Geschäftsführer jederzeit abberufen – unabhängig davon, ob es sich um Gesellschafterinnen oder Gesellschafter oder um Dritte handelt. Soweit den an der Gesellschaft beteiligten Personen die Befugnis zur Geschäftsführung ohne Wahl durch die Gesellschafterversammlung zusteht (sei es nach Art. 809 Abs. 1 E OR oder nach den Statuten), ist eine Abberufung nur auf dem Weg einer statutarischen Neuregelung der Geschäftsführung möglich.

Abs. 2 enthält eine Sicherheitsklausel für Problemfälle: Liegen wichtige Gründe vor, so kann das Gericht einer Geschäftsführerin oder einem Geschäftsführer die Geschäftsführungs- und Vertretungsbefugnis entziehen oder beschränken. Antragsberechtigt ist jede Gesellschafterin und jeder Gesellschafter. Ein Grund für die Entziehung der Geschäftsführungs- und Vertretungsbefugnis liegt insbesondere dann vor, wenn die betreffende Person ihre Pflichten grob verletzt oder die Fähigkeiten zu einer guten Geschäftsführung verloren hat.

Um eine rasche Reaktion auf Probleme zu ermöglichen, räumt *Abs. 3* den Geschäftsführerinnen und Geschäftsführern das Recht ein, Direktorinnen und Direktoren, Prokuristinnen und Prokuristen sowie Handlungsbevollmächtigte jederzeit in ihrer Funktion einzustellen (durch einen Entscheid gemäss Art. 809 Abs. 3 E OR). Dies muss aus Sicherheitsgründen auch dann gelten, wenn es sich um Personen handelt, die durch die Gesellschafterversammlung ernannt wurden (vgl. Art. 804 Abs. 3 E OR). In diesem Fall muss jedoch nach *Abs. 4* unverzüglich eine Gesellschafterversammlung einberufen werden (vgl. Art. 726 Abs. 1 und 2 OR für die Aktiengesellschaft). Allfällige Entschädigungsansprüche der Betroffenen bleiben gemäss *Abs. 5* vorbehalten.

Die Vorschriften zur Abberufung von Geschäftsführerinnen und Geschäftsführern sowie zur Entziehung der Vertretungsbefugnis sind in dem Sinne als zwingend zu verstehen, als die vorgesehenen Vorkehren durch

Kapitel 1: Neue Gesetzesbestimmungen und Erläuterungen

die Statuten nicht erschwert werden dürfen, da sie der Erhaltung der Funktionstauglichkeit der Gesellschaftsorgane dienen.

VIII. Nichtigkeit von Beschlüssen

Art. 816

Für die Beschlüsse der Geschäftsführer gelten sinngemäss die gleichen Nichtigkeitsgründe wie für die Beschlüsse der Generalversammlung der Aktiengesellschaft.

Für die Beschlüsse der Geschäftsführerinnen und Geschäftsführer sollen sinngemäss die gleichen Nichtigkeitsgründe gelten wie für die Beschlüsse der Generalversammlung und des Verwaltungsrates in der Aktiengesellschaft (s. Art. 706*b* und 714 OR).

IX. Haftung

Art. 817

Die Gesellschaft haftet für den Schaden aus unerlaubten Handlungen, die eine zur Geschäftsführung oder zur Vertretung befugte Person in Ausübung ihrer geschäftlichen Verrichtungen begeht.

Die Gesellschaft haftet für den Schaden aus unerlaubten Handlungen, die eine zur Geschäftsführung oder zur Vertretung befugte Person in Ausübung ihrer geschäftlichen Verrichtungen begeht (ebenso Art. 814 Abs. 4 OR im geltenden Recht sowie Art. 722 OR für die Aktiengesellschaft).

C. Revisionsstelle

Art. 818

1 Für die Revisionsstelle sind die Vorschriften des Aktienrechts entsprechend anwendbar.

2 Ein Gesellschafter, der einer Nachschusspflicht unterliegt, kann eine ordentliche Revision der Jahresrechnung verlangen.

Das geltende GmbH-Recht kennt keine Pflicht, die Jahresrechnung von einer unabhängigen Revisorin oder einem unabhängigen Revisor prüfen zu lassen (Art. 819 OR). Es steht der Gesellschaft damit frei, eine Revisionsstelle zu bezeichnen oder davon abzusehen.

Nach dem Vorentwurf der Professoren Peter Böckli, Peter Forstmoser und Jean-Marc Rapp zur Revision des Rechts der GmbH sollte für Gesellschaften mit beschränkter Haftung eine allgemeine Pflicht zur Prüfung der Jahresrechnung geschaffen werden (Art. 819 VE OR; für kleinere Gesellschaften wurden an die Revisorinnen und Revisoren wie im Aktienrecht keine bestimmten fachlichen Anforderungen gestellt)[109]. Dieser Vorschlag wurde in der Vernehmlassung zwar in einigen Stellungnahmen begrüsst, stiess aber andernorts auf heftige Kritik, dies hauptsächlich auf Grund der Kosten, die der Gesellschaft aus einer Revisionspflicht entstehen. Es wurde angeregt, eine Lösung zu treffen, die nach der Grösse des Unternehmens differenziert, wie dies im Vorentwurf zum Bundesgesetz über die Rechnungslegung und Revision (VE RRG)[110] vorgesehen wurde.

Der Bundesrat schlug in der Folge im Entwurf zur Revision des Rechts der GmbH eine nuancierte Regelung[111] vor. Im Rahmen der Beratungen dieses Entwurfs setzte sich die Kommission für Rechtsfragen des Nationalrates jedoch zum Ziel, die Revisionsstelle nicht nur für die GmbH neu zu regeln, sondern ein aktualisiertes und harmonisiertes Gesamtkonzept der Revisionsstelle für sämtliche Rechtsformen des Privatrechts zu schaffen ist. Die Zusatzbotschaft trägt diesem Anliegen Rechnung. Entsprechend dem vorliegenden Entwurf muss auch die Bestimmung zur Revisionsstelle in der GmbH angepasst werden. Der Regelungsvorschlag zu Artikel 818 E OR ersetzt die entsprechende Vorschrift im Entwurf zur Revision des Rechts der GmbH.

---

109 PETER BÖCKLI/PETER FORSTMOSER/JEAN-MARC RAPP, Reform des GmbH-Rechts, Expertenentwurf vom 29. November 1996 für eine Reform des Rechts der Gesellschaft mit beschränkter Haftung, Zürich 1997, 40, 59.

110 Art. 43 VE RRG, in: Revision des Rechnungslegungsrechts, Vorentwürfe und Begleitbericht vom 29.6.1998 (Bezugsquelle: Bundesamt für Bauten und Logistik, Vertrieb Publikationen, 3003 Bern).

111 01.082 Botschaft zur Revision des Obligationenrechts (GmbH-Recht sowie Anpassungen im Aktien-, Genossenschafts-, Handelsregister- und Firmenrecht) vom 19. Dezember 2001, BBl 2002 3148, 3164 f., 3217 ff., 3285.

Der Entwurf schlägt ein Neukonzept für die Revisionspflicht und die Revisionsstelle vor, das für alle Rechtsformen grundsätzlich gleichermassen gilt. Soweit keine sachlichen Gründe für eine abweichende Regelung gegeben sind, ist die Revisionspflicht in der GmbH nach denselben Kriterien zu umschreiben wie in der Aktiengesellschaft.

Abs. 1 verweist daher für die Revisionspflicht und die Revisionsstelle auf die Vorschriften des Aktienrechts (vgl. Art. 727 ff. E OR), welche sinngemäss zur Anwendung kommen. Diese für das Gesellschaftsrecht typische Querverweisung auf das Recht einer andern Rechtsform ist als sog. dynamischer Verweis zu verstehen.

Die GmbH muss ihre Jahresrechnung und ihre Konzernrechnung demnach ordentlich durch ein staatlich beaufsichtigtes Revisionsunternehmen (s. Art. 727*b* Abs. 1 E OR) prüfen lassen, wenn sie:

– Anleihensobligationen ausstehend hat (Art. 727 Abs. 1 Ziff. 1 lit. b E OR); oder

– mindestens 20% der Aktiven oder des Umsatzes zur Konzernrechnung einer Gesellschaft beiträgt, die über kotierte Beteiligungspapiere verfügt oder Anleihensobligationen ausstehend hat (Art. 727 Abs. 1 Ziff. 1 lit. c E OR; die GmbH kann selbst keine kotierten Beteiligungspapiere ausgeben, s. Art. 784 ff. E OR sowie die Ausführungen dazu in der Botschaft zur Revision des GmbH-Rechts[112]).

Sie muss ihre Jahresrechnung und ihre Konzernrechnung ausserdem ordentlich durch eine zugelassene Revisionsexpertin oder einen zugelassenen Revisionsexperten prüfen lassen (s. Art. 727*b* Abs. 2 E OR), wenn:

– zwei der drei in Artikel 727 Abs. 1 Ziff. 2 E OR vorgesehenen Grenzwerte in zwei aufeinander folgenden Geschäftsjahren überschritten werden;

– sie zur Erstellung einer Konzernrechnung verpflichtet ist (Art. 801 E OR in der Fassung gemäss Botschaft zur Revision des Rechts der GmbH i.V.m. Art. 663*e* Abs. 3 und Art. 727 Abs. 1 Ziff. 3 E OR);

– Gesellschafter, die zusammen mindestens 10% des Stammkapitals vertreten, dies verlangen (Art. 727 Abs. 2 E OR);

– die Statuten dies vorsehen (Art. 727 Abs. 3 E OR); oder

---

112 BBl 2002 3159 f., 3184 ff., 3271 f.

– die Gesellschafterversammlung dies beschliesst (Art. 727 Abs. 3 E OR).

Ist keine ordentliche Revision erforderlich, so besteht grundsätzlich eine Pflicht zur eingeschränkten Revision der Jahresrechnung (Art. 727*a* i.V.m. 818 Abs. 1 E OR), wobei den Gesellschaften die Möglichkeit eines Opting-out (s. Art. 727*a* Abs. 2 i.V.m. 818 Abs. 1 E OR; eröffnet wird.

Abs. 2 enthält die einzige Besonderheit, die für die Revisionspflicht in der GmbH im Vergleich mit dem Aktienrecht vorgesehen ist: Jeder Gesellschafterin und jedem Gesellschafter, die oder der einer Nachschusspflicht unterliegt (vgl. dazu im geltenden GmbH-Recht Art. 803 OR und im Entwurf zur Revision des GmbH-Rechts Art. 795 ff. E OR[113]), wird das Recht eingeräumt, eine ordentliche Revision zu verlangen. Ein entsprechender Schutz erscheint im Hinblick auf das mit der Nachschusspflicht verbundene finanzielle Risiko unabdingbar.

Die vorgesehene Lösung ermöglicht es aber auch, ungeachtet bestehender Nachschusspflichten auf eine Revisionsstelle zu verzichten, wenn die Gesellschafterinnen und Gesellschafter einem Opting-out zustimmen (s. Art. 727*a* Abs. 2 E OR); dies wird häufig dann möglich sein, wenn die zum Nachschuss verpflichteten Personen selber in die Geschäftsführung einbezogen sind. Der Umfang der Revision wird sich somit in der Praxis nach den konkreten Verhältnissen bestimmen.

D. Mängel in der Organisation der Gesellschaft

Art. 819

Bei Mängeln in der Organisation der Gesellschaft sind die Vorschriften des Aktienrechts entsprechend anwendbar.

Die neue Regelung von Mängeln in der Organisation der Aktiengesellschaft kann auch für die GmbH herangezogen werden. Es wird dazu auf den Kommentar zu Artikel 731*b* E OR verwiesen.

---

113 BBl 2002 3194 ff., 3274 f.

E. Kapitalverlust und Überschuldung

Art. 820

1 Für die Anzeigepflichten bei Kapitalverlust und Überschuldung der Gesellschaft sowie für die Eröffnung und den Aufschub des Konkurses sind die Vorschriften des Aktienrechts entsprechend anwendbar.

2 Das Gericht kann den Konkurs auf Antrag der Geschäftsführer oder eines Gläubigers aufschieben, namentlich wenn ausstehende Nachschüsse unverzüglich einbezahlt werden und Aussicht auf Sanierung besteht.

Abs. 1 verweist für die Anzeigepflichten bei Kapitalverlust und Überschuldung der Gesellschaft sowie für die Eröffnung und den Aufschub des Konkurses auf die entsprechenden Vorschriften des Aktienrechts (s. Art. 725 f. OR). Die bisherige Verweisungsnorm (Art. 817 Abs. 1 OR) wird durch die Neuformulierung vervollständigt und mit der aktienrechtlichen Umschreibung des Kapitalverlustes in Übereinstimmung gebracht. Die Pflichten des Verwaltungsrates obliegen in der GmbH den Geschäftsführerinnen und Geschäftsführern. Muss eine Zwischenbilanz erstellt werden, ist diese in der GmbH nur dann der Revisionsstelle vorzulegen, wenn die Gesellschaft eine solche bezeichnen muss oder freiwillig eine solche bezeichnet hat.

Nach *Abs. 2* kann das Gericht den Konkurs auf Antrag der Geschäftsführerinnen und Geschäftsführer oder auf Antrag einer Gläubigerin oder eines Gläubigers aufschieben, so namentlich wenn ausstehende Nachschüsse unverzüglich einbezahlt werden und Aussicht auf Sanierung besteht. Diese Bestimmung trägt der Möglichkeit statutarischer Nachschüsse in der GmbH-Rechnung (s. Art. 795 ff. E OR).

Vierter Abschnitt: Auflösung und Ausscheiden

A. Auflösung

I. Gründe

Art. 821

1 Die Gesellschaft mit beschränkter Haftung wird aufgelöst:

1. **wenn ein in den Statuten vorgesehener Auflösungsgrund eintritt;**
2. **wenn die Gesellschafterversammlung dies beschliesst;**
3. **wenn der Konkurs eröffnet wird;**
4. **in den übrigen vom Gesetz vorgesehenen Fällen.**

2 Beschliesst die Gesellschafterversammlung die Auflösung, so bedarf der Beschluss der öffentlichen Beurkundung.

3 Jeder Gesellschafter kann beim Gericht die Auflösung der Gesellschaft aus wichtigem Grund verlangen. Das Gericht kann statt auf Auflösung auf eine andere sachgemässe und den Beteiligten zumutbare Lösung erkennen, so insbesondere auf die Abfindung des klagenden Gesellschafters zum wirklichen Wert seiner Stammanteile.

Abs. 1 führt die verschiedenen Gründe auf, die zur Auflösung der Gesellschaft führen (im geltenden Recht Art. 820 OR):

- Die Statuten dürfen Sachverhalte vorsehen, welche die Auflösung der Gesellschaft zur Folge haben (*Ziff. 1*).

- Die Gesellschafterversammlung kann mit qualifizierter Mehrheit die Auflösung beschliessen (*Ziff. 2*; s. Art. 804 Abs. 2 Ziff. 16 und Art. 808*b* Abs. 1 Ziff. 10 E OR). Der Beschluss ist öffentlich zu beurkunden (*Abs. 2*).

- Die Eröffnung des Konkurses hat die Auflösung zur Folge (*Ziff. 3*).

- Vorbehalten bleiben weitere Fälle der Auflösung, soweit dafür eine gesetzliche Grundlage besteht (*Ziff. 4*), so insbesondere die Auflösung aus wichtigen Gründen (nachfolgend Abs. 3), die Auflösung wegen Mängeln in der Organisation (Art. 731*b* i.V.m. 819 E OR), die Auflösung wegen Verfolgung unsittlicher oder widerrechtlicher Zwecke (Art. 57 Abs. 3

ZGB) und die Tatbestände der Auflösung ohne Liquidation nach dem zukünftigen Fusionsgesetz[114].

Nach *Abs. 3* kann jede Gesellschafterin und jeder Gesellschafter wie schon im geltenden Recht (Art. 820 Ziff. 4 und Art. 822 Abs. 2 OR) beim Gericht die Auflösung der Gesellschaft aus wichtigem Grund verlangen. Neu wird dem Gericht in Anlehnung an das neue Aktienrecht (s. Art. 736 Ziff. 4 OR) die Möglichkeit eingeräumt, statt auf Auflösung auf eine andere sachgemässe und den Beteiligten zumutbare Lösung zu erkennen. Ein derartiger Handlungsspielraum erscheint im Hinblick auf die Folgen einer Auflösung der Gesellschaft für die Beteiligten und Dritte gerechtfertigt. Es soll dem Gericht ermöglicht werden, eine nach den Umständen angemessene Lösung zu erwirken, wobei den Interessen aller Betroffenen Rechnung zu tragen ist.

II. Folgen

Art. 821a

1 Für die Folgen der Auflösung sind die Vorschriften des Aktienrechts entsprechend anwendbar.

2 Die Auflösung einer Gesellschaft muss ins Handelsregister eingetragen werden. Die Auflösung durch Urteil ist vom Gericht dem Handelsregister unverzüglich zu melden. Die Auflösung aus anderen Gründen muss die Gesellschaft beim Handelsregister anmelden.

Für die Rechtsfolgen der Auflösung verweist *Abs. 1* auf die Vorschriften des Aktienrechts (s. Art. 738 OR). Unter Vorbehalt der Fälle der Fusion, der Aufspaltung sowie der Übertragung ihres Vermögens auf eine Körperschaft des öffentlichen Rechts tritt die Gesellschaft mit der Auflösung in Liquidation[115].

Nach *Abs. 2* muss die Auflösung ins Handelsregister eingetragen werden. Die Meldung oder Anmeldung beim Handelsregister erfolgt bei der Auflösung durch Urteil durch das Gericht, in allen andern Fällen durch die Gesellschaft.

---

114 s. Art. 3 Abs. 2 und 29 lit. a E FusG; BBl 2000 4533 und 4543.
115 So gemäss der Neufassung von Art. 738 im Anhang zum Fusionsgesetz; BBl **2000** 4494 und 4568.

B. Ausscheiden von Gesellschaftern

I. Austritt

Art. 822

1 Ein Gesellschafter kann aus wichtigem Grund beim Gericht auf Bewilligung des Austritts klagen.

2 Die Statuten können den Gesellschaftern ein Recht auf Austritt einräumen und dieses von bestimmten Bedingungen abhängig machen.

Abs. 1 sieht vor, dass eine Gesellschafterin oder ein Gesellschafter aus wichtigem Grund beim Gericht auf Bewilligung des Austritts klagen kann (im geltenden Recht Art. 822 Abs. 2 OR[116]). Während in der Aktiengesellschaft ein Ausscheiden grundsätzlich nur auf dem Weg der Übertragung der Aktien möglich ist, vermag die Abtretbarkeit der Stammanteile in der GmbH nicht zu genügen. Im Hinblick auf den engen Personenbezug der Gesellschafterstellung darf die Zulässigkeit der Abtretung durch die Statuten stark eingeschränkt oder ausgeschlossen werden (s. Art. 786 E OR). In Kleingesellschaften ist die Abtretung von Stammanteilen zudem meist auch faktisch schwierig, da der Kreis potentieller Erwerber eng begrenzt ist. Das Recht der GmbH sichert ein Ausscheiden aus wichtigen Gründen daher durch ein entsprechendes Austrittsrecht. Relevante wichtige Gründe können sowohl in der Sphäre der Gesellschaft als auch im persönlichen Bereich einer Gesellschafterin oder eines Gesellschafters vorliegen. Das Gericht hat bei seinem Entscheid den Interessen aller betroffenen Personen Rechnung zu tragen. Zu berücksichtigen ist auch, ob die Abtretung der Stammanteile aus rechtlichen oder faktischen Gründen erschwert ist.
Die Möglichkeit zum Austritt aus wichtigen Gründen darf durch die Statuten nicht eingeschränkt werden. *Abs. 2* erlaubt aber, den Gesellschafterinnen und Gesellschaftern in den Statuten ein weitergehendes Austrittsrecht einzuräumen und die Bedingungen dafür festzulegen (im geltenden Recht Art. 822 Abs. 1 OR). Der Austritt aus statutarischen Gründen erfolgt durch Erklärung an die Gesellschaft, es sei denn, die Statuten treffen eine andere Regelung.

---

116 Nun aOR.

Kapitel 1: Neue Gesetzesbestimmungen und Erläuterungen

II. Anschlussaustritt

Art. 822a

1 Reicht ein Gesellschafter eine Klage auf Austritt aus wichtigem Grund ein oder erklärt ein Gesellschafter seinen Austritt gestützt auf ein statutarisches Austrittsrecht, so müssen die Geschäftsführer unverzüglich die übrigen Gesellschafter informieren.

2 Falls andere Gesellschafter innerhalb von drei Monaten nach Zugang dieser Mitteilung auf Austritt aus wichtigem Grund klagen oder ein statutarisches Austrittsrecht ausüben, sind alle austretenden Gesellschafter im Verhältnis des Nennwerts ihrer Stammanteile gleich zu behandeln. Wurden Nachschüsse geleistet, so ist deren Betrag dem Nennwert zuzurechnen.

Wird eine Klage auf Austritt aus wichtigem Grund eingereicht oder ein statutarisches Austrittsrecht geltend gemacht, so müssen die Geschäftsführerinnen und Geschäftsführer die übrigen Gesellschafterinnen und Gesellschafter unverzüglich informieren (*Abs. 1*). Diese haben dann die Möglichkeit, sich die Gleichbehandlung mit der austretenden Gesellschafterin oder dem austretenden Gesellschafter zu sichern, wenn sie sich innerhalb von 3 Monaten dem Austritt anschliessen (*Abs. 2*). Eine Überlegungsfrist von 3 Monaten erscheint erforderlich, weil in kleineren Unternehmen die Beteiligung an der Gesellschaft häufig mit dem Arbeitserwerb der beteiligten Personen verbunden ist. Die vorliegende Regelung will die Gleichbehandlung mehrerer austretender Personen gewährleisten und zudem vermeiden, dass sich aus den Umständen ein gewisser Druck zum Austritt ergibt, weil ein möglichst rascher Austritt eine Privilegierung namentlich in Bezug auf die Ausbezahlung der Abfindung zur Folge haben könnte (vgl. Art. 825*a* E OR). Die Gleichbehandlung erfolgt im Verhältnis der Nennwerte der Stammanteile unter Einschluss bereits geleisteter Nachschüsse.

III. Ausschluss

Art. 823

1 Liegt ein wichtiger Grund vor, so kann die Gesellschaft beim Gericht auf Ausschluss eines Gesellschafters klagen.

2 Die Statuten können vorsehen, dass die Gesellschafterversammlung Gesellschafter aus der Gesellschaft ausschliessen darf, wenn bestimmte Gründe vorliegen.

3 Die Vorschriften über den Anschlussaustritt sind nicht anwendbar.

Nach *Abs. 1* kann die Gesellschaft beim Gericht auf Ausschluss einer Gesellschafterin oder eines Gesellschafters klagen, wenn dafür ein wichtiger Grund vorliegt. Diese Ausschlussmöglichkeit trägt den meist engen persönlichen Beziehungen in der GmbH Rechnung und bietet eine Lösung für Fälle, in denen das Zusammenwirken mit einer Gesellschafterin oder einem Gesellschafter unzumutbar geworden ist. Zur Klage legitimiert ist nur die Gesellschaft, nicht aber die Gesellschafterinnen und Gesellschafter. Die Anhebung der Klage setzt einen Beschluss der Gesellschafterversammlung voraus, der einer qualifizierten Mehrheit bedarf (Art. 804 Abs. 2 Ziff. 14 und Art. 808*b* Abs. 1 Ziff. 8 E OR).

Abs. 2 räumt die Möglichkeit ein, in den Statuten besondere Ausschlussgründe vorzusehen. Zum Schutze aller Beteiligten müssen die Gründe in den Statuten bestimmt umschrieben werden. Generalklauseln sind demnach nicht zulässig und unklare Formulierungen im Zweifelsfalle eng auszulegen. Liegt ein statutarisch genannter Grund vor, so entscheidet die Gesellschafterversammlung mit qualifizierter Mehrheit über den Ausschluss (Art. 804 Abs. 2 Ziff. 15 und Art. 808*b* Abs. 1 Ziff. 8 E OR; der Rechtsweg bleibt vorbehalten).

Abs. 3 stellt klar, dass die Vorschriften über den Anschlussaustritt (Art. 822*a* E OR) beim Ausschluss einer Gesellschafterin oder eines Gesellschafters nicht anwendbar sind. Ein analoges Verfahren erscheint nicht erforderlich: Das Ausscheiden erfolgt hier unfreiwillig, und die Information der übrigen Gesellschafterinnen und Gesellschafter ist ohnehin gewährleistet, weil der Ausschluss stets einen Beschluss der Gesellschafterversammlung voraussetzt.

Kapitel 1: Neue Gesetzesbestimmungen und Erläuterungen

IV. Vorsorgliche Massnahmen

Art. 824

In einem Verfahren betreffend das Ausscheiden eines Gesellschafters kann das Gericht auf Antrag einer Partei bestimmen, dass einzelne oder alle mitgliedschaftlichen Rechte und Pflichten der betroffenen Person ruhen.

Vorsorgliche Massnahmen sind im Allgemeinen Sache des kantonalen Zivilprozessrechts, zumindest was Massnahmen zur Aufrechterhaltung des bestehenden Zustandes betrifft (sog. Sicherungsmassnahmen). *Artikel 824* dient jedoch auch dazu, das Verhältnis des Gesellschafters zur Gesellschaft für die Dauer des Prozesses zu regeln (sog. Regelungsmassnahmen). Solche bedürfen nach herrschender Lehre und Rechtsprechung einer bundesrechtlichen Grundlage, die mit der vorliegenden Bestimmung geliefert wird. Mit Blick auf die Mitwirkungsrechte einerseits und verschiedene statutarische Pflichten andererseits (so insbes. Nachschusspflichten, Nebenleistungspflichten, Konkurrenzverbote) kann eine entsprechende vorsorgliche Massnahme sowohl zur Wahrung der Interessen der Gesellschaft als auch jeder der ausscheidenden Person erforderlich sein. Entsprechend den konkreten Umständen sollen sowohl einzelne Rechte oder Pflichten als auch deren Gesamtheit suspendiert werden können.

V. Abfindung

1. Anspruch und Höhe

Art. 825

1 Scheidet ein Gesellschafter aus der Gesellschaft aus, so hat er Anspruch auf eine Abfindung, die dem wirklichen Wert seiner Stammanteile entspricht.

2 Für das Ausscheiden auf Grund eines statutarischen Austrittsrechts können die Statuten die Abfindung abweichend festlegen.

Das geltende Recht bestimmt die Ansprüche ausscheidender Gesellschafterinnen und Gesellschafter nicht näher. Die Schliessung dieser Gesetzeslücke erscheint sowohl im Interesse der Rechtssicherheit als auch für den Rechtsschutz ausscheidender Personen dringend (vgl. Art. 822 Abs. 4 OR). Nach *Abs. 1* steht ausscheidenden Gesellschafterinnen und Gesellschaftern ein Anspruch auf eine Abfindung zu, die dem wirklichen Wert ihrer Stammanteile entspricht. Dieser Anspruch besteht nicht nur beim Austritt sowie beim Ausscheiden im Rahmen einer Klage auf Auflösung der Gesellschaft (vgl. Art. 821 Abs. 3 E OR), sondern ebenfalls beim Ausschluss aus wichtigen oder in den Statuten vorgesehenen Gründen. Dem Ausschluss darf keinerlei konfiskatorischer Charakter zukommen. Bei der Ausrichtung der Abfindung geht es ohne Rücksicht auf den Grund des Ausscheidens lediglich darum, den wirtschaftlichen Gegenwert einer aufzugebenden Beteiligung an der Gesellschaft zu vergüten.

Abs. 2 räumt die Möglichkeit ein, für statutarische Austrittsrechte in den Statuten eine vom wirklichen Wert der Stammanteile abweichende Abfindung festzulegen. Es soll insbesondere zulässig sein, einerseits die Voraussetzungen für einen Austritt herabzusetzen, dafür aber andererseits eine vom wirklichen Wert abweichende Abfindung vorzusehen. Der Raum für individuelle Gestaltungen bleibt freilich durch die relevanten allgemeinen Rechtsgrundsätze begrenzt. Die Abfindung darf demnach nicht willkürlich bemessen werden. Es ist aber beispielsweise möglich, aus Praktikabilitätsgründen auf den Steuerwert (kantonale Bewertung der Stammanteile für die Zwecke der Vermögenssteuer) oder auf den Substanzwert abzustellen. Es steht zudem offen, in den Statuten besondere Modalitäten der Abfindung vorzusehen; so kann die Ausrichtung der Abfindung gestaffelt oder an Stelle einer Barabfindung eine andere Art der Entschädigung bestimmt werden.

Ein entsprechender Freiraum zur Festsetzung der Abfindung wird nur für den Austritt, nicht aber für den Ausschluss vorgesehen, weil beim Ausschluss eine einvernehmliche Grundlage fehlt und statutarische Regelungen zu enteignungsähnlichen Tatbeständen führen könnten.

Kapitel 1: Neue Gesetzesbestimmungen und Erläuterungen

2. Auszahlung

Art. 825a

1 Die Abfindung wird mit dem Ausscheiden fällig, soweit die Gesellschaft:
1. **über verwendbares Eigenkapital verfügt;**
2. **die Stammanteile der ausscheidenden Person veräussern kann;**
3. **ihr Stammkapital unter Beachtung der entsprechenden Vorschriften herabsetzen darf.**

2 Ein zugelassener Revisionsexperte muss die Höhe des verwendbaren Eigenkapitals feststellen. Reicht dieses zur Auszahlung der Abfindung nicht aus, so muss er zudem zur Frage Stellung nehmen, wie weit das Stammkapital herabgesetzt werden könnte.

3 Für den nicht ausbezahlten Teil der Abfindung hat der ausgeschiedene Gesellschafter eine unverzinsliche nachrangige Forderung. Diese wird fällig, soweit im jährlichen Geschäftsbericht verwendbares Eigenkapital festgestellt wird.

4 Solange die Abfindung nicht vollständig ausgezahlt ist, kann der ausgeschiedene Gesellschafter verlangen, dass die Gesellschaft eine Revisionsstelle bezeichnet und die Jahresrechnung ordentlich revidieren lässt.

Die Regelung der Auszahlung macht deutlich, wie ausserordentlich komplex sich das Ausscheiden einzelner Gesellschafterinnen und Gesellschafter aus einer Kapitalgesellschaft gestaltet. Es gilt dabei eine Schädigung der Gläubigerinnen und Gläubiger auszuschliessen und die Interessen der Gesellschaft sowie der ausscheidenden und der verbleibenden Gesellschafterinnen und Gesellschafter gegeneinander abzugrenzen.

Abs. 1 regelt die Fälligkeit der Abfindung:

- Die Abfindung wird grundsätzlich mit dem Ausscheiden einer Gesellschafterin oder eines Gesellschafters fällig, aber nur soweit die Gesellschaft über verwendbares Eigenkapital verfügt (*Ziff. 1*). Im Rahmen der Vorschriften zum Erwerb eigener Stammanteile steht es der Gesellschaft offen, die Anteile der ausscheidenden Person bis zur

Höchstgrenze von 35% des Stammkapitals zu übernehmen. Anders als bei den Voraussetzungen für den Erwerb eigener Stammanteile (s. Art. 783 Abs. 1 E OR) wird für die Fälligkeit der Abfindung nicht auf «frei verwendbares Eigenkapital» abgestellt, sondern auf «verwendbares Eigenkapital»: Für die Auszahlung der Abfindung sollen alle über das Stammkapital, die Reserve für eigene Stammanteile, gegebenenfalls die Aufwertungsreserve und den gesperrten Teil der Allgemeinen Reserven hinausgehenden Teile des Eigenkapitals verwendet werden können. Für besondere Zwecke vorgesehene Reserven – wie insbesondere Dividenden- und Wiederbeschaffungsreserven – sind demnach für die Auszahlung von Abfindungen heranzuziehen, obschon es sich dabei um Eigenkapital handelt, das nicht frei verwendbar ist. Auf diese Weise wird vermieden, dass die Auszahlung einer Abfindung durch die Bildung besonderer Reserven vereitelt werden kann.

– Nach *Ziff. 2* wird die Abfindung fällig, soweit die Gesellschaft die Stammanteile der ausscheidenden Person veräussern kann. Diese Regelung schliesst eine Berufung auf die Möglichkeit der Verweigerung der Zustimmung zur Abtretung von Stammanteilen ohne Angabe von Gründen (vgl. Art. 786 E OR) sachlich aus. Die Gelegenheit zur Veräusserung der Stammanteile bewirkt ohne weiteres die Fälligkeit der Abfindung.

– Nach *Ziff. 3* wird die Abfindung fällig, soweit die Gesellschaft ihr Stammkapital unter Beachtung der gesetzlichen Vorschriften herabsetzen darf (vgl. Art. 782 E OR).

Der Entscheid darüber, ob für die Auszahlung der Abfindung genügend verwendbares Eigenkapital vorhanden ist, kann nicht den Geschäftsführerinnen und Geschäftsführern bzw. den Gesellschafterinnen und Gesellschaftern allein überlassen bleiben; nach *Abs. 2* muss daher eine besonders befähigte Revisorin oder ein besonders befähigter Revisor die Höhe des verwendbaren Eigenkapitals feststellen (vgl. Abs. 1 Ziff. 1). Reicht dieses zur Auszahlung der Abfindung nicht aus, so muss die Revisorin oder der Revisor zudem zur Frage Stellung nehmen, wie weit das Stammkapital unter Beachtung der gesetzlichen Vorschriften herabgesetzt werden darf (vgl. Abs. 1 Ziff. 3; das Erfordernis einer besonders befähigten Revisorin oder eines besonders befähigten Revisors entspricht Art. 732 Abs. 2 i.V.m. 782 Abs. 4 E OR).

Falls die Abfindung im Zeitpunkt des Ausscheidens nicht vollständig ausbezahlt wird, steht der ausgeschiedenen Gesellschafterin oder dem ausgeschiedenen Gesellschafter nach *Abs. 3* eine unverzinsliche nachrangige Forderung in der Höhe des nicht ausbezahlten Teils zu. Das Guthaben für die Abfindung soll den übrigen Forderungen im Rang nachgehen, weil es sich um die Rückleistung einer Beteiligung am Eigenkapital handelt.

Der nicht ausbezahlte Teil der Abfindung wird fällig, soweit im jährlichen Geschäftsbericht verwendbares Eigenkapital (vgl. dazu die Ausführungen zu Abs. 1 Ziff. 1) festgestellt wird. Die Ausrichtung einer geschuldeten Abfindung geht somit der Ausschüttung von Dividenden vor. Dadurch wird ein gewisser Druck für eine rasche Abwicklung des Ausscheidens geschaffen. Es ist zudem dem Umstand Rechnung zu tragen, dass die Abfindung nicht verzinst werden muss.

So lange ihre Abfindung noch nicht vollständig ausbezahlt ist, können ausgeschiedene Gesellschafterinnen und Gesellschafter nach *Abs. 4* verlangen, dass die Gesellschaft eine Revisionsstelle bezeichnen muss. Diese optionale Revisionspflicht dient dazu, die Zuverlässigkeit des Geschäftsberichts im Hinblick auf die Regelung von *Abs. 3* zu gewährleisten.

In steuerlicher Hinsicht ist der durch die GmbH abzugeltende Abfindungsanspruch sowohl bei der direkten Bundessteuer als auch bei der Verrechnungssteuer Beteiligungsertrag.

Gemäss dem Entwurf zur Revision des GmbH-Rechts regelt Artikel 825*a* E OR die Auszahlung der Abfindung einer ausscheidenden Gesellschafterin oder eines ausscheidenden Gesellschafters[117]. Die Neuregelung der Revisionsstelle bedingt in dieser Bestimmung zwei redaktionelle Modifikationen:
In *Abs. 2* muss der Begriff der besonders befähigten Revisorin bzw. des besonders befähigten Revisors durch jenen der zugelassenen Revisionsexpertin bzw. des zugelassenen Revisionsexperten ersetzt werden (vgl. dazu die Erläuterungen zu Art. 4 E RAG).

In *Abs. 4* ist klarzustellen, welcher Art (eingeschränkt oder ordentlich) die verlangte Revision ist: Solange eine fällige Abfindung nicht vollständig ausbezahlt ist, kann eine ausgeschiedene Gesellschafterin bzw. ein ausgeschiedener Gesellschafter zu ihrem oder seinem Schutz verlangen, dass die Gesellschaft eine Revisionsstelle bezeichnet. Der neue Abs. 4 verlangt unter Berücksichtigung der Interessen der Betroffenen eine ordentliche Revision. Dies entspricht auch dem Entwurf zur Revision des GmbH-

---

117 BBl **2002** 3223 f., 3287.

Rechts, der den Begriff der Revision stets für eine ordentliche Revision verwendet.

C. Liquidation

Art. 826

1 Jeder Gesellschafter hat Anspruch auf einen Anteil am Liquidationsergebnis, der dem Verhältnis der Nennwerte der Stammanteile entspricht. Wurden Nachschüsse geleistet, so ist deren Betrag dem Nennwert zuzurechnen; die Statuten können eine abweichende Regelung vorsehen.

2 Für die Auflösung der Gesellschaft mit Liquidation sind die Vorschriften des Aktienrechts entsprechend anwendbar.

Abs. 1 räumt jeder Gesellschafterin und jedem Gesellschafter einen Anspruch auf einen Anteil am Liquidationsergebnis ein. Die Aufteilung erfolgt im Verhältnis der Nennwerte der Stammanteile, wobei geleistete Nachschüsse dem Nennwert zuzurechnen sind. Die Regelung der Aufteilung ist dispositiver Natur: Die Statuten können auf die Berücksichtigung geleisteter Nachschüsse verzichten oder so genannte Vorzugsstammanteile vorsehen, die Vorrechte betreffend den Liquidationsanteil vermitteln (Art. 776a Abs. 1 Ziff. 5 und 799 E OR sowie Art. 654 und 656 OR). Für die Auflösung der Gesellschaft mit Liquidation finden nach *Abs. 2* im Übrigen die Vorschriften des Aktienrechts entsprechende Anwendung (s. Art. 739 ff. OR).

Fünfter Abschnitt: Verantwortlichkeit

Art. 827

Für die Verantwortlichkeit der Personen, die bei der Gründung mitwirken oder mit der Geschäftsführung, der Revision oder der Liquidation befasst sind, sind die Vorschriften des Aktienrechts entsprechend anwendbar.

Kapitel 1: Neue Gesetzesbestimmungen und Erläuterungen

Für die Verantwortlichkeit von Personen, die bei der Gründung mitwirken oder mit der Geschäftsführung, der Revision oder der Liquidation befasst sind, wird (wie bisher) auf die entsprechenden Bestimmungen des Aktienrechts verwiesen. Für die Verantwortlichkeit soll auch in der GmbH ein materieller Organbegriff massgebend sein. Eine Verweisung auf die Haftung für den Emissionsprospekt fehlt (vgl. Art. 752 OR), da in der GmbH ein öffentliches Angebot zur Zeichnung der Stammanteile nicht möglich ist (s. Art. 781 Abs. 3 E OR).

§ 3 Das Recht der Genossenschaft

Erster Abschnitt: Begriff und Errichtung

A. Genossenschaft des Obligationenrechts

Art. 828

1 Die Genossenschaft ist eine als Körperschaft organisierte Verbindung einer nicht geschlossenen Zahl von Personen oder Handelsgesellschaften, die in der Hauptsache die Förderung oder Sicherung bestimmter wirtschaftlicher Interessen ihrer Mitglieder in gemeinsamer Selbsthilfe bezweckt.

2 Genossenschaften mit einem zum voraus festgesetzten Grundkapital sind unzulässig.

B. Genossenschaften des öffentlichen Rechts

Art. 829

Öffentlich-rechtliche Personenverbände stehen, auch wenn sie genossenschaftlichen Zwecken dienen, unter dem öffentlichen Recht des Bundes und der Kantone.

C. Errichtung

I. Erfordernisse

1. Im Allgemeinen

Art. 830

Die Genossenschaft entsteht nach Aufstellung der Statuten und deren Genehmigung in der konstituierenden Versammlung durch Eintragung in das Handelsregister.

2. Zahl der Mitglieder

Art. 831

1 Bei der Gründung einer Genossenschaft müssen mindestens sieben Mitglieder beteiligt sein.

2 Sinkt in der Folge die Zahl der Genossenschafter unter diese Mindestzahl, so sind die Vorschriften des Aktienrechts über Mängel in der Organisation der Gesellschaft entsprechend anwendbar.

Kennzeichnend für die Rechtsform der Genossenschaft ist die Förderung wirtschaftlicher Interessen ihrer Mitglieder in gemeinsamer Selbsthilfe (s. Art. 828 Abs. 1 OR)[118, 119]. Der Zweck der gemeinsamen Selbsthilfe setzt jedoch wesensnotwendigerweise eine Mehrzahl von Personen voraus. Anders als in der GmbH und in der Aktiengesellschaft (s. die Ausführungen zu Art. 625 und 775 E OR) erscheinen die Gründung und der Bestand von Einpersonenunternehmen als Genossenschaften demzufolge nicht sachgerecht. Von der Zulassung von Einpersonen-Genossenschaften ist daher abzusehen.

---

118 Dazu statt vieler PETER FORSTMOSER, in: Berner Kommentar VII/4, Bern 1972, Art. 828 N 93 ff. und Art. 831 N 26.
119 Vorbehalten bleibt die Genossenschaft mit gemeinnützigem Zweck gemäss Art. 92 Abs. 2 HRegV. Für gemeinnützige Ziele stehen aber auch andere Rechtsformen zur Verfügung.

Die vorliegende Bestimmung muss aber der Neuregelung für die Behebung von Mängeln in der Organisation angepasst werden (s. Art. 731*b* i.V.m. 910*a* E OR). Die Durchsetzung einer Personenmehrheit ist im Hinblick auf den bewusst beschränkten Verwendungszweck der Rechtsform der Genossenschaft unabdingbar.

II. Statuten

1. Gesetzlich vorgeschriebener Inhalt

Art. 832

Die Statuten müssen Bestimmungen enthalten über:

1. **den Namen (die Firma) und den Sitz der Genossenschaft;**
2. **den Zweck der Genossenschaft;**
3. **eine allfällige Verpflichtung der Genossenschafter zu Geld- oder andern Leistungen sowie deren Art und Höhe;**
4. **die Organe für die Verwaltung und für die Kontrolle und die Art der Ausübung der Vertretung;**
5. **die Form der von der Genossenschaft ausgehenden Bekanntmachungen.**

2. Weitere Bestimmungen

Art. 833

Zu ihrer Verbindlichkeit bedürfen der Aufnahme in die Statuten:

1. **Vorschriften über die Schaffung eines Genossenschaftskapitals durch Genossenschaftsanteile (Anteilscheine);**
2. **Bestimmungen über nicht durch Einzahlung geleistete Einlagen auf das Genossenschaftskapital (Sacheinlagen), deren Gegenstand und deren Anrechnungsbetrag, sowie über die Person des einlegenden Genossenschafters;**

3. Bestimmungen über Vermögenswerte, die bei der Gründung übernommen werden, über die hiefür zu leistende Vergütung und über die Person des Eigentümers der zu übernehmenden Vermögenswerte;
4. von den gesetzlichen Bestimmungen abweichende Vorschriften über den Eintritt in die Genossenschaft und über den Verlust der Mitgliedschaft;
5. Bestimmungen über die persönliche Haftung und die Nachschusspflicht der Genossenschafter;
6. von den gesetzlichen Bestimmungen abweichende Vorschriften über die Organisation, die Vertretung, die Abänderung der Statuten und über die Beschlussfassung der Generalversammlung;
7. Beschränkungen und Erweiterungen in der Ausübung des Stimmrechtes;
8. Bestimmungen über die Berechnung und die Verwendung des Reinertrages und des Liquidationsüberschusses.

III. Konstituierende Versammlung

Art. 834

1 Die Statuten sind schriftlich abzufassen und einer von den Gründern einzuberufenden Versammlung zur Beratung und Genehmigung vorzulegen.

2 Überdies ist ein schriftlicher Bericht der Gründer über allfällige Sacheinlagen und zu übernehmenden Vermögenswerte der Versammlung bekanntzugeben und von ihr zu beraten.

3 Diese Versammlung bestellt auch die notwendigen Organe.

4 Bis zur Eintragung der Genossenschaft in das Handelsregister kann die Mitgliedschaft nur durch Unterzeichnung der Statuten begründet werden.

IV. Eintragung ins Handelsregister

1. Gesellschaft

Art. 835

Die Gesellschaft ist ins Handelsregister des Ortes einzutragen, an dem sie ihren Sitz hat.

Neben dem Grundsatz der Eintragung der Genossenschaft ins Handelsregister (Abs. 1) regelt das geltende Recht in dieser Bestimmung auch die Anmeldung beim Handelsregister, deren Unterzeichnung (Abs. 3 und 4) sowie die Anmeldung der Mitglieder der Verwaltung und der Personen, welche die Genossenschaft vertreten (Abs. 2). Der Entwurf sieht dazu eine einheitliche Regelung für alle Rechtsformen vor, wobei eine Teilnormierung auf Verordnungsstufe ermöglicht wird (s. Art. 929 Abs. 1 und 931*a* E OR sowie die Ausführungen zu diesen Bestimmungen). Die bisherigen *Abs. 2 bis 4* können daher gestrichen werden.

2. Zweigniederlassungen

Art. 836

Zweigniederlassungen sind unter Bezugnahme auf die Eintragung der Hauptniederlassung ins Handelsregister des Ortes einzutragen, an dem sie sich befinden.

Im geltenden Recht regelt die vorliegende Bestimmung den Inhalt der Eintragung im Handelsregister, die Veröffentlichung eines Auszugs dieser Eintragung im Schweizerischen Handelsamtsblatt sowie die Einsichtnahme in das Verzeichnis der Genossenschafterinnen und Genossenschafter. Die Regelung des Inhalts der Eintragung wird vom Entwurf für alle Rechtsformen in die Handelsregisterverordnung verwiesen (s. Art. 929 Abs. 1 E OR). Die heutige Anordnung einer bloss teilweisen Veröffentlichung der Eintragung weicht ohne überzeugenden Grund von den Vorschriften für andere Rechtsformen ab (vgl. Art. 931 OR) und hat sich als nicht praxisgerecht herausgestellt; der Entwurf verzichtet daher auf eine Sonderregelung. Das Verzeichnis der Genossenschafterinnen und

Genossenschafter wird neu in der nachfolgenden Bestimmung vorgesehen (s. Art. 837 E OR).

Da der bisherige Inhalt entfällt, wird im vorliegenden Artikel die Eintragung von Zweigniederlassungen geregelt (bisher Art. 837 OR). Die Regelung der Anmeldung (bisher Art. 837 Abs. 2 OR) erfolgt neu für alle Rechtsformen im Handelsregisterrecht (s. Art. 929 und 931*a* sowie Art. 778*a* E OR).

3. Verzeichnis der Genossenschafter

Art. 837

Genossenschaften, deren Statuten eine persönliche Haftung oder Nachschusspflicht vorsehen, müssen dem Handelsregisteramt ein Verzeichnis der Genossenschafter einreichen. Dieses wird nicht ins Handelsregister eingetragen, steht jedoch zur Einsicht offen.

Wie bisher (s. Art. 836 Abs. 3 OR) haben Genossenschaften dem Handelsregisteramt ein Verzeichnis der Genossenschafterinnen und Genossenschafter einzureichen, sofern die Statuten eine persönliche Haftung oder Nachschusspflicht vorsehen. Dieses wird nicht ins Handelsregister eingetragen, steht aber weiterhin zur Einsicht offen.

V. Erwerb der Persönlichkeit

Art. 838

1 Die Genossenschaft erlangt das Recht der Persönlichkeit erst durch die Eintragung in das Handelsregister.

2 Ist vor der Eintragung im Namen der Genossenschaft gehandelt worden, so haften die Handelnden persönlich und solidarisch.

3 Wurden solche Verpflichtungen ausdrücklich im Namen der zu bildenden Genossenschaft eingegangen und innerhalb einer Frist von drei Monaten nach der Eintragung in das Handelsregister von der Genossenschaft übernommen, so werden die Handelnden befreit, und es haftet die Genossenschaft.

Kapitel 1: Neue Gesetzesbestimmungen und Erläuterungen

Zweiter Abschnitt: Erwerb der Mitgliedschaft

A. Grundsatz

Art. 839

1 In eine Genossenschaft können jederzeit neue Mitglieder aufgenommen werden.

2 Die Statuten können unter Wahrung des Grundsatzes der nicht geschlossenen Mitgliederzahl die nähern Bestimmungen über den Eintritt treffen; sie dürfen jedoch den Eintritt nicht übermässig erschweren.

B. Beitrittserklärung

Art. 840

1 Zum Beitritt bedarf es einer schriftlichen Erklärung.

2 Besteht bei einer Genossenschaft neben der Haftung des Genossenschaftsvermögens eine persönliche Haftung oder eine Nachschusspflicht der einzelnen Genossenschafter, so muss die Beitrittserklärung diese Verpflichtungen ausdrücklich enthalten.

3 Über die Aufnahme neuer Mitglieder entscheidet die Verwaltung, soweit nicht nach den Statuten die blosse Beitrittserklärung genügt oder ein Beschluss der Generalversammlung nötig ist.

C. Verbindung mit einem Versicherungsvertrag

Art. 841

1 Ist die Zugehörigkeit zur Genossenschaft mit einem Versicherungsvertrag bei dieser Genossenschaft verknüpft, so wird die Mitgliedschaft erworben mit der Annahme des Versicherungsantrages durch das zuständige Organ.

689

² Die von einer konzessionierten Versicherungsgenossenschaft mit den Mitgliedern abgeschlossenen Versicherungsverträge unterstehen in gleicher Weise wie die von ihr mit Dritten abgeschlossenen Versicherungsverträge den Bestimmungen des Bundesgesetzes vom 2. April 1908[120] über den Versicherungsvertrag.

Dritter Abschnitt: Verlust der Mitgliedschaft

A. Austritt

I. Freiheit des Austrittes

Art. 842

¹ Solange die Auflösung der Genossenschaft nicht beschlossen ist, steht jedem Genossenschafter der Austritt frei.

² Die Statuten können vorschreiben, dass der Austretende zur Bezahlung einer angemessenen Auslösungssumme verpflichtet ist, wenn nach den Umständen durch den Austritt der Genossenschaft ein erheblicher Schaden erwächst oder deren Fortbestand gefährdet wird.

³ Ein dauerndes Verbot oder eine übermässige Erschwerung des Austrittes durch die Statuten oder durch Vertrag sind ungültig.

II. Beschränkung des Austrittes

Art. 843

¹ Der Austritt kann durch die Statuten oder durch Vertrag auf höchstens fünf Jahre ausgeschlossen werden.

² Auch während dieser Frist kann aus wichtigen Gründen der Austritt erklärt werden. Die Pflicht zur Bezahlung einer angemessenen

---

120 SR **221.229.1**

Auslösungssumme unter den für den freien Austritt vorgesehenen Voraussetzungen bleibt vorbehalten.

III. Kündigungsfrist und Zeitpunkt des Austrittes

Art. 844

1 Der Austritt kann nur auf Schluss des Geschäftsjahres und unter Beobachtung einer einjährigen Kündigungsfrist stattfinden.

2 Den Statuten bleibt vorbehalten, eine kürzere Kündigungsfrist vorzuschreiben und den Austritt auch im Laufe des Geschäftsjahres zu gestatten.

IV. Geltendmachung im Konkurs und bei Pfändung

Art. 845

Falls die Statuten dem ausscheidenden Mitglied einen Anteil am Vermögen der Genossenschaft gewähren, kann ein dem Genossenschafter zustehendes Austrittsrecht in dessen Konkurse von der Konkursverwaltung oder, wenn dieser Anteil gepfändet wird, vom Betreibungsamt geltend gemacht werden.

B. Ausschliessung

Art. 846

1 Die Statuten können die Gründe bestimmen, aus denen ein Genossenschafter ausgeschlossen werden darf.

2 Überdies kann er jederzeit aus wichtigen Gründen ausgeschlossen werden.

3 Über die Ausschliessung entscheidet die Generalversammlung. Die Statuten können die Verwaltung als zuständig erklären, wobei dem Ausgeschlossenen ein Rekursrecht an die Generalversammlung zusteht. Dem Ausgeschlossenen steht innerhalb drei Monaten die Anrufung des Richters offen.

4 Das ausgeschlossene Mitglied kann unter den für den freien Austritt aufgestellten Voraussetzungen zur Entrichtung einer Auslösungssumme verhalten werden.

C. Tod des Genossenschafters

Art. 847

1 Die Mitgliedschaft erlischt mit dem Tode des Genossenschafters.

2 Die Statuten können jedoch bestimmen, dass die Erben ohne weiteres Mitglieder der Genossenschaft sind.

3 Die Statuten können ferner bestimmen, dass die Erben oder einer unter mehreren Erben auf schriftliches Begehren an Stelle des verstorbenen Genossenschafters als Mitglied anerkannt werden müssen.

4 Die Erbengemeinschaft hat für die Beteiligung an der Genossenschaft einen gemeinsamen Vertreter zu bestellen.

D. Wegfall einer Beamtung oder Anstellung oder eines Vertrages

Art. 848

Ist die Zugehörigkeit zu einer Genossenschaft mit einer Beamtung oder Anstellung verknüpft oder die Folge eines Vertragsverhältnisses, wie bei einer Versicherungsgenossenschaft, so fällt die Mitgliedschaft, sofern die Statuten es nicht anders ordnen, mit dem Aufhören der Beamtung oder Anstellung oder des Vertrages dahin.

Kapitel 1: Neue Gesetzesbestimmungen und Erläuterungen

E. Übertragung der Mitgliedschaft
I. Im Allgemeinen

Art. 849

1 Die Abtretung der Genossenschaftsanteile und, wenn über die Mitgliedschaft oder den Genossenschaftsanteil eine Urkunde ausgestellt worden ist, die Übertragung dieser Urkunde machen den Erwerber nicht ohne weiteres zum Genossenschafter. Der Erwerber wird erst durch einen dem Gesetz und den Statuten entsprechenden Aufnahmebeschluss Genossenschafter.

2 Solange der Erwerber nicht als Genossenschafter aufgenommen ist, steht die Ausübung der persönlichen Mitgliedschaftsrechte dem Veräusserer zu.

3 Ist die Zugehörigkeit zu einer Genossenschaft mit einem Vertrage verknüpft, so können die Statuten bestimmen, dass die Mitgliedschaft mit der Übernahme des Vertrages ohne weiteres auf den Rechtsnachfolger übergeht.

II. Durch Übertragung von Grundstücken oder wirtschaftlichen Betrieben

Art. 850

1 Die Mitgliedschaft bei einer Genossenschaft kann durch die Statuten vom Eigentum an einem Grundstück oder vom wirtschaftlichen Betrieb eines solchen abhängig gemacht werden.

2 Die Statuten können für solche Fälle vorschreiben, dass mit der Veräusserung des Grundstückes oder mit der Übernahme des wirtschaftlichen Betriebes die Mitgliedschaft ohne weiteres auf den Erwerber oder den Übernehmer übergeht.

3 Die Bestimmung betreffend den Übergang der Mitgliedschaft bei Veräusserung des Grundstückes bedarf zu ihrer Gültigkeit gegenüber Dritten der Vormerkung im Grundbuche.

Teil F: Rechtliche Aspekte / Legal aspects

F. Austritt des Rechtsnachfolgers

Art. 851

Bei Übertragung und Vererbung der Mitgliedschaft gelten für den Rechtsnachfolger die gleichen Austrittsbedingungen wie für das frühere Mitglied.

Vierter Abschnitt: Rechte und Pflichten der Genossenschafter

A. Ausweis der Mitgliedschaft

Art. 852

1 Die Statuten können vorschreiben, dass für den Ausweis der Mitgliedschaft eine Urkunde ausgestellt wird.

2 Dieser Ausweis kann auch im Anteilschein enthalten sein.

B. Genossenschaftsanteile

Art. 853

1 Bestehen bei einer Genossenschaft Anteilscheine, so hat jeder der Genossenschaft Beitretende mindestens einen Anteilschein zu übernehmen.

2 Die Statuten können bestimmen, dass bis zu einer bestimmten Höchstzahl mehrere Anteilscheine erworben werden dürfen.

3 Die Anteilscheine werden auf den Namen des Mitgliedes ausgestellt. Sie können aber nicht als Wertpapiere, sondern nur als Beweisurkunden errichtet werden.

Kapitel 1: Neue Gesetzesbestimmungen und Erläuterungen

C. Rechtsgleichheit

Art. 854

Die Genossenschafter stehen in gleichen Rechten und Pflichten, soweit sich aus dem Gesetz nicht eine Ausnahme ergibt.

D. Rechte
I. Stimmrecht

Art. 855

Die Rechte, die den Genossenschaftern in den Angelegenheiten der Genossenschaft, insbesondere in Bezug auf die Führung der genossenschaftlichen Geschäfte und die Förderung der Genossenschaft zustehen, werden durch die Teilnahme an der Generalversammlung oder in den vom Gesetz vorgesehenen Fällen durch schriftliche Stimmabgabe (Urabstimmung) ausgeübt.

II. Kontrollrecht der Genossenschafter
1. Bekanntgabe der Bilanz

Art. 856

1 Spätestens zehn Tage vor der Generalversammlung oder der Urabstimmung, die über die Abnahme der Betriebsrechnung und der Bilanz zu entscheiden hat, sind die Betriebsrechnung und die Bilanz mit dem Revisionsbericht zur Einsicht der Genossenschafter am Sitz der Genossenschaft aufzulegen.

2 Die Statuten können bestimmen, dass jeder Genossenschafter berechtigt ist, auf Kosten der Genossenschaft eine Abschrift der Betriebsrechnung und der Bilanz zu verlangen.

2. Auskunfterteilung

Art. 857

1 Die Genossenschafter können die Revisionsstelle auf zweifelhafte Ansätze aufmerksam machen und die erforderlichen Aufschlüsse verlangen.

2 Eine Einsichtnahme in die Geschäftsbücher und Korrespondenzen ist nur mit ausdrücklicher Ermächtigung der Generalversammlung oder durch Beschluss der Verwaltung und unter Wahrung des Geschäftsgeheimnisses gestattet.

3 Der Richter kann verfügen, dass die Genossenschaft dem Genossenschafter über bestimmte, für die Ausübung des Kontrollrechts erhebliche Tatsachen durch beglaubigte Abschrift aus ihren Geschäftsbüchern oder von Korrespondenzen Auskunft zu erteilen hat. Durch diese Verfügung dürfen die Interessen der Genossenschaft nicht gefährdet werden.

4 Das Kontrollrecht der Genossenschafter kann weder durch die Statuten noch durch Beschlüsse eines Genossenschaftsorgans aufgehoben oder beschränkt werden.

Aus Gründen einer einheitlichen Terminologie wird die Kontrollstelle der Genossenschaft neu als «Revisionsstelle» bezeichnet. Siehe dazu auch die Ausführungen zu Art. 906 OR.

III. Allfällige Rechte auf den Reinertrag

1. Feststellung des Reinertrages

Art. 858

1 Die Berechnung des Reinertrages erfolgt auf Grund der Jahresbilanz, die nach den Vorschriften über die kaufmännische Buchführung zu erstellen ist.

2 Kreditgenossenschaften und konzessionierte Versicherungsgenossenschaften stehen unter den für die Aktiengesellschaft geltenden Bilanzvorschriften.

2. Verteilungsgrundsätze

Art. 859

1 Ein Reinertrag aus dem Betriebe der Genossenschaft fällt, wenn die Statuten es nicht anders bestimmen, in seinem ganzen Umfange in das Genossenschaftsvermögen.

2 Ist eine Verteilung des Reinertrages unter die Genossenschafter vorgesehen, so erfolgt sie, soweit die Statuten es nicht anders ordnen, nach dem Masse der Benützung der genossenschaftlichen Einrichtungen durch die einzelnen Mitglieder.

3 Bestehen Anteilscheine, so darf die auf sie entfallende Quote des Reinertrages den landesüblichen Zinsfuss für langfristige Darlehen ohne besondere Sicherheiten nicht übersteigen.

3. Pflicht zur Bildung und Äufnung eines Reservefonds

Art. 860

1 Soweit der Reinertrag in anderer Weise als zur Äufnung des Genossenschaftsvermögens verwendet wird, ist davon jährlich ein Zwanzigstel einem Reservefonds zuzuweisen. Diese Zuweisung hat während mindestens 20 Jahren zu erfolgen; wenn Anteilscheine bestehen, hat die Zuweisung auf alle Fälle so lange zu erfolgen, bis der Reservefonds einen Fünftel des Genossenschaftskapitals ausmacht.

2 Durch die Statuten kann eine weitergehende Äufnung des Reservefonds vorgeschrieben werden.

3 Soweit der Reservefonds die Hälfte des übrigen Genossenschaftsvermögens oder, wenn Anteilscheine bestehen, die Hälfte des Genossenschaftskapitals nicht übersteigt, darf er nur zur Deckung von

Verlusten oder zu Massnahmen verwendet werden, die geeignet sind, in Zeiten schlechten Geschäftsganges die Erreichung des Genossenschaftszweckes sicherzustellen.

4. Reinertrag bei Kreditgenossenschaften

Art. 861

1 Kreditgenossenschaften können in den Statuten von den Bestimmungen der vorstehenden Artikel abweichende Vorschriften über die Verteilung des Reinertrages erlassen, doch sind auch sie gehalten, einen Reservefonds zu bilden und den vorstehenden Bestimmungen gemäss zu verwenden.

2 Dem Reservefonds ist alljährlich mindestens ein Zehntel des Reinertrages zuzuweisen, bis der Fonds die Höhe von einem Zehntel des Genossenschaftskapitals erreicht hat.

3 Wird auf die Genossenschaftsanteile eine Quote des Reinertrages verteilt, die den landesüblichen Zinsfuss für langfristige Darlehen ohne besondere Sicherheiten übersteigt, so ist von dem diesen Zinsfuss übersteigenden Betrag ein Zehntel ebenfalls dem Reservefonds zuzuweisen.

5. Fonds zu Wohlfahrtszwecken

Art. 862

1 Die Statuten können insbesondere auch Fonds zur Gründung und Unterstützung von Wohlfahrtseinrichtungen für Angestellte und Arbeiter des Unternehmens sowie für Genossenschafter vorsehen.
2–4 ...[121]

---

[121] Aufgehoben durch Ziff. I lit. *b* des BG vom 21. März 1958 (AS **1958** 379; BBl **1956** II 825).

6. Weitere Reserveanlagen

Art. 863

¹ Die dem Gesetz und den Statuten entsprechenden Einlagen in Reserve- und andere Fonds sind in erster Linie von dem zur Verteilung gelangenden Reinertrag in Abzug zu bringen.

² Soweit die Rücksicht auf das dauernde Gedeihen des Unternehmens es als angezeigt erscheinen lässt, kann die Generalversammlung auch solche Reserveanlagen beschliessen, die im Gesetz oder in den Statuten nicht vorgesehen sind oder über deren Anforderungen hinausgehen.

³ In gleicher Weise können zum Zwecke der Gründung und Unterstützung von Wohlfahrtseinrichtungen für Angestellte, Arbeiter und Genossenschafter sowie zu andern Wohlfahrtszwecken Beiträge aus dem Reinertrag auch dann ausgeschieden werden, wenn sie in den Statuten nicht vorgesehen sind; solche Beitrage stehen unter den Bestimmungen über die statutarischen Wohlfahrtsfonds.

IV. Abfindungsanspruch

1. Nach Massgabe der Statuten

Art. 864

¹ Die Statuten bestimmen, ob und welche Ansprüche an das Genossenschaftsvermögen den ausscheidenden Genossenschaftern oder deren Erben zustehen. Diese Ansprüche sind auf Grund des bilanzmässigen Reinvermögens im Zeitpunkt des Ausscheidens mit Ausschluss der Reserven zu berechnen.

² Die Statuten können dem Ausscheidenden oder seinen Erben ein Recht auf gänzliche oder teilweise Rückzahlung der Anteilscheine mit Ausschluss des Eintrittsgeldes zuerkennen. Sie können die Hinausschiebung der Rückzahlung bis auf die Dauer von drei Jahren nach dem Ausscheiden vorsehen.

3 Die Genossenschaft bleibt indessen auch ohne statutarische Bestimmung hierüber berechtigt, die Rückzahlung bis auf drei Jahre hinauszuschieben, sofern ihr durch diese Zahlung ein erheblicher Schaden erwachsen oder ihr Fortbestand gefährdet würde. Ein allfälliger Anspruch der Genossenschaft auf Bezahlung einer angemessenen Auslösungssumme wird durch diese Bestimmung nicht berührt.

4 Die Ansprüche des Ausscheidenden oder seiner Erben verjähren in drei Jahren vom Zeitpunkt an gerechnet, auf den die Auszahlung verlangt werden kann.

2. Nach Gesetz

Art. 865

1 Enthalten die Statuten keine Bestimmung über einen Abfindungsanspruch, so können die ausscheidenden Genossenschafter oder ihre Erben keine Abfindung beanspruchen.

2 Wird die Genossenschaft innerhalb eines Jahres nach dem Ausscheiden oder nach dem Tode eines Genossenschafters aufgelöst und wird das Vermögen verteilt, so steht dem Ausgeschiedenen oder seinen Erben der gleiche Anspruch zu wie den bei der Auflösung vorhandenen Genossenschaftern.

E. Pflichten

I. Treuepflicht

Art. 866

Die Genossenschafter sind verpflichtet, die Interessen der Genossenschaft in guten Treuen zu wahren.

Kapitel 1: Neue Gesetzesbestimmungen und Erläuterungen

II. Pflicht zu Beiträgen und Leistungen

Art. 867

1 Die Statuten regeln die Beitrags- und Leistungspflicht.

2 Sind die Genossenschafter zur Einzahlung von Genossenschaftsanteilen oder zu andern Beitragsleistungen verpflichtet, so hat die Genossenschaft diese Leistungen unter Ansetzung einer angemessenen Frist und mit eingeschriebenem Brief einzufordern.

3 Wird auf die erste Aufforderung nicht bezahlt und kommt der Genossenschafter auch einer zweiten Zahlungsaufforderung innert Monatsfrist nicht nach, so kann er, sofern ihm dies mit eingeschriebenem Brief angedroht worden ist, seiner Genossenschaftsrechte verlustig erklärt werden.

4 Sofern die Statuten es nicht anders ordnen, wird der Genossenschafter durch die Verlustigerklärung nicht von fälligen oder durch die Ausschliessung fällig werdenden Verpflichtungen befreit.

III. Haftung

1. Der Genossenschaft

Art. 868

Für die Verbindlichkeiten der Genossenschaft haftet das Genossenschaftsvermögen. Es haftet ausschliesslich, sofern die Statuten nichts anderes bestimmen.

2. Der Genossenschafter

a. Unbeschränkte Haftung

Art. 869

1 Die Statuten können, ausgenommen bei konzessionierten Versicherungsgenossenschaften, die Bestimmung aufstellen, dass nach dem Genossenschaftsvermögen die Genossenschafter persönlich unbeschränkt haften.

2 In diesem Falle haften, soweit die Gläubiger im Genossenschaftskonkurse zu Verlust kommen, die Genossenschafter für alle Verbindlichkeiten der Genossenschaft solidarisch mit ihrem ganzen Vermögen. Diese Haftung wird bis zur Beendigung des Konkurses durch die Konkursverwaltung geltend gemacht.

b. Beschränkte Haftung

Art. 870

1 Die Statuten können, ausgenommen bei konzessionierten Versicherungsgenossenschaften, die Bestimmung aufstellen, dass die Genossenschafter über die Mitgliederbeiträge und Genossenschaftsanteile hinaus für die Verbindlichkeiten der Genossenschaft nach dem Genossenschaftsvermögen persönlich, jedoch nur bis zu einem bestimmten Betrage haften.

2 Wenn Genossenschaftsanteile bestehen, ist der Haftungsbetrag für die einzelnen Genossenschafter nach dem Betrag ihrer Genossenschaftsanteile zu bestimmen.

3 Die Haftung wird bis zur Beendigung des Konkurses durch die Konkursverwaltung geltend gemacht.

Kapitel 1: Neue Gesetzesbestimmungen und Erläuterungen

c. Nachschusspflicht

Art. 871

1 Die Statuten können die Genossenschafter an Stelle oder neben der Haftung zur Leistung von Nachschüssen verpflichten, die jedoch nur zur Deckung von Bilanzverlusten dienen dürfen.

2 Die Nachschusspflicht kann unbeschränkt sein, sie kann aber auch auf bestimmte Beträge oder im Verhältnis zu den Mitgliederbeiträgen oder den Genossenschaftsanteilen beschränkt werden.

3 Enthalten die Statuten keine Bestimmungen über die Verteilung der Nachschüsse auf die einzelnen Genossenschafter, so richtet sich diese nach dem Betrag der Genossenschaftsanteile oder, wenn solche nicht bestehen, nach Köpfen.

4 Die Nachschüsse können jederzeit eingefordert werden. Im Konkurse der Genossenschaft steht die Einforderung der Nachschüsse der Konkursverwaltung zu.

5 Im Übrigen sind die Vorschriften über die Einforderung der Leistungen und über die Verlustigerklärung anwendbar.

d Unzulässige Beschränkungen

Art. 872

Bestimmungen der Statuten, welche die Haftung auf bestimmte Zeit oder auf besondere Verbindlichkeiten oder auf einzelne Gruppen von Mitgliedern beschränken, sind ungültig.

e. Verfahren im Konkurs

Art. 873

1 Im Konkurs einer Genossenschaft mit persönlicher Haftung oder mit Nachschusspflicht der Genossenschafter hat die Konkursverwal-

tung gleichzeitig mit der Aufstellung des Kollokationsplanes die auf die einzelnen Genossenschafter entfallenden vorläufigen Haftungsanteile oder Nachschussbeträge festzustellen und einzufordern.

2 Uneinbringliche Beträge sind auf die übrigen Genossenschafter im gleichen Verhältnis zu verteilen, Überschüsse nach endgültiger Feststellung der Verteilungsliste zurückzuerstatten. Der Rückgriff der Genossenschafter unter sich bleibt vorbehalten.

3 Die vorläufige Feststellung der Verpflichtungen der Genossenschafter und die Verteilungsliste können nach den Vorschriften des Schuldbetreibungs- und Konkursgesetzes[122] durch Beschwerde angefochten werden.

4 Das Verfahren wird durch eine Verordnung des Bundesgerichts geregelt.

f. Änderung der Haftungsbestimmungen

Art. 874

1 Änderungen an den Haftungs- oder Nachschussverpflichtungen der Genossenschafter sowie die Herabsetzung oder Aufhebung der Anteilscheine können nur auf dem Wege der Statutenrevision vorgenommen werden.

2 Auf die Herabsetzung oder Aufhebung der Anteilscheine finden überdies die Bestimmungen über die Herabsetzung des Grundkapitals bei der Aktiengesellschaft Anwendung.

3 Von einer Verminderung der Haftung oder der Nachschusspflicht werden die vor der Veröffentlichung der Statutenrevision entstandenen Verbindlichkeiten nicht betroffen.

4 Die Neubegründung oder Vermehrung der Haftung oder der Nachschusspflicht wirkt mit der Eintragung des Beschlusses zugunsten aller Gläubiger der Genossenschaft.

---

122 SR **281.1**

Kapitel 1: Neue Gesetzesbestimmungen und Erläuterungen

g. Haftung neu eintretender Genossenschafter

Art. 875

1 Wer in eine Genossenschaft mit persönlicher Haftung oder mit Nachschusspflicht der Genossenschafter eintritt, haftet gleich den andern Genossenschaftern auch für die vor seinem Eintritt entstandenen Verbindlichkeiten.

2 Eine entgegenstehende Bestimmung der Statuten oder Verabredung unter den Genossenschaftern hat Dritten gegenüber keine Wirkung.

h. Haftung nach Ausscheiden oder nach Auflösung

Art. 876

1 Wenn ein unbeschränkt oder beschränkt haftender Genossenschafter durch Tod oder in anderer Weise ausscheidet, dauert die Haftung für die vor seinem Ausscheiden entstandenen Verbindlichkeiten fort, sofern die Genossenschaft innerhalb eines Jahres oder einer statutarisch festgesetzten längern Frist seit der Eintragung des Ausscheidens in das Handelsregister in Konkurs gerät.

2 Unter den gleichen Voraussetzungen und für die gleichen Fristen besteht auch die Nachschusspflicht fort.

3 Wird eine Genossenschaft aufgelöst, so bleiben die Mitglieder in gleicher Weise haftbar oder zu Nachschüssen verpflichtet, falls innerhalb eines Jahres oder einer statutarisch festgesetzten längere Frist seit der Eintragung der Auflösung in das Handelsregister der Konkurs über die Genossenschaft eröffnet wird.

i. Anmeldung von Ein- und Austritt im Handelsregister

Art. 877

1 Sind die Genossenschafter für die Genossenschaftsschulden unbeschränkt oder beschränkt haftbar oder sind sie zu Nachschüssen

verpflichtet, so hat die Verwaltung jeden Eintritt oder Austritt eines Genossenschafters innerhalb drei Monaten beim Handelsregisteramt anzumelden.

2 Überdies steht jedem austretenden oder ausgeschlossenen Mitgliede sowie den Erben eines Mitgliedes die Befugnis zu, die Eintragung des Austrittes, des Ausschlusses oder des Todesfalles von sich aus vornehmen zu lassen. Das Handelsregisteramt hat der Verwaltung der Genossenschaft von einer solchen Anmeldung sofort Kenntnis zu geben.

3 Die konzessionierten Versicherungsgenossenschaften sind von der Pflicht zur Anmeldung ihrer Mitglieder beim Handelsregisteramt befreit.

k. Verjährung der Haftung

Art. 878

1 Die Ansprüche der Gläubiger aus der persönlichen Haftung der einzelnen Genossenschafter können noch während der Dauer eines Jahres vom Schlusse des Konkursverfahrens an von jedem Gläubiger geltend gemacht werden, sofern sie nicht nach gesetzlicher Vorschrift schon vorher erloschen sind.

2 Der Rückgriff der Genossenschafter unter sich verjährt ebenfalls in einem Jahre vom Zeitpunkt der Zahlung an, für die er geltend gemacht wird.

Kapitel 1: Neue Gesetzesbestimmungen und Erläuterungen

Fünfter Abschnitt: Organisation der Genossenschaft

A. Generalversammlung

I. Befugnisse

Art. 879

1 Oberstes Organ der Genossenschaft ist die Generalversammlung der Genossenschafter.

2 Ihr stehen folgende unübertragbare Befugnisse zu:

1. **die Festsetzung und Änderung der Statuten;**
2. **die Wahl der Verwaltung und der Revisionsstelle;**
3. **die Abnahme der Betriebsrechnung und der Bilanz und gegebenenfalls die Beschlussfassung über die Verteilung des Reinertrages;**
4. **die Entlastung der Verwaltung;**
5. **die Beschlussfassung über die Gegenstände, die der Generalversammlung durch das Gesetz oder die Statuten vorbehalten sind.**

Aus Gründen einer einheitlichen Terminologie wird der Ausdruck «Kontrollstelle» durch den Begriff «Revisionsstelle» ersetzt.

II. Urabstimmung

Art. 880

Bei Genossenschaften, die mehr als 300 Mitglieder zählen oder bei denen die Mehrheit der Mitglieder aus Genossenschaften besteht, können die Statuten bestimmen, dass die Befugnisse der Generalversammlung ganz oder zum Teil durch schriftliche Stimmabgabe (Urabstimmung) der Genossenschafter ausgeübt werden.

III. Einberufung

1. Recht und Pflicht

Art. 881

1 Die Generalversammlung wird durch die Verwaltung oder ein anderes nach den Statuten dazu befugtes Organ, nötigenfalls durch die Revisionsstelle einberufen. Das Einberufungsrecht steht auch den Liquidatoren und den Vertretern der Anleihensgläubiger zu.

2 Die Generalversammlung muss einberufen werden, wenn wenigstens der zehnte Teil der Genossenschafter oder, bei Genossenschaften von weniger als 30 Mitgliedern, mindestens drei Genossenschafter die Einberufung verlangen.

3 Entspricht die Verwaltung diesem Begehren nicht binnen angemessener Frist, so hat der Richter auf Antrag der Gesuchsteller die Einberufung anzuordnen.

Aus Gründen einer einheitlichen Terminologie wird der Ausdruck «Kontrollstelle» durch den Begriff «Revisionsstelle» ersetzt.

2. Form

Art. 882

1 Die Generalversammlung ist in der durch die Statuten vorgesehenen Form, jedoch mindestens fünf Tage vor dem Versammlungstag einzuberufen.

2 Bei Genossenschaften von über 30 Mitgliedern ist die Einberufung wirksam, sobald sie durch öffentliche Auskündigung erfolgt.

Kapitel 1: Neue Gesetzesbestimmungen und Erläuterungen

3. Verhandlungsgegenstände

Art. 883

1 Bei der Einberufung sind die Verhandlungsgegenstände, bei Abänderung der Statuten der wesentliche Inhalt der vorgeschlagenen Änderungen bekanntzugeben.

2 Über Gegenstände, die nicht in dieser Weise angekündigt worden sind, können Beschlüsse nicht gefasst werden, ausser über einen Antrag auf Einberufung einer weitern Generalversammlung.

3 Zur Stellung von Anträgen und zu Verhandlungen ohne Beschlussfassung bedarf es der vorgängigen Ankündigung nicht.

4. Universalversammlung

Art. 884

Wenn und solange alle Genossenschafter in einer Versammlung anwesend sind, können sie, falls kein Widerspruch erhoben wird, Beschlüsse fassen, auch wenn die Vorschriften über die Einberufung nicht eingehalten wurden.

IV. Stimmrecht

Art. 885

Jeder Genossenschafter hat in der Generalversammlung oder in der Urabstimmung eine Stimme.

V. Vertretung

Art. 886

1 Bei der Ausübung seines Stimmrechts in der Generalversammlung kann sich ein Genossenschafter durch einen andern Genossenschafter vertreten lassen, doch kann kein Bevollmächtigter mehr als einen Genossenschafter vertreten.

2 Bei Genossenschaften mit über 1000 Mitgliedern können die Statuten vorsehen, dass jeder Genossenschafter mehr als einen, höchstens aber neun andere Genossenschafter vertreten darf.

3 Den Statuten bleibt vorbehalten, die Vertretung durch einen handlungsfähigen Familienangehörigen zulässig zu erklären.

VI. Ausschliessung vom Stimmrecht

Art. 887

Bei Beschlüssen über die Entlastung der Verwaltung haben Personen, die in irgendeiner Weise an der Geschäftsführung teilgenommen haben, kein Stimmrecht.

Bei der Beschlussfassung über die Entlastung der Verwaltung haben Personen, die in irgendeiner Weise an der Geschäftsführung teilgenommen haben, kein Stimmrecht; sie haben von Gesetzes wegen in den Ausstand zu treten (Art. 887 Abs. 1 OR). Der Revisionsstelle ist es auf Grund der verschärften Vorschriften zur Unabhängigkeit generell verboten, an der Geschäftsführung der von ihr geprüften Gesellschaft mitzuwirken (Art. 728 Abs. 2 Ziff. 1 und Art. 729 Abs. 1 E OR).

Abs. 2 ist mit dem Gebot der Unabhängigkeit nicht vereinbar und daher aufzuheben (vgl. auch Art. 695 Abs. 2 E OR zum Aktienrecht).

VII. Beschlussfassung

1. Im Allgemeinen

Art. 888

1 Die Generalversammlung fasst ihre Beschlüsse und vollzieht ihre Wahlen, soweit das Gesetz oder die Statuten es nicht anders bestimmen, mit absoluter Mehrheit der abgegebenen Stimmen. Dasselbe gilt für Beschlüsse und Wahlen, die auf dem Wege der Urabstimmung vorgenommen werden.

2 Für die Auflösung der Genossenschaft sowie für die Abänderung der Statuten bedarf es einer Mehrheit von zwei Dritteln der abgegebenen Stimmen. Die Statuten können die Bedingungen für diese Beschlüsse noch erschweren.[123]

2. Bei Erhöhung der Leistungen der Genossenschafter

Art. 889

1 Beschlüsse über die Einführung oder die Vermehrung der persönlichen Haftung oder der Nachschusspflicht der Genossenschafter bedürfen der Zustimmung von drei Vierteilen sämtlicher Genossenschafter.

2 Solche Beschlüsse sind für Genossenschafter, die nicht zugestimmt haben, nicht verbindlich, wenn sie binnen drei Monaten seit der Veröffentlichung des Beschlusses den Austritt erklären. Dieser Austritt ist wirksam auf den Zeitpunkt des Inkrafttretens des Beschlusses.

3 Der Austritt darf in diesem Falle nicht von der Leistung einer Auslösungssumme abhängig gemacht werden.

---

[123] Fassung gemäss Anhang Ziff. 2 des Fusionsgesetzes vom 3. Okt. 2003, in Kraft seit 1. Juli 2004 (SR **221.301**).

VIII. Abberufung der Verwaltung und Revisionsstelle

Art. 890

1 Die Generalversammlung ist berechtigt, die Mitglieder der Verwaltung und der Revisionsstelle sowie andere von ihr gewählte Bevollmächtigte und Beauftragte abzuberufen.

2 Auf den Antrag von wenigstens einem Zehntel der Genossenschafter kann der Richter die Abberufung verfügen, wenn wichtige Gründe vorliegen, insbesondere wenn die Abberufenen die ihnen obliegenden Pflichten vernachlässigt haben oder zu erfüllen ausserstande waren. Er hat in einem solchen Falle, soweit notwendig, eine Neuwahl durch die zuständigen Genossenschaftsorgane zu verfügen und für die Zwischenzeit die geeigneten Anordnungen zu treffen.

3 Entschädigungsansprüche der Abberufenen bleiben vorbehalten.

Aus Gründen einer einheitlichen Terminologie wird der Ausdruck «Kontrollstelle» durch den Begriff «Revisionsstelle» ersetzt.

IX. Anfechtung der Generalversammlungsbeschlüsse

Art. 891

1 Die Verwaltung und jeder Genossenschafter können von der Generalversammlung oder in der Urabstimmung gefasste Beschlüsse, die gegen das Gesetz oder die Statuten verstossen, beim Richter mit Klage gegen die Genossenschaft anfechten. Ist die Verwaltung Klägerin, so bestimmt der Richter einen Vertreter für die Genossenschaft.

2 Das Anfechtungsrecht erlischt, wenn die Klage nicht spätestens zwei Monate nach der Beschlussfassung angehoben wird.

3 Das Urteil, das einen Beschluss aufhebt, wirkt für und gegen alle Genossenschafter.

X. Delegiertenversammlung

Art. 892

1 Genossenschaften, die mehr als 300 Mitglieder zählen oder bei denen die Mehrheit der Mitglieder aus Genossenschaften besteht, können durch die Statuten die Befugnisse der Generalversammlung ganz oder zum Teil einer Delegiertenversammlung übertragen.

2 Zusammensetzung, Wahlart und Einberufung der Delegiertenversammlung werden durch die Statuten geregelt.

3 Jeder Delegierte hat in der Delegiertenversammlung eine Stimme, sofern die Statuten das Stimmrecht nicht anders ordnen.

4 Im Übrigen gelten für die Delegiertenversammlung die gesetzlichen Vorschriften über die Generalversammlung.

XI. Ausnahmebestimmungen für Versicherungsgenossenschaften

Art. 893

1 Die konzessionierten Versicherungsgenossenschaften mit über 1000 Mitgliedern können durch die Statuten die Befugnisse der Generalversammlung ganz oder zum Teil der Verwaltung übertragen.

2 Unübertragbar sind die Befugnisse der Generalversammlung zur Einführung oder Vermehrung der Nachschusspflicht, zur Auflösung, zur Fusion, zur Spaltung und zur Umwandlung der Rechtsform der Genossenschaft.[124]

---

[124] Fassung gemäss Anhang Ziff. 2 des Fusionsgesetzes vom 3. Okt. 2003, in Kraft seit 1. Juli 2004 (SR **221.301**).

Teil F: Rechtliche Aspekte / Legal aspects

B. Verwaltung

I. Wählbarkeit

1. Mitgliedschaft

Art. 894

1 Die Verwaltung der Genossenschaft besteht aus mindestens drei Personen; die Mehrheit muss aus Genossenschaftern bestehen.

2 Ist an der Genossenschaft eine juristische Person oder eine Handelsgesellschaft beteiligt, so ist sie als solche nicht als Mitglied der Verwaltung wählbar; dagegen können an ihrer Stelle ihre Vertreter gewählt werden.

2. Nationalität und Wohnsitz

Art. 895

Aufgehoben

Das Nationalitätserfordernis für Mitglieder der Verwaltung wird aufgehoben (s. dazu die Ausführungen zu Art. 708 E OR) und durch eine Bestimmung bezüglich der Vertretung der Gesellschaft durch eine Person mit Wohnsitz in der Schweiz ersetzt (Art. 898 E OR).

II. Amtsdauer

Art. 896

1 Die Mitglieder der Verwaltung werden auf höchstens vier Jahre gewählt, sind aber, wenn die Statuten nicht etwas anderes bestimmen, wieder wählbar.

2 Bei den konzessionierten Versicherungsgenossenschaften finden für die Amtsdauer der Verwaltung die für die Aktiengesellschaft geltenden Vorschriften Anwendung.

III. Verwaltungsausschuss

Art. 897

Die Statuten können einen Teil der Pflichten und Befugnisse der Verwaltung einem oder mehreren von dieser gewählten Verwaltungsausschüssen übertragen.

IV. Geschäftsführung und Vertretung
1. Übertragung

Art. 898 (ursprünglicher Botschaftsentwurf)

1 Die Statuten können die Generalversammlung oder die Verwaltung ermächtigen, die Geschäftsführung oder einzelne Zweige derselben und die Vertretung an eine oder mehrere Personen, Geschäftsführer oder Direktoren zu übertragen, die nicht Mitglieder der Genossenschaft zu sein brauchen.

2 Die Genossenschaft muss durch ein Mitglied der Verwaltung, einen Geschäftsführer oder einen Direktor mit Wohnsitz in der Schweiz vertreten werden können.

Art. 898 (durch den Nationalrat bereinigte Version)

2 Die Genossenschaft muss durch eine Person vertreten werden können, die Wohnsitz in der Schweiz hat. Dieses Erfordernis kann durch ein Mitglied der Verwaltung, einen Geschäftsführer oder einen Direktor erfüllt werden.

Der neue *Abs. 2* tritt an die Stelle der Regelung von Art. 895 OR und stimmt inhaltlich mit den Vorschriften für die GmbH und die Aktiengesellschaft überein. Es kann auf die Ausführungen zu Art. 814 Abs. 3 E OR verwiesen werden (vgl. auch Art. 718 Abs. 3 E OR).[125]

2. Umfang und Beschränkung

Art. 899

1 Die zur Vertretung befugten Personen sind ermächtigt, im Namen der Genossenschaft alle Rechtshandlungen vorzunehmen, die der Zweck der Genossenschaft mit sich bringen kann.

2 Eine Beschränkung dieser Vertretungsbefugnis hat gegenüber gutgläubigen Dritten keine Wirkung, unter Vorbehalt der im Handelsregister eingetragenen Bestimmungen über die ausschliessliche Vertretung der Hauptniederlassung oder einer Zweigniederlassung oder über die gemeinsame Führung der Firma.

3 Die Genossenschaft haftet für den Schaden aus unerlaubten Handlungen, die eine zur Geschäftsführung oder zur Vertretung befugte Person in Ausübung ihrer geschäftlichen Verrichtungen begeht.

3. Verträge zwischen der Genossenschaft und ihrem Vertreter

Art. 899a

Wird die Genossenschaft beim Abschluss eines Vertrages durch diejenige Person vertreten, mit der sie den Vertrag abschliesst, so muss der Vertrag schriftlich abgefasst werden. Dieses Erfordernis gilt nicht für Verträge des laufenden Geschäfts, bei denen die Leistung der Gesellschaft den Wert von 1000 Franken nicht übersteigt.

Die vorliegende Regelung entspricht Art. 718*b* E OR; es kann auf die Ausführungen zu dieser Bestimmung verwiesen werden.

---

[125] Die vorliegenden Erläuterungen beziehen sich ausschliesslich auf die ursprüngliche bundesrätliche Gesetzesversion und nicht auf die bereinigte Fassung durch den Nationalrat.

4. Zeichnung

Art. 900

Die zur Vertretung der Genossenschaft befugten Personen haben in der Weise zu zeichnen, dass sie der Firma der Genossenschaft ihre Unterschrift beifügen.

5. Eintragung

Art. 901

Die zur Vertretung der Genossenschaft befugten Personen sind von der Verwaltung zur Eintragung in das Handelsregister anzumelden unter Vorlegung einer beglaubigten Abschrift des Beschlusses. Sie haben ihre Unterschrift beim Handelsregisteramt zu zeichnen oder die Zeichnung in beglaubigter Form einzureichen.

V. Pflichten

1. Im Allgemeinen

Art. 902

1 Die Verwaltung hat die Geschäfte der Genossenschaft mit aller Sorgfalt zu leiten und die genossenschaftliche Aufgabe mit besten Kräften zu fördern.

2 Sie ist insbesondere verpflichtet:

1. die Geschäfte der Generalversammlung vorzubereiten und deren Beschlüsse auszuführen;
2. die mit der Geschäftsführung und Vertretung Beauftragten im Hinblick auf die Beobachtung der Gesetze, der Statuten und allfälliger Reglemente zu überwachen und sich über den Geschäftsgang regelmässig unterrichten zu lassen.

3 Die Verwaltung ist dafür verantwortlich, dass ihre Protokolle und diejenigen der Generalversammlung, die notwendigen Geschäftsbücher sowie das Genossenschafterverzeichnis regelmässig geführt werden, dass die Betriebsrechnung und die Jahresbilanz nach den gesetzlichen Vorschriften aufgestellt und der Revisionsstelle zur Prüfung unterbreitet und die vorgeschriebenen Anzeigen an das Handelsregisteramt über Eintritt und Austritt der Genossenschafter gemacht werden.

Aus Gründen einer einheitlichen Terminologie wird der Ausdruck «Kontrollstelle» durch den Begriff «Revisionsstelle» ersetzt.

2. Anzeigepflicht bei Überschuldung und bei Kapitalverlust

Art. 903

1 Besteht begründete Besorgnis einer Überschuldung, so hat die Verwaltung sofort auf Grund der Veräusserungswerte eine Zwischenbilanz aufzustellen.

2 Zeigt die letzte Jahresbilanz und eine daraufhin zu errichtende Liquidationsbilanz oder zeigt eine Zwischenbilanz, dass die Forderungen der Genossenschaftsgläubiger durch die Aktiven nicht mehr gedeckt sind, so hat die Verwaltung den Richter zu benachrichtigen. Dieser hat die Konkurseröffnung auszusprechen, falls nicht die Voraussetzungen eines Aufschubes gegeben sind.

3 Bei Genossenschaften mit Anteilscheinen hat die Verwaltung unverzüglich eine Generalversammlung einzuberufen und diese von der Sachlage zu unterrichten, wenn die letzte Jahresbilanz ergibt, dass die Hälfte des Genossenschaftskapitals nicht mehr gedeckt ist.

4 Bei Genossenschaften mit Nachschusspflicht muss der Richter erst benachrichtigt werden, wenn der durch die Bilanz ausgewiesene Verlust nicht innert drei Monaten durch Nachschüsse der Mitglieder gedeckt wird.

5 Auf Antrag der Verwaltung oder eines Gläubigers kann der Richter, falls Aussicht auf Sanierung besteht, die Konkurseröffnung aufschieben. In diesem Falle trifft er die zur Erhaltung des

Vermögens geeigneten Massnahmen, wie Inventaraufnahme, Bestellung eines Sachwalters.

6 Bei konzessionierten Versicherungsgenossenschaften gelten die Ansprüche der Mitglieder aus Versicherungsverträgen als Gläubigerrechte.

VI. Rückerstattung entrichteter Zahlungen

Art. 904

1 Im Konkurse der Genossenschaft sind die Mitglieder der Verwaltung den Genossenschaftsgläubigern gegenüber zur Rückerstattung aller in den letzten drei Jahren vor Konkursausbruch als Gewinnanteile oder unter anderer Bezeichnung gemachten Bezüge verpflichtet, soweit diese ein angemessenes Entgelt für Gegenleistungen übersteigen und bei vorsichtiger Bilanzierung nicht hätten ausgerichtet werden sollen.

2 Die Rückerstattung ist ausgeschlossen, soweit sie nach den Bestimmungen über die ungerechtfertigte Bereicherung nicht gefordert werden kann.

3 Der Richter entscheidet unter Würdigung aller Umstände nach freiem Ermessen.

VII. Einstellung und Abberufung

Art. 905

1 Die Verwaltung kann die von ihr bestellten Ausschüsse, Geschäftsführer, Direktoren und andern Bevollmächtigten und Beauftragten jederzeit abberufen.

2 Die von der Generalversammlung bestellten Bevollmächtigten und Beauftragten können von der Verwaltung jederzeit in ihren Funktionen eingestellt werden unter sofortiger Einberufung einer Generalversammlung.

3 Entschädigungsansprüche der Abberufenen oder in ihren Funktionen Eingestellten bleiben vorbehalten.

C. Revisionsstelle

I. Im Allgemeinen

Art. 906

1 Für die Revisionsstelle sind die Vorschriften des Aktienrechts entsprechend anwendbar.

2 Eine ordentliche Revision der Jahresrechnung durch eine Revisionsstelle können verlangen:

1. 10 Prozent der Genossenschafter;
2. Genossenschafter, die zusammen mindestens 10 Prozent des Anteilscheinkapitals vertreten;
3. Genossenschafter, die einer persönlichen Haftung oder einer Nachschusspflicht unterliegen.

Der Entwurf schlägt ein Neukonzept für die Revisionspflicht und die Revisionsstelle vor, das für alle Rechtsformen des Privatrechts gleichermassen gilt. Aus diesem Grund sollen für die Revisionspflicht in der Genossenschaft soweit möglich dieselben Kriterien ausschlaggebend sein wie bei der Aktiengesellschaft.

Abs. 1 sieht vor, dass für die Revisionsstelle die Vorschriften des Aktienrechts entsprechend anwendbar sind. Dabei handelt es sich um eine sog. dynamische Verweisnorm (s. dazu die Ausführungen zu Art. 818 Abs. 1 E OR).

Auf Grund dieser Verweisung muss eine Genossenschaft ihre Jahresrechnung und gegebenenfalls ihre Konzernrechnung ordentlich durch ein staatlich beaufsichtigtes Revisionsunternehmen prüfen lassen (s. Art. 727*b* Abs. 1 E OR), wenn sie:

- Beteiligungspapiere (insbes. Partizipationsscheine) ausgegeben hat, die an einer Börse kotiert sind (Art. 727 Abs. 1 lit. a E OR)[126];
- Anleihensobligationen ausstehend hat (lit. b);
- mindestens 20% der Aktiven oder des Umsatzes zur Konzernrechnung einer Gesellschaft beiträgt, die ihrerseits zu einer ordentlichen Revision durch ein staatlich beaufsichtigtes Revisionsunternehmen verpflichtet ist (lit. c).

Eine Genossenschaft muss ihre Jahresrechnung und ihre Konzernrechnung ordentlich durch eine zugelassene Revisionsexpertin oder einen zugelassenen Revisionsexperten prüfen lassen (s. Art. 727*b* Abs. 2 E OR), wenn:

- zwei der drei in Art. 727 Abs. 1 Ziff. 2 E OR vorgesehenen Grenzwerte in zwei aufeinander folgenden Geschäftsjahren überschritten werden;
- sie zur Erstellung einer Konzernrechnung verpflichtet ist (Art. 858 Abs. 2 OR i.V.m. Art. 663*e* Abs. 3 und Art. 727 Abs. 1 Ziff. 3 E OR);
- die Statuten dies vorsehen (Art. 727 Abs. 3 E OR); oder
- die Generalversammlung dies beschliesst (Art. 727 Abs. 3 E OR).

Gemäss *Abs. 2* können zudem folgende Personengruppen bzw. Personen eine ordentliche Revision durch eine zugelassene Revisionsexpertin oder einen zugelassenen Revisionsexperten (s. Art. 727*b* Abs. 2 i.V.m. Art. 906 Abs. 1 E OR) verlangen:

- *Ziff. 1:* 10% der Genossenschafter;
- *Ziff. 2:* Genossenschafter, die zusammen mindestens 10% des Anteilscheinkapitals vertreten;
- *Ziff. 3:* Genossenschafter, die einer persönlichen Haftung oder einer Nachschusspflicht unterliegen (vgl. Art. 869 ff. OR).

Abs. 2 stellt eine der Rechtsform der Genossenschaft angepasste Sonderbestimmung dar, die an die Stelle der Regelung von Art. 727 Abs. 2 E OR tritt. Da Genossenschaften häufig über kein Anteilscheinkapital verfügen, würde eine Regelung des Minderheitenschutzes, die ausschliesslich an die Kapitalbeteiligung anknüpft (so Ziff. 2), zum Teil ins Leere stossen. Aus

---

[126] Nach Auskunft der Schweizer Börse SWX sind derzeit keine Beteiligungspapiere von Genossenschaften an der SWX kotiert; dennoch soll diese Möglichkeit nicht grundsätzlich ausgeschlossen werden.

diesem Grund und auch weil das Kopfprinzip (eine Stimme pro beteiligte Person) einen der prägenden Grundsätze des Genossenschaftsrechts darstellt, wird als Alternative auf eine prozentuale Anzahl von Genossenschafterinnen und Genossenschafter abgestellt (so Ziff. 1). Für die Anwendung von Ziff. 1 ist unerheblich, ob die Genossenschaft über ein Anteilscheinkapital verfügt oder nicht. Auch in der Genossenschaft soll eine erhebliche Beteiligung am Eigenkapital aber in jedem Fall den erforderlichen Schutz erfahren. Die alternativen Voraussetzungen der Ziff. 1 und 2 sind daher sachlich begründet und gerechtfertigt.

Die Regelung der Revision auf Begehren der Genossenschafterinnen und Genossenschafter bedarf zudem in *Ziff. 3* der Ergänzung zum Schutz von Personen, die mit den Risiken belastet sind, die sich aus einer persönlichen Haftung oder einer Nachschusspflicht ergeben. Die vorgesehene Lösung ermöglicht es aber, auch beim Bestehen einer persönlichen Haftung oder einer Nachschusspflicht auf eine Revisionsstelle zu verzichten, so etwa wenn die Verpflichteten selber in die Geschäftsführung eingebunden sind.

Abs. 1 verweist für die übrigen Fragen zur Revision auf das Aktienrecht (Art. 727 ff. E OR). Genossenschaften, die ihre Jahresrechnung nicht ordentlich revidieren lassen müssen, sind somit zu einer eingeschränkten Revision durch eine zugelassene Revisorin oder einen zugelassenen Revisor verpflichtet. In der Genossenschaft besteht aber auch die Möglichkeit eines Opting-out (Art. 727*a* Abs. 2 i.V.m. Art. 906 Abs. 1 E OR).

Mit der Neuordnung der Revisionsstelle in der Genossenschaft werden zwei bisherige Differenzen zum Aktienrecht aufgegeben:

– Art. 906 Abs. 1 OR sieht vor, dass die Revisionsstelle auch die Geschäftsführung der Verwaltung kontrolliert. Dies ist der Grund dafür, dass die genossenschaftliche Revisionsstelle im geltenden Recht «Kontrollstelle» genannt wird. Die Prüfung der Geschäftsführung ist allerdings in der Praxis weitgehend toter Buchstabe geblieben[127]. Einer objektiven Überprüfung sind ohnehin nur die Ordnungsmässigkeit und die Legalität der Geschäftsführung zugänglich. Die Zweckmässigkeit von Geschäftsführungsentscheiden kann durch die Revisionsstelle naturgemäss nicht über-

---

[127] JEAN NICOLAS DRUEY, Das Recht der Abschlussprüfung, in: Gauch/Schmid (Hrsg.), Die Rechtsentwicklung an der Schwelle zum 21. Jahrhundert, Zürich 2001, 493 ff., 493 Fn 1; ROLF WATTER, in: Honsell/Vogt/Watter (Hrsg.), Basler Kommentar zum Schweizerischen Privatrecht, Obligationenrecht II, Art. 530–1186 OR, 2. Aufl., Basel 2002, Art. 906 N 3.

prüft werden[128]. Der Entwurf hält aus diesen Gründen nicht an der Prüfung der Geschäftsführung fest. Eine entsprechende Änderung blieb in der Vernehmlassung zum Vorentwurf RRG unbestritten. Falls jedoch in einer Genossenschaft das Bedürfnis nach einer Prüfung der Geschäftsführung durch die Revisionsstelle besteht, können deren Aufgaben in den Statuten oder durch Beschluss der Generalversammlung im gewünschten Ausmass erweitert werden (vgl. die Ausführungen zu Art. 731*a* E OR).
– Die Vorschriften zur Unabhängigkeit der Revisionsstelle lassen es im Gegensatz zum geltenden Recht (s. Art. 906 Abs. 3 OR) nicht mehr zu, dass Genossenschafterinnen oder Genossenschafter ihre eigene Genossenschaft revidieren (Art. 728 Abs. 2 Ziff. 2 und Art. 729 Abs. 1 E OR); die dadurch entstehenden Interessenkonflikte sind zur Sicherung der Verlässlichkeit der Revision zu vermeiden.

II. Prüfung des Genossenschafterverzeichnisses

Art. 907

Bei Genossenschaften mit persönlicher Haftung oder Nachschusspflicht der Genossenschafter hat die Revisionsstelle festzustellen, ob das Genossenschaftsverzeichnis korrekt geführt wird. Verfügt die Genossenschaft über keine Revisionsstelle, so muss die Verwaltung das Genossenschaftsverzeichnis durch einen zugelassenen Revisor prüfen lassen.

Art. 907 des geltenden Genossenschaftsrechts schreibt vor, welche Prüfungshandlungen die genossenschaftliche Revisionsstelle vorzunehmen hat.

Nach der allgemeinen Verweisung von Art. 906 Abs. 1 E OR bestimmt sich neu auch die Tätigkeit der Revisionsstelle nach der Regelung im Aktienrecht (vgl. dazu die Ausführungen zu Art. 728*a* und Art. 729*a* E OR). Art. 907 ist daher grundsätzlich aufzuheben.

---

128 Überprüft werden können nur die Vereinbarkeit der Tätigkeit der Genossenschaft mit den Statuten, der Aufbau der Geschäftsführung ihren Aufgaben entsprechend und das Vorliegen der Voraussetzungen für eine gesetzes- und statutenkonforme Geschäftsführung: Schweizer Handbuch der Wirtschaftsprüfung, Band 2, Zürich 1998, 75 f.

Nach dem geltenden Recht hat die Revisionsstelle zu prüfen, ob das Genossenschafterverzeichnis bei Genossenschaften mit persönlicher Haftung oder Nachschusspflicht korrekt geführt wird (Art. 907 Abs. 1 OR). Durch den Verweis des Entwurfs auf das Aktienrecht würde diese Aufgabe wegfallen. Die Bonität der Genossenschafterinnen und Genossenschafter, die persönlich haften oder zu Nachschüssen verpflichtet sind, ist jedoch für die Beurteilung der wirtschaftlichen Substanz der Genossenschaft durch Dritte relevant. Der Entwurf sieht daher in Art. 907 vor, dass die Revisionsstelle weiterhin prüft, ob das Genossenschaftsverzeichnis korrekt geführt wird. Verfügt die Genossenschaft über keine Revisionsstelle (s. Art. 727a Abs. 2 i.V.m. 906 Abs. 1 E OR), so muss die Verwaltung das Genossenschaftsverzeichnis durch eine zugelassene Revisorin oder einen zugelassenen Revisor prüfen lassen.

Ob die Prüfung des Genossenschaftsverzeichnisses durch die Revisionsstelle aufgegeben werden soll, wird im Rahmen einer zukünftigen Revision des Genossenschaftsrechts zu prüfen sein. Es ist darauf hinzuweisen, dass das Recht der GmbH keine vergleichbare Regelung kennt, obschon auch die Gesellschafterinnen und Gesellschafter einer GmbH mit einer Nachschusspflicht belastet werden können.

D. Mängel in der Organisation

Art. 908

Bei Mängeln in der Organisation der Genossenschaft sind die Vorschriften des Aktienrechts entsprechend anwendbar.

Art. 908 des geltenden Genossenschaftsrechts enthält Vorschriften zur Berichterstattung der Revisionsstelle und kann infolge der Verweisung von Art. 906 Abs. 1 E OR aufgehoben werden.

Der Entwurf zur Revision des Rechts der GmbH regelt in Art. 731*b* E OR wie vorzugehen ist, wenn einer Gesellschaft eines der vorgeschriebenen Organe fehlt oder eines dieser Organe nicht rechtmässig zusammengesetzt ist[129]. Gemäss Entwurf zur GmbH-Revision soll diese Regelung auch für die GmbH und die Genossenschaft gelten (vgl. Art. 819 und Art. 910*a* E

---

129 BBl **2002** 3231 ff., 3292.

OR[130]). Da die Art. 908–910 OR durch den vorliegenden Entwurf aufgehoben werden, muss die mit der GmbH-Revision vorgeschlagene Bestimmung (Art. 910*a* E OR) in Art. 908 verschoben werden.

Art. 909

Aufgehoben

Die Bestimmung kann infolge der Verweisung von Art. 906 Abs. 1 E OR aufgehoben werden.

Art. 910

Aufgehoben

Abs. 1 des geltenden Rechts kann infolge der Verweisung von Art. 906 Abs. 1 E OR aufgehoben werden.

Abs. 2 sieht im geltenden Recht vor, dass die Statuten neben der ordentlichen Kontrolle die periodische Revision der gesamten Geschäftsführung durch Revisionsverbände oder durch besondere Revisorinnen und Revisoren anordnen können. Dieser Abs. fällt ebenfalls weg, weil eine entsprechende Sonderregelung als «Kann-Vorschrift» nicht erforderlich und eher verwirrend ist: Soweit keine gesetzlich zwingend einem Organ zugewiesene Aufgaben berührt werden (vgl. Art. 731*a* Abs. 2 i.V.m. 906 Abs. 1 E OR), sind ohne weiteres zusätzliche Prüfungen möglich.

Sechster Abschnitt: Auflösung der Genossenschaft

A.   Auflösungsgründe

Art. 911

Die Genossenschaft wird aufgelöst:

1. **nach Massgabe der Statuten;**
2. **durch einen Beschluss der Generalversammlung;**

---

130   BBl **2002** 3285, 3294.

Teil F: Rechtliche Aspekte / Legal aspects

3. durch Eröffnung des Konkurses;
4. in den übrigen vom Gesetze vorgesehenen Fällen.

B. Anmeldung beim Handelsregister

Art. 912

Erfolgt die Auflösung der Genossenschaft nicht durch Konkurs, so ist sie von der Verwaltung zur Eintragung in das Handelsregister anzumelden.

C. Liquidation, Verteilung des Vermögens

Art. 913

1 Die Genossenschaft wird, unter Vorbehalt der nachfolgenden Bestimmungen, nach den für die Aktiengesellschaft geltenden Vorschriften liquidiert.

2 Das nach Tilgung sämtlicher Schulden und Rückzahlung allfälliger Genossenschaftsanteile verbleibende Vermögen der aufgelösten Genossenschaft darf nur dann unter die Genossenschafter verteilt werden, wenn die Statuten eine solche Verteilung vorsehen.

3 Die Verteilung erfolgt in diesem Falle, wenn die Statuten nicht etwas anderes bestimmen, unter die zur Zeit der Auflösung vorhandenen Genossenschafter oder ihre Rechtsnachfolger nach Köpfen. Der gesetzliche Abfindungsanspruch der ausgeschiedenen Genossenschafter oder ihrer Erben bleibt vorbehalten.

4 Enthalten die Statuten keine Vorschrift über die Verteilung unter die Genossenschafter, so muss der Liquidationsüberschuss zu genossenschaftlichen Zwecken oder zur Forderung gemeinnütziger Bestrebungen verwendet werden.

5 Der Entscheid hierüber steht, wenn die Statuten es nicht anders ordnen, der Generalversammlung zu.

Kapitel 1: Neue Gesetzesbestimmungen und Erläuterungen

Art. 914[131]

E. Übernahme durch eine Körperschaft des öffentlichen Rechts

Art. 915

1 Wird das Vermögen einer Genossenschaft vom Bunde, von einem Kanton oder unter Garantie des Kantons von einem Bezirk oder von einer Gemeinde übernommen, so kann mit Zustimmung der Generalversammlung vereinbart werden, dass die Liquidation unterbleiben soll.

2 Der Beschluss der Generalversammlung ist nach den Vorschriften über die Auflösung zu fassen und beim Handelsregisteramt anzumelden.

3 Mit der Eintragung dieses Beschlusses ist der Übergang des Vermögens der Genossenschaft mit Einschluss der Schulden vollzogen, und es ist die Firma der Genossenschaft zu löschen.

Siebenter Abschnitt: Verantwortlichkeit

A. Haftung gegenüber der Genossenschaft

Art. 916

Alle mit der Verwaltung, Geschäftsführung, Revision oder Liquidation befassten Personen sind der Genossenschaft für den Schaden verantwortlich, den sie ihr durch absichtliche oder fahrlässige Verletzung der ihnen obliegenden Pflichten verursachen.

Diese Vorschrift wird redaktionell angepasst. Zum einen wird aus Gründen der einheitlichen Terminologie der Ausdruck «Kontrolle» durch den

---

131 Aufgehoben durch Anhang Ziff. 2 des Fusionsgesetzes vom 3. Okt. 2003, mit Wirkung seit 1. Juli 2004 (SR **221.301**).

Begriff «Revision» sowie «betraut» durch «befasst» (s. dazu die entsprechenden Bestimmung im Aktienrecht, Art. 754 Abs. 1 OR und im Entwurf zur Revision der GmbH, Art. 827 E OR, BBl *2002* 3288) ersetzt. Zum anderen wird eine grammatikalische Unklarheit im geltenden Wortlaut beseitigt, aus dem geschlossen werden könnte, dass der Organbegriff bei der Verwaltung, Geschäftsführung und Revision ein materieller, bei der Liquidation jedoch ein formeller sei. Durch die aufeinander folgende Aufzählung aller verantwortlichen Funktionen wird klar, dass in jedem die materiellen Organe erfasst sind.

B. Haftung gegenüber Genossenschaft, Genossenschaftern und Gläubigern

Art. 917

1 Die Mitglieder der Verwaltung und die Liquidatoren, welche die für den Fall der Überschuldung der Genossenschaft vom Gesetz aufgestellten Pflichten absichtlich oder fahrlässig verletzen, haften der Genossenschaft, den einzelnen Genossenschaftern und den Gläubigern für den entstandenen Schaden.

2 Der Ersatz des Schadens, der den Genossenschaftern und den Gläubigern nur mittelbar durch Schädigung der Genossenschaft verursacht wurde, ist nach den für die Aktiengesellschaft aufgestellten Vorschriften geltend zu machen.

C. Solidarität und Rückgriff

Art. 918

1 Sind mehrere Personen für denselben Schaden verantwortlich, so haften sie solidarisch.

2 Der Rückgriff unter mehreren Beteiligten wird vom Richter nach dem Grade des Verschuldens des einzelnen bestimmt.

Kapitel 1: Neue Gesetzesbestimmungen und Erläuterungen

D. Verjährung

Art. 919

1 Der Anspruch auf Schadenersatz gegen die nach den vorstehenden Bestimmungen verantwortlichen Personen verjährt in fünf Jahren von dem Tage an, an dem der Geschädigte Kenntnis vom Schaden und von der Person des Ersatzpflichtigen erlangt hat, jedenfalls aber mit dem Ablaufe von zehn Jahren, vom Tage der schädigenden Handlung an gerechnet.

2 Wird die Klage aus einer strafbaren Handlung hergeleitet, für die das Strafrecht eine längere Verjährung vorschreibt, so gilt diese auch für den Zivilanspruch.

E. Bei Kredit- und Versicherungsgenossenschaften

Art. 920

Bei Kreditgenossenschaften und konzessionierten Versicherungsgenossenschaften richtet sich die Verantwortlichkeit nach den Bestimmungen des Aktienrechts.

Achter Abschnitt: Genossenschaftsverbände

A. Voraussetzungen

Art. 921

Drei oder mehr Genossenschaften können einen Genossenschaftsverband bilden und ihn als Genossenschaft ausgestalten.

B. Organisation
I. Delegiertenversammlung

Art. 922

1 Oberstes Organ des Genossenschaftsverbandes ist, sofern die Statuten es nicht anders ordnen, die Delegiertenversammlung.

2 Die Statuten bestimmen die Zahl der Delegierten der angeschlossenen Genossenschaften.

3 Jeder Delegierte hat, unter Vorbehalt anderer Regelung durch die Statuten, eine Stimme.

II. Verwaltung

Art. 923

Die Verwaltung wird, sofern die Statuten es nicht anders bestimmen, aus Mitgliedern der angeschlossenen Genossenschaften gebildet.

III. Überwachung. Anfechtung

Art. 924

1 Die Statuten können der Verwaltung des Verbandes das Recht einräumen, die geschäftliche Tätigkeit der angeschlossenen Genossenschaften zu überwachen.

2 Sie können der Verwaltung des Verbandes das Recht verleihen, Beschlüsse, die von den einzelnen angeschlossenen Genossenschaften gefasst worden sind, beim Richter durch Klage anzufechten.

Kapitel 1: Neue Gesetzesbestimmungen und Erläuterungen

IV. Ausschluss neuer Verpflichtungen

Art. 925

Der Eintritt in einen Genossenschaftsverband darf für die Mitglieder der eintretenden Genossenschaft keine Verpflichtungen zur Folge haben, denen sie nicht schon durch das Gesetz oder die Statuten ihrer Genossenschaft unterworfen sind.

Neunter Abschnitt:
Beteiligung von Körperschaften des öffentlichen Rechts

Art. 926

1 Bei Genossenschaften, an denen Körperschaften des öffentlichen Rechts, wie Bund, Kanton, Bezirk oder Gemeinde, ein öffentliches Interesse besitzen, kann der Körperschaft in den Statuten der Genossenschaft das Recht eingeräumt werden, Vertreter in die Verwaltung oder in die Revisionsstelle abzuordnen.

2 Die von einer Körperschaft des öffentlichen Rechts abgeordneten Mitglieder haben die gleichen Rechte und Pflichten wie die von der Genossenschaft gewählten.

3 Die Abberufung der von einer Körperschaft des öffentlichen Rechts abgeordneten Mitglieder der Verwaltung und der Revisionsstelle steht nur der Körperschaft selbst zu. Diese haftet gegenüber der Genossenschaft, den Genossenschaftern und den Gläubiger für diese Mitglieder, unter Vorbehalt des Rückgriffs nach dem Rechte des Bundes und der Kantone.

Aus Gründen einer einheitlichen Terminologie wird der Ausdruck «Kontrollstelle» sowohl in *Abs. 1* als auch in *Abs. 3* durch den Begriff «Revisionsstelle» ersetzt. Im Weiteren erfolgt die erforderliche Anpassung von Abs. 1 an den Wortlaut des Art. 762 Abs. 1 OR, die anlässlich der Aktienrechtsrevision von 1991 unterblieben ist. Körperschaften des öffentlichen Rechts können bei Aktiengesellschaften und neu auch bei Genossenschaften nur Vertreter in den Verwaltungsrat bzw. Verwaltung *oder* in die Revisionsstelle entsenden, nicht aber in beide Organe.

§ 4 Änderung anderer Bestimmungen des Obligationenrechts

Erste Abteilung: Allgemeine Bestimmungen

Fünfter Titel: Die Abtretung von Forderungen und die Schuldübernahme

B. Schuldübernahme

V. Übernahme eines Vermögens oder eines Geschäftes

Art. 181

1 Wer ein Vermögen oder ein Geschäft mit Aktiven und Passiven übernimmt, wird den Gläubigern aus den damit verbundenen Schulden ohne weiteres verpflichtet, sobald von dem Übernehmer die Übernahme den Gläubigern mitgeteilt oder in öffentlichen Blättern ausgekündigt worden ist.

2 Der bisherige Schuldner haftet jedoch solidarisch mit dem neuen noch während dreier Jahre, die für fällige Forderungen mit der Mitteilung oder der Auskündigung und bei später fällig werdenden Forderungen mit Eintritt der Fälligkeit zu laufen beginnen.[132]

3 Im übrigen hat diese Schuldübernahme die gleiche Wirkung wie die Übernahme einer einzelnen Schuld.

4 Die Übernahme des Vermögens oder des Geschäfts von Handelsgesellschaften, Genossenschaften, Vereinen, Stiftungen und Einzelunternehmen, die im Handelsregister eingetragen sind, richtet sich nach den Vorschriften des Fusionsgesetzes vom 3. Oktober 2003[133].

---

[132] Fassung gemäss Anhang Ziff. 2 des Fusionsgesetzes vom 3. Okt. 2003, in Kraft seit 1. Juli 2004 (SR **221.301**).
[133] SR **221.301**; AS **2004** 2617

Der Bundesrat hat im Rahmen der Revision des Rechts der GmbH beschlossen, den Begriff der «Einzelfirma» durch denjenigen des «Einzelunternehmens» zu ersetzen, um eine missverständliche Verwendung des Begriffs der «Firma» zu vermeiden[134].
Im Bundesgesetz vom 3. Oktober 2003 über Fusion, Spaltung, Umwandlung und Vermögensübertragung[135] sowie in den Änderungen des bisherigen Rechts gemäss Anhang wird demgegenüber noch die Bezeichnung «Einzelfirma» verwendet. Mit dem vorliegenden Entwurf wird die Anpassung an die neue Terminologie vorgenommen.

Zweite Abteilung: Die Einzelnen Vertragsverhältnisse

Sechster Titel: Kauf und Tausch

Vierter Abschnitt: Besondere Arten des Kaufes

C. Teilzahlungsgeschäfte

II. Der Vorauszahlungsvertrag

5. Geltungsbereich

Art. 227i

Die Art. 227a–227h finden keine Anwendung, wenn der Käufer als Einzelunternehmen oder als Zeichnungsberechtigter eines Einzelunternehmens oder einer Handelsgesellschaft im Handelsregister eingetragen ist oder wenn sich der Kauf auf Gegenstände bezieht, die nach ihrer Beschaffenheit vorwiegend für einen Gewerbebetrieb oder vorwiegend für berufliche Zwecke bestimmt sind.

Der Entwurf sieht terminologische Anpassungen vor; s. dazu auch die Ausführungen zu Art. 181 Abs. 4 E OR.

---

134 BBl **2002** 3240 3296.
135 SR **221.301**; AS **2004** 2617.

Zwanzigster Titel: Die Bürgschaft

A. Voraussetzungen

III. Zustimmung des Ehegatten

Art. 494

1 Die Bürgschaft einer verheirateten Person bedarf zu ihrer Gültigkeit der im einzelnen Fall vorgängig oder spätestens gleichzeitig abgegebenen schriftlichen Zustimmung des Ehegatten, wenn die Ehe nicht durch richterliches Urteil getrennt ist.

2 ...[136]

3 Für nachträgliche Abänderungen einer Bürgschaft ist die Zustimmung des andern Ehegatten nur erforderlich, wenn der Haftungsbetrag erhöht oder eine einfache Bürgschaft in eine Solidarbürgschaft umgewandelt werden soll, oder wenn die Änderung eine erhebliche Verminderung der Sicherheiten bedeutet.

4 Die gleiche Regelung gilt bei eingetragenen Partnerschaften sinngemäss.

Der Entwurf sieht eine terminologische Anpassung vor; s. dazu die Ausführungen zu Art. 181 Abs. 4 E OR.

---

136 Aufgehoben durch Ziff. II 2 des BG vom 5. Okt. 1984 über die Änderung des ZGB (AS **1986** 122; BBl **1979** II 1191).

Kapitel 1: Neue Gesetzesbestimmungen und Erläuterungen

Dritte Abteilung: Die Handelsgesellschaften und die Genossenschaft

Vierundzwanzigster Titel: Die Kollektivgesellschaft

Erster Abschnitt: Begriff und Errichtung

C. Registereintrag

I. Ort und Inhalt

Art. 554

Die Gesellschaft ist ins Handelsregister des Ortes einzutragen, an dem sie ihren Sitz hat.

Der Inhalt der Eintragung ins Handelsregister soll neu für alle Gesellschaftsformen in der Handelsregisterverordnung geregelt werden, da es sich dabei um Einzelheiten eher technischer Natur handelt. Eine entsprechende Delegation wird im Handelsregisterrecht in Art. 929 Abs. 1 E OR vorgesehen (s. dazu die Ausführungen zu dieser Bestimmung). Der bisherige Abs. 2 von Art. 554 OR kann demnach entfallen. Die Bestimmung bleibt im Übrigen unverändert (abgesehen von einer redaktionellen Änderung in der französischen Fassung).

Fünfundzwanzigster Titel: Die Kommanditgesellschaft

Erster Abschnitt: Begriff und Errichtung

C. Registereintrag

I. Ort der Eintragung und Sacheinlagen

Art. 596

1 Die Gesellschaft ist in das Handelsregister des Ortes einzutragen, an dem sie ihren Sitz hat.

2 ...

3 Soll die Kommanditsumme nicht oder nur teilweise in bar entrichtet werden, so ist die Sacheinlage in der Anmeldung ausdrücklich und mit bestimmtem Wertansatz zu bezeichnen und in das Handelsregister einzutragen.

Abs. 2 kann gestrichen werden, da der Inhalt des Handelsregisters neu in der Handelsregisterverordnung geregelt werden soll (s. dazu die Ausführungen zu Art. 929 Abs. 1 E OR). *Abs. 3* ist beizubehalten, weil die Eintragung ins Handelsregister für Sacheinlagen eine materielle Gültigkeitsvoraussetzung darstellt (s. auch Art. 642 E OR).

Siebenundzwanzigster Titel: Die Kommanditaktiengesellschaft

B. Verwaltung

I. Bezeichnung und Befugnisse

Art. 765

1 Die unbeschränkt haftenden Mitglieder bilden die Verwaltung der Kommanditaktiengesellschaft. Ihnen steht die Geschäftsführung und die Vertretung zu. Sie sind in den Statuten zu nennen.

2 Der Name, der Wohnsitz, der Heimatort und die Funktion der Mitglieder der Verwaltung sowie der zur Vertretung befugten Personen sind in das Handelsregister einzutragen.

3 Für Änderungen im Bestande der unbeschränkt haftenden Mitglieder bedarf es der Zustimmung der bisherigen Mitglieder und der Änderung der Statuten.

Die vorliegende Bestimmung soll in Anlehnung an die unbestrittene Handelsregisterpraxis vervollständigt werden. Die Mitglieder der Verwaltung und die zur Vertretung befugten Personen sind unter Angabe ihres Namens, Wohnsitzes, Heimatortes sowie gegebenenfalls ihrer Funktion ins Handelsregister einzutragen.

Kapitel 1: Neue Gesetzesbestimmungen und Erläuterungen

Vierte Abteilung: Handelsregister, Geschäftsfirmen und kaufmännische Buchführung

Dreissigster Titel: Das Handelsregister

A. Zweck und Einrichtung

III. Verordnung des Bundesrates

Art. 929

1 Der Bundesrat erlässt die Vorschriften über die Einrichtung, die Führung und die Beaufsichtigung des Handelsregisters sowie über das Verfahren, die Anmeldung zur Eintragung, die einzureichenden Belege und deren Prüfung, den Inhalt der Eintragungen, die Gebühren und die Beschwerdeführung.

2 Die Gebühren sollen der wirtschaftlichen Bedeutung des Unternehmens angepasst sein.

Das geltende Recht sieht auf Gesetzesstufe Bestimmungen zur Anmeldung beim Handelsregisteramt, zu den einzureichenden Belegen und zum Inhalt des Registereintrags vor. Im Gesetz finden sich entsprechende Listen, die bei den verschiedenen Gesellschaftsformen wiederholt werden (s. Art. 554, 596, 640 f., 780 f., 835 f. OR). Demgegenüber sind der Inhalt der Eintragung und die Belege für den Verein und die Stiftung in der Handelsregisterverordnung vorgesehen (vgl. Art. 61 und 81 Abs. 2 ZGB; Art. 97 ff. und 101 ff. HRegV).

Die aufgeführten Regelungsgegenstände sind materiellrechtlich und politisch nur von beschränkter Bedeutung, wobei selbst für die Bestimmung des Registerinhalts sachlich nur ein enger Entscheidungsspielraum besteht. Es erscheint daher möglich, diese Punkte an den Bundesrat zu delegieren. Eine Verweisung auf Verordnungsebene erlaubt, das Gesetz von eher technischen Listen zu entlasten und die Regelung der Einzelheiten der Eintragung in der Handelsregisterverordnung zusammenzufassen, ohne dass gesetzliche Bestimmungen (wie bisher) in der Verordnung wiederholt werden müssen (vgl. bspw. Art. 836 OR und Art. 93 HRegV).

Die geltende Delegationsnorm in Art. 929 Abs. 1 OR ist sehr weit gefasst und ermächtigt den Bundesrat unter anderem zum Erlass von Vorschriften über die Einrichtung und die Führung des Handelsregisters sowie über das Verfahren. Gestützt auf diese Aufgabenzuweisung hat der Bundesrat bereits heute die notwendigen Vorschriften zur Anmeldung, zu den Belegen und zum Registerinhalt in der Handelsregisterverordnung vorgesehen, soweit dazu für einzelne Rechtsformen gesetzliche Bestimmungen fehlen. Da diese Sachfragen für die Rechtsformen des Obligationenrechts bisher zumindest zum Teil im Gesetz geregelt wurden, ist es vorzuziehen, die Delegationsnorm entsprechend zu ergänzen. Dabei handelt es sich jedoch lediglich um eine Klarstellung. Die vorgeschlagenen Modifikationen sollen die bisherige umfassende Delegation in keiner Weise einschränken.

B. Eintragungen

I. Anmeldung

Art. 931a

1 Bei juristischen Personen obliegt die Anmeldung zur Eintragung ins Handelsregister dem obersten Leitungs- oder Verwaltungsorgan. Spezialgesetzliche Vorschriften betreffend öffentlich-rechtliche Körperschaften und Anstalten bleiben vorbehalten.

2 Die Anmeldung muss von zwei Mitgliedern des obersten Leitungs- oder Verwaltungsorgans oder von einem Mitglied mit Einzelzeichnungsberechtigung unterzeichnet werden. Die Anmeldung ist beim Handelsregisteramt zu unterzeichnen oder mit den beglaubigten Unterschriften einzureichen.

Die Unterzeichnung der Anmeldung von Eintragungen ins Handelsregister soll neu für alle juristischen Personen in einer einzigen Bestimmung geregelt werden. Die bisher für die verschiedenen Rechtsformen vorgesehenen, teilweise uneinheitlichen Vorschriften können in der Folge aufgehoben werden (Art. 640 Abs. 2, Art. 642 Abs. 2, Art. 647 Abs. 2, Art. 780 Abs. 2, Art. 782 Abs. 2, Art. 835 Abs. 3, Art. 837 Abs. 2 OR).

Nach *Abs. 1* obliegt die Anmeldung zur Eintragung ins Handelsregister dem obersten Leitungs- oder Verwaltungsorgan. Dieser Begriff wird aus dem Entwurf zum Fusionsgesetz übernommen; es handelt sich dabei in der Aktiengesellschaft um den Verwaltungsrat, in der GmbH um die Geschäftsführerinnen und Geschäftsführer, in der Genossenschaft und in der Kommanditaktiengesellschaft um die Verwaltung, im Verein um den Vorstand und in der Stiftung um den Stiftungsrat[137]. Spezialgesetzliche Vorschriften zur Anmeldung beim Handelsregister betreffend öffentlich-rechtliche Körperschaften und Anstalten bleiben vorbehalten.

Nach *Abs. 2* muss die Anmeldung von zwei Mitgliedern des obersten Leitungs- oder Verwaltungsorgans oder von einem Mitglied mit Einzelzeichnungsberechtigung unterschrieben werden. Wie im geltenden Recht ist die Anmeldung entweder beim Handelsregisteramt zu unterzeichnen oder mit den beglaubigten Unterschriften einzureichen.

II. Beginn der Wirksamkeit

Art. 932 Randtitel

III. Wirkungen

Art. 933 Randtitel

Art. 932 und 933 Randtitel

Geändert wird nur die Nummerierung der Randtitel.

IV. Eintragung ins Handelsregister

1. Recht und Pflicht

Art. 934

1 Wer ein Handels-, Fabrikations- oder ein anderes nach kaufmännischer Art geführtes Gewerbe betreibt, ist verpflichtet, dieses am Ort der Hauptniederlassung ins Handelsregister eintragen zu lassen.

---

137 BBl **2000** 4406 und 4470.

2 Wer unter einer Firma ein Gewerbe betreibt, das nicht eingetragen werden muss, hat das Recht, dieses am Ort der Hauptniederlassung ins Handelsregister eintragen zu lassen.

Der Randtitel und der Gesetzestext dieser Bestimmung werden rein redaktionell umformuliert, um eine missverständliche Verwendung des Begriffs der «Firma» zu vermeiden (zum Begriff der Firma im Rechtssinn vgl. Art. 944 ff. OR).

3. Ausführungsbestimmungen

b. Identifikationsnummer

Art. 936a

1 Die im Handelsregister eingetragenen Einzelunternehmen, Kollektiv- und Kommanditgesellschaften, Kapitalgesellschaften, Genossenschaften, Vereine, Stiftungen und Institute des öffentlichen Rechts erhalten eine Identifikationsnummer.

2 Die Identifikationsnummer bleibt während des Bestehens des Rechtsträgers unverändert, so insbesondere auch bei der Sitzverlegung, der Umwandlung und der Änderung des Namens oder der Firma.

3 Der Bundesrat erlässt Ausführungsvorschriften. Er kann vorsehen, dass die Identifikationsnummer nebst der Firma auf Briefen, Bestellscheinen und Rechnungen anzugeben ist.

Der Entwurf sieht eine terminologische Anpassung vor; siehe dazu die Ausführungen zu Art. 181 Abs. 4 E OR.

V. Änderung

Art. 937 Randtitel

Kapitel 1: Neue Gesetzesbestimmungen und Erläuterungen

Art. 937 Randtitel

Geändert wird nur die Nummerierung des Randtitels.

VI. Löschung

1. Pflicht zur Löschung

Art. 938

Wenn ein im Handelsregister eingetragenes Gewerbe zu bestehen aufhört oder auf eine andere Person übergeht, so sind die bisherigen Inhaber oder deren Erben verpflichtet, die Eintragung löschen zu lassen.

Die Bestimmung wird rein redaktionell umformuliert, um eine missverständliche Verwendung des Begriffs «Firma» zu vermeiden.

2. Löschung von Amtes wegen

Art. 938a

1 Weist eine Gesellschaft keine Geschäftstätigkeit mehr auf und hat sie keine verwertbaren Aktiven mehr, so kann sie der Handelsregisterführer nach dreimaligem ergebnislosem Rechnungsruf im Handelsregister löschen.

2 Macht ein Gesellschafter beziehungsweise ein Aktionär oder Genossenschafter oder ein Gläubiger ein Interesse an der Aufrechterhaltung der Eintragung geltend, so entscheidet der Richter.

3 Der Bundesrat regelt die Einzelheiten.

Es kommt in der Praxis vor, dass Gesellschaften, die ihre Geschäftstätigkeit aufgegeben haben und die faktisch liquidiert wurden, im Handelsregister nicht gelöscht werden. Die Handelsregisterverordnung sieht daher in Art. 89 seit langem die Möglichkeit der Löschung von Amtes wegen vor. Die entsprechende Regelung hat sich grundsätzlich bewährt, soll aber auf Grund ihrer materiellrechtlichen Bedeutung ins Gesetz aufgenommen werden. Sie wird nicht in die Bestimmung über die Mängel in der Organisation der Gesellschaft integriert (Art. 731b E OR), weil meist kein gerichtliches Verfahren notwendig ist.

Eine Löschung von Amtes wegen setzt stets kumulativ voraus, dass die Gesellschaft ihre Geschäftstätigkeit vollumfänglich eingestellt hat, dass – nach den Umständen zu schliessen – keine verwertbaren Aktiven mehr vorhanden sind und dass ein dreimaliger Rechnungsruf ergebnislos geblieben ist *(Abs. 1).* Falls eine Gläubigerin, ein Gläubiger oder eine an der Gesellschaft beteiligte Person ein Interesse an der Aufrechterhaltung der Eintragung geltend macht, soll nicht wie bisher die Aufsichtsbehörde in Handelsregistersachen, sondern das Zivilgericht über die Löschung entscheiden *(Abs. 2).*

In Ergänzung der neuen gesetzlichen Grundlagen wird der Bundesrat mit der Regelung der Einzelheiten der Löschung von Amtes wegen beauftragt *(Abs. 3).* Er kann dabei insbesondere auch die Verfahrenskosten Personen auferlegen, die ihre Pflicht zur Löschung der Gesellschaft nach Art. 938 OR verletzt haben (dies auch dann, wenn sie inzwischen aus den Organen der Gesellschaft ausgeschieden sind).

3. Organe und Vertretungsbefugnisse

Art. 938b

1 Scheiden im Handelsregister als Organ eingetragene Personen aus ihrem Amt aus, so muss die betroffene juristische Person unverzüglich deren Löschung verlangen.

2 Die ausgeschiedenen Personen können ihre Löschung auch selbst anmelden. Der Registerführer teilt der juristischen Person die Löschung unverzüglich mit.

3 Diese Vorschriften sind für die Löschung eingetragener Zeichnungsberechtigter ebenfalls anwendbar.

Der Entwurf sieht eine Neuregelung der Löschung von Organmitgliedern und Vertretungsbefugnissen vor, die an die Stelle der uneinheitlichen Vorschriften für die verschiedenen Rechtsformen tritt. Grundsätzlich obliegt es der Gesellschaft, im Handelsregister als Organ eingetragene Personen unverzüglich löschen zu lassen, wenn diese aus ihrem Amt ausscheiden

(*Abs. 1*). Weil das Mandat von Organen in jedem Fall zwingend mit ihrer rechtsgenügenden Demission beendet wird, haben sowohl die ausscheidenden Personen als auch Dritte ein grosses Interesse an einer umgehenden Bereinigung des Handelsregistereintrags, da unrichtig gewordene Eintragungen zu Täuschungen führen können. Ausgeschiedene Personen müssen daher ihre Löschung auch selbst erwirken können (*Abs. 2*). Es gibt keinen überzeugenden Grund, ihnen dieses Recht wie bisher erst zuzugestehen, wenn die Gesellschaft 30 Tage untätig geblieben ist (vgl. Art. 711 Abs. 2 OR; Art. 25*a* HRegV); vielmehr kann eine möglichst rasche Löschung in Problemfällen auch im Interesse Dritter von erheblicher Bedeutung sein. Der betroffenen Gesellschaft ist die Löschung jedoch unverzüglich mitzuteilen.

Die Regelung der Löschung von Organmitgliedern kann auch für die Löschung von im Handelsregister eingetragenen Zeichnungsberechtigungen Anwendung finden (*Abs. 3*). Dabei bleibt unbeachtlich, ob es sich um eine Zeichnungsberechtigung für eine juristische Person, eine Personengesellschaft oder eine Einzelfirma handelt.

VII. Konkurs von Handelsgesellschaften und Genossenschaften

Art. 939 Randtitel

VIII. Pflichten des Registerführers
1. Prüfungspflicht

Art. 940 Randtitel

Art. 939 und 940 Randtitel

Geändert wird nur die Nummerierung der Randtitel.

3. Überweisung an den Richter oder an die Aufsichtsbehörde

Art. 941a[138] *(ursprünglicher Botschaftsentwurf)*

1 Bei Mängeln in der gesetzlich zwingend vorgeschriebenen Organisation der Gesellschaft stellt der Registerführer den Antrag, die erforderlichen Massnahmen zu treffen.

2 Sind die zwingenden Vorschriften über die Revisionsstelle im Verein oder in der Stiftung verletzt, so stellt der Registerführer dem Richter beziehungsweise der Aufsichtsbehörde den Antrag, die erforderlichen Massnahmen zu ergreifen.

Art. 941a *(durch den Nationalrat bereinigte Version, neuer Abs. 1bis)*

1 Bei Mängeln in der gesetzlich zwingend vorgeschriebenen Organisation der Gesellschaft stellt der Registerführer dem Richter den Antrag, die erforderlichen Massnahmen zu ergreifen.

1bis Bei Mängeln in der gesetzlich zwingend vorgeschriebenen Organisation der Stiftung stellt der Registerführer der Aufsichtsbehörde den Antrag, die erforderlichen Massnahmen zu ergreifen.

2 Sind die zwingenden Vorschriften über die Revisionsstelle im Verein verletzt, so stellt der Registerführer dem Richter den Antrag, die erforderlichen Massnahmen zu ergreifen.

Der Entwurf zur Revision des Rechts der GmbH enthält eine Neuregelung des Vorgehens bei Mängeln in der Organisation von Gesellschaften (s. Art. 731*b*, 819, 910*a* E OR; vgl. dazu die Ausführungen zu Art. 908 E OR sowie zu Art. 69*c* und 83*d* E ZGB).

Abs. 1 knüpft an diese Regelung an und macht es der Registerführerin oder dem Registerführer zur Aufgabe, bei Mängeln in der gesetzlich zwingend vorgeschriebenen Organisation der Gesellschaft das Gericht zu benachrichtigen und diesem zu beantragen, die erforderlichen Massnah-

---

[138] Ersetzt Art. 941*a* des Entwurfs zur Revision des Rechts der GmbH vom 19. Dezember 2001 (BBl **2002** 3296).

men zu ergreifen. Die Vorschrift entspricht Art. 941*a* E OR des Entwurfes zur Revision des Rechts der GmbH[139]. Lediglich der Begriff «Handelsregisterführer» wird durch den Ausdruck «Registerführer» ersetzt.
Die im Rahmen der Revision des Rechts der GmbH vorgesehene Regelung ist um einen *Abs. 2* zu ergänzen, weil sie davon ausgeht, dass für Vereine und Stiftungen keine zwingenden Vorschriften zur Bestellung einer Revisionsstelle bestehen. Mit dem vorliegenden Entwurf werden Vereine und Stiftungen jedoch unter bestimmten Voraussetzungen revisionspflichtig (s. Art. 69*b* und Art. 83*b* E ZGB). Sind die zwingenden Vorschriften über die Revisionsstelle im Verein oder in der Stiftung verletzt, so muss die Registerführerin oder der Registerführer dem Gericht (im Falle des Vereins) beziehungsweise der Aufsichtsbehörde (im Falle einer Stiftung) beantragen, die erforderlichen Massnahmen zu ergreifen. Das Gericht bzw. die Aufsichtsbehörde entscheidet über das weitere Vorgehen.

Der Erweiterung des Artikels entsprechend muss auch der Randtitel angepasst werden.[140]

IX. Nichtbefolgung der Vorschriften

1. Haftung für Schaden

Art. 942 Randtitel

Art. 942 Randtitel

Geändert wird nur die Nummerierung des Randtitels.

---

139 BBl **2002** 3239 f., 3296.
140 Die vorliegenden Erläuterungen beziehen sich ausschliesslich auf die ursprüngliche bundesrätliche Gesetzesversion und nicht auf die bereinigte Fassung durch den Nationalrat.

Teil F: Rechtliche Aspekte / Legal aspects

Einunddreissigster Titel: Die Geschäftsfirmen

A. Grundsätze der Firmenbildung

II. Einzelunternehmen

1. Wesentlicher Inhalt

Art. 945 Randtitel

Im Randtitel wird der Begriff «Einzelfirma» durch «Einzelunternehmen» ersetzt, um eine missverständliche Verwendung des Begriffs der «Firma» zu vermeiden.

III. Gesellschaftsfirmen

2. Gesellschaft mit beschränkter Haftung

Art. 949

Aufgehoben

Diese Bestimmung wird aufgehoben, weil die Firmenbildung für die GmbH, die Aktiengesellschaft und die Genossenschaft in Art. 950 E OR einheitlich geregelt werden soll.

2. Aktiengesellschaft, Gesellschaft mit beschränkter Haftung und Genossenschaft

Art. 950

Aktiengesellschaften, Gesellschaften mit beschränkter Haftung und Genossenschaften können unter Wahrung der allgemeinen Grundsätze der Firmenbildung ihre Firma frei wählen. In der Firma muss die Rechtsform angegeben werden.

Im geltenden Recht ist die Firmenbildung für die GmbH anders geregelt als für die Aktiengesellschaft und die Genossenschaft. Während diese die

Bezeichnung der Rechtsform nur beifügen müssen, wenn die Firma Personennamen enthält, ist die Angabe der Rechtsform für die GmbH stets erforderlich (vgl. Art. 949 f. OR). Da abweichende Vorschriften zur Firma nicht plausibel erscheinen, gilt es im Rahmen der Revision des GmbH-Rechts eine einheitliche Ordnung zu schaffen.

Wie bisher sollen die Aktiengesellschaft, die GmbH und die Genossenschaft ihre Firma unter Wahrung der allgemeinen Grundsätze zur Firmenbildung frei wählen dürfen. Weil das Firmenrecht nur beschränkt kodifiziert ist, sei hier darauf hingewiesen, dass die allgemeinen Grundsätze neben den Vorschriften des Obligationenrechts und der Handelsregisterverordnung auch die Kriterien umfassen, die in der Rechtsprechung des Bundesgerichts und in der Praxis der Handelsregisterbehörden herausgebildet wurden[141].

Ein selbstverständliches und daher im Gesetz nicht erwähntes Erfordernis der Firmenbildung liegt in der Erkennbarkeit als Firma: Die Firma dient als Zeichen für ein Rechtssubjekt oder einen andern Rechtsträger; sie kann dieser Zeichenfunktion aber nur gerecht werden, wenn sie im Rechtsverkehr ohne weiteres als Firma erkannt wird. Ausdrücke, die nach dem Sprachgebrauch nicht zweifelsfrei als Firma verstanden werden (so bspw. blosse Buchstabenkombinationen wie «WBR») können nicht als Firma dienen, weil ihnen keine firmenspezifische Zeichenfunktion zukommt und sie daher keine Firma im Rechtssinne darstellen. 1998 hat das Eidgenössische Amt für das Handelsregister eine Liberalisierung der früheren strengen Praxis im Firmenrecht realisiert. Dabei zeigte sich, dass die Angabe der Rechtsform eine Voraussetzung für eine liberale Praxis im Firmenrecht darstellt, weil dadurch die Erkennbarkeit eines Zeichens als Firma sichergestellt wird (Bsp. «WBR AG»). Die Angabe der Rechtsform in der Firma entspricht zudem den Informationserfordernissen der Praxis im Rechtsverkehr und aus diesem Grund auch der internationalen Rechtsentwicklung[142].

---

141 Das Eidgenössische Amt für das Handelsregister (EHRA) hat die in der Rechtsprechung und Praxis seit langer Zeit entwickelten Regeln zur Firmenbildung 1998 liberalisiert und in der Anleitung und Weisung an die Handelsregisterbehörden betreffend die Prüfung von Firmen und Namen zusammengestellt (Bezugsquelle: Bundesamt für Bauten und Logistik, Vertrieb Publikationen, 3003 Bern, Art.-Nr. 401.020 d).

142 Art. 4 der 1. Richtlinie (68/151/EWG; ABl. Nr. L 065 vom 14.03.1968, S.8 ff.) verlangt die Angabe der Rechtsform im Rechtsverkehr. Diese Vorgabe wird durch das Landesrecht am einfachsten im Rahmen der Vorschriften zur Firmenbildung umgesetzt.

Der Entwurf sieht deshalb vor, dass die Aktiengesellschaft und die Genossenschaft in gleicher Weise wie bisher die GmbH generell die Rechtsform in der Firma angeben müssen. Wirklich relevante Nachteile ergeben sich daraus keine: Nach wie vor dürfen Logos und andere Schriftzüge verwendet werden, die keinen Rechtsformzusatz enthalten. Die obligatorische Angabe der Rechtsform bleibt von vornherein auf den Rahmen der Firmengebrauchspflicht (s. Art. 954*a* E OR) beschränkt. Erforderlich ist demnach nur, dass im formellen Geschäftsverkehr irgendwo auf dem Briefpapier die Firma samt Rechtsformzusatz verwendet wird. Dies kann beispielsweise bei der Unterschrift oder in einer Fusszeile erfolgen; eine Abänderung des Briefpapiers erübrigt sich daher (zum Übergangsrecht s. die Ausführungen zu Art. 2 Abs. 4 UeB).

3. Ausschliesslichkeit der eingetragenen Firma

Art. 951

1 Die Vorschriften über die Ausschliesslichkeit der eingetragenen Firma von Einzelunternehmen gelten auch für die Firma der Kollektivgesellschaft, der Kommanditgesellschaft und der Kommanditaktiengesellschaft.

2 Die Firmen der Aktiengesellschaften, der Gesellschaften mit beschränkter Haftung und der Genossenschaften müssen sich von allen in der Schweiz bereits eingetragenen Firmen von Gesellschaften in einer dieser Rechtsformen deutlich unterscheiden.

In der Praxis ist wenig bekannt, dass nach dem geltenden Recht für die Firma der GmbH eine andere Regelung der Ausschliesslichkeit gilt als für die Aktiengesellschaft: Enthält die Firma einer GmbH Personennamen, so bleibt ihre Ausschliesslichkeit auf den Ort des Sitzes beschränkt (Art. 951 Abs. 1 i.V.m. Art. 946 Abs. 1 OR). Daraus können sich jedoch Verwechslungen mit der Firma anderer GmbH ergeben. Eine Harmonisierung der Vorschriften für die GmbH mit denjenigen für die Aktiengesellschaft ist daher geboten. Ungeachtet ihrer Zusammensetzung soll die Firma der GmbH zukünftig wie die Firma der Aktiengesellschaft und der Genossenschaft für die ganze Schweiz das Recht der Ausschliesslichkeit geniessen.

Die Revision der vorliegenden Bestimmung muss weiter klarstellen, wie sich die Ausschlusswirkungen der Firmen von Unternehmen mit unterschiedlicher Rechtsform zueinander verhalten. Dies ist erforderlich, weil der Rechtsformzusatz nach der Rechtsprechung nicht als unterscheidungskräftig gilt[143]. Der Entwurf definiert zwei Kategorien von Rechtsformen, denen unterschiedliche räumliche Schutzkreise zugeordnet werden, wobei eine Ausschliesslichkeit nur innerhalb der beiden Kategorien beachtet werden muss[144]: Die Firmen von Einzelunternehmen, Personengesellschaften und Kommanditaktiengesellschaften haben sich von den eingetragenen Firmen von Unternehmen deutlich zu unterscheiden, die am selben Orte ansässig sind und eine der erwähnten Rechtsformen aufweisen (Art. 951 Abs. 1 E OR i.V.m. 946 Abs. 1 OR). Die Firmen von Aktiengesellschaften, GmbH und Genossenschaften müssen sich von allen Firmen von Gesellschaften mit Sitz in der Schweiz deutlich unterscheiden, die eine dieser drei Rechtsformen aufweisen (Art. 951 Abs. 2 E OR). Ist in der Schweiz bereits eine «Muster AG» im Handelsregister eingetragen, darf demzufolge keine «Muster GmbH» eingetragen werden. Hingegen steht der Eintragung einer «Gertrud Muster GmbH» grundsätzlich nicht entgegen, dass bereits ein Einzelunternehmen unter der Firma «Gertrud Muster» eingetragen ist (dies selbst dann nicht, wenn beide Unternehmen am gleichen Ort ansässig sind); vorbehalten bleiben jedoch firmen- und wettbewerbsrechtliche Ansprüche von Unternehmen mit ähnlichen Firmen.

B.   Firmen- und Namensgebrauchspflicht

Art. 954a (ursprünglicher Botschaftsentwurf)

1 In der Korrespondenz, auf Bestellscheinen und Rechnungen sowie in Bekanntmachungen muss die im Handelsregister eingetragene Firma vollständig und unverändert angegeben werden.

2 Zusätzlich können Kurzbezeichnungen, Logos, Geschäftsbezeichnungen, Enseignes und ähnliche Angaben verwendet werden.

---

143 vgl. das in der Amtlichen Sammlung nicht veröffentlichte Urteil des Schweizerischen Bundesgerichts vom 11.9.1998, in: REPRAX 2/99, S. 69 ff., insb. S. 75.
144 Im geltenden Recht ist das Verhältnis zwischen Abs. 1 und Abs. 2 von Art. 951 OR unklar.

Teil F: Rechtliche Aspekte / Legal aspects

Art. 954a (durch den Ständerat bereinigte Version)

1 In der Korrespondenz, auf Bestellscheinen und Rechnungen sowie in Bekanntmachungen muss die im Handelsregister eingetragene Firma oder der im Handelsregister eingetragene Name vollständig und unverändert angegeben werden.

Art. 326ter StGB sanktioniert die Verwendung von Firmen, die nicht mit dem im Handelsregister eingetragenen Wortlaut übereinstimmen und die irreführen können. Die zivilrechtliche Firmengebrauchspflicht ist jedoch im geltenden Obligationenrecht nicht ausdrücklich festgehalten, da sie wohl als selbstverständlich erachtet wurde. Im nur unvollständig kodifizierten, alten Rechtsbereich des Firmenrechts ist der Firmengebrauchspflicht bisher gewohnheitsrechtlicher Charakter beizumessen. Mit Blick auf die Strafnorm wurde sie vor wenigen Jahren in der Handelsregisterverordnung erwähnt (s. Art. 47 HRegV). Es erscheint aber angezeigt, die Firmengebrauchspflicht im Gesetz inhaltlich klar zu umschreiben.

Nach *Abs. 1* der vorliegenden Bestimmung muss die im Handelsregister eingetragene Firma in der Geschäftskorrespondenz, auf Bestellscheinen und Rechnungen sowie in öffentlichen Bekanntmachungen vollständig und unverändert angegeben werden. Der Form der Korrespondenz kann für die Massgeblichkeit der Firmengebrauchspflicht keine Relevanz zukommen; die eingetragene Firma muss insbesondere auch im Internet in rechtskonformer Weise verwendet werden.

Aus der Firmengebrauchspflicht ergeben sich für die Praxis im Rahmen einer seriösen Geschäftätigkeit kaum Einschränkungen: Der Entwurf stellt in *Abs. 2* klar, dass Kurzbezeichnungen, Logos, Geschäftsbezeichnungen, Enseignes und ähnliche Angaben selbstverständlich auch zukünftig verwendet werden dürfen. Einzige Voraussetzung ist, dass in den von *Abs. 1* umschriebenen Texten zugleich die im Handelsregister eingetragene Firma angegeben wird.

Kapitel 1: Neue Gesetzesbestimmungen und Erläuterungen

C. Überwachung

Art. 955 Randtitel

D. Schutz der Firma

Art. 956 Randtitel

Geändert wird nur die Nummerierung der Randtitel.

Fünfte Abteilung: Die Wertpapiere

Vierunddreissigster Titel: Anleihensobligationen

Zweiter Abschnitt: Gläubigergemeinschaft bei Anleihensobligationen
D. Gemeinschaftsbeschlüsse
I. Eingriffe in die Gläubigerrechte
2. Beschränkungen
c. Status und Bilanz

Art. 1175

Ein Antrag auf Ergreifung der in Art. 1170 genannten Massnahmen darf vom Schuldner nur eingebracht und von der Gläubigerversammlung nur in Beratung gezogen werden auf Grund eines auf den Tag der Gläubigerversammlung aufgestellten Status oder einer ordnungsgemäss errichteten und gegebenenfalls von der Revisionsstelle als richtig bescheinigten Bilanz, die auf einen höchstens sechs Monate zurückliegenden Zeitpunkt abgeschlossen ist.

Aus Gründen einer einheitlichen Terminologie wird der Ausdruck «Kontrollstelle» durch den Begriff «Revisionsstelle» ersetzt.

§ 5 Das Recht des Vereins[145]

A. Gründung

I. Körperschaftliche Personenverbindung

Art. 60

1 Vereine, die sich einer politischen, religiösen, wissenschaftlichen, künstlerischen, wohltätigen, geselligen oder andern nicht wirtschaftlichen Aufgabe widmen, erlangen die Persönlichkeit, sobald der Wille, als Körperschaft zu bestehen, aus den Statuten ersichtlich ist.

2 Die Statuten müssen in schriftlicher Form errichtet sein und über den Zweck des Vereins, seine Mittel und seine Organisation Aufschluss geben.

II. Eintragung ins Handelsregister

Art. 61

1 Sind die Vereinsstatuten angenommen und ist der Vorstand bestellt, so ist der Verein befugt, sich in das Handelsregister eintragen zu lassen.

2 Der Verein ist zur Eintragung verpflichtet, wenn er:

1. für seinen Zweck ein nach kaufmännischer Art geführtes Gewerbe betreibt;
2. revisionspflichtig ist.

3 Der Anmeldung sind die Statuten und das Verzeichnis der Vorstandsmitglieder beizufügen.

---

145 Die Artikelangaben beziehen sich auf das Schweizerische Zivilgesetzbuch (ZGB).

Vereine sind nach dem geltenden Recht nur dann verpflichtet, sich im Handelsregister eintragen zu lassen, wenn sie ein kaufmännisches Gewerbe betreiben (vgl. dazu Art. 934 Abs. 1 OR und Art. 52 ff. HRegV, SR *221.411*).

Der Entwurf übernimmt diese bisherige Regelung in *Abs. 2 Ziff. 1* und ergänzt sie in *Ziff. 2* durch eine Eintragungspflicht für alle revisionspflichtigen Vereine (zur Revisionspflicht s. Art. 69*b* E ZGB). Diese Ergänzung ist allerdings nur von beschränkter Tragweite: Die meisten Vereine, die nach Art. 69*b* E ZGB zu einer Revision verpflichtet werden, betreiben ein kaufmännisches Gewerbe und müssen daher ohnehin bereits im Handelsregister eingetragen sein. Es ist aber denkbar, dass einzelne Vereine, welche die im Entwurf vorgesehenen Grössenmerkmale (Art. 69*b* Abs. 1 Ziff. 1 E ZGB) erreichen, kein kaufmännisches Gewerbe betreiben (z.B. Spenden sammelnde Organisationen von erheblicher Grösse). In diesen Fällen erscheint die Eintragung in das Handelsregister im öffentlichen Interesse und zum Schutz Dritter sachlich dennoch dringend angezeigt. Diese eng beschränkte Erweiterung der Eintragungspflicht entspricht zudem der neuen Konzeption der Revisionsstelle: Soweit das Gesetz eine Revisionsstelle verlangt, muss diese im Interesse der Durchsetzung der Revisionspflicht im Handelsregister eingetragen werden. Dies bedingt aber, dass die betroffenen Vereine selbst alle im Handelsregister eingetragen sind.

Der Eintrag ins Handelsregister gemäss Art. 61 Abs. 2 E ZGB ist wie unter geltendem Recht deklaratorischer Natur. Die Gründung des Vereins erfolgt also weiterhin durch die Genehmigung der schriftlichen Statuten durch die Gründerversammlung (Art. 60 Abs. 1 und 2 ZGB).

III. Vereine ohne Persönlichkeit

Art. 62

Vereine, denen die Persönlichkeit nicht zukommt, oder die sie noch nicht erlangt haben, sind den einfachen Gesellschaften gleichgestellt.

IV. Verhältnis der Statuten zum Gesetz

Art. 63

1 Soweit die Statuten über die Organisation und über das Verhältnis des Vereins zu seinen Mitgliedern keine Vorschriften aufstellen, finden die nachstehenden Bestimmungen Anwendung.

2 Bestimmungen, deren Anwendung von Gesetzes wegen vorgeschrieben ist, können durch die Statuten nicht abgeändert werden.

B. Organisation

I. Vereinsversammlung

1. Bedeutung und Einberufung

Art. 64

1 Die Versammlung der Mitglieder bildet das oberste Organ des Vereins.

2 Sie wird vom Vorstand einberufen.

3 Die Einberufung erfolgt nach Vorschrift der Statuten und überdies von Gesetzes wegen, wenn ein Fünftel der Mitglieder die Einberufung verlangt.

2. Zuständigkeit

Art. 65

1 Die Vereinsversammlung beschliesst über die Aufnahme und den Ausschluss von Mitgliedern, wählt den Vorstand und entscheidet in allen Angelegenheiten, die nicht andern Organen des Vereins übertragen sind.

2 Sie hat die Aufsicht über die Tätigkeit der Organe und kann sie jederzeit abberufen, unbeschadet der Ansprüche, die den Abberufenen aus bestehenden Verträgen zustehen.

3 Das Recht der Abberufung besteht, wenn ein wichtiger Grund sie rechtfertigt, von Gesetzes wegen.

3. Vereinsbeschluss

a. Beschlussfassung

Art. 66

1 Vereinsbeschlüsse werden von der Vereinsversammlung gefasst.

2 Die schriftliche Zustimmung aller Mitglieder zu einem Antrag ist einem Beschlusse der Vereinsversammlung gleichgestellt.

b. Stimmrecht und Mehrheit

Art. 67

1 Alle Mitglieder haben in der Vereinsversammlung das gleiche Stimmrecht.

2 Die Vereinsbeschlüsse werden mit Mehrheit der Stimmen der anwesenden Mitglieder gefasst.

3 Über Gegenstände, die nicht gehörig angekündigt sind, darf ein Beschluss nur dann gefasst werden, wenn die Statuten es ausdrücklich gestatten.

c. Ausschliessung vom Stimmrecht

Art. 68
Jedes Mitglied ist von Gesetzes wegen vom Stimmrechte ausgeschlossen bei der Beschlussfassung über ein Rechtsgeschäft oder einen Rechtsstreit zwischen ihm, seinem Ehegatten oder einer mit ihm in gerader Linie verwandten Person einerseits und dem Vereine anderseits.

II. Vorstand

1. Rechte und Pflichten im Allgemeinen

Art. 69
Der Vorstand hat das Recht und die Pflicht, nach den Befugnissen, die die Statuten ihm einräumen, die Angelegenheiten des Vereins zu besorgen und den Verein zu vertreten.

Die Modifikation dieses Artikels betrifft lediglich den Randtitel.

2. Buchführung

Art. 69a
Der Vorstand führt Buch über die Einnahmen und Ausgaben sowie über die Vermögenslage des Vereins. Ist der Verein zur Eintragung in das Handelsregister verpflichtet, so finden die Vorschriften des Obligationenrechts[146] **über die kaufmännische Buchführung Anwendung.**

Vereine sind bereits nach geltendem Recht eingeschränkt buchführungspflichtig: Der Vorstand hat die Angelegenheiten des Vereins zu besorgen und ist damit auch verpflichtet, als Teil der Geschäftsführung beispielsweise die Mitgliederbeiträge zu verwalten (Art. 69 i.V.m. Art. 71 ZGB)

---

146 SR **220**

sowie über Einnahmen, Ausgaben und Vermögensstand nach Auftragsrecht getreu und sorgfältig Rechnung abzulegen (s. Art. 398 OR)[147]. In der Praxis dürfte es daher nur wenige Vereine geben, die tatsächlich auf jede Art von Buchführung verzichten.

Der Entwurf sieht eine auf die übrigen Rechtsformen des Privatrechts abgestimmte (eng begrenzte) Revisionspflicht des Vereins vor (Art. 69*b* E OR). Dies setzt aber voraus, dass das Gesetz auch die Anforderungen an die Rechnungslegung klarstellt. Der Entwurf sieht dafür – entsprechend den Gegebenheiten in Vereinen – eine sehr behutsame Regelung vor:

Der Vorstand ist gemäss *Satz 1* verpflichtet, über die Einnahmen und Ausgaben sowie über die Vermögenslage des Vereins Buch zu führen. Der Entwurf orientiert sich mit dieser Vorgabe an der Praxis, und er verlangt somit nichts, was ein korrekt geführter Verein nicht bereits heute schon tut.

Für die Buchführung ist der Vorstand verantwortlich; das schliesst allerdings nicht aus, dass dieser die eigentliche Buchführungstätigkeit an Vorstandsmitglieder oder Dritte delegiert.

In Bezug auf die Art und Weise der Buchführung macht der Entwurf grundsätzlich keine Vorschriften. Der Vorstand ist verantwortlich dafür, dass die Art und Weise der Buchführung der Grösse des Vereins und der Komplexität der Buchungen angemessen ist. Bei vielen Kleinvereinen dürfte somit eine sog. «Milchbuchrechnung», also eine blosse Gegenüberstellung von Einnahmen und Ausgaben, genügen.

Ist der Verein zur Eintragung in das Handelsregister verpflichtet, so finden gemäss *Satz 2* die Vorschriften von Art. 957 ff. OR über die kaufmännische Buchführung Anwendung. Gemäss Art. 61 Abs. 2 E ZGB ist dies der Fall, wenn ein kaufmännisches Gewerbe betrieben wird oder wenn der Verein revisionspflichtig ist. In beiden Fällen sind die etwas erhöhten Anforderungen an die Buchführung sachlich gerechtfertigt.

---

147 KARL KÄFER, in: Berner Kommentar zum schweizerischen Privatrecht, Band VIII/2, Bern 1976, Art. 957 N 99 f., m.w.N.; MICHAEL RIEMER, in: Berner Kommentar zum schweizerischen Privatrecht, Band I/3, Bern 1990, Art. 61 N 75, Art. 71 N 7, m.w.N.

III. Revisionsstelle

Art. 69b (ursprünglicher Botschaftsentwurf)

1 Der Verein muss seine Buchführung durch eine Revisionsstelle ordentlich prüfen lassen, wenn:

1. zwei der nachstehenden Grössen in zwei aufeinander folgenden Geschäftsjahren überschritten werden:

    a. Bilanzsumme von 6 Millionen Franken,

    b. Umsatzerlös von 12 Millionen Franken,

    c. 50 Vollzeitstellen im Jahresdurchschnitt;

2. ein Vereinsmitglied, das einer persönlichen Haftung oder einer Nachschusspflicht unterliegt, dies verlangt;

3. 10 Prozent der Mitglieder dies verlangen.

2 Auf die ordentliche Revision sind die Vorschriften des Obligationenrechts[148] über die Revisionsstelle bei Aktiengesellschaften entsprechend anwendbar.

3 In den übrigen Fällen sind die Statuten und die Generalversammlung in der Ordnung der Revision frei.

4 Für Vereine, die gesetzliche Aufgaben wahrnehmen, kann die Eidgenössische Finanzkontrolle oder eine kantonale Finanzkontrolle als Revisionsstelle bezeichnet werden.

Art. 69b (durch den Nationalrat bereinigte Version)

1 Der Verein muss seine Buchführung durch eine Revisionsstelle ordentlich prüfen lassen, wenn:

1. zwei der nachstehenden Grössen in zwei aufeinander folgenden Geschäftsjahren überschritten werden:

    a. Bilanzsumme von 10 Millionen Franken,

---

[148] SR **220**

Kapitel 1: Neue Gesetzesbestimmungen und Erläuterungen

    b. Umsatzerlös von 20 Millionen Franken,

4 ...gestrichen

Art. 69b (durch den Ständerat bereinigte Version, neuer Abs. 1bis)

1 Der Verein muss seine Buchführung durch eine Revisionsstelle ordentlich prüfen lassen, wenn zwei der nachstehenden Grössen in zwei aufeinanderfolgenden Geschäftsjahren überschritten werden:

1. Bilanzsumme von 6 Millionen Franken;
2. Umsatzerlös von 12 Millionen Franken;
3. 50 Vollzeitstellen im Jahresdurchschnitt;

1bis Der Verein muss seine Buchführung durch eine Revisionsstelle eingeschränkt prüfen lassen, wenn ein Vereinsmitglied, das einer persönlichen Haftung oder einer Nachschusspflicht unterliegt, dies verlangt.

2 Die Vorschriften des Obligationenrechts über die Revisionsstelle bei Aktiengesellschaften sind entsprechend anwendbar.

Das geltende Vereinsrecht sieht keine gesetzliche Revisionspflicht vor. Es steht den Vereinen jedoch offen, freiwillig in den Statuten eine Revisionsstelle einzusetzen. In der Praxis verfügen wohl die meisten Vereine über eine Revisorin oder einen Revisor, wobei die Revision häufig von Vereinsmitgliedern durchgeführt wird.

Der Vorentwurf RRG schlug vor, dass Vereine, die im Handelsregister eingetragen sind oder sich eintragen lassen müssen (also ein kaufmännisches Gewerbe betreiben, Art. 61 Abs. 2 ZGB) und die an zwei aufeinander folgenden Bilanzstichtagen zwei von drei Grössen (Bilanzsumme von 4 Millionen Franken; Umsatzerlös von 8 Millionen Franken; 50 Vollzeitstellen) erreichen, revisionspflichtig sein sollen (Art. 2 Abs. 1 i.V.m. Art. 43 Abs. 1 VE RRG). Die Revisionspflicht für Grossvereine blieb in der Vernehmlassung weitgehend unbestritten.

Der Entwurf folgt dem Vorentwurf RRG insofern, als er ein Konzept für die Revisionspflicht und die Revisionsstelle vorsieht, das in den Grundlinien für alle Rechtsformen des Privatrechts massgebend ist. Für die Revisionspflicht des Vereins sind grundsätzlich dieselben Kriterien heranzuziehen wie bei den Körperschaften des Obligationenrechts, da sie sich auch hier als sachgerecht erweisen (vgl. Art. 727 E OR). Von Gesetzes wegen revisionspflichtig sollen jedoch nur wirtschaftlich bedeutsame Grossvereine sein, welche die Kriterien von Art. 727 Abs. 1 Ziff. 2 E OR erfüllen. Eine Ungleichbehandlung wirtschaftlich bedeutender Rechtsträger auf Grund ihrer Rechtsform wäre sachlich nicht zu rechtfertigen, da die Schutzziele der Revision hier identisch sind. Der Harmonisierungsbedarf betreffend die Regelung der Revision von Vereinen mit den entsprechenden Vorschriften für Körperschaften des Obligationenrechts beschränkt sich aber auf wirtschaftlich bedeutende Organisationen. Für kleinere Vereine kann demgegenüber eine sehr offene Regelung getroffen werden (s. dazu die Ausführungen zu Abs. 3).

Abs. 1 Ziff. 1 regelt die Pflicht zur Revision für grosse Vereine. Vereine müssen ihre Buchführung durch eine Revisionsstelle ordentlich prüfen lassen, wenn zwei der drei nachstehenden Grössen in zwei aufeinander folgenden Geschäftsjahren überschritten werden:

– eine Bilanzsumme von 6 Millionen Franken;

– ein Umsatzerlös von 12 Millionen Franken;

– 50 Vollzeitstellen im Jahresdurchschnitt.

Der Entwurf verwendet den Begriff «Geschäftsjahr» als Gegenbegriff zum «Kalenderjahr». Der Begriff wird bereits im geltenden Recht bei den Grundsätzen der kaufmännischen Buchführung in Art. 958 Abs. 1 OR gebraucht. Er nimmt Bezug auf die allgemeine Geschäftstätigkeit des Vereins im weiteren Sinne und spricht somit nicht eine wirtschaftliche Tätigkeit an. Aus der Formulierung der vorliegenden Bestimmung darf daher keine Ausdehnung der Zulässigkeit wirtschaftlicher Tätigkeiten in der Rechtsform des Vereins abgeleitet werden.

Zuständig für die Wahl der Revisionsstelle ist die Mitgliederversammlung (Art. 64 Abs. 1 ZGB).

Ein Verein unterliegt zudem gemäss *Ziff. 2* der Revisionspflicht, wenn ein Vereinsmitglied, das einer persönlichen Haftung oder einer Nachschusspflicht unterliegt, dies verlangt. Dieses Recht der haftungs- oder nachschusspflichtigen Vereinsmitglieder zu einem Opting-in rechtfertigt sich durch das Risiko, das diese mit der Übernahme einer Haftungs- oder Nachschusspflicht eingehen. Die vorgesehene Regelung ermöglicht es aber auch, ungeachtet bestehender Haftungs- oder Nachschusspflichten auf eine Revisionsstelle zu verzichten, so etwa wenn die Verpflichteten selber in den Vorstand oder in die Geschäftsleitung eingebunden sind.

Gemäss *Ziff. 3* ist weiter eine ordentlich prüfende Revisionsstelle zu bezeichnen, wenn 10% aller Vereinsmitglieder dies verlangen. Diese Bestimmung entspricht in ihrer Zielsetzung sinngemäss Art. 727 Abs. 2 E OR für die Aktiengesellschaft. Da im Verein eine Bezugnahme auf das Eigenkapital nicht möglich ist und weil das Kopfprinzip im Vereinsrecht eine tragende Rolle spielt, wird für den Minderheitenschutz auf einen prozentualen Anteil der Mitglieder abgestellt. Der Entwurf verlangt für eine ordentliche Revision ein entsprechendes Begehren von mindestens 10% der Mitglieder. Es ist zu beachten, dass sich dieses Erfordernis nicht etwa auf die an einer Generalversammlung anwesenden Personen bezieht, sondern auf sämtliche Vereinsmitglieder.

Abs. 2 verweist für die ordentliche Revision auf die Vorschriften des Aktienrechts, welche sinngemäss zur Anwendung kommen. Diese Verweisung betrifft die fachlichen Anforderungen an die Revisionsstelle (s. Art. 727*b* Abs. 2 E OR), die Vorschriften zur Unabhängigkeit, die Aufgaben der Revisionsstelle und die gemeinsamen Bestimmungen nach Art. 730 ff. E OR. Bei Abs. 2 handelt es sich um eine sog. dynamische Verweisnorm (s. dazu vorne die Ausführungen zu Art. 818 E OR).

Soweit nicht nach Abs. 1 eine ordentliche Revision erforderlich ist, steht es den Vereinen nach *Abs. 3* frei, ob sie eine Revision durchführen wollen und wie diese gegebenenfalls auszugestalten ist. Sie können eine Revision sowohl in den Statuten als auch durch einen Generalversammlungsbeschluss vorsehen. Es ist daher ohne weiteres möglich, eine eingeschränkte Revision durch ein Vereinsmitglied durchführen zu lassen, das über keine bestimmte Ausbildung verfügen muss. Es darf auch gänzlich von einer Revision abgesehen werden.

Diese sehr liberale Regelung beruht darauf, dass kleinere Vereine nur sehr beschränkt am wirtschaftlichen Handeln teilnehmen und dass die Rechtsform des Vereins von vornherein zwingend nur für ideale Zwecke (s. Art. 60 ZGB; zur beschränkten Verwendbarkeit für wirtschaftliche Ziele s. BGE *90* II 333 ff.) verwendet werden darf[149]. Personenvereinigungen, welche den gesetzlich vorgegebenen Verwendungszweck der Rechtsform des Vereins nicht beachten oder überschreiten, dürfen nicht als Verein in das Handelsregister eingetragen werden und sind von den

---

[149] s. dazu ARTHUR MEIER-HAYOZ/PETER FORSTMOSER, Schweizerisches Gesellschaftsrecht, 9. Aufl., Bern 2004, § 20 N 3 f. und 11–22.

Registerbehörden zurückzuweisen[150]. Nur so kann sichergestellt werden, dass der allgemeinen Neuordnung der Revisionspflicht nicht dadurch ausgewichen werden kann, dass eine Rechtsform für wirtschaftliche Zwecke verwendet wird, die nicht dafür konzipiert ist.

Für Vereine, die gesetzliche Aufgaben wahrnehmen, kann gemäss *Abs. 4* die Eidgenössische Finanzkontrolle (EFK) oder eine kantonale Finanzkontrolle als Revisionsstelle bezeichnet werden. Die Vorschriften des Obligationenrechts und des Revisionsaufsichtsgesetzes zur Unabhängigkeit, zu den fachlichen Anforderungen und zur Zulassung der Revisorinnen und Revisoren kommen nicht zur Anwendung. Durch diese Ausnahmebestimmung werden bestehende Synergien im Bereich der öffentlichen Finanzaufsicht sichergestellt. Abs. 4 ist jedoch nicht dahingehend zu verstehen, dass die genannten Vereine ein Anrecht auf eine Revision durch eine öffentliche Finanzkontrolle haben; sofern keine spezialgesetzliche Vorschrift besteht, muss die EFK oder die betreffende kantonale Finanzkontrolle die Wahl als Revisionsstelle durch die Mitgliederversammlung des Vereins zuerst annehmen. Die Regelung der Eintragung der EFK oder einer kantonalen Finanzkontrolle in das Handelsregister erfolgt in der Handelsregisterverordnung. Als Revisionsstelle wird die EFK oder die kantonale Finanzkontrolle eingetragen, was aber nichts an der Haftung desjenigen Gemeinwesens ändert, dem die Finanzkontrolle angehört.[151]

IV. Mängel in der Organisation

Art. 69c

1 Fehlt dem Verein eines der vorgeschriebenen Organe, so kann ein Mitglied oder ein Gläubiger dem Gericht beantragen, die erforderlichen Massnahmen zu ergreifen.

2 Das Gericht kann dem Verein insbesondere eine Frist zur Wiederherstellung des rechtmässigen Zustandes ansetzen und, wenn nötig, einen Sachwalter ernennen.

---

150 In gleicher Weise wird auch sichergestellt, dass die Genossenschaft nicht für genossenschaftsfremde Zwecke verwendet wird. Entsprechendes gilt ebenfalls für die Stiftung.
151 Die vorliegenden Erläuterungen beziehen sich ausschliesslich auf die ursprüngliche bundesrätliche Gesetzesversion und nicht auf die bereinigte Fassung durch den Nationalrat.

3 Der Verein trägt die Kosten der Massnahmen. Das Gericht kann den Verein verpflichten, den ernannten Personen einen Vorschuss zu leisten.

4 Liegt ein wichtiger Grund vor, so kann der Verein vom Gericht die Abberufung von Personen verlangen, die dieses eingesetzt hat.

Die vorliegende Bestimmung entspricht Art. 69*a* E ZGB, der im Rahmen des Entwurfes zur Revision des GmbH-Rechts vorgeschlagen wird[152].

C. Mitgliedschaft

I. Ein- und Austritt

Art. 70

1 Der Eintritt von Mitgliedern kann jederzeit erfolgen.

2 Der Austritt ist von Gesetzes wegen zulässig, wenn er mit Beobachtung einer halbjährigen Frist auf das Ende des Kalenderjahres oder, wenn eine Verwaltungsperiode vorgesehen ist, auf deren Ende angesagt wird.

3 Die Mitgliedschaft ist weder veräusserlich noch vererblich.

II. Beitragspflicht

Art. 71

Beiträge können von den Mitgliedern verlangt werden, sofern die Statuten dies vorsehen.

---

[152] BBl **2002** 3243, 3301.

III. Ausschliessung

Art. 72

1 Die Statuten können die Gründe bestimmen, aus denen ein Mitglied ausgeschlossen werden darf, sie können aber auch die Ausschliessung ohne Angabe der Gründe gestatten.

2 Eine Anfechtung der Ausschliessung wegen ihres Grundes ist in diesen Fällen nicht statthaft.

3 Enthalten die Statuten hierüber keine Bestimmung, so darf die Ausschliessung nur durch Vereinsbeschluss und aus wichtigen Gründen erfolgen.

IV. Stellung ausgeschiedener Mitglieder

Art. 73

1 Mitglieder, die austreten oder ausgeschlossen werden, haben auf das Vereinsvermögen keinen Anspruch.

2 Für die Beiträge haften sie nach Massgabe der Zeit ihrer Mitgliedschaft.

V. Schutz des Vereinszweckes

Art. 74

Eine Umwandlung des Vereinszweckes kann keinem Mitgliede aufgenötigt werden.

VI. Schutz der Mitgliedschaft

Art. 75

Beschlüsse, die das Gesetz oder die Statuten verletzen, kann jedes Mitglied, das nicht zugestimmt hat, von Gesetzes wegen binnen Monatsfrist, nachdem es von ihnen Kenntnis erhalten hat, beim Gericht anfechten.

D. Auflösung
I. Auflösungsarten
1. Vereinsbeschluss

Art. 76

Die Auflösung des Vereins kann jederzeit durch Vereinsbeschluss herbeigeführt werden.

2. Von Gesetzes wegen

Art. 77

Die Auflösung erfolgt von Gesetzes wegen, wenn der Verein zahlungsunfähig ist, sowie wenn der Vorstand nicht mehr statutengemäss bestellt werden kann.

3. Urteil

Art. 78

Die Auflösung erfolgt durch das Gericht auf Klage der zuständigen Behörde oder eines Beteiligten, wenn der Zweck des Vereins widerrechtlich oder unsittlich ist.

II. Löschung des Registereintrags

Art. 79

Ist der Verein im Handelsregister eingetragen, so hat der Vorstand oder das Gericht dem Registerführer die Auflösung behufs Löschung des Eintrages mitzuteilen.

§ 6 Das Recht der Stiftung

A. Errichtung

I. Im Allgemeinen

Art. 80

Zur Errichtung einer Stiftung bedarf es der Widmung eines Vermögens für einen besondern Zweck.

II. Form der Errichtung

Art. 81

1 Die Errichtung erfolgt in der Form einer öffentlichen Urkunde oder durch letztwillige Verfügung.

2 Die Eintragung in das Handelsregister erfolgt auf Grund der Stiftungsurkunde und nötigenfalls nach Anordnung der Aufsichtsbehörde unter Angabe der Mitglieder der Verwaltung.

Kapitel 1: Neue Gesetzesbestimmungen und Erläuterungen

III. Anfechtung

Art. 82

Eine Stiftung kann von den Erben oder den Gläubigern des Stifters gleich einer Schenkung angefochten werden.

B. Organisation
I. Im Allgemeinen

Art. 83

Die Organe der Stiftung und die Art der Verwaltung werden durch die Stiftungsurkunde festgestellt.

Der *Randtitel* wird dem neuen Aufbau der Regelung der Organisation der Stiftung angepasst. Der bisherige *Abs. 1* bleibt unverändert. Die *Abs. 2 und 3* werden überarbeitet und in den neuen Art. 83*d* E ZGB verschoben.

II. Buchführung

Art. 83a

1 Das oberste Stiftungsorgan führt die Geschäftsbücher der Stiftung nach den Vorschriften des Obligationenrechts über die kaufmännische Buchführung.

2 Betreibt die Stiftung für ihren Zweck ein nach kaufmännischer Art geführtes Gewerbe, so sind die Vorschriften des Obligationenrechts über die Rechnungslegung und die Offenlegung der Jahresrechnung für Aktiengesellschaften entsprechend anwendbar.

Abs. 1 sieht vor, dass das oberste Stiftungsorgan die Geschäftsbücher der Stiftung führt. Stiftungen werden damit ausdrücklich zur Buchführung verpflichtet, was eine unabdingbare Voraussetzung für die Revision der Jahresrechnung gemäss Art. 83*c* E ZGB darstellt. Nach der Rechtsprechung des Bundesgerichts[153] zum geltenden Recht sind Stiftungen trotz des Wortlauts von Art. 957 OR nur dann buchführungspflichtig, wenn sie ein Handels-, Fabrikations- oder ein anderes nach kaufmännischer Art geführtes Gewerbe (i.S.v. Art. 934 Abs. 1 OR und Art. 52 ff. HRegV) betreiben. Dies vermag allerdings sachlich kaum zu befriedigen: Zur Absicherung ihrer Zweckerfüllung haben Stiftungen auch dann zumindest eine einfache Rechnung zu erstellen, wenn sie kein nach kaufmännischer Art geführtes Gewerbe betreiben. Der Entwurf sieht daher eine Buchführungspflicht für alle Stiftungen vor. Inhaltlich richtet sich diese nach den Vorschriften von Art. 957 ff. OR.

Für Stiftungen, die ein nach kaufmännischer Art geführtes Gewerbe betreiben, vermögen diese geringen Anforderungen jedoch nicht zu genügen; nach *Abs. 2* finden daher die aktienrechtlichen Vorschriften über die Rechnungslegung und die Offenlegung der Jahresrechnung (Art. 662 ff. und 697*h* OR) entsprechende Anwendung. Diese einlässlichere Regelung ist gerechtfertigt, weil Begünstigte, Gläubigerinnen und Gläubiger sowie Spenderinnen und Spender in diesen Fällen ein erhöhtes Interesse an einem Nachweis der Verwendung der eingenommenen Mittel haben.

Die vorliegende Bestimmung wurde im Wesentlichen dem Vorentwurf entnommen, der die Kommission für Wirtschaft und Abgaben des Ständerates im Rahmen der Arbeiten an der parlamentarischen Initiative «Schiesser» zur Revision des Stiftungsrechts[154] vorgelegt hat. Im Vernehmlassungsverfahren wurden dazu keine grundsätzlichen Einwände geltend gemacht.

III. Revisionsstelle

1. Revisionspflicht und anwendbares Recht

Art. 83b (ursprünglicher Botschaftsentwurf)

1 Das oberste Stiftungsorgan bezeichnet eine Revisionsstelle.

2 Die Aufsichtsbehörde kann eine Stiftung von der Pflicht befreien, eine Revisionsstelle zu bezeichnen. Der Bundesrat legt die Voraussetzungen der Befreiung fest.

---

153 BGE **110** Ib 17 ff., 19 (E. 2a).
154 00.461s.

Kapitel 1: Neue Gesetzesbestimmungen und Erläuterungen

³ Soweit für Stiftungen keine besonderen Vorschriften bestehen, sind die Vorschriften des Obligationenrechts[155] über die Revisionsstelle bei Aktiengesellschaften entsprechend anwendbar.

⁴ Für Stiftungen, die gesetzliche Aufgaben wahrnehmen, kann die Eidgenössische Finanzkontrolle oder eine kantonale Finanzkontrolle als Revisionsstelle bezeichnet werden.

Art. 83b (durch den Nationalrat bereinigte Version)
⁴ ...gestrichen

Art. 83b (durch den Ständerat bereinigte Version, neuer Abs. 3bis)
⁴ Ist die Stiftung zu einer eingeschränkten Revision verpflichtet, so kann die Aufsichtsbehörde eine ordentliche Revision verlangen, wenn dies für die zuverlässige Beurteilung der Vermögens- und Ertragslage der Stiftung notwendig ist.

Grundsätzlich ist gemäss *Abs. 1* jede Stiftung verpflichtet, eine Revisionsstelle zu bezeichnen. Diese Aufgabe kommt dem obersten Stiftungsorgan zu. Spezialgesetzliche Vorschriften, beispielsweise im Bereich der Vorsorgestiftungen, bleiben vorbehalten (s. Art. 89bis Abs. 6 ZGB). Die Pflicht zur Bezeichnung einer Revisionsstelle wurde bereits im Vorentwurf für die Revision des Stiftungsrechts von 1993, im Vorentwurf RRG und im Vorentwurf der Kommission für Wirtschaft und Angaben des Ständerates zur parlamentarischen Initiative Schiesser vorgeschlagen. In allen drei Vernehmlassungsverfahren waren die Reaktionen in dieser Frage positiv.

Zumindest auf Bundesebene verlangt die Stiftungsaufsicht bereits heute, dass eine Revisionsstelle bezeichnet wird. In der Praxis hat sich gezeigt,

---

[155] SR **220**

dass die Revision der Jahresrechnung ein unentbehrliches Instrument zur Beaufsichtigung der Stiftungen[156] darstellt.

Vom vorgesehenen Obligatorium einer Revisionsstelle werden nur die so genannten «klassischen Stiftungen» erfasst; Familienstiftungen und kirchliche Stiftungen werden davon in Art. 87 Abs. 1bis E ZGB ausdrücklich ausgenommen.

Nach *Abs.* 2 kann die Aufsichtsbehörde die Stiftung von der Pflicht zur Bezeichnung einer Revisionsstelle befreien, wenn bestimmte Voraussetzungen gegeben sind, die der Bundesrat in einer Verordnung festlegt. Die Befreiung von der Revision wird allerdings die Ausnahme darstellen und nur für jene Stiftungen möglich sein, die nur ein kleines Vermögen oder eine sehr beschränkte Geschäftstätigkeit aufweisen. Mit der Bestimmung von Abs. 2 kann den Bedürfnissen der Praxis Rechnung getragen; wo eine Revision nach den Umständen nicht erforderlich ist, kann davon abgesehen werden. Im Vernehmlassungsverfahren zum Vorentwurf der Kommission für Wirtschaft und Angaben des Ständerates wurde dieses Modell grundsätzlich begrüsst.

Soweit für Stiftungen keine besonderen Vorschriften bestehen, sind nach *Abs.* 3 die Vorschriften des Obligationenrechts über die Revisionsstelle bei Aktiengesellschaften (Art. 727 ff. E OR) sinngemäss anwendbar. Es handelt sich dabei um eine sog. dynamische Verweisnorm (s. die Ausführungen zu Art. 818 E OR).

Aus dieser Verweisung ergeben sich die zwingenden gesetzlichen Anforderungen an die Revision; so richtet sich beispielsweise die Art der Revision (ordentliche oder eingeschränkte Revision) nach den Bestimmungen des Aktienrechts. Die Frage der Revisionspflicht wird in Art. 83*b* Abs. 1 und 2 E ZGB abschliessend geregelt; es steht den Stiftungen also nicht offen, vom Opting-out in Art. 727*a* Abs. 2 E OR Gebrauch zu machen.

Die Aufsichtsbehörde kann zwar eine Stiftung von der allgemeinen Revisionspflicht befreien. Falls die Voraussetzungen eines Verzichts auf die Revision nicht gegeben sind, kann sie aber die zwingenden gesetzlichen Anforderungen an die Revision nicht modifizieren, weil dadurch die Revision ihre Verlässlichkeit für Dritte einbüssen würde. Die inhaltlichen Vorschriften zur Revision sind daher auch für die Aufsichtsbehörde verbindlich.

---

156 Ende 2003 waren in den kantonalen Handelsregistern 19 355 Stiftungen eingetragen (Quelle: Schweizerisches Handelsamtsblatt Nr. 22 vom 3. Februar 2004, S. 30).

Die Stiftung muss ihre Buchführung durch eine zugelassene Revisionsexpertin oder einen zugelassenen Revisionsexperten ordentlich prüfen lassen, wenn zwei der drei nachstehenden Grössen in zwei aufeinander folgenden Geschäftsjahren überschritten werden (s. Art. 727 Abs. 1 Ziff. 2 und 727*b* Abs. 2 E OR i.V.m. Art. 83*b* Abs. 3 E ZGB):

– eine Bilanzsumme von 6 Millionen Franken;

– ein Umsatzerlös von 12 Millionen Franken;

– 50 Vollzeitstellen im Jahresdurchschnitt.

Überschreitet eine Stiftung diese Schwellenwerte nicht, so muss sie ihre Jahresrechnung *eingeschränkt* durch eine zugelassene Revisorin oder einen zugelassenen Revisor prüfen lassen (Art. 727*a* und 727*c* E OR i.V.m. Art. 83*b* Abs. 3 E ZGB). Vorbehalten bleibt dabei die Befreiung von der Revision durch die Aufsichtsbehörde.

Auf Grund der Verweisung von *Abs. 3* gelten für die Revisionsstelle der Stiftung auch die Anzeigepflichten von Art. 728*c* und 729*c* E OR sinngemäss. Art. 728*c* Abs. 2 E OR betreffend Meldepflichten an die Generalversammlung kann allerdings nicht zur Anwendung gelangen, weil ein entsprechendes Organ bei der Stiftung fehlt. Die Verstösse, die gemäss dieser Bestimmung der Generalversammlung gemeldet werden müssten, sind aber in jedem Fall in den Revisionsbericht aufzunehmen (Art. 728*b* Abs. 1 und Abs. 2 Ziff. 1 bzw. Art. 729*b* Abs. 1 Ziff. 2 E OR). Die Aufsichtsbehörde erhält dadurch Kenntnis davon, ohne dass eine besondere Anzeigepflicht an die Aufsichtsbehörde erforderlich wäre (s. Art. 83*c* E ZGB). Was die Anzeigepflichten an das Gericht betrifft, sei darauf hingewiesen, dass der Entwurf zur parlamentarischen Initiative Schiesser besondere Vorschriften für die Fälle der Zahlungsunfähigkeit und der Überschuldung der Stiftung vorsieht. Der vorliegende Entwurf wurde so konzipiert, dass entsprechende Ergänzungen eingepasst werden können.

Für Stiftungen, die gesetzliche Aufgaben wahrnehmen, kann gemäss *Abs. 4* die Eidgenössische Finanzkontrolle oder eine kantonale Finanzkontrolle als Revisionsstelle bezeichnet werden. Vgl. im Übrigen die Ausführungen zu Art. 69*b* Abs. 4 E ZGB.[157]

---

157 Die vorliegenden Erläuterungen beziehen sich ausschliesslich auf die ursprüngliche bundesrätliche Gesetzesversion und nicht auf die bereinigte Fassung durch den Nationalrat.

2. Verhältnis zur Aufsichtsbehörde

Art. 83c

Die Revisionsstelle übermittelt der Aufsichtsbehörde eine Kopie des Revisionsberichts sowie aller wichtigen Mitteilungen an die Stiftung.

Wie bereits in den Erläuterungen zu Art. 83*b* E ZGB ausgeführt wurde, sind die Aufsichtsbehörden oft nicht in der Lage, ihre Aufgaben ohne Unterstützung durch eine Revisionsstelle zu bewältigen. Der Entwurf schreibt daher vor, dass die Revisionsstelle der Aufsichtsbehörde eine Kopie des Revisionsberichts übermittelt. Wurde von der Revisionsstelle eine ordentliche Revision durchgeführt, so ist unter dem Revisionsbericht der umfassende Revisionsbericht zu verstehen (s. Art. 728*b* Abs. 1 E OR). Hat die Revisionsstelle eingeschränkt geprüft, so hat sie der Aufsichtsbehörde den zusammenfassenden Revisionsbericht zuzustellen (s. Art. 729*b* E OR). Diese Bestimmung wurde sowohl im Vorentwurf zur Revision des Stiftungsrechts von 1993 als auch im Vorentwurf der Kommission für Wirtschaft und Angaben des Ständerates im Rahmen der parlamentarischen Initiative Schiesser vorgesehen. In der Vernehmlassung zum Vorentwurf von 1993 wurde gefordert, dass die Revisionsstelle nur den Stiftungsorganen gegenüber meldepflichtig sein soll. Verschiedene Ereignisse haben jedoch vor Augen geführt, wie wichtig die Aufsichtstätigkeit im Stiftungsbereich ist. Die direkte Weiterleitung des umfassenden Revisionsberichts an die zuständige Stiftungsaufsicht erscheint für deren Effizienz unabdingbar. Im Vernehmlassungsverfahren zur parlamentarischen Initiative Schiesser ist der vorliegenden Bestimmung kein Widerspruch mehr erwachsen.

Die Revisionsstelle übermittelt der Aufsichtsbehörde zudem eine Kopie aller wichtigen Mitteilungen an die Stiftung. Hierunter fallen die Meldungen im Rahmen der Anzeigepflichten gemäss Art. 728*c* Abs. 1 und 2 E OR, aber auch andere wichtige Mitteilungen. Was die Anzeigepflicht der Revisionsstelle an das Gericht im Falle der Überschuldung betrifft, wird mit der Vorlage zur parlamentarischen Initiative Schiesser eine besondere Regelung geschaffen.

IV. Mängel in der Organisation

Art. 83d (ursprünglicher Botschaftsentwurf)

¹ Ist die vorgesehene Organisation nicht genügend, fehlt der Stiftung eines der vorgeschriebenen Organe oder ist eines dieser Organe nicht rechtmässig zusammengesetzt, so muss die Aufsichtsbehörde die erforderlichen Massnahmen ergreifen. Sie kann insbesondere:
1. der Stiftung eine Frist ansetzen, binnen derer der rechtmässige Zustand wieder herzustellen ist; oder
2. das fehlende Organ oder einen Sachwalter ernennen.

² Kann eine zweckdienliche Organisation nicht gewährleistet werden, so hat die Aufsichtsbehörde das Vermögen einer anderen Stiftung mit möglichst gleichartigem Zweck zuzuwenden, sofern der Stifter keinen Einspruch erhebt oder nicht eine Bestimmung der Stiftungsurkunde entgegensteht.

³ Die Stiftung trägt die Kosten der Massnahmen. Die Aufsichtsbehörde kann die Stiftung verpflichten, den ernannten Personen einen Vorschuss zu leisten.

⁴ Liegt ein wichtiger Grund vor, so kann die Stiftung von der Aufsichtsbehörde die Abberufung von Personen verlangen, die diese eingesetzt hat.

Art. 83d (durch den Nationalrat bereinigte Version)

² Kann eine zweckdienliche Organisation nicht gewährleistet werden, so hat die Aufsichtsbehörde das Vermögen einer anderen Stiftung mit möglichst gleichartigem Zweck zuzuwenden.

Die vorliegende Bestimmung entspricht Art. 83 Abs. 2–5 E ZGB gemäss dem Entwurf zur Revision des GmbH-Rechts[158]. Durch den Einbau der Vorschriften zur Buchführungspflicht (Art. 83*a* E ZGB) und zur Revisi-

---

158 BBl **2002** 3243 f., 3301 f.

onsstelle (Art. 83*b* und Art. 83*c* E ZGB) ergibt sich eine Verschiebung in Art. 83*d* E ZGB.[159]

C. Aufsicht

Art. 84

1 **Die Stiftungen stehen unter der Aufsicht des Gemeinwesens (Bund, Kanton, Gemeinde), dem sie nach ihrer Bestimmung angehören.**

1bis **Die Kantone können die ihren Gemeinden angehörenden Stiftungen der kantonalen Aufsichtsbehörde unterstellen.**

2 **Die Aufsichtsbehörde hat dafür zu sorgen, dass das Stiftungsvermögen seinen Zwecken gemäss verwendet wird.**

Art. 84b

Aufgehoben

D. Umwandlung der Stiftung

I. Änderung der Organisation

Art. 85

Die zuständige Bundes- oder Kantonsbehörde kann auf Antrag der Aufsichtsbehörde oder des obersten Stiftungsorgans den Zweck der Stiftung ändern, wenn die Erhaltung des Vermögens oder die Wahrung des Stiftungszwecks die Änderung dringend erfordert.

---

[159] Die vorliegenden Erläuterungen beziehen sich ausschliesslich auf die ursprüngliche bundesrätliche Gesetzesversion und nicht auf die bereinigte Fassung durch den Nationalrat.

Kapitel 1: Neue Gesetzesbestimmungen und Erläuterungen

II. Änderung des Zweckes

Art. 86

1 Die zuständige kantonale Behörde oder, wo die Stiftung unter der Aufsicht des Bundes steht, der Bundesrat[160] darf auf Antrag der Aufsichtsbehörde und nach Anhörung des obersten Stiftungsorganes den Zweck der Stiftung abändern, wenn ihr ursprünglicher Zweck eine ganz andere Bedeutung oder Wirkung erhalten hat, so dass die Stiftung dem Willen des Stifters offenbar entfremdet worden ist.

2 Unter den gleichen Voraussetzungen können Auflagen oder Bedingungen, die den Stiftungszweck beeinträchtigen, aufgehoben oder abgeändert werden.

E. Familienstiftungen und kirchliche Stiftungen

Art. 87

1 Die Familienstiftungen und die kirchlichen Stiftungen sind unter Vorbehalt des öffentlichen Rechtes der Aufsichtsbehörde nicht unterstellt.

1bis Sie sind von der Pflicht befreit, eine Revisionsstelle zu bezeichnen.

2 Über Anstände privatrechtlicher Natur entscheidet das Gericht.

Stiftungen sind gemäss Art. 83*b* E ZGB grundsätzlich verpflichtet, eine Revisionsstelle zu bezeichnen. Familienstiftungen und kirchliche Stiftungen geniessen im geltenden Stiftungsrecht jedoch eine Sonderstellung, die vor allem darin gründet, dass diesen Stiftungen ein privatimer Charakter

---

[160] Heute: das zuständige Dep. des BR (Art. 47 des Regierungs- und Verwaltungsorganisationsgesetzes vom 21. März 1997 – SR **172.010**). Gegen die Entscheide des Dep. sowie der kantonalen Aufsichtsbehörden ist die Verwaltungsgerichtsbeschwerde an das BGer zulässig (Art. 97 ff. OG – SR **173.110**).

zukommt; zudem nehmen sie kaum am Rechtsverkehr teil[161]. Dementsprechend besteht kein Bedürfnis, diese Stiftungen einer Revision zu unterziehen. Familienstiftungen und kirchliche Stiftungen werden daher gemäss *Abs. 1bis* von der Pflicht befreit, eine Revisionsstelle zu bezeichnen.

Der Verzicht auf eine Revision entspricht dem Vorentwurf von 1993 und dem Vorentwurf zur parlamentarischen Initiative Schiesser. Im Vernehmlassungsverfahren wurde dieser Regelungsvorschlag mit einer Ausnahme begrüsst.[162]

F. Aufhebung und Löschung im Register

I. Aufhebung durch die zuständige Behörde

Art. 88

1 Die zuständige Bundes- oder Kantonsbehörde hebt die Stiftung auf Antrag oder von Amtes wegen auf, wenn:

1. deren Zweck unerreichbar geworden ist und die Stiftung durch eine Änderung der Stiftungsurkunde nicht aufrechterhalten werden kann; oder

2. deren Zweck widerrechtlic oder unsittlich geworden ist.

2 Familienstiftungen und kirchliche Stiftungen werden durch das Gericht aufgehoben.

---

161 Dazu HAROLD GRÜNINGER, in: Honsell/Vogt/Geiser (Hrsg.), Basler Kommentar zum schweizerischen Privatrecht, Zivilgesetzbuch I, Art. 1–456 ZGB, 2. Aufl., Basel 2002, Art. 87 N 9; HANS MICHAEL RIEMER, in: Berner Kommentar zum schweizerischen Privatrecht, Band I/3, Die Stiftungen, Systematischer Teil und Kommentar zu Art. 80–89bis ZGB, Bern 1975, syst. Teil N 113.

162 Die vorliegenden Erläuterungen beziehen sich ausschliesslich auf die ursprüngliche bundesrätliche Gesetzesversion und nicht auf die bereinigte Fassung durch den Nationalrat.

Kapitel 1: Neue Gesetzesbestimmungen und Erläuterungen

II. Antrags- und Klagerecht, Löschung im Register

Art. 89

1 Zur Antragsstellung oder zur Klage auf Aufhebung der Stiftung berechtigt ist jede Person, die ein Interesse hat.

2 Die Aufhebung ist dem Registerführer zur Löschung des Eintrages anzumelden.

G. Personalfürsorgestiftungen[163]

Art. 89bis[164]

1 Für Personalfürsorgeeinrichtungen, die gemäss Art. 331 des Obligationenrechts[165] in Form der Stiftung errichtet worden sind, gelten überdies noch folgende Bestimmungen.[166]

2 Die Stiftungsorgane haben den Begünstigten über die Organisation, die Tätigkeit und die Vermögenslage der Stiftung den erforderlichen Aufschluss zu erteilen.

3 Leisten die Arbeitnehmer Beiträge an die Stiftung, so sind sie an der Verwaltung wenigstens nach Massgabe dieser Beiträge zu beteiligen; soweit möglich haben die Arbeitnehmer ihre Vertretung aus dem Personal des Arbeitgebers zu wählen.[167]

4 ...[168]

5 Die Begünstigten können auf Ausrichtung von Leistungen der Stiftung klagen, wenn sie Beiträge an diese entrichtet haben oder wenn ihnen nach den Stiftungsbestimmungen ein Rechtsanspruch auf Leistungen zusteht.

---

163 Fassung gemäss Ziff. II Art. 2 Ziff. 1 des BG vom 25. Juni 1971, in Kraft seit 1. Jan. 1972 (SR **220** am Schluss, Schl- und UeB zum X. Tit.).
164 Eingefügt durch Ziff. II des BG vom 21. März 1958, in Kraft seit 1. Juli 1958 (AS **1958** 379 381; BBl **1956** II 825).
165 SR **220**
166 Fassung gemäss Ziff. II Art. 2 Ziff. 1 des BG vom 25. Juni 1971, in Kraft seit 1. Jan. 1972 (SR **220** am Schluss, Schl- und UeB zum X. Tit.).
167 Fassung gemäss Ziff. II Art. 2 Ziff. 1 des BG vom 25. Juni 1971, in Kraft seit 1. Jan. 1972 (SR **220** am Schluss, Schl- und UeB zum X. Tit.).
168 Aufgehoben durch Ziff. III des BG vom 21. Juni 1996 (AS **1996** 3067; BBl **1996** I 564 580).

6 Für Personalfürsorgestiftungen, die auf dem Gebiet der Alters-, Hinterlassenen- und Invalidenvorsorge tätig sind, gelten überdies die folgenden Bestimmungen des Bundesgesetzes vom 25. Juni 1982[169] über die berufliche Alters-, Hinterlassenen- und Invalidenvorsorge über:

1. die Definition und Grundsätze der beruflichen Vorsorge sowie des versicherbaren Lohnes oder des versicherbaren Einkommens (Art. 1),

2. die zusätzlichen Einkäufe für den Vorbezug der Altersleistung (Art. 13a Abs. 8[170]),

3. die Begünstigten bei Hinterlassenenleistungen (Art. 20a),

4. die Anpassung der reglementarischen Leistungen an die Preisentwicklung (Art. 36 Abs. 2 und 3),

5. die Verjährung von Ansprüchen und die Aufbewahrung von Vorsorgeunterlagen (Art. 41),

6. die Verantwortlichkeit (Art. 52),

7. die Kontrolle (Art. 53),

8. die Interessenkonflikte (Art. 53a),

9. die Teil- oder Gesamtliquidation (Art. 53b–53d),

10. die Auflösung von Verträgen (Art. 53e),

11. den Sicherheitsfonds (Art. 56 Abs. 1 lit. c und Abs. 2–5, Art. 56a, 57 und 59),

12. die Aufsicht (Art. 61, 62 und 64),

13. die Gebühren (Art. 63a),

14. die finanzielle Sicherheit (Art. 65 Abs. 1 und 3, Art. 66 Abs. 4, Art. 67 und 69),

15. die Transparenz (Art. 65a),

16. die Rückstellungen (Art. 65b),

17. die Versicherungsverträge zwischen Vorsorgeeinrichtungen und Versicherungseinrichtungen (Art. 68 Abs. 3 und 4),

---

169 SR **831.40**
170 Art. 13*a* tritt mit einer 11. AHV-Revision in Kraft.

18. die Vermögensverwaltung (Art. 71),
19. die Rechtspflege (Art. 73 und 74),
20. die Strafbestimmungen (Art. 75–79),
21. den Einkauf (Art. 79b),
22. den versicherbaren Lohn und das versicherbare Einkommen (Art. 79c),
23. die Information der Versicherten (Art. 86b).[171]

§ 7 Änderung bisherigen Rechts

I. Zivilgesetzbuch

Erster Teil: Das Personenrecht

Zweiter Titel: Die juristischen Personen

Erster Abschnitt: Allgemeine Bestimmungen

D. Sitz

Art. 56

Der Sitz der juristischen Personen befindet sich, wenn ihre Statuten es nicht anders bestimmen, an dem Orte, wo ihre Verwaltung geführt wird.

Der Randtitel und der bisherige Gesetzestext sprechen vom «Wohnsitz» juristischer Personen. Es wird vorgeschlagen, stattdessen den üblichen Begriff «Sitz» zu verwenden.

---

171 Eingefügt durch Anhang Ziff. 1 des BG vom 25. Juni 1982 über die berufliche Alters-, Hinterlassenen- und Invalidenvorsorge (SR **831.40**). Fassung gemäss Anhang Ziff. 1 des BG vom 3. Okt. 2003 (1. BVG-Revision), Ziff. 6, 7, 10–12, 14 (mit Ausnahme von Art. 66 Abs. 4), 15, 17–20 und 23 in Kraft seit 1. April 2004, Ziff. 3–5, 8, 9, 13, 14 (Art. 66 Abs. 4) und 16 in Kraft seit 1. Jan. 2005, Ziff. 1, 21 und 22 in Kraft seit 1. Jan. 2006 (AS **2004** 1677 1700; BBl **2000** 2637).

Zweiter Teil: Das Familienrecht

Dritte Abteilung: Die Vormundschaft

Zehnter Titel: Die allgemeine Ordnung der Vormundschaft

Fünfter Abschnitt: Die Beistandschaft

A. Fälle der Beistandschaft

II. Vermögensverwaltung

1. Kraft Gesetzes

Art. 393

Fehlt einem Vermögen die nötige Verwaltung, so hat die Vormundschaftsbehörde das Erforderliche anzuordnen und namentlich in folgenden Fällen einen Beistand zu ernennen:

1. **bei längerer Abwesenheit einer Person mit unbekanntem Aufenthalt;**
2. **bei Unfähigkeit einer Person, die Verwaltung ihres Vermögens selbst zu besorgen oder einen Vertreter zu bestellen, falls nicht die Vormundschaft anzuordnen ist;**
3. **bei Ungewissheit der Erbfolge und zur Wahrung der Interessen des Kindes vor der Geburt;**
4. ...
5. **bei öffentlicher Sammlung von Geldern für wohltätige und andere dem öffentlichen Wohle dienende Zwecke, solange für die Verwaltung oder Verwendung nicht gesorgt ist.**

Der Vorentwurf zur Revision des Vormundschaftsrechts sieht vor, dass vormundschaftliche Massnahmen nur noch auf natürliche Personen Anwendung finden sollen. An Stelle der Ernennung eines Beistandes tritt für juristische Personen die Einsetzung einer Sachwalterin oder eines Sachwalters. Die vorliegende Bestimmung wird durch eine umfassende Neuregelung des Vorgehens bei Mängeln in der Organisation juristischer Personen ersetzt (s. Art. 731*b* E OR sowie Art. 69*a* und 83 E ZGB); sie ist daher zu streichen. Zur neuen Regelung wird im Weiteren auf die Ausführungen zu Art. 731*b* E OR verwiesen.

Kapitel 1: Neue Gesetzesbestimmungen und Erläuterungen

Vierter Teil: Das Sachenrecht

Zweite Abteilung: Die beschränkten dinglichen Rechte

Dreiundzwanzigster Titel: Das Fahrnispfand

Zweiter Abschnitt: Das Pfandrecht an Forderungen und andern Rechten

C. Wirkung

II. Vertretung verpfändeter Aktien und Stammanteile von Gesellschaften mit beschränkter Haftung

Art. 905

1 Verpfändete Aktien werden in der Generalversammlung durch die Aktionäre und nicht durch die Pfandgläubiger vertreten.

2 Verpfändete Stammanteile einer Gesellschaft mit beschränkter Haftung werden in der Gesellschafterversammlung durch die Gesellschafter und nicht durch die Pfandgläubiger vertreten.

Das geltende Recht regelt nur die Vertretung verpfändeter Aktien. Die gleiche Ordnung soll auch für verpfändete Stammanteile einer GmbH vorgesehen werden: In der Gesellschafterversammlung sind verpfändete Stammanteile durch die Gesellschafterin oder den Gesellschafter zu vertreten, da den Pfandgläubigerinnen und Pfandgläubigern lediglich ein Recht auf Befriedigung aus dem Erlös der Verwertung der Pfandsache zusteht (s. Art. 891 Abs. 1 i.V.m. Art. 899 Abs. 2 ZGB).

II. Schlusstitel: Anwendungs- und Einführungsbestimmungen

Erster Abschnitt: Die Anwendung bisherigen und neuen Rechts

B. Personenrecht

III. Juristische Personen

1. Im Allgemeinen

Art. 6a Randtitel

Der Randtitel von Art. 6*a* SchlT ZGB muss der Tatsache angepasst werden, dass mit dem neuen Art. 6*b* E SchlT ZGB (s. dazu nachstehend) eine neue Übergangsvorschrift in das Zivilgesetzbuch eingeführt werden muss.

2. Buchführung und Revisionsstelle

Art. 6b

Die Bestimmungen der Änderung vom ... betreffend die Buchführung und die Revisionsstelle gelten für Vereine und Stiftungen vom ersten Geschäftsjahr an, das mit dem Inkrafttreten dieses Gesetzes oder danach beginnt.

Die Bestimmungen der vorliegenden Änderungen des Zivilgesetzbuchs betreffend die Buchführung und die Revisionsstelle gelten für Vereine und Stiftungen vom ersten Geschäftsjahr an, das mit dem Inkrafttreten dieses Gesetzes oder danach beginnt. Es wird dazu auf die Ausführungen zu Art. 7 E ÜB und Art. 44 E RAG verwiesen. Falls ein Verein bisher kein klar definiertes Geschäftsjahr festgelegt hat, liegt es beim Vereinsvorstand, ein solches zu bestimmen. Aus sachlogischen Gründen hat er dies innerhalb eines Jahres zu tun. Die Pflicht zur Buchführung beginnt daher spätestens ein Jahr nach dem Inkrafttreten der neuen Vorschriften.

Kapitel 1: Neue Gesetzesbestimmungen und Erläuterungen

III. Bundesgesetz über Schuldbetreibung und Konkurs[172]

Zweiter Titel: Schuldbetreibung

I. Arten der Schuldbetreibung

B. Konkursbetreibung

1. Anwendungsbereich

Art. 39 Abs. 1 Ziff. 5

Aufgehoben

Nach dieser Bestimmung werden geschäftsführende Gesellschafterinnen und Gesellschafter einer GmbH der Konkursbetreibung unterstellt[173]. Demgegenüber unterliegen die Mitglieder des Verwaltungsrates einer Aktiengesellschaft oder der Verwaltung einer Genossenschaft der Konkursbetreibung nicht. Überzeugende Gründe für eine abweichende Regelung der Betreibung geschäftsführender Gesellschafterinnen und Gesellschafter der GmbH bestehen jedoch keine. In einer Motion von Herrn Ständerat Toni Dettling wird daher zu Recht die Abschaffung dieser Sondervorschrift verlangt[174]. Der Entwurf sieht die entsprechende Modifikation des Bundesgesetzes über Schuldbetreibung und Konkurs vor. Wie die anderen juristischen Personen bleibt die GmbH als solche selbstverständlich weiterhin der Konkursbetreibung unterstellt (Art. 39 Abs. 1 Ziff. 9 SchKG).

---

172 SR **281.1**.
173 Betreibungen gegen Geschäftsführerinnen und Geschäftsführer, die nicht an der Gesellschaft beteiligt sind, sowie gegen nicht geschäftsführende Gesellschafterinnen und Gesellschafter werden auf dem Weg der Pfändung fortgesetzt.
174 Motion 97.3668, SchKG und geschäftsführender Gesellschafter einer GmbH.

Teil F: Rechtliche Aspekte / Legal aspects

IV. Bundesgesetz über Fusion, Spaltung, Umwandlung und Vermögensübertragung

1. Kapitel: Gegenstand und Begriffe

Gegenstand

Art. 1 Abs. 1

1 Dieses Gesetz regelt die Anpassung der rechtlichen Strukturen von Kapitalgesellschaften, Kollektiv- und Kommanditgesellschaften, Genossenschaften, Vereinen, Stiftungen und Einzelunternehmen im Zusammenhang mit Fusion, Spaltung, Umwandlung und Vermögensübertragung.

Der Entwurf ersetzt den Begriff der «Einzelfirma» durch denjenigen des «Einzelunternehmens»; s. dazu die Ausführungen zu Art. 181 Abs. 4 E OR.

Begriffe

Art. 2 lit. a

In diesem Gesetz gelten als:

a. *Rechtsträger:* **Gesellschaften, Stiftungen, im Handelsregister eingetragene Einzelunternehmen und Institute des öffentlichen Rechts;**

Der Entwurf ersetzt den Begriff der «Einzelfirma» durch denjenigen des «Einzelunternehmens»; s. dazu die Ausführungen zu Art. 181 Abs. 4 E OR.

Kapitel 1: Neue Gesetzesbestimmungen und Erläuterungen

2. Kapitel: Fusion von Gesellschaften

1. Abschnitt: Allgemeine Bestimmungen

Fusion von Gesellschaften im Fall von Kapitalverlust oder Überschuldung

Art. 6 Abs. 2

2 **Das oberste Leitungs- oder Verwaltungsorgan muss dem Handelsregisteramt eine Bestätigung einer zugelassenen Revisionsexpertin oder eines zugelassenen Revisionsexperten einreichen, wonach die Voraussetzungen nach Abs. 1 erfüllt ist.**

Der Entwurf ersetzt den Begriff der besonders befähigten Revisorin bzw. des besonders befähigten Revisors durch jenen der zugelassenen Revisionsexpertin bzw. des zugelassenen Revisionsexperten (vgl. dazu die Erläuterungen zu Art. 4 E RAG).

4. Abschnitt: Fusionsvertrag, Fusionsbericht und Prüfung

Prüfung des Fusionsvertrags und des Fusionsberichts

Art. 15 Abs. 1, 3 und 4 Einleitungssatz

1 **Die an der Fusion beteiligten Gesellschaften müssen den Fusionsvertrag, den Fusionsbericht und die der Fusion zu Grunde liegende Bilanz von einer zugelassenen Revisionsexpertin oder einem zugelassenen Revisionsexperten prüfen lassen, falls die übernehmende Gesellschaft eine Kapitalgesellschaft oder eine Genossenschaft mit Anteilscheinen ist. Sie können eine gemeinsame Revisionsexpertin oder einen gemeinsamen Revisionsexperten bestimmen.**

3 **Die beteiligten Gesellschaften müssen der Revisionsexpertin oder dem Revisionsexperten alle zweckdienlichen Auskünfte und Unterlagen geben.**

4 **Die Revisionsexpertin oder der Revisionsexperte legt in einem schriftlichen Prüfungsbericht dar:**

...

Siehe dazu die Ausführungen zu Art. 6 Abs. 2 FusG.

5. Abschnitt: Fusionsbeschluss und Eintragung ins Handelsregister

Fusionsbeschluss

Art. 18 Abs. 1 lit. c

1 Bei den Kapitalgesellschaften, den Genossenschaften und den Vereinen muss das oberste Leitungs- oder Verwaltungsorgan den Fusionsvertrag der Generalversammlung zur Beschlussfassung unterbreiten. Folgende Mehrheiten sind erforderlich:

c. bei Gesellschaften mit beschränkter Haftung mindestens zwei Drittel der an der Generalversammlung vertretenen Stimmen und die absolute Mehrheit des gesamten Stammkapitals; mit dem ein ausübbares Stimmrecht verbunden ist.

Die Vorschriften des zukünftigen Fusionsgesetzes[175] betreffend die Anforderungen an die Beschlussfassung durch die Gesellschafterversammlung müssen den neu festgelegten Mehrheitserfordernissen für wichtige Beschlüsse im GmbH-Recht angepasst werden (s. Art. 808*b* Abs. 1 Ziff. 10 E OR und Art. 704 Abs. 1 Ziff. 8 E OR).

7. Abschnitt: Gläubiger- und Arbeitnehmerschutz

Sicherstellung der Forderungen

Art. 25 Abs. 2 zweiter Satz

2 ... Sie können von einer Publikation absehen, wenn eine zugelassene Revisionsexpertin oder ein zugelassener Revisionsexperte bestätigt, dass keine Forderungen bekannt oder zu erwarten sind, zu deren Befriedigung das freie Vermögen der beteiligten Gesellschaften nicht ausreicht.

---

175 Botschaft: BBl. **2000**, S. 4337 ff.; Entwurf: BBl. **2000**, S. 4531 ff.

Kapitel 1: Neue Gesetzesbestimmungen und Erläuterungen

Siehe dazu die Ausführungen zu Art. 6 Abs. 2 FusG.

4. Kapitel: Umwandlung von Gesellschaften

1. Abschnitt: Allgemeine Bestimmungen

Sonderregelung für die Umwandlung von Kollektiv- und Kommanditgesellschaften

Art. 55 Abs. 3
³ Die Fortführung einer Kollektiv- oder Kommanditgesellschaft als Einzelunternehmen nach Art. 579 des Obligationenrechts[176] bleibt vorbehalten.

Der Entwurf ersetzt den Begriff der «Einzelfirma» durch denjenigen des «Einzelunternehmens»; s. dazu die Ausführungen zu Art. 181 Abs. 4 E OR.

4. Abschnitt: Umwandlungsplan, Umwandlungsbericht und Prüfung

Prüfung des Umwandlungsplans und des Umwandlungsberichts

Art. 62 Abs. 1, 3 und 4
1 Die Gesellschaft muss den Umwandlungsplan, den Umwandlungsbericht und die der Umwandlung zu Grunde liegende Bilanz von einer zugelassenen Revisionsexpertin oder einem zugelassenen Revisionsexperten prüfen lassen.

3 Die Gesellschaft muss der Revisionsexpertin oder dem Revisionsexperten alle zweckdienlichen Auskünfte und Unterlagen geben.

4 Die Revisionsexpertin oder der Revisionsexperte muss prüfen, ob die Voraussetzungen für die Umwandlung erfüllt sind, insbesondere, ob die Rechtsstellung der Gesellschafterinnen und Gesellschafter nach der Umwandlung gewahrt bleiben.

---

[176] SR **220**

Siehe dazu die Ausführungen zu Art. 6 Abs. 2 FusG.

5. Abschnitt: Umwandlungsbeschluss und Eintragung ins Handelsregister

Umwandlungsbeschluss

Art. 64 Abs. 1 lit. c

1 Bei den Kapitalgesellschaften, den Genossenschaften und den Vereinen muss das oberste Leitungs- oder Verwaltungsorgan den Umwandlungsplan der Generalversammlung zur Beschlussfassung unterbreiten. Folgende Mehrheiten sind erforderlich:

c. Gesellschaften mit beschränkter Haftung mindestens zwei Drittel der an der Generalversammlung vertretenen Stimmen und die absolute Mehrheit des gesamten Kapitals; mit dem ein ausübbares Stimmrecht verbunden ist.

Die Vorschriften des zukünftigen Fusionsgesetzes[177] betreffend die Anforderungen an die Beschlussfassung durch die Gesellschafterversammlung müssen den neu festgelegten Mehrheitserfordernissen für wichtige Beschlüsse im GmbH-Recht angepasst werden (s. Art. 808*b* Abs. 1 Ziff. 10 E OR und Art. 704 Abs. 1 Ziff. 8 E OR).

6. Kapitel: Fusion und Vermögensübertragung von Stiftungen

1. Abschnitt: Fusion

Prüfung des Fusionsvertrags

Art. 81 Abs. 1

1 Die Stiftungen müssen den Fusionsvertrag sowie die Bilanzen von einer zugelassenen Revisorin oder einem zugelassenen Revisor prüfen lassen.

---

177 Botschaft: BBl. **2000**, S. 4337 ff.; Entwurf: BBl. **2000**, S. 4531 ff.

Der Entwurf übernimmt im *Abs. 1* die neue Bezeichnung der zugelassenen Revisorinnen und Revisoren (s. dazu auch die Ausführungen zu Art. 6 Abs. 2 FusG). Inhaltlich erfolgt insofern eine Modifikation, als die fachlichen Anforderungen an zugelassene Revisorinnen und Revisoren klar definiert sind, während dies für die Revisorinnen und Revisoren des geltenden Rechts nicht der Fall war.

Genehmigung und Vollzug der Fusion

Art. 83 Abs. 1 dritter Satz

1 ... Mit dem Antrag sind der Aufsichtsbehörde die von der zugelassenen Revisorin oder dem zugelassenen Revisor geprüften Bilanzen der beteiligten Stiftungen sowie der Revisionsbericht einzureichen.

Siehe dazu die Ausführungen zu Art. 81 Abs. 1 FusG.

Gläubiger- und Arbeitnehmerschutz

Art. 85 Abs. 2

2 Die Aufsichtsbehörde oder, bei Familienstiftungen und kirchlichen Stiftungen, das oberste Stiftungsorgan kann von einer Aufforderung an die Gläubigerinnen und Gläubiger absehen, wenn auf Grund des Berichts der zugelassenen Revisorin oder des zugelassenen Revisors keine Forderungen bekannt oder zu erwarten sind, zu deren Befriedigung das Stiftungsvermögen der beteiligten Stiftungen nicht ausreicht.

Siehe dazu die Ausführungen zu Art. 81 Abs. 1 FusG.

8. Kapitel: Fusion, Umwandlung und Vermögensübertragung unter Beteiligung von Instituten des öffentlichen Rechts

Anwendbares Recht

Art. 100 Abs. 2 dritter Satz

2 ... Das Inventar muss von einer zugelassenen Revisionsexpertin oder einem zugelassenen Revisionsexperten geprüft werden, sofern nicht in anderer Weise sichergestellt ist, dass die Erstellung und die Bewertung des Inventars den anerkannten Rechnungslegungsgrundsätzen entsprechen.

Siehe dazu die Ausführungen zu Art. 6 Abs. 2 FusG.

V. Bundesgesetz über das Internationale Privatrecht[178]

10. Kapitel: Gesellschaftsrecht
VI. Verlegung, Fusion, Spaltung und Vermögensübertragung
1. Verlegung der Gesellschaft vom Ausland in die Schweiz
b. Massgeblicher Zeitpunkt

Art. 162 Abs. 3

3 Eine Kapitalgesellschaft hat vor der Eintragung durch den Bericht einer zugelassenen Revisionsexpertin oder eines zugelassenen Revisionsexperten im Sinne des Revisionsaufsichtsgesetzes vom 16. Dezember 2005[179] über die Zulassung und Beaufsichtigung der Revisorinnen und Revisoren nachzuweisen, dass ihr Grundkapital nach schweizerischem Recht gedeckt ist.

Siehe dazu die Ausführungen zu Art. 6 Abs. 2 FusG. Da die fachlichen Qualifikationen an die zugelassenen Revisionsexpertinnen und Revisions-

---

178 SR **291**.
179 SR ...; AS ... (BBl **2004** 4139)

experten zukünftig im Revisionsaufsichtsgesetz normiert sind, wird neu auf Letzteres und nicht mehr auf das Obligationenrecht verwiesen.

5. Gemeinsame Bestimmungen

a. Löschung im Handelsregister

Art. 164 Abs. 1 und 2 lit. b[180]

1 Eine im schweizerischen Handelsregister eingetragene Gesellschaft kann nur gelöscht werden, wenn durch einen Bericht einer zugelassenen Revisionsexpertin oder eines zugelassenen Revisionsexperten bestätigt wird, dass die Forderungen der Gläubiger im Sinne von Art. 46 des Fusionsgesetzes vom 3. Oktober 2003[181] sichergestellt oder erfüllt worden sind oder dass die Gläubiger mit der Löschung einverstanden sind.

2 Übernimmt eine ausländische Gesellschaft eine schweizerische, schliesst sie sich mit ihr zu einer neuen ausländischen Gesellschaft zusammen oder spaltet sich eine schweizerische Gesellschaft in ausländische Gesellschaften auf, so muss überdies:

b. eine zugelassene Revisionsexpertin oder ein zugelassener Revisionsexperte bestätigen, dass die ausländische Gesellschaft den anspruchsberechtigten Gesellschaftern der schweizerischen Gesellschaft die Anteils- oder Mitgliedschaftsrechte eingeräumt oder eine allfällige Ausgleichszahlung oder Abfindung ausgerichtet oder sichergestellt hat.

Siehe dazu die Ausführungen zu Art. 6 Abs. 2 FusG.

---

180 Art. 164 Abs. 1 und Abs. 2 lit. b in der Fassung des Fusionsgesetzes vom 3. Oktober 2003, in Kraft ab 1. Juli 2004, AS **2004** 2617
181 SR **221.301**; AS **2004** 2617

VI. Bundesgesetz über die Stempelabgaben[182]

Einleitung

I. Gegenstand des Gesetzes

Art. 1 Abs. 1 lit. a Ziff. 2 und lit. b Ziff. 3

1 Der Bund erhebt Stempelabgaben:

a. auf der Ausgabe folgender inländischer Urkunden:

2. **Stammanteile von Gesellschaften mit beschränkter Haftung und Anteilscheine von Genossenschaften,**

b. auf dem Umsatz der folgenden inländischen und ausländischen Urkunden:

3. **Stammanteile von Gesellschaften mit beschränkter Haftung und Anteilscheine von Genossenschaften,**

Erster Abschnitt: Emissionsabgabe

I. Gegenstand der Abgabe

Beteiligungsrechte

Art. 5 Abs. 1 lit. a zweites Lemma und Abs. 2 lit. b

1 Gegenstand der Abgabe sind:

a. die entgeltliche oder unentgeltliche Begründung und Erhöhung des Nennwertes von Beteiligungsrechten in Form von:

– Stammanteilen inländischer Gesellschaften mit beschränkter Haftung;

2 Der Begründung von Beteiligungsrechten in Sinne von Abs. 1 lit. a sind gleichgestellt:

---

[182] SR **641.10**.

b. Der Handwechsel der Mehrheit der Aktien, Stammanteilen oder Genossenschaftsanteile an einer inländischen Gesellschaft oder Genossenschaft, die wirtschaftlich liquidiert oder in liquide Form gebracht worden ist;

II. Entstehung der Abgabeforderung

Art. 7 Abs. 1 lit. a

1 Die Abgabeforderung entsteht:

a. bei Aktien, Partizipationsscheinen und bei Stammanteilen von Gesellschaften mit beschränkter Haftung: im Zeitpunkt der Eintragung der Begründung oder der Erhöhung der Beteiligungsrechte im Handelsregister;

III. Abgabesätze und Berechnungsgrundlage

Besondere Fälle

Art. 9 Abs. 1 lit. e[183]

1 Die Abgabe beträgt:

e. auf Beteiligungsrechten, die in Durchführung von Beschlüssen über die Fusion, Spaltung oder Umwandlung von Einzelunternehmen, Handelsgesellschaften ohne juristische Persönlichkeit, Vereinen, Stiftungen oder Unternehmen des öffentlichen Rechts begründet oder erhöht werden, sofern der bisherige Rechtsträger während mindestens fünf Jahren bestand: 1 Prozent des Nennwerts, vorbehältlich der Ausnahmen in Art. 6 Abs. 1 lit. h. Über den Mehrwert wird nachträglich abgerechnet, soweit während den der Umstrukturierung nachfolgenden fünf Jahren die Beteiligungsrechte veräussert werden.

---

[183] Art. 9 Abs. 1 lit. e in der Fassung des Fusionsgesetzes vom 3. Oktober 2003, in Kraft ab 1. Juli 2004, AS **2004** 2617

Der Entwurf ersetzt den Begriff der «Einzelfirma» durch denjenigen des «Einzelunternehmens»; s. dazu die Ausführungen zu Art. 181 Abs. 4 E OR.

Zweiter Abschnitt: Umsatzabgabe

I. Gegenstand der Abgabe

Regel

Art. 13 Abs. 2 lit. a Ziff. 2

2 Steuerbare Urkunden sind:

a. die von einem Inländer ausgegebenen
   2. Aktien, Stammanteile von Gesellschaften mit beschränkter Haftung, Anteilscheine von Genossenschaften, Partizipationsscheine, Genussscheine,

Ausnahmen

Art. 14 Abs. 1 lit. a und b

1 Von der Abgabe sind ausgenommen:

a. die Ausgabe inländischer Aktien, Stammanteile von Gesellschaften mit beschränkter Haftung, Anteilscheine von Genossenschaften, Partizipationsscheine, Genussscheine, Anteilscheine von Anlagefonds, Obligationen und Geldmarktpapiere, einschliesslich der Festübernahme durch eine Bank oder Beteiligungsgesellschaft und der Zuteilung bei einer nachfolgenden Emission;

b. die Sacheinlage von Urkunden zur Liberierung in- oder ausländischer Aktien, Stammanteile von Gesellschaften mit beschränkter Haftung, Genossenschaftsanteile, Partizipationsscheine und Anteile an kollektiven Kapitalanlagen gemäss KAG;

Kapitel 1: Neue Gesetzesbestimmungen und Erläuterungen

In allen aufgeführten Bestimmungen wird die Terminologie des Entwurfs zur Revision des GmbH-Rechts übernommen. Insbesondere wird der bisher verwendete Begriff der «Stammeinlagen» durch den neuen Begriff «Stammanteile» ersetzt. Diese redaktionellen Anpassungen sind nur beim deutschen Text notwendig.

VII. Bundesgesetz über die Verrechnungssteuer[184]

Erster Abschnitt: Steuererhebung

A. Gegenstand der Steuer

I. Kapitalerträge

1. Regel

Art. 4 Abs. 1 lit. b

1 Gegenstand der Verrechnungssteuer auf dem Ertrag beweglichen Kapitalvermögens sind die Zinsen, Renten, Gewinnanteile und sonstigen Erträge:

b. der von einem Inländer ausgegebenen Aktien, Stammanteile an Gesellschaften mit beschränkter Haftung, Genossenschaftsanteile, Partizipationsscheine und Genussscheine.

Entsprechend der Terminologie des Entwurfs zur Revision des GmbH-Rechts wird der bisher verwendete Begriff der «Anteile» durch jenen der «Stammanteile» ersetzt. Diese redaktionelle Anpassung betrifft nur den deutschen Text.

1a Erwerb eigener Beteiligungsrechte

Art. 4a Abs. 1 und 2

1 Erwirbt eine Gesellschaft oder eine Genossenschaft gestützt auf einen Beschluss über die Herabsetzung des Kapitals oder im Hinblick auf eine Herabsetzung ihres Kapitals eigene Beteiligungsrechte (Ak-

---

184 SR **642.21**.

tien, Stammanteile von Gesellschaften mit beschränkter Haftung, Anteilscheine, Partizipationsscheine oder Genussscheine), so unterliegt die Differenz zwischen dem Erwerbspreis und dem einbezahlten Nennwert dieser Beteiligungsrechte der Verrechnungssteuer. Dasselbe gilt, soweit der Erwerb eigener Beteiligungsrechte den Rahmen der Art. 659 oder 783 des Obligationenrechts[185] überschreitet.

2 Erwirbt eine Gesellschaft oder eine Genossenschaft im Rahmen der Art. 659 oder 783 des Obligationenrechts eigene Beteiligungsrechte, ohne anschliessend ihr Kapital herabzusetzen, so gilt Abs. 1 sinngemäss, wenn die Gesellschaft oder die Genossenschaft diese Beteiligungsrechte nicht innerhalb von sechs Jahren wieder veräussert.

Auch die vorliegende Bestimmung wird terminologisch angeglichen. Zudem wird neu auf Art. 783 E OR hingewiesen, der den Erwerb eigener Stammanteile durch Gesellschaften mit beschränkter Haftung regelt.

VIII. Bundesgesetz über die direkte Bundessteuer[186]

Zweiter Teil: Besteuerung der natürlichen Personen

Zweiter Titel: Einkommenssteuer

1. Kapitel: Steuerbare Einkünfte

3. Abschnitt: Selbständige Erwerbstätigkeit

Umstrukturierungen

Art. 19 Abs. 1 Einleitungssatz[187]

1 Stille Reserven einer Personenunternehmung (Einzelunternehmen, Personengesellschaft) werden bei Umstrukturierungen, insbesondere im Fall der Fusion, Spaltung oder Umwandlung, nicht besteuert, soweit die Steuerpflicht in der Schweiz fortbesteht und die bisher für

---

185 SR **220**
186 SR **642.11**
187 Art. 19 Abs. 1 Einleitungssatz in der Fassung des Fusionsgesetzes vom 3. Oktober 2003, in Kraft ab 1. Juli 2004, AS **2004** 2617

die Einkommenssteuer massgeblichen Werte übernommen werden:
...

Der Entwurf ersetzt den Begriff der «Einzelfirma» durch denjenigen des «Einzelunternehmens»; s. dazu die Ausführungen zu Art. 181 Abs. 4 E OR.

IX. Bundesgesetz über die Harmonisierung der direkten Steuern der Kantone und Gemeinden[188]

Zweiter Titel: Steuern der natürlichen Personen

2. Kapitel: Einkommenssteuer

1. Abschnitt: Einkünfte

Selbständige Erwerbstätigkeit

Art. 8 Abs. 3[189]

3 Stille Reserven einer Personenunternehmung (Einzelunternehmen, Personengesellschaft) werden bei Umstrukturierungen, insbesondere im Fall der Fusion, Spaltung oder Umwandlung, nicht besteuert, soweit die Steuerpflicht in der Schweiz fortbesteht und die bisher für die Einkommenssteuer massgeblichen Werte übernommen werden:
...

Der Entwurf ersetzt den Begriff der «Einzelfirma» durch denjenigen des «Einzelunternehmens»; s. dazu die Ausführungen zu Art. 181 Abs. 4 E OR.

---

188 SR **642.14**

189 Art. 8 Abs. 3 Einleitungssatz in der Fassung des Fusionsgesetzes vom 3. Oktober 2003, in Kraft ab 1. Juli 2004, AS **2004** 2617

Teil F: Rechtliche Aspekte / Legal aspects

§ 8 Übergangsbestimmungen zum Gesetzesentwurf 01.082

A. Allgemeine Regel

Art. 1

1 Der Schlusstitel des Zivilgesetzbuches gilt für dieses Gesetz, soweit die folgenden Bestimmungen nichts anderes vorsehen.

2 Die Bestimmungen des neuen Gesetzes werden mit seinem Inkrafttreten auf bestehende Gesellschaften anwendbar.

Abs. 1 verweist auf den Schlusstitel des Zivilgesetzbuches, soweit in den Übergangsbestimmungen des Entwurfs nichts anderes vorgesehen wird. Nach Art. 1 SchlT ZGB richten sich die rechtlichen Wirkungen von Tatsachen, die vor dem Inkrafttreten des neuen Rechts eingetreten sind, auch nachher nach dem bisherigen Recht. Diese Regel der Nichtrückwirkung für abgeschlossene Sachverhalte erfasst indessen nach allgemein anerkannter Auffassung so genannte Dauertatbestände nicht (d.h. Sachverhalte, die unter dem neuen Recht andauern). Im Gesellschaftsrecht sind derartige Dauertatbestände von grosser Bedeutung: Sowohl die Organisation der Gesellschaft als auch die Rechtsstellung der beteiligten Personen folgen als Dauertatbestände vom Zeitpunkt des Inkrafttretens an grundsätzlich dem neuen Recht. *Abs. 2* hält daher fest, dass die Bestimmungen des neuen Gesetzes mit seinem Inkrafttreten auf bestehende Gesellschaften Anwendung finden (vgl. auch Art. 3 SchlT ZGB).

B. Anpassungsfrist

Art. 2

1 Gesellschaften mit beschränkter Haftung, die im Zeitpunkt des Inkrafttretens dieses Gesetzes im Handelsregister eingetragen sind, jedoch den neuen Vorschriften nicht entsprechen, müssen innerhalb von zwei Jahren ihre Statuten und Reglemente den neuen Bestimmungen anpassen.

2 Bestimmungen der Statuten und Reglemente, die mit dem neuen Recht nicht vereinbar sind, bleiben bis zur Anpassung, längstens aber noch zwei Jahre, in Kraft.

3 Für Gesellschaften mit beschränkter Haftung, die im Zeitpunkt des Inkrafttretens dieses Gesetzes im Handelsregister eingetragen sind, finden die Art. 808a und 809 Abs. 4 zweiter Satz erst nach Ablauf der Frist zur Anpassung der Statuten Anwendung.

4 Aktiengesellschaften und Genossenschaften, die im Zeitpunkt des Inkrafttretens dieses Gesetzes im Handelsregister eingetragen sind und deren Firma den neuen gesetzlichen Vorschriften nicht entspricht, müssen ihre Firma innerhalb von zwei Jahren den neuen Bestimmungen anpassen. Nach Ablauf dieser Frist ergänzt das Handelsregisteramt die Firma von Amtes wegen.

Eine unmittelbare Anwendung des neuen Rechts, wie sie Art. 1 Abs. 2 vorsieht, ist jedoch nur sachgerecht, soweit bisherige Gesetzesbestimmungen durch neue zwingende Regelungen ersetzt werden. Soweit die rechtliche Ausgestaltung von Gesellschaften in den Statuten konkretisiert wurden, muss den Gesellschaften eine adäquate Frist zur Anpassung ihrer rechtlichen Grundordnung an das neue Recht eingeräumt werden.

Abs. 1 räumt Gesellschaften, die im Zeitpunkt des Inkrafttretens des neuen Rechts bereits im Handelsregister eingetragen sind, für die Anpassung ihrer Statuten und Reglemente eine Frist von 2 Jahren ein. Bei der Revision des Aktienrechts von 1991 wurde eine Anpassungsfrist von 5 Jahren vorgesehen. Diese Frist hat sich jedoch in der Praxis als erheblich zu lange herausgestellt: Sie hatte zur Folge, dass die nötigen Anpassungen vergessen gingen, und wurde in der Literatur daher zu Recht kritisiert. Bei der vorliegenden Revision des GmbH-Rechts wird im Unterschied zur Aktienrechtsrevision auf eine Anpassung des Mindestkapitals verzichtet. Auch im Übrigen dürfte der Anpassungsbedarf auf Grund der dispositiven Natur zahlreicher gesetzlicher Normen eher gering sein. Eine Anpassungsfrist von 2 Jahren erscheint daher sachgerecht.

Bestimmungen der Statuten und Reglemente, die den neuen Vorschriften nicht entsprechen, bleiben nach *Abs. 2* höchstens bis zum Ablauf der Anpassungsfrist in Kraft. Werden sie nicht fristgerecht angepasst, fallen sie ersatzlos dahin, soweit nicht dispositive gesetzliche Regelungen an ihre Stelle treten.

Ein Bedarf zur Anpassung der Statuten kann sich auch daraus ergeben, dass eine Gesellschaft die neue dispositive Regelung des Stichentscheids in der Gesellschafterversammlung ausschliessen will. Wird die Frage des Stichentscheids in den Statuten bisher nicht geregelt, so muss eine entsprechende Anordnung aufgenommen werden. *Abs. 3* sieht daher vor, dass die neue Bestimmung zum Stichentscheid (Art. 808a E OR) für Gesellschaften, die im Zeitpunkt des Inkrafttretens des revidierten Rechts im Handelsregister eingetragen sind, erst nach der allgemeinen Frist für die Anpassung der Statuten zur Anwendung gelangt. Es steht den betroffenen Gesellschaften somit offen, während einer Frist von 2 Jahren den Stichentscheid ausdrücklich auszuschliessen, um eine Änderung der bisherigen Verhältnisse zu vermeiden. Das Gleiche muss auch für die Regelung des Stichentscheids der Vorsitzenden oder des Vorsitzenden der Geschäftsführerinnen und Geschäftsführer gelten (s. Art. 809 Abs. 4 Satz 2 E OR).

Abs. 4 enthält eine besondere Übergangsregelung zu Art. 950 E OR betreffend die Angabe der Rechtsform in der Firma. Aktiengesellschaften und Genossenschaften, deren Firmen keine entsprechende Angabe enthalten, müssen innert 2 Jahren einen Rechtsformzusatz hinzufügen. Der Rechtszwang für diese Anpassung soll jedoch zurückhaltend ausgestaltet werden[190]: Bleibt eine Gesellschaft untätig, so ergänzt das Handelsregisteramt die Firma von Amtes wegen. Die Statuten müssen in diesem Fall erst mit der nächsten ohnehin durchzuführenden Statutenrevision zwingend der neuen Firma angepasst werden. Für die Firmengebrauchspflicht (Art. 954*a* E OR) ist nach der amtlich angeordneten Änderung jedoch sofort die neue im Handelsregister eingetragene Firma massgebend.

C. Leistung der Einlagen

Art. 3

1 Wurden in Gesellschaften mit beschränkter Haftung, die im Zeitpunkt des Inkrafttretens dieses Gesetzes im Handelsregister eingetragen sind, keine dem Ausgabebetrag aller Stammanteile entsprechenden Einlagen geleistet, so müssen diese innerhalb von zwei Jahren erbracht werden.

---

[190] Die erforderliche Statutenänderung bedingt ein Tätigwerden der Generalversammlung und lässt sich daher nicht auf direktem Weg erzwingen.

2 Bis zur vollständigen Leistung der Einlagen in der Höhe des Stammkapitals haften die Gesellschafter nach Art. 802 des Obligationenrechts in der Fassung vom 18. Dezember 1936[191].

Während das neue Recht eine vollständige Liberierung der Stammanteile verlangt (Art. 777c Abs. 1 E OR), war es bisher zulässig, nur die Hälfte des Stammkapitals einzubezahlen. Im Hinblick auf die Rechtssicherheit im Geschäftsverkehr mit GmbH und weil die Vollliberierung eine Voraussetzung verschiedener Neuerungen der Revision darstellt (insbes. der Aufhebung der bisherigen subsidiären Solidarhaftung), ist es unerlässlich, Gesellschaften, deren Stammkapital nicht voll einbezahlt ist, zur Liberierung des noch ausstehenden Teils anzuhalten. *Abs. 1* verlangt daher die vollständige Leistung des Ausgabebetrages aller Stammanteile innerhalb von 2 Jahren. Von dieser Anpassung wird nur eine beschränkte Minderheit der Gesellschaften betroffen. Da das Mindestkapital auf 20 000 Franken belassen wird, beträgt die zu leistende Liberierung bei Gesellschaften mit minimaler Kapitalausstattung lediglich 10 000 Franken, wobei es sich um die Erfüllung einer ohnehin bestehenden Verbindlichkeit handelt. Die noch zu leistende Einlage des Stammkapitals kann sowohl durch nachträgliche Einzahlung oder Sacheinlage als auch durch die Umwandlung von Reserven in Stammkapital erfolgen.

Das Übergangsrecht zur Revision des Aktienrechts von 1991 sah beim Unterbleiben der Anpassung an die neuen Vorschriften zur Mindesteinlage die Auflösung durch das Gericht vor (Art. 2 Abs. 2 SchlB OR 1991). Der Entwurf verzichtet auf einen derart drakonischen Rechtszwang: *Abs. 2* beschränkt sich darauf, die subsidiäre solidarische Haftung der Gesellschafterinnen und Gesellschafter nach Art. 802 OR bis zur vollständigen Leistung der Einlagen andauern zu lassen. Es liegt somit im Interesse der Gesellschafterinnen und Gesellschafter, sich durch eine rasche Liberierung des Stammkapitals von dieser Haftung zu befreien. Die Befreiung tritt erst mit der vollständigen Liberierung sämtlicher Stammanteile ein.

Werden nicht vollständig einbezahlte Stammanteile abgetreten, so geht die subsidiäre solidarische Haftung gemäss dem bisherigen Recht auf die Erwerberinnen oder Erwerber über. Es obliegt diesen, zum eigenen Schutz die Liberierung zu überprüfen.

---

191 BS 53 185

D. Partizipationsscheine und Genussscheine

Art. 4

1 Anteile an Gesellschaften mit beschränkter Haftung, die einen Nennwert aufweisen und in den Passiven der Bilanz ausgewiesen werden, die aber kein Stimmrecht vermitteln (Partizipationsscheine), gelten nach Ablauf von zwei Jahren als Stammanteile mit gleichen Vermögensrechten, wenn sie nicht innerhalb dieser Frist durch Kapitalherabsetzung vernichtet werden. Werden die Anteile vernichtet, so muss den bisherigen Partizipanten eine Abfindung in der Höhe des wirklichen Werts ausgerichtet werden.

2 Die erforderlichen Beschlüsse der Gesellschafterversammlung können mit der absoluten Mehrheit der vertretenen Stimmen gefasst werden, auch wenn die Statuten etwas anderes vorsehen.

3 Für Anteile an Gesellschaften mit beschränkter Haftung, die nicht in den Passiven der Bilanz ausgewiesen werden, finden nach dem Inkrafttreten dieses Gesetzes die Vorschriften über die Genussscheine Anwendung, dies auch dann, wenn sie als Partizipationsscheine bezeichnet sind. Sie dürfen keinen Nennwert angeben und müssen als Genussscheine bezeichnet werden. Die Bezeichnung der Titel und die Statuten sind innerhalb von zwei Jahren anzupassen.

Die Ausgabe von Partizipationsscheinen durch Gesellschaften mit beschränkter Haftung ist im geltenden Recht nicht geregelt und war bisher auch nie gerichtlich zu beurteilen. Im Handelsregister ist nur in wenigen Einzelfällen ein Partizipationskapital eingetragen, wobei die Eintragung im Rahmen der beschränkten Kognition der Registerbehörden erfolgte.

Die Ausgabe von Partizipationsscheinen dient in der Praxis zwei verschiedenen Zielen:

– Sie erlaubt die Beschaffung von Eigenkapital auf dem Kapitalmarkt, ohne dass dadurch die bisherigen Beherrschungsverhältnisse berührt werden.

– Namentlich im Rahmen einer Unternehmensnachfolge kann sie dazu verwendet werden, die Mehrheitsverhältnisse dadurch zu beeinflussen, dass einer Gruppe von Beteiligten keine Stimmrechte gewährt werden.

Wie im geltenden Recht ist die GmbH als nicht kapitalmarktfähige Rechtsform ausgestaltet, damit mit Rücksicht auf die Bedürfnisse kleinerer Unternehmen von den strukturellen Anforderungen abgesehen werden kann, die für eine öffentliche Kapitalaufnahme vorauszusetzen wären. Die GmbH ist demnach für die Aufnahme von nicht stimmberechtigtem Eigenkapital auf dem Kapitalmarkt nicht geeignet.

Partizipantinnen und Partizipanten sind am Risikokapital der Gesellschaft beteiligt. Ihre Investition ist weder fest verzinslich noch kündbar. Da ihnen kein Stimmrecht zusteht, vermögen sie zudem in keiner relevanten Weise auf die Geschäftstätigkeit der Gesellschaft und die Bestellung der Organe Einfluss zu nehmen. Die Partizipantinnen und Partizipanten verfügen demzufolge über eine ausserordentlich prekäre Rechtsstellung und sind daher in erheblichem Masse auf allgemeine gesellschaftsrechtliche Schutzvorkehren angewiesen. Für einen minimalen Schutz vorauszusetzen wären insbesondere das Obligatorium einer Revisionsstelle sowie das Rechtsinstitut der Sonderprüfung. Der Entwurf sieht jedoch von einer entsprechenden Ausgestaltung des GmbH-Rechts ab, um kleinen und mittleren Unternehmen eine möglichst einfache und wenig kostenintensive Rechtsform zur Verfügung zu stellen.

Die Ausgabe von Partizipationsscheinen würde die Übernahme der aktienrechtlichen Schutzmechanismen bedingen. Da in der Praxis jedoch nur ein sehr beschränktes Bedürfnis besteht, erscheint eine entsprechende Regelung für die Zulassung von Partizipationsscheinen in der GmbH nicht als sinnvoll. Soll eine stimmrechtslose Beteiligung am Risikokapital der Gesellschaft geschaffen werden, so ist sachgerechterweise die Rechtsform der Aktiengesellschaft zu wählen (eine einfache Umwandlung wird vom zukünftigen Fusionsgesetz gewährleistet[192]). Der Entwurf sieht aus diesen Gründen von der Möglichkeit der Ausgabe von Partizipationsscheinen in der GmbH ab (es handelt sich dabei um ein qualifiziertes Schweigen des Gesetzes).

Für die wenigen GmbH, die ein Partizipationskapital aufweisen, ist eine Übergangsregelung zu schaffen. Da die Struktur der GmbH für ein stimmrechtsloses Eigenkapital nicht geeignet ist, sieht *Abs. 1* vor, dass Partizipationsscheine nach Ablauf von 2 Jahren grundsätzlich als Stammanteile gelten. Es wird jedoch nur verlangt, dass die Vermögensrechte der bisherigen Kapitalbeteiligung entsprechen; für die Festsetzung des Stimmrechts stehen die Gestaltungsmöglichkeiten von Art. 806 E OR zur Verfügung. Die Gesellschaft kann die Umwandlung der Partizipationsscheine in

---

192 s. Art. 53 ff. E FusG; BBl **2000** 4446 ff. und 4550 ff.

Stammanteile dadurch vermeiden, dass sie die Partizipationsscheine vor Ablauf der Anpassungsfrist durch eine Kapitalherabsetzung vernichtet und den bisherigen Partizipantinnen und Partizipanten eine Abfindung in der Höhe des wirklichen Werts ausrichtet. Eine weitere Möglichkeit besteht in der Umwandlung der GmbH in eine Aktiengesellschaft unter Beibehaltung eines Partizipationskapitals. Es liegt an der Gesellschaft, die nach den konkreten Umständen am besten geeignete Lösung zu treffen.

Zur Erleichterung der nach *Abs. 1* erforderlichen Anpassungen sieht *Abs. 2* vor, dass die notwendigen Beschlüsse der Gesellschafterversammlung mit der absoluten Mehrheit der vertretenen Stimmen gefasst werden können, und zwar auch dann, wenn die Statuten andere Mehrheitserfordernisse vorsehen. Dies gilt jedoch nicht für die im Gesetzestext nicht erwähnte Möglichkeit der Umwandlung in eine Aktiengesellschaft.

Abs. 3 stellt die Abgrenzung zwischen Partizipations- und Genussscheinen klar: Anteile, die nicht in den Passiven der Bilanz ausgewiesen werden, unterstehen zwingend den Vorschriften für Genussscheine (s. Art. 774*a* E OR). Sie dürfen keinen Nennwert angeben und müssen als Genussscheine bezeichnet werden. Die Statuten und allfällige Titel sind innerhalb von zwei Jahren entsprechend anzupassen.

E. Eigene Stammanteile

Art. 5

Haben Gesellschaften mit beschränkter Haftung vor dem Inkrafttreten dieses Gesetzes eigene Stammanteile erworben, so müssen sie diese, soweit sie zehn Prozent des Stammkapitals übersteigen, innerhalb von zwei Jahren veräussern oder durch Kapitalherabsetzung vernichten.

Das geltende Recht sieht für den Erwerb eigener Stammanteile keine Beschränkung vor (s. Art. 807 OR). Der Entwurf enthält demgegenüber eine Begrenzung auf 10% des Stammkapitals; für besondere Tatbestände gilt eine erhöhte Schwelle von 35% (s. Art. 783 E OR). Über 10% des Stammkapitals hinaus erworbene eigene Stammanteile sind innerhalb von 2 Jahren zu veräussern oder durch Kapitalherabsetzung zu vernichten (Art. 783 Abs. 2 E OR). Die vorliegende Bestimmung bringt diese Regelung auch für eigene Stammanteile zur Anwendung, die vor dem Inkrafttreten des neuen Rechts erworben wurden, wobei die Frist von 2 Jahren mit dem Inkrafttreten beginnt.

F. Nachschusspflicht

Art. 6

1 Statutarische Verpflichtungen zur Leistung von Nachschüssen, die vor dem Inkrafttreten dieses Gesetzes begründet wurden und die das Doppelte des Nennwerts der Stammanteile übersteigen, bleiben rechtsgültig und können nur im Verfahren nach Art. 795c herabgesetzt werden.

2 Im Übrigen finden nach dem Inkrafttreten dieses Gesetzes die neuen Vorschriften Anwendung, so namentlich für die Einforderung der Nachschüsse.

Das geltende Recht sieht für statutarische Nachschusspflichten keine gesetzliche Begrenzung vor (s. Art. 803 OR). Der Entwurf beschränkt Nachschusspflichten auf das Doppelte des Nennwerts der Stammanteile, mit denen sie verbunden sind (Art. 795 Abs. 2 E OR).

Unter dem alten Recht begründete Nachschusspflichten, welche die neue gesetzliche Schranke übersteigen, bleiben nach *Abs. 1* rechtsgültig und dürfen nur im Verfahren nach Art. 795c E OR herabgesetzt werden. Die Fortdauer bestehender Nachschusspflichten in ihrer bisherigen Höhe erscheint zum Schutz der Gläubigerinnen und Gläubiger unabdingbar. Erwerberinnen und Erwerber von Stammanteilen werden dadurch nicht gefährdet, da sie sich ohnehin in den Statuten über allfällige Nachschusspflichten informieren müssen.

Abgesehen von der neuen gesetzlichen Begrenzung finden für unter dem alten Recht begründete Nachschusspflichten nach dem Inkrafttreten gemäss *Abs. 2* die neuen Vorschriften Anwendung, so namentlich für die Einforderung der Nachschüsse.

Der Entwurf verzichtet auf eine übergangsrechtliche Regelung statutarischer Nebenleistungspflichten. In Abweichung vom bisherigen Recht (vgl. Art. 777 Ziff. 2 OR) werden Nebenleistungspflichten mit der Revision in ihrem Verwendungszweck geringfügig beschränkt (s. Art. 796 Abs. 2 E OR sowie die Ausführungen zu dieser Bestimmung). Da es sich um eine sachlich gebotene Eingrenzung auf für die Gesellschaft relevante Pflichten handelt, erscheint es angezeigt, unter dem alten Recht begründete Nebenleistungspflichten, die mit der neuen Regelung nicht vereinbar sind, nach Ablauf der Frist zur Anpassung der Statuten entfallen zu lassen (s. Art. 2 ÜBest). In den wenigen Fällen, die von dieser Regelung betroffen sind, steht es offen, bisherige statutarische Anordnungen während der Anpassungsfrist durch vertragliche Vereinbarungen abzulösen.

G. Revisionsstelle

Art. 7[193]

Die Bestimmungen dieses Gesetzes zur Revisionsstelle gelten vom ersten Geschäftsjahr an, das mit dem Inkrafttreten dieses Gesetzes oder danach beginnt.

Der vorliegende Entwurf ist aus normtechnischen Gründen als Zusatzbotschaft zur Botschaft über die Revision des GmbH-Rechts konzipiert. Dementsprechend gilt das Übergangsrecht des Entwurfs zur Revision des GmbH-Rechts auch für die Vorschriften des vorliegenden Entwurfs[194].
Somit kommt als Grundregel das Prinzip der Nichtrückwirkung nach Art. 1 SchlT ZGB zur Anwendung (Art. 1 Abs. 1 E ÜBest GmbH-Revision): Die rechtlichen Wirkungen von Tatsachen, die vor dem Inkrafttreten des neuen Rechts eingetreten sind, richten sich auch nachher nach dem bisherigen Recht. Umgekehrt sind Tatsachen, die nach diesem Zeitpunkt eintreten, gemäss Art. 1 Abs. 3 SchlT ZGB nach dem neuen Recht zu beurteilen, sofern das Gesetz keine Ausnahme vorsieht.

Nach dem Inkrafttreten neu eintretende Ereignisse und neu gefasste Beschlüsse der Gesellschaftsorgane unterstehen demnach den neuen Vorschriften. Wo das Gesetz eine besondere Bestätigung oder eine Prüfung durch eine zugelassene Revisorin, einen zugelassenen Revisor, eine zugelassene Revisionsexpertin oder einen zugelassenen Revisionsexperten verlangt (s. bspw. Art. 732 Abs. 2 E OR betreffend Prüfung der Kapitalherabsetzung in der Aktiengesellschaft), findet somit das neue Recht mit

---

193 Ersetzt Art. 7 der Übergangsbestimmungen des Entwurfs zur Revision des Rechts der GmbH vom 19. Dezember 2001 (BBl **2002** 3299).
194 01.082 Botschaft zur Revision des Obligationenrechts (GmbH-Recht sowie Anpassungen im Aktien-, Genossenschafts-, Handelsregister- und Firmenrecht) vom 19. Dezember 2001, BBl **2002** 3148, 3297 ff.

dem Inkrafttreten Anwendung[195]. Falls die Revisionsstelle nicht über die für die Revisionsdienstleistung erforderliche Zulassung verfügt, muss die Gesellschaft eine Fachperson oder ein Revisionsunternehmen mit entsprechender Zulassung mit der Prüfung beauftragen.

Die Regel der Nichtrückwirkung für abgeschlossene Sachverhalte erfasst nach allgemein anerkannter Auffassung so genannte Dauertatbestände nicht (d.h. Sachverhalte, die unter dem neuen Recht andauern). Im Gesellschaftsrecht sind solche Dauertatbestände von grosser Bedeutung: Sowohl die Organisation der Gesellschaft als auch die Rechtsstellung der beteiligten Personen folgen als Dauertatbestände vom Zeitpunkt des Inkrafttretens an grundsätzlich dem neuen Recht. Art. 1 Abs. 2 E ÜBest GmbH-Revision hält daher fest, dass die Bestimmungen des neuen Gesetzes mit seinem Inkrafttreten auf bestehende Gesellschaften Anwendung finden (vgl. auch Art. 3 SchlT ZGB).

Zu dieser Vorschrift besteht innerhalb der Übergangsbestimmungen zum GmbH-Recht eine mit Blick auf den vorliegenden Entwurf bedeutsame Ausnahme: Gemäss Art. 7 E ÜBest GmbH-Recht gilt die Pflicht zur Bezeichnung einer Revisionsstelle erst vom ersten Geschäftsjahr an, das mit dem Inkrafttreten des Gesetzes oder danach beginnt.

Diese Ausnahme erklärt sich dadurch, dass die Prüfung von Jahres- und Konzernrechnungen kein punktuelles Ereignis (s. dazu vorne Art. 1 SchlT ZGB), sondern einen Dauertatbestand darstellt, der sich über die ganze Zeitspanne der Rechnungsperiode erstreckt[196]. Als Gesamttatsache sind die in ihr widergespiegelten Einzeltatsachen erst am letzten Tag der Rechnungsperiode vollendet. Eine Aufspaltung der Rechtsfolgen (Anwendung von altem Revisionsrecht auf Ereignisse vor Inkrafttreten der vorliegenden Gesetzesänderung, von neuem auf die Ereignisse danach) wäre nicht praktikabel. Durch Art. 7 E ÜBest GmbH-Recht wird daher sichergestellt, dass die Revision einer Jahres- oder Konzernrechnung in Übereinstimmung mit dem zu Grunde liegenden Geschäftsjahr vollumfänglich unter neuem Revisionsrecht erfolgen kann.

Allerdings trägt Art. 7 E Übest in der Fassung, wie er im Rahmen der GmbH-Revision vorgesehen wurde, nur der Tatsache Rechnung, dass die Revisions*pflicht* mit dem Inkrafttreten der Revision des GmbH-Rechts für einzelne Gesellschaften ändern kann. Der vorliegende Entwurf enthält jedoch eine Neuordnung des gesamten Revisionsrechts. Aus diesem

---

195 s. dazu PETER BÖCKLI, Schweizer Aktienrecht, 2. Aufl., Zürich 1996, N 2147.
196 s. dazu und zum Folgenden PETER BÖCKLI, Schweizer Aktienrecht, 2. Aufl., Zürich 1996, N 2145.

Grund muss Art. 7 E ÜBest GmbH-Revision in seinem Anwendungsbereich erweitert werden. Der modifizierte Art. 7 E ÜBest schreibt daher vor, dass die Bestimmungen des neuen Rechts zur Revisionsstelle vom ersten Geschäftsjahr an gelten, das mit dem Inkrafttreten des neuen Rechts oder danach beginnt. Unter die Bestimmungen zur Revisionsstelle fallen die Art. 727 ff. E OR sowie die entsprechenden Vorschriften zu den übrigen Rechtsformen.

Für die Umschreibung der Revisionspflicht stellt der Entwurf in Art. 727 Abs. 1 Ziff. 2 E OR auf bestimmte Grössenkriterien ab. Für die Beurteilung der Frage, ob diese in zwei aufeinander folgenden Geschäftsjahren überschritten wurden, ist im Zeitpunkt des Inkrafttretens aus sachlichen Gründen auf die zwei letzten Geschäftsjahre abzustellen, die dem Inkrafttreten vorangegangen sind. Dabei liegt keine Rückwirkung vor, da die vorangehenden Geschäftsjahre lediglich zur Ermittlung der neurechtlichen Revisionspflicht dienen, diese aber ausschliesslich Geschäftsjahre betrifft, die nach dem Inkrafttreten beginnen.

H. Stimmrecht

Art. 8

1 Gesellschaften mit beschränkter Haftung, die das Stimmrecht vor dem Inkrafttreten dieses Gesetzes unabhängig vom Nennwert der Stammanteile festgelegt haben, müssen die entsprechenden Bestimmungen nicht an die Anforderungen von Art. 806 anpassen.

2 Bei der Ausgabe neuer Stammanteile muss Art. 806 Abs. 2 zweiter Satz in jedem Fall beachtet werden.

Das geltende Recht hält lediglich fest, dass die Statuten das Stimmrecht auch anders ordnen können, als das Gesetz dies vorsieht (Art. 808 Abs. 4 OR). Der Entwurf gibt demgegenüber für die statutarische Regelung des Stimmrechts klarere Konturen vor. Er setzt damit für Abweichungen von der für Kapitalgesellschaften typischen Parallelität zwischen der Beteiligung am Stammkapital und der Stimmkraft gewisse Grenzen (s. Art. 806 Abs. 1 E OR sowie die Ausführungen zu dieser Bestimmung).

Ein Eingriff in bisherige Beherrschungsverhältnisse wäre ausserordentlich problematisch. Gesellschaften, die unter dem geltenden Recht ihr Stimmrecht abweichend von der gesetzlichen Regelung festgelegt haben, sollen daher nach *Abs. 1* die betreffenden Statutenbestimmungen nicht den Anforderungen von Art. 806 E OR anpassen müssen. Setzen die Statuten das Stimmrecht unabhängig vom Nennwert auf eine Stimme pro Stammanteil fest, so dürfen *nach Abs. 2* nach dem Inkrafttreten des neuen Rechts keine zusätzlichen Stammanteile ausgegeben werden, deren Nennwert mehr als das Zehnfache des kleinsten oder weniger als einen Zehntel des grössten Nennwerts der ausstehenden Stammanteile beträgt. Diese Regelung verhindert, dass eine nicht mehr zulässige Ausgestaltung nach dem Inkrafttreten der neuen Vorschriften noch verstärkt wird (so bereits Art. 5 der Schlussbest. zum neuen Aktienrecht von 1991).

J. Anpassung statutarischer Mehrheitserfordernisse

Art. 9

Hat eine Gesellschaft mit beschränkter Haftung durch blosse Wiedergabe von Bestimmungen des alten Rechts Vorschriften in die Statuten aufgenommen, die für die Beschlussfassung der Gesellschafterversammlung qualifizierte Mehrheiten vorsehen, so kann die Gesellschafterversammlung innerhalb von zwei Jahren mit der absoluten Mehrheit der vertretenen Stimmen die Anpassung dieser Bestimmungen an das neue Recht beschliessen.

Gesellschaften, die durch blosse Wiedergabe von Bestimmungen des bisherigen Rechts Vorschriften in die Statuten aufgenommen haben, welche für bestimmte Beschlüsse qualifizierte Mehrheiten vorsehen (s. Art. 784 Abs. 2 und 3, Art. 791 Abs. 2, Art. 822 Abs. 3 OR), können diese innerhalb von zwei Jahren mit einfachem Mehr an die neuen gesetzlichen Mehrheitserfordernisse anpassen (so bereits Art. 6 der Schlussbestimmungen zum neuen Aktienrecht von 1991). Diese Regelung will die Übernahme der neu festgelegten Mindestanforderungen an die Beschlussfassung erleichtern.

Teil F: Rechtliche Aspekte / Legal aspects

K. Vernichtung von Aktien und Stammanteilen im Fall einer Sanierung

Art. 10
Wurde das Aktienkapital oder das Stammkapital vor dem Inkrafttreten dieses Gesetzes zum Zwecke der Sanierung auf null herabgesetzt und anschliessend wieder erhöht, so gehen die Mitgliedschaftsrechte der früheren Aktionäre oder Gesellschafter mit dem Inkrafttreten unter.

Wird das Aktienkapital zum Zweck der Sanierung unter Vernichtung der Aktien auf null herabgesetzt und zugleich wieder erhöht, so kommt den bisherigen Aktionärinnen und Aktionären nach der Rechtsprechung auch dann noch ein minimales Stimmrecht zu, wenn sie am Aktienkapital nicht mehr beteiligt sind[197]. Der Entwurf lässt demgegenüber das Stimmrecht mit der Vernichtung der Aktien untergehen (es wird auf die Ausführungen zu Art. 732*a* E OR verwiesen). Da die erwähnte Rechtsprechung in der Praxis zu ernsthaften Problemen führen kann, sieht die vorliegende Bestimmung vor, dass allfällige «nackte» Stimmrechte früherer Aktionäre mit dem Inkrafttreten des neuen Rechts untergehen. Das Gleiche muss auch für die GmbH gelten.

L. Ausschliesslichkeit eingetragener Firmen

Art. 11
Die Ausschliesslichkeit von Firmen, die vor dem Inkrafttreten dieses Gesetzes im Handelsregister eingetragen wurden, beurteilt sich nach Art. 951 des Obligationenrechts in der Fassung vom 18. Dezember 1936[198].

Im bisherigen Recht gilt für die Ausschliesslichkeit der Firmen von Gesellschaften mit beschränkter Haftung eine unterschiedliche Regelung, je nachdem ob sie einen Personennamen enthalten oder nicht (s. Art. 951 OR). Nach den geltenden Vorschriften können mehrere GmbH die gleiche Firma führen, sofern diese einen Personennamen enthält und der Sitz der

---

197 BGE **121** III 420 ff., insbes. S. 429 ff., Erwägung 4c.
198 BS **53** 185

Kapitel 1: Neue Gesetzesbestimmungen und Erläuterungen

betreffenden Gesellschaften nicht am selben Orte liegt. Demgegenüber soll die Firma der GmbH nach dem Entwurf in jedem Fall für die ganze Schweiz das Recht der Ausschliesslichkeit geniessen. Für bereits im Handelsregister eingetragene Firmen darf die Rechtslage aber nicht verändert werden. Im Verhältnis zwischen Firmen, die beim Inkrafttreten des neuen Rechts im Handelsregister eingetragen sind, ist die Ausschliesslichkeit daher nach dem bisherigen Recht zu beurteilen.

Referendum und Inkrafttreten

Referendum und Inkrafttreten

1 Dieses Gesetz untersteht dem fakultativen Referendum.

2 Der Bundesrat bestimmt das Inkrafttreten.

Die vorliegende Gesetzesrevision untersteht dem fakultativen Referendum. Der Bundesrat bestimmt ihr Inkrafttreten.

§ 9 Das Bundesgesetz über die Zulassung und Beaufsichtigung der Revisorinnen und Revisoren und damit einhergehende Änderungen bisherigen Rechts

I. Das Bundesgesetz über die Zulassung und Beaufsichtigung der Revisorinnen und Revisoren

1. Abschnitt: Gegenstand und Begriffe

Gegenstand und Zweck

Art. 1

1 Dieses Gesetz regelt die Zulassung und die Beaufsichtigung von Personen, die Revisionsdienstleistungen erbringen.

2 Es dient der ordnungsgemässen Erfüllung und der Sicherstellung der Qualität von Revisionsdienstleistungen.

3 Spezialgesetzliche Vorschriften bleiben vorbehalten.

Das Revisionsaufsichtsgesetz regelt gemäss *Abs. 1* die Zulassung und die Beaufsichtigung von Personen, die Revisionsdienstleistungen erbringen (der Begriff der Revisionsdienstleistungen wird in Art. 2 lit. a E RAG definiert). Es dient nach *Abs. 2* der ordnungsgemässen Erfüllung und der Sicherstellung der Qualität von Revisionsdienstleistungen.

Die Umschreibung von Gegenstand und Zweck der vorliegenden Bestimmung ist für die Auslegung des Revisionsaufsichtsgesetzes heranzuziehen. Bei der Interpretation und der Rechtsanwendung ist auch den völkerrechtlichen Verpflichtungen der Schweiz Rechnung zu tragen.

Abs. 3 behält spezialgesetzliche Vorschriften vor. Zu denken ist an weitergehende Anforderungen an externe Revisionsstellen sowie an branchenspezifische externe Qualitätssicherungssysteme, wie sie beispielsweise in den Bundesgesetzen über die Banken und Sparkassen (BankG, SR *952.0*) und zur Bekämpfung der Geldwäscherei im Finanzsektor (GwG, SR *955.0*) enthalten sind. Vorbehalten bleiben namentlich auch die Bestimmungen zur Revision im Bundesgesetz über die Schweizerische Nationalbank (NBG, SR *951.11*).

Begriffe

Art. 2

In diesem Gesetz gelten als:

a. **Revisionsdienstleistungen:** Prüfungen und Bestätigungen, die nach bundesrechtlichen Vorschriften durch eine zugelassene Revisionsexpertin, einen zugelassenen Revisionsexperten, eine zugelassene Revisorin oder einen zugelassenen Revisor vorgenommen werden müssen;

b. **Revisionsunternehmen:** im Handelsregister eingetragene Einzelunternehmen, Personengesellschaften oder juristische Personen, die Revisionsdienstleistungen erbringen;

c. Publikumsgesellschaften: Gesellschaften nach Art. 727 Abs. 1 Ziff. 1 Obligationenrecht[199].

Art. 2 enthält Definitionen verschiedener im Entwurf verwendeter Begriffe.

lit. a: Als *Revisionsdienstleistungen* gelten Prüfungen und Bestätigungen, die nach bundesrechtlichen Vorschriften durch eine zugelassene Revisionsexpertin bzw. einen zugelassenen Revisionsexperten oder durch eine zugelassene Revisorin bzw. einen zugelassenen Revisor vorgenommen werden müssen. Darunter fallen namentlich folgende Prüfungen und Bestätigungen:

Zivilgesetzbuch (ZGB, SR *210*)

– Art. 69*b* E ZGB: ordentliche Prüfung der Jahresrechnung eines Vereins durch die Revisionsstelle;

– Art. 83*b* E ZGB: ordentliche oder eingeschränkte Prüfung der Jahresrechnung einer Stiftung durch die Revisionsstelle (Art. 83*b* Abs. 3 E ZGB verweist auf Art. 727 ff. E OR).

Obligationenrecht (OR, SR *220*)

– Art. 635*a* E OR: Prüfung des Gründungsberichts einer Aktiengesellschaft;

– Art. 652*a* Abs. 3 E OR: Prüfung der Jahresrechnung, der Konzernrechnung und allenfalls des Zwischenabschlusses einer Aktiengesellschaft im Hinblick auf die Erstellung eines Emissionsprospekts, wenn die Gesellschaft über keine Revisionsstelle verfügt;

– Art. 652*d* Abs. 2 E OR: Prüfung der Kapitalerhöhung aus Eigenkapital einer Aktiengesellschaft;

– Art. 652*f* Abs. 1 E OR: Prüfung des Kapitalerhöhungsberichts einer Aktiengesellschaft;

– Art. 653*f* Abs. 1 E OR: Prüfung der Ausgabe von Aktien im Rahmen der bedingten Kapitalerhöhung einer Aktiengesellschaft;

– Art. 653*i* Abs. 1 E OR: Prüfung der Erlöschung von Wandel- und Optionsrechten bei der bedingten Kapitalerhöhung einer Aktiengesellschaft;

---

[199] SR **220**

- Art. 670 Abs. 2 E OR: Prüfung der Aufwertung bei einer Unterbilanz einer Aktiengesellschaft;
- Art. 725 Abs. 2 E OR: Prüfung der Zwischenbilanz einer Aktiengesellschaft bei begründeter Besorgnis einer Überschuldung;
- Art. 727 Abs. 1, 2 oder 3 E OR: ordentliche Prüfung der Jahresrechnung und der Konzernrechnung einer Aktiengesellschaft;
- Art. 727a Abs. 1 E OR: eingeschränkte Prüfung der Jahresrechnung einer Aktiengesellschaft;
- Art. 732 Abs. 2 E OR: Prüfung der Kapitalherabsetzung einer Aktiengesellschaft;
- Art. 745 Abs. 3 E OR: Prüfung der Zulässigkeit einer vorzeitigen Verteilung des Liquidationserlöses einer Aktiengesellschaft;
- Art. 795b E OR: Prüfung der Zulässigkeit der Rückzahlung von Nachschüssen in der GmbH;
- Art. 818 E OR: ordentliche oder eingeschränkte Prüfung der Jahresrechnung und der Konzernrechnung einer GmbH durch die Revisionsstelle (Art. 818 Abs. 1 E ZGB verweist auf Art. 727 ff. E OR);
- Art. 825a Abs. 2 E OR: Feststellung der Höhe des verwendbaren Eigenkapitals für die Abfindung von ausgeschiedenen Gesellschafterinnen und Gesellschaftern;
- Art. 825a Abs. 4 E OR: ordentliche Revision der Jahresrechnung einer GmbH auf Verlangen von ausgeschiedenen Gesellschafterinnen und Gesellschaftern;
- Art. 906 E OR: ordentliche oder eingeschränkte Prüfung der Jahresrechnung und Konzernrechnung einer Genossenschaft (Art. 906 Abs. 1 E ZGB verweist auf Art. 727 ff. E OR);
- Art. 907 E OR: Prüfung des Genossenschafterverzeichnisses durch die Revisionsstelle.

Fusionsgesetz (FusG, SR *221.301*; AS *2004* 2617)
- Art. 6 Abs. 2 FusG: Prüfung der Zulässigkeit der Fusion von Gesellschaften, wenn ein Kapitalverlust oder eine Überschuldung vorliegt;
- Art. 15 Abs. 1 FusG: Prüfung des Fusionsvertrags, des Fusionsberichts und der Fusionsbilanz;

- Art. 25 Abs. 2 FusG: Prüfung des Verzichts auf eine Information der Gläubigerinnen und Gläubiger betreffend die Sicherstellung ihrer Forderungen bei einer Fusion;
- Art. 40 FusG: Prüfung des Spaltungsvertrags, des Spaltungsplans und der Spaltungsbilanz;
- Art. 62 Abs. 1 FusG: Prüfung des Umwandlungsplans, des Umwandlungsberichts und der Umwandlungsbilanz;
- Art. 81 Abs. 1 FusG: Prüfung des Fusionsvertrages sowie der Fusionsbilanzen bei der Fusion von Stiftungen;
- Art. 85 Abs. 2 FusG: Prüfung des Verzichts auf eine Information der Gläubigerinnen und Gläubiger betreffend die Sicherstellung ihrer Forderungen bei der Fusion von Stiftungen;
- Art. 92 Abs. 1 FusG: Prüfung des Fusionsvertrages, des Fusionsberichts und der Fusionsbilanz bei der Fusion von Vorsorgeeinrichtungen;
- Art. 97 Abs. 3 FusG: Prüfung des Umwandlungsplans, des Umwandlungsberichts und der Umwandlungsbilanz bei der Umwandlung von Vorsorgeeinrichtungen (Art. 97 Abs. 3 FusG verweist auf Art. 89 ff. FusG);
- Art. 100 Abs. 1 FusG: Prüfung der Pläne, Berichte und Bilanzen bei Fusionen, Spaltungen und Umwandlungen, an denen ein Institut des öffentlichen Rechts beteiligt ist (Art. 100 Abs. 1 FusG verweist auf die entsprechenden Vorschriften im Fusionsgesetz);
- Art. 100 Abs. 2 FusG: Prüfung des Inventars bei Fusionen, Umwandlungen und Vermögensübertragungen, an denen ein Institut des öffentlichen Rechts beteiligt ist.

Bundesgesetz über das Internationale Privatrecht **(IPRG, SR *291*)**

- Art. 162 Abs. 3 E IPRG: Prüfung der Deckung des Grundkapitals einer Kapitalgesellschaft bei einer Sitzverlegung vom Ausland in die Schweiz;
- Art. 163*d* Abs. 1 E IPRG: Prüfung des Spaltungsvertrags, des Spaltungsplans und der Spaltungsbilanz bei der Spaltung einer Gesellschaft im internationalen Verhältnis (Art. 163*d* Abs. 1 E IPRG verweist auf Art. 29 ff. FusG);

- Art. 164 Abs. 1 E IPRG: Prüfung der Zulässigkeit der Löschung einer Gesellschaft im schweizerischen Handelsregister im Falle einer grenzüberschreitenden Fusion, Spaltung oder Vermögensübertragung;
- Art. 164 Abs. 2 lit. b E IPRG: Prüfung der Abgeltung der schweizerischen Gesellschafterinnen und Gesellschafter bei grenzüberschreitender Fusion oder Spaltung.

Lit. b: Als *Revisionsunternehmen* gelten im Handelsregister eingetragene Einzelunternehmen, Personengesellschaften oder juristische Personen, die Revisionsdienstleistungen i.S.v. lit. a erbringen.

Lit.c: Für den Begriff der *Publikumsgesellschaft* verweist der Entwurf zum Revisionsaufsichtsgesetz auf die Definition in Art. 727 Abs. 1 Ziff. 1 E OR (s. dazu die Ausführungen zu dieser Bestimmung).

2. Abschnitt: Allgemeine Bestimmungen über die Zulassung zur Erbringung von Revisionsdienstleistungen

Grundsatz

Art. 3

1 Natürliche Personen und Revisionsunternehmen, die Revisionsdienstleistungen im Sinne von Art. 2 lit. a erbringen, bedürfen einer Zulassung.

2 Natürliche Personen werden unbefristet, Revisionsunternehmen für die Dauer von fünf Jahren zugelassen.

Abs. 1 hält den Grundsatz fest, wonach natürliche Personen und Revisionsunternehmen, die Revisionsdienstleistungen i.S.v. Art. 2 lit. a E RAG erbringen, einer Zulassung durch die Aufsichtsbehörde bedürfen (s. dazu Art. 16 Abs. 1 E RAG).

Revisionsdienstleistungen, die das Gesetz nicht zwingend vorschreibt – beispielsweise die Revision der Jahresrechnung eines kleinen oder mittelgrossen Vereins (s. Art. 69*b* E ZGB) – können weiterhin durch Personen erbracht werden, die über keine Zulassung verfügen.

Die Zulassung für natürliche Personen gilt gemäss *Abs. 2* unbefristet, weil die gesetzlichen Anforderungen an die Ausbildung und an die Fachpraxis

(s. dazu Art. 4 und 5 E RAG) durch eine einmalige Kontrolle seitens der Aufsichtsbehörde geprüft werden können. Verliert eine zugelassene Person später Eigenschaften, die für die Zulassung erforderlich sind – so insbes. den unbescholtenen Leumund –, so kann die Zulassung entzogen werden (s. dazu Art. 18 Abs. 1 E RAG).

Demgegenüber werden Revisionsunternehmen bloss für eine beschränkte Dauer von 5 Jahren zugelassen, weil die Erfüllung der Voraussetzungen von den (möglicherweise wechselnden) Personen abhängt, die für ein Unternehmen arbeiten, und weil Revisionsunternehmen zusätzliche organisatorische Voraussetzungen erfüllen müssen, um als Revisionsexperte oder Revisor zugelassen zu werden (s. Art. 6 E RAG). Alle 5 Jahre soll von Amtes wegen überprüft werden, ob noch alle Zulassungsvoraussetzungen erfüllt sind.

Voraussetzungen für Revisionsexpertinnen und Revisionsexperten

Art. 4 (ursprünglicher Botschaftsentwurf)

1 Eine natürliche Person wird als Revisionsexpertin oder Revisionsexperte zugelassen, wenn sie die Anforderungen an Ausbildung und Fachpraxis erfüllt und über einen unbescholtenen Leumund verfügt.

2 Die Anforderungen an Ausbildung und Fachpraxis erfüllen:

a. **eidgenössisch diplomierte Wirtschaftsprüferinnen und Wirtschaftsprüfer;**

b. **eidgenössisch diplomierte Treuhandexpertinnen und Treuhandexperten, Steuerexpertinnen und Steuerexperten sowie Buchhalterinnen/Controllerinnen und Buchhalter/Controller, je mit mindestens fünf Jahren Fachpraxis;**

c. **Absolventinnen und Absolventen eines Universitäts- oder Fachhochschulstudiums in Betriebs-, Wirtschafts- oder Rechtswissenschaften an einer schweizerischen Hochschule, Fachleute Finanz- und Rechnungswesen mit eidgenössischem Fachausweis sowie Treuhänderinnen und Treuhänder mit eidgenössischem Fachausweis, je mit mindestens zwölf Jahren Fachpraxis;**

d. **Personen, die eine den lit. a, b oder c vergleichbare ausländische Ausbildung abgeschlossen haben, die entsprechende Fachpraxis aufweisen und die notwendigen Kenntnisse des schweizerischen**

Rechts nachweisen, sofern ein Staatsvertrag mit dem Herkunftsstaat dies so vorsieht oder der Herkunftsstaat Gegenrecht hält.

3 Der Bundesrat kann weitere gleichwertige Ausbildungsgänge zulassen und die Dauer der notwendigen Fachpraxis bestimmen.

4 Die Fachpraxis muss vorwiegend auf den Gebieten des Rechnungswesens und der Rechnungsrevision erworben worden sein, davon mindestens zwei Drittel unter Beaufsichtigung durch eine zugelassene Revisionsexpertin oder einen zugelassenen Revisionsexperten oder durch eine ausländische Fachperson mit vergleichbarer Qualifikation. Fachpraxis während der Ausbildung wird angerechnet, wenn diese Voraussetzungen erfüllt sind.

Art. 4 (durch den Nationalrat bereinigte Version)

2 Die Anforderungen an Ausbildung und Fachpraxis erfüllen:

b. eidgenössisch diplomierte Treuhandexpertinnen und Treuhandexperten, Steuerexpertinnen und Steuerexperten sowie Expertinnen und Experten in Rechnungslegung und Controlling, je mit mindestens fünf Jahren Fachpraxis;

c. Absolventinnen und Absolventen eines Universitäts- oder Fachhochschulstudiums in Betriebs-, Wirtschafts- oder Rechtswissenschaften an einer schweizerischen Hochschule, Fachleute im Finanz- und Rechnungswesen mit eidgenössischem Fachausweis sowie Treuhänderinnen und Treuhänder mit eidgenössischem Fachausweis, je mit mindestens zwölf Jahren Fachpraxis;

Art. 4 (durch den Ständerat bereinigte Version)

2 Die Anforderungen an Ausbildung und Fachpraxis erfüllen:

b. eidgenössisch diplomierte Treuhandexpertinnen und Treuhandexperten, Steuerexpertinnen und Steuerexperten sowie Expertinnen und Experten in Rechnungslegung und Controlling, je mit mindestens drei Jahren Fachpraxis;

c. Absolventinnen und Absolventen eines Universitäts- oder Fachhochschulstudiums in Betriebs-, Wirtschafts- oder Rechtswissenschaften an einer schweizerischen Hochschule, Fachleute im Finanz- und Rechnungswesen mit eidgenössischem Fachausweis sowie Treuhänderinnen und Treuhänder mit eidgenössischem Fachausweis, je mit mindestens drei Jahren Fachpraxis;

Abs. 1 verlangt für die Zulassung einer natürlichen Person als Revisionsexpertin oder Revisionsexperte, dass sie die Anforderungen an die Ausbildung und an die Fachpraxis erfüllt und über einen unbescholtenen Leumund verfügt.

Die Anforderungen an Ausbildung und Fachpraxis werden in *Abs. 2* umschrieben. Der Entwurf verfolgt ein liberales Konzept und ermöglicht Personen mit verschiedenen Ausbildungen den Zugang zu Arbeit als Revisionsexpertinnen und Revisionsexperten. Dabei werden weniger spezifisch auf die Revisionstätigkeit ausgerichtete Ausbildungen durch das Erfordernis einer längeren Fachpraxis im Bereich des Rechnungswesens und der Revision ausgeglichen. Die Anforderungen an Ausbildung und Fachpraxis erfüllen:

- *lit. a*: Eidgenössisch diplomierte Wirtschaftsprüferinnen und Wirtschaftsprüfer. Weil Personen mit diesen Diplomen im Rahmen ihrer Ausbildung bereits die erforderliche Fachpraxis erwerben, haben sie keine zusätzliche Praxis nachzuweisen.

- *lit. b*: Eidgenössisch diplomierte Treuhandexpertinnen und Treuhandexperten, Steuerexpertinnen und Steuerexperten sowie Buchhalterinnen/Controllerinnen und Buchhalter/Controller, je mit mindestens fünf Jahren Fachpraxis.

- *lit. c*: Absolventinnen und Absolventen eines Universitäts- oder Fachhochschulstudiums in Betriebs-, Wirtschafts- oder Rechtswissenschaften an einer schweizerischen Hochschule, Fachleute Finanz- und Rechnungswesen mit eidgenössischem Fachausweis sowie Treuhänderinnen und Treuhänder mit eidgenössischem Fachausweis, je mit mindestens 12 Jahren Fachpraxis.

- *lit. d*: Personen, die eine den lit. a, b oder c vergleichbare ausländische Ausbildung abgeschlossen haben und über die entsprechende Fachpraxis verfügen; sie haben zudem die notwendigen Kenntnisse des schweizerischen Rechts nachzuweisen. Die Bedingung des Nachweises der erforderlichen Kenntnisse des schweizerischen Rechts ist im Wirtschaftsvölkerrecht anerkannt und stellt keine verpönte Diskriminierung ausländischer Personen dar.

Der Entwurf setzt zudem voraus, dass eine staatsvertragliche Regelung vorliegt (eine solche besteht insbesondere mit der Europäischen Union und mit der Europäischen Freihandelsassoziation [EFTA][200]) oder dass der Herkunftsstaat Gegenrecht für Schweizer Bürgerinnen und Bürger hält.

Abs. 3 Satz 1 stellt genauere Anforderungen an die Fachpraxis auf. Diese muss vorwiegend auf den Gebieten des Rechnungswesens und der Rechnungsrevision erworben worden sein, davon mindestens zwei Drittel unter Beaufsichtigung durch eine zugelassene Revisionsexpertin, einen zugelassenen Revisionsexperten oder eine ausländische Fachperson mit vergleichbarer Qualifikation. Der Wortlaut dieser Bestimmung wurde aus der Verordnung des Bundesrates vom 15. Juni 1992 über die fachlichen Anforderungen an besonders befähigte Revisoren (SR *221.302*) übernommen und geringfügig angepasst.

Fachpraxis, die vor dem Abschluss einer der in Abs. 2 aufgeführten Ausbildungsgänge erworben wurde (insbesondere die im Rahmen dieser Ausbildungen zu absolvierenden Praktika), wird gemäss *Abs. 3 Satz 2* angerechnet, wenn die erwähnten Voraussetzungen erfüllt sind. Zur übergangsrechtlichen Anerkennung von Fachpraxis siehe die Ausführungen zu Art. 44 Abs. 4 E RAG.

Voraussetzungen für Revisorinnen und Revisoren

Art. 5

1 Eine natürliche Person wird als Revisorin oder Revisor zugelassen, wenn sie:

a. **über einen unbescholtenen Leumund verfügt;**

b. **eine Ausbildung nach Art. 4 Abs. 2 abgeschlossen hat;**

---

200 Abkommen vom 21. Juni 1999 zwischen der Schweizerischen Eidgenossenschaft einerseits und der Europäischen Gemeinschaft und ihren Mitgliedstaaten andererseits über die Freizügigkeit (SR **0.142.112.681**) sowie Übereinkommen vom 4. Januar 1960 zur Errichtung der Europäischen Freihandelsassoziation, EFTA (SR **0.632.31**).

c. eine Fachpraxis von einem Jahr nachweist.

2 Die Fachpraxis muss vorwiegend auf den Gebieten des Rechnungswesens und der Rechnungsrevision erworben worden sein, dies unter Beaufsichtigung durch eine zugelassene Revisorin oder einen zugelassenen Revisor oder durch eine ausländische Fachperson mit vergleichbarer Qualifikation. Fachpraxis während der Ausbildung wird angerechnet, wenn diese Voraussetzungen erfüllt sind.

Eine natürliche Person wird gemäss *Abs. 1* als Revisorin oder Revisor zugelassen, wenn sie:

- *Lit.a*: über einen unbescholtenen Leumund verfügt;
- *Lit.b*: eine Ausbildung nach Art. 4 Abs. 2 E RAG abgeschlossen hat;
- *Lit.c*: eine Fachpraxis von einem Jahr nachweist.

Lit.c geht den Bestimmungen zur Fachpraxis von Art. 4 Abs. 2 E RAG vor und wird von *Abs. 2* konkretisiert. Demnach muss die Fachpraxis vorwiegend auf den Gebieten des Rechnungswesens und der Rechnungsrevision erworben worden sein, und zwar unter Beaufsichtigung durch eine zugelassene Revisorin oder einen zugelassenen Revisor oder durch eine ausländische Fachperson mit vergleichbarer Qualifikation. Fachpraxis während der Ausbildung wird angerechnet, wenn diese Voraussetzungen erfüllt sind.

Zur übergangsrechtlichen Anerkennung von Fachpraxis siehe die Ausführungen zu Art. 44 Abs. 5 E RAG.

Voraussetzungen für Revisionsunternehmen

Art. 6 (ursprünglicher Botschaftsentwurf)

Ein Revisionsunternehmen wird als Revisionsexperte oder als Revisor zugelassen, wenn:

a. **die Mehrheit der Mitglieder seines obersten Leitungs- oder Verwaltungsorgans sowie seines Geschäftsführungsorgans über die entsprechende Zulassung verfügt;**

b. mindestens ein Fünftel der Personen, die an der Erbringung von Revisionsdienstleistungen beteiligt sind, über die entsprechende Zulassung verfügt;

c. sichergestellt ist, dass alle Personen, die Revisionsdienstleistungen leiten, über die entsprechende Zulassung verfügen;

d. die Führungsstruktur gewährleistet, dass die einzelnen Mandate genügend überwacht werden.

Art. 6 (durch den Nationalrat bereinigte Version, neuer Abs. 2)
2 Finanzkontrollen der öffentlichen Hand werden als Revisionsunternehmen zugelassen, wenn sie die Anforderungen nach Abs. 1 erfüllen. Die Zulassung als staatlich beaufsichtigte Revisionsunternehmen ist nicht möglich.

Ein Revisionsunternehmen wird als Revisionsexpertin oder als Revisorin zugelassen, wenn es die folgenden Voraussetzungen nachweist:

– Nach *lit. a* muss die Mehrheit der Mitglieder des obersten Leitungs- oder Verwaltungsorgans sowie des Geschäftsführungsorgans über die entsprechende Zulassung (als Revisionsexpertin oder Revisionsexperte bzw. als Revisorin oder Revisor) verfügen. Besteht das Organ aus zwei Personen, so muss zumindest eine dieser beiden Personen über die notwendige Zulassung verfügen. Durch diese Vorschrift wird sichergestellt, dass die Unternehmensleitung in den Händen von Personen mit ausreichender fachlicher Befähigung liegt.

– *Lit. b* schreibt vor, dass mindestens ein Fünftel der Personen, die an der Erbringung von Revisionsdienstleistungen beteiligt sind, über die entsprechende Zulassung verfügt. Mit dieser Bestimmung wird ein Mindestverhältnis zwischen Fachleuten und anderen Mitarbeiterinnen und Mitarbeitern festgelegt, das eine angemessene fachliche Anleitung derjenigen Personen sicherstellt, die als Nichtfachleute zu einer bestimmten Revisionsdienstleistung beitragen. Der Begriff der beteiligten Personen deckt sich mit demjenigen in den Vorschriften zur Unabhängigkeit (s. Art. 728 Abs. 3 E OR).

- Auf Grund von *lit. c* muss das Revisionsunternehmen sicherstellen, dass alle Personen, die für Revisionsdienstleistungen verantwortlich sind (in der Fachsprache sog. leitende Prüferinnen und leitende Prüfer) über die entsprechende Zulassung verfügen. Wie bereits im geltenden Recht (s. Art. 727*d* Abs. 2 OR) wird mit dieser Vorschrift verlangt, dass jedes Revisionsmandat ausschliesslich durch Personen geleitet wird, die über die entsprechende Zulassung verfügen.

- Das Revisionsunternehmen hat gemäss *lit. d* eine Führungsstruktur nachzuweisen, die gewährleistet, dass die einzelnen Mandate genügend überwacht werden. Das Unternehmen muss somit über ein minimales internes Qualitätssicherungssystem verfügen.

Nach Art. 2 lit. b E RAG können auch Einzelunternehmen als Revisionsunternehmen zugelassen werden, sofern sie im Handelsregister eingetragen sind. Die Voraussetzungen von Art. 6 gelangen auch für Einzelunternehmen zur Anwendung; allerdings kann lit. a nur sinngemäss herangezogen und so verstanden werden, dass die Einzelunternehmerin oder der Einzelunternehmer über die entsprechende Zulassung verfügen muss.

3. Abschnitt: Besondere Bestimmungen über die Zulassung zur Erbringung von Revisionsdienstleistungen für Publikumsgesellschaften

Grundsatz

Art. 7

1 Revisionsunternehmen, die Revisionsdienstleistungen für Publikumsgesellschaften erbringen, bedürfen einer besonderen Zulassung und stehen unter staatlicher Aufsicht (staatlich beaufsichtigte Revisionsunternehmen).

2 Andere Revisionsunternehmen werden auf Gesuch hin ebenfalls als staatlich beaufsichtigte Revisionsunternehmen zugelassen, wenn sie die gesetzlichen Voraussetzungen erfüllen.

Abs. 1 schreibt vor, dass Revisionsunternehmen (s. dazu Art. 2 lit. b E RAG), die Revisionsdienstleistungen (s. dazu Art. 2 lit. a E RAG) für Publikumsgesellschaften (s. dazu Art. 2 lit. c E RAG) erbringen, einer besonderen Zulassung bedürfen und unter staatlicher Aufsicht stehen.

Solche Revisionsunternehmen werden als «staatlich beaufsichtigte Revisionsunternehmen» bezeichnet.

Die Beschränkung von Revisionsdienstleistungen für Publikumsgesellschaften auf staatlich beaufsichtigte Revisionsunternehmen schliesst natürliche Personen nicht von vornherein aus: Natürliche Personen gelten nach Art. 2 lit. b E RAG als Revisionsunternehmen, wenn sie sich als Einzelunternehmen in das Handelsregister eintragen lassen. Diese Eintragungspflicht ist für eine griffige Aufsichtstätigkeit unabdingbar. Unter Erfüllung der Voraussetzungen für staatlich beaufsichtigte Revisionsunternehmen steht es daher auch natürlichen Personen offen, beispielsweise die Jahresrechnung einer Untergesellschaft eines börsenkotierten Konzerns zu revidieren (vgl. Art. 727 Abs. 1 Ziff. 1 E OR; die Revision einer Publikumsgesellschaft dürfte dagegen aus sachlichen Gründen stets ein grösseres Revisionsunternehmen erfordern).

Andere Revisionsunternehmen werden gemäss *Abs. 2* auf Gesuch hin ebenfalls als staatlich beaufsichtigte Revisionsunternehmen zugelassen, wenn sie die gesetzlichen Voraussetzungen erfüllen. Von dieser Möglichkeit einer freiwilligen Beaufsichtigung dürften vor allem drei Gruppen von Revisionsunternehmen Gebrauch machen:

– Freiwillig unterstellen werden sich Revisionsunternehmen, die künftig Revisionsdienstleistungen für (schweizerische oder ausländische) Publikumsgesellschaften erbringen wollen und zur Akquisition entsprechender Revisionsmandate auf eine entsprechende Zulassung angewiesen sind. Die Bearbeitung eines Zulassungsgesuchs kann eine gewisse Zeit in Anspruch nehmen; das Zulassungsgesuch (s. Art. 10 E RAG) muss auch daher frühzeitig eingereicht werden können, wenn der Markteintritt neuer Revisionsunternehmen nicht erschwert werden soll.

– An einer Unterstellung dürften zudem Revisionsunternehmen mit Sitz in der Schweiz interessiert sein, die ausschliesslich unter der Aufsicht einer ausländischen Aufsichtsbehörde stehen. Dies ist dann der Fall, wenn sie Revisionsdienstleistungen an Gesellschaften erbringen, die im Ausland kotiert sind. Das Gleiche gilt für Untergesellschaften eines im Ausland kotierten Unternehmens.

Revisionsunternehmen mit entsprechenden Mandaten profitieren mit der Unterstellung unter die Schweizer Aufsicht vom formalisierten Amts- und Rechtshilfeverfahren zwischen der Schweizer Aufsichtsbehörde und ihren ausländischen Partnerbehörden (s. dazu die Ausführungen zu Art. 27 ff. E RAG). Sie können sich mit einer freiwilligen Unterstellung unter die schweizerische Aufsicht vor direkten Amtshandlungen durch ausländische Revisionsaufsichtsbehörden schützen. Konflikte zwischen den Erfordernissen einer ausländischen Aufsicht und schweizerischen Geheimhaltungsvorschriften können somit vermieden werden.

– Schliesslich dürften sich auch Revisionsunternehmen mit Sitz im Ausland der schweizerischen Aufsicht unterstellen, wenn sie für Gesellschaften, die am Schweizer Kapitalmarkt aktiv sind (s. dazu Art. 8 E RAG), Revisionsdienstleistungen anbieten möchten.

Für die Unterstellung unter die schweizerische Revisionsaufsicht ist nicht massgebend, ob ein Revisionsunternehmen seinen Sitz in der Schweiz oder im Ausland hat. Unter der Bedingung, dass sämtliche Zulassungsvoraussetzungen erfüllt werden, können sich auch ausländische Revisionsunternehmen der schweizerischen Aufsicht unterstellen. Für die Übernahme von Revisionsmandaten ist aber stets Art. 730 Abs. 3 E OR zu beachten.

Die Durchsetzung der Vorschriften zur Revisionsaufsicht wird einerseits durch die Art. 731b und 941a E OR abgesichert; sie obliegt aber insbesondere auch den zuständigen Börsenorganen (s. dazu die Ausführungen zu Art. 8 Abs. 3bis E BEHG).

Sonderfälle im internationalen Verhältnis

Art. 8

1 Einer Zulassung als staatlich beaufsichtigtes Revisionsunternehmen bedürfen auch Revisionsunternehmen, die Revisionsdienstleistungen im Sinne von Art. 2 lit. a oder diesen vergleichbare Dienstleistungen nach ausländischem Recht erbringen für:

a. Gesellschaften nach ausländischem Recht, deren Beteiligungspapiere an einer Schweizer Börse kotiert sind;

b. Gesellschaften nach ausländischem Recht, die in der Schweiz Anleihensobligationen ausstehend haben;

c. Gesellschaften nach schweizerischem oder ausländischem Recht, die mindestens 20 Prozent der Aktiven oder des Umsatzes zur Konzernrechnung einer Gesellschaft nach lit. a oder b beitragen;

d. Gesellschaften nach ausländischem Recht, die mindestens 20 Prozent der Aktiven oder des Umsatzes zur Konzernrechnung einer schweizerischen Publikumsgesellschaft im Sinne von Art. 727 Abs. 1 Ziff. 1 lit. a oder b Obligationenrecht[201] beitragen.

2 Die Zulassungspflicht entfällt, wenn das Revisionsunternehmen einer vom Bundesrat anerkannten ausländischen Revisionsaufsichtsbehörde untersteht.

3 Die Zulassungspflicht gemäss Abs. 1 lit. b entfällt zudem, wenn die Anleihensobligationen durch eine Gesellschaft garantiert werden, die über ein Revisionsunternehmen verfügt, das entweder Abs. 1 oder 2 erfüllt.

Der Entwurf zum Revisionsaufsichtsgesetz bezweckt die Gewährleistung der ordnungsgemässen Erfüllung und die Sicherung der Qualität von Revisionsdienstleistungen (s. Art. 1 Abs. 2 E RAG). Er unterstellt deshalb Revisionsunternehmen, die Revisionsdienstleistungen an Publikumsgesellschaften erbringen (Art. 7 Abs. 1 E RAG), einer laufenden Aufsicht. Der Kapitalmarkt hat sich allerdings in den letzten Jahren zunehmend internationalisiert und globalisiert. Es sind daher nicht nur Schweizer Unternehmen, sondern auch ausländische Gesellschaften am Schweizer Kapitalmarkt aktiv. Die für diese Gesellschaften tätigen Revisionsunternehmen müssen ebenfalls angemessen beaufsichtigt werden, wenn die Qualität der Revision für alle am Schweizer Kapitalmarkt tätigen Gesellschaften gewährleistet werden soll.

Aus diesem Grund bedürfen nach *Abs. 1* auch Revisionsunternehmen von ausländischen Gesellschaften einer Zulassung als staatlich beaufsichtigte Revisionsunternehmen, sofern sie Gesellschaften prüfen, die direkt oder indirekt den Schweizerischen Kapitalmarkt in Anspruch nehmen. Damit wird der Geltungsbereich von Art. 727 Abs. 1 Ziff. 1 E OR ins internationale Verhältnis abgebildet. Erfasst werden diejenigen Revisionsunternehmen, die Revisionsdienstleistungen nach Art. 2 lit. a E RAG oder diesen vergleichbare Dienstleistungen nach ausländischem Recht an folgende Gesellschaften erbringen:

– *Lit. a:* Gesellschaften mit Sitz im Ausland, deren Beteiligungspapiere an einer Schweizer Börse kotiert sind (diese Bestimmung entspricht Art. 727 Abs. 1 Ziff. 1 lit. a E OR).

---

[201] SR **220**

- *Lit.b:* Gesellschaften mit Sitz im Ausland, die in der Schweiz Anleihensobligationen ausstehend haben (diese Bestimmung entspricht Art. 727 Abs. 1 Ziff. 1 lit. b E OR).

- *Lit.c:* Gesellschaften mit Sitz in der Schweiz oder im Ausland, die mindestens 20% der Aktiven oder des Umsatzes zur Konzernrechnung einer Gesellschaft nach lit. a oder lit. b beitragen (diese Bestimmung entspricht Art. 727 Abs. 1 Ziff. 1 lit. c E OR). Erfasst werden nicht nur wesentliche ausländische, sondern auch wesentliche inländische Tochtergesellschaften. Es ist möglich, dass eine solche Gesellschaft nicht unter den Geltungsbereich von Art. 7 Abs. 1 E RAG fällt, weil sie nicht direkt, sondern nur indirekt über eine ausländische Muttergesellschaft am Schweizer Kapitalmarkt aktiv ist.

- *Lit.d:* Gesellschaften mit Sitz im Ausland, die mindestens 20% der Aktiven oder des Umsatzes zur Konzernrechnung einer schweizerischen Publikumsgesellschaft i.S.v. Art. 727 Abs. 1 Ziff. 1 lit. a oder b E OR beitragen. Gemeint sind damit wesentliche ausländische Tochtergesellschaften von Schweizer Konzernen.

Zum Schutz der Anlegerinnen und Anleger erfasst das Revisionsaufsichtsgesetz mit Abs. 1 Revisionsdienstleistungen an ausländische Gesellschaften, soweit diese den schweizerischen Kapitalmarkt in Anspruch nehmen. Diese Schutzregelung im Interesse des Finanzplatzes entspricht dem Konzept des US-amerikanischen Sarbanes-Oxley Act. Anknüpfungspunkt einer umfassenden Umschreibung des Geltungsbereichs der Aufsichtsvorschriften ist stets eine Kotierung von Beteiligungspapieren oder Anleihensobligationen an der Schweizer Börse. Eine entsprechende Regelung führt allerdings unvermeidlich dazu, dass die Revisionsstelle eines internationalen Konzerns von der Revisionsaufsicht mehrerer Staaten erfasst wird. Zur Vermeidung von Doppelspurigkeiten und zur Abstimmung auf ausländische Ordnungen der Revisionsaufsicht sieht *Abs. 2* vor, dass die Zulassungspflicht nach Abs. 1 entfällt, wenn ein Revisionsunternehmen einer vom Bundesrat anerkannten ausländischen Revisionsaufsichtsbehörde untersteht.

Einer ausländischen Gesellschaft, die ihre Beteiligungspapiere an der Schweizer Börse kotiert hat, stehen damit folgende Möglichkeiten zur Verfügung:

- Sie kann sich durch ein staatlich beaufsichtigtes Revisionsunternehmen mit Sitz in der Schweiz prüfen lassen (s. Art. 7 Abs. 1 E RAG).

- Sie kann sich von einem Revisionsunternehmen mit Sitz im Ausland revidieren lassen, das in der Schweiz zugelassen ist und von der Schweizer Aufsichtsbehörde beaufsichtigt wird (s. Art. 7 Abs. 2 E RAG; vgl. zur Amts- und Rechtshilfe sowie zu grenzüberschreitenden Prüfungshandlungen Art. 27 f. E RAG).

- Sie kann sich von einem Revisionsunternehmen mit Sitz im Ausland revidieren lassen, das von einer ausländischen Revisionsaufsichtsbehörde beaufsichtigt wird, die vom Bundesrat als gleichwertig anerkannt wurde (Art. 8 Abs. 2 E RAG).

Die gleichen Möglichkeiten haben auch ausländische Untergesellschaften börsenkotierter schweizerischer Konzerne.

Ausländische Publikumsgesellschaften, die ihre Beteiligungspapiere in der Schweiz kotiert haben und deren Sitz in einem Staat liegt, in dem keine Revisionsaufsicht besteht, müssen sich durch ein Revisionsunternehmen prüfen lassen, das der schweizerischen Revisionsaufsicht untersteht. Dieses Prüfungsunternehmen kann seinen Sitz in der Schweiz oder im Ausland haben.

Die Durchsetzung der Vorschriften zur Revisionsaufsicht in internationalen Verhältnissen obliegt vorrangig den zuständigen Börsenorganen (s. dazu die Ausführungen zu Art. 24 E RAG und Art. 8 Abs. 3bis E BEHG); die Art. 731*b* und 941*a* E OR können für Gesellschaften mit Sitz im Ausland nicht zum Tragen kommen.

Abs. 3 enthält eine weitere Ausnahme von der Zulassungspflicht nach Abs. 1: Diese entfällt mit Blick auf Art. 1 lit. b, wenn die Anleihensobligationen durch eine Gesellschaft garantiert werden, die über ein Revisionsunternehmen verfügt, das entweder Abs. 1 oder 2 erfüllt. Der Entwurf nimmt damit Rücksicht darauf, dass ausländische Anleihensobligationen oftmals von Emittenten mit Sitz in Off-Shore Staaten begeben, aber von einer Muttergesellschaft in einem On-Shore Staat garantiert werden. Der Entwurf begnügt sich in diesem Fall mit der Beaufsichtigung des Revisionsunternehmens der Muttergesellschaft bzw. mit der Aufsicht durch die Aufsichtsbehörde des Sitzstaates der garantierenden Gesellschaft. Den Investorinnen und Investoren erwächst hierdurch kein Nachteil, weil die Anleihensobligationen vollständig durch die Muttergesellschaft garantiert werden und sichergestellt wird, dass deren Revisionsunternehmen beaufsichtigt wird.

Mit Art. 8 E RAG werden Revisionsdienstleistungen an gewisse ausländische Gesellschaften dem Revisionsaufsichtsgesetz und damit teilweise dem schweizerischem Recht unterstellt. Diese Regelung stellt eine lex specialis zu den Regeln des IPRG dar (insbes. Art. 154 ff. IPRG), welche im Übrigen anwendbar bleiben.

Voraussetzungen

Art. 9

1 Revisionsunternehmen werden zur Erbringung von Revisionsdienstleistungen für Publikumsgesellschaften zugelassen, wenn sie:

a. die Voraussetzungen für die Zulassung als Revisionsexperten erfüllen;

b. gewährleisten, dass sie die gesetzlichen Vorschriften einhalten;

c. für die Haftungsrisiken ausreichend versichert sind.

2 Die Aufsichtsbehörde kann die Zulassung eines Revisionsunternehmens auf der Grundlage einer ausländischen Zulassung erteilen, wenn die Anforderung dieses Gesetzes erfüllt sind.

Für die Zulassung zur Revision von Publikumsgesellschaften hat ein Revisionsunternehmen verschiedene Bedingungen zu erfüllen:

– Auf Grund von *lit. a* ist nachzuweisen, dass das Revisionsunternehmen die Voraussetzungen für die Zulassung als Revisionsexperte i.S.v. Art. 6 i.V.m. Art. 4 E RAG erfüllt. Gewisse organisatorische Voraussetzungen werden bereits bei der Zulassung als Revisionsexpertin oder Revisionsexperte sichergestellt.

– Das Revisionsunternehmen hat nach *lit. b* zu gewährleisten, dass es die gesetzlichen Vorschriften einhält. Darunter sind die Vorschriften des Obligationenrechts und des Revisionsaufsichtsgesetzes zu verstehen, die für staatlich beaufsichtigte Revisionsunternehmen zur Anwendung kommen. Die Gesuchstellerin hat beispielsweise nachzuweisen, dass die Massnahmen zur Qualitätssicherung gemäss Art. 12 E RAG bereits ergriffen wurden. Liegen Umstände vor, die darauf schliessen lassen, dass andere Pflichten nicht eingehalten werden (z.B. die Vorschriften zur Unabhängigkeit nach Art. 728 E OR oder Art. 11 E RAG), wird der Gesuchstellerin die Zulassung als staatlich beaufsichtigtes Revisionsunternehmen verweigert.

– *Lit.c* schreibt schliesslich vor, dass das Revisionsunternehmen seine Haftungsrisiken ausreichend versichert.

Gesuch

Art. 10

1 Der Aufsichtsbehörde muss ein Gesuch um Zulassung als staatlich beaufsichtigtes Revisionsunternehmen eingereicht werden.

2 Der Bundesrat regelt die Einzelheiten, insbesondere die dem Gesuch beizulegenden Unterlagen.

Für die Zulassung als staatlich beaufsichtigtes Revisionsunternehmen muss nach *Abs. 1* bei der Aufsichtsbehörde ein Gesuch eingereicht werden.

Nach *Abs. 2* regelt der Bundesrat die Einzelheiten der Gesuchstellung und insbesondere die dem Gesuch beizulegenden Unterlagen. Er trägt bei deren Festlegung rechtsvergleichenden Gesichtspunkten Rechnung.

4. Abschnitt: Pflichten staatlich beaufsichtigter Revisionsunternehmen

Unabhängigkeit

Art. 11 (ursprünglicher Botschaftsentwurf)
Über die allgemeinen gesetzlichen Vorschriften zur Unabhängigkeit der Revisionsstelle hinaus (Art. 728 Obligationenrecht[202]) müssen staatlich beaufsichtigte Revisionsunternehmen bei der Erbringung von Revisionsdienstleistungen für Publikumsgesellschaften folgende Grundsätze einhalten:

a. Die jährlichen Honorare aus Revisions- und anderen Dienstleistungen für eine einzelne Gesellschaft und die mit ihr durch einheitliche Leitung verbundenen Gesellschaften (Konzern) dürfen 10 Prozent ihrer gesamten Honorarsumme nicht übersteigen.

---

202 SR **220**

b. Treten Personen, die in einer Gesellschaft eine Entscheidfunktion innehatten oder in leitender Stellung in der Rechnungslegung tätig waren, in ein Revisionsunternehmen über und übernehmen sie dort eine leitende Stellung, so darf dieses während zwei Jahren ab Übertritt keine Revisionsdienstleistungen für diese Gesellschaft erbringen.

c. Treten Personen, die in einer Gesellschaft in der Rechnungslegung mitgewirkt haben, in ein Revisionsunternehmen über, so dürfen sie während zwei Jahren ab Übertritt keine Revisionsdienstleistungen für diese Gesellschaft leiten.

d. Treten Personen, die in einem Revisionsunternehmen eine Entscheidfunktion innehatten, in eine andere Gesellschaft über und übernehmen sie dort eine leitende Stellung, so darf das Revisionsunternehmen während zwei Jahren ab Übertritt keine Revisionsdienstleistungen für diese Gesellschaft erbringen. Das Gleiche gilt, wenn Personen, die im Revisionsunternehmen Revisionsdienstleistungen geleitet haben, eine leitende Stellung in einer von ihnen geprüften Gesellschaft übernehmen.

Art. 11 (durch den Nationalrat bereinigte Version, neuer Abs. 2)
1 Über die allgemeinen gesetzlichen Vorschriften zur Unabhängigkeit der Revisionsstelle hinaus (Art. 728 Obligationenrecht[203]) müssen staatlich beaufsichtigte Revisionsunternehmen bei der Erbringung von Revisionsdienstleistungen für Publikumsgesellschaften folgende Grundsätze einhalten:

d. *...gestrichen*

2 Eine Publikumsgesellschaft darf keine Personen beschäftigen, die während der zwei vorangehenden Jahre Revisionsdienstleistungen für diese Gesellschaft geleitet haben oder im betreffenden Revisionsunternehmen eine Entscheidfunktion innehatten.

---

[203] SR **220**

Über die allgemeinen gesetzlichen Vorschriften zur Unabhängigkeit der Revisionsstelle (s. Art. 728 E OR) hinaus müssen staatlich beaufsichtigte Revisionsunternehmen bei der Erbringung von Revisionsdienstleistungen für Publikumsgesellschaften die folgenden Grundsätze einhalten:

- Nach *lit. a* dürfen die jährlichen Honorare aus Revisions- und anderen Dienstleistungen für eine einzelne geprüfte Gesellschaft und die mit ihr durch einheitliche Leitung verbundenen Gesellschaften (Konzern) 10% der gesamten Honorarsumme des Revisionsunternehmens nicht übersteigen. Damit wird die Vorschrift von Art. 728 Abs. 2 Ziff. 5 E OR konkretisiert, wonach ein Revisionsunternehmen keine Aufträge entgegennehmen darf, die zu einer wirtschaftlichen Abhängigkeit von der zu prüfenden Gesellschaft führen.

- Treten nach *lit. b* Personen, die in einer Gesellschaft eine Entscheidfunktion innehatten oder in leitender Stellung in der Rechnungslegung tätig waren, in ein Revisionsunternehmen über und übernehmen sie dort eine leitende Stellung, so darf dieses während zwei Jahren ab Übertritt keine Revisionsdienstleistungen für diese Gesellschaft erbringen.

- Treten nach *lit. c* Personen, die in einer Gesellschaft in der Rechnungslegung mitgewirkt haben, in ein Revisionsunternehmen über, so dürfen sie während 2 Jahren ab Übertritt keine Revisionsdienstleistungen für diese Gesellschaft leiten.

- Treten nach *lit. d* Personen, die in einem Revisionsunternehmen eine Entscheidfunktion innehatten, in eine andere Gesellschaft über und übernehmen sie dort eine leitende Stellung, so darf das Revisionsunternehmen während 2 Jahren ab Übertritt keine Revisionsdienstleistungen für diese Gesellschaft erbringen. Das Gleiche gilt, wenn Personen, die im Revisionsunternehmen Revisionsdienstleistungen geleitet haben, eine leitende Stellung in einer von ihnen geprüften Gesellschaft übernehmen.

Die lit. b, c und d sehen Wartefristen (sog. *Cooling-off Periods*) vor, welche eine zu grosse Vertrautheit verhindern, die durch personelle Wechsel zwischen dem Revisionsunternehmen und der zu prüfenden Gesellschaft entstehen kann. Das staatlich beaufsichtigte Revisionsunternehmen kann sich allenfalls gegen sensitive personelle Wechsel in den Arbeitsverträgen absichern. Die EU sieht ebenfalls eine Karenzfrist von zwei Jahren, der Sarbanes-Oxley Act eine solche von einem Jahr vor[204]. Sowohl die EU als auch die USA regulieren lediglich den personellen Wechsel von der Revisionsstelle zur geprüften Gesellschaft. Der Entwurf geht mit der Vorschrift in den lit. b und c etwas weiter und macht auch für den personellen Wechsel von der geprüften Gesellschaft zur Revisionsstelle angemessene Auflagen, da sachlich dieselbe Problematik vorliegt wie im umgekehrten Fall.[205]

Sicherung der Qualität

Art. 12

1 Die staatlich beaufsichtigten Revisionsunternehmen treffen alle Massnahmen, die zur Sicherung der Qualität ihrer Revisionsdienstleistungen notwendig sind.

2 Sie stellen eine geeignete Organisation sicher und erlassen insbesondere schriftliche Weisungen über:

a. die Anstellung, die Aus- und Weiterbildung, die Beurteilung, die Zeichnungsberechtigung und das gebotene Verhalten der Mitarbeiterinnen und Mitarbeiter;

b. die Annahme neuer und die Weiterführung bestehender Aufträge für Revisionsdienstleistungen;

c. die Überwachung der Massnahmen zur Sicherung der Unabhängigkeit und der Qualität.

3 Sie gewährleisten bei den einzelnen Revisionsdienstleistungen insbesondere:

a. die sachgerechte Zuteilung der Aufgaben;

b. die Überwachung der Arbeiten;

---

204 Empfehlung der Kommission vom 16. Mai 2002 zur Unhängigkeit des Abschlussprüfers in der EU, Grundprinzipien, ABl. Nr. L 191 vom 19.7.2002, S. 22 ff., Ziff. B3.3. und 3.5., und neu Art. 40 lit. c des Vorschlags der EU-Kommission zur neuen Prüferrichtlinie (vgl. dazu hinten Ziff. 5) vom 16. März 2004; Sec. 206 Sarbanes-Oxley Act.

205 Die vorliegenden Erläuterungen beziehen sich ausschliesslich auf die ursprüngliche bundesrätliche Gesetzesversion und nicht auf die bereinigte Fassung durch den Nationalrat.

c. **die Einhaltung der massgebenden Vorschriften und Standards zur Prüfung und zur Unabhängigkeit;**

d. **eine qualifizierte und unabhängige Nachkontrolle der Prüfungsergebnisse.**

Abs. 1 schreibt vor, dass die staatlich beaufsichtigten Revisionsunternehmen alle erforderlichen unternehmensbezogenen (s. Abs. 2) und mandatsbezogenen Massnahmen (s. Abs. 3) treffen müssen, die zur Sicherung der Qualität ihrer Revisionsdienstleistungen notwendig sind. In den *Abs. 2 und 3* werden diese Massnahmen in nicht abschliessender Weise konkretisiert.

Nach *Abs. 2* müssen sich staatlich beaufsichtigte Revisionsunternehmen so organisieren, dass die Einhaltung der gesetzlichen und anderweitigen Pflichten durch das Revisionsunternehmen, seine Mitarbeitenden und geschäftlich verbundene Personen sichergestellt ist. Dies betrifft die Organisation sowohl der Struktur als auch der Abläufe, da die Qualität der Revisionsdienstleistungen durch beides mittelbar oder unmittelbar beeinflusst wird. Revisionsunternehmen haben insbesondere Weisungen zu folgenden Punkten zu erlassen:

– *Lit.a:* Weisungen zur Anstellung, zur Aus- und Weiterbildung, zur Beurteilung, zur Zeichnungsberechtigung und zum gebotenen Verhalten der Mitarbeiterinnen und Mitarbeiter.

– *Lit.b:* Weisungen zur Annahme neuer und zur Weiterführung bestehender Aufträge für Revisionsdienstleistungen.

– *Lit.c:* Weisungen zur Überwachung der Massnahmen zur Sicherung der Unabhängigkeit des Revisionsunternehmens und seiner Mitarbeitenden (Art. 11 E RAG) sowie zur Qualität der Revisionsdienstleistungen (Art. 12 E RAG).

Während Abs. 2 allgemeine strukturelle Massnamen zur Sicherung der Qualität verlangt, enthält *Abs. 3* Vorschriften zur Qualitätssicherung im Hinblick auf die einzelnen konkreten Revisionsdienstleistungen. Die Revisionsunternehmen gewährleisten insbesondere:

– *Lit.a:* Massnahmen zur sachgerechten Zuteilung der Aufgaben. Zu gewährleisten ist sowohl eine angemessene Zuteilung der Revisionsmandate auf die verschiedenen Arbeitseinheiten als auch eine sachgerechte Aufteilung der Prüfungshandlungen innerhalb dieser Arbeitseinheiten.

- *Lit.b:* Massnahmen zur Überwachung der Arbeiten. Hierunter fallen beispielsweise die kritische Durchsicht aller erstellten Arbeitspapiere und eine Überprüfung aller wesentlichen Vorgehensschritte durch erfahrene Personen. Zu überwachen ist auch die Zusammenarbeit mit Personen, die zur Erbringung einer Revisionsdienstleistung beigezogen werden.

  Als Personen, die zur Erbringung einer Revisionsdienstleistung beigezogen werden, sollen insbesondere die beiden nachfolgend beschriebenen Personenkreise erfasst werden:

  - Ist das Revisionsunternehmen nicht in der Lage, einen Rechnungsposten oder einen Sachverhalt abschliessend zu beurteilen, so zieht es Fachleute bei, die über das notwendige Fachwissen verfügen. Zu denken ist an die Bewertung von Grundstücken, Maschinen oder Kunstgegenständen oder an versicherungsmathematische Bewertungen durch Expertinnen oder Experten.

  - Wo Untergesellschaften (insbesondere im Zusammenhang mit der Revision von Konzernrechnungen), Zweigniederlassungen oder andere Unternehmensteile nicht von staatlich beaufsichtigten Revisionsunternehmen, sondern von anderen zugelassenen Revisorinnen, Revisoren, Revisionsexpertinnen oder Revisionsexperten geprüft werden, stellt das Revisionsunternehmen häufig auf deren Prüfungsarbeiten ab.

  Für die Seriosität und fachliche Qualität beider Kategorien von beigezogenen Personen ist das Revisionsunternehmen verantwortlich; es hat dazu die geeigneten Massnahmen zur Qualitätssicherung zu treffen.

- *Lit.c:* Massnahmen zur Einhaltung der massgebenden Standards zur Prüfung und zur Unabhängigkeit. Diese Standards ergeben sich aus dem Regelwerk, das die zu prüfende Gesellschaft für ihre Rechnungslegung gewählt hat. Beispielsweise gelten für Jahresrechnungen, die nach den International Financial Reporting Standards (IFRS, vormals IAS) erstellt wurden, die International Standards on Auditing (ISA).

- *Lit.d:* Massnahmen zur qualifizierten und unabhängigen Nachkontrolle der Prüfungsergebnisse. Qualifiziert ist eine Nachkontrolle, wenn sie durch eine zugelassene Revisionsexpertin oder einen zugelassenen

Revisionsexperten erfolgt. Die nachkontrollierende Person ist dann unabhängig, wenn sie an der Erbringung der Revisionsdienstleistung in keiner Weise beteiligt war.

Dokumentation und Aufbewahrung

Art. 13 (ursprünglicher Botschaftsentwurf, gestrichen durch den Nationalrat)

1 Die staatlich beaufsichtigten Revisionsunternehmen müssen sämtliche Revisionsdienstleistungen dokumentieren und die Revisionsberichte sowie alle wesentlichen Unterlagen mindestens während zehn Jahren aufbewahren. Elektronische Daten müssen während der gleichen Zeitperiode wieder lesbar gemacht werden können.

2 Die Unterlagen müssen der Aufsichtsbehörde ermöglichen, die Einhaltung der gesetzlichen Vorschriften in effizienter Weise zu prüfen.

Staatlich beaufsichtigte Revisionsunternehmen sind auf Grund von *Abs. 1 Satz 1* verpflichtet, sämtliche Revisionsdienstleistungen zu dokumentieren und die Revisionsberichte sowie alle wesentlichen Unterlagen mindestens während 10 Jahren aufzubewahren. Ausschlaggebend ist das Datum des betreffenden Dokumentes.

Zu dokumentieren sind insbesondere auch die Planung und die Durchführung der Arbeiten für eine bestimmte Revisionsdienstleistung und die Umsetzung von Anweisungen der Aufsichtsbehörde (s. dazu die Ausführungen zu Art. 17 Abs. 4 E RAG). Die Dokumente sind zu datieren und mit einem Vermerk des Autors sowie derjenigen Person zu versehen, die das Revisionsmandat leitet. (vgl. Amtl. Bulletin vom 02.03.2005, 15.00 h, Anmerkung NR Leutenegger Oberholzer: Da es sich um eine Vielzahl von Dokumenten handelt, wäre es völlig unverhältnismässig, wenn hier ein Doppelvermerk bestehen würde. Es sei zuhanden der Materialien festzuhalten, dass der Vermerk des Autors ausreichend sei.)

Aufbewahrt werden müssen nicht nur die Revisionsberichte, welche die Schlussfolgerungen der Prüfung beinhalten, sondern auch sämtliche Papiere, die der Erarbeitung der Schlussfolgerung des Prüfungsberichts dienen, also auch interne Arbeitspapiere.

Die Dokumentations- und Aufbewahrungspflicht dient einerseits der internen Qualitätssicherung, andererseits aber auch der Aufsichtsbehörde, welche die Einhaltung der gesetzlichen Pflichten durch das Revisionsunternehmen überprüfen muss (s. dazu Art. 14 und Art. 17 E RAG). Die Dokumente können ferner in allfälligen zivil- und strafrechtlichen Verfahren als Beweismittel herangezogen werden.

Gemäss *Satz 2* müssen elektronische Daten ebenfalls während 10 Jahren wieder lesbar gemacht werden können.

Die Unterlagen müssen der Aufsichtsbehörde nach *Abs.* 2 ermöglichen, die Einhaltung der gesetzlichen Vorschriften in effizienter Weise zu prüfen. Diese Vorschrift auferlegt den staatlich beaufsichtigten Revisionsunternehmen die Pflicht, die Dokumente so zu erstellen, dass die Aufsichtsbehörde beurteilen kann, ob die Vorschriften des Revisionsaufsichtsgesetzes und des Obligationenrechts eingehalten werden. Die staatlich beaufsichtigten Revisionsunternehmen müssen durch die Art und die Organisation der Aufbewahrung weiter sicherstellen, dass sie Auskunfts- und Einsichtsbegehren der Aufsichtsbehörde innert angemessener Frist nachkommen können (s. Art. 14 und 17 E RAG). Damit soll verhindert werden, dass Verfahren in wichtigen Fällen verzögert werden, weil die erforderlichen Dokumente erst noch zusammengetragen werden müssen.

Auskunftspflicht und Zutrittsgewährung

Art. 13

1 Staatlich beaufsichtigte Revisionsunternehmen, ihre Mitarbeiterinnen und Mitarbeiter, die Personen, die sie für Revisionsdienstleistungen beiziehen, und die geprüften Gesellschaften müssen der Aufsichtsbehörde die Auskünfte erteilen und Unterlagen herausgeben, die diese für die Erfüllung ihrer Aufgabe benötigt.

2 Staatlich beaufsichtigte Revisionsunternehmen müssen der Aufsichtsbehörde jederzeit Zutritt zu ihren Geschäftsräumen gewähren.

Revisionsunternehmen, ihre Mitarbeiterinnen und Mitarbeiter sowie Personen, die für Revisionsdienstleistungen beigezogen wurden (s. dazu die Ausführungen zu Art. 12 Abs. 3 lit. b E RAG), müssen der Aufsichtsbehörde nach *Abs. 1* alle Auskünfte erteilen, die diese zur Erfüllung ihrer

Aufgabe benötigt. Sie haben auch die erforderlichen Unterlagen herausgeben.

Die von einem beaufsichtigten Revisionsunternehmen geprüften Publikumsgesellschaften sind ebenfalls der Auskunfts- und Herausgabepflicht unterworfen. Dies erlaubt der Aufsichtsbehörde Referenzprüfungen und ermöglicht ihr, Unterlagen einzusehen, die beim staatlich beaufsichtigten Revisionsunternehmen nicht oder nicht mehr vorhanden sind. Die geprüften Unternehmen werden vor zu weit gehenden Einsichtsrechten der Aufsichtsbehörde dadurch geschützt, dass diese nur Informationen erheben darf, die sie für ihre Aufsichtstätigkeit braucht. An die Notwendigkeit der Auskünfte und Unterlagen für die Aufsichtstätigkeit dürfen allerdings keine zu strengen Anforderungen gestellt werden: Das heisst, dass der Aufsichtsbehörde alle von ihr verlangten Informationen zugänglich gemacht werden müssen, die im Zusammenhang mir ihrer gesetzlichen Aufgabe stehen. Die Informationen können sowohl konkrete Revisionsdienstleistungen als auch das Revisionsunternehmen als solches betreffen.

Staatlich beaufsichtigte Revisionsunternehmen müssen der Aufsichtsbehörde gemäss *Abs. 2* jederzeit Zutritt zu den Geschäftsräumen gewähren. Eine vorgängige Anmeldung wird im Interesse der Effizienz der Aufsicht nicht vorausgesetzt. Soweit das Revisionsunternehmen auf Grund von Abs. 1 zur Herausgabe von Akten verpflichtet ist, ist im Rahmen einer Inspektion auch eine Sicherstellung von Unterlagen möglich.

Die Pflichten staatlich beaufsichtigter Revisionsunternehmen nach Art. 14 E RAG gelten auch gegenüber Drittpersonen, die von der Aufsichtsbehörde für die Erfüllung ihrer Aufgaben beigezogen werden (s. Art. 21 E RAG).

Meldungen an die Aufsichtsbehörde

Art. 14

1 Staatlich beaufsichtigte Revisionsunternehmen müssen die Zulassungsunterlagen jedes Jahr jeweils per 30. Juni aktualisieren und bis zum 30. September bei der Aufsichtsbehörde einreichen. Unverändert gültige Unterlagen müssen nicht erneut eingereicht werden.

2 Staatlich beaufsichtigte Revisionsunternehmen müssen die Aufsichtsbehörde überdies unverzüglich schriftlich über wichtige Vor-

kommnisse unterrichten, die für die Aufsicht relevant sind. Zu melden sind insbesondere:

a. Änderungen der Zusammensetzung ihres obersten Leitungs- oder Verwaltungsorgans sowie ihres Geschäftsführungsorgans;

b. Wechsel einer Person, die eine Revisionsdienstleistung leitet, unter Angabe der Gründe;

c. die vorzeitige Auflösung oder der Verzicht auf die Verlängerung eines Revisionsauftrags, unter Angabe der Gründe.

Die vorliegende Bestimmung sieht aktive Meldepflichten der staatlich beaufsichtigten Revisionsunternehmen gegenüber der Aufsichtsbehörde vor. Der Entwurf unterscheidet periodische Meldepflichten (Abs. 1) und solche in Einzelfällen (Abs. 2).

Nach *Abs. 1* haben staatlich beaufsichtigte Revisionsunternehmen die Zulassungsunterlagen (s. dazu Art. 10 E RAG) jährlich jeweils per 30. Juni zu aktualisieren. Die aktualisierten Unterlagen sind jeweils bis zum 30. September bei der Aufsichtsbehörde einzureichen. Unverändert gültige Unterlagen müssen nicht erneut eingereicht werden; es genügt ein Hinweis, dass sie nicht verändert worden sind.

Das Stichdatum für die Erneuerung der Zulassungsunterlagen wurde bewusst nicht auf das Ende des Kalenderjahres gelegt, weil es auf diesen Termin üblicherweise zu personellen Mutationen kommt.

Werden die aktualisierten Zulassungsunterlagen versehentlich nicht rechtzeitig eingereicht, so hat dies nicht zwingend den Entzug der Registrierung zur Folge (s. dazu Art. 18 E RAG). Die Aufsichtsbehörde kann aber von allen ihr zur Verfügung stehenden Sanktionen Gebrauch machen.

Abs. 2 enthält die Vorschrift, dass staatlich beaufsichtigte Revisionsunternehmen die Aufsichtsbehörde schriftlich und unverzüglich über wichtige, für die Aufsicht relevante Vorkommnisse unterrichten müssen. Anzuzeigen sind insbesondere die folgenden Tatbestände:

– *Lit.a:* Zu melden sind Änderungen der Zusammensetzung des obersten Leitungs- oder Verwaltungsorgans sowie des Geschäftsführungsorgans des Revisionsunternehmens. Dadurch kann überprüft werden, ob die Zulassungsvoraussetzungen nach Art. 6 lit. a E RAG eingehalten werden.

- *Lit.b:* Ebenfalls mitgeteilt werden müssen Wechsel einer Person, die eine Revisionsdienstleistung leitet, und zwar unter Angabe der Gründe. Damit wird die Einhaltung folgender Bestimmungen sichergestellt:
    - das Erfordernis der Leitung der Revisionsdienstleistungen ausschliesslich durch zugelassene Revisionsexpertinnen und -experten (Art. 6 lit. c E RAG);
    - die Rotationspflicht der leitenden Prüferinnen und Prüfer (Art. 730a Abs. 2 E OR).
- Die Gründe, die zum Wechsel einer leitenden Prüferin oder eines leitenden Prüfers geführt haben, sind für die Aufsichtsbehörde von Interesse, da sie auf Schwierigkeiten in der internen Organisation oder auf Meinungsverschiedenheiten über Massnahmen zur Qualitätssicherung hinweisen können.
- *Lit.c:* Zu melden sind auch die vorzeitige Auflösung oder der Verzicht auf eine Verlängerung eines Revisionsauftrags, beides unter Angabe der Gründe. Es ist für die Erfüllung der Aufgaben der Aufsichtsbehörde erforderlich, dass sie erfährt, warum ein der Aufsicht unterstehendes Revisionsverhältnis beendet wurde.

5. Abschnitt: Zulassung und Aufsicht

Zulassung und Registrierung

Art. 15

1 **Die Aufsichtsbehörde entscheidet auf Gesuch hin über die Zulassung von:**

a. **Revisorinnen und Revisoren;**

b. **Revisionsexpertinnen und Revisionsexperten;**

c. **staatlich beaufsichtigten Revisionsunternehmen.**

2 Sie führt ein Register über die zugelassenen natürlichen Personen und Revisionsunternehmen. Das Register ist öffentlich und wird auf dem Internet publiziert. Der Bundesrat regelt den Inhalt des Registers.

| Kapitel 1: | Neue Gesetzesbestimmungen und Erläuterungen |

3 Die registrierten natürlichen Personen und Revisionsunternehmen müssen der Aufsichtsbehörde jede Änderung von eingetragenen Tatsachen mitteilen.

Die Aufsichtsbehörde entscheidet gemäss *Abs. 1* auf Gesuch hin über die Zulassung von Revisionsexpertinnen, Revisionsexperten, Revisorinnen und Revisoren sowie von staatlich beaufsichtigten Revisionsunternehmen.

Abs. 2 sieht vor, dass die Aufsichtsbehörde ein Register über die zugelassenen natürlichen Personen und Revisionsunternehmen führt. Das Register ist öffentlich zugänglich und wird auf dem Internet publiziert. Damit wird jeder revisionspflichtigen Gesellschaft die Möglichkeit gegeben, sich vor der Wahl oder der Beauftragung eines Revisors, einer Revisionsexpertin oder eines Revisionsunternehmens über deren Qualifikationen zu informieren. Auch Dritte – so insbesondere Gläubigerinnen und Gläubiger, aber auch Behörden – können auf einfache Weise prüfen, welche Voraussetzungen die Revisionsstelle einer Gesellschaft erfüllt.

Der Bundesrat regelt den Inhalt des Registers. Er trägt dabei rechtsvergleichenden Gesichtspunkten Rechnung. Beispielsweise kann er bei natürlichen Personen die Eintragung des Arbeitgebers und bei Revisionsunternehmen deren Zugehörigkeit zu einem Netzwerk vorsehen. Zudem wird die Möglichkeit eröffnet, besondere Qualifikationen, beispielsweise im Bereich der Bankenrevision, in das Register aufzunehmen.

Abs. 3 schreibt vor, dass die registrierten natürlichen Personen und Revisionsunternehmen der Aufsichtsbehörde jede Änderung von eingetragenen Tatsachen mitteilen müssen.

Überprüfung staatlich beaufsichtigter Revisionsunternehmen

Art. 16

1 Die Aufsichtsbehörde unterzieht die staatlich beaufsichtigten Revisionsunternehmen mindestens alle drei Jahre einer eingehenden Überprüfung. Bei Verdacht auf Verstösse gegen gesetzliche Pflichten nimmt sie eine entsprechende Überprüfung vor.

2 Sie überprüft:

a. die Richtigkeit der Angaben in den Zulassungsunterlagen;

b. die Einhaltung der gesetzlichen Pflichten sowie die Beachtung der Berufsgrundsätze, der Standesregeln und gegebenenfalls des Kotierungsreglements;

c. die Qualität der erbrachten Revisionsdienstleistungen durch einzelne Stichproben;

d. die Einhaltung und Umsetzung der von ihr erteilten Anweisungen.

3 Sie erstellt zuhanden des obersten Leitungs- oder Verwaltungsorgans des Revisionsunternehmens einen schriftlichen Bericht über das Ergebnis der Überprüfung.

4 Stellt sie Verstösse gegen gesetzliche Pflichten fest, so erteilt sie dem staatlich beaufsichtigten Revisionsunternehmen einen schriftlichen Verweis, gibt Anweisungen zur Wiederherstellung des ordnungsgemässen Zustands und setzt ihm dafür eine Frist von höchstens zwölf Monaten. Aus wichtigen Gründen kann sie die Frist angemessen verlängern.

Abs. 1 Satz 1 verpflichtet die Aufsichtsbehörde, die zu beaufsichtigenden Revisionsunternehmen zumindest alle drei Jahre einer eingehenden Überprüfung zu unterziehen. Die Vorschrift gibt der Aufsichtsbehörde somit eine minimale Kadenz der Überprüfung vor. Eine starre Regelmässigkeit ist allerdings zu vermeiden. Es steht der Aufsichtsbehörde insbesondere frei, Revisionsunternehmen häufiger zu überprüfen, was namentlich dann angezeigt ist, wenn bei einer Überprüfung Mängel festgestellt wurden.

Gemäss *Abs. 1 Satz 2* nimmt die Aufsichtsbehörde bei Verdacht auf Verstösse gegen gesetzliche Pflichten eine Überprüfung vor. Es steht jedermann und insbesondere der Börse offen, die Aufsichtsbehörde über zweifelhafte Sachverhalte zu informieren. Ergibt sich aus den vorgebrachten Hinweisen ein begründeter Verdacht auf einen Verstoss gegen zwingende Vorschriften, so ist die Aufsichtsbehörde verpflichtet, entsprechende Abklärungen vorzunehmen. Es ist darauf hinzuweisen, dass unter einem begründeten Verdacht keine qualifizierte Art des Verdachts zu verstehen ist.

Gemäss *Abs. 2* hat die Aufsichtsbehörde folgende Punkte zu überprüfen:

– *Lit.a:* die Richtigkeit der Angaben in den Zulassungsunterlagen (s. Art. 10 E RAG);

- *Lit.b:* die Einhaltung der gesetzlichen Pflichten sowie die Beachtung der Berufsgrundsätze, der Standesregeln und gegebenenfalls des Kotierungsreglements.

Unter Berufsgrundsätzen werden die von der Branche geschaffenen technischen Anleitungen und unter dem Standesrecht die übrigen Normen der Selbstregulierung verstanden. Die Vorschriften des Kotierungsreglements sind nur dann zu befolgen, wenn die Gesellschaft, für welche das Revisionsunternehmen Revisionsdienstleistungen erbringt, Beteiligungspapiere oder Anleihensobligationen an der Börse kotiert hat.

Der Entwurf unterscheidet zwischen der Einhaltung der gesetzlichen Pflichten einerseits und der Beachtung der Berufsgrundsätze, Standesregeln und gegebenenfalls des Kotierungsreglements andererseits. In Bezug auf die zweite Gruppe von Normen wird damit zum Ausdruck gebracht, dass der Aufsichtsbehörde ein gewisses Ermessen zukommt, ob sie Verstösse gegen diese Normen sanktionieren will oder nicht.

- *Lit.c:* die Qualität der erbrachten Revisionsdienstleistungen. Die Überprüfung der Qualität kann und soll nicht «flächendeckend» im Sinne einer Zweitrevision erfolgen, sondern nur durch eine stichprobenweise Überprüfung einzelner von der Revisionsstelle geprüfter Sachverhalte bei zufällig ausgewählten Mandaten. Die Überprüfung durch die Aufsichtsbehörde bezweckt nicht eine integrale Nachprüfung konkreter Revisionsmandate, sondern die Kontrolle, ob die Vorgaben des Revisionsaufsichtsgesetzes für die Revisionsunternehmen in zufällig ausgewählten Einzelfällen eingehalten werden. Daraus kann sich jedoch keinerlei staatliche Garantie für die Fehlerlosigkeit der Arbeit der Revisionsstelle ergeben.

- *Lit.d:* die Einhaltung und Umsetzung der von ihr erteilten Anweisungen (s. Art. 17 Abs. 4 E RAG).

Was die Revisionsaufsicht bei internationalen Verhältnissen (s. Art. 8 E RAG) betrifft, sei darauf hingewiesen, dass sich aus lit. b keine Folgerungen für das anwendbare Recht ergeben. Bei der Anwendung dieser Bestimmung ist jedoch zu beachten, dass das Verhältnis zwischen der schweizerischen Aufsichtsbehörde und einem ausländischen Revisionsunternehmen, das sich dieser Aufsichtsbehörde unterstellt hat, aus sachlichen Gründen dem schweizerischen Recht unterstehen muss, weil sonst die Aufsicht gar nicht zum Tragen kommen könnte (vgl. insbes. die Art. 11 ff. E RAG).

Die Aufsichtsbehörde hat nach *Abs. 3* zuhanden des obersten Leitungs- oder Verwaltungsorgans des Revisionsunternehmens einen schriftlichen Bericht über das Ergebnis der Überprüfung zu erstellen, sodass sich das Revisionsunternehmen ein umfassendes Bild vom Resultat der Prüfung machen kann.

Stellt die Aufsichtsbehörde Verstösse gegen gesetzliche Pflichten fest, so erteilt sie dem Revisionsunternehmen nach *Abs. 4 Satz 1* einen schriftlichen Verweis, gibt Anweisungen zur Wiederherstellung des ordnungsgemässen Zustands und setzt ihm dafür eine Frist von höchstens 12 Monaten.

Die Aufsichtsbehörde bestimmt die Umsetzungsfristen nach freiem Ermessen, berücksichtigt dabei aber die organisatorischen und finanziellen Folgen, die eine Anweisung für das Revisionsunternehmen und die betroffenen Personen haben kann (Grundsatz der Verhältnismässigkeit). Ist Gefahr im Verzug, so können auch sehr kurze Fristen angemessen sein. Demgegenüber kann die Aufsichtsbehörde die Frist gemäss *Satz 2* aus wichtigen Gründen angemessen verlängern. Dies ist beispielsweise dann der Fall, wenn die angeordneten Massnahmen aus sachlichen Gründen nicht vor Ablauf der Einjahresfrist umgesetzt werden können.

Beispiele für Anweisungen an ein Revisionsunternehmen sind:
- die Ansetzung einer Frist zum Erlass bestimmter Weisungen gemäss Art. 12 Abs. 2 E RAG;
- die Anweisung, einen bestimmten Auftrag für Revisionsdienstleistungen zu beenden;
- Anweisungen zur Wiederherstellung der Unabhängigkeit, beispielsweise durch Verkauf einer wesentlichen Beteiligung an einem geprüften Unternehmen;
- die Anweisung, eine Person zu ersetzen, die eine Revisionsdienstleistung leitet;
- ein Verbot, bestimmte Personen zur Erbringung von Revisionsdienstleistungen beizuziehen.

Kapitel 1: Neue Gesetzesbestimmungen und Erläuterungen

Entzug der Zulassung

Art. 17

1 Erfüllt eine Revisorin, ein Revisor, eine Revisionsexpertin oder ein Revisionsexperte die Zulassungsvoraussetzungen der Art. 4–6 nicht mehr, so kann die Aufsichtsbehörde die Zulassung befristet oder unbefristet entziehen. Soweit die Zulassungsvoraussetzungen wiederhergestellt werden können, ist der Entzug vorher anzudrohen.

2 Erfüllt ein staatlich beaufsichtigtes Revisionsunternehmen die Zulassungsvoraussetzungen nicht mehr oder verletzt es die gesetzlichen Vorschriften wiederholt oder in grober Weise, so kann ihm die Aufsichtsbehörde die Zulassung befristet oder unbefristet entziehen. Der Entzug ist vorher anzudrohen; dies gilt nicht bei groben Verstössen gegen das Gesetz.

3 Die Aufsichtsbehörde informiert die betroffenen Gesellschaften und die Börse über den Entzug der Zulassung.

Erfüllt eine Revisorin, ein Revisor, eine Revisionsexpertin oder ein Revisionsexperte die Zulassungsvoraussetzungen der Art. 4–6 E RAG nicht mehr, so kann die Aufsichtsbehörde nach *Abs. 1* die Zulassung befristet oder unbefristet entziehen. Soweit die Zulassungsvoraussetzungen wiederhergestellt werden können, ist der Entzug vorher anzudrohen.

Erfüllt ein staatlich beaufsichtigtes Revisionsunternehmen die Zulassungsvoraussetzungen nicht mehr oder verletzt es die gesetzlichen Vorschriften wiederholt oder in grober Weise, so kann ihm die Aufsichtsbehörde nach *Abs. 2* die Zulassung befristet oder unbefristet entziehen. Der Entzug der Zulassung ist auch hier im Allgemeinen vorher anzudrohen. Bei gravierenden Verstössen gegen das Gesetz würde das Erfordernis einer vorangehenden Mahnung allerdings den gefährdeten Interessen Dritter nicht gerecht; verletzt eine Revisionsstelle einer Publikumsgesellschaft gesetzliche Vorschriften in grober Weise, hat sie den sofortigen Entzug der Zulassung zu gewärtigen.

Abs. 3 auferlegt der Aufsichtsbehörde die Pflicht, die vom Entzug betroffenen Gesellschaften sowie die Börse über den Entzug der Zulassung zu informieren. Dies gilt auch für den Entzug von Zulassungen von nicht staatlich beaufsichtigten Revisionsunternehmen oder von Revisorinnen,

Revisoren, Revisionsexpertinnen und Revisionsexperten, wobei sich die Informationspflicht auf diejenigen Revisionsmandate beschränkt, die der Aufsichtsbehörde bekannt sind. Auf diese Weise wird sichergestellt, dass die Gesellschaften möglichst rasch eine neue Revisionsstelle wählen können. Bei dieser Mitteilung handelt es sich um keine anfechtbare Verfügung (zum Beschwerderecht s. die Ausführungen zu Art. 40 E RAG).

Massnahmen gegenüber natürlichen Personen, die für staatlich beaufsichtigte Revisionsunternehmen tätig sind

Art. 18
Verletzt eine natürliche Person, die für ein staatlich beaufsichtigtes Revisionsunternehmen tätig ist, die gesetzlichen Vorschriften, so erteilt ihr die Aufsichtsbehörde einen schriftlichen Verweis. Bei wiederholten oder groben Verstössen kann ihr die Aufsichtsbehörde die Ausübung ihrer Tätigkeit befristet oder unbefristet verbieten und gegebenenfalls die Zulassung nach Art. 18 Abs. 1 entziehen.

Verletzt eine natürliche Personen, die für ein staatlich beaufsichtigtes Revisionsunternehmen tätig ist, die gesetzlichen Vorschriften, so erteilt ihr die Aufsichtsbehörde gemäss *Satz 1* einen schriftlichen Verweis. Liegen wiederholte oder grobe Verstösse vor, so kann ihr die Aufsichtsbehörde die Ausübung ihrer Tätigkeit nach *Satz 2* befristet oder unbefristet verbieten und gegebenenfalls die Zulassung nach Art. 18 Abs. 1 entziehen. Unbefristete Tätigkeitsverbote werden dabei nur bei schweren Verstössen ausgesprochen.

Art. 19 E RAG will vor allem Personen erfassen, die Revisionsdienstleistungen leiten (leitende Prüferinnen und Prüfer); aber auch Mitglieder des obersten Leitungs- oder Verwaltungsorgans und des Geschäftsführungsorgans müssen erforderlichenfalls mit Sanktionen belegt werden können. Für Personen, die als Revisorin, Revisor, Revisionsexpertin oder Revisionsexperte zugelassen sind, bleibt eine Sanktionierung nach Art. 18 Abs. 1 vorbehalten. Die Aufsichtsbehörde kann damit Verfehlungen einzelner verantwortlicher Personen direkt und ohne Bestrafung des Revisionsunternehmens sanktionieren.

Im Rahmen allfälliger Strafverfahren (s. Art. 42 E RAG) kann zudem das Gericht Berufsverbote aussprechen (s. den geltenden Art. 54 StGB, der durch Art. 67 nStGB[206] ersetzt wird).

Information der Öffentlichkeit

Art. 19

1 Die Aufsichtsbehörde veröffentlicht jährlich einen Bericht über ihre Tätigkeit und Praxis.

2 Über laufende und abgeschlossene Verfahren informiert sie nur, wenn dies aus Gründen überwiegender öffentlicher oder privater Interessen erforderlich ist.

Abs. 1 verpflichtet die Aufsichtsbehörde, jährlich einen Bericht über ihre Tätigkeit und ihre Praxis zu veröffentlichen.

Die Aufsichtsbehörde informiert nach *Abs. 2* grundsätzlich nicht über laufende oder abgeschlossene Verfahren. Ausgenommen bleiben Fälle, in denen eine Information aus Gründen überwiegender öffentlicher oder privater Interessen erforderlich ist. Eine Information kann etwa dann angezeigt sein, wenn falsche oder irreführende Nachrichten zu berichtigen sind und betroffene Personen, Revisionsunternehmen oder Publikumsgesellschaften zu schützen sind oder wenn die Glaubwürdigkeit der Aufsichtstätigkeit zum Schaden des Kapitalmarktes angezweifelt wird. Im Rahmen der vorzunehmenden Abwägung der berührten Interessen ist zu berücksichtigen, ob das in Frage stehende Verfahren bereits öffentlich bekannt ist.

Beizug von Drittpersonen

Art. 20

1 Die Aufsichtsbehörde kann zur Erfüllung ihrer Aufgaben Drittpersonen beiziehen.

---

206 SR **311.0** bzw. BBl **2002** 8240 ff., 8266.

2 Die beauftragten Drittpersonen müssen vom staatlich beaufsichtigten Revisionsunternehmen und von Gesellschaften, für die dieses Revisionsdienstleistungen erbringt, unabhängig sein.

3 Sie haben über Feststellungen, die sie im Rahmen ihrer Tätigkeit machen, das Geheimnis zu wahren.

Abs. 1 ermächtigt die Aufsichtsbehörde, zur Erfüllung ihrer Aufgaben Drittpersonen beizuziehen. Damit wird der Aufsichtsbehörde ermöglicht, das Know-how und die Ressourcen von qualifizierten Drittpersonen zu Aufsichtszwecken zu nutzen. Dies dürfte vor allem bei komplizierten Sachlagen von Bedeutung sein, die mit den Mitteln der Aufsichtsbehörde nicht zu bewältigen sind.

Abs. 2 schreibt vor, dass die beauftragten Drittpersonen vom Revisionsunternehmen unabhängig sein müssen, für dessen Beaufsichtigung sie herangezogen werden. Sie dürfen aber auch nicht von Gesellschaften abhängig sein, für die das zu beaufsichtigende Revisionsunternehmen Revisionsdienstleistungen erbringt. Zur Interpretation des Begriffs der Unabhängigkeit sind die Bestimmungen des Obligationenrechts (s. Art. 728 E OR) und des Revisionsaufsichtsgesetzes zur Unabhängigkeit der Revisionsstelle (s. Art. 11 E RAG) sinngemäss heranzuziehen.

Die beauftragten Drittpersonen sind nach *Abs. 3* verpflichtet, über Feststellungen, die sie im Rahmen ihrer Tätigkeit machen, das Geheimnis zu wahren. Art. 42 Abs. 1 lit. d E RAG stellt die Verletzung dieser Schweigepflicht unter Strafe.

Finanzierung

Art. 21

1 Die Aufsichtsbehörde erhebt für ihre Verfügungen, Überprüfungen und Dienstleistungen Gebühren.

2 Zur Deckung der Aufsichtskosten, die nicht durch Gebühren gedeckt sind, erhebt die Aufsichtsbehörde von den staatlich beaufsichtigten Revisionsunternehmen eine jährliche Aufsichtsabgabe. Diese wird auf der Grundlage der Kosten des Rechnungsjahres

Kapitel 1: Neue Gesetzesbestimmungen und Erläuterungen

erhoben und trägt der wirtschaftlichen Bedeutung der staatlich beaufsichtigten Revisionsunternehmen Rechnung.

3 Der Bundesrat regelt die Einzelheiten, insbesondere die Gebührenansätze, die Bemessung der Aufsichtsabgabe und deren Aufteilung auf die beaufsichtigten Revisionsunternehmen.

Gemäss *Abs. 1* erhebt die Aufsichtsbehörde für ihre Verfügungen, Überprüfungen und Dienstleistungen Gebühren.

Die Erhebung der Gebühren wird im Rahmen von Art. 46a RVOG erfolgen, der im Zusammenhang mit dem Entlastungsprogramm 2003 eingeführt worden ist. Für die Einzelheiten, insbesondere für die Gebührenbemessung anhand des Äquivalenz- und des Kostendeckungsprinzips, kann auf die entsprechenden Ausführungen in der Botschaft verwiesen werden[207]. Einer besonderen Erwähnung bedarf es, dass Gebühren nicht bloss für Verfügungen und Dienstleistungen, sondern auch für die Überprüfungen durch die Aufsichtsbehörde (s. dazu Art. 17 E RAG) erhoben werden. Die Kriterien für die Bemessung der Gebühren für Überprüfungen sind dieselben wie für die übrigen Gebühren.

Abs. 2 sieht vor, dass zur Deckung der allgemeinen Kosten der Aufsicht, soweit diese nicht durch die Gebühren nach Abs. 1 gedeckt sind, von den staatlich beaufsichtigten Revisionsunternehmen eine jährliche Aufsichtsabgabe erhoben wird (z.B. für die Kosten allgemeiner internationaler Absprachen, die nicht einem bestimmten Aufsichtsmandat zugeordnet werden können). Diese Aufsichtsabgabe wird auf der Grundlage der angefallenen Kosten erhoben und trägt der wirtschaftlichen Bedeutung der staatlich beaufsichtigten Revisionsunternehmen Rechnung. Die Finanzierung der Aufsichtsstelle hat jedoch so weit wie möglich über Gebühren nach Abs. 1 zu erfolgen; diese dürfen durchaus eine Aufteilung der allgemeinen Fixkosten der Aufsichtsbehörde einschliessen.

Die staatlich überwachten Revisionsunternehmen können die ihnen auferlegten Kosten auf die von ihnen geprüften Publikumsgesellschaften abwälzen. Die Aufsichtskosten dürften demnach letztlich von den Publikumsgesellschaften zu tragen sein. Dieser zusätzlichen Belastung steht ein Gewinn an Glaubwürdigkeit und Qualität der Rechnungslegung und Revi-

---

207 Regierungs- und Verwaltungsorganisationsgesetz vom 21. März 1997 (SR **172.010**; RVOG); Botschaft vom 2. Juli 2003 zum Entlastungsprogramm 2003 für den Bundeshaushalt, BBl **2003** 5615, 5760 ff.).

sion gegenüber, der zu einer positiven Entwicklung des schweizerischen Kapitalmarktes beitragen wird.

Gemäss *Abs. 3* regelt der Bundesrat die Einzelheiten, namentlich die Gebührenansätze, die Bemessung der Aufsichtsabgabe und deren Aufteilung auf die beaufsichtigten Revisionsunternehmen.

6. Abschnitt: Amts- und Rechtshilfe

Spezialgesetzliche Aufsichtsbehörden

Art. 22

1 Die Aufsichtsbehörde und die spezialgesetzlichen Aufsichtsbehörden müssen einander alle Auskünfte erteilen und Unterlagen übermitteln, die sie für die Durchsetzung der jeweiligen Gesetzgebung benötigen. Sie koordinieren ihre Aufsichtstätigkeiten, um Doppelspurigkeiten zu vermeiden.

2 Sie informieren sich gegenseitig über hängige Verfahren und Entscheide, die für die jeweilige Aufsichtstätigkeit von Belang sein können.

Nach *Abs. 1 Satz 1* müssen die Revisionsaufsichtsbehörde und die spezialgesetzlichen Aufsichtsbehörden einander alle Auskünfte erteilen und Unterlagen übermitteln, die sie für die Durchsetzung der jeweiligen Gesetzgebung benötigen. Zu denken ist beispielsweise an die EBK im Bankensektor oder an das Bundesamt für Privatversicherungen im Bereich der Versicherungsaufsicht (bzw. dereinst an die noch zu schaffende Eidgenössische Finanzmarktaufsicht FINMA).

Durch diese Bestimmung wird der Informationsaustausch zwischen der Behörde, die mit der Revisionsaufsicht betraut ist, und den anderen Aufsichtsbehörden am Finanzmarkt ermöglicht. Auf diese Weise soll auf eine hinreichende Verknüpfung mit den übrigen Finanzmarktaufsichtsbehörden hingewirkt und eine umfassende Aufsicht sichergestellt werden. Durch eine Zusammenarbeit lässt sich zudem der Aufwand sowohl für die verschiedenen Aufsichtsbehörden als auch für die beaufsichtigten Gesellschaften senken.

Kapitel 1: Neue Gesetzesbestimmungen und Erläuterungen

Die Revisionsaufsichtsbehörde und die spezialgesetzlichen Aufsichtsbehörden sind nach *Satz 2* gehalten, ihre Tätigkeiten zu koordinieren, um Doppelspurigkeiten in der Aufsicht zu vermeiden. Soweit erforderlich kann der Bundesrat die Einzelheiten der Zusammenarbeit auf Verordnungsstufe regeln. Im Rahmen der Schaffung der zukünftigen FINMA können zudem auch auf Gesetzesstufe weitere Punkte der Zusammenarbeit geordnet werden. Zum heutigen Zeitpunkt können hierzu keine Ausführungen gemacht werden, da die organisatorische Ausgestaltung der FINMA noch nicht feststeht.

Die in Abs. 1 genannten Aufsichtsbehörden informieren sich gemäss *Abs. 2* gegenseitig über hängige Verfahren und Entscheide, die für die jeweilige Aufsichtstätigkeit von Belang sein können. Die Information hat bereits über hängige Verfahren und nicht erst über Verfahren abschliessende Entscheide zu erfolgen, damit gewährleistet ist, dass bei Problemfällen auch die andern allenfalls betroffenen Aufsichtsbehörden rechtzeitig die erforderlichen Massnahmen anordnen können.

Börsen

Art. 23

1 Die Börse und die Aufsichtsbehörde koordinieren ihre Aufsichtstätigkeiten, um Doppelspurigkeiten zu vermeiden.

2 Sie informieren sich gegenseitig über hängige Verfahren und Entscheide, die für die jeweilige Aufsichtstätigkeit von Belang sein können.

3 Können Sanktionen der Aufsichtsbehörde bei Verstössen gegen die Art. 7 und 8 nicht durchgesetzt werden, so ergreift die Börse die erforderlichen Sanktionen.

Da die Börsenorgane nicht als spezialgesetzliche Behörden nach Art. 23 E RAG gelten können, ist eine spezifische Vorschrift zur Zusammenarbeit zwischen der Revisionsaufsichtsbehörde und den Organen der Schweizer Börse notwendig.

Die Börse und die Aufsichtsbehörde koordinieren gemäss *Abs. 1* ihre Aufsichtstätigkeiten, um Doppelspurigkeiten zu vermeiden. Eine wesentliche Massnahme zur Zusammenarbeit ordnet das Gesetz mit dem nachstehend erläuterten Abs. 3 selbst an. Eine Vorschrift analog zu Art. 23 Abs. 1 Satz 1 E RAG erübrigt sich, weil die Aufsichtsbehörde nach Art. 14 E RAG in der Lage ist, alle Informationen direkt bei den Revisionsunternehmen und Emittenten einzuholen.

Die Aufsichtsbehörde und die Börse informieren sich nach *Abs. 2* gegenseitig über hängige Verfahren und Entscheide, die für ihre Aufsichtstätigkeit von Belang sein können.

Können Sanktionen der Aufsichtsbehörde bei Verstössen gegen die Art. 7 und 8 E RAG nicht durchgesetzt werden, so ergreift die Börse gemäss *Abs. 3* die erforderlichen Sanktionen. Zu denken ist in diesem Zusammenhang vor allem an Revisionsunternehmen mit Sitz im Ausland, die von der Schweizer Revisionsaufsichtsbehörde nicht sanktioniert werden können, weil das Schweizer Recht keine extraterritorialen Wirkungen entfalten kann. Es liegt daher an der Börse, die Einhaltung des Revisionsaufsichtsgesetzes sicherzustellen; sie sanktioniert (ausländische) Emittenten, deren Revisorinnen und Revisoren Vorschriften des schweizerischen Rechts missachten (s. dazu auch die Ausführungen zu Art. 8 Abs. 3bis E BEHG). Die Befugnis der Börse zur Sanktionierung in- und ausländischer Emittenten bleibt in jedem Fall unabhängig von der Sanktionierung der Revisionsunternehmen durch die Revisionsaufsichtsbehörde gewahrt.

Gemäss Art. 82 des Kotierungsreglements stehen der Schweizer Börse SWX folgende Sanktionsmöglichkeiten gegen Emittenten zur Verfügung: Verweis, Publikation von Tatsachen, Busse bis 200 000 Franken, Sistierung des Handels, Streichung der Kotierung (Dekotierung), Ausschluss von weiteren Kotierungen und Publikation von Sanktionen. Art. 24 Abs. 3 E RAG überlässt die Wahl der angemessenen Sanktion der Börse. Das Beschwerderecht der Emittenten gegen Sanktionsentscheide der Börse richtet sich auf Grund des Prinzips der Selbstregulierung nach dem Kotierungsreglement.

Strafverfolgungsbehörden

Art. 24

1 Die Aufsichtsbehörde und die Strafverfolgungsbehörden müssen einander alle Auskünfte erteilen und Unterlagen übermitteln, die sie für die Durchsetzung dieses Gesetzes benötigen.

2 Die Strafverfolgungsbehörde darf von der Aufsichtsbehörde erhaltene Auskünfte und Unterlagen nur im Rahmen des Strafverfahrens verwenden, für das Rechtshilfe gewährt wurde. Sie darf Auskünfte und Unterlagen nicht an Dritte weitergeben.

3 Erhält die Aufsichtsbehörde in Ausübung ihrer dienstlichen Pflichten Kenntnis von strafbaren Handlungen, so benachrichtigt sie die zuständigen Strafverfolgungsbehörden.

4 Die Strafverfolgungsbehörden melden der Aufsichtsbehörde sämtliche Verfahren, die im Zusammenhang mit einer von einem staatlich beaufsichtigten Revisionsunternehmen erbrachten Revisionsdienstleistung stehen; sie übermitteln ihr die Urteile und die Einstellungsbeschlüsse. Zu melden sind insbesondere Verfahren, die folgende Bestimmungen betreffen:

a. die Art. 146, 152, 153, 161, 166, 251, 253–255 und 321 des Strafgesetzbuches[208];

b. Art. 47 des Bankengesetzes vom 8. November 1934[209];

c. Art. 43 des Börsengesetzes vom 24. März 1995[210].

Die Aufsichtsbehörde und die Strafverfolgungsbehörden müssen einander nach *Abs. 1* alle für die Durchsetzung dieses Gesetzes notwendigen Auskünfte erteilen und Unterlagen übermitteln.

Die Strafverfolgungsbehörde darf die von der Aufsichtsbehörde erhaltenen Auskünfte und Unterlagen nach *Abs. 2* nur im Rahmen desjenigen Strafverfahrens verwenden, für das die Aufsichtsbehörde Rechtshilfe gewährt hat. Sie darf Auskünfte und Unterlagen nicht an Dritte weitergeben, worunter auch am Verfahren beteiligte Drittpersonen zu verstehen sind.

Diese Bestimmungen zur Rechts- und Amtshilfe werden ergänzt durch *Abs. 3*, der eine Meldepflicht der Aufsichtsbehörde statuiert. Erhält diese in Ausübung ihrer dienstlichen Pflichten Kenntnis von strafbaren Handlungen (insbesondere von solchen gemäss Art. 42 E RAG), so muss sie die zuständigen Strafverfolgungsbehörden darüber informieren.

---

[208] SR **311.0**
[209] SR **952.0**
[210] SR **954.1**

Abs. 4 statuiert eine Meldepflicht der Strafverfolgungsbehörden betreffend aufsichtsrelevante Verfahren: Die Strafverfolgungsbehörden melden der Aufsichtsbehörde sämtliche Verfahren, die im Zusammenhang mit einer Revisionsdienstleistung stehen, die von einem staatlich beaufsichtigten Revisionsunternehmen erbracht wurde. Sie übermitteln der Aufsichtsbehörde die Urteile und die Einstellungsbeschlüsse. Die Meldepflicht gilt auch für Verfahren gegen Mitarbeiterinnen und Mitarbeiter eines staatlich beaufsichtigten Revisionsunternehmens oder gegen Personen, die von einem solchen zur Erbringung einer Revisionsdienstleistung beigezogen wurden.

Zu informieren ist insbesondere über Verfahren, die folgende Bestimmungen betreffen:

– *Lit.a:* Gemeldet werden müssen Strafverfahren wegen Betrug (Art. 146 StGB[211]), unwahren Angaben über kaufmännische Gewerbe (Art. 152 StGB), unwahren Angaben gegenüber Handelsregisterbehörden (Art. 153 StGB), Ausnützen der Kenntnis vertraulicher Tatsachen (Art. 161 StGB), Unterlassen der Buchführung (Art. 166 StGB), Urkundendelikten (Art. 251, 253, 254 und 255) sowie wegen Verletzungen des Berufsgeheimnisses (Art. 321 StGB).
– *Lit.b:* Meldepflichtig sind auch Verletzungen des Bankengeheimnisses (Art. 47 BankG[212]).
– *Lit.c:* Anzuzeigen sind zudem Verstösse gegen das Börsengeheimnis (Art. 43 BEHG[213]).

Die Information hat bereits über hängige Verfahren und nicht erst über die Verfahren abschliessende Entscheide zu erfolgen, damit gewährleistet ist, dass die Aufsichtsbehörde bei Problemfällen rechtzeitig die erforderlichen Massnahmen anordnen kann.

Zivilgerichte

Art. 25

Die kantonalen Zivilgerichte und das Bundesgericht melden der Aufsichtsbehörde sämtliche Verfahren betreffend die Revisions-

---

[211] SR **311.0**.
[212] SR **952.0**.
[213] SR **954.1**.

haftung (Art. 755 Obligationenrecht[214]) im Zusammenhang mit einer von einem staatlich beaufsichtigten Revisionsunternehmen erbrachten Revisionsdienstleistung und stellen ihr die Urteile sowie andere Entscheide zu, welche ein solches Verfahren abschliessen.

Art. 26 statuiert eine Meldepflicht der Zivilgerichte betreffend aufsichtsrelevante Verfahren: Die kantonalen Zivilgerichte und das Bundesgericht melden der Aufsichtsbehörde sämtliche Verfahren betreffend die Revisionshaftung (s. Art. 755 OR) für eine Dienstleistung, die von einem staatlich beaufsichtigten Revisionsunternehmen erbracht wurde. Sie stellen der Aufsichtsbehörde die Urteile und andere Verfahren abschliessende Entscheide zu.

Die Meldepflicht gilt auch für Verfahren gegen Mitarbeiterinnen und Mitarbeiter eines staatlich beaufsichtigten Revisionsunternehmens oder gegen Personen, die von einem solchen zur Erbringung einer Revisionsdienstleistung beigezogen wurden.

Zusammenarbeit mit ausländischen Revisionsaufsichtsbehörden

Art. 26 (ursprünglicher Botschaftsentwurf)

1 Die Aufsichtsbehörde kann zur Durchsetzung dieses Gesetzes ausländische Revisionsaufsichtsbehörden um Auskünfte und Unterlagen ersuchen.

2 Sie darf ausländischen Revisionsaufsichtsbehörden nicht öffentlich zugängliche Auskünfte und Unterlagen übermitteln, sofern diese Behörden:

a. die übermittelten Informationen ausschliesslich zur direkten Beaufsichtigung von Personen und Unternehmen verwenden, die Revisionsdienstleistungen erbringen;

b. an das Amts- oder Berufsgeheimnis gebunden sind;

c. die Informationen nur auf Grund einer Ermächtigung in einem Staatsvertrag oder mit vorgängiger Zustimmung der Aufsichtsbehörde an Behörden und an Organe weiterleiten, die im

---

[214] SR **220**

öffentlichen Interesse liegende Aufsichtsaufgaben wahrnehmen und an das Amts- und Berufsgeheimnis gebunden sind.

3 Die Aufsichtsbehörde verweigert die Zustimmung, wenn die Informationen an Strafbehörden weitergeleitet werden sollen und die Rechtshilfe in Strafsachen wegen der Art der Tat ausgeschlossen wäre. Die Aufsichtsbehörde entscheidet im Einvernehmen mit dem Bundesamt für Justiz.

4 Der Bundesrat ist im Rahmen von Abs. 2 befugt, die Zusammenarbeit mit ausländischen Revisionsaufsichtsbehörden in Staatsverträgen zu regeln.

Art. 26 (durch den Nationalrat bereinigte Version)

3 Die Aufsichtsbehörde verweigert die Zustimmung, wenn die Informationen an Strafbehörden oder an Behörden und Organe mit verwaltungsrechtlichen Sanktionsbefugnissen weitergeleitet werden sollen und die Rechtshilfe in Strafsachen wegen der Art der Tat ausgeschlossen wäre. Die Aufsichtsbehörde entscheidet im Einvernehmen mit dem Bundesamt für Justiz.

Den Amts- und Rechtshilfebestimmungen kommt auf Grund der Internationalität des Kapitalmarktes eine grosse Bedeutung zu. Im Ausland bestehen bereits Revisionsaufsichtsbehörden (z.B. das Public Company Accounting Oversight Board in den USA [PCAOB]) oder sind im Entstehen begriffen (z.B. in der EU). Ein griffiges Amts- und Rechtshilfesystem dient nicht nur einer effizienten Aufsicht, sondern erleichtert auch die internationale Zusammenarbeit und trägt zur Verhinderung von Normkonflikten zwischen den beteiligten Rechtsordnungen bei.

Abs. 1 sieht vor, dass die Aufsichtsbehörde zur Durchsetzung dieses Gesetzes ausländische Revisionsaufsichtsbehörden um Auskünfte und Unterlagen ersuchen kann. Ob die entsprechenden Aufschlüsse erteilt werden, richtet sich nach dem für die ausländischen Revisionsaufsichtsbehörden massgebenden Recht.

Die Aufsichtsbehörde darf gemäss *Abs. 2* ausländischen Revisionsaufsichtsbehörden Auskünfte und Unterlagen übermitteln, die nicht öffentlich zugänglich sind, wenn drei Bedingungen erfüllt sind:

- Gemäss *lit. a* dürfen die übermittelten Informationen nur zur direkten Beaufsichtigung von Personen und Unternehmen verwendet werden, die Revisionsdienstleistungen erbringen.
- *Lit.b* setzt voraus, dass die ersuchende ausländische Behörde an das Amts- oder Berufsgeheimnis gebunden ist.
- Nach *lit. c* dürfen die übermittelten Informationen von der ausländischen Behörde nur auf Grund einer Ermächtigung in einem Staatsvertrag oder mit vorgängiger Zustimmung der schweizerischen Aufsichtsbehörde an andere Behörden und Organe weitergeleitet werden, die im öffentlichen Interesse liegende Aufsichtsaufgaben wahrnehmen und ihrerseits an das Amts- und Berufsgeheimnis gebunden sind.

Abs. 2 wurde in redaktionell leicht modifizierter Form aus dem Entwurf zum Versicherungsaufsichtsgesetz (BBl *2003* 3789 ff., 3898) übernommen. Letzterer basiert wiederum auf den Vorgaben im Bankengesetz.

Nach *Abs. 3* muss die Aufsichtsbehörde die Zustimmung zur Weiterleitung von Auskünften oder von Unterlagen an Strafbehörden verweigern, wenn die Rechtshilfe in Strafsachen wegen der Art der Tat ausgeschlossen wäre. Somit sind für die Gewährung der Rechtshilfe nur die Ausschlussgründe bezüglich der Art der Tat (entsprechend Art. 3 Rechtshilfegesetz, IRSG, beispielsweise im Bereich der Fiskaldelikte) zu prüfen und nicht die Voraussetzung der beidseitigen Strafbarkeit; Letztere schliesst nicht die Rechtshilfe an sich aus, sondern nur die Anordnung von Zwangsmassnahmen (vgl. Art. 64 IRSG). Die Aufsichtsbehörde entscheidet im Einvernehmen mit dem Bundesamt für Justiz. Damit wird klargestellt, dass sowohl die Aufsichtsbehörde als auch das Bundesamt für Justiz der Übermittlung von Informationen zustimmen müssen.

Der Bundesrat ist gemäss *Abs. 4* befugt, die Zusammenarbeit mit ausländischen Revisionsaufsichtsbehörden in Staatsverträgen zu regeln. In diesen Verträgen erfolgt sinngemäss auch die Anerkennung ausländischer Behörden im Sinne von Art. 8 Abs. 2 E RAG. Entsprechende Abkommen müssen vom Parlament nicht mehr genehmigt werden. Der Bundesrat hat jedoch die in Abs. 2 aufgestellten Rahmenbedingungen zwingend zu beachten. Der Gesetzesentwurf macht die Amtshilfe nicht vom Vorhandensein derartiger Verträge abhängig, um zu vermeiden, dass eine grosse Anzahl entsprechender Abkommen abgeschlossen werden müssen. Dennoch sind staatsvertragliche Regelungen sinnvoll, da in ihnen die gegenseitigen Amtshilfepflichten verankert und Einzelheiten geregelt werden können.[215]

Grenzüberschreitende Prüfungshandlungen

Art. 27

1 Die Aufsichtsbehörde kann zur Durchsetzung dieses Gesetzes ausländische Revisionsaufsichtsbehörden um die Vornahme von Prüfungshandlungen im Ausland ersuchen. Auf Grund einer Ermächtigung in einem Staatsvertrag oder mit vorgängiger Zustimmung der ausländischen Revisionsaufsichtsbehörde kann sie Prüfungshandlungen im Ausland selbst vornehmen.

2 Auf Ersuchen ausländischer Revisionsaufsichtsbehörden nimmt die Aufsichtsbehörde für diese Prüfungshandlungen im Inland vor, wenn der ersuchende Staat Gegenrecht hält. Art. 27 Abs. 2 und 3 finden entsprechende Anwendung.

3 Auf Grund einer Ermächtigung in einem Staatsvertrag oder mit vorgängiger Zustimmung der Aufsichtsbehörde können ausländische Revisionsaufsichtsbehörden Prüfungshandlungen in der Schweiz selbst vornehmen, wenn der ersuchende Staat Gegenrecht hält. Art. 27 Abs. 2 und 3 findet entsprechende Anwendung.

4 Die Aufsichtsbehörde kann die ausländische Revisionsaufsichtsbehörde bei deren Aufsichtshandlungen in der Schweiz begleiten. Die betroffene Person oder das betroffene Unternehmen kann eine solche Begleitung verlangen.

5 Der Bundesrat ist im Rahmen der Abs. 2 und 3 befugt, die Zusammenarbeit mit ausländischen Revisionsaufsichtsbehörden in Staatsverträgen zu regeln.

Die Bestimmung enthält die gesetzliche Grundlage für eine Kontrolle vor Ort durch die schweizerische Aufsichtsbehörde im Ausland. Diese Rege-

---

215 Die vorliegenden Erläuterungen beziehen sich ausschliesslich auf die ursprüngliche bundesrätliche Gesetzesversion und nicht auf die bereinigte Fassung durch den Nationalrat.

lung entspricht der Internationalität der Kapitalmärkte. Spiegelbildlich wird auch eine Vorortkontrolle durch ausländische Revisionsaufsichtsbehörden in der Schweiz ermöglicht. Es wird dabei sichergestellt, dass die schweizerische Revisionsaufsichtsbehörde Gegenrecht erhält.

Abs. 1 Satz 1 sieht vor, dass die Aufsichtsbehörde zur Durchsetzung dieses Gesetzes ausländische Revisionsaufsichtsbehörden um die Vornahme von stellvertretenden Prüfungshandlungen im Ausland ersuchen kann. Auf Grund einer Ermächtigung in einem Staatsvertrag oder mit vorgängiger Zustimmung der ausländischen Revisionsaufsichtsbehörde kann sie gemäss *Satz 2* in eigener Verantwortung direkt Prüfungshandlungen im Ausland vornehmen.

Abs. 2 enthält die Komplementärnorm zu Abs. 1 Satz 1: Auf Ersuchen ausländischer Revisionsaufsichtsbehörden nimmt die Aufsichtsbehörde stellvertretend für diese Prüfungshandlungen im Inland vor, wenn der ersuchende Staat Gegenrecht hält. Damit wird auf das sog. materielle Gegenrecht Bezug genommen, wonach das Gegenrecht nicht zwingend durch einen Staatsvertrag, sondern durch tieferrangiges Recht oder durch Rechtsprechung gewährleistet ist. Art. 27 Abs. 2 und 3 E RAG finden entsprechende Anwendung. Die dort aufgestellten Bedingungen für die Gewährung der Amts- bzw. der Rechtshilfe bleiben somit vorbehalten.

Abs. 3 enthält die Komplementärnorm zu Abs. 1 Satz 2: Auf Grund einer Ermächtigung in einem Staatsvertrag oder mit vorgängiger Zustimmung der Aufsichtsbehörde können ausländische Revisionsaufsichtsbehörden Prüfungshandlungen in der Schweiz selbst vornehmen, wenn der ersuchende Staat (sog. materielles) Gegenrecht hält. Art. 27 Abs. 2 und 3 E RAG finden entsprechende Anwendung. Auch hier bleiben die dort aufgestellten Bedingungen für die Gewährung der Amts- bzw. der Rechtshilfe vorbehalten.

Nach *Abs. 4* kann die Aufsichtsbehörde eine ausländische Revisionsaufsichtsbehörde bei deren Aufsichtshandlungen in der Schweiz begleiten. Die von der Aufsichtshandlung betroffene Person oder das betroffene Unternehmen haben das Recht, eine solche Begleitung zu verlangen. Die Aufsichtsbehörde steht es frei, zur Erfüllung dieser Pflicht auf Drittpersonen zurückgreifen (s. Art. 21 E RAG).

Der Bundesrat ist nach *Abs. 5* befugt, die Zusammenarbeit mit ausländischen Revisionsaufsichtsbehörden in Staatsverträgen zu regeln. Er hat sich dabei allerdings an die in den Abs. 2 und 3 aufgestellten Rahmenbedingungen zu halten.

7. Abschnitt: Organisation der Aufsichtsbehörde, Verfahren und Rechtsschutz

Aufsichtsbehörde

Art. 28

1 Die Aufsicht nach diesem Gesetz obliegt der Eidgenössischen Revisionsaufsichtsbehörde.

2 Die Aufsichtsbehörde ist eine öffentlich-rechtliche Anstalt mit eigener Rechtspersönlichkeit. Sie übt die Aufsicht unabhängig aus.

3 Sie ist in ihrer Organisation sowie in ihrer Betriebsführung selbstständig und führt eine eigene Rechnung.

Die Aufsicht nach diesem Gesetz obliegt nach *Abs. 1* der Eidgenössischen Revisionsaufsichtsbehörde.

Die Eidgenössische Revisionsaufsichtsbehörde wird auf Grund von *Abs. 2* als öffentlich-rechtliche Anstalt mit eigener Rechtspersönlichkeit ausgestaltet. Als solche übt sie die Aufsicht über die Revisionsbranche unabhängig aus, wobei die Unabhängigkeit sowohl gegenüber den politischen Behörden wie auch gegenüber der Wirtschaft gegeben sein muss.

Die Aufsichtsbehörde wird deshalb nicht als Verwaltungsstelle innerhalb der zentralen Bundesverwaltung konzipiert, sondern gemäss *Abs. 3* als selbständige öffentlich-rechtliche Anstalt mit eigener Rechtspersönlichkeit. Die eigene Rechtspersönlichkeit hat insbesondere zur Folge, dass die Aufsichtsbehörde selber Rechte und Pflichten erwerben kann. So kann sie etwa Eigentum an ihren Einrichtungen erwerben und sich Dritten gegenüber vertraglich verpflichten.

Abs. 3 sieht vor, dass die Aufsichtsbehörde in ihrer Organisation sowie in ihrer Betriebsführung selbständig ist und eine eigene Rechnung ausserhalb des Finanzhaushalts des Bundes führt. Die Tätigkeit der Aufsichtsbehörde soll nicht von aussen über die Zuteilung und Verwaltung der Ressourcen für die Aufgabenerfüllung beeinflusst werden. Voraussetzung dafür ist die Eigenfinanzierung. Diese soll dadurch realisiert werden, dass die Aufsichtsbehörde sich vollständig über Gebühren und eine Aufsichtsabgabe finanziert, die von den zugelassenen und beaufsichtigten Personen und Unternehmen erhoben werden (vgl. dazu Art. 22 E RAG). Eine ausrei-

Kapitel 1: Neue Gesetzesbestimmungen und Erläuterungen

chende und unabhängige Finanzierung wird eine der zentralen Voraussetzungen dafür bilden, dass die Schweizer Revisionsaufsichtsbehörde von ihren ausländischen Partnerbehörden als gleichwertig anerkannt wird. Diese Anerkennung wiederum bringt den Schweizer Revisorinnen und Revisoren sowie Revisionsunternehmen administrative Vorteile, weil damit voraussichtlich die Registrierung in einigen ausländischen Revisionsregistern entfällt.

Organe

Art. 29

Die Organe der Aufsichtsbehörde sind:

a. der Aufsichtsrat;

b. die Direktorin oder der Direktor;

c. die Revisionsstelle.

Als Organe der Aufsichtsbehörde sind der Aufsichtsrat, die Direktorin oder der Direktor und die Revisionsstelle vorgesehen. Die Organisation der Aufsichtsbehörde entspricht damit derjenigen von diversen vergleichbaren Institutionen (vgl. beispielsweise Art. 3 des Bundesgesetzes vom 24. März 1995 über Statut und Aufgaben des Eidgenössischen Instituts für Geistiges Eigentum, IGEG, SR *172.010.31*; oder Art. 71 des Bundesgesetzes vom 15. Dezember 2000 über Arzneimittel und Medizinprodukte, Heilmittelgesetz, HMG, SR *812.21*).

Aufsichtsrat

Art. 30

1 Der Bundesrat wählt den Verwaltungsrat, bestimmt das Präsidium sowie das Vizepräsidium und legt die Entschädigung fest.

2 Der Aufsichtsrat besteht aus höchstens fünf Mitgliedern. Er wird für eine Amtsdauer von vier Jahren gewählt. Die Mitglieder müssen fachkundig und von der Revisionsbranche unabhängig sein.

3 Der Aufsichtsrat ist das oberste Organ der Revisionsaufsichtsbehörde. Er hat folgende Aufgaben:

a. Er regelt die Organisation und erlässt Vorschriften über weitere Angelegenheiten, deren Regelung der Aufsichtsbehörde übertragen ist.

b. Er wählt die Direktorin oder den Direktor unter Vorbehalt der Genehmigung durch den Bundesrat.

c. Er überwacht die Erfüllung der Aufgaben durch die Direktorin oder den Direktor.

d. Er genehmigt die Tätigkeitsberichte.

e. Er genehmigt den Voranschlag und die Jahresrechnung.

4 Für das Honorar der Mitglieder des Aufsichtsrates und die weiteren mit diesen Personen vereinbarten Vertragsbedingungen findet Art. 6a Abs. 1–5 des Bundespersonalgesetzes vom 24. März 2000[216] entsprechende Anwendung.

Gemäss *Abs. 1* wählt der Bundesrat den Aufsichtsrat und bestimmt, wer das Präsidium und das Vizepräsidium innehat.

Angesichts der eng umschriebenen Aufgabenstellung der Aufsichtsbehörde und der notwendigen fachlichen Spezialisierung der für diese tätigen Personen sollte der Aufsichtsrat nicht zu gross sein. Zudem wird die Aufsichtsbehörde im Vergleich zu anderen Anstalten des Bundes einen relativ kleinen Personalbestand aufweisen. *Abs. 2* sieht daher vor, dass die Aufsichtsbehörde von maximal fünf Aufsichtsrätinnen oder Aufsichtsräten geleitet werden soll.

Da die Aufsichtsbehörde über eine hohe Sachkompetenz im Bereich der Revision verfügen muss, rechtfertigt es sich, auch an die Mitglieder des Aufsichtsrates fachliche Anforderungen zu stellen und als Wählbarkeitsvoraussetzung das erforderliche Fachwissen zu statuieren.

Nur eine unabhängige Revisionsaufsicht ist glaubwürdig; daher dürfen bei den Mitgliedern des Aufsichtsrates keine Interessenkollisionen vorliegen. Zudem bildet die Unabhängigkeit von der Revisionsbranche eine wesent-

---

216 SR **172.220.1**

liche Voraussetzung der Gleichwertigkeitsanerkennung der Schweizer Revisionsaufsichtsbehörde durch ihre ausländischen Partnerbehörden.

Die Aufsichtsrätinnen und Aufsichtsräte dürfen insbesondere keine Revisionsdienstleistungen erbringen oder Organe bzw. Angestellte eines Revisionsunternehmens sein. Nicht unabhängig wäre beispielsweise auch eine Person, die im Auftragsverhältnis als Beraterin oder Berater für ein Revisionsunternehmen tätig ist. Die Amtsdauer der Aufsichtsrätinnen und Aufsichtsräten beträgt vier Jahre, was die Unabhängigkeit der Mitglieder der Aufsichtsbehörde unterstreicht.

In *Abs. 3* werden die Aufgaben des Aufsichtsrates aufgeführt. Der Aufsichtsrat hat im Gegensatz zu Behördenkommissionen wie der EBK keine materiellen Einzelfall-Entscheide zu fällen oder Verwaltungsverfügungen zu erlassen.

In *lit. a* wird dem Aufsichtsrat die Kompetenz zur Regelung der Organisation der Aufsichtsbehörde im Einzelnen übertragen. Die damit verbundene Autonomie im organisatorischen Bereich soll die Unabhängigkeit der Aufsichtsbehörde unterstützen. Soweit der Aufsichtsbehörde der Erlass von Ausführungsbestimmungen übertragen wird (s. dazu Art. 43 Satz 2 E RAG), ist hierfür der Aufsichtsrat und nicht der Direktor oder die Direktorin zuständig.

Die weit gehende Autonomie der Aufsichtsbehörde wird in *lit. b* dadurch bekräftigt, dass nicht der Bundesrat, sondern der Aufsichtsrat die Direktorin oder den Direktor wählt. Da es sich beim Direktor oder der Direktorin um das oberste vollziehende Organ handelt, rechtfertigt es sich jedoch, die Wahl des Aufsichtsrates unter den Vorbehalt der Genehmigung durch den Bundesrat zu stellen.

In den *lit. c, d und e* werden die wesentlichen Instrumente aufgezählt, mit denen der Aufsichtsrat als oberstes Organ seine Verantwortung für die Aufsichtsbehörde wahrnimmt: die Überwachung der Aufgabenerfüllung durch den Direktor oder die Direktorin, die Genehmigung der Berichte über die Tätigkeit und die Praxis der Aufsichtsbehörde (vgl. Art. 20 Abs. 1 und Art. 39 Abs. 2 E RAG) sowie die Genehmigung des Voranschlags und der Jahresrechnung.

In *Abs. 4* wird für die Entschädigung der Aufsichtsrätinnen und Aufsichtsräte die sinngemässe Anwendung von Art. *6a* des Bundespersonalgesetzes (BPG, SR *172.220.1*) statuiert. Dies ist notwendig, weil das BPG grundsätzlich für den Aufsichtsrat der Aufsichtsbehörde gelten soll (zum Personal siehe Art. 34 E RAG).

Mit dem Bundesgesetz vom 20. Juni 2003 über die Entlöhnung und weitere Vertragsbedingungen des obersten Kaders und der Mitglieder leitender Organe von Unternehmen und Anstalten des Bundes (AS *2002* 297) wurde die Regelung der Anstellungsbedingungen der obersten Führungskräfte, der Mitglieder der Verwaltungsräte und analoger Leitungsgremien vereinheitlicht (vgl. BBl *2002* 7514). Mit Abs. 4 wird das Revisionsaufsichtsgesetz an das genannte Gesetz angepasst.

Direktorin oder Direktor

Art. 31

1 Die Direktorin oder der Direktor ist oberstes vollziehendes Organ und erfüllt alle Aufgaben gemäss diesem Gesetz, die nicht dem Aufsichtsrat vorbehalten sind.

2 Sie oder er erarbeitet die Entscheidgrundlagen des Aufsichtsrates und berichtet ihm regelmässig, bei besonderen Ereignissen ohne Verzug.

3 Sie oder er kann in internationalen Organisationen und Gremien mitwirken, die Angelegenheiten der Revisionsaufsicht behandeln.

Diese Bestimmung enthält den Aufgabenkatalog der Direktorin oder der Direktors.

Gemäss *Abs. 1* stellt die Direktorin oder der Direktor das oberste vollziehende Organ der Aufsichtsbehörde dar und erfüllt alle Aufgaben gemäss Gesetz, die nicht dem Aufsichtsrat vorbehalten sind. Sie oder er ist insbesondere für den Erlass der für die Zulassungs- und Aufsichtstätigkeit der Aufsichtsbehörde notwendigen Verfügungen zuständig. Der Aufsichtsrat kann jedoch abweichende Unterschriftsregelungen vorsehen (s. Art. 31 Abs. 2 lit. a E RAG).

Nach *Abs. 2* erarbeitet die Direktorin oder der Direktor die Entscheidgrundlagen des Aufsichtsrates und berichtet diesem regelmässig, bei besonderen Ereignissen ohne Verzug.

Die Direktorin oder der Direktor kann gemäss *Abs. 3* in internationalen Organisationen und Gremien mitwirken, welche Angelegenheiten der Revisionsaufsicht behandeln. Die Vertretung der Schweiz gegen aussen fällt ohne besondere Anordnung in die Zuständigkeit des Bundesrates (vgl. Art. 184 BV). Es erscheint jedoch sinnvoll, dass der Direktor oder die Direktorin im Namen der Aufsichtsbehörde in internationalen Gremien mitwirken kann, in denen aufsichtsrelevante Themen behandelt werden. Was den Abschluss von völkerrechtlichen Verträgen angeht, sollen jedoch weiterhin die regulären Zuständigkeiten gelten (vgl. dazu Art. 8 Abs. 2, Art. 27 Abs. 4 und Art. 28 Abs. 5 E RAG sowie Art. 24 Parlamentsgesetz, SR *171.10*, und Art. 7a Regierungs- und Verwaltungsorganisationsgesetz, SR *172.010*).

Revisionsstelle

Art. 32
Die Eidgenössische Finanzkontrolle besorgt die Revision der Aufsichtsbehörde nach Massgabe des Finanzkontrollgesetzes vom 28. Juni 1967[217].

Die Eidgenössische Finanzkontrolle (EFK) besorgt die Revision der Jahresrechnung der Aufsichtsbehörde nach Massgabe des Finanzkontrollgesetzes vom 28. Juni 1967 (FKG; SR *614.0*). Die Rechnungsprüfung kann nicht an ein privates Revisionsunternehmen übertragen werden, da dies mit der Unabhängigkeit der Aufsichtsbehörde nicht vereinbar wäre.

Die EFK nimmt allerdings eine genauere Kontrolle vor, als dies im Rahmen einer privatrechtlichen Revision der Fall wäre. Die EFK nimmt insbesondere auch eine Wirtschaftlichkeitsprüfung vor (vgl. Art. 5 Abs. 2 FKG). Um sicherzustellen, dass in diesem Rahmen nicht die Aufsichtstätigkeit der Aufsichtsbehörde Gegenstand der Prüfung durch die EFK wird, empfiehlt es sich, die Revision durch die EFK entsprechend einzuschränken (vgl. dazu die Ausführungen zu Art. 8 Abs. 2 E FKG).

Personal

Art. 33

1 Die Aufsichtsbehörde stellt ihr Personal öffentlich-rechtlich an.

---

217 SR **614.0**

2 Der Bundesrat erlässt die erforderlichen Vorschriften, insbesondere zur Vermeidung von Interessenkonflikten.

3 Für den Lohn der Direktorin oder des Direktors sowie der Angehörigen des geschäftsleitenden Kaders und des weiteren Personals, das in vergleichbarer Weise entlöhnt wird, sowie für die weiteren mit diesen Personen vereinbarten Vertragsbedingungen findet Art. 6*a* Abs. 1–5 des Bundespersonalgesetzes vom 24. März 2000[218] entsprechende Anwendung.

Nach *Abs. 1* stellt die Aufsichtsbehörde ihr Personal öffentlich-rechtlich an.

Der Handlungsspielraum der Aufsichtsbehörde bei den Anstellungsbedingungen des Personals muss grösser sein als derjenige, den das Bundespersonalrecht zur Verfügung stellt. Insbesondere muss die Aufsichtsbehörde bei der Entlöhnung von Fachleuten über die Ansätze des Bundespersonalrechts hinausgehen können. In *Abs. 2* wird daher der Erlass eines eigenständigen Personalstatuts durch den Bundesrat vorgesehen. Die Revisionsaufsichtsbehörde ist demnach in Übereinstimmung mit Art. 2 Abs. 1 lit. e BPG vom Geltungsbereich des BPG ausgenommen.

Wie bei den Mitgliedern des Aufsichtsrats (s. Art. 31 Abs. 2 Satz 2 E RAG) stellt sich auch für das Personal der Aufsichtsbehörde die Problematik der Unabhängigkeit von der Revisionsbranche: Die Direktorin oder der Direktor sowie das restliche Personal der Aufsichtsbehörde müssen von der Revisionsbranche hinreichend unabhängig sein. Der Bundesrat erlässt hierfür die entsprechenden Vorschriften.

In *Abs. 3* wird die sinngemässe Anwendung von Art. 6*a* BPG auf die Löhne der Direktorin oder des Direktors sowie der Angehörigen des geschäftsleitenden Kaders der Aufsichtsbehörde statuiert (vgl. dazu die Ausführungen zu Art. 31 Abs. 4 E RAG).

---

218 SR **172.220.1**

Amtsgeheimnis

Art. 34

Die Organe der Aufsichtsbehörde und ihr Personal unterstehen dem Amtsgeheimnis.

Die Organe der Aufsichtsbehörde und ihr Personal unterstehen dem Amtsgeheimnis.

Die Verletzung des Amtsgeheimnisses ist nach Art. 320 StGB.

Zur Geheimhaltungspflicht von Personen, die von der Aufsichtsbehörde im Auftragsverhältnis beigezogen werden, wird auf die Ausführungen zu Art. 21 Abs. 3 und Art. 42 Abs. 1 lit. d E RAG verwiesen.

Rechnungswesen

Art. 35

1 Der Voranschlag und die Jahresrechnung der Aufsichtsbehörde werden unabhängig vom Voranschlag und von der Rechnung des Bundes geführt.
2 Auf die Rechnungslegung finden die Bestimmungen der Art. 662a–663b des Obligationenrechts[219] entsprechende Anwendung.
3 Die Aufsichtsbehörde bildet die für die Ausübung ihrer Aufsichtstätigkeit erforderlichen Reserven im Umfang von höchstens einem Jahresbudget.

Die Art. 36 und 37 E RAG betreffen die finanztechnischen Aspekte, die als Folge der betrieblich-organisatorischen und rechnungsmässigen Verselbständigung der Aufsichtsbehörde geregelt werden müssen (s. Art. 29 Abs. 3 E RAG).

Abs. 1 sieht vor, dass der Voranschlag und die Jahresrechnung der Aufsichtsbehörde aus dem Budget und der Rechnung des Bundes ausge-

---

[219] SR 220

klammert werden. Auf die Rechnungslegung der Aufsichtsbehörde finden gemäss *Abs. 2* die Art. 662a–663b OR sinngemässe Anwendung.

Die Aufsichtsbehörde bildet nach *Abs. 3* die für die Ausübung ihrer Aufsichtstätigkeit erforderlichen Reserven im Umfang von höchstens einem Jahresbudget. Die Reserven dienen dazu, unvorhergesehene Risiken und Einnahmeschwankungen auszugleichen und geplante Investitionen, beispielsweise in den Bereichen der Informatik oder des Mobiliars, zu tätigen. Da die Äufnung dieser Reserven über einen längeren Zeitraum erfolgt, ist sie für die Revisionsbranche wirtschaftlich tragbar.

Tresorerie

Art. 36

1 Die Aufsichtsbehörde verfügt beim Bund über ein Kontokorrent und legt die überschüssigen Gelder beim Bund zu Marktzinsen an.

2 Der Bund gewährt der Aufsichtsbehörde zur Sicherstellung ihrer Zahlungsbereitschaft Darlehen zu Marktzinsen.

Die Aufsichtsbehörde verfügt gemäss *Abs. 1* über ein Kontokorrent beim Bund und legt die überschüssigen Gelder beim Bund zu Marktzinsen an. *Abs. 2* sieht vor, dass der Bund der Aufsichtsbehörde zur Sicherstellung ihrer Zahlungsbereitschaft Darlehen zu Marktzinsen gewährt.

Da die Aufsichtsbehörde öffentliche Aufgaben erfüllt, muss unter allen Umständen ihre Zahlungsbereitschaft sichergestellt und daher eine entsprechende Verpflichtung des Bundes zur Gewährung von Darlehen statuiert werden. Im Gegenzug soll die Aufsichtsbehörde überschüssige Gelder beim Bund anlegen.

Steuerbefreiung

Art. 37

Die Aufsichtsbehörde ist von jeder Besteuerung durch den Bund, die Kantone und die Gemeinden befreit.

Die Aufsichtsbehörde ist von jeder Besteuerung durch den Bund, die Kantone und die Gemeinden befreit. Die Mittel der im öffentlichen Interesse tätigen Revisionsaufsichtsbehörde sollen nicht durch die Entrichtung von Steuern geschmälert werden. Demgegenüber ist die Aufsichtsbehörde nicht von der Entrichtung von Gebühren und Kausalabgaben dispensiert.

Aufsicht

Art. 38 (ursprünglicher Botschaftsentwurf)

1 Die Aufsichtsbehörde untersteht der Aufsicht des Bundesrates. Sie tritt mit dem Bundesrat über das Eidgenössische Finanzdepartement in Kontakt.

2 Sie erstattet dem Bundesrat und der Bundesversammlung jährlich Bericht über ihre Tätigkeit.

Art. 38 (durch den Ständerat bereinigte Version)

1 Die Aufsichtsbehörde untersteht der Aufsicht des Bundesrates. Dieser entscheidet über die administrative Zuordnung.

Die Aufsichtsbehörde untersteht nach *Abs. 1 Satz 1* der Aufsicht des Bundesrates. Der Umfang der Aufsicht ist nicht derart umfassend wie bei der zentralen Bundesverwaltung. Er ist vielmehr beschränkt auf die dem Bundesrat gesetzlich eingeräumten Befugnisse wie namentlich die Wahl des Aufsichtsrates (Art. 31 Abs. 1 E RAG), den Erlass des Personalstatuts (Art. 34 Abs. 2 E RAG), die Gebührenregelung (Art. 22 Abs. 3 E RAG) oder die Information durch Berichte der Aufsichtsbehörde (Art. 39 Abs. 2 E RAG). Der Bundesrat wahrt die Unabhängigkeit der Aufsichtsbehörde nach diesem Gesetz.

Da ein Direktkontakt mit dem Bundesrat praktisch zu schwerfällig ist, tritt die Aufsichtsbehörde gemäss *Satz 2* mit dem Bundesrat über das Eidgenössische Finanzdepartement in Kontakt.

Auf Grund der Oberaufsicht der Bundesversammlung (s. Art. 169 BV) erstattet die Aufsichtsbehörde dem Bundesrat und der Bundesversammlung gemäss *Abs. 2* jährlich Bericht über ihre Tätigkeit. Zum öffentlichen Bericht über die Tätigkeit und die Praxis siehe die Ausführungen zu Art. 20 Abs. 1 E RAG.

8. Abschnitt: Strafbestimmungen

Der Entwurf unterscheidet zwei Gruppen von Delikten:

- Übertretungen werden von der Aufsichtsbehörde unter Anwendung des Verwaltungsstrafrechts sanktioniert;

- Vergehen werden von den kantonalen Strafgerichten beurteilt.

Die Doppelrolle der Aufsichtsbehörde als untersuchende Behörde einerseits und als sanktionierende Behörde andererseits sowie die Aufspaltung der Zuständigkeiten ist mit gewissen Nachteilen verbunden. Falls im Rahmen der Arbeiten zur Integrierten Finanzmarktaufsicht (FINMA) eine sinnvolle Lösung für diese Probleme erarbeitet wird, wird zu prüfen sein, ob diese auch auf das Sanktionswesen im Bereich der Revisionsaufsicht zu übertragen ist.

Die Bussenrahmen werden relativ hoch angesetzt. Der Entwurf sieht vor, dass Übertretungen mit Busse bis zu 100 000 Franken und Vergehen mit Gefängnis oder mit Busse bis zu 1 000 000 Franken bestraft werden können. Die vorgeschlagenen Bussenhöhen entsprechen den Vorschlägen zum neuen Versicherungsaufsichtsgesetz (Art. 83 f. E VAG, BBl *2003* 3900 ff.). Die Bussenhöhe beim Vergehenstatbestand (Art. 42 E RAG) entspricht dem neuen Allgemeinen Teil zum Strafgesetzbuch, wonach künftig Geldstrafen bis zu 1 080 000 Franken verhängt werden können (Art. 34 Abs. 1 und 2 nStGB). Die Bussenhöhe beim Übertretenstatbestand nach Art. 41 E RAG geht deutlich über die im neuen Allgemeinen Teil festgelegte Höchstbusse für Übertretungen von 10 000 Franken hinaus (Art. 106 Abs. 1 nStGB). Diese höhere Bussenobergrenze ist hier jedoch angesichts der wirtschaftlichen Realitäten ohne weiteres angemessen. Im Nebenstrafrecht geht die Entwicklung zudem allgemein in Richtung höhere Bussen.

Art. 41 E RAG (Übertretungen) ist prinzipiell nur auf natürliche Personen anwendbar. Die am 1. Oktober 2003 in Kraft getretene Bestimmung zur strafrechtlichen Verantwortlichkeit des Unternehmens (Art. 100quater StGB [AS *2003* 3043 f.]) gilt nur bei Vergehen und Verbrechen. Für ausgesprochene Bagatellfälle bleibt aber die Ausnahmevorschrift von Art. 7 des Verwaltungsstrafrechts (VStrR; SR *313.0*) vorbehalten. Dieser zufolge kann bei Straftaten, für die eine Busse von höchstens 5000 Franken in Betracht kommt und bei denen die Ermittlung der strafbaren Person Untersuchungsmassnahmen bedingen, die im Hinblick auf die verwirkte Strafe unverhältnismässig wären, direkt das Unternehmen zur Bezahlung der Busse verurteilt werden.

Wird in einem Unternehmen hingegen ein Vergehenstatbestand im Sinne von Art. 42 Abs. 1 E RAG begangen, ist Art. 100^{quater} StGB anwendbar. Demnach kann ein solches Vergehen dem Unternehmen zugerechnet und das Unternehmen mit Busse bis zu 5 Millionen Franken bestraft werden (Art. 100^{quater} Abs. 1 StGB), wenn diese Tat wegen einer mangelhaften Organisation des Unternehmens keiner natürlichen Person zugerechnet werden kann. In Bezug auf Art. 41 Abs. 2 E RAG, welcher bei fahrlässiger Begehung keine Gefängnisstrafe, sondern eine Busse bis zu 50 000 Franken androht, verbleibt wiederum nur die Möglichkeit der Anwendung von Art. 7 VStrR.

Übertretungen

Art. 39

1 Mit Busse bis zu 100 000 Franken wird bestraft, wer:

a. gegen die Grundsätze zur Unabhängigkeit nach Art. 11 sowie nach Art. 728 Obligationenrecht[220] verstösst;

b. gegen die Meldepflichten nach Art. 15 verstösst;

c. gegen die Mitteilungspflicht nach Art. 16 Abs. 3 verstösst;

d. gegen eine Ausführungsbestimmung zu diesem Gesetz verstösst, deren Übertretung vom Bundesrat für strafbar erklärt wird;

e. gegen eine Verfügung oder Massnahme der Aufsichtsbehörde verstösst, die unter Hinweis auf die Strafdrohung dieses Artikels erlassen wurde.

2 Handelt der Täter fahrlässig, so wird er mit Busse bis zu 50 000 Franken bestraft.

---

220 SR **220**

3 Die Aufsichtsbehörde verfolgt und beurteilt diese Widerhandlungen nach den Vorschriften des Bundesgesetzes vom 22. März 1974[221] über das Verwaltungsstrafrecht.

4 Die Verfolgung von Übertretungen verjährt nach sieben Jahren.

Diese Bestimmung erfasst Delikte von geringerer Schwere. Mit einer Busse bis zu 100 000 Franken wird gemäss *Abs. 1* bestraft, wer:

- *Lit.a:* gegen die Grundsätze zur Unabhängigkeit nach Art. 11 bzw. Art. 728 des OR verstösst;
- *Lit.b:* gegen die Meldepflichten nach Art. 15 verstösst;
- *Lit.c:* gegen die Mitteilungspflicht nach Art. 16 Abs. 3 verstösst;
- *Lit.d:* gegen eine Ausführungsbestimmung zu diesem Gesetz verstösst, deren Übertretung vom Bundesrat für strafbar erklärt wurde;
- *Lit.e:* gegen eine Verfügung oder Massnahme der Aufsichtsbehörde verstösst, die unter Hinweis auf die Strafdrohung dieses Artikels erlassen wurde; bei der Verfügung kann es sich auch um eine Anweisung i.S.v. Art. 17 Abs. 4 E RAG handeln.

Der Entwurf verzichtet auf eine Strafnorm betreffend Verstösse gegen die Pflichten zur Qualitätssicherung nach Art. 12 E RAG, weil das zu bestrafende Verhalten für einen Straftatbestand nicht in allgemeiner Weise hinreichend klar und konkret umschrieben werden kann (strafrechtlicher Bestimmtheitsgrundsatz). Die Aufsichtsbehörde kann jedoch Missstände im Bereich der Qualitätssicherung dadurch strafrechtlich sanktionieren, dass sie konkrete Anweisungen erlässt und diese mit einer Strafdrohung nach Abs. 1 lit. e E RAG verbindet.

Handelt der Täter bei einem der in Abs. 1 aufgeführten Delikte fahrlässig, so wird er gemäss *Abs. 2* mit Busse bis zu 50 000 Franken bestraft.

Die Verfolgung und Beurteilung dieser Übertretungen liegt gemäss *Abs. 3* in der Kompetenz der Aufsichtsbehörde und erfolgt unter Anwendung der Vorschriften des VStrR.

Die Verfolgung der Übertretungen verjährt gemäss geltendem Recht nach vier Jahren (Art. 11 Abs. 1 VStrR i.V.m. Art. 333 Abs. 5 lit. b StGB; nach Inkrafttreten der Änderung vom 13. Dezember 2002 des Strafgesetzbuchs

---

221 SR **313.0**

[BBl *2002* 8240] Art. 11 Abs. 1 VStrR i.V.m. Art. 333 Abs. 6 lit. b nStGB). Diese Verjährungsfrist wird mit *Abs. 4* auf 7 Jahre erhöht und damit an die Verjährungsfrist von Vergehen angepasst (vgl. dazu die Ausführungen zu Art. 42 E RAG).

Vergehen

Art. 40 (ursprünglicher Botschaftsentwurf)
1 Mit Gefängnis oder mit Busse bis zu 1 000 000 Franken wird bestraft, wer[222]:

a. eine Revisionsdienstleistung ohne die erforderliche Zulassung oder trotz Verbot zur Ausübung seiner Tätigkeit erbringt;

b. der Aufsichtsbehörde die verlangten Auskünfte nicht erteilt oder ihr die verlangten Unterlagen nicht herausgibt, ihr gegenüber falsche oder unvollständige Angaben macht oder ihr keinen Zutritt zu seinen Geschäftsräumlichkeiten gewährt (Art. 13);

c. gegen die Pflichten zur Dokumentation und zur Aufbewahrung verstösst (Art. 13);

d. während oder nach Beendigung der Tätigkeit als von der Aufsichtsbehörde beauftragte Drittperson (Art. 21) ein Geheimnis offenbart, das ihr in dieser Eigenschaft anvertraut worden ist oder das sie in dieser Eigenschaft wahrgenommen hat; vorbehalten bleiben die eidgenössischen und kantonalen Bestimmungen über die Zeugnispflicht und die Auskunftspflicht gegenüber einer Behörde.

2 Wird die Tat fahrlässig begangen, so ist die Strafe Busse bis zu 100 000 Franken.[223].

3 Strafverfolgung und Beurteilung sind Sache der Kantone.

---

222 Bei Inkrafttreten der Änderung vom 13. Dezember 2002 des Strafgesetzbuches (BBl **2002** 8240) erhält der Ingress von Artikel 42 Abs. 1 die folgende Fassung:1 Mit Freiheitsstrafe bis zu drei Jahren oder mit Geldstrafe wird bestraft, wer ...:

223 Bei Inkrafttreten der Änderung vom 13. Dezember 2002 des Strafgesetzbuches (BBl **2002** 8240) erhält Artikel 42 Abs. 2 die folgende Fassung:2 Handelt der Täter fahrlässig, so wird er mit Busse bestraft.

Art. 40 (durch den Nationalrat bereinigte Version)

1 Mit Gefängnis oder mit Busse bis zu 1 000 000 Franken wird bestraft, wer:

c. als staatlich beaufsichtigtes Revisionsunternehmen gegen die Pflichten zur Dokumentation und zur Aufbewahrung verstösst (Art. 730c des Obligationenrechtes);

Diese Vorschrift erfasst schwerere Delikte. Mit Gefängnis oder einer Busse bis zu 1 000 000 Franken werden die nachfolgenden, in *Abs. 1* umschriebenen Delikte geahndet:

– Nach *lit. a* wird bestraft, wer eine Revisionsdienstleistung ohne die erforderliche Zulassung (s. Art. 4–8 E RAG) oder trotz Verbot zur Ausübung dieser Tätigkeit (s. Art. 18 f. E RAG, aber auch Art. 54 StGB und Art. 67 nStGB) erbringt.

– Nach *lit. b* wird bestraft, wer gegenüber der Aufsichtsbehörde die verlangten Auskünfte nicht erteilt, die verlangten Unterlagen nicht herausgibt oder ihr gegenüber falsche oder unvollständige Angaben macht oder ihr keinen Zutritt zu seinen Geschäftsräumlichkeiten gewährt (s. Art. 14 E RAG). Die Strafbarkeit setzt die Missachtung einer rechtskräftigen Verfügung voraus. Diese Vorschrift gilt auch für von der Aufsichtsbehörde beauftragte Drittpersonen (s. Art. 21 E RAG).

– Nach *lit. c* wird bestraft, wer gegen die Pflichten zur Dokumentation und zur Aufbewahrung nach Art. 13 E RAG verstösst. Diese Bestimmung steht in einem engen sachlichen Zusammenhang mit den in lit. b erfassten Straftatbeständen. Die Ahndung als Vergehen trägt der Bedeutung Rechnung, die der Dokumentations- und Aufbewahrungspflicht gerade in Problemfällen zukommen kann.

– Nach *lit. d* wird bestraft, wer während oder nach Beendigung der Tätigkeit als von der Aufsichtsbehörde beauftragte Drittperson (s. Art. 21 E RAG) ein Geheimnis offenbart, das ihr in dieser Eigenschaft anvertraut worden ist oder das sie in dieser Eigenschaft wahrgenommen hat. Vorbehalten bleiben die eidgenössischen und kantonalen Bestimmungen über die Zeugnispflicht und die Auskunftspflicht gegenüber einer Behörde.

Bei Inkrafttreten der Änderung vom 13. Dezember 2002 des StGB (BBl *2002* 8240) erhält der Ingress von Art. 42 Abs. 1 E RAG die folgende Fassung:

«¹ Mit Freiheitsstrafe bis zu drei Jahren oder mit Geldstrafe wird bestraft, wer ...»

Die vorsätzliche Tatbegehung wird mit Gefängnis oder mit Busse bis zu 1 000 000 Franken bestraft. Unter Berücksichtigung der wirtschaftlichen Realitäten und der Höhe des immensen Schadens, der durch mangelhafte Revisionsarbeiten entstehen kann, erscheint der hohe Bussenrahmen gerechtfertigt.

Handelt der Täter fahrlässig, so wird er gemäss *Abs. 2* mit Busse bis zu 100 000 Franken bestraft.

Bei Inkrafttreten der Änderung vom 13. Dezember 2002 des StGB (BBl *2002* 8240) erhält Art. 42 Abs. 2 E RAG die folgende Fassung:

«² Handelt der Täter fahrlässig, so wird er mit Busse bestraft.»

Die Untersuchung und Strafverfolgung der Vergehenstatbestände obliegt gemäss *Abs. 3* den Kantonen. Zur Rechtshilfe zwischen den Strafverfolgungsbehörden und der Aufsichtsbehörde wird auf Art. 25 Abs. 1 und 2 E RAG verwiesen.

Die Vergehen gemäss Abs. 1 verjähren nach sieben Jahren (s. Art. 70 Abs. 1 lit. c StGB bzw. Art. 97 Abs. 1 lit. c nStGB).[224]

9. Abschnitt: Schlussbestimmungen

Vollzug

Art. 41

Der Bundesrat erlässt die Ausführungsbestimmungen. Er kann die Aufsichtsbehörde ermächtigen, weitere Ausführungsbestimmungen zu erlassen.

---

[224] Die vorliegenden Erläuterungen beziehen sich ausschliesslich auf die ursprüngliche bundesrätliche Gesetzesversion und nicht auf die bereinigte Fassung durch den Nationalrat.

Der Bundesrat erlässt gemäss *Satz 1* die Ausführungsbestimmungen zu diesem Gesetz. Die grosse Dynamik am Kapitalmarkt erfordert eine hohe Flexibilität beim Erlass der in diesem Bereich notwendigen generell-abstrakten Regelungen. Eine Kompetenzdelegation an den Bundesrat zum Erlass von Ausführungsbestimmungen drängt sich daher auf. Die vorliegende Delegationsnorm ermöglicht es aber nicht, Bestimmungen zu erlassen, die von ihrer Bedeutung her auf Gesetzesstufe zu regeln wären.

Der Bundesrat kann auf Grund von *Satz 2* die Aufsichtsbehörde ermächtigen, weitere Ausführungsbestimmungen zu erlassen. Die Detailregelung der Aufsicht umfasst komplexe technische Fragen, die auf Grund der grösseren Sachnähe bei Bedarf der Aufsichtsbehörde übertragen werden sollen. Der Aufsichtsbehörde dürfen jedoch nur Sachverhalte von untergeordneter Bedeutung zur Regelung überlassen werden.

Änderungen bisherigen Rechts

Art. 42

Die Änderung bisherigen Rechts wird im Anhang geregelt.

Übergangsbestimmungen

Art. 43

1 Erfüllt eine natürliche Person oder ein Revisionsunternehmen die Aufgaben einer Revisionsstelle, so gelten die Vorschriften dieses Gesetzes, sobald auf die zu prüfende juristische Person die neuen Vorschriften zur Revisionsstelle vom … Anwendung finden.

2 Erbringen natürliche Personen oder Revisionsunternehmen andere Revisionsdienstleistungen, so findet das neue Recht mit Inkrafttreten dieses Gesetzes Anwendung.

3 Natürliche Personen und Revisionsunternehmen, die bis vier Monate nach Inkrafttreten dieses Gesetzes bei der Aufsichtsbehörde ein Gesuch um Zulassung als Revisorin, Revisor, Revisionsexpertin, Revisionsexperte oder staatlich beaufsichtigtes Revisionsunternehmen

einreichen, dürfen bis zum Entscheid über die Zulassung Revisionsdienstleistungen im Sinne von Art. 2 lit. a erbringen. Die Aufsichtsbehörde bestätigt der Gesuchstellerin oder dem Gesuchsteller schriftlich die fristgerechte Einreichung des Gesuchs. Sie macht der Börse Mitteilung über die eingereichten Gesuche um Zulassung als staatlich beaufsichtigtes Revisionsunternehmen.

4 Fachpraxis, die bis zwei Jahre nach Inkrafttreten dieses Gesetzes unter der Beaufsichtigung von Personen erworben wurde, welche die Voraussetzungen nach der Verordnung vom 15. Juni 1992[225] über die fachlichen Anforderungen an besonders befähigte Revisoren erfüllen, gilt als Fachpraxis im Sinne von Art. 4.

5 Fachpraxis, die bis zwei Jahre nach Inkrafttreten dieses Gesetzes unter der Beaufsichtigung von Personen erworben wurde, welche die Voraussetzungen an die Ausbildung nach Art. 4 Abs. 2 erfüllen, gilt als Fachpraxis im Sinne von Art. 5.

6 Die Aufsichtsbehörde kann in Härtefällen auch Fachpraxis anerkennen, die den gesetzlichen Anforderungen nicht genügt, sofern eine einwandfreie Erbringung von Revisionsdienstleistungen auf Grund einer langjährigen praktischen Erfahrung nachgewiesen wird.

Erfüllt eine natürliche Person oder ein Revisionsunternehmen die Aufgaben einer Revisionsstelle, so gelten gemäss *Abs. 1* die Vorschriften des Revisionsaufsichtsgesetzes, sobald auf die zu prüfende juristische Person (also Gesellschaften, Vereine und Stiftungen) die neuen Vorschriften des Obligationenrechts bzw. des Zivilgesetzbuches zur Revisionsstelle Anwendung finden.

Erbringen natürliche Personen oder Revisionsunternehmen andere Revisionsdienstleistungen als die in Abs. 1 erfasste Prüfung der Jahres- und Konzernrechnung, so findet das Revisionsaufsichtsgesetz gemäss *Abs. 2* mit seinem Inkrafttreten Anwendung.

Das intertemporale Recht des Revisionsaufsichtsgesetzes wird durch die Abs. 1 und 2 auf die Übergangsbestimmungen des Entwurfs zur Revision des Rechts der GmbH abgestimmt (wobei Art. 7 E ÜBest in der Fassung des Entwurfs zur GmbH-Revision durch den vorliegenden Entwurf modi-

---

225 SR **221.302**

fiziert wird; siehe dazu die Ausführungen zu Art. 7 E ÜBest in der neuen Fassung).

Dies bedeutet, dass sich eine Revisionsstelle nach Abs. 1 so lange nicht den Bestimmungen des Revisionsaufsichtsgesetzes anpassen muss, als die zu prüfende Gesellschaft, der zu prüfende Verein oder die zu prüfende Stiftung nicht verpflichtet ist, ihre Jahres- bzw. Konzernrechnung nach neuem Revisionsrecht prüfen zu lassen.

Umgekehrt ist das Revisionsaufsichtsgesetz für besondere, punktuelle Prüfvorgänge gemäss Abs. 2 (z.B. eine Kapitalherabsetzungsprüfung nach Art. 732 Abs. 2 E OR) sofort anwendbar. Wer als Fachperson oder als Revisionsunternehmen mit einer solchen Prüfung beauftragt ist, muss demnach über die von diesem Gesetz vorgeschriebene Zulassung verfügen. Das Gleiche ergibt sich aus dem Fehlen einer besonderen Übergangsregelung auch für die entsprechenden neuen Vorschriften des Obligationenrechts (s. Art. 1 Abs. 3 SchlT ZGB i.V.m. Art. 1 Abs. 1 E ÜBest OR). Die vorgesehene übergangsrechtliche Ordnung entspricht derjenigen des neuen Aktienrechts von 1991[226].

Während die Abs. 1 und 2 den Zeitpunkt bestimmen, von welchem an die neuen Vorschriften grundsätzlich Anwendung finden, sieht *Abs. 3* für den Übergang zum neuen Recht eine Erleichterung betreffend das Zulassungsverfahren vor: Natürliche Personen und Revisionsunternehmen, die bis 4 Monate nach Inkrafttreten dieses Gesetzes bei der Aufsichtsbehörde ein Gesuch um Zulassung als Revisorin, Revisor, Revisionsexpertin, Revisionsexperte oder staatlich beaufsichtigtes Revisionsunternehmen einreichen, dürfen bis zum Entscheid über die Zulassung Revisionsdienstleistungen i.S.v. Art. 2 lit. a erbringen. Die fristgerechte Einreichung eines Zulassungsgesuchs bewirkt somit eine provisorische Zulassung. Die Aufsichtsbehörde bestätigt der Gesuchstellerin oder dem Gesuchsteller schriftlich die fristgerechte Einreichung des Gesuchs. Gesuche, die offensichtlich nicht vollständig oder aussichtslos sind, können von der Aufsichtsbehörde umgehend abgewiesen werden. Die Aufsichtsbehörde macht der Börse Mitteilung über die eingereichten Gesuche um Zulassung als staatlich beaufsichtigte Revisionsunternehmen.

Die in Abs. 3 vorgesehene Frist dient der zeitlichen Begrenzung der privilegierenden Übergangsregelung zum neuen Recht. Zulassungsgesuche, die nach Ablauf dieser Frist eingereicht werden, bewirken keine provisorische

---

[226] s. dazu PETER BÖCKLI, Schweizer Aktienrecht, 2. Aufl., Zürich 1996, N 2144–2150.

Zulassung mehr: Die betreffenden Gesuchstellerinnen und Gesuchsteller dürfen demnach Revisionsdienstleistungen i.S.v. Art. 2 lit. a erst erbringen, wenn die Aufsichtsbehörde ihnen die beantragte Zulassung erteilt hat.

Nach *Abs. 4* gilt Fachpraxis, die bis 2 Jahre nach Inkrafttreten dieses Gesetzes unter der Beaufsichtigung von Personen erworben wurde, welche die Voraussetzungen nach der Verordnung vom 15. Juni 1992[227] über die fachlichen Anforderungen an besonders befähigte Revisoren erfüllen, als Fachpraxis i.S.v. Art. 4 E RAG. Mit dieser Regelung wird die Anrechnung der unter dem bisherigen Recht erworbenen Fachpraxis sichergestellt. Zudem wird gewährleistet, dass noch unter dem bisherigen Recht begonnene Praktika ohne Nachteile bis 2 Jahre nach dem Inkrafttreten des neuen Rechts fortgesetzt werden können, auch wenn sie unter Beaufsichtigung einer Person absolviert werden, welche kein Gesuch um Zulassung nach neuem Recht stellt. Es wird in diesem Zusammenhang aber darauf hingewiesen, dass Personen, welche die Voraussetzungen für besonders befähigte Revisorinnen und Revisoren erfüllen, auch diejenigen des neuen Rechts für zugelassene Revisionsexpertinnen und Revisionsexperten erfüllen.

Für die Zulassung als Revisorin oder Revisor gilt Fachpraxis, die bis 2 Jahre nach Inkrafttreten dieses Gesetzes unter der Beaufsichtigung von Personen erworben wurde, welche die Voraussetzungen an die Ausbildung gemäss Art. 4 Abs. 2 E RAG erfüllen, nach *Abs. 5* als Fachpraxis i.S.v. Art. 5 E RAG. Für den Nachweis der Fachpraxis wird hierbei lediglich auf die Ausbildung derjenigen Personen abgestellt, unter deren Beaufsichtigung die praktische Erfahrung erworben wurde. Verzichtet wird jedoch auf den Nachweis, dass die beaufsichtigenden Personen ihrerseits über eine praktische Erfahrung verfügen, die unter Beaufsichtigung entsprechender Fachpersonen erworben wurde. Die Anforderungen an die Beaufsichtigung des Erwerbs der praktischen Erfahrung würden sich sonst endlos in die Vergangenheit fortsetzen. Eine entsprechende übergangsrechtliche Sonderregelung ist daher aus sachlichen Gründen unabdingbar.

Nach *Abs. 6* kann die Aufsichtsbehörde in Härtefällen auch Fachpraxis anerkennen, die nicht der gesetzlichen Regelung entspricht, falls eine einwandfreie Erbringung von Revisionsdienstleistungen auf Grund einer langjährigen praktischen Erfahrung nachgewiesen wird. Unter bestimmten Umständen kann es sich als schwierig erweisen, die notwendigen Nachweise für die erworbene Fachpraxis zu erbringen. So ist denkbar, dass die

---

[227] SR **221.302**

Fachpraxis bei Personen erworben wurde, die verstorben sind und deren Fachdiplome nicht mehr beigebracht werden können. Für entsprechende Fälle enthält der Entwurf die vorliegende Härteklausel. Unter Berücksichtigung des Normzwecks hat die Aufsichtsbehörde jedoch nur restriktiv Gebrauch von dieser Sondervorschrift zu machen: Die Ausnahmeregelung soll insbesondere nicht ermöglichen, Praktikerinnen und Praktiker ohne eine abgeschlossene Ausbildung nach Art. 4 Abs. 2 E RAG oder ohne qualifizierte Berufserfahrung als Revisionsexpertinnen, Revisionsexperten, Revisorinnen oder Revisoren zuzulassen. Sie muss auf Personen beschränkt bleibt, die über ein Diplom und eine langjährige praktische Erfahrung verfügen (dies gilt auch für zuzulassende Revisorinnen und Revisoren); andernfalls wäre die Durchsetzung der Neuordnung nicht gewährleistet.

Übergangsbestimmungen zum Rechtsschutz

Art. 44

Bis zum Inkrafttreten des Verwaltungsgerichtsgesetzes vom 17. Juni 2005 wird der Rechtsschutz in Ergänzung zu den allgemeinen Bestimmungen über die Bundesrechtspflege wie folgt geregelt: Die Rekurskommission EVD beurteilt Beschwerden gegen Verfügungen der Aufsichtsbehörde.

Referendum und Inkrafttreten

Art. 45

1 Dieses Gesetz untersteht dem fakultativen Referendum.

2 Der Bundesrat bestimmt das Inkrafttreten.

Das Gesetz untersteht nach *Abs. 1* dem fakultativen Referendum.

Der Bundesrat bestimmt auf Grund von *Abs. 2* über das Inkrafttreten. Es steht ihm dabei offen, auch ein gestaffeltes Inkrafttreten des Gesetzes festzulegen. Insbesondere könnte es sich unter Umständen als vorteilhaft erweisen, Art. 8 E RAG nach den übrigen Bestimmungen in Kraft setzen: Die Beaufsichtigung der Revisionsunternehmen von ausländischen Gesellschaften soll gemäss Art. 8 Abs. 2 E RAG soweit möglich an die Aufsichtsbehörden in deren Sitzstaaten delegiert werden. Da es denkbar ist, dass sich diese Aufsichtsbehörden beim Inkrafttreten des RAG noch im Aufbau befinden, kann der Bundesrat auf diese Tatsache Rücksicht nehmen. Art. 8 E RAG soll erst dann in Kraft treten, wenn in den relevanten Staaten Aufsichtsbehörden bestehen, die vom Bundesrat anerkannt werden können.

II. Änderungen bisherigen Rechts

1. Bundesgesetz über die Eidgenössische Finanzkontrolle[228]

II. Aufgaben, Bereich und Durchführung der Kontrolle

Bereich der Aufsicht

Art. 8 Abs. 2

² Die eidgenössischen Gerichte und die Eidgenössische Revisionsaufsichtsbehörde unterstehen der Finanzaufsicht durch die Eidgenössische Finanzkontrolle, soweit sie der Ausübung der Oberaufsicht durch die Bundesversammlung dient.

Die eidgenössischen Gerichte und die Eidgenössische Revisionsaufsichtsbehörde unterstehen gemäss *Abs. 2* der Finanzaufsicht durch die Eidgenössische Finanzkontrolle (EFK), soweit sie der Ausübung der Oberaufsicht durch die Bundesversammlung dient.

Diese Ergänzung verfolgt den Zweck, den Umfang der Finanzaufsicht der EFK zu beschränken. Es handelt sich nur um eine administrative und finanzielle Kontrolle, nicht jedoch um eine Beurteilung der Aufsichtstätigkeit (vgl. auch die Ausführungen zu Art. 33 E RAG).

---

[228] SR **614**

2. Börsengesetz[229]

2. Abschnitt: Börsen

Zulassung von Effekten

Art. 8 Abs. 3bis

3bis Es macht die Zulassung von Beteiligungspapieren und Anleihensobligationen davon abhängig, dass die Art. 7 und 8 des Bundesgesetzes vom ...[230] über die Zulassung und Beaufsichtigung der Revisorinnen und Revisoren eingehalten werden.

Die Vorschrift von Art. 8 Abs. 1 des BEHG hält den Grundsatz der Selbstregulierung durch die Börse fest. Das Modell der Selbstregulierung hat sich in diesem Bereich bewährt. Aus übergeordneten Interessen muss jedoch mit dem neuen *Abs. 3bis* eine beschränkte Ausnahme statuiert werden.

Neu schreibt das Börsengesetz vor, dass das Kotierungsreglement der Börse die Zulassung von Beteiligungspapieren und Anleihensobligationen davon abhängig machen muss, dass die Art. 7 und 8 RAG eingehalten werden.

Soll die Schweizer Revisionsaufsichtsbehörde die auf dem Börsenplatz Schweiz aktiven Investorinnen und Investoren glaubwürdig vor qualitativ unbefriedigenden Revisionsdienstleistungen schützen, so muss sie allfällige Verstösse sanktionieren können. Dies ist mit dem befristeten und unbefristeten Entzug der Zulassung für staatlich beaufsichtigte Revisionsunternehmen (s. Art. 18 Abs. 2 E RAG), mit Verboten der Tätigkeitsausübung gegenüber natürlichen Personen (s. Art. 19 E RAG) und mit den Straftatbeständen nach den Art. 41 und 42 E RAG für Revisionsgesellschaften mit Sitz in der Schweiz gewährleistet.

Schwieriger gestaltet sich die Sanktionierung, wenn ein Revisionsunternehmen mit Sitz im Ausland gegen die Bestimmungen dieses Gesetzes verstösst. Gegen diese Unternehmen können grundsätzlich keine Sanktionen durchgesetzt werden.

---

229 SR **954.1**
230 SR ...; AS ... (BBl **2004** 4139)

Die einzige Sanktion, die ein ausländisches Revisionsunternehmen dazu zwingt, die Prüfung gemäss den in der Schweiz massgebenden Grundsätzen vorzunehmen, ist die Androhung, dass andernfalls die geprüfte Gesellschaft von der Schweizer Börse im Rahmen der Kompetenzen der Selbstregulierung sanktioniert wird. Das geprüfte Unternehmen wird damit indirekt dazu gezwungen, nur Revisionsunternehmen mit Revisionsdienstleistungen zu beauftragen, die in der Schweiz registriert sind oder durch eine vom Bundesrat anerkannte Aufsichtsbehörde beaufsichtigt werden (s. dazu die Ausführungen zu Art. 8 E RAG).

Die Zulassungsbehörde der Börse wird daher von Gesetzes wegen verpflichtet, die Einhaltung der Art. 7 und 8 E RAG als Bedingung der Erstkotierung von Beteiligungspapieren und Anleihensobligationen zu behandeln. Aus Gründen der Gleichbehandlung gilt diese Vorschrift sowohl für inländische als auch für ausländische Effekten. Die Kotierung von Beteiligungspapieren und Anleihensobligationen, deren Emittenten diese Bedingung nicht erfüllen, ist demnach nicht statthaft. Erfüllt eine emittierende Gesellschaft diese Bedingung nachträglich nicht mehr, so ergreift die Schweizer Börse die erforderlichen Sanktionen gegen die Emittentin (s. dazu Art. 24 Abs. 3 E RAG).

Diese Sanktionierung ist grundsätzlich nur für ausländische Emittenten notwendig; für Publikumsgesellschaften mit Sitz in der Schweiz sind die Sanktionsmöglichkeiten der Revisionsaufsichtsbehörde genügend.

Teil F: Rechtliche Aspekte / Legal aspects

Teil G

Anhänge und Unterlagen / Appendices and Documents

Kapitel 1:
Bilanz, Erfolgsrechnung, Anhang, Vollständigkeitserklärung, Geschäftsbericht als Muster

§ 1   Bilanz

AKTIVEN

Umlaufvermögen:
- Flüssige Mittel
- Forderungen aus Lieferungen und Leistungen
- Andere Forderungen
- Forderungen gegenüber Aktionären
- Nicht einbezahlter Teil des Aktienkapitals
- Vorräte
- Transitorische Aktiven

Anlagevermögen:
- Finanzanlagen
- Beteiligungen
- Sachanlagen
- Immaterielle Anlagen
- Aktivierte Gründungskosten

PASSIVEN

Fremdkapital:
- Schulden aus Lieferungen und Leistungen
- Andere kurzfristige Schulden

Kapitel 1: Bilanz, Erfolgsrechnung, Anhang, Vollständigkeitserklärung, Muster

- Langfristige Verbindlichkeiten
- Verbindlichkeiten gegenüber Aktionären
- Rückstellungen
- Transitorische Passiven

Eigenkapital:

- Aktienkapital
- Allgemeine gesetzliche Reserven
- Andere Reserven
- Fakultativ: Aufwertungsreserve
- Bilanzgewinn/-verlust

§ 2 Erfolgsrechnung

ERTRAG

- Umsatz (Erlöse aus Lieferungen und Leistungen)
- Finanzertrag
- Veräusserungsgewinne (aus Anlagevermögen)
- Ausserordentlicher Ertrag
- Betriebsfremder Ertrag
- Verlust

AUFWAND

- Material- und Warenaufwand
- Personalaufwand
- Finanzaufwand
- Aufwand für Abschreibungen

Teil G: Anhänge und Unterlagen / Appendices and documents

- Aufwand für Rückstellungen
- Übrige Betriebsaufwendungen
- Ausserordentliche Aufwendungen
- Betriebsfremder Aufwand
- Gewinn

§ 3 Anhang

1. Bürgschaften, Garantieverpflichtungen, Pfandbestellungen zu Gunsten Dritter

- Bürgschaften CHF
- Garantieverpflichtungen CHF
- Pfandbestellungen zu Gunsten Dritter CHF

2. Verpfändete Aktiven/Aktiven unter Eigentumsvorbehalt

- Zur Sicherung eigener Verpflichtungen verpfändete oder abgetretene Aktiven CHF
- Aktiven unter Eigentumsvorbehalt CHF

3. Nicht bilanzierte Leasingverpflichtungen

- Vorräte CHF
- Maschinen CHF
- Mobiliar CHF
- Geräte CHF
- Werkzeuge CHF
- Fahrzeuge CHF
- Übrige CHF

Kapitel 1: Bilanz, Erfolgsrechnung, Anhang, Vollständigkeitserklärung, Muster

4. Brandversicherungswerte
- Immobilien CHF
- Bewegliche Sachanlagen CHF

5. Verbindlichkeiten gegenüber Vorsorgeeinrichtungen
- Schuld CHF

6. Anleihensobligationen
- i.d.R. keine Angabe

7. Wesentliche Beteiligungen
- Firma
- Sitz
- Zweck
- Quote
- Aktienkapital

8. Aufgelöste stille Reserven
- Wiederbeschaffungsreserven CHF
- Darüber hinausgehende stille Reserven CHF

9. Aufwertungen
- Immobilien: Anschaffungswert, Verkehrswert, Aufwertung CHF
- Beteiligungen: Anschaffungswert, Verkehrswert, Aufwertung CHF

10. Eigene Aktien (inkl. Tochtergesellschaften)
- i.d.R. keine Angabe

11. Kapitalerhöhungen
- i.d.R. keine Angabe

Teil G: Anhänge und Unterlagen / Appendices and documents

12. Risikobeurteilung

- Analytischer Bericht über die Risikobeurteilung

13. Rücktritt der Revisionsstelle

- Allfällige Angaben des Grundes für den Rücktritt der Revisionsstelle

14. Andere Angaben

Abweichungen von Grundsätzen ordnungsmässiger Rechnungslegung

- Unternehmensfortführung
- Stetigkeit der Darstellung
- Bewertungen
- Verrechnungsverbot
- Information zur steuerlichen Situation

§ 4 Gewinnverwendungsvorschlag

Gewinn des Geschäftsjahres	10'000.–
Gewinnvortrag	10'000.–
Zur Verfügung der Generalversammlung	20'000.–

Einlage 1: Gesetzliche Reserven 500.–

5 % des Jahresgewinnes sind den allgemeinen gesetzlichen Reserven zuzuweisen, bis diese 20 % des einbezahlten Aktienkapitals erreicht haben (Art. 671 Abs. 1 OR).

Einlage 2: Gesetzliche Reserven 1'000.–

10 % der Beträge, die nach Bezahlung einer Dividende von 5 % als Gewinnanteil ausgerichtet werden (Art. 671 Abs. 2 Ziff. 3 OR).

Dividende 15 % auf dem Aktienkapital von 100'000.– 15'000.–

Kapitel 1:   Bilanz, Erfolgsrechnung, Anhang, Vollständigkeitserklärung, Muster

Vortrag auf neue Rechnung   3'500.–

Detail zur Einlage 2: 5 % Dividende = 5'000.–

Ausgeschüttet: 15 % Dividende = 15'000.–

Übersteigender Betrag zu 5 %-Normaldividende: 10'000.–

davon 1/10 = 1'000.–

§ 5   Vollständigkeitserklärung

Aus den RHB 1992:

Vollständigkeitserklärung der XY AG an die ABC-Prüfungsgesellschaft zur Jahresrechnung [Datum]

Wir bestätigen nach bestem Wissen die unten aufgeführten Auskünfte, die wir Ihnen im Zusammenhang mit der Prüfung der Jahresrechnung gegeben haben. Im Übrigen ist uns bekannt, dass es uns obliegt, die Jahresrechnung zu erstellen und dass wir für sie verantwortlich sind.

1. *In der Ihnen vorgelegten Jahresrechnung sind alle Geschäftsvorfälle erfasst, die für das genannte Geschäftsjahr buchungspflichtig sind. Den zuständigen Personen ist die Weisung erteilt worden, Ihnen die Bücher und Belege sowie alle übrigen Unterlagen des Unternehmens vollständig zur Verfügung zu stellen.*

2. *In der von Ihnen geprüften und von uns unterzeichneten Jahresrechnung sind alle bilanzierungspflichtigen Vermögenswerte und Verpflichtungen berücksichtigt.*

3. *Allen bilanzierungspflichtigen Risiken und Werteinbussen ist bei der Bewertung und der Festsetzung der Wertberichtigungen und der Rückstellungen genügend Rechnung getragen worden.*

4. *Die Angaben im Anhang zur Jahresrechnung i.S.v. Art. 663b Ziff. 12 OR sind vollständig und richtig.*

5. *Andere Verträge, Rechtsstreitigkeiten oder andere Auseinandersetzungen, die für die Beurteilung der Jahresrechnung des Unternehmens*

> von wesentlicher Bedeutung sind, bestanden nicht/sind in der Beilage angeführt.
> 6. Über die stillen Reserven und deren Veränderung ist Ihnen i.S.v. Art. 669 Abs. 4 OR Aufschluss erteilt worden.
> 7. Alle bis zum Zeitpunkt der Beendigung Ihrer Prüfung bekannt gewordenen und bilanzierungspflichtigen Ereignisse sind in der vorliegenden Jahresrechnung angemessen berücksichtigt.
> 8. Alle bis zum Zeitpunkt der Generalversammlung bekannt werdenden und bilanzierungspflichtigen Ereignisse werden wir Ihnen unverzüglich mitteilen.
>
> Ort und Datum   Firmenunterschrift
>
> Beilagen:
> – Unterzeichnete Jahresrechnung bestehend aus Erfolgsrechnung, Bilanz und Anhang
> – Angaben und übrige Zusammenstellungen zu Punkt 5 und 6.

§ 6 Rangrücktritt

> **Vertrag zwischen A und B**
>
> *Präambel*
>
> Es wurde ein Zwischenabschluss der Aktiengesellschaft erstellt. Dieser weist ein Aktienkapital von CHF 100'000.– aus. Nach Vornahme aller notwendigen Abschreibungen wird ein Verlust von CHF 120'000.– ausgewiesen. Die Liquidität ist angespannt (freie Limite bei Bank: CHF 10'000.–). Die Aktionäre haben ein Darlehen von CHF 100'000.– in die

Kapitel 1: Bilanz, Erfolgsrechnung, Anhang, Vollständigkeitserklärung, Muster

Gesellschaft eingebracht. Oder: Die Aktionäre werden der Gesellschaft CHF 100'000.– nachrangiges Darlehen zur Verfügung stellen.

An der Verwaltungsratssitzung vom [Datum] haben die Aktionäre beschlossen, ihre Darlehen nachrangig der Gesellschaft zur Verfügung zu stellen.

Aktionär 1 CHF 30'000.–

Aktionär 2 CHF 20'000.–

Aktionär 3 CHF 50'000.–

Die Parteien vereinbaren was folgt.

Darlehenshingabe

Der Aktionär 1 verpflichtet sich unwiderruflich, der Darlehensnehmerin als nachrangiges Darlehen CHF 30'000.– zur Verfügung zu stellen. Die Einzahlung ist bereits erfolgt. Oder: Die Einzahlung hat bis [Datum] zu erfolgen.

Der Aktionär 2 verpflichtet sich unwiderruflich, der Darlehensnehmerin als nachrangiges Darlehen CHF 20'000.– zur Verfügung zu stellen. Die Einzahlung ist bereits erfolgt. Oder: Die Einzahlung hat bis [Datum] zu erfolgen.

Der Aktionär 3 verpflichtet sich unwiderruflich, der Darlehensnehmerin als nachrangiges Darlehen CHF 50'000.– zur Verfügung zu stellen. Die Einzahlung ist bereits erfolgt. Oder: Die Einzahlung hat bis [Datum] zu erfolgen.

Verzinsung

Dieses Darlehen wird zum Maximalzinssatz verzinst, den die eidgenössische Steuerverwaltung für Vorschüsse an Aktionäre toleriert (gemäss Merkblatt). Der Aktionär verzichtet auf eine Verzinsung, soweit dies bei der Darlehensnehmerin zu einem Verlust führt.

Oder: Das Darlehen wird nicht verzinst.

Kündigung

Das Darlehen kann vom Aktionär so lange nicht gekündigt werden, als die Hälfte des Aktienkapitals und der gesetzlichen Reserven der Darlehens-

nehmerin bei einer Bilanzierung zu Fortführungswerten nicht gedeckt ist und die Liquidität durch die Rückzahlung nicht mehr gewährleistet ist.

Stundung

Das Darlehen wird vom Aktionär so lange gestundet, als die Hälfte des Aktienkapitals und der gesetzlichen Reserven der Darlehensnehmerin bei einer Bilanzierung zu Fortführungswerten nicht gedeckt ist.

Abtretung

Die Darlehensforderung kann nicht:

- verpfändet
- abgetreten
- als Sicherstellung zur Verfügung gestellt
- einem Dritten übertragen

werden.

Dauer

Der nachrangige Darlehensvertrag besteht so lange, als die Hälfte des Aktienkapitals und der gesetzlichen Reserven der Darlehensnehmerin bei einer Bilanzierung zu Fortführungswerten nicht gedeckt ist und die Liquidität durch die Rückzahlung nicht mehr gewährleistet ist. Danach kann der Vertrag mit einer Frist von 3 Monaten auf den nächsten Bilanzstichtag gekündigt werden.

Exemplare

Dieser Vertrag existiert in vier Exemplaren (Darlehensnehmerin, Aktionär 1, 2, und 3).

Gerichtsstand

Gerichtsstand ist der Sitz der Darlehensnehmerin.

Ort, Datum, Unterschriften.

(Teilw. aus RHB 1992)

Kapitel 1: Bilanz, Erfolgsrechnung, Anhang, Vollständigkeitserklärung, Muster

§ 7 Geschäftsbericht

Nachfolgend wird ein kurzes Raster für einen Geschäftsbericht vorgeschlagen.

Geschäftsbericht

1. *Bericht über die Vermögens- und Ertragslage*
2. *Aktuelle Organisation und Führungsstruktur*
3. *Bericht über das Leistungsangebot*
4. *Aktuelle Marktsituation*
5. *Bericht über die Stellung des Unternehmens in der Region*
6. *Bericht über die Investitionen*
7. *Bericht über das Personalwesen*
8. *Bericht über wesentliche Änderungen*
9. *Zukunftsperspektiven*

§ 8 Die Generalversammlung

Einladung zur ordentlichen Generalversammlung:

X AG
Adresse

An die Aktionäre der X AG sowie
die Revisionsstelle Y AG

Ort und Datum

EINLADUNG

zur

ORDENTLICHEN GENERALVERSAMMLUNG

am .... um .... Uhr

am Sitze der Gesellschaft X AG in ....

Der Geschäftsbericht, der Revisionsbericht sowie das Protokoll der letzten Generalversammlung liegen am Sitz der Gesellschaft während der Geschäftszeit zur Einsicht auf. Den Aktionären werden diese Unterlagen separat zugestellt, soweit die Zustellung nicht bereits erfolgt ist.

TRAKTANDEN:

1. Protokoll der Generalversammlung vom ....

   Antrag des Verwaltungsrates: Genehmigung

2. Bericht des Verwaltungsrates über das Geschäftsjahr 2004/2005 und den Rechnungsabschluss per ....

3. Kenntnisnahme vom Bericht der Revisionsstelle

   Antrag des Verwaltungsrates: Kenntnisnahme vom Bericht der Revisionsstelle vom ....

4. Beschlussfassungen

   4.a.   Jahresbericht 2004/2005

   Antrag des Verwaltungsrates: Genehmigung

   4.b.   Jahresrechnung 2004/2005

   Antrag des Verwaltungsrates: Genehmigung der Jahresrechnung, welche einen Bilanzgewinn von insgesamt Fr. .... ausweist, bestehend aus .... Jahresgewinn und Fr. .... Gewinnvortrag.

4.c. Entlastung des Verwaltungsrates

Antrag des Verwaltungsrates: Den Mitgliedern des Verwaltungsrates sei in globo für das Geschäftsjahr 2004/2005 Décharge zu erteilen

4.d. Verwendung des Jahresergebnisses

Antrag des Verwaltungsrates: Der Verlust-/Gewinnsaldo von Fr. .... sei auf die neue Rechnung vorzutragen.

5. Wahlen

Antrag des Verwaltungsrates: Wahl von .... zum alleinigen Verwaltungsrat. Wahl von XY AG als Revisionsstelle.

6. Diverses

        Mit freundlichen Grüssen

        Für den Verwaltungsrat:

        ....

        X. Y.

Protokoll

PROTOKOLL

über die ordentliche Generalversammlung der

....

Teil G: Anhänge und Unterlagen / Appendices and documents

abgehalten am .... um .... Uhr, am Sitze der Gesellschaft ....

.... übernimmt den Vorsitz. Sie/Er bestimmt Herrn .... zum Protokollführer.

Die/Der Vorsitzende stellt fest, dass die Gesellschafter gültig vertreten sind. Sie/Er beantragt die Versammlung mit den nachstehend protokollierten Traktanden durchzuführen.

Variante: Auf Antrag des Vorsitzenden wird beschlossen, diese Generalversammlung als Universalversammlung durchzuführen, somit kann auch über nicht traktandierte Traktanden Beschluss gefasst werden (es bedarf der Zustimmung aller Aktionäre).

1. Protokoll der Generalversammlung vom..............

Das Protokoll der Generalversammlung vom .... wird der Versammlung vorgelegt und von dieser einstimmig genehmigt.

2. Bericht des Verwaltungsrates über das Geschäftsjahr 2004/2005 und den Rechnungsabschluss per ....

Geschäftsbericht sowie Bilanz und Erfolgsrechnung per .... liegen vor. Die Rechnung schliesst mit einem Verlust/Gewinn von Fr. .... Unter Verrechnung des Gewinnvortrages von Fr. .... ergibt sich ein Verlust-/Gewinnsaldo von Fr. .... zur Verfügung der Generalversammlung.

Der Verwaltungsrat erstattet Bericht über das abgelaufene Jahr.

3. Kenntnisnahme vom Bericht der Revisionsstelle

Die Firma .... weist einen Verlust-/Gewinnsaldo von Fr. .... aus. Die Generalversammlung nimmt davon Kenntnis, dass der Bericht der Revisionsstelle keine Einschränkung enthält.

4. Beschlussfassungen

4.a.   Jahresbericht 2004/2005

Der Verwaltungsrat beantragt Genehmigung des Jahresberichtes 2004/2005. Die Versammlung beschliesst einstimmig Annahme.

4.b.   Jahresrechnung 2004/2005

Der Verwaltungsrat beantragt Genehmigung der Jahresrechnung 2004/2005. Die Versammlung beschliesst einstimmig Annahme.

4.c.   Entlastung des Verwaltungsrates

Der Verwaltungsrat beantragt die Entlastung der Mitglieder des Verwaltungsrates für die Tätigkeit im Geschäftsjahr 2004/2005. Die Versammlung beschliesst einstimmig Décharge.

4.d.   Verwendung des Jahresergebnisses

Der Verwaltungsrat beantragt den Verlust-/Gewinnsaldo von Fr. .... auf die neue Rechnung vorzutragen.

Die Versammlung stimmt dem Antrag zu.

5. Wahlen

Der Verwaltungsrat beantragt der Generalversammlung die Wahl von .... zum alleinigen Verwaltungsrat. Die Versammlung bestätigt .... für das Geschäftsjahr 2005/2006 als alleiniger Verwaltungsrat.

Die XY AG wird auf Antrag des Verwaltungsrates als Revionsstelle gewählt.

6. Diverses

Es liegen keine weiteren Wortbegehren vor, so dass der Vorsitzende die Versammlung um [Uhrzeit] schliessen kann.

Teil G: Anhänge und Unterlagen / Appendices and documents

Basel, ...

Die Vorsitzende: Der Protokollführer:

....

§ 9   Mittelflussrechnung

1. Betriebliche Mittelerarbeitung

   Erfolg

   + Abschreibungen

   = Cashflow (+) / Cash loss (–)

2. Mittel der Bilanzaktiven

   Veränderung des Umlaufvermögens

   Veränderung des Anlagevermögens

   = Mittelfreisetzung (+) / Mittelbindung (–)

3. Mittel der Bilanzpassiven

   Veränderung Fremdkapital

   Veränderung Eigenkapital

   = Mittelzufluss (+) / Mittelabfluss (–)

Kapitel 1:   Bilanz, Erfolgsrechnung, Anhang, Vollständigkeitserklärung, Muster

4. Mittelfluss (1–3)

Cashflow / Cash loss

Mittelfreisetzung / Mittelbindung

Mittelzufluss / Mittelabfluss

= Mittelfluss

§ 10   Geschäfts- und Organisationsreglement

GESCHÄFTSREGLEMENT

1. Grundlagen

Dieses Reglement regelt die Aufgaben und Befugnisse des Verwaltungsrates.

2. Exekutivorgane der Gesellschaft

Exekutivorgan der Gesellschaft ist der Verwaltungsrat.

3. Der Verwaltungsrat

3.1. Konstituierung

Der Verwaltungsrat wählt jährlich in der ersten Sitzung nach der ordentlichen Generalversammlung aus seiner Mitte den Präsidenten sowie einen Sekretären.

3.2. Sitzungen und Sitzungsrhythmus, Einberufung und Traktandierung

Der Verwaltungsrat tagt, so oft es die Geschäfte erfordern. Die Einberufung erfolgt durch den Präsidenten oder – im Falle seiner Verhinderung – durch ein anderes Mitglied des Verwaltungsrates. Jedes Mitglied des

Verwaltungsrates ist berechtigt, die unverzügliche Einberufung unter Angabe des Zwecks zu verlangen.

Die Einberufung erfolgt mindestens zehn Tage im Voraus schriftlich und unter Angabe der Traktanden.

Der Präsident oder – im Falle seiner Verhinderung – ein anderes Mitglied des Verwaltungsrates führt den Vorsitz.

3.3. Beschlussfähigkeit, Beschlussfassung und Protokollierung

Der Verwaltungsrat ist beschlussfähig, wenn die Mehrheit seiner Mitglieder anwesend ist. Der Verwaltungsrat fasst seine Beschlüsse mit der Mehrheit der abgegebenen Stimmen. Bei Stimmengleichheit hat der Vorsitzende den Stichentscheid.

Beschlüsse können auch auf dem Zirkularweg oder telefonisch gefasst werden, es sei denn, ein Mitglied verlange innert zehn Tagen seit Erhalt des entsprechenden Antrages die Beratung in einer Sitzung.

Alle Beschlüsse sind zu protokollieren. Das Protokoll ist vom Vorsitzenden und vom Sekretären zu unterzeichnen. Es ist vom Verwaltungsrat, in der Regel in der nächsten Sitzung, zu genehmigen.

3.4. Aufgaben und Kompetenzen

Die vom Verwaltungsrat zu entscheidenden Geschäfte werden wie folgt vorbereitet und dem Gesamtverwaltungsrat zur Beschlussfassung vorgelegt:

Verwaltungsrat 1:

- Marketing, Verkauf, Einkauf
- Zukunftsperspektiven
- etc.

Verwaltungsrat 2:

- Investitionen
- Finanzielle Situation
- etc.

Kapitel 1: Bilanz, Erfolgsrechnung, Anhang, Vollständigkeitserklärung, Muster

Verwaltungsrat 3:

- Buchhaltung
- Personalwesen
- etc.

3.5. Auskunftsrecht und Berichterstattung

Jedes Mitglied des Verwaltungsrates kann Auskunft über alle Angelegenheiten der Gesellschaft verlangen.

3.6. Entschädigung

Der Verwaltungsrat bestimmt die Höhe der seinen Mitgliedern zukommenden festen Entschädigung nach Massgabe ihrer Beanspruchung und Verantwortlichkeit.

4. Gemeinsame Bestimmungen

4.1. Zeichnungsberechtigung

Der Präsident und die vom Verwaltungsrat bestimmten weiteren Mitglieder des Verwaltungsrates sind kollektiv zu zweien zeichnungsberechtigt.

4.2. Ausstand

Die Mitglieder des Verwaltungsrates sind verpflichtet, in den Ausstand zu treten, wenn Geschäfte behandelt werden, die ihre eigenen Interessen oder die Interessen von ihnen nahe stehenden natürlichen oder juristischen Personen berühren.

4.3. Geheimhaltung, Aktenrückgabe

Die Mitglieder des Verwaltungsrates sind verpflichtet, gegenüber Dritten Stillschweigen über Tatsachen zu bewahren, die ihnen in Ausübung ihres Amtes zur Kenntnis gelangen.

5. Schlussbestimmungen

5.1. Inkrafttreten

Dieses Reglement tritt am [Datum] in Kraft. Es ersetzt dasjenige vom [Datum].

Ort, Datum

Der Präsident des Verwaltungsrates   Der Sekretär des Verwaltungsrates

(Teilweise übernommen aus P&SC_on;eter&SC_off; F&SC_on; Forstmoser&SC_off;, Organisation und Organisationsreglement nach neuem Aktienrecht, in: Schriften zum neuen Aktienrecht, J. N. Druey und P. Forstmoser [Hrsg.], Zürich, 1992)

ORGANISATIONS- UND GESCHÄFTSREGLEMENT

1. Grundlagen

Dieses Reglement wird gestützt auf Art. XX der Statuten erlassen.

Es regelt die Aufgaben und Befugnisse des Verwaltungsrats und der Geschäftsstelle.

2. Exekutivorgane der Gesellschaft

Die Exekutivorgane der Gesellschaft sind der Verwaltungsrat, der Präsident des Verwaltungsrates und die Geschäftsleitung.

3. Der Verwaltungsrat

3.1. Konstituierung

Kapitel 1: Bilanz, Erfolgsrechnung, Anhang, Vollständigkeitserklärung, Muster

Der Verwaltungsrat wählt jährlich in der ersten Sitzung nach der ordentlichen Generalversammlung aus seiner Mitte den Präsidenten und den Vizepräsidenten. Er bezeichnet ferner einen Sekretären, der nicht Mitglied des Verwaltungsrates zu sein braucht.

3.2. Sitzungen und Sitzungsrhythmus, Einberufung und Traktandierung

Der Verwaltungsrat tagt, sooft es die Geschäfte erfordern, mindestens aber viermal jährlich. Die Einberufung erfolgt durch den Präsidenten oder – im Falle seiner Verhinderung – den Vizepräsidenten oder ein anderes Mitglied des Verwaltungsrates. Jedes Mitglied des Verwaltungsrates ist berechtigt, die unverzügliche Einberufung unter Angabe des Zweckes zu verlangen.

Die Einberufung erfolgt mindestens zehn Tage im Voraus schriftlich und unter Angabe der Traktanden.

Der Präsident oder – im Falle seiner Verhinderung – ein anderes Mitglied des Verwaltungsrates führt den Vorsitz.

3.3. Beschlussfähigkeit, Beschlussfassung und Protokollierung

Der Verwaltungsrat ist beschlussfähig, wenn die Mehrheit seiner Mitglieder anwesend ist.

Der Verwaltungsrat fasst seine Beschlüsse mit der Mehrheit der abgegebenen Stimmen. Bei Stimmengleichheit hat der Vorsitzende den Stichentscheid.

Beschlüsse können auch auf dem Zirkularweg gefasst werden, es sei denn, ein Mitglied verlange innert zehn Tagen seit Erhalt des entsprechenden Antrages telefonisch die Beratung in einer Sitzung.

Alle Beschlüsse sind zu protokollieren. Das Protokoll ist vom Vorsitzenden zu unterzeichnen. Es ist vom Verwaltungsrat, in der Regel in der nächsten Sitzung, zu genehmigen. Zirkulationsbeschlüsse sind in das nächste Protokoll aufzunehmen.

3.4. Aufgaben und Kompetenzen

Der Verwaltungsrat delegiert die Geschäftsführung vollumfänglich an die Geschäftsleitung, soweit nicht das Gesetz, die Statuten oder dieses Reglement etwas anderes vorsehen.

Der Verwaltungsrat übt die Oberleitung und die Aufsicht und Kontrolle über die Geschäftsführung aus. Er erlässt Richtlinien für die Geschäftspolitik und lässt sich über den Geschäftsgang regelmässig orientieren.

Insbesondere kommen dem Verwaltungsrat die folgenden Aufgaben zu:

- *die Oberleitung der Gesellschaft und die Erteilung der nötigen Weisungen;*
- *die Festlegung der Organisation;*
- *die Ausgestaltung des Rechnungswesens, der Finanzkontrolle und der Finanzplanung;*
- *die Ernennung und Abberufung der mit der Geschäftsführung und der Vertretung betrauten Personen und die Regelung der Zeichnungsberechtigung;*
- *die Oberaufsicht über die mit der Geschäftsführung betrauten Personen, auch im Hinblick auf die Befolgung der Gesetze, Statuten, Reglemente und Weisungen;*
- *die Erstellung des Geschäftsberichtes sowie die Vorbereitung der Generalversammlung und die Ausführung ihrer Beschlüsse;*
- *die Benachrichtigung des Richters im Falle der Überschuldung;*
- *die Beschlussfassung über die nachträgliche Leistung von Einlagen auf nicht voll liberierte Aktien;*
- *die Beschlussfassung über die Erhöhung des Aktienkapitals, soweit diese in der Kompetenz des Verwaltungsrates liegt (Art. 651 Abs. 1 OR), sowie die Feststellung von Kapitalerhöhungen und entsprechende Statutenänderungen;*
- *die Prüfung der fachlichen Voraussetzungen der Auswahl der Revisoren*

Der Verwaltungsrat ist befugt, über die Angelegenheiten Beschluss zu fassen, die nicht der Generalversammlung oder einem anderen Organ der Gesellschaft durch Gesetz, Statuten oder Reglemente vorbehalten oder übertragen sind.

Der Verwaltungsrat führt die Geschäfte der Gesellschaft, soweit er die Geschäftsführung nicht übertragen hat.

Er fasst Beschluss über alle Angelegenheiten, die nicht der Generalversammlung oder einem anderen Organ der Gesellschaft durch Gesetz, Statuten oder Reglemente vorbehalten oder übertragen sind.

3.5. Auskunftsrecht und Berichterstattung

Jedes Mitglied des Verwaltungsrates kann Auskunft über alle Angelegenheiten der Gesellschaft verlangen.

In jeder Sitzung ist der Verwaltungsrat von der Geschäftsleitung über den laufenden Geschäftsgang und die wichtigeren Geschäftsvorfälle zu orientieren.

3.6. Entschädigung

Der Verwaltungsrat bestimmt die Höhe der seinen Mitgliedern zukommenden festen Entschädigung nach Massgabe ihrer Beanspruchung und Verantwortlichkeit.

4. Die Geschäftsleitung

Im Rahmen des gesetzlich und statutarisch Zulässigen überträgt der Verwaltungsrat die gesamte Geschäftsführung an die Geschäftsleitung. Vorbehalten bleiben die in diesem Reglement vorgesehenen Ausnahmen.

Die Geschäftsleitung ist ferner mit der Vorbereitung und Ausführung der Beschlüsse des Verwaltungsrates beauftragt. Über die ihr vom Verwaltungsrat zugewiesenen Geschäfte entscheidet sie in eigener Kompetenz, soweit sich der Verwaltungsrat nicht den Entscheid oder die Genehmigung vorbehalten hat.

5. Gemeinsame Bestimmungen

5.1. Zeichnungsberechtigung

Der Präsident und der Vizepräsident des Verwaltungsrates sowie die vom Verwaltungsrat bestimmten weiteren Mitglieder des Verwaltungsrates sind kollektiv zu zweien zeichnungsberechtigt.

5.2. Ausstand

> *Die Mitglieder des Verwaltungsrates sind verpflichtet, in den Ausstand zu treten, wenn Geschäfte behandelt werden, die ihre eigenen Interessen oder die Interessen von ihnen nahe stehenden natürlichen oder juristischen Personen berühren.*
>
> *5.3. Geheimhaltung, Aktenrückgabe*
>
> *Die Mitglieder des Verwaltungsrates sind verpflichtet, gegenüber Dritten Stillschweigen über Tatsachen zu bewahren, die ihnen in Ausübung ihres Amtes zur Kenntnis gelangen.*
>
> **6. Schlussbestimmungen**
>
> *Dieses Reglement tritt am [Datum] in Kraft und ersetzt dasjenige vom [Datum].*
>
> *Ort, Datum*
>
> *Der Präsident des Verwaltungsrates   Der Sekretär des Verwaltungsrates*

(Auszugsweise übernommen von Peter Forstmoser, Organisation und Organisationsreglement nach neuem Aktienrecht, in: Schriften zum neuen Aktienrecht, J. N. Druey und P. Forstmoser [Hrsg.], Zürich, 1992)

§ 11   Auftragsbestätigung

> *Auftrag*
>
> *An den Verwaltungsrat*
>
> *der MUSTER AG*

Kapitel 1: Bilanz, Erfolgsrechnung, Anhang, Vollständigkeitserklärung, Muster

Sehr geehrte Damen und Herren

An der Generalversammlung/Gründerversammlung Ihrer Gesellschaft vom [Datum] sind wir als Revisionsstelle (Art. 729 ff. OR) für die Durchführung einer eingeschränkten Revision gewählt worden. Wir danken Ihnen für das uns entgegengebrachte Vertrauen.

Das Honorar für unsere Dienstleistung errechnet sich aufgrund des tatsächlichen Zeitaufwands unserer Mitarbeiter und deren Qualifikationen. Die Mitarbeiterstundenansätze ergeben sich aus der Honorarempfehlung unseres Berufsstandes. Für die Prüfung der Jahresrechnung schätzen wird das Honorar auf CHF [Betrag], zuzüglich Barauslagen und Mehrwertsteuer.

Wir freuen uns auf eine gute Zusammenarbeit mit Ihnen und Ihren Mitarbeitern.

Die Revisionsstelle.

Kapitel 2:
Standardrevisionsunterlagen bei der AG für den Review

Je mehr Ja-Antworten Sie ankreuzen, desto eher können Sie den Bericht abgeben. Verneinende Fragen sind mit Ja – Bestätigung der Verneinung – zu beantworten (Haben Sie keine Probleme? – Ja, ich habe keine Probleme). Wenn Sie aufgrund von Nein-Antworten unsicher sind, zeigen Sie diese Arbeitspapiere einer Zweitperson. Sie kann Ihnen helfen, zu einem Urteil und zu Ihrem Revisionsbericht zu gelangen.

FIRMA	AG
Bereich	

Revisionsfirma	
Name des leitenden Revisors	
Name des zweiten Revisors	
Mandat	Jahr

Allgemeine Fragen	Ja	Nein
Sind Sie als Revisionsstelle im Handelsregister eingetragen?		
Sind Sie gemäss GV-Protokoll als Revisionsstelle gewählt?		
Haben Sie eine kaufmännische Berufsausbildung?		
Haben Sie Erfahrung auf dem Gebiet der Revision?		
Sind Sie fähig, aufgrund ihrer Kenntnisse die vorliegende Rechnungslegung im Hinblick auf Umfang und Schwierigkeitsgrad zu prüfen?		
Sind Sie unabhängig im Hinblick auf die Revision?		

Kapitel 2: **Standardrevisionsunterlagen bei der AG für den Review**

Führen Sie nur Arbeiten für die AG aus, die mit der Revision vereinbar sind?		
Sind Sie nicht im Verwaltungsrat der AG?		
Führen Sie nicht die Buchhaltung, die Sie revidieren?		
Ist der Buchhalter nicht mit Ihnen verwandt?		
Ist der Verwaltungsrat nicht mit Ihnen verwandt?		
Können Sie auf dieses Mandat bei Schwierigkeiten verzichten, ohne dass Sie ihre Büroorganisation ändern müssen?		
Können Sie auf dieses Mandat bei Schwierigkeiten verzichten, ohne dass Sie der Honorarverlust allzu sehr schmerzt?		
Können Sie – sofern es die Situation erfordert – die Jahresrechnung zur Nicht-Genehmigung empfehlen, ohne dass Sie ein schlechtes Gewissen gegenüber der Verwaltung haben?		
Haben Sie einen aktuellen Handelsregisterauszug (1–3 Jahre alt)?		
Kennen Sie alle Verwaltungsräte?		
Kennen Sie den verantwortlichen Buchhalter der AG?		
Haben Sie die Statuten der AG?		
Gibt es in den Statuten keine besonderen Bestimmungen für die Revisionsstelle?		
Existiert ein Protokoll zur letzten o/GV?		
Wurde die letzte Jahresrechnung genehmigt?		
Gab es keine a/o GV?		
Gibt es ein Organisationsreglement?		
Haben Sie keine Fragen mehr zur letztjährigen Revision?		
Haben Sie keine offenen Kontrollen mehr vom letzten Jahr?		
Ist die Buchhaltungsperson nicht alleine unterschriftsberechtigt?		

Teil G: Anhänge und Unterlagen / Appendices and documents

Ist die Buchhaltungsperson nicht für den Zahlungsverkehr alleine verantwortlich?		

Grundlagen	Ja	Nein
Ist die Bilanz rechtsgültig unterzeichnet?		
Ist die Erfolgsrechnung rechtsgültig unterzeichnet?		
Ist der Anhang rechtsgültig unterzeichnet?		
Liegt eine unterzeichnete Vollständigkeitserklärung vor?		
Liegt ein unterzeichneter Gewinnverwendungsvorschlag vor?		
Liegt ein Jahresbericht (Text zum Geschäftsjahr) vor?		
Erfolgt die Revision innerhalb von 6 Monaten seit Bilanzstichtag?		
Erfolgt die Revision innerhalb von 12 Monaten seit Bilanzstichtag?		
Existiert ein Budget?		

Buchhaltung	Ja	Nein
Liegt ein kompletter Ausdruck aller Kontoblätter, Journale, Bilanzen und der Erfolgsrechnung des Vorjahres vor?		
Liegt eine Bilanz vor?		
Liegt eine Erfolgsrechnung vor?		
Wenn eine Abschrift existiert, stimmt diese mit der EDV überein?		
Wenn eine Abschrift vorliegt, stimmt die Addition?		
Stimmt die Eröffnungsbilanz des laufenden Jahres mit der Schlussbilanz des Vorjahres überein?		
Sind die Hauptbuchkonti ausgedruckt?		

Ist das Journal vorliegend?		
Ist die Buchhaltung auf einem Datenträger gespeichert?		
Haben Sie 1–2 Kontoblätter addiert (rechnerische Kontrolle)?		
Ist die Belegablage geordnet?		
Finden Sie zu jedem Beleg eine Buchung? (Antwort aufgrund von Stichproben)		
Sind die Belege des Vorjahres vorhanden?		
Bewahrt die Gesellschaft ihre Akten der letzten 10 Jahre auf?		
Wurde das letzte Mal innerhalb eines Monats gebucht?		
Wurde das letzte Mal innerhalb zweier Monate gebucht?		
Wurde das letzte Mal innerhalb dreier Monate gebucht?		
Ist die Buchhaltung à jour?		
Sind die Buchungen mit Buchungstexten versehen?		
Sind die Konti klar geführt?		
Wurde dem Verrechnungsverbot Rechnung getragen?		

BILANZ	Eröffnungssaldo	Schlusssaldo	**Ja**	**Nein**
Es empfiehlt sich eine lückenlose Prüfung der Bilanz, wobei einzelne Bilanzposten nach dem Stichprobenprinzip geprüft werden. Lückenlos: Bank; Stichprobe: Debitoren	Buchsaldi oder geprüfte Bilanz	Buchsaldi oder geprüfte Bilanz		
AKTIVEN				

Teil G: Anhänge und Unterlagen / Appendices and documents

Umlaufvermögen				
Umlaufvermögen. Wie hoch ist der Anteil an der Bilanzsumme?	......%			
Kasse 1				
Buchsaldi:	CHF	CHF		
Haben Sie den Bestand geprüft?				
Haben Sie den Verkehr kritisch gesichtet?				
Hat nur eine Person Zugang zur Kasse?				
Bemerkung				
Kasse 2				
Buchsaldi:	CHF	CHF		
Haben Sie den Bestand geprüft?				
Haben Sie den Verkehr kritisch gesichtet?				
Bemerkung				
Kasse 3 Fremdwährung				
Buchsaldi umgerechnet:	CHF	CHF		
Haben Sie den Bestand geprüft?				
Haben Sie den Verkehr kritisch gesichtet?				
Bemerkung				

Postkonto 1				
Buchsaldi:	CHF	CHF		
Haben Sie den Bestand geprüft?				
Haben Sie den Verkehr kritisch gesichtet?				
Bemerkung				

Postkonto 2				
Buchsaldi:	CHF	CHF		
Haben Sie den Bestand geprüft?				
Haben Sie den Verkehr kritisch gesichtet?				
Bemerkung				

Bank 1				
Buchsaldi:	CHF	CHF		
Haben Sie den Bestand geprüft?				
Haben Sie den Verkehr kritisch gesichtet?				
Bemerkung				

Bank 2				
Buchsaldi:	CHF	CHF		
Haben Sie den Bestand geprüft?				
Haben Sie den Verkehr kritisch gesichtet?				

Teil G: Anhänge und Unterlagen / Appendices and documents

Bemerkung				
Sparkonto				
Buchsaldi:	CHF	CHF		
Haben Sie den Bestand geprüft?				
Haben Sie den Verkehr kritisch gesichtet?				
Bemerkung				
Bank Fremdwährung				
Buchsaldi umgerechnet	CHF	CHF		
Haben Sie den Bestand geprüft?				
Haben Sie den Verkehr kritisch gesichtet?				
Bemerkung				
Festgeldanlagen				
Buchsaldi:	CHF	CHF		
Haben Sie den Bestand geprüft?				
Haben Sie den Verkehr kritisch gesichtet?				
Bemerkung				
Aktien				
Buchsaldi:	CHF	CHF		
Haben Sie den Bestand geprüft?				
Ist die Bewertung korrekt?				

Kapitel 2: Standardrevisionsunterlagen bei der AG für den Review

Haben Sie einen Depotauszug der Bank?				
Haben Sie den Verkehr kritisch gesichtet?				
Bemerkung				

Obligationen

Buchsaldi:	CHF	CHF		
Haben Sie den Bestand geprüft?				
Haben Sie einen Depotauszug der Bank?				
Haben Sie den Verkehr kritisch gesichtet?				
Bemerkung				

Wertberichtigungen auf Wertschriften

Buchsaldi:	CHF	CHF		
Haben Sie den Bestand (Bewegungen) geprüft?				
Ist die Bewertung korrekt?				
Haben Sie den Verkehr kritisch gesichtet?				
Bemerkung				

Geldtransferkonto

Buchsaldi:	CHF	CHF		
Haben Sie den Bestand geprüft?				
Ist die Bewertung korrekt? (Saldo				

Teil G: Anhänge und Unterlagen / Appendices and documents

meistens 0.-)				
Haben Sie den Verkehr kritisch gesichtet?				
Bemerkung				

Forderungen aus Lieferungen und Leistungen: Debitoren

Buchsaldi:	CHF	CHF		
Haben Sie den Bestand (Debitorenliste) geprüft?				
Ist die Bewertung korrekt (5% Delkredere CH und 10% Ausland)?				
Haben Sie den Verkehr kritisch gesichtet?				
Liegt eine unterzeichnete Debitorenliste vor?				
Wissen Sie, wie viele der Debitoren am Bilanzstichtag bezahlt sind?				
Bemerkung				

Forderung gegenüber Tochtergesellschaft

Buchsaldi:	CHF	CHF		
Haben Sie den Bestand geprüft?				
Ist die Bewertung korrekt?				
Haben Sie den Verkehr kritisch gesichtet?				
Bemerkung				

Forderung gegenüber Aktionär/en

Kapitel 2: Standardrevisionsunterlagen bei der AG für den Review

Buchsaldi:	CHF	CHF		
Haben Sie den Bestand geprüft?				
Ist die Bewertung korrekt?				
Haben Sie den Verkehr kritisch gesichtet?				
Bemerkung				

Andere kurzfristige Forderungen

Buchsaldi:	CHF	CHF		
Haben Sie den Bestand geprüft?				
Ist die Bewertung korrekt?				
Haben Sie den Verkehr kritisch gesichtet?				
Bemerkung				

Kurzfristige Darlehen

Buchsaldi:	CHF	CHF		
Haben Sie den Bestand geprüft?				
Ist die Bewertung korrekt?				
Haben Sie den Verkehr kritisch gesichtet?				
Bemerkung				

Darlehen gegenüber Tochtergesellschaften

Buchsaldi:	CHF	CHF		
Haben Sie den Bestand geprüft?				
Ist die Bewertung korrekt?				

Teil G: Anhänge und Unterlagen / Appendices and documents

Haben Sie den Verkehr kritisch gesichtet?				
Bemerkung				

Mehrwertsteuer				
Buchsaldi:	CHF	CHF		
Haben Sie den Bestand geprüft?				
Ist die Bewertung korrekt?				
Haben Sie die Mehrwertsteuerabrechnungen eingesehen?				
Stimmt der MwSt-Umsatz mit der Buchhaltung überein?				
Bemerkung				

Guthaben Verrechnungssteuer				
Buchsaldi:	CHF	CHF		
Haben Sie den Bestand geprüft?				
Ist die Bewertung korrekt?				
Wurde das Formular 25 Rückerstattung eingereicht?				
Haben Sie den Verkehr kritisch gesichtet?				
Bemerkung				

Guthaben AHV				
Buchsaldi:	CHF	CHF		
Haben Sie den Bestand geprüft?				
Ist die Bewertung korrekt?				

Haben Sie den Verkehr kritisch gesichtet?				
Bemerkung				

Guthaben SUVA (UVG)

Buchsaldi:	CHF	CHF		
Haben Sie den Bestand geprüft?				
Ist die Bewertung korrekt?				
Haben Sie den Verkehr kritisch gesichtet?				
Bemerkung				

Guthaben BVG

Buchsaldi:	CHF	CHF		
Haben Sie den Bestand geprüft?				
Ist die Bewertung korrekt?				
Haben Sie den Verkehr kritisch gesichtet?				
Bemerkung				

Nicht einbezahltes Aktienkapital

Buchsaldi:	CHF	CHF		
Haben Sie den Bestand geprüft?				
Ist die Bewertung korrekt?				
Gab es keinen Verkehr?				
Bemerkung				

Teil G: Anhänge und Unterlagen / Appendices and documents

WIR Forderungen				
Buchsaldi:	CHF	CHF		
Haben Sie den Bestand geprüft?				
Ist die Bewertung korrekt?				
Haben Sie den Verkehr kritisch gesichtet?				
Bemerkung				

Barkautionen				
Buchsaldi:	CHF	CHF		
Haben Sie den Bestand geprüft (Liste)?				
Ist die Bewertung korrekt?				
Haben Sie den Verkehr kritisch gesichtet?				
Bemerkung				

Vorauszahlungen				
Buchsaldi:	CHF	CHF		
Haben Sie den Bestand geprüft?				
Ist die Bewertung korrekt?				
Haben Sie den Verkehr kritisch gesichtet?				
Bemerkung				

Vorräte 1

Buchsaldi:	CHF	CHF		
Haben Sie den Bestand geprüft?				
Ist die Bewertung korrekt?				
Haben Sie den Verkehr kritisch gesichtet?				
Gibt es ein Wareninventar?				
Waren Sie bei der Inventur anwesend?				
Haben Sie das aktuelle Warenlager gesehen?				
Bemerkung				

Vorräte 2

Buchsaldi:	CHF	CHF		
Haben Sie den Bestand geprüft?				
Ist die Bewertung korrekt?				
Haben Sie den Verkehr kritisch gesichtet?				
Gibt es ein Wareninventar?				
Waren Sie bei der Inventur anwesend?				
Haben Sie das aktuelle Warenlager gesehen?				
Bemerkung				

Wertberichtigung Vorräte

Buchsaldi:	CHF	CHF		
Haben Sie den Bestand geprüft?				

Teil G: Anhänge und Unterlagen / Appendices and documents

Ist die Bewertung korrekt?				
Hat sich die Warenlagerreserve verändert?				
Haben Sie den Verkehr kritisch gesichtet?				
Bemerkung				

Angefangene Arbeiten (kurzfristig)

Buchsaldi:	CHF	CHF		
Haben Sie den Bestand geprüft?				
Ist genügend Liquidität vorhanden, um die Arbeiten zu Ende zu führen?				
Ist die Bewertung korrekt?				
Haben Sie den Verkehr kritisch gesichtet?				
Bemerkung				

Transitorische Aktiven

Buchsaldi:	CHF	CHF		
Haben Sie den Bestand geprüft?				
Ist die Bewertung korrekt?				
Haben sich die TA des Vorjahres aufgelöst?				
Bemerkung				

Anlagevermögen

Langfristige Finanzanlagen

Kapitel 2: Standardrevisionsunterlagen bei der AG für den Review

Buchsaldi:	CHF	CHF		
Haben Sie den Bestand geprüft?				
Ist die Bewertung korrekt?				
Haben Sie den Verkehr kritisch gesichtet?				
Bemerkung				

Beteiligungen

Buchsaldi:	CHF	CHF		
Haben Sie den Bestand geprüft?				
Ist die Bewertung korrekt?				
Haben Sie den Verkehr kritisch gesichtet?				
Bemerkung				

Langfristige Darlehen

Buchsaldi:	CHF	CHF		
Haben Sie den Bestand geprüft?				
Ist die Bewertung korrekt?				
Haben Sie den Verkehr kritisch gesichtet?				
Bemerkung				

Maschinen

Buchsaldi:	CHF	CHF		
Haben Sie den Bestand geprüft (Zugang/Abgang)?				

Teil G: Anhänge und Unterlagen / Appendices and documents

Existiert eine Anlagekartei?				
Haben Sie bei wesentlichen Neuzugängen den Kaufvertrag eingesehen?				
Ist die Bewertung korrekt?				
Wurden Abschreibungen vorgenommen?				
Bemerkung				

Apparate

Buchsaldi:	CHF	CHF		
Haben Sie den Bestand geprüft (Zugang/Abgang)?				
Existiert eine Anlagekartei?				
Haben Sie bei wesentlichen Neuzugängen den Kaufvertrag eingesehen?				
Ist die Bewertung korrekt?				
Wurden Abschreibungen vorgenommen?				
Bemerkung				

Produktionsanlagen

Buchsaldi:	CHF	CHF		
Haben Sie den Bestand geprüft (Zugang/Abgang)?				
Existiert eine Anlagekartei?				
Haben Sie bei wesentlichen Neuzugängen den Kaufvertrag eingesehen?				
Ist die Bewertung korrekt?				

Wurden Abschreibungen vorgenommen?				
Bemerkung				

Mobiliar

Buchsaldi:	CHF	CHF		
Haben Sie den Bestand geprüft (Zugang/Abgang)?				
Existiert eine Anlagekartei?				
Haben Sie bei wesentlichen Neuzugängen den Kaufvertrag eingesehen?				
Ist die Bewertung korrekt?				
Wurden Abschreibungen vorgenommen?				
Bemerkung				

Einrichtungen

Buchsaldi:	CHF	CHF		
Haben Sie den Bestand geprüft (Zugang/Abgang)?				
Existiert eine Anlagekartei?				
Haben Sie bei wesentlichen Neuzugängen den Kaufvertrag eingesehen?				
Ist die Bewertung korrekt?				
Wurden Abschreibungen vorgenommen?				
Bemerkung				

Büromaschinen				
Buchsaldi:	CHF	CHF		
Haben Sie den Bestand geprüft (Zugang/Abgang)?				
Existiert eine Anlagekartei?				
Haben Sie bei wesentlichen Neuzugängen den Kaufvertrag eingesehen?				
Ist die Bewertung korrekt?				
Wurden Abschreibungen vorgenommen?				
Bemerkung				
EDV				
Buchsaldi:	CHF	CHF		
Haben Sie den Bestand geprüft (Zugang/Abgang)?				
Existiert eine Anlagekartei?				
Haben Sie bei wesentlichen Neuzugängen den Kaufvertrag eingesehen?				
Ist die Bewertung korrekt?				
Wurden Abschreibungen vorgenommen?				
Bemerkung				
Fahrzeuge				
Buchsaldi:	CHF	CHF		
Haben Sie den Bestand geprüft (Zugang/Abgang)?				

Existiert eine Anlagekartei?				
Haben Sie bei wesentlichen Neuzugängen den Kaufvertrag eingesehen?				
Ist die Bewertung korrekt?				
Wurden Abschreibungen vorgenommen?				
Bemerkung				

Werkzeug und Geräte

Buchsaldi:	CHF	CHF		
Haben Sie den Bestand geprüft (Zugang/Abgang)?				
Existiert eine Anlagekartei?				
Haben Sie bei wesentlichen Neuzugängen den Kaufvertrag eingesehen?				
Ist die Bewertung korrekt?				
Wurden Abschreibungen vorgenommen?				
Bemerkung				

Lagereinrichtungen

Buchsaldi:	CHF	CHF		
Haben Sie den Bestand geprüft (Zugang/Abgang)?				
Existiert eine Anlagekartei?				
Haben Sie bei wesentlichen Neuzugängen den Kaufvertrag eingesehen?				
Ist die Bewertung korrekt?				

Wurden Abschreibungen vorgenommen?				
Bemerkung				

Übriges Anlagegut

Buchsaldi:	CHF	CHF		
Haben Sie den Bestand geprüft (Zugang/Abgang)?				
Existiert eine Anlagekartei?				
Haben Sie bei wesentlichen Neuzugängen den Kaufvertrag eingesehen?				
Ist die Bewertung korrekt?				
Wurden Abschreibungen vorgenommen?				
Bemerkung				

Liegenschaft/en

Buchsaldi:	CHF	CHF		
Haben Sie den Bestand geprüft (Zugang/Abgang)?				
Existiert eine Anlagekartei (Grundbuchauszug)?				
Ist die Bewertung korrekt?				
Wurden Abschreibungen vorgenommen?				
Bemerkung				

Patente, Know-how, Rezepte

Buchsaldi:	CHF	CHF		
Haben Sie den Bestand geprüft (Zugang/Abgang)?				
Existiert eine Anlagekartei?				
Ist die Bewertung korrekt?				
Wurden Abschreibungen vorgenommen?				
Bemerkung				

Marken, Muster, Modelle, Pläne

Buchsaldi:	CHF	CHF		
Haben Sie den Bestand geprüft (Zugang/Abgang)?				
Existiert eine Anlagekartei?				
Ist die Bewertung korrekt?				
Wurden Abschreibungen vorgenommen?				
Bemerkung				

Lizenzen, Konzessionen, Nutzungsrechte, Firmenrechte

Buchsaldi:	CHF	CHF		
Haben Sie den Bestand geprüft (Zugang/Abgang)?				
Existiert eine Anlagekartei?				
Ist die Bewertung korrekt?				
Wurden Abschreibungen vorgenommen?				
Bemerkung				

Urheberrechte, Verlagsrechte, Vertragsrechte

Buchsaldi:	CHF	CHF		
Haben Sie den Bestand geprüft (Zugang/Abgang)?				
Existiert eine Anlagekartei?				
Ist die Bewertung korrekt?				
Wurden Abschreibungen vorgenommen?				
Bemerkung				

Goodwill

Buchsaldi:	CHF	CHF		
Haben Sie den Bestand geprüft (Zugang/Abgang)?				
Existiert eine Anlagekartei?				
Ist die Bewertung korrekt?				
Wurden Abschreibungen vorgenommen?				
Bemerkung				

Aktivierter Aufwand: Gründungskosten

Buchsaldi:	CHF	CHF		
Haben Sie den Bestand geprüft (Zugang/Abgang)?				
Ist die Bewertung korrekt?				
Wurden Abschreibungen vorgenommen?				

Ist das Abschreibungsziel in 5 Jahren erreicht?				
Bemerkung				

Aktivierter Aufwand: Forschung und Entwicklung

Buchsaldi:	CHF	CHF		
Haben Sie den Bestand geprüft (Zugang/Abgang)?				
Existiert eine Anlagekartei?				
Ist die Bewertung korrekt?				
Wurden Abschreibungen vorgenommen?				
Bemerkung				

Angefangene Arbeiten (Langfristig)

Buchsaldi:	CHF	CHF		
Haben Sie den Bestand geprüft (Zugang/Abgang)?				
Existiert eine Anlagekartei?				
Ist die Bewertung korrekt?				
Wurden Abschreibungen vorgenommen?				
Sind genügend Liquidität und Kapital vorhanden, um die Arbeiten zu Ende zu führen?				
Bemerkung				
Entspricht die Darstellung der Konti, mit Ausnahme von Neuem und Weg-				

gefallenem, dem Vorjahr (Prinzip der Stetigkeit)?				

PASSIVEN

Fremdkapital

Verbindlichkeiten aus Lieferungen und Leistungen: Kreditoren

Buchsaldi:	CHF	CHF		
Haben Sie den Bestand geprüft?				
Haben Sie die Kreditoren des Vorjahres aufgelöst?				
Haben Sie den Verkehr kritisch gesichtet?				
Bemerkung				

Verbindlichkeiten aus Lieferungen und Leistungen gegenüber Aktionären

Buchsaldi:	CHF	CHF		
Haben Sie den Bestand geprüft?				
Haben Sie den Verkehr kritisch gesichtet?				
Bemerkung				

Bankverbindlichkeiten 1

Buchsaldi:	CHF	CHF		
Haben Sie den Bestand geprüft?				
Haben Sie den Verkehr kritisch ge-				

Kapitel 2: Standardrevisionsunterlagen bei der AG für den Review

sichtet?				
Bemerkung				

Bankverbindlichkeiten 2

Buchsaldi:	CHF	CHF		
Haben Sie den Bestand geprüft?				
Haben Sie den Verkehr kritisch gesichtet?				
Bemerkung				

WIR-Schulden

Buchsaldi:	CHF	CHF		
Haben Sie den Bestand geprüft?				
Haben Sie den Verkehr kritisch gesichtet?				
Bemerkung				

Sonstige Verbindlichkeiten gegenüber Dritten

Buchsaldi:	CHF	CHF		
Haben Sie den Bestand geprüft?				
Haben Sie den Verkehr kritisch gesichtet?				
Bemerkung				

Sonstige Verbindlichkeiten gegenüber Aktionären

Buchsaldi:	CHF	CHF		
Haben Sie den Bestand geprüft?				

Teil G: Anhänge und Unterlagen / Appendices and documents

Haben Sie den Verkehr kritisch gesichtet?				
Bemerkung				

Verbindlichkeiten gegenüber Vorsorgeeinrichtungen

Buchsaldi:	CHF	CHF		
Haben Sie den Bestand geprüft?				
Haben Sie den Verkehr kritisch gesichtet?				
Bemerkung				

Andere Verbindlichkeiten

Buchsaldi:	CHF	CHF		
Haben Sie den Bestand geprüft?				
Haben Sie den Verkehr kritisch gesichtet?				
Bemerkung				

Transitorische Passiven

Buchsaldi:	CHF	CHF		
Haben Sie den Bestand geprüft?				
Haben Sie den Verkehr kritisch gesichtet?				
Haben sich die TP des Vorjahres aufgelöst?				
Bemerkung				

Rückstellungen

Buchsaldi:	CHF	CHF		
Haben Sie den Bestand geprüft?				
Haben Sie den Verkehr kritisch gesichtet?				
Bemerkung				

Eigenkapital

Aktienkapital

Buchsaldi:	CHF	CHF		
Gab es keine Veränderung?				
Ist das Kapital 100% vorhanden?				
Besteht kein Kapitalverlust?				
Bemerkung				

Gesetzliche Reserven

Buchsaldi:	CHF	CHF		
Wurde die Gewinnverteilung des Vorjahres verbucht?				
Sind das Kapital und die Reserven 100% vorhanden?				
Bemerkung				

Freie Reserven

Buchsaldi:	CHF	CHF		
Wurde die Gewinnverteilung des Vorjahres verbucht?				

Teil G: Anhänge und Unterlagen / Appendices and documents

Sind das Kapital und die Reserven 100% vorhanden?			
Bemerkung			
Entspricht die Darstellung der Konti, mit Ausnahme von Neuem und Weggefallenem, dem Vorjahr (Prinzip der Stetigkeit)?			

ERFOLGSRECHNUNG

Ertrag

Die Belegstichprobe muss nicht für jedes Konto durchgeführt werden. Es genügt eine Auswahl.			

Produktionsertrag

Buchsaldo:	CHF		
Haben Sie eine Belegstichprobe gemacht (von der Buchung zum Beleg)?			
Bemerkung			

Handelsertrag

Buchsaldo:	CHF		
Haben Sie eine Belegstichprobe gemacht (von der Buchung zum Beleg)?			
Bemerkung			

Dienstleistungsertrag

Kapitel 2: Standardrevisionsunterlagen bei der AG für den Review

Buchsaldo:	CHF		
Haben Sie eine Belegstichprobe gemacht (von der Buchung zum Beleg)?			
Bemerkung			

Übriger Ertrag

Buchsaldo:	CHF		
Haben Sie eine Belegstichprobe gemacht (von der Buchung zum Beleg)?			
Bemerkung			

Bestandesänderungen

Buchsaldo:	CHF		
Ergibt sich die Bestandesänderung durch das Inventar?			
Bemerkung			

Finanzertrag

Buchsaldo:	CHF		
Haben Sie eine Belegstichprobe gemacht (von der Buchung zum Beleg)?			
Bemerkung			
Sind die Ertragskonti rein geführt, ohne direkte Verrechnung von Aufwand (Bruttoprinzip/Verrechnungsverbot)?			

Teil G: Anhänge und Unterlagen / Appendices and documents

Aufwand			
Materialaufwand			
Buchsaldo:	CHF		
Haben Sie eine Belegstichprobe gemacht (von der Buchung zum Beleg)?			
Bemerkung			
Bestandesänderungen			
Buchsaldo:	CHF		
Ist die Warenlagerreserve unverändert (1/3)?			
Bemerkung			
Handelswarenaufwand			
Buchsaldo:	CHF		
Haben Sie eine Belegstichprobe gemacht (von der Buchung zum Beleg)?			
Bemerkung			
Aufwand für Drittleistungen			
Buchsaldo:	CHF		
Haben Sie eine Belegstichprobe gemacht (von der Buchung zum Beleg)?			
Bemerkung			
Personalaufwand (Löhne)			

Kapitel 2: Standardrevisionsunterlagen bei der AG für den Review

Buchsaldo:	CHF		
Haben Sie eine Belegstichprobe gemacht (von der Buchung zum Beleg) ?			
Haben Sie die AHV-Jahreslohnbescheinigung eingesehen?			
Bemerkung			

Sozialversicherungsaufwand

Buchsaldo:	CHF		
Haben Sie eine Belegstichprobe gemacht (von der Buchung zum Beleg)?			
Bemerkung			

Übriger Personalaufwand

Buchsaldo:	CHF		
Haben Sie eine Belegstichprobe gemacht (von der Buchung zum Beleg)?			
Bemerkung			

Raumaufwand

Buchsaldo:	CHF		
Haben Sie eine Belegstichprobe gemacht (von der Buchung zum Beleg)?			
Bemerkung			

Unterhalt und Reparaturen

Buchsaldo:	CHF		
Haben Sie eine Belegstichprobe gemacht			

Teil G: Anhänge und Unterlagen / Appendices and documents

(von der Buchung zum Beleg)?			
Bemerkung			

Leasing			
Buchsaldo:	CHF		
Haben Sie eine Belegstichprobe gemacht (von der Buchung zum Beleg)?			
Bemerkung			

Fahrzeugaufwand			
Buchsaldo:	CHF		
Haben Sie eine Belegstichprobe gemacht (von der Buchung zum Beleg)?			
Bemerkung			

Sachversicherungsaufwand			
Buchsaldo	CHF		
Haben Sie eine Belegstichprobe gemacht (von der Buchung zum Beleg)?			
Bemerkung			

Abgaben, Gebühren, Bewilligungen			
Buchsaldo:	CHF		
Haben Sie eine Belegstichprobe gemacht (von der Buchung zum Beleg)?			
Bemerkung			

Kapitel 2: Standardrevisionsunterlagen bei der AG für den Review

Energieaufwand			
Buchsaldo:	CHF		
Haben Sie eine Belegstichprobe gemacht (von der Buchung zum Beleg)?			
Bemerkung			
Entsorgungsaufwand			
Buchsaldo:	CHF		
Haben Sie eine Belegstichprobe gemacht (von der Buchung zum Beleg)?			
Bemerkung			
Verwaltungsaufwand			
Buchsaldo:	CHF		
Haben Sie eine Belegstichprobe gemacht (von der Buchung zum Beleg)?			
Bemerkung			
Informatikaufwand			
Buchsaldo:	CHF		
Haben Sie eine Belegstichprobe gemacht (von der Buchung zum Beleg)?			
Bemerkung			
Werbeaufwand			
Buchsaldo:	CHF		
Haben Sie eine Belegstichprobe gemacht			

Teil G: Anhänge und Unterlagen / Appendices and documents

(von der Buchung zum Beleg)?			
Bemerkung			
Zinsaufwand			
Buchsaldo:	CHF		
Haben Sie eine Belegstichprobe gemacht (von der Buchung zum Beleg)?			
Bemerkung			
Abschreibungen			
Buchsaldo:	CHF		
Sind alle Anlagekonti abgeschrieben worden?			
Bemerkung			
Übriger Aufwand			
Buchsaldo:	CHF		
Haben Sie eine Belegstichprobe gemacht (von der Buchung zum Beleg)?			
Bemerkung			
Steueraufwand			
Buchsaldo:	CHF		
Haben Sie eine Belegstichprobe gemacht (von der Buchung zum Beleg)?			
Sind die 35% Verrechnungssteuer der letzten Dividende nicht als Aufwand verbucht?			
Wurde die Steuererklärung einge-			

reicht?			
Bemerkung			
Sind die Aufwandkonti rein geführt, ohne direkte Verrechnung von Ertrag (Bruttoprinzip/Verrechnungsverbot)?			

ANHANG	Ja	Nein
Haben Sie geprüft, ob der Anhang alle ausweispflichtigen Angaben enthält?		
1. Bürgschaften etc. für Dritte		
2. Abgetretene Aktiven für eigene Verbindlichkeiten		
3. nicht-bilanzierte Leasingverbindlichkeiten		
4. Brandversicherungswerte der Sachanlagen		
5. Verbindlichkeiten gegenüber Vorsorgeeinrichtungen		
6. Anleihensobligationen		
7. Beteiligungen		
8. Nettobetrag der aufgelösten Reserven		
9. Aufwertungen		
10. Eigene Aktien		
11. Kapitalerhöhung		
12. Risikobeurteilung		
13. Rücktritt der Revisionsstelle		
14. Andere Angaben		

Kontrollfragen zum Anhang:

1. Besteht kein Rückstellungsbedarf für Bürgschaften?		

Teil G: Anhänge und Unterlagen / Appendices and documents

2. Besteht kein Rückstellungsbedarf für Pfandbestellungen zugunsten Dritter?		
3. Besteht kein Rückstellungsbedarf für Garantieverträge?		
4. Existiert kein Bankkredit mit Debitorenzession, der im Anhang nicht aufgeführt ist?		
5. Existiert kein aktiviertes Mietzinsdepotkonto, das im Anhang nicht aufgeführt ist?		
6. Bestehen keine Auflösungen von wesentlichen stillen Reserven?		
7. Bestehen keine Abweichungen zu den Bewertungsvorschriften?		
8. Bestehen keine Abweichungen zur Stetigkeit?		
9. Müssen keine wesentlichen Informationen in den Anhang aufgenommen werden?		
Abschliessende Fragen		
1. Haben Sie den Gewinnverwendungsvorschlag geprüft?		
2. Sind keine ungewöhnlichen Veränderungen gegenüber dem Vorjahr vorhanden, für die keine Erklärung vorliegt?		
3. Gibt es keine wesentlichen Ereignisse nach Bilanzstichtag, die das Gesamtbild verändern?		
4. Ist eine zuverlässige Beurteilung der Vermögens- und Ertragslage möglich?		
5. Ist eine zuverlässige Beurteilung der Finanzlage möglich?		
6. Entsprechen Bilanz und Erfolgsrechnung den Mindestgliederungsvorschriften?		
Schlussbemerkung		

Kapitel 2: Standardrevisionsunterlagen bei der AG für den Review

Datum und Unterschrift des Revisors oder der Revisoren		

Kapitel 3:
Kurzfassung der Standardrevisionsunterlagen bei der AG für den Review

Je mehr Ja-Antworten Sie ankreuzen, desto eher können Sie den Bericht abgeben. Verneinende Fragen sind mit Ja – Bestätigung der Verneinung – zu beantworten (Haben Sie keine Probleme? – Ja, ich habe keine Probleme). Wenn Sie aufgrund von Nein-Antworten unsicher sind, zeigen Sie diese Arbeitspapiere einer Zweitperson. Sie kann Ihnen helfen, zu einem Urteil und zu Ihrem Revisionsbericht zu gelangen.

FIRMA	AG
Bereich	

Revisionsfirma
Name des leitenden Revisors
Name des zweiten Revisors
Mandat   Jahr

Allgemeine Fragen	Ja	Nein
Sind Sie als Revisionsstelle im Handelsregister eingetragen?		
Sind Sie gemäss GV-Protokoll als Revisionsstelle gewählt?		
Haben Sie eine kaufmännische Berufsausbildung?		
Haben Sie Erfahrung auf dem Gebiet der Revision?		
Sind Sie fähig, aufgrund ihrer Kenntnisse die vorliegende Rechnungslegung im Hinblick auf Umfang und Schwierigkeitsgrad zu prüfen?		
Sind Sie unabhängig im Hinblick auf die Revision?		
Führen Sie nur Arbeiten für die AG aus, die mit der Revision		

Kapitel 3: Kurzfassung der Standardrevisionsunterlagen

vereinbar sind?		
Sind Sie nicht im Verwaltungsrat der AG?		
Führen Sie nicht die Buchhaltung, die Sie revidieren?		
Ist der Buchhalter nicht mit Ihnen verwandt?		
Ist der Verwaltungsrat nicht mit Ihnen verwandt?		
Können Sie auf dieses Mandat bei Schwierigkeiten verzichten, ohne dass Sie ihre Büroorganisation ändern müssen?		
Können Sie auf dieses Mandat bei Schwierigkeiten verzichten, ohne dass Sie der Honorarverlust allzu sehr schmerzt?		
Können Sie – sofern es die Situation erfordert – die Jahresrechnung zur Nicht-Genehmigung empfehlen, ohne dass Sie ein schlechtes Gewissen gegenüber der Verwaltung haben?		
Haben Sie einen aktuellen Handelsregisterauszug (1–3 Jahre alt)?		
Kennen Sie alle Verwaltungsräte?		
Kennen Sie den verantwortlichen Buchhalter der AG?		
Haben Sie die Statuten der AG?		
Gibt es in den Statuten keine besonderen Bestimmungen für die Revisionsstelle?		
Existiert ein Protokoll zur letzten o/GV?		
Wurde die letzte Jahresrechnung genehmigt?		
Gab es keine a/o GV?		
Gibt es ein Organisationsreglement?		
Haben Sie keine Fragen mehr zur letztjährigen Revision?		
Haben Sie keine offenen Kontrollen mehr vom letzten Jahr?		
Ist die Buchhaltungsperson nicht alleine unterschriftsberechtigt?		
Ist die Buchhaltungsperson nicht für den Zahlungsverkehr		

Teil G: Anhänge und Unterlagen / Appendices and documents

alleine verantwortlich?		

Grundlagen	Ja	Nein
Ist die Bilanz rechtsgültig unterzeichnet?		
Ist die Erfolgsrechnung rechtsgültig unterzeichnet?		
Ist der Anhang rechtsgültig unterzeichnet?		
Liegt eine unterzeichnete Vollständigkeitserklärung vor?		
Liegt ein unterzeichneter Gewinnverwendungsvorschlag vor?		
Liegt ein Jahresbericht (Text zum Geschäftsjahr) vor?		
Erfolgt die Revision innerhalb von 6 Monaten seit Bilanzstichtag?		
Erfolgt die Revision innerhalb von 12 Monaten seit Bilanzstichtag?		
Existiert ein Budget?		

Buchhaltung	Ja	Nein
Liegt ein kompletter Ausdruck aller Kontoblätter, Journale, Bilanzen und der Erfolgsrechnung des Vorjahres vor?		
Liegt eine Bilanz vor?		
Liegt eine Erfolgsrechnung vor?		
Wenn eine Abschrift existiert, stimmt diese mit der EDV überein?		
Wenn eine Abschrift vorliegt, stimmt die Addition?		
Stimmt die Eröffnungsbilanz des laufenden Jahres mit der Schlussbilanz des Vorjahres überein?		
Sind die Hauptbuchkonti ausgedruckt?		
Ist das Journal vorliegend?		

Kapitel 3: Kurzfassung der Standardrevisionsunterlagen

Ist die Buchhaltung auf einem Datenträger gespeichert?		
Haben Sie 1-2 Kontoblätter addiert (rechnerische Kontrolle)?		
Ist die Belegablage geordnet?		
Finden Sie zu jedem Beleg eine Buchung? (Antwort aufgrund von Stichproben)		
Sind die Belege des Vorjahres vorhanden?		
Bewahrt die Gesellschaft ihre Akten der letzten 10 Jahre auf?		
Wurde das letzte Mal innerhalb eines Monats gebucht?		
Wurde das letzte Mal innerhalb zweier Monate gebucht?		
Wurde das letzte Mal innerhalb dreier Monate gebucht?		
Ist die Buchhaltung à jour?		
Sind die Buchungen mit Buchungstexten versehen?		
Sind die Konti klar geführt?		
Wurde dem Verrechnungsverbot Rechnung getragen?		

BILANZ	Eröffnungssaldo	Schlusssaldo		
Es empfiehlt sich eine lückenlose Prüfung der Bilanz, wobei einzelne Bilanzposten nach dem Stichprobenprinzip geprüft werden. Lückenlos: Bank; Stichprobe: Debitoren	Buchsaldi oder geprüfte Bilanz	Buchsaldi oder geprüfte Bilanz		
AKTIVEN				

Teil G: Anhänge und Unterlagen / Appendices and documents

Umlaufvermögen				
Umlaufvermögen. Wie hoch ist der Anteil an der Bilanzsumme?	......%			
Kasse				
Buchsaldi:	CHF	CHF		
Haben Sie den Bestand geprüft?				
Haben Sie den Verkehr kritisch gesichtet?				
Hat nur eine Person Zugang zur Kasse?				
Bemerkung				
Postkonto				
Buchsaldi:	CHF	CHF		
Haben Sie den Bestand geprüft?				
Haben Sie den Verkehr kritisch gesichtet?				
Bemerkung				
Bank				
Buchsaldi:	CHF	CHF		
Haben Sie den Bestand geprüft?				
Haben Sie den Verkehr kritisch gesichtet?				
Bemerkung				
Wertschriften				

Kapitel 3: Kurzfassung der Standardrevisionsunterlagen

Buchsaldi:	CHF	CHF		
Haben Sie den Bestand geprüft?				
Ist die Bewertung korrekt?				
Haben Sie einen Depotauszug der Bank?				
Haben Sie den Verkehr kritisch gesichtet?				
Bemerkung				

Wertberichtigungen auf Wertschriften

Buchsaldi:	CHF	CHF		
Haben Sie den Bestand (Bewegungen) geprüft?				
Ist die Bewertung korrekt?				
Haben Sie den Verkehr kritisch gesichtet?				
Bemerkung				

Forderungen aus Lieferungen und Leistungen: Debitoren

Buchsaldi:	CHF	CHF		
Haben Sie den Bestand (Debitorenliste) geprüft?				
Ist die Bewertung korrekt (5% Delkredere CH und 10% Ausland)?				
Haben Sie den Verkehr kritisch gesichtet?				
Liegt eine unterzeichnete Debitorenliste vor?				
Wissen Sie, wie viele der Debitoren				

am Bilanzstichtag bezahlt sind?				
Bemerkung				

Forderung gegenüber Aktionär/en

Buchsaldi:	CHF	CHF	
Haben Sie den Bestand geprüft?			
Ist die Bewertung korrekt?			
Haben Sie den Verkehr kritisch gesichtet?			
Bemerkung			

Mehrwertsteuer

Buchsaldi:	CHF	CHF	
Haben Sie den Bestand geprüft?			
Ist die Bewertung korrekt?			
Haben Sie die Mehrwertsteuerabrechnungen eingesehen?			
Stimmt der MwSt-Umsatz mit der Buchhaltung überein?			
Bemerkung			

Guthaben Verrechnungssteuer

Buchsaldi:	CHF	CHF	
Haben Sie den Bestand geprüft?			
Ist die Bewertung korrekt?			
Wurde das Formular 25 Rückerstattung eingereicht?			

Kapitel 3: Kurzfassung der Standardrevisionsunterlagen

Haben Sie den Verkehr kritisch gesichtet?				
Bemerkung				
Guthaben AHV/BVG/SUVA				
Buchsaldi:	CHF	CHF		
Haben Sie den Bestand geprüft?				
Ist die Bewertung korrekt?				
Haben Sie den Verkehr kritisch gesichtet?				
Bemerkung				
WIR Forderungen				
Buchsaldi:	CHF	CHF		
Haben Sie den Bestand geprüft?				
Ist die Bewertung korrekt?				
Haben Sie den Verkehr kritisch gesichtet?				
Bemerkung				
Vorräte				
Buchsaldi:	CHF	CHF		
Haben Sie den Bestand geprüft?				
Ist die Bewertung korrekt?				
Haben Sie den Verkehr kritisch gesichtet?				
Gibt es ein Wareninventar?				

Teil G: Anhänge und Unterlagen / Appendices and documents

Waren Sie bei der Inventur anwesend?				
Haben Sie das aktuelle Warenlager gesehen?				
Bemerkung				

Wertberichtigung Vorräte

Buchsaldi:	CHF	CHF		
Haben Sie den Bestand geprüft?				
Ist die Bewertung korrekt?				
Hat sich die Warenlagerreserve verändert?				
Haben Sie den Verkehr kritisch gesichtet?				
Bemerkung				

Transitorische Aktiven

Buchsaldi:	CHF	CHF		
Haben Sie den Bestand geprüft?				
Ist die Bewertung korrekt?				
Haben sich die TA des Vorjahres aufgelöst?				
Bemerkung				

Anlagevermögen

Maschinen

Buchsaldi:	CHF	CHF		

Kapitel 3: Kurzfassung der Standardrevisionsunterlagen

Haben Sie den Bestand geprüft (Zugang/Abgang)?				
Existiert eine Anlagekartei?				
Haben Sie bei wesentlichen Neuzugängen den Kaufvertrag eingesehen?				
Ist die Bewertung korrekt?				
Wurden Abschreibungen vorgenommen?				
Bemerkung				

Produktionsanlagen

Buchsaldi:	CHF	CHF		
Haben Sie den Bestand geprüft (Zugang/Abgang)?				
Existiert eine Anlagekartei?				
Haben Sie bei wesentlichen Neuzugängen den Kaufvertrag eingesehen?				
Ist die Bewertung korrekt?				
Wurden Abschreibungen vorgenommen?				
Bemerkung				

Mobiliar

Buchsaldi:	CHF	CHF		
Haben Sie den Bestand geprüft (Zugang/Abgang)?				
Existiert eine Anlagekartei?				
Haben Sie bei wesentlichen Neuzugängen den Kaufvertrag eingesehen?				

Teil G: Anhänge und Unterlagen / Appendices and documents

Ist die Bewertung korrekt?				
Wurden Abschreibungen vorgenommen?				
Bemerkung				
Büromaschinen				
Buchsaldi:	CHF	CHF		
Haben Sie den Bestand geprüft (Zugang/Abgang)?				
Existiert eine Anlagekartei?				
Haben Sie bei wesentlichen Neuzugängen den Kaufvertrag eingesehen?				
Ist die Bewertung korrekt?				
Wurden Abschreibungen vorgenommen?				
Bemerkung				
EDV				
Buchsaldi:	CHF	CHF		
Haben Sie den Bestand geprüft (Zugang/Abgang)?				
Existiert eine Anlagekartei?				
Haben Sie bei wesentlichen Neuzugängen den Kaufvertrag eingesehen?				
Ist die Bewertung korrekt?				
Wurden Abschreibungen vorgenommen?				
Bemerkung				

Kapitel 3: Kurzfassung der Standardrevisionsunterlagen

Fahrzeuge				
Buchsaldi:	CHF	CHF		
Haben Sie den Bestand geprüft (Zugang/Abgang)?				
Existiert eine Anlagekartei?				
Haben Sie bei wesentlichen Neuzugängen den Kaufvertrag eingesehen?				
Ist die Bewertung korrekt?				
Wurden Abschreibungen vorgenommen?				
Bemerkung				
Werkzeug und Geräte				
Buchsaldi:	CHF	CHF		
Haben Sie den Bestand geprüft (Zugang/Abgang)?				
Existiert eine Anlagekartei?				
Haben Sie bei wesentlichen Neuzugängen den Kaufvertrag eingesehen?				
Ist die Bewertung korrekt?				
Wurden Abschreibungen vorgenommen?				
Bemerkung				
Liegenschaft/en				
Buchsaldi:	CHF	CHF		
Haben Sie den Bestand geprüft (Zu-				

Teil G: Anhänge und Unterlagen / Appendices and documents

gang/Abgang)?				
Existiert eine Anlagekartei (Grundbuchauszug)?				
Ist die Bewertung korrekt?				
Wurden Abschreibungen vorgenommen?				
Bemerkung				

PASSIVEN

Fremdkapital

Verbindlichkeiten aus Lieferungen und Leistungen: Kreditoren

Buchsaldi:	CHF	CHF	
Haben Sie den Bestand geprüft?			
Haben Sie den Verkehr kritisch gesichtet?			
Bemerkung			

Verbindlichkeiten aus Lieferungen und Leistungen gegenüber Aktionären

Buchsaldi:	CHF	CHF	
Haben Sie den Bestand geprüft?			
Haben Sie den Verkehr kritisch gesichtet?			
Bemerkung			

Bankverbindlichkeiten

Kapitel 3: Kurzfassung der Standardrevisionsunterlagen

Buchsaldi:	CHF	CHF		
Haben Sie den Bestand geprüft?				
Haben Sie den Verkehr kritisch gesichtet?				
Bemerkung				

Sonstige Verbindlichkeiten gegenüber Dritten

Buchsaldi:	CHF	CHF		
Haben Sie den Bestand geprüft?				
Haben Sie den Verkehr kritisch gesichtet?				
Bemerkung				

Sonstige Verbindlichkeiten gegenüber Aktionären

Buchsaldi:	CHF	CHF		
Haben Sie den Bestand geprüft?				
Haben Sie den Verkehr kritisch gesichtet?				
Bemerkung				

Verbindlichkeiten gegenüber Vorsorgeeinrichtungen

Buchsaldi:	CHF	CHF		
Haben Sie den Bestand geprüft?				
Haben Sie den Verkehr kritisch gesichtet?				
Bemerkung				

Teil G: Anhänge und Unterlagen / Appendices and documents

Transitorische Passiven				
Buchsaldi:	CHF	CHF		
Haben Sie den Bestand geprüft?				
Haben Sie den Verkehr kritisch gesichtet?				
Haben sich die TP des Vorjahres aufgelöst?				
Bemerkung				

Rückstellungen				
Buchsaldi:	CHF	CHF		
Haben Sie den Bestand geprüft?				
Haben Sie den Verkehr kritisch gesichtet?				
Bemerkung				

Eigenkapital				

Aktienkapital				
Buchsaldi:	CHF	CHF		
Gab es keine Veränderung?				
Ist das Kapital 100% vorhanden?				
Besteht kein Kapitalverlust?				
Bemerkung				

Gesetzliche Reserven				

Kapitel 3: Kurzfassung der Standardrevisionsunterlagen

Buchsaldi:	CHF	CHF		
Wurde die Gewinnverteilung des Vorjahres verbucht?				
Sind das Kapital und die Reserven 100% vorhanden?				
Bemerkung				

Freie Reserven

Buchsaldi:	CHF	CHF		
Wurde die Gewinnverteilung des Vorjahres verbucht?				
Sind das Kapital und die Reserven 100% vorhanden?				
Bemerkung				
Entspricht die Darstellung der Konti, mit Ausnahme von Neuem und Weggefallenem, dem Vorjahr (Prinzip der Stetigkeit)?				

ERFOLGSRECHNUNG

Ertrag

Ertragskonto 1

Buchsaldo:		CHF		
Haben Sie eine Belegstichprobe gemacht (von der Buchung zum Beleg)?				
Bemerkung				

Teil G: Anhänge und Unterlagen / Appendices and documents

Ertragskonto 2

Buchsaldo:	CHF		
Haben Sie eine Belegstichprobe gemacht (von der Buchung zum Beleg)?			
Bemerkung			

Ertragskonto 3

Buchsaldo:	CHF		
Haben Sie eine Belegstichprobe gemacht (von der Buchung zum Beleg) ?			
Bemerkung			

Ertragskonto 4

Buchsaldo:	CHF		
Haben Sie eine Belegstichprobe gemacht (von der Buchung zum Beleg)?			
Bemerkung			

Ertragskonto 5

Buchsaldo:	CHF		
Haben Sie eine Belegstichprobe gemacht (von der Buchung zum Beleg)?			
Bemerkung			

Aufwand

Aufwandkonto 1

Buchsaldo:	CHF		
Haben Sie eine Belegstichprobe gemacht (von der Buchung zum Beleg)?			
Bemerkung			

Aufwandkonto 2

Buchsaldo:	CHF		
Haben Sie eine Belegstichprobe gemacht (von der Buchung zum Beleg)?			
Bemerkung			

Aufwandkonto 3

Buchsaldo:	CHF		
Haben Sie eine Belegstichprobe gemacht (von der Buchung zum Beleg)?			
Bemerkung			

Aufwandkonto 4

Buchsaldo:	CHF		
Haben Sie eine Belegstichprobe gemacht (von der Buchung zum Beleg)?			
Bemerkung			

Aufwandkonto 5

Buchsaldo:	CHF		
Haben Sie eine Belegstichprobe gemacht (von der Buchung zum Beleg)?			

Teil G: Anhänge und Unterlagen / Appendices and documents

Bemerkung			

Aufwandkonto 6			
Buchsaldo:	CHF		
Haben Sie eine Belegstichprobe gemacht (von der Buchung zum Beleg)?			
Bemerkung			

Aufwandkonto 7			
Buchsaldo:	CHF		
Haben Sie eine Belegstichprobe gemacht (von der Buchung zum Beleg)?			
Bemerkung			

Aufwandkonto 8			
Buchsaldo:	CHF		
Haben Sie eine Belegstichprobe gemacht (von der Buchung zum Beleg)?			
Bemerkung			

Aufwandkonto 9			
Buchsaldo:	CHF		
Haben Sie eine Belegstichprobe gemacht (von der Buchung zum Beleg)?			
Bemerkung			

Aufwandkonto 10			

Kapitel 3: Kurzfassung der Standardrevisionsunterlagen

Buchsaldo:	CHF	
Haben Sie eine Belegstichprobe gemacht (von der Buchung zum Beleg)?		
Bemerkung		

ANHANG	Ja	Nein
Haben Sie geprüft, ob der Anhang alle ausweispflichtigen Angaben enthält?		
1. Bürgschaften etc. für Dritte		
2. Abgetretene Aktiven für eigene Verbindlichkeiten		
3. nicht bilanzierte Leasingverbindlichkeiten		
4. Brandversicherungswerte der Sachanlagen		
5. Verbindlichkeiten gegenüber Vorsorgeeinrichtungen		
6. Anleihensobligationen		
7. Beteiligungen		
8. Nettobetrag der aufgelösten Reserven		
9. Aufwertungen		
10. Eigene Aktien		
11. Kapitalerhöhung		
12. Risikobeurteilung		
13. Rücktritt der Revisionsstelle		
14. Andere Angaben		
Kontrollfragen zum Anhang		
1. Besteht kein Rückstellungsbedarf für Bürgschaften?		

2. Besteht kein Rückstellungsbedarf für Pfandbestellungen zugunsten Dritter?		
3. Besteht kein Rückstellungsbedarf für Garantieverträge?		
4. Existiert kein Bankkredit mit Debitorenzession, der im Anhang nicht aufgeführt ist?		
5. Existiert kein aktiviertes Mietzinsdepotkonto, das im Anhang nicht aufgeführt ist?		
6. Bestehen keine Auflösungen von wesentlichen stillen Reserven?		
7. Bestehen keine Abweichungen zu den Bewertungsvorschriften?		
8. Bestehen keine Abweichungen zur Stetigkeit?		
9. Müssen keine wesentlichen Informationen in den Anhang aufgenommen werden?		

Abschliessende Fragen

1. Haben Sie den Gewinnverwendungsvorschlag geprüft?		
2. Sind keine ungewöhnlichen Veränderungen gegenüber dem Vorjahr vorhanden, für die keine Erklärung vorliegt?		
3. Gibt es keine wesentlichen Ereignisse nach Bilanzstichtag, die das Gesamtbild verändern?		
4. Ist eine zuverlässige Beurteilung der Vermögens- und Ertragslage möglich?		
5. Ist eine zuverlässige Beurteilung der Finanzlage möglich?		
6. Entsprechen Bilanz und Erfolgsrechnung den Mindestgliederungsvorschriften?		

Schlussbemerkung

Kapitel 3: Kurzfassung der Standardrevisionsunterlagen

| Datum und Unterschrift des Revisors oder der Revisoren | | |

Kapitel 4:
Standardrevisionsunterlagen (Kurzfassung für Vereine etc.)

J e mehr Ja-Antworten Sie ankreuzen, desto eher können Sie den Bericht abgeben. Verneinende Fragen sind mit Ja – Bestätigung der Verneinung – zu beantworten (Haben Sie keine Probleme? – Ja, ich habe keine Probleme). Wenn Sie aufgrund von Nein-Antworten unsicher sind, zeigen Sie diese Arbeitspapiere einer Zweitperson. Sie kann Ihnen helfen, zu einem Urteil und zu Ihrem Revisionsbericht zu gelangen.

FIRMA	AG

Mandat	Jahr

Name und Adresse des Revisors

Allgemeine Fragen	Ja	Nein
Haben Sie die Statuten?		
Gibt es in den Statuten keine besonderen Bestimmungen für die Revisionsstelle?		
Sind Sie gemäss Mitgliederversammlungs-Protokollen als Revisionsstelle gewählt?		
Haben Sie kaufmännische Grundkenntnisse?		
Fühlen Sie sich fähig, die Bilanz und Erfolgsrechnung zu revidieren?		
Sind Sie unabhängig für die Durchführung der Prüfung?		
Können Sie jedem Vorstandsmitglied/Verwaltungsrat Unstimmigkeiten mitteilen?		

Kapitel 4: Standardrevisionsunterlagen (Kurzfassung für Vereine etc.)

Sind Sie frei von jeder Verpflichtung für eine unabhängige Revision?		

Grundlagen		
Ist die Bilanz rechtsgültig unterzeichnet?		
Ist die Erfolgsrechnung rechtsgültig unterzeichnet?		

Buchhaltung		
Liegt ein kompletter Ausdruck aller Kontoblätter, Journale, Bilanzen und der Erfolgsrechnung des Vorjahres vor?		
Liegt eine Bilanz vor?		
Liegt eine Erfolgsrechnung vor?		
Wenn eine Abschrift existiert, stimmt diese mit der EDV überein?		
Wenn eine Abschrift vorliegt, stimmt die Addition?		
Stimmt die Eröffnungsbilanz des laufenden Jahres mit der Schlussbilanz des Vorjahres überein?		
Sind die Hauptbuchkonti ausgedruckt?		
Ist das Journal vorliegend?		
Ist die Buchhaltung auf einem Datenträger gespeichert?		

DIE EINZELNEN KONTI				
BILANZ	**Eröffnungssaldo**	**Schluss-saldo**		
Es empfiehlt sich eine lückenlose Prüfung der Bilanz, wobei einzelne Bilanzposten nach dem Stichprobenprinzip geprüft werden.	Buchsaldi oder geprüfte Bilanz	Buch-saldi oder geprüf-		

Teil G: Anhänge und Unterlagen / Appendices and documents

		te Bi-lanz		
Umlaufvermögen				
Kasse				
Buchsaldi:		CHF	CHF	
Haben Sie den Bestand geprüft				
Haben Sie den Verkehr kritisch gesichtet				
Bemerkung				
Post				
Buchsaldi:		CHF	CHF	
Haben Sie den Bestand geprüft?				
Haben Sie den Verkehr kritisch gesichtet?				
Bemerkung				
Bank				
Buchsaldi:		CHF	CHF	
Haben Sie den Bestand geprüft?				
Haben Sie den Verkehr kritisch gesichtet?				
Bemerkung				
Wertschriften				

972

Kapitel 4: Standardrevisionsunterlagen (Kurzfassung für Vereine etc.)

Buchsaldi:	CHF	CHF		
Haben Sie den Bestand geprüft?				
Haben Sie den Verkehr kritisch gesichtet?				
Bemerkung				

Guthaben

Buchsaldi:	CHF	CHF		
Haben Sie den Bestand geprüft?				
Haben Sie den Verkehr kritisch gesichtet?				
Bemerkung				

Forderung

Buchsaldi:	CHF	CHF		
Haben Sie den Bestand geprüft?				
Haben Sie den Verkehr kritisch gesichtet?				
Bemerkung				

Vorräte

Buchsaldi:	CHF	CHF		
Haben Sie den Bestand geprüft?				
Ist die Bewertung korrekt?				
Haben Sie den Verkehr kritisch gesichtet?				
Gibt es ein Wareninventar?				

Teil G: Anhänge und Unterlagen / Appendices and documents

Waren Sie bei der Inventur anwesend?				
Haben Sie das aktuelle Warenlager gesehen?				
Bemerkung				
Haben Sie den Bestand geprüft (Abschreibungen)?				
Bemerkung				

Wertberichtigung Vorräte				
Buchsaldi:	CHF	CHF		
Haben Sie den Bestand geprüft?				
Ist die Bewertung korrekt?				
Hat sich die Warenlagerreserve verändert?				
Haben Sie den Verkehr kritisch gesichtet?				
Bemerkung				

Angefangene Arbeiten				
Buchsaldi:	CHF	CHF		
Haben Sie den Bestand geprüft?				
Ist genügend Liquidität vorhanden, um die Arbeiten zu Ende zu führen?				
Ist die Bewertung korrekt?				
Haben Sie den Verkehr kritisch gesichtet?				
Bemerkung				

Kapitel 4: Standardrevisionsunterlagen (Kurzfassung für Vereine etc.)

Transitorische Aktiven				
Buchsaldi:	CHF	CHF		
Haben Sie den Bestand geprüft?				
Ist die Bewertung korrekt?				
Haben sich die TA des Vorjahres aufgelöst?				
Bemerkung				
Anlagevermögen				
Maschinen				
Buchsaldi:	CHF	CHF		
Haben Sie den Bestand geprüft (Zugang/Abgang)?				
Existiert eine Anlagekartei?				
Haben Sie bei wesentlichen Neuzugängen den Kaufvertrag eingesehen?				
Ist die Bewertung korrekt?				
Wurden Abschreibungen vorgenommen?				
Bemerkung				
Mobiliar/Einrichtungen				
Buchsaldi:	CHF	CHF		
Haben Sie den Bestand geprüft (Zugang/Abgang)?				
Existiert eine Anlagekartei?				

Haben Sie bei wesentlichen Neuzugängen den Kaufvertrag eingesehen?				
Ist die Bewertung korrekt?				
Wurden Abschreibungen vorgenommen?				
Bemerkung				

Fahrzeuge

Buchsaldi:	CHF	CHF		
Haben Sie den Bestand geprüft (Zugang/Abgang)?				
Existiert eine Anlagekartei?				
Haben Sie bei wesentlichen Neuzugängen den Kaufvertrag eingesehen?				
Ist die Bewertung korrekt?				
Wurden Abschreibungen vorgenommen?				
Bemerkung				

Fremdkapital

Kreditoren

Buchsaldi	CHF	CHF		
Haben Sie den Bestand geprüft (Kreditorenliste)?				
Wurden alle Kreditoren des Vorjahres bezahlt?				
Bemerkungen				

Kapitel 4:   Standardrevisionsunterlagen (Kurzfassung für Vereine etc.)

Sonstige Verbindlichkeiten				
Buchsaldi	CHF	CHF		
Haben Sie den Bestand geprüft?				
Bemerkungen				
Darlehen				
Buchsaldi	CHF	CHF		
Haben Sie den Bestand geprüft?				
Bemerkungen				
Bankschuld				
Buchsaldi	CHF	CHF		
Haben Sie den Bestand geprüft?				
Bemerkungen				
Eigenkapital				
Kapital				
Buchsaldi:	CHF	CHF		
Gab es keine Veränderung?				
Ist das Kapital 100% vorhanden?				
Besteht kein Kapitalverlust?				
Bemerkung				
Reserven 1				

Teil G: Anhänge und Unterlagen / Appendices and documents

Buchsaldi:	CHF	CHF		
Wurde die Gewinnverteilung des Vorjahres verbucht?				
Sind das Kapital und die Reserven 100% vorhanden?				
Bemerkung				

Reserven 2

Buchsaldi:	CHF	CHF		
Wurde die Gewinnverteilung des Vorjahres verbucht?				
Sind das Kapital und die Reserven 100% vorhanden?				
Bemerkung				

ERFOLGSRECHNUNG

Ertrag

Ertragskonto 1

Buchsaldo:	CHF		
Haben Sie eine Belegstichprobe gemacht (von der Buchung zum Beleg)?			
Bemerkung			

Ertragskonto 2

Buchsaldo:	CHF		
Haben Sie eine Belegstichprobe gemacht (von			

Kapitel 4: Standardrevisionsunterlagen (Kurzfassung für Vereine etc.)

der Buchung zum Beleg)?			
Bemerkung			
Ertragskonto 3			
Buchsaldo:	CHF		
Haben Sie eine Belegstichprobe gemacht (von der Buchung zum Beleg)?			
Bemerkung			
Ertragskonto 4			
Buchsaldo:	CHF		
Haben Sie eine Belegstichprobe gemacht (von der Buchung zum Beleg)?			
Bemerkung			
Ertragskonto 5			
Buchsaldo:	CHF		
Haben Sie eine Belegstichprobe gemacht (von der Buchung zum Beleg)?			
Bemerkung			
Aufwand			
Aufwandkonto 1			
Buchsaldo:	CHF		
Haben Sie eine Belegstichprobe gemacht (von der Buchung zum Beleg)?			

Teil G: Anhänge und Unterlagen / Appendices and documents

Bemerkung			

Aufwandkonto 2

Buchsaldo:	CHF		
Haben Sie eine Belegstichprobe gemacht (von der Buchung zum Beleg)?			
Bemerkung			

Aufwandkonto 3

Buchsaldo:	CHF		
Haben Sie eine Belegstichprobe gemacht (von der Buchung zum Beleg)?			
Bemerkung			

Aufwandkonto 4

Buchsaldo:	CHF		
Haben Sie eine Belegstichprobe gemacht (von der Buchung zum Beleg)?			
Bemerkung			

Aufwandkonto 5

Buchsaldo:	CHF		
Haben Sie eine Belegstichprobe gemacht (von der Buchung zum Beleg)?			
Bemerkung			

Aufwandkonto 6

Buchsaldo:	CHF		
Haben Sie eine Belegstichprobe gemacht (von der Buchung zum Beleg)?			
Bemerkung			

Aufwandkonto 7

Buchsaldo:	CHF		
Haben Sie eine Belegstichprobe gemacht (von der Buchung zum Beleg)?			
Bemerkung			

Aufwandkonto 8

Buchsaldo:	CHF		
Haben Sie eine Belegstichprobe gemacht (von der Buchung zum Beleg)?			
Bemerkung			

Aufwandkonto 9

Buchsaldo:	CHF		
Haben Sie eine Belegstichprobe gemacht (von der Buchung zum Beleg)?			
Bemerkung			

Aufwandkonto 10

Buchsaldo:	CHF		
Haben Sie eine Belegstichprobe gemacht (von der Buchung zum Beleg)?			
Bemerkung			

Teil G: Anhänge und Unterlagen / Appendices and documents

Schlussbemerkung			
Datum und Unterschrift des Revisors			

Kapitel 5:
Contents of Swiss Handbook on Auditing (HWP, MSA)

The Schweizer Handbuch der Wirtschaftsprüfung (HWP), Manuel Suisse d'Audit (MSA) contains about 1,650 pages. It was issued 1998 by the Swiss Institute of Certified Auditors (Treuhhand-Kammer), Zurich, in German and French. A revised version is in preparation for the year 2009. Below the contents of the current 1998 issues are summarised.

Wichtigste Bestandteile: Main contents:

Original titles (German)   **English translation**

Band 1 HWP (378 Seiten)	**Volume 1 (378 pages)**
1 Einführung	Introduction
2 Buchführung und Rechnungslegung	Accounting and reporting
Allgemeine Anforderungen an das Rechnungswesen	General requirements for accounting
2.2 Buchführungs- und Rechnungslegungsvorschriften nach schweizerischem Recht	Accounting and reporting rules under Swiss legal requirements
3.3 Buchführungs- und Rechnungslegungspraxis in der Schweiz	Accounting and reporting practice in Switzerland
3.4 Verwendung des Bilanzgewinnes und offene Reserven	Appropriation of retained earnings and other reserves

Teil G: Anhänge und Unterlagen / Appendices and documents

Band 2 HWP (462 Seiten)	Volume 2 (462 pages)
3 Prüfung	Auditing
3.1 Grundlage der Prüfung	Basis of auditing
3.2 Prüfungsansatz	Audit approach
3.3 Prüfungstechnik	Audit techniques
3.4 Prüfung von Konzernrechnungen	Audit of consolidated financial statements
4 Berichterstattung	Reporting
4.1 Berichterstattung gemäss Aktienrecht	Reporting according to Swiss Corporation Law
4.2 Berichterstattung für andere Rechtsformen	Reporting for other types of organisations
4.3 Berichterstattung allgemein	Reporting generally
5 Interne Revision	Internal auditing
5.1 Allgemeines	General
5.2 Aufgaben, Kompetenzen und Verantwortung	Objectives, competencies and responsibilities
5.3 Organisatorisches Konzept	Organisational concept

Kapitel 5: Contents of Swiss Handbook on Auditing (HWP, MSA)

5.4	Fachliches Konzept	Professional concept
5.5	Prüfungsunterstützung und Fachwissen	Audit support and professional know how
5.6	Zusammenarbeit mit internen Stellen	Cooperation with internal departments
5.7	Zusammenarbeit mit externen Stellen	Cooperation with external organisations
5.8	Wachsende Anforderungen und Bedeutung	Increasing requirements and importance
Band 3 HWP (378 Seiten)		**Volume 3 (378 pages)**
6	Prüfung in der Finanzbranche	Auditing in financial institutions
6.1	Banken	Banks
6.2	Anlagefonds	Investments funds
6.3	Effektenhändler	Brokers and dealers
6.4	Versicherungsgesellschaften	Insurance companies
Band 4 HWP (424 Seiten)		**Volume 4 (424 pages)**
7	Andere Prüfungen	Other audits

Teil G: Anhänge und Unterlagen / Appendices and documents

7.1	Gründungsprüfung	Foundation audit
7.2	Kapitalerhöhungsprüfung	Capital increase audit
7.3	Kapitalherabsetzungsprüfung	Capital decrease audit
7.4	Sitzverlegung einer ausländischen Gesellschaft in die Schweiz	Transfer of domicile of a foreign company to Switzerland
7.5	Sonderprüfung	Special examination
8	Prüfung in besonderen Branchen	Auditing of special organisations
8.1	Personalvorsorgeeinrichtungen	Pension funds
8.2	Sozialversicherung (AHV/IV/EO/EL)	Governmental social insurance (old age insurance etc.)
9	Öffentliche Verwaltung	Governmental bodies
9.1	Einleitung	Introduction
9.2	Organisation der Finanzaufsicht	Organsiation of financial control
9.3	Der Finanzhaushalt	Governmental accounting
9.4	Prüfungen in der öffentlichen Verwaltung	Audits of governmental bodies

10. Berufswesen	The accounting profession
10.1 TREUHAND-KAMMER	The Swiss Institute of Certified Auditors
10.2 Berfusbilder und höhere Fachprüfungen	Professions and professional examinations
10.3 Fach- und Bildungsarbeit der Treuhand-Kammer	Professional and educational efforts of the Swiss Institute of Certified Auditors

Kapitel 6:
Comparison of International Standards on Auditing (ISA) and Swiss Auditing Standards (SAS) / Schweizer Prüfungsstandards (PS) / Normes d'audit suisses (NAS)

Contents	Inhaltsverzeichnis
Handbook of International Auditing, Assurance, and Ethics Pronouncements (IFAC Handbook 2006 Edition)	
Code of Ethics for Professional Accountants (June 2005)	
International Standards on Quality Control (ISCQs):	
ISCQ 1:	
Quality Control for Firms that Perform Audits and Reviews of Historical Financial Information, and Other Assurance and Related Services Engagements (2005)	
International Framework for Assurance Engagements	
100-999 International Standards on Auditing (ISAs)	Schweizer Prüfungsstandards (PS) (Edition 2004, ISAs status as of 30 June 2003)

Kapitel 6: Comparison of standards

100-199	Introductory Matters	Einführung
120	Framework of ISAs	Konzeptioneller Rahmen der PS

200-299	Responsibilities	Aufgaben
200	Objective and General Principles Governing an Audit of Financial Statements	Ziel und allgemeine Grundsätze der Abschlussprüfung
210	Terms of Audit Engagement	Auftragsbedingungen des Abschlussprüfers
220	Quality Control for Audits of Historical Information (2005)	Qualitätssicherung in der Wirtschaftsprüfung
230	Documentation	Dokumentation
240	The Auditors' Responsibility to Consider in an Audit of Financial Statements (2005)	Deliktische Handlungen und Fehler – Verantwortung des Abschlussprüfers
250	Consideration of Laws and Regu-lations in an Audit of Financial Statements	Gesetzliche und andere Vorschriften – Berücksichtigung bei der Abschlussprüfung
260	Communications of Audit Matters with those Charged with Governance	Kommunikation über die Abschlussprüfung mit den Verantwortlichen für die Leitung und Überwachung
		Pflichten der gesetzlichen Revisionsstelle bei Kapitalverlust und Überschuldung

300-499	Risk Assessment and Response to Assessed Risks	Planung
300	Planning an Audit of Financial Statements	Planung

310	Knowledge of the Business (withdrawn 2004)	Kenntnisse der Tätigkeit und des Umfelds des Unternehmens
315	Understanding the Entity and Its Environment and Assessing the Risk of Material Misstatement (2005)	
320	Audit Materiality	Wesentlichkeit bei der Abschlussprüfung
330	The Auditor's Procedures in Response to Assessed Risks (2005)	

400-499		Interne Kontrolle
400	Risk Assessment and Internal Control (withdrawn 2004)	Risikobeurteilung und interne Kontrolle
401	Auditing in a Computer Information Systems Environment (withdrawn 2004)	Prüfung im Umfeld der Informations- und Kommunikationstechnologie
402	Audit Considerations Relating to Entities Using Service Organisations	Unternehmen, die Dienstleistungsorganisationen in Anspruch nehmen – Auswirkung auf die Abschlussprüfung

500-599	Audit Evidence	Prüfungsnachweise
500	Audit Evidence	Prüfungsnachweise
501	Audit Evidence – Additional Considerations for Specific Items	Prüfungsnachweise – Zusätzliche Überlegungen zu bestimmten Positionen

505	External Confirmations	Bestätigungen Dritter
510	Initial Engagements – Opening Balances	Erstprüfungen – Eröffnungsbestände
520	Analytical Procedures	Analytische Prüfungshandlungen
530	Audit Sampling and Other Means of Testing	Stichproben- und andere Auswahlverfahren bei der Abschlussprüfung
540	Audit of Accounting Estimates	Prüfung von Schätzungen im Abschluss
545	Auditing Fair Value Measurements and Disclosures	Prüfung von Fair Values (Bewertung und Angaben)
550	Related Parties	Nahe stehende Parteien
560	Subsequent Events	Ereignisse nach dem Bilanzstichtag
570	Going Concern	Unternehmensfortführung (Going Concern)
580	Management Representations	Erklärungen der Unternehmensleitung
600-699	**Using Work of Others**	**Verwendung von Arbeiten Dritter**
600	Using the Work of Another Auditor	Verwendung der Arbeiten eines anderen Wirtschaftsprüfers
610	Considering the Work of Internal Auditing	Interne Revision – Auswirkungen auf die Abschlussprüfung
620	Using the Work of an Expert	Verwendung der Arbeiten eines Experten

Teil G: Anhänge und Unterlagen / Appendices and documents

700-799	**Audit Conclusions and Reporting**	**Schlussfolgerungen und Berichterstattung**
700	The Auditor's Report on Financial Statements	Bericht des Abschlussprüfers
701	Modifications ot the Independent Aduitor's Report	
710	Comparatives	Vergleichsinformationen
720	Other Information in Documents Containing Audited Financial Statements	Andere Informationen in Dokumenten, die den geprüften Abschluss enthalten

800-899	**Specialized Areas**	**Spezielle Bereiche**
800	The Auditor's Report on Special Purpose Audit Engagements	Berichte über Spezialprüfungen
810	The Examination of Prospective Financial Information (replaced by ISAE 3400)	Prüfung zukunftsorientierter Finanzinformationen

900-999	**Related Services**	**Verwandte Dienstleistungen**
910	Engagements to Review Financial Statements (replaced by ISRE 2400)	Review (prüferische Durchsicht) von Abschlüssen
920	Engagements to Perform Agreed-Upon Procedures Regarding Financial Information (replaced by ISRS 4400)	Vereinbarte Prüfungshandlungen bezüglich Finanzinformationen

930	Engagements to Compile Financial Information (replacec by ISRS 4410)	Erstellung von Finanzinformationen (Compilation)
1000-1100	**International Auditing Practice Statements (IAPSs)**	
1000	Inter-Bank Confirmation Procedures	
1005	The Special Considerations in the Audit of Small Entities	
1006	Audits of the Financial Statements of Banks	
1010	The Consideration of Environmental Matters in the Audit of Financial Statements	
1012	Auditing Derivative Financial Instruments	
1013	Electronic Commerce – Effect on the Audit of Financial Statements	
1014	Reporting by Auditors on Compliance with International Financial Reporting Standards	
2000-2699	**International Standards on Review Engagements (ISREs)**	
2400	Engagements to Review Financial Statements (Previously ISA 910)	

993

2410	Review of Interim Financial Statements Performed by the Independent Auditor of the Entity

Assurance Engagements other than Audits or Reviews of Historical Financial Information

3000-3699	**International Standards on Assurance Engagements (ISAEs)**
3000	Assurance Engagements Other than Audits or Reviews of Historical Financial Statements
3400-3699	**Subject Specific Standards**
3400	The Examination of Prospective Financial Information (previously ISA 810)
4000-4699	**International Standards on Related Services (ISRSs)**
4400	Engagements to Perform Agreed-Upon Procedures Regarding Financial Information (Previously ISA 920)
4410	Engagements ot Compile Financial Intormation (Previously ISA 930)

Kapitel 7:
Financial reporting and audit oversight institutions in Switzerland

- **Swiss GAAP FER – Swiss Accounting and Reporting Recommendations (ARR)**

  P.O. Box 892
  8025 Zurich

  Fax: +41 044 267 75 85
  Internet: www.fer.ch

  Main publication:
  Swiss Accounting and Reporting Recommendations
  - Edition 2007
  - about 200 pages
  - ISBN 3-908159-55-5
  - Annual publication of all published standards, booklet available in German, French, Italian and English. This includes a CD with the full text.

- **Swiss Institute of Swiss Certified Accountants and Tax Consultants**
  Treuhand-Kammer

  Limmatquai 120
  8025 Zurich

  Phone: +41 044 267 75 75
  Fax: +41 044 267 75 85
  Internet: www.treuhand-kammer.ch

  Main publication:
  Schweizer Handbuch der Wirtschaftsprüfung (Swiss Auditing Handbook)
  - 4 Volumes
  - approximately 2,000 pages
  - in German and French only
  - Edition 1998

Teil G: Anhänge und Unterlagen / Appendices and documents

- o ISBN 3-908567-63-7
- o Volume I about 500 pages on Accounting Issues including Consolidated Financial Statements
- o The four volumes are also available on Compact Disc (CD)
- o A new edition is under preparation for 2009

- **Swiss Federal Auditor Oversight Authority**
  *Schweizerische Revisionsaufsichtsbehörde (*RAB**)**

  Established 17 Octobre 2006, in office as of 1 November 2008

  Berne

  Main publication:

  Federal Act on the Licensing and Oversight of Auditors - Swiss Auditor Oversight Act (AOA) of 16 Decembre 2006

  Bundesgesetz über die Zulassung und Beaufsichtigung der Revisorinnen und Revisoren - Revisionsaufsichtsgesetz (RAG)

  Loi fédérale sur l'agrément et la surveillance des réviseurs – loi sur la surveillance des réviseurs (LSR)

Kapitel 8:
Accounting glossary USA – UK – CH – D

Verein. Staaten (USA)	England (UK)	Schweiz (CH)	Deutschland (D)
Accounts payable	Creditors	Kreditoren	Verpflichtungen
Accounts receivable	Debtors	Debitoren	Forderungen
Bylaws	Articles of association	Statuten	Satzungen
Capital surplus	Share premium	Agio	Kapitalrücklagen
Certified Public Accountant (CPA)	Chartered Accountant (CA)	Dipl. Wirtschaftsprüfer (dipl. WP)	Wirtschaftsprüfer (WP)
Common stock	Ordinary shares	Stammaktien	Stammaktien
Current rate method	Closing rate method	Jahresendkursumrechnung	Stichtagsumrechnung
Deferred income tax credits	Deferred tax	Latente Steuern	Aufgeschobene Steuern
Depreciation	Depreciation	Abschreibungen	Abschreibungen
Fiscal year	Financial year	Geschäftsjahr	Geschäftsjahr
Income	Profit	Jahresgewinn	Jahresüberschuss
Income statement (IS)	Profit and loss account (P&L)	Erfolgsrechnung (ER)	Gewinn- und Verlustrechnung (GuV)
Inventories	Stocks	Warenlager	Vorräte
Notes	Bills	Wechsel	Wechsel

Paid-in surplus	Share premium	Agio	Kapitalrücklage
Legal pooling-of-interests	Legal merger	Fusion	Verschmelzung
Preferred stock	Preference shares	Vorzugsaktien	Vorzugsaktie
Property, plant and equipment	Tangible fixed assets	Sachanlagen	Sachanlagen
Real estate/ Property	Land and buildings	Liegenschaften	Grundstücke und Bauten
Sales	Turnover	Umsatz	Verkaufserlöse
Shareholders' meeting	Annual General Meeting (AGM)	Generalversammlung (GV)	Hauptversammlung (HV)
Statement of financial position	Balance sheet	Bilanz	Jahresbilanz
Stocks	Shares	Aktien	Aktien
Stock dividend	Bonus shares	Gratisaktien	Gratisaktien
Stockowners' equity	Shareholders' funds	Eigenkapital	Eigenkapital
Treasury stock	Own shares	Eigene Aktien	Eigene Aktien

Kapitel 9:
Accounting terms German - English

(German expression, if different, in brackets)

German	English
Abschreibung (Sachanlagen)	depreciation (tangible fixed assets)
Agio (Aufgeld, Kapitalreserven)	additional paid-in capital
Aktienkapital (Gezeichnetes Kapital)	share capital
Akquisition (Firmenkauf)	acquisition of a company
Aktuelle Werte (Tageswerte)	current cost
Aktiven	assets
Aktueller Wert	current cost, current value
Amortisation (immaterielle Aktiven)	amortisation (intangible assets)
angefangene Arbeiten	work in progress
anglo-amerikanische Kapitalkonsolidierung (Erwerbsmethode)	purchase or acquisition method
Anhang	annex with notes to financial statements

Anlagespiegel (Anlagegitter)	grid with changes of fixed assets
Anleihe, Obligationsanleihe (Schuldverschreibung)	debenture bond
Anschaffungskosten	historical acquisition cost
Assoziierte Gesellschaften (Gesellschaften mit Beteiligungsverhältnis)	associated companies
Aufträge in Arbeit (Unfertige Leistungen)	work in progress
Aufwand	expenses, charges

Badwill (passivischer Unterschiedsbetrag)	excess of net assets over cost, negative goodwill
Belastete Aktiven	encumbered, pledged assets
Beteiligungen	investments in subsidiaries and affiliates
Beteiligungsliste	list of subsidiaries and affiliates
Bewertung (Bilanzansatz)	valuation method
Bilanz	balance sheet
Bilanzstichtag	balance sheet date
Bilanzverlust	accumulated losses

Kapitel 9: Accounting terms German - English

Darlehen (Ausleihungen)	loans
Dekonsolidierung (End- oder Entkonsolidierung)	deconsolidation
Direkte Methode (Cash flow)	direct method
Dividenden (Ausschüttungen)	dividends

Eigene Aktien	own shares, treasury stock
Eigenkapitalnachweis	changes of shareholders' equity
Einheitliche Leitung	control
Einzelabschluss	individual (company) accounts
Eliminierung der Zwischengewinne	elimination of interim profits
Erfolgsrechnung	income statement, profit and loss account
Ertragssteuern	income taxes
Erläuterung	(foot) note
Eventualverbindlichkeiten (Haftungsverhältnisse)	contingent liabilities

Fertigfabrikate (fertige Erzeugnisse)	finished products, finished goods
Finanzinstrumente	financial instruments

Flüssige Mittel (Zahlungsmittel)	cash, liquid assets
Forderungen	accounts receivable, debtors
Fortführung	going concern
Fremdwährungsumrechnung	foreign currency translation
Fusion (Verschmelzung)	merger
Garantie	guarantee
Geldflussrechnung	cash flow statement
Geldnahe Mittel	cash equivalents
Gemeinschaftsunternehmen	joint venture
Gesamtkostenverfahren der Erfolgsrechnung	income statement with cost types, period based costing method
Gesetzliche Reserven	legal reserves
Gewinn pro Aktie	earnings (profit) per share
Gewinnreserven (Gewinnrücklagen)	retained earnings
Gewinnverwendung, Gewinnausschüttung	distribution of profits, dividend distribution, appropriation of profits
Goodwill (Firmen- oder Geschäftswert, aktivischer Unterschiedsbetrag)	excess of cost over net assets acquired

German	English
Gratisaktien	stock split, stock dividends
Halbfabrikate (Unfertige Erzeugnisse)	half-finished products
Herstellkosten, Herstellungskosten	production cost, manufacturing cost
Historischer Kurs	historical exchange rate
Historischer Wert	historical cost, historical value
Holdinggesellschaft (Mutter- oder Obergesellschaft)	parent
Hypothek	mortgage
Immaterielle Aktiven, Anlagen, Werte (Immaterielle Vermögensgegenstände)	intangible assets
Indirekte Methode (Cash flow)	indirect method
Inhaberaktie	bearer share
Interessenzusammenführung	pooling of interests
Jahresabschluss, Jahresrechnung	individual annual accounts
Kapitalreserven, Agio (Kapitalrücklagen)	additional paid-in capital, capital reserves

Konglomerat (Mischkonzern)	conglomerate
Konsolidierungskreis	scope of consolidation, composition of consolidation
Konsolidierungspflicht	obligation, duty to consolidate
Konzern (Gruppe)	group
Konzernbilanz	consolidated balance sheet
Konzernerfolgsrechnung (Konzern-Gewinn- und Verlustrechnung)	consolidated income statement
Konzerngesellschaft (verbundenes Unternehmen, Konzernuntergesellschaft)	consolidated company, group company, subsidiary, subsidiary company
Konzerngewinn (Konzernjahresüberschuss)	consolidated net income
Konzernhandbuch	accounting manual
Konzerninterner Umsatz (Innenumsatz)	inter company sales
Konzernrechnung (Konzernabschluss)	group accounts, consolidated financial statements
Konzernprüfer	group auditors
Kontinuität (Stetigkeit)	consistency
Kurzfristiges Fremdkapital	current liabilities

Langfristiges Fremdkapital	long-term debt, non-current liabilities
Latente Ertragssteuern (aufgeschobene Steuern)	deferred taxes
Leasing (Gebrauchsüberlassung)	lease, hire purchase contract
Lebensdauer	useful life
Liegenschaften (Grundstücke und Gebäude)	real estate, property, land and buildings
Lizenzen	royalties, license fees
Liquidationswert (Veräusserungswert)	liquidation, net realisable value
Materialaufwand	raw material expense
Massgeblicher Einfluss	significant control
Minderheitsanteile (Drittanteile, Anteile in Fremdbesitz)	minority interests
Muttergesellschaft (Obergesellschaft)	parent company
Nahestehende Gesellschaften (verbundene Gesellschaften)	related companies
Namenaktie	registered shares

Nettoerlös	net sales, turnover net
Neubewertungsreserven	revaluation reserves
Obergesellschaft	parent company
Offenlegung	disclosure
Passiven	liabilities and shareholders' equity
Pensionsverpflichtung (Verpflichtung aus Altersvorsorge)	pension liability
Personalaufwand	personnel expense
Proportionale Konsolidierung	pro rate consolidation, proportionate consolidation, quota consolidation
Publikumsgesellschaften	quoted, public companies
Quotenkonsolidierung	proportional, proportionate or quota consolidation
Rechnungsabgrenzung (aktiv)	prepayments and accrued income
Rechnungsabgrenzung (passiv)	accrued liabilities and deferred income
Rechnunslegungsgrundsätze	accounting policies

Reserve für eigene Aktien	reserve for own shares, treasury shares
Rückstellungen	provisions

Sachanlagen	tangible fixed assets, property, plant and equipment
Sacheinlagen	in-kind contributions
Saldierungsverbot (Verrechnungsverbot)	prohibition to net out amounts
Stammaktien	common shares
Stetigkeit, Kontinuität	consistency
Stichtagskurs, Jahresendkurs	current exchange rate, balance sheet rate
Stille Reserven	hidden, latent, undisclosed, silent reserves
Subkonzern (Teilkonzern)	subgroup
Subkonzernabschluss (Teilkonzernabschluss)	sub consolidated financial statements
Subventionen (Regierungszuschüsse)	subsidies, government grants
Subkonzernabschluss	subgroup accounts

Tageskurs (Sichtagskurs)	current rate

Teil G: Anhänge und Unterlagen / Appendices and documents

Tageswert	current, actual value
Tochtergesellschaft (Untergesellschaft, Tochterunternehmen)	subsidiary company

Umlaufvermögen	current assets
Umrechnungsdifferenz	currency translation difference
Umsatzkostenverfahren (Absatzerfolgsrechnung)	sales income statement, activity-based costing method

Verbindlichkeiten	liabilities
Verkehrswert (Tageswert)	fair market value, market value
Verkauf von Tochtergesellschaften	disposal of subsidiaries
Vertriebsaufwand	selling expense
Verwaltungsaufwand	administrative expense
Versicherungswert	insurance value
Vollkonsolidierung	full consolidation
Vorauszahlungen	advance payments, prepayments
Vorjahresvergleich	prior year, comparative information
Vorräte	stocks, inventories

Vorsichtsprinzip	prudence, conservatism
Vorzugsaktie	preferred share, preference stock

Wahlrechte	options
Wertberichtigung	value adjustment
Wesentlichkeit	materiality
Wiederbeschaffungskosten	replacement cost

Zwischenabschlüsse	interim financial statements
Zwischengewinne (Zwischenergebnisse)	interim profits, inter company profits
Zwischenholding	intermediate holding company

Kapitel 10:
Glossary to the Swiss Auditing Supervisory Act (RAG)

German	English	French
Absolvent	graduate	Être titulaire d'un diplôme
Anleihensobligation	bond	Emprunt par obligation
Aufsichtsabgabe	oversight dues	Redevance de surveillance
Aufsichtsbehörde	oversight authority	Autorité de surveillance
Auskunftspflicht	duty to inform	Obligation de renseigner
Ausländische Revisionsaufsichtsbehörde	foreign oversight authority	Surveillance d'une autorité étrangère
Beaufsichtigung	oversight	Surveillance
Berufsgrundsätze	professional standards	Éthique professionnelle
Bestätigung	attestation	Attestation
Einstellungsbeschluss	resolution to discontinue proceedings	Ordonnance de classement
Entschädigung	remuneration	Dédommagement

Kapitel 10: Glossary to the Swiss Auditing Supervisory Act (RAG)

Entscheidfunktion	decision making function	Fonction décisionnelle
Erfüllung	performance	Exécution
Fachpraxis	professional experience	Pratique professionnelle
Führungsstruktur	management structure	Structure de direction
Gebührenansatz	fee schedule	Montant des émoluments
Kotierungsreglement	listing rules	Règlement de cotation
Leumund (unbescholten)	spotless record	Réputation
Meldepflicht	duty to notify	Obligation de communiquer
Prüfung	examination	Vérification
Publikumsgesellschaft	public company	Société ouverte au public
Revisionsaufsichtsgesetz	Law on Auditor Oversight	Loi sur la surveillance de la revision
Revisionsbranche	audit profession	Branche de la révision
Revisionsdienstleistungen	audit services	Fournir des prestations en matière de revision
Revisionsexperte	Audit expert	Expert-réviseur
Revisionsstelle	auditors	Organe de révision
Revisionsunternehmen	audit firm	Entreprise de révision

Sicherung der Qualität	quality assurance	Assurance-qualité
Staatlich beaufsichtigtes Revisionsunternehmen	auditing firm under government oversight	Enterprise de revision soumise à la surveillance de l'Etat
Standesregel	professional rules	Déontologie
Steuerexperte	tax expert	Expert fiscal
Unabhängigkeit	independence	Indépendance
Zulassung	licensing	Agrément, Être agrée
Zulassungspflicht	obligation to be licensed	Obligation de se faire agréer
Zulassungsunterlagen	licensing documents	Document qu'on a joint à son demande d'agrément
Zutrittsgewährung	Obligation to admit to premises	Obligation d'accorder l'accès aux locaux

Kapitel 11:
Syllabus of Swiss law test for foreign CPAs, CAs, WPs, RAs etc.

Swiss Accountancy Academy (a division of Educaris Ltd., Lausanne Branch, a subsidiary of the Swiss Institute / Chamber) offering the following course (first time in November/December 2007 in Berne). There was also another course in May/June 2008. Therefore, it is anticipated that the course will be held twice a year thereafter.

§ 1   Proof of the required Knowledge of Swiss Law according to the Swiss Federal Auditor Oversight Act (AOA)

- Studies and Exam for Public Accountants with foreign Diplomas - officially recognised by the "Swiss PCAOB" (FAOA)
- Course language: English (only)
- The course takes 4 1/2 days, the exam two hours
- Course Location: Bern

§ 2   Oversight of Auditors - The legal position of the auditors in Switzerland

- Legal sources and rules under the AOA
    - Legal basis of AOA
    - Organisation of the FAOA
    - Inspections by the FAOA
- Banking Law
    - Federal Law on Banks and Saving Banks (BA)
    - Swiss Federal Banking Commission (SFBC) / FINMA
    - Supervision of Banks and Security Dealers (Authorisation)

Teil G: Anhänge und Unterlagen / Appendices and documents

- o Audit related Matters, Recognized Bank Auditors, Independence Rules
- Anti-Money Laundering Act (AMLA)
  - o Federal Act on Combating Money Laundering in the the Financial Sector
  - o For fiancial intermediaries (Banks, fund and asset managers, insurance, security dealers etc.)
  - o Recognised Self Regulatory Organisations (SRO)
  - o AML Control Authority under direction of Federal Finance Administration for Direct Subordinated Financial Intermediaries (DSFI)
  - o Audit related matters (for SROs) by accredited auditors / firms
- Federal Act on Stock Exchanges and Securities Trading (SESTA)
  - o Self regulation / Soft law for Swiss Stock Exchange (SIX)
  - o Public Takeover Offers (listed Swiss targets) must be reviewed by Take-over Board (TOB)
  - o and related audit matters
  - o Supervisory authority (Swiss Federal Banking Commission/ FINMA)

§ 3 Business law, general part und special part (Contract law)

- Contract law, special contracts, contracts not treated in the law (e.g. Leasing), dissensus vs. error, breach of contracts, unjust enrichment, statute of limitations, sale contracts, work contracts, differences between employment contract and agency contracts, audit contracts as agency

§ 4 Company law

Partnerships:
- Simple, general and limited partnerships

- limited liability companies under Swiss Law, Organisation of the Swiss Corporation (AG, SA), Liability of board members and auditors, Basis of Stock Exchange and Merger Law.

§ 5 Social insurance law

- Basis of the Swiss social insurance laws
  - EU conventions: Subjection to the Swiss social security system with EU member states
  - First pillar Swiss Old Age Insurance (AHV)
  - Second pillar pension fund laws (BVG)
  - Third pillar fiscal : 3a linked individual provident measures and policies encouraging of home ownership (EPL); 3b private savings

§ 6 VAT

- Basis of Swiss Value Added Taxes on sale transactions

§ 7 Swiss and international corporate tax laws

- Examples of taxation of partnerships and corporations, direct and indirect taxes, calculation of taxable profits and relation to bookkeeping, special tax status, double tax treaties, transfer pricing etc.

§ 8 What is special about Swiss audit reports

- Presentation and discussion of different types of audit reports and special situations that influence the reports, PS 700 the report of the auditor, PS 290 Duties of statutory auditors in the case of loss of (half of) the capital and overindebtment (CO 725), PS 570 Going concern

Teil G: Anhänge und Unterlagen / Appendices and documents

§ 9 Special audits

- for foundations, capital increase and reduction, liquidation, mergers

§ 10 Ordinary audit and limited statutory examination (ER)

- including examination whether an internal control system (IKS) exists and detailled (long form) audit report to the board

§ 11 Test

- multiple choice on the above subjects
- in Berne from 10.00 to 12.00 (two hours)
- All courses have to be attended. Only one day absence can be tolerated with indication of reasons (sickness).

Kapitel 12:
Glossary Swiss Legal Terms (German-French-English) – unofficial

Glossar Schweizer Rechtsbegriffe	Glossary Swiss Legal Terms – unofficial
Nachweis der notwendigen Kenntnisse des schweizerischen Rechts gemäss Revisionsaufsichtsgesetz für Inhaber ausländischer Prüfer-Diplome (Art. 4 Abs. 2 lit. d RAG) *(Connaissances requises du droit suisse)*	Required knowledge of Swiss Law under the new Swiss Auditor Oversight Act (AOA) for foreign holders of audit diplomas
ohne Begriffe des Rechnungswesens *(sans expressions de comptabilité)*	without accounting terms

Inhalt *(contenu)*	Contents
1. Revisionsrecht (im Aktienrecht) *(droit de révision)*	Auditing Law (in Company Law)
2. Revisionsaufsicht *(surveillance des réviseurs)*	Auditor Oversight
3. Gesellschaftsrecht *(droits des sociétés)*	Company Law, Corporate Law (US)

Teil G: Anhänge und Unterlagen / Appendices and documents

4.	Aktienrecht *(droit des sociétés anonymes)*	Corporation Law
5.	Geldwäschereigesetz (GWG) *(loi sur le blanchiment d'argent, LBA)*	Anti-Money Laundering Act (AMLA)
6.	Vertragsrecht *(droit des contrats)*	Contract Law
7.	Bundesverfassung (BV) *(constitution fédérale, Cst)*	Swiss Federal Constitution (SFC, Cons.)
8.	Handelsregister (HR) *(registre du commerce, RC)*	Commercial register (CR)
9.	Zivilgesetzbuch (ZGB) *(code civil Suisse, CC)*	Civil Code (CC)
10.	Fusionsgesetz (FusG) *(loi sur la fusion, LFus)*	Merger Act (MA)
11.	Konkursrecht *(droit des poursuites et faillites)*	Insolvency and bankruptcy act
12.	Bankengesetz (BankG) *(loi fédérale sur les banques, LB)*	Banking Act (BA)
13.	Börsengesetz (BEHG) *(loi sur les bourses)*	Stock Exchange Act (SESTA)
14.	Kollektivanlagegesetz (KAG) *(placements collectifs, LPPC)*	Collective Investment Schemes Act (CISA)

15.	Sozialversicherungsrecht *(sécurité sociale)*	Social security laws
16.	AHV-Gesetz *(AVS)*	Old age insurance
17.	Krankenversicherung *(assurance-maladie, LAMal)*	Sickness insurance and maternity insurance
18.	Unfallversicherung *(assurance-accidents, LAA)*	Accident and occupational disease insurance
19.	Familienzulagen *(allocation familiales)*	Family allowances
20.	Arbeitslosenversicherung (AVIG) *(assurance- chômage)*	Unemployment insurance
21.	Berufsvorsorgegesetz (BVG) *(prèvoyance professionelle)*	Pension Law
22.	Versicherungsaufsichtsgesetz (VAG) *(surveillance des assurances, LSA)*	Insurance Oversight Act (IOA)
23.	Mehrwertsteuern (MWST) *(taxe sur la valeur ajoutée, TVA)*	Value Added Tax (VAT)
24.	Bundessteuern (DBG) *(impôt fédéral direct)*	Swiss Corporate Tax, company taxation

Teil G: Anhänge und Unterlagen / Appendices and documents

25. Verrechnungssteuern (VStG) *(impot anticipé)*	Withholding tax
26. Stempelsteuern (StG) *(droits de timbres)*	Stamp taxes, stamp duties
27. Strafgesetzbuch (StGB) *(code penal)*	Penal Code (SPC, PC)

Deutsch, German *(kursiv: Französisch, italics: French)*	**English (UK, US)**
(DE=Deutschland, Germany, *Allemagne*)	
1. Revisionsrecht (im Aktienrecht)	**Auditing Law (in Company Law)**
Ordentliche Revision, volle Prüfung (OR 727) *(contrôle ordinaire)*	Ordinary audit, full (statutory, legal) audit
Prüfbericht, Bericht der Revisionsstelle, Testat an Generalversammlung (OR 728b Abs. 2) *(rapport de révision à l'assemblée générale)*	Audit opinion, (summary) audit report to general short form report
Umfassender Revisionsbericht, Detailbericht an Verwaltungsrat (OR 728b Abs. 1) *(rapport détaillé au conseil d'administration)*	Comprehensive audit report, long from, detailed report to board of directors

Sachregister

Eingeschränkte Prüfung (OR 727a) *(contrôle restraint, succinct)*	Limited examination (audit)
Befragungen, analytische Prüfungshandlungen und angemessene Detailprüfungen (OR 729a Abs. 2) *(auditions, opérations de contrôle analytiques, vérifications detaillées appropriées)*	Interviews, analytical examinations and adequate examinations (tests) of details
Negativbestätigung *(assurance negative)*	Negative
Internes Kontrollsystem (IKS) (OR 728a Abs.1 Ziff. 3) *(système du contrôle interne)*	Internal Control System (ICS)
Unabhängigkeit (OR 728) *(independance)*	Independence
Tatsächliche Unabhängigkeit (OR 728) *(independance dans les faits)*	Independence in fact
Unabhängigkeit dem Anschein nach (OR 728) *(independance en apparance)*	Independence in appearance

1021

Teil G: Anhänge und Unterlagen / Appendices and documents

Wahl der Revisionsstelle (OR 730) *(élection de l'organe de révision)*	Election of statutory auditors
Kapitalverlust (OR 725 Abs. 1) *(perte de capital)*	Capital loss (50% of share capital and legal reserves lost)
Dokumentation und Aufbewahrung der Arbeitspapiere der Revisionsstelle (OR 730c) *(documentation et conservation des pièces)*	Documentation and archiving of audit working papers
Besorgnis einer Überschuldung (OR 725 Abs. 2) *(raisons sérieuses d'un surendettement)*	Substantiated concern of overindebtedness
Überschuldung (OR 725 Abs. 2) *(surendettement)*	Overindebtedness, overindebtment, excess of liabilities over assets
Benachrichtigung des Konkursrichters durch die Revisionsstelle bei Untätigkeit des Verwaltungsrates (OR 728c Abs. 3) *(avis du juge de faillite par l'organe de révision si le conseil d'administration leomet)*	Notification of bankruptcy judge by the statutory auditors in case the board of directors fails to do so
Rangrücktrittsvereinbarung (OR 725 Abs. 2) *(convention de subordination, postposition)*	Subordination agreement

Forderungsverzicht eines Gläubigers *(abandon de crédit)*	Waiver of claim
Stille Reserven (OR 669 Abs. 3) *(réserves latentes)*	Hidden reserves, undisclosed reserves, silent reserves
Gewinnverwendung, Gewinnverteilung (OR 731) *(emploi du bénéfice)*	Use of profits, losses, distribution, allocation of profits
Allgemeine (gesetzliche) Reserven (OR 671) *(réserves generales)*	General (legal) reserves
Agio, Kapitalreserven (OR 671 Abs. 2 Ziff. 1), *(agio)*	Capital reserves, share premium (UK), additional paid-in capital (APIC)
Reserve für eigene Aktien (OR 671a) *(réserve pour actions propres)*	Reserve for own shares
Aufwertungsreserve (OR 670) *(réserve de réévaluation)*	Revaluation reserves
Kapitalherabsetzung (OR 732) *(réduction du capital-actions)*	Capital decrease, reduction of share capital

Teil G: Anhänge und Unterlagen / Appendices and documents

Kapitalherabsetzung mit gleichzeitiger Wiedererhöhung (OR 732a) *(réduction du capital avec augmentation)*	Capital reduction followed by immediate increase, „accordéon"
Sonderprüfung (OR 697a) *(contrôle spécial)*	Special audit, special investigation
Verantwortlichkeit, Haftung der Organe, des Revisionsstelle (OR 754) *(résponsabilité de l'organe de révision)*	Responsibility, liability of corporate organs, of the board of directors
Verantwortlichkeit, Haftung der Organe des Verwaltungsrates (OR 755) *(résponsabilité des réviseurs)*	Responsibility, liability of corporate organs, of the statutory auditors
Angabe von Vergütungen (OR 663b bis)/Transparenzgesetz *(indications des indemnités)*	Disclosure of management and board compensation / loans
2. Revisionsaufsicht *(surveillance des réviseurs)*	**Auditor Oversight**
Revisionsaufsichtsgesetz (RAG)	Audit Oversight Act (AOA)
Bundesgesetz über die Zulassung und Beaufsichtigung der Revisorinnen und Revisoren vom	Federal Act on the Licensing and Oversight of Auditors

16. Dezember 2007 *(Loi fédérale sur l'agrément et la surveillance des réviseurs, LSR)*	
Revisionsaufsichtsbehörde (RAB) (RAG 28), Bern *(Autorité des surveillance)*	Federal Auditor Oversight Authority (FAOA)
Verordnung zum RAG (VRAG) *(Ordonance LSR)*	Ordinance of AOA
Revisoren (RAG 15 Abs. 1 a) *(réviseurs)*	Auditors
Revisionsexperten (RAG 15 Abs. 1 b) *(expert-réviseurs)*	Audit experts
Revisionsunternehmen (RAG 2 b und 15 Abs. 1c) *(entreprises de révision)*	Audit firms
Revisionsunternehmen unter staatlicher Aufsicht (RAG 7) *(entreprises de révision soumises à la surveillance de l'Etat)*	Audit firms under state oversight (AFUSO)
Revisionsdienstleistungen (RAG 2 a) *(prestations en matière de révision)*	Audit services
Leumundszeugnis (RAG 5 Abs. 1 a) *(réputation irréprochable)*	Spotless record, irreproachable reputation, proper and good standing

Teil G: Anhänge und Unterlagen / Appendices and documents

Eidgenössisch diplomierter Wirtschaftsprüfer (dipl. WP) (RAG 4 Abs. 2 a) *(expert-comptable diplomé)*	(Swiss) Federally Certified Accountant
Publikumsgesellschaft (RAG 2 c) *(société ouvert aux public)*	Public company
Leitender Revisor, Mandatsleiter (OR 728b) *(personne qui a dirigé la révision, chef de mandat)*	Person who leads the audit, auditor in-charge, lead auditor
Kundenannahme und Weiterführung (RAG 12 Abs. 2 b) *(acceptation et poursuite des mandats)*	Client acceptance and continuance
3. Gesellschaftsrecht *(droits des sociétés)*	**Company Law, Corporate Law (US)**
Einzelfirma, Einzelunternehmen (OR 945) *(enterprise individuelle, raison individuelle)*	Sole proprietor, owner managed business (OMB), personal business, small business, one-man business
Einfache Gesellschaft (OR 530) *(société simple, de personnes)*	Simple partnership, unregistered partnership
Kollektivgesellschaft (& Co.) (OR 552) *(société en nom collectif, & Cie)*	General partnership (GP)

Sachregister

Komanditgesellschaft (& Co.) (OR 594) *(société en commandite, & Cie)*	Limited partnership (LP)
Aktiengesellschaft (AG) (OR 620) *(société anonyme, SA)*	Corporation, joint stock company
Kommanditaktiengesellschaft (OR 764) *(société en commandite par action)*	Corporation with unlimited partner(s)
Gesellschaft mit beschränkter Haftung (GmbH) (OR 772) *(société à responsabilité limitée, Sàrl)*	Limited liability company (LLC)
Genossenschaft (OR 828) *(société coopérative, Scoop)*	Cooperative, COOP

4. Aktienrecht *(droit des sociétés anonymes)*	**Corporation Law**
Aktiengesellschaft (OR 620), AG *(société anonyme, SA)*	Limited company (UK), (stock) corporation (US), Inc.
Gesellschaftsorgane (OR 698) *(organes de la société)*	Corporate bodies, organes

1027

Teil G: Anhänge und Unterlagen / Appendices and documents

Aktienkapital (AK) (OR 620) *(capital-actions)*	Share capital
Minimumkapital (OR 621) *(capital-actions minimum)*	Minimum capital (CHF 100,000)
Mindesteinlage (OR 632), einbezahltes Aktienkapital (20% des Nominalwertes und CHF 50,000) für Namenaktien *(apport minium, au moins 20 pour cent de la valeur nominale et CHF 50,000 pour les actions nominatives)*	Paid-in capital (minimal 20% of nominal value and CHF 50,000) for registered shares
Mindestnennwert pro Aktie (OR 662 Abs. 4) *(valeur nominal minimal par action, 1 centime)*	Minimal par value per share (CHF 0.01, 1 Cent)
Beschränkte Haftung (OR 620 Abs. 1) *(responsabilité limitée)*	Limited liability
Aktionäre (OR 660) *(actionnaires)*	Shareholders (SH), members (UK)
Gründung (OR 629) *(fondation, constitution)*	Formation, establishment, foundation, creation
Eintragung in Handelsregister (OR 640)	Entry in the commercial register, incorporation

(inscription au registre du commerce)	
Statuten (OR 626), Satzung (DE) *(statuts)*	Articles of incorporation, statutes
Firma, Name der Gesellschaft (OR 641) *(raison sociale)*	Legal name of company, firm name
Sitz, Domizil (OR 640) *(siège de la société)*	Legal domicile
Generalversammlung der Aktionäre (GV) (OR 698) *(assemblée générale des actionnaires)*	Shareholders' meeting (AGM)
Ordentliche Generalversammlung (o GV) (OR 699 Abs. 2) *(assemblée générale ordinaire, annuelle)*	Ordinary (annual) shareholders' meeting (AGM)
Ausserordentliche Generalversammlung (ao GV) (OR 699 Abs. 2) *(assemblé générale extraordinaire)*	Extraordinary shareholders meeting
Verwaltungsrat (VR) (OR 707) *(conseil d'administration, CA)*	Board of directors (BoD)

Teil G: Anhänge und Unterlagen / Appendices and documents

Organisationsreglement (OGR) (OR 716b) *(règlement d'organisation)*	Organisational regulation
Verwaltungsratspräsident (VRP) (OR 712) *(président du conseil d'administration)*	Chairman of the board, president of BoD
Delegierter des Verwaltungsrates (DelVR) (OR 718 Abs. 2) *(délégué du conseil d'administration)*	Managing director (UK), delegate of the board
Revisionsstelle (OR 727), Abschlussprüfer (DE) *(organe de révision)*	Statutory auditors, legal auditors
Aktien (OR 622), Anteile (DE) *(actions)*	Shares, stocks (US)
Zeichnung von Aktien (OR 630) *(souscrption d'actions)*	subscription of shares, share subscription
Stimmrechtsaktien (OR 693) *(actions à droit de vote privilégié)*	Shares with privileged voting rights
Partizipationsscheine (PS) (OR 656a) *(bons de participations)*	Participation certificates (PC), nonvoting shares

Genussscheine (GS) (OR 657) *(bons de jouissance)*	Profit sharing certificates
Inhaberaktien (IA) (OR 622) *(actions nominatives)*	Bearer shares (unregistered)
Namensaktien (NA) (OR 622) *(actions au porteur)*	Registered shares (nominative)
Aktienbuch, Aktienregister (OR 686) *(registre des actions)*	Share register
Sacheinlagen (OR 628) *(apports en nature)*	In-kind contribution, qualified contribution
Beabsichtige Sachübernahme von einem Aktionär oder ihm Nahestehenden (OR 628) *(reprise de biens envisagé d'un actionnaire ou personne qui lui est proche)*	Acquisition of assets from shareholder or party related to him
Kapitalerhöhung durch Verrechnung mit Schulden (OR 635) *(compensation avec dette)*	Capital increase with set-off with existing debt
Gründervorteile (OR 628) *(avantages particuliers en faveur des fondateurs)*	Special, particular benefits to founder shareholders

Teil G: Anhänge und Unterlagen / Appendices and documents

Genehmigtes Aktienkapital (OR 651) *(capital-actions autorisé)*	Authorised share capital
Bedingtes Aktienkapital (OR 653) *(Capital-actions conditionnel)*	Contingent share capital
Bezugsrecht des Aktionärs (OR 652b) *(droits de souscription préférentiel)*	Preemptive rights (to purchase new shares), subscription rights
Liquidation (OR 739), Auflösung, Abwicklung der Gesellschaft (DE) *(liquidation)*	Liquidation, winding-up of a company (UK), dissolution
Löschung im Handelsregister (OR 746) *(radiation du registre du commerce)*	Cancellation in the commercial register, striking-off (UK) deletion, deregistration
Aufbewahrungsfrist von Akten 10 Jahre (OR 962) *(delai de conservation des documents, pièces, dix ans)*	archiving, retention period for (legal and accounting documents) 10 years
5. Geldwäschereigesetz (GWG) *(loi sur le blanchiment d'argent, LBA)*	**Anti-Money Laundering Act (AMLA)**

Bundesgesetz zur Bekämpfung der Geldwäscherei im Finanzsektor vom 10. Oktober 1997 *(loi fédérale concernant la lutte contre le blanchiment d'argent dans le secteur financier)*	Federal Act on Combating (Money) Laundering in 1997
Finanzintermediäre (Banken, Fondsleitungen, Investmentgesellschaften, Versicherungseinrichtungen, Effektenhändler, Spielcasinos, usw.) (GWG 2) *(intermédiaires financiers – banques, directions de Fonds, sociétés d'investissment, institutions d'assurance, négociant en valeurs mobilières, maisons de jeu etc.)*	Financial intermediaries (banks, fund managers, investment companies, insurance companies, securities traders, gambling casinos, etc.)
Selbstregulierungsorganisation (SRO) (GWG 24) *(organisme d'autorégulation)*	Self-regulatory organisation (SRO)
Kontrollstelle für die Bekämpfung der Geldwäscherei, Kontrollstelle (GWG 17) *(autorité de contrôle en matière de lutte contre le blanchiment d'argent)*	Anti-Money Laundering Control Authority (AMLCA) AML Control Authority
Eidgenössische Finanzverwaltung, Bern (GWG 17) *(administration fédérale des finances)*	Federal Finance Administration (FFA)

Teil G: Anhänge und Unterlagen / Appendices and documents

Meldestelle für Geldwäscherei Bern, (GWG 23) *(bureau de communication en matière de blanchiment d'argent)*	Money Laundering Reporting Office (MROS)
Bundesamt für Polizei, Bern (GWG 23) *(office fédérale de police)*	Federal Police Department (FDP)
Amtshilfe (GWG 29) *(entreaide administrative)*	Mutual assistance
Zusammenarbeit mit ausländischen Behörden (GWG 30) *(collaboration avec les autorités étrangers)*	Cooperation with foreign authorities, administrative assistance, cooperation with domestic and foreign authorities
Identifzierung der Vertragspartei (GWG 3) *(vérification de l'identité du concontractant)*	Identification of client, Know your client (KYI), verification of customers
Offizieller Identiätsnachweis (Pass, Identitätskarte, Fahrausweis) *(pièce d'identification officielle – passport, carte d'identité, permit de conduire)*	Official prove of identiy (passport, ID card, driving licence)
Formular A *(formulaire A)*	Form A Establishment of the beneficial owner's identity
Wirtschaftlich Berechtigter (WB)	Ultimate beneficial owner (BO)

(bénéficiaire, propriétaire économique)	
Vollmacht *(pouvoir, procuration)*	Power of attorney, proxy
Meldung bei begründetem Verdacht von Geldwäscherei (GWG 9) *(rapport en cas de soupçon de blanchiment d'argent)*	Suspicious activity report in case of money laundering duty to file report to MROS
Unverzügliche Vermögenssperre für fünf Werktage (GWG 10) *(blocage immédiat des avoirs durant cinq jours ouvrables)*	Immediate freezing of assets for five working days, arrest
Politisch exponierte Person *(person exposé politiquement)*	Politicically Exposed Person (PEP)
Sorgfaltspflichtvereinbarung (VSB 08) der Bankiervereinigung *(convention relative à l'obligation de diligence des banques, CDB 08)*	Code of Conduct with Regard to the Exercise of Due Diligence (CDB 08) of the Swiss Banks

6. Vertragsrecht *(droit des contrats)*	**Contract Law**
OR allgemeiner Teil und Vertragsverhältnisse *(droit des contrats)*	CO General provisions and type of contracts

Teil G: Anhänge und Unterlagen / Appendices and documents

Entstehung der Obligationen, Schulden (OR 1) *(formation des obligations)*	Origin of obligations, debts
Entstehung durch Vertrag (OR 1) *(obligation resultant d'un contrat)*	Origin from contract
Übereinstimmende Willensäusserung (OR 1 Abs. 1) *(accord des parties)*	Manifestation of mutual assent, consensus
Antrag und Annahme (OR 3 Abs. 1) *(offre et acceptation)*	Offer and acceptance
Vertragsmängel (OR 23) *(vices du consentement)*	Defects of contracts, vitigating factors
Wesentlicher Irrtum (OR 23) *(erreur essentielle)*	Material error
Entstehung durch unerlaubte Handlung (OR 41) *(obligations résultant d'actes illicites)*	Origin from tort, illegal acts
Entstehung aus ungerechtfertigter Bereicherung (OR 62) *(obligations résultant de l'enrichissement illégitime)*	Origin from unjust enrichment

1036

Erlöschen der Obligationen (OR 114) *(extinction des obligations)*	Extinction of obligations, debt
Solidarhaftung (OR 143) *(solidarité passive)*	Joint and several liability and claim
Konventionalstrafen (OR 160) *(montant de la peine)*	Liquidated damages
Abtretung von Forderungen, Zession von Forderungen (OR 164) *(cession des créances)*	Assignment of claims
Vertragsrecht (OR 1) *(loi de contrats)*	Contract law
Obligationenrecht (OR) *(code des obligations)*	Code of obligations (CO)
Vertrag (OR 1) *(contrat)*	Contract, agreement
Vertragsfreiheit (OR 19) *(liberté de contrat?)*	Freedom of contract
Haftpflichtrecht (OR 41) *(droit de responsabilité)*	Law of tort

Konkludentes Verhalten *(comportment implicite?)*	Concludent, implicit, tacit, act implying consent
Notar *(notaire)*	Notary public
Urkunde *(document, pièce justificative)*	document, deed, legal document
Unerlaubte Handlung (OR 41) *(acte illicite, défendu)*	Tort, tortious act, illegal act
Handlungsfähigkeit (ZGB 12, 27) *(capacité)*	Capacity
Nichtiger Vertrag (OR 20) *(nullité du contrat)*	Void contract
Anfechtbarer Vertrag (OR 20 Abs. 2) (contrat contestable)	Voidable contract
Antrag Offerte, (OR 3), Angebot (DE) *(offre)*	Offer, bid, proposal, tender, quote
Annahme eines Angebotes (OR 3) *(acceptation)*	Acceptance

Sachregister

Anbieter, Offertsteller, Antragsteller (OR 7) *(l'auteur de l'offre)*	Offeror
Wesentliche Punkte, lateinisch: Essentialia (OR 2) *(points essentiels)*	Crucial elements of a contract, main points
Vertrauensprinzip, guter Glaube (ZGB 2) *(bonne foi)*	Principle of confidence, good faith, bona fide
Grundlagenirrtum (OR 24) *(erreur essentiel, fondamental)*	Material error
Motivirrtum (OR 25) *(erreur de motif)*	Error in motive
Rechnungsfehler (OR 24 Abs. 3) *(erreur de calcule)*	Calculation error
Wie ist rechtlich zu entscheiden, zu urteilen? *(comment à juger?)*	Quid juris? What is the law? How to legally judge the case?
Vertragsmängel (OR 23) *(vices du consentement, du contrat)*	Defects of contract conclusions, vitiating elements of contract

1039

Leistung, Kaufpreis, Entgelt (OR 21) *(prestation)*	Consideration
Betrug (OR 28 I, StGB 146) *(fraude)*	Fraud
Furchterregung, Drohung (OR 29 I und 30 I) Nötigung (DE) *(crainte fondée)*	Duress
Schadenersatz (OR 41, 97) *(dommage, responsabilité)*	Damages
Verzug (OR 102) *(demeure)*	Delay, default
Verjährung (OR 60, 127, 210) *(prescription)*	Statute limitations, statutory time bar
Kaufvertrag (OR 184) *(contrat de vente)*	Purchase contract
Verschulden (OR 97) *(faulte)*	Fault
Fahrniskauf, Kauf von beweglichen Vermögensgegenständen	Purchase of chattels, movable goods

(OR 187) *(vente mobilière)*	
Grundstückkauf, Kauf von Immobilien, Land und Gebäuden (OR 216) *(vente d'immeubles)*	Purchase of real estate, real property, immovable goods, land and buildings
Tauschvertrag (OR 237) *(contrat d'échange)*	Barter contract
Schenkung (OR 239) *(donation)*	Donation, gift
Miete, Mietvertrag (OR 253) *(bail à loyer)*	Rental agreement, operating lease
Pacht (OR 275) *(bail à ferme)*	Usufructuary lease
Leihe, Ausleihung (OR 305) *(prêt à usage)*	Lending, loan of and object for use
Arbeitsvertrag (OR 319), Anstellungsverhältnis (DE) *(contrat de travail)*	Employment contract, hire agreement
Auftrag, Mandat (OR 394),	Mandate, (professional) engagement, agency contract

(mandat)	
Bürgschaft Garantie, Kaution (OR 492), *(cautionnement)*	Guarantee, guaranty, surety, warranty, indemnity
7. Bundesverfassung (BV) *(constitution fédérale, Cst)*	**Swiss Federal Constitution (SFC, Cons.)**
Bund *(Confédération)*	Confederation, Federal State, CH (Confoederatio Helvetica)
Kantone *(cantons)*	Swiss cantons, states
Gemeinden *(communes)*	Municipalities, communities, local authorities
Staatliche Organisationen: Bund / Eidgenossenschaft, Kantone, Gemeinden *(instituts de droit public: Etat féderale/Conféderation, cantons, communes)*	Governmental entities, government units: Federation, Cantons, Communities
Bundesparlament *(parlament suisse)*	Swiss Federal Parliament
Nationalrat *(conseil national)*	National council, House of representatives
Ständerat *(conseil d'états)*	Council of States, Senate

Bundesgericht (BGer), Lausanne *(Tribunal fédéral suisse)*	Swiss Federal Tribunal, Supreme Court of Switzerland
Bundesgerichtsentscheid (BGE) *(Arrêt du Tribunal Fédéral Suisse, ATF)*	Decision of the Federal Tribunal
Gesamtbundesrat *(Conseil Fédéral)*	Federal Council
Bundesrat, Bundesrätin *(Conseiller Féderal)*	Federal Councellor

8. Handelsregister (HR)

Handelsregister (HR) *(registre du commerce)*	**Commercial register (CR),** commercial registry (UK)
Kantonales Handelsregisteramt *(registre du commerce cantonal)*	Cantonal Commerical Register Office
Handelsregisterführer *(préposé du registre du commerce)*	Head, officer of commercial register
Geschäftsfirma (OR 944) *(raison de commerce, raison sociale)*	Trade name, legal (statutory) company name as registered in commercial register
Handelsregisterverordnung (HRV) *(ordonance de registre de commerce)*	Commerical register ordinance
Zweigniederlassung, Filiale, Sitz	Branch (office), permanent esta-

(OR 641, 952) *(succursale, établissment stable, bureau)*	blishment
Schweizerisches Handelsamtsblatt (SHAB) www.shab.ch *(Feuille officielle suisse de commerce, FOSC)*	Swiss Official Commercial Gazette
Prokurist (ppa) (OR 721) *(fondé de procuration, procuriste)*	Holder of procuration, manager
Kollektivunterschrift zu zweien (KU), Zeichnungsberechtigung (DE) *(signature à deux, collective)*	Dual signatures, collective signatures, authorised joint signatories
Handlungsbevollmächtiger (i.V.) (OR 721) *(mandataire commercial)*	Commercial mandate holder
9. Zivilgesetzbuch (ZGB) vom 10. Dezember 1907 *(code civil suisse, CC)*	**Civil Code (CC)**
Personenrecht (ZGB 11 ff.) *(loi des personnes)*	Law of persons
Natürliche Personen (ZGB 11) *(personnes physiques)*	Natural persons

Sachregister

Juristische Personen (ZGB 52) *(personnes morales)*	Legal entities, legal persons
Verein, Vereinigung, Verband (ZGB 60), *(association)*	Association, club, society
Stiftung (ZGB 80) *(foundation)*	Foundation, charity (fund)
Pensionskasse, Personalvorsorgstiftung (BVG) *(caisse de pension, fonds de prévoyance)*	Pension fund, pension scheme, occupational pension plan, superannuation fund (UK), retirement fund
(patronaler) Wohlfahrtsfonds *(fonds de bienfaisance, fonds patronal)*	Welfare fund (voluntary) of employer
Familienrecht (Ehe, Scheidung); (ZGB 90) *(droit de la famille, marriage, divorce)*	Family law (marriage, divorce)
Erbrecht (ZGB 457) *(droit de successions, héritiers)*	Inheritance law, law of succession (UK)
Erbschaft, Erbmasse, Nachlass *(biens de la succession)*	Estate (of the deceased), estate of inheritance
Sachenrecht (ZGB 655 und 713) *(propriété foncière et mobilière)*	Property law, real estate law

Eigentum (ZGB 641) *(propriété)*	Ownership, (legal) title, property, freehold property (UK), freehold real estate (UK)
Beschränkte dingliche Rechte (ZGB 730) *(autres droits réels)*	Limited rights in rem
Grunddienstbarkeit, Servitut (ZGB 730) *(servitude foncière)*	Easement of real estate, encumbrance, pledge
Nutzniessung (ZGB 745) *(usufruit)*	Usufruct, right to use
Grundpfandverschreibung, Hypothek (ZGB 824) *(hypothèque)*	Mortgage
Faustpfand, Pfandrecht (ZGB 884) *(gage mobilier, nantissement)*	Chattel pledge, pawn, security, lien, collateral (US)
Retentionsrecht (ZGB 895) Einbehaltung (DE) *(droit de rétention)*	Right of retention, withholding (of goods)
Besitz (ZGB 919) *(possession)*	Possession

Sachregister

Grundbuch (ZGB 942) Grundstücksregister (DE) *(régistre foncier)*	Real estate register public land register
Grundbuchamt *(bureau du régistre foncier)*	Office of the real estate register
10. Fusionsgesetz (FusG) *(loi sur la fusion, LFus)*	**Merger Act (MA)**
Bundesgesetz über Fusion, Spaltung, Umwandlung und Vermögensübertragung vom 3. Oktober 2003 *(Loi féderale sur la fusion, la scission, la transformation et le transfert de patrimoine)*	Federal Law on Merger, Demerger, Conversion and Transfer of Assets and Liabilities
Fusionsrecht *(droit de fusion)*	Merger law
Absorbtionsfusion, Übernahme (FusG 3 Abs. 1 a) *(fusion par absorption, reprise)*	Absorption, annexion, legal take over
Kombinationsfusion, Zusammenschluss (FusG Abs. 1 b) *(fusion par combinaison, réunion, concentration)*	Combination, amalgamation, legal merger
Übernehmende Gesellschaft (FusG 9) *(société reprenante)*	Absorbing company, entity taking over, surviving company

1047

Teil G: Anhänge und Unterlagen / Appendices and documents

Übertragende Gesellschaft (FusG 9) *(société transférante)*	Transferring company, entity
Umtauschverhältnis, Austauschverhältnis (FusG 14 Abs. 2 c) *(échange)*	Exchange ratio
Fusionsvertrag (FusG 13) *(contrat de fusion)*	Merger agreement
Fusionsbericht (FusG 14) *(rapport de fusion)*	Merger report
Kapitalerhöhung (FusG 9, OR 650) *(augmentation de capital)*	Capital increase
Sanierungsfusion (FusG 6) *(fusion de sociétés en cas de perte en capital ou de surendettement)*	Restructuring merger
Zwischenbilanz (FusG 11) *(bilan intermédiaire)*	Interim balance sheet
Prüfung durch Fusionsprüfer (FusG 15) *(vérification)*	Verification by merger auditors, examination

Abfindung (FusG 8 Abs. 2) *(dédommagement)*	Cash consideration
Universalsukzession, Übernahme eines Geschäftes mit Aktiven und Passiven (OR 181) *(cession universelle)*	Universal transfer
Gläubigerschutz (FusG 45) *(protection des créanciers)*	Creditor protection
Mitarbeiterschutz (FusG 45) *(protection des travailleurs)*	Protection of employees
Vereinfachte Fusion (FusG 23) *(fusion simplifiée)*	Simplified merger
Gruppeninterne Fusionen (FusG 23) *(fusion dans un group)*	Intra-group mergers
Klein- und Mittelunternehmen (KMU) (FusG 2) *(petites et moyennes entreprises, PME)*	Small and medium enterprises (SME)
Spaltung (FusG 29) *(scission)*	Demerger, spin-off, splitting

Aufspaltung (FusG 29 a) *(scission par division)*	Division
Abspaltung (FusG 29 b) *(séparation, scission par transfert)*	Separation, carve-out
Spaltungsvertrag (FusG 37) *(contrat de scission)*	Demerger agreement
Spaltungsplan (FusG 37) *(projet de scission)*	Demerger plan
Spaltungsbericht (FusG 39) *(rapport de scission)*	Demerger report
Öffentliche Urkunde (FusG 20, OR 629) *(acte authentique)*	Public deed
Kapitalherabesetzung *(réduction de capital)*	Capital decrease
Anteils- und Mitgliedschaftsrechte (FusG 56) *(parts sociales et droits de sociétariat)*	participation and membership rights
Schuldenruf (dreimaliger) in Handelsamtblatt (SHAB)	Notices to creditors (three times) in commercial

(FusG 25 Abs. 2) *(avis aux créanciers, trois fois dans le FOSC)*	
Umwandlung (FusG 59) *(transformation)*	Conversion, change of legal form, transformation
Übertragung von Aktiven *(transfert des actifs)*	Asset deal, transfer of assets
Inventar (FusG 37 und 71) *(inventaire)*	Inventory, list of assets and liabilities
Vermögensübertragung (FusG 69) *(transfert de patrimoine)*	Transfer of assets and liabilities
Haftung, Verantwortlichkeit (FusG 108) *(responsabilité)*	Liability

11. Konkursrecht	**Insolvency and bankruptcy act**
Schuldbetreibungs- und Konkursgesetz (SchKG) vom 11. April 1889 *(Droit des poursuites et faillites)*	Swiss Federal Code of Debt Enforcement and Bankruptcy
Arrest, Beschlagnahmung (SchKG 8 und 271) *(séquestre)*	Seizure of assets

Teil G: Anhänge und Unterlagen / Appendices and documents

Betreibungs- und Konkursamt (SchKG 2) *(office des poursuites)*	Debt enforcement (execution) and bankruptcy office, authority
Betreibungsbeamter (SchKG 2) *(préposé aux poursuites)*	Debt enforcement official
Gläubiger *(créancier)*	Claimant, creditor
Schuldner *(débiteur)*	Debtor
Betreibungsbegehren (SchKG 67) *(réquisition de pousuite)*	Enforcement request
Gebühr (SchKG 16) *(emolument)*	Fees
Rechtsvorschlag (SchKG 74) *(opposition)*	Objection
Insolvenzerklärung (SchKG 191) *(déclaration d'insolvabilité)*	Insolvency declaration
Überschuldungsanzeige von juristischen Personen durch Verwaltungsrat beim Konkursrichter (Konkursgericht) (OR 725 Abs. 2) *(avis du juge par le conseil d'administration d'un surendettment)*	Declaration of overindebtedness (of companies) by court (judge)

Rangrücktritt auf Darlehen (OR 725 Abs. 2) *(prêt de rang subordonné, en rang inférieur)*	Subordination of claims, subordinated loan
Forderungsverzicht, à fonds perdu *(abandon de crédit)*	Waiver of claim, loan
Nachlassstundung (SchKG 298) *(sursit concordataire)*	Debt restructuring moratorium
Konkursverwalter (SchKG 240) *(administrateur)*	Administrator, receiver (UK)
Kollokationsplan *(état de collocation)*	Schedule, inventory of claims, ranking
Klassen von Gläubigern: Gesicherte Schulden (durch Pfänder) Erste Klasse: Mitarbeiter Zweite Klasse: Sozialversicherung Dritte Klasse: alle übrigen	Classes of creditors: Secured claims (satisfied by collateral) First class: employees Second class: social security Third class: all others
Konkursmasse (SchKG 197) *(masse de faillite)*	bankruptcy estate
Lastenverzeichnis (SchKG 247) *(état de charges)*	Inventory of claims
Pfändung (SchKG 95) *(saisie)*	Pledge

Retentionsrecht (OR 268, SchKG 283) *(droit de retention)*	Retention right
Zwangsversteigerung (SchKG 257) *(vente forcée aux enchères publiques)*	Compulsory auction
Zahlungsbefehl (SchKG 69) *(commandement de payer)*	Default summons
Zahlungsunfähigkeit (OR 725a, SchKG 192) Insolvenz (DE) *(insolvabilité)*	Illiquidity, insolvency (UK)
Zuschlag (SchKG 126 und 258) *(adjudication)*	Fall of the hammer
Anfechtungsklage (SchKG 285) *(plainte pauliana)*	law suit to claim moneys paid shortly before bankruptcy
12. Bankengesetz (BankG) *(loi fédérale sur les banques, LB)*	**Banking Act (BA)**
Bundesgesetz über die Banken und Sparkassen vom 8. November 1934 *(loi fédérale sur les banques et les caisses d'epargne)*	Federal Law on Banks and Savings, Banking Act

Eidgenössische Bankenkommission (EBK) / FINMA *(Commission Fédérale de Banques, CFB) / FINMA*	Swiss Federal Banking Commission (FBC) / FINMA
Bankzulassung (BankG 3) *(licence de banque)*	Banking license
Gewähr für eine einwandfreie Geschäftsführung (BankG 3 Abs. 2 c) *(réputation irreprochable)*	proper conduct of business, irreproachable reputation

13. Börsengesetz (BEHG) *(loi sur les bourses, LBVM)*	**Stock Exchange Act (SESTA)**
Bundesgesetz über die Börsen und den Effektenhandel vom 24. März 1995 *(loi fédérale sur les bourses et la commerce des valeurs mobilières)*	Federal Act on Stock Exchanges and Securities
Effektenhändler, Wertschriftenhändler (BEHG 14) *(commerçant de titres professionel)*	Securities dealers
Öffentliches Übernahmeangebot (BEHG 22) *(offre publique d'acquisition, d'achat, OPA)*	Public takeover offer

Übernahmekommission (BEHG 23) *(Commision des offers publiques d'acquisition, COPA)*	Takeover Board (TOB), commission on public take overs
Zielgesellschaft (BEHG 22) *(société visée.)*	Offeree, target (company)
Übernehmer (BEHG 24) *(offrant)*	Offeror
Kotierungsreglement *(règlement de cotisation)*	Listing rules (of 24 January 1996)
Zulassungsstelle der Börse *(d'admission)*	Admission board of SIX
Ad hoc-Publizität *(publicité ad-hoc)*	Ad hoc publicity
Publikumsgesellschaft mit Aktien, kotiert an Börse (BEHG 22) notiert (DE) *(société avec titres (actions) cotés en Suisse)*	Public company with shares on a Swiss
Offenlegung von Beteiligungen (BEHG 20) *(obligation de declarer des particpations)*	Disclosure of participations, shareholding threshold at 3, 5, 10, 15, 20, 25, 33.3, 50 and 66.6%

14. Kollektivanlagegesetz (KAG) *(loi fédérale sur les placements collectifs de Capitaux, LPPC)*	**Collective Investment Schemes Act (CISA)**
Anlagefonds, Investment-Fonds *(fonds de placement)*	Mutual fund, investment fund, investment trust
Investmentgesellschaft mit variablem Kapital *(société d'investissements avec du capital variable, SICAV)*	Company with variable share capital
Investmentgesellschaft mit festem Kapital *(société d'investissements avec du capital fixe, SICAF)*	Company with fixed share capital

15. Sozialversicherungsrecht *(sécurité sociale)*	**Social security laws**
Dreisäulensystem: 1. Staatliche Vorsorge (Sicherung des Existenz 2. Berufliche Vorsorge (Sicherstellung des gewohnten Lebensstandards in angemessener Weise) 3. Individuelle Vorsorge (private Ersparnisse) *(trois piliers)*	Three pillar system, three columns principle: 1. Basic federal insurance system (secure livelihood) 2. Occupational pension scheme (maintain previous standard of living) 3. Individual provident measures (individual savings)

Teil G: Anhänge und Unterlagen / Appendices and documents

Schutz vor sozialen Risiken *(protection contre les risques sociales)*	Protection against social risks
16. AHV-Gesetz *(AVS)*	**Old age insurance**
Gesetz über die Alters-, Hinterbliebenen und Invaliditätsversicherung (AHV / IV / EO) vom 20. Dezember 1946 *(Assurance-vieillesse et survivants et assurance invalidité, assurance perte de gain, LAVS AVS / AI / APG)* www.ahv-iv.info	Old-age, survivors' and invalidity insurance
Zweck (BV 113): Deckung des Existenzbedarfs *(but: couvrir les besoins vitaux de manière approprié)*	Purpose: Must cover the basic needs in appropriate way, secure livelyhood
Erste Säule (staatlich) *(premier pilier, Etat)*	First pillar, 1st column (governmental pension scheme)
Bundesamt für Sozialversicherung (BSV), Bern www.bsv.admin.ch *(office fédéral des assurances sociales, OFAS)*	Federal Social Insurance Office
Abkommen über die Personalfreizügigkeit (CH / EU / EFTA / EEA Reg. 1408/71 and 574/72) *(traité sur l'échange des personnes)*	Agreement on the free movement of persons

Erwerbstätigkeit *(activité lucrative)*	Gainful employment
Wohnort *(domicile, résidence)*	Residence
Selbständige Erwerbstätigkeit *(activité indépendante)*	Self-employment
Unselbständigerwerbener *(dependant, salarié)*	Employed (person)
Ort der Arbeit, Lateinisch: Lex loci laboris *(endroit du travail)*	Contribution payable in country of work, where employer has its head office (domicile)
Ausgleichskasse (AK), kantonal *(caisse suisse de compensation)*	Compensation fund office, cantonal
AHV-Ausweis *(carte AVS)*	Personal insurance certificate card
AHV-Nummer *(numéro AVS)*	Personal social security number, code
Individuelles Konto (IK) *(compte individuel AVS)*	Individual account
Beiträge als Prozentsatz des Salärs *(cotisations)*	Contributions as percentage of earned income
Arbeitgeber *(employeur)*	Employer
Arbeitnehmer *(salarié)*	Employee

Teil G: Anhänge und Unterlagen / Appendices and documents

für Alters- und Hinterlassene (AHV) *(vielleisse et survivants)*	for old age and survivors' insurance
Invalidität (IV) *(invalidité)*	Invalidity insurance
Erwerbsersatz und Mutterschaft (EO) *(perte de gain en cas de service et maternité)*	EO and maternity insurance
Selbständigerwerbender *(indépendant)*	Self-employed (person)
Nichterwerbstätiger *(sans activité lucrative)*	Not gainfully employed (person), not engaged in paid employment
Leistungen *(prestations)* Alterspensionen *(pensions de vieillesse)* Witwen- und Witwerrenten *(veuves)* Kinder- und Waisenrenten *(enfants et orphelins)* Invaliditätsmassnahme *(invalidité)*	Benefits old age pensions Widows and widower pensions Children and orphan pensions Invalidity measures, rehabilitation
Erwerbsersatzordnung (EO) *(perte de gain en cas de service et de maternité)*	Compensation for temporary loss or income (during army and other service and maternity leave)

17. Krankenversicherung (assurance-maladie)	**Sickness insurance and maternity insurance**
Krankenversicherungsgesetz (KVG)	**Federal health insurance (FHIA)**
Bundesgesetz über die Krankenversicherung (Loi fédérale sur l'assurance-maladie, LAMal)	Federal health insurance act
Gemeinsame Einrichtung KVG www.assurancessociales.admin.ch www.kvg.org	Common institution under FIHA
18. Unfallversicherung	**Accident and occupational disease insurance**
Unfallversicherungsgesetz (UVG)	Accident Insurance Act
Bundesgesetz über die Unfallversicherung vom 20. März 1981 (Loi fédérale sur l'assurance-accidents, LAA)	Federal Law on Accident Insurance
Schweizerische Unfallversicherungsanstalt (SUVA), Luzern www.suva.ch (Caisse nationale suisse d'assurances en cas d'accidents, CNA)	Swiss National Accident Insurance Fund, Lucerne
Betriebsunfallversicherung (BU) (assurance accident du travail)	Occupational accident insurance

Nichtbetriebsunfallversicherung (NBU) *(assurance accident du non-travail)*	non-occupational accident insurance, private accidents, non-work accidents

19. Familienzulagen *(allocations familiales)*	**Family allowances**
Familienausgleichskassen (FAK), kantonal *(caisse de compensation pour allocations familiales, cantonale)*	Family compensation funds, cantonal

20. Arbeitslosenversicherung (AVIG) *(assurance-chômage)*	**Unemployment insurance**
Staatsekretariat für Wirtschaft, Bern (seco) www.seco.admin.ch *(Secrétariat d'Etat à l'économie)*	State secretariat for Economic Affairs

21. Berufsvorsorgegesetz (BVG) *(prévoyance professionnelle)*	**Pension Law**
Bundesgesetz über die berufliche Alters-, Hinterlassenen- und Invalidenvorsorge (BVG) www.sfbvg.ch	Federal Law on Occupational Benefit Plans Concerning old-age, survivors and invalidity, employee insurance

(Loi fédéral sur la prévoyance professionelle, LPP)	
Zweite Säule *(deuxième pilier)*	Second pillar, 2nd column
Zweck: *(but)*	Purpose: To maintain the previous standard of living in an appropriate way
Organisiert von *(organisé par)* Arbeitgeber (AG) *(employeur)* 2a obligatorisch *(obligatoire)* 2b überobligatorisch	Organised by: Employers 2a mandatory 2b above and beyond mandatory
Altersguthaben *(actifs veillesse)*	Retirement assets
Leistungen: Altersrenten und/oder Kapitalabfindung (maximal 25%) *(préstations)*	Benefits: Old-age pensions and/or capital benefits (maximum 25%)
Umwandlungssatz (7.1% der Altersguthaben) *(taux de conversion)*	Conversion rate (7.1% of retirement assets)
Vorzeitige Pensionierung *(retraite anticipée)*	Early retirement
Freizügigkeitsleistungen (FZG) *(libre passage, prestation de sortie)*	Entitlement to a departure benefit, vested benefit, pension, cash surrender value

Wohneigentumsförderung (WEF) *(encouragement à la propriété du logement, EPL)*	Encouragement of home ownership, promotion of home ownership
Auffangeinrichtung BVG *(Insitution supplétive LPP)*	Substitute Occupational Benefit Institution (for those not insured elsewere)
Sicherheitsfonds BVG, Bern *(Fonds de garantie LPP)*	Guarantee Fund (if pension fund gets bankrupt)
Dritte Säule: Individuelle Vorsorge (steuerbefreit) (BBV 3) *(prévoyance individuelle)*	Third pillar, 3rd column: Linked individual provident measures (tax deductible)
3a gebundene Selbstvorsorge mit Bankstiftung oder Versicherungseinrichtung (Sperrkonto, gesperrte Versicherungspolice) *(prévoyance individuelle liée avec fondation bancaire ou assurance) (compte bloqué, police d'assurance bloquée)*	3a qualified pension plans with bank foundation or insurance organization, qualified fiscally privileged (escrow, blocked accounts, blocked insurance policy)
3b persönliche Ersparnisse *(prévoyance individuelle libre)*	3b individual savings

22. Versicherungsaufsichtsgesetz (VAG) *(surveillance des assurances, LSA)*	**Insurance Oversight Act (IOA)**
Bundesgesetz betreffend die Aufsicht über Versicherungsunternehmen vom 17. Dezember 2004 *(loi fédérale sur la surveillance des assurances, LSA)*	Federal Act on the Oversight of Insurance Companies
Bundesamt für Privatversicherung (BPV) *(office fédérale des assurances)*	Swiss Federal Office of Private Insurance (OPI)
23. Mehrwertsteuern (MWST) *(Taxe sur la valeur ajoutée, TVA)*	**Value Added Tax (VAT)**
Gesetz über die Mehrwertsteuer vom 2. September 1999 *(Loi fédérale régissant la taxe sur la valeur ajoutée, LTVA)* www.estv.admin.ch	Value Added Tax Law (VATL)
Eidgenössische Steuerverwaltung (ESTV), Haupabteilung Mehrwertsteuer (MWST), Bern *(Administration fédérale des contributions (AFC), Division principale de la taxe sur la valeur ajoutée (TVA))*	Federal Tax Authority (FTA), Department VAT
Indirekte Steuern *(impôts indirecte)*	Indirect tax

MWST-Pflicht (MWSTG 21) *(assujettissement à la TVA)*	VAT liability
Lieferungen von Gegenständen (MWSTG 6) *(livraison des biens)*	VAT on delivery of goods
Erbringung von Dienstleistungen (MWSTG 7) *(prestation des services)*	VAT on procurement of services
Eigenverbrauch (MWSTG 9) *(prestation à soi-même)*	VAT for own use
MWST-Sätze: *(taux de l'impôt)* - Normal 7.6% - Reduzierter Satz 2.4% (Lebensmittel, Medikamente usw.) *(taux réduit de 2.4 % (comestibles, médicaments etc.)* - Spezialsatz 3.6% (Hotelunterkunft) *(taux spécial de 3.6 % (hébergement)*	VAT Tax rates: - Normal rate 7.6% - Reduced rate 2.4% (food, medicine etc.) - Special rate 3.6% (hotel accommodation)
Gruppenbesteuerung (MWSTG 22) *(imposition de groupe)*	Group taxation (Swiss companies only)
Gruppenträger (MWSTG 22 Abs. 4) *(Chef de groupe)*	Controlling company
Mithaftung solidarische Haftung der Gruppenmitglieder	Joint liability of the VAT group members

Sachregister

(MWSTG 32 Abs. 1 e) *(responsabilité solidaire des partenaires du groupe)*	
Steuerbare Umsätze (MWSTG 5) *(opérations imposables)*	Taxable revenues, vatable revenues
Unecht steuerbefreite Umsätze wie Gesundheitswesen, Bildung, Kultur, Sport, Versicherung, Banken Zahlungsverkehr usw. (MWSTG 18) *(opérations exclues comme santé, éducation, culture, sport, assurances, banques etc.)*	Unreal VAT exempt revenues like services for health, education, culture, sports, insurance, banks etc.
Nullsteuer (z.B. Exporte) (MWSTG 19) *(opérations exonérées par example exports)*	Zero-rated revenues, (e.g. exports)
Nicht steuerpflichtige Erträge in Umsatzsteuerabstimmung *(gains non-imposable)*	Non-VAT revenues (e.g. dividends, interest etc.)
Freiwillige Optionen für die Steuerpflicht (MWSTG 27) *(option pour l'assujettissement à titre volontaire)*	Voluntary VAT option
MWST auf Eigenverbrauch (MWSTG 9) *(TVA sur prestations à soi-même)*	VAT on self-supply

Teil G: Anhänge und Unterlagen / Appendices and documents

Vorsteuerabzug (MWSTG 38) (déduction de l'impôt préalable)	Input VAT deduction
Steuerschuld (MWSTG 43) (créance fiscale)	Tax liability (quarterly)
Rückerstattung von Steuern (MWSTG 48) (remboursement de l'impôt)	Repayment of tax
Verjährung der Steuerforderung nach fünf Jahren (MWSTG 49) (prescription de la créance fiscale par cinq ans)	statute of limitations for five years
Abrechnungsperiode, Quartal (MWSTG 45) (période fiscale)	Fiscal period, measurement period
Selbstdeklarierung nach 60 Tagen nach Quartalsende (MWSTG 46) (auto-taxation)	Self declaration after 60 days after the end of the quarter
Umsatzabstimmung, Plausibilitätstest (prevue de plausibilité du chiffre d'affairs)	Revenue reconciliation (with quarterly) VAT tax returns, plausibility check
Kauf von Dienstleistungen im Ausland (MWSTG 10) über CHF 10,000	Purchase of services abroad of more than CHF 10,000 per year

Sachregister

(MWSTG 24) *(préstations de services fournie par une enterprise ayant son siege à l'étranger)*	
MWSt Satz (MWSTG 36) *(taux de l'impôt)*	VAT tax rate
Exportnachweis, zollamtlich (MWSTG 20) *(prevue de exportation attestée par l'autorité douanière)*	Proof of export by customs office
Korrekturformular *(formulaire de correction)*	Corrective VAT tax return (Form No. 535)
Vorentscheid der MWSt-Behörde	VAT Ruling
24. Unternehmensbesteuerung in der Schweiz www.admin.ch **Direktes Bundessteuergesetz (DBG)**	**Swiss Corporate Tax, company taxation (UK)** Direct Tax Law (DTL)
Bundesgesetz über die direkte Bundessteuer vom 14. Dezember 1990 *(Loi sur l'impôt fédérale direct, LIFD)*	Swiss Law on the Direct Federal Tax
Steuerharmonisierungsgesetz *(Loi sur l'harmonisation fiscale, LHID)*	Federal Tax Harmonisation Law, to coordinate tax basis for cantonal taxes, but not tax rates

1069

Besteuerung juristischer Personen (DBG 49) *(Taxation des personnes morales)*	Taxing jurisdictions for legal entities:
Bund (Reingewinn, Verrechnungssteuern) *Confédération (bénéfice net, impôt anticipé)*	Swiss federal government (net profit, withholding tax)
Kantone (Reingewinn und Eigenkapital) *Cantons (bénéfice net, patrimoine net)*	Swiss cantons (net profit, equity)
Steuererklärung (DBG 124) *(déclaration d'impôt)*	tax return, tax declaration
Massgeblichkeitsprinzip der Handelsbilanz für die Steuerbilanz *(equivalence du bilan commercial avec le bilan fiscal)*	authoritative character of commercial / statutory accounting also for tax purposes
stille Reserven (DBG 61) *(réserves latentes)*	Hidden, undisclosed, silent reserves
Einlagen der Aktionäre (DBG 60 a) *(apports des actionaires, agio)*	Shareholder contributions e.g. contribution of APIC

Verlustverrechnung 7 Jahre kein Verlustrücktrag (DBG 67) *(deduction des pertes, sept excercices)*	Loss carry forwards 7 preceeding years no carry back
Umstrukturierungen (DBG 61) *(restructurations)*	Restructuring, deferral of book values (hidden reserves)
Doppelbesteuerung der Gesellschaft und Aktionärs *(double taxation)*	Double taxation of company and shareholder
Verdeckte Gewinnausschüttung (DBG 58) *(distribution dissimulée)*	Hidden profit distribution, deemed dividend
Bundessteuersatz für Kapitalgesellschaften, 8.5% des Gewinns vor Steuern (DBG 68) *(taux d'impôt, 8.5 pour cent du bénéfice net)*	Federal income tax rate 8.5% statutory rate
Effektiver Steuersatz, da Steuern abziehbar *(taux effectif)*	Effective tax rate (7.8%), as taxes are deductible
Holdinggesellschaft (DGB 69) *(société de participation, holding)*	Holding company
Beteiligungsabzug (DBG 69) *(reduction pour participations)*	Participation reduction

Hilfsgesellschaft, Verwaltungsgesellschaft *(société auxiliaire, de gestion)*	Auxiliary company, administrative company
Gemischte Gesellschaft *(société mixte)*	Mixed company
Domizilgesellschaft *(société de domicile)*	Domiciliary company, domicile company
Ersatzbeschaffung, Übertragung von stillen Reserven (DBG 64) *(remploi)*	Replacement, transfer of hidden reserves to replaced asset (e.g. real estate)
Ausländische Filialen, Betriebsstätte (DBG 51) *(succursale suisse d'une société étrangère)*	Foreign Branch, Swiss permanent establishment of a foreign company
Doppelbesteurungsabkommen (DBA) *(accord de double imposition de bénéfice)*	Double Tax Agreement (DTA), Double Tax Treaty
Pauschalbesteuerung, Besteuerung von ausländische Privatpersonen nach Aufwand (DBG 14) *(imposition forfaitaire, imposition d'après la dépense des personnes physiques étrangers, forfait fiscal)*	Lump-sum taxation of unemployed „leisured foreigners (e.g. retirees or „idle rich") based on lifestyle (e.g. five times rent) for high net worth individuals (HNWI)

Indirekte Teilliquidation (DBG 20a Abs. 1a) *(liquidation particiel indirecte)*	Indirect partial liquidation theory
Transponierung (DBG 201 Abs. 1b) *(théorie de la transposition)*	Transposition theory
Quellensteuern für ausländische Mitarbeiter (DBG 83) *(impôt à la source pour travailleurs étrangers)*	Salary withholding tax, source tax for foreign employees working in Switzerland
25. Verrechnungssteuern (VStG) *(impot anticipé)*	**Withholding Tax (WHT)**
Verrechnungssteuergesetz vom 13. Oktober 1965 *(Loi fédérale sur l'impôt anticipé, LIA)*	Swiss Federal Withholding Tax Law
Verrechnungssteuersatz (35%) auf Dividenden, Zinsen auf Bankkonten, Anleihen usw.	Withholding tax rate (35%) on dividends, interest on bank deposits, bonds etc.
Gewinnausschüttung (VStG 4) *(distribution de bénéfice)*	dividend payment
Geldwerte Leistungen an Aktionäre, verdeckte Gewinnausschüttung *(prestations appréciables en argent, distribution dissimulée de bénéfice)*	deemed, hidden, constructive dividends

Gratisaktien (DBG 20) *(actions gratuites)*	bonus shares
26. Stempelsteuern (StG) *(droits de timbres)*	**Stamp taxes, stamp duties**
Bundesgesetz über die Stempelabgaben vom 27. Juni 1973 *(Loi fédérale sur les droits de timbre, LT)*	Swiss Federal Stamp Tax Law
Emissionsabgabe auf Beteiligungsrechten (StG 5), Emissionsstempelsteuern (1% des ausgegebenen Kapitals inkl. Agio über CHF 1 Mio.) *(droits de timbres d'émission, 1 pour cent des actions émises y inclus un agio qui dépassent CHF 1 million)*	Issuance stamp tax (1% of issue share capital and premium above CHF 1 million), share stamp
Umsatzabgabe von Wertschriftenhändlern (StG 13) *(droit de timbre de négociation)*	Transfer stamp tax of security dealers
27. Strafgesetzbuch (StGB) *(code pénal suisse, CPS)*	**Penal Code (SPC, PC)**
Schweizerisches Strafgesetzbuch vom 21. Dezember 1937	Swiss Penal Code, Federal Criminal Code

Sachregister

Keine Sanktion (Strafe), ohne Gesetz (StGB 1) *(pas de sanction sans loi (pénale))*	no punishment, penalty without legal justification Latin: nulla poena sine lege (scripta), nullum crimen sine lege (stricta)
Verbrechen (StGB 1) → Freiheitsstrafe von mehr als drei Jahren (StGB 10 Abs. 2), Gefängnisstrafe *(crime → peine privative de liberté de plus de trois ans, emprisonment)*	Crimes → prison, jail of more than three years imprisonment, detention
Vergehen (StGB 1) *(délit → peine privative de liberté de moins de trois ou peine pécuniaire)*	Offence → prison of less than three years or (money) fines, penalty
Vorsatz und Fahrlässigkeit (StGB 10) *(intention et négligence)*	Intention and negligence
Sachverhalt (StGB 13) *(faits)*	facts and circumstances
Strafbare Handlungen gegen Leib und Leben *(infraction contre la vie et l'intégralité corporelle)*	Offenses against life and limb
Strafbare Handlungen gegen das Vermögen (StGB 137) *(infraction contre le patrimoine)*	Offenses against property

Unrechtmässige Aneignung (StGB 138) *(appropriation illégitime)*	Embezzlement
Betrug (StGB 146) *(escroquerie)*	Fraud
Unwahre Angaben über kaufmännische Gewerbe (StGB 152) *(faux renseignments sur des entreprises commerciales)*	False statement about commercial entreprises
Erpressung (StGB 156) *(extorsion et chantage)*	Extortion, black mail
Wucherei (StGB 157) *(usure)*	Usuary
Verbot des Insiderhandels (StGB 161) und Kursmanipulation (StGB 161bis) *(exploitation de la connaissance de faits confidentiel, prohibition de manipulation de cours)*	Prohibition of insider trading (in listed securities) and price manipulation
Betrügerischer Konkurs (StGB 163) *(banquerote frauduleuse)*	Fraudulent bankruptcy
Urkundenfälschung (StGB 251) *(faux dans le titres)*	Forgery of documents

Geldwäscherei (StGB 305bis) *(blanchiment d'argent)*	Money laundering
Bestechung (StGB 322ter), Korruption aktiv und passiv, Bestechungsgelder *(corruption, active et passive, commission occultes)*	Corruption, (actively) bribing and being bribed (receiving), bribes
Ordnungswidrige Führung der Geschäftsbücher (StGB 325) *(inobservation des prescriptions légales sur la comptabilité)*	Irregular keeping of books

Sachregister

	Text[231]	Gesetzestext[232]
A		
Abberufung		
- von Organen und Bevollmächtigten der AG		705, 716a, 726, 731b, 740, 762
- von Geschäftsführern der GmbH		815
- von Verwaltung und Revisionsstelle der Genossenschaft		890
- durch die Verwaltung		905
Abfindung		
- GmbH		825 f.
- Genossenschaft		864 f.
Abnahme der Rechnung		731
Abschreibungen		663, 665, 669, 732
- linear	86	
- degressiv	87	
- Sofortabschreibungen	88	

---

[231] Die Zahlen in der Spalte „Text" sind als Seitenzahlen zu verstehen.
[232] Falls nicht anders vermerkt, beziehen sich die Artikelangaben der Spalte „Gesetzestext" auf das Obligationenrecht (OR).

	Text	Gesetzestext
Abstimmung		
- AG		703
- GmbH		808
- Genossenschaft		855, 880, 888
Abtretung		
- der Genossenschaftsanteile		849
- der Stammanteile		785 ff.
Abweichungen		
Agio		624
AHV	110	
Aktien		620, 622 ff.
- Arten		622
- Zerlegung und Zusammenlegung		621
- Zeichnung		652
- kotierte, Beteiligungsverhältnisse		663c
- Vernichtung im Fall einer Sanierung		732a
Aktienbuch		686 f.
Aktiengesellschaft		620 ff.
- Begriff		620
- Organisation		698 ff.
Aktienkapital		620 ff.; 650 ff.
- Erhöhung		650 ff.
- Herabsetzung, vgl. auch Herabsetzung		732 ff.
Aktienzeichnung		630, 644

Sachregister

	Text	Gesetzestext
Aktionär		
- Rechte und Pflichten		660 ff.
- Anzahl zur Gründung		625
Aktionärbindungsvertrag		
Aktiven		
- verpfändete	121	
- abgetretene	121	
- unter Eigentumsvorbehalt zur Sicherstellung eigener Gesellschaftsverbindlichkeiten	119	
Amtsdauer		
- Verwaltungsrat		710
- der Revisionsstelle		730a
- der Verwaltung der Genossenschaft		896
Amtsgeheimnis		35 RAG
Amtshilfe, vgl. Rechtshilfe		
Änderung		
- der Statuten		647
- der Haftungsbestimmungen (Genossenschaft)		874
Anfechtung		
- der Generalversammlungsbeschlüsse der AG		706 f.
- der Gesellschafterversammlungsbeschlüsse der GmbH		808c
- der Generalversammlungsbeschlüsse der Genossenschaft		891
- von Beschlüssen durch Genossenschaftsverbände		924

	Text	Gesetzestext
- der Stiftung		82 ZGB
Anhang		663b
Anlagespiegel	89	
Anlagevermögen		665 f.
Anleihensobligationen	124	
Anteil		
- der Aktionäre der AG		660 ff.
- des Verwaltungsrates der AG		677
- der Gesellschafter der GmbH		804
Anteilbuch der GmbH		790
Anteilschein des Genossenschafters		849, 852 f.
Anschlussaustritt		822a
Anzahlungen von Kunden	99	
Anzeigepflichten		
- bei der ordentlichen Revision		728c
- bei der eingeschränkten Revision (Review)		729c
Arbeitspapiere		
Aufbewahrung der Geschäftsbücher		747
Aufbewahrungspflicht der Revisionsstelle		730c
Auflösung		
- der AG		736 ff.
- mit Liquidation		739 ff.
- ohne Liquidation		751
- der GmbH		821 ff.
- der Genossenschaft		911 ff.

Sachregister

	Text	Gesetzestext
- des Vereins		76 ff. ZGB
- der Stiftung		88 f. ZGB
Aufsicht		
- bei Stiftungen		84 ZGB
- der Aufsichtsbehörde		39 RAG
Aufsichtsbehörde		16 ff. RAG
Aufsichtsrat, Organ der Aufsichtsbehörde		31 RAG
Auftragsbestätigung		
Aufwand		
- aktivierter	98	
- Materialaufwand	109	
- Handelswarenaufwand	109	
- Aufwand für Dienstleistungen	109	
- Personalaufwand	110	
- Lohnaufwand	110	
- Sozialversicherungsaufwand	110	
- Raumaufwand	112	
- Fahrzeug- und Transportaufwand	113	
- Versicherungsaufwand	113	
- Energieaufwand	113	
- Verwaltungs- und Informatikaufwand	113	
- Werbeaufwand	114	
- Übriger Betriebsaufwand	114	
- Ausserordentlicher und betriebsfremder Aufwand	117	

	Text	Gesetzestext
Aufwertung		670
- von immobilen Sachanlagen	96	
Aufwertungsreserve		671b
Ausgabebetrag		624
Auskunft		
- Recht des Aktionärs		697
- Recht der Verwaltungsräte		715a
- Recht der Revisionsstelle		730b
- GmbH		802
- Recht des Genossenschafters		857
Auskunftspflicht		
- des Revisionsunternehmens gegenüber der Aufsichtsbehörde		14 RAG
Ausscheiden		
- aus der GmbH		822 ff.
- aus der Genossenschaft		842 ff., 864, 876
Ausschliessung		
- eines Gesellschafters der GmbH		823
- eines Genossenschafters		846
Austrittbedingungen		
- bei Übertragung und Vererbung der Mitgliedschaft		851
Austrittsbeschränkung		843
Austrittsfreiheit		842

	Text	Gesetzestext
B		
Bankengerechtes Verhalten	414	
Bankguthaben	72	
Bankverbindlichkeiten	100	
Bauzinsen		
- bei der AG		676
- Rückerstattung		678
Beitragspflicht		71 ZGB
Beitrittserklärung		840
Belegablage	53	
Belege	53	
- AG		631
- GmbH		777b
Berater, externe	128	
Berichterstattung	305 ff.	
Berichtigungsposten, aktive	98	
Beschlussfassung		
- Generalversammlung der AG		703 f.
- Gesellschafterversammlung der GmbH		808 ff.
- Generalversammlung der Genossenschaft		888 f.
Bestandesänderungen	80	
Beteiligung von Körperschaften des öffentlichen Rechts		762
Beteiligungen		665a

	Text	Gesetzestext
Beteiligungspapiere	90	
Beteiligungsverhältnisse bei Gesellschaften mit kotierten Aktien		663c
Bevollmächtigte		721
Bewertungsrichtlinien	67	
Bezugsrecht		
- des Aktionärs		652b, 656g
- bei der GmbH		652b
Bilanz		
- der AG		663a, 742
- der GmbH		801
- der Genossenschaft		856
Bilanzgewinn	106	
Bilanzverlust	106	
Brandversicherungswerte	123	
Bruttoprinzip	50	
Buchführung	51	
- Formelle Erfordernisse	51	
- Personelle Erfordernisse	55	
- Organisatorische Erfordernisse	56	
- kaufmännische		858, 69a, 83a ZGB
Buchführungsvorschriften	51 ff.	
Bürgschaften	119	
BVG	123	

	Text	Gesetzestext
D		
Datenverarbeitung	61	
Debitoren	76	
Décharge, vgl. Entlastung	413	
Delegation	901	
Delegiertenversammlung		
- der Genossenschaft		892
- der Genossenschaftsverbände		922
Delegierter, Sorgfalts- und Treuepflicht		717
Depotvertreter		689d
Didaktik		
Direktor		
- bei der AG		708, 718, 726
- bei der GmbH		776a, 804, 814, 815
- bei der Genossenschaft		898, 905
- bei der Aufsichtsbehörde		32 RAG
Dividende		
- AG		675
- GmbH		798
Dokumentationspflicht der Revisionsstelle		730c
Domizil, vgl. Sitz		
Doppelbesteuerungsrecht	380	
Drittpersonen, Beizug		21 RAG

	Text	Gesetzestext
E		
Ehevertrag	415	
Eigene Aktien		
- Erwerb		659 ff.
Eigenkapital		652d
Einlagen		632 ff.
- Prüfung (AG)		635 f.
- Leistung (AG)		652c
- bei der GmbH		777c
- Leistung (GmbH)		793
Einmanngesellschaft		625
Einschränkungen	346	
Einsichtsrecht		
- des Aktionärs		696 f.
- bei der GmbH		802
- des Genossenschafters		857
Eintritt		
- in die Genossenschaft		893 f., 875
- vgl. auch Selbsteintritt		
Einzahlung der Aktien		681 f.
Einzelgesellschaft	259	
Emissionsprospekt		
- Haftung		652
Entlastung		

Sachregister

	Text	Gesetzestext
- der Verwaltung der AG		758
- GmbH		804, 806a
- Genossenschaft		887
Entzug		
- der Geschäftsführung bei der GmbH		815
- vgl. auch Abberufung und Widerruf		
EO	110	
Erbvertrag	415	
Erfolg		
- ausserordentlicher	118	
- betriebsfremder	118	
Erfolgsrechnung		663
Erläuterungsbericht	354	
Eröffnungsbilanz	52	
Errichtungsakt		
- AG		629 f.
- GmbH		777
- Genossenschaft		830 ff.
- Stiftung		80 ff. ZGB
Ertrag	117	
Ertragssteuer	115	
F		
Familienstiftungen		87 ZGB
Finanzanlagen	90	

Sachregister

	Text	Gesetzestext
Finanzerfolg	118	
Finanzierung der Aufsichtsbehörde		22 RAG
Firma		
- der AG		626, 641, 719, 739, 746, 751, 776
- der GmbH		814
- der Genossenschaft		832, 899, 900, 915
Fonds der Genossenschaft		862
Forderungen	76	
- kurzfristige	77	
- langfristige	91	
Fortführung		
Fremdkapital	99	
- kurzfristiges	99	
- langfristiges	103	
Fusion		
- bei der AG		vgl. FusG
- zweier Genossenschaften		Vg. FusG
G		
Garantieverpflichtungen	119	
Geheimhaltung		
- Revisionsstelle		730b

1089

Sachregister

	Text	Gesetzestext
Generalversammlung		
- der AG		698 ff.
- Befugnisse		698
- Einberufung und Traktandierung		699 ff.
- Protokoll		702
- Beschlussfassung und Wahlen		703 f.
- der Genossenschaft		879 ff.
- Einberufung		881 ff.
- Stimmrecht		885
- Vertretung		886
- Beschlussfassung		888 f.
Genossenschaft, Begriff		828
Genossenschafter		
- Rechte		855 ff.
- Pflichten		866 ff.
Genossenschafterverzeichnis		907
Genossenschaftsanteil		853
- Übertragung		849
Genossenschaftsverbände		921 ff.
Genussschein		
- bei der AG		657
- bei der GmbH		774a
Geschäftsabschluss	354	
Geschäftsbericht	895	
- AG		662 ff.

	Text	Gesetzestext
- Bewertung		664 ff.
- GmbH		801
- Zustellung		801a
- Muster	895	
Geschäftsbesorgung, vgl. Geschäftsführung		
Geschäftsfirmen, vgl. Firma		
Geschäftsführung		
- der AG		627, 695, 715a, 716 ff., 729a, 731a, 754
- Übertragung		716b
- der GmbH		776a, 809 ff.
- Aufgaben		810
- Genehmigung durch die Gesellschafterversammlung		811
- Vertretung		814
- Nichtigkeit		816
- Haftung		817
- der Genossenschaft		887, 898 ff., 916
Geschäftslage	347	
Geschäftsreglement	901	
Geschäftsvermögen	68 f.	
Gesellschaft mit beschränkter Haftung		772 ff.
Gesellschafter		
- Anzahl		775

Sachregister

	Text	Gesetzestext
- Rechte und Pflichten		784 ff.
Gesellschafterversammlung der GmbH		804 ff., 810
- Aufgaben		804
- Einberufung und Durchführung		805
- Stimmrecht		806 ff.
Gesellschaftsform, Wahl	406	
Gesetzesverstösse	350	
Gewinnanteil		660 f.
Gewinnausschüttung	379/282	
- verdeckte		
Gewinnverwendung		731
Gewinnverwendungsvorschlag	890	
Gläubigerschutz		744
Gleichbehandlung der Gesellschafter (GmbH)		813
GOD (Grundsatz ordnungsmässiger Datenverarbeitung)	61	
Going Concern	86 ff.	
Gründerverantwortlichkeit		
- AG		752 ff.
- GmbH		827
- Genossenschaft		916 ff.
Grundkapital der AG, vgl. Aktienkapital	104	
Grundstück, Erwerb durch Ausländer	95	
Gründung		
- der AG		620 ff., 625, 629 ff.

	Text	Gesetzestext
- der GmbH		772 ff., 775, 777 ff.
- der Genossenschaft		828 ff., 831
- des Vereins		60 ff. ZGB
Gründungsbericht bei der AG		635 ff.
- Prüfungsbestätigung		635a
Gründungshaftung		753
Gründungskosten		664
H		
Haftung		752 ff.
- für Verwaltung, Geschäftsführung und Liquidation (AG)		754
- bei der GmbH		794
- von Geschäftsführern (GmbH)		817
- der Genossenschaft		868
- der Genossenschafter		869 ff.
- bei Neueintritt		875
- nach Ausscheiden oder nach Auflösung		876
Handelsregister		
- Eintragung bei der AG		640 ff.
- Löschung		746
- Eintragung bei der GmbH		778, 791
- Eintragung bei der Genossenschaft		835 ff., 877
- Eintragung beim Verein		61 ZGB
- Löschung		79 ZGB

1093

	Text	Gesetzestext
- Eintragung bei der Stiftung		81 ZGB
- Löschung		89 ZGB
Handlungspflichten	304	
Hauptbuch	51	
Herabsetzung des Aktienkapitals		732 ff.
- Aufforderung an die Gläubiger		733
- Durchführung		734
- Im Fall einer Unterbilanz		735
Herabsetzungsbeschluss		732
Hinterlegung bei Liquidation der AG		744
Hinweise		
I		
Immobilien	92	
Imparitätsprinzip	49	
Indossament		684
Inhaberaktien		622, 683
Interimsscheine		688
Investitionsrechnung	139	
IV	110	
J		
Jahresbericht		
- im Aktienrecht		663d
- der Aufsichtsbehörde		20 RAG

	Text	Gesetzestext
Jahresrechnung	52	
Journal	51	
K		
Kapital		
- AG		620 f.
- GmbH		772 f.
Kapitalerhöhung		
- ordentliche		650
- genehmigte		651 f.
- bedingte		653 ff.
- Durchführung		653e ff.
Kapitalerhöhungsbericht		652e
- Prüfungsbestätigung		652f
Kapitalerhöhungskosten		664
Kapitalsteuer	115	
Kapitalverlust		
- AG		725 f.
- GmbH		820
Kasse	71	
Kaufpreis	93	
Kaufvertrag	93	
Kennzahlen	129 ff.	
Kirchliche Stiftungen		87
Klagerecht		89 ZGB

Sachregister

	Text	Gesetzestext
Klarheit	48	
Kollektivgesellschaft	407	
Kommanditgesellschaft	407	
Konkurrenzverbot (GmbH)		776a, 777a, 803, 804, 806a, 808b, 812
Konkurs		
- bei der AG		736
- bei der GmbH		795a, 795d, 820, 821
- des ausscheidenden Genossenschafters		845
- der Genossenschaft		873
Konkursaufschub	321	
Kontenrahmen	70	
Kontrollrechte		
- der Aktionäre		696 f.
- der Genossenschafter		856 f.
Konventionalstrafe		
- bei der AG		627, 681, 682
- bei der GmbH		776a, 777a
Konzern		663e ff., 697h
Konzernabschlüsse		
Konzernrechnung		663e ff.
Kostenartenrechnung	137	

1096

Sachregister

	Text	Gesetzestext
Kostenrechnung	137	
Kostenstellenrechnung	137	
Kostenträgerrechnung	138	
Kreditgenossenschaften		
- Reingewinn		861
- Verantwortlichkeit		920
Kreditoren	99	
Kündigungsfrist		844
L		
Leasingverbindlichkeiten, nicht bilanziert	122	
Leistungsertrag	117	
Leistungspflicht des Aktionärs		
- des Aktionärs		680 ff.
- des Genossenschafters		867
Liegenschaftsertrag	118	
Liquidation		
- AG		739 ff.
- GmbH		826
- Genossenschaft		913
Liquidationsanteil		660 f.
Liquidationstätigkeit		742 ff.
Liquidatoren		
- Bestellung		740
- Abberufung		741

1097

Sachregister

	Text	Gesetzestext
Lohnbuchhaltung	110	
Löschung		
- der Gesellschaften		746, 826, 913
- der Firma		938 ff.
M		
Mandat		
- bestehendes	281	
- Überwachung	298	
Mängel in der Organisation		
- AG		731b
- GmbH		819
- Genossenschaft		908
- Verein		69c ZGB
- Stiftung		83d ZGB
Mantelhandel	380	
Marktsituation	94	
Mehrheitsbeschlüsse		
- qualifizierte, der AG		704
- der GmbH		808, 808b, 809
- der Genossenschaft		888, 889
Mehrwertsteuer	115	
Meldepflichten	303	
Meldung		

	Text	Gesetzestext
- an die Aufsichtsbehörde		15 RAG
- bezüglich Abweichung von der Standardberichterstattung	342 ff.	
Minderheitenschutz in der AG		709
Mindestkapital		621
Mitgliederverzeichnis der Genossenschafter		837
Mitgliedschaft		
- Erwerb (Genossenschaft)		839
- Verlust (Genossenschaft)		842 ff.
- Übertragung (Genossenschaft)		849 f.
- Ein- und Austritt (Verein)		70 ZGB
- Ausschliessung		72 ZGB
Mitgliedschaftsrechte, persönliche		689 ff.
Mittel, flüssige	71	
Mittelflussrechnung	132	
N		
Nachfolge		
- familiäre	416	
- ausserfamiliäre	420	
Nachschüsse		
- bei der GmbH		795 ff.
- nachträgliche Einführung		797
- der Genossenschafter		871
Namenaktien		622, 684

	Text	Gesetzestext
- nicht börsenkotierte		685b f.
- börsenkotierte		685d ff.
- nicht voll einbezahlte		687
Nationalität		
- bei der AG		718
- bei der GmbH		814
- bei der Genossenschaft		898
Nebenleistungen bei der GmbH		796
- nachträgliche Einführung		797
Nennwert		622 ff.
Neumandate	279	
Nichtigkeit		
- von Beschlüssen der Generalversammlung der AG		706b
- von Beschlüssen der Geschäftsführer der GmbH		816
Niederlassung, vgl. Haupt- und Zweigniederlassung		
Niederstwertprinzip	50	
Nutzniessung		
- an Stammanteilen		789a
- Stimmrecht		806b
O		
Obligationen	90	
Obligationenrecht	257	

	Text	Gesetzestext
Offenlegung		801
Öffentlich-rechtliche Körperschaften		
- Übernahme einer AG		751
- Beteiligung an einer AG		762
- Übernahme einer Genossenschaft		915
- Beteiligung an einer Genossenschaft		926
Öffentlich-rechtliche Personenverbände		829
Optionsrecht		653d
Organe		
- der AG		698 ff.
- der GmbH		804 ff.
- der Genossenschaft		879 ff.
- der Aufsichtsbehörde		30 RAG
Organhaftung		722
Organvertreter		689c
Organisation		
- GmbH		804 ff.
- Genossenschaft		879 ff.
- Verein		64 ff. ZGB
- Stiftung		83 ff. ZGB
- Aufsichtsbehörde		29 RAG
Organisationskosten		664
Organisationsreglement	901	

Sachregister

	Text	Gesetzestext
P		
Partizipationsschein		656a f.
Partizipant		656c ff.
Passiven	99	
Personal der Aufsichtsbehörde		34 RAG
Personalfürsorgestiftung		89bis ZGB
Personengesellschaft	340	
Persönlichkeit		
- AG		643 ff.
- GmbH		779 f.
- Genossenschaft		838
Pfandbestellung zugunsten Dritter	119	
Pfandrecht		
- an Aktien, Stimmrecht		689b
- an Stammanteilen		789b
Pflichten		
- der Gesellschafter		784 ff.
- der Verwaltung der Genossenschaft		902 f.
- staatlich beaufsichtigter Revisionsunternehmen		11 ff. RAG
Planungsrechnung		
- kurzfristig	139	
- langfristig	139	
Postkonto	72	
Privatvermögen	377	

Sachregister

	Text	Gesetzestext
Prokura		
- bei der AG		721
- bei der GmbH		815
Prospekt		652a
Protokoll		
- der Generalversammlung		702
- der Verwaltung		713
Prüfung		
- direkte	296	
- indirekte	296	
- systematische	296	
- logische	297	
Prüfungshandlungen		
- grenzüberschreitende		28 RAG
Prüfungsmethoden	295	
Prüfungspflichten	303	
Prüfungsstandards	306 ff.	
Prüfungstechniken	296	
Prüfungsumfang	295	
Prüfungsverhalten	352	
Prüfungsweg	295	
Publikumsgesellschaften		2 RAG
Q		
Qualitätssicherung	257 ff.	

	Text	Gesetzestext
- der staatlich beaufsichtigten Revisionsunternehmen		12 RAG
R		
Rangrücktritt	319 f./351	
Realisationsprinzip	49	
Rechnungsabgrenzung		
- aktive	85	
- passive	101	
Rechnungslegung		
- ordnungsmässige		662a
- Abweichung von den Grundsätzen ordnungsmässiger Rechnungslegung	128	
Rechnungswesen		36 RAG
Rechte der Gesellschafter		784
Rechtshilfe		23 ff. RAG
Rechtsschutz im RAG		40 RAG
Rechtsübergang bei Abtretung von Stammanteilen		787
Reingewinn		
- der AG		660 f.
- der Genossenschaft		858 ff.
Reservefonds		860
Reserven		
- AG		671 ff.
- gesetzliche		671 ff.

Sachregister

	Text	Gesetzestext
- statutarische		672 f.
- GmbH		801
- Genossenschaft		860, 863
- stille, Auflösung	128	
Review		729 ff.
Revision, eingeschränkte (Review)		727a, 729 ff.
- Aufgaben der Revisionsstelle		729a ff.
Revision, ordentliche		
- AG		727, 728 ff.
- Aufgaben der Revisionsstelle		728a ff.
- GmbH	266	
- Genossenschaft	267	
- Spezialerlasse	268	
- Verein	269	
- Stiftung	273	
- Vertragliche Revisionen	274	
- gesetzliche	274	
- interne	274	
Revisionsbericht		
- bei der ordentlichen Revision		728b
- bei der eingeschränkten Revision (Review)		729b
- vorbehaltsfeindlicher	343	
Revisionsdienstleistungen		2 RAG
Revisionsexperte		4 RAG
Revisionshaftung		755

1105

	Text	Gesetzestext
Revisionspflicht	303	727 f.
Revisionsrecht	257	
Revisionsstelle		
- Ziele	257	
- Pflichten	303	
- AG		727 ff.
- Anforderungen		727b f.
- GmbH		818
- Genossenschaft		906 f.
- Verein		69b ZGB
- Stiftung		83b f. ZGB
- Aufsichtsbehörde		33 RAG
- Rücktritt	287	
- Empfehlung	313/352	
- Verantwortlichkeit	356	
Revisionsunternehmen		2 RAG
- Voraussetzungen		6 RAG
Revisoren		5 RAG
Risikobeurteilung	128	
Rückerstattungspflicht		
- von Leistungen im allgemeinen		678
- von Tantiemen im Konkurs		679
- der Gesellschafter der GmbH		800
- bei der Genossenschaft		904
Rückgriff		

Sachregister

	Text	Gesetzestext
- bei aktienrechtlicher Verantwortlichkeit		759
- bei genossenschaftlicher Verantwortlichkeit		918
Rückstellungen		669
- für absehbare Verpflichtungen	102	
- für künftige Ersatzinvestitionen	102	
- langfristig	104	
S		
Sachanlagen		
- mobile	91	
- immobile	92	
- immaterielle	96	
Sacheinlage		
- bei Gründung der AG		628, 634, 642
- bei Gründung der GmbH		777b f.
Sachenrecht	92	
Sachübernahmen		628, 642
Schadenersatz bei der AG		756 ff.
- Ansprüche ausser Konkurs		756
- Ansprüche im Konkurs		757
Schlussbilanz	52	
Schuldenruf		742
Sitz		
- der Kollektivgesellschaft		554

1107

Sachregister

	Text	Gesetzestext
- der Kommanditgesellschaft		596
- der AG		626, 640
- der GmbH		776, 778, 808b
- der Genossenschaft		832, 835, 856
Sofortabschreibungen	88	
Solidarität		918
Sonderprüfung		697a ff.
- mit Genehmigung der Generalversammlung		697a
- bei Ablehnung durch die Generalversammlung		697b
- Einsetzung		697c
Sorgfaltspflicht		
- des Verwaltungsrates der AG		717
- GmbH		812
- Genossenschaft		902
Stammanteile		784 ff.
- Zeichnung		777a
- Erwerb eigener Stammanteile		783
- Übertragung		785 ff.
- Abtretung		785 ff.
- Nutzniessung		789a
- gemeinschaftliches Eigentum		792
Stammeinlagen		774
Stammkapital		773
- Erhöhung		781

	Text	Gesetzestext
- Herabsetzung		782
Standardbericht		
- Treuhandkammer	306	
- für Review (versch. Sprachen)	307	
- für Review bei Stiftungen	329	
- für Vereine	331	
- für Subventionierte (Kanton BS)	336	
- für Genossenschaften	337	
- für GmbH	339	
- für Kollektivgesellschaften	340	
Standardberichterstattung, Abweichungen	348	
Standardrevisionsunterlagen		
- bei der AG für den Review	910	
- bei der AG für den Review (Kurzfassung)	948	
- bei Vereinen etc. (Kurzfassung)	970	
Statuten		
- der AG		626 ff.
- der GmbH		776 f.
- der Genossenschaft		832 f.
Statutenänderung		
- bei der AG		647, 652g
- Eintragung in das Handelsregister		652h
- bei der GmbH		780
Stetigkeit	50/128	
Steuerbefreiung		38 RAG

Sachregister

	Text	Gesetzestext
Steuererklärung	376	
Steuern	115	
Stichentscheid		
- bei Gesellschafterversammlung der GmbH		808a
Stiftung		80 ff. ZGB
Stimmrecht		
- in der AG		626, 627, 692 ff.
- Entstehung		694
- Ausschliessung		695
- in der GmbH		806 ff.
- Bemessung		806
- Ausschliessung		806a
- bei Nutzniessung		806b
- in der Genossenschaft		855, 885, 887
- im Verein		67 f. ZGB
- Ausschliessung		68 ZGB
Stimmrechtsaktien		693
Strohmänner		691
T		
Tantiemen		
- AG		677
- GmbH		798b
Teilnahme, unbefugte		691

Sachregister

	Text	Gesetzestext
Tod		
- des Gesellschafters der GmbH		788
- des Genossenschafters		847, 864, 876
Tresorerie	90 f.	
Treuepflicht		37 RAG
- GmbH		803, 812
- Genossenschaft		866
U		
Übernahme		
- einer AG durch eine öffentlich-rechtliche Körperschaft		751
Überprüfung staatlich beaufsichtigter Revisionsunternehmen		17 RAG
Überschuldung		
- einer AG		725 f.
- einer GmbH		820
- einer Genossenschaft		903
Überschuldungsanzeige	319	
Übertragung		
- der Aktien		627, 684
- der Stammanteile		785 ff.
Übertragbarkeit, Beschränkung		685 ff.
- gesetzliche		685
- statutarische		685a ff.

Sachregister

	Text	Gesetzestext
Übertretungen		41 RAG
Überwachung der Genossenschaftsverbände		924
Umlaufvermögen	71	
Umwandlung		
- von Aktien		622
- der Stiftung		85 f. ZGB
Unabhängigkeit der Revisionsstelle		
- persönlich	284	
- finanziell	285	
- strukturell	286	
- bei der ordentlichen Revision		728
- bei der eingeschränkten Revision (Review)		729
- der staatlich beaufsichtigten Revisionsunternehmen		11 RAG
Unerlaubte Handlung		
- der Liquidatoren		743
- der GmbH		817
- der Genossenschaft		899
Universalversammlung		
- der AG		701
- der Genossenschaft		884
Unterbilanz		725, 735
Unterlassungspflichten	304	
Unternehmensnachfolge	415 ff.	
Urabstimmung		880

	Text	Gesetzestext
Urkunde		784
UVG	110	
V		
Verantwortlichkeit		
- AG		752 ff.
- GmbH		827
- Genossenschaft		916 ff.
- Revisionsstelle	356	
Verbindlichkeiten		
- gegenüber Aktionären	99	
- andere kurzfristige Verbindlichkeiten	101	
- gegenüber Vorsorgeeinrichtungen	123	
Verein		60 ff. ZGB
Vereinsversammlung		64 ff. ZGB
- Bedeutung und Einberufung		64 ZGB
- Zuständigkeit		65 ZGB
- Vereinsbeschluss		66 ff. ZGB
Vereinszweck		74 ZGB
Vergehen		42 RAG
Verjährung		
- aus Verantwortlichkeit (AG)		760
- aus Verantwortlichkeit (GmbH)		827
- Rückerstattung bei GmbH		800
- bei der Genossenschaft		864, 878

Sachregister

	Text	Gesetzestext
- aus Verantwortlichkeit (Genossenschaft)		919
Vernichtung von Aktien		732a
Verrechnungssteuer, eidgenössische	116	
Verrechnungsverbot	50	
Versammlung, konstituierende		834
Versicherungsgenossenschaften		
- Generalversammlung		893
- Verantwortlichkeit		920
Versicherungsvertrag		841
Vertretung		
- der AG		718 ff.
- des Aktionärs		689b ff.
- des Aktionärs im Verwaltungsrat		709
- der GmbH		809 ff.
- der Gesellschaft durch die Geschäftsführung		814
- Entziehung		815
- der Genossenschaft		898 ff.
Verwaltung		
- der Genossenschaft		894 ff.
- Pflichten		902 f.
- der Genossenschaftsverbände		923
Verwaltungsausschuss		897
Verwaltungsrat		707 ff.
- Wählbarkeit		707
- Organisation		712 ff.

1114

	Text	Gesetzestext
- Aufgaben		716 ff.
Vetorecht		807
Vinkulierung		685a ff.
Vollständigkeit	48	
Vollständigkeitserklärung	276	
Vorbehalte	343	
Vorräte		666
Vorteile, besondere		628, 642
Vorsicht	49	
Vorsorgliche Massnahmen		
- bei Ausscheiden eines Gesellschafters (GmbH)		824
Vorstand		69 f. ZGB
Vorzugsaktie		654 f.
Vorzugsstammanteile		799
W		
Wahl der Revisionsstelle		730
Wahlen		
- Generalversammlung der AG		703 f.
- Verwaltung der Genossenschaft		894
Wandelrecht		653d
Warenlager	80	
Wertberichtigungen		669
Wertschriften		667
Wesentlichkeit	51	

	Text	Gesetzestext
Wichtige Beschlüsse, Generalversammlung der AG		704
Wohlfahrtszwecke		
- Reserven		673
- Fonds		862
Wohnsitz		
- der Verwaltungsräte der AG		708
- der Geschäftsführer der GmbH		791, 814
- der Verwaltung der Genossenschaft		898
Z		
Zahl		
- der Aktionäre		625
- der Gesellschafter m.b.H.		775
- der Genossenschafter		831
Zeichnungsscheine		
- bei Gründung der AG		652
Zinse		
- AG		675 f., 678
- GmbH		798a
- Genossenschaft		859
Zulassung bez. Revisionsdienstleistungen		16 ff. RAG
- Entzug		18 RAG
Zusammenarbeit mit ausländischen Revisionsaufsichtsbehörden		27 RAG

	Text	Gesetzestext
Zustimmungserfordernisse bei Abtretung von Stammanteilen		786
Zutrittsgewährung der Aufsichtsbehörde		14 RAG
Zweckänderung der Stiftung		86 ZGB
Zweigniederlassung		
- der AG, Eintragung im Handelsregister		641
- der GmbH, Eintragung im Handelsregister		778a
- der Genossenschaft, Eintragung im Handelsregister		836
Zwischengesellschaft		663f